## Basic *sa* Tasks

### Starting and Stopping the Server

```
startserver -d master_device -f runserver_file -c
configuration_file [-m] [-p]
```
- *runserver_file* contains the SQL Server command with appropriate options for locations of the master device, interfaces file, SQL Server name, and so on.
- *configuration_file* contains SQL Server configuration parameters.
- d specifies the master device name.
- f specifies an alternative runserver file.
- c specifies the location of the configuration file.
- m specifies single-user mode.
- p generates a password for the sso account.

```
shutdown [with  nowait]
```

### Granting Access to the Server

```
sp_addlogin login_name, password [ ,default_db
              [ ,language]]
```
- *password* required, 6 characters minimum.
  *Note:* Only the user with sso_role can add logins.
```
sp_password caller_password, new_password, [ ,
login_name]
```
  *Note:* Only the user with sso_role should specify *login_name*.
```
sp_droplogin login_name
```
- Drops specified *login_name*.
```
sp_locklogin login_name, {"lock ¦ "unlock"}
```
- Locks the specified *login_name*.
```
sp_configure "password expiration interval", #_of_days
```
- Sets the number of days before passwords will expire after they are changed.
- A value of 0 means no password expiration.
  *Note:* Only the user with sso_role can set the password expiration interval.
```
sp_modifylogin login_name, options, value
```
- *options* are defdb, deflanguage, and fullname.

### Defining Physical Resources

```
disk init name = 'logical_name',
          physname = "phys_name",
          vdevno = dev_num,
          size = dev_size
```
- *logical_name* must be unique throughout the server.
- *phys_name* indicates the disk location of the device.
- *dev_num* is the unique integer < sp_configure devices.
- *dev_siz* indicates the size in pages—2KB, except Stratus (4KB).
```
disk reinit name = 'logical_name',
          physname = "phys_name",
          vdevno = dev_num,
          size = dev_size
```
- Used to rebuild sysdevices to reestablish a database device after restoring a damaged master database if the device was added since the last database dump of the master database.

---

```
disk refit
```
- Used after disk reinit sysdatabases to reestabl since the last database backup of master.
```
disk mirror name = 'logical_name', mirror = 'phys_name'
```
- Keeps a copy of the device *logical_name* on *phys_name*.
```
disk unmirror name = "logical_name"
            [ , side = {primary ¦ secondary}]
            [ , mode = {retain ¦ remove}]
```
- Defaults are side=secondary and mode=retain.
```
disk remirror name = "logical_name"
sp_adddumpdevice 'disk' ¦ 'tape', logical_name,
              physical_name, tape_size
```
- Adds dump devices.
- *logical_name* is a unique name within the server for the dump device.
- *physical_name* is the physical location of the device of the disk file.
- *tape_size* is the capacity of the tape dump device in megabytes.
```
sp_help device [logical_name]
```
- Reports information about the specified or all database and dump devices.
```
sp_diskdefault logical_name, defaulton ¦ defaultoff
sp_dropdevice logical_name
```
- Removes the device definition if the device is not in use.

## Database Management

```
create database db_name [on device_name = size [ , ...] ]
              [log on device_name = size [, ...] ]
              [with override]
              [for load]
```
- with override enables the specification of the same device name for the on and log on clauses; enables dumping of transaction log even though it is not a separate device.
- for load invokes a streamlined version of create database. Use when recovering from media failure, and database will be loaded from backup immediately following creation.
- *size* is in megabytes.
- *device_name* is any database device in sysdevices.
- A separate log device is highly recommended.
```
drop database db_name
alter database db_name [on device_name = size [ , ...]]
              [log on device_name = size [ , ...]]
              [with override]
              [for load]
sp_changedbowner login_name
sp_dboption database, options, true ¦ false
```
- *options* are select into/bulkcopy, read only, single user, dbo use only, no chkpt on recovery, trunc log on chkpt, abort tran on log full, allow nulls by default, ddl in tran, and no free space acctg.
```
checkpoint
```
- checkpoint a database (must be in database to be checkpointed).
```
sp_helpdb [database_name]
```

### Granting *create database* Permission

```
use master
sp_adduser login_name
grant create database to login_name
```

### Memory and Resource Allocation

```
sp_configure [option, [new_value] ¦ config_group_name]
```

- *option* is any value in the description column of sysconfigures.
- *new_value* is any value in the valid range for the parameter.
- *config_group_name* is the name of the configuration parameter group.
- sp_configure without arguments lists valid options and ranges.

## Monitoring CPU and I/O Usage

### Basic Commands

```
sp_monitor
```

- Shows CPU usage, I/O usage, and so on, since server came up and also since last sp_monitor call.

```
set statistics io on ¦ off
```

- Quantity of logical and physical I/O.

```
set statistics time on ¦ off
```

- Elapsed system and CPU time for parse, compile, and execute.

```
set forceplan on ¦ off
```

### Managing Remote Access

```
sp_addserver server_name, {local ¦ null}, network_name
sp_dropserver server_name [ , droplogins]
sp_addremotelogin server_name [ , local_name
                  [, remote_name]]
sp_remoteoption [server_name, login_name, remote_name,
'trusted', true ¦ false]
sp_serveroption [servername, options, {true ¦ false}]
```

- *options* are net password encryption and time-outs.

```
sp_helpremotelogin [servername [, remotename]]
```

### Managing System-Defined Roles

```
sp_role {"grant" ¦ "revoke"}, {sa_role ¦ sso_role ¦
oper_role ¦ oper_role}, login_name
```

- *login_name* must be a valid SQL Server login.
- User must have sa_role to grant sa_role.
- User must have sso_role to grant sso_role and oper_role.
- sa_role performs SQL Server management tasks:
  - Server configuration
  - Manage database devices
  - Create/drop databases
  - Shut down SQL Server
  - Kill processes
- sso_role performs security related tasks:
  - Add/drop/lock logins
  - Change passwords
  - Set password expiration interval
  - Manage auditing system
- oper_role can back up and restore any database within SQL Server.

```
set role {"sa_role" ¦ "sso_role" ¦ "oper_role"}
{on ¦ off}
```

- Disable/enable the role for current session.

## Basic *dbo* Tasks

### User and Group Maintenance

```
sp_adduser login_name [ , name_within_db
              [ , group_name]]
```

- *login_name* is from syslogins.
- *name_within_db* is an optional different name within database.
- *group_name* is the name of the group in which to place the user.
- Specifying a group name requires specifying a non-null *name_within_db*.
- guest is a special case of user; it gives database access to any nonuser.
- Adds a row to sysusers.

```
sp_addalias login_name, current_user
```

- *login_name* is the user to add to the database.
- *current_user* is the existing user to whom *login_name* will alias.
- Adds a row to sysusers.

```
sp_addgroup group_name
```

- Adds the group *group_name* to sysusers.

```
sp_changegroup group_name, user_name
```

- Places the user *user_name* in group *group_name*.

```
sp_dropuser user_name
```

- Removes the user *user_name* from sysusers and any aliased users from sysalternates.

```
sp_dropalias login_name
```

- Removes *login_name* from sysalternates.

```
sp_dropgroup group_name
```

- Removes group *group_name* from sysusers.

```
sp_helpuser [user_name]
```

- Displays the list of database users or detailed user information.

### Granting and Revoking Permission

```
grant {all ¦ permission_list} on object [(column_list)]
to {public ¦ name_list ¦ role_name}
[with grant option]
grant {all ¦ command_list} to {public ¦ name_list ¦
          role_name}
```

- *permission_list* may be any combination of select, insert, update, and delete.
- *name_list* may be any combination of users and groups.
- *command_list* may include any of the create commands (create rule/table/view/procedure/default).
- with grant option enables the user to grant specified permissions to other users.

```
revoke [grant option for]
            {all ¦ permission_list ¦ execute}
            on object [ (column_list)]
            from {public ¦ name_list ¦ role_name}
[cascade]
revoke {all ¦ command_list} from {public ¦ name_list ¦
          role_name}
```

- grant option for revokes the user's permission to grant specified permissions.
- cascade is required with grant option for if the user has granted permissions to other users.
- Revokes those permissions.

# Sybase® SQL Server™ 11

# UNLEASHED

Ray Rankins
Jeffrey R. Garbus
David Solomon
Bennett Wm. McEwan

**SAMS**
PUBLISHING

201 West 103rd Street
Indianapolis, IN 46290

*To the two shining beacons in my sea of life, Elizabeth and Jason, without whose love, understanding, and most of all, patience, I would be lost.—Ray Rankins, Northern Lights Consulting*

*I dedicate this book to my wife, Penny, without whose help and support I would never have finished my chapters; and to my children, Brandon, Devon, Max, and Gillian, for the space they gave me to write.—Jeffrey Garbus*

*This book is for you, Rosemarie (if you can still stand to look at it!).—David Solomon*

*"To the love of work, where the line between leisure and toil is no line at all."— Bennett Wm. McEwan*

# Copyright © 1996 by Sams Publishing

FIRST EDITION

International Standard Book Number: 0-672-30909-2

Library of Congress Catalog Card Number: 95-72919

99        10  9  8  7  6  5

Interpretation of the printing code: the rightmost double-digit number is the year of the book's printing; the rightmost single-digit, the number of the book's printing. For example, a printing code of 96-1 shows that the first printing of the book occurred in 1996.

*Composed in AGaramond and MCPdigital by Macmillan Computer Publishing*

*Printed in the United States of America*

| | |
|---:|:---|
| **Publisher** | Richard K. Swadley |
| **Acquisitions Manager** | Greg Wiegand |
| **Development Manager** | Dean Miller |
| **Managing Editor** | Cindy Morrow |
| **Marketing Manager** | Gregg Bushyeager |
| **Assistant Marketing Manager** | Kristina Perry |

**Acquisitions Editor**
Rosemarie Graham

**Development Editor**
Todd Bumbalough

**Software Development Specialist**
Steve Flatt

**Production Editor**
Bart Reed

**Copy Editors**
Nancy Albright, Anne Barret, Mary Ann Faughnan, Kimberly K. Hannel, Philip Hanover, Kris Simmons

**Technical Reviewers**
Ramesh Chandak, John Scott

**Editorial Coordinator**
Bill Whitmer

**Technical Edit Coordinator**
Lynette Quinn

**Resource Coordinator**
Deborah Frisby

**Formatter**
Frank Sinclair

**Editorial Assistants**
Carol Ackerman, Andi Richter, Rhonda Tinch-Mize

**Cover Designer**
Tim Amrhein

**Book Designer**
Gary Adair

**Copy Writer**
Peter Fuller

**Production Team Supervisor**
Brad Chinn

**Production**
Stephen Adams, Carol Bowers, Gina Brown, Michael Brumitt, Jama Carter, Jeanne Clark, Judy Everly, Trey Frank, Jason Hand, George Hanlin, Sonja Hart, Michael Henry, Ayanna Lacey, Clint Lahnen, Paula Lowell, Louisa Klucznik, Steph Mineart, Diana Moore, Nancy Price, Erich J. Richter, Laura Robbins, Bobbi Satterfield, Laura Smith, SA Springer, Andrew Stone, Tim Tate, Chris Van Camp, Susan Van Ness, Mark Walchle, Todd Wente, Suzanne Whitmer, Colleen Williams, Jeff Yesh

# Overview

## Part IV  System Administration

## Part V  Introduction to Open Client Programming

## PART VI  Appendixes

# Contents

# Acknowledgments

I wish to thank my wife, Elizabeth, and son, Jason, for their understanding and patience during the long, late hours put in to make this book a reality. I would also like to acknowledge the teachers I have had in my lifetime who instilled in me a joy of learning and the importance of good writing and communication skills.—Ray Rankins

I'd like to thank the people from Sybase who gave us early access to the products we're describing; SAMS Publishing staff for helping us get these books finished; our clients for giving us the "War Stories" we're sharing with you herein; my co-authors and other employees at Northern Lights for their support and very hard work; and last but not least my family, for understanding.—Jeffrey Garbus

This book would hardly say anything about System 11 without the diligence and attention of Ray Rankins. A lot of the material regarding system administration is based on work done for our *Sybase DBA Survival Guide* by Brian Tretter. I acknowledge both of them for their hard work. I want to thank my students, clients, and associates for helping me to understand the ins and outs of SQL Server, and for presenting gnarly problems whose solutions gave greater insight into the product. Emphatic thanks once more to Rosemarie Graham at SAMS, who worked harder on this book than on any other book I know about—checking, verifying, and reviewing. I only hope it was worth it.—David Solomon

# About the Authors

## Ray Rankins

Ray Rankins is currently a Managing Consultant for Northern Lights Consulting and a Certified Sybase Professional Database Administrator. Prior to joining Northern Lights, he worked for Sybase Professional Services as a consultant and instructor and was involved in the development of the Sybase Performance and Tuning class. Ray has been working with Sybase and Microsoft SQL Server since 1987 as a DBA, application developer, database designer, project manager, consultant, and instructor and has worked in a variety of industries including financial, manufacturing, health care, retail, insurance, communications, and state and federal government. His expertise is in SQL Server performance and tuning, SQL Server application design and development, client/server architecture, and very large database (VLDB) design and implementation.

## Jeffrey R. Garbus

Jeffrey R. Garbus is President of Northern Lights Software, Ltd. Since 1989, Jeff has taught thousands of programmers, systems administrators, and database designers about Sybase administration and tuning, based on his experience as a consultant to some of the most complex Sybase installations in the world. His current interests are in design, tuning, and maintenance of very large databases in Sybase.

## David Solomon

David Solomon, President of metis technologies, llc., of Troy, NY, writes, speaks, teaches, and consults on SQL Server design, application, and implementation. With more than five years of experience in SQL Server, he is an expert on query analysis and troubleshooting, logical database design, and application design and implementation. He specializes in advanced SQL techniques and physical database design.

## Ben McEwan

Ben McEwan is the Manager of Software Development for Northern Lights Software. He has been responsible for the development of the Aurora Utilities suite since February 1995. Ben teaches classes on SQL Server, Open Client, and Visual Basic/SQL Server integration. His specialty is the practical use of emerging technologies.

# Introduction

## Welcome to Sybase System 11 SQL Server

Congratulations! You have bought the premier multi-platform database management product on the market today. System 11 SQL Server continues to provide the performance, scalability, and value characteristic of Sybase database products.

System 11 SQL Server is a relational database management system (RDMS or RDBMS, depending on where you grew up!) that is capable of handling large amounts of data and many concurrent users while preserving data integrity and providing many advanced administration and data distribution capabilities.

Here are a few of the capabilities of SQL Server:

- Complete data integrity protection, from complex transaction support and advanced security to objects that support your business rules as an implicit part of your database.
- Fast and efficient multi-tasking and multi-threading on any platform, including support for symmetric multi-processing on SMP systems. System 11 SQL Server runs on operating systems from NetWare and Windows NT to OSF, Solaris, AIX and HP/UX.
- Outstanding price/performance.

## Is This Book for Me?

This *Unleashed* book is meant for anyone who is responsible for designing, building, administering and tuning systems that rely on SQL Server. Among other things, this book contains performance information you may not find anywhere else, including tuning methods and advanced SQL techniques that are undocumented or not well described.

- *System Administrators* will learn how to install and administer SQL Server. You will also learn about important standards and protocols to ensure that SQL Server applications can be maintained and supported for the long haul.
- *Database Administrators* will learn to make the best use of SQL Server objects and datatypes and will learn to write effective stored procedures and triggers. The "Performance And Tuning" section of the book will help you understand what's going on under the hood of the server, including a detailed analysis of the query optimizer and the physical storage mechanisms used by SQL Server. You can start to understand what performance you can reasonably expect with SQL Server so that you can focus on problems that you can really fix and on practical solutions.

■ *Programmers* will learn how to write code that runs well on SQL Server and will acquire a complete understanding of how the server interprets SQL statements when running. We also provide a solid foundation for your work in C and Visual Basic with DB-Library, ct-Library, and ODBC in the "Introduction to Open Client Programming" section of this book.

# What Will I Learn from This Book?

Understanding SQL Server starts with understanding—both functionally and conceptually—the tasks an administrator or programmer must perform. There are several third-party tools available in the market for working with SQL Server, but few tools that ship with the core SQL Server product. For this reason, this book is *task-oriented*, not tool-oriented—concentrating on the tools and commands available in the core SQL Server product. In this book, we will explain the important tasks and the concepts behind them, describe when they need to occur, then show you how to perform them in the core product. You will then have a better understanding of what the tools you may choose to use are doing behind the scenes.

# What's in This Book?

This book consists of five sections:

■ Part I, "SQL Server Architecture," discusses client/server architecture in general and looks closely at how Sybase SQL Server implements a client/server database system.

■ Part II, "Transact-SQL Programming," discusses the language constructs of Transact-SQL and discusses how objects are created and maintained. You will learn about the different datatypes in SQL Server and how their use can affect performance, data maintenance, and capacity. We look closely at programming issues in writing procedures and triggers, examine cursor programming, and explain the ins and outs of transaction programming.

■ Part III, "Performance and Tuning," describes in detail how SQL Server stores data, how it decides on optimization strategies, and how locking and multi-user issues impact overall performance. Perhaps the most important point here is that you can start to understand the kinds of expectations you should have for the system: when the query performance is as good as you can expect, and when it can get a lot better. Chapter 22, "Common Performance and Tuning Problems," describes some performance pitfalls that are easy for newcomers to SQL Server to miss, but also easy to avoid once you know they are there.

■ Part IV, "System Administration," describes the tasks needed to get SQL Server up the first time and to keep it running all the time. (The Performance and Tuning section worries about making SQL Server fast; the System Administration section worries about making it reliable.) You will learn to make backups, how to restore them, and how to develop a backup and maintenance regimen that ensures your data is safe. Chapter 35, "Administering Very Large SQL Server Databases," looks at some of the issues associated with building very large databases (VLDBs).

■ Part V, "Introduction to Open Client Programming," provides a first look at the programming issues with SQL Server. Of course, this is a topic for a whole other book, but you learn in these chapters the basics of DB-Library, ODBC, and ct-Library programming for both Visual Basic and C++.

# What's Next?

If SQL Server is not yet installed, you may want to start with Chapter 24, "SQL Server Installation and Connectivity," to get SQL Server up and running, then continue on to the other sections of this book.

## If You Are New to SQL Server...

Start at the beginning and read about how this stuff is built. (You will never make the time later and you really need to understand this stuff to make good use of the server.)

As a System Administrator, you should read Chapter 3, "Introduction to Transact-SQL," because you will need to know some SQL. Then you can jump right to Chapter 23, "Overview of System Administration," and work through the administration section.

As a Database Administrator, you will need to understand Transact-SQL programming, so work through the book in order from Chapter 3 to about Chapter 14. Before you design a system ready to go into production, you should finish the performance section and try some stuff using a hands-on approach. Then you need to understand thoroughly Chapters 28 (on database logging) and 31 (on server configuration and performance). Read Chapter 22, "Common Performance and Tuning Problems," before you take a production system online. If you are working with large databases, be sure to read Chapter 35.

As a programmer, you should probably read the chapters in order through Chapter 10, then make the time to look at Chapters 12 through 16 to make sure you understand the kinds of performance issues and problems you might run into. If you will be writing in Visual Basic or C, read the section on Open Client Programming. (It may help you choose the best architecture for your application.) Finally, make the time to read 19, "Application Design for Performance," and Chapter 20, "Advanced Transact-SQL Programming."

# Conventions Used in This Book

We've tried to be consistent in our use of conventions here. Names of commands and stored procedures are presented in a special monospaced, `computer` typeface. In the text itself, we have tried to present all SQL keywords in the text in upper case, but because SQL Server does not make a distinction between upper- and lowercase for SQL keywords in actual SQL code, many code examples show SQL keywords in lowercase.

We have purposely not capitalized the names of objects, databases, or logins/users where that would be incorrect. That may have left sentences starting like this, "`sysdatabases` includes…" with an initial lowercase character.

Code and output examples are presented separately from regular paragraphs and also are in a monospaced, computer typeface. Here is an example:

```
select id, name, audflags
from sysobjects
where type != "S"

id            name                               audflags
- - - - - - - - - -   - - - - - - - - - - - - - - - - - - - - - - - - - - -   - - - - - - - - - -
144003544    marketing_table                    130
```

When we provide *syntax* for a command, we've attempted to follow the following conventions:

| *Key* | *Definition* |
| --- | --- |
| `command` | Command names, options, and other keywords |
| `variable` | Indicates values you provide |
| `{}` | Indicates you must choose at least one of the enclosed options |
| `[]` | Means the value/keyword is optional |
| `()` | Parentheses are part of the command |
| ¦ | Indicates you can select only one of the options shown |
| , | Means you can select as many of the options shown, separated by commas |
| ... | Indicates the previous option can be repeated |

Consider the following example:

```
grant {all ¦ permission_list} on object [(column_list)]
     to {public ¦ user_or_group_name [, …]}
```

In this case, the `object` value is required, but the `column_list` is optional. Note also that items shown in plain computer type, such as `grant`, `public`, or `all`, should be entered literally as shown. Placeholders are presented in italics, such as *permission_list* and *user_or_group_name*; a placeholder is a generic term for which you must supply a specific value or values. The ellipses in the square brackets following *user_or_group_name* indicates that multiple user or group names can be specified separated by commas. You can specify either the keyword `public` or one or more user or group names, but not both.

Our editors were enormously helpful in finding inconsistencies in how we used these conventions. We apologize for any that remain; they are entirely the fault of the authors.

# Disclaimer

Please note that much of the material in this book was based upon a pre-release version of System 11 SQL Server. The syntax or output of some of the SQL Server commands and procedures may be different in the final General Availability (GA) release of System 11 SQL Server.

# Good Luck!

You are in good shape now. You have chosen a fine platform for building database applications, one that can provide outstanding performance and rock-solid reliability at a reasonable cost. And you now have the information you need to make the best of it.

We wish you all the best with SQL Server.

# SQL Server Architecture

**PART**

**I**

# Overview of
# Client/Server

**1**

# Roots of Client/Server Computing

Strictly speaking, *client/server* is a style of computing where a client process requests services from a server process. Client/server computing is a broad area within *cooperative processing*, a field that looks at interactive computing between systems. What most distinguishes client/server computing is how processing is distributed between independent applications.

That's all well and good, but in the real world of business computing, the term client/server has come to describe the interaction between fourth generation language (4GL) front-end applications and relational database management systems (RDBMS). That is how the term is used in this book.

Client/server computing represents the marriage of two older processing models: mainframe or host-based computing, and PC/LAN-based computing. Let's look more closely at these two models to understand the purpose of client/server.

For this discussion, a typical business data processing application is broken down into four components:

- User interface
- Application program
- Logical data processing
- Physical data processing

User interface elements control keyboard and screen features, including the implementation of function keys, the field-to-field behavior of the cursor, and the display of data.

Application program elements manage screen-to-screen behavior of the system and menuing, as well as mapping field information to a logical data model.

Logical data processing is the application of *business rules* to application data. This includes data validation and referential integrity. *Data validation* involves ensuring that a provided value is in a valid format or within a valid range of values. (Is the `price` greater than $0.00? Is `social_security_number` in the format ###-##-####?) *Referential integrity* (RI) involves verifying that the data "referenced" in one table exists in a "related" table. (Does the `pub_id` value in the `titles` table exist in the `publishers` table? Is `item_number` found in the `items` table?) It also includes rules particular to a specific organization or application (for example, promised ship dates are always seven days from the date of order, only managers may fill in an "override" column, and so forth).

Physical data processing maps logical data to a physical storage structure. It handles locking, data caching, and indexing, as well as the actual reads and writes from media.

# Host-Based Computing

In the host-based environment, almost all processing occurs on the central host. What little local processing does occur (for instance, with an advanced terminal) is restricted to cursor handling from field to field and handling individual keystrokes. Once a screen of data is transmitted, the host resumes control.

In this environment, applications and data are centralized and exist solely on the host computer. Communications are virtually eliminated as a bottleneck, even when the host and the terminal are separated by hundreds of miles and only share a relatively slow asynchronous connection. Application development and maintenance is also centralized, providing an important measure of control and security. Administration of the system (backup, data maintenance) is handled centrally as well.

Host-based computing has been the platform for most business database applications for the past 20 years. Mainframes and traditional minicomputers have provided solid, reliable performance, but at a tremendous cost. Purchase prices are stratospheric compared to PCs, but the intolerable burden of mainframes has been the cost of maintenance. The combined effect of high purchase prices and exorbitant maintenance fees was that processing cycles centralized on the host became far more expensive than the processing cycles on a PC.

# PC/LAN–Based Computing

When those central mainframe costs were billed to a department manager's budget, the manager turned to a PC to solve departmental problems. The low cost and high availability of PC computing was extremely attractive to people who were forced to wait in line to pay high prices for mainframe processing.

Of course, the real nightmare of host processing has always been the tremendous backlog of applications waiting to be developed and maintained. PC users found that they could build their own applications (admittedly amateur, but often more usable than the enterprise applications) faster than they could fill out the forms requesting apps from the central MIS group.

> **NOTE**
>
> Years ago, a colleague of mine switched to a PC to do all his data analysis and number crunching, even though his data sets were typically large and fairly complex. He explained, "It takes my PC seven minutes to do what the mainframe can do in one-half second, but I have to wait a week to run my job on the mainframe."

Small, private, PC-based databases started to grow into multiuser, LAN-based databases because it made sense—users found ways to share data and be more efficient. Although fileserver-based LANs are well-qualified to handle most office automation (OA) tasks (word processing document storage, shared printing devices, and central OA application maintenance), performance is problematic when managing databases with large amounts of data and/or increasing numbers of concurrent users.

The performance problem relates to the breakdown of application processing on the LAN. User interface processing is performed entirely on the local PC, as is application processing. Logical data processing also occurs on the PC, which can create a data integrity problem (discussed later in this chapter). Physical data processing is split between the local PC and the central fileserver.

A fileserver is a lot like a hard drive attached to your computer by a very long cable (the network), and that cable is usually shared by many users. When your application needs to find a particular record in a database, it retrieves a set of physical blocks from the fileserver file. It is up to the application to find the required record in the data stream that is transmitted.

The efficiency of each request (defined as the ratio of data required to data returned) depends significantly on the capabilities of the application programmer. Using clever indexing strategies, a skilled programmer can write applications in the fileserver environment that support hundreds of thousands and even millions of records.

On the other hand, ad hoc query performance can be disastrous. Users without a sophisticated understanding of how to manipulate indexes to improve performance can initiate queries that—although accurate—require that the system return all records for review by the local PC. Not only is this time-consuming, but it also can lock up system resources for the hours it takes to retrieve the results.

The problem is that the fileserver doesn't know anything about the data itself. All it understands is the physical storage of information on the hard drive. The result is that a simple query could take hours, filling the network with useless traffic and slowing down every other operation at the same time.

---

**NOTE**

Here is a useful analogy to help you understand LAN-DBMS computing.

If you call information to get a telephone number for John Murphy on Cedar Street, the conversation might go like this:

| | |
|---|---|
| OPERATOR: | "Information. What city, please?" |
| YOU: | "Murphysville, please. I would like a number for John Murphy on Cedar Street." |
| OPERATOR: | "Please hold for the number." |

[Pause]

RECORDING:    "Abbott, James, 555-1234."
              "Abbott, Martin, 555-1299."
              "Abby, Philip, 555-9999."
              ...

[Two hours later]

OPERATOR:     "Are you still waiting?"

RECORDING:    "Murphy, James, 555-8888."
              "Murphy, John, 555-6666."
              ...

Of course, by this time, John Murphy has probably moved to another city.

You didn't call to have someone play a recorded telephone book—you called to get a specific number. With LAN-based databases, the server sends your application the telephone book and it's up to the application program to find the number you need.

The other problem with the PC/LAN-based approach to database applications is as much cultural as technical. There are plenty of outstanding PC programmers and sophisticated power users, but every shop seems to have its share of dBASE programmers whose background in computer systems left them with no understanding of the craft of software development.

This latter group tends to be very productive in the early stages of development, but software maintenance is another issue. Because data integrity checks are housed in the application software and application software is distributed, version control and related data integrity control can often fall victim to deadlines and software enhancements.

The fact of life is that application development, report development, and data analysis are gravitating toward individuals with less experience and less training in the information disciplines. This means that the "system" (to be better defined later) needs to become more intelligent, more protective of data integrity, and more efficient.

The host-versus-LAN dichotomy is summarized in the following table:

| Host | LAN |
| --- | --- |
| High speed | Low cost |
| Central administration | Local processing |
| Geographical distribution | High-speed communication |
| High maintenance cost | Graphical User Interfaces |
| Maturity | Opportunity |

The issue of maturity versus opportunity is where a lot of people are stuck right now. Mainframes represent a stable, predictable environment, with dependable utilities, well-developed infrastructures, and large budgets. PCs represent a dynamic, uncontrolled world, short on administrative utilities, long on risk, and with very low cost expectations from management.

# Client/Server to the Rescue!

Client/server computing seeks to merge the best of both worlds: the sheer power and central control of mainframes with the lower cost and better processing balance of PCs. Let's look at how this is achieved.

First, what is client/server computing? For many, client/server is another way of saying cooperative processing. By that definition, any time two separate computers are communicating, you are in a client/server world. Broadly speaking, client/server is a subset of cooperative processing, which is a peer-to-peer architecture.

In the real world (that is, when you see the words in the classified ads), client/server refers to the interaction between user workstations and central database servers. The workstations run application programs that query and update data stored centrally on the database server.

The following are the key points about this client/server model:

- The client process and server process may be (but are not required to be) connected by a LAN or a Wide Area Network (WAN). They both can be running on the same computer.
- The basic language used to communicate between the client and a database server is through Structured Query Language (SQL).

> **NOTE**
>
> SQL is a highly abstract language, in which the programmer or user describes his requirements (add a row of data to a particular table, display rows having the following characteristics, and so forth) without needing to understand or define the physical approach to answering the question. The database server is fully responsible for interpreting an abstract request, finding the fastest method to retrieve the data, and managing the locking and data integrity.
>
> Because SQL is so abstract, the implementation of client and server software tools and client/server applications does not require the close coordination ordinarily required for cooperative processing. In client/server, both sides write to a common API with some confidence that the final result will provide sufficient functionality and good performance.

Client/server provides a new approach to the central/local distribution of work and responsibility. Like a host-based system, client/server is capable of exerting stringent central control over data integrity, administration, and security. Because data is stored centrally, client/server enables you (the administrator) to back up work centrally and to perform periodic maintenance against data stored in a central and secure location.

Because application programs run entirely on the client systems and only database requests are handled centrally, intricate and processor-intensive user interfaces (for example, Windows applications and highly graphical data presentations) are performed by using local processors and local memory.

> **NOTE**
>
> The other resource that can become a bottleneck is the network, especially in a multiuser environment with graphical applications. Anyone who has tried to execute intricate X-Windows applications with multiple X-terminals on a busy network will tell you that executing graphical application processing on a host can cause serious performance degradation on a LAN. (With lots of users, CPU and memory resources on the server can quickly run dry.)
>
> Local application and interface processing (using local CPUs and local memory) make the client/server model work.

Client/server is particularly efficient (when properly implemented) at responding to ad hoc queries. A LAN DBMS often responds to simple requests by delivering huge amounts of useless data, but client/server systems return an answer. This answer, called a *result set,* is only the rows and columns of data you requested from the server in an SQL statement.

As mentioned before, SQL should not dictate a specific method of answering a query; it only defines the data required. How does the server know how to answer the question?

SQL Server includes a *query optimizer,* whose responsibility is to analyze the SQL query, consider the data it is to act on, and decide on an *optimization plan.* The SQL Server optimizer is very powerful and a major factor in the success of the product. (The optimizer is also a fascinating part of the system, and understanding how it works can have a major impact on system performance. For more on the optimizer, take a look at Chapter 12, "Understanding the Query Optimizer.")

The other implication of client/server computing (particularly under the SQL Server model) is that application programming can be distributed without creating complete havoc in the database. SQL Server (and now other competitive products) provides several data integrity structures to perform server-side validation and processing within the database.

Because the server is able to manage data integrity, this burden can be lifted (in part or in whole) from the application development at the client. Consider each item in this list. Where was this processing taking place before? Data integrity was managed within the application, not the database. Application programmers were fully responsible for data integrity. An error in implementing data integrity in an application would likely result in having "bad" data in the database. The detection, identification, and cleanup of this data could require hundreds (or thousands!) of hours. DBAs (Database Administrators) could do no more than provide guidelines, review code, and hope for the best.

The DBA is able to become more active now. The database has extensive capabilities, and the DBA can use the data integrity objects to enforce guidelines on the server side. In many cases, this enables the elimination of thousands of lines of redundant code within applications. Applications become simpler, they are faster to develop, and it is less likely to be a disaster when they contain an error.

# The Critical Factor: Cost

Of course, the driving force behind the move to client/server is the cost difference. Mainframe hardware and software is expensive to buy and expensive to keep. Annual maintenance costs alone make MIS managers see red (instead of black), and the rightsizing trend is intended to bring systems' costs to an acceptable level. For some organizations, this can mean the elimination of a mainframe or not having to perform an expensive mainframe upgrade to handle new application requirements.

> **NOTE**
>
> There is some discussion of using mainframes as giant database servers, and some organizations are already doing this. Because NT systems are now able to provide more storage options in hundreds of gigabytes, they will be more attractive as superservers. As of this writing, mainframe DASD storage costs approximately 30 times what NT drives cost for the same capacity (and that gap is actually widening).
>
> Mainframes as database servers represent an enormous integration problem as well: there is a very limited choice of RDBMS software, and sophisticated connectivity on the mainframe is substantially more difficult than on Windows NT. The proprietary architecture of mainframes imposes a substantial burden on an integrator because of the problems in transferring knowledge and tools from one environment to the other.

Cost issues extend beyond the purchase and maintenance costs of computing equipment. LANs are not cheap, and they can become enormously complex. On the other hand, most organizations are building LANs and WANs for other uses, including office automation, telephony, and videoconferencing. Client/server creates substantially less traffic on the network than some of these other systems.

Many businesses have bought into client/server to gain access to advanced development tools, such as PowerBuilder, Visual Basic, Visual C++, and many useful query and analysis products as well. The opportunity to develop products in less time does more than reduce development costs; it also enables an organization to move more rapidly into new markets, improve customer service, and be more competitive.

> **WARNING**
>
> It is crucial that you understand the business case for client/server in your organization in order to gauge management's expectations of your new systems. Many MIS shops have succeeded in implementing newer technologies, but they have failed in the eyes of management because of a marked difference between what was implemented and what management expected.

This book looks at Sybase from several perspectives. In Part I, "SQL Server Architecture," you'll learn about the fundamental architecture of Sybase SQL Server. In Part II, "Transact-SQL Programming," you'll learn the basic structures that SQL Server supports and how to address those structures. In Part III, "Performance and Tuning," you'll begin to understand how SQL Server uses those structures in order to implement the system to get the best performance. Part IV, "System Administration," looks at SQL Server from an administrative standpoint so that you can understand the strengths and weaknesses of the product, along with the background you'll need to develop an aggressive approach to maintaining and tuning the server. In the final section, Part V, "Introduction to Open Client Programming," you can look at some programming interfaces for writing client applications.

# Summary

You and your organization have traded in the maturity and stability you were used to with mainframe systems for the dynamism and opportunity of the client/server environment. Maybe you decided to step up from a LAN DBMS to a database capable of supporting hundreds and thousands of users and hundreds of gigabytes of information.

This book provides you with the information you need to bolster the system and to provide the reliable service your organization expects from its data resources.

# Understanding the Sybase Client/Server Architecture

**2**

**IN THIS CHAPTER**

Since the time that "client/server" became an over-used, misinterpreted computer buzzword, different vendors have been attempting to refine their implementations of the concepts discussed in Chapter 1, "Overview of Client/Server." In this section, I walk through a comparison of different database engine architectures—the heart of any client/server DBMS. From that comparison, the history of the Sybase/Microsoft client/server architecture, starting in 1986 with the first release of SQL Server 1.0, will be more understandable. The chapter culminates with a discussion of how Sybase System 11 SQL Server has emerged and a brief review of its most interesting features and capabilities.

# Comparative Database Architectures 101

In the current client/server world, there are two dominant architectures for writing database engines. Understanding both architectures aids in understanding how yours works, so let's take a look at both.

The first type is the multi-process engine, which is characterized by multiple executables running simultaneously. Typically, these engines consume significantly higher system resources than the other type, but appear (with limited testing) to scale to dramatically larger platforms more easily than their counterparts.

Second is the single-process, multi-threaded architecture, which is used by SQL Server. Instead of running distinct executables or applications for each task, this architecture relies on multi-threading work within a single application. The benefit is substantially lower hardware requirements for a given performance level.

## Multi-Process Database Engines

Some database engines rely on multiple executable applications to perform user-query work. In this architecture, each time a user logs in, it actually starts a separate instance of the database engine itself. Each user login, therefore, is running its own instance of the database application. In order to coordinate many users accessing the same sets of data, these executables work with other "global coordinator" tasks to schedule operations among these various users. Applications in a database of this type communicate using a proprietary *inter-process communication* (IPC) facility. Although not necessarily efficient, Dynamic Data Exchange under Microsoft Windows is one IPC.

Multi-process database engines typically are used on mainframe databases, and are popular on the MVS operating system, because MVS provides IPC facilities for applications.

The most popular example of a multi-process database engine typically isn't run on mainframes. Oracle Corporation's Oracle Server is a true multi-process database engine. Sixteen different types of executables are loaded by the Oracle Server to perform different tasks. User connections start user database executables. System executables manage multi-user access to data tables, transaction logging and versioning, and other features, such as distributed transactions, data replication, and so on.

Each time a user connects to an Oracle database, it loads a distinct instance of the Oracle database executable. Queries are passed to that executable, which works in concert with the other executables on the server to return result sets, manage locking, and other necessary data access functions. Figure 2.1 illustrates how multiple database engines require multiple instances of the database executable. This requires substantial system resources to provide the memory resources and handles to operating system resources.

**FIGURE 2.1.**

*Multi-process database engines start many instances of the database executable to provide access to data for multiple users.*

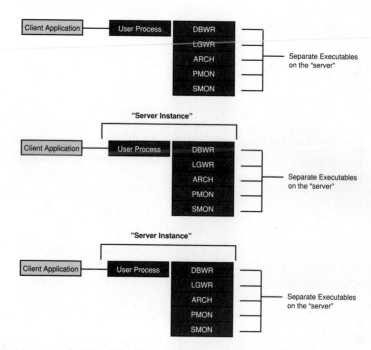

# The Pros and Cons of Multi-Process Database Engines

Most multi-process database engines were developed before operating systems supported features such as threads and preemptive scheduling. As a result, "breaking down" a single operation meant writing a distinct executable to handle that operation. This enabled two important benefits for database processing: First, a database could support multiple simultaneous users, providing for data centralization on a network; second, it provided for scalability through the addition of more CPUs and the physical machine.

In a multi-tasking operating system, the OS divides processing time among multiple applications (tasks) by giving each task a "slice" of the CPU's available work time. In this way, there still is only one task executing at one time. However, the tasks share the processor because the OS grants a particular percentage of the CPU's time to each task. As a result, multiple applications appear to be running simultaneously on a single CPU. The real advantage, however, comes when multiple CPUs can be used by the operating system.

Applications love operating systems that support multi-tasking as well as symmetric multi-processing. The capability to schedule distinct tasks to distinct processors gives applications the true capability to run simultaneously. As a result, today's multi-process database management systems scale to larger numbers of processors more readily than their counterparts. Most industry polls and publications acknowledge that Oracle Server can scale to large numbers of processors and do so efficiently—that is, as new processors are added, Oracle takes advantage of that processor, so that there is a net gain in processing power for the database. As you'll see in the discussion on multi-threaded DBMSs, next, that may or may not be what your business really needs.

# Single-Process, Multi-Threaded Database Engines

Multi-threaded database engines tackle the thorny issue of multi-user access in a different way, but use similar principles. Instead of relying on a multi-tasking operating system to schedule applications on a CPU, a multi-threaded database engine takes on this responsibility for itself. In theory, the database engine's capability to "fend for itself" gives it greater portability, because the database manages scheduling individual task execution, memory, and disk access.

Multi-threaded systems are more efficient for a given hardware platform. Whereas a multi-process database uses between 500KB and 1MB of memory for each user connection (remember, that memory is protected and dedicated to an executable file), a multi-threaded DBMS uses only 50KB to 100KB of RAM. In addition, because the database executable itself manages these multiple threads, there is no need for a costly and inefficient inter-process communication mechanism.

Instead, the database engine itself coordinates the multiple operations it must perform, and sends these instructions to the operating system for final execution. In this way, the database time-slices individual operations by taking individual threads, one at a time, and sending the user instructions on those threads to the operating system. Instead of the OS time-slicing applications, the DBMS time-slices threads. (See Figure 2.2.)

In this way, the database uses a finite element of work (a thread) for a variety of operations (user instructions, locking data pages, disk I/O, cache I/O, and so on) instead of a multi-process DBMS, which uses specialized applications for each.

This architecture forms the heart of all Sybase SQL Server versions through System 11 and, without the multi-processing features, also for SQL Server on OS/2. (In fact, Sybase developers wrote the code that Microsoft distributed for its then-new operating system, OS/2. Microsoft has since assumed more and more responsibility for this code base, but the underlying architecture is identical to the one Sybase developed in its first release of SQL Server.)

**FIGURE 2.2.**

*Multi-threaded database engines can provide access to data for multiple users with only a single database engine.*

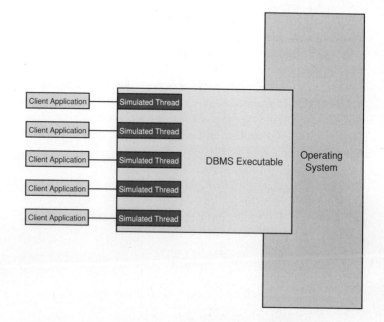

# Pros and Cons of Multi-Threading Database Engines

Sybase was quick to point out the performance it could achieve on relatively small hardware platforms when SQL Server first debuted. In fact, SQL Server was typically one of the fastest, if not the fastest, DBMS for any given database size or hardware platform. That performance is derived, in part, from the efficiency of a multi-threaded DBMS relative to other multi-process competitors. A single executable running multiple internal threads consumes far fewer system resources, and it uses those it consumes much more effectively than in other architectures.

> **NOTE**
>
> As a developer using SQL Server 1.0 for OS/2 a few years ago, I was able to convince my management to buy what was, at the time, the hottest PC available: a 486/DX33 with 16 MB of RAM, and three SCSI hard disks. With a 16Mbps Token Ring adapter, we were able to support 50 simultaneous users with almost instantaneous query response using databases as large as a full gigabyte (remember, this was 1991). We thought this performance was amazing from a hardware platform that cost only $12,000 (again, this was 1991) but could run "real" applications.
>
> Today, that $12,000 could buy a two-processor Intel machine with 64MB of RAM, a Fast Ethernet (100Mbps) network card, and a stack of 1.0GB or 2.0GB SCSI fixed disks, and support literally dozens if not hundreds of users and a 10GB database!

One major benefit from this enhanced efficiency is the reduction in RAM requirements for the server, saving precious megabytes for data and procedure caching. Cache is a critical element for any serious database application, and maximizing both the quantity and usage of that cache is an important performance factor. Although the need for such efficiency has been somewhat mitigated by falling RAM prices, memory still is a precious commodity. As you'll see in Chapter 30, "Configuring and Tuning the SQL Server," there's no such thing as too much memory!

The most significant detractor of a multi-threaded DBMS is more implementational than architectural, but it still reflects choices the database vendor may make.

Scalability with multi-threaded DBMSs can be an issue, if only because the degree to which a multi-threaded database is scalable is a function of the database vendor's ability to take a single operation and break it down so that multiple threads can work on that single operation.

Single-process DBMSs are not inherently restricted from using SMP hardware. Quite the contrary: Their efficient use of threads makes them better candidates for such platforms, because of their ability to squeeze the most from the least. However, SMP support competes with portability, because different hardware vendors implement SMP support in different ways.

As a result, Sybase has implemented an operating system–neutral means of accessing hardware- and operating system–level SMP support. This has contributed some overhead to SQL Server, and has limited its ability to scale to larger numbers of processors. This is more a function of the parallelization of threads than anything else. SQL Server has implemented user connections as individual threads—but only as single thread operations, not multi-thread operations. Therefore, when a user executes a query that scans a 4GB table, that user has only one thread of execution to do the scanning. Because threads are the most finite element of work in SQL Server, only a single thread can be scheduled to one CPU at any given time. Therefore, there is no parallelization of work for this user; there is a single task, running on a single CPU, at any given time. Any performance benefits resulting from SMP are the result of another processor being made available before the existing processor would be—which is a scheduling benefit, not a true processing benefit.

Sybase originally promised that it would address this problem with the 11.0 release of SQL Server. While Sybase did find ways to get better performance on an SMP platform, multi-threading of individual query operations has been postponed at least until the 11.1 release.

## System 11 Features

System 10 provided a host of new features to help administrators and programmers run SQL Server databases with less administrative overhead. SQL Server added support for declarative data integrity checks (data protection schemes that were *declared* (hence the name) instead of requiring programming. The introduction of the Backup Server substantially improved both the flexibility and the performance of the backup and restore subsystem. New datatypes were added and new syntactic structures were provided.

System 11 addresses more fundamental performance issues, particularly those encountered when running SQL Server with large numbers of users or large amounts of data. Here are some of the most important new features of System 11:

- *Named caches* allow the administrator to separate memory into smaller pools for use with specific databases or objects.
- *Improved optimization* provides substantially better performance on certain complex queries.
- *Larger block sizes* for memory storage provide better table scan performance.
- *Table partitioning* allows data loads to run somewhat in parallel.
- *Revised configuration control* simplifies one administrative task.
- *Private log caches* for each active session allow high-transaction systems to run more efficiently.

Most of the changes are deep within the system. Some, like improved optimization or private log caches, work right out of the box. Others, like named caches or large block sizes, require proper configuration and administration to get a substantial performance benefit.

# The Two APIs of Any Client/Server Database

Most computer professionals are familiar with some form of database technology because most business applications are worthless without some central data store. Accessing that data is the job of programmers, who require two distinctly different languages. There is a host language, which for ages now has been COBOL. However, COBOL isn't a database language; it's a generic programming language with file-access capabilities. To access a database, you need a language to get to that database.

Through most of the 1970s, database access came through embedded languages and precompilers. Statements that accessed the database were inserted using special codes or function calls that marked the source code as a flag for the precompiler. The source code was fed to the precompiler first, and the database-specific code was compiled into separate instructions. The host-language compiler took the standard COBOL code, turned it into a binary object, and linked it so the operating system could understand it as an executable.

## Host Language APIs for SQL Server

That same process goes into writing SQL Server applications, with an interesting twist: There is no precompiler. Instead, the database-specific calls reside in the source code of the application merely as strings—and they stay that way through the host language's compilation process. In the resulting executable, all of the database queries still are stored as strings. In fact, those queries won't run on the SQL Server until the source code is properly compiled and runs for the first time!

**NOTE**

Of course, it's a really good idea to always check your SQL as soon as possible using some kind of interactive query tool like isql, which is provided with SQL Server.

Most books and documentation written about SQL Server (or any client/server database, for that matter) don't address this issue. They discuss SQL syntax, and they discuss client library API calls. However, integrating the two is a topic most people just assume. It's a dangerous assumption. Improperly using DB Library or ct-Library or Transact-SQL calls can contribute to bad applications just as easily as can bad design.

This fundamental difference between interface types defines what a call-level interface is. Both DB Library and ct-Library are *call-level interfaces*: The host application makes native language calls into a library of database functions. The data manipulation statements are stored as strings, instead of being marked for precompilation like those in embedded languages.

For SQL Server, there are two different APIs that every application uses. The client host-language API that has traditionally been the SQL Server standard is DB Library, although more and more organizations are standardizing now on ct-Library. Sybase introduced DB Library with the original version of SQL Server, and Microsoft used DB Library for all versions of SQL Server. Marking a change in SQL Server's focus, ct-Library actually is now the strategic API for Sybase.

## SQL Is an API?

Transact-SQL is the second of the two APIs for SQL Server. Why define T-SQL as an API? Most importantly, it fits the definition! An API is an access point to the resources of an operating system or application that provides a specific set of services. Transact-SQL, through its enhancements to the SQL standard (in the form of functions, datatypes, logical operators, and branching logic), is the access point to SQL Server's data processing resources and services. It is the second of two APIs for SQL Server, because DB Library and ct-Library also are access points to a different, but still necessary, set of resources and services.

SQL Server applications need both in order to function. A standard SELECT statement is useless unless it can be passed to SQL Server. A sqllogin C-language function is used to open a connection to SQL Server, but that connection is equally useless unless T-SQL statements can be passed over that connection, prompting SQL Server to pass results back to the client.

Sound like fun? It gets better. As mentioned above, Transact-SQL is a dialect of ANSI standard SQL. ANSI has two primary standards: one codified in 1989, the other in 1992. SQL Server is ANSI 1989–compliant, and System 11 is now technically ANSI 92–compliant.

# How Does SQL Server Process Queries?

SQL Server doesn't process SQL statements until they are passed to the server over the network. There are some implicit assumptions here: first, that the client application is capable of formulating queries; second, that there is a network for transporting these query instructions to the server; and third, that the server is capable of using the network to return the results of the query.

These assumptions form the architecture that makes up the SQL Server Client/Server Architecture. With any query you execute, whether interactively through isql, or within an application, all of these steps take place:

1. ct-Library receives an SQL string from the client application.

2. ct-Library associates that string with a particular user connection opened at the server.

3. ct-Library passes the string along that connection to the network library.

4. SQL Server's Network Library "disassembles" the SQL string into a data packet for the network you are running. The data chunk of the packet conforms to SQL Server's formatting, which is called *tabular data stream.*

5. The network delivers those packets to SQL Server.

6. SQL Server has a network library, too, which listens for queries to arrive.

7. The server-side network library re-assembles the query into a string, and passes that string to the SQL Server query processor.

8. SQL Server processes the query and, if it is a select statement, generates a result set.

9. SQL Server passes the result set to the server-side network library, which disassembles the result set into tabular data stream packets.

10. The client-side network library receives the packets, and reassembles them into a result set, which resides on the client in a connection-specific memory region.

11. ct-Library API calls access the memory region, extracting the data held there, and putting it into host-language variables (variables that are local to the client application) for display to the user.

While this may seem like too many steps, the process has been broken down to a very low level. You'll see this process in more detail in Chapters 36, "DB-Library Programming," and 37, "ct-Library Programming," when I discuss DB Library and ct-Library programming for SQL Server.

What is most significant about this process is that, regardless of the operating system, these steps are followed every time you send a query to SQL Server.

# Summary

Sybase has taken important steps with the System 11 release of SQL Server toward providing a truly scalable, multi-processing engine for processing huge data and handling enormous transaction volumes.

While all client/server databases make use of two APIs for developing applications, only SQL Server using DB Library or ct-Library, and Transact-SQL provide the two necessary means to access SQL Server's powerful features.

PART

**II**

**IN THIS PART**

# Transact-SQL Programming

# Introduction to Transact-SQL

The next several chapters describe the building blocks of Transact-SQL, the programming language used to create, manage, and manipulate data and data objects in SQL Server. Although application programmers use a variety of products and programming languages to build applications for SQL Server data, whenever an application needs to change or retrieve the data, it must transmit a T-SQL query to the server. This chapter introduces the fundamental commands that allow you to retrieve or modify data. In later chapters, you will learn to use the T-SQL constructs to create and manage SQL Server data objects.

# What Is Transact-SQL?

To communicate with the SQL Server and to manipulate objects stored in SQL Server, client programs and stored procedures use a variety of Structured Query Language (SQL) called Transact-SQL, or T-SQL. T-SQL provides most of the capabilities of the standard 1989 version of SQL as published by the American National Standards Institute (ANSI SQL 89), as well as several extensions that allow greater programmability and flexibility in the language.

## Structured Query Language

SQL provides a language for accessing data objects using substantially less programming code than required by a third-generation language. An SQL query addresses data in sets rather than requiring the programmer to construct a typical loop. For example, the following pseudo-code resembles the code required to modify a set of rows in a table:

```
open file
while not(eof)
begin
    lock record
    read record
    if column-value = value
    write record
    unlock record
end
close file
```

Using SQL, you can accomplish the same task with a single statement like this:

```
update table-name
set column-name = new-value
where column-value = value
```

The atomic SQL statement is far more likely to represent a work unit than the atomic line of code in a third-generation language. This greater level of abstraction means better reliability, easier maintenance, and more readable, meaningful code.

SQL provides some additional benefits:

- There's no need for explicit locking statements: the server manages all locking.

- There's no reference to the physical location of the data: the server translates a logical name into a linked set of physical locations.

- There's no specification of indexing or search strategy: the server identifies the most efficient method of finding the requested data.

In later chapters we'll explore the mechanics of locking in SQL Server, the method the server uses to manage table storage, and query-optimization strategies. For now, we'll continue to discuss the basics of T-SQL.

## T-SQL and ANSI SQL

Standard SQL provides mechanisms to manipulate and manage data. Some components of SQL include:

- Data Definition Language (DDL) to create and drop data structures and to manage object level security

- Data Modification Language (DML) to add, modify, and remove data from tables

- Data Control Language (DCL) to secure table data

Standard SQL was originally conceived as a query and execution language, not as a full-fledged programming language. Transact-SQL extends SQL by adding program flow-control constructs (if and while, for example), local variables, and other capabilities to allow the DBA to build code-based objects, including stored procedures and triggers.

## Statements, Batches, and Elements of T-SQL

A Transact-SQL statement (almost) always includes at least one keyword: a verb indicating an action. For example, select asks the server to retrieve rows of data, while update tells the server to change the contents of the specified rows. In this chapter we'll look closely at four commands, select, insert, update, and delete.

> **NOTE**
>
> The one case in which a keyword is not required is in the execution of a stored procedure. When the name of a stored procedure is the first element of a batch submitted to SQL Server, the execute keyword is optional.

Other keywords introduce new elements of a statement. For example, the from keyword tells the server that a list of source tables follows. The where keyword introduces a list of logically connected conditions specifying the rows affected by a query.

T-SQL statements are submitted to the server in *batches*. A batch is a set of statements sent to the server at a single time. Every SQL Server application has a mechanism for telling the server to execute a batch of statements. For example, in the following isql session, the go directive tells isql to submit the three preceding lines as a batch to the server:

```
1> select au_lname, au_fname, phone
2> from authors
3> where state = "CA"
4> go
```

## Server Processing Steps

When you submit an SQL batch to the server, the batch is parsed as a whole, optimized and compiled as a whole, then executed statement by statement.

Take a closer look at each of these steps. The server *parses* the batch to check the syntax of each command and keyword, and to validate table and column names. During optimization, the server determines the most efficient method for resolving a query. (There's much more on optimization in Part III, "Performance and Tuning.") *Compilation* creates an executable version of the batch. *Execution* is the step-by-step performance of each statement in the batch.

If parsing or compilation fails for any reason (for example, a syntax error or a type mismatch), the batch fails and no statements are executed. If the batch fails because of an error during execution, some subset of the entire batch may have been executed.

## Who Uses SQL and Transact-SQL?

The short answer is, "Everybody."

If you want to interact with SQL Server data, you must submit a query in SQL. If you want to write a program to store as an SQL Server stored procedure, you must write Transact-SQL code.

Whether you are working from PowerBuilder; writing a C application in UNIX, Windows, or MS-DOS; or using Microsoft Access or Visual Basic, or any of the thousand other products that interact with SQL Server, you ultimately submit an SQL query to the server. Some tools do the dirty work for you by providing a visual interface to let you identify the components of the ultimate query, then submit the query behind the scenes. You may never see the SQL, but it's still there.

In this chapter we'll discuss the basic SQL data-retrieval and data-modification capabilities. Chapters 4, "Transact-SQL Datatypes," and 5, "Creating and Altering Database Objects," explore SQL datatypes and the creation of tables and views. In Chapter 6, "Transact-SQL Programming Constructs," you learn how to use the programming constructs with T-SQL, and in Chapter 7, "Transact-SQL Program Structures," we'll review how to build objects based on SQL code.

> **NOTE**
>
> If you already know SQL, you may want to skim most of this chapter. Look at the notes, which highlight performance characteristics of SQL on SQL Server. Be sure to read about the use of worktables in ordering data and in performing aggregate functions.
>
> If you are just learning SQL, plow through this and try executing some of the queries presented to get a "feel" for the language.
>
> This book is not intended to be a detailed text on SQL syntax. There already are several excellent books to help you learn the intricate details of SQL programming. Instead, I give you some SQL background, then forge into those areas where the Transact-SQL language differs from standard SQL.

## How Do I Test SQL Queries?

If SQL Server is installed on your network, you need an SQL editor that enables you to write SQL statements and submit them to the server. There are two obvious choices:

- Use the Aurora Desktop product included on the CD-ROM in the back of this book. (I think it's a really cool and easy way to execute SQL. But I'm biased, as I wrote it.) Instructions for installation and use of Aurora are included in a readme file on the CD-ROM.

- Use the character-based utility, `isql`. This is included in the installation of the server in the bin subdirectory. To run `isql`, you must set some environmental variables. (See Chapter 24, "SQL Server Installation and Connectivity," for more on this.)

For now, let's assume that you can login to a server. For the following examples, use the `pubs2` database. (I discuss what actually happens when you "use" a database later.) Type this command, then execute it:

```
use pubs2
```

To execute the query, press a button that says Execute; or, if you are using `isql`, type the word `go` on its own line. Now you're ready to execute the examples in this chapter.

# Retrieving Data with *select*

When people think of SQL, they think first of the `select` statement. A `select` statement asks the server to prepare a result and return it to the client. In standard SQL, `select` is used to retrieve data from tables and views. In T-SQL, `select` also permits the user to retrieve information from the system and to set the values of local variables.

# Tables, Rows, and Columns

Most SQL statements retrieve data from tables. Logically, a *table* is a two-dimensional structure consisting of *rows* (or instances) of data, each having one or many *columns* (or attributes). In the next chapter you learn how to create tables. For now, you can retrieve data from the tables in the pubs2 database.

# The *pubs2* Database

When SQL Server was installed, you had the option to install the pubs2 database. This is a collection of tables containing sample data related to a fictitious book-distribution company.

> **TIP**
>
> If the pubs2 database is not installed on your server, you should install it or ask your administrator to do so. All of the examples in the Sybase documentation, as well as many of the examples in this book, are based on that database.
>
> To install pubs2 now, you need to run the script file, instpbs2, on your server. Type this command at the operating system prompt in the scripts subdirectory within the sybase install directory:
>
> ```
> isql -Usa -Sservername -iinstpbs2 -oinstpbs2.out -e
> ```
>
> Then provide your sa password when prompted. Note that the -Sservername parameter is optional. (Substitute the name of your server.)
>
> This command starts isql, logs you in as the sa, passes the name of an input and output file, and instructs the server to include the executed commands with the server response in the output file. If you have disabled the sa account, pass the name of the new account with the sa role.

The database contains several tables, each listing information about a single type of entity. There's a publishers table, with the names of the publishers who publish books; an authors table contains the names of the authors who wrote the books; a titles table contains titles (these are the books themselves); and a stores table contains the names of stores that sell the books. There also are tables stating the relationship between the tables: the titleauthor table shows which author(s) wrote which title(s), the sales table lists the stores' purchases, and the salesdetail table provides the details about which title(s) were included as part of each sale.

> **NOTE**
>
> There are other tables with special characteristics to demonstrate additional features of the server, including the `blurbs` table to demonstrate binary large objects (BLOBs) consisting of text, the `au_pix` table to demonstrate binary BLOBs for images, and the `discount` and `royalty` tables to show how to perform more off-beat join operations and other kinds of queries.

# Selecting Data from a Table

To retrieve data from a table, you submit a `select` statement. The (extremely) simplified syntax for a `select` statement is

```
select <column-list>
from <table-name>
```

The following example retrieves the last and first names of all rows in the `authors` table:

```
select au_lname, au_fname
from authors
```

> **NOTE**
>
> After you write an SQL statement, you need to execute it. The method of executing statements depends on your SQL editor. If you are using the `isql` utility provided with SQL Server, you must add the word go on its own line after the SQL, like this:
>
> ```
> select au_lname, au_fname
> from authors
> go
> ```
>
> Note that go *is not an SQL command or keyword.* It is an instruction to the `isql` utility to execute everything typed since the last go.
>
> If you are using some other query program, you need to find out how that program executes queries. Look for a button or menu choice labeled `execute` or `go`.

The first and most important point about SQL is that it operates on *sets* of data, not on individual rows. This statement returns all rows specified—in this case, all rows in the table. (Shortly, we'll explore how to limit affected rows with a `where` clause.)

# SQL Result Sets

Let's take a look at the results returned from this query. Because you specified two columns in the select list, the result set contains two columns:

```
au_lname                                         au_fname
-------------------------------------------      --------------------
Bennet                                           Abraham
Blotchet-Halls                                   Reginald
Carson                                           Cheryl
DeFrance                                         Michel
Dull                                             Ann
Green                                            Marjorie
Greene                                           Morningstar
Gringlesby                                       Burt
Hunter                                           Sheryl
Karsen                                           Livia
Locksley                                         Chastity
MacFeather                                       Stearns
McBadden                                         Heather
O'Leary                                          Michael
Panteley                                         Sylvia
Ringer                                           Albert
Ringer                                           Anne
Smith                                            Meander
Straight                                         Dick
Stringer                                         Dirk
White                                            Johnson
Yokomoto                                         Akiko
del Castillo                                     Innes

(23 rows affected)
```

> **NOTE**
>
> This is a complete result set, with each of the 23 rows displayed. Most of the result sets that follow are truncated, with ellipses (...) to stand for the missing rows. I've included complete results sets only when it was necessary for you to see all of the data to understand the example.

The results returned by most queries actually are tables themselves, consisting of one or more columns, with zero or more rows of data.

> **NOTE**
>
> Standard result sets can be redirected into a new table using the into keyword. Some keywords yield a result set that is not a pure table. For instance, the compute keyword (described in detail later in this chapter) produces additional result rows that don't fit the column/row structure. You cannot direct a result set into a new table in combination with a compute clause.

# Column-Based Expressions

You can manipulate the contents of columns in the select list as in the next example, where the proposed increase in the price of books is 10 percent of the current price:

```
select title_id, type, price, price * .1
from titles
```

Here is the result set, containing four columns of data. The fourth column is an expression derived from price:

```
title_id type          price

BU1032   business              19.99              1.99900
BU1111   business              11.95              1.19500
BU2075   business               2.99              0.29900
BU7832   business              19.99              1.99900
MC2222   mod_cook              19.99              1.99900
...
PS7777   psychology             7.99              0.79900
TC3218   trad_cook             20.95              2.09500
TC4203   trad_cook             11.95              1.19500
TC7777   trad_cook             14.99              1.49900

(18 rows affected)
```

The basic arithmetic operators (+, -, *, and /) are available in expressions, as well as modulo (%), bitwise logical operators (AND &, OR ¦, XOR ^, NOT ~), and string concatenation (∪).

Here is an example of string concatenation, combining the contents of two columns and a constant string expression:

```
select au_lname +", " + au_fname
from authors
```

```
-------------------------------------------------------------
Bennet, Abraham
Blotchet-Halls, Reginald
Carson, Cheryl
DeFrance, Michel
Dull, Ann
Green, Marjorie
Greene, Morningstar
Gringlesby, Burt
Hunter, Sheryl
...
White, Johnson
Yokomoto, Akiko
del Castillo, Innes

(23 rows affected)
```

# Manipulating Column Names in the Select List

Look closely at the column headings for each of the result sets provided above. Wherever a column appears unmodified in the select list, the column name is provided as the default column heading. Where any kind of expression or manipulation takes place, the column heading is blank.

To provide a column heading for a blank column, or to replace the default heading, you specify a *column alias*. Here are a couple of examples:

```
select title_id, type, price "original price", price * .1 discount
from titles
```

```
title_id type           original price        discount
-------- ----------   ------------------------ -------------------------
BU1032   business                  19.99             1.99900
BU1111   business                  11.95             1.19500
BU2075   business                   2.99             0.29900
BU7832   business                  19.99             1.99900
MC2222   mod_cook                  19.99             1.99900
...
TC4203   trad_cook                 11.95             1.19500
TC7777   trad_cook                 14.99             1.49900

(18 rows affected)
```

```
select "Full Author Name" = au_lname +", " + au_fname
from authors
```

```
Full Author Name
-----------------------------------------------------------------
Bennet, Abraham
Blotchet-Halls, Reginald
Carson, Cheryl
DeFrance, Michel
Dull, Ann
...
White, Johnson
Yokomoto, Akiko
del Castillo, Innes

(23 rows affected)
```

These two examples do the same thing in different ways. The first, which is the ANSI SQL standard method, states the alias after the column expression. Note that "original price" appears in quotes because the alias itself contains two words. The quotes do not appear in the result heading. In the second example, the alias precedes the column expression with an equals (=) sign. The two aliasing methods have the same effect.

> **TIP**
>
> Newcomers to SQL often forget commas in the select list, which is a difficult and subtle problem to catch unless you know it can happen. For example, look at this query and the result:
>
> ```
> select city state from publishers
> state
> --------------------
> Boston
> Washington
> Berkeley
>
> (3 rows affected)
> ```
>
> What happened to the state column? Without the comma between `city` and `state`, the word "state" was interpreted as a column heading for the `city` column. Unless you knew to look for this problem, you could spend hours trying to fix your server, your network, and your workstation, without looking at the query.
>
> A simple solution to troubleshooting SQL is to always ask an easy question first: how many columns did I request? How many came back? If those numbers differ, look at the query and make certain you really asked for the right number of columns of data.

## Using *distinct*

The `distinct` keyword removes duplicate rows from the result set. Without `distinct`, this query returns one row per row in the source table:

```
select type
from titles
type
------------
business
business
business
business
mod_cook
mod_cook
UNDECIDED
popular_comp
popular_comp
popular_comp
psychology
psychology
psychology
psychology
psychology
trad_cook
trad_cook
trad_cook

(18 rows affected)
```

Adding `distinct` instructs the server to remove duplicate rows from the result set:

```
select distinct type
from titles

type
------------
UNDECIDED
business
mod_cook
popular_comp
psychology
trad_cook
```

The scope of the `distinct` keyword is over the entire select list, not over a single column. In the next query, containing two columns, the `distinct` keyword identifies unique *combinations* of `city` and `state` in the `authors` table. Here is the complete list of cities and states in the authors table:

```
select city, state
from authors

city                  state
--------------------- ----
Menlo Park            CA
Oakland               CA
Berkeley              CA
San Jose              CA
Oakland               CA
Lawrence              KS
Berkeley              CA
Palo Alto             CA
Covelo                CA
San Francisco         CA
Nashville             TN
Corvallis             OR
Walnut Creek          CA
Ann Arbor             MI
Gary                  IN
Oakland               CA
Oakland               CA
Oakland               CA
Rockville             MD
Palo Alto             CA
Vacaville             CA
Salt Lake City        UT
Salt Lake City        UT

(23 rows affected)
```

Here is the same result set, with `distinct`:

```
select distinct city, state
from authors

city                  state
--------------------- ----
Gary                  IN
Covelo                CA
Oakland               CA
```

```
Berkeley         CA
Lawrence         KS
San Jose         CA
Ann Arbor        MI
Corvallis        OR
Nashville        TN
Palo Alto        CA
Rockville        MD
Vacaville        CA
Menlo Park       CA
Walnut Creek     CA
San Francisco    CA
Salt Lake City   UT

(16 rows affected)
```

In the result set, note that many rows may contain the same value for a specific city or state; the `distinct` operator removes only duplicate combinations.

> **TIP**
>
> Don't use `distinct` if you don't have to. It forces the server to perform an extra sorting and processing step that will slow your work when it is not necessary.

# Using *select* *

You can include an asterisk (*) in the select list in the place of a column or columns. The asterisk stands for all columns in a table. For example:

```
select *
from publishers
```

This is a convenient shortcut for ad hoc queries, because it displays all columns in logical order and the user does not have to know the names of columns to display information.

```
pub_id pub_name                                city           state
------ ----------------------------------      ----------     -----
0736   New Age Books                           Boston         MA
0877   Binnet & Hardley                        Washington     DC
1389   Algodata Infosystems                    Berkeley       CA

(3 rows affected)
```

> **WARNING**
>
> Using `select *` is not recommended in programs of any type because it may lead to unexpected program behavior, or to runtime application failures. The problem is that the server expands the * into a list of all columns in the table during the parsing stage. If a database administrator adds an additional column to a four-column table, queries that once returned four columns now will return five.

The problem created by using select * becomes even more complex if the user is restricted from viewing the contents of the new column. Parsing of the * occurs prior to permissions being checked. Therefore, a user expecting a four-column result may be refused access to a result set previously accessed because of permissions problems on a column the user never knew existed.

# Filtering Rows with where

SQL is a set-processing language, so data modification and data retrieval statements act on all rows in a table unless a where clause limits the scope of the query. The where clause must follow the from clause:

```
select <column-list>
from <table-name>
where <condition>
```

In the following example, the where clause restricts the result set to authors from California:

```
select au_lname, au_fname
from authors
where state = "CA"
```

This section examines the methods available for limiting the number of rows affected by a query.

## Equality and Inequality Operators

In the preceding example, the condition is in the form

```
<column name> = <constant expression>
```

The server evaluates each row to determine whether the search expression is true for that row.

> **NOTE**
>
> The server does not always have to examine every row in a table to find rows that match a query. It can use indexes to speed searches if it decides that that is more efficient. The various search methods used by the server are described in detail in Chapter 12, "Understanding the Query Optimizer."

The search condition is more generally in the form

```
<expression> <operator> <expression>
```

where either expression is any valid combination of constant, variable, and column-based expressions; and where the operator is

- ◼ =
- ◼ <> or != (equivalent symbols meaning "not equal to")
- ◼ >
- ◼ <
- ◼ >=
- ◼ <=
- ◼ !<
- ◼ !>

For example, the following query compares price, total unit sales, and advance in the `titles` table:

```
select type, title_id, price
from titles
where price * total_sales < advance
```

## Inequalities and Character Data

When you use inequalities to compare character strings, the server determines which string would appear first in the current server *sort order*. Using the default sort order, which is based on the ASCII character set, cp-850, the server selects and orders character data based on the standard ASCII character set. For example, the condition

```
type < "mod_cook"
```

would find the value `business`, but would also find `UNDECIDED`, because uppercase characters appear before lowercase characters in the ASCII character set.

## Logical OR and AND

You can connect multiple search conditions with the `OR` and `AND` keywords. This example displays authors from California or from Salt Lake City:

```
select au_id, city, state
from authors
where state = "CA" or city = "Salt Lake City"
```

| au_id | city | state |
| --- | --- | --- |
| 172-32-1176 | Menlo Park | CA |
| 213-46-8915 | Oakland | CA |
| 238-95-7766 | Berkeley | CA |
| 267-41-2394 | San Jose | CA |
| 274-80-9391 | Oakland | CA |
| 409-56-7008 | Berkeley | CA |
| 427-17-2319 | Palo Alto | CA |

```
472-27-2349 Covelo              CA
486-29-1786 San Francisco       CA
672-71-3249 Walnut Creek        CA
724-08-9931 Oakland             CA
724-80-9391 Oakland             CA
756-30-7391 Oakland             CA
846-92-7186 Palo Alto           CA
893-72-1158 Vacaville           CA
899-46-2035 Salt Lake City      UT
998-72-3567 Salt Lake City      UT

(17 rows affected)
```

## *between* and Ranges of Data

You can search for data in a range using a condition in the form

```
<expression> between <expression> and <expression>
```

In this query, the search condition compares a column to a specific range. This is the most common use of the between operator.

```
select title_id, price
from titles
where price between $5 and $10
```

Note that between includes the endpoint values; thus, between has the same effect as two conditions connected with AND:

```
select title_id, price
from titles
where price >= $5 and price <= $10
```

Use not between to identify rows outside the range, as in this example:

```
select title_id, price
from titles
where price not between $5 and $10
```

Note that not between *excludes* endpoint values; not between has the same effect as two conditions connected with OR:

```
select title_id, price
from titles
where price < $5 or price > $10
```

## Lists of Possible Values with *in (...)*

Use in to provide a list of possible values for a column or expression:

```
select title_id, price
from titles
where type in ("mod_cook", "trad_cook", "business")
```

The server reviews the value of type in each row; if the value appears in the list, the condition is true for the row. Note that in has the same effect as multiple equality conditions (one per value in the list) connected with OR:

```
select title_id, price
from titles
where type = "mod_cook"
    or type = "trad_cook"
    or type = "business"
```

Use not in to provide a list of ineligible values:

```
select title_id, price
from titles
where type not in ("mod_cook", "trad_cook", "business")
```

The value must not be found in the list for the condition to be true. Note that not in has the same effect as multiple inequality conditions (one per value in the list) connected with AND:

```
select title_id, price
from titles
where type <> "mod_cook"
    and type <> "trad_cook"
    and type <> "business"
```

# Wildcards with *like*

SQL also provides a pattern-matching method for string expressions using the like keyword and three wildcard mechanisms: the percent sign (%), the underscore character (_), and characters in brackets ([ ]). Table 3.1 shows the effect of these wildcard mechanisms with the like operator.

## Table 3.1. Wildcard mechanisms with the `like` operator.

| Wildcard | Meaning |
|---|---|
| % | Any number (0 to many) of any character(s) |
| _ | Any single character |
| [ ] | Any single character listed in the brackets |

You can freely combine wildcards in a single expression.

**NOTE**

The % and _ methods are supported by ANSI SQL; the [ ] pattern is recognized only by the SQL Server.

Let's look at some uses of the wildcard. In the first example, the where clause matches any row where the city starts with the word "Spring" (including Spring Hill, Springdale, Springfield, and even Spring itself):

```
select au_lname, au_fname, city, state
from authors
where city like "Spring%"
```

In the following example, the underscore matches only a single character in an expression, so the query finds only rows with a single character between the "B" and "1342" in the title_id.

```
select type, title_id, price
from titles
where title_id like "B_1342"
```

Possible matches for title_id include BA1342 to BZ1342, but also include numerics (for example, B71342) and other non-alphanumeric characters (B*1342 or even B%1342). Notice that B1342 and BAB1342 do not match the pattern because the underscore stands for a single character.

The bracket notation enables you to define a set of valid values for a position in a string. For example, the next example specifies the value for title_id more accurately than does the previous example, with only the specific alphabetic characters U, A, or N permitted in the position shown:

```
select type, title_id, price
from titles
where title_id like "B[UAN]1342"
```

Note that this query could also be written as a set of equality statements, much like an in clause:

```
select type, title_id, price
from titles
where title_id = "BU1342"
    or title_id = "BA1342"
    or title_id = "BN1342"
```

Within the brackets, you can list specific characters, or you can specify a range of values with a hyphen, as in this example which permits any alphabetic character (upper- or lowercase) in the same position of the earlier titles query:

```
select type, title_id, price
from titles
where title_id like "B[A-Za-z]1342"
```

---

**NOTE**

This last example could conceivably be written with lots of equality conditions connected by OR …:

```
where title_id = "BA1342"
    or title_id = "BB1342"
    or ...
    or title_id = "Bz1342"
```

It would require 52 `where` clauses. The pattern-matching strengths of the `[]` become increasingly clear as the number of permutations and combinations increases:

```
where title_id like "[A-Z][A-Z][0-9][0-9][0-9][0-9]"
```

This example would require more than 6 million `where` clauses!

### WARNING

Remember, the wildcard characters are only meaningful after the `like` keyword. In all other circumstances, the wildcard characters are treated as actual characters, usually with odd results. In this query, only rows with individuals whose names ended in a percent sign (probably very few) would be returned:

```
select au_lname, au_fname
from authors
where au_lname = "G%"
```

Chapter 4 describes the column, variable, and expression datatypes available to the DBA and programmer. Look for information there on the interaction of specific datatypes with the comparison operators.

# Ordering Result Sets with *order by*

In most cases, you cannot count on SQL Server data being sorted in any particular order. The rows returned in an unsorted result set are ordered according to the most efficient method for resolving the query. In order to force the output to be sorted by a particular value, you must specify an `order by` clause:

```
select au_lname, au_fname
from authors
order by au_lname
```

You also can sort based on two or more columns, separating the sort keys with commas:

```
select au_lname, au_fname
from authors
order by au_lname, au_fname
```

### NOTE

Sorting result sets introduces a performance cost because the server adds an additional sorting step subsequent to preparing the set of rows to be returned. This additional step can be circumvented if the server can make use of an index on the sort columns.

You can specify the sort column by name or by position in the select list. In the following example, titles are sorted by total dollar sales, derived from price and total_sales (unit sales):

```
select title_id, price, total_sales, price*total_sales "total dollar sales"
from titles
order by 4
```

If you wish to sort by an expression in the select list, you should make certain that the expression in the order by clause matches exactly the expression in the select list:

```
select title_id, price, total_sales, price*total_sales "total dollar sales"
from titles
order by price*total_sales
```

> **TIP**
>
> I usually prefer to name the full column or expression in the order by clause. Otherwise, a programmer making a change to the select statement (adding type after title_id, for example) inadvertently could change the sort column.

## Ascending and Descending Ordering

In the example above, it might be more common to sort the data by sales in descending order, showing best-performing items first. To reverse the sort order (highest items displayed first) use the desc keyword:

```
select title_id, price, total_sales, price*total_sales "total dollar sales"
from titles
order by price*total_sales desc
```

> **NOTE**
>
> By default, sort order is ascending. The asc keyword (for "ascending") is included as part of SQL for completeness, but seldom is used.

asc and desc ordering only affects a single column. The following query displays best-selling books by type (ascending), then quantity sales (descending):

```
select title_id, type, total_sales
from titles
order by type, total_sales desc
```

## Ordering by Columns Not Appearing in the Select List

Every example so far has demonstrated sorting by a column or columns, included in the select list. ANSI SQL requires that sort columns be included in the select list, but SQL Server does not. Sometimes, this leads to confusing results, as in the following query, where the data is sorted by the invisible `city` and `state` columns:

```
select au_lname, au_fname
from authors
order by city, state
```

```
au_lname                                        au_fname
---------------------------------------------   --------------------
del Castillo                                    Innes
Carson                                          Cheryl
Bennet                                          Abraham
Blotchet-Halls                                  Reginald
Gringlesby                                      Burt
DeFrance                                        Michel
Smith                                           Meander
White                                           Johnson
Greene                                          Morningstar
Karsen                                          Livia
Straight                                        Dick
Stringer                                        Dirk
Green                                           Marjorie
MacFeather                                      Stearns
Dull                                            Ann
Hunter                                          Sheryl
Panteley                                        Sylvia
Ringer                                          Anne
Ringer                                          Albert
Locksley                                        Chastity
O'Leary                                         Michael
McBadden                                        Heather
Yokomoto                                        Akiko

(23 rows affected)
```

A user trying to determine the sort order of these results would be driven nuts trying to find the pattern.

Ordering by a column not in the select list may allow better performance. In the following example, the query displays a discount derived from price but sorts by the `price` column itself:

```
select title_id, discount = price * .15
from titles
where price between $10.50 and $15.00
order by price
```

The logical result of the query is the same as if you had ordered by the expression `price * .15`. However, because you create indexes only on columns (not expressions), it's always better to sort by a column than on an expression derived from that column. If there were an index on the `price` column, this query probably would be generated without the intermediate work-table, providing substantially better performance.

By now, you probably have noticed that the behavior of the server cannot always be predicted—that it "probably" will use an index or "in many cases" will make use of an intermediate worktable. Even given a specific table structure and query, you cannot predict universally how the server will answer a question until you also understand the distribution of the data. It is the work of the query optimizer to decide, on a query-by-query basis, what is the most effective method for resolving queries. You learn about the query optimizer in Chapter 12.

Experienced programmers often have a difficult time getting used to the idea that the server makes these decisions for them, but this is one of the primary benefits of the SQL Server implementation. Programmers can worry about how to logically define their requirements; database administrators worry about how to efficiently satisfy those requirements.

## Retrieving Aggregate Data

SQL provides functions for describing data as a whole rather than as a set of rows. Table 3.2 lists the *aggregate* functions (so named because they "aggregate" many rows of data into a single row).

**Table 3.2. The aggregate functions.**

| Function | Description |
| --- | --- |
| sum() | Totals numeric expressions |
| avg() | Averages numeric expressions |
| min() | Returns the lowest numeric expression, the lowest sorting string expression, or the earliest datetime expression |
| max() | Returns the highest numeric expression, the highest sorting string expression, or the latest datetime expression |
| count() | Returns the number of non-null expressions |
| count(*) | Returns the number of rows found |

Take a look at the following query and result set. The avg() function returns a single average for all title rows in the table:

```
select avg(price)
from titles
```

```
 -----------------------
                  14.77
```

```
(1 row affected)
```

Notice that the query examined all rows of the titles table, but returned only a single row.

> **TIP**
>
> The result column for the aggregate has no default column heading. It is useful to assign headings like "sum" and "avg" to SQL result sets, but you must assign these headings in quotes because these are reserved words as names of functions:
>
> ```
> select avg(price) "avg" ...
> ```

Combine where clauses with aggregates to specify the rows to be included in the aggregate. In this example, the query asks for the average price of business books:

```
select avg(price) "avg"
from titles
where type = "business."
```

Include many aggregates in the same select list if they relate to the same rows within a table:

```
select avg(price) "avg", sum(price) "sum"
from titles
where type in ("business", "mod_cook")
```

```
avg                      sum
------------------------- -----------------------
                  12.98                    77.90
```

```
(1 row affected)
```

# Counting Rows with *count(\*)*

An important aggregate function is count(*), which counts rows matching a set of conditions. This query determines the number of authors in California:

```
select count(*)
from authors
where state = "CA"
```

```
 ----------
         15
```

```
(1 row affected)
```

## Aggregates and Null Values

Aggregate functions do not include null values. Consider a table, `test_table`, containing four rows, with these values in the c2 column:

```
c2
----
100
150
200
null
```

This example displays the behavior of each of the aggregate functions on a table containing a null value:

```
select sum(c2) "sum", count(c2) "count", avg(c2) "avg",
       min(c2) "min", max(c2) "max", count(*) "count(*)"
from test_table
```

| sum | count | avg | min | max | count(*) |
|-----|-------|-----|-----|-----|----------|
| 450 | 3 | 150 | 100 | 200 | 4 |

```
(1 row affected)
```

Null values imply no value—not even zero. Notice that the count(c2) is 3, meaning that three rows in the table contain non-null values in the c2 column. The average disregards the null value and the minimum is 100, not zero or null, because nulls are disregarded.

Note, however, that the count(*) column includes all rows, regardless of nulls.

## Sub-Aggregates with *group by*

The previous query provides the overall average and sum of prices for business and modern cooking books, but how do you determine the average and sum of each of these individual types of books? The answer is to return subaverages and subtotals by type, using group by, like this:

```
select type, avg(price) "avg", sum(price) "sum"from titles where type in
➥("_business", "mod_cook")
group by type
```

| type | avg | sum |
|------|-----|-----|
| business | 13.73 | 54.92 |
| mod_cook | 11.49 | 22.98 |

```
(2 rows affected)
```

The result set includes one row per type value among the selected rows. Aggregates return a single row for each unique value in the column specified in the group by clause.

When two or more columns are included in the group by statement, aggregates are based on unique combinations of those columns. In this example, the server returns the average and total price for business and modern cooking books for each combination of type and publisher ID:

```
select type, pub_id, avg(price) "avg", sum(price) "sum"
from titles
where type in ("business", "mod_cook")
group by type, pub_id
```

| type | pub_id | avg | sum |
| --- | --- | --- | --- |
| business | 0736 | 2.99 | 2.99 |
| business | 1389 | 17.31 | 51.93 |
| mod_cook | 0877 | 11.49 | 22.98 |

(3 rows affected)

## Aggregates Without *group by*

In order for aggregates to properly subtotal (or subaverage or subcount) by non-aggregate values, all non-aggregate columns in the select list must be repeated in the group by clause.

Consider these two queries and results:

```
select state, count(*)
from publishers
group by state
```

| state | |
| --- | --- |
| CA | 1 |
| DC | 1 |
| MA | 1 |

(3 rows affected)

```
select state, count(*)
from publishers
```

| state | |
| --- | --- |
| MA | 3 |
| DC | 3 |
| CA | 3 |

(3 rows affected)

The count(*) column in the first example shows the distribution of the data by state. The second count(*) column is the overall total for the table, with one row in the result set per row in the publishers table. (This might lead the user to believe that there are nine rows in the table, overall.)

In an example considered earlier, the select list contains two non-aggregate expressions (type and pub_id) and two aggregate expressions. The non-aggregate expressions must appear in the group by clause in order to get the correct values for the avg and sum functions. What if the group by clause is missing one or more of the non-aggregate expressions? In this example (based on the previous select statement), the pub_id column has been omitted from the group by clause:

```
select type, pub_id, avg(price) "avg", sum(price) "sum"
from titles
where type in ("business", "mod_cook")
group by type
```

| type | pub_id | avg | sum |
|------|--------|-----|-----|
| business | 1389 | 13.73 | 54.92 |
| business | 1389 | 13.73 | 54.92 |
| business | 0736 | 13.73 | 54.92 |
| business | 1389 | 13.73 | 54.92 |
| mod_cook | 0877 | 11.49 | 22.98 |
| mod_cook | 0877 | 11.49 | 22.98 |

(6 rows affected)

To a user, this is a pretty confusing result. The subtotals and subaverages relate to type (not pub_id), and are repeated for each row in the table that matches the where clause. To fully understand this result set, you must walk through the logical steps taken to resolve this query.

> **NOTE**
>
> Often, it's useful to understand the *logical* steps to resolve a query, but you must consider that those logical steps are usually different from the *physical* steps taken by the server, which are chosen in order to make the query more efficient.

The server first identifies the rows matching the where clause (six rows in all), then determines the subtotal and subaverage for each type (business and modern cooking). That intermediate result set would look like this:

| type | avg | sum |
|------|-----|-----|
| business | 13.73 | 54.92 |
| mod_cook | 11.49 | 22.98 |

The server then displays one row in the result set per row matching the where clause, matching those rows by type.

> **WARNING**
>
> In ANSI SQL, the failure to match non-aggregates in the select list in the group by clause is a syntax error. In SQL Server, this is a more insidious error because it may produce spurious results.

# Filtering Results with *having*

You can use the having keyword to select rows from the result set. If you wanted to display, by type, the average price of books costing more than $10, you would use a where clause:

```
select type, avg(price)
from titles
where price > $10
group by type
```

```
type
------------- -------------------------
business                  17.31
mod_cook                  19.99
popular_comp              21.48
psychology                17.51
trad_cook                 15.96

(5 rows affected)
```

The where clause selects rows from the table before averaging takes place.

A having clause enables you to select rows from the result set. In this example, you display only those types with an average price greater than $20:

```
select type, avg(price)
from titles
where price > $10
group by type
having avg(price) > $20
```

```
type
------------- -------------------------
popular_comp              21.48

(1 row affected)
```

---

**TIP**

One useful application of the having keyword is to identify rows in a table having duplicate keys. (Keys are unique identifiers. Duplicate keys are a terrible idea, but they often crop up during a data transfer from older systems.)

To find all rows in the authors table sharing the same key, use this query:

```
select au_id, count(*)
from authors
group by au_id
having count(*) > 1
```

## Worktables and Aggregate Functions

In order to resolve a query containing a group by clause, the server uses an intermediate work-table. Figure 3.1 shows the role of the worktable in the resolution of a query. The server resolves where clauses and grouping while building the intermediate worktable. distinct, having, and order by are resolved after the worktable is generated, while preparing the final result set.

**FIGURE 3.1.**

*The worktable helps the server resolve complex queries involving grouping and ordering.*

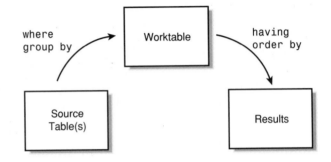

The server must use an intermediate result set to resolve this query:

```
select type, avg(price)
from titles
where pub_id = "1289"
group by type
having avg(price) > $15
order by avg(price) desc
```

First, rows matching the where clause are averaged into a worktable. The server then filters and sorts the result set.

## Join Operations

So far, all of the queries I have discussed address only one table at a time, but most SQL queries have to address multiple tables at one time. For example, to display the titles of books and the names of publishers in a single query, you must draw information from both the titles and publishers tables.

Let's look more closely at how you would write a query to join the titles and publishers tables.

When two tables are joined, they must share a *common key* or *join key*, which defines how rows in the tables correspond to each other. For example, in the case of titles and publishers, the tables share a common key, pub_id. In the publishers table, the pub_id uniquely identifies a row in that table. In the titles table, the pub_id uniquely identifies a row in the publishers table; it says, "titles with this pub_id belong to publishers having the same pub_id."

When you join two or more tables in SQL Server, the server does not implicitly understand the relationship between tables; you must tell the server about common keys. In the following example, the selection is drawn from two tables (see the `from` clause), and the `where` clause of the query defines how those tables relate to each other:

```
select title, pub_name
from titles, publishers
where titles.pub_id = publishers.pub_id
```

Notice that the `from` clause now names two tables. Also, notice that the join condition specifies a table name, `titles.pub_id`, before each column name. Column names must be *qualified* (that is, you must specify the exact table name) whenever there is possible ambiguity because of duplicate column names in multiple tables.

In this case, because `pub_id` appears in both titles and publishers, the `pub_id` column needed to be qualified. On the other hand, the `title` and `pub_name` columns are not qualified because each only appears in a single table among those named in the `from` clause.

## What Happens When You Fail to Specify a Common Key?

When you write a join without specifying a common key, the server returns all the possible combination of rows between the tables. In the example just cited, if the `where` clause were left out, the server would return a list containing each title many times: once for each publisher. This is a meaningless result, because only a single publisher would have published each book.

A result set based on a query missing a proper join condition is called a *Cartesian product*. Cartesian products can take forever to resolve—and, once resolved, are usually utterly useless.

## Recipe for Writing Queries Containing Join

Here is a simple recipe for writing joins if you have been assigned to write a specific query or report:

1. Build the select list, naming each column or expression.
2. Name the tables where the columns in the select list reside, as well as any tables required to connect those tables.
3. Provide the join conditions to connect the tables.

For example, imagine writing a query to determine the average price of all books sold by a single publisher. In that case, the select list might look like this:

```
select pub_name, avg(price)
```

> **NOTE**
>
> In this example I'm using an aggregate expression based on the price column. In spite of this added wrinkle, the join method is the same as elsewhere, and the recipe described here is valid.

The next step is to determine the tables where these columns are found, and any tables that must be identified between them.

```
from titles t, publishers p
```

> **NOTE**
>
> Earlier, you saw how column aliases allowed the user to specify a substitution column name. In the previous example I included *table aliases,* which do not affect the final results but do enable you to simplify the SQL syntax. Later in the book you see how self-joins require table aliases; in all other circumstances, table aliases are completely optional. For the present, any reference to those tables for this SQL statement requires the table alias rather than the full name.

The final step is to name the where clauses and complete the SQL. Here is the complete query:

```
select pub_name, title
from titles t, publishers p
where t.pub_id = p.pub_id
group by pub_name
```

> **NOTE**
>
> You can combine joins with every other aspect of SQL, including grouping, ordering, having, and other complex where conditions.

## Dealing with More than Two Tables

You can join up to 16 tables at a time. In this example, you join the titles and authors tables to determine which author wrote each psychology title. Following the recipe for a join, here is the select list:

```
select au_lname, au_fname, title
```

In the `from` clause, you could simply name the `authors` and `titles` tables, but note that the tables do not share a common key. In order to connect these tables, you must include the `titleauthor` table, which shares a common key with both tables:

```
from authors a, titles t, titleauthor ta
```

> **NOTE**
>
> Does the order in which the tables are named have an effect on the overall behavior of the server or on performance? In a few cases, and only in cases where more than four tables are named, table order can have an impact on performance. See Chapter 12, Chapter 14, "Analyzing Query Plans," and Chapter 16, "Overriding the SQL Server Optimizer," for more on performance issues and how they relate to the actual syntax of a select statement.

Now you must name the join conditions. Because there are three joins, there are two required join conditions.

> **TIP**
>
> When joining two tables, in order to avoid a Cartesian product, you must specify one join condition. When joining three tables, you must specify two join conditions. As a general rule, when joining *N* tables, you must specify *N*-1 join conditions.

```
where ta.title_id = t.title_id
and a.au_id = ta.au_id
```

Now all that's required is to put the whole query together and add the condition to limit the result set to psychology books, and you're done:

```
select au_lname, au_fname, title
from authors a, titles t, titleauthor ta
where ta.title_id = t.title_id
and a.au_id = ta.au_id
and type = "psychology"
```

# The Meaning of * in a Multi-Table Query

In a multi-table query, an unqualified asterisk (*) means "all columns from all tables." For example, in the following query, * means "every column from both the `titles` and `publishers` tables":

```
select *
from titles t, publishers p
where t.pub_id = p.pub_id
```

If you qualify the * as in this example, you get only the columns from a single table:

```
select t.*, pub_name
from titles t, publishers p
where t.pub_id = p.pub_id
```

# Subqueries

With SQL Server you can use a *subquery* in place of a constant expression to tell the server to derive a result before processing the remainder of the query. In this example, you ask the server to show you all books published by a specific publisher. Note that a subquery may only return a single column of data:

```
select title
from titles
where pub_id =
    (select pub_id
     from publishers
     where pub_name = "Algodata Infosystems")
```

> **NOTE**
>
> The subquery must always appear in parentheses.

When a subquery appears as part of an equality condition (for example, pub_id = (...)), the server expects to resolve the subquery before it starts work on the main query, and the subquery must return only a single row.

> **TIP**
>
> To be certain to return only a single row, use a unique key or other unique identifier in the where clause of the subquery, or use an aggregate.

## Subqueries with *in*

While a subquery may only return a single column of data, when used with in and not in, it may return multiple rows of data. In this example, the server displays all publishers of business books:

```
select pub_name
from publishers
where pub_id in
    (select pub_id
     from titles
     where type = "business")
```

The server returns a list of valid publisher IDs to the main query, then determines whether each publisher's `pub_id` is in that list. Here is the result set from the query:

```
pub_name
----------------------------------------
New Age Books
Algodata Infosystems
Algodata Infosystems
Algodata Infsystems
(4 rows affected)
```

## Subqueries versus Joins

The SQL Server treats the subquery the same way it treats a join. Here is a query using a join condition to return a result similar to the previous example of a subquery:

```
select pub_name
from publishers p, titles t
where p.pub_id = t.pub_id and type = "business"
```

Here is the result set:

```
pub_name
----------------------------------------
New Age Books
Algodata Infosystems
Algodata Infosystems
Algodata Infosystems
(4 rows affected)
```

## Subqueries with *exists*

Why does the server return duplicate rows in the result set? Because each query asks for all matching rows. There are two ways to solve this problem. The first method is to use the `distinct` keyword to force the server to find only unique results. The problem with `distinct` is that it requires an additional sorting step using a worktable, with an often severe performance penalty on large data sets.

The second method is to use the `exists` keyword to find only rows matching the condition, and to stop looking for results once the first match is found for a particular value. Here's the same query as the previous example, but this example uses an `exists` clause. Look at the example, then step through it and understand how it is written and resolved:

```
select pub_name
from publishers p
where exists
    (select *
    from titles t
    where p.pub_id = t.pub_id
    and type = "business")
```

There are a number of syntactic oddities to observe. First, note that exists takes neither an equals nor an in, and it does not apply to a relationship between columns but to a relationship between tables. Because of that, you do not specify a column name in the select list of the subquery; always write select * instead.

Finally, notice that the subquery refers to a table alias, p, in the where condition (p.pub_id), even though this table alias is not declared in the from clause of the subquery itself. The table alias p, of course, relates to the publishers table, which is declared in the outer portion of the query.

exists uses a *correlated subquery*, in which the subquery would not run on its own. In order to resolve the correlated subquery, the server must execute the subquery once for each row in the outer query, testing for a match on pub_id.

Here is the result set of the query with exists:

```
pub_name
-------------------------------------------
New Age Books
Algodata Infosystems

(2 rows affected)
```

The duplicates are eliminated without an intermediate worktable.

> **TIP**
>
> Always use exists rather than joining tables and using distinct. The performance benefits are dramatic.

## not exists and not in

Certain results, such as non-membership and non-existence, can be defined only with a subquery. For example, which publishers do not publish business books? You cannot express this query with a join, but you can using not exists or not in:

```
select pub_name
from publishers p
where not exists
    (select *
     from titles t
     where t.pub_id = p.pub_id
     and type = "business")

select pub_name
from publishers
where pub_id not in
    (select pub_id
     from titles
     where type = "business")cx
```

> **TIP**
>
> In most cases, not in and not exists are identical in their behavior. However, using not exists you can compare tables where the join condition consists of multiple columns.

## Subqueries with Aggregates in *where* Clauses

One specific case where a subquery is required appears when you want to use an aggregate function in a where clause. In this next example, you return the type and price of all books with a price below the average price. This condition in a where clause would be illegal:

```
where price < avg(price)
```

The server requires that the average price be derived in a subquery:

```
select type, price
from titles
where price <
    (select avg(price)
     from titles)
```

## *union* Operations

The SQL union keyword enables you to request a logical union of two or more result sets, listing rows where values are found in either result. This query requests the city and state of each author and each publisher in a single result set:

```
select city, state
from authors
union
select city, state
from publishers
```

The server resolves each element of the union, placing the results in an intermediate worktable. Once all of the results are available, the server automatically removes duplicate rows from the final result.

> **TIP**
>
> To prevent the server from removing duplicates, use union all to force all result rows to be returned.

Each result set must have the same number of columns as the first result set, and each column must be of the same datatype as one in the corresponding position in the first result set. The name of each column is drawn from the column names in the first result set.

You can sort the result of a union operation. The order by clause appears after the final select statement, but it references the column names or expressions in the first select list. In this sample query, authors' and publishers' cities and states are sorted by state, then city:

```
select city, state
from authors
union
select city, state
from publishers
order by state, city
```

The union operation is most often used to connect active and archive data, or data that has been separated by year into a single result set. This example draws data from two fictional tables, salescurrent and saleshistory, that have the same structure:

```
select 95 "year", month, sum(dollar_sales)
from salescurrent
group by month
union
select 94, month, sum(dollar_sales)
from saleshistory
group by month
order by year, month
```

Notice that the union operator enables you to create result sets using group by and where clauses, each of which is specific to its own select operation. Also, note that the order by clause may reference the column aliases defined in the first result clause.

# Using *select* with *into*

The select statement may be directed to create a table consisting of the rows in the result set "on the fly," instead of returning the output to the user. This is a common mechanism for creating temporary tables that will be used for subsequent reporting. The structure of the table is defined by the select list itself. The columns are created in the order of the select list, with column names and datatypes drawn from the select list as well.

This example instructs the server to create a table with each of the book types included in the titles table:

```
select distinct type
into type_lookup
from titles
```

The resulting type_lookup table has one column, named type, with a datatype that is the same as the datatype stored in the titles table.

You can use any of the SQL syntax you have seen. This query prepares a master list of all California cities for publishers, authors, and stores:

```
select city
into cal_cities
from publishers
where state = "CA"
union
select city
from authors
where state = "CA"
union
select city
from stores
where state = "CA"
```

**NOTE**

The into statement must be stated after the first select list when combined with a union statement.

It often is useful to create an empty copy of an existing table. This query creates an empty copy of salesdetail:

```
select *
into new_salesdetail
from salesdetail
where 1 = 2
```

Even though no rows are found, a table with no rows is created.

# Adding Rows with *insert*

So far, you have seen only SQL for retrieving data. In the next couple of sections, you get a look at queries that modify the data in tables using the keywords insert, update, and delete.

To add rows to a table, use the insert statement. You can either insert specific values that you state in the query, or you can insert based on a selection from another table.

# Inserting Specific Values

The following query inserts a row in the `authors` table, providing values for four of the nine columns in the table:

```
insert authors
    (au_id, au_lname, au_fname, phone)
values
    ("123-45-6789", "Jones", "Mary", "415 555-1212")
```

In the `insert` statement, the number of columns in the values list must match those in the column list. The datatype of the values must allow an implicit conversion to the datatype of each corresponding column. Columns that are not specified are set to their default value, where one is defined; if there is no default value for a column, and the column is not specified in the column list, a null value is inserted for the column. (See Chapter 5 for information on default values.)

> **NOTE**
>
> However, if a column does not allow null values and has no default value or identity property or is a timestamp column, then an error will result. A column must have a value specified under those circumstances.

The `insert` statement, in which you provide specific values, only inserts one row at a time. Each additional row requires that you specify the `insert` keyword again, providing again the name of the table and related columns.

# Inserting Several Rows with *select*

In addition to inserting individual rows with a values list, you can also insert one row or many rows based on the result set from a `select` query embedded in the `insert` statement. In this example, the query inserts rows in the fictitious `authors_archive` table based on rows in the `authors` table:

```
insert authors_archive
    (au_id, au_lname, au_fname, phone, city, state, zip)
select au_id, au_lname, au_fname, phone, city, state, zip
from authors
where state = "CA"
```

> **NOTE**
>
> A single `insert` statement can insert zero, one, or many rows. This is an important point to remember about inserting rows when writing insert triggers. For more on this, see Chapter 7.

# Omitting the Column List

The column list in an insert statement is optional, but when you leave it out, you must provide values for each column in the table in the order in which the columns were defined. If you fail to provide the correct number of columns, the server returns a syntax error and the insert fails. This query inserts a row in the publishers table, but does not specify any column names:

```
insert publishers
values
    ("1235", "New World Books and Prints", "Atlanta", "GA")
```

If you specify values in an incorrect order, the server traps invalid datatypes where appropriate. Otherwise, the wrong data simply appears in each column. For example, this insert to the publishers table has the city and state in the wrong order:

```
insert publishers
values
    ("1235", "New World Books and Prints", "GA", "Atlanta")
```

The server will not catch this error because all of the columns are character or variable-character datatypes, allowing implicit conversions and length adjustments. In this case, the value GA would be inserted as the city, and the value At (truncated to two characters to match the state column definition) would be inserted for the state.

> **WARNING**
>
> Omitting column names from insert statements, particularly when the statements are embedded in application programs, stored procedures, and triggers, can result in ugly code-maintenance problems. What if someone added a column, zip, to the publishers table? An insert statement including the column names to be inserted would succeed, although zip would be stored as a null value. But an insert without column names would fail, because the statement now requires five values instead of four.
>
> Here's an important coding standard for your organization: all insert statements will name the columns to be inserted.

# Modifying Rows with *update*

To modify values within tables, use the update statement. update statements consist of three main components:

- The table to be updated
- The columns to be updated, with the new values
- The rows to be updated, in the form of a where clause

This statement changes the name of a publisher to "Joe's Press":

```
update publishers
set pub_name = "Joe's Press"
where pub_id = "1234"
```

An unqualified update statement (one without a `where` clause) modifies every row in the table:

```
update titles
set price = price * 2
```

---

**TIP**

By far the hardest element of SQL for experienced database programmers to grasp is the need for a `where` clause to define the set of rows to be updated. This is particularly true when writing an online update system where the row to be modified is visible on screen.

When you pass the update statement, SQL Server has no idea which row, or rows, you might have on screen; each statement is taken on its own, without a reference to other processing. Therefore, the statement

```
update publishers
set name = "Joe's Books and Prints"
```

instructs the server to change every row in the table.

---

You can update only one table at a time, but you can set values for many columns at a single time. This statement updates the entire address record for a contact:

```
update contacts
set address1 = "5 West Main St.",
    address2 = "Apartment 3D",
    city = "Hartford",
    state = "CT",
    zip = "03838"
where contact_id = 17938
```

---

**TIP**

It's always much more efficient to set many columns in a single statement than to issue many update statements.

---

# Removing Rows with *delete*

To remove rows from a table, issue the `delete` statement. `delete` statements include the name of the table and a `where` clause defining the rows to delete. This example removes all business books from the titles table:

```
delete titles
where type = "business"
```

An unqualified `delete` statement removes every row from the table:

```
delete titles
```

You will usually want to define which rows to delete: (see the Tip in the section on "Modifying Rows with `update`"). Deleting all the rows in a table is usually unintended; if it wasn't, see the next section.

You can delete rows from only a single table at a time.

# Clearing a Table with *truncate table*

There are times when you want to clear all rows from a table, but leave the table definition as is. To clear a table, issue the `truncate table` command:

```
truncate table titles
```

`truncate table` simply deallocates all space allocations to a table and its indexes, instead of removing each row from the table one by one. This is substantially faster than an unqualified `delete`, especially on large tables.

---

**WARNING**

You probably aren't ready for this information, but I'll remind you of it later, when you learn about transaction logs and data backup.

`truncate table` is fast, because it does not log individual row deletions as it deallocates space. Your ability to recover your database in case of disaster is compromised after `truncate table` until you run a backup, and you will not be able to run an incremental backup (`dump transaction …`) until you first run a full backup (`dump database …`).

---

`truncate table` is most commonly used when moving large blocks of test data in and out of the server and when preparing the server for a rollout.

# Summary

SQL provides a flexible, English-like method of retrieving and modifying data in tables. The query language is fairly simple yet powerful. It is the only way to access data in a SQL Server and is supported by every product that supports SQL Server itself.

In the following chapters you get a look at Transact-SQL: the extensions to the standard SQL language that allow SQL Server to store programmatic, SQL-based objects and to manage data integrity at the server.

# Transact-SQL
# Datatypes

**4**

In this chapter, you'll look at the datatypes supported by SQL Server. *Datatypes* are predefined, named methods for storing, retrieving, and interpreting categories of data values. As in most programming environments, the system defines the datatypes available to you and you are not permitted to improvise your own.

> **NOTE**
>
> SQL Server supports user-defined datatypes, but these enable the user only to subclass an existing datatype, not to define a new type with new storage and retrieval characteristics. For more on user-defined datatypes, please see Chapter 5, "Creating and Altering Database Objects."

You must choose a datatype when you create a column in a table or declare a local variable. In each case, the choice of a datatype determines the following:

- The kind of data that may be stored in the column (numbers, strings, binary strings, bit values, or dates)
- In the case of numeric and date datatypes, the range of values permitted in the column
- In the case of strings and binary data, the maximum length of data you may store in the column

> **WARNING**
>
> Column datatype selection is one of those incredibly important topics that has ramifications in space utilization, performance, reliability, and manageability of your system. Unfortunately, it is also something you need to do very early in the process of implementing SQL Server, long before you really understand the ramifications of your choices.
>
> Be certain you understand this point:
>
> *Once you create a column and declare its datatype, you cannot change that datatype without dropping and re-creating the table. The more data in the table, the more time that process takes and the more disruption it causes in system availability.*
>
> There will be references to advanced material appearing in other chapters in this book. Do your best to understand the issues if you must define your table and column structures long before you have time to read those other chapters. If you are planning to build very large tables or tables that need to perform extremely well, take the time now to read those other chapters.

# Nullability and Datatypes

When you define a column, you must also decide whether or not to allow null values in that column. A column that allows nulls requires more space to store a value and may have other performance or storage implications. In this chapter, be sure to notice any special concerns related to nullability for each datatype.

> **NOTE**
>
> This chapter will probably be more helpful if you understand the context in which you will define a datatype. Here is a brief example of a table creation statement:
>
> ```
> create table my_table
> (id int not null,
> value float not null,
> description varchar(30) null)
> ```
>
> This query creates a three-column table named my_table. Each column is assigned a datatype, and the variable-length column description is also assigned a maximum length of 30 characters.
>
> For much more about table definition, see Chapter 5.

# Character and Binary Datatypes

Store strings by using character datatypes. There are five valid datatypes for storing strings:

- char, for storing fixed-length strings
- varchar, for variable-length strings
- nchar, for multi-byte character strings (specifically for handling alphabets such as Kanji, where there are many more than 255 character symbols)
- nvarchar, for variable-length, multi-byte character strings
- text, for strings of virtually unlimited size (up to 2GB of text per row)

Binary datatypes store *binary* strings (strings consisting of binary values rather than characters). The most common uses of binary data are for timestamp and image datatypes:

- binary, for fixed-length binary strings
- varbinary, for variable-length binary strings
- image, for storing large binary strings (up to 2GB of image data per row)

# char and varchar

The most common string datatypes are fixed-length (`char`) and variable-length (`varchar`) character types. Columns defined as `char` (character) store trailing blanks to fill out a fixed number of characters. Columns defined as `varchar` (character varying) truncate trailing blanks to save space.

## Column Length

The maximum length of a character column is 255 characters. When you define a `char` or `varchar` column, you must also specify a column length to indicate the maximum number of characters the column will store. Here are some column definitions and likely datatypes:

```
name varchar(40)
state char(2)
title varchar(80)
comments varchar(255)
title_id char(6)
```

In the examples, `name`, `title`, and `comments` will vary in length. The server will not reserve space to handle trailing blanks, so a value of `"George"` in the SQL Server will store only the first six characters in the `name` column. The columns `title_id` and `state` are fixed-length `char` types because the user is likely to (or may be restricted to) insert only strings of the stated length.

---

### TIP

The decision to use `char` or `varchar` depends on how frequently the user will provide data of *exactly* the length specified in the column definition. Variable-length structures require additional overhead for their storage (1 extra byte per row to store the length of the variable-length data). In addition, SQL Server must store 1 extra byte per row if there is any variable-length data at all in the table definition. Finally, certain operations are more efficient with fixed-length data.

The extra cost in overhead of storing variable-length data is often worth the substantial space savings provided by not storing trailing blanks. If a column is defined as `char(20)` but averages only 8 bytes of data per row, SQL Server still stores (on average) 12 additional padding spaces per row. That may not seem like much, but over a million rows, that's at least 12MB of additional space. More importantly, smaller rows means greater *row density* (measured in rows stored per 2KB page) and better performance on almost all operations on the table.

Until you have a firmer understanding of how SQL Server stores data, you may not make the correct choice between `char` and `varchar`. As a rule of thumb, the more the data varies in length, the more important it is to use `varchar`. Note that there is no reason at all to define a `varchar(1)` column.

Chapter 10, "Understanding SQL Server Storage Structures," discusses the details of physical storage of data in more detail. (For example, you will find there the specifics on variable-length column overhead.)

**NOTE**

Nullable character columns are stored and treated as variable-length columns. For example, the `description` column in this table is stored exactly like a `varchar(50)` column:

```
create table null_char_example
    (id int not null,
    description char(50) null)
```

The `description` column is not stored with trailing blanks, and the server will use extra overhead in each row to keep track of the actual length of the data.

## Character Insert Format

When inserting character data to the server or searching for a value in a `where` clause, pass the value in single or double (matched) quotations. The following `insert` statement provides four character values:

```
insert publishers
    (pub_id, pub_name, city, state)
values
    ("1234", "Stendahl Publishing", "Paris", "France")
```

**NOTE**

For some reason, when the `pubs2` database was defined, the `publisher`, `title`, `store`, and `author id` columns were all defined as character data. This is not usually as good a choice for a key as an integer or other numeric type, which can be stored far more efficiently. (See the section "Numeric Datatypes," later in this chapter.)

Here is an example of an `update` statement with character data:

```
update publishers
    set pub_name = "Press of St. Martins-in-the-Field"
    where pub_id = "1234"
```

# Truncation with Character Strings

SQL Server truncates character strings that are longer than the column definition, without reporting an error. Let's create a table with four rows to demonstrate the behavior of character strings under a variety of circumstances:

```
create table chars
(id int not null,
c1 char(6) not null)
```

Here are the `insert` statements. Note that the second `insert` includes a character string that is longer than the defined length of the c1 column. The server truncates the string after six characters, but returns no error message or warning:

```
insert chars values (1, "abc")
insert chars values (2, "abcdefg")
insert chars values (3, "   ef")
insert chars values (4, "ab ef")
```

Now retrieve the rows to see how the server stored them:

```
select id, c1, ">" + c1 + "<" c1_too
from chars


id            c1      c1too
-----------   ------  --------
1             abc     >abc   <
2             abcdef  >abcdef<
3                 ef  >   ef<
4             ab ef   >ab ef<
```

As expected, the server has truncated the g from the end of the second entry. Notice also how blanks are treated in a non-null `char()` column. The server stores the trailing blanks in the first row.

## *sysname* Datatypes

Earlier in the chapter, you learned that user-defined datatypes enable you to subclass an existing system datatype to provide a common structure for many columns sharing a single type and having consistent data integrity requirements. When you install SQL Server, two user-defined datatypes are already available: `sysname` and `timestamp`. (For more on `timestamp` data, see the section "Timestamps," later in this chapter.)

# *binary* and *varbinary*

SQL Server binary datatypes are similar to character datatypes. When you specify a column as `binary` or `varbinary` (binary varying), you must also specify a maximum data length for the column. The server truncates binary values that are too long. As with character columns, variable-length columns have some overhead, but fixed-length ones pad shorter values with trailing hex zeros.

To specify a binary column, use the `binary` datatype, as in this example:

```
create table binary_example
      (id int not null,
      bin_column binary(4) not null)
```

## Binary Data Insert Format

To insert binary data in a column, specify it without quotation marks, starting with `0x` and providing two hexadecimal characters for each byte of data. This `insert` statement adds a row containing a 4-byte value into the example table specified previously:

```
insert binary_example
      (id, bin_column)
values
      (19, 0xa134c2ff)
```

Treatment of binary columns is similar to character types in terms of null or non-null columns (see the section on nullability of character data earlier in this chapter). Null columns require an additional byte of storage where a value exists, but consume less storage space if no value is available.

## Timestamps

The most common use of binary columns is in the application of another preinstalled user-defined datatype, `timestamp`. Timestamp columns enable the user uniquely to identify *versions* of each row in the table.

> **NOTE**
>
> If you don't understand that statement, you probably are not alone. Keep reading and it will probably make more sense.

There are three important steps involving timestamps:

- Creation of a table with a timestamp column
- Automatic updating of a timestamp column
- Optimistic locking using the timestamp value

To create a table with a timestamp column, use the `timestamp` datatype in the table creation statement. Note that in this example, the column is named `ts`, but you may use any legal column name:

```
create table timestamp_example
      (id int not null,
      code char(3) not null,
      ts timestamp not null)
```

> **NOTE**
>
> A single table may have only one timestamp column.

To insert a row in a table and update the timestamp value, just insert the row. All updating of `timestamp` is automatic, so you don't have to indicate a timestamp value. This `insert` statement creates a row with an `id` of 17. The server will provide a unique timestamp:

```
insert timestamp_example
    (id, code)
values
    (17, "AAA")
```

When you retrieve the rows from the table, you should see that `timestamp` has been assigned a binary value. Look at the output after inserting a row into the `timestamp_example` table:

```
select id, code, ts
    from timestamp_example
id          code ts
----------- ---- ------------------
         17 AAA  0x0000000010000198a
```

> **NOTE**
>
> How does the server provide a unique timestamp for each row? Every modification to a row in a SQL Server table is written first to the transaction log. The server uses the unique row identifier in the transaction log as the timestamp value for that row.
>
> You can see the timestamp values steadily escalate if you execute the `timestamp` insert several times. When you retrieve the rows, you should see that the unique log identifier is incrementing by 3 or 4 per row. (The increment is not 1 because the log has additional work to record during an insert.) For more on log writes, see Chapter 12, "Understanding the Query Optimizer."

In fact, *the server does not allow you to specify a timestamp value.* This command generates an error message:

```
insert timestamp_example
    (id, code, ts)
values
    (18, "BBB", 0x01)
```

The third step in the use of the timestamp column is with optimistic locking. Here's a brief description of how you implement optimistic locking, but see Chapter 15, "Locking and Performance," for a more in-depth discussion of this technique.

Optimistic locking uses a new system function, `tsequal()` (pronounced *Tee-Ess-equal*, for *timestamp equal* ). Most locking techniques warn concurrent users when they attempt to retrieve a record for modification. Optimistic locking warns users when they are performing conflicting modifications.

Consider two users, Mary and Al, each attempting to modify a row in the `timestamp_example` table used earlier. Each retrieves the row with a `select` statement, planning later to update the row:

```
select id, code, ts
from timestamp_example
where id = 17
```

Each user retrieves the current, unchanged value of the timestamp column. Mary then modifies the code value of the row with an `update` statement, using the `tsequal()` function to be certain that the row has not changed since she retrieved it:

```
update timestamp_example
set code = "BBB"
where id = 17
and tsequal(ts, 0x000000010000198a)
```

It's important to understand why this where clause is written as it is. In order to use the `tsequal()` function, the rest of the `where` clause must identify a unique row. The `id` column is a primary key for the table (and has a unique index, as it turns out), so the `where` clause specifies only one row. (If the value of 17 were not found in the table, the `update` statement would complete and SQL Server would report that no rows were processed by the query.)

Once the rest of the query identifies the row, SQL Server evaluates the `tsequal()` function for that row. It retrieves the value of the timestamp column (`ts`, in this example) and compares it to the constant expression passed with the function (`0x000000010000198a`, in this example). If those values are the same, the update is allowed.

If you retrieve a `timestamp` value from the server and then return that value to the server at the next step, why would the `tsequal()` function ever fail to match? Mary's update worked because the `timestamp` failed, but during the update the server automatically updates the `timestamp` value again. Now think about poor Al, who is about to update the same row in the table:

```
update timestamp_example
set code = "CCC"
where id = 17
and tsequal(ts, 0x000000010000198a)
```

Al's update fails in this example because the `timestamp` value he retrieved when he originally read the record is no longer the current value. When Mary updated the row, the `timestamp` value changed. Al gets error number 532:

```
The timestamp (changed to 0x000000010000387c) shows that the row has been updated
by another user.
```

**TIP**

If you are writing applications and planning to use optimistic locking, you should definitely plan to trap this error and document for users how to work around it.

# Text and Image Data

The longest variable-length column is only 255 characters. The maximum row length in SQL Server is limited by the size of the data page, which is 2KB.

**NOTE**

The rows themselves are restricted to 1,962 bytes maximum because of page and transaction log overhead. Chapter 10 discusses row storage in detail and helps you understand the actual row-length limitations (there are many).

Many applications need to store much larger data than a 255-byte column or a 2KB page will allow. Long comments, detailed descriptions, telephone call-log notes, and graphical objects such as digitized photos, screen shots, and online images all need much larger capacity than 2KB. SQL Server provides a mechanism for storing *binary large objects (BLOBs)* as large as 2GB per row by using the text and image datatypes.

## Defining Text and Image Columns

The example table, texts, has three columns, including a text column, textstring:

```
create table texts
    (id numeric(5,0) identity,
     item int not null,
     textstring text null)
```

Let's insert four rows in the table, then look at the characteristics of the text columns. You can insert a string into a text column exactly as you do a regular char or varchar column:

```
insert texts (item, textstring) values
    (1, null)
insert texts (item) values
    (2)
insert texts (item, textstring) values
    (3,"the rain in spain falls mainly on the plain")
insert texts (item, textstring) values
    (4,replicate("the rain in spain falls mainly on the plain", 7)
```

The first two text values inserted are null, the following two rows are not. The last row uses the replicate function to write a fairly long value. Notice that the insert statement will not insert a text value longer than about 1,200 bytes.

> **TIP**
>
> Most string functions return only 255 characters because they are limited to the maximum length of a varchar. String concatenation of text data is also illegal.

## writetext and readtext

SQL Server provides two statements to enable manipulation of long string and binary data, to improve performance, and to simplify access to text and image columns. Text and image data are stored in a chain of separate 2KB pages, apart from the rest of the row data. In the row data itself, SQL Server stores a pointer to the page where the chain of text or image data begins. The text/image statements, writetext and readtext, use that pointer to find the page chain and can write directly to that chain without modifying the underlying row. (In order to do this, you must already have a non-null page pointer stored in the row itself.)

To retrieve the page pointer for a row, use the textptr() function. Here are the page pointers for the rows already inserted in the example table, texts, along with the length of the text data (using the datalength() function):

```
select id, textptr(textstring) textptr,
      datalength(textstring) datalength
from texts
id          textptr                                          datalength
----------  ------------------------------------------------ ----------
1           (null)                                           0
2           (null)                                           0
3           0x6901000000000000010000009a080000 43
4           0x6a0100000000000001000000a1080000 225

(4 row(s) affected)
```

> **NOTE**
>
> The page pointers for the first two rows are null. Before you can use either of the two text/image statements, you should either update the column with data or a null value, or insert data into the text or image column during the original insert statement.

Let's write a new textstring value to the third row using the writetext statement. Here is the syntax for writetext:

```
writetext table_name.column_name text_ptr
[with log] data
```

> **NOTE**
>
> The `writetext` statement allows *nonlogged* modifications to text columns, which can substantially improve the performance of text operations (see Chapter 21, "Miscellaneous Performance Topics"). If the database option `select into/bulkcopy` has not been set, you must include `with log` to allow the modifications to be logged.

`writetext` completely replaces the existing text or image value with the new value. This `writetext` statement replaces the existing string with the replacement string. Notice that you must first retrieve the page pointer, then pass it to the `writetext` statement in a variable:

```
declare @pageptr varbinary(16)
select @pageptr = textptr(textstring)
      from texts
      where id = 3
writetext texts.textstring @pageptr
"Mary had a little lamb, its fleece was white as snow"
```

> **NOTE**
>
> All text and image operations, whether performed manually with `writetext` or automatically with `insert` or `update` statements, require two physical steps: SQL Server must first find a page pointer in the row itself, then go to that page and perform the requested operation.

A `select` statement returns only the first 255 bytes of a text column, but you can use `readtext` to retrieve any sequence of characters in the column. This `readtext` statement retrieves the 50 bytes starting in position `40000` into the result set:

```
declare @pageptr varbinary(16)
select @pageptr = textptr(textstring)
      from texts
      where id = 3
readtext texts.textstring @pageptr 40000 50
textstring
-------------------------------------------------
go.Mary had a little lamb, its fleece was white as
```

> **WARNING**
>
> Before you use `text` and `image` datatypes, please see Chapter 21 for more information about the drawbacks of BLOBs and alternative implementation methods.

# Date/Time Datatypes

SQL Server enables you to store date and time values and supports two date storage types, datetime and smalldatetime. Columns using datetime or smalldatetime store both a date and a time value for each row. This create table statement creates a two-column table, consisting of an int and a datetime column:

```
create table date_example
    (id int not null,
     dateval datetime not null)
```

## datetime versus smalldatetime

Generally speaking, smalldatetime is less precise and covers a smaller range of dates, but it occupies less space. The details are outlined in Table 4.1.

### Table 4.1. Comparison of date storage types.

| Feature | datetime | smalldatetime |
|---------|----------|---------------|
| Minimum value | Jan 1, 1753 | Jan 1, 1900 |
| Maximum value | Dec 31, 9999 | Jun 6, 2079 |
| Precision | 3 milliseconds | 1 minute |
| Storage size | 8 bytes | 4 bytes |

> **NOTE**
>
> Here's a question to stump your friends while watching *Jeopardy!*. Why does Sybase start tracking datetime values with Jan 1, 1753? The answer is that the Gregorian and Julian calendars were 13 days apart until they were synchronized in September 1752. Date accuracy prior to 1753 is meaningless using our calendars.

## Date/Time Inserts

Datetime values are passed to the server in a character string. SQL Server is responsible for conversion and validation of datetime data. This statement inserts a date and time into the sample table created previously:

```
insert date_example
    (id, dateval)
values
    (19, "September 25, 1996 3:15PM")
```

SQL Server permits entry of many date formats. Table 4.2 summarizes the entry value and the return value for several date formats.

## Table 4.2. Date format entry and return values.

| *Insert Format* | datetime *Value* | smalldatetime *Value* |
|---|---|---|
| Sep 3, 1995 13:17:35.332 | Sep  3 1995  1:17:35:333PM | Sep  3 1995  1:18PM |
| 9/3/95 1pm | Sep  3 1995  1:00:00:000PM | Sep  3 1995  1:00PM |
| 9.3.95 13:00 | Sep  3 1995  1:00:00:000PM | Sep  3 1995  1:00PM |
| 3 sep 95 13:00 | Sep  3 1995  1:00:00:000PM | Sep  3 1995  1:00PM |
| 13:25:19 | Jan  1 1900  1:25:19:000PM | Jan  1 1900  1:25PM |
| 3 september 95 | Sep  3 1995 12:00:00:000AM | Sep  3 1995 12:00AM |
| 4/15/46 | Apr 15 2046 12:00:00:000AM | Apr 15 2046 12:00AM |

Let's look at each of these examples. The first example demonstrates the complete date specification—including the month, day, and year—as well as time in hours, minutes, seconds, and milliseconds. Note that the datetime value is rounded to the nearest 3 milliseconds and the smalldatetime value is rounded to the nearest minute.

Lines 2 through 4 show alternative methods of entering dates, with slashes and periods, and with the name of the month specified as well. Dashes (-) are also a legitimate delimiter in this format.

Line 5 demonstrates how the server handles a time without a date value. When you specify a time without a date, the server provides the default date, Jan 1, 1900.

> **TIP**
>
> In general, it makes no sense to enter a time without a date in SQL Server.

In line 6, the server uses the default value of 12:00 midnight (AM) for the time when none is provided. You almost always need to use a range search method (between x and y) when searching for specific dates (see the section "Search Behavior with Dates," later in this chapter).

Line 7 shows how the server treats two-digit year values less than 50. As you can see, all two-digit years less than 50 are assumed to be in the twenty-first century (20*xx*), and two-digit years greater than or equal to 50 are treated as twentieth-century dates (19*xx*).

## *dateformat* Option, Languages, and Date Formatting

By default, the server treats a date in the format *xx/yy/zz* as a month/day/year sequence. Sybase calls this the *mdy* date format. SQL Server also supports several other date orderings. Using the set dateformat command, you can choose other date orders. Valid choices are *mdy*, *dmy*, *ymd*, *ydm*, *myd*, or *dym*.

This is a session-level option, which means that it must be set when the user logs in to the server. For example, to change your date ordering from the default to *yy/mm/dd* formatting, execute this statement:

```
set dateformat ymd
```

> **NOTE**
>
> When a user's language option is changed, it also changes the user's default date format. The server supports us_english (this is the default language), french, german, and japanese. A user's language option can be set at the server level for all users, as a characteristic of an individual's login account, or within a session by executing the set language statement.

## Search Behavior with Dates

How do you find rows having a specific date or time value? Consider a table having the values listed in Table 4.2 in a date column. The where clause of the select statement needs to specify a date range, not a single date value. The next three select statements might be expected to bring back the same date, but the first returns rows only when the time is exactly midnight. The second and third select statements properly state a range of times within a single day:

```
/* this won't work ... only matches on time = midnight */
select *
from date_table
where date = "9/3/95"
/* this will work ... it states a range of times for the date */
select *
from date_table
where date between "9/3/95" and "9/3/95 23:59:59.999"
/* this will work ... and it might be easier to type */
select *
from date_table
where date >= "9/3/95" and date < "9/4/95"
```

In the last example, notice that the upper boundary is open (less than) and the lower bound is closed (greater than or equals). This is a general formula for returning a range of dates. Here are some other examples of search conditions returning a range of dates:

```
/* month */ where date >= "9/1/95" and date < "10/1/95"
/* year */ where date >= "1/1/95" and date < "1/1/96"
```

> **TIP**
>
> As you work with SQL Server, you will discover other techniques for date manipula-
> tion, including the date parsing functions, `datename()` and `datepart()`, and the
> `convert()` function, which are all covered in this book in the "Date Functions" section
> of Chapter 6, "Transact-SQL Programming Constructs." These functions can be used
> in search conditions to determine whether a date falls in a range. For example, you can
> use `datepart()` to determine the month and year of a date, as in this `select` statement,
> which finds rows with a date in September of 1995:
>
> ```
> select *
> from date_table
> where datepart(mm,date) = 9
> and datepart(yy,date) = 95
> ```
>
> The problem with using parsing functions in the search condition of a query is that the
> server cannot use an advanced performance strategy to speed the query. For example, if
> there were an index on the `date` column of this table, the range searches (`date between
> x and y` and `date >= x and date < y`) might provide a faster access path to the specific
> rows that match the search condition.
>
> When you ask the server to perform a function on a column in a search condition, the
> only way the server can resolve the query is to step through each row of the table,
> convert the `date` column in each row, and test its value. This method of query resolu-
> tion is called a *table scan* and usually takes much longer than index access, particularly
> when tables are large.
>
> In general, to get better performance, avoid using parsing functions in your search
> conditions. For much more on this and related topics, see Chapter 12 and Chapter 14,
> "Analyzing Query Plans."

# Logical Datatype: *bit*

SQL Server supports a logical datatype of `bit` for flag columns that store a value of 1 or 0. `bit`
columns are used for on/off or true/false columns. The following table includes a `bit` column:

```
create table bit_sample
     (id int not null,
      description varchar(30) null,
      active bit not null)
```

`bit` columns have several unique characteristics:

- They do not permit null values.
- They may not be indexed.

■ Several `bit` columns can occupy a single byte (SQL Server collects up to eight `bit` columns into a single byte of physical storage).

> **NOTE**
>
> There are many uses for `bit` columns, including status flags, active account indicators, and item availability. Advanced data warehousing systems can use `bit` columns to stand for larger columns to shorten data rows and improve performance substantially.
>
> There are many instances where a `bit` column is inappropriate. For example, inexperienced database administrators will create a `bit` column to indicate whether an account is active as well as a `date` column to store the activation date. The `active bit` column depends on the activation date in this example. This not only violates basic normalization rules, but also requires additional overhead to keep the two columns in sync.

# Numeric Datatypes

SQL Server provides many ways to store numeric values, providing flexibility in precision, range of values, and data storage size. Numeric types fall into four basic categories:

■ Integers—`int`, `smallint`, and `tinyint`

■ Floating-point datatypes—`float` and `real`

■ Exact numeric datatypes—`numeric` and `decimal`

■ Money datatypes—`money` and `smallmoney`

## Integer Datatypes

Integer columns store exact, scalar values. There are three integer datatypes for storing varying ranges of values: `int` (or `integer`), `smallint`, and `tinyint` (see Table 4.3).

### Table 4.3. Comparison of integer datatypes.

| Feature | int | smallint | tinyint |
|---------|-----|----------|---------|
| Minimum value | $-2^{31}$ (-2,147,483,647) | $-2^{15}$ (-32,768) | 0 |
| Maximum value | $2^{31}$ (2,147,483,647) | $2^{15-1}$ (32,767) | 255 |
| Storage size | 4 bytes | 2 bytes | 1 byte |
| bits | 31 | 15 | 8 |
| sign | yes | yes | no |

Integers make useful keys because they can record a large number of exact values in very few bytes. Where possible, use integers for numeric columns because of the efficient storage mechanism. Here is a `create` statement including all three integer types:

```
create table auto_sales
     (id int not null,
     make varchar(25) not null,
     model varchar(25) not null,
     year smallint not null,
     age_at_purchase tinyint not null)
```

Consider how each of the integer type columns is used in this example. The `id` column should be an `int` column in order to enable up to 2 billion unique row keys in this table.

In the example, the year of the car is a good use of `smallint` because the range of values is likely to be from about 1900 to 20*xx*.

> **NOTE**
>
> By the way, this is a terrible place to use a `smalldatetime` column. You are not recording the date of the car's manufacture (which requires date and time specificity), but the model year of the car. Aside from inefficient storage (`smallint` requires only 2 bytes and `smalldatetime` requires 4), `smalldatetime` does not permit date entry with only a year. For example, to find all orders in 1990, you have to parse the order date:
>
> ```
> select order_id, ...
> from orders
> where datepart(yy, order_date) = 1990
> ```
>
> In the case of a model year, where the date specifics are not required, an integer value for the year is much easier to search for:
>
> ```
> select make, model
> from auto_sales
> where year = 1990
> ```

The age column in the `auto_sales` example is a good example of `tinyint` (until people start living for 256 years!).

> **WARNING**
>
> Remember that you cannot change the datatype of a column. If you discover late in the game that a `decode` table requires more than 256 unique keys, and therefore `tinyint` was a bad choice for a primary key, you'll need to drop the table (as well as any other table that references that key) and re-create it with the proper datatype.

> **NOTE**
>
> An integer should be transmitted to the server as a number with no decimal place, as in this `insert` statement:
>
> ```
> insert auto_sales
>       (make, model, year, age_at_purchase)
> values
>       ("Ford", "Taurus", 1995, 42)
> ```
>
> Pass integers in search conditions the same way:
>
> ```
> select make, model
> from auto_sales
> where year >= 1993
> and age_at_purchase between 18 and 25
> ```

# Floating-Point Datatypes

SQL Server provides two approximate numeric datatypes, `float` (or `double precision`) and `real`, for handling numbers with a very large range of values requiring the same precision no matter how large or small the number. In Table 4.4, you can see that `float` and `real` differ only in precision and storage size.

**Table 4.4. Comparison of two floating-point datatypes.**

| Feature | float | real |
|---------|-------|------|
| Minimum value | $\pm 2.23E-308$ | $\pm 1.18E-38$ |
| Maximum value | $\pm 1.79E308$ | $\pm 3.40E38$ |
| Precision | Up to 15 digits | Up to 7 digits |
| Storage size | 8 bytes | 4 bytes |

`float` and `real` datatypes are useful for scientific and statistical data, where absolute accuracy is not required and where the data in a single column might vary from extremely large to extremely small.

> **NOTE**
>
> `float` columns use an internal algorithm to store numbers as a mantissa and exponent. The algorithm is not perfectly precise: What you put in is not always *exactly* what you get back. For example, a number with 15 significant digits entered in a `float` column may see some variance in the last digit.
>
> That was why I was surprised to learn from a client at one of the New York City financial trading companies that they had adopted a standard of using `float` for all stocks and bonds share prices. I had assumed that they used `money` or `smallmoney` instead (see the section "Money Datatypes," later in this chapter).
>
> The problem with using `money` and `smallmoney` was that they were rounding to the fourth decimal place, which was inaccurate when dealing with shares trading at $1/32$ of a dollar ($0.03125) or $1/64$ of a dollar ($0.015125). In spite of the fact that a `float` is an approximate money type, it was perfectly exact in this case, where the number of significant digits in the value did not approach the precision of the datatype.
>
> Remember that what you commonly think of as precision is the number of decimal places that are accurately returned. In the case of approximate datatypes, precision is the number of significant digits in the value. The value of $1/32$ (or 0.03125) requires five decimal places for storage, but a `real` or `float` datatype sees only four significant digits in the mantissa, 3.125, as well as an exponent, $10^{-2}$. The value of $325^{-1/32}$ (or 325.03125) also requires only five decimal places, but it requires eight-digit precision in a `real` or `float` datatype to record all the significant digits.
>
> This means that the decimal precision of `float` and `real` data decreases as the number to store increases. A `real` column is sufficient to store $1/32$ exactly, but it will not store $325^{-1/32}$ precisely.

## Inserting *float* and *real* Data

To insert `float` or `real` data, merely supply the number (always include a decimal). If you need to specify both a mantissa and an exponent, use standard scientific notation in the form, $\pm m.mmmE\pm ee$, where $m.mmm$ is the mantissa (up to 15 digits precision) and $ee$ is the base-ten exponent, as in the following example:

```
insert float_example
     (id, float_col)
values
     (1, 1.395E3)
```

# Precision of *float*

float permits the user to specify an optional precision, ranging from 1 to 15. A float column with a precision of 1 to 7 is stored as a real in 4 bytes; one with a precision of 8 to 15 bytes is stored as a float (without a specified precision) in 8 bytes.

# Exact Numeric Datatypes

SQL Server supports two exact numeric datatypes: decimal (or dec) and numeric. The two are mostly synonymous, but note that only numeric may be used in combination with identity columns. Use numeric data where the precision (number of significant digits) and scale (number of decimal positions) are known from the start. This is a useful datatype for handling monetary columns.

To create an exact numeric column, specify in the table creation statement the datatype, along with the precision (maximum is 28) and scale (less than or equal to the precision) for the column, as in this example:

```
create table numeric_example
     (id numeric(8,0) identity,
     num_col numeric(7,2))
```

The column, num_col, will store numbers up to ±99,999.99, with two digits following the decimal place.

> **NOTE**
>
> The identity keyword tells the server to maintain an automatic counter using this column. The server wastes some counter values because of failed insertions, so even if you know exactly how many rows will be contained in a table, you need to make a provision for the counter to grow to a higher value. SQL Server allows the use of only the numeric datatype of scale 0 with identity columns. Using too low a precision for the numeric type for the key in this example can result in the server being unable to insert rows in the table once the next available value is higher than the maximum value for the datatype.
>
> For more on identity and other characteristics of tables, see Chapter 5.

The storage size for a numeric column depends on the precision. A 28-digit numeric column will occupy 13 bytes per row.

# Money Datatypes

In the previous sections, you saw that `float` and `numeric` datatypes are useful options for monetary values. SQL Server also provides two datatypes specifically for this purpose: `money` and `smallmoney`. Both `money` and `smallmoney` are exact datatypes with four-digit decimal precision (see Table 4.5). (Some Sybase tools round up two decimal places for display.)

## Table 4.5. Comparison of money datatypes.

| Feature | money | smallmoney |
|---------|-------|------------|
| Range | ±922,337,203,685,477.5808 | ±214,748.3647 |
| Storage size | 8 bytes | 4 bytes |

**NOTE**

You probably noticed that the maximum `smallmoney` value is the same as the maximum integer value, but the decimal is shifted four positions to the left. `money` and `smallmoney` are treated essentially as integers for arithmetic operations; then the decimal shifts to the correct position for output.

Remember also that the correct format for entering money is with a dollar sign ($) and no commas:

```
insert dollar_table
      (id, dollars)
values
      (95, $12345.93)
```

**Important:** Your language option does not affect the currency symbol or choice of decimal separator.

The following table summarizes the datatypes discussed in this chapter:

| Datatype | Range of Values | Size in Bytes | Sample Input |
|---|---|---|---|
| **Character Datatypes** | | | |
| char[(n)] (character) | 1<=n<=255 | n (default is 1) | 'Fred' |
| varchar[(n)] (character varying) | 1<=n<=255 | data length (default is 1) | '14 Main St.' |
| nchar(n) (national char or national character) | 1<=n<=255 (and n <=255 / @ @ncharsize) | n*a @ @ncharsize | |
| nchar(n) (national char or varying or national charactervarying or nchar varying) | 1<=n<=255 (and n <=255 / @ @ncharsize) | n*a @ @ncharsize | |
| text | BLOB up to 2,147,483,647 chars | 16 + multiple of 2KB | 'Fred' |
| **Binary Datatypes** | | | |
| binary(n) | 1<=n<=255 | n | 0xa1b3 |
| varbinary(n) | 1<=n<=255 | n + 1 | 0xf1 |
| image | BLOB up to 2,147,483,647 bytes | 16 + multiple of 2KB | 0xf1... |
| timestamp | Used for change management | 16 | N/A |
| **Data Datatypes** | | | |
| datetime | Jan 1, 1753 to Dec 31, 9999 accuracy 3-millisecond interval | 8 | 'jan 2, 1770 13:15:17.12' |
| smalldatetime | Jan 1, 1990 to Jun 6, 2079 accuracy minute | 4 | 'jan 2, 1970 15:18' |
| **Logical Datatype** | | | |
| bit | 0 or 1 | 1 (up to 8-bit columns/byte) | 1 |
| **Numeric Datatype** | | | |
| int (integer) | ±2,147,483,647 | 4 | 1234567 |
| smallint | ±32767 | 2 | 2134 |
| tinyint | 0 through 255 | 1 | 32 |
| float [(precision)] | machine-dependent | 4 (precision < 16) 8 (precision>=16) | 123.1397864 |
| double precision | machine-dependent | 8 | 123.1397864 |
| real | machine-dependent | 4 | 123.1324 |
| numeric(p,s) decimal(p,s) (dec) | ±10 to 38th power, p is precision (total digits, 1-38) s is scale (decimal digits, <= p) | 2 through 17 | 12345.55 |
| money | ±$922,337,203,685,477.5807 | 8 | $1596980.23 |
| smallmoney | ±$214,748.3647 | 4 | $10000.25 |

# System Tables and Datatypes

SQL Server datatypes are not keywords; instead, they are stored as *data values* in a database-level system table, systypes. The systypes table contains both system- and user-defined datatypes.

If you view all the names of the types, you will see all the entries described in this chapter. You also will see entries for nullable versions of many datatypes. For example, systypes includes both money and moneyn—one for non-null and one for nullable versions of the money datatype.

# Summary

Datatype selection is one of the truly critical decisions the DBA must make when defining a database. Because a column datatype cannot be easily modified after a table is created, you need to anticipate the changing needs of your system and understand the ramifications of your datatype choices.

In the next chapters you build SQL Server objects, referring to columns and variables belonging to these datatypes.

# Creating and Altering Database Objects

# An Approach to Learning to Manage Objects

In this chapter you learn how to develop and maintain SQL Server objects by writing Transact-SQL statements. Because there are useful tools that enable you to maintain objects simply by using a graphical interface, you might wonder why you should bother learning the syntactic approach. There are two reasons. First, as you become more accomplished with the language, you will find it easier to create a fast example for testing by writing code than by using the tool. Second, and more importantly, when you are finished designing your database using any tool, you will need to make a backup version of that design, and you might even want to distribute that design (perhaps with minor modifications). The method of backing up and publishing a database *design* (as opposed to a database and its *data*) is to generate SQL scripts that can automatically reproduce the database structure.

# Creating Database Objects

All objects created within SQL Server require a frame of reference—a logical way of putting your arms around all the related objects. This logical grouping of objects is referred to as a *database*. We assume you are working, now, in an existing database. Do *not* begin playing in the master or model databases; instead, create one of your own if you are experimenting or learning.

> **NOTE**
>
> If you don't have a test database and you are working on a server where it's acceptable to make some mistakes, here are some quick instructions on how to create a new test database. If it's not acceptable to make mistakes on your server, you should carefully read Chapter 26, "Defining, Altering, and Maintaining Databases and Logs," before creating a test database. (You will need to be able to log in as sa to do this. If you can't log in as sa, ask your SQL Server administrator to create a database for you.)
>
> To create a test database, use isql/w to execute this command:
>
> ```
> sp_helpdb test
> ```
>
> If you get an error message saying that the database "test" does not exist, that's good. (If not, try "test1" and "test2" and so forth until you find an unused name.)
>
> Now execute this statement to create the database:
>
> ```
> create database test on default = 2
> ```
>
> This creates a 2MB database named test on a device that was set up for default use. If you get an error message saying that there is not enough space on the default disk, or if no default disk is found, there is more work to do and you need to read Chapter 28, "Database Logging and Recovery."

SQL Server supports a variety of database objects that enable you to better utilize, access, and care for your data. In this chapter, you learn the use and creation of the various SQL Server object types:

- Tables, to store SQL Server data.
- Temporary tables, to store temporary result sets.
- Views, to provide a logical depiction of data from one or more tables.
- Rules, to validate column data.
- Defaults, to provide a column value when none is provided by the client application.
- Constraints, to validate column data and to maintain consistency between tables.

In this chapter, you also learn about other structures (not properly *objects*, but relevant to this discussion):

- User-defined datatypes, to maintain consistent rule and default enforcement among related columns.
- Indexes, to maintain uniqueness and improve performance.
- Keys, to document the structure of individual tables and relationships among tables.

SQL Server also supports two code-based object types, which are discussed in Chapter 7, "Transact-SQL Program Structures":

- Stored procedures
- Triggers

# Tables

*Tables* are logical constructs used for storage and manipulation of data in the databases. Tables contain *columns*, which describe data, and *rows*, which are unique instances of data. Basic relational database design (in conjunction with your shop standards) determines table and column names, as well as distribution of columns within the tables.

Table creation is accomplished by using Transact-SQL's `create table` statement. Here is the fundamental syntax:

```
create table table_name
(column name datatype {identity | null | not null}
[, ...]
)
```

For example, you could create a four-column table called `demographics` using this statement:

```
create table demographics
(user_id numeric(10,0) identity,
last_name varchar(30) not null,
first_name varchar(30) not null,
comments varchar(255) null)
```

Table names are unique for a user within a database; this means that each user could potentially have his own table entitled `demographics`. (It also means that each user can have only one table called `demographics`.)

To remove a table and its structure, use the `drop` command.

**NOTE**

The basic syntax to remove most database objects is `drop` *object_type object_name*.

```
drop table table_name

drop table demographics
```

**WARNING**

There is no `UNDROP`. Once it is gone, it is gone. The only way to get a dropped object back into the database is to have the system administrator restore it from a dump. If that object did not exist in its entirety at the time of that dump, you are completely out of luck.

You can get information on the table you have created by executing the `sp_help` system stored procedure.

**NOTE**

`sp_help` is the Swiss Army knife of SQL Server. Without any parameters, it provides a list of all objects and user-defined datatypes in a database. If you pass a table name, it will show you the structure of the table (see the next example). If you pass a procedure name, it will show you the parameters.

```
sp_help table name

sp_help demographics

Name            Owner    Type         When_created
------------    ------   ---------    --------------------
demographics    dbo      user table   Nov 13 1995  8:50PM
( 0 rows affected)
Name                          Owner            Type
------------------------      ----------       ------------
 demographics                 dbo              user table

 Data_located_on_segment      When_created
 ----------------------       ----------------------
 default                      Jan 17 1996 11:46AM
```

```
Column_name    Type      Length Prec Scale Nulls Default_name Rule_name Identity
------------   --------  ------ ---- ----- ----- ------------ --------- --------
user_id        numeric        6   10     0     0 NULL         NULL             1
last_name      varchar       30 NULL  NULL     0 NULL         NULL             0
first_name     varchar       30 NULL  NULL     0 NULL         NULL             0
comments       varchar      255 NULL  NULL     1 NULL         NULL             0
Object does not have any indexes.
No defined keys for this object.
Object is not partitioned.
```

Alternatively, sp_help without an object name gives you a list of all objects in the database:

```
sp_help

Name              Owner             Object_type
---------------   ---------------   ----------------------
A                 dbo               user table
B                 dbo               user table
C                 dbo               user table
demographics      dbo               user table
insmessages       dbo               user table
smessages         dbo               user table
tr_A_ins          dbo               trigger
sysalternates     dbo               system table
sysattributes     dbo               system table
syscolumns        dbo               system table
syscomments       dbo               system table
sysconstraints    dbo               system table
sysdepends        dbo               system table
sysgams           dbo               system table
sysindexes        dbo               system table
syskeys           dbo               system table
syslogs           dbo               system table
sysobjects        dbo               system table
syspartitions     dbo               system table
sysprocedures     dbo               system table
sysprotects       dbo               system table
sysreferences     dbo               system table
sysroles          dbo               system table
syssegments       dbo               system table
systhresholds     dbo               system table
systypes          dbo               system table
sysusermessages   dbo               system table
sysusers          dbo               system table
p1                dbo               stored procedure

User_type         Storage_type      Length Nulls Default_name    Rule_name
---------------   ---------------   ------ ----- --------------- ---------------
```

This information is particularly useful if you are trying to identify what objects are within a database, if you think you created a database object and don't remember what you called it, or if you are sure you created one and it does not appear to be there.

Tables are comprised of up to 250 user-defined columns, each of which has three characteristics: a name, a datatype, and a property.

# SQL Server Object Names

All SQL Server object names can be up to 30 characters in length and are case-sensitive. The 30-character limitation is imposed by the maximum length of the name columns in the `sysobjects` and `syscolumns` system tables. Note that keywords, by definition, are case-insensitive.

The following is the full name of any SQL Server object:

```
database_name.owner_name.object_name
```

Note that the `database_name` defaults to the database you are in, and does not need to be explicitly named. `owner_name` defaults to the user name within the database of the person who signed in. If there is no object owned by the person who signed in, the server defaults to the database owner (`dbo`).

For example, this

```
pubs.dbo.authors
```

is a table named `authors`, owned by the `dbo`, in the `pubs` database (included with installation). The object

```
pubs.user1.authors
```

can coexist in that database and be owned by `user1`, and

```
user1.authors.au_lname
```

is the name of a column in the table `authors` owned by `user1` in the current database; however, you know this only by looking at the names and making sense of them. If you look at this by convention only, it could as easily be a table called `au_lname` owned by `authors` in the database `user1`.

> **TIP**
>
> In a production database, all objects should be owned by the `dbo` to simplify ownership, avoid confusion, and ease a permission scheme (see Chapter 27, "Security and User Administration").

# Column Properties

Columns can have the following properties:

- Null (a value does not need to be specified for a column)
- Not null (a value must be specified for the column)
- Identity (the server is to maintain a row counter on the table)

A value of null (in the column) means that the column has not been assigned a value. This is *not* equivalent to having a value of zero (for a numeric type) or spaces (for a character type). In fact, from a boolean standpoint, a null column value is not equal to a null column value because null is not a value at all; it is the absence of a value.

If a column has a property of not null, a value must be assigned at insert time or the row will not be inserted.

Identity columns are used for sequential, unique numbering of rows being inserted into the table:

```
create table table_name
(column_name {int ¦ smallint ¦ tinyint ¦ numeric(p,0)} identity [,...] )
```

Here is an example of a table with an identity column:

```
/* this table has first, last names and an automatic key */
create table names2
 (auto_key numeric(7,0)identity,
 first varchar(30) not null,
 last varchar(30) not null
 )
```

You may have a maximum of one identity column per table, which will be (by default) not null. Identity columns must use the numeric datatype and have a scale of 0 (for example, `numeric(7,0)`).

The right choice of datatype for an identity column is very important, because it is difficult to modify the datatype after the table has been created and rows have been added. In addition, identity columns are limited to the range of values for that particular datatype. In simpler terms, a column of type `tinyint` can store only 256 distinct values in the range of 0 through 255. By using an identity column, you have effectively limited your table to holding 256 rows!

If an upper or lower limit is reached for a datatype, inserts can no longer be processed on that table. SQL Server does not automatically reuse values that have been skipped or deleted, nor does the counter cycle back to the beginning to hunt for available values. In that way, your identity fields are limited by the datatype you select.

---

**TIP**

If your tables require an identity column and you anticipate that the identity value will grow to be quite large, remember that any whole-number datatype will suffice. A `numeric` column allows you up to 38 decimal places for storing numbers. When specifying the datatype for such a column, use `numeric (38,0)` for the datatype. You'll have 38 decimal places, which should be plenty of row numbers (but if you don't use all those numbers, you might be wasting a lot of empty space in each row).

---

To insert rows into a table with an `identity` column, do not specify the `identity` column in the `insert` statement. In the first example insert statement, the column names have been omitted and SQL Server expects values for all the columns in the table except the identity column. In the second example, the column names are specified; SQL Server expects values for only the named columns.

```
insert names values ("John", "Smith")
insert names (first, last) values ("Tom", "Jones")
select * from names
go
```

```
auto_key first            last
-------- ---------------- -----------------
1        John             Smith
2        Tom              Jones
```

The last value applied to an identity column for a session is available in the @@identity global variable (see more on global variables in Chapter 6, " Transact-SQL Programming Constructs"). @@identity retains its value until the session inserts another row into a table with an identity column.

You can use the syb_identity keyword in other SQL statements to refer to the identity column (or you can identify it by the column name):

```
select auto_key, first, last
     from names
/* OR */
select syb_identity, first, last from names

/* update a row in names2 table */
update names2
     set first = "John"
     where identitycol = 2
```

## Notes on *identity* Columns

Updates to identity columns are never allowed. You have to delete the old row and insert the new row.

> **WARNING**
>
> identity column values are not row numbers. SQL Server attempts to use sequential numbers for identity column values, but might not be able to because values are lost when rows fail to be inserted into the table after they are assigned an identity value when a transaction fails to complete. You can end up with gaps in the identity values SQL Server generates. SQL Server does not support internal row-numbering operations, and identity columns are not a 100-percent-reliable method of implementing such processing!

The table owner, database owner, or sa can explicitly insert identity values if the following set option is enabled:

```
set identity_insert table_name on

set identity_insert names on
insert names (10, "Jane", "Doe")
set identity_insert names off
go
```

This option enables you to set a seed value for identity columns or to fill in gaps in identity sequences.

> **WARNING**
>
> It is possible, with this option on, to insert duplicate identity values into a table if there is no unique index or unique constraint defined on the `identity` column. `identity` columns do not validate unique values—they merely generate numbers according to a sequence!

# Views

*Views* are a logical way of looking at the physical data located in the tables. In fact, to a `select` statement, a view looks exactly like a table.

> **NOTE**
>
> A view does not represent any physical data; it is merely a window into the physical data. Dropping a view has no effect on the underlying table(s).

Creating a view is as simple as writing a `select` statement. Views (like other objects) require unique names *among all objects in the database.*

```
create view view_name [ (col_name, ...) ]
as select statement
[ with check option ]
```

If you omit the column names in a view, the view columns inherit the column names from the base table(s) at the time the view is created.

```
/* make view with two columns from authors table */
create view author_name as
    select last = au_lname, first = au_fname
    from authors
```

If you use column headings, as in this example, the column headings become the column names in the view.

In almost all ways, you can treat a view like a table:

```
/* retrieve all rows and columns from view */
select * from author_name
last                                     first
---------------------------------------- --------------------
White                                    Johnson
Green                                    Marjorie
Carson                                   Cheryl
O'Leary                                  Michael
Straight                                 Dean
Smith                                    Meander
Bennet                                   Abraham
Dull                                     Ann
Gringlesby                               Burt
Locksley                                 Charlene
Greene                                   Morningstar
Blotchet-Halls                           Reginald
Yokomoto                                 Akiko
del Castillo                             Innes
DeFrance                                 Michel
Stringer                                 Dirk
MacFeather                               Stearns
Karsen                                   Livia
Panteley                                 Sylvia
Hunter                                   Sheryl
McBadden                                 Heather
Ringer                                   Anne
Ringer                                   Albert
( 23 rows affected)
```

To remove a view, use the drop view statement:

```
drop view view_name

/* drop the author_name view */
(d)drop view author_name
```

# Views as Security—Vertical

You can use a view to limit access to selected *columns* in a base table. (See Figure 5.1.) This is a normal approach to restricting access to a user while not requiring the user to write a lot of SQL. In this example, the view includes only three of the four columns in the titleauthor table.

```
/* create a view to show 3 of 4 titleauthor columns */
create view ta_limited as
    select au_id, title_id, au_ord
    from titleauthor
```

**FIGURE 5.1.**

*The view displays only the named columns. Those columns not named are invisible to users accessing the table through the view.*

| au_id | title_id | au_ord | royaltyper |
|-------|----------|--------|------------|
| 172-32-1176 | PS3333 | 1 | 100 |
| 213-46-8915 | BU1032 | 2 | 40 |
| 213-46-8915 | BU2075 | 1 | 100 |
| ... | ... | ... | ... |
| 998-72-3567 | PS2106 | 1 | 100 |

When you select from the view, you will only see the columns specified in the view. The royaltyper column in the titleauthor table is not displayed here and is unavailable from this view:

```
select * from ta_limited

au_id       title_id au_ord
----------- -------- ------
172-32-1176 PS3333   1
213-46-8915 BU1032   2
213-46-8915 BU2075   1
238-95-7766 PC1035   1
267-41-2394 BU1111   2
...
899-46-2035 PS2091   2
998-72-3567 PS2091   1
998-72-3567 PS2106   1
( 25 rows affected)
```

When you use a view for security, grant the user permission to select from the view but not from the base table.

This view can now be used to join titles and authors:

```
/* select title and author name using ta_limited view */
select au_lname, title
from authors a, titles t, ta_limited ta
where a.au_id = ta.au_id and t.title_id = ta.title_id

au_lname             title
-------------------- ----------------------------------------
Green                The Busy Executive's Database Guide
Bennet               The Busy Executive's Database Guide
O'Leary              Cooking with Computers: Surreptitious Balance Sheets
MacFeather           Cooking with Computers: Surreptitious Balance Sheets
Green                You Can Combat Computer Stress!
Straight             Straight Talk About Computers
del Castillo         Silicon Valley Gastronomic Treats
DeFrance             The Gourmet Microwave
Ringer               The Gourmet Microwave
Carson               But Is It User Friendly?
```

```
Dull                  Secrets of Silicon Valley
Hunter                Secrets of Silicon Valley
Locksley              Net Etiquette
MacFeather            Computer Phobic AND Non-Phobic Individuals: Behavior Varia
Karsen                Computer Phobic AND Non-Phobic Individuals: Behavior Varia
Ringer                Is Anger the Enemy?
Ringer                Is Anger the Enemy?
Ringer                Life Without Fear
White                 Prolonged Data Deprivation: Four Case Studies
Locksley              Emotional Security: A New Algorithm
Panteley              Onions, Leeks, and Garlic: Cooking Secrets of the Mediterr
Blotchet-Halls        Fifty Years in Buckingham Palace Kitchens
O'Leary               Sushi, Anyone?
Gringlesby            Sushi, Anyone?
Yokomoto              Sushi, Anyone?
( 25 rows affected)
```

# Views as Security—Horizontal

You can use a view to limit access to specific *rows* in a base table by writing a where clause in the view that restricts rows to those a user should see. In this example, the `cal_publishers` view contains only rows where the state has the value CA:

```
/* create view with only California publishers */
create view cal_publishers as
    select *
    from publishers
    where state = "CA"
```

When you select from the view, only publishers from California are displayed:

```
/* retrieve all rows and columns from the view */
select * from cal_publishers

pub_id pub_name                    city                   state country
------ --------------------------- ---------------------- ---- ----------------
1389   Algodata Infosystems        Berkeley               CA   USA
( 1 row affected)
```

# Views to Ease SQL

Views can be used to simplify queries. It has been my direct and personal experience that the best programmers are the lazy ones; they find efficient ways of doing things and are therefore more productive. Views are useful for hiding complex joins or denormalized tables from end users and easing the SQL for programmers. In this example, the view joins three tables, allowing users to query a complex data structure as if the data were stored in a single, flat table:

```
/* create a view to handle a three-way join */
create view titles_and_authors as
    select title, au_lname, au_fname, type
    from titles t, ta_limited ta, authors a
    where t.title_id = ta.title_id
    and a.au_id = ta.au_id
```

```
/* retrieve all rows and columns from the view */
select *
    from titles_and_authors
    where type = "business"
```

```
title                                        au_lname        au_fname    type
-------------------------------------------- --------------- ----------- --------
The Busy Executive's Database Guide          Green           Marjorie    business
The Busy Executive's Database Guide          Bennet          Abraham     business
Cooking with Computers: Surreptitious Balanc O'Leary         Michael     business
Cooking with Computers: Surreptitious Balanc MacFeather      Stearns     business
You Can Combat Computer Stress!              Green           Marjorie    business
Straight Talk About Computers                Straight        Dean        business
( 6 rows affected)
```

> **NOTE**
>
> This view contains the `ta_limited` view that was created earlier. A view is permitted to refer to other views.

Views can contain the following:

- Aggregate functions and groupings
- Joins
- Other views (up to 16 levels of nesting)
- A `distinct` clause

Views cannot include the following:

- `select into`
- A `compute` clause
- A `union`
- An `order by` clause

You can use an `order by` statement when selecting from the view, however.

The inability to use a `union` has design implications when it comes time to segment data tables horizontally.

# Data Modifications and Views

SQL Server allows you to insert into, update, and delete from views, with some restrictions.

`insert` adds rows to one base table. `update` and `delete` affect rows in one base table:

```
/* delete rows from a view ...
** corresponding rows in the table are deleted */
delete author_name
    where last = "Smith" and first = "Joseph"
```

```
/* change the name of a publisher */
update cal_publishers
 set pub_name = "Joe's Books and Magazines"
 where pub_id = "1389"
```

When a view includes columns from more than one table, you may not do the following:

■ Delete rows from the view (this would affect multiple base tables).

■ Update columns from more than one table in a single update statement:

```
/* this is NOT permitted */
update titles_and_authors
   set type = "mod_cook", au_fname = "Mary"
   where title = "The Gourmet Microwave"
/* INSTEAD, update each table in turn */
update titles_and_authors
   set type = "mod_cook"
   where title = "The Gourmet Microwave"
update titles_and_authors
   set au_fname = "Mary"
   where title = "The Gourmet Microwave"
```

Inserts are not allowed into views unless all underlying columns in the base table not included in the view either are defined to allow NULL values or have a default defined on the columns.

Inserts are allowed on views containing joins as long as all columns being inserted into the view belong to a single base table.

Finally, you cannot update, delete, or insert into a view containing the distinct clause.

## Views with check option

In previous releases of SQL Server, it was possible for users to insert or update a row, creating a row they could not retrieve with select:

```
insert into cal_publishers
     (pub_id, pub_name, city, state)
values
     ("1234", "Joe's Books", "Canton", "OH")

/* update creates an "invisible" row */
update cal_publishers
  set state = "OH"
/* would make ALL rows "Invisible" */
```

The with check option flag prevents insertion or updating of rows that will subsequently not meet the view criteria. Notice that with check option appears as the last element of the query:

```
create view view_name [ ( colname, ... ) ]
     as select_statements
     [with check option]
```

In this example,

```
/* create view with only California publishers */
create view cal_publishers_ck as
```

```
      select *
      from publishers
      where state = "CA"
with check option

update cal_publishers_ck
  set state = "OH"
```

the update fails because, after the update, the modified rows would fail to appear in the view. Here is the actual error message:

```
Msg 550, Level 16, State 2
The attempted insert or update failed because the target view was
either created WITH CHECK OPTION or spans another view created
WITH CHECK OPTION.  At least one resultant row from the command
would not qualify under the CHECK OPTION constraint.

Command has been aborted.
```

# Getting View Information

sp_help lists all objects in a database, including views and tables. To get a list of just the views in a database, run the following select statement:

```
select name from sysobjects
     where type = "V"


name
------------------------------
titleview
author_name
ta_limited
cal_publishers
titles_and_authors
cal_publishers_ck
( 6 rows affected)
```

To see a list of columns in a view, use sp_help:

```
sp_help view_name

Name                Owner    Type   When_created
------------------- -------- ------ --------------------------
cal_publishers_ck   dbo      view   Nov 14 1995  6:12PM
( 0 rows affected)


Data_located_on_segment
-----------------------
not applicable
( 0 rows affected)


Column_name  Type     Length Prec  Scale Nullable
-----------  -------- ------ ----- ----- -----------
pub_id       char     4                  no
pub_name     varchar  40                 yes
```

```
city          varchar    20              yes
state         char       2               yes
country       varchar    30              yes
( 0 rows affected)
...
 ( 0 rows affected)
```

# Renaming Objects

You may not change the owner of an object or its database, but you can change its name. To rename an object (for example, a table or a view), use sp_rename. In the example, the table name is changed from names2 to new_names2.

> **NOTE**
>
> Even though the name of the table has changed, objects like views and procedures that refer to the table by name are not affected by the change in the name. That's because SQL-based objects like views and procedures are stored both as text in the syscomments table and as a pre-parsed *query tree* identifying related objects by ID instead of name. When a table name changes, a dependent view still works because the object ID of the table (stored in sysobjects) does not change.

```
sp_rename old_name, new_name

/* change the table names2 to new_names2 */
sp_rename names2, new_names2
```

Once a table has been created, columns may not be removed, datatypes may not be changed, and null status may not be changed. However, columns may be renamed by using sp_rename. Here is the basic syntax for renaming a column:

```
sp_rename 'table_name.old_col_name', new_col_name
```

In this example, the au_lname column in the authors table is renamed last_name:

```
/* change the au_lname column to "last_name" */
sp_rename 'authors.au_lname', 'last_name'
```

> **NOTE**
>
> Quotation marks are optional when passing character data to stored procedures unless the character string includes punctuation or spaces (for example, authors.au_lname). Note that the original column name must include a table name, but the new column name is not permitted to specify one.

# Adding Columns to a Table

Columns can be added to an existing table using the `alter table` command. Here is a simplified version of the `alter table` syntax that shows you how to add a column to a table:

```
alter table table_name add
    col_name datatype { null ¦ identity } [, ...]
```

In this example, the `alter table` command adds two new columns to the `names2` table:

```
/* add middle name and fax columns to names table */
alter table names2 add
middle_name varchar(20) null,
fax varchar(15) null
```

New columns must either be `identity` columns or they must allow null values; otherwise, rows existing in the database would become invalid. The keyword `null` is required in the command.

A table can have only one `identity` column. When you add an `identity` column with `alter table`, SQL Server generates identity values for all existing rows.

# Temporary Tables

*Temporary tables* are real tables created in the `tempdb` database, usually for the purpose of holding an intermediate result set. Temporary tables are identified by a number sign (#) before the table name. They exist only for the duration of a user session or the stored procedure in which they are created. If the server crashes unexpectedly, these tables are lost, with no recovery possible. All SQL Server users have permission to create temporary tables.

One way to create a temporary table is to use the `create table` statement:

```
/* create temp table in tempdb for use in this session */
create table #temp (a int, b int)
```

More typically, temporary tables are created with `select into`:

```
/* create titles and authors table in tempdb
** for use in this session */
select au_lname, au_fname, title, pub_id
    into #titles_and_authors
    from authors a, titleauthor ta, titles t
    where a.au_id = ta.au_id
    and t.title_id = ta.title_id
```

Now, a two-table join can be made between `publishers` and `#titles_and_authors` to find out which publishers use which authors.

## Permanent Temporary Tables

Ordinary temporary tables only last as long as your session, and are only available to your session. You can create a *permanent* temporary table in `tempdb` by fully qualifying the table name with the name of the database:

```
select *
into tempdb..titles
from pubs2..titles
```

Permanent temporary tables exist until explicitly dropped or until the SQL Server is restarted (that is, after a shutdown or a crash). They are useful for nonpermanent data that needs to be shared between multiple users.

# Rules

Rules provide a mechanism for enforcing domain constraints for columns or user-defined datatypes. The rules are applied before an `insert` or `update`, prior to the execution of the command.

## Creating Rules

A rule is created in much the same way as any other database object:

```
create rule rule_name as
     @variable operator expression
     [{and¦or} ...]
```

Here are some examples of rules:

```
/* orders must fall into a range */
create rule order_quantity as
     @quantity between 100 and 150000


/* specify a list of valid colors */
create rule color_rule as
     @color in ('black', 'brown', 'red')


/* provide a rule for pub_id */
create rule pub_id_rule as
     @pubid like ('99[0-9][0-9]')
     or @pubid in ('0736', '0877', '1389')


/* date must be >= to current date */
create rule date_rule as
     @date >= getdate(
```

The variable (@date in the last example) is a placeholder and has no bearing on the column name. It must be no more than 30 characters in length, including the @.

Rules can use any of the comparison operators available in a where clause as long as the comparison operator works for the underlying datatype of the field to which the rule will be bound. In other words, a like clause works only with strings, so creating a rule that uses like as a comparison operator wouldn't be much use on a column that stores integers. For further information on this, see Chapter 3, "Introduction to Transact-SQL," on using the where clause, datatypes, and datatype conversions.

Rules are a Transact-SQL method for implementing *domain integrity*, which is the capability to maintain a valid list of values for a column. Domain integrity can also be implemented using ANSI-standard SQL syntax, which is discussed in the "Check Constraints" section later in this chapter. ANSI SQL syntax enables data object definitions to be portable to other ANSI-supported platforms, but using Transact-SQL statements means the data definition language can be used only with SQL Server.

If a rule is not bound to any columns or user-defined datatypes, you can drop it with drop rule:

```
drop rule rule_name

/* remove rule from database */
drop rule key_rule
```

# Rule Usage

A rule is a separate and distinct database object. In order for a rule to take effect, you must bind the rule to a column in a table or tables by using sp_bindrule:

```
sp_bindrule rule_name, 'table.column_name'
```

> **TIP**
>
> Remember that the quotation marks are necessary because of the separator, the period (.) in the parameter being passed to the sp_bindrule stored procedure.

This example binds the rule, key_rule, to the column user_id in demographics.

```
/* bind key_rule to user_id column in demographics table */
sp_bindrule key_rule, 'demographics.user_id'
```

You can instruct the server to stop applying a rule (unbind a rule) by using sp_unbindrule.

```
sp_unbindrule 'table.column_name'

/* unbind rule from user_id in demographics table */
sp_unbindrule 'demographics.user_id'
```

# Rule Limitations

A rule can deal only with constants, SQL Server functions, and edit masks. It cannot perform a table lookup (use a trigger if this is necessary), nor can it compare a column against other columns in the table.

Only one rule can be bound per column. If you bind a rule to a column and there is an existing rule bound to the column, it is replaced by the new rule.

A rule will not be retroactively applied to existing data in a table, but it will be applied when an existing row is updated.

A rule cannot be dropped if it is bound to a column or user-defined datatype; you must first unbind it from all columns and datatypes.

> **WARNING**
>
> Rules are not applied when you bulk-copy data into the system.

> **TIP**
>
> Make sure the values in the rule are compatible with the datatype of the column to which it is bound.

# Defaults

Defaults provide a value for a column when one is not supplied at insert time. Like rules, they exist only as database objects and after creation, they must be subsequently bound to columns.

To create a default, use the `create default` statement:

```
create default default_name
    as constant_expression
```

Here are some examples of defaults:

```
/* default country value is "USA" */
create default country_default as
    'USA'


/* default age is 16 */
create default age_default as
    16
```

```
/* default time is the current system time */
create default time_default as
   getdate()
```

> **NOTE**
>
> There are *no quotation marks* around the value 16. It is dangerously easy to make a mistake about the datatype of a default value. The server will not catch datatype mismatches until the first time the value is used in an `insert` statement.

To drop a default, use the `drop default` statement.

```
drop default default_name
```

```
/* remove default definition from database */
drop default age_default
```

# Default Usage

You bind a default to columns in a table or tables by using `sp_bindefault`. Here is the syntax for binding a default to a column:

```
sp_bindefault default_name, 'table.column_name'
```

In this example, the default `country_default` is bound to the column `country` in the table `country`:

```
/* apply the default to country in demographics */
sp_bindefault country_default, 'demographics.country'
```

To unbind a default, use `sp_unbindefault`.

```
sp_unbindefault 'table.column_name'
```

```
/* remove default from country in demographics */
sp_unbindefault 'demographics.country'
```

> **NOTE**
>
> How many d's in `sp_unbindefault`? Only one. The standard naming system always removes duplicated letters when they occur between words in the names of system procedures. So, `bind` + `default` becomes `sp_bindefault` and `help` + `protect` becomes `sp_helpprotect`. `add` + `dump` + `device` becomes `sp_addumpdevice`, however! (Only one d is removed.)

# Declarative Defaults

SQL Server also permits the declaration of a default value for a column during table creation. Note that the `default` expression falls between the datatype and the nullability:

```
create table table_name
(col_name datatype
     [default expression]
     [{null | not null | identity}]
[, ... ]
)
```

Here the definition of the price column includes a default value of $12.95:

```
create table items
(item_id char(6) not null,
price money default $12.95 not null)
```

Use the `alter table` statement to add or drop a default clause from a table:

```
/* To remove the default defined on price */
alter table items
     replace price default null

/* To define a default on ssn */
alter table items
     replace item_code default "N/A"
```

# Default Limitations

A column can have a default defined by a `default` clause or a default bound to the column, but not both.

A default can set only one constant or SQL Server function value; it cannot make a decision or perform a table lookup (use a trigger if this is necessary).

Only one default may be bound per column. If you attempt to bind a second default to a column, you get an error message from SQL Server (`Error 15103 (Severity 16)`). You cannot bind a default to a column that was created with, or altered to have, a default value.)

Make sure the datatype of the value in the default is compatible with the datatype of the column to which it is bound. Like rules, a default is not retroactively applied to existing data in a table.

Make sure that defaults are consistent with any rule on the column; otherwise, rows with defaults will not be inserted (although this might be a way of forcing a nullable column to be made not null).

The default is applied before the rule is checked; this enables the rule to be applied to the default rather than to the null value.

Defaults are applied during bulkcopy.

A default cannot be dropped if it is bound to a column or user-defined datatype; you must first unbind the default from all columns or datatypes before dropping it.

## When a Default Is Applied

Defaults are applied only when no value is specified for a column during insert. Consider this example:

```
/* define table with two columns */
create table table1
(id int not null,
price smallmoney null)

/* define a default price of $15 */
create default price_default as $15


/* bind the default */
sp_bindefault price_default, "table1.price"
```

In order to use the default value, the column must be assigned no value in the `insert` statement. An insert that does not specify columns must provide all values. In this example (where no columns are specified), a default will not be used:

```
/* value is provided for price, default not applied */
insert table1
values (1, $30)
```

The following insert format uses the default:

```
/* default is applied */
insert table1 (id)
values (5)
```

Inserting an explicit null overrides the default:

```
/* Explicit null value provided for price, default not applied */
insert table1 (id, price)
values (1, null)
```

# Examining Rules and Defaults

To list rules and defaults, along with all other objects in a database, use `sp_help`.

To list all rules or defaults in a database, use the following:

```
select name from sysobjects
    where type in ( "R", "D" )
```

To examine the rules and defaults bound to columns in a table, use this:

```
sp_help table_name
```

In the output of sp_help, the names of defaults and rules are displayed in the Default_name and Rule_name columns:

```
sp_help authors
```

| Name | Owner | Type |
| --- | --- | --- |
| authors | dbo | user table |

| Data_located_on_segment | When_created |
| --- | --- |
| default | Jan 17 1996 11:56AM |

| Column_name | Type | Length | Prec | Scale | Nulls | Default_name | Rule_name | Identity |
| --- | --- | --- | --- | --- | --- | --- | --- | --- |
| au_id | id | 11 | NULL | NULL | 0 | NULL | NULL | 0 |
| au_lname | varchar | 40 | NULL | NULL | 0 | NULL | NULL | 0 |
| au_fname | varchar | 20 | NULL | NULL | 0 | NULL | NULL | 0 |
| phone | char | 12 | NULL | NULL | 0 | phonedflt | NULL | 0 |
| address | varchar | 40 | NULL | NULL | 1 | NULL | NULL | 0 |
| city | varchar | 20 | NULL | NULL | 1 | NULL | NULL | 0 |
| state | char | 2 | NULL | NULL | 1 | NULL | NULL | 0 |
| country | varchar | 12 | NULL | NULL | 1 | NULL | NULL | 0 |
| postalcode | char | 10 | NULL | NULL | 1 | NULL | NULL | 0 |

| index_name | index_description | index_keys | index_m |
| --- | --- | --- | --- |
| auidind | clustered, unique located on default | au_id | 0 |
| aunmind | nonclustered located on default | au_lname, au_fname | 0 |

```
(2 rows affected)
```

| keytype | object | related_object | object_keys | related_ |
| --- | --- | --- | --- | --- |
| foreign | au_pix | authors | au_id, *, *, *, *, * | au_id, * |
| primary | authors | -- none -- | au_id, *, *, *, *, * | *, *, *, |
| foreign | blurbs | authors | au_id, *, *, *, *, * | au_id, * |
| foreign | titleauthor | authors | au_id, *, *, *, *, * | au_id, * |

```
Object is not partitioned.
```

You can get a wealth of information from the system tables if you know how. For example, to list all columns in a database bound to a rule, use this SQL:

```
/* list tables and columns for a rule */
select "table" = o.name, "column" = c.name,
    "user" = user_name(uid), "rule" = object_name(domain)
from syscolumns c, sysobjects o
    where o.id = c.id
    and object_name(domain) = "insert rule_name"
order by 1, 2
```

To list all columns in a database bound to a *default*, use the following:

```
/* list tables and columns for a default */
select "table" = o.name, "column" = c.name,
  "user" = user_name(uid), "default" = object_name(cdefault)
from syscolumns c, sysobjects o
```

```
where o.id = c.id
  and object_name(cdefault) = "insert default_name"
order by 1, 2
```

The text used to create a rule or default can be examined by using the `sp_helptext` stored procedure:

```
sp_helptext object_name
```

# User-Defined Datatypes

A *user-defined* datatype is not really a new datatype; it is a way of describing an existing datatype. It provides a mechanism for enforcing datatype consistency across and within a database or server. It also can simplify management of frequently used rules and defaults.

> **NOTE**
>
> A datatype is not a database object and therefore is not listed in `sysobjects`; it is listed in `systypes`, but follows object naming conventions.

## Creating User-Defined Datatypes

Define and remove user-defined datatypes with `sp_addtype` and `sp_droptype`:

```
sp_addtype type_name,
    system_type,
    {null ¦ "not null" ¦ identity}

sp_droptype type_name
```

> **NOTE**
>
> System types that include separators (for example, parentheses in `char` or commas in `numeric`) must be enclosed in quotes.

Here are some examples of user-defined datatypes:

```
/* add a social security number datatype */
sp_addtype ssn_type, 'char(9)', "not null"

/* add a price datatype */
sp_addtype price_type, money, null


/* drop the datatype */
sp_droptype price_type
```

## User-Defined Datatype Notes

You cannot drop a user-defined datatype if it is used in the definition of an existing column; you first have to drop all tables using the defined datatype.

You bind rules and defaults directly to the datatypes by using sp_bindrule and sp_bindefault:

```
/* bind price_rule to price datatype */
sp_bindrule price_rule, price_type


/* bind price_default to price datatype */
sp_bindefault price_default, price_type
```

Any column created with the price_type datatype automatically inherits the rule and default through the datatype, unless a rule or default has been explicitly bound to the column itself.

## Defining and Using User-Defined Datatypes

The following is a typical sequence of events when using datatypes:

Create a user-defined datatype:

```
sp_addtype ssn_type, 'char(9)', 'not null'
```

Create a rule and default:

```
create rule ssn_rule as
   @ssn between '000001111' and '999999999'
   or @ssn = 'N / A'
create default ssn_default as
   'N / A'
```

Bind the rule and default to the datatype:

```
exec sp_bindrule ssn_rule, ssn_type
exec sp_bindefault ssn_default, ssn_type
```

Create the tables using the datatype:

```
create table test_table
(ssn ssn_type, name varchar(30) )
```

Typically, user-defined datatypes are defined in the model database and propagated to the user databases as the new databases are created.

# Binding Precedence with Rules and Defaults

Rules and defaults are maintained with a single pointer, so if you unbind a rule or default from a column, no binding remains. The following example demonstrates this point. The last sp_unbindrule statement results in no remaining rule being bound to the column:

```
/* bind a rule to a column */
sp_bindrule "rule_r", "table_t.col_c"
/* bind another rule to the column */
/* the first rule is replaced */
sp_bindrule "rule_s", "table_t.col_c"
/* unbind the rule - no rule is bound now*/
sp_unbindrule "table_t.col_c"
```

A rule or default bound explicitly to a column overrides a rule or default bound to a datatype. A subsequent bind to the datatype replaces the bind to the column as long as the column and datatype have the same rule or default prior to modification. If you unbind a rule or default from a column, future binds to the datatype apply to the column.

# Indexes

The primary purpose of an index is to provide faster access to data pages than scanning every page. Secondarily, it is sometimes used as a mechanism for enforcing uniqueness.

## Index Types

SQL Server provides two types of indexes, *clustered* and *nonclustered*. Both are B-tree indexes. For clustered indexes, data is maintained in clustered index order; as a result, only one clustered index per table may exist (because data can be physically sorted only one way!). Alternatively, you can have 249 nonclustered indexes per table because nonclustered indexes maintain pointers to rows (not data pages).

An index can contain from 1 to 16 columns, but the total index entry width must be no greater than 255 bytes. Indexes are maintained and used internally by the server to improve performance or to enforce uniqueness. Under normal circumstances, the application programmer does not usually refer to indexes.

## Clustered Index Mechanism

With a clustered index, there is one entry on the last intermediate index level page for each data page. This means that the data page is the leaf, or bottom, level of the index. (See Figure 5.2.)

In Figure 5.2, which diagrams a clustered index on last name, to find Fred Amundsen you look first in the root page. Because Amundsen is between Albert and Jones, you follow the Albert pointer to the appropriate intermediate page. There, Amundsen is between Albert and Brown, so you again follow the Albert pointer to the data page. Note that the data page must be scanned (which is very quick) to find the actual data row.

**FIGURE 5.2.**

*A clustered index stores pointers matching the physical sort of the data. At the lowest index level, rows in the index point to pages in the table itself.*

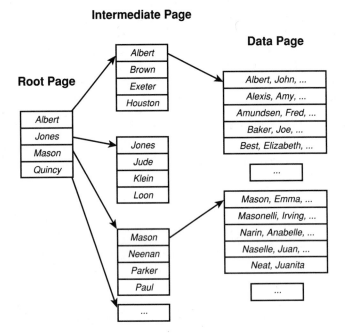

## Nonclustered Index Mechanism

The nonclustered index has an extra leaf index level for page/row pointers. (See Figure 5.3.)

**FIGURE 5.3.**

*The nonclustered index introduces an extra leaf level with one row of index for every row in the table.*

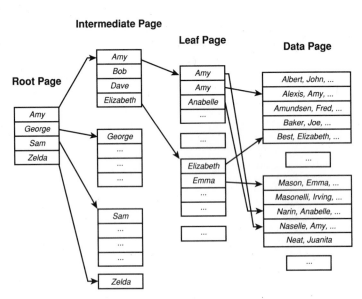

Figure 5.3 depicts a nonclustered index on first name (but a clustered index on last name). Let's find all the Amy entries. First, look into the root page. Amy is between Amy and George, therefore you follow the Amy pointer. Proceed like this until you get to the leaf page. At this point, read from the leaf page(s) the list of row IDs (page number and row number combinations) and read each of the Amy entries, retrieving rows as appropriate.

## Clustered versus Nonclustered

A clustered index *tends to be* one I/O faster than a nonclustered index for a single-row lookup because there tend to be fewer index levels. Clustered indexes are excellent for retrieving ranges of data because the server can narrow down a range of data, retrieve the first row, and scan the data without returning to the index for more information.

Nonclustered indexes are a bit slower and take up much more disk space, but are the next best alternative to a table scan. Nonclustered indexes may cover the query for maximal retrieval speed. This means that if the data required is in the index, the server does not need to return the data row.

> **WARNING**
>
> When creating a clustered index, you need *free space* in your database approximately equal to 120 percent of the table size. This enables space for the table to coexist in the database while it is being sorted.

## Creating Indexes

Create your clustered indexes before creating nonclustered indexes so that the nonclustered index entries will not need to be resorted or reshuffled during the data sort. (In reality, SQL Server actually drops and re-creates these indexes.)

```
create [unique] [clustered ¦ nonclustered] index
    index_name on table_name (column [, ...])
```

Here are some examples of index creation statements:

```
create unique clustered index name_index
    on authors (au_lname, au_fname)

create index fname_index
    on authors (au_fname, au_lname)
```

By default (unless otherwise specified), an index is nonunique and nonclustered.

# Notes on Indexes

Only one index can be defined on an ordered set of columns in a table (this is a new feature).

When an index is defined as unique, no two rows can have the same index value (null counts as one value!). The uniqueness check is performed at index creation, on insert, and on update.

Often, a clustered index is used for the primary key; this is not always the best performance selection. It is a good idea to have a clustered index on all tables; otherwise, space will not be reused from deleted rows. If there is no clustered index on the table, all new rows (and updated rows!) are placed at the end of the table.

As the number of indexes increases (past five or so) the overhead at update to maintain the indexes gets excessive; in an *executive information system* (EIS) where there is virtually no real-time update, the only constraint on the number indexes is disk space.

An OLTP system usually is configured with as few indexes as possible to speed update, insert, and delete activity.

Watch out for datatype mismatches in where clauses, especially char and varchar. They cannot be optimized effectively because the optimizer might be unable to use the data distribution statistics for the index. This is easy to do unintentionally in stored procedures. Using user-defined datatypes can help avoid this problem.

# Constraints

*Constraints* provide an alternative method for defining data-integrity requirements (to rules and defaults). SQL Server enforces three general types of constraints:

- Primary-key and unique constraints
- Check constraints
- Referential-integrity constraints

## Primary Key and Unique Constraints

SQL Server permits the declaration of a primary key or a unique constraint at table definition time. Unique constraints require that all non-null values be unique and allow a single null value for the column in the table. At definition, SQL Server automatically creates a unique index, nonclustered by default.

Primary-key constraints require that all values in a table be unique, and the column(s) cannot allow null values. They also automatically create a unique index, which is clustered by default.

All standard index-creation options are available as part of the syntax for primary key and unique constraints. Here is the syntax for creating the constraints:

```
create table table_name
 ( col datatype [ {identity ¦ null ¦ not null} ]
     [ constraint constraint_name ]
         {unique ¦ primary key}
             [ {clustered ¦ nonclustered} ]
  [ , ... ]
 [ [, constraint constraint_name ]
    {unique ¦ primary key}
         [{clustered ¦ nonclustered}]
             (col [, ...] )
 [, ... ] ] )
```

Primary-key and unique constraints can be defined at the column level or the table level. A table-level constraint can apply to a single column or multiple columns in the table. If you are defining a primary-key or unique constraint on multiple columns (a composite key), the constraint must be defined at the table level:

```
/* create names table: primary key on ssn (table level) */
create table names
 (ssn varchar(9) not null,
 name varchar(20) not null,
 constraint names_pk primary key (ssn) )


/* create names2 table: primary key on ssn (column level),
   nonclustered, unique key on name, ssn, clustered (table level) */
create table names
 (ssn varchar(9) not null
     constraint ssn_pk primary key nonclustered,
 name varchar(20) not null,
 constraint name_key unique clustered (name, ssn))
```

# Check Constraints

*Check constraints* specify a domain for columns (similar to rules) and may be slightly faster. They are defined for a table by using the `create table` or `alter table` command. Check constraints can be defined at the column level or the table level. Table-level constraints can perform multi-column checks.

Multiple constraints can be associated with a single column. Check constraints cannot compare column values to values in other tables (use triggers to do this), but they can look at other columns in the current row. Check constraints cannot contain aggregates:

```
create table table_name
 ( col datatype
     [ default constant_expression ]
     [ {identity ¦ null ¦ not null} ]
     [ [ constraint constraint_name ]
         check (search_condition) ]
  [ , ... ]
 [ [, constraint constraint_name ]
     [ [ constraint constraint_name ]
         check (search_condition) ]
  [ , ... ]
 )
```

Here are some examples of check constraints. The first example checks an `item_code` to make certain that inserted values consist of four characters, all numeric:

```
/* two column table with column level check
** constraint on key and default on price */
create table prices
 (item_code char(4) not null
    constraint item_code_constraint
    check (item_code like "[0-9][0-9][0-9][0-9]"),
  price smallmoney default $15 not null
)
```

The inventory table created here consists of three columns. Note that the high and low columns each have a constraint requiring that the value be above zero; then a table-level constraint requires that the high and low volumes have a specific relationship to each other (high must be greater than low and they must be no more than 1000 apart):

```
/* inventory table with column level check
** constraints and table level constraint comparing
** two columns */
create table inventory
 (item_code char(4) not null
    constraint item_code_constraint
    check (item_code like "[0-9][0-9][0-9][0-9]"),
  high_volume int not null
    check (high_volume > 0),
  low_volume int not null
    check (low_volume > 0),
  constraint check hi_lo_check
    (high_volume >= low_volume
      and high_volume - low_volume < 1000)
 )
```

# Referential-Integrity Constraints

*Referential integrity* (RI) in a database is the property of all foreign keys having an associated primary key in the related tables. For example, if there is a pub_id in the titles table, there should be a corresponding publisher in the publishers table. You can also add constraints to enforce referential integrity at table creation time or later with an alter table statement. Referential-integrity constraints prevent data modifications that would leave foreign keys pointing at nonexistent primary keys. For example, no title is permitted to have a pub_id that does not match an existing pub_id in the publishers table. (See Figure 5.4.)

Constraints can enforce both primary- and foreign-key integrity checks without programming; this is called *declarative referential integrity*. Constraints can support both column-level (single-part) keys and table-level (multi-part) keys.

Single-part keys can also be defined as table-level constraints.

*Declarative* constraints roll back an update or insert when the RI constraint is violated. More advanced RI options currently require using triggers or SQL transactions.

**FIGURE 5.4.**

*Referential integrity defines the relationship between two tables. The referencing table contains a foreign key, pub_id, that references a primary key in the referenced table.*

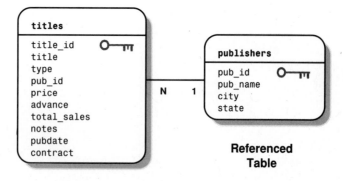

Referencing
Table

Referenced
Table

# Primary-Key Constraints

*Primary-key constraints* require that all values in a table be unique, and require a value in each column identified in the primary key (no nulls) for every row. They automatically create a unique clustered index, and all standard index-creation options are available:

```
create table table_name
 ( col datatype [ {identity ¦ null ¦ not null} ]
    [ constraint constraint_name ]
         primary key [ {clustered ¦ nonclustered} ]
  [ , ... ]
 [ [, constraint constraint_name ]
                 primary key [{clustered ¦ nonclustered}]
             (col [, ...] )
 [, ... ] ] )
```

In each of these examples, ssn is defined as the primary key for the names table. A unique, clustered index will be created on that column automatically:

```
/* primary key on ssn (table level) */
create table names
 (ssn varchar(9) not null,
  name varchar(20) not null,
  constraint names_pk primary key (ssn) )

/* primary key on ssn (column level, nonclustered)*/
create table names
 (ssn varchar(9) not null
     constraint ssn_pk primary key nonclustered,
  name varchar(20) not null)
```

# Foreign-Key Constraints

Foreign keys are declared using the reference constraint in the create table or alter table statement. Foreign-key constraints can be defined at the column level (single-part key) or at the table level (single- or multi-part keys):

```
create table table_name
 (column_name datatype
     [ [ constraint constraint_name ]
        references ref_table [(ref_col)] ]
  [, ... ]
  [, [ constraint constraint_name ]
     foreign key (column_name[, ...])
        references ref_table [(ref_col[, ...])] ]
 )
```

Here a `salesdetail` table is created that references two tables, `titles` and `sales`. Note that the `titles` reference is a column-level constraint on the `title_id` column, but the `sales` reference is a table-level constraint because the foreign key consists of two columns, `stor_id` and `ord_num`:

```
create table salesdetail
 (stor_id char(6),
  ord_num char(10),
  title_id tid
     constraint tid_fk_constraint
     references titles (title_id),
  qty int,
  discount real,
  constraint sales_fk_constraint
     foreign key (stor_id, ord_num)
     references sales (stor_id, ord_num)
 )
```

## Constraint Notes

Reference constraints currently are restrictive only. Tables named in a `references` statement cannot have rows deleted if there are existing rows in the referencing table matching the primary key. Primary key columns cannot be updated if they are referenced by a reference constraint and there are matching foreign-key entries in the referencing table.

Inserts or updates of foreign-key values into a referencing table is not allowed if the value of the new foreign-key entry does not exist in the primary-key column of the referenced table. No reference checks are performed when primary keys are inserted.

Tables referenced in reference constraints must have a primary-key constraint defined on the referenced columns or a unique index via a unique constraint or `create index` statement. If you do not provide the referenced column names in a reference constraint, there must be a primary-key constraint on the appropriate columns in the referenced table.

The datatypes of the referencing table columns must exactly match the datatypes of the referenced table columns.

Constraint names must be unique within the current database. If the constraint name is not supplied, SQL Server generates a unique system-generated name.

To reference a table you do not own, you must have references permission on the table. (This is new!)

A table can include a reference constraint on itself. A referenced table cannot be dropped until the referencing table or reference constraint is dropped. Tables referenced in constraints must exist.

If tables are to cross-reference one another, use `alter table` to add a reference after the tables have been created or use the `create schema` command.

## Modifying Constraints

You can add and drop primary- and foreign-key constraints by using `alter table`:

```
alter table table_name add      [constraint constraint_name ]
    { primary_key [ clustered ¦ nonclustered ]
        ( col_name [, ...] ) }
    ¦ foreign key (col [, ...])
        references ref_table [(ref_col [, ...])] }

alter table table_name
    drop constraint constraint_name
```

This example adds a primary-key constraint to the `publishers` table and automatically creates a unique, clustered index on `pub_id`. Even though the primary key is a single column, this is considered a table-level constraint because it was added at the table level using an `alter table` statement:

```
alter table publishers
    add constraint pub_pk_constraint
        primary key (pub_id)
```

This `alter table` statement adds a foreign-key constraint to the `titles` table, referencing the primary key established in the prior example. No rows can be added to `titles` if a corresponding `pub_id` cannot be found in the `publishers` table:

```
alter table titles
    add constraint pub_fk_constraint
        foreign key (pub_id)
        references publishers (pub_id)
```

The foreign key constraint on the `titles` table has been dropped and the restrictions on the table are lifted:

```
alter table titles
    drop constraint pub_fk_constraint
```

## Adding Constraints

To add a constraint to an existing table, use the `alter table` statement. All new constraints are defined as table-level constraints; column-level constraints can be created only at table or column creation time:

```
alter table table_name add
    [constraint constraint_name ]
```

```
{ {unique ¦ primary_key }
     [ clustered ¦ nonclustered ]
     ( col_name [, ...] )
   ¦ check (search_condition) }
```

Here a check constraint is added to the `prices` table, requiring the `price` to be greater than zero:

```
/* add a table level check constraint: prices > 0
** note that constraint is table-level,
** but only checks a single column */
alter table prices add
     constraint price_chk
     check (price > $0)
```

As with any object, to modify a constraint, you must drop and re-create it.

## Removing Constraints

To remove a constraint from a table, use the `alter table` command:

```
alter table table_name drop
     constraint constraint_name

/* remove the item_code constraint */
alter table prices
     drop constraint price_chk
```

## Information on Constraints

For information on the constraints on a table, use `sp_helpconstraint`. Here is sample output from the stored procedure:

```
name           defn
------------   ----------------------------------------------------------
cfk            titles FOREIGN KEY (pub_id) REFERENCES publishers(pub_id)
cpk            PRIMARY KEY INDEX ( pub_id) : CLUSTERED, FOREIGN REFERENCE
```

When you are defining primary-key constraints, remember that the primary key requires a unique index in order to work. Therefore, the primary key represents the unique row identifier for each row in a table. If you are defining primary keys that are to be referenced by other tables, make sure you are defining foreign keys on those other tables.

When you define foreign-key constraints, remember that you are working from the current table, and that it holds *foreign-key records that relate to a different primary-key table*. For example, the `titles` table in the `pubs` database serves as a primary key table for a relationship with the `titleauthor` table. However, the `titles` table is also a foreign-key table in relation to the `publishers` table. As a result, to establish the proper key relationships, you have to create a primary key on the `publishers` table and then create a foreign key on the `titles` table. You also have to create a primary key on the `titles` table and then a foreign key on the `titleauthor` table that references `titles`. Understanding proper key-creation order can prevent many headaches when dealing with large numbers of table relationships!

When defining unique and check constraints, you need only worry about the current table with which you are working. Because these two constraint types enforce domain integrity (the valid values possible for a column or set of columns), you don't need to worry about their creation order.

## Guidelines on Constraints

Rules and check constraints both enforce domains.

Tables can have both rules and check constraints. The set of allowable values will be the intersection of the rules and check constraints. Constraints enable you to define data integrity requirements as part of a table creation statement. Table-level check constraints can access other columns in the table.

Using datatypes with rules and defaults, you can centrally manage the data-integrity requirements of many columns through a single mechanism.

Constraint names must follow SQL Server object naming conventions, if named. If you do not name your constraint, it will be named for you:

- `tablename_colname_uniquenumber` for column constraint
- `tablename_uniquenumber` for table level constraint

For ease of maintenance, it is recommended that you explicitly name constraints.

# Comparing Data-Integrity Methods

Rules, defaults, and indexes are T-SQL extensions to the ANSI-89 SQL standard. Rules and defaults are reusable database objects and can be bound to many datatypes or columns. User-defined datatypes can simplify maintenance of rules and defaults for common columns and datatypes. Indexes can be created on columns other than primary-key and unique columns to improve query performance.

## Constraints

Constraints are ANSI-89 SQL-compliant. They are specific to the table in which they are defined. Check constraints can perform multi-column checks within a table. Because they are stored in the table definition, this documents data integrity checks within the table. Constraints also enable the display of custom error messages when the constraint is violated.

## Keys

SQL Server enables the definition of logical keys for a database design within the database. The key definitions are for documentation purposes only. The server does not use these for any purpose whatsoever. (As a result, the discussion here is short.) Their only practical application is that some applications (for example, APT-Forms) use the key information to help define join candidates between tables within the application. These differ from constraints (which enforce referential integrity) and indexes (which enforce uniqueness—for example, of primary keys).

Do not confuse keys with indexes. Keys are logical entities that have meaning to logical database designers. Indexes are physical database objects, whose purpose is performance:

| *Key Type* | *Description* |
|---|---|
| Primary key | Unique row identifier |
| Foreign key | Primary key from another table, typically used for joins |
| Common key | Usually an alternate, shorter primary key, used for joins |

Use these stored procedures to identify keys in your tables:

```
sp_primarykey table_name, col1 [, col2, ...]

sp_foreignkey table_name, pk_table_name,
    col1 [, col2, ...]

sp_commonkey table1_name, table2_name,
    col1a, col2a [, col1b, col2b , ...]

sp_helpkey table_name
```

# Which One Should You Use?

Which one should you use? As with all things, the simple answer is "it depends." There are some important distinctions. First, constraints have proved to be consistently faster than T-SQL data validation objects such as rules and defaults. The reason for this is that constraint-based validation of data happens as a code path within the SQL Server executable, and data-validation object processes require fetches from disk to read the validation object. For example, if you establish a check constraint and a rule on a column, the check constraint is always faster.

This is because the constraint is part of the SQL Server executable, meaning its instructions are always in working memory. With a rule, the instructions for validating data are out in the disk subsystem or, at best, reside in cache. Either way, instead of simply jumping to the code path, SQL Server must search for the resolved rule, execute the rule's instructions, and process the results. Because this involves reads to cache or disk, the process is inherently less efficient than using a check constraint. This principle also holds true for default constraints. As a general rule, constraints are always faster than the equivalent T-SQL data validation object.

In the case of referential-integrity constraints, there are some other issues to consider. As of System 11, SQL Server is only base-level ANSI 92-compliant. As a result, its referential integrity features support "restrict-only" operations. Therefore, if you have orders that you want deleted from the orders table whenever the corresponding customer is deleted, constraints do not work. Constraints work only when the goal is to *prevent* any multi-table operations. SQL Server constraints will not automatically *cascade* any multi-table operations.

> **NOTE**
>
> Data modifications are said to *cascade* when changes made in one table are automatically made to referenced rows in another table. The orders/customers situation referred to in the previous paragraph is an example of a cascade operation; a deletion to the customers table would result in possibly many deletions of related orders. Cascading operations are available within some RDBMSs and are considered part of the ANSI standard at this time.
>
> In order to implement cascading multi-table operations in Sybase SQL Server, you must write triggers using Transact-SQL coding. Creating triggers, particularly referential-integrity triggers, is discussed in Chapter 7. Until SQL Server's ANSI 92 compliance is expanded to support declarative referential integrity with cascade options, triggers are your only choice for implementing cascading RI functions at the database level.

The issue of portability is important for some shops as well. In areas where multiple relational databases are used, the capability to move quickly from one server platform to another can be an issue. As a result, some shops insist on ANSI 92 SQL compatibility for data definition language. In such cases, your only choice is to use ANSI constraints because SQL Server data validation objects are, by definition, proprietary enhancements to the ANSI 89 SQL standard. They do not work on any other server platform.

In the end, the issues boil down to functionality, performance, and portability. Based on the requirements of your applications, deciding on constraints versus T-SQL objects breaks down along these lines. If one doesn't work, the other probably will.

# Summary

In this chapter, you explored the creation and use of several database objects, all of which center on the manipulation and control of user data in tables. You could probably start designing a database with what you know right now, but there is a great deal more to learn about how these tables and indexes are physically stored in the server, what kinds of database design choices you need to make to provide the best `select` versus `update` performance, how SQL Server really uses indexes, and so forth. Proper database design and implementation is a major factor in the long-term performance and usefulness of a system, and it turns out to be fairly difficult to change the design of a production system. So keep reading!

In the next chapter, you learn about the extensions to the basic SQL language that make up Transact-SQL. These extensions are the building blocks for stored procedures and triggers, which you need to understand to begin designing effective databases for SQL Server.

# Transact-SQL Programming Constructs

**6**

A myriad of books are available that discuss the relative merits of the ANSI standard SQL language, not the lightest of which is the one published by ANSI. SQL Server supports 98 to 100 percent of the ANSI standard, but the ANSI standard does not really provide the ability to do anything other than query the database.

Because the SQL Server is much more robust and programmers demand more, SQL Server provides extensions to the standard for things such as extended functions and programming constructs. These extensions to the standard SQL are called Transact SQLs (abbreviated T-SQLs).

This section will cover the following topics:

- ■ SQL Server extensions to ANSI standard
- ■ Built-in mathematical, string, and date manipulation functions
- ■ Extensions to insert, update, and delete
- ■ Programming constructs (if, while, and so on)
- ■ Cursors

# SQL Server Functions

ANSI-89 SQL allows standard arithmetic operators (+ - * / ^) in both select and data modification statements.

## Examples

```
/* display 10% of each price */
select title, price, price / 10
from titles
```

| title | price | |
|---|---|---|
| The Busy Executive's Database Guide | 19.99 | 2.00 |
| Cooking with Computers: Surreptitious Balance Sheets | 11.95 | 1.20 |
| You Can Combat Computer Stress! | 2.99 | 0.30 |
| Straight Talk About Computers | 19.99 | 2.00 |
| Silicon Valley Gastronomic Treats | 19.99 | 2.00 |
| The Gourmet Microwave | 2.99 | 0.30 |
| The Psychology of Computer Cooking | | |
| But Is It User Friendly? | 22.95 | 2.30 |
| Secrets of Silicon Valley | 20.00 | 2.00 |
| Net Etiquette | | |
| Computer Phobic AND Non-Phobic Individuals: Behavior Variations | 21.59 | 2.16 |
| Is Anger the Enemy? | 10.95 | 1.10 |
| Life Without Fear | 7.00 | 0.70 |
| Prolonged Data Deprivation: Four Case Studies | 19.99 | 2.00 |
| Emotional Security: A New Algorithm | 7.99 | 0.80 |
| Onions, Leeks, and Garlic: Cooking Secrets of the Mediterranean | 20.95 | 2.10 |
| Fifty Years in Buckingham Palace Kitchens | 11.95 | 1.20 |
| Sushi, Anyone? | 14.99 | 1.50 |

```
( 18 rows affected)

/* use an operator in an update statement */

update titles
    set price = price * 1.1
    where type = "business"

/* perform concatenation with "+" */
select location = city + ', ' + state
    from publishers

location
- - - - - - - - - - - - - - - - - - - - - - -
Boston, MA
Washington, DC
Berkeley, CA
Chicago, IL
Dallas, TX
München,
New York, NY
Paris,
( 8 rows affected)
```

SQL Server provides advanced data manipulation through its string functions, math functions, date functions, and system functions.

# String Functions

Table 6.1 lists the SQL Server string functions, which can be used as part of any character expression. SQL Server string functions allow manipulation, parsing, and conversion of character strings.

### Table 6.1. SQL Server string functions.

| Function | Definition |
|---|---|
| **Length and Parsing** | |
| datalength(*char_expr*) | Returns integer number of characters in *char_expr*, ignoring trailing spaces |
| substring (*expression, start, length*) | Returns part of string |
| right (*char_expr, int_expr*) | Returns *int_expr* characters from right of *char_expr* |
| **Basic String Manipulation** | |
| upper (*char_expr*) | Converts *char_expr* to uppercase |
| lower (*char_expr*) | Converts *char_expr* to lowercase |
| space (*int_expr*) | Generates string of *int_expr* spaces |

*continues*

**Table 6.1. continued**

| Function | Definition |
|---|---|
| **Basic String Manipulation** | |
| replicate (*char_expr*, *int_expr*) | Repeats *char_expr*, *int_expr* times |
| stuff (*expr1*, *start*, *length*, *expr2*) | Replaces *length* characters from *expr1* at *start* with *expr2* |
| reverse (*char_expr*) | Reverses text in *char_expr* |
| ltrim (*char_expr*) | Removes leading spaces |
| rtrim (*char_expr*) | Removes trailing spaces |
| **Conversions** | |
| ascii (*char_expr*) | Returns ASCII value of first character in *char_expr* |
| char (*int_expr*) | Converts ASCII code to character |
| str (*float_expr* [, *length* [, *decimal*]]) | Performs numeric to character conversion |
| soundex (*char_expr*) | Returns soundex value of *char_expr* |
| difference (*char_expr1*, *char_expr2*) | Returns difference between soundex values of expressions |
| **In-String Searches** | |
| charindex (*char_expr*, *expression*) | Returns the starting position of the specified *char_expr*, else 0 |
| patindex ("*%pattern%*", *expression*) | Returns the starting position of the specified pattern, else 0 |

# Basic String Manipulation and Parsing

The important thing to understand is that all of the string manipulation and parsing functions you used in other languages are available in T-SQL. Of those listed in Table 6.1, note the following special uses:

datalength is useful for determining the length of a variable string.

right returns the rightmost *n* characters, but there is no "left" function; for a "left" function, use the substring function and start in position 1.

upper and lower are case conversion, which are useful for text comparisons.

# Conversions

The `soundex` function is useful in determining whether character strings sound similar. It's a nifty function that returns a value something like the following:

```
select soundex('Jeff')

----
J100
( 1 row affected)
```

This has useful but sometimes limited application. For example, `'Phone'` is more likely to match with `'Pen'` than with `'Fun'`. The `difference` function returns a value between `0` and `4`, with `0` being the least similar and `4` being the most similar.

```
select soundex('Phone'), soundex('Fun'), soundex ('Pen')
select 'Phone-Fun ' , difference ('Phone', 'Fun')
select 'Phone-Pen ' , difference ('Phone', 'Pen')


----- ----- -----
P500  F500  P500
( 1 row affected)


---------- ----------
Phone-Fun  3
( 1 row affected)


---------- ----------
Phone-Pen  4
( 1 row affected)
```

You can form your own opinion about the usefulness of the `difference` function.

# String Functions—Wildcards

SQL Server provides wildcards to allow pattern matching in text searches. This is roughly like the matching you use in Windows File Manager to look for a missing file. Table 6.2 outlines the wildcards, which you must use with the `like` operator.

## Table 6.2. SQL Server wildcards.

| Wildcard | Description |
|----------|-------------|
| % | Matches any quantity of characters, or no characters |
| _ | (Underscore) Matches any single character (a place holder) |
| [ ] | Specifies a range of valid characters, or an "or" condition (this is an SQL Server extension) |

# Examples

```
[ABG]       /* matches "A" or "B" or "G" */

[A-CE-G]    /* matches "A", "B", "C", "E", "F", "G" */

[^ABG]      /* matches any except "A", "B", "G" */

[^A-C]      /* matches any except "A", "B", "C" */
```

> **WARNING**
>
> It is very important to use wildcards with the `like` operator instead of `=`.
>
> ```
> /* this will work */
> select * from authors
>     where au_lname like "[Ss]mith%"
> /* this will not work as expected! */
> select * from authors
>     where au_lname = "[Ss]mith%"
> ```
>
> In the first example, the server will return rows with values like 'Smith', 'smith', 'Smithers', and 'Smithsonian'. In the last example, the server is being instructed to look for an author whose last name is '[Ss]mith%'. I would not expect any rows to be returned.

## The *escape* Clause

To include wildcard characters as literals in a search string, use an escape character.

SQL Server by default uses the square brackets ([]) to escape a wildcard, which means that you should use the wildcard as a literal character.

## Example

```
/* find a string containing the value 20% */
select * from test_tab
    where description like "%20[%]%"
```

The ANSI-89 SQL Standard defines the escape clause to specify an escape character.

## Syntax

```
like char_expression escape escape_character
```

## Example

```
/* find a string containing the value 20% */
```

```
select * from test_tab
    where description like "%20#%%" escape "#"
```

An escape character retains its special meaning inside square brackets (unlike wildcard characters). It is only valid within its `like` predicate and does not affect other `like` predicates in the same statement. Finally, it affects only the single character following it.

# String Functions—Examples

In this example, we build a name column from two columns, using the concatenation operator, +.

```
select au_lname + "," + au_fname
    from authors
```

Here are the results of the query:

```
-------------------------------------------------------------
White,Johnson
Green,Marjorie
Carson,Cheryl
O'Leary,Michael
Straight,Dean
Smith,Meander
Bennet,Abraham
Dull,Ann
Gringlesby,Burt
Locksley,Charlene
Greene,Morningstar
Blotchet-Halls,Reginald
Yokomoto,Akiko
del Castillo,Innes
DeFrance,Michel
Stringer,Dirk
MacFeather,Stearns
Karsen,Livia
Panteley,Sylvia
Hunter,Sheryl
McBadden,Heather
Ringer,Anne
Ringer,Albert
( 23 rows affected)
```

This example finds all rows where the last name has an identical soundex value to the name Green. The results of the query follow immediately after.

```
select au_id, au_lname, au_fname
    from authors
    where difference (au_lname, "Green") = 4
```

```
au_id        au_lname                                    au_fname
----------   -----------------------------------------   --------------------
213-46-8915  Green                                       Marjorie
527-72-3246  Greene                                      Morningstar
( 2 rows affected)
```

The soundex function returns the same results as the `difference` function in this example.

```
select au_id, au_lname, au_fname
    from authors
    where soundex (au_lname) = soundex ("Green")
```

| au_id | au_lname | au_fname |
|-------|----------|----------|
| 213-46-8915 | Green | Marjorie |
| 527-72-3246 | Greene | Morningstar |
| ( 2 rows affected) | | |

Here is an `update` statement using the `stuff` function to replace the fourth character of the phone column with a hyphen:

```
/* replace characters within a string */
update authors
    set phone = stuff(phone, 4, 1, "-")
```

This example displays all titles containing the word computer, using the `like` operator and wildcards to identify many rows.

```
select title
    from titles
    where title like "%Computer%"
```

```
title
-------------------------------------------------------------------
Computer Phobic AND Non-Phobic Individuals: Behavior Variations
Cooking with Computers: Surreptitious Balance Sheets
Straight Talk About Computers
The Psychology of Computer Cooking
You Can Combat Computer Stress!
( 5 rows affected)
```

# Mathematical Functions

SQL Server performs standard arithmetic operations using normal precedence (functions and parentheses are evaluated first, then multiplication, division, addition, and subtraction, all from left to right). Also, SQL Server supports all standard trigonometric functions and a number of other useful ones.

## Table 6.3. SQL Server mathematic functions.

| Function | Description |
|----------|-------------|
| abs (*numeric_expr*) | Returns the absolute value of the specified value |
| ceiling (*numeric_expr*) | Returns the smallest integer greater than or equal to the specified value |
| exp (*float_expr*) | Provides the exponential value of the specified value |
| floor (*numeric_expr*) | Returns the largest integer less than or equal to the specified value |

| *Function* | *Description* |
|---|---|
| pi () | Returns the constant value of 3.1415926… |
| power (*numeric_expr, power*) | Returns the value of *numeric_expr* to the power of *power* |
| rand ([*int_expr*]) | Returns a random float number between 0 and 1, optionally using *int_expr* as a seed |
| round (*numeric_expr, int_expr*) | Rounds off a numeric expression to the precision specified in *int_expr* |
| sign (*int_expr*) | Returns the positive (+1), zero (0), or negative (-1) |
| sqrt (*float_expr*) | Provides the square root of the specified value |

**WARNING**

The randomizer function needs a random seed in order to provide a random value.

# Date Functions

SQL Server includes date functions for performing date parsing and date arithmetic. This is extremely useful for identifying (for example) how old invoices are.

**Table 6.4. Date functions.**

| *Function* | *Description* |
|---|---|
| getdate ( ) | Returns current system date and time |
| datename(*datepart, date_expr*) | Returns specified part of *date_expr* value as a string, converted to a name (e.g. June) if appropriate |
| datepart(*datepart, date_expr*) | Returns specified part of *date_expr* value as an integer |
| datediff(*datepart, date_expr1, date_expr2*) | Returns *date_expr2 – date_expr1*, as measured by specified *datepart* |
| dateadd(*datepart, number, date_expr*) | Returns the date produced by adding specified *number* of date parts to *date_expr* |

# Date Parts (for Use with Date Functions)

Date parts are used in conjunction with the date functions to specify an element of a date value for parsing or date arithmetic.

**Table 6.5. SQL Server date parts.**

| Date Part | Abbreviation | Value Range (in datepart) |
|-----------|--------------|---------------------------|
| year | yy | 1753–9999 |
| quarter | qq | 1–4 |
| month | mm | 1–12 |
| dayofyear | dy | 1–366 |
| day | dd | 1–31 |
| week | wk | 1–54 |
| weekday | dw | 1–7 (1=Sunday) |
| hour | hh | 0–23 |
| minute | mi | 0–59 |
| second | ss | 0–59 |
| millisecond | ms | 0–999 |

# Examples

```
/* what is the current date and time */
select getdate()
```

```
---------------------------
Nov 15 1995 10:39AM
( 1 row affected)
```

```
/* how old are unpaid invoices? */
select invoice_no,
    datediff (dd, date_shipped, getdate())
    from invoices
    where balance_due > 0
```

In this previous example, notice the sequence date_shipped, get_date, which avoids a negative number.

```
/* what month were these books published? */
select title, datename ( mm, pubdate )
    from titles
```

```
title
```

```
- - - - - - - - - - - - - - - - - - - - - - - - - - - - - - - - - - - - - - - - - - - - - - - - - - - - - - - - -
The Busy Executive's Database Guide                                     June
Cooking with Computers: Surreptitious Balance Sheets                   June
You Can Combat Computer Stress!                                         June
Straight Talk About Computers                                          June
Silicon Valley Gastronomic Treats                                      June
The Gourmet Microwave                                                  June
The Psychology of Computer Cooking                                     November
But Is It User Friendly?                                               June
Secrets of Silicon Valley                                             June
Net Etiquette                                                         November
Computer Phobic AND Non-Phobic Individuals: Behavior Variations       October
Is Anger the Enemy?                                                    June
Life Without Fear                                                     October
Prolonged Data Deprivation: Four Case Studies                         June
Emotional Security: A New Algorithm                                   June
Onions, Leeks, and Garlic: Cooking Secrets of the Mediterranean       October
Fifty Years in Buckingham Palace Kitchens                             June
Sushi, Anyone?                                                        June
( 18 rows affected)
```

## convert

The convert function is used to change data from one type to another when SQL Server cannot implicitly understand a conversion (for example, float, real, and integer values are all dynamically converted for comparison purposes).

## Syntax

```
convert (datatype [(length)], expression)
```

## Example

```
/* return one column of data ...the conversion is
** required to allow concatenation of literal
** string with a numeric */

select "Advance = "
    + convert (char(12), advance)
from titles
```

```
- - - - - - - - - - - - - - - - - - - - - - - - -
Advance =        5000.00
Advance =        5000.00
Advance =       10125.00
Advance =        5000.00
Advance =           0.00
Advance =       15000.00
Advance =
Advance =        7000.00
Advance =        8000.00
Advance =
```

```
Advance =      7000.00
Advance =      2275.00
Advance =      6000.00
Advance =      2000.00
Advance =      4000.00
Advance =      7000.00
Advance =      4000.00
Advance =      8000.00
( 18 rows affected)
```

SQL Server will make any reasonable conversion; if you choose an unreasonable conversion, you will get an error message. For example, you can't convert a binary value to a date!

# Date Conversions

A special version of the `convert` function allows date datatypes to be converted to character types.

## Syntax

```
convert (datatype [(length)], expression, format)
```

The *format* parameter tells SQL Server which date format to provide in the converted string.

## Table 6.6. Date formats available with the `convert` function.

| Without Century | With Century | Format of Date in Converted String |
|---|---|---|
|  | 0 or 100 | mon dd yyyy hh:miAM (or PM) |
| 1 | 101 | mm/dd/yy |
| 2 | 102 | yy.mm.dd |
| 3 | 103 | dd/mm/yy |
| 4 | 104 | dd.mm.yy |
| 5 | 105 | dd-mm-yy |
| 6 | 106 | dd mon yy |
| 7 | 107 | mon dd, yy |
| 8 | 108 | hh:mm:ss |
|  | 9 or 109 | mon dd, yyyy hh:mi:ss:mmmAM (or PM) |
| 10 | 110 | mm-dd-yy |
| 11 | 111 | yy/mm/dd |
| 12 | 112 | yymmdd |

Notice that you can display dates in almost any kind of format without resorting to string manipulation.

## Example

```
/* return pubdate in mon dd, yyyy format*/
select "Pubdate" = convert (char(12), pubdate, 107)
    from titles

Pubdate
------------
Jun 12, 1991
Jun 09, 1991
Jun 30, 1991
Jun 22, 1991
Jun 09, 1991
Jun 18, 1991
Nov 13, 1995
Jun 30, 1991
Jun 12, 1994
Nov 13, 1995
Oct 21, 1991
Jun 15, 1991
Oct 05, 1991
Jun 12, 1991
Jun 12, 1991
Oct 21, 1991
Jun 12, 1991
Jun 12, 1991
( 18 rows affected)
```

# System Functions

System functions are used to display information about the SQL Server, database, or user. These tend to be used a lot by programmers and DBAs, but not very often by users.

## Useful System Functions

System functions with optional parameters will return values for current user, database, and process if a parameter is not specified. System functions allow quick conversion of system and object information without writing several join clauses. They are heavily used in system stored procedures.

## Table 6.7. SQL Server system functions.

| Function | Definition |
| --- | --- |
| **Access and Security Information** | |
| host_id ( ) | Current host process ID number of client process |
| host_name ( ) | Current host computer name of client process |
| suser_id (["*login_name*"]) | User's SQL Server ID number |
| suser_name ([*server_user_id*]) | User's SQL Server login name |
| user_id (["*name_in_db*"]) | User's ID number in database |
| user_name ([*user_id*]) | User's name in database |
| user | User's name in database |
| show_role() | Current active roles for user |
| **Database and Object Information** | |
| db_id (["*db_name*"]) | Database ID number |
| db_name ([*db_id*]) | Database name |
| object_id ("*objname*") | Database object ID number |
| object_name (*obj_id*) | Database object name |
| col_name (*obj_id,col_id*) | Column name of object |
| col_length ("*objname*", "*colname*") | Length of column |
| index_col ("*objname*", *index_id*, *key #*) | Indexed column name |
| valid_name (*char_expr*) | Returns 0 if *char_expr* is not a valid identifier |
| **Data Functions** | |
| datalength (*expression*) | Returns length of *expression* in bytes |
| tsequal (*timestamp1*, *timestamp2*) | Compares timestamp values. Returns error if timestamp values do not match |

# System Function Examples

```
/* return current user ID*/
select user_id ()

------
1
```

```
( 1 row affected)

/* return login name of the login whose ID is 10 */
select suser_name (1)

- - - - - - - - - - - - - - - - - - - - - - - - - - - - - -
sa
( 1 row affected)
```

> **NOTE**
>
> The system user ID (suid) of the sa is always 1 because sa is the first login added to the syslogins table during installation. SQL Server automatically assigns suid values sequentially starting with the value 1.
>
> Likewise, the user ID (uid) of the dbo is always 1 (user_name("dbo") is always 1) because the dbo is the first user added to the sysusers table in every database when the database is created.

```
/* Return name of the object specified by the ID */
select object_name (112003430)


- - - - - - - - - - - - - - - - - - - - - - - - - - - - - -
publishers
( 1 row affected)

/* Return list of all indexes for titles table */
select name from sysindexes
    where id = object_id("titles")

name
- - - - - - - - - - - - - - - - - - - - - - - - - - - - - -
UPKCL_titleidind
titleind
( 2 rows affected)

/* compare timestamps for update */
update titles
    set price = $10.95
    where title_id = "BU1032"
    and tsequal(timestamp, 0x0010000000002ea8)
```

# compute and compute by

The compute and compute by keywords allow you to include both detail and summary information in a single result set.

## compute

A compute clause reports overall aggregates for a result set.

# Example

```
/*list titles and prices, show overall max price*/
select title, price
    from titles
    compute max(price)
```

| title | price |
| --- | --- |
| The Busy Executive's Database Guide | 19.99 |
| Cooking with Computers: Surreptitious Bal | 11.95 |
| You Can Combat Computer Stress! | 2.99 |
| Straight Talk About Computers | 19.99 |
| Silicon Valley Gastronomic Treats | 19.99 |
| The Gourmet Microwave | 2.99 |
| The Psychology of Computer Cooking | |
| But Is It User Friendly? | 22.95 |
| Secrets of Silicon Valley | 20.00 |
| Net Etiquette | |
| Computer Phobic AND Non-Phobic Individual | 21.59 |
| Is Anger the Enemy? | 10.95 |
| Life Without Fear | 7.00 |
| Prolonged Data Deprivation: Four Case Stu | 19.99 |
| Emotional Security: A New Algorithm | 7.99 |
| Onions, Leeks, and Garlic: Cooking Secret | 20.95 |
| Fifty Years in Buckingham Palace Kitchens | 11.95 |
| Sushi, Anyone? | 14.99 |
| | 23 |

```
( 19 rows affected)
```

In this output, the most expensive book is listed as 23 (note the last line). The format of this output will vary from one reporting tool to the next. Some tools (including isql) produce a header in the line before the output, but this is completely dependent on the application program. The server merely returns rows marked as compute columns and it is up to the application to determine a format. Here is what the isql output might look like:

```
max
        ========================
                22.95
```

A compute by clause displays subtotals within a result set, but not totals.

# Example

```
/* display type, title and price,
** and show the maximum price for each type */
select type, title, price
    from titles
    order by type
    compute max(price) by type
```

| type | title | price |
| --- | --- | --- |
| UNDECIDED | The Psychology of Computer Cook | |
| | | 0 |
| business | Straight Talk About Computers | 19.99 |

```
business      You Can Combat Computer Stress!      2.99
business      The Busy Executive's Database G     19.99
business      Cooking with Computers: Surrept     11.95
                                                  20
mod_cook      The Gourmet Microwave                2.99
mod_cook      Silicon Valley Gastronomic Trea    19.99
                                                  20
popular_comp Net Etiquette
popular_comp But Is It User Friendly?             22.95
popular_comp Secrets of Silicon Valley            20.00
                                                  23
psychology    Life Without Fear                    7.00
psychology    Is Anger the Enemy?                 10.95
psychology    Emotional Security: A New Algor      7.99
psychology    Prolonged Data Deprivation: Fou     19.99
psychology    Computer Phobic AND Non-Phobic      21.59
                                                  22
trad_cook     Sushi, Anyone?                      14.99
trad_cook     Fifty Years in Buckingham Palac     11.95
trad_cook     Onions, Leeks, and Garlic: Cook     20.95
                                                  21

( 24 rows affected)
```

Looking at the results, you should see a maximum price reported for each type.

To show subtotals and totals, combine compute by and compute in one select statement. Note the subtotals and final total in this example:

```
/*display details with subtotals and grand totals*/
select pub_id, title_id, ytd_sales
    from titles
    order by pub_id
    compute sum(ytd_sales) by pub_id
    compute sum(ytd_sales)
```

```
pub_id   title_id   ytd_sales   sum(ytd_sales)   sum(ytd_sales)
0736     BU2075     18722
0736     PS2091     2045
0736     PS2106     111
0736     PS3333     4072
0736     PS7777     3336        28286
0877     MC3026
0877     MC2222     2032
0877     MC3021     22246
0877     PS1372     375
0877     TC3218     375
0877     TC4203     15096
0877     TC7777     4095        44219
1389     PC9999
1389     BU1032     4095
1389     BU1111     3876
1389     BU7832     4095
1389     PC1035     8780
1389     PC8888     4095        24941            97446
```

## *compute* and *compute by* Notes

Whenever you use compute by, you must also use order by. Although all of the ordering columns do not need to be named in the compute by clause, the columns that are named must match *one for one* the order columns in left-to-right order without skipping.

An example often clarifies this point. If you had a select statement with the following order by clause:

```
order by a, b, c
```

the only allowed compute by clauses would be:

- compute by a, b, c
- compute by a, b
- compute by a

If you try to perform a compute by operation without a corresponding order by clause, the server returns this message:

```
A compute-by item was not found in the order-by list.
All expressions in the compute-by list must also be present in the order-by list
```

Expressions in a compute or compute by clause must match exactly the corresponding expression in the select list.

## Example

```
select type, price, price*2
from titles
    where type = "business"
    compute sum(price), sum(price*2)
```

```
type         price
----------   -------------------------   --------------------------
business     19.99                       39.98
business     11.95                       23.90
business     2.99                        5.98
business     19.99                       39.98
                                         110

( 5 rows affected)
```

# *isnull* Function

Sometimes, when calculating aggregates or printing reports to end users, you want to have null values treated as if they are something else. To make them that "something else," you can use the isnull function. The isnull function substitutes a specified value for a null value in a column in a query or an aggregate.

This is easier if you consider an example. Consider an `invoices` table containing four rows, and the value of the `total_order` column in those rows is $15, $20, $25, and `null`. Compare the value of these three SQL statements:

```
/* average of orders excluding nulls */
select avg ( total_order )
    from invoices

/* average of orders using $0 for orders
** that have a null  total */
select avg ( isnull ( total_order, $0 ) )
    from invoices

/* average of orders using $10 for orders
** that have a null total */
select avg ( isnull ( total_order, $10 ) )
    from invoices
```

The avg function (like all aggregate functions) ignores null values, so the first example returns the value $20 (($15 + $20 + $25) / 3 non-null values). The second example substitutes the value $0 for all null values, so the result is $15 (($15 + $20 + $25 + $0) / 4 non-null values). The last example substitutes $10 for nulls, so the result is $17.50 (($15 + $20 + $25 + $10) / 4 non-null values). The isnull function provides a method of substituting a value for a non-null value for the duration of the query.

# Programming Constructs

As previously mentioned, it is sometimes necessary to do more than is available in the ANSI standard—it is necessary to program. To that end, we will address the following topics:

- Batches
- Comments
- Variables
- Message handling
- Error handling
- While loops
- If...Then
- Begin...End

## Batches

A batch is the entire packet passed from the client to the server and can contain several SQL statements. Statements in a batch are parsed, compiled, and executed as a group. This means that none of the statements in the batch is executed if there are any syntax errors in the batch.

> **NOTE**
>
> If a stored procedure is not the first statement in a batch, it must be preceded by the
> exec keyword (which is otherwise optional).

## Examples

```
/* this batch performs two selections */
select * from authors
select * from titles
go

/* this batch binds defaults to several columns at once */
sp_bindefault "my_default", "my_table.col_3"
exec sp_bindefault "my_default", "my_table.col_2"
go

/* this batch sets security on a table */
grant select, insert to mary on mytable
revoke select, insert from mary on mytable(col_3)
go
```

A batch represents everything shipped to the server. If you are going to separate your batches
(which you often will because some tasks require their own batch), you will either need to send
twice or use some sort of separator that instructs the front end to ship separate batches. In many
tools, this is the keyword go. go is not T-SQL. It is an instruction to the front end to ship
everything up until the go out to the server.

## Comments

Comments may be included in batches, and it is a good practice to include descriptive comments in stored procedures.

## Syntax

```
/* single or multi-line comment
[...]
*/

-- single-line comment
```

Two hyphens (--) precede a single-line comment that is terminated with an end-of-line (CR-
LF) sequence.

Multi-line comments (with /*) must be explicitly terminated (*/).

## Local Variables

Variables for use in a batch or stored procedure are defined with the declare statement.

> **WARNING**
>
> Local variables exist only for the life of the batch. When the batch is complete, all information stored in the local variables is deleted.

## Syntax

```
declare @variable_name datatype [, ...]
```

## Example

```
/* declare two variables in a single statement */
declare @name varchar(30), @type int
```

Variable names must be preceded by a single @. Note that this limits variable names to 29 characters plus the @. Local variables are assigned values with a select statement, generally referred to as an assignment select.

## Syntax

```
select @variable_name = expression
[, ...] [from ... [where ...]]
```

## Examples

```
/* set a variable equal to a constant expression */
declare @int_var int
select @int_var = 12
go

/* multiple variables set in a select statement */
declare @single_auth varchar(40),
        @curdate datetime
select @single_auth = au_lname,
       @curdate = getdate()
    from authors
    where au_id = '123-45-6789'
```

## Notes on Local Variables

A single select statement may be for data retrieval or variable setting, but not both. They last for the duration of the batch or stored procedure in which they are declared and are not available to other processes.

From a compilation point of view, it is more efficient to declare multiple variables in a single declare statement and set multiple variables in a single select statement.

If an assignment `select` that retrieves data returns multiple rows, the local variable is assigned the value for the last row returned. If an assignment `select` that retrieves data returns no rows, the local variable will retain the value it had prior to the execution of the `select` statement. Note that this may not have been the expected result.

# Global Variables

The server uses global variables to track server-wide and session-specific information. They cannot be explicitly set or declared. Global variables cannot be defined by users and are not used to pass information across processors by applicants (as defined in many third and fourth generation languages).

## Some Useful Global Variables

| Function | Description |
| --- | --- |
| `@@rowcount` | Number of rows processed by preceding command |
| `@@error` | Error number reported for last SQL statement |
| `@@trancount` | Transaction nesting level |
| `@@transtate` | Current state of a transaction |
| `@@tranchained` | Current transaction mode (chained or unchained) |
| `@@servername` | Name of local SQL Server |
| `@@version` | SQL Server and O/S release level |
| `@@spid` | Current process ID |
| `@@identity` | Last identity value used in an insert |
| `@@nestlevel` | Number of levels nested in a stored procedure or trigger |
| `@@sqlstatus` | Status of previous fetch statement in a cursor |

From a programming standpoint, three of these global variables are important. Applications and stored procedures should check `@@error` after every SQL statement. If there is an error, the value is non-zero. Usually, this means you will need to take some special action.

During an open transaction, `@@trancount` will be greater than 0. At other times, the value will be zero. (For more information about `@@trancount`, see Chapter 8, "Transaction Management.")

`@@version` provides the current release and operating system for the server. This is useful for technical support and sometimes helpful to identify an unnamed server in your network.

# print

The `print` statement is used to pass a message to the client program's message handler. Messages may include up to 255 characters of text. You can also pass variables into the text in much the same way C does it.

## Syntax

```
print {character_string ¦ @local_variable ¦
    @@global_variable }
```

## Examples

```
/* send a string to the message handler */
print "This is a message"
This is a message
/* send a variable to the message handler
** the variable needs to be of a character type */
declare @msg varchar(30)
select @msg = "Hello " + user_name()
print @msg

Hello dbo
```

## *raiserror*

It is useful to be able to return or identify an error condition to a calling procedure or batch. To create an error condition programmatically, use the `raiserror` command. `raiserror` places the error number in the `@@error` global variable.

Error messages cannot exceed 255 characters. Error numbers must exceed 20,000 because the values between 0 and 20,000 are reserved for SQL Server use.

## Syntax

```
raiserror error_number { character_string ¦ @local_variable }
```

## Examples

```
/* raise the error and send a message */
raiserror 52345 'Row not found'
```

## Conditional Execution: *if...else*

Statements to be conditionally executed are identified with the `if...else` construct. This permits a statement or statement block (delineated with a `begin...end` pair) to be executed only if the condition in the `if` clause is true.

## Syntax

```
if boolean_expression
    {statement ¦ statement_block}
[else
    {statement ¦ statement_block}]
```

## Example

```
/* check for average price of business books
** and return a message */
if (select avg(price) from titles
        where type = "business") > $19.95
    print "The average price of business books is greater than $19.95"
else
    print "The average price of business books is less than $19.95"

The average price of business books is less than $19.95
```

# if exists

The `if exists` test is used to check for the existence of data, without regard to the number of matching rows. The existence test is superior to a `count(*) > 0` for an existence check because the server stops processing the `select` when the first matching row is found.

## Syntax

```
if [not] exists (select_statement)
    {statement ¦ statement_block}
[else
    {statement ¦ statement_block}]
```

## Example

```
/* check for authors named Smith */
declare @lname varchar(40), @msg varchar(255)
select @lname = "Smith"
if exists (select * from titles
        where au_lname = @lname)
    begin
    select @msg = "There are authors named " + @lname
    print @msg
    end
else
    begin
    select @msg = "There are no authors named " + @lname
    print @msg
    end
go
```

Note that using a `print` statement causes the information to be returned to the client's message handler (perhaps a pop-up dialog box) rather than as data.

## Notes on *if...else*

If the Boolean expression contains a `select` statement, the `select` statement must be enclosed in parentheses.

if statements can be nested up to 150 levels (if you are going to be nesting deeply, make sure your system administrator has configured your stack size adequately. Also, consider whether you should be using a case statement).

if exists is useful when performing referential integrity checks.

The if condition affects exactly one succeeding statement or statement block.

# Statement Blocks: *begin...end*

To treat multiple SQL statements as a single block, use the begin...end construct.

## Syntax

```
begin
    SQL Statements
end
```

## Example

```
/* check for a smith and do two things */
if exists (select * from authors
        where au_lname = "Smith")
    begin
        print "Smith exists"
        exec found_proc
    end
else
    begin
        print "Smith not found"
        exec not_found_proc
    end
```

Although begin...end can be used almost anywhere, it is most commonly used in combination with while and if...else.

# Repeated Execution: *while*

To execute statements multiple times, use the while construct.

## Syntax

```
while boolean_condition
    [{statement | statement_block}]

[break]

[continue]
```

break unconditionally exits the while loop and continues processing with the first statement after the end statement. continue reevaluates the Boolean condition and begins processing from the top of the loop if the condition is true.

Here is an example of a loop using while, begin, and continue. Notice that the SQL processing statements are actually executed *one time per iteration of the loop.*

```
/* loop until average price equals or exceeds $25*/
while (select avg (price) from titles) < $25
    begin
        update titles set price = price * 1.05
        /* if fewer than 10 books are less than
        ** $15, continue processing */
        if (select count(*) from titles
                where price < $15) < 10
            continue
        else
        /* If maximum price of single book exceeds
        ** $50, exit loop */
          if (select max(price) from titles) > $50
            break
    end
```

Comments describing the processing of the batch help you to understand the processing of this loop. It's important to remember that the condition governing the while loop is evaluated once before any processing begins. (There is no do ... while *condition* structure in SQL Server.)

# Repeated Execution: *goto*

We include goto for the sake of completeness.

## Syntax

```
goto label
...

label:
```

## Example

```
declare @counter tinyint
select @counter = 0
top:
select @counter = @counter + 1
print "Structured programming scoffs at the goto"
if @counter <= 10
goto top

Structured programming scoffs at the goto
Structured programming scoffs at the goto
```

```
Structured programming scoffs at the goto
Structured programming scoffs at the goto
Structured programming scoffs at the goto
Structured programming scoffs at the goto
Structured programming scoffs at the goto
Structured programming scoffs at the goto
Structured programming scoffs at the goto
Structured programming scoffs at the goto
Structured programming scoffs at the goto
```

## Parsing Notes

Note that SQL Server has a single-pass parser and cannot therefore resolve forward references to objects that have not been created.

## Example

```
goto label2
label1:
    insert into #mytemp values (1)
    return
label2:
    create table #mytemp  (a int)
    goto label1

error 208 invalid object name #mytemp
```

This example fails because the server cannot resolve the backward references.

# Event Handling: *waitfor*

The `waitfor` statement is used to cause a query to pause for a period of time or until an event occurs. It is an event handler.

## Syntax

```
waitfor {delay "time" ¦ time "time" ¦ errorexit ¦ processexit ¦ mirrorexit}
```

- ■ `delay` pauses for the specified amount of time.
- ■ *time* waits until the specified time of day. The time specified for `delay` and *time* is in "hh:mm:ss" format; you cannot specify dates. Also, the time value cannot exceed a 24-hour period, and you cannot specify a variable.
- ■ `mirrorexit` waits for a mirrored device failure.
- ■ `errorexit` waits until a kernel or user process terminates abnormally.
- ■ `processexit` waits until a kernel or user process terminates for any reason.

**TIP**

Although you cannot use a variable in the `waitfor time` or `waitfor delay` statement, you can use the execute statement to formulate a variable execution string such as the following, which performs an action (in this case, reports who is online) once per hour on the hour for a day.

```
declare @exec_string char(255),
    @start datetime,
    @ctr tinyint
select @start = getdate(),
    @ctr = datepart(hh, getdate())
while datediff(hh, @start, getdate()) < 24
    begin
    select @exec string = "waitfor time '"
        + str(@ctr) + ":00:00'"
    execute (@exec_string)
    execute sp_who
    end
```

## Examples

```
/* Pauses until 10pm */
waitfor time "22:00:00"
/* display current logins every 30 seconds */
while 1 < 2
begin
    waitfor delay "00:00:30"
    exec sp_who
end
```

**NOTE**

Note that 1 will be less than 2 for a very, very long time—this is an infinite loop!

## return

To unconditionally exit a batch, use the `return` statement.

## Syntax

```
return
```

# Examples

```
select * from authors
print "finishing now"
return

/* return can be used with a conditional statement
** to terminate processing */
if not exists (select * from inventory
            where item_num = @item_num)
    begin
        raiserror 51345 "Not found"
        return
    end
print "No error found"
return
```

# Set Options

Options affect the way the server handles specific conditions. Options exist for the duration of your connection or for the duration of a stored procedure if used in a stored procedure.

# Syntax

```
set condition {on ¦ off ¦ value}
```

# Examples

```
/* instruct the server to return only the first 100 rows of data */
set rowcount 100

/* asks the server for the number of logical and physical page requests */
set statistics io on

/* requests execution time */
set statistics time on

/* tells the server to stop reporting the number of rows returned */
set nocount on

/* asks the server for the final optimization plan for the query */
set showplan on

/* parse and optimize, but don't execute the query (often used in conjunction
** with showplan for looking at a plan without running a query) */
set noexec on

/* checks the batch for syntax, and then stops. */
set parseonly on
```

# Cursors

ANSI SQL provides the ability to address a set of rows individually, one row at a time, by means of a *cursor*. A cursor is a pointer that identifies a specific working row within a set. In this section, we will discuss the syntactic structures used to define and use cursors.

Before looking at how to use a cursor, you need to understand what cursors can do for your application. Most SQL operations are set operations; a where clause defines the set of rows to address and the rest of the statement provides definitive instructions on what to do with the rows.

Consider a typical reporting requirement in which the sales manager wants to evaluate the probable value of all sales opportunities for the next three months.

> **NOTE**
>
> I have to say that it's extremely difficult to come up with compelling examples of cursor programming. The problem is that cursors introduce a fantastic performance problem in your applications and nearly always need to be avoided.

A typical table to track sales opportunities would contain these columns:

```
create table leads
 (id int identity,
  cust int not null,
  est_sale int not null,
  close_date smalldatetime
     default dateadd(dd, 30, getdate()) not null,
  prob tinyint default 20 not null,
  sales_id char(3) not null,
  descr varchar(30) not null)
```

Here is some sample data that might occur in the leads table:

| id | cust | est_sale | close_date | prob | sales_id | descr |
| --- | --- | --- | --- | --- | --- | --- |
| 1 | 1 | 5000 | Jan 17 1996 12:00AM | 25 | JJJ | software |
| 2 | 1 | 9000 | Jan 28 1996 12:00AM | 60 | DDD | hardware |
| 3 | 1 | 9000 | Jan 30 1995 12:00AM | 70 | RRR | hardware |
| 4 | 2 | 2000 | Jan 31 1995 12:00AM | 60 | XXX | hardware |
| 5 | 3 | 8000 | Jan 20 1995 12:00AM | 5 | MMM | misc |
| 6 | 12 | 2000 | Jan 24 1995 12:00AM | 95 | PPP | software |
| 7 | 3 | 8000 | Jan 19 1995 12:00AM | 70 | DDD | software |
| 8 | 1 | 2000 | Jan 29 1995 12:00AM | 50 | JJJ | hardware |
| 9 | 23 | 4000 | Feb 5 1995 12:00AM | 55 | DDD | hardware |
| 10 | 1 | 2000 | Jan 30 1995 12:00AM | 55 | SSS | hardware |
| 11 | 43 | 4000 | Jan 16 1995 12:00AM | 25 | RRR | software |
| 12 | 2 | 6000 | Feb 5 1995 12:00AM | 50 | AAA | misc |

A simple sales projection method is to multiply the estimated sale (est_sale) by the probability of a sale occurring (prob) and then total those discounted projections:

```
select est_total = sum(est_sale * prob)
from leads
```

Suppose that you wanted to write a sales projection that was far more scientific. Here are some facts you need to add to your sales projection:

- Some of the salespeople are way too optimistic; others too conservative. JJJ's probabilities are always 20 percent high, and DDD is always 50 percent low.

- Customer number 2 is known for asking for bids he never buys. His projections should also be lowered by 80 percent (except on JJJ's, which are already sufficiently discounted).

- Anything projected for February should be discounted by an additional 20 percent.

- Salespeople have been selling more hardware than they expect, so increase the sale amount in the projection by 15 percent.

## Some Approaches

You could certainly write a program using a client-side application program, and many of these programs are written that way. However, what if there are 5 million lead rows? What impact will that have on your application?

You could use a set of temporary tables and build a standard query or set of queries to perform this step, but it might be easier to write a query that uses cursors, examine each row to see if it fits any of the rules, and make any necessary adjustments.

> **NOTE**
>
> See my earlier note. I really do not like cursors because they are substantially slower than the typical set processing mechanisms. In this chapter, I come not to praise cursors but to bury them (that is, describe them).

## Cursor Example and Some Syntax

Take a look at the code in Listing 6.1. This is the actual cursor program to execute the sales projection, given the functional requirements stated above.

### Listing 6.1. Sample cursor application.

```
declare leads_curs cursor for
select  cust_id, est_sale, close_date, prob, sales_id, descr
from leads
```

*continues*

### Listing 6.1. continued

```
for read only

go

declare
  @cust_id int,
  @est_sale int,
  @close_date smalldatetime,
  @prob tinyint,
  @sales_id char(3),
  @descr varchar(30),
@sum_sales int

select @sum_sales = 0

open leads_curs
fetch leads_curs into
  @cust_id, @est_sale, @close_date, @prob, @sales_id, @descr

while (@@sqlstatus = 0)
begin
  if @sales_id = "DDD"          /* increase DDD's sales */
    select @prob = @prob * 1.5
  if @sales_id = "JJJ"          /* decrease JJJ's sales */
    select @prob = @prob * .8
  else
    if @cust_id = 2             /* decrease cust 2's sales */
      select @prob = @prob * .8
  if datepart(mm, @close_date) = 2 /* decrease feb sales */
    select @prob = @prob * .8
  if @descr = "hardware"        /* increase hardware sales */
    select @est_sale = @est_sale * 1.15

  select @sum_sales = @sum_sales + @est_sale * @prob / 100
  fetch leads_curs into
    @cust_id, @est_sale, @close_date, @prob, @sales_id, @descr
end

close leads_curs
select @sum_sales "Weighted projected sales"
deallocate leads_curs
go
```

Let's review in detail each element of the sample program.

## Declaring Cursors

You will notice that the sample program consists of two batches. The first batch creates the cursor and the second batch uses it:

```
declare leads_curs cursor for
select cust_id, est_sale, close_date, prob, sales_id, descr
from leads
for read only

go
```

The example declares a cursor that selects from a single table. The cursor will only be used to read values, not for updating rows (FOR READ ONLY).

The cursor is optimized and compiled when it is declared. If the cursor contains a where clause and could use an index, it is a good idea to make it a SARG and support it with an index.

Cursor names are restricted by the same rules as object names: 30 characters and no reserved characters. The select statement is a normal select statement. (There are some restrictions detailed below.)

## Declaring Variables

You will see in the section "Fetching Rows" that you may do one of two things with cursor data:

- You can return the row to the user, in which case the data looks just like a one-row result set from a select statement.

- You can retrieve the data into variables.

```
declare
   @cust_id int,
   @est_sale int,
   @close_date smalldatetime,
   @prob tinyint,
   @sales_id char(3),
   @descr varchar(30),
   @sum_sales int

select @sum_sales = 0
```

In order to retrieve the data into variables, you first need to declare the variables. Also, the variables should be of the same type and length as the columns specified in the select list of the select statement (no implicit conversion is allowed).

> **TIP**
>
> As a convention, we usually name the variables exactly the same as the column names in the select list. In the example, the columns were cust_id, est_sale, and so on, and the variables are @cust_id, @est_sale, and so on.

# Opening Cursors

When you open a cursor with Sybase SQL Server, the server begins execution of the select statement, but membership and ordering of the cursor set is not fixed at that time (only the method of identifying the next row). When you open the cursor, the row pointer is above the first row in the cursor; you must fetch a row to move the pointer to the first row.

```
open leads_curs
```

You may repeatedly close and open a cursor. If you do, the cursor select will be reexecuted to determine a revised ordering and membership for the set, and the row pointer will move above the first row in the new set.

# Fetching Rows

Once a cursor is open, you can fetch rows from the cursor set. In this case, the cursor is retrieving into variables. Note that one variable is required for every column in the select list.

```
fetch leads_curs into
  @cust_id, @est_sale, @close_date, @prob, @sales_id, @descr
```

The fetch keyword is forward-going only. This means that each subsequent fetch statement moves you one row forward in the keyset.

# The Main Loop

This is the reason for writing a cursor, right? This is the main loop, where you retrieve all the rows one at a time, perform some conditional processing on each one, and then move on to the next.

```
while (@@sqlstatus = 0)
begin
    if @sales_id = "DDD"           /* increase DDD's sales */
      select @prob = @prob * 1.5
    if @sales_id = "JJJ"           /* decrease JJJ's sales */
      select @prob = @prob * .8
    else
      if @cust_id = 2              /* decrease cust 2's sales */
        select @prob = @prob * .8
    if datepart(mm, @close_date) = 2 /* decrease feb sales */
      select @prob = @prob * .8
    if @descr = "hardware"         /* increase hardware sales */
      select @est_sale = @est_sale * 1.15

    select @sum_sales = @sum_sales + @est_sale * @prob / 100
    fetch leads_curs into
      @cust_id, @est_sale, @close_date, @prob, @sales_id, @descr
  end
```

**NOTE**

You know, this code looks a lot like old-fashioned programming—something you might do in COBOL or PASCAL or BASIC. The problem is that SQL Server is rotten at old-fashioned programming.

By the way, the example reviewed here took about 8 seconds to run against 12 rows on my Pentium. (That's a long time for 12 rows!)

The moral of the story is that old-fashioned programming is typically a bad choice in SQL Server. You want to write set-based programs whenever you can, even (most of the time) if it means making multiple passes of a single table or set of tables.

You should note the global variable, `@@sqlstatus`, which has three states after you execute a `fetch` statement:

- 0 means that a row was successfully fetched.
- 1 means that the fetch failed because of an error.
- 2 means that there are no more rows.

**TIP**

Some additional code is required in the main loop to handle the case when `@@sqlstatus` is 1 and do other appropriate error checking before this code can go into production.

## Closing the Cursor

Close the cursor when you are finished working with it and then do your end-of-process programming. Some open cursors hold locks that block others' work and an open cursor uses up other resources as well. You can reopen a closed cursor; the row pointer will return to the top of the set.

```
close leads_curs
select @sum_sales "Weighted projected sales"
```

## Deallocating Cursors

When you are finished working with a cursor, deallocate it. The cursor optimization plan takes up space in memory, so it should be deallocated as soon as possible. Once a cursor is deallocated, you will need to declare it again before issuing the `open` statement.

```
deallocate leads_curs
```

# Updating with Cursors

The sales projection example only demonstrates how to read data using a cursor. Cursors may also be used to modify (update or delete) rows in a table. In order to allow update and delete statements to deal with the current row in a cursor set, SQL Server includes the WHERE CURRENT OF *cursor_name* condition:

```
UPDATE table_name
SET column = expression [, column = expression[, ...]]
WHERE CURRENT OF cursor_name

DELETE table_name
WHERE CURRENT OF cursor_name
```

Here are a couple of examples:

```
update leads
set est_sale = est_sale * .8
where current of leads_curs

delete leads
where current of leads_curs
```

## Cursor Declaration for Update

In order to update or delete using a cursor, you need to declare the cursor for update. Here is the complete syntax for the declare statement:

```
DECLARE cursor_name CURSOR
   FOR select_statement
   [FOR {READ ONLY ¦ UPDATE [OF column_list]}]
```

Let's look at the last line of the statement, where you set up the cursor as a read-only cursor or as an updatable cursor. If a cursor is declared as READ ONLY, you may only fetch rows. You may not use the WHERE CURRENT OF construction to modify the contents of the set.

In the example of the leads_curs, the updatable version would look like this:

```
declare leads_curs cursor for
select cust_id, est_sale, close_date, prob, sales_id, descr
from leads
```

You may declare a cursor FOR UPDATE or FOR UPDATE OF *column_list*. If you do not specify a list of columns, all columns in all tables are considered updatable. This means that you can update the contents of several tables during the processing of a cursor containing a join.

---

**NOTE**

Is it a good idea to update many tables using a single cursor? Possibly, but it is easy to become confused.

If you plan to update only one table in the cursor, but need to access information in another, declare the cursor FOR UPDATE. You can use the SHARED keyword to indicate from which tables you will read and which tables will be modified. In this example, you need to access the pub- lishers table to increase prices on titles published in Massachusetts, but no modifications will be made to the publishers table:

```
declare tp cursor for
select title_id, type, price
from titles t, publishers p shared
where t.pub_id = p.pub_id
and state = "MA"
for update of price
```

In addition to limiting updates to the price column of the titles table, this cursor also maintains only shared locks on the publishers table, improving multiuser operations.

# Avoiding Cursors

In general, you should try to avoid using cursors. The sample cursor program took 8 seconds to process 12 rows. For the record, here is how you could use a complex expression in a select statement to replace the cursor processing:

```
select "Sum of Sales" = sum(
    est_sale * prob * .01
/* increase hardware estimates by 15% */
    * (charindex("hardware", descr, 1) * .15 + 1)
/* discount February sales */
    * (1 - (1 - abs(sign(2-datepart(mm, close_date)))) * .2)
/* discount JJJ projections but increase DDD projections */
    * (1. - charindex("JJJ", sales_id, 1) * .2 +
        charindex("DDD", sales_id, 1) * .5)
/* discount projections for customer 2 */
    * (1 - (1 - abs(sign(2-cust_id)))
/* already discounted JJJ projections */
        * (.8 + charindex("JJJ", sales_id, 1) * .2))
    )
from leads
```

How does this work? Let's just look at one element of one of the column expressions in the select list above:

```
(1 - (1 - abs(sign(2-datepart(mm, close_date)))) * .2)
```

This expression applies a twenty percent discount to February sales. Here's how the expression is derived (follow along in Table 6.8 throughout this discussion).

1. The datepart function determines whether the close_date falls in the month of February.

2. Subtract the datepart value from 2 to set only February expressions to zero. Others will be some other (non-zero) value.

3. Next force all the values into one of two sets, zero or 1, by using a combination of the abs() and sign() functions.

4. Now reverse the zeros and ones by subtracting the result from 1.

5. Finally, multiply the result by .2 and that is your discount percentage. If the value was zero, the discount is zero; if the value was 1, the discount is 20%.

**Table 6.8. Derivation of the February discount expression.**

| Datepart | 2-datepart | ABS(sign()) | 1-abs(sign()) | () *.2 |
|----------|-----------|-------------|---------------|--------|
| 1 | 1 | 1 | 0 | 0 |
| 2 | 0 | 0 | 1 | 1 |
| 3 | -1 | 1 | 0 | 0 |
| 4 | -2 | 1 | 0 | 0 |
| 5 | -3 | 1 | 0 | 0 |

The query presented without cursors took less than a second to run. On a large data set, gaining a performance improvement of more than 80 percent by removing cursor processing is well worth a little hard work.

# Summary

This chapter has considered the syntactic extensions and special features of the Transact-SQL. In the next chapters, we will look at using these structures to manage transactions and write stored procedures and triggers.

## Syntax Summary: Programming Structures

**Table 6.9. Summary of syntax presented in this chapter.**

| Task | Syntax |
|------|--------|
| Insert a comment | `/* multi-line comment`<br>`[...]`<br>`*/`<br>`-- single-line comment` |
| Unconditional end of batch or procedure | `return` |
| Send a message | `print {character_string ¦`<br>`@local_variable`<br>`¦ @@global_variable } [ , arg_list ]` |

| Task | Syntax |
|---|---|
| Send an error message | `raiserror error_number`<br>`    { character_string ¦ @local_variable}`<br>`    [, arg_list]` |
| Register an error message | `sp_addmessage message_number,`<br>`message_text` |
| Bind an error message to a constraint | `sp_bindmsg constraint_name, msg_number` |
| Declare a local variable | `declare @variable_name datatype`<br>`[, ...]` |
| Set a local variable | `select @variable_name = expression`<br>`[, ...] [from ... [where ...]]` |
| Evaluate a condition | `if boolean_expression`<br>`    {statement ¦ statement_block}`<br>`[else`<br>`    {statement ¦ statement_block}]` |
| Check for existence of rows | `if [not] exists (select_statement)`<br>`    {statement ¦ statement_block}`<br>`[else`<br>`    {statement ¦ statement_block}]` |
| Create a statement block with `if` or `while` | `begin`<br>`    SQL_Statements`<br>`end` |
| Execute repeatedly | `while boolean_condition`<br>`    {statement ¦ statement_block}` |
| Declare a label execute from a labeled spot | `goto label`<br>`...`<br>`label:` |
| Wait for an event | `waitfor {delay "time" ¦ time "time" ¦`<br>`    errorexit ¦ processexit ¦ mirrorexit}` |
| Modify the environment | `set condition {on ¦ off ¦ value}` |

# Transact-SQL
# Program Structures

# 7

Now that you understand how to code batches, you need to find ways to make these batches permanent. This is done with triggers and stored procedures. Triggers are database objects that are bound directly to tables. Stored procedures exist independently from tables (although they typically reference tables).

# Typical Trigger Uses

Why would you want to bind a collection of T-SQL statements directly to a table? There are a variety of good applications. The most common use, probably, is enforcing referential integrity (RI). Using a trigger, you can cascade updates and deletes of primary keys. Alternatively, you can use triggers for complex domain enforcement—for example, if a column's data integrity requires a table lookup comparison to another table or comparison to another column in the table.

Another common trigger use is enforcing complex business rules—for example, you want to make sure salary increases do not exceed 25 percent. The trigger has access to before and after images of the data, which enable you to make the comparison and the calculation, and, if necessary, undo (roll back) the changes.

Triggers are also used to maintain complex defaults (conditional defaults, for example). They are also useful for maintaining duplicate data. Duplicate data might be exact copies of data in other tables, for performance reasons, or perhaps summary information (such as ytd_sales in the titles table).

## When Is a Trigger Executed (Fired)?

A trigger is an integral part of the statement that fires it. This means that a statement is not complete until the trigger completes, and that any work done in the trigger will be part of the same transaction (unit of work) as the statement that caused the trigger to fire (see next section).

Without a trigger, a data modification command works like this:

| Command | Result |
| --- | --- |
| delete publishers where | Any existing RI constraints are checked. |
| | Row(s) are deleted if not referenced. |

With a trigger, a data modification command works like this:

| Command | Result |
| --- | --- |
| delete publishers where | Any existing RI constraints are checked. |
| | Row(s) are deleted if not referenced. |
| | Execute commands in trigger and either roll back or allow deletion. |

Triggers are executed only once for a single data modification statement regardless of the number of rows affected (zero to many). This means that if you delete, insert, or update multiple rows, any trigger code must take into account the possibility that multiple rows were affected.

# Trigger Creation

A table can have up to three triggers—one each for insert, update, and delete—or a single trigger may be defined for any combination of the three. Here is the syntax:

```
create trigger trigger_name
  on table_name
  for {insert ¦ update ¦ delete} [, ...]
as
SQL_Statements
[return]
```

Simplified example:

```
create trigger titles_trigger
     on titles
     for insert
as
print "title inserted"
return
```

When a row is inserted into the titles table, the "title inserted" message is passed to the front-end's message handler.

To delete a trigger, use the drop trigger command. When you drop a trigger, users will be able to perform modifications to the table without the restrictions originally enforced by the trigger. Here's the syntax:

```
drop trigger trigger_name
```

> **NOTE**
>
> You must be the table owner to modify an object's schema, which is what you are doing when you create a trigger on the table. Triggers do not take parameters and cannot be explicitly called or executed. This can make them difficult to debug. Be thorough.

# Deleted and Inserted Tables

The inserted and deleted tables are special views of the transaction log that last for the duration of a trigger. They reflect the changes made in the table by the statement that causes the trigger to execute. The structure of the inserted and deleted tables exactly matches the structure of the table on which the trigger is created.

The inserted table contains the new rows that resulted from an insert or update. The deleted table contains the old rows that were removed as the result of a delete or update. You may have discerned that SQL Server treats an update as a delete followed by an insert, which is correct!

> **NOTE**
>
> SQL Server typically treats an update as a delete followed by an insert. It can be used inside a trigger to determine which event caused the trigger to fire. Typically, the trigger joins to the inserted and deleted tables to maintain foreign keys and RI.
>
> The inserted and deleted tables can be seen only inside a trigger and are unavailable once the trigger completes.

## What Happens on *delete*?

Figure 7.1 illustrates what happens when a delete trigger executes. After the T-SQL is issued, the trigger executes. The trigger sees the existing table, as modified; this table has an exclusive lock on it that keeps other processes from reading the page until the lock is released. The trigger also sees the contents of the inserted and deleted tables, which are identical in structure to the publishers table. The deleted table has a row in it that corresponds to the row removed, and the inserted table is empty, due to the nature of the statement that caused it to fire.

**FIGURE 7.1.**

*During execution of a* delete *trigger, the inserted table is empty, but a deleted table contains a copy of each deleted row.*

publishers

| pub_id | pub_name | city | state |
|--------|----------|------|-------|
| 0736 | New Age Books | Boston | MA |
| 0877 | Binnet & Hardley | Washington | DC |
| 1389 | Algodata Infosystems | Berkeley | CA |

**1. Command executes:**

```
delete publishers where pub_id = "0736"
```

**1. The trigger sees:**

publishers

| pub_id | pub_name | city | state |
|--------|----------|------|-------|
| 0877 | Binnet & Hardley | Washington | DC |
| 1389 | Algodata Infosystems | Berkeley | CA |
| | | | |

deleted

| pub_id | pub_name | city | state |
|--------|----------|------|-------|
| 0736 | New Age Books | Boston | MA |
| | | | |

inserted

| pub_id | pub_name | city | state |
|--------|----------|------|-------|
| | | | |
| | | | |

# *delete* Trigger Example

Task: *Write a* delete *trigger for* publishers *that cascades deletions to the* titles *table.*

Remember to check the number of rows affected (via @@rowcount), because the delete statement itself causes the trigger to fire whether any rows were deleted or not.

Here is the solution:

```
create trigger cascade_del_trigger
     on publishers
     for delete
as

if @@rowcount = 0  -- no rows deleted
     return

/* cascade delete of pub_id(s) to related */
/* rows in titles table */
delete titles
     from titles t, deleted d
     where t.pub_id = d.pub_id

if @@error != 0
     begin
     print "Error occurred deleting related titles"      rollback tran
     end

return
```

Note some key features of the code. First, check to see whether any rows were modified. Remember, the trigger fires whether data was modified or not; execution is dependent on execution of the T-SQL statement, not on whether any potential where clause was executed.

Next, because the list of modified rows is no longer available in the table, you look in the deleted table. In fact, you join the titles table (the dependent table) to the deleted table so that you can remove the appropriate rows.

Finally—and this is very important—you check the return code of your T-SQL statement to trap any error conditions.

This code does *not* check for any dependencies of the titles table. You have to write a trigger on the titles table to affect tables such as sales and titleauthor, which contain the title_id.

# What Happens on *insert?*

Figure 7.2 illustrates the inserted and deleted tables during an insert. At insert time, you see the modified titles table (though nobody else can) and the inserted row in the inserted table.

**FIGURE 7.2.**

*When a trigger executes during an* insert, *the inserted table contains the row(s) inserted by the operation. The deleted table is always empty.*

titles

| title_id | title_name | type | pub_id | ... |
|----------|------------|------|--------|-----|
| BU1032 | The Busy Executive's... | business | 1389 | ... |
| BU1111 | Cooking With Comput... | business | 1389 | ... |
| BU2075 | You Can Combat Com... | business | 0736 | ... |
| ... | ... | ... | ... | ... |

**1. Command executes:**

```
Insert titles
    values ("BU1234", "Tuning SQL Server", "business", "0877",...)
```

**1. The trigger sees:**

titles

| title_id | title_name | type | pub_id | ... |
|----------|------------|------|--------|-----|
| BU1032 | The Busy Ex... | business | 1389 | ... |
| BU1111 | Cooking With... | business | 1389 | ... |
| BU1234 | Tuning SQL Server | business | 0877 | ... |
| BU2075 | You Can Com... | business | 0736 | ... |
| ... | ... | ... | ... | ... |

deleted

| title_id | title | type | pub_id | ... |
|----------|-------|------|--------|-----|
|  |  |  |  |  |
|  |  |  |  |  |
|  |  |  |  |  |

inserted

| title_id | title_name | type | pub_id | ... |
|----------|------------|------|--------|-----|
| BU1234 | Tuning SQL Server | business | 0877 | ... |
|  |  |  |  |  |
|  |  |  |  |  |

# Handling Multi-Row *insert* and *update* Statements

SQL Server allows multi-row inserts in a single insert statement via the insert... select... syntax. If inserting or updating multiple foreign key values, the trigger should compare the count of all rows inserted or updated against a count of those that are valid keys. This can be accomplished by using the count(*) aggregate with a join between the inserted table and the primary key table. You must compare the value of select count(*)... against the value of @@rowcount at the beginning of the trigger. @@rowcount must be checked (and preferably stored in a local variable) before any operations are performed within the trigger that can affect @@rowcount. If the number of rows in the inserted table that join successfully with rows in the primary key table doesn't equal the total number of rows inserted or updated, at least one of the rows is invalid.

Here is an example:

```
create trigger tr1
on ...
for insert, update
as
declare @rows int
select @rows = @@rowcount
...
if (select count(*) from inserted i, pkey_tab p
    where i.fkey = p.pkey) != @rows
/* At least one of the inserted/updated rows
   does not match a primary key */
/*  begin error processing */
...
```

This is another very useful piece of code. Because every SQL statement modifies `@@rowcount`, you must save the value of the number of rows modified as soon as you enter the trigger if you want to reference it later. (`declare` is the only SQL statement that does not modify `@@rowcount`.)

Here, you join the inserted table (that is, each row that is newly entering the table) to the list of *valid* foreign keys (that is, the primary keys in the `parent` table). If the count of this join matches the number of rows inserted, you have RI.

## *if update* Test

Any `insert` or `update` on a table causes the corresponding `insert` or `update` trigger to fire. If the trigger is designed to maintain referential integrity, you may want to act only if a primary or foreign key column is updated or inserted. The `if update` test provides a mechanism to find out whether a specific column has been modified or inserted. Here is the syntax:

```
if update (col_name)
    [ { and ¦ or } update (col_name) ...]
```

The test is true when either of the following conditions is true:

- A non-null value has been inserted into the column.
- The column was named in the set clause of an `update` statement (this does *not* necessarily mean the column's value changed!).

## *insert* Trigger Example

Task: *Verify the referential integrity of the* `titles` *row(s) inserted into* `titles` *against the* `publishers` *table. Roll back the* `insert` *transaction if any rows violate RI.*

Here is the solution:

```
create trigger tr_titles_i
on titles
for insert
as
declare @rows int  -- create variable to hold @@rowcount
select @rows = @@rowcount

if @rows = 0        -- no rows inserted, exit trigger
return

/* check if pub_id was inserted and if all pub_ids
   inserted are valid pub_ids in the publishers table */
if update(pub_id) -- was an explicit pub_id inserted?
  and (select count(*)
      from inserted i, publishers p
      where p.pub_id = i.pub_id ) != @rows
  begin
     raiserror 33333 "Invalid pub_id inserted"
     rollback transaction
  end

return
```

In this example, you act only if rows were modified. You also act only if the column you care about (the foreign key) is affected by the SQL statement. This is true for either insert or update. As in the prior join example, you want the count of the join to match the count of the rows affected, thus demonstrating RI.

# Conditional *insert* Trigger Example

Task: *Verify the referential integrity of the* titles *row(s) inserted into* titles *against the publishers table. Remove any rows from* titles *that violate RI and allow the rest to remain in the table.*

Here is the solution:

```
create trigger tr_titles_i
on titles
for insert
as
declare @rows int  -- create variable to hold @@rowcount
select @rows = @@rowcount

if @rows = 0       -- no rows inserted, exit trigger
return

/* check if pub_id was inserted and if all pub_ids
   inserted are valid pub_ids in the publishers table
   delete any invalid rows from titles */
if update(pub_id)  -- was an explicit pub_id inserted?
  and (select count(*)
      from inserted i, publishers p
      where p.pub_id = i.pub_id ) != @rows
  begin
  delete titles
    from titles t, inserted i
    where t.pub_id = i.pub_id
    and i.pub_id not in
         (select pub_id from publishers)
  raiserror 33334 "Some Invalid pub_id(s) not inserted"
  end

return
```

The only code in this example you haven't seen yet is one that identifies the rows that failed the criteria and that are being removed from the base table in the delete. The subquery identifies valid rows, and that list is compared to the rows in the inserted table to identify nonmatching rows. This is different from a rollback transaction statement, which reverses all modifications so that no rows are added, even if some are valid.

# What Happens on *update?*

Remember, the update is a delete followed by an insert. As a result, you get a row in both the inserted and deleted tables (see Figure 7.3). The nifty thing about this is the capability of comparing before and after images of the data.

**FIGURE 7.3.**

*During an* update *trigger, there will always be the same number of rows in the deleted table as in the inserted table. The deleted table contains the rows prior to the update, and the inserted table contains the modified rows.*

salesdetail

| stor_id | ord_num | title_id | qty | discount |
|---------|---------|----------|-----|----------|
| 7896 | 234518 | TC3218 | 75 | 40.0 |
| 7896 | 234518 | TC7777 | 75 | 40.0 |
| 7131 | Asoap432 | TC3218 | 50 | 40.0 |
| ... | ... | ... | ... | ... |

**1. Command executes:**

```
update salesdetail
  set qty = 100
  where stor_id = 7896
  and ord_num = 234518
  and title_id = TC3218
```

**1. The trigger sees:**

salesdetail

| stor_id | ord_num | title_id | qty | discount |
|---------|---------|----------|-----|----------|
| 7896 | 234518 | TC3218 | 75 | 40.0 |
| 7896 | 234518 | TC7777 | 75 | 40.0 |
| 7131 | Asoap432 | TC3218 | 50 | 40.0 |
| ... | ... | ... | ... | ... |

deleted

| stor_id | ord_num | title_id | qty | discount |
|---------|---------|----------|-----|----------|
| 7896 | 234518 | TC3218 | 75 | 40.0 |
| | | | | |
| | | | | |
| | | | | |

inserted

| stor_id | ord_num | title_id | qty | discount |
|---------|---------|----------|-----|----------|
| 7896 | 234518 | TC3218 | 100 | 40.0 |
| | | | | |
| | | | | |
| | | | | |

# *update* Trigger Example

Task: *When a* salesdetail *row is inserted or updated, update the corresponding summary value,* total_sales, *in the* titles *table.*

Here is the solution:

```
create trigger tr_total_sales
on salesdetail
for update, insert
as
declare @rows int  -- create variable to hold @@rowcount
select @rows = @@rowcount
if @rows = 0        -- no rows inserted, exit trigger
   return
if exists (select * from deleted) and @rows > 1
  begin
  print "Multi-row updates to sales not allowed!"
  rollback tran
  return
  end
/* update the totals in titles with qty
** in modified salesdetail rows */
if update(qty)
  begin
  update titles
     set total_sales = isnull(total_sales, 0)
```

```
/* use isnull function in case of no value */
/* use subqueries to get total inserts and deletions */
    + (select isnull(sum(i.qty), 0)
          from inserted i
          where i.title_id = titles.title_id)
    - (select isnull(sum(d.qty), 0)
          from deleted d
          where d.title_id = titles.title_id)
  end
return
```

First, you automatically reject, out of hand, any modifications to more than one row simultaneously, because matching becomes impossible. Then, you subtract rows from the deleted and add rows from the inserted for your new net value to the summary data.

## Trigger Limitations

The following SQL statements are not permitted in triggers:

- Any create command (this includes creation of temp tables; if you need to create a temporary table in a trigger, call a stored procedure that does that work)
- Any drop command
- alter table/database
- grant
- revoke
- select into (table creation!)
- truncate table
- update statistics
- reconfigure
- load database/transaction
- disk init/mirror/reinit/refit/remirror/unmirror

## Triggers During Transactions

A trigger is an integral part of the statement that fired it and of the transaction in which that statement occurs. A rollback tran inside a trigger rolls back all work to the outermost begin tran, completes processing in the trigger, and *aborts* the current batch:

```
/* trigger on the table called on insert */
create trigger tr_titles_i on titles for insert as
declare @rows int  -- create variable to hold @@rowcount
select @rows = @@rowcount
if @rows = 0 return
if update(pub_id) and (select count(*)
      from inserted i, publishers p
      where p.pub_id = i.pub_id ) != @rows
```

```
    begin
        rollback transaction
        raiserror 33333 "Invalid pub_id inserted"
    end
return

/* transaction inserts rows into a table */
begin tran add_titles
insert titles (title_id, pub_id, title)
    values ('BU1234', '0736', 'Tuning SQL Server')
insert titles (title_id, pub_id, title)
    values ('BU1235', 'abcd', 'Tuning SQL Server')
insert titles (title_id, pub_id, title)
    values ('BU1236', '0877', 'Tuning SQL Server')
commit tran
```

How many rows are inserted if 'abcd' is an invalid pub_id? No rows are inserted, because unlike a rollback tran in a procedure, a rollback tran in a trigger aborts the rest of the batch.

Statements subsequent to a rollback tran in a trigger are executed. Remember to return following a rollback tran in a trigger to prevent unwanted results. Do not issue begin tran statements in a transaction. A transaction is already active at the time the trigger is executed.

You can set a savepoint in a trigger and roll back to the savepoint. Only the statements in the trigger subsequent to the savepoint are rolled back. The transaction will still be active until subsequently committed or rolled back; the batch will continue.

Do *not* roll back to a named transaction from within a trigger. This generates a runtime error, rolls back all work, and aborts the batch. For best results, include save tran or rollback tran statements in triggers. For finer transaction control in triggers, SQL Server provides the rollback trigger command.

## *rollback trigger*

The rollback trigger statement rolls back all work inside the trigger and any data modifications performed in any nested triggers. It also rolls back the data modification statement that caused the trigger to fire. Trigger execution stops and returns to the calling process. The calling process continues—prior and subsequent modifications can still be committed or rolled back. Here is the syntax:

```
rollback trigger [with raiserror error_num [message]]
```

## Programming Recommendations

Because rollback trigger does not abort the batch, processing continues. Always raise an error with rollback trigger and always check for errors after *each individual data modification statement* to see whether a rollback trigger occurred and programmatically determine whether to rollback the entire transaction or not. Here is a trigger that performs several data validations and checks for a specific error after each one:

```
/* Here's the trigger */
/* trigger on the table called on insert */
create trigger tr_titles_i on titles for insert as
declare @rows int  -- create variable to hold @@rowcount
select @rows = @@rowcount
if @rows = 0 return
if update(pub_id) and (select count(*)
      from inserted i, publishers p
      where p.pub_id = i.pub_id ) != @rows
  begin
        rollback trigger
            with raiserror 33333 "Invalid pub_id inserted"
  end
/* the following statements will be skipped if the
   rollback trigger command is executed */
print "Insert successful!"
return
/* Here's the batch that starts everything */
/* transaction inserts rows into a table */
begin tran add_titles
insert titles (title_id, pub_id, title)
     values ('BU1234', '0736', 'Tuning SQL Server')
if @@error = 33333
  begin
  rollback tran
  return
  end
insert titles (title_id, pub_id, title)
     values ('BU1235', 'abcd', 'Tuning SQL Server')
if @@error = 33333
  begin
  rollback tran
  return
  end
insert titles (title_id, pub_id, title)
     values ('BU1236', '0877', 'Tuning SQL Server')
if @@error = 33333
  begin
  rollback tran
  return
  end
commit tran
```

# Nested Triggers

If a trigger performs an insert, update, or delete on another table that has a trigger defined for that action, by default, that trigger will also fire. This is called a *nested trigger* (see Figure 7.4).

**FIGURE 7.4.**

*A nested trigger on* `table_b` *fires as part of the transaction on* `table_a`.

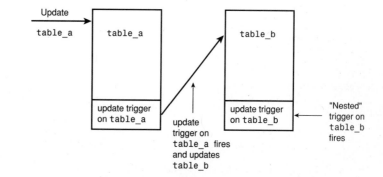

Triggers are limited to 16 levels of nesting. Check `@@nestlevel` to avoid exceeding limits. Nested triggers cannot see the contents of the inserted and deleted tables for other triggers. Nesting of triggers can be disabled at the server level by a system administrator with `sp_configure`.

Here are some things you need to know about trigger maintenance and performance:

- Triggers typically are not "recursive"; that is, they will not fire if the trigger modifies its own table.

- If more than one trigger is defined for a given action on a table, the most recently defined trigger takes precedence. A trigger does not have to be dropped before being re-created for the same single action (one of `insert`, `update`, or `delete`) on a table.

- Triggers do not override existing permissions; instead, they take advantage of the existing permission structure. If a user does not have permission to update a table directly, it cannot be updated via a trigger on another table on which the user has update permission.

- Triggers cannot be defined on temporary tables or views. If modifying data through a view, any triggers on the underlying tables are executed.

- Triggers can execute stored procedures, including remote stored procedures.

- Cursors can be used in triggers. Some uses for cursors in triggers include custom logging, maintaining duplicate data, and performing actions in individual rows in the inserted and deleted tables.

- Trigger overhead, like stored procedure overhead, is relatively low.

- An `insert` trigger will not fire during a `bcp` load. A `delete` trigger will not fire on a `truncate table` command.

- *Do not* use `select` statements that return result sets to the end user within a trigger. An application issuing an `insert` command will most likely not expect or be coded to process result rows. Return information from triggers via `print` or `raiserror`.

SQL Server allows recursive triggers if you use the set `self_recursion` on option inside the trigger definition. Data modification statements inside a trigger do not affect the values of the inserted or deleted tables for that trigger.

# Examining Triggers

List all tables and their triggers with this select statement:

```
/* display user tables and triggers */
select name, user_name(uid),
    "insert trigger" = object_name(instrig),
    "update trigger" = object_name(updtrig),
    "delete trigger" = object_name(deltrig)
  from sysobjects
  where type = "U"
  order by name
```

| name ➥update trigger | delete trigger | insert trigger |
|---|---|---|
| ➥------- | | |
| authors | dbo | |
| discounts | dbo | |
| employee | dbo | employee_insupd |
| employee_insupd | | |
| jobs | dbo | |
| pub_info | dbo | |
| publishers | dbo | |
| roysched | dbo | |
| sales | dbo | tr_total_sales |
| tr_total_sales | | |
| stores | dbo | |
| titleauthor | dbo | |
| titles | dbo | tr_titles_i |

```
( 11 rows affected)
```

```
Sort Order:  name
```

Display trigger text with the following:

```
sp_helptext trigger_name
```

```
sp_helptext tr_total_sales
```

To list all objects referenced within a trigger, use this:

```
sp_depends trigger_name
```

```
sp_depends tr_total_sales
```

```
In the current database the specified object references the following:
```

| name | type | updated | selected |
|---|---|---|---|
| dbo.jobs | user table | no | no |
| dbo.employee | user table | no | no |

```
( 1 row affected)
```

To list all triggers and stored procedures that reference a table, use the following:

```
sp_depends table_name

sp_depends employee
```

```
In the current database the specified object is referenced by the following:
name                                      type
----------------------------------------- ----------------
dbo.employee_insupd                       trigger
( 1 row affected)
```

# Stored Procedures

A stored procedure is a database object that exists independently of a table. It can be called from a client, parameters may be passed and returned, and error codes may be checked. This section explores the following topics:

- Creating stored procedures
- Passing parameters in and out
- Handling return codes
- Effects on the optimizer

The following list summarizes the advantages of stored procedures:

- *Faster execution.* Stored procedures, after their first execution, become memory-resident and do not need to be reparsed, reoptimized, or recompiled.
- *Reduced network traffic.* Less SQL needs to cross busy network lines.
- *Modular programming.* You now have a way of breaking up things into digestible pieces.
- *Restricted, function-based access to tables.* You can grant permissions in such a way as to allow a user access to tables *only* through the stored procedure.
- *Reduced operator error.* Less information to pass.
- *Enforced consistency.* If users are accessing tables only through your stored procedures, ad-hoc modifications go away.
- *Automated complex or sensitive transactions.* Obviously.

## Running Stored Procedures

Stored procedures improve overall system performance by reducing network traffic and the optimization and compilation by the SQL Server:

| First Execution | Subsequent Executions |
|---|---|
| Locate stored procedure on disk and load into cache. | Locate stored procedure in cache. |
| Substitute parameter values. | Substitute parameter values. |
| Develop optimization plan. | |
| Compile optimization plan. | |
| Execute from cache. | Execute from cache. |

Note that the second time the stored procedure is run, it is in memory and is that much faster to locate. You do not need to parse, optimize, or create an executable, and that saves time as well.

> **NOTE**
>
> Later, you'll see that skipping the optimize step is not always a good thing!

# Creating Stored Procedures

You create stored procedures by executing a batch starting with the keywords create procedure (or create proc). The procedure will be the entire batch transmitted to the server as a single unit.

```
create proc procedure_name
as
SQL statements
[return [status_value]]
```

Here is an example of a stored procedure:

```
create proc pub_titles
as
select t.title, p.pub_name
  from publishers p, titles t
  where p.pub_id = t.pub_id
return
```

To execute a stored procedure, just type the name of the procedure:

```
pub_titles
```

Use the execute keyword if the call to the stored procedure is not the first statement in the batch. Here's the syntax:

```
[exec[ute]] proc_name
```

Here are some examples:

```
exec pub_titles

title      pub_name
The Busy Executive's Database Guide       Algodata Infosystems
Cooking with Computers: Surreptitious Balance Sheets      Algodata Infosystems
You Can Combat Computer Stress!      New Moon Books
Straight Talk About Computers      Algodata Infosystems
Silicon Valley Gastronomic Treats      Binnet & Hardley
The Gourmet Microwave      Binnet & Hardley
The Psychology of Computer Cooking      Binnet & Hardley
But Is It User Friendly?      Algodata Infosystems
Secrets of Silicon Valley      Algodata Infosystems
Net Etiquette      Algodata Infosystems
Computer Phobic AND Non-Phobic Individuals: Behavior Variations      Binnet &
Hardley
Is Anger the Enemy?      New Moon Books
Life Without Fear      New Moon Books
Prolonged Data Deprivation: Four Case Studies      New Moon Books
Emotional Security: A New Algorithm      New Moon Books
Onions, Leeks, and Garlic: Cooking Secrets of the Mediterranean      Binnet &
Hardley
Fifty Years in Buckingham Palace Kitchens      Binnet & Hardley
Sushi, Anyone?      Binnet & Hardley
```

You can drop stored procedures with the drop procedure (or drop proc) statement:

```
drop proc proc_name
```

> **NOTE**
>
> You cannot alter a procedure. You must drop and re-create the stored procedure in order to change it.

# Display and Maintenance

Procedures can be renamed by using sp_rename. To modify a stored procedure, drop the procedure and re-create it; a stored procedure must be dropped before it can be re-created with the same name by the same user.

You cannot drop and re-create an object in the same batch. This example will fail during parsing because the parser will refuse to create a procedure that already exists. (Don't forget that at parse time, the drop proc statement hasn't been executed yet!)

```
/* this batch will fail to execute ... why?
Objects cannot be dropped and created in the same batch */
drop proc titles_for_a_pub
create proc titles_for_a_pub
as ...
```

A better method is the following:

```
/* check if the procedure exists and drop it */
if exists (select * from sysobjects
     where name = "titles_for_a_pub"
     and type = "P" and uid = user_id())
  drop proc titles_for_a_pub
go
create proc titles_for_a_pub
as ...
```

Why do we even worry about this? It is a standard and very important practice to maintain copies of your stored procedures in scripts, both for documentation and so that you can modify the procedures (there is no "modify procedure" or "alter procedure" statement).

To display text of a stored procedure in the database in which it was created, use the following:

sp_helptext *procedure_name*

**NOTE**

The Sybase utility, defncopy, as well as many third-party tools will reverse-engineer the text of stored procedures, triggers, views, rules, and defaults from the system tables in much the same way as sp_helptext.

sp_help reports parameters' names and datatypes for a stored procedure:

sp_help *procedure_name*

sp_help titles_for_a_pub

| Name | Owner | Type |
|---|---|---|
| When_created | | |
| ---- | ---- | ---- |
| titles_for_a_pub | dbo | stored procedure |
| Nov 16 1995  3:58PM | | |
| ( 0 rows affected) | | |

```
Data_located_on_segment
-----------------------
not applicable
( 0 rows affected)
```

| Parameter_name | Type | Length | Prec | Scale |
|---|---|---|---|---|
| ➥Param_order | | | | |
| ---- | ---- | ---- | ---- | ---- |
| ➥-------- | | | | |
| @pub_name | varchar | 40 | 40 | 1 |
| ( 0 rows affected) | | | | |

# Procedures and Parameters

Stored procedures can accept parameters to improve their usefulness and flexibility. To pass a parameter, include a list of parameters in parentheses (optional) after the name of the procedure. Here's the syntax:

```
create proc procedure_name
    (parameter_name datatype [, ...])
as
SQL Statements
[return [status_value]][exec[ute]] procedure_name [expression] [, ... ]
```

Here is an example of a stored procedure that takes one parameter, @pub_name:

```
create proc titles_for_a_pub
    (@pub_name varchar(40))
as
select t.title from publishers p, titles t
    where p.pub_id = t.pub_id
    and pub_name like @pub_name
return
```

In this procedure, you pass in a publisher name and perform a lookup based on that publisher name. Note that you use the like operator and therefore can do some pattern matching.

Here are two examples of how the procedure might be used. In the second example, the exec keyword is used because the stored procedure execution is not the first statement in the batch:

```
titles_for_a_pub 'Algo%'
title
-------------------------------------------------------------------------
The Busy Executive's Database Guide
Cooking with Computers: Surreptitious Balance Sheets
Straight Talk About Computers
But Is It User Friendly?
Secrets of Silicon Valley
Net Etiquette
( 6 rows affected)

declare @my_pub_name varchar(40)
select @my_pub_name = "New Moon Books"
exec titles_for_a_pub @my_pub_name

title
-------------------------------------------------------------------------
You Can Combat Computer Stress!
Is Anger the Enemy?
Life Without Fear
Prolonged Data Deprivation: Four Case Studies
Emotional Security: A New Algorithm
( 5 rows affected)
```

Here's some information about stored procedure parameters:

■ Parameter names, like local variables, may be up to 29 characters in length, and they follow SQL Server naming guidelines.

- Up to 255 parameters may be defined.
- Wildcards can be contained in values passed to stored procedures if the parameter is used in a `like` clause.
- Parameter datatypes can be either system datatypes or user-defined datatypes.
- Rules, defaults, and column properties do not apply to parameters defined with user-defined datatypes.
- Microsoft SQL Server can use text and image datatypes as *read-only* stored procedure parameters.

## Executing with Parameters

At execution time, parameters may be specified by position or by name. If passed by name, parameters can be passed in any order. Here's the syntax:

```
[exec[ute]] procedure_name
     [[@parm_name = ]expression] [, ... ]
```

Here is an example of a procedure with several parameters. When the procedure is invoked, the user may pass the procedures by name or by position:

```
create proc mypro
     (@val1 int, @val2 int, @val3 int)
as
...
go

/* parameters passed by position here */
exec myproc 10,20,15

/* parameter passed by name here */
exec myproc @val2 = 20, @val1 = 10, @val3 = 15
```

Once you start passing parameters by name, all subsequent parameters must be passed by name; if you want to skip any parameters and have them take default values, you pass parameters by name unless they are the last parameters in the procedure.

Passing parameters by name is recommended in programming environments because it is more flexible and self-documenting than passing parameters by position.

## Default Parameter Values

Stored procedure parameters can be assigned default values if no value is supplied during execution. You can improve your stored procedure code by defining *defaults* for all parameters. To define a default, provide the value of the default after the datatype of the parameter:

```
create proc procedure_name
     (parameter_name datatype = default_value
     [,...])
as
```

```
SQL Statements
[return [status_value]]
```

In this example, the procedure defaults the value of the parameter to `null`. This is a common way to trap errors in the invocation of the stored procedure inside the procedure instead of allowing the standard server message to report that parameters are missing:

```
/* check for a pub_name before executing query */
create proc titles_for_a_pub
     (@pub_name varchar(40) = null)
as
if @pub_name = null
  begin
  print "Pass in the pub_name as a parameter"
  return
  end
select t.title from publishers p, titles t
     where p.pub_id = t.pub_id
     and pub_name like @pub_name + "%"
return
```

Here, you pass in a parameter and verify that the parameter has actually been passed. If you do not specify a default, you get an error (the procedure will not execute) if no procedure name is passed. If you specify a default, you can check the default and take action within the stored procedure.

Here we see the stored procedure in action. In the first example, the user neglects to pass a parameter and receives an error message. In the second example, the user passes a parameter and receives a list of titles for that publisher name:

```
/* without a parameter, you get the message */
titles_for_a_pub
go

Pass in the pub_name as a parameter

/* with a parameter, you get the results */
titles_for_a_pub "Algo%"
go

title
-------------------------------------------------
The Busy Executive's Database Guide
Cooking with Computers:Surreptitious Balance Sheets
Straight Talk About Computers
But is it User Friendly
Secrets of Silicon Valley
Net Etiquette
```

# Passing Parameters In and Out

The `output` keyword may be specified in the stored procedure creation statement if the parameters can be passed both in and out of the stored procedure. When passing parameters out, the `output` keyword *must also be specified* in the execution statement. Here's the syntax:

```
create proc procedure_name
  [ (parm_name datatype = default_value [output]
   [, ... ] )]
as
SQL Statements
[return [status_value]]
[exec[ute]] procedure_name
      [[parm_name = ] expression [output] [, ... ]
```

# Output Parameters

Here is an example of a procedure that includes an output parameter, @ytd_sales:

```
/* passing a parameter back to calling batch */
create proc ytd_sales
  (@title varchar(80) = null,
   @ytd_sales int output)
as
if @title = null
  begin
  print "Syntax: ytd_sales title, @variable [output]"
  return
  end
select @ytd_sales = ytd_sales
  from titles
  where title = @title
return
```

Note that it is reasonable to display correct syntax if a user misuses the parameters.

In the following queries, a user executes the stored procedure. In the first example, the parameter is passed by position; in the second, it is passed by name. Note the use of the output keyword in both the procedure and the batch that calls it:

```
/* variable must be set up first to accept output value
** in this example, total sales are returned by position */
declare @sales_figure int
exec ytd_sales 'But Is It User Friendly?', @sales_figure output
select 'ytd sales of But Is It User Friendly?  = ', @sales_figure
go
```

```
----------------------------------------- ----------
ytd sales of But Is It User Friendly?  =   8780
( 1 row affected)
```

```
/* in this example, total sales are returned by name */
declare @sales_figure int
exec total_sales @title= 'But Is It User Friendly?',
            @total_sales = @sales_figure output
print "total sales of But Is It User Friendly?= %1!", @sales_figure
go
```

# Returning Procedure Status

Every stored procedure automatically returns an integer status value: 0 is returned on success-ful completion, -1 through -99 are returned for SQL Server detected errors. Use a return state-ment to specify a return value greater than 0 or less than -99. The calling program can set up a local variable to receive and check the return status. Here's the syntax:

```
create proc procedure_name
 [ (parm_name datatype = default_value [output]
   [, ... ] ) ]
as
SQL Statements
return [integer_status_value]
[execute] [@status_var = procedure_name
     [[parm_name = ] expression [output] [, ... ]
```

Here is an example of a stored procedure that returns a different stored procedure status de-pending on the reason for the procedure to return. If the return value is non-zero, then some-thing unusual has happened:

```
/* procedure sets an error status on error */
create proc titles_for_a_pub
     (@pub_name varchar(40) = null ) as
if @pub_name = null
     return 15
if not exists (select * from publishers
          where pub_name = @pub_name)
     return -101
select t.title from publishers p, titles t
     where p.pub_id = t.pub_id
     and pub_name = @pub_name
return 0
```

In this example of a batch to interact with the return status, the user needs to check the return status to be certain that the procedure ran to completion without error. The @status local vari-able is used here to retrieve the status. The user then checks its value in case a non-zero value was returned:

```
/* check for status and report errors */
declare @status int
exec @status = titles_for_a_pub 'New Age Books'
if @status = 15
     print "Invalid Syntax"
else if @status = -101
     print "No publisher by that name found"
```

# SQL Server Status Codes

The following is a list of return status codes currently in use by SQL Server:

| Status Code | Meaning |
| --- | --- |
| 0 | Successful return |
| –1 | Missing object referenced |
| –2 | Datatype mismatch error |
| –3 | Process chosen as deadlock victim |
| –4 | Permission error |
| –5 | Syntax error |
| –6 | Miscellaneous user error |
| –7 | Resource error, such as out of space |
| –8 | Non-fatal internal problem (bug) |
| –9 | System limit reached |
| –10 | Fatal internal inconsistency (bug) |
| –11 | Fatal internal inconsistency (bug) |
| –12 | Table or index corrupted |
| –13 | Database corrupt |
| –14 | Hardware error |

# Stored Procedures and Transactions

SQL Server notes the transaction nesting level before calling a stored procedure. If the transaction nesting level when the procedure returns is different from the level when executed, SQL Server displays the following message: `Transaction count after EXECUTE indicates that a COMMIT or ROLLBACK TRAN is missing`. This message indicates that transaction nesting is out of whack. Because a stored procedure does not abort the batch on a `rollback tran`, a `rollback tran` inside the procedure could result in a loss of data integrity if subsequent statements are executed and committed.

A `rollback tran` rolls back all statements to the outermost transaction, including any work performed inside nested stored procedures that have not been fully committed (that is, `@@trancount > 0`). A `commit tran` within the stored procedure decreases the `@@trancount` by only one.

## Stored Procedures and Transactions: Guidelines

Develop a consistent error handling strategy for failed transactions or other errors that occur within transactions. Implement this strategy consistently across procedures and applications.

Implement transaction control in nested stored procedures. Check whether the procedure is being called from within a transaction before issuing a `begin tran`.

Determine whether procedures are to operate in chained or unchained mode (these are described in more detail in Chapter 8, "Transaction Management"). If the stored procedure is created under a different mode, SQL Server generates an error message. Under chained mode, a stored procedure may be unexpectedly called from within a transaction.

Because a `rollback tran` from a procedure does not abort the batch calling the procedure, follow these guidelines:

- Procedures should make no net change to `@@trancount`.

- Issue a `rollback tran` only if the stored procedure issues the `begin tran` statement.

If you are managing transactions both within stored procedures and outside of them, you may want to work from a template stored procedure similar to the one in the following example. This procedure performs a complete `rollback transaction` after an error only if there is no transaction underway when the procedure starts. Otherwise, it returns control to the calling batch and alerts it (through the return status value) that a `rollback` is required at that level:

```
/* proc to demonstrate no net change to @@trancount
** but rolls back changes within the proc
** VERY IMPORTANT: return an error code
** to tell the calling procedure rollback occurred */

create proc p1
as
declare @trncnt int

select @trncnt = @@trancount   -- save @@trancount value

if @trncnt = 0    -- transaction has not begun
  begin tran p1   -- begin tran increments nest level to 1

else              -- already in a transaction
  save tran p1    -- save tran doesn't increment nest level

/* do some processing */

if (@@transtate = 2) -- or other error condition
  begin
  rollback tran p1  -- rollback to savepoint, or begin tran
  return 25         -- return error code indicating rollback
  end

/* more processing if required */

if @trncnt = 0     -- this proc issued begin tran
  commit tran p1   -- commit tran, decrement @@trancount to 0
                   -- commit not required with save tran

return 0 /* successful return */
```

Here is what the batch that calls the stored procedure might look like. The batch needs to check the return status value to determine whether the stored procedure completed properly. If not, the batch may need to roll back any partial work:

```
/* Retrieve status code to determine if proc was successful */
...

declare @status_val int, @trncnt int

select @trncnt = @@trancount   -- save @@trancount value

if @trncnt = 0     -- transaction has not begun
  begin tran t1    -- begin tran increments nest level to 1
else               -- otherwise, already in a transaction
  save tran t1     -- save tran doesn't increment nest level

/* do some processing if required */

if (@@transtate = 2) -- or other error condition
  begin
  rollback tran t1   -- rollback to savepoint,or begin tran
  return             -- and exit batch/procedure
  end

execute @status_val = p1  --exec procedure, begin nesting

if @status_val = 25 -- if proc performed rollback
  begin             -- determine whether to rollback or continue
  rollback tran t1
  return
  end

/* more processing if required */

if @trncnt = 0      -- this proc/batch issued begin tran
  commit tran t1    -- commit tran, decrement @@trancount to 0
return              -- commit not required with save tran
```

# Cursors in Stored Procedures

In stored procedures, the declare cursor statement does not have to be in a separate batch (these are called server cursors). As Figure 7.5 illustrates, if stored procedures are nested, they can access cursors declared in higher-level stored procedures in the call tree.

Here is an example of a stored procedure cursor:

```
create proc title_price_update
as
declare @total_sales int, @price money
/*declare cursor*/
declare titles_curs cursor for
  select total_sales, price from titles
  for update of price
open titles_curs
fetch titles_curs into @total_sales, @price
```

```
if (@@sqlstatus = 2)
  begin
     print "No books found"
     close titles_curs
     deallocate cursor titles_curs
     return
  end
while (@@sqlstatus = 0)
  begin
     if @total_sales = null
        begin
        update titles set price = @price * .75
           where current of titles_curs
        end
     else
        if @price > $15
           update titles set price = @price * .9
              where current of titles_curs
        else
           update titles set price = @price * 1.15
              where current of titles_curs
           fetch titles_curs into @total_sales, @price
  end
if (@@sqlstatus = 1)
  raiserror 55555 "Fetch of titles_curs failed"
close titles_curs
deallocate cursor titles_curs
return
```

## FIGURE 7.5.

*If stored procedures are nested, they can access cursors declared in higher-level stored procedures in the call tree.*

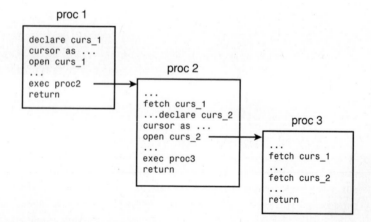

## Procedure Limitations and Notes

A stored procedure may not create views, defaults, rules, triggers, or procedures or issue the use statement. (If you want a stored procedure to operate within the context of the database it is called from, create a system stored procedure.) You can create tables in stored procedures. Typically, you create temporary tables for storing intermediate results or as work tables. Temporary tables used within stored procedures are dropped at procedure termination. A table cannot be created, dropped, and re-created with the same name in a single procedure.

Stored procedures are parsed in a single pass and will not resolve forward or backward references. For example, when defining a stored procedure that references a temporary table, either the stored procedure must create the temporary table prior to referencing it, or the temporary table must exist at the time the stored procedure is created.

Procedures are reusable, but not reentrant. Stored procedures can be recursive.

Stored procedures may reference objects in other databases and call other procedures to a nesting level of 16 deep.

# Objects Referenced in Procedures

To display a list of objects referenced by stored procedures, use sp_depends:

```
exec sp_depends procedure_name
```

To display a list of stored procedures that reference a specific table or view, use sp_depends:

```
exec sp_depends {table_name | view_name}
```

If you rename an object referenced by a stored procedure, the stored procedure still references the original object. If you drop the original object and create a new object with the original object's name, the stored procedure is recompiled to reference the new object. If you create a new object with the original object's name and the original object still exists, you should drop and re-create the stored procedure to reference the new object.

If you drop any object referenced by the stored procedure and do not re-create it with the same name, you get a run-time error. If you drop an index used by the query plan of a stored procedure, SQL Server generates a new query plan the next time it is executed.

# Optimizing Stored Procedures

The SQL Server optimizer generates a query plan for a stored procedure based on the parameters passed in the first time it is executed. This query plan is then run from cache for subsequent executions. To force a new query plan to be generated, use the with recompile option either at creation time or execution time. with recompile specified at procedure creation time causes the optimizer to generate a new query plan for every execution. If it is specified at procedure execution time, it causes the optimizer to generate a new query plan for that execution only and is used for subsequent executions. Here are some examples:

```
create proc advance_range
     (@low money, @high money)
     with recompile
     as
select * from titles
  where advance between @low and @high
return
go
```

```
/* if the procedure has not been created with the
** 'with recompile' option, execute as follows to
** recompile */
exec advance_range $1000,$2000 with recompile
```

Here is when to use `with recompile`:

- When a stored procedure can generate widely different query plans depending on the parameters passed in and there is no way of predicting the best query plan for all executions

- When statistics have been updated on a table and you want the stored procedure to generate a new query plan based on the updated statistics

- When an index has been added to a table that you want the optimizer to consider to generate a new query plan for the stored procedure

If the procedure contains `select * from tablename` and `alter table` has been used to add a column to the table, `with recompile` will not force all the columns to be displayed. Instead, you have to drop and re-create the stored procedure to display the new column.

# Remote Stored Procedures

Remote stored procedures are procedures residing on other servers. Fully qualify the stored procedure name with the server name to execute procedures on other servers. Here's the syntax:

```
[exec[ute]] server_name.db_name.owner.proc_name
```

Both servers must be configured for remote access. This is a cookbook procedure your sa will understand, but there are many steps and the server needs to be cycled.

Transaction control statements do not affect work performed in remote procedure calls.

# Stored Procedure Guidelines

Stored procedures should be solid, because they are server-resident and called frequently. Check parameters for validity and return an error if there is a problem. Ensure that the parameter datatypes match the column datatypes they are compared against to avoid datatype mismatches. Check `@@error` after each SQL statement. Comment your code. Always use a `return` statement. Develop a method for maintaining versions of stored procedure source code.

# Stored Procedure Debugging Techniques

Write it as a batch first. To get the syntax right on a stored procedure, write small parts of it as a batch first, then store the procedure once the whole operation starts working.

Get SHOWPLAN output with recompile. SHOWPLAN and DBCC output are generated by the optimizer, which operates only when a procedure is recompiled. To see the effect of different parameters on optimization, create the procedure with recompile, then drop and re-create the procedure without it when you go into production.

---

**TIP**

Use FlushMessage to see debugging Print statements. Print statements are returned to the client only when a network packet fills in the process of returning results or when the result set is complete. To instruct the server to return a network packet whenever a print message is sent to the client, use the Sybase session-level option, flushmessage:

```
set flushmessage on
```

---

# Summary

When SQL Server was first introduced, stored procedures and triggers helped differentiate the product from competitive database products. Even now, the capability of writing effective stored procedures and triggers will make your system operate better, with better integrity and usually better performance.

Understand the capabilities and limitations of stored procedures and triggers before writing lots of code. Well-written applications run fast and clean; poorly written code makes the server run sluggishly and inefficiently.

# Transaction Management

# 8

A *transaction* is a set of operations to be completed at one time, as though they were a single operation. A transaction must be fully completed, or not performed at all. Standard examples of transactions include bank transfers (withdraw $500 from checking, add $500 to savings) and order-entry systems (write an order for five widgets, remove five widgets from inventory).

# Transaction Mechanisms

There are four aspects of transaction processing:

- SQL Server maintains a transaction log.
- SQL Server locks table pages during transactions so other users cannot access the changing data.
- SQL Server performs automatic recovery upon restart.
- Transaction control statements in Transact-SQL determine when a transaction begins and commits or rolls back.

The *transaction log* is actually a system table, syslogs, that records all changes to data within a database. The log is used to maintain database consistency. The role of the log and how it is implemented and maintained are discussed in detail in Chapter 28, "Database Logging and Recovery."

Transactions *automatically* lock data to allow data modifications to occur in isolation from each other. There is a brief discussion of the interaction between locks and transactions in this chapter, but a more detailed discussion of locking can be found in Chapter 15, "Locking and Performance."

SQL Server performs *automatic recovery* on a database every time the server is started. This process guarantees that the data is consistent with itself and that all changes logged to the transaction log are completely executed in the data. Chapter 28 looks more closely at the issues surrounding recovery.

*Transaction control statements* allow you, the programmer, to define transactions. This chapter looks closely at how to use transaction control statements to guarantee that data matches the consistency rules appropriate to your business.

# Transaction Control

All SQL statements are inherently transactions, from GRANT and CREATE statements to the data-modification statements INSERT, UPDATE, and DELETE. Consider the following UPDATE example:

```
update titles
set price = price * 1.02
```

This statement modifies all rows in the `titles` table. SQL Server guarantees that, regardless of the size of the `titles` table, all rows will be processed or no rows will be processed at all. What if half the rows are modified and the server fails? When the server comes back up (but before the database is available for use), it rolls back the incomplete transaction, removing all evidence that it ever began. That's part of the recovery process, which is discussed in Chapter 28.

SQL Server also includes transaction control syntax to group sets of SQL statements together into single logical work units:

- `BEGIN TRANSACTION` starts a unit of work.
- `COMMIT TRANSACTION` completes a unit of work.
- `ROLLBACK TRANSACTION` cancels a unit of work.

The following example enters an order and depletes inventory in a single transaction:

```
begin transaction
    update inventory
        set in_stock = in_stock - 5
        where item_num = "14141"
    insert orders (cust_num, item_num, qty)
        values ("ABC151", "14141", 5)
commit transaction
```

SQL Server guarantees that the inventory will not change unless the order is also entered.

Look at the same example, but with the `ROLLBACK TRANSACTION` statement instead of `COMMIT`:

```
begin transaction
    update inventory
        set in_stock = in_stock - 5
        where item_num = "14141"
    insert orders (cust_num, item_num, qty)
        values ("ABC151", "14141", 5)
rollback transaction
```

When the server encounters the `ROLLBACK` statement, it discards all changes in the transaction and returns the data to the state it was in before work began.

# Transaction Programming

The programming issues associated with writing transactional SQL are fairly straightforward. Once you issue a `BEGIN TRANSACTION` (or `BEGIN TRAN`) statement, the server performs all the subsequent work without formally writing a final record of the work. At any time after issuing a `BEGIN TRAN` statement, you can roll back the entire transaction or commit it.

The SQL Server implicitly commits work executed outside of explicit transactional control. For example, this set of statements includes no explicit transactional syntax:

```
insert publishers (pub_id, pub_name, city, state)
    values ("1111", "Joe and Mary's Books", "Northern Plains", "IA")
update titles
```

```
    set pub_id = "1111"
    where pub_id = "1234"
delete authors
    where state = "CA"
```

Each of these statements will be treated as its own transaction. Thus the server issues *implicit* instructions on transaction control for each individual SQL statement. The server would treat the preceding batch like this:

```
[implicit BEGIN TRANSACTION]
insert publishers (pub_id, pub_name, city, state)
    values ("1111", "Joe and Mary's Books", "Northern Plains", "IA")
[implicit COMMIT TRANSACTION]

[implicit BEGIN TRANSACTION]
update titles
    set pub_id = "1111"
    where pub_id = "1234"
[implicit COMMIT TRANSACTION]

[implicit BEGIN TRANSACTION]
delete authors
    where state = "CA"
[implicit COMMIT TRANSACTION]
```

Each statement would include implicit BEGIN and COMMIT instructions.

What does that mean for the integrity of this batch? Each statement is guaranteed to be carried to completion or rolled back to the beginning. If the server goes down unexpectedly after the titles update starts but before it is complete, the server rolls back any work already performed by the UPDATE statement. On the other hand, the work associated with the insert to publishers would have already been completed and committed (by the implicit COMMIT operation), so only part of the batch would be complete.

## Transactions and Batches

In the previous example, you may have wanted the whole operation to complete or nothing at all. The obvious solution is to wrap the entire operation in a single transaction, like this:

```
begin transaction
insert publishers (pub_id, pub_name, city, state)
    values ("1111", "Joe and Mary's Books", "Northern Plains", "IA")
update titles
    set pub_id = "1111"
    where pub_id = "1234"
delete authors
    where state = "CA"
commit transaction
```

Now the server treats all three operations performed in the batch as a single modification.

There is no inherent transactional quality to batches. As you saw earlier, unless you provide the syntax to form a transaction out of several statements, each statement in a batch is its own transaction, and each statement is carried to completion or failure individually.

Transactions also can span batches. For example, you can write an application that begins a transaction in one batch and then asks for user verification during a second batch. The SQL might look like this:

*First Batch:*

```
/* DON'T DO THIS ... EVER!!! */
begin transaction
insert publishers (pub_id, pub_name, city, state)
    values ("1111", "Joe and Mary's Books", "Northern Plains", "IA")
if @@error = 0
    print "publishers insert was successful. Please go on."
else
    print "publisher insert failed. Please roll back"
```

*Second Batch:*

```
update titles
    set pub_id = "1111"
    where pub_id = "1234"
delete authors
    where state = "CA"
commit transaction
```

In the "Transactions and Locking" section later in this chapter, you'll look at the locking issues associated with transactions. You'll see that transactions force data modifications (INSERT, UPDATE, DELETE) to hold locks that persist until a COMMIT TRANSACTION or ROLLBACK TRANSACTION statement is encountered.

Writing transactions that span multiple batches is usually bad. The locking problems can get very complicated, with awful performance implications. (What if this waited for a user to say "OK" before going on, but the user went to Cancun and didn't come back for two weeks? Locks would be held until the user got back and said "OK.") In general, you want to enclose each transaction in a single batch, using conditional programming constructs to handle situations like the previous one. Here is a better way to write that program:

```
/* DO THIS INSTEAD !! */
begin transaction
insert publishers (pub_id, pub_name, city, state)
    values ("1111", "Joe and Mary's Books", "Northern Plains", "IA")
if @@error = 0
begin
    print "publishers insert was successful. Continuing."
    update titles
        set pub_id = "1111"
        where pub_id = "1234"
    delete authors
        where state = "CA"
    commit transaction
end
else
begin
    print "publisher insert failed. rolling back transaction"
    rollback transaction
end
```

The important point in this example is that the transaction now takes place within a single batch.

# Savepoints

SQL Server allows you to mark a *savepoint* in a transaction. Savepoints enable you to do some work inside a transaction and then roll back just that work, based on other circumstances. In this example, the program sells several items and then tests inventory (which is automatically updated through a trigger) and rolls back a portion of the work if there is insufficient inventory:

```
begin tran

save tran item111     /* mark a savepoint before each insert */
insert order (ord_no, item_no, qty)
    values ("2345", "111", 15)
if (select in_stock from inventory where item_no = '111') < 0
begin
    rollback tran item111   /* roll back just this item if incorrect */
    print "Item 111 would be back-ordered, cancelling order"
end

save tran item999
insert order (ord_no, item_no, qty)
    values ("2345", "999", 5)
if (select in_stock from inventory where item_no = '999') < 0
begin
    rollback tran item999
    print "Item 999 would be back-ordered, cancelling order"
end

save tran item444
    insert order (ord_no, item_no, qty)
values ("2345", "444", 25)
if (select in_stock from inventory where item_no = '444') < 0
begin
    rollback tran item444
    print "Item 444 would be back-ordered, cancelling order"
end

commit tran
```

By wrapping the insert statements in a transaction, the programmer gets two benefits. First, the overall effect of each insert can be observed before the work is committed, which makes it very easy to reverse the effects of problem update statements. The second benefit is that all the legitimate insert statements included in the batch will go in, and the rest will be rejected. (This approach may not match the needs of your business.)

The scope of transaction savepoint names is local, so you don't have to worry about generating unique names for your savepoints. Savepoints and related rollback statements do not affect program flow. Note also that rolling back to a savepoint enables processing to continue forward from that point.

# Nested Transactions

It is important to note that SQL Server does not implicitly commit work when you log out. For example, what if you issue the following statement and then log out?

```
begin transaction
insert publishers (pub_id, pub_name, city, state)
    values ("1111", "Joe and Mary's Books", "Northern Plains", "IA")
```

Any uncommitted transactions are rolled back automatically when you log out.

How does the server know you have uncommitted transactions? SQL Server retains a *transaction nesting level* for each user connection.

---

**NOTE**

SQL Server maintains a list of active connections in master..sysprocesses. The primary key of that table is spid (server process ID). You can retrieve the server process ID for your current connection by using the global variable @@spid:

```
select @@spid
```

---

The transaction nesting level can be retrieved for your connection with the global variable, @@trancount. You should understand how each transactional statement affects the contents of @@trancount in order to write properly nested transactions and to manage transactions through triggers and stored procedures. Table 8.1 summarizes the effect of transactional statements on @@trancount.

**Table 8.1. How transaction control statements affect @@trancount.**

| *Statement* | *Effect on @@trancount* |
| --- | --- |
| BEGIN TRAN | @@trancount = @@trancount + 1 |
| COMMIT TRAN | @@trancount = @@trancount − 1 |
| SAVE TRAN | (no effect) |
| ROLLBACK TRANSACTION | @@trancount = 0 |
| ROLLBACK TRIGGER | |
| ROLLBACK TRANSACTION *save_name*\* | (no effect) |

Here is a summary of how transactional control relates to @@trancount:

- When you log in to SQL Server, your session @@trancount is zero.
- Each time you execute BEGIN TRANSACTION, SQL Server increments @@trancount.

- Each time you execute COMMIT TRANSACTION, SQL Server decrements @@trancount.

- Actual work is committed only when @@trancount reaches 0 again.

- When you execute ROLLBACK TRANSACTION, the transaction is canceled and @@trancount returns to 0. Notice that ROLLBACK TRANSACTION cuts straight through any number of nested transactions, canceling the overall main transaction. This means that you need to be careful how you write code that contains a ROLLBACK statement.

- Savepoints and rolling back to a savepoint do not affect @@trancount or transaction nesting in any way.

- If a user connection is disconnected for any reason when @@trancount is greater than zero, any pending work for that connection is automatically rolled back. The server requires that transactions be explicitly committed.

The following is an example of how the server handles transaction nesting. In this example, transactions are nested two levels deep:

```
begin tran
    update titles
        set price = price * 1.1
        from titles
        where pub_id = "1234"
    begin tran
        update titles
            set advance = advance * 1.15
            where pub_id in
              (select pub_id from publishers
                where state = "MA")
    commit tran
    delete titles
        where type = "UNDECIDED"
commit tran
```

Let's track @@trancount through each statement. Assuming that @@trancount starts at zero, Table 8.2 shows the effect of each statement on @@trancount.

**Table 8.2. How statements in the example affect @@trancount.**

| Statement | Effect on @@trancount |
|---|---|
| BEGIN TRAN | @@trancount = @@trancount + 1 = 1 |
| UPDATE TITLES | @@trancount = 1 |
| BEGIN TRAN | @@trancount = @@trancount + 1 = 2 |
| UPDATE TITLES | @@trancount = 2 |
| COMMIT TRAN | @@trancount = @@trancount − 1 = 1 |
| DELETE TITLES | @@trancount = 1 |
| COMMIT TRAN | @@trancount = @@trancount − 1 = 0 |

Nested transactions are *syntactic only.* The only COMMIT TRAN statement that has an impact on real data is the last one, the statement returning @@trancount to 0, which forces physical data to be written to disk.

# Transactions and Locking

In order to ensure data integrity, SQL Server places exclusive locks on data pages (2KB blocks of table data or index information) involved in a transaction. In the previous example, pages in both the titles and publishers tables are involved. As SQL Server progresses through the query, locks are acquired on each table modified by a statement and are then held until SQL Server reaches a COMMIT TRAN that sets @@trancount to 0 (or a ROLLBACK TRAN). A long-running transaction performing data modifications to many different tables can effectively block the work of all other users in the system (see the section "Long-Running Transactions," later in this chapter).

Because of this, you need to be aware of the performance and concurrency issues involved with writing transactions. When writing transactional code, here are some things to keep in mind:

- Keep transactions as short as your application allows.
- Avoid returning data with a SELECT in the middle of a transaction.
- Try to write all transactions within stored procedures.
- Avoid transactions that span multiple batches.

For more information on locking and performance, please read Chapter 15.

# Transactions and Triggers

Triggers are considered part of the transaction in which a data modification is executed. In this example, an update trigger on the titles table fires as part of the transaction:

```
begin tran
    update titles
        set price = $99
        where title_id = "BU1234"
commit tran
```

## @@trancount and Implicit Transactions

What is the value of @@trancount as SQL Server processes each of these statements? If @@trancount starts at 0, BEGIN TRAN makes it 1, the UPDATE statement leaves it at 1, and it returns to 0 with the COMMIT TRAN statement.

What is the value of @@trancount inside the update trigger? To determine that, you need a trigger that prints out the contents of @@trancount during execution. Here is an example:

```
/* DON'T LEAVE THIS KIND OF TRIGGER LYING AROUND!! */
create trigger tr_stores_upd
on stores
for update
as
declare @tc varchar(80)
select @tc = "Trancount = " + convert(char(1), @@trancount)
print @tc
raiserror 99999 "this update statement will never commit ... test trigger in place"
rollback tran
return
```

Here is what the isql session looks like when you update the stores table:

```
1> update stores
2> set city = "Pittsburgh"
3> go
Trancount = 1
Msg 99999, Level 16, State 1:
this update statement will never commit ... test trigger in place
```

The output from the print statement shows that, inside the trigger, @@trancount is equal to 1. Recall that each individual SQL statement is a transaction in and of itself. From this example, you can see that SQL Server uses the same transaction nesting methods with implicit and explicit transaction control. You also can see that any work completed in the trigger is part of the UPDATE statement itself. (See Figure 8.1.)

**FIGURE 8.1.**

*A simple SQL data modification statement includes implicit transactional control to make certain that the whole statement is executed. Any triggers associated with that statement are executed as part of the implicit transaction as well.*

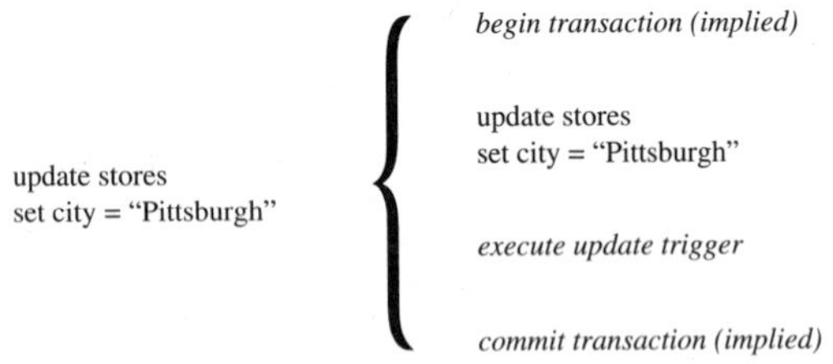

update stores
set city = "Pittsburgh"

begin transaction (implied)

update stores
set city = "Pittsburgh"

execute update trigger

commit transaction (implied)

Watch what happens as the same trigger executes when the UPDATE runs as part of an explicit transaction:

```
1> begin tran
2> select "Before Update Trancount " , @@trancount
3> update stores
4> set city = "Pittsburgh"
5> select "After Update Trancount " , @@trancount
6> commit tran
7> go
```

```
------------------------ ----------
Before Update Trancount          1
```

```
(1 row affected)
Trancount = 2
Msg 99999, Level 16, State 1:
this update statement will never commit ... test trigger in place
```

When the first begin tran executes, @@trancount is set to 1, as reported by the SELECT statement. The UPDATE statement executes and the update trigger fires. The update trigger reports that @@trancount is 2 (again reflecting the effect on @@trancount of implicit transactions).

> **NOTE**
>
> Please don't allow this section to confuse you about transaction control and individual SQL statements. It is critical to understand that data modification statements (INSERT, UPDATE, and DELETE) have *no net effect* on @@trancount.

## *rollback transaction* in a Trigger

In the previous example, you should note that the SELECT statement after the UPDATE is not executed. ROLLBACK TRANSACTION statements, in addition to reversing the effect of the current data-modification statement, immediately return from the trigger and abort the batch, returning no automatic error message.

Consider this example in which three INSERT statements are submitted as a batch to a table, trigger_test. The INSERT statements are not stated as a transaction. Here is the insert trigger for the table, which ensures that the integer column, c1, is always less than c2:

```
create trigger tr_1
on trigger_test
for insert
as
if exists (select * from inserted
    where c1 > c2)
begin
    raiserror 99998 "c1 exceeds c2 -- rolling back"
    rollback transaction
end
return
```

Here is the insert batch and the results:

```
1> insert trigger_test (c1, c2) values (1, 3)
2> insert trigger_test (c1, c2) values (3, 1)
3> insert trigger_test (c1, c2) values (1, 4)
4> go
(1 row affected)
Msg 99998, Level 16, State 1:
c1 exceeds c2 -- rolling back
1> select * from trigger_test
2> go
```

```
c1          c2
----------- -----------
          1           3
```

**(1 row affected)**

As you can see, only the first INSERT statement is executed successfully. The trigger returns an error when the second statement fails the validation test. The error raised in the text of the trigger is returned, but notice that there is no error returned from the ROLLBACK statement itself. Finally, note that the final statement, which would pass the validation test if executed, is not executed.

Let's run the same INSERT (into an empty table) as a single transaction:

```
1> begin tran
2> insert trigger_test (c1, c2) values (1, 3)
3> insert trigger_test (c1, c2) values (3, 1)
4> insert trigger_test (c1, c2) values (1, 4)
5> commit tran
6> go
(1 row affected)
Msg 99998, Level 16, State 1:
c1 exceeds c2 -- rolling back
1> select * from trigger_test
2> go
 c1          c2
----------- -----------
```

**(0 rows affected)**

Again, note that the trigger ROLLBACK cancels the batch, so the third INSERT is never executed. When the statement firing the trigger executes from within a transaction, the ROLLBACK in the trigger rolls back the whole transaction.

> **WARNING**
>
> Suppose you had this error trap in a trigger:
> ```
> if exists (...)
> begin
>    rollback tran
>    raiserror 99998 "This is an error!"
> end
> ```
> This error message would never be returned to the user. In most circumstances, the user would never learn that his or her batch had aborted, because the ROLLBACK TRAN in the trigger *immediately ceases processing on the batch.*
>
> Be absolutely certain to raise necessary errors prior to rolling back.

Please note that ROLLBACK TRANSACTION aborts only a batch from inside a trigger. *In all other cases, transactional syntax has no effect on program execution.*

# ROLLBACK TRIGGER

System 10 introduced a new syntactic construct with ROLLBACK TRIGGER. It provides a method within a trigger for rolling back a single statement in a transaction without affecting the rest of the transaction.

Consider this simplified transaction from a typical order-entry system:

```
begin tran
    insert order_header (cust_id, po_num, date)
        values (1234, "9993532", "3/1/96")
    insert order_detail (cust_id, po_num, item_seq, item_id, qty)
        values (1234, "9993532", 1, 343, 1)
    insert order_detail (cust_id, po_num, item_seq, item_id, qty)
        values (1234, "9993532", 2, 998, 2)
    insert order_detail (cust_id, po_num, item_seq, item_id, qty)
        values (1234, "9993532", 3, 7773, 8)
    insert order_detail (cust_id, po_num, item_seq, item_id, qty)
        values (1234, "9993532", 4, 422, 15)
commit tran
```

This transaction inserts a single order_header row and then four rows in order_detail. The header contains control information about the order; the details contain individual items on the order. Here is a trigger checking each inserted row to make certain that no order contains more than a stated maximum qty for each item (specified in the item table):

```
create trigger tr_order_detail_ins_upd
for order_detail
on insert, update
as
if exists (select * from inserted i, item it
        where i.item_id = it.item_id
        and i.qty > it.max_qty)
begin
    raiserror 99999 "maximum quantity exceeded"
    rollback tran
end
return
```

The effect of this trigger is to roll back *the entire transaction* and abort processing of that batch immediately. Let's rewrite the trigger with ROLLBACK TRIGGER and see what effect that has on processing:

```
create trigger tr_order_detail_ins_upd_rt
for order_detail
on insert, update
as
if exists (select * from inserted i, item it
        where i.item_id = it.item_id
        and i.qty > it.max_qty)
    rollback trigger with raiserror 99999 "maximum quantity exceeded"
return
```

`ROLLBACK TRIGGER` has the following effect inside a trigger:

- It rolls back any work performed by the trigger.
- It rolls back any work performed by the statement that fired the trigger.
- It rolls back any work performed by nested triggers.
- It resets `@@trancount` to the value before the current statement was executed.
- It issues the error, if specified.
- It continues processing the current batch with the next statement.

> **NOTE**
>
> It's worth noting that `RAISERROR` is optional with `ROLLBACK TRIGGER`, but if you don't raise an error, there is absolutely no way for the batch to know that anything went wrong in the trigger.

Let's look at how this code changes the way a sample batch might operate. Here is the batch repeated:

```
begin tran
   insert order_header (cust_id, po_num, date)
      values (1234, "9993532", "3/1/96")
   insert order_detail (cust_id, po_num, item_seq, item_id, qty)
      values (1234, "9993532", 1, 343, 1)
   insert order_detail (cust_id, po_num, item_seq, item_id, qty)
      values (1234, "9993532", 2, 998, 2)
   insert order_detail (cust_id, po_num, item_seq, item_id, qty)
      values (1234, "9993532", 3, 7773, 8)
   insert order_detail (cust_id, po_num, item_seq, item_id, qty)
      values (1234, "9993532", 4, 422, 15)
commit tran
```

`ROLLBACK TRIGGER` allows the dba to determine that (in this case) it is permissible to record partial transactions in the database. If your application cannot permit partial transactions, but the database does, you need to include error-handling code in your batch to check for the reported error and abort processing of the batch:

```
begin tran
   insert order_header (cust_id, po_num, date)
      values (1234, "9993532", "3/1/96")
   if @@error = 99999
   begin
      rollback tran
      return
   end
   insert order_detail (cust_id, po_num, item_seq, item_id, qty)
      values (1234, "9993532", 1, 343, 1)
   if @@error = 99999
```

```
      begin
         rollback tran
         return
      end
      insert order_detail (cust_id, po_num, item_seq, item_id, qty)
         values (1234, "9993532", 2, 998, 2)
      if @@error = 99999
      begin
         rollback tran
         return
      end
      if @@error = 99999
      begin
         rollback tran
         return
      end
      insert order_detail (cust_id, po_num, item_seq, item_id, qty)
         values (1234, "9993532", 3, 7773, 8)
      insert order_detail (cust_id, po_num, item_seq, item_id, qty)
         values (1234, "9993532", 4, 422, 15)
      if @@error = 99999
      begin
         rollback tran
         return
      end
commit tran
```

Using ROLLBACK TRANSACTION in a trigger does not require all this error-checking code in the SQL because ROLLBACK TRAN during a trigger immediately aborts a batch. ROLLBACK TRIGGER requires substantially greater care to ensure referential integrity in your database.

# Transactions and Stored Procedures

Writing all your transactions in stored procedures can provide better performance by avoiding partial transactions, especially because the server provides error messages to help you manage the transaction nesting level within procedures. The biggest concern you have is how to handle ROLLBACK TRANSACTION statements within stored procedures. Mistakes in using ROLLBACK statements in procedures can result in data integrity problems.

Consider this stored procedure, which inserts a row in a table, tests the table after the INSERT, and rolls back that INSERT if more than three rows exist with that value:

```
/* stored procedure example coded improperly (see below) */
create proc p2
(@parm int)
as
begin tran
insert tally_table (c1) values (@parm)
if (select count(*) from tally_table
    where c1 = @parm) > 3
begin
    raiserror 99997 "too many rows with that value - rolling back"
    rollback tran
    return 99997    /* error ... rolled back */
end
```

```
else
begin
    commit tran
    return 0         /* no error */
end
```

If you execute the stored procedure when the table contains only two rows with $c_1 = 1$, the procedure runs properly and the INSERT is entered:

```
1> exec p2 1
2> go
1> select * from tally_table
2> go
 c1
 -----------
           1
           1
           1
```

**(3 rows affected)**

When you run the procedure again, the ROLLBACK statement executes and you receive the error message:

```
1> exec p2 1
2> go
Msg 99997, Level 16, State 1:
too many rows with that value - rolling back
1> select * from tally_table
2> go
 c1
 -----------
           1
           1
           1
```

**(3 rows affected)**

As expected, the procedure works properly and there are only three rows in the table after the INSERT fails.

The problem with this procedure arises only when it is executed from within a transaction. Consider this example:

```
begin tran
    exec p2 1
    exec p2 2
commit tran
```

What you intend by writing this as a transaction is that the INSERT statements with value 2 will not occur unless you can make the related INSERT with value 1: both INSERT should go in as a unit or no INSERT should take place. Let's look at the output when the table contains three rows with value 1:

```
1> select * from tally_table
2> go
```

```
  c1
  ----------
           1
           1
           1

(3 rows affected)
1> begin tran
2>     exec p2 1
3>     exec p2 2
4> commit tran
5> go
Msg 99997, Level 16, State 1:
too many rows with that value - rolling back
Msg 266, Level 16, State 1:
Transaction count after EXECUTE indicates that a COMMIT or ROLLBACK
TRAN is missing. Previous count = 1, Current count = 0.
Msg 3902, Level 16, State 1:
The commit transaction request has no corresponding BEGIN TRANSACTION.
1> select * from tally_table
2> go
  c1
  ----------
           1
           1
           1
           2

(4 rows affected)
```

Before the batch, the table contains three rows; afterward, it contains four rows. The new row contains the value 2, so only half the transaction was executed. The integrity of the transaction has been lost. Let's look at the output from the batch closely to understand what has occurred, then write the stored procedure and batch properly:

```
Msg 99997, Level 16, State 1:
too many rows with that value - rolling back
```

This is the error message, generated because the first INSERT failed:

```
Msg 266, Level 16, State 1:
Transaction count after EXECUTE indicates that a COMMIT or ROLLBACK
TRAN is missing. Previous count = 1, Current count = 0.
```

This error occurs because the transaction nesting level (that is, the value of @@trancount) is different when the procedure starts from when it ends. Why? ROLLBACK TRANSACTION returns @@trancount to 0 regardless of the prior transaction nesting level. Clearly, this is a problem if the calling batch is unaware of the nesting level. Table 8,3 steps through the batch a statement at a time, understanding the impact of each statement on @@trancount (and on the transaction).

## Table 8.3. Tracking @@trancount during procedure execution.

| Calling Batch | Procedure | @@trancount |
|---|---|---|
| begin tran | | 1 |
| exec p2 1 | | 1 |
| | begin tran | 2 |
| | insert tally_table (c1) values (@parm) | 2 |
| | if (select count(*) from tally_table | 2 |
| |     where c1 = @parm) > 3 | |
| | begin | 0 (A) |
| |     raiserror 99997 "too many rows with that | |
| | value - rolling back" | |
| |     rollback tran | |
| |     return 99997    /* error ... rolled back */ | |
| | end | |
| exec p2 2 | | 0 |
| | begin tran | 1 |
| | insert tally_table (c1) values (@parm) | 1 |
| | if (select count(*) from tally_table | 1 |
| |     where c1 = @parm) > 3 | |
| | begin | |
| |     commit tran | 0 (B) |
| |     return 0    /* no error */ | |
| | end | |
| commit tran | | 0 (C) |

There are three specific events—noted in the table as A, B, and C—that help you understand the problems in data integrity. Note A points out the problems caused by ROLLBACK TRANSACTION in a procedure. When you write the procedure, you should make allowances so that a user can execute it whether a transaction is currently running or not. Note B shows that the second execution of the procedure, when it reaches the COMMIT statement, forces @@trancount to 0, performing an actual COMMIT of the data modifications since the prior BEGIN TRAN statement. Note C, finally, shows that the COMMIT statement tries to decrement @@trancount, which is already 0. When this happens, the server returns the message you saw earlier:

```
Msg 3902, Level 16, State 1:
The commit transaction request has no corresponding BEGIN TRANSACTION.
```

These two messages (3902 and 266) are your warnings that the transaction nesting is not properly managed in the stored procedure.

There are several methods of coding stored procedures with transactions to ensure that the procedure works properly as a standalone transaction or as a part of a larger, nested transaction. Here is one example of how to write a stored procedure with transaction control:

```
/* proc to demonstrate no net change to @@trancount
** while still rolling back changes within the proc
** VERY IMPORTANT: return an error code
** to tell the calling procedure rollback occurred */

create proc p1
as
declare @trncnt int
```

```
select @trncnt = @@trancount   -- save @@trancount value

if @trncnt = 0    -- transaction has not begun
   begin tran p1  -- begin tran increments nest level to 1

else               -- already in a transaction
   save tran p1    -- save tran doesn't increment nest level

/* do some processing */

if (@@transtate = 2) -- or other error condition
   begin
   rollback tran p1  -- rollback to savepoint, or begin tran
   return 25         -- return error code indicating rollback
   end

/* more processing if required */

if @trncnt = 0     -- this proc issued begin tran
   commit tran p1  -- commit tran, decrement @@trancount to 0
                   -- commit not required with save tran

return 0 /* successful return */
```

As important as it is to write the stored procedure properly, it is equally important to write the batch calling the procedure to make proper use of the information provided by the stored procedure return codes. Here is an example of how to manage nested procedures from the calling batch:

```
/* Retrieve status code to determine if proc was successful */
...

declare @status_val int, @trncnt int

select @trncnt = @@trancount   -- save @@trancount value

if @trncnt = 0    -- transaction has not begun
   begin tran t1  -- begin tran increments nest level to 1
else               -- otherwise, already in a transaction
   save tran t1    -- save tran doesn't increment nest level

/* do some processing if required */

if (@@transtate = 2) -- or other error condition
   begin
   rollback tran t1  -- rollback to savepoint,or begin tran
   return            -- and exit batch/procedure
   end

execute @status_val = p1 --exec procedure, begin nesting

if @status_val = 25 -- if proc performed rollback
   begin           -- determine whether to rollback or continue
   rollback tran t1
   return
   end

/* more processing if required */
```

```
if @trncnt = 0      -- this proc/batch issued begin tran
  commit tran t1    -- commit tran, decrement @@trancount to 0
return              -- commit not required with save tran
```

Whether you choose to adhere to the coding standards or not, the important point is that stored procedures and the batches that call those procedures need to be consistent with each other to provide you with proper data integrity control. You must establish coding standards for both that enable transactional control to work whether the transaction commits successfully or whether the transaction is rolled back.

# Chained Transactions

With System 10, Sybase introduced some alternative transaction-processing capabilities to provide better compatibility with other front-ends and greater ANSI compliance in the area of transaction processing. The major change is in the option to use *chained transactions,* an alternative transactional mode available to SQL programmers.

These are the major differences between chained and unchained (the default) modes:

- ■ Chained mode eliminates transaction nesting.
- ■ In chained mode, every SQL data retrieval (SELECT) or data modification (INSERT, UPDATE, DELETE) statement initiates a transaction that needs subsequently to be closed with a COMMIT statement or canceled with a ROLLBACK.

Turn on chained mode with the following:

```
set chained on
```

Select the global variable, @@tranchained, to determine whether you are working in chained (= 1) or unchained (= 0) mode. Unchained mode is the default.

Let's look quickly at a couple of examples. This example runs differently if it is run in chained or unchained mode:

```
insert order_header (cust_id, po_num, date)
    values (1234, "9993532", "3/1/96")
begin tran
   insert order_detail (cust_id, po_num, item_seq, item_id, qty)
    values (1234, "9993532", 1, 343, 1)
rollback tran
```

If you are working in unchained mode, the first INSERT is committed implicitly because the statement is its own transaction. The second INSERT is rolled back because it is part of an explicit transaction.

If the same query is run in chained mode, both INSERTs are rolled back. First, the initial INSERT initiates a transaction, but it contains no implicit COMMIT TRAN. The explicit BEGIN TRAN is essentially ignored because there is no transaction nesting. The second INSERT is part of the initial transaction. The ROLLBACK statement rolls back both INSERTs.

Here is another example that clarifies the differences between chained and unchained mode, this time looking at syntactically nested transactions:

```
begin tran
    insert order_header (cust_id, po_num, date)
            values (1234, "9993532", "3/1/96")
        begin tran
            insert order_detail (cust_id, po_num, item_seq, item_id, qty)
                    values (1234, "9993532", 1, 343, 1)
        commit tran
    insert order_detail (cust_id, po_num, item_seq, item_id, qty)
            values (1234, "9993532", 1, 343, 1)
rollback tran
```

In this example, using unchained mode, no rows are committed. The first explicit COMMIT TRAN statement is nested two levels deep, so it only reduces @@trancount to 1 (actual COMMITs occur only when @@trancount hits 0). The ROLLBACK statement rolls back all the work of the batch.

Using chained mode, the COMMIT TRAN commits all the work that preceded the COMMIT statement (regardless of how many BEGIN TRAN statements have been executed) because there is no transaction nesting in chained mode. The ROLLBACK statement applies only to the final INSERT statement immediately preceding it.

# Procedure Transaction Mode

If you are working in both modes from time to time and especially if you plan to use chained mode in production, look closely at the problems presented with transaction handling in stored procedures. The differences in transaction nesting syntax in either mode mean that your stored procedures need to be especially aware of the transaction mode when they are executed.

SQL Server provides you with the capability of identifying each stored procedure by the transaction modes it can support. The system procedure, sp_procxmode, enables you to assign a transaction mode to each stored procedure and to report the modes assigned to procedures. This example reports the transaction mode for procedure p1:

```
1> sp_procxmode p1
2> go
procedure name                   user name                        transaction mode
-------------------------------- -------------------------------- -----------------
p1                               dbo                              Unchained
```

To set the transaction mode, pass a transaction mode: "Unchained", "Chained", or "Any Mode". Here is an example:

```
sp_procxmode p1, "Any Mode"
```

For more on stored procedures and transactions, refer to the earlier section on that topic.

# Long-Running Transactions

There is no specific definition of a long-running transaction, but as transactions get longer, problems arise. Long-running transactions are not inherently different from shorter ones, but they do stress elements of the system that otherwise run quite well. In particular, you may encounter performance or concurrency problems because of issues related to the transaction log, the caching system, and locking.

Here are some of the symptoms of long-running transactions:

- Your transaction log fills up. Some transactions can actually exceed the size of your transaction log. Unlike some other database systems, SQL Server does not enable you to define a temporary emergency overflow log to handle this situation. Instead, you need to assign—permanently—a transaction log large enough to hold all of your largest transaction. (Why not just clear half the transaction and continue? The DUMP TRAN commands and other transaction log maintenance methods, such as "trunc. log on checkpoint" do not enable the server to prune pending, uncommitted transactions.)

- You are holding blocking locks that prevent all work from continuing by other users. You may be able to resolve this specific problem by looking at your lock escalation level (see Chapter 15).

- Ordinarily, all transactional work is performed in memory. Only when a COMMIT is executed are the changes to the transaction log flushed to disk, and changes to tables and indexes wait until a system-initiated checkpoint. If a transaction gets too long, the caching system may run out of unused memory and initiate a checkpoint to release additional memory. This could slow down your transaction as well, and a rollback following a checkpoint is far more disk-intensive than one that is executed only in memory.

It is usually helpful to reduce the size of your transactions when you start to encounter performance or blocking problems. There are two ways to reduce transaction size. One is to reduce the size of the logical unit of work. For example, you can take a single-transaction task and execute it in two steps, each its own transaction. This may require that you write program code to handle the data integrity in cases where the first part works but the second does not (in effect, writing your own transaction handler).

Before changing the definition of a unit of work, you should look for technical fixes to your code to reduce the amount of log work required for each step. For example, if you can get the server to perform an update in place rather than a deferred update, you can substantially reduce the amount of information recorded in the transaction log to perform the same work (see Chapter 12, "Understanding the Query Optimizer"). Reducing the number of indexes on a table also reduces the number of log writes required to handle complex modifications.

# Summary

A transaction is a logical unit of work. SQL Server provides several automatic and programmatic mechanisms including Transact-SQL transaction control statements, the transaction log, and transaction isolation through locking to preserve data integrity while transactions are running. Transactions allow you to tie together logically related operations, allowing the server to maintain data integrity. Remember, when writing applications that include transaction control, you need to pay special attention to how you write and work with triggers and stored procedures.

Here is a summary of the programming keywords related to transactions:

| Keyword | Purpose |
| --- | --- |
| begin tran | Alerts the SQL Server that a transaction is beginning. You can optionally name the transaction. |
| save tran | Marks this point in the transaction for potential rollback. |
| rollback tran | Undoes the changes—rolls back to the savepoint transaction or the beginning of the transaction. |
| commit tran | Ends the transaction and ensures the changes to the database will be reflected in the database. |
| set chained | Sets the transaction mode to chained (on) or unchained (off) mode. Unchained is the default mode. |
| @@tranchained | Has one of two values: |
|  | 0 means chained mode is off |
|  | * 1 means chained mode is on |

# Performance and Tuning

# Defining Performance Expectations and Variables

9

The first problem in tuning the performance of a SQL Server is understanding what performance can be reasonably expected from the server.

There are physical constraints on the server's performance, so some things are clearly improbable. For example, with today's technology SQL Server cannot scan a 2T table from SCSI disks (the most common type of magnetic storage device used today) in under one second. In fact, the server can scan at best only about 2MB per second from a single disk. Later in this chapter you will learn to measure the physical constraints of your server.

On the other hand, certain basic performance capabilities are clearly expected. For example, if you have a properly indexed table, you should be able to retrieve a single specified row (random row retrieval) in under one second. (You actually should be able to retrieve hundreds to thousands of individual rows in under a second.)

Somewhere between what is improbable and what is easily expected, you should understand what is possible and what is not possible on your server. In addition, you need to be able to develop expectations as to what amount of elapsed time a specific query will cost (this book defines the cost of a query as the total elapsed time it takes the query to run—this is the same performance measure your users probably use).

# Definition of Performance

You may not define performance the same way as the dba you meet at the local user's group. There are three basic ways of defining SQL Server performance. Other definitions are simply combinations of the following:

1. *Response time for queries*

   This means that what is important for you is that you want answers back to your queries in a specific amount of elapsed time. At many shops, the standard is the old "subsecond response" standard. Of course, more complex queries take longer than a second, but measuring the response time for specific queries is an important measure of performance.

   > **NOTE**
   >
   > As the story goes, ergonomic studies were done at IBM years ago (in my IBM-bashing days I might have suggested that these were performed by the hardware sales group) that demonstrated a substantial drop-off of productivity if users had to wait more than a second for a response.

2. *Throughput*

   This is typically measured in "transactions per minute" or TPM. There are a variety of industry-standard benchmarks (TPC-A, -B, and -C for example). These benchmarks help you compare the performance of database servers running on various platforms, but they will not help you define or predict the actual performance of the system, because they do not reflect your own transactions.

Perform your own performance benchmarking with your own queries and data to get meaningful throughput measures. You still need to make sure that your database and server are up to the challenge of managing the number of queries in the amount of time you need.

3. *Concurrency*

   This may reasonably be considered a subset of throughput. Here's the basic question: Can your system handle 5000 users? Answering this question is usually a substantial task, requiring you to profile predicted query and throughput traffic, then to answer the response time and throughput questions under load. You need to configure for this (and test for this) differently than for throughput.

4. *Combination: Running OLTP (On-Line Transaction Processing), DSS (Decision Support Systems, also called Data Warehousing), and Batch (Management and Off-Line Report Systems) simultaneously*

   This is the hardest thing to tune for, particularly on single-processor SQL Servers. These issues are covered in the subsequent performance and tuning chapters.

# Performance Tradeoffs

You will find it reasonably simple to tune for a single performance need. Approaches that solve single performance problems include the following:

- Normalization (eliminating duplicate data)
- Denormalization (storing duplicate data)
- Creation or removal of indexes
- Database segmenting to move specific objects onto specific physical devices
- Partitioning tables across databases

You might even need to buy additional hardware or software.

Although solving a single problem is fairly straightforward, finding a way to solve multiple performance needs is usually a delicate balancing act. For example, you may choose to speed throughput by removing indexes used to improve query performance. Without the additional indexes, modifications to tables are much faster, so transactions require less work and the system can handle more transactions per second. The tradeoff is that queries previously supported by an index now must perform a table scan. A query that used to take three minutes may now take several hours!

There are some common tradeoffs you need to consider when you are looking at performance issues. None of these tradeoffs is simple or has a standard solution. As you evaluate your performance options, it is vital that you be able to state clearly what you are getting and what you are giving up.

# Normalization versus Performance

Most database administrators develop database designs by using a two-step approach—starting with a logical design, then moving to a physical design. A *logical database design* is a representation of data intended to remove all duplication and to express clearly the relationship between data elements.

The *physical design* is a plan for how to store the data represented by the logical design on a particular system. One of the first hurdles to overcome in physical design is understanding that it has a separate purpose from the logical design. Logical design is for understanding the data. The primary purpose of a physical design is performance.

> **NOTE**
>
> Making SQL Server run fast is not a popularity contest or a beauty pageant. Some database administrators are unhappy that they have to trade off their beautiful logical designs for less aesthetically pleasing physical designs to make the system fast. Al Davis says, "Just win, baby!" It's probably good advice.

The first tradeoff is normalization versus performance. A normalized database is easy to understand. It also requires more joins to resolve multi-entity queries, and joins can be costly. If you denormalize, you can reduce joins and many queries may run faster. (For more information on modifying the database design for performance, see Chapter 17, "Database Design and Performance".)

# Storage versus Cost

This brings up the next tradeoff: storage versus cost. Denormalizing frequently requires more storage because it requires the storage of duplicate data, and that isn't free; however, it is often cheap compared to the cost of unresolved performance issues.

# Retrieval versus Update

Duplication implies the next tradeoff: if you have redundant (denormalized) data, it is going to take more time and resources to update the redundant data.

Remember, redundancy helps retrieval, but it adds overhead during updates.

## Fast Execution versus Ad Hoc Access

Fast execution versus access is a specialized tradeoff problem. Before you can address your performance issues, you should define your requirements and boundaries. You need to provide a physical design to enable the response times that you want to achieve. Over the next several chapters, you learn how to set and adjust these parameters.

# Performance Expectations

Let's take a look at some specific queries and try to identify what the performance expectations are. These queries are based on a table and index defined as follows (tables are partial—forget for a moment that you do not yet understand how SQL Server manages indexes):

```
create table orders( ...
    item_num int,
    warehouse int,
...)
create index ord_index on orders (item_num, warehouse)
```

Here are the queries and some hypothetical response times:

A.  (response time subsecond)
```
select sum(qty) from orders
    where item_num = 1234 and warehouse = 432
```

B.  (response time 600 seconds)
```
select sum(qty) from orders
where warehouse = 432
```

C.  (response time 50 seconds)
```
select sum(qty) from orders
where item_num in (1234,2345) and warehouse = 432
```

Which queries have acceptable response times? Which queries have expected response times? These are extremely important questions, and it is crucial to understand that they are different questions.

Look first at query A. Is the response time acceptable? Clearly, if you have subsecond response time, it is silly to waste time trying to decide whether response time is acceptable. Move on to the next problem. Is the response time expected? If you have a reasonable amount of data for the test, the answer again is to look for real problems elsewhere.

Query B has response time that is unacceptable for most real-time operations. The next question is whether the response time is expected. Should this query take 600 seconds?

This is more difficult to determine because it requires an understanding of the data, the physical design, and how the server uses the physical design. Let's handle this in reverse order of the questions just posed. First, how can the server handle the physical design? Can SQL Server use the index to resolve the query? Because you are indexed on `item_num` and do not have `item_num` in the WHERE clause, the server cannot use the index. Therefore, the only way to resolve the query is with a table scan. A table scan is the process of reading every page in the table. Next comes your understanding of the data: How many pages of data do you have to read to resolve the query? It also opens up a hardware question. How many pages of data can you read in a second? Depending on the platform, you can read between 90 and 1000 pages per second (typically) from a SCSI disk drive. This is a huge discrepancy and makes another point clear: You must understand the physical limitations of your system to be able to have reasonable expectations and from there, make physical design decisions.

In query B, how many pages of data must you read? (By default, SQL Server reads a page at a time.) If the amount of data needed to be read takes several hundred seconds and you are willing to allow a few seconds for overhead, 600 seconds may be an expected result, even though it is not an acceptable result. During your physical design phase, you need to identify that you have a potential problem query, with expected results that are unacceptable. Then you figure out a way to improve performance (this may be an additional index, a summary table, or one of many other possible decisions—read the following performance and tuning chapters for tips on ways to improve performance).

Query C gets a bit trickier. It looks like a subset of query A. (The IN is treated as an OR clause.) Why does this take (at least) 50 times the elapsed time of query A? Go back to the basics—is the response time acceptable? Let's assume no.

One of the first things to do is break up the query. You need to make some assumptions—namely, that the server is able to use an index to resolve this particular query. If both components of the query are each resolved in a subsecond, it's time to get on the horn with technical support and report a possible bug. If one component takes a subsecond to resolve (which we know from query A) and the other takes 49 seconds, what is the cause of the performance problem? The most likely cause is that you suddenly have substantially more data for this item_num in the warehouse. Here, it becomes necessary again to understand the bias of your data.

> **NOTE**
>
> There is a demo product, Aurora Distribution Viewer, on the CD-ROM included with this book that will help you understand what the server thinks is the bias of your data.

# Defining and Tracking Down Bottlenecks

A *bottleneck* is a resource that is limiting the throughput of the rest of your processing because of inherent limitations. Typically, the elimination of one bottleneck has the net effect of shifting the bottleneck to another resource. With any luck, though, this new bottleneck will be wider.

A typical bottleneck is a physical disk drive. You might need to get data off of the disk drive a bit faster and be limited by the speed of data retrieval off the drive. Is this the real problem, however? Is the problem the disk drive, the controller, or the operating system? Are you even using operating system I/O?

It is essential to understand where bottlenecks *can* occur and also where they *tend* to occur and under what circumstances. These potential bottlenecks are your performance variables, those things you adjust and tune and balance in order to get the best possible performance for your application.

# Performance Variables

There are a number of variables that affect SQL Server performance at various levels within the SQL Server and its operating environment. These include the following:

- System Architecture Issues
  CPU/Symmetric Multi-Processing (SMP) utilization and management
  Disk I/O performance
  Network performance and throughput capabilities
  Concurrent processing capabilities
- Application Issues
  Query design
  Logical database design
  Physical database design
- SQL Server Issues
  Configuration options
  Query optimization
  Locking management and contention
- Concurrency Issues
  Impact of maintenance activity
  Impact of batch processing
  Management of concurrent processes

As you look over this list, at categories and subcategories, you find that there are some variables that you can affect and some that are fixed, which require hardware upgrades to change.

The intent of this section is not to identify how to fix all the problems associated with these variables (you learn how do this throughout the subsequent chapters in this book), but to identify potential problem areas that you should start to consider.

# System Architecture Issues

Each subcategory has subcategories. For example, under CPU/SMP management, how fast is your CPU? Can you make it faster? Probably not without an upgrade, but how about changing the number of CPU cycles needed by a transaction? (See Chapters 19, "Application Design for Performance," and 20, "Advanced Transact-SQL Programming.") This enables transactions to run with fewer CPU cycles, giving you a virtual CPU upgrade merely by writing better code.

Symmetric multiprocessing is an issue requiring an understanding of the underlying software. For example, can you affect the number of CPU engines for a single query? Currently, this is not a configurable option. You can, however, affect the number of concurrent user processes SQL Server can handle by configuring the number of engines available to SQL Server (see Chapters 30, "Configuring and Tuning the SQL Server," and 31, "Optimizing SQL Server Configuration Options").

You cannot change the I/O rate for a physical device. You can, however, change the physical I/O requirements of a transaction by changing the physical design of the database or by reducing the amount of requested data. (For example, you can limit the maximum number of rows to be retrieved from the database. Does a user really need all 4,000,000 rows? Usually not.) System 11 also allows for the capability to affect the amount of pages retrieved per fetch. For more information on improving I/O performance, see Chapter 18, "Database Object Placement and Performance," and Chapters 30 and 31.

The network is a whole new world. In a client/server environment, it should always be regarded as a bottleneck, and you should make a point of reducing network traffic when and wherever possible. You can do this by reducing the number of packets transmitted or by increasing the TDS packet size. (For more information on improving network performance, see Chapter 19, Chapter 30, and Chapter 31.) Finally, you can also consider using a different network topology that better suits your requirements.

Concurrent processing capabilities at the system architecture level are not directly tunable, but they are sometimes containable. For example, if logging overhead is causing problems, you can try committing less frequently or putting the log on a higher-speed device. Additionally, if sequential reads are slower than you expect, you may be able to redistribute the data on your disks. Overall server architecture is also going to affect concurrent processing capabilities. For example, additional memory is going to be necessary to allow more operations to occur in cache. Along those lines, some dedicated hardware is normal for high transaction volume or high concurrency systems.

# Application Issues

The most important issue from an application point is to be sure your user asks the right query. (I frequently suggest providing substantial user training, particularly where there are ad hoc queries involved, because horrid SQL is probably the number one cause of bad performance.)

Bad queries can come in a variety of flavors: unnecessary joins, insufficient joins, lack of optimizable search arguments, or no capability of taking advantage of server features (for example, updates in place). See Chapters 12, 20, 21, and 22 for tips on improving query performance.

Logical design issues might involve changing table normalization to reduce joins, or vertical segmentation to take infrequently referenced data out of the scanned table (see Chapter 17).

When you decide to tune performance, you tend to fix physical design problems most often. Correct index selection can often fix (improve the performance of) otherwise problematic queries (see Chapter 11, "Designing Indexes for Performance"). This includes adding or removing indexes. Adding indexes tends to help queries but hurt update performance. You also can provide summary data or redundant data (see Chapter 17). Finally, you can physically segment your data for the purpose of scanning multiple physical disks and spreading throughput across devices (see Chapter 18).

Cursors are a favorite way programmers can foul up performance, particularly concurrency. A poorly written cursor can lock huge amounts of data. Tell your programmers that cursors are a way of treating a set-processing language like a row-processing language, and that it is usually the wrong approach.

Batch programming tends to be the Achilles tendon of applications. When the server engine decides it is time to swap out a process, it needs to perform overhead to be able to come back to the point it left. The more processing involved, the more overhead. As a result, as batch processes get longer and longer, the swapping takes more and more CPU time. This means less CPU time available for OLTP processes.

## SQL Server Issues

The database server is another tunable component of your application. For example, you can configure and reconfigure memory, cache, locks, disk resource dissemination, connections, and dozens of other things (see Chapters 30 and 31). There are also some components you cannot easily tune.

For example, you cannot rewrite the optimizer. The optimizer is going to pick its own path, join order, and other search tactic.

> **NOTE**
>
> You can, for a particular query or session, force a join order or index selection on the optimizer. This is covered in Chapter 16, "Overriding the SQL Server Optimizer." However, you first need to understand what the optimizer is doing and why before saying, "I think that is a bad idea. Do it my way instead." Note that it is often unlikely you'll pick a better join order than the optimizer picks. To better understand how the optimizer works, see Chapters 11 through 15.

Lock management is handled automatically by the server. The number of concurrent locks allowed is configurable by the SQL Server system administrator. Use of the locks is managed by the SQL Server. You can favorably affect the server locking by keeping transactions short, and by *not changing* transaction isolation levels. Avoid situations where deadlocking becomes likely. (For more in locking and performance, see Chapter 15.)

SQL Server overhead issues can sometimes be handled with hardware—for example, by using a solid state device for the log to increase transaction throughput where the log has been positively identified as a bottleneck. The audit queue, as a bottleneck, can sometimes be managed by throwing memory at the situation (that is, configuring the audit queue for more rows—see Chapters 30 and 31).

## Concurrency Issues

You will probably want to identify a batch processing window for performing, among other things, maintenance activity (such as DBCC commands and database dumps), index creations and re-creations (no, this is not something you normally need to do periodically), or other batch processing (reporting, generating mailing labels, long-running ad hoc queries). All these activities are of the type that tend to hog an entire processor (or set of processors) or generate a significant amount of I/O and adversely impact the performance of other concurrent processes. They are also the types of activities that can lock tables or databases, which reduces OLTP concurrency.

Fitting all your work into a batch window is sometimes a highly specialized art form, particularly in 24×7 shops (shops that require 24-hour/day, 7-day/week operation).

# Defining a Tuning Approach

Before beginning to tune the performance of SQL Server, you should gather as much information as possible about the circumstances surrounding the perceived performance problem. Remember, you can't tune for everything, and tradeoffs will have to be made. You need to identify and prioritize problems before addressing them, and make the tradeoffs where necessary.

For example, you have a problem report that runs for 40 hours. You can fix the problem by denormalizing the database design and adding additional indexes to the tables. The cost of this is additional storage requirements, additional time required for performing backups, and additional processing required to maintain the denormalized data. It may also adversely impact the performance of online transactions.

Ask yourself whether it is worth the cost. How critical is this report to the application? What level of user are you tuning this query for? Is it for the CEO of the company, who needs this report updated every two hours, or is this query being run every six months by an associate accountant, who has completely fouled up your expense checks for the past four months? Sometimes the decisions are easy to make, sometimes they are more difficult.

The next step is to spotlight obvious performance problems. Over the course of the next several chapters, you will get a feel for what are going to be common performance problems, if you haven't had that type of experience already. If you are tuning a SQL Server, consider changes to improve performance that are transparent to users, such as indexes and segments.

One of the most important steps in tuning is to estimate your performance requirements prior to final roll-out and to identify potential performance problems before going into production. The best way to do this is to find or build a tool that will simulate production levels of user activity and run them against representative samples and volumes of production data.

> **NOTE**
>
> You can often assume that whatever volumes your users say they are going to use are off by an order of magnitude, but at least you can turn back to them later when they complain about system performance and say, "I tuned for what you told me. Now that I can see what you really need, I will tune accordingly."

When you have specific performance problems to address, follow these steps:

1. Identify baseline response times for your CPU, disks, network, and controllers so that you can identify *expected* results.

2. Identify whether the results are expected but undesired, or unexpected and undesired.

3. Examine the problem query. Is it too complex? Does the query resolve the user's actual need? (Frequently, the answer is no. More than once, I've seen 25 pages of stored procedure doing what could have been done by four `select` statements.)

4. Are the indexes appropriately selected in the physical design? Is the optimizer using the indexes you think it should? (Refer to Chapter 11.)

5. Is the optimizer selecting the correct path, join plan, or approach? (See Chapter 14, "Analyzing Query Plans.")

6. When in doubt, break down the query. Do the individual components take too long? How might this query be rewritten? (See Chapters 19 and 20.)

Finally, prioritize the problem. Does the situation, user, application, or so forth warrant physical database design changes or other work on your part in order to improve the query performance, or is it of a lower priority?

# Summary

Tuning the performance of SQL Server is often a balancing act. You cannot tune for everything, and you'll need to make a number of tradeoffs to balance out the performance of the system to meet user requirements and expectations. Often, you will need to set your users' expectations appropriately, based on a thorough understanding of your system's strengths and limitations as well an understanding of which items can be tuned to improve SQL Server performance.

This chapter has given you an overview of the issues and components of SQL Server that can be tuned to improve performance. In the subsequent performance and tuning chapters in this book, you'll learn about how these items affect performance and how you can affect them to improve (or if you are not careful, degrade) SQL Server performance.

# Understanding SQL Server Storage Structures

# 10

In order to get the best performance out of a high-performance vehicle, you occasionally need to tune the engine. However, before you can begin tuning a high-performance vehicle, you need to have a good understanding of the internals of the engine and how they work. Likewise, in order to tune SQL Server effectively, you need to have a good understanding of the internal storage structures and how SQL Server stores and manages objects and data within the database.

In this chapter, you explore the basic storage structures in SQL Server and how they are managed and maintained. This information will help you better understand performance issues raised in the subsequent chapters.

# SQL Server Storage Structures

SQL Server doesn't see storage in exactly the same way a DBA or end user does. A DBA sees initialized devices, device fragments allocated to databases, segments defined within databases, tables defined within segments, and rows stored in tables. SQL Server views storage at a lower level as device fragments allocated to databases, pages allocated to tables and indexes within the database, and information stored on pages.

There are two basic types of storage structures in a database, linked data pages and index trees. All information in SQL Server is stored at the page level. When a database is created, all space allocated to it is divided into a number of 2KB pages. There are five types of pages within SQL Server:

- Data and log pages
- Index pages
- Text/image pages
- Allocation pages
- Distribution pages

All pages in SQL Server contain a page header. The page header is 32 bytes and contains the logical page number, the next and previous logical page numbers in the page linkage, the object_id of the object the page belongs to, the minimum row size, the next available row number within the page, and the byte location of the start of the free space on the page.

The contents of a page header can be examined by using the dbcc page command. The syntax is as follows:

```
dbcc page (dbid ¦ db_name, page_no [, 0 ¦ 1 ¦ 2 ])
```

The display options (0, 1, 2) determine how the page contents will be displayed. 0 is the default and displays only the page header without the page contents. 1 displays the page header and a hex dump of the page contents individually by row. 2 displays the same information as 1, but displays the page contents as a single block of data.

**NOTE**

You need to run the dbcc traceon(3604) command prior to running dbcc page, or dbcc page will print its output to the SQL Server errorlog rather than to the terminal.

Here is a sample page header:

```
PAGE HEADER:
Page header for page 0xac0000
pageno=424 nextpg=0 prevpg=0 objid=288004057 timestamp=0001 00000b46
nextrno=25 level=0 indid=0  freeoff=832 minlen=2
page status bits: 0x1
```

The following is an explanation of the fields visible in the page header:

- pageno is the current page number (the logical page number assigned when a page is allocated to the database).
- nextpg is the pointer to the next page in the page linkage.
- prevpg is the pointer to the previous page in the page linkage.
- objid is the object ID of the object to which this page belongs.
- indid is the index ID of the index to which this page belongs.
- level is the level within the index in which this page is found.
- nextrno is the row number of the next row to be inserted on this page.
- freeoff is the location of the free space at the end of the page.
- minlen is the minimum allowable length of any row on the page.

If indid is 0, this is a data or nonindex page. If it is an index page (indid != 0), level will indicate the level within the index in which this page is found. Index levels and index structures are covered in more detail later in this chapter.

With five different types of pages within a database, how does SQL Server keep track of what object a page belongs to, if any? The allocation of pages within SQL Server is managed through the use of allocation units and allocation pages.

# Allocation and Object Allocation Map (OAM) Pages

The allocation of pages to objects within a database is managed using *allocation pages* and *object allocation map* (OAM) pages.

# Allocation Pages

Space is allocated to an SQL Server database by the create/alter database commands. The space allocated to a database is divided into a number of 2KB pages. Each page is assigned a logical page number, starting at page 0 and increasing sequentially. The pages are then divided into allocation units of 256 contiguous 2KB pages, or 512 bytes (1/2MB) each. The first page of each allocation unit is an allocation page, which controls the allocation of all pages within the allocation unit (see Figure 10.1). The first allocation page is logical page number 0, and subsequent allocation pages are stored at each multiple of 256.

**FIGURE 10.1.**

*Allocation units within an SQL Server database.*

| 0 | 1 | 2 | 3 | 4 | 5 | 6 | 7 |
|---|---|---|---|---|---|---|---|
| 8 | 9 | 10 | 11 | 12 | 13 | 14 | 15 |
| 16 | 17 | 18 | 19 | 20 | 21 | 22 | 23 |
| 24 | 25 | 26 | 27 | 28 | 29 | 30 | 31 |
| 32 | 33 | 34 | 35 | 36 | 37 | 38 | 39 |
| 40 | 41 | 42 | 43 | 44 | 45 | 46 | 47 |
| ... | | | | | | | |
| ... | | | | | | | |
| ... | | | | | | | |
| 248 | 249 | 250 | 251 | 252 | 253 | 254 | 255 |

| 256 | 257 | 258 | 259 | 260 | 261 | 262 | 263 |
|---|---|---|---|---|---|---|---|
| 264 | 265 | 266 | 267 | 268 | 269 | 270 | 271 |
| 272 | 273 | 274 | 275 | 276 | 277 | 278 | 279 |
| 280 | 281 | 282 | 283 | 284 | 285 | 286 | 287 |
| 288 | 289 | 290 | 291 | 292 | 293 | 294 | 295 |
| 296 | 297 | 298 | 299 | 300 | 301 | 302 | 303 |
| ... | | | | | | | |
| ... | | | | | | | |
| ... | | | | | | | |
| 504 | 505 | 506 | 507 | 508 | 509 | 510 | 511 |

| 512 | 513 | 514 | 515 | 516 | 517 | 518 | 519 |
|---|---|---|---|---|---|---|---|
| 520 | 521 | 522 | 523 | 524 | 525 | 526 | 527 |
| 528 | 529 | 530 | 531 | 532 | 533 | 534 | 535 |
| 536 | 537 | 538 | 539 | 540 | 541 | 542 | 543 |
| 544 | 545 | 546 | 547 | 548 | 549 | 550 | 551 |
| 552 | 553 | 554 | 555 | 556 | 557 | 558 | 559 |
| ... | | | | | | | |
| ... | | | | | | | |
| ... | | | | | | | |
| 760 | 761 | 762 | 763 | 764 | 765 | 766 | 767 |

...

■ = Allocation page

The allocation pages control the allocation of pages to tables and indexes within the database. Pages are allocated in contiguous blocks of eight pages called *extents*. The minimum unit of allocation within a database is an extent. When a table is created, it is initially assigned a single extent, or 16KB, even if the table contains no rows. There are 32 extents within an allocation unit (see Figure 10.2).

**FIGURE 10.2.**

*Extents within an allocation unit.*

| 256 | 257 | 258 | 259 | 260 | 261 | 262 | 263 |
|-----|-----|-----|-----|-----|-----|-----|-----|
| 264 | 265 | 266 | 267 | 268 | 269 | 270 | 271 |
| 272 | 273 | 274 | 275 | 276 | 277 | 278 | 279 |
| 280 | 281 | 282 | 283 | 284 | 285 | 286 | 287 |
| 288 | 289 | 290 | 291 | 292 | 293 | 294 | 295 |
| 296 | 297 | 298 | 299 | 300 | 301 | 302 | 303 |
| ... | | | | | | | |
| ... | | | | | | | |
| ... | | | | | | | |
| 504 | 505 | 506 | 507 | 508 | 509 | 510 | 511 |

← Extent

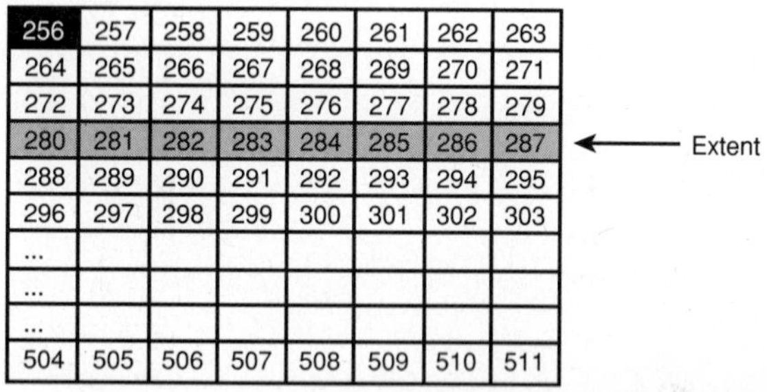

An allocation page contains 32 extent structures for each extent within that allocation unit. Each extent structure is 16 bytes and contains the following information about each extent:

- The object ID of the object to which the extent is allocated
- The next extent ID in the chain
- The previous extent ID in the chain
- The allocation bitmap
- The deallocation bitmap
- The index ID (if any) to which the extent is allocated
- The status

The allocation bitmap indicates which pages within the extent are in use by the table (see Figure 10.3). If the allocation bit is on, the page is currently in use by the table/index. If the allocation bit is off, the page is reserved, but not currently in use. The deallocation bitmap is used to identify pages that have become empty during a transaction that has not yet completed. The actual marking of the page as unused will not occur until the transaction is committed to prevent another transaction from allocating the page before the transaction is complete.

**FIGURE 10.3.**

*Diagram of the extent structures in allocation page 0 showing the allocation bitmap for extent ID 24.*

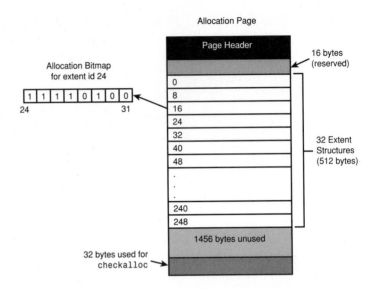

Pages not currently in use are reserved for use by that table or index and cannot be used by any other table or index within the database. This is the information you see reported by the `sp_spaceused` stored procedure. For example, consider the following output:

```
sp_spaceused  titles
name          rows      reserved  data    index_size  unused
------------- --------- --------- ------- ----------- ---------
titles        18        48 KB     6 KB    8 KB        34 KB
```

`reserved` is the total number of kilobytes allocated to the table and its indexes (it should be a factor of 8), `data` is the total number of kilobytes in use for data, `index_size` is the total number of kilobytes in use for all indexes on the table, and `unused` is allocated pages for the table and its indexes that are currently not being used. `unused` indicates the amount of space that can be used for the table or its indexes before additional extents need to be allocated. The `titles` table has 24 pages allocated to it: 3 used for data, 4 used for its indexes, and 17 allocated pages that currently are not in use.

This information is obtained from the Object Allocation Map (OAM) page for the table.

# OAM Pages

OAM pages are used to keep a map of which allocation pages are controlling extents allocated to a table or indexes. The OAM pages provide SQL Server with an accurate picture of the allocation data for a table or index. In addition to a list of all the allocation pages on which there are extents allocated to the table or index, there is also data on how many pages are used and unused in the extents allocated. This information is stored in the OAM structure contained on the first OAM page for a table or index (see Figure 10.4), and it is updated automatically by most SQL Server processes when pages are allocated and deallocated. Some of the dbcc commands validate and update these values as well when they perform consistency checks.

**FIGURE 10.4.**

*Example of an OAM page.*

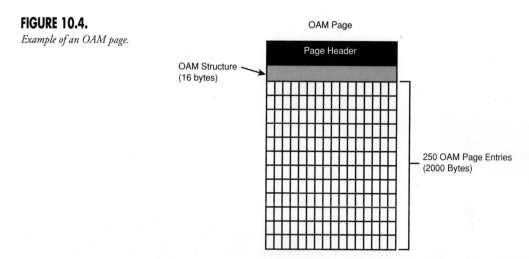

The OAM pages provide SQL Server with an efficient way to determine which pages are allocated to a table or index and help in allocating new pages near other pages already allocated to the table or index. All tables have at least one OAM page or a series of OAM pages except for the syslogs and sysgams tables and tables that reside only in memory (for example, sysprocesses and syslocks).

The OAM structure contains summary information, such as the total number of rows and total used and unused pages allocated to the table or index. Each OAM page entry contains the address of each allocation page controlling extents allocated to the table or index and the number of used and unused pages in that allocation unit. The OAM entries are stored in sorted order based on allocation page numbers. Each OAM page entry is 8 bytes and there are 250 OAM entries ((2048 – 32 – 16) / 8) stored in an OAM page.

With 250 OAM entries on an OAM page, a single OAM page can reference from 2,000 to 63,750 data pages. The actual number depends on how much the table is spread across allocation units. If the table is spread so that it uses only a single extent per allocation unit, the OAM entries will point to 250 * 8, or 2,000 data pages. If the table is very compact and uses all 255 available pages within an allocation unit, the OAM entries will point to 255 * 8 or 63,750 data pages. If a table is spread across more than 250 allocation units, additional OAM pages will be linked with the first OAM page as needed.

The advantage of the OAM pages is that SQL Server doesn't have to scan all the allocation pages in a database to allocate new pages or extents to a table or index.

# Allocating New Space for a Table or Index

When a table or index requires more space, it will make use of the OAM pages, allocation pages, and the Global Allocation Map (GAM) pages to determine where free pages and extents exist that can be allocated to the table or index.

The GAM pages are created when a database is created. A GAM page contains a bitmap to record which allocation units in a database contain free extents (see Figure 10.5). One bit is used for each allocation unit in the database. If the bit is set to 1, there are no more free extents within that allocation unit. Each GAM page contains 16,128 bits, or $(2048 - 32) \times 8$. A single GAM page can hold allocation unit information for a database up to 8GB in size. If a database is larger than 8GB, additional GAM pages, as needed, will be linked to the first GAM page.

**FIGURE 10.5.**

*Example of the first GAM page in a database.*

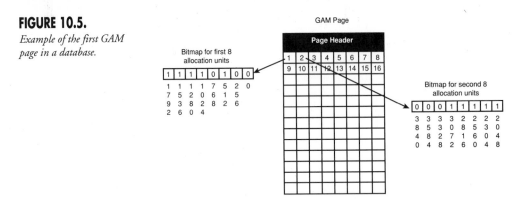

When additional space (that is, a new page) is needed for a table or index, the following steps are performed by SQL Server:

1. Find an unused page in the extent for the current page to be linked to the new page by first checking the OAM page entry for the allocation unit containing the extent to see whether any unused pages exist, and then checking the extent bitmap on the allocation page to see which specific page is available. If a page is available, that page is linked into the page chain, it is marked as used in the extent bitmap on the allocation page, and the OAM page information is updated for that allocation unit and the summary information.

2. If no pages are available in the target extent, SQL Server will check the OAM page to see whether there are any other extents with unused pages within the same allocation unit. If so, that page is linked into the page chain, it is marked as used in the extent bitmap on the allocation page, and the OAM page information is updated for that allocation unit and the summary information.

3. If no pages are unused in the same allocation unit, SQL Server will scan the OAM page to find the first allocation unit for that object with an unused page in one of its extents. That page is then linked into the page chain, it is marked as used in the extent

bitmap on the allocation page, and the OAM page information is updated for that allocation unit and the summary information.

4. If there are no unused pages in any of the extents already allocated to the table, the OAM page will be scanned to find an allocation unit already controlling space for the table with a free extent available. If a free extent is found, the extent is allocated to the table, the first page in the extent is linked into the page chain, the extent bitmap is updated in the allocation page, and the OAM page information is updated for that allocation unit and the summary information.

5. If there are no free extents in any of the allocation units currently assigned to the table, SQL Server will scan the GAM page in the database to find the first allocation page with a free extent. The extent is then allocated to the table, the first page in the extent is linked into the page chain, the extent bitmap is updated in the allocation page, an entry for the allocation page is added to the OAM page, and the OAM page information is updated for that allocation unit and the summary information.

The location of the first OAM page for a table or index is contained in the sysindexes table along with other information about the table or index. The sysindexes table is described in Table 10.1.

**Table 10.1. Description of the sysindexes table and its contents.**

| Column | Datatype | Description |
| --- | --- | --- |
| name | varchar(30) | If indid >= 1 and <= 250, name of index. If indid = 0 or 255, name of table. |
| id | int | ID of table related to this sysindexes row. |
| indid | smallint | Index ID: 0 = table, no clustered index. 1 = table and clustered index. > 1 and <= 250, nonclustered index. 255, text or image data. |
| doampg | int | Page number of the OAM page for the table if indid = 0 or indid = 1; otherwise, doampg = 0 for nonclustered index. |
| ioampg | int | Page number of the OAM page for the indid >= 1 and indid <= 255; otherwise, ioampg = 0 for a table. |
| oampgtrips | int | Ratio of OAM page to data page residency in cache. |
| status2 | int | Bitmap status field for index: 1 - Index supports foreign key constraint. 2 - Index supports primary key/unique declarative constraint. |

*continues*

## Table 10.1. continued

| Column | Datatype | Description |
|--------|----------|-------------|
| | | 4 - Index contains an identity column. |
| | | 8 - No constraint name specified. |
| | | 16 - (System 11 only). Large I/Os (prefetch) enabled for table, index, or text chain. |
| | | 32 - (System 11 only) MRU cache strategy enabled for table, index, or text chain. |
| ipgtrips | int | Ratio of index page to data page residency in cache. |
| first | int | If indid <= 1 or = 255, pointer to first data or text/image page. If indid > 1 and <= 250, pointer to first leaf index page. |
| root | int | If indid >= 1 and < 250, pointer to the root page of index. If indid = 0 or 255, pointer to the last page in data or text/image chain. In System 11, if a table is partitioned, root is unused—root page information for partitions is obtained from syspartitions table. |
| distribution | int | If indid >= 1 and < 255, pointer to distribution page for that index. |
| usagecnt | smallint | Reserved for future use by Sybase. |
| segment | smallint | Segment ID for segment from which this object is currently allocating space. |
| status | smallint | Bitmap status for index: 1 - Abort command if attempt to insert duplicate key (IGNORE_DUP_KEY not specified). 2 - Unique index. 4 - Abort command if attempt to insert duplicate row in nonunique, clustered index (IGNORE_DUP_ROW not specified). 16 - Clustered index. 64 - Clustered index enables duplicate rows (ALLOW_DUP_ROW set). 128 - Sorted object; not set for tables without clustered index. 512 - with sorted data option used in create index command. |

| Column | Datatype | Description |
|--------|----------|-------------|
| | | 1024 - Index being created. |
| | | 2048 - Index defined by PRIMARY KEY constraint. |
| | | 4096 - Index defined by UNIQUE constraint. |
| | | 32768 - Index marked suspect or created under a different sort order. |
| rowpage | smallint | Maximum allowable number of rows per page. (Renamed maxrowsperpage in System 11.) |
| minlen | smallint | Minimum row width. |
| maxlen | smallint | Maximum row width. |
| maxirow | smallint | Maximum width of a nonleaf index row. |
| keycnt | smallint | Number of columns in clustered index. Number of columns + 1 in nonclustered index |
| keys1 | varbinary(255) | If indid > 0 and <= 250, description of index columns. |
| keys2 | varbinary(255) | If indid > 0 and <= 250, description of index columns. |
| soid | tinyint | ID of sort order that the index was created with (0 if no character data in the index). |
| csid | tinyint | ID of character set (0 if no character data in the index). |

Using the information in the sysindexes table and the data_pgs() and reserved_pgs() built-in system functions in SQL Server, you can write your own custom version of sp_spaceused. For example, the following query lists the reserved and used data and index pages for all user tables and their indexes in a database:

```
select "Table" = o.name, "Index" = i.name,
       "Data used" = data_pgs(i.id, doampg),
       "Data resrvd" = reserved_pgs(i.id, doampg),
       "Index used" = data_pgs(i.id, ioampg),
       "Index resrvd" = reserved_pgs(i.id, ioampg)
from sysobjects o, sysindexes i
where o.id = i.id
and o.type = "U"
```

# Changes to Page Allocation Strategy for System 11

The OAM page provides a more efficient method of allocating pages to a table or index than having to scan the allocation pages in a database. However, with very large tables or indexes, OAM page scans can become expensive. As a minimum, a new page allocation requires two OAM page scans—one to find the first unused page and associated allocation page, and a second scan once the allocation page is updated to update the used/unused counts on the associated OAM page pointing to that allocation page. Depending on the availability of new unused pages, multiple scans of the OAM pages may be required to find the first available unused page. Three OAM page scans are not uncommon and, in the worst case, as many as five scans could occur. If a new extent needs to be allocated, this also requires a scan of the GAM pages to find an available extent.

As a database becomes larger, the number of GAM pages increases. As a table becomes larger, the number of OAM pages increases as well. If a table is spread across many allocation units, the number of OAM pages is even greater. For example, a 1GB table with each extent belonging to a different allocation unit requires scans of 256 OAM pages.

These performance issues for very large databases and tables prompted some changes to the allocation scheme used in System 11:

- Direct OAM page access
- More efficient OAM page scans allocation hints
- More efficient page utilization

## Direct OAM Page Access

Currently in System 10, SQL Server keeps no record of which OAM pages are referencing the extents managed by the allocation page. When an extent structure is modified, SQL Server must scan all the associated OAM pages for a table to update the used/unused counts contained on the OAM page pointing to that allocation page. To avoid this scan, SQL Server 11 now stores the OAM page number for each allocated extent on the allocation page (see Figure 10.6). When an extent structure is updated, SQL Server can now access the OAM page associated with that extent directly, avoiding a scan of the OAM pages.

**FIGURE 10.6.**

*Structure of the allocation page in System 11.*

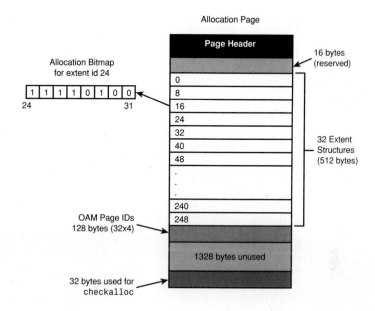

Allocation Page

Page Header

Allocation Bitmap for extent id 24

`1 1 1 1 0 1 0 0`

24                31

0
8
16
24
32
40
48
.
.
.
240
248

16 bytes (reserved)

32 Extent Structures (512 bytes)

OAM Page IDs 128 bytes (32x4)

1328 bytes unused

32 bytes used for checkalloc

# Allocation Hints

To help avoid excessive OAM page scans, SQL Server System 11 now stores allocation hints on the first OAM page (see Figure 10.7). The allocation hints are used to store the last 15 extents that were allocated or had pages that were deallocated from the table. These extents are the ones most likely to contain unused pages. In addition, the location of the last OAM page accessed where an available page was found is also stored on the first OAM page. In System 10, finding a new unused page requires a full scan of all OAM pages. The next time an unused page is required, it is most likely on, or after, the last OAM page scanned during the previous page allocation. By keeping track of this page, SQL Server can begin the search for an unused page beginning at that OAM page rather than scanning all OAM pages.

**FIGURE 10.7.**

*The OAM page in System 11.*

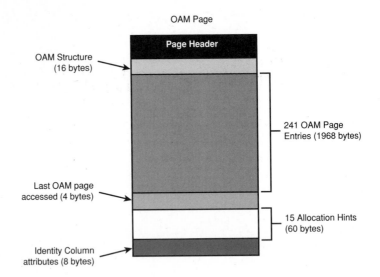

OAM Page

Page Header

OAM Structure (16 bytes)

241 OAM Page Entries (1968 bytes)

Last OAM page accessed (4 bytes)

15 Allocation Hints (60 bytes)

Identity Column attributes (8 bytes)

# Page Utilization

Another new feature in System 11 is the capability of configuring the page utilization percentage for tables. Normally, SQL Server will perform an OAM page scan to find any unused pages before it allocates an additional extent to the table. Setting page utilization percent in System 11 determines when SQL Server will perform an OAM scan or simply allocate a new extent when a page allocation is requested.

Consider a table with 200 OAM pages and one unused page. Is it more efficient to scan all 200 pages to find the one page or to allocate another extent to the table? Essentially, it depends on whether performance is more important than maintaining high page utilization.

Page utilization is specified as a percentage of used pages allocated to the table. If page utilization is set to 100, all unused pages are used before additional extents are allocated. This is similar to pre-System 11 behavior. If page utilization is set to a value less than 100, SQL Server compares the page utilization percentage to the ratio of used pages to used plus unused pages (that is, total reserved pages). The ratio of used to total reserved pages is determined as follows:

```
100 × used pages / (used pages + unused pages)
```

If the percentage setting is lower than the ratio, SQL Server will allocate a new extent rather than search for the unused pages. A lower setting results in more unused pages in a table. A higher setting results in fewer unused pages, but slower page allocations in large tables.

**NOTE**

The default setting for page utilization percent in System 11 is 95.

Consider the following page utilization setting:

```
sp_configure 'page utilization percent', 90
```

This sets page utilization to 90 percent. For a 1GB table, SQL Server will allocate new extents to the table rather than perform an OAM scan when there are less than 56,888 unused pages allocated to the table—that is, when more than 90 percent of the reserved pages are utilized:

```
100 × 512,000 / (512,000 + 56,888)
= 100 × 512,000 / 568,888
= 90%
```

When less than 90 percent of the pages are utilized—that is, more than 568,888 pages are allocated but marked unused—SQL Server will perform OAM scans to use the unused pages.

Although, at times, there may be a high number of unused pages allocated to a table, the unused pages will eventually be used. SQL Server simply doesn't spend the time to find those pages when performing a large number of new page allocations. If you run out of available extents, SQL Server will fall back to performing OAM page scans to find the unused pages and use them.

> **NOTE**
>
> When performing a bcp load, the bulk copy facility always ignores the page utilization percent setting and allocates new extents rather than performing OAM page scans until there are no more extents in the database.

# Data Pages

A data page is the basic unit of storage within SQL Server. All the other types of pages within a database are essentially variations of the data page. Figure 10.8 shows the basic structure of a data page.

All data pages contain a 32-byte header as described earlier. With a 2KB page (2,048 bytes) this leaves 2,016 bytes for storing data within the data page. In SQL Server, data rows cannot cross page boundaries. A data row must fit entirely within the data page. If there is not enough space at the end of a page to hold the entire row, it will be stored on the next page in the page linkage. The maximum size of a single row within SQL Server is 1,962 bytes, because pages in the transaction log are 2KB pages as well.

When a data row is logged—for example, during an insert—the entire row is written to a log page along with some logging information. This log information is 54 bytes per log record. Like data rows, log records cannot cross page boundaries. Because there are only 2,016 bytes available to store the log record, 2,016 bytes minus 54 bytes of overhead leaves 1,962 bytes for the data row—therefore, the limit of 1,962 bytes for the maximum data row size.

**FIGURE 10.8.**

*Structure of an SQL Server data page.*

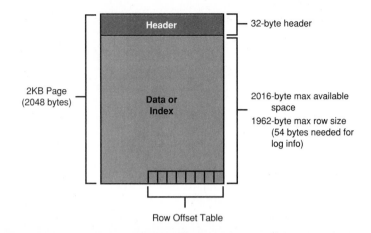

**TIP**

SQL Server will enable you to create a table with data rows that could exceed 1,962 bytes if it contains variable-length columns. SQL Server will create the table but give you a warning message such as the following:

```
The total row size, 2575, for table 't3' exceeds the maximum number of ➡bytes
per row, 1962.
```

If you attempt to insert a data row that actually exceeds 1,962 bytes, or update the row so that its updated length exceeds 1,962 bytes, you will receive the following error message, and the insert or update will fail:

```
Msg 511, Level 16, State 2
Updated or inserted row is bigger than maximum size (1962 bytes) allowed ➡for
this table.
```

Data pages are linked to one another by using the page pointers (prevpg, nextpg) contained in the page header (see Figure 10.9). This page linkage enables SQL Server to locate all rows in a table by scanning all pages in the link. Data page linkage can be thought of as a two-way linked list, because each page contains the previous and next page pointer. This enables SQL Server to link new pages into or unlink pages from the page linkage easily by adjusting the page pointers. If nextpg = 0, the current page is the last page in the page chain. If prevpg = 0, the current page is the first page in the page chain.

**FIGURE 10.9.**

*Linked data pages.*

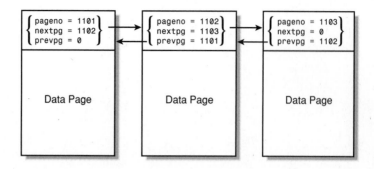

In addition to the page header, each data page also contains data rows and a row offset table (refer to Figure 10.8). The row offset table grows backward from the end of the page and contains the location of each row on the data page. Each entry in the row offset table is 2 bytes wide.

# Data Rows

Data is stored on data pages in data rows. The size of each data row is a factor of the sum of the size of the columns plus the row overhead. Each record in a data page is assigned a row number. A single byte is used within each row to store the row number. Therefore, SQL Server has a maximum limit of 256 rows per page, because that is the largest value that can be stored in a single byte. Figure 10.10 displays the structure of a data row.

**FIGURE 10.10.**

*Structure of a data row.*

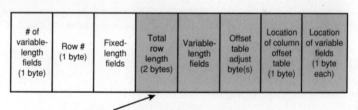

Shaded areas represent data present only when table contains variable-length columns.

For a data row containing all fixed-length columns, there are 4 bytes of overhead per row:

- 1 byte to store the number of variable-length columns (in this case, 0)
- 1 byte to store the row number
- 2 bytes in the row offset table at the end of the page to store the location of the row on the page

If a data row contains variable-length columns, there is additional overhead per row. A data row size is variable if any column is defined as varchar, varbinary, or allows null values. In addition to the 4 bytes of overhead described previously, the following bytes are required to store the actual row width and location of columns within the data row:

- 2 bytes to store the total row width
- 1 byte per variable-length column to store the starting location of the column within the row
- 1 byte for the column offset table
- 1 additional byte for each 256-byte boundary passed (adjust table)

Within each row containing variable-length columns, SQL Server builds a column offset table backward from the end of the row for each variable-length column in the table. Because only 1 byte is used for each column with a maximum offset of 255, an adjust byte must be created for each 256-byte boundary crossed as an additional offset. Variable-length columns are always stored after all fixed-length columns, regardless of the order of the columns in the table definition.

Figure 10.11 demonstrates what the row structure looks like for the following table with all fixed-length fields:

```
create table t1
        (cola char(10),
        colb char(25),
        colc int)
```

**FIGURE 10.11.**

*Diagram of a row with all fixed-length fields.*

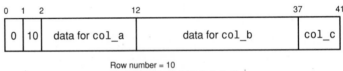

Row number = 10
No variable-length fields (byte 0 =0)
No row length stored
Data row is 41 bytes wide

Figure 10.12 demonstrates what the row structure looks like for the following table:

```
create table t2
        (col_a char(10),
        col_b varchar(25),
        col_c int,
        col_d varchar(10))
```

**FIGURE 10.12.**

*Diagram of a row with variable-length fields.*

Row number = 12 (stored in byte 1)
2 variable-length fields (stored in byte 0)
Data row is 47 bytes wide (stored in bytes 16 and 17)
Adjust byte location at byte 43 (stored in byte 44)
Two bytes at end of record to store location of variable-length columns

# Estimating Row and Table Sizes

Knowing the size of a data row and the corresponding overhead per row helps you determine the number of rows that can be stored per page. The number of rows per page is important as you explore performance issues in this section of the book. In a nutshell, a greater number of rows per page can help query performance by reducing the number of pages that need to be read to satisfy the query. Conversely, fewer rows per page helps improve performance for concurrent transactions by reducing the chances of two or more users accessing rows on the same page that may be locked.

These topics are explored in greater detail in other chapters, but for now, let's take a look at how you can estimate your row and table sizes.

If you have only fixed-length fields in your table and none that allow null values, it is easy to estimate the row size:

```
sum of column widths
+ 1 byte to store the row number
+ 1 byte to store the number of variable length columns
+ 2 bytes per row in the row offset table
```

There is a minimum amount of overhead of 4 bytes for every data row. For example, consider table t1, described previously, which contains three fixed-length columns (char(10), char(25), int). The total row size is the following:

```
(10 + 25 + 4) + 4 = 43 bytes per row
```

If the table contains any variable-length fields or nullable columns, the row width is determined as follows:

```
sum of all fixed column widths
+ 1 byte to store the row number
+ 1 byte to store the number of variable length columns
+ 2 bytes per row in the row offset table
+ sum of average size of variable length columns
+ number of variable length columns ( 1 byte per column )
+ 1 byte ( for column offset table within row )
+ 2 bytes ( for row length )
= subtotal
+ subtotal/256 rounded up to next integer
= average row size
```

Each row containing variable-length columns has a minimum 4 bytes of overhead plus a minimum of 5 bytes of overhead if it contains at least one nullable or variable-length field. Let's examine table t2, shown previously, which contains two fixed-length columns (char(10), int) and two variable-length columns (varchar(25), varchar(10)). Let's assume the average data size for both col_b and col_d is half the column size—13 and 5 bytes, respectively. The calculation of the average row size is as follows:

```
(10 + 4) (for fixed fields)
+ 4 (for overhead)
+ (13 + 5) (for sum of average size of variable fields)
+ 2 (number of variable fields)
+ 1 ( for columns offset table )
+ 2 ( for row length)
= 41 (subtotal)
+ round(41/256) (adjust table bytes)
= 42 bytes (average row size)
```

> **NOTE**
>
> For a listing of SQL Server datatypes and their corresponding sizes, refer to Chapter 4, "Transact-SQL Datatypes."

Once you know the average data row size, you can determine the number of rows per page by dividing the row size into the available space on the data page, 2,016 bytes. For example, if your average row size is 42 bytes, the average number of rows per page is the following:

```
2016 / 42 = 48 rows per page
```

Remember to round "down" any fractions, because you cannot have only a portion of a row on a data page. If the calculation worked out to something like 24.8 rows per page, it would actually require two pages to store 25 rows, because the 25th row would not fit entirely on the first data page. If you are using a fillfactor other than the default (covered later in this chapter), you also need to multiply the number of rows per page times the fillfactor percentage as well. For this example, assume the default fill factor of 0 is being used, which indicates that the data pages are 100 percent full.

Once you know the average number of rows per page, you can next calculate the number of pages required to store the data by dividing the total number of rows in the table by the number of rows per page. To follow this example, if you have 100,000 rows in the table, the number of pages required to store the data is the following:

```
100,000 / 48 = 2083.333...
```

In this case, you round "up" the value to get the actual number of pages (2,084) required to store all the data rows. The size of the table in pages is also the cost in number of page I/Os to perform a table scan. A table scan involves reading the first page of the table and following the page pointers until all pages in the table have been read. The table scan, as you will explore in

Chapter 11, "Designing Indexes for Performance," and Chapter 12, "Understanding the Query Optimizer," is the fallback technique employed by the SQL Server optimizer to satisfy a query when there is no less expensive alternative, such as a clustered or nonclustered index, to find the matching data rows.

# The Row Offset Table

The location of a row within a page is determined by using the row offset table at the end of the page (see Figure 10.13).

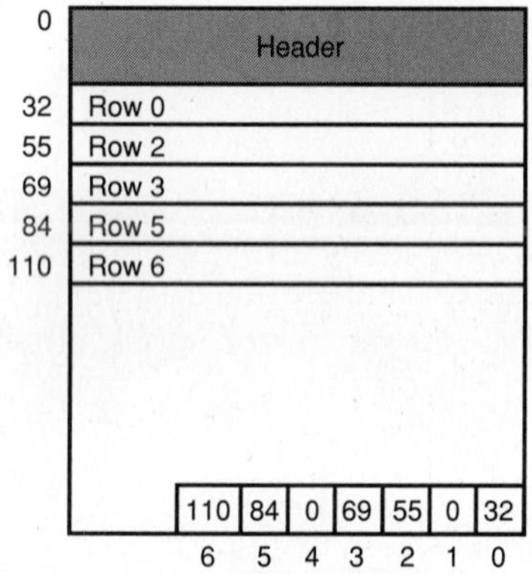

**FIGURE 10.13.**

*Row offset table on data page.*

To find a specific row within the data page, SQL Server looks up in the row offset table the starting byte address within the data page for that row ID.

Note that SQL Server keeps all free space at the end of the data page, shifting rows up to fill in where a previous row was deleted, ensuring no space fragmentation within the page. However, the row IDs for the remaining rows do not change. This helps reduce the amount of overhead involved to maintain row ID pointers in nonclustered indexes (to be covered later in this chapter).

If the offset table contains a zero value for a row ID, that indicates the row has been deleted. The next row to be inserted into the table will reuse the first available row ID, and the row offset will be set accordingly. Whether the new row is inserted at the end of the page or between existing rows depends on whether there is a clustered index created on the table that requires the rows to be in sorted order. Let's examine both scenarios, first looking at a table without a clustered index.

A table without a clustered index is stored as a heap structure. All new rows are added at the end of the table on the last data page. No sorting of the data rows is maintained. Assume that the page displayed in Figure 10.14 is the last page in the table.

**FIGURE 10.14.**

*Deletion and insertion of a row without clustered index.*

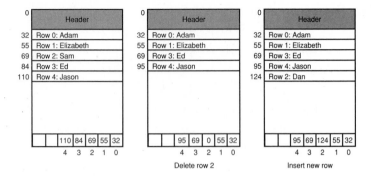

Delete row 2          Insert new row

As row 2 is deleted, all remaining rows on the page are shifted upward, the offsets are adjusted, and the offset for row 2 in the row offset table is set to 0. As a new row is inserted back into the page, it is assigned row ID 2, but inserted after the last existing row on the page. The offset for row 2 is set to the location of the new row on the page.

If the table has a clustered index defined on it, the rows must be kept in physically sorted order within the data page. Figure 10.15 demonstrates the sequence of events when deleting and inserting rows into a sorted table.

**FIGURE 10.15.**

*Deletion and insertion of a row with clustered index.*

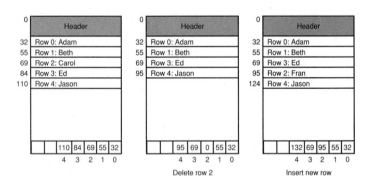

Delete row 2          Insert new row

Again, notice that all rows below row 2 were moved up on the page when row 2 was deleted, but the row IDs didn't change. The row offsets were adjusted to reflect the new row locations within the page, and the row offset for row 2 was set to 0. When a new row was inserted into the page, it was inserted in the proper sort order between rows 3 and 4, and row 4 was shifted down on the page. The new row, however, is reassigned row ID 2, and the offset table is adjusted accordingly for rows 2 and 4. Although the row IDs may not be in physical order, the actual data values are. The advantage of this approach, to reiterate, is to minimize updates to row pointers in the nonclustered indexes. If the row ID for an existing row does not change, the index row pointing to that data row does not need to be updated.

# Text and Image Pages

Occasionally, you have the need to store large text values or binary large objects (BLOBs) in a database, data values that could be millions of bytes in size. However, SQL Server is limited to a maximum row size of 1,962 bytes.

To address the need to store large data values, SQL Server provides the text and image datatypes that enable you to store data values up to 2GB. This is accomplished by storing the text/image data across a number of linked pages separate from the page containing the data row itself.

The data row contains a 16-byte field, defined as a varbinary(16), containing a pointer to the first page containing the text/image data for that column. The text/image data is then spread across as many pages as necessary to store the data, up to 2GB (see Figure 10.16). Each text/image page contains an embedded pointer to the next linked text/image page for that column.

**FIGURE 10.16.**

*Text/image pages.*

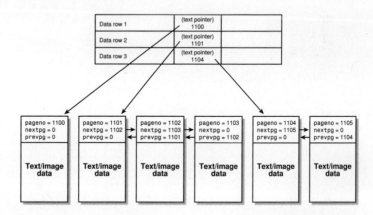

A text/image page is a standard data page with a 32-byte header plus an additional 112 bytes of overhead per page. A text page can store up to 1,800 bytes of information. Therefore, a data value that is 1,801 bytes requires two 2KB pages to store the data.

If a row is inserted into a table containing a text/image column that allows null values and the column is initially null, the column is not initialized with a text page pointer, saving 2KB of storage for that row. However, once the text value for that row is updated to something other than null, at least one text/image page will be linked to that row even if the text/image column is subsequently set to NULL.

Text/image data is retrieved by reading the pointer in the data row, reading the data from the page pointed to by the text/image pointer, and following the embedded page pointers in the text/image pages until nextpg = 0, signaling the end of the text data for that column.

For any table containing any text/image columns, an additional row is added to the sysindexes table with an indid of 255. The name of the index is system-generated by prepending a t to the table name. For example, the name in sysindexes for the table `titles` is `ttitles`. This row is used for allocating and maintaining the text/image pages for that table. Text/image pages are allocated from a different set of extents than the data or index pages.

# Indexes and the B-Tree Structure

To this point, you have examined only the table structure. A table with no clustered index is stored as a heap structure. All data is added at the end of the table. You can think of it as a single file where all new records are simply added to the bottom of the file.

This structure is the fastest way of adding data to the table. When there is no clustered index on the table, there is a row in sysindexes with an `indid` of `0`. The root column of this row points to the last page in the table where inserts are to occur (see Figure 10.17). SQL Server simply adds records to this page until the page is full and then links in a new page to the table.

**FIGURE 10.17.**

*SQL Server heap storage.*

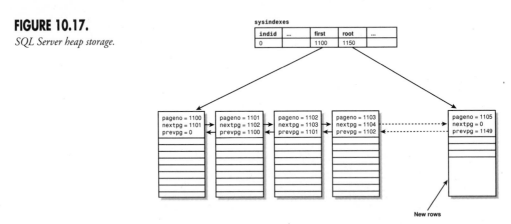

Needless to say, this is not a very efficient method for retrieving data. To find a specific record, you have to start at the top of the pile and read through each record until you find the requested record. This is what is referred to as a table scan. Because SQL Server doesn't know whether the first record found is the only record to be found, it continues reading all records until it reaches the end of the table. If a table was of sufficient size—for example, 100,000 pages—you probably wouldn't want to have to scan all 100,000 pages to read or modify a single record.

You need a mechanism to identify specific records within a table quickly and easily. SQL Server provides this mechanism through two types of indexes: clustered and nonclustered.

Indexes are storage structures separate from the data pages in the table itself. The primary functions of indexes are to provide faster access to the data and provide a means for enforcing uniqueness of your data rows.

All SQL Server indexes are B-tree, or Balanced-tree structures (see Figure 10.18). There is a single root page at the top of the tree, branching out into *N* number of pages at each intermediate level until it reaches the bottom, or leaf level, of the index. The index tree is traversed by following pointers from the upper-level pages down through the lower-level pages. In addition, each index level is a separate page chain.

There may be many intermediate levels in an index. The number of levels is dependent on the index key width, the type of index, and the number of rows and/or pages in the table. The number of levels is important in relation to index performance, as you shall see later in this chapter.

**FIGURE 10.18.**

*B-tree structure.*

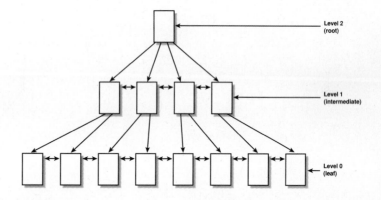

SQL Server indexes are limited to a maximum of 16 columns in the index, with a maximum total index key width of 255 bytes.

# Clustered Indexes

When a clustered index is created on a table, the data in the table is physically sorted in clustered index key order. SQL Server allows only one clustered index per table, because there is only one way to sort the data in the table physically. A clustered index can be thought of like a filing cabinet. The data pages are like the folders in a file drawer in alphabetical order, and the data rows are like the records in the file folder, also in sorted order.

The intermediate index levels can be thought of as the file drawers themselves, also in alphabetical order at a higher level up, assisting you in finding the appropriate file folder. Figure 10.19 shows an example of a clustered index.

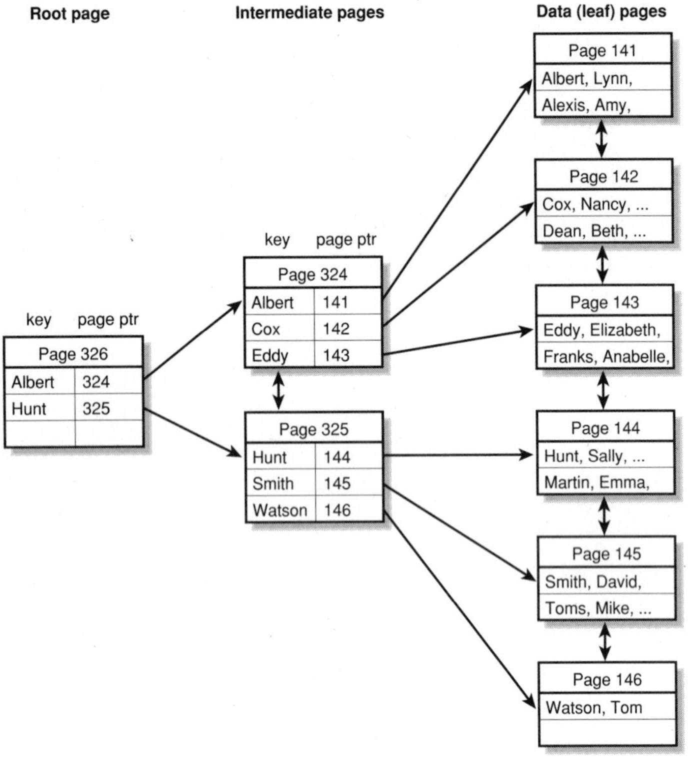

**FIGURE 10.19.**

*Clustered index structure.*

Root page     Intermediate pages     Data (leaf) pages

Notice how the data is stored in clustered index order in Figure 10.19. This feature makes clustered indexes useful for range retrieval queries, because the rows within the range will be physically located in the same or adjacent data pages.

The data pages and clustered index are tightly coupled to each other. The clustered index contains a pointer to every data page in the table. In essence, the data page is the leaf level of the clustered index. To find all instances of a clustered index key value, you must eventually access the data page and scan the rows on that page.

SQL Server performs the following steps when searching for a data row using the clustered index:

1. Query sysindexes for the table where indid = 1 and get the address of the root page.
2. Compare the search value against the key values on the root page.
3. Find the highest key value on the page where the key value is less than or equal to the search value.
4. Follow that page pointer to the next level down in the index.
5. Continue following page pointers as in steps 3 and 4 until the data page is reached.

6. Search the rows on the data page to locate a match for the search value. If a matching row is not found on that data page, there are no matching rows in the table.

Because clustered indexes contain only page pointers, the size and number of levels in a clustered index are dependent on the width of the index key and the number of pages in the table. The structure of a clustered index row is detailed in Figure 10.20.

**FIGURE 10.20.**

*Clustered index row structure.*

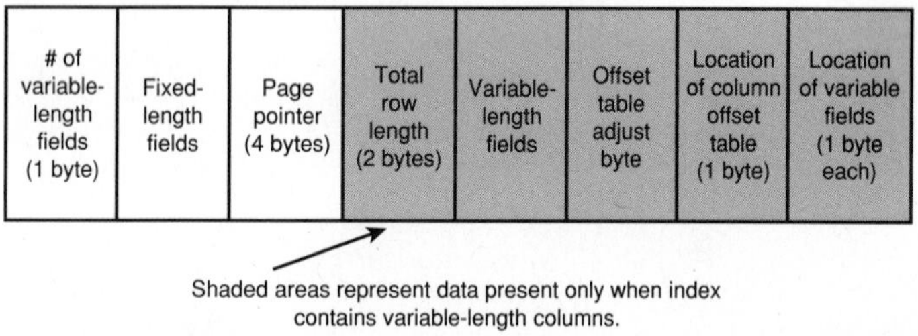

| # of variable-length fields (1 byte) | Fixed-length fields | Page pointer (4 bytes) | Total row length (2 bytes) | Variable-length fields | Offset table adjust byte | Location of column offset table (1 byte) | Location of variable fields (1 byte each) |
|---|---|---|---|---|---|---|---|

Shaded areas represent data present only when index contains variable-length columns.

# Estimating Clustered Index Size

The formula for determining clustered index row width with all fixed-length fields is the following:

```
Sum of fixed length fields
+ 1 byte (number of variable columns)
+ 4 bytes (page pointer)
```

The formula for determining clustered index row width with variable-length fields is the following:

```
Sum of fixed length fields
+ 1 byte (number of variable columns)
+ 4 bytes (page pointer)
+ 2 bytes (index row width)
+ sum of average width variable columns
+ 1 byte (adjust table)
+ 1 byte (location of offset table)
+ 1 byte per variable length column
```

Let's assume a clustered index on a char(10) column that doesn't allow null values. The index row size is this:

```
10 bytes
+ 4 bytes (page pointer)
+ 1 byte (number of variable columns = 0 in this case)
= 15 bytes per index row
```

Because the clustered index contains a pointer to each data page in the table, the number of rows at the bottom level of the index is equal to the number of pages in the table.

If the data row size is 42 bytes, you can get 48 data rows per data page. With 100,000 rows in the table, you have 2,084 pages in the table. Therefore, you have 2,084 rows in the bottom level of the clustered index. Each index page, like a data page, has 2,016 bytes available for storing index row entries. To determine the number of clustered index rows per page, divide the index row size into 2,016 bytes and multiply by the fill factor. For this example, assume the default fill factor is being applied, which fills clustered index pages about 75 percent full:

```
2016 / 15 = 134.4 rounded down to 134 rows per page × .75
= 100 rows per page
```

At 100 rows per page, you need the following:

```
2084 / 100 = 20.84 rounded up to 21 pages
```

to store all the rows at the bottom level of the index.

The top level of the index must be a single root page. You need to build levels on top of one another in the index until you reach a single root page. To determine the total number of levels in the index, use the following algorithm:

```
N = 0
divide number of data pages by number of index rows per page
while number of index pages at level N is > 1
begin
    divide number of pages at level N by number of rows per page
    N = N+1
end
```

When the number of pages at level N equals 1, you are at the root page and N+1 equals the number of levels in the index. The total size of the clustered index in number of pages is the total sum of all pages at each level.

The following applies this algorithm to the example:

```
Level 0: 2084 / 100 = 21 pages
Level 1: 21 / 100 = 1 page
```

Thus, the index contains two levels for a total size of 22 pages, or 44KB.

The I/O cost of retrieving a single row using the index is the number of levels in the index plus a single data page. Contrast this with the cost of a table scan for the example:

```
2 index levels + 1 data page = 3 page I/Os
Table scan = 2084 page I/Os
```

You can easily see the performance advantage during a select that having an index on the table can provide. An index is also helpful during data modifications to identify quickly the rows specified to be updated or deleted.

## Nonclustered Indexes

A nonclustered index is a separate index structure independent of the physical sort order of the data in the table, as shown in Figure 10.21. SQL Server allows up to 249 nonclustered indexes per table. Without a clustered index, the data is stored in the table as a heap structure, with no specific sort order applied.

**FIGURE 10.21.**

*Nonclustered index structure.*

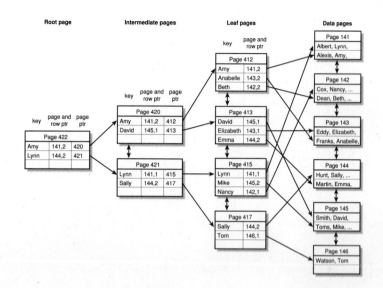

You can think of a nonclustered index as an index in the back of a road atlas. The towns are not located in any sort of structured order within a road atlas; rather they seem to be randomly spread throughout the maps. To find a specific town, you look up the name of the town in the index, which contains all towns in alphabetical order. For the town name you are looking for, you will find a page number and the coordinates on that page where the town can be found.

A nonclustered index works in a similar fashion. The data rows may be randomly spread throughout the table. The nonclustered index tree contains the index keys in sorted order, with the leaf level of the index containing a pointer to the data page and the row number within the page where the index key value can be found. There is a row in the leaf level for every data row in the table.

The intermediate- and root-level pages contain the entire leaf-level row information plus an additional page pointer to the page at the next level down containing the key value in the first row.

SQL Server performs the following steps when searching for a data row by using the nonclustered index:

1. Query sysindexes for the table where indid > 1 and <= 250 and get the address of the root page for this index.
2. Compare the search value against the key values on the root page.
3. Find the highest key value on the page where the key value is less than or equal to the search value.
4. Follow that page pointer to the next level down in the index.
5. Continue following page pointers as in steps 3 and 4 until the leaf page is reached.

6. Search the rows on the leaf page to locate a match for the search value. If a matching row is not found on that leaf page, there are no matching rows in the table.

7. If a match is found on the leaf page, follow the pointer to the data page and row ID to retrieve the requested data row.

Because nonclustered indexes contain page and row pointers, the size and number of levels in a nonclustered index depends on the width of the index key and the number of rows in the table. The structure of an nonclustered index row is detailed in Figure 10.22.

**FIGURE 10.22.**

*Nonclustered index leaf row structure.*

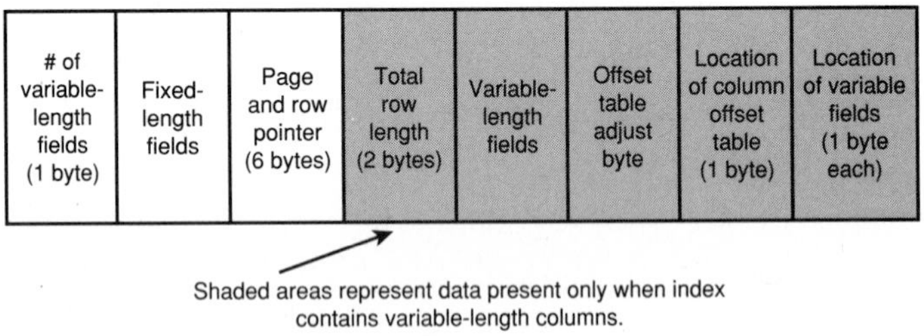

| # of variable-length fields (1 byte) | Fixed-length fields | Page and row pointer (6 bytes) | Total row length (2 bytes) | Variable-length fields | Offset table adjust byte | Location of column offset table (1 byte) | Location of variable fields (1 byte each) |
|---|---|---|---|---|---|---|---|

Shaded areas represent data present only when index contains variable-length columns.

The nonleaf rows of a nonclustered index contain the entire leaf row information, index key plus page and row pointer, and an additional page pointer to point to the pages at the next lower level. The nonleaf rows of a clustered index are constructed similar to a clustered index (see Figure 10.23).

**FIGURE 10.23.**

*Nonclustered index nonleaf row structure.*

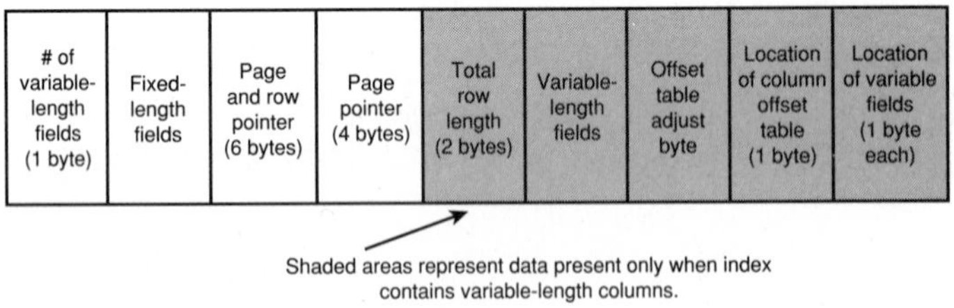

| # of variable-length fields (1 byte) | Fixed-length fields | Page and row pointer (6 bytes) | Page pointer (4 bytes) | Total row length (2 bytes) | Variable-length fields | Offset table adjust byte | Location of column offset table (1 byte) | Location of variable fields (1 byte each) |
|---|---|---|---|---|---|---|---|---|

Shaded areas represent data present only when index contains variable-length columns.

## Estimating Nonclustered Index Size

The formula for determining nonclustered leaf index row width with all fixed-length fields is the following:

```
Sum of fixed length fields
+ 1 byte (number of variable columns)
+ 6 bytes (page and row pointer)
```

The formula for determining nonclustered leaf index row width with variable-length fields is this:

```
Sum of fixed length fields
+ 1 byte (number of variable columns)
+ 6 bytes (page and row pointer)
```

```
+ 2 bytes (index row width)
+ sum of average width variable columns
+ 1 byte (adjust table)
+ 1 byte (location of offset table)
+ 1 byte per variable length column
```

Let's assume you have a nonclustered index on a char(10) column that doesn't allow null values. The leaf index row size is the following:

```
10 bytes
+ 6 bytes (page and row pointer)
+ 1 byte (number of variable columns = 0 in this case)
= 17 bytes per leaf index row
```

Because the leaf level of a nonclustered index contains a pointer to each data row in the table, the number of rows at the leaf level of the index is equal to the number of rows in the table.

If you have 100,000 rows in the table, you'll have 100,000 rows in the nonclustered leaf level. Each nonclustered index page, like a data page, has 2,016 bytes available for storing index row entries. To determine the number of nonclustered leaf index rows per page, divide the leaf index row size into 2,016 bytes. Here is an example:

```
2016 / 17 = 118.6 rounded down to 118 rows per page × .75
= 88 rows per page
```

At 88 rows per page, you need the following:

```
100,000 / 88 = 1136.4 rounded up to 1137 pages
```

to store all the rows at the leaf level of the index.

The nonleaf rows of a nonclustered index are like clustered index rows in that they contain pointers to all pages at the next level down in the index. Each nonleaf row contains the full index row from the leaf level plus an additional page pointer, 4 bytes in size. Therefore, the size of the nonleaf rows equals the following:

```
Size of leaf row
+ 4 bytes (page pointer)
```

Here are the nonleaf rows for the example:

```
17 bytes (leaf index row size)
+ 4 bytes (page pointer)
= 21 bytes per nonleaf index row
```

To determine the number of nonclustered nonleaf index rows per page, divide the nonleaf index row size into 2,016 bytes and multiply by the fill factor. For this example, let's use a fill factor of 75 percent:

```
2016 / 21 = 96 rows per page × .75
= 72 nonleaf rows per page
```

Like the clustered index, the top level of the index must be a single root page. You need to build levels on top of one another in the index until you reach a single root page. To determine the total number of levels in the nonclustered index, use the following algorithm:

```
N = 0
divide number of data rows by number of index rows per page
while number of index pages at level N is > 1
begin
    divide number of pages at level N by number of rows per page
    N = N+1
end
```

When the number of pages at level N equals 1, you are at the root page, and N+1 equals the number of levels in the index. The total size of the nonclustered index in number of pages is the total sum of all pages at each level.

The following applies this algorithm to the example:

```
Level 0: 100,000 / 88 = 1137 pages
Level 1: 1137 / 72 = 16 pages
Level 2: 16 / 72 = 1 page
```

Thus, the nonclustered index contains three levels, for a total size of 1,154 pages, or 2,308KB.

The I/O cost of retrieving a single row using the index is the number of levels in the index plus a single data page. Contrast this with the cost of table scan for the example:

```
3 index levels + 1 data page = 4 page I/Os
Table scan = 2084 page I/Os
```

Although a nonclustered index defined on the same column as a clustered index typically consists of one additional level, resulting in one additional I/O, it is still significantly faster than a table scan. You can easily see the performance advantage during a select that having an index on the table can provide. An index is also helpful during data modifications to identify quickly the rows specified to be updated or deleted.

## Estimating Table and Index Sizes Using *sp_estspace*

SQL Server provides a system stored procedure that can be used to estimate the size of a table and its corresponding index within an SQL Server database. This stored procedure is the sp_estspace stored procedure. The following is the syntax for the sp_estspace stored procedure:

```
sp_estspace table_name, est # of rows [, fill factor [, cols_to_max [, textbin_len
➡[, iosec ]]]]
```

The parameters passed to sp_estspace are as follows:

- table_name is the name of an existing table in the current database.
- est_#_of_rows is the estimated number of rows the table will contain.

- ◼ `fill_factor` is the fill factor to be used for the index and data pages. If omitted or set to NULL, the SQL Server default fill factor will be used.

- ◼ `cols_to_max` is a comma-separated list of the variable-length column names in quotation marks (for example, `"col1, col2, col3"`) that uses the maximum column width rather than the average column width in the size calculations. If omitted or set to NULL, the default value is the average length (column width / 2).

- ◼ `textbin_len` is the average total size of all text and image columns per row. If omitted or set to NULL, the default value of `0` is used.

- ◼ `iosec` is the number of disk I/Os per second for the current platform. If omitted or set to NULL, the default value of `30` I/Os per second is used. This value is used in determining the estimated index creation times.

> **NOTE**
>
> Curiously, no matter what value you supply for `iosec`, you get the same time estimate generated each time. This is because, for some inexplicable reason, the stored procedure contains an assignment select that sets the `iosec` parameter to `0`, replacing any other specified value. This appears to be a minor bug in the `sp_estspace` stored procedure code, which still persists even in System 11.
>
> It is not a major loss, however, because the time estimates are not all that accurate. You can get better time estimates by benchmarking the time it takes to create the indexes on a smaller version of the table and scaling up the estimates based upon the estimated table size. Index creation time appears to scale up in a linear fashion proportional to overall table size.
>
> For example, if it takes 10 minutes to create a nonclustered index on a 10MB table, it should take approximately 100 minutes to create the same index on a 100MB table.

For example, to estimate the size of the `titles` table with 10,000 rows, you can simply enter the following:

```
sp_estspace titles, 10000
```

However, if you want to estimate the size of the `titles` table using the maximum column width for the `title` and `description` columns and a 75-percent fill factor, you enter the following:

```
sp_estspace titles, 10000, 75, "title, notes"
```

Here is the output:

| name | type | idx_level | Pages | Kbytes |
| --- | --- | --- | --- | --- |
| titles | data | 0 | 2256 | 4513 |
| titleidind | clustered | 0 | 13 | 26 |
| titleidind | clustered | 1 | 1 | 2 |

```
titleind              nonclustered 0              668        1334
titleind              nonclustered 1               36          72
titleind              nonclustered 2                3           4
titleind              nonclustered 3                1           2

Total_Mbytes
----------------
           5.81

name                        type       total_pages  time_mins
-------------------------   ----------  -----------  -----------
titleidind                  clustered   2270                 6
titleind                    nonclustered 708                 2
```

According to this output, the total size of the table with 10,000 rows and a clustered index on `title_id` and a nonclustered index on `title` is 5.81MB. The number of lines in the detail output for each index indicates the number of index levels. In this example, there are two levels in the clustered index (13 pages at level 0 and 1 root page at level 1) and three levels in the nonclustered index (668 pages at the leaf level 0, 36 pages at level 1, and 1 root page at level 3). The table alone will take up 2256 pages. The last two lines of the output indicate the estimated time to create the indexes, based on 30 I/Os per second.

> **NOTE**
>
> Although using sp_estspace can save you a lot of hand calculations, the main disadvantage to using sp_estspace for estimating table and index sizes is that the table and its indexes must be created first. If you are attempting to get size estimates to plan the capacity of a production system, you will need to create a scratch copy of the production database and create all tables and indexes to be able to use sp_estspace. You then need to run it for every table and sum up the total size estimates manually.

## Indexes and Performance

You've seen so far how indexes, by their nature, can help speed data retrieval by giving you a direct path to the desired data and avoiding a costly table scan. However, indexes have an adverse impact on update performance because the indexes need to be maintained "on the fly" by SQL Server in order to maintain the proper sort order within the index and table.

The disadvantage of clustered indexes is that, during inserts, the rows must be inserted into the appropriate location to maintain the sort order. This is just like a filing system. If you don't put the files away in alphabetical order, your filing system becomes worthless. Similarly, SQL Server maintains the sort order of your data when you update, insert, and delete data rows.

If there is not a clustered index on the table, rows are added at the end of the table as a heap. Any nonclustered indexes have the new row added in the appropriate location within the index leaf page, depending on the index key value.

With or without a clustered index on a table, every time you insert, delete, or update a row and it causes the row to move within the table, all nonclustered indexes on the table need to be updated to reflect the new row location. With a large number of indexes on a table, the overhead during data modification may become excessive. For tables involved in Online Transaction Processing (OLTP) types of applications, you should try to keep the number of indexes to less than five.

Let's now examine what occurs in SQL Server when you modify data with indexes on the table.

# SQL Server Index Maintenance

SQL Server indexes are self-maintaining structures. That is, they allocate additional space as needed and deallocate space as rows are deleted, all the while maintaining the sort order of the index tree. Typically, you do not need to perform a "reorg" on SQL Server indexes, because SQL Server typically keeps the index tree balanced.

# 50–50 Page Splits

Normally, when inserting data into a table with a clustered index, the row is inserted into the appropriate position within the appropriate data and/or index page. If the data or index page is full, SQL Server will perform a 50–50 page split (see Figure 10.24).

Whenever a page split occurs, the following also occur:

1. A new page is linked into the page chain.
2. Half the rows on the affected page are moved to a new page.
3. The new row is inserted into the appropriate location.
4. The clustered index is updated to reflect the new data page; entries for new index pages are added to the next higher index level.
5. An entry for the new data row is added to all nonclustered indexes on the table.
6. All nonclustered indexes on the table are updated for each row that moved as a result of the page split.

A 50–50 page split obviously does incur index maintenance overhead and slows insert/update performance when it occurs. However, it will help to improve subsequent inserts and updates, because the affected pages now are, on average, only about 50 percent full. This leaves free space for additional rows before another page split will occur. SQL Server index and table pages typically average out to about 75 percent full for any table that is sufficiently active. This is desirable in an OLTP environment so that 50–50 page splits are not occurring excessively.

Be aware, that on occasion, a page split may cascade up multiple levels within the index tree, if the index pages are full as well. If the root page splits, a new root page is created and the index tree grows an additional level.

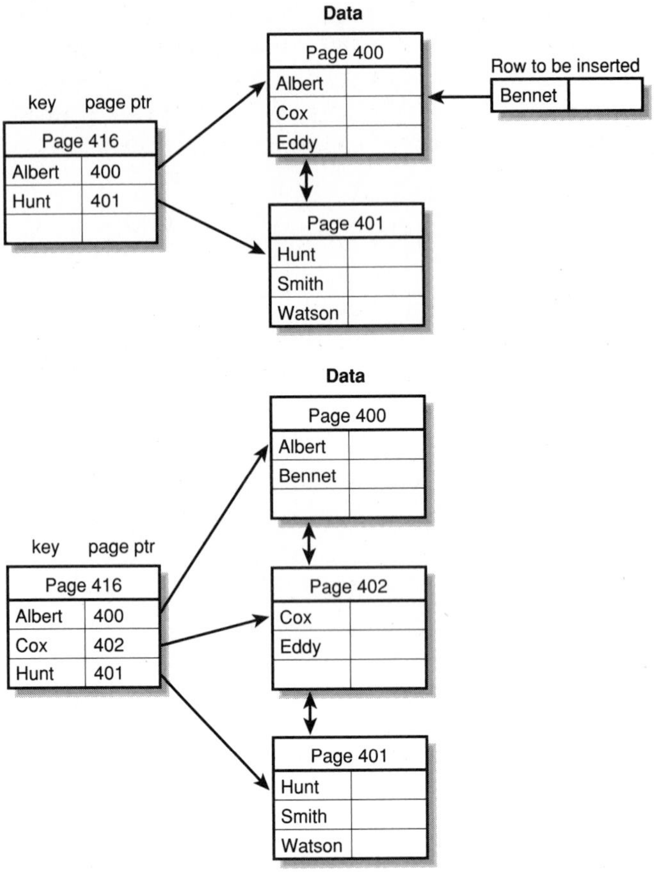

**FIGURE 10.24.**

*50–50 page split.*

## Monotonic (100–0) Page Splits

If the table has no clustered index, or the clustered index is on a sequential key and data rows are inserted in sequential key order, all new rows are added to the end of the last page in the table. When a data or index page is full and a new row needs to be added to the end of the page, SQL Server performs a monotonic page split (see Figure 10.25).

When a monotonic page split occurs, the following also occur:

1. A new page is linked into the page chain.
2. The new row is added to the new page.
3. An entry for the new data page is added to the clustered index; entries for new index pages are added to the next higher index level.
4. An entry is added for the new data row to all nonclustered indexes on the table.

As you can see, when you have a monotonic page split, there is less index maintenance and overhead involved. The downside to monotonic page splits or storage in a heap structure is that free space on previous pages is not reused, because all new rows are added at the end of the page chain. The only way to recover this "lost" space is to rebuild the clustered index and reapply a new fill factor, which you will learn about shortly.

**FIGURE 10.25.**

*Monotonic (100–0) page split.*

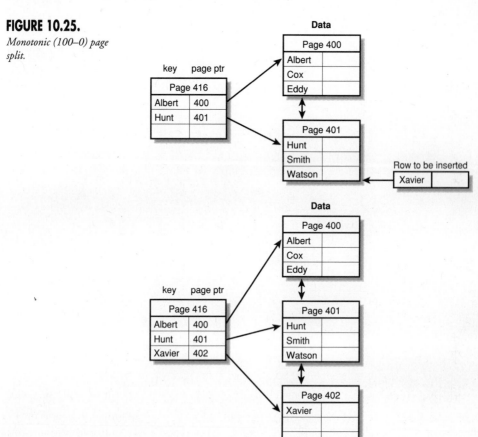

## Overflow Pages

First, let's examine what happens if you have a nonunique clustered index that allows duplicate rows, and you need to add a duplicate value to the end of the page (see Figure 10.26).

**FIGURE 10.26.**

*Overflow page.*

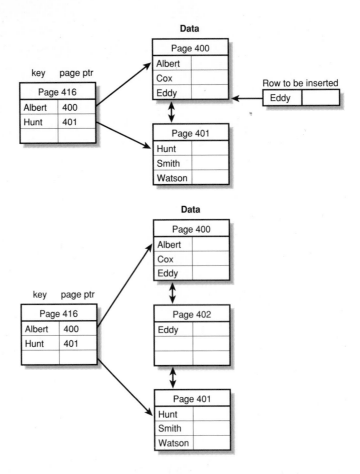

At first, this insert looks similar to a monotonic page split, but it is slightly different because the new page does not get recorded in the clustered index. In essence, it is an "overflow" of a duplicate value from the previous page. An overflow page is generated only if the duplicate key value matches the last data row on the page and there is no more room to store additional rows on that page. The clustered index still points to the original data page, and the data page points to the overflow page.

Theoretically, this violates the normal B-tree scheme but gives you a way of handling duplicate key values in a clustered index. If duplicate key values were split across normal data pages, you could miss the rows on a preceding data page if you used the normal method of traversing the index tree. For example, in Figure 10.26, if you had an index pointer to page 402 for the key value Eddy, you would traverse the index tree directly to page 402 and scan for all values of Eddy from that point forward, missing the entry for Eddy on page 400.

With all the overhead involved in maintaining a sort order, why would you want to use clustered indexes? True, there is an overhead penalty paid when a page split occurs, but clustered indexes also provide a number of advantages:

- Because clustered indexes maintain a sort order and insert data into the appropriate location within the table, clustered indexes make use of free space in pages throughout the table, resulting in less wasted space.

- Clustered indexes can help improve performance for certain types of queries such as range retrievals and queries with order by, as you'll see in Chapter 11.

- Clustered indexes take up much less space than nonclustered indexes defined on the same column(s).

- Clustered indexes typically provide a faster access path to the data than a similarly created nonclustered index, unless the nonclustered index can cover the query (which is also covered in Chapter 11).

- Clustered indexes are updated less often than nonclustered indexes. Review the previous examples. Every time you performed some form of operation on a data row, you had to update the nonclustered indexes. However, the clustered indexes needed to be updated only if you allocated or deallocated a data page.

I once had a customer who somehow became convinced that clustered indexes were a bad thing and got rid of all clustered indexes within his database. When I outlined the previous five points for him, he realized the error of his thinking and redefined his indexing scheme. In general, if you have one and only one index for a table, it is best to define it as a clustered index. If you have multiple candidates for a clustered index and are not sure which column(s) to create the clustered index on, read Chapter 11, which covers index selection and provides guidelines on how to determine what indexes will best support your queries and transactions.

# Page Merges

As you delete data rows from pages, the remaining rows are shuffled upward on the page to keep all free space at the end of the page. However, if the clustered index key does not cause random inserts into these pages, the free space will not be reused. This occurs if the clustered index is defined on a key value, which tends to concentrate inserts to a specific portion of the table, such as at the end of the table if defined on a sequential key.

With no clustered index at all, the table is a heap structure and all inserts occur at the end of the page, with no preceding space being reused at all.

When all rows are deleted from a data page, the following also occur:

1. The page is removed from the page linkage.

2. The page is marked as unused in the extent structure bitmap on the allocation page for the allocation unit within which the page is located.

This page is still reserved for use by the table to which it is allocated. Unused pages are not deallocated from the table until all eight pages within the extent are marked as unused. At that point, the extent is deallocated and may be used by any object within the database that requires additional storage. Until the extent is deallocated, the table or index will reuse the unused pages before a new extent is allocated to the table.

Pages within an index are managed similarly to data pages when rows are deleted—with one exception. When only one row is left on an index page, SQL Server merges the index row into an adjacent index page at the same level and removes the now empty page from the index. This behavior helps keep the index tree smaller and more efficient.

If the empty space within data and/or index pages is not reused, your table can become fragmented and may result in the table taking up more space than anticipated. It can also cause your index tree to become unbalanced, with a crowding of data values at the end of the tree and the pages at the beginning of the tree being rather sparse.

This scenario is one of the few times you may have to perform a sort of "reorg" on your indexes. The way to do this is to drop and re-create your clustered index, reapplying a fill factor to the data to even out the distribution across the data pages.

# Fill Factor

The fill factor is a percentage specifying how full you want your index and/or data pages when the index is created. A lower fill factor has the effect of spreading data and index across more pages by leaving more free space in the pages. This reduces page splitting and dynamic reorganization, which can improve performance in environments where there are a lot of inserts and updates to the data. A higher fill factor has the effect of packing more data and indexes per page by leaving less free space in the pages. This is useful in environments where the data is relatively static, because it reduces the number of pages required for storing the data and its indexes and helps to improve performance for queries by reducing the number of pages that need to be accessed.

The fill factor applies only at index creation time and is *not* maintained by the SQL Server. Once you begin updating and inserting data, the fill factor will eventually be lost. To reintroduce fill factor, the index must be dropped and rebuilt. Providing a fill factor when creating a clustered index will apply to the data pages for the table as well. A fill factor on a nonclustered index will not affect the data pages.

## Setting Fill Factor

The default fill factor is set at the server level, but is typically provided at index creation. The typical default fill factor set at the server level is 0. A fill factor of 0 indicates that data and leaf pages are to be completely filled (100 percent) and the nonleaf pages filled to approximately 75 percent. This minimizes your data storage requirements, but it leaves some free space within the index tree to prevent excessive page splits within the nonleaf pages.

If you wish to change the server-wide default for the fill factor, use the `sp_configure` command:

```
sp_configure 'fill factor',N
reconfigure
```

Typically, you specify the fill factor to be used for the index within the index creation statement:

```
create index idx_name on table (column)
with fillfactor=N
```

In both cases, N is the fill factor percentage to be applied. N can range from any valid integer between 0 and 100. 100 is typically used for static tables and all data in index pages will be completely filled, except for the root page. For an OLTP environment, you may choose to use a fill factor value of 50, leaving your index and data pages only half full.

Because SQL Server indexes are self-maintaining and self-balancing, there is typically no need to reapply a fill factor to the index and/or data, because with random activity and normal 50–50 page splits occurring, the data and indexes will average out to about 75 percent full.

When might you need to reestablish the fill factor for your indexes or data? Some shops in intensive update situations will drop and reload indexes periodically to spread the data out and minimize page splits during heavy OLTP activity.

How might you determine whether you are experiencing excessive page splits? One way is to count the number of page splits recorded in your transaction log by running the following query:

```
select count(*) from syslogs where op = 16
```

By monitoring this value over time, you can determine when your page split count is increasing and also evaluate the effectiveness of various fill factor settings in reducing page splits.

If a table becomes very large and then very small, it is possible that rows may have become isolated within data pages. This space will not be recovered until the last row on the page is deleted and the page is marked as unused. To reclaim this space, you may choose to drop and re-create the clustered index.

# Updates and Performance

The last thing you will examine in this chapter is what occurs during updates to data rows within SQL Server.

All updates within SQL Server are essentially a `delete` followed by an `insert`, unless performed as a direct update in-place. With a clustered index on the table, the row is reinserted to the appropriate location on the appropriate data page relative to its physical sort order. Without a clustered index, the row is inserted into one of three locations:

- The same physical location on the same data page
- The same data page if there is room

■ The last page in the heap

SQL Server performs two distinct types of updates:

■ Deferred updates
■ Direct updates

Direct updates can occur as updates in-place or not-in-place.

# Deferred Updates

A deferred update is a multistep process, which occurs when the conditions are not met for a direct update to occur. Deferred updates are always required for the following:

■ Updates that include a join
■ Updates to columns used for referential integrity
■ When a variable-length column is updated
■ When the update would move the row to a new page, and the query is being processed via a table scan or clustered index
■ When the index used to find the data row is not unique, and the update causes the row to move due to a change in the clustered index key or because the row no longer fits on the current page
■ When the data modification statement can have a cascading effect on a unique index column

For example, consider a table with a unique index on an integer column and sequential data values stored in that column, with the following update performed:

```
update invoices set invoice_num = invoice_num + 1
```

If SQL Server were to start at the first row and update invoice_num from 1 to 2, and there was already a row with an invoice_num of 2, it would violate the uniqueness of the index and the update would fail.

In order to perform this sort of update, SQL Server uses the deferred update method. With deferred updates, the following steps are performed:

1. All records to be modified are copied to the transaction log to reflect the old and new values for the column(s) to be modified.

2. SQL Server then reads the transaction log and deletes the affected rows from the data pages and deletes any affected index rows.

3. SQL Server then rereads the transaction log and inserts the new rows from the log into the table and inserts any affected index rows.

This method will typically have the effect of generating more than the usual number of log records than a direct update. It will also incur the following additional overhead:

- Three data page accesses for each data row
- Four log records generated for each updated row
- Two log records generated for each affected index row
- Two index traversals for each affected index
- Two scans of the log records

SQL Server may also apply the deferred method for inserts and deletes. Consider running the following `insert` on a table with no clustered index:

```
insert authors select * from authors
```

Because the table is a heap structure, all new rows will be added at the end of the table. How does SQL Server know which rows are newly inserted rows and which are existing rows? SQL Server uses a deferred method of inserting the records by copying the data rows to be inserted into the transaction log, and then reading the records in the transaction log and inserting them into the table and inserting into any affected indexes as well.

Due to the additional processing overhead incurred when performing deferred updates, SQL Server will attempt to perform direct updates whenever possible.

# Direct Updates

Direct updates can be performed either in-place or not-in-place. A direct update not-in-place is still a `delete` followed by an `insert`, but the updates can be applied in a single pass. A direct update not-in-place can be classified as a cheap direct update or an expensive direct update.

A *cheap direct update* is when an in-place update cannot take place, but the updated row does not move to a new page or cause row ids to change on the current page. The advantage to cheap direct updates is that only indexes whose key fields are modified by the update need to be updated (see Figure 10.27). Because no row IDs change, none of the other nonclustered indexes pointing to that row need to be updated. Cheap direct updates will occur when all of the following are true:

- Only fixed-length columns are modified.
- The table has an update trigger or is marked for replication.
- No join clauses are used in the `update` statement.
- The affected columns are not used for referential integrity.
- The index used to find the row is not being modified by the update.
- The update does not change a clustered index key value, which would force the row to be reinserted into a different data page.

**FIGURE 10.27.**

*Cheap direct update not-in-place.*

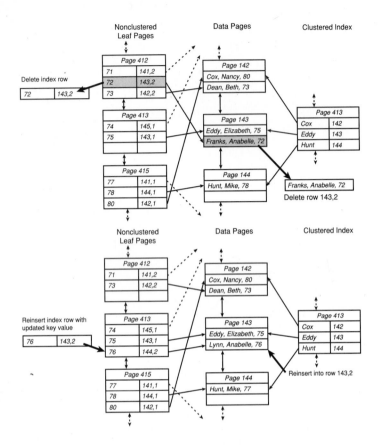

A cheap direct update can also be performed for multiple rows as long as no index key fields are modified.

If a cheap direct update cannot be performed, SQL Server next attempts to perform an expensive direct update. An *expensive direct update* occurs when all the qualifications for a cheap direct update have been met except that the update causes a change to a clustered index key value, forcing the row to be reinserted into a different data page. Figure 10.28 demonstrates an expensive direct update not-in-place.

Even if the data row is reinserted back into the same data page, it may be assigned a different row number than previously if there are any unused row numbers (entry in row offset table = 0) less than the previous row ID for the affected row. This behavior necessitates that all index rows pointing to the data row be deleted and reinserted as well, in order to reflect the new page/row pointer information.

**FIGURE 10.28.**

*Expensive direct update not-in-place.*

Update ... set lname = "Lynn" where lname = "Franks"

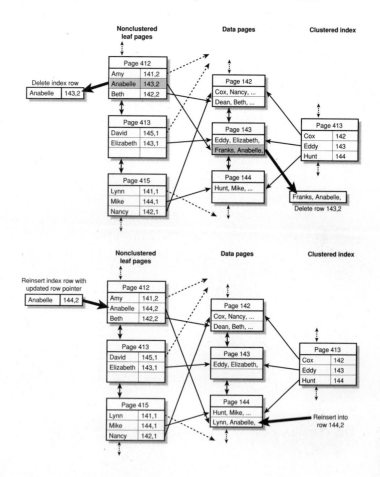

A direct update not-in-place will produce the following overhead:

- A single data page access for each data row updated
- Two log records (DELETE, INSERT) generated for each updated data row
- Two log records (IDELETE, IINSERT) generated for each affected index row

If the column being modified is not part of an index and the row is deleted and reinserted into the same page with the same row ID, no index maintenance is required because no index pointers need to be updated.

Although they are slowest direct update, expensive direct updates still incur less overhead and are faster than deferred updates. Cheap direct updates are more efficient and are almost as fast as direct updates in-place.

# Direct Updates in Place

SQL Server handles both expensive and cheap direct updates as a `delete` followed by an `insert`. An update in-place is a method for modifying the record directly, without the necessity for the delete. Because the row is modified in-place and doesn't move, updates in-place will be faster than updates not-in-place because they will incur fewer log writes and fewer index updates.

In SQL Server 10, all of the following criteria must be met for a direct update in-place to occur:

- The `UPDATE` cannot modify a clustered index column because this will obviously require the data row to move.
- An `UPDATE` trigger cannot exist on the table because the trigger requires the before and after image of the row.
- The table cannot be marked for replication.
- The column(s) being updated must be fixed-length.
- The column(s) being updated can be part of a nonunique, nonclustered index if the index key column being modified is a fixed-width column.
- The column(s) being updated can be part of a unique, nonclustered index if the index key column being modified is fixed-width and the `WHERE` clause criteria matches only one row.

SQL Server 10 also now allows direct updates in-place for multi-row updates if the following additional criteria are met:

- The column being updated cannot be part of a nonclustered index.
- The index used to find the rows does not contain a column to be updated.
- The table does not contain a timestamp column.

A direct update in-place will produce the following overhead:

- A single data page access for each data row updated
- A single log record (`MODIFY`) generated for each updated data row
- Two log records (`IDELETE`, `IINSERT`) generated for any affected index row (only if a column being updated is part of a nonclustered index)

Direct updates in-place incur the least amount of overhead of all the update methods. Direct updates in-place result in the fewest number of log records generated and the smallest opportunity for any index rows to need to be updated. SQL Server will perform direct updates in-place rather than updates not-in-place whenever possible.

# System 11 and Direct Updates

Because of the minimal logging and reduced index maintenance overhead, it is desirable for in-place updates or cheap direct updates to occur as often as possible. To this end, System 11 SQL Server has improved the optimizer algorithms to allow in-place updates and cheap direct updates to occur more often. In System 11, in-place updates can now also take place for the following types of updates as long as the existing criteria for updates-in-place are also met:

- The column(s) being updated are of variable-length as long as the total row width doesn't change.
- Multiple rows are updated affecting unique/nonunique indexes as long as the clustered index is unaffected.

In addition, cheap direct updates rather than deferred updates can occur when the following are true:

- Variable-length columns are updated but the row still fits on the current page.
- Multiple rows are updated affecting unique/nonunique indexes, even if the index used to satisfy the query, as long as the clustered index is unaffected.

# Confirming Updates in Place

One of the trickier tasks is determining whether a direct update occurs in-place or not-in-place. The SQL Server query optimizer reports only whether an update was direct or deferred, not whether it was in-place or not in-place.

The only way to determine accurately whether a direct update occurs in-place or not-in-place is to examine the transaction log for the update in question.

The easy way to examine the transaction log records is to execute the update statement in question and execute the following immediately:

```
select * from syslogs
```

As long as no one else has run a logged operation in that database between the time you execute your update statement and run the select against the syslogs table, the last rows retrieved should be the rows related to the update in question.

If you are hoping for an update in-place, you will see a row where op = 9 is sandwiched between a 0 and a 30. Table 10.2 lists some common op code values and the type of log record to which they relate.

## Table 10.2. Transaction log op codes.

| Op | Description |
| --- | --- |
| 0 | BEGIN TRANSACTION |
| 4 | INSERT |
| 5 | DELETE |
| 6 | INSIND (indirect insert) |
| 7 | IINSERT (index insert) |
| 8 | IDELETE (index delete) |
| 9 | MODIFY (update in-place) |
| 11 | INOOP (deferred insert) |
| 12 | DNOOP (deferred delete) |
| 13 | ALLOC (page) |
| 15 | EXTENT (allocation) |
| 16 | PAGE SPLIT |
| 17 | CHECKPOINT |
| 30 | END TRANSACTION (commit or rollback) |

If you are like me and have trouble remembering what the different op codes relate to, there is another way to examine the transaction log by using the dbcc log command. You have to log in as sa to run this command.

### WARNING

Do not run DBCC LOG in a database if you have the 'trunc. log on chkpt.' option set to true for that database. There apparently is a rare situation where, if you are running dbcc log at the same time that the SQL Server is attempting to truncate the log, you could end up with a corrupted transaction log and your database will become marked suspect.

If your log ever gets corrupted, you'd better hope you have a fairly recent backup of your database, because there is no way to fix a bad transaction log other than to restore your database to a point prior to the log's getting corrupted.

DBCC LOG displays a translated hex dump of the log contents, and one of the nice things it does is translate the op codes into a textual representation of the type of operation.

To examine the transaction log, execute the following steps:

1. Log in as sa or a user with the sa role.

2. Put the database in single-user mode to avoid having other users add additional log records (not required, but recommended).

3. Run dbcc traceon(3604) to route dbcc output to your terminal.

4. Truncate the transaction log to make it as small as possible (again not required, but recommended because dbcc log can generate tons of output if the log hasn't been pruned recently).

5. Execute the update statement in question.

6. Execute dbcc log to print out the contents of the transaction log (this output can be quite large and you may want to redirect it to a file).

7. Examine the last few log records, which should correspond to your update command.

The BEGINXACT and ENDXACT records in the dbcc log output represent the beginning and end of the transaction. If an update in-place occurred, a MODIFY record should be between the BEGINXACT and ENDXACT records. You can match the transaction records to their corresponding BEGINXACT and ENDXACT records via the transaction ID (xactid). The following is sample output for a single-row update in-place:

```
BEGINXACT (555, 16)
attcnt=1 rno=16 op=0 padlen=0 xactid=(555, 16) len=60 status=0x201d
masterid=(0, 0) lastrec=(0, 0)
xstat=XBEG_ENDXACT,
spid=1 suid=1 uid=1 masterdbid=0 mastersite=0 endstat=3
name=upd    time=Dec 17 1995  6:30AM

MODIFY (555, 17)
attcnt=1 rno=17 op=9 padlen=2 xactid=(555, 16) len=68 status=0x0000
oampg=376 pageno=576 offset=1263 status=0x201f
old ts=0x0001 0x000012ea    new ts=0x0001 0x000012e xvallen=10
oldval:
203eff3a:  41424344 45464748 494a          ABCDEFGHIJH
newval:
203eff44:  48656c6c 6f202020 2020          Hello        .

ENDXACT (555, 18)
attcnt=1 rno=18 op=30 padlen=0 xactid=(555, 16) len=28 status=0x0000
endstat=COMMIT time=Dec 17 1995  6:30AM
```

If the update was not in-place, there should be at least two records, a DELETE followed by an INSERT record.

The following output is an example of a single-row update not-in-place:

```
BEGINXACT (593, 10)
attcnt=1 rno=10 op=0 padlen=0 xactid=(593, 10) len=60 status=0x201d
masterid=(0, 0)  lastrec=(0, 0)
xstat=XBEG_ENDXACT,
spid=1 suid=1 uid=1 masterdbid=0 mastersite=0 endstat=3
name=upd    time=Dec 17 1995  6:38AM
```

```
DELETE (593, 11)
attcnt=1 rno=11 op=5 padlen=0 xactid=(593, 10) len=340 status=0x0000
oampg=376 pageno=576 offset=1258 status=0x00
old ts=0x0001 0x000012ed    new ts=0x0001 0x00001330
xrow:
203c2c70:   01040000 0a48656c 6c6f2020 20202059   .....Hello      Y
203c2c80:   58575655 54535251 504f4e4d 4c4b4a49   XWVUTSRQPONMLKJI
203c2c90:   48474645 44434241 20202020 20202020   HGFEDCBA
203c2ca0:   20202020 20202020 20202020 20202020
203c2cb0:   20202020 20202020 20202020 20202020
203c2cc0:   20202020 20202020 20202020 20202020
203c2cd0:   20202020 20202020 20202020 20202020
203c2ce0:   20202020 20202020 20202020 20202020
203c2cf0:   20202020 20202020 20202020 20202020
203c2d00:   20202020 20202020 20202020 20202020
203c2d10:   20202020 20202020 20202020 20202020
203c2d20:   20202020 20202020 20202020 20202020
203c2d30:   20202020 20202020 20202020 20202020
203c2d40:   20202020 20202020 20202020 20202020
203c2d50:   20202020 20202020 20202020 20202020
203c2d60:   20202020 20202020 20202020 20202020
203c2d70:   20202020 20202020 20202020 20203130              10
203c2d80:   20204142 43444546 4748494a 20280168   ABCDEFGHIJ (.h
203c2d90:   616c6c6f 0201241f                     allo..$..

INSERT (593, 12)
attcnt=1 rno=12 op=4 padlen=0 xactid=(593, 10) len=340 status=0x0000
oampg=376 pageno=576 offset=1258 status=0x00
old ts=0x0001 0x00001330   new ts=0x0001 0x00001331
xrow:
203c2dc4:   01040000 0a48656c 6c6f2020 20202059   .....Hello      Y
203c2dd4:   58575655 54535251 504f4e4d 4c4b4a49   XWVUTSRQPONMLKJI
203c2de4:   48474645 44434241 20202020 20202020   HGFEDCBA
203c2df4:   20202020 20202020 20202020 20202020
203c2e04:   20202020 20202020 20202020 20202020
203c2e14:   20202020 20202020 20202020 20202020
203c2e24:   20202020 20202020 20202020 20202020
203c2e34:   20202020 20202020 20202020 20202020
203c2e44:   20202020 20202020 20202020 20202020
203c2e54:   20202020 20202020 20202020 20202020
203c2e64:   20202020 20202020 20202020 20202020
203c2e74:   20202020 20202020 20202020 20202020
203c2e84:   20202020 20202020 20202020 20202020
203c2e94:   20202020 20202020 20202020 20202020
203c2ea4:   20202020 20202020 20202020 20202020
203c2eb4:   20202020 20202020 20202020 20202020
203c2ec4:   20202020 20202020 20202020 20203130              10
203c2ed4:   20204142 43444546 4748494a 20280168   ABCDEFGHIJ (.h
203c2ee4:   616c6c6f 0201241f                     allo..$..

ENDXACT (593, 13)
attcnt=1 rno=13 op=30 padlen=0 xactid=(593, 10) len=28 status=0x0000
endstat=COMMIT time=Dec 17 1995  6:38AM
```

If you see any IINSERT and IDELETE records, these represent index row updates. The following output is an example of an update in-place on a nonclustered index column resulting in the corresponding nonclustered index row update:

```
BEGINXACT (597, 16)
attcnt=1 rno=16 op=0 padlen=0 xactid=(597, 16) len=60 status=0x201d
masterid=(0, 0)  lastrec=(0, 0)
xstat=XBEG_ENDXACT,
spid=1 suid=1 uid=1 masterdbid=0 mastersite=0 endstat=3
name=upd   time=Dec 17 1995  6:47AM


IDELETE (597, 17)
attcnt=1 rno=17 op=8 padlen=2 xactid=(597, 16) len=68 status=0x0000
oampg=376 pageno=621 offset=1044 status=0x00
old ts=0x0001 0x00001340   new ts=0x0001 0x00001377
xrow:
203c35a4:  0048656c 6c6f2020 20202020 20202020    .Hello
203c35b4:  40020000 0400                          @......


DELETE (597, 18)
attcnt=1 rno=18 op=5 padlen=0 xactid=(597, 16) len=340 status=0x0000
oampg=376 pageno=576 offset=1258 status=0x00
old ts=0x0001 0x0000133f   new ts=0x0001 0x00001378
xrow:
203c35e8:  01040000 0a48656c 6c6f2020 20202059    .....Hello       Y
203c35f8:  58575655 54535251 504f4e4d 4c4b4a49    XWVUTSRQPONMLKJI
203c3608:  48474645 44434241 20202020 20202020    HGFEDCBA
203c3618:  20202020 20202020 20202020 20202020
203c3628:  20202020 20202020 20202020 20202020
203c3638:  20202020 20202020 20202020 20202020
203c3648:  20202020 20202020 20202020 20202020
203c3658:  20202020 20202020 20202020 20202020
203c3668:  20202020 20202020 20202020 20202020
203c3678:  20202020 20202020 20202020 20202020
203c3688:  20202020 20202020 20202020 20202020
203c3698:  20202020 20202020 20202020 20202020
203c36a8:  20202020 20202020 20202020 20202020
203c36b8:  20202020 20202020 20202020 20202020
203c36c8:  20202020 20202020 20202020 20202020
203c36d8:  20202020 20202020 20202020 20202020
203c36e8:  20202020 20202020 20202020 20204865                    He
203c36f8:  6c6c6f20 20202020 20202020 20280168    llo            (.h
203c3708:  616c6c6f 0201241f                      allo..$..


INSERT (598, 0)
attcnt=1 rno=0 op=4 padlen=0 xactid=(597, 16) len=340 status=0x0000
oampg=376 pageno=576 offset=1258 status=0x00
old ts=0x0001 0x00001378   new ts=0x0001 0x00001379
xrow:
203c404c:  01040000 0a48656c 6c6f2020 20202059    .....Hello       Y
203c405c:  58575655 54535251 504f4e4d 4c4b4a49    XWVUTSRQPONMLKJI
203c406c:  48474645 44434241 20202020 20202020    HGFEDCBA
203c407c:  20202020 20202020 20202020 20202020
203c408c:  20202020 20202020 20202020 20202020
203c409c:  20202020 20202020 20202020 20202020
203c40ac:  20202020 20202020 20202020 20202020
203c40bc:  20202020 20202020 20202020 20202020
203c40cc:  20202020 20202020 20202020 20202020
203c40dc:  20202020 20202020 20202020 20202020
203c40ec:  20202020 20202020 20202020 20202020
203c40fc:  20202020 20202020 20202020 20202020
203c410c:  20202020 20202020 20202020 20202020
```

```
203c411c:   20202020 20202020 20202020 20202020
203c412c:   20202020 20202020 20202020 20202020
203c413c:   20202020 20202020 20202020 20202020
203c414c:   20202020 20202020 20202020 20204865                     He
203c415c:   6c6c6f20 576f726c 64202020 20280168  llo World        (.h
203c416c:   616c6c6f 0201241f                     allo..$..

IINSERT (598, 1)
attcnt=1 rno=1 op=7 padlen=2 xactid=(597, 16) len=68 status=0x0000
oampg=376 pageno=621 offset=1044 status=0x00
old ts=0x0001 0x00001377   new ts=0x0001 0x0000137c
xrow:
203c41a0:   0048656c 6c6f2057 6f726c64 20202020  .Hello World
203c41b0:   40020000 0400                         @......

ENDXACT (598, 2)
attcnt=1 rno=2 op=30 padlen=0 xactid=(597, 16) len=28 status=0x0000
endstat=COMMIT time=Dec 17 1995  6:47AM
```

# Summary

By now, you should have a reasonable understanding of SQL Server storage structures and how they are maintained and manipulated. This will help you further understand the topics discussed in the rest of this section of the book.

Now that you have a good understanding of the internals of your high-performance vehicle, SQL Server, it is time to starting tuning it to get the best possible performance for your applications.

# Designing Indexes for Performance

# 11

There are a number of ways to improve SQL Server performance, but the greatest speed improvement results from having indexes that the query optimizer can use to avoid table scans and reduce the I/O costs of resolving queries. (See Chapter 12, "Understanding the Query Optimizer," for more information.) Proper index design is the most important issue in tuning SQL Server performance.

In this chapter you will examine the SQL Server criteria for utilizing indexes and explore the issues and factors that influence index design.

# Why Use Indexes?

There are two primary reasons for creating indexes in SQL Server:

- To maintain uniqueness of the indexed column(s)
- To provide fast access to the tables

If you have primary-key constraints, you need unique indexes to ensure the integrity of the primary key and avoid duplicates.

You do not have to have indexes in order to access the data; SQL Server can always perform a table scan to retrieve data rows. Table scans, however, are not an efficient mechanism to retrieve a single row from a million-row table. If the table could store 50 rows per page, it would require 200,000 page reads to access a single row. You need to have a more direct access path to the data.

Indexes can provide this direct-access path. The tricky part is deciding which indexes to create, and which type of index to create: clustered or nonclustered. In order to make appropriate decisions, you must know when SQL Server can use indexes and how it uses them. You also should understand the performance and size implications of indexes.

# Index Usage Criteria

To effectively determine what indexes to create, you must know whether and how SQL Server will use them. If an index isn't being used, it's just wasting space and creating unnecessary overhead during updates.

The main criteria to remember is that SQL Server cannot use an index defined on a table unless either of the following is true:

- The query contains a column in a valid search argument (SARG).
- The query contains a column in a join clause that matches at least the first column of the index.

Keep this in mind when choosing the column order for composite indexes. For example, if you create an index on the `employee` table as follows:

```
create index idx1 on employee (division, dept, empl_type)
```

each of the following queries could make use of the index:

```
select * from employee
where division = 'accounting'
and empl_type = 'exempt'

select * from employee
where division = 'accounting'
  and empl_type = 'exempt'

select * from employee
where division = 'accounting'
```

However, this query:

```
select * from employee
where empl_type = 'exempt'
```

would not be able to use the index because it doesn't specify the first column of the index. In order for the index `idx1` to be used for this query, you would have to reorder the columns so that `empl_type` was first. However, the index then wouldn't be useful for any queries specifying only `division`, `dept_num`, or both. Satisfying all queries in this case would require defining multiple indexes on the `employee` table.

You might think the easy solution is to index all columns on a table. This might work in a decision support system (DSS) environment, although it would take up a significant amount of space. However, too many indexes can have an adverse impact on performance in an online transaction processing (OLTP) environment.

# Indexes and Performance

Although indexes provide a performance benefit for queries, they can be a hindrance to good performance for updates. This is due to the overhead incurred to keep indexes up-to-date when data is modified, inserted, or deleted. This is a common problem in databases that must support both OLTP and decision support-type applications.

In a DSS, having too many indexes isn't much of an issue because the data is relatively static. You typically load the data, create the indexes, and forget about it until the next data load. As long as you have the indexes to support the user queries, and those queries are getting decent response time, the only penalty for having too many indexes is the space wasted for indexes that are not used.

In an OLTP environment, too many indexes can lead to significant performance degradation, especially if the number of indexes on a table exceeds four or five. Think about it for a second. Every single row insert is one data page write and one or more index page writes (depending on whether a page split occurs or not) for every index on the table. With eight nonclustered indexes, that would be a minimum of nine writes to the database. For a "not-in-place" update of a single row, which is a delete followed by an insert, you'd be looking at potentially 17 writes to the database (for a discussion of in-place and not-in-place updates, refer to Chapter 10, "Understanding SQL Server Storage Structures"). Therefore, for an OLTP environment you would want as few indexes as possible; typically, only the indexes required to support the update transactions and enforce your uniqueness constraints.

Meeting the index needs of DSS and OLTP requirements is an obvious balancing act, with no easy solution. It often involves making hard decisions as to which queries have to get by with a table scan and which updates have to contend with additional overhead.

One solution is to have two separate databases, one for DSS applications and another for OLTP applications. Obviously, this would require some mechanism to keep the databases synchronized. The mechanism chosen would depend on how up-to-date the DSS database has to be. If you can afford some lag time, consider using a dump-and-load mechanism. If the DSS system requires up-to-the-minute concurrency, you probably would want to consider using Sybase Replication Server to keep the databases synchronized.

I wouldn't recommend triggers as a method to keep two databases synchronized. I once saw a system designed using this approach. The performance overhead of the trigger in the OLTP environment was much greater than any overhead caused by having the indexes on the tables. Believe me, replication is a much cleaner, behind-the-scenes approach.

Another possible alternative is to have only the required indexes in place during normal processing to support the OLTP requirements. At the end of the business day, create the indexes necessary to support the DSS queries to be run as batch jobs after normal processing hours. When the DSS reports are complete, drop the additional indexes and you'll be prepared for the next day's processing.

# Index Selection

Determining which indexes to define involves performing a detailed query analysis. This means examining the search clauses to see what columns are referenced, knowing the bias of the data to determine the usefulness of the index, and ranking the queries in order of importance. You have to be careful not to examine individual queries and develop indexes to support one query without considering the other queries that are executed on the table.

Because it's usually not possible to index for everything, you want to index for the queries that are most critical to your applications, or the queries that are run frequently by a large number of users. Is it worth it to create an index to support a query that's run only once a month when you would have to maintain that index throughout the rest of the month? The sum of the additional processing time throughout the month could conceivably exceed the time it takes to perform a single table scan to satisfy that one query.

If, due to processing requirements, you must have the index in place when the query is run, you might consider creating the index only when you run the query, and then dropping the index for the remainder of the month.

# Evaluating Index Usefulness

When the SARGs or join clauses in a query match the indexes on a table, SQL Server evaluates all possible indexes and compares them to each other and to the cost of a table scan. This is to determine the least-expensive method of processing the query in terms of page I/Os. The SQL Server uses an index only if the index is more efficient than a table scan, depending on the type of query and the data in the table.

Also, SQL Server typically uses only one index per table to satisfy a query. The only exception to this rule is when a query contains an OR clause and SQL Server can apply the OR strategy. (This topic is covered in Chapter 12.) If a query has multiple where clauses that can be satisfied by an index, SQL Server evaluates all alternatives and chooses to use only the index that will yield the most efficient query plan.

How does SQL Server determine the cheapest index to use, you might ask? For example, how does it know how many rows will be returned by the following query?

```
select * from table
    where key between 1000000 and 2000000
```

If the table contains 10,000,000 rows with values ranging between 0 and 20,000,000, how does the query optimizer know whether to use an index or table scan? There could be 10 rows in the range, or 900,000 rows in the range. How does the SQL Server estimate how many rows there are between 1,000,000 and 2,000,000?

# The Distribution Page

The SQL Server keeps distribution information for each index on a separate page in the database, called the *distribution page*. The location of this page is stored in the distribution column in the sysindexes table. The query optimizer uses the information on the distribution page to estimate the number of rows that would match a search argument or join clause for a query.

The query optimizer stores two types of information in the distribution page:

- Sample data values for the first column of the index in a structure similar to a histogram
- The density, also referred to as selectivity, of the index columns

The distribution page is built at index-creation time if the table contains data. If the table is empty, no distribution page is created. In addition, the distribution page is not maintained by SQL Server as data is inserted, updated, and deleted from the table. In order to update (or, if necessary, create) the distribution page, the DBA or table owner must run the `update statistics` command:

```
update statistics table_name [index_name]
```

If you specify only the table name, `update statistics` updates statistics for all indexes on the table. If you want to update the statistics for an individual index, specify the index name after the table name.

The general rule of thumb is that if your data volume changes by more than 10 to 20 percent, or if more than 10 to 20 percent of your indexed values have been modified, it's a good time to run `update statistics`.

The distribution page contains two types of information: a distribution table and a density table. The distribution table contains information about the distribution of index key values in the index. The density table contains information about the average proportion of duplicate values in the index. Figure 11.1 shows a graphic representation of a distribution page.

For the distribution table, only the key values for the first column in the index are stored. The number of values, or *steps*, that can be stored in the distribution table depends on the width of the first column in the index. The width of each step is divided into the space available on the distribution page to determine the number of steps it can store. SQL Server then stores sample values for the first index column at each step.

The total space available on the distribution page for the distribution table is 2,016 bytes (2,048 minus the 32-byte header), minus the additional space required for the index density table. The index density table is stored at the end of the page and requires two bytes for each density stored. There are at least two density values stored on each distribution page. (See the section titled "Index Densities" for a more detailed discussion of the index density table.) This leaves a maximum of 2,012 bytes available to store the distribution steps for a single-column index.

The size of each step depends on the size of the first column in the index and whether it is a fixed- or variable-length column. For a fixed-length column, the size of each distribution step is the width of the column plus two bytes of overhead. For an index with a variable-length column as the first column, the width of each distribution step is the actual data width for the value stored in the step, plus 7 bytes of overhead. The additional overhead is the extra bytes used to store the row width plus the size of the data value, just like a row with variable-length columns on a data page. (See Chapter 10 for a discussion of how variable length data is stored.)

The number of distribution steps for a fixed-length column would then be calculated as this:

```
(2016 - 2 - (number of key columns * 2) )
/ (column width + 2)
```

# FIGURE 11.1.

*A graphical representation of a distribution page.*

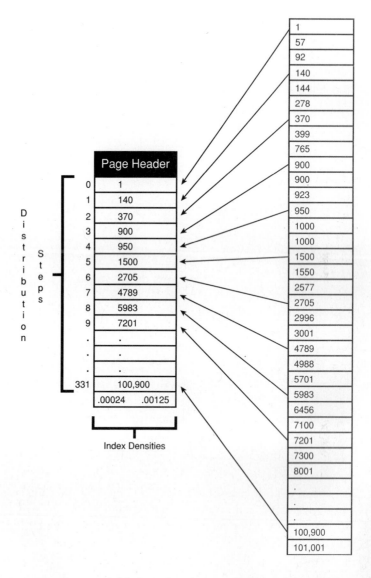

The number of distribution steps for a variable-length column would be determined as follows:

```
(2016 - 2 - (number of key columns * 2) )
/ (maximum column width + 2)
```

Let's consider an example of an index defined on an integer column that doesn't allow null values. The following calculates the number of steps that could be stored for this column:

```
 (2016 - 2 - (1 * 2)) / (4 + 2)
= 2012 / 6
= 335 steps
```

With 10,000,000 rows in the table and 335 steps on the page, SQL Server can store a sample value for every

```
10,000,000 rows / 335 steps = 29,850 rows
```

The SQL Server then populates the distribution table by walking the index and storing the key value in each step for every 29,850 rows, starting with the first row in the table.

How does the query optimizer then use this information to determine the effectiveness of the index? Consider, again, the query discussed previously:

```
select * from table
where key between 1000000 and 2000000
```

SQL Server estimates the number of rows within the range of values by determining which distribution steps the data values fall on or between. It then multiplies the total number of steps times the number of rows per step, to estimate the total number of rows within the range of values.

In this example, SQL Server compares the search values 1,000,000 and 2,000,000 to the values stored on the distribution page. If it finds 1,000,000 at step 157 and 2,000,000 at step 182, the estimated number of rows would be calculated as follows:

```
182 - 157 = 25 steps
25 steps × 29,850 rows per step =  746,250 rows
```

If an index contains a number of duplicate values, the search value could be stored on multiple steps. For an equality search, if a search value matched a number of steps on the distribution page, the estimated number of matching rows would be equal to the number of matching steps multiplied by the number of rows per step.

This is why a composite index with many duplicate values in the first column may sometimes result in a higher estimated row count for the query when using the distribution steps to estimate the number of matching rows. If it's possible, it's often better to put the most unique column as the first column in a composite index. This results in more selective distribution steps being stored on the distribution page. However, it also makes the index useless for certain queries where the first column of the index is not specified in a SARG, so you may have to make a trade-off here.

Distribution steps can be used only for search clauses when a constant expression is compared against an indexed column and the value of the constant expression is known at query compile time. In SQL Server, this includes only explicitly specified constant values or stored procedure parameters. Arithmetic expressions, system functions, string concatenation operations, local variables, join clauses, and subqueries represent constant values that are not known until query execution. Examples of expressions where distribution steps cannot be used include:

```
where col_a = getdate()
where monthly_sales < 10000 / 12
where l_name like "Smith" + "%"
where price = @avg_price
```

```
where total_sales > (select sum(qty) from sales)
where titles.pub_id = publishers.pub_id
```

For these types of statements, SQL Server needs some other way of estimating the number of matching rows. Additionally, because distribution steps are kept only on the first column of the index, the query optimizer must use a different method for determining the number of rows matching search arguments specifying more than the single column of a multi-column key. In these cases, the query optimizer uses the index density values to estimate the number of matching rows.

# Index Densities

When the query optimizer doesn't use distribution steps for equality searches, it uses a value called the *density*. The density is the average proportion of duplicates for the index key(s). Essentially, this can be calculated as the inverse of the number of unique values in the table. For example, an index on a 10,000-row table with 2,500 unique values would have a density of

```
1/2500 = .0004
```

The index density is applied against the number of rows in the table to estimate the average number of rows that would match any given value. Therefore, any single value compared against the index key on a 10,000-row table with an index density of .0004 would be expected to match:

```
10,000 × .0004 = 4 rows
```

The lower the density value, the more selective the index is; the higher the density, the less selective. If an index consisted of all duplicates, the density would be 1, or 100 percent.

For multi-column indexes, SQL Server now stores multiple densities for each sequential combination of columns. For example, if you had an index on columns A, B, and C, SQL Server would store densities for

```
A alone
A and B combined
A, B, and C combined
```

Typically, the density value should become smaller (that is, more selective) as you add more columns to the index. For example, if the densities were as follows:

```
A         .05
A, B      .004
A, B, C   .0001
```

and you had 10,000 rows in the table and a single search value comparing against A alone, you would estimate it to match:

```
.05 * 10,000 = 500 rows
```

If the query provided values for both A and B, you would expect it to match:

```
.004 * 10,000 = 40 rows
```

If A, B, and C all are specified, the query would be estimated to match:

```
.0001 * 10,000 = 1 row
```

> **NOTE**
>
> Prior to SQL Server 10, the distribution page contained only a single density value for all columns in the index.

All density values are stored at the end of the distribution page. (Refer to Figure 11.1.) There are at least two densities stored, even for single-column indexes. One is used for determining join selectivity, or for search arguments with unknown values, and is referred to as the alldensity value. This density value is based on all rows in the table, because the join or search value could match a value with a large number of duplicates.

The other density is used for search clauses when the value being searched for falls between two distribution steps. If there were a few values in the table with a large number of duplicates, the alldensity value could conceivably refer to a greater number of rows than would exist between the two steps. For example, consider a table with 10,000 rows with an index on a char(8) key:

```
8 bytes plus 2 = 10 bytes per step
2012 bytes / 10 bytes per step = 200 steps
10,000 rows / 200 steps = 50 rows per step
```

Assume you have 150 unique values in the table. The alldensity would be

```
1 / 150 = .0067
```

If a search value was found to be between two steps and the query optimizer applied the alldensity value, it would estimate that

```
.0067 * 10,000 = 67
```

rows would match. However, there are only 50 rows per step in the distribution table. If the search value falls between two steps, there cannot be more than 50 instances of the data value. For this reason, SQL Server stores an additional density value that excludes some values with a high number of duplicates, essentially those values that would span multiple steps in the distribution table. Therefore, when there are a lot of duplicates, the alldensity value is likely to be higher and the regular density value is likely to be lower.

## Viewing Distribution Page Values

Over time in an environment where the data is modified, your index statistics become out-of-date. You have to run the update statistics command to generate new statistics based on the current data values in the table because SQL Server does not automatically maintain the information on the distribution page.

You can use the dbcc page command to examine the current contents of the distribution page to determine whether they accurately represent the data values stored in the table. (Refer to Chapter 10 for more information on using dbcc page.) The address of the distribution page is stored in the distribution column of the sysindexes table. To determine the location of the distribution page for the index idx1 on table table1, you could run the following query:

```
select distribution from sysindexes
    where name = 'idx1' and id = object_id('table1')
```

Use the value returned for distribution as the page number in the dbcc page command. For example, if the page number is 330 and the database name is pubs2, execute the following to display a dump of the distribution page:

```
dbcc page (pubs2, 330, 1)
```

Unfortunately, dbcc page displays the contents of the distribution page in hexadecimal format, which is difficult to read. In addition, it doesn't display the index density values. If you prefer to see the distribution steps for an index displayed in a graphical format, check out the demonstration copy of Aurora Distribution Viewer on the included CD-ROM. In addition to providing multiple ways of graphing distribution page values, it also can keep a history of distribution page values for tracking the effectiveness of your update statistics strategy. The advantage of a graphical display is that it can help you track down spikes or anomalies in your data distribution.

# Index Design Guidelines

Now that you should have an understanding of how the optimizer uses indexes and index statistics to optimize queries, let's examine some guidelines to consider when developing your index strategy.

## Clustered Index Indications

One thing that I've found in my travels is that, too often, the database designer (or, as is more often the case, the database design tool) automatically assigns the clustered index to the primary key. This may be correct if the primary key is the primary access path for that table, but there are other good candidates for the clustered index to consider:

- Range searches
- Columns containing a number of duplicate values
- Columns frequently referenced in an ORDER BY
- Columns other than the primary key referenced in join clauses

In most applications, the primary-key column on a table is almost always retrieved in single-row lookups. For single-row lookups, a nonclustered index usually is only going to cost you one I/O more than a similar clustered index. Are you or the users going to notice a difference between three page reads and four page reads? Not at all. However, if you also have a retrieval, such as a lookup on last name, will you notice a difference between scanning 10 percent of the table versus a full table scan? Most definitely.

Clustered indexes can improve performance for range retrievals because the clustered index can be used to set the bounds of a search, even if the query involves a large percentage of the rows in the table. Because the data is in sorted order, SQL Server can use the clustered index to find the starting and ending points of the range, and scan only the data pages within the range. Without a clustered index, the rows could be randomly spread throughout the table, and SQL Server would have to perform a table scan to find all rows within the range.

Assume you have 2,000,000 book titles in a table, with an estimated 1,000,000 books in the price range between $5 and $10, and you want to run the following query:

```
Select title from titles
where price between $5. and $10.
```

If you had a clustered index on the table, the rows would be grouped together by price and you could start your search at the first row where the price is more than $5, scanning the rows in order until you find the last row within the range. Figure 11.2 illustrates this kind of clustered index range retrieval.

**FIGURE 11.2.**

*Clustered index range retrieval.*

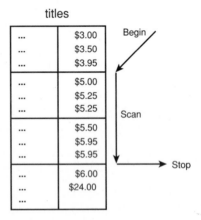

If there are 40 rows per page, with 1,000,000 rows within the range, it would cost you approximately

```
1,000,000 / 40 = 25,000 data page reads
```

plus the number of index page reads required to find the first row in the range. This value should be equal to the number of levels in the index.

The same concept holds true for indexes on columns with a large number of duplicates. With a clustered index, the duplicate values are grouped together. This minimizes the number of pages that would have to be read to retrieve them.

Another good candidate for a clustered index is a column used frequently in queries for sorting the result set. Most sorts require that the table be copied into a *work table* in tempdb for sorting purposes. This incurs additional I/O overhead, and also increases the potential for I/O and locking contention in tempdb. However, if you are performing an order by on clustered index column(s) on a table, you can avoid creating a work table even if the query contains no search arguments. True, the query optimizer performs a table scan at this point. However, the query optimizer recognizes that the rows are in sorted order by the nature of the clustered index, and so can avoid the additional processing to sort the results.

> **NOTE**
>
> If you have a search clause on the table that will be satisfied by a nonclustered index, and an order by on a clustered index column(s), SQL Server must use a work table to sort the results. This is because the data in this case is being retrieved in nonclustered index order, not clustered index order. Therefore, rows are not sorted in the order specified by the order by clause when retrieved.

You also want to try to keep your clustered indexes on relatively static columns to minimize the resorting of data rows when an indexed column is updated. Any time a clustered index row moves, all nonclustered indexes pointing to that row also must be updated.

Clustered indexes also can be more efficient for joins that are nonclustered indexes, because clustered indexes usually are much smaller in size; typically, they are at least one level less. (Refer to Chapter 10 for a detailed discussion of index structures and sizes.) A single page read may not seem like much for a single row retrieval, but add that one additional page to 100,000 join iterations and you're looking at 100,000 additional page reads.

If you require only a single index on a table, it typically is advantageous to make it a clustered index, as the resulting overhead of maintaining clustered indexes during updates, inserts, and deletes can be considerably less than the overhead incurred by nonclustered indexes.

Try to avoid creating clustered indexes on sequential key fields that are inserted monotonically, such as on an identity column. This can create a "hot spot" at the end of the table, which results in locking contention on the last page of the table and the index. Additionally, the clustered index is not reusing available space on preceding data pages, as all new rows sort to the end of the table. This results in wasted space, and your table growing larger than anticipated. I typically recommend that you try to cluster on a data value that is somewhat randomly distributed throughout your table. Some candidates for clustered index keys to randomize your data include the following:

- Date of birth
- Last name, first name
- Zip code
- A random hash key

Spreading your data throughout the table helps minimize page contention as well as space utilization. If the sequential key is your primary key, you still can use a unique, nonclustered index to provide an access path using the index, and maintain the uniqueness of the primary key.

Because there is only one way to physically sort the data in a table, you can have only one clustered index. Any other columns you want to index must be defined with nonclustered indexes.

# Nonclustered Index Indications

Until tables become extremely large, the actual space taken up by a nonclustered index is a minor expense compared to the increased access performance. However, you must remember the impact on performance in an OLTP environment of each additional index defined on a table.

Also, when defining nonclustered indexes, you typically want to define indexes on columns with a low number of duplicates (that is, with low density values) so that they can be used by the query optimizer effectively. A high number of duplicates on a nonclustered index often can make it more expensive in terms of I/O to process the query using the nonclustered index than a table scan. Let's look at an example:

```
Select title from titles
where price between $5. and $10.
```

Again, if you have 1,000,000 rows within the range, those 1,000,000 rows could be randomly scattered throughout the table. Although the index leaf level has all the index rows in sorted order, reading all data rows one at a time would require at least 1,000,000 page reads. Figure 11.3 illustrates this.

**FIGURE 11.3.**

*Nonclustered index range retrieval.*

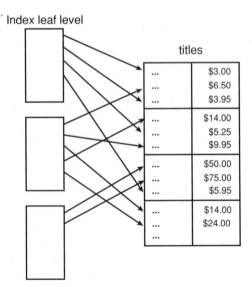

Thus, the I/O estimate for range retrievals using a clustered index is

```
number of matching rows
+ number of index levels
+ number of index pages to be scanned to find rows
```

In this example, if you have 1,000,000 rows in the table, the page cost estimate would be

```
1,000,000 data pages + index pages
```

Contrast this with the cost of a table scan. At 40 rows per page, and with 2,000,000 rows in the table, a full table scan would cost only 50,000 pages. Therefore, a clustered index (25,000 pages) would be most efficient. However, if a clustered index already is defined on a better candidate column, a table scan actually would be more efficient than a nonclustered index for this type of query.

This same principle holds true for nonclustered indexes with a large number of duplicate values (that is, where index density is high). As a general rule of thumb, nonclustered indexes are more effective if less than 10 to 20 percent of the data is to be accessed through the nonclustered index.

Nonclustered indexes also can help improve performance for certain range retrievals by avoiding the need for a work table. This occurs when the column(s) in the order by clause match the column(s) in the nonclustered index, and the index is chosen to satisfy the query. For example, if you had a nonclustered index on city, SQL Server could choose to use the nonclustered index to satisfy the following query:

```
select * from authors
    where city in ("Boston", "San Francisco", "Chicago",
        "New York", "Indianapolis")
    order by city.
```

If the index is used, the data rows are retrieved in nonclustered index order, and you can avoid the additional step of sorting the rows in a work table.

In general, nonclustered indexes are useful for single row lookups, joins, queries on columns that are highly selective, or for queries with small range retrievals. Although they may incur one additional page read per row lookup than a clustered index, they typically are preferable to table scans.

Also, when considering your nonclustered index design, don't overlook the benefits of index covering.

# Index Covering

*Index covering* is a mechanism for using the leaf level of a nonclustered index the way the data page of a clustered index would work. Index covering occurs when all columns referenced in a query are contained in the index itself. Because the nonclustered index contains a leaf row corresponding to every data row in the table, SQL Server can satisfy the query from the leaf rows of the nonclustered index without having to read the data pages.

Because all leaf index pages point to the next page in the leaf-page chain, the leaf level of the index can be scanned just like the data pages in a table. Because the leaf index rows typically are much smaller than the data rows, a nonclustered index that covers a query will be faster than a clustered index on the same columns, due to the fewer number of pages that must be read. Figure 11.4 illustrates scanning the leaf level of the index on `price` to determine the `sum` of `price`.

**FIGURE 11.4.**

*Scanning the leaf pages of a nonclustered index to retrieve data values (index covering).*

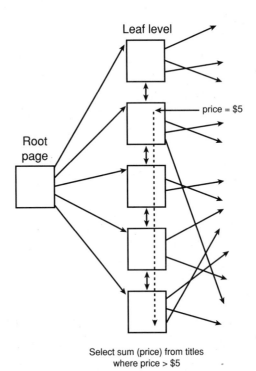

Nonclustered index on price

Leaf level

price = $5

Root page

Select sum (price) from titles
where price > $5

Adding columns to nonclustered indexes to get index covering to occur is a common method of reducing query time. Consider the following query:

```
Select royalty from titles
where price between $10 and $20
```

If you create an index on only the `price` column, SQL Server could find the rows in the index where the price is between $10 and $20, but would have to access the data rows to retrieve `royalty`. If there were 100 rows in the range, the page cost would be 100 data pages plus the number of index pages that would have to be scanned. With an index on `price`, a money field (which in this case is assumed to be not null), the index-row width would be

```
8 bytes + 7 bytes overhead = 15 bytes per row
```

With 15 bytes per row, SQL Server could store approximately 100 rows per page with a 75-percent fill factor, costing one additional index page to be scanned, plus the number of nonleaf pages necessary to reach the leaf page.

> **NOTE**
>
> If you are not clear on how to arrive at these values at this point, please read Chapter 10 for a detailed discussion about index structures and size estimation.

However, if you were to create the index on `price` and `royalty`, the query could be completely satisfied by the index. The number of pages required in this case would be a factor of the number of index leaf pages you would need to scan. An index on `price` and `royalty`, both money fields, would be 16 bytes wide:

```
16 + 7 bytes = 23 bytes per row
```

At 23 bytes per row, SQL Server could store approximately 65 rows per page with a 75-percent fill factor. Because you can scan all 100 qualifying index rows in order in the leaf pages of the index, the I/O cost for this query would be only two leaf pages plus the number of nonleaf levels in the index.

Index covering also provides a number of performance benefits for queries containing aggregates. Typically, for SQL Server to use an index to satisfy a query, at least the first column of the index must be referenced in the `where` clause. However, with aggregates, SQL Server can recognize when an aggregate can be satisfied by a nonclustered index without any `where` clause at all. Consider the following queries:

```
select avg(price) from titles
select count(*) from titles where price > $7.95
select count(*) from titles
```

The first query can use a nonclustered index on `price` and scan all the index leaf rows to calculate the average price. The second query can again use the nonclustered index on `price` to find the first leaf row where the price is greater than $7.95, and then just scan to the end of the index counting the number of leaf rows along the way.

The third query is even more interesting: you just want a count of all the rows in the table. You are not providing any `where` clauses to cause it to use an index, so it must perform a table scan, right? Actually, SQL Server is somewhat clever with this one. Because it knows that any nonclustered index on the table has as many rows as the table itself, it uses the nonclustered index with the smallest row size (and, therefore, the fewest number of pages), and simply counts all the rows in the leaf level of that index.

> **WARNING**
>
> When considering padding your indexes to take advantage of index covering, beware making the index too wide. As index row width approaches data row width, the benefits of covering are lost as the number of pages in the leaf level increases. As the number of pages approaches the number of pages in the table, the number of index levels increases and index scan time begins to approach table scan time.
>
> Also, if you add volatile columns to an index, remember that any changes to the columns in the data rows will cascade into indexes as well.

## Composite Indexes versus Multiple Indexes

At times it may be more beneficial to have many narrow indexes than to have one or more larger composite index(es) on a table. Having more indexes gives the query optimizer more alternatives to look at in deriving a more optimal plan. Remember from earlier in this chapter that distribution steps are stored only for the first column in a composite index. If the first column has poor selectivity, SQL Server may not choose to use the composite index.

Also remember that composite (compound) indexes are selected by SQL Server to satisfy a query only if at least the first column of the index is specified in the where clause. Also, because of the increased width of composite indexes, the index structure consists of more levels and pages than in a narrower index.

On the flip side of things, each additional index negatively impacts update performance.

So how do you determine the optimal index(es) for a table? Here's an example:

```
select pub_id, title, notes from titles
where type = 'Computer'
and price > $15.
```

The index candidates include the following:

- Clustered or nonclustered on type only
- Clustered or nonclustered on price only
- Clustered on type, nonclustered on price
- Nonclustered on type, clustered on price
- Clustered or nonclustered index on type and price
- Clustered or nonclustered index on price and type
- Clustered or nonclustered index on pub_id, title, notes, type, and price

Which are the best options under different circumstances? The answer is entirely dependent on the data distribution and whether the indexes would be unique enough to be worthwhile.

For example, neither `type` nor `price` are unique values, so would a nonclustered index help in any case for either of them? Probably not, if this is a representative sample of the types of queries going against this table. If you had other queries that could take advantage of index covering (for example, `select avg(price)`), a nonclustered index might help.

What about a clustered index? That's the logical choice when a column contains a large number of duplicate values, or if a column is involved in range retrievals. On which column should you create the clustered index, though? The `price` column would probably be the better candidate, as there are more distinct prices than there are book types. Actually, there are very few book types—only six out of a thousand titles. Would an index on `type` be helpful at all? How much I/O would an index on `type` save you in comparison to a table scan? Would the corresponding overhead be worth the minimal time savings?

What if you went the route of creating a composite index on `type` and `price`? That would help you if you were searching on `type` alone, and would help further narrow down the result set when you are searching on `type` and `price`. Unfortunately, that index won't help you when you are searching on just `price`. Conversely, an index on `price` and `type` won't help you when you search on `type` alone.

The question that must be asked at this point is: Which type of query is most critical? Which query must have good response time?

The last index suggested barely rates consideration. The attempt is to get index covering to take place. However, the index row is so wide that any I/O savings from index covering versus accessing the data in the table directly would be negligible.

As you can see from many of the questions raised in this exercise, you cannot examine just one query and devise the best indexing strategy. You must examine all queries going against the database and design your indexes appropriately to support multiple queries.

# Indexing for Multiple Queries

Indexing for multiple queries involves asking many of the questions raised in the previous section. It really requires that you sit down and perform a detailed query analysis and transaction analysis for all applications going against a database.

Once the information has been gathered, you then must begin ranking the queries/transactions in order of importance. The more critical queries should get a higher priority.

Once you have ranked your indexes and decided which ones you are going to tune the system for, you must examine the `where` clauses and see what types of indexes you should create to support those queries. In order to evaluate the index's usefulness, you also need a good understanding of the data and the data distribution. Determine what queries will actually make effective use of an index on a column. Don't assume that just because a column is referenced in a `where` clause it needs an index. Consider, also, whether other columns that are more selective are already indexed, or whether the index, based upon the selectivity, would even be used.

Start out by devising an indexing strategy for each query independently, then begin comparing strategies. Look for overlap between them to find indexes that satisfy more than one query or transaction. This is the point at which you may find a composite index is more useful, or you may find that multiple smaller indexes would be better. Look for crossover between queries on a significant sort column, or a common range retrieval between queries to identify a good candidate for the clustered index. Look for instances, such as aggregates, where you may be able to take advantage of index covering for a number of queries. Keep in mind the issues of over-indexing if you have OLTP activity as well.

Once you have devised your indexing strategy, go ahead and implement and test it, but be prepared to make changes. Few of us rarely, if ever, predict all query performance accurately the first time out. I have actually found trial and error to be an acceptable approach to aiding in index design, as well as an excellent learning process.

Let's look at a simple example and apply this strategy. Assume you have the following customer table:

```
create table customer
   (cust_id   char(6) not null,
    lname     varchar(15) not null,
    fname     varchar(15) not null,
    address   varchar(30) not null,
    city      varchar(30) not null,
    state     char(2) not null,
    zip       char(5) not null,
    zone      char(1) not null)
```

The customer table has 100,000 rows and six distinct zones, with a data distribution as follows:

```
Zone A 70,000 rows
Zone B 15,000 rows
Zone C 10,000 rows
Zone D 3,000 rows
Zone E 1,5000 rows
Zone F 500 rows
```

cust_id is the unique primary key, and states exist entirely within zones; for example, New York is in Zone A only. Here are samples of the critical queries run against the customer table:

```
select * from customer where zone = 'A'
select * from customer where zone = 'C' and state = 'NY'
select * from customer where cust_id = '345678'
select cust_id from customer where lname like "Smith%"
```

Select indexes for each query individually:

■ `select * from customer where zone = 'A'`

For this query, because zone is not a unique value, you have the option of either a clustered index on zone or no index at all. For now, choose the clustered index on zone.

■ `select * from customer where zone = 'C' and state = 'NY'`

Again, `zone` is not a very unique value, and there is also `state`. Because states exist within a zone, you can always query `state` by limiting the result set to `zone` first. This is a good candidate for a composite index, and again, due to the poor selectivity, you can opt for a clustered index.

■ `select * from customer where cust_id = '345678'`

   `cust_id` is a unique primary key. Let's follow the normal trend and choose a clustered index on the primary key.

■ `select cust_id from customer where lname like "Smith%"`

   Again, you have a range-type retrieval with, more than likely, poor selectivity. Again, choose a clustered index on `lname`.

Let's examine what we've got so far:

■ Clustered on `zone`
■ Clustered on `zone, state`
■ Clustered on `cust_id`
■ Clustered on `lname`

Obviously, there's some overlap here. Make the trade-offs and decide which one should be your clustered index. Because `cust_id` is a unique key involved in a single-row lookup, there is no appreciable benefit of having a clustered index on it when there are other candidates for the clustered index.

Next, you must decide between a clustered index on `zone` and `lname`. If you look closely at the `lname` query, you see that it's only retrieving a list of `cust_id`s from `customer` for a list of last names. You could get away with a nonclustered index on `lname, cust_id`, which would cover the query. An index that covers a query is actually more efficient than a similarly defined clustered index.

Now you're left with a decision on the clustered index on `zone`. Because you have two queries that rely on `zone`, but one that needs to limit the result to a state within a zone, make the clustered index on `zone` and `state`. This way, one composite index can effectively satisfy two different queries.

To summarize, the indexes you create initially will be

■ Clustered index on `zone, state`
■ Nonclustered index on `lname, cust_id`
■ Unique nonclustered index on `cust_id`

Remember, you cannot tune for everything and everyone. You won't be able to make everyone happy. At some point you will have to make a trade-off of some sort:

■ OLTP performance needs versus DSS response time
■ Critical query versus noncritical query

- Frequently run query versus rarely run query
- Online queries versus batch queries

The art is balancing the trade-offs effectively such that the system is deemed a success.

# Summary

The most important aspect to improving SQL Server performance is proper index design. Choosing the appropriate indexes that will be used by SQL Server to process queries involves thoroughly understanding the queries and transactions being run against the database, understanding the bias of the data, understanding how SQL Server uses indexes, and staying aware of the performance implications of overindexing tables in an OLTP environment. In general, consider using clustered indexes to support range retrievals or when data needs to be sorted in clustered index order; use nonclustered indexes for single or discrete row retrievals or when you can take advantage of index covering.

You also will need to have a good understanding of the SQL Server query optimizer to know how it uses indexes and index statistics to develop query plans. This might be a good time to read the next chapter, "Understanding the Query Optimizer."

And always remember: Keep your index statistics up-to-date!

# Understanding the Query Optimizer

# 12

*Query optimization* is the process of analyzing individual queries and determining the best way to process them. This involves understanding the underlying storage structures, and the indexes defined on them, to determine if there is a way to process the query more efficiently. To achieve this end, SQL Server uses a cost-based query optimizer. *Cost-based* means the query optimizer determines the query plan that can access the data with the least accumulated elapsed time. The query optimizer examines parsed SQL queries and, based on information about the objects involved, outputs a query plan. The query plan is the set of steps to be carried out to execute the query.

To allow the query optimizer to do its job properly, you must understand what types of queries can be optimized, and learn techniques to help the query optimizer choose the best query path. Having a good understanding of the query optimizer will help you to write better queries, choose better indexes, and detect potential performance problems.

> **NOTE**
>
> To better understand the concepts to be presented in this chapter, you should have a reasonable understanding of how SQL Server manages data objects and indexes, and how indexes affect performance. If you haven't already read Chapters 10, "Understanding SQL Server Storage Structures," and 11, "Designing Indexes for Performance," you should review them now.

# Optimization Goals

The primary goal of the query optimizer is to find the cheapest access path to minimize the total time to process the query. To achieve this goal, the query optimizer analyzes the query and searches for access paths and techniques primarily to:

- Minimize logical page access
- Minimize physical page access

Disk I/O is the most significant factor in query-processing costs. Therefore, the fewer number of physical and logical I/Os performed, the faster the query plan.

# Query Optimization Steps

When SQL Server processes the query, it performs the following steps:

1. Parses and normalizes the query validating syntax and object references
2. Optimizes the query and generates the query plan
3. Compiles the query plan
4. Executes the query plan and returns the results to the user

The optimization step (step 2) is broken down into multiple phases:

Phase 1—Query Analysis

1. Find the SARG.

2. Find the ORs.

3. Find the joins.

Phase 2—Index Selection

4. Choose the best index for each SARG.

5. Choose the best method for ORs.

6. Choose the best indexes for any join clauses.

7. Choose the best index to use for each table.

Phase 3—Join Order Selection

8. Evaluate join orders.

9. Compute the costs.

10. Evaluate other server options for resolving joins (using reformatting strategy). See the section on "Reformatting Strategy" for more information.

Phase 4—Plan Selection

If a query is a single-table query containing no join clauses, SQL Server skips Phase 3, "Join Order Selection," and jumps directly to Phase 4, "Plan Selection."

# Query Analysis

The first step in query optimization is to analyze each table in the query to identify all search arguments (SARGs), OR clauses, and join clauses. The SARGs, OR clauses, and join clauses are used in the next phase to select useful indexes to satisfy a query. For SQL Server to use an index to satisfy a query, at least the first column of the index must match a SARG, OR clause, or join column.

## Identifying SARGs

SARGs exist to enable the optimizer to limit the rows searched to satisfy a query. The general goal is to match a SARG with an index to avoid a table scan. A search argument is defined as a where clause comparing a column to a constant. The format of a SARG is this:

```
Column operator constant_expression [AND...][MC1]
```

The valid operators for a SARG are =, >, <, >=, and <=. The inequality operator (!= or <>) is a valid operator but is a SARG that cannot be optimized by the query optimizer. If you use an inequality operator, the optimizer recognizes that statement as a SARG, but the statement cannot be used to match a value against an index. The optimizer will always use a table scan to resolve an inequality SARG unless the query can be solved by index covering. (See Chapter 11 for more detail on index covering.)

> **TIP**
>
> If you have a search clause containing an inequality operator, try to rewrite it as a SARG so that it can be recognized as a search argument by the query optimizer. For example, consider the following query:
>
> ```
> select title from titles where price != 0
> ```
>
> If there is a business rule enforced on the table to prevent any rows where the price is less than zero, the query could be rewritten as
>
> ```
> select title from titles where price > 0
> ```
>
> and still return the same result set. The difference is that the second version contains a valid SARG that the optimizer can recognize and consider for matching with an index to satisfy the query. True, it may still result in a table scan, but at least it gives the query optimizer the option to consider, which wouldn't have happened with the inequality operator.

Multiple SARGs can be combined with the AND clause. If an OR clause is specified, the SARG is treated differently, as you see in a little bit. Here are examples of valid search arguments:

- `flag = 7`
- `salary > 100000`
- `city = 'Saratoga' and state = 'NY'`

As I stated before, an inequality operator is a non-optimizable search argument. Additionally, if any operation is performed on the column, the column is ignored as a search argument by the query optimizer. Some examples of invalid SARGs:

- `gender != 'M'`
- `lname = fname` (comparison against a column, not a constant)
- `ytd/months > 1000` (operation performed on column)
- `ytd/12 = 1000` (operation performed on the column)

> **TIP**
>
> The last SARG, `ytd/12 = 1000`, can be rewritten to be treated as `ytd = 12000`. When tuning system performance, keep an eye out for non-optimizable or invalid SARGs. They are a common cause of poor performance, as they prevent an index from being used. Many times, invalid SARGs can be rewritten as valid SARGs.

# Improvising SARGs

Some SQL statements do not appear to follow the syntax for a valid SARG, but can be improvised as SARGs by the query optimizer. Here are some clauses that can be improvised as SARGs:

- BETWEEN becomes >= AND <=

  ```
  price between $10 and $20 becomes:
  price > = $10 and price <= $20
  100 between lo_val and hi_val becomes:
  lo_val <= 100 and hi_val >= 100
  ```

- LIKE becomes >= AND <

  ```
  au_lname like "Sm%" becomes:
  au_lname >= "Sm" and au_lname < "Sn"
  ```

The LIKE clause can be improvised as a SARG as long as the first character in the string is a constant. The following statement cannot be improvised into a SARG:

```
au_lname like "%son"
```

Also, in SQL Server 10.0 and later, be careful of the following BETWEEN clause:

```
price BETWEEN $20 and $10
```

This will be improvised by the query optimizer into

```
price >= $20 and <= $10
```

which is an empty result set. SQL Server doesn't generate any error or warning message when this code is encountered.

> **TIP**
>
> In releases of SQL Server prior to 10.0, the optimizer would switch the upper and lower bounds of a BETWEEN, if necessary, so that the higher value was the upper bound. Unfortunately, this behavior is in violation of the ANSI standard. It was changed in version 10.0 to comply.
>
> If you are porting an existing application from a previous version of SQL Server to System 10 or 11, you may want to check any queries containing BETWEEN clauses to verify that the lesser value is always defined as the lower bound.

In some cases, the column in a SARG may be compared with a constant expression rather than a single constant value. The constant expression can be an arithmetic operation, built-in function, string concatenation, local variable, or subquery result. As long as the left side of the SARG contains a column alone, it's still a valid SARG.

## Constant Expressions in SARGs

The issue with a SARG containing a constant expression is that the query optimizer does not know the value of the expression prior to optimization. The value is not known until the query is executed. Therefore, the query optimizer cannot make use of the distribution steps, and must use the density value for the index to estimate the number of matching rows. These types of SARGs typically contain subqueries, local variables, built-in functions, or arithmetic operations.

The following are examples of constant expressions that cannot be evaluated prior to optimization:

- `due_date > getdate()`
- `ytd_sales < 100000/12`
- `lname like "Smith" + "%"%`
- `price < (select avg(price) from titles)`
- `qty < @inventory`

## OR Clauses

The next statement the query optimizer looks for in the query is an OR clause. OR clauses are SARGs combined with an OR statement rather than an AND statement, and are treated differently than a standard SARG. The format of an OR clause is

```
SARG or SARG [or ...]
```

with all columns involved in the OR belonging to the same table.

The IN statement

```
column IN ( constant1, constant2, ...)
```

also is treated as an OR clause, becoming:

```
column = constant1 OR column = constant2 OR ...
```

Examples of OR clauses include the following:

- `where au_lname = 'Smith'  or au_fname = 'Fred'`
- `where (type = 'business' and price > $25) OR pub_id = "1234"`
- `where au_lname in ('Smith', 'Jones', 'N/A')`

An OR clause is a disjunction: all rows matching either of the two criteria appear in the result set. Any row matching both criteria should appear only once.

# The *OR* Strategy

An OR clause can be handled by either a table scan or by using the OR strategy. Using a table scan, SQL Server reads every row in the table and applies all search criteria to each row. Any row that matches one of the criteria is put into the result set.

However, if indexes exist on both columns in the OR clause, SQL Server evaluates the possibility of applying the OR strategy.

The OR strategy essentially breaks the query into two or more parts, executes each part using the available index, and retrieves the matching row IDs, unioning the row IDs together to remove duplicates. Finally, SQL Server uses the row IDs as a dynamic index to retrieve the final result set from the base table.

If any one of the parts of an OR clause requires a table scan to be processed, or if a table scan is cheaper than using the available index, SQL Server simply uses a table scan to resolve the whole query, rather than applying the OR strategy.

Let's see how SQL Server would handle the following query, given that an index exists on both au_lname and state:

```
select * from authors
  where au_lname = "Smith"
    or state = "NY"
```

The OR strategy would be applied as follows:

1. Estimate the cost of a table scan.
2. Break the query into multiple parts, for example:
   ```
   select * from authors where au_lname = "Smith"
   select * from authors where state = "NY"
   ```
3. Execute each query and get the row IDs into a work table in tempdb as a dynamic index.
4. Union the row IDs to remove any duplicates.
5. Use the dynamic index to retrieve all qualifying rows from the work table.

Figure 12.1 illustrates using a dynamic index to resolve an OR clause.

SQL Server applies the OR strategy only if the sum of the total I/Os to use the OR strategy is less than the number of I/Os required to perform a table scan.

**FIGURE 12.1.**

*Using a dynamic index to resolve an OR clause.*

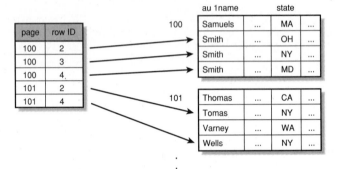

**Join Clauses**

The last type of statement the query optimizer looks for during the query analysis phase is the join clause. A join clause is a where clause in the format

```
Table1.Column Operator Table2.Column
```

A join clause involves two tables, except in the case of a self-join. Even in a self-join, however, you must specify the table twice in the query; for example

```
select "Employee" = e.name, "Manager" = m.name
    from empl e, empl m
    where e.empl_id = m.mgr_id
```

In some cases, certain types of subqueries can be flattened and treated as an *existence join*. Other types of subqueries must be processed differently. The next section discusses how SQL Server processes subqueries.

# Subquery Processing

The query optimizer can use multiple approaches to processing subqueries to improve performance. Subqueries can be processed as:

- Flattened subqueries
- Materialized subqueries
- Correlated subqueries

## Flattening Subqueries

SQL Server will sometimes attempt to flatten a subquery into a join when possible to allow the optimizer to select the optimal join order, rather than being forced to process the query inside-out. In SQL Server versions 10.0 and later, any query containing a subquery introduced with an IN, ANY, or EXISTS predicate is flattened into an existence join. This occurs unless the outer query also contains an OR clause, or unless the subquery is correlated or contains one or more aggregates. This allows the query optimizer to select the optimal join order, rather than being forced to process the query inside-out. (See the section on "Correlated Subqueries" for more about correlated subqueries.)

An existence join can be optimized the same way as a regular join—except that, with an existence join, as soon as a matching row is found in the inner table the value TRUE is returned and SQL Server stops looking for further matches for that row in the outer table, moving on to the next row. For example, the following query would be converted to an existence join:

```
select pub_name from publishers
    where pub_id in (select pub_id from titles where type = "business")
```

This behavior was modified in SQL Server version 10.0 from previous versions of SQL Server. Prior to 10.0, the preceding query would have been flattened into a normal join like the following:

```
select pub_name from publishers p, titles t
where p.pub_id = t.pub_idand t.type = "business"
```

These joins would be processed essentially the same way, but the result sets would be different.

If there are four rows in the titles table, and you use a regular join where type is equal to business, you get four rows in the result set. However, you get only two distinct publisher names. Using an existence join, you get only the two rows for the publishers who have a match in the titles table.

If SQL Server cannot flatten the subquery into an existence join, the query must be processed inside-out; that is, the subquery result set must be formed first and then joined with the outer query. Inside-out processing is used whenever the subquery is introduced with the quantified predicates of NOT IN, ALL, or NOT EXISTS. These types of queries require the creation of a work table to process the subquery. For example, the following query:

```
select pub_name from publishers
where pub_id not in (select pub_id from titles where type = "business")
```

actually is processed by the SQL Server query optimizer as follows:

```
select p.pub_id, enny = any(t.pub_id)
    into #worktable
    from publishers p, title t
    where p.pub_id = t.pub_id
    and t.type = 'business'

select pub_name
    from publishers p, #worktable w
    where p.pub_id = w.pub_id
    and enny = 0
```

A subquery also must be processed inside-out if it is an expression subquery that must be materialized first.

## Flattening Expression Subqueries

SQL Server can also treat subqueries contained in a query's select list or that are introduced by >, >=, <, <=, =, or != as expression subqueries. Expression subqueries can be flattened into equijoins if the following are true:

- ■ The subquery joins on unique columns or returns unique columns.
- ■ There is a unique index on the columns.

## Materialized Subqueries

If the outer query compares a column against the result of a subquery using any of the comparison operators (=, >, <, >=, <=, or !=) and the subquery cannot be flattened into an expression subquery, the results of the subquery must be resolved—that is, *materialized*—before comparison against the outer table column. The query optimizer must process these types of queries "inside-out."

Here is an example of this type of query:

```
select title from titles
    where total_sales = (select max(total_sales) from titles)
```

The subquery must be resolved first to find the value to compare against total_sales in the outer query. The subquery expression is processed only once, and can be treated as an optimizable SARG. These types of subqueries are materialized in this way only if the subquery is not correlated.

# Correlated Subqueries

A correlated subquery contains a reference to an outer table in a join clause in the subquery. For example, the following is a correlated subquery:

```
select col_a from table_1 t1
    where col_b = (select sum(col_x)
                        from table_2 where col_y = t1.col_c)
```

To process a correlated subquery in System 10, SQL Server processes them inside-out, using an intermediate work table to hold the subquery results. The work table is grouped on the correlation columns. For example, the previous query becomes this:

```
select t1.col_c, summ=sum(t2.col_x)
    into #worktable
    from table_1 t1, table_2 t2
    where t2.col_c = t1.col_c

select t1.col_a from table_1 t1, #worktable w
    where t1.col_c = w.col_c
    and t1.col_b = w.summ
```

# System 11 Subquery Performance Enhancements

In the System 10 SQL Server, there were some performance issues with how the query optimizer handled certain types of subqueries. Essentially, SQL Server used two types of processing strategies: change the subquery to an existence join, or process the subquery inside out (that is, form a subquery result set first, then join with the outer query). These strategies resulted in the following performance issues:

- System 10 subqueries provided poor response time when using inside-out strategy due to work-table processing.
- The result set for a subquery could be larger than necessary if there was a restrictive join in outer query.
- Inside-out processing required two join operations: one to form the subquery result set, another to form the outer result.

The query optimizer has been modified in System 11 to address these performance issues. It still materializes and flattens subqueries when those are the appropriate strategies, but also now considers using the following optimization techniques for subqueries:

- Treat unflattened subqueries as expressions.
- Apply "short circuiting" to avoid unnecessary subquery processing.
- Use subquery-results caching.

These are explored next.

## Subqueries as Expressions

In System 11, unflattened subqueries are modeled as expressions. The subquery expression is evaluated once for every row in the outer table in the query and returns a value every time it is evaluated. This method addresses some correctness problems with System 10 subqueries because it more closely matches the ISO/ANSI definition of subqueries.

This is an "outside-in" approach to processing subqueries. The subquery is evaluated for every qualifying row in the outer table. Using an "inside-out" processing strategy, most nested aggregates and subqueries were evaluated first before executing the outer query. Thus, the subquery was evaluated at least once before using any join restrictions from the outer query.

## Short-Circuiting Subqueries

Short-circuiting is a method used to avoid unnecessary execution of unflattened (that is, expression) subqueries. If the expression subquery is combined with other search arguments, the other search arguments are evaluated first, before the subquery is executed. The query optimizer shuffles the where clauses so that the subquery is at the end. If the subquery is part of an AND list, and any other clause is FALSE, the subquery execution is skipped. If the subquery is part of an OR list, and any other clause is TRUE, the subquery execution is skipped. For example, the following query:

```
select col1 from table1
where not exists (select * from table2
                      where col2 = table1.col3)
  and col4 = 10
```

is transformed to this:

```
select col1 from table1
where col4 = 10
  and not exists (select * from table2
                      where col2 = table1.col3)
```

Processing of the subquery is skipped for any row where col4 is not equal to 10.

## Subquery-Results Caching

For outside-in subquery processing, System 11 uses an in-memory subquery cache to store the result values of each subsequent execution of the subquery. This helps improve performance when there may be duplicate values in join or correlation columns, especially if the correlation values are ordered or contain few distinct values. (A correlation column is a column used in a subquery from a table in the from clause of the outer query.) If the correlation or join columns are unique, caching neither hurts nor helps query processing. The cache pages are tacked onto the query plan for the subquery, so the query plan is a bit larger.

The subquery-results cache contains a combination of the values in the correlation columns and the join columns in a quantified predicate subquery. These correlation or join column cache values are used as lookup keys for subsequent executions of the subquery. When a query runs, it checks first to see whether a needed subquery-result value is found in the subquery-results cache before going against the table. This can save unnecessary subquery processing if the value for the outer row join or correlation column was found previously.

While processing the subquery, the query optimizer evaluates the effectiveness of the subquery cache. If the cache hit ratio is low (that is, if the lookup values are not being found in the cache), the query optimizer determines that the subquery cache is not useful, and reduces it in size. You can examine the size and usefulness of the subquery cache by executing the set statistics subquerycache on command. For example:

```
select count(*) from titles
where price > all (select price from titles where advance > 1000)


----------0


Statement: 1  Subquery: 1  cache size: 12  hits: 6  misses: 12
```

You can see that for this query the subquery cache was used. Twelve rows were stored in the cache (cache size: 12). There were six hits and 12 misses against the cache rows.

# Index Selection

Once the query-analysis phase of optimization is complete and all SARGs, OR clauses, and join clauses have been identified, the next step is to match them up with any available indexes and estimate the I/O costs. The index I/O costs are compared with each other and against the cost of a table scan to determine the least expensive access path.

If no useful indexes are found to match a SARG, OR clause, or join, a table scan must be performed on the table. A table scan is the fall-back tactic for the query optimizer to use if there is no better way of resolving a query.

## Evaluating Indexes for SARGs or OR clauses

To estimate the I/O costs of using an index for a SARG or OR clause, the optimizer uses the index statistics stored on the distribution page for the index. If no distribution page is available, or if there is no index on the column in the SARG, the query optimizer uses built-in percentages for estimating the number of matching rows. Here are the built-in percentages the query optimizer assumes for the different equality operators:

| Operator | Row Estimate Percentage |
|---|---|
| = | 10% |
| BETWEEN, > AND < | 25% |
| >, <, >=, <= | 33% |

So, for example, consider a query containing the following search clause:

```
lname = "Smith"
```

Without any index statistics, the query optimizer would assume that 10 percent of the rows in the table would match the search value of Smith. If index statistics are available and the SARG contains a constant value, the query optimizer would use the distribution-step information to estimate the number of rows that match the constant value. If the SARG contains a constant expression that cannot be resolved until query execution, the query optimizer bases its estimates on the index density.

> **NOTE**
>
> In previous releases of SQL Server, certain data-type mismatches also prevented the query optimizer from using distribution steps to estimate the number of matching rows in a query.
>
> With all current releases and for any of the arithmetic data types, if a legal implicit conversion can take place, SQL Server performs the datatype conversion on the search value so that it matches the column datatype. The query optimizer then uses the distribution steps for its row estimates. This also is true for comparing a character string against a datetime column.
>
> However, this is not the case when comparing a varchar against a char. This is easy to do in a stored procedure. Remember, also, that a char column that allows nulls actually is stored as a varchar. Define any stored-procedure parameter used in a SARG to match such a column as a varchar.
>
> Also, do not use the convert function in a SARG to try to match datatypes. Remember that any system function used in a SARG does not have its value evaluated until execution time, and index densities are used rather than distribution steps.

If a SARG contains the equality (=) operator and there is a unique index matching the SARG, the query optimizer estimates that one and only one row matches the SARG.

> **NOTE**
>
> For a more thorough discussion of index selection and index statistics, please refer to the preceding chapter.

# Evaluating Indexes for Join Clauses

If the query contains a join clause, SQL Server determines whether any usable indexes exist that match the column(s) in the join clause. Because the query optimizer has no way of determining what value(s) will join between rows in the table at optimization time, it cannot use the distribution steps to estimate the number of matching rows. Instead, it uses the index density, which is an estimate of the number of matching rows in the table for any given value.

If the index density is not available, the query optimizer estimates the number of matching rows as this:

```
1 / number of rows in smaller table
```

For example, if the query is joining an orders table with 1 million rows to a customers table containing 5,000 rows, the join selectivity would be this:

```
1/5000 or .0002
```

Therefore, for every row in the customers table, you would expect to find

```
1,000,000 * .0002 = 200
```

matching rows in the orders table (200 orders/per customer × 5000 customers = 1,000,000 orders).

If there is an index on the join column(s), the index density value would be used to estimate the number of rows per join between the two tables. Index density is based on the percentage of the number of unique values in an index. If you had 1,000 unique values in the orders table, the density would be

```
1/1,000 or .001
```

Using this density value, for each row in the customers table you would expect

```
1,000,000 * .001 = 1,000
```

rows to match for any single customer.

A lower density value indicates a more selective index. As the density approaches 1, the index becomes less selective and approaches uselessness as a possible access path.

# Ranking Indexes

Unless the OR strategy is applied, SQL Server uses only one index per table to satisfy a query. The index chosen is the one that provides the most efficient access path to the table—that is, the index that requires the fewest number of I/Os to solve the query for that table.

Using available or built-in statistics, the query optimizer estimates the number of page reads necessary to retrieve the estimated number of rows using the candidate index. It then ranks candidate indexes to determine the index that results in the least amount of I/O.

Keep in mind that there are instances (for example, large-range retrievals on a nonclustered-index column) where a table scan may be cheaper than a candidate index in terms of total I/O.

# Estimating Page I/O

If there is no usable index, the query optimizer performs a table scan. The estimate of the total I/O cost is the number of pages in the table, which is stored in the object allocation map (OAM) page for the table.

If there is a clustered index, the I/O cost estimate is the number of index levels in the clustered index plus the number of pages to scan. The number of pages to scan is based on the estimated number of rows multiplied by the number of rows per page.

For a nonclustered index, I/O cost estimate is

> the number of index levels
> + the number of leaf pages
> + the number of qualifying rows (number of data page reads)

The number of leaf pages is based upon the estimated number of rows multiplied by the number of leaf index rows per page. Because each leaf-index row requires a separate data-page lookup to retrieve the data row, the number of data-page reads is equal to the number of matching rows in the leaf-index level. (See Chapter 11 for more information on leaf pages and leaf indexes.)

For a unique index and an equality join, the I/O cost estimate is one data page plus the number of index levels traversed to access the data page.

# Index Covering

When analyzing a query, the query optimizer also considers any possibility to take advantage of index covering. *Index covering* is a mechanism for using the leaf level of a nonclustered index in the same way as the data page of a clustered index. The leaf level of the nonclustered index must contain all the data necessary to satisfy the query (that is, all columns contained in the select list and SARGs). (Index covering is explored in Chapter 11.)

This can save a significant amount of I/O if the query does not have to access the data page. In most cases, a nonclustered index that covers a query will be faster than a similarly defined clustered index.

Index covering has particular benefits with aggregates. SQL Server attempts to solve aggregates using index covering whenever possible, even when the query contains no SARGs. For example, this query:

```
select avg (price) from titles
```

can be satisfied by scanning the leaf rows of a nonclustered index on price to determine the average.

If index covering can take place in a query, the query optimizer considers it and estimates the I/O cost of using the nonclustered index to cover the query. The estimated I/O cost of index covering is the number of index levels plus the number of leaf index pages to scan. The number of leaf index pages to scan is based on the estimated number of rows multiplied by the number of leaf index rows per page.

# Join Order Processing

If the query contains any join clauses, the next phase in query optimization is to determine the best possible join order.

The query optimizer evaluates all possible join orders and, for each join order considered, estimates the cost of the different index alternatives for each table in the join. If no useful indexes are available on one or more of the tables involved in the join, SQL Server also considers applying the reformatting strategy to solve the query efficiently. (This topic is covered in the section on "Reformatting Strategy.")

The optimal query plan for a join involves picking the best indexes for each table and the most efficient order to process the tables in the join.

## Determining Join Order

Joins are performed as a set of nested loops, often referred to as *nested iterations*. Essentially, for each matching row in the outer table, SQL Server performs a nested iteration on the inner table to find all rows matching the current outer row. This is repeated for each row in the outer table.

To process a nested iteration, SQL Server needs to determine the optimal order in which to process the tables. Consider the following query:

```
select au_lname, au_fname, title
   from authors a, titleauthor ta, titles t
   where a.au_id = ta.au_id
   and ta.title_id = t.title_id
```

Figure 12.2 shows the possible join orders that could be used to process this query.

**FIGURE 12.2.**

*Possible join orders for a query joining the* titles*,* titleauthor, *and* authors *tables.*

```
titles  ———▶  titleauthor  ———▶  authors

authors  ———▶  titleauthor  ———▶  titles
```

Because the SQL Server query optimizer is a cost-based optimizer, the order of the tables in the from clause does not dictate the order in which the tables are joined. When processing a join, the query optimizer evaluates all reasonable join permutations and estimates the total I/O cost, in terms of I/O time. The plan resulting in the lowest estimate of I/O time is the plan chosen.

However, as the number of tables increases, the number of permutations that the query optimizer must evaluate increases as a factorial of the number of tables in the query. Table 12.1 shows this.

**Table 12.1. Number of possible join permutations based upon number of tables in the query.**

| # of Tables | # of Join Permutations |
| --- | --- |
| 2 | 2! = 2 |
| 3 | 3! = 6 |
| 4 | 4! = 24 |
| 5 | 5! = 120 |
| 6 | 6! = 720 |
| 7 | 7! = 5,040 |
| 8 | 8! = 40,320 |
| 9 | 9! = 362,880 |
| 10 | 10! = 3,628,800 |
| 11 | 11! = 39,916,800 |
| 12 | 12! = 479,001,600 |
| 13 | 13! = 6,227,020,800 |
| 14 | 14! = 87,178,291,200 |
| 15 | 15! = 1,307,674,368,000 |
| 16 | 16! = 20,922,789,888,000 |

## Large, Multi-Table Queries

To minimize the number of permutations that must be examined, SQL Server breaks up joins of more than four tables into all possible groups of four to evaluate the join permutations within each group of four. This is an iterative approach, repeated until the join order for all the tables is determined. The purpose of this approach is to limit the number of permutations the query optimizer has to consider.

The algorithm used by SQL Server to process joins of more than four tables is as follows:

1. Group the tables into all possible groups of four.
2. For each group of four tables, estimate the join cost for each permutation possible.

3. Determine the group of four with the cheapest permutation. The first table of that permutation is marked as the outer table and taken out of the list of tables.

4. Repeat steps 1 through 3 for the remaining tables until only four tables remain, and estimate the join cost for those four as one final step.

Let's look at an example of this algorithm in practice. Assume a query that joins six tables: T1, T2, T3, T4, T5, and T6. Breaking the six tables into all possible groups of four, you would have

```
T1T2T3T4, T1T2T3T5, T1T2T3T6, T1T2T4T5, T1T2T4T6,
T1T2T5T6, T1T3T4T5, T1T3T4T6, T1T3T5T6, T1T4T5T6,
T2T3T4T5, T2T3T4T6, T2T3T5T6, T2T4T5T6, T3T4T5T6
```

For each group of four, find the lowest cost permutation and make that table the outermost. Assuming that the best permutation is T3T5T4T2, table T3 is set as the outermost table. The remaining tables are regrouped into all possible groups of four, giving us

```
T1T2T4T5, T1T2T4T6, T1T2T5T6, T1T4T5T6, T2T4T5T6
```

Assume that the lowest cost permutation out of each group of four is T4T2T5T6. Table T4 now becomes the second-outermost table in the query.

You now are left with four tables, which the query optimizer evaluates as if they were in a normal, four-table join. Assume that the best join order for the remaining four tables is T5T2T1T6. This join order then is appended to the two previously determined outer tables (T3 and T4), resulting in the final join order for the entire query being

```
T3,T4,T5,T2,T1,T6
```

This may seem like a lot of work, but the actual number of permutations examined can be substantially less, especially when the number of tables in the query exceeds eight or more tables. And, as the query optimizer still is looking at all possible combinations of four tables for all tables listed in the from clause, the order of the tables in the from clause is irrelevant.

The main benefit to this approach is the savings in CPU time to identify the best join order. The resulting number of combinations examined with this approach is the sum of

```
N! / (N-4)!
```

for each iteration. For this example, the number of permutations considered would be

```
6!/(6-4)! = 720/2 = 360
5!/(5-4)! = 120/1 = 120
4! = 24
```

The total sum of all permutations considered is

```
360 + 120 + 24 = 504 permutations
```

This represents a savings of 30 percent. As the number of tables increases, the savings become even more significant, as shown in Table 12.2.

**Table 12.2. Savings in number of permutations examined using modified approach to evaluate the join order.**

| # of tables (N) | N! | Optimizer method | Savings |
|---|---|---|---|
| 6 | 720 | 504 | 30% |
| 7 | 5040 | 1,344 | 73.3% |
| 8 | 40320 | 3,024 | 92.5% |
| 9 | 362880 | 6,048 | 98.3% |
| 10 | 3628800 | 11,088 | 99.7% |
| 16 | 20922789888000 | 148,512 | 99.999% |

**TIP**

Even using the modified approach to identifying join permutations, large multi-table queries still are rather costly to optimize. Sometimes the time spent optimizing the query can be greater than the time spent processing the query.

In some earlier releases of SQL Server, the query optimizer didn't do such a good job of handling queries with more than four tables. The order of the tables in the from clause would sometimes influence the query plan chosen. This forced developers to write queries in a specific manner, or sometimes to break queries with more than four tables into smaller queries.

The more recent releases of SQL Server, however, seem to handle multi-table queries quite well. In testing that I and others have done, the query optimizer consistently tends to arrive at the most optimal plan regardless of the table order. It's typically not necessary to break up large queries anymore.

What you may be concerned with, however, is the time spent optimizing the query. In order to reduce the optimization time, you might consider putting the query into a stored procedure. With the query in a stored procedure, the query plan is determined only for the first execution, and then reused for subsequent executions. This can provide significant time savings if the query is repeatedly executed.

Another alternative is to override the join ordering phase of the query optimizer using the forceplan option once you have determined the optimal join order for a query. For details and warnings on using the forceplan option, please read Chapter 16, "Overriding the SQL Server Optimizer."

# Increasing the Number of Tables in Join Permutations

System 11 provides the ability to have the optimizer evaluate join permutations using more than four tables at a time. You can increase the number of tables examined at a time using the set table count option:

```
set table count number_of_tables
```

You can specify an integer value between 1 and 8. If you decrease the value, you reduce the chances of the optimizer finding the most efficient query plan. Increasing the value increases the number of tables the optimizer considers at one time to evaluate join orders. However, it also may increase the amount of time it takes to optimize the query. For example, for a query joining eight tables, the optimizer would look at 3,024 total permutations using the four-tables-at-a-time approach, but would have to examine 40,320 permutations examining all eight tables at a time. For more information on using this option, refer to Chapter 16.

## Estimating Join Order Costs

For each join permutation considered, the query optimizer must estimate the cost of that particular join order in terms of total I/O. For comparison purposes, the query optimizer estimates the total logical I/Os per table and the total number of physical I/Os per table. It then sums the total logical and physical I/Os for the entire permutation, and translates that into an estimate of total elapsed time. The total elapsed time estimate is used only for comparison purposes, and does not reflect the actual time it would take for the query to run.

Currently, SQL Server rates a logical read as 2 ms and a physical read as 18 ms, a ratio between logical and physical of 1 to 9. These are fixed values regardless of which platform you are running on.

The relative performance of a nested iteration is directly proportional to the number of times the inner query is done and the number of pages per lookup. The algorithm for determining the total number of I/Os for a nested iteration is as follows:

```
number of pages accessed in outer table
+ (number of matching rows in outer table
      × number of pages per lookup in inner table)
```

The total cost of the nested iteration is the total number of logical reads multiplied by 2, plus the total number of physical reads multiplied by 18.

When determining the total I/O cost, SQL Server makes no assumptions as to whether the table currently resides in cache or not (by the time the query actually executes, the table could have been flushed from cache). It always assumes the first access of the table will be a physical page read, and any subsequent accesses or iterations on the table will be logical page reads. For every physical page read, there is a corresponding logical page read.

The only time that the data cache is considered is when there is insufficient cache to keep the inner table in memory. When this is the case, the query optimizer assumes that, because the table cannot stay in cache, all accesses to the inner table will be physical I/Os.

> **NOTE**
>
> System 11 provides a number of enhancements including defining cache partitions, binding tables to cache partitions, and prefetch strategies for performing large I/Os. The query optimizer in System 11 does make assumptions based upon the cache configuration whether a table will remain in cache or whether large I/Os can be used when performing physical I/Os. These strategies will be factored into the total I/O cost of a query. The effect of cache and prefetch strategies on query cost estimates are covered later in this chapter in the "System 11 Query Optimization Enhancements" section.

## Join Cost Estimating Examples

Let's consider a few examples of possible join permutations the query optimizer would consider for the following query:

```
select * from titles t, titleauthor ta
 where t.title_id = ta.title_id and royaltyper < 50
```

For these examples, make the following assumptions:

- 15,000 rows in titles (15 rows/page), 1,000 pages
- 25,000 rows in titleauthor (50 rows/page), 500 pages
- Clustered index statistics on royaltyper in the titleauthor table indicate that 20 percent of the rows have a royaltyper that is less than 50.
- There is sufficient data cache to keep both tables in memory.

### Example 1: *titles* to *titleauthor*, no indexes

The first plan the query optimizer looks at is joining from the first table in the query to the second table in the query, using no indexes at all; in other words, performing a table scan on each table for each lookup.

For the outer table, titles, this would be single scan costing 1,000 pages. For each row in titles, SQL Server has to look up the matching row(s) in titleauthor, using a table scan each time, and check to see if royaltyper for the joined row is less than 50. Because there are 15,000 rows in the titles table and no SARG to limit that further, SQL Server performs 15,000 iterations on the titleauthor table. Each iterative table scan on titleauthor costs 500 pages.

The total number of I/Os for this query would be estimated as

```
   1000 pages in titles
+ (15000 rows in titles × 500 pgs/lookup in titleauthor)
= 7,501,000 I/Os
```

Next, SQL Server calculates the relative I/O cost for this permutation. Because SQL Server performs one scan of `titles`, the first scan incurs 1,000 physical and logical reads. For the `titleauthor` table, as it can fit entirely in cache, only the first iteration incurs physical page reads. All subsequent iterations are logical I/Os only. Therefore, there are 500 physical and logical I/Os on the first iteration, and 14,999 times 500 logical I/Os on the subsequent iterations. The following factors this all out into the relative I/O cost:

```
1,000 physical reads on titles: 18 × 1000              =      18,000
1,000 logical reads on titles: 2 × 1000               =       2,000
500 physical reads on titleauthor: 18 × 500           =       9,000
7,500,000 logical reads on  titleauthor: 2 × 7,500,000 = 15,000,000
Total                                                  = 15,029,000
```

The total cost (15,029,000) is the value that the query optimizer uses to compare the query plan against the other alternatives.

Let's examine some other hypothetical alternatives.

### Example 2: *titles to titleauthor, clustered index on titleauthor.title_id*

For this example, the I/O cost on the `titles` table remains the same. The difference is on the `titleauthor` table. Instead of having to perform a table scan on `titleauthor` for each iteration, SQL Server can use the clustered index to find the matching rows. Assume the following:

- The index density indicates that, for any join value, one row will match in the `titleauthor` table.
- The clustered index consists of two levels.
- The I/O cost per lookup on the `titleauthor` table will be three pages (two index levels plus a data-page lookup).

The total number of I/Os for this query would be estimated as

```
   1000 pgs in titles
+ (15000 rows in titles × 3 pgs per lookup on titleauthor)
= 46,000 I/Os
```

Because SQL Server still has no way of limiting the query any further at the beginning by `royaltyper`, it still must join with every row in the `titleauthor` table during query processing to check the value of `royaltyper`. Therefore, at the end of query processing SQL Server will still have examined every page in the `titleauthor` table, for a total of 500 physical page reads. However, each iteration only costs three pages, which are assumed to be logical page reads.

The relative I/O cost would be as follows:

```
1,000 physical reads on titles: 18 × 1000      =   18,000
1,000 logical reads on titles: 2 × 1000        =    2,000
```

```
500 physical reads on titleauthor: 18 × 500    =   9,000
45,000 logical reads on titleauthor: 2 × 45,000 = 90,000
Total                                          = 119,000
```

As you easily can see, this plan (119,000) is much cheaper than the previous plan (15,029,000). However, there are still other plans to consider. What if you also had a nonclustered index on `title_id` in the `titleauthor` table?

### Example 3: *titles* to *titleauthor*, nonclustered index on *titleauthor.title_id*

Again, the I/O costs on titles remains the same. The only real difference between this query and the last one, which used the clustered index, is that the nonclustered index has one more level than the clustered index, and would cost us one extra I/O per lookup.

The total number of I/Os for this query would be estimated as:

```
1000 pgs in titles
+ (15000 rows in titles × 4 pgs per lookup on titleauthor)
= 61,000 I/Os
```

The relative I/O cost would be as follows:

```
1,000 physical reads on titles: 18 × 1000       =  18,000
1,000 logical reads on titles: 2 × 1000         =   2,000
500 physical reads on titleauthor: 18 × 500     =   9,000
60,000 logical reads on titleauthor: 2 × 60,000 = 120,000
Total                                           = 149,000
```

This plan (149,000) is more expensive than the plan using the clustered index (119,000), but still is substantially cheaper than the table-scan plan (15,029,000). If you only had a choice between a table scan and using the nonclustered index, the nonclustered index would still be much cheaper.

This pretty much exhausts the alternatives joining from `titles` to `titleauthor`. Note that even if there were an index on `titles`, it wouldn't have aided any of these three plans because there is no SARG on `titles` to limit the rows to join with `titleauthor`.

However, there is a SARG on `titleauthor`. Let's examine some cost-estimating examples where `titleauthor` is the outer table.

### Example 4: *titleauthor* to *titles*, no indexes

With no indexes used, SQL Server must perform a table scan for the outer table, `titleauthor`, to find the rows where `royaltyper` is less than 50. This is a single scan costing 500 pages. Because there are no indexes used on `titles`, either, SQL Server must perform a table scan for each lookup on `titles`, costing 1,000 pages per lookup.

The question at this point is, how many lookups would SQL Server have to perform on the `titles` table? Remember back a bit: If there are no statistics available to estimate the rows matching a search argument, the built-in percentages are used. For the search argument:

```
royaltyper < 50
```

the built-in estimate is that 33 percent of the rows will match.

Therefore, SQL Server estimates a join will be performed only on the `titles` table for 33 percent, or 8,250, of the rows in the `titleauthor` table. If a row read during the table scan on `titleauthor` doesn't have a `royaltyper` under 50, SQL Server simply skips that row and compares against the next one. Therefore, the query optimizer estimates that you will perform 8,250 iterations on `titles`, rather than 25,000.

The total number of I/Os for this query would be estimated as:

```
    500 pages in titleauthor
+ (8250 rows in titleauthor × 1000 pgs/lookup in titles)
= 8,250,500 I/Os
```

Because the `titles` table can fit entirely in cache, the relative I/O cost for this plan would be

```
500 physical reads on titleauthor: 18 × 500           =       9,000
500 logical reads on titleauthor: 2 × 500             =       1,000
1000 physical reads on titles: 18 × 1000              =      18,000
8,250,000 logical reads on titleauthor: 2 × 8,250,000 = 16,500,000
Total                                                 = 16,528,000
```

Next, let's look at a plan for when you have a clustered index on `title_id` on the `titles` table.

## Example 5: *titleauthor* to *titles*, unique clustered index on *titles.title_id*

Again, the I/O costs on `titleauthor` remain the same. However, rather than iterative table scans on `titles`, SQL Server uses the clustered index. Because there is a unique clustered index on `title_id`, SQL Server knows that one, and only one, row will match a single join value in the `titles` table. Each single-row lookup using the clustered index on `titles` costs three pages (two index levels plus the data page). SQL Server uses the built-in percentage of 33 percent to estimate the number of rows in which `royaltyper` is under 50.

Therefore, the total number of I/Os for this query would be estimated as:

```
    500 pgs in titleauthor
+ (8250 rows in titleauthor × 3 pgs per lookup on titles)
= 25,250 I/Os
```

Because SQL Server assumes that only 33 percent, or 8,250, of the rows in `titleauthor` match (where `royaltyper` is under 50), and only one row in the `titles` table joins with a single value in the `titleauthor` table, SQL Server expects to access only 8,250 rows in the `titles` table. At 15 rows per page, that works out to:

```
8250 / 15 = 550
```

data pages that are read during processing of this query. This translates into the total physical page estimate for the `titles` table. Based on this information, the relative I/O cost would be as follows:

```
500 physical reads on titleauthor: 18 × 500  =   9,000
500 logical reads on titleauthor: 2 × 500    =   1,000
550 physical reads on titles: 18 × 550       =   9,900
```

```
24,750 logical reads on titles: 2 × 24,750   = 49,500
Total                                         = 69,400
```

This is the cheapest plan so far, but you're not done yet! Next, consider the plan cost with a clustered index on royaltyper.

### Example 6: *titleauthor* to *titles*, clustered index on *titleauthor.royaltyper*, unique clustered index on *titles.title_id*

Because there is a clustered index on royaltyper, SQL Server can use the index statistics to estimate the number of rows where royaltyper is under 50. In this example, the statistics indicate 20 percent of the rows have a royaltyper under 50. Therefore, SQL Server estimates that

```
25,000 * .20 = 5,000
```

rows in titleauthor have a royaltyper under 50. Also, because it can use the clustered index to find the rows, SQL Server doesn't have to scan the entire table. It can start at the beginning of the table and scan the data pages until it finds the first row where royaltyper is equal to or greater than 50. At 50 rows per page, that would be

```
5000 rows / 50 rows per page = 100 pages.
```

Also, because there is a unique clustered index on titles, only one row will match for every matching row in titleauthor: 5,000 rows. At 15 rows per page, SQL Server will access

```
5000/15 = 334
```

data pages in titles while processing this query. Each single-row lookup is still going to cost three pages per lookup. Armed with this information, SQL Server estimates the query cost as follows:

```
    100 pgs in titleauthor+ (5000 rows in titleauthor × 3 pgs per lookup on titles)
= 15,500 I/Os
```

```
100 physical reads on titleauthor: 18 × 100   =   1,800
100 logical reads on titleauthor: 2 × 100     =     200
334 physical reads on titles: 18 × 334        =   6,012
15,000 logical reads on titles: 2 × 15,000    =  30,000
Total                                         =  38,012
```

By far, this is the cheapest plan of all the ones considered, as long there actually is a clustered index on royaltyper in the titleauthor table and a unique, clustered index on title_id in the titles table.

This example also underscores the reason you must understand how the query optimizer works. By knowing how the query optimizer examines search arguments, index statistics, and join orders to process your queries, you can make better-informed decisions about your index design, and write better queries.

For example, having a clustered index on titleauthor.royaltyper and a unique, clustered index on titles.title_id was the cheapest plan (38,012), but wasn't that much cheaper than using no index on titleauthor (69,400) compared to the cheapest plan that uses no indexes at all

(15,029,000). This could help you decide whether to create a clustered index on the `royaltyper` column in `titleauthor`, or create the clustered index on a different column where the cost savings would be more substantial for other critical queries.

# Reformatting Strategy

As you saw in the previous set of examples, the worst-case cost scenario for joins is joining a table scan to a table scan. The resulting I/O cost is this:

```
  number of pages in the outer table
+ (rows in outer table * number of pgs in the inner table)
```

This can be a significantly large I/O cost, even with tables where the page and row counts number only in the hundreds.

Occasionally, it may be cheaper to build a temporary, clustered index on the inner table and use the index to process the query than to repeatedly scan the table. This is known as the *reformatting strategy.*

When reformatting occurs, SQL Server copies the contents of the inner table into a temporary work table in `tempdb`, and creates a clustered index on the join columns specified in the index. SQL Server then uses the clustered index when processing the join to retrieve the qualifying rows from the temporary work table.

The cost of applying the reformatting strategy is the cost of the I/O required to create the temporary work table and build the clustered index on it. The I/O cost of the reformatting strategy alone (that is, copying the table and building the clustered index) is

$P2 + P2\log_2 * P2$

where $P2$ = number of pages in inner table.

The reformatting strategy is not used unless the estimated cost of processing the query using the reformatting strategy is less than the cost of a join using a table scan on the inner table. The total I/O cost for processing the query would be the reformatting cost plus the number of pages in the outer table (P1), plus the number of rows in the outer table (R1) multiplied by the number of scans on the outer table. (For a normal, nested iteration there is only a single scan of the outer table.) The full equation to estimate total I/O for a query using the reformatting strategy would be

$(P2 + P2\log_2 * P2) + P1 + R1$

If your outer table consists of 300 rows and 200 pages, and the inner table consists of 100 pages, the cost of reformatting would be

$(100 + 100\log_2 * 100) + 200 + 300 = 1{,}300$ I/Os

The cost of processing this query using table scans would be

$200 + (300 * 100) = 30{,}200$ I/Os

In this example, the query optimizer would choose to apply the reformatting strategy because it's substantially cheaper than a join with table scans.

> **TIP**
>
> It's nice that the query optimizer has the capability to create a temporary clustered index "on the fly" to process queries on tables without supporting indexes. However, if you see the reformatting strategy being applied, it should set off a number of bells and whistles in your head alerting you that you probably don't have the appropriate indexes defined on your tables. True, while reformatting is cheaper than joining a table scan to table scan, it's still quite a bit more expensive than if the appropriate index were defined on the table(s) in the first place.

## Outer Joins

An asterisk (*) on either side of a join operator in the query indicates that all rows from the table on the side of the asterisk are to be included in the result set, whether or not that table joins successfully with the inner table.

For example, to see all publishers, whether or not you currently carry any of their titles, you could write the following query:

```
select pub_name, title from publishers p, titles t
where p.pub_id *= t.pub_id
```

This query retrieves all pub_names from publishers. For any row that doesn't join successfully with titles, the title column will contain a null for that row in the output.

This syntax is referred to as an *outer* join. The table on the side of the asterisk is forced to be treated as the outer table; that is, it is to be the first table accessed in a nested iteration.

For this type of query, the query optimizer does not evaluate the reverse join order.

# ORDER BY, GROUP BY, and DISTINCT Clauses

In addition to determining the best indexes and join orders, the query optimizer also determines whether work tables are required to further process a query. These are typically queries containing an ORDER BY, GROUP BY, or DISTINCT clause. Because work tables incur additional processing and I/O, the query optimizer makes the determination of whether or not a work table is required.

For a GROUP BY, a work table must always be created to perform the grouping and hold any aggregate values being generated for each group.

Because the DISTINCT clause applies across the entire row, a work table is created to sort and remove duplicates. In versions of SQL Server prior to System 11, a work table always is used to resolve any query containing a DISTINCT clause, even if the select list contains all columns of a unique index, regardless of the fact that the unique index itself guarantees that each row is unique.

In System 11, the query optimizer has gotten a little bit smarter. If a unique index exists on the table and all columns in the unique index are included in the result set, a work table can be avoided as the unique index guarantees that each row is distinct. For an ORDER BY clause, the determination of whether a work table is required is dependent on the indexes on the table and the query containing the ORDER BY clause.

Consider the situation in which a clustered index exists on a table, the order by clause specifies at least the first column in the clustered index, and no columns are not part of the index. In this case, no work table is required as long as the query is resolved using either the clustered index or a table scan. This is because the rows in the table already are sorted in clustered-index order, and are returned in clustered-index order. For example, if a clustered index exists on price, the following queries avoid a work table for an ORDER BY:

```
select * from titles order by price
```

```
select * from titles where
```

However, if a nonclustered index exists on title, and that index was used to process the query, a work table would be required for the following query:

```
select * from titles where title like "Cooking in %" order by price
```

This is because the rows are retrieved in nonclustered-index order, by title, rather than in price order.

For this same reason, no work table is needed if the ORDER BY clause specifies at least the first column of a nonclustered index, no columns are not part of the index, and the nonclustered index is used to satisfy the query by matching a SARG. For example, no work table is required for the following query because a nonclustered index exists on title and the index, rather than a table scan, is used to resolve the query:

```
select * from titles where title like "Cooking in %" order by title
```

In addition, no work table is required if there is a nonclustered index on the table and the query is resolved using index covering, as long as the order by clause specifies at least the first column of the nonclustered index and no columns not part of the index. Again, this is because the rows are retrieved in nonclustered-index order.

# Potential Optimizer Problems and Solutions

So you've written the query and read the plan, and the query optimizer is not choosing the plan you think is best. What's wrong with this query? Before we get into a detailed discussion about analyzing and debugging query plans (which is covered in detail in Chapter 14, "Analyzing Query Plans"), let's look at some of the more common problems that lead to the use of poor query plans.

## Making Sure the Statistics Are Up-to-Date

One of the more common problems encountered with performance in new production systems is the fact that no index statistics are available, or are woefully out-of-date. Before you start tearing queries apart, or your hair out, run update statistics on the tables in question and rerun your query.

## Checking the SARGs

Look closely at your where clauses. Are what appear to be SARGs actual or optimizable SARGs in the eye of the query optimizer? Watch out for inequality operators, operations on columns, and constant expressions that cannot be evaluated at query compile time.

## Ensuring that the Index Covers the Query

If you were expecting index covering to take place, double-check the query and index in question to make sure all columns in the query are contained in the index. It's easy for a nonindexed column to sneak into a query, forcing a data-row retrieval.

## Checking Stored Procedures for Current Parameters

Query plans for stored procedures are compiled once and placed into the procedure cache. The query plan created is based on the parameters passed during the first execution. It's possible that the best plan for those parameters may not be the best plan for the current parameters. The next chapter, "Stored Procedure Optimization," contains a complete discussion on how to deal with this problem.

## Checking the Query Plan for "Reformatting"

If reformatting is taking place, either there are no supporting indexes for the query or the query contains invalid or nonoptimizable SARGs that cannot use any available indexes. At this point, you must reevaluate your indexing decisions, or rewrite the query to take advantage of an available index.

# System 11 Query Optimization Enhancements

In SQL Server version 11.0, Sybase has made a number of enhancements to the query optimizer in an effort to improve query performance. These enhancements take into account the current cache and buffer strategies, which are completely new in System 11.

## Buffer Management

The System 11 SQL Server contains a number of enhancements to improve performance. The changes were designed to improve performance by minimizing I/O, allowing larger than 2KB I/Os, and using memory more efficiently in mixed environments (for example, OLTP and DSS). Two of the methods implemented in System 11 to support these goals are the ability to partition the data cache and assign objects to different cache partitions, and the ability to perform I/Os up to 16KB in size (the size of an extent). (See Chapters 30, "Configuring and Tuning the SQL Server," and 31, "Optimizing SQL Server Configuration Options," for more detailed discussions of how to configure and tune these options.)

Large I/Os can improve performance for queries retrieving a large number of sequential pages by minimizing the total number of disk I/Os required. Queries that can benefit from large I/Os include:

- Table scans
- Range queries using clustered indexes
- Queries covered by a nonclustered index

In System 11, if SQL Server has been configured to use large I/Os, the query optimizer now also attempts to determine the optimal I/O size for processing a query.

If the cache space used by the table or index is configured for large I/Os, the query optimizer now is able to recognize this, and attempts to use large I/Os for these three types of queries. The query optimizer also compares the I/O cost of performing a table scan using large I/Os versus the cost of using an index and performing 2KB I/Os, and chooses the cheapest alternative.

For example, assume the `titles` table contains 2,000 rows on 1,000 data pages. A table scan using 2KB I/Os would therefore require 1,000 physical page reads. A nonclustered index exists on `price`. For the following query:

```
select * from titles where price > $20
```

The index statistics indicate that 30 percent of the rows have a price greater than $20. Using the nonclustered index to find the data rows would require 620 I/Os (2,000 rows multiplied by 30 percent equals 600 data page reads, plus 20 index page reads). This would be fewer page reads than a table scan using 2KB I/Os.

However, the query optimizer recognizes that this table is bound to a data cache with a 16KB buffer pool configured. This allows it to perform 16KB I/Os—that is, each physical I/O request can read eight pages at a time. Reading eight 2KB pages at a time would incur only 125 (1,000 divided by 8) physical I/O requests. This is considerably fewer I/O requests than using the nonclustered index. For this example, the query optimizer would choose to perform a table scan rather than use the nonclustered index to process the query.

# Cache Strategies

Another new feature of System 11 is the ability of the query optimizer to determine whether or not to use a fetch-and-discard strategy for pages read in from disk. In previous releases of SQL Server, all pages read in from disk went onto the most recently used (MRU) end of the cache chain. As you read more pages into memory, other pages would be pushed off the least recently used (LRU) end of the chain. This essentially was a first-in-first-out (FIFO) replacement strategy, and all pages in cache would travel the same number of hops before being replaced. This would, in some cases, hurt performance, such as when a large table scan would fill up the data cache, pushing frequently needed pages out of memory.

In System 11, the query optimizer now can determine whether a query is a fetch-and-discard type of query; that is, one in which it reads the data in once and doesn't need to access it again. If the query is a fetch-and-discard type, the query optimizer puts the page near the LRU end of the cache chain so that it doesn't push out pages that should remain in cache. Essentially, the query optimizer designates pages likely to be reused as "hot" pages, and pages unlikely to be reused as "cold" pages. It then attempts to keep the "hot" pages in cache longer. This can help improve the cache-hit ratio for some applications.

The types of queries to which the System 11 query optimizer applies the fetch-and-discard strategy include:

- Table scans
- Range queries using clustered indexes
- Covered queries that scan nonclustered leaf pages
- The outer table of a join (only a single scan required)
- The inner table of a join if the table is larger than the available cache space

Also, with the ability in System 11 of binding tables to a cache space, the query optimizer now can recognize situations where a query on a table is guaranteed to incur no physical I/Os, or when a table scan may deplete more than half the cache space. Using this information, the query optimizer makes intelligent decisions on the optimal cache and I/O strategy to employ.

> **NOTE**
>
> If you suspect the query optimizer is choosing the wrong I/O or cache strategy, there are options you can set within a session or for a specific query to override the query optimizer's decisions. These methods are described in Chapter 16.

# Summary

The SQL Server query optimizer has continuously improved over the years, taking advantage of new techniques and algorithms to improve its ability to find the cheapest plan. Most of the time, the query optimizer makes the correct decision. There are occasions when the query optimizer can make the wrong decision due to inaccurate or incomplete information in the index statistics. When you suspect that the query optimizer is making the wrong decision, use the tools provided by SQL Server to analyze the query plans generated and determine the source of the problem. These tools are described in Chapter 14.

# Stored Procedure Optimization

# 13

The stored procedure is one of the primary features of SQL Server. Almost any application developed on SQL Server makes use of stored procedures at some point. As a matter of fact, most administrative tasks in SQL Server are performed with stored procedures. For these reasons, it is important to understand how stored procedures are managed and processed by SQL Server in order to understand the performance benefits and issues when using stored procedures.

# Stored Procedures and Performance Benefits

A *stored procedure* is parsed and compiled SQL code that resides in a database and may be called by name from a client application or from within another stored procedure. There are a number of advantages to using stored procedures in SQL Server:

- Faster execution of SQL
- Reduced network traffic
- Modular programming and code reusability
- Restricted, function-based access to tables
- Reduced operator error
- Enforced consistency and data integrity
- Automation of complex or sensitive transactions

Two of the main advantages of using stored procedures are reduced network traffic and faster execution of SQL.

In a client/server environment, the network must always be considered a potential bottleneck, because all communications between clients and servers occur over the network. Using stored procedures can help reduce network traffic. A stored procedure can contain large complex queries or SQL operations that are compiled and stored within an SQL Server database. They are then executed on the SQL Server when the client issues a request to execute the stored procedure. The SQL statements are executed locally within the SQL Server and typically only the final results are sent back to the client application. With the programming features (if...else, while, goto, local variables, and so forth) built into Transact-SQL, the SQL Server itself can evaluate intermediate results and perform any necessary code branching, without having to send intermediate results back to the client for processing.

Another performance gain that stored procedures provide over dynamic SQL is that all object references and SQL syntax are checked at the time the stored procedure is created. This parse tree is stored on disk in the sysprocedures table in the database where the stored procedure is created. When the stored procedure is executed, this parsing doesn't need to be performed. With dynamic SQL, the SQL statements must be parsed and all object references checked for each execution, even if the same SQL statements are executed repeatedly.

The main performance gain realized by using stored procedures, however, is the capability of SQL Server to save the optimized query plan generated by the first execution of the stored procedure in procedure cache memory and to reuse it for subsequent executions. Avoiding the optimization and compilation phase for subsequent executions can result in significant time savings on procedure execution, especially for complex queries or transactions. See Table 13.1, which compares the differences between the first execution of a stored procedure and subsequent executions.

**Table 13.1. Comparison between first and subsequent stored procedure executions.**

| First Execution | Subsequent Executions |
| --- | --- |
| Locate stored procedure on disk and load into cache | Locate stored procedure in cache |
| Substitute parameter values | Substitute parameter values |
| Develop optimization plan | |
| Compile optimization plan | |
| Execute from cache | Execute from cache |

# Stored Procedure Optimization

The SQL Server query optimizer generates a query plan for a stored procedure based on the parameters passed in the first time it is executed. The stored procedure parse tree is read in from disk, and SQL Server generates a query tree for the procedure in the procedure cache. The parameters are then substituted and the optimizer generates a query plan in the procedure cache (see Figure 13.1).

**FIGURE 13.1.**

*Stored procedure query plans are read in from disk and a query plan is generated in cache for each concurrent user.*

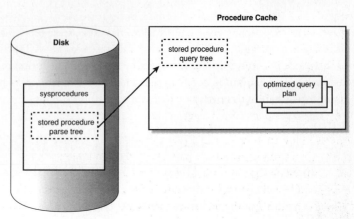

The stored procedure query plan remains in cache after execution for subsequent execution by the same or other SQL Server users, providing there is sufficient cache space available for the query plan to remain in cache.

> **NOTE**
>
> If the procedure cache size is not configured large enough, there may not be enough free space in the procedure cache to load another query tree or plan for all users needing to run query plans at the same time. Procedure cache space can be freed only if a query tree or plan is not currently in use. If all query plans are currently in use and there is insufficient space to load another query tree or plan, error 701, `There is insufficient system memory to run this query.`, occurs.
>
> There is a maximum number of stored procedures or other compiled objects allowed in the procedure cache concurrently. (Remember, the procedure cache is also used for compiled objects such as triggers, rules, and constraints.) If the number of stored procedures or compiled objects in use concurrently exceeds the maximum, error 701 occurs.
>
> The maximum number of compiled objects allowed in the procedure cache is based on the number of proc buffers allocated. The total number of proc buffers is a function of the procedure cache size and is displayed as the number of available `'proc buffers'` during SQL Server startup in the errorlog. SQL Server sets aside a number of pages to manage the compiled objects in the procedure cache. Because 21 proc buffers can fit in a single page, the total number of pages required to manage the compiled objects is the number of proc buffers divided by 21. The actual number of pages set aside can be viewed with the DBCC MEMUSAGE command. The pages required to manage the proc buffers is taken from the total amount of memory allocated to the procedure cache.
>
> Please refer to Chapter 31, " Optimizing SQL Server Configuration Options," for guidelines on estimating procedure cache space requirements.

It is important to note at this point that stored procedure query plans in SQL Server are reusable, but not reentrant. What this means is that a query plan in cache can be in use by only one user at a time. If multiple users execute the same stored procedure concurrently, SQL Server generates newly optimized copies of the stored procedure query plan in cache for each concurrent user for whom a copy is not available.

# The Stored Procedure Dilemma

The advantage of using a cost-based optimizer is that it has the capability of generating the optimal query plan for all queries based on the search criteria. For certain types of queries (for example, range retrievals) the query optimizer may at times generate different query plans based on the supplied search arguments and the estimated number of matching rows. Consider the following example:

```
select * from orders where saledate between @lowdate and @highdate
```

If there is a nonclustered index on `saledate`, the query optimizer has the option of resolving the query by using the nonclustered index or performing a table scan. This decision is based on the available distribution statistics and the estimated number of rows where `saledate` is between `@lowdate` and `@highdate`. For an execution of the query where there is a small number of rows within the range, the optimizer may choose to process the query by using the nonclustered index. For a subsequent execution with a large number of values in the range, the optimizer may choose to process the query by using a table scan.

However, the behavior of stored procedures for subsequent executions is to reuse the query plan residing in the procedure cache that was generated for the first execution of the stored procedure. This provides a performance gain for queries that consistently use the same query plan, but it can be a performance loss if the wrong query plan is used for subsequent executions.

Consider the previous SQL example and put it into a stored procedure as follows:

```
create proc get_orders (@lowdate datetime, @highdate datetime)
as
select * from orders
  where saledate between @lowdate and @highdate
return
```

Suppose the first time that procedure gets executed each day, it is passed parameter values to retrieve all order records for the previous day and is resolved via a table scan. This is the query plan that is placed in the procedure cache for subsequent executions. Subsequent executions for the remainder of the day retrieve order records only since the last time the procedure was executed to provide for real-time monitoring of the orders being received throughout the day. Assuming the procedure is run every five minutes, the number of records to be retrieved is minimal, which can be sufficiently resolved by using the nonclustered index. The query plan from the first execution of this stored procedure still exists in the procedure cache, however, so a new query plan is not generated. The procedure ends up performing a table scan for each execution, and therefore does not provide the expected response time performance for the query. You need somehow to get the SQL Server to recompile a new query plan for the subsequent executions.

# Recompiling Stored Procedures

So how do you go about generating a new query plan when a stored procedure is using the wrong one for a particular execution? Fortunately, SQL Server gives us a couple of options. The first option is to create the stored procedure with the WITH RECOMPILE option as follows:

```
CREATE PROC get_orders (@lowdate datetime, @highdate datetime)
WITH RECOMPILE
as
select * from orders
  where saledate between @lowdate and @highdate
return
```

This option forces the SQL Server query optimizer to generate a new query plan for each execution. As you might suspect, this creates a lot of overhead with the optimizer, and you lose the performance gains typically realized with stored procedures by avoiding the query plan compilation phase for subsequent executions. However, if you are looking at a few milliseconds extra each execution versus the minutes or possibly hours a stored procedure may run if the wrong query plan is used, it's probably a worthwhile tradeoff. You can be virtually guaranteed that the proper query plan is being chosen based on the parameters passed on each execution.

The second alternative creates the procedure normally, but uses the WITH RECOMPILE option on procedure execution:

```
EXEC get_orders @lowdate = "12/15/94", @highdate = "12/16/94" WITH RECOMPILE
```

Using WITH RECOMPILE on stored procedure execution causes the SQL Server optimizer to generate a new query plan based on the supplied parameters only for the current execution. Other existing query plans in cache, except for the one it is replacing, remain unchanged. This method lets you then explicitly specify when you want to use the optimizer to examine your parameters and generate a new query plan rather than create a new query plan for each execution, as the CREATE PROC … WITH RECOMPILE option does. You typically use this method when you are running a specific instance of a stored procedure with atypical parameters.

> **WARNING**
>
> If there are multiple copies of a stored procedure query plan in the procedure cache, the stored procedure currently being executed reuses the first available query plan that the SQL Server finds in cache. There is no guarantee that specific users will get the query plans they generated previously with the 'EXEC … WITH RECOMPILE' on subsequent executions. Likewise, other users may unexpectedly get the recompiled query plan, which may not be appropriate for the parameters they are passing in. The SQL Server still will return the appropriate results, but possibly not in the most efficient manner.
>
> Unfortunately, SQL Server provides no mechanism to flush query plans out of the procedure cache explicitly. The only way to remove all query plans for a specific stored procedure from the procedure cache is to drop and re-create the stored procedure.

## Automatic Recompilation

What happens if you drop an index from a table referenced by a stored procedure, and the procedure query plan is using that index to resolve the query? In this instance, SQL Server detects that the index is no longer available and automatically recompiles a new query plan. However, adding additional indexes or running the UPDATE STATISTICS statement does not cause automatic recompilation of stored procedures.

# Using *sp_recompile*

If you've updated statistics for a table or added additional indexes and want the query optimizer to reexamine the new statistics and/or indexes and generate new query plans for all stored procedures that reference that table, use the sp_recompile stored procedure as follows:

```
sp_recompile tablename
```

Using sp_recompile causes all query plans in cache that reference the specified table to be recompiled.

Use the WITH RECOMPILE option when the following is true:

- A stored procedure can generate widely different query plans depending on the parameters passed in and there is no way of predicting the best query plan for all executions.

Use the sp_recompile option when the following is true:

- Statistics have been updated on a table and you want the stored procedure to generate a new query plan based on the updated statistics.
- An index has been added to a table that you want the optimizer to consider and possibly generate new query plans for all stored procedures that reference the table.

## When Recompilation Doesn't Work

If a stored procedure contains a SELECT * FROM *tablename...* statement and ALTER TABLE has been used to add a column to the table, the stored procedure will not pick up the new column(s), even if executed by using the WITH RECOMPILE option. This is because the columns that SELECT * resolves to are stored in the parse tree. To pick up the new columns, a new parse tree should be created. The only way to do this is to drop and re-create the stored procedure.

This same situation applies when you rename tables referenced by a stored procedure. Because the stored procedure resolves object references by object ID rather than name, the stored procedure can still reference the original table. For example, if you rename the customer table old_customer, your stored procedure continues to work, performing operations on what is now the old_customer table. If you subsequently create a new customer table, your stored procedures do not recompile and operate on the new customer table as long as the old_customer table exists. If you drop the old_customer table, the stored procedures that reference it are automatically recompiled and a new parse tree is generated to reference the new customer table. If you want to force the stored procedures to reference the new customer table without dropping old_customer, you need to drop and re-create all stored procedures that reference customer.

## Alternatives to Recompiling

Because of the performance issues identified earlier with using the WITH RECOMPILE option, avoid using WITH RECOMPILE whenever possible.

Instead of creating a procedure with the WITH RECOMPILE option, consider the following solution:

```
create proc get_orders_smallrange (@lowdate datetime, @highdate datetime)
as
select * from orders
  where saledate between @lowdate and @highdate
return
go

create proc get_orders_bigrange (@lowdate datetime, @highdate datetime)
as
select * from orders
  where saledate between @lowdate and @highdate
return
go

create proc range_value (@lowdate datetime, @highdate datetime)
as
if datediff(hh, @highdate, @lowdate) >= 12
    exec get_orders_bigrange @lowdate, @highdate
else
    exec get_orders_smallrange @lowdate, @highdate
```

By using this approach, each subprocedure (get_orders_smallrange and get_orders_bigrange) is optimized on first execution with the appropriate query plan for the different range values specified in the parameters passed to it by the get_orders procedure. Thus, if a user executes get_orders with date values that are greater than 12 hours apart, get_orders executes the get_orders_bigrange procedure that is optimized for processing large range retrievals, possibly using a table scan. For a user executing get_orders with date values that are less than 12 hours apart, get_orders executes the get_orders_smallrange procedure that is optimized for processing smaller range retrievals, possibly using an available nonclustered index. This approach should result in more consistent response times for queries by minimizing the possibility of a user executing a stored procedure with an inappropriate query plan for the parameters specified.

> **NOTE**
>
> Using this approach requires sufficient knowledge of the bias of your data to know when certain range values result in different query plans to design the stored procedure effectively.
>
> This technique may increase your procedure cache memory requirements. Users will now have at least two procedure query plans (get_orders and either get_orders_smallrange or get_orders_bigrange) in cache. However, this approach is typically preferred over coding your application to check the range values and execute the appropriate stored procedure.
>
> If the range check is hard-coded into your application source code and the bias of your data changes, you have to modify your application source code and recompile it. By

performing the range check within the top level stored procedure, you can easily drop, modify, and re-create the stored procedure to reflect changes in the bias of the data without having to change and recompile the application program.

One other programming consideration with stored procedures related to performance and optimal query plan generation occurs when stored procedures perform different SELECT statements based on condition branching. Let's examine the following stored procedure:

```
create proc get_order_data (@flag tinyint, @value int)
as
if @flag = 1
    select * from orders where price = @value
else
    select * from orders where qty = @value
```

At query compile time, the optimizer doesn't know which branch will be followed, because the if...else construct isn't evaluated until runtime. On the first execution, the optimizer generates a query plan for all SELECT statements in the stored procedure, regardless of the conditional branching. The query plan for each SELECT statement is based on the passed-in parameters.

Having distinctly different queries in the stored procedure can result in having the wrong query plan generated for one of the SELECT statements, because its query plan may be based on inappropriate values for that query.

Remember, a better approach is to break the different SELECT statements into two separate stored procedures and execute the appropriate stored procedure for the type of query to be executed. Here's an example:

```
create proc get_orders_by_price(@price int)
as
    select * from orders where price = @value
return
go

create proc get_orders_by_qty(@qty int)
as
    select * from orders where qty = @qty
return
go

create proc get_order_data (@flag tinyint, @value int)
as
if @flag = 1
    exec get_orders_by_price
else
    exec get_orders_by_qty
return
```

# Summary

Stored procedures can provide a number of performance benefits within SQL Server. Having a good understanding of how stored procedures are optimized by the SQL Server helps you develop efficient stored procedures and achieve the maximum performance benefits that stored procedures provide.

# Analyzing Query Plans

# 14

The SQL Server's cost-based query optimizer typically does a good job of determining the best query plan to process a query. However, there are times when you may be a little skeptical about the plan the optimizer is generating. At least, you'll want to know the specifics about the query plan it is using to determine the following:

- Is the optimizer using the indexes you have defined or is it performing table scans?
- Are worktables being used to process the query?
- Is the reformatting strategy being applied?
- What join order is the optimizer using?
- What are the actual statistics and cost estimates on which the optimizer is basing its decisions?
- How do the optimizer's estimates compare to actual I/O costs?

Fortunately, SQL Server gives you some tools to answer just these questions.

# Using and Understanding *showplan*

To determine the query plan the optimizer has chosen to process a query, SQL Server provides the set `showplan` on option to display the query plan that will be executed. By examining the `showplan` output, you can determine, among other things, which indexes (if any) are being used, what join order was selected, and whether any worktables are required to resolve the query. Interpreting and understanding this output assists you in writing more efficient queries and choosing the appropriate indexing strategy for your tables.

The `showplan` option is a session-level setting. It will not affect other users and, by default, is off when you first log in to SQL Server. To turn the `showplan` option on, execute the following statement in SQL Server:

```
set showplan on
```

When using `showplan` to debug queries, you may also want to use it in conjunction with the `noexec` option. The `noexec` option tells SQL Server to generate a query plan, but not submit it for execution. This option is useful when you are trying to rewrite a long-running query in order to get it to use a more efficient query plan. You don't want to have to wait hours for the query to run or wade through thousands of rows of data just to see whether a query would use an index. Setting `noexec` on prevents the query from actually executing, but SQL Server still generates a query plan and displays it if `showplan` is turned on.

To turn on the `noexec` option, run the following command:

```
set noexec on
```

Like `showplan`, `noexec` is a session-level setting that is off by default. It won't affect any other users or sessions that you may have open.

**TIP**

When the `noexec` option is turned on, the only command SQL Server will execute is `set noexec off`. Always remember to set all your other session settings, trace flags, and so forth before setting `noexec` on. Otherwise you'll be pulling your hair out trying to figure out why you're not seeing the `showplan` output! Remember also to turn it off when you want to execute the query or another command.

**TIP**

When the `showplan`, `statistics io`, or `statistics time` options are turned on and you run a system stored procedure, the `showplan` or `statistics` output is often rather voluminous, making it difficult to read the stored procedure output. Sometimes, depending on the query tool being used, the amount of output exceeds the tool's results buffer. Many of the system stored procedures are very large and complex (for example, run `sp_helptext` on a procedure such as `sp_help` sometime).

To avoid generating all that output, you'd have to keep switching the `showplan`/`noexec`/ `statistics` options off and on. If you're a lazy typer like me, this is not a viable plan. I recommend in this situation that you open a second session to the SQL Server for running system stored procedures, such as `sp_help` and `sp_helpindex`, where you don't have any of these options turned on. Use the other session where you have the options on for debugging your SQL code.

The following is an example of the information displayed by `showplan` for System 10 and earlier versions of SQL Server:

```
/*QUERY for a simple join with SHOWPLAN ON*/
select sum(total_sales)from titles t, publishers p
where t.pub_id = p.pub_id
and p.pub_name = "New Age Books"

STEP 1
The type of query is SELECT
Scalar Aggregate
FROM TABLE
publishers
Nested iteration
Table Scan
FROM TABLE
titles
Nested iteration
Table Scan
STEP 2
The type of query is SELECT
Table Scan
```

```
----------
28286

(1 row(s) affected)
```

For System 11, Sybase has attempted to make the `showplan` output more readable. In addition, it has added information to display new optimizer strategies incorporated in System 11. (Refer to Chapter 12, "Understanding the Query Optimizer," for a discussion of these new strategies.) The `showplan` output for the same query appears as follows:

```
QUERY PLAN FOR STATEMENT 1 (at line 1).


    STEP 1
        The type of query is SELECT.
        Evaluate Ungrouped SUM OR AVERAGE AGGREGATE.

        FROM TABLE
            publishers
        Nested iteration.
        Table Scan.
        Ascending scan.
        Positioning at start of table.
        Using I/O Size 2 Kbytes.
        With LRU Buffer Replacement Strategy.

        FROM TABLE
            titles
        Nested iteration.
        Table Scan.
        Ascending scan.
        Positioning at start of table.
        Using I/O Size 2 Kbytes.
        With LRU Buffer Replacement Strategy.

    STEP 2
        The type of query is SELECT.


----------
28286
```

Let's break down the `showplan` output and examine the statements displayed. Those that are new for System 11 will be noted.

# QUERY PLAN for STATEMENT # (at line #) (System 11 Only)

QUERY PLAN for STATEMENT # (at line #) is printed once for each statement in a SQL batch as a visual clue to separate the `showplan` output for one statement from another. The line number and statement number help you match the `showplan` output with the original statements.

# STEP #

Sometimes, SQL Server cannot process the entire query in a single step and must break it down into multiple pieces. The STEP statement displays which component of the query the optimizer is processing.

Typical queries that require multiple steps are queries with aggregates, GROUP BY or ORDER BY clauses, or occasions when a worktable is required to execute the query. The SQL Server must first retrieve the results from the base table(s) into a worktable in tempdb in the first step in order to calculate the aggregate or group or to sort the result set. In the second step, it retrieves the result set from the worktable.

If you examine the sample query, you'll see an aggregate in the query. In the first step, SQL Server performs the SELECT...FROM TABLEs. The value for SUM (amount) is stored and calculated in a worktable in tempdb. In the second step, SQL Server retrieves the calculated sum from the worktable.

# The type of query is XXXXXXX

The type of query is *XXXXXXX* merely states what type of command is being executed at each step. If the SQL statement is not the typical SELECT, INSERT, UPDATE, or DELETE, showplan reports the type of statement being executed. For example, executing a stored procedure displays the following:

```
exec proc_1

STEP 1
The type of query is EXECUTE
...
```

# The type of query is SELECT (into a worktable)

The type of query is SELECT (into a worktable) indicates that SQL Server needs to select results into a worktable for processing—for example, when a GROUP BY clause is used:

```
select sum(total_sales), type from titles
group by type
```

The showplan output for System 10 and earlier appears as follows:

```
STEP 1
The type of query is SELECT (into a worktable)
GROUP BY
Vector Aggregate
FROM TABLE
titles
Nested iteration
Table Scan
TO TABLE
Worktable 1
```

```
STEP 2
The type of query is SELECT
FROM TABLE
Worktable 1
Nested iteration
Table Scan
```

For System 11, the showplan output is this:

```
QUERY PLAN FOR STATEMENT 1 (at line 1).


    STEP 1
        The type of query is SELECT (into Worktable1).
        GROUP BY
        Evaluate Grouped SUM OR AVERAGE AGGREGATE.

        FROM TABLE
            titles
        Nested iteration.
        Table Scan.
        Ascending scan.
        Positioning at start of table.
        Using I/O Size 2 Kbytes.
        With LRU Buffer Replacement Strategy.
        TO TABLE
            Worktable1.

    STEP 2
        The type of query is SELECT.

        FROM TABLE
            Worktable1.
        Nested iteration.
        Table Scan.
        Ascending scan.
        Positioning at start of table.
        Using I/O Size 16 Kbytes.
        With MRU Buffer Replacement Strategy.
```

Notice that this query is a two-step one. The results are first retrieved from the titles table into a worktable to do the grouping and calculate the aggregate; then the final result set is retrieved from the worktable in the second step.

# *GROUP BY*

GROUP BY indicates that the query contains a GROUP BY clause. All queries with a GROUP BY are two-step queries because a worktable must be used to calculate the vector or scalar aggregate.

# Evaluate Grouped/Ungrouped *TYPE* Aggregate

SQL Server versions prior to System 11 only reported whether a Vector Aggregate or Scalar Aggregate was used to process a query containing one or more aggregate functions with or without a GROUP BY clause.

A vector aggregate is created when the query contains one or more aggregates in conjunction with a GROUP BY clause (see previous query example). The vector aggregate is essentially a multi-column table created in tempdb with one column for each column you are grouping on and another column to hold the computed aggregate for each distinct group. There is a row in the worktable for each distinct instance of the column(s) in the GROUP BY clause (see Figure 14.1).

**FIGURE 14.1.**

*Worktable for vector aggregate.*

| type | avg (price) |
|------|-------------|
| UNDECIDED | NULL |
| business | 13.73 |
| mod_cook | 11.49 |
| popular_comp | 21.48 |
| psychology | 13.50 |
| trad_cook | 15.96 |

**NOTE**

In a lot of the classes I teach, students have a tendency to misread the showplan output for queries with scalar and vector aggregates. They see the Table Scan output in the second step and assume the optimizer performed a table scan on the base table; actually, it is the query against the worktable that is performing the table scan. SQL Server has to do a table scan on the worktable because it is not indexed.

Be careful not to make this same mistake. To determine the access path used by the optimizer, note the access path listed right after the FROM TABLE statement for the table in question.

A scalar, or ungrouped, aggregate contains a single value for the aggregate when the query does not contain a GROUP BY clause. A scalar aggregate is still a two-step query. The scalar aggregate is essentially a single-column, single-row worktable in tempdb used to keep a running total for each aggregate as the result rows are processed in the first step. In the second step, SQL Server retrieves the value stored in the scalar aggregate.

Here is the showplan output for System 10:

```
select sum(total_sales), avg(price)
from titles
```

```
The type of query is SELECT
Scalar Aggregate
FROM TABLE
titles
Nested iteration
Table Scan
STEP 2
The type of query is SELECT
Table Scan
```

For System 11, the showplan output has been changed to indicate whether a grouped or ungrouped aggregate was performed and the type of aggregate(s) contained in the query. The rather non-descriptive Vector Aggregate and Scalar Aggregate clauses have now been replaced with one or more of the following:

■ Evaluate Grouped SUM OR AVERAGE AGGREGATE.

■ Evaluate Grouped COUNT AGGREGATE.

■ Evaluate Grouped MIN AGGREGATE.

■ Evaluate Grouped MAX AGGREGATE.

■ Evaluate Ungrouped COUNT AGGREGATE.

■ Evaluate Ungrouped SUM OR AVERAGE AGGREGATE.

■ Evaluate Ungrouped SUM OR AVERAGE AGGREGATE.

■ Evaluate Ungrouped MIN AGGREGATE.

■ Evaluate Ungrouped MAX AGGREGATE.

For example, examine the System 11 showplan output for a query containing both a sum and an average, without a GROUP BY clause:

```
select sum(total_sales), avg(price)
from titles

QUERY PLAN FOR STATEMENT 1 (at line 1).


    STEP 1
        The type of query is SELECT.
        Evaluate Ungrouped COUNT AGGREGATE.
        Evaluate Ungrouped SUM OR AVERAGE AGGREGATE.
        Evaluate Ungrouped SUM OR AVERAGE AGGREGATE.

        FROM TABLE
            titles
        Nested iteration.
        Table Scan.
        Ascending scan.
        Positioning at start of table.
        Using I/O Size 2 Kbytes.
        With LRU Buffer Replacement Strategy.

    STEP 2
        The type of query is SELECT.
```

**NOTE**

Why are three ungrouped aggregates listed when there are only two in the query (sum, avg)? The COUNT AGGREGATE is done internally by the optimizer to get the total number of rows in the result set in order to determine the average price.

Valid values for the type of grouped and ungrouped aggregates include COUNT, SUM OR AVERAGE, MINIMUM, and MAXIMUM. If the query contains a compute clause, you see the clause

```
Evaluate Grouped ASSIGNMENT OPERATOR
```

along with the aggregate types. For min and max queries, the optimizer also reports whether a shortcut can be used to satisfy the aggregate. For a min query, you may see the message

```
Scanning only up to the first qualifying row.
```

if the optimizer can solve the query by going directly to the first row in the table.

For a max query, you may see the message

```
Scanning only the last page of the table.
```

if the optimizer can solve the query by going directly to the last page in the table. (See Chapter 22, "Common Performance and Tuning Problems," for a discussion of how and when these shortcuts can be used.)

## FROM TABLE tablename

The FROM TABLE line typically is followed on the next line with the name of the table from which data is being selected. This can be a table in the FROM clause in the query or it can be a work-table. The order of the FROM TABLE information in the showplan information indicates the join order used to process the query. In the following System 10 showplan example, the publishers table is the first or outer table in the join, and the titles table is the second or inner table:

```
STEP 1
The type of query is SELECT
Scalar Aggregate
FROM TABLE
publishers
Nested iteration
Table Scan
FROM TABLE
titles
Nested iteration
Table Scan
STEP 2
The type of query is SELECT
```

In System 10 or 11, if an insert or update is performed on a table with a foreign key constraint, a lookup is required on the referenced table and this information is shown in the showplan output. For System 10, it is the following:

```
insert titles (title_id, title, type, pub_id, price, contract)
    values ("BU1234", "My Computer Book", "computing", "1234", $10, 1)

STEP 1
The type of query is INSERT.
The update mode is direct.
Table Scan
```

```
FROM TABLE
publishers
EXISTS TABLE : nested iteration
Using Clustered Index
TO TABLE
titles
```

Notice the `Table Scan` on the `publishers` table, as required by the foreign key constraint. However, the `showplan` output doesn't give any indication that that is what it is doing. In System 11, `showplan` gives additional information when a foreign key check is performed:

```
QUERY PLAN FOR STATEMENT 1 (at line 1).


    STEP 1
        The type of query is INSERT.
        The update mode is direct.

        FROM TABLE
            publishers
        Using Clustered Index.
        Index : pubind
        Ascending scan.
        Positioning by key.
        Keys are:
            pub_id
        Using I/O Size 2 Kbytes.
        With LRU Buffer Replacement Strategy.
        TO TABLE
            titles
```

As you can see, the System 11 output indicates that the lookup on `publishers` was by the key on pub_id.

## TO TABLE tablename

`TO TABLE` *tablename* merely indicates—for an `insert`, `update`, `delete`, or `select into`—what the target table is for the query. The target table may be a worktable.

## Nested iteration

As covered in Chapter 12, all joins are processed as a series of nested iterations, looping on the inner table for each row in the outer table. Essentially, all retrievals from a table are one or more sets of loops on the table to retrieve the matching data rows. When you see the `Nested iteration` statement in the `showplan` output, it indicates one or more passes were made on the table.

## Table Scan

`Table Scan` indicates that the access method used to retrieve data from the table listed above it was a table scan.

# Using Clustered Index

Using Clustered Index indicates that the data was retrieved from the table by using the clustered index. This typically indicates that the query contains a search argument that can be satisfied by using the clustered index. In System 10 and earlier versions of SQL Server, the name of the index is not displayed because there can be only one clustered index on a table. In System 11, the name of the clustered index follows this statement in the Index: *index_name* statement.

# Index : index_name

Index : *index_name* displays the name of the index used to satisfy the query. In System 10 and earlier versions of SQL Server, this indicated that a nonclustered index was used to satisfy the query. In System 11, it is used to show the clustered index name as well as whether the clustered index is chosen.

A nonclustered index may be used to satisfy the query if there is a SARG that matches the index or if the query is covered by the nonclustered index. If the index covers the query, showplan in System 11 displays that information:

```
select au_fname, au_lname from authors where au_lname like "Gr%"

QUERY PLAN FOR STATEMENT 1 (at line 1).


    STEP 1
        The type of query is SELECT.

        FROM TABLE
            authors
        Nested iteration.
        Index : aunmind
        Ascending scan.
        Positioning by key.
        Index contains all needed columns. Base table will not be read.
        Keys are:
            au_lname
        Using I/O Size 2 Kbytes.
        With LRU Buffer Replacement Strategy.
```

The line

```
Index contains all needed columns. Base table will not be read.
```

indicates that the index covered the query.

# Additional Access Method Statements in System 11

System 11 also includes additional information about how the optimizer is using the various access methods (table scan, clustered index, nonclustered index) for each table. These statements are summarized in Table 14.1.

**Table 14.1. System 11 `showplan` messages describing access methods used to process queries.**

| Statement | Definition |
|---|---|
| Ascending scan | Indicates the direction of the table or index scan. Currently, SQL Server supports only ascending scans. A descending scan requires a worktable. |
| Positioning at start of table | Indicates that the table scan is starting at the first row in the table. |
| Positioning by key | Indicates that the index is being used to find the first qualifying row. It will appear for covered or noncovered range queries, index access for joins, and individual row lookups. |
| Positioning at index start | Indicates that a nonmatching, nonclustered index scan is being performed (that is, the index covers the query). |
| Positioning by Row Identifier (RID) | Printed when the query uses a Dynamic Index to resolve an OR. |
| Keys are: | Indicates the keys used by SQL Server to match a clustered or nonclustered index. |
| Log Scan. | Insert, update, or delete statement caused a trigger to fire that needed to scan the log to populate the inserted and deleted tables for the trigger. |
| Using I/O size # bytes | Indicates the I/O size used for disk reads and writes (see Chapter 12). |
| With LRU/MRU buffer replacement strategy | Indicates which caching strategy was used for this query (see Chapter 12). |

# Using Dynamic Index

If you see the statement Using Dynamic Index in your showplan output, it indicates that the query contains an OR statement and the query optimizer applied the OR strategy to solve the query rather than a table scan. Refer to Chapter 12 for a discussion of SQL Server's OR strategy.

# Worktable created for ORDER BY or DISTINCT

If the query contains an ORDER BY, a worktable may need to be created to sort the final result set if the data cannot be retrieved in sorted order by using an index.

If the query contains a DISTINCT clause, it requires sorting to eliminate the duplicate rows (prior to System 11, the DISTINCT clause always required a worktable, even if the result row contained a unique key!). The result rows are copied into a worktable and sorted so that the duplicate rows can be removed.

If sorting is required on the worktable to retrieve the final result set, you will see the following statements in the step where the final result set is retrieved from the worktable:

```
This step involves sorting

...

Using GETSORTED
```

The following is an example of the showplan output for an ORDER BY in System 10 SQL Server and earlier versions:

```
select * from titles
order by price
go

STEP 1
The type of query is INSERT
The update mode is direct
Worktable created for ORDER BY
FROM TABLE
titles
Nested iteration
Table Scan
TO TABLE
Worktable 1
STEP 2
The type of query is SELECT
This step involves sorting
FROM TABLE
Worktable 1
Using GETSORTED
Table Scan
```

In this example, the rows are retrieved from the titles table into a worktable in tempdb in the first step. In the second step, the rows are retrieved from the worktable in sorted order by using a table scan on the worktable.

The following is an example of the showplan output in System 10 and earlier versions of SQL Server for a query containing a distinct clause:

```
select distinct title_id, title from titles
go
```

```
STEP 1
The type of query is INSERT
The update mode is direct
Worktable created for DISTINCT
FROM TABLE
titles
Nested iteration
Table Scan
TO TABLE
Worktable 1
STEP 2
The type of query is SELECT
This step involves sorting
FROM TABLE
Worktable 1
Using GETSORTED
Table Scan
```

If you look at the following `showplan` output for System 11, you see that the worktable is not required because the optimizer recognizes the unique key, `title_id`, in the result row, which guarantees that each row in the result set will be unique as well:

```
QUERY PLAN FOR STATEMENT 1 (at line 1).


    STEP 1
        The type of query is SELECT.

        FROM TABLE
            titles
        Nested iteration.
        Table Scan.
        Ascending scan.
        Positioning at start of table.
        Using I/O Size 2 Kbytes.
        With LRU Buffer Replacement Strategy.
```

# Worktable created for REFORMATTING

The reformatting strategy is an alternative used by the query optimizer when no useful indexes are available on either of two tables involved in a join. Joining two tables without an index on either can be very costly. SQL Server compares the cost of joining the tables without an index to the cost of making a copy of one of the tables, creating a clustered index on it, and using the clustered index on the worktable to join it with the other table. The following is an example of the `showplan` output when the reformatting strategy is used:

```
/* no indexes exist on either table */
Select * from table1, table2
where table1.number = table2.number
go

STEP 1
The type of query is INSERT
The update mode is direct
Worktable created for REFORMATTING
```

```
FROM TABLE
table2
Nested Iteration
Table Scan
TO TABLE
Worktable

STEP 2
The type of query is SELECT
FROM TABLE
table1
Nested Iteration
Table Scan
FROM TABLE
Worktable
Nested Iteration
Using Clustered Index
```

Let's walk through the showplan output step-by-step to get an understanding of what's taking place.

In STEP 1, the worktable is being created in tempdb and the rows from table2 are copied into the worktable. A clustered index is then created on the worktable. In STEP 2, table1 is joined to the worktable, using the clustered index on the worktable to find the matching rows for the join.

## Worktable created for SELECT_INTO

When you run a SELECT_INTO statement, a new table is created in the specified database with the same structure as the table(s) from which you are selecting. This statement in the showplan output is somewhat misleading in that it's not actually a worktable that gets created, but an actual table in the specified database. Unlike worktables created within other query plans, this table is not dropped when query execution completes:

```
select * into newtitles from titles
go
```

```
STEP 1
The type of query is CREATE TABLE.
STEP 2
The type of query is INSERT.
The update mode is direct.
Worktable created for SELECT_INTO.
FROM TABLE
titles
Nested iteration
Table Scan
TO TABLE
Worktable
```

In System 11, the showplan output for a select_into is a bit less cryptic:

```
select * into newtitles from titles
go
```

```
QUERY PLAN FOR STATEMENT 1 (at line 1).


    STEP 1
        The type of query is CREATE TABLE.

    STEP 2
        The type of query is INSERT.
        The update mode is direct.

        FROM TABLE
            titles
        Nested iteration.
        Table Scan.
        Ascending scan.
        Positioning at start of table.
        Using I/O Size 2 Kbytes.
        With LRU Buffer Replacement Strategy.
        TO TABLE
            newtitles
```

# The update mode is DEFERRED/DIRECT

When you perform an update operation (UPDATE, DELETE, INSERT, SELECT_INTO), SQL Server can perform the update as direct or deferred. Refer to Chapter 10, "Understanding SQL Server Storage Structures," for a full discussion of direct and deferred updates. This statement in the showplan output indicates which update method is being used on the specified table.

In System 11, two additional messages have been added to showplan to indicate when an update command may result in a deferred index update:

```
    The update mode is deferred_varcol
    The update mode is deferred_index
```

The deferred_var_col mode is used when updating one or more variable length columns, and the update affects the index rows (that is, the data rows move on the data pages). The update to the data page may be direct or deferred, but the index row update will be deferred.

The deferred_index mode is used when the update command affects the index row directly, or the index used to find the row is a unique index. In this case, the index row is deleted in direct mode, but the reinsert of the index row is deferred.

# WITH CHECK OPTION

WITH CHECK OPTION indicates that data is being inserted or updated in a view that was defined with the WITH CHECK OPTION clause.

# EXISTS TABLE : nested iteration

EXISTS TABLE : nested iteration is very similar to a standard nested iteration, except that the nested iteration is being performed on a table in a subquery that is part of an existence check in the query, so an existence join is used. An existence join is used when the subquery contains an EXISTS, IN, or = ANY clause. For example, the following is the System 10 `showplan` output for an existence join subquery using an `in` clause:

```
select pub_name from publishers
where pub_id in (select pub_id from titles
where type = "business")
STEP 1
The type of query is SELECT
FROM TABLE
publishers
Nested iteration
Table Scan
FROM TABLE
titles
EXISTS TABLE : nested iteration
Table Scan
```

Refer to Chapter 12 for a discussion on how subqueries are optimized.

# Additional *showplan* Messages for Subqueries in System 11

Because subqueries can contain many of the same clauses that regular queries contain, the `showplan` output contains many of the same clauses discussed to this point. However, in System 10 and earlier releases of SQL Server, it can be difficult to determine from the `showplan` output which clauses belong to the subquery and which belong to the outer query. Table 14.2 describes the new `showplan` messages.

**Table 14.2. System 11 `showplan` messages for subqueries.**

| Message | Description |
|---|---|
| Run subquery # (at nesting level #) | Indicates the point in the query where the subquery is actually processed. |
| NESTING LEVEL # SUBQUERIES FOR STATEMENT # | Displays the nesting level of the subquery. Maps the subquery back to the nesting level in the Run subquery... message. |
| QUERY PLAN FOR SUBQUERY # (at line #) | Indicates the start of the `showplan` output for each subquery. |
| END OF QUERY PLAN FOR SUBQUERY # | Indicates the end of the `showplan` output for subquery #. |
| Correlated Subquery. | Indicates that it is a correlated subquery. |

*continues*

## Table 14.2. continued

| Message | Description |
|---------|-------------|
| Non-Correlated Subquery. | Indicates that the subquery is not correlated. |
| Subquery under a *type* predicate | Indicates how the subquery is introduced. Valid values for *type* include IN, ANY, ALL, EXISTS, and EXPRESSION. |
| Evaluate Grouped *type* AGGREGATE | The subquery contains an internal aggregate that is grouped. Valid values for *type* include ONCE, ONCE-UNIQUE, and ANY. |
| Evaluate Ungrouped *type* AGGREGATE | The subquery contains an internal aggregate that is not grouped. Valid values for *type* include ONCE, ONCE-UNIQUE, and ANY. |

Let's look at a query containing a subquery and examine its showplan output:

```
select title from titles
    where price > all (select price from titles
                        where type = "business")
go
```

```
QUERY PLAN FOR STATEMENT 1 (at line 1).


    STEP 1
        The type of query is SELECT.

        FROM TABLE
            titles
        Nested iteration.
        Table Scan.
        Ascending scan.
        Positioning at start of table.

        Run subquery 1 (at nesting level 1).
        Using I/O Size 2 Kbytes.
        With LRU Buffer Replacement Strategy.

NESTING LEVEL 1 SUBQUERIES FOR STATEMENT 1.

    QUERY PLAN FOR SUBQUERY 1 (at nesting level 1 and at line 2).
```

```
    Correlated Subquery.
    Subquery under an ALL predicate.


STEP 1
    The type of query is SELECT.
    Evaluate Ungrouped ANY AGGREGATE.

    FROM TABLE
        titles
    EXISTS TABLE : nested iteration.
    Table Scan.
    Ascending scan.
    Positioning at start of table.
    Using I/O Size 2 Kbytes.
    With LRU Buffer Replacement Strategy.

END OF QUERY PLAN FOR SUBQUERY 1.
```

In this output, you see that the query contains a single subquery that runs at nesting level 1. It maps to the first statement in the batch (STATEMENT 1). The subquery is correlated under an ALL predicate and is evaluating an ANY AGGREGATE. A table scan is used to satisfy the subquery as well as the outer query.

# Using *dbcc* Trace Flags for Analyzing Query Plans

showplan is a very useful tool for determining the query plan that the optimizer has chosen to process the query, but it doesn't give any indication how or why that plan was chosen. Unfortunately, sometimes it may not be clear why a particular plan is being used, or it may appear that the wrong query plan was chosen. How exactly do you determine whether the optimizer is choosing the appropriate plan?

The hard way is to force the optimizer to use different query plans and let it execute the various query plans to see which one actually results in the least amount of I/O and query processing time. (See Chapter 16, "Overriding the SQL Server Optimizer," for a discussion of how to force specific query plans.) This obviously is very time-consuming, and it might help you determine whether the optimizer was choosing the correct query plan, but still not necessarily why.

What you really want to know is whether the optimizer is recognizing your search arguments and join clauses and what information it is using to come up with the row and page I/O estimates on which it is basing its decision.

Fortunately, SQL Server provides some dbcc trace flags that give exactly that information. Useful trace flags and the information they provide are listed in Table 14.3.

**Table 14.3. Useful `dbcc traceon` commands for interpreting query plans.**

| Trace Flag | Effect |
|---|---|
| -1 | Causes trace flags to apply to all user sessions |
| 302 | Displays information on the index selection process for each table in the query |
| 310 | Displays information on the join order selection process |
| 3604 | Sends trace output to the client session |
| 3605 | Sends trace output to the SQL Server errorlog |

You must be logged in as sa or a user with the sa role assigned to have the necessary permissions to run the dbcc traceon command. These traceon options apply only to the current session unless the -1 trace flag is applied. The trace flag options can be turned off with the dbcc traceoff command.

## dbcc traceon (-1)

Most dbcc traceon commands, such as the 302 and 310 trace flags, display information only for the current user process in which they were executed. If, as the sa or a user with the sa role, you want to turn a trace flag on globally for all user sessions, you can use the dbcc traceon (-1) command. The dbcc traceon (-1) command causes all dbcc traceon or dbcc traceoff commands to apply to all *currently* open user sessions globally. In order for new connections to pick up the trace flags, you need to rerun the dbcc traceon (-1) command periodically.

## dbcc traceon 3604 and dbcc traceon 3605

By default, most dbcc traceon flags send their output to the SQL Server errorlog. To route the output to the client session, run the following command:

```
dbcc traceon (3604)
```

To turn off output to the client session, use the dbcc traceoff command:

```
dbcc traceoff (3604)
```

## dbcc traceon (302) and dbcc traceon (310)

The 302 and 310 trace flags give you a look into the cost analysis process that the query optimizer goes through when determining the best query plan. These are the ones concentrated on in this chapter. (There are other trace flags that peak into the query optimization process, but I have not found them to generate very readable output or be of much benefit.) The 302 and 310 trace flags currently provide the most useful information regarding optimizer query plan selection.

The 302 trace flag displays information about the index selection phase of the query optimizer. You can examine the search arguments and join clauses identified by the query optimizer, determine whether an index is found on the column(s) that matches the SARG or join clause or whether the statistics page is used, and learn what the row and page I/O estimates are for each candidate index.

The 310 trace flag is most often used in conjunction with the 302 trace flag, but it's not required. The 310 output displays the join selection phase of the query optimizer, which takes place after the index selection phase. Here, you can examine the possible join permutations and costs associated with each one that the optimizer is considering.

As with the other dbcc trace flags, you must be logged into SQL Server as sa or a user with the sa role to turn on the 302 and 310 trace flags. However, these can be turned on for all users by using the dbcc traceon (-1) command. You also need to issue a dbcc traceon (-1, 3604) command to have the trace output returned to the client application: otherwise, the output will go to the SQL Server errorlog.

As sa, or user with the sa role, run the following commands to turn on the 302 and 310 trace flags for your current session:

```
dbcc traceon (3604, 302,310)
```

If you want to turn the trace flag on for all user sessions, run the following commands as sa or a user with the sa role:

```
dbcc traceon (-1, 3604)
dbcc traceon (-1, 302, 310)
```

# Interpreting the *dbcc traceon (302)* Output

The 302 and 310 trace flags provide a textual representation of the query optimization process. However, this output obviously was originally intended for the developers of SQL Server to debug the query optimizer code. Over the years, the output has become somewhat more readable, but still can be a bit cryptic. In this section, you examine the output from the dbcc (302) trace facility and decipher what each of the statements you may see actually represents. In places where the output has changed for System 11 (because the optimizer in System 11 considers other factors such as prefetch size and cache strategy), you examine the differences.

## Scoring Search and Join Clauses

The first part of the 302 output is the search clause and join clause scoring phase. The process is performed for each valid search argument and join clause identified in the query. If no search arguments are identified by the query optimizer for a table, there is no search clause information displayed. If there are no join clauses found, there is no join clause information displayed.

For each table on which the optimizer identifies one or more search or join clauses, you see its information displayed between two strings of asterisks. The following is a sample of the output from System 10 for a search clause:

```
*******************************
Entering q_score_index() for table 'titles' (objectid 208003772).
The table has 18 rows and 3 pages.
Scoring the SEARCH CLAUSE:
    price GT

Base cost: indid: 0 rows: 18 pages: 3

Cheapest index is index 0, costing 3 pages and generating 5 rows per scan.
Search argument selectivity is 0.330000.
*******************************
```

For System 11, the output for the same query looks like the following:

```
*******************************
Entering q_score_index() for table 'titles' (objectid 208003772, varno = 0).
The table has 18 rows and 3 pages.
Scoring the SEARCH CLAUSE:
    price GT

Base cost: indid: 0 rows: 18 pages: 3 prefetch: N
    I/O size: 2 cacheid: 0 replace: LRU

Cheapest index is index 0, costing 3 pages and
    generating 6 rows per scan, using no data prefetch (size 2)
    on dcacheid 0 with LRU replacement
Search argument selectivity is 0.330000.

*******************************
```

As you can see, the System 11 output contains a bit more information. Let's take a look at the important pieces of the 302 output to determine what the optimizer is doing.

## Entering q_score_index() for table 'table_name'

`Entering q_score_index() for table 'table_name'` indicates that you are in a scoring routine for the specified table to find the best index to use for a table, depending on the search arguments or join clauses. If a search argument or join clause does not show up in a `q_score_index()` analysis, the optimizer is not recognizing it as a valid search argument or join clause.

The optimizer evaluates all search clauses for all tables in the query first, followed by all join clauses for each table in the query.

# varno = # (System 11 Only)

varno = # indicates the location of the table in the from list in the query. 0 is the first table, 1 is the second table, 2 is the third table, and so on.

# The table has N rows and n pages

The table has N rows and n pages is the estimate of the overall table size. These values are taken from the table's first OAM page. Essentially, this is the base cost of a table scan against which the cost of using any indexes will be compared to find the cheapest approach. Be sure to double-check these values because there are instances where they could be inaccurate or out-of-date, resulting in the wrong query plan being selected.

# Scoring the SEARCH CLAUSE:

Scoring the SEARCH CLAUSE: indicates that the optimizer is scoring a search clause on the specified table. The output following this line displays the column name and the type of comparison operator in the search argument. Table 14.4 displays the types of comparison operators and the two-character codes that refer to them.

**Table 14.4. Operator codes used in dbcc traceon (302) output.**

| Operator code | Comparison Operator |
| --- | --- |
| EQ | Equal to (=) |
| LT | Less than (<) |
| GT | Greater than (>) |
| LE | Less than or equal to (<=) |
| GE | Greater than or equal to (>=) |
| NE | Not equal (<>, !=) (System 11 only) |
| ISNULL | is null comparison in query |
| ISNOTNULL | is not null comparison (System 11 only) |

NE (<>, !=) and ISNOTNULL are not considered valid search arguments prior to System 11 and do not generate the q_score_index() output for that search argument.

**NOTE**

Range queries, such as queries containing the following types of clauses:

```
between loval and highval
like "k%"
col1 >= 100 and col1 < 200
```

are treated as a single search argument for the purpose of estimating the number of rows within the range of values. The following is the q_score_index() output for a between clause:

```
*******************************
Entering q_score_index() for table 'titles' (objectid 208003772, varno = 0).
The table has 18 rows and 3 pages.
Scoring the SEARCH CLAUSE:
     price LE
     price GE

Base cost: indid: 0 rows: 18 pages: 3 prefetch: N
     I/O size: 2 cacheid: 0 replace: LRU

Cheapest index is index 0, costing 3 pages and
     generating 5 rows per scan, using no data prefetch (size 2)
     on dcacheid 0 with LRU replacement
Search argument selectivity is 0.250000.

*******************************
```

Be careful when dealing with BETWEEN clauses in SQL Server 10 and later. In previous releases, it didn't matter whether you put the lower bound on the left or right of the search clause. SQL Server swapped the values to ensure that the lower bound was always the smaller value. With the release of SQL Server 10, the ANSI standard does not allow this treatment of a BETWEEN statement. If you state the query as the following:

```
BETWEEN upper_bound AND lower_bound
```

SQL Server still processes the query, but the row estimate is always 0.

For any LIKE clause where the first character of the matching string is a wildcard character, it is not treated as a search argument.

## *Scoring the JOIN CLAUSE:*

Scoring the JOIN CLAUSE: indicates that the optimizer is scoring a join clause on the specified table. The output following this line displays the column name and the type of comparison operator in the join clause. Refer to Table 14.3 for a list of the types of comparison operators and the two-character codes that refer to them. The following is an example of the join clause output for System 11:

```
********************************
Entering q_score_index() for table 'publishers' (objectid 48003202, varno = 1).
The table has 3 rows and 1 pages.
Scoring the JOIN CLAUSE:
     pub_id EQ


Base cost: indid: 0 rows: 3 pages: 1 prefetch: N
     I/O size: 2 cacheid: 0 replace: LRU
Unique clustered index found--return rows 1 pages 2

Cheapest index is index 1, costing 2 pages and
     generating 1 rows per scan, using no data prefetch (size 2)
     on dcacheid 0 with LRU replacement
Join selectivity is 3.000000.

********************************
```

# Forcing Indexes

If the user forces the use of an index by specifying the ID of the index to be used or including the index clause in System 11, the 302 output indicates this and displays the ID of the forced index. For example, here is an example using the clustered index (index 1):

```
select * from titles (1) where title like "Cook%"
```

```
********************************
Entering q_score_index() for table 'titles' (objectid 208003772).
The table has 18 rows and 3 pages.
Scoring the SEARCH CLAUSE:
     title LT
     title GE
```

**User forces index 1**

```
Cheapest index is index 1, costing 3 pages and generating 4 rows per scan.
Search argument selectivity is 0.250000.
********************************
```

In System 11, if the user also forces a prefetch size or cache strategy in the index clause, that is also indicated:

```
select * from car_sales (index car_sales prefetch 16 lru)
where make = "Ford"
```

```
********************************
Entering q_score_index() for table 'car_sales' (objectid 16003088, varno = 0).
The table has 1000 rows and 334 pages.
Scoring the SEARCH CLAUSE:
     make EQ
```

```
User forces index 0
User forces data prefetch of 16K
User forces LRU buffer replacement strategy

Cheapest index is index 0, costing 334 pages and
    generating 100 rows per scan, using sequential data prefetch (size 16)
    on dcacheid 0 with LRU replacement
Search argument selectivity is 0.100000.


********************************
```

In this example, the optimizer is forced to use a table scan to process the query (index 0), and to use a prefetch size of 16K and the LRU buffer replacement strategy. For more information on overriding the query optimizer, see Chapter 16.

# Estimating Index Costs

The next section of the q_score_index routine is the cost analysis of the cheapest access path for the search or join clause. This includes estimating the costs of a table scan as well as the cheapest index.

## Base cost: indid: # rows: ## pages: #

Base cost: indid: # rows: ## pages: # displays the cost of performing a table scan. A table scan is always the base cost against which the I/O cost of using any available indexes is compared. The values reported here should match the table size reported earlier.

For example, the following output tells you that a table scan (index 0) costs 3 pages to return 18 rows:

```
Base cost: indid: 0 rows: 18 pages: 3
```

In System 11, the base cost also gives additional information on prefetch sizes and buffer replacement strategy for the table (see Table 14.5):

```
Base cost: indid: 0 rows: 18 pages: 3 prefetch: N
    I/O size: 2 cacheid: 0 replace: LRU
```

**Table 14.5. Description of the additional base cost output variables for System 11.**

| Variable | Meaning |
| --- | --- |
| prefetch | Whether prefetch is being considered for this table |
| I/O size | I/O size to be used for physical I/Os (2, 4, 8, or 16) |
| cacheid | ID of the named data cache to be used |
| replace | Buffer replacement strategy to be used (LRU or MRU) |

After displaying the base cost, the optimizer next evaluates any available indexes and compares the cost against the base cost.

## Unique type index found -- return rows 1 pages #

If the search argument is an equality operation (=) on a unique index, the optimizer knows that only a single row can match a single value. The index type can be either clustered or nonclustered. The page cost is estimated to be a single data page read plus a number of index page reads equal to the number of levels in the index. Consider the following example:

```
********************************
Entering q_score_index() for table 'pt_sample' (objectid 304004114, varno = 0).
The table has 5772 rows and 243 pages.
Scoring the SEARCH CLAUSE:
    id EQ

Base cost: indid: 0 rows: 5772 pages: 243 prefetch: N
    I/O size: 2 cacheid: 0 replace: LRU
Unique clustered index found--return rows 1 pages 2

Cheapest index is index 1, costing 2 pages and
    generating 1 rows per scan, using no data prefetch (size 2)
    on dcacheid 0 with LRU replacement
Search argument selectivity is 0.000173.

********************************
```

A unique index was found on the id column for the table 'pt_sample' and the search argument is an equality operator. The cost of finding a single row for this table is 2 pages—one index page read to find the data page plus one data page read.

If the index is not a unique index, the optimizer must estimate the number of matching rows using the index statistics.

## Relop bits are: #

You can ignore the line Relop bits are: #. It merely is reiterating the integer bitmap value of the conditional operator. It is used for debugging by SQL Server engineers.

# Using Index Statistics to Estimate I/O Costs

The next few lines of output give information on which index statistics are used (distribution steps, density, or built-in percentages) to estimate the page and row count for an identified index that matches the search or join clause. (Refer to Chapter 11, "Designing Indexes for Performance," for a discussion of index statistics and the distribution page.) Let's examine the different alternatives and what the output looks like.

# Qualifying stat page; pgno: NNNN steps: nnn

`Qualifying stat page; pgno:` *NNNN* `steps:` *nnn* indicates that a valid statistics page was found for this index at logical page address *NNNN*. The statistics page has *nnn* steps on it. The information on this statistics page is what the optimizer will base its decisions on when evaluating that index.

> **TIP**
>
> One of the more common errors made by newcomers to SQL Server is creating a table and all indexes on it before loading the data. If the `update statistics` command is not run subsequent to the data load, there will be no statistics page for any of the indexes. SQL Server does not create a statistics page for an index created on any empty table because there is nothing with which to populate the statistics page.
>
> Remember to keep your statistics up-to-date so that the optimizer can make more valid assumptions about your data distribution when it is estimating the number of matching rows. The rough rule of thumb is to run `update statistics` for the table when more than 10–20 percent of the data has been modified, inserted, or deleted.

If you want to examine the contents of the distribution page, you can use the `dbcc page` command (refer to Chapter 10), but the contents are displayed in hexadecimal format and not very useful unless you are handy at reading hex data. If the first column of the index is on a character column, it is somewhat more readable.

If you prefer to see the index statistics in a graphical format, check out the demonstration copy of Aurora Distribution Viewer on the included CD-ROM. In addition to providing multiple ways of graphing the distribution page values, it also can keep a history of distribution page values for tracking the effectiveness of your `update statistics` strategy.

# Search value: NNNNNNNN

`Search value:` *NNNNNNNN* displays the value being compared in the search clause if the search argument is a constant value. This is the value that is used for comparison against the index statistics.

If you see the following message:

```
Search value: *** CAN'T INTERPRET ***
```

this merely indicates that the routine used to display the `302` output isn't wasting time trying to build the search value's printable representation. It doesn't mean that the optimizer cannot interpret the search value.

# Distribution Page Matching

The next line of output indicates whether the search value matches a distribution page value exactly or whether it falls between steps on the distribution page.

## Match found on statistics page

An exact match of the search value was found on the distribution page. This will be followed by one of the following four messages to indicate where within the distribution page the match was found and the number of steps it matched:

- `equal to a single row (1st or last) -- use endsingleSC`

  The search value matched the first or last step on the distribution page.

- `equal to several rows including 1st or last -- use endseveralSC`

  The search value matched multiple steps near the beginning or end of the distribution page.

- `equal to single row in middle of page -- use midsingleSC`

  The search value matched a single row in the middle of the distribution page.

- `equal to several rows in middle of page -- use midseveralSC`

  The search value matched multiple rows in the middle of the distribution page.

If no exact match is found on the distribution page, SQL Server looks to see between which steps the search value will fall.

## No steps for search value -- qualpage for LT search value finds

`No steps for search value — qualpage for LT search value finds` indicates that no exact match for the search value was found on the distribution page. Based on where within the distribution steps the search value falls, SQL Server displays one of the following three messages:

- `value between step K and K + 1 -- use betweenSC`

  The search value falls between the two steps listed.

- `value < first step -- use outsideSC`

  The search value is less than the first distribution step value.

- `value > last step -- use outsideSC`

  The search value is greater than the last distribution step value.

If the search value falls less than the first step or greater than the last step, this indicates that statistics are out-of-date, especially if the index is created on a sequential key value.

This is a potential problem if there are a large number of rows outside the distribution steps but the optimizer estimates there are only a few rows. If the estimate of the steps where the search value falls between seems inconsistent with your knowledge of the actual data, it is probably time to run update statistics for that table or index.

Because SQL Server knows the number of rows between steps, it can make an estimate of the number of rows that match the search value, depending on which of the matches listed previously is applied.

The betweenSC or outsideSC statement indicates the algorithm that is applied to estimate the number of matching rows. The row estimate is determined as a factor of the number of distribution steps matched and the index density. For example, if a search value falls between two step values, SQL Server cannot determine exactly how many duplicates there may be for the search value between the two steps. The estimate will be either the smaller of the index density times the number of rows in the table or the number of rows between the steps.

Consider a table with 100,000 rows, 333 steps on the distribution page, and an index density of .00025. The search clause is an equality search (column = constant). If a search value is found between two steps, the number of candidate rows is one of these:

- 100,000 rows / 333 steps – 2 = 298 rows between 2 steps
- 100,000 rows × .00025 = 25 rows based on index density

In this case, SQL Server would use the density estimate that 25 rows would match the search argument rather than 298. This is the typical case for an equality search when the search value falls between two steps.

For search arguments other than equality searches (column = constant), when the search value falls between two steps, the row estimates are determined as follows:

- column < constant     selectivity = ((stepnum + .5 / numsteps) – (density /2))
- column <= constant    selectivity = ((stepnum + .5 / numsteps) + (density / 2))
- column > constant     selectivity = 1 – ((stepnum + .5 / numsteps) – (density / 2))
- column >= constant    selectivity = 1 + ((stepnum + .5 / numsteps) – (density / 2))

## Range Queries

If the search argument was a closed range query (for example, a between search clause), the optimizer uses the index statistics to score both the upper and lower bounds to estimate the number of rows between the two values:

```
********************************
Entering q_score_index() for table 'pt_sample' (objectid 304004114, varno = 0).
The table has 5772 rows and 243 pages.
Scoring the SEARCH CLAUSE:
      id LE
      id GE
```

```
Base cost: indid: 0 rows: 5772 pages: 243 prefetch: S
    I/O size: 16 cacheid: 0 replace: MRU
Relop bits are: c
Qualifying stat page; pgno: 2809 steps: 321
Search value: 2000
No steps for search value--qualpage for LT search value finds
value between step K, K + 1, K = 16--use betweenSC
Scoring SARG interval, lower bound.
Qualifying stat page; pgno: 2809 steps: 321
Search value: 1000
No steps for search value--qualpage for LT search value finds
value between step K, K + 1, K = 12--use betweenSC
Net selectivity of interval: 1.262891e-002
Estimate: indid 1, selectivity 0.012629, rows 73 pages 6

Cheapest index is index 1, costing 6 pages and
    generating 73 rows per scan, using sequential data prefetch (size 16)
        on dcacheid 0 with LRU replacement
Search argument selectivity is 0.012629.

********************************
```

## Scoring SARG interval, lower bound

The optimizer first determines the location of the upper bound on the distribution page. Following that, it looks for the location of the lower bound on the distribution page.

## Net selectivity of interval: #.###

`Net selectivity of interval: #.###` displays the selectivity as a decimal representation of the number of rows within the range, divided by the total number of rows in the table. This is used to determine the number of rows within the specified range of values.

# When Distribution Steps Cannot Be Used

A common problem for the optimizer is search arguments that are valid, but don't have known values until run time. This occurs when the constant expression in the search argument contains a local variable, arithmetic expression, or built-in function, or is compared against a subquery—for example, this:

```
select count(*) from pt_tx_CIamountNCamount
    where amount > (select avg(amount) from pt_tx_CIamountNCamount)
```

or this:

```
declare @max_amt money
select @max_amt = max(amount) from pt_tx_CIamountNCamount
select count(*) from pt_tx_CIamountNCamount
    where amount = @max_amt
```

or this:

```
select title from titles
   where pubdate > dateadd(yy, -1, getdate())
```

There is no way for the optimizer to know what value the subquery, local variable, arithmetic expression, or built-in function will have at runtime, because the value cannot be determined until the query is executed. The query cannot be executed until a query plan is generated.

Sounds like a bit of a Catch-22, doesn't it? Actually, the only limitation on the optimizer in these cases is that it cannot use the distribution steps to estimate row counts for equality operations; it has to use the index density. Index density is the percentage of unique values in the table. For any other type of operator (for example, > or <), it has to use built-in, or "magic" percentages. The magic percentages used are dependent on the type of operator:

- equality (=)                              10 percent
- closed interval (>= AND <, BETWEEN)       25 percent
- open interval (>, <, <=, >=)              33 percent

When the distribution steps cannot be used, the 302 output contains the following:

```
SARG is a subbed VAR or expr result or local variable (constat=number)-- use
magicSC or densitySC
```

In most cases, it is preferable for the optimizer to compare values against the distribution steps rather than use the index density, and especially preferable over using the magic percentages. Consider the following example:

- 100,000 rows
- .00025 index density (4,000 unique values)
- 20,000 rows where id = 100

```
declare @id int
select @id = 100
select count(*) from table_1 where id = @id
```

If the distribution steps were used, SQL Server would estimate that approximately 20,000 rows would match the search argument where id = 100. However, because this example uses a local variable, SQL Server uses the index density instead to estimate the number of rows. In this case, it is 100,000 × .00025, or 25 rows. That's quite a significant difference in row estimates between the two approaches, possibly resulting in a less-than-efficient query plan being chosen.

Another situation where the optimizer is forced to use the magic percentages is when the distribution page is unavailable, or no index exists on the column specified in the search argument. With no index on the column, SQL Server automatically uses the magic percentages, and no information on index selection is displayed:

```
select count(*) from titles
where price between 10 and 20
go
```

```
*******************************
Entering q_score_index() for table 'titles' (objectid 208003772, varno = 0).
The table has 18 rows and 3 pages.
Scoring the SEARCH CLAUSE:
      price LE
      price GE

Base cost: indid: 0 rows: 18 pages: 3 prefetch: N
      I/O size: 2 cacheid: 0 replace: LRU

Cheapest index is index 0, costing 3 pages and
      generating 5 rows per scan, using no data prefetch (size 2)
      on dcacheid 0 with LRU replacement
Search argument selectivity is 0.250000.

*******************************
```

Notice that this query contains a closed range search (`between`). The last line states that the `Search argument selectivity is 0.250000`, or 25 percent—the magic percentage for a closed range search.

If an index exists but no distribution page has been created, the following text is displayed:

```
No statistics page -- use magicSC
```

# Determining Final Cost Estimates and Selectivity of Indexes

Once the row estimates have been determined by using one of these described methods, the next step is to determine the I/O cost estimates and overall selectivity of the indexes. Let's examine the 302 output for the following query, which has two indexes from which to choose:

```
select count(id) from pt_tx
where amount > 20000
go
```

```
*******************************
Entering q_score_index() for table 'pt_tx' (objectid 176003658,
 varno = 0).
The table has 7282 rows and 88 pages.
Scoring the SEARCH CLAUSE:
      amount GT

Base cost: indid: 0 rows: 7282 pages: 88 prefetch: S
      I/O size: 16 cacheid: 0 replace: LRU
Relop bits are: 10
Qualifying stat page; pgno: 1977 steps: 197
Search value: *** CAN'T INTERPRET ***
No steps for search value--qualpage for LT search value finds
value between step K, K + 1, K = 32--use betweenSC
Estimate: indid 1, selectivity 0.834957, rows 6080 pages 75
Relop bits are: 1810
```

```
Qualifying stat page; pgno: 881 steps: 197
Search value: *** CAN'T INTERPRET ***
No steps for search value--qualpage for LT search value finds
value between step K, K + 1, K = 32--use betweenSC
Estimate: indid 2, selectivity 0.834957, rows 6080 pages 6127

Cheapest index is index 1, costing 75 pages and
     generating 6080 rows per scan, using sequential data prefetch (size 16)
     on dcacheid 0 with LRU replacement
Search argument selectivity is 0.834957.


********************************
```

# Estimate: indid I, selectivity #.###, rows R pages P

Estimate: indid `I`, selectivity `#.###`, rows `R` pages `P` is displayed for each index considered, showing the estimated number of matching rows, the page I/O estimate to retrieve the rows, and the overall selectivity of the index expressed as a floating-point value of the percentage of matching rows.

In the example, you see this information twice for the one search argument because there are two indexes on the amount column that can be considered.

For the clustered index, indid `1`, you see the estimate of the number of matching rows to be `6080`, costing `75` pages to retrieve them. The selectivity is `.834957`, or approximately 83.5 percent of the rows in the table.

For the nonclustered index, indid `2`, the number of matching rows is the same and selectivity is the same, but the I/O cost is `6127` pages.

The page estimates for each of these alternatives is compared against the cost of a table scan, which is equal to the total number of pages in the table. The access path resulting in the fewest number of page I/Os is selected as the cheapest approach and is the next bit of information displayed by the optimizer.

### NOTE

Although at this point, the optimizer may determine that a nonclustered index is the cheapest access path, a table scan may still be used to execute the query. The actual decision of which access path to use is deferred until the join order is evaluated.

This happens because the actual query cost is not known until the optimizer determines the ratio of physical versus logical I/Os. This is dependent on the join order, and in System 11, the available cache space and `prefetch` size.

# Cheapest index is index I, costing P pages and generating R rows per scan

Cheapest index is index `I`, costing `P` pages and generating `R` rows per scan merely reiterates the cost estimates for the index resulting in the cheapest access path. Note that if the index ID equals `0`, a table scan is the cheapest access path.

In the previous example, the cheapest index is the clustered index (indid 1), resulting in 75 page I/Os. Note that this is only slightly less than a table scan (88 pages), due to the high number of matching rows. If there were no clustered index on the table, a table scan would have been cheaper than the nonclustered index (6,127 pages).

## Search argument selectivity is N

Search argument selectivity is `N` displays the selectivity of the chosen index for a search argument as a `float` value.

# Scoring Join Clauses

After scoring all search arguments for the query, the next step is to score any join clauses. With joins, a specific value cannot be looked up on the distribution page, because the value to be compared is entirely dependent on the row being joined at run time.

Therefore, similar to how it deals with search arguments with unknown values, the optimizer uses the index density to estimate the number of rows which match any single row in a join clause. If index density is not available, the join selectivity is determined as the following:

> 1/# of rows in smaller table

The following is an example of a query with join clauses and the resulting dbcc traceon (302) output:

```
select company, amount from pt_sample s, pt_tx t
where t.id = s.id


*******************************
Entering q_score_index() for table 'pt_sample' (objectid 16003088, varno = 0).
The table has 5772 rows and 243 pages.
Scoring the JOIN CLAUSE:
     id EQ id

Base cost: indid: 0 rows: 5772 pages: 243 prefetch: S
     I/O size: 16 cacheid: 0 replace: MRU
Unique clustered index found--return rows 1 pages 2

Cheapest index is index 1, costing 2 pages and
     generating 1 rows per scan, using no data prefetch (size 2)
     on dcacheid 0 with LRU replacement
Join selectivity is 5772.000000.
```

```
********************************


********************************
Entering q_score_index() for table 'pt_tx' (objectid 48003202, varno = 1).
The table has 7282 rows and 118 pages.
Scoring the JOIN CLAUSE:
     id EQ id

Base cost: indid: 0 rows: 7282 pages: 118 prefetch: S
     I/O size: 16 cacheid: 0 replace: LRU
Relop bits are: 4
Estimate: indid 1, selectivity 0.000198, rows 1 pages 2

Cheapest index is index 1, costing 2 pages and
     generating 1 rows per scan, using no data prefetch (size 2)
     on dcacheid 0 with LRU replacement
Join selectivity is 5041.153847.

********************************
```

## Scoring the JOIN CLAUSE:

Scoring the JOIN CLAUSE: indicates that the optimizer is now scoring a join clause rather than a search clause for this query. Notice that the output is nearly identical to the search clause output, except that it does not use distribution steps to estimate the query cost.

## Join selectivity is #####

Join selectivity is ##### displays the join selectivity as an integer representation of the denominator of the index density in the System 10 SQL Server and earlier versions. In System 11, the join selectivity is expressed as a float representation of the join selectivity. This allows for more accurate row estimates. In the example, the clustered index on pt_sample is a unique index. Because the index density is determined as 1/# of unique values in the table, it is 1/5772 for pt_sample. In System 10, the join selectivity is the denominator of the index density, or 5,772. In System 11, the join selectivity is displayed as a float value: 5772.000000.

For the pt_tx table, the index is not unique, so the index density information is used to determine the number of distinct values in the table. In this example, the index density is displayed as .000198 and the join selectivity is 5041.153847 (1/5041.153847 = .000198367). In other words, there are approximately 5,041 unique values for id in the pt_tx table. The join selectivity in System 10 would be displayed as 5,041.

Once you examine the search clause and join clause index selection process, the next step is to examine the join order processing phase by using the dbcc traceon (310) command.

# Interpreting the *dbcc traceon (310)* Output

The dbcc traceon (310) trace flag displays the cost analysis of the possible join permutations for the query. Here's an example of the 310 output for a simple two-table join:

```
select company, amount from pt_sample s, pt_tx t
where t.id = s.id


QUERY IS CONNECTED

 0 - 1 -
NEW PLAN (total cost = 1010754):

varno=0 (pt_sample) indexid=0 ()
path=0x20e66920 pathtype=sclause method=NESTED ITERATION
outerrows=1 rows=5772 joinsel=1.000000 cpages=243 prefetch=N iosize=2
replace=LRU lp=243 pp=243 corder=95

varno=1 (pt_tx) indexid=0 ()
path=0x20e66b80 pathtype=sclause method=NESTED ITERATION
outerrows=5772 rows=7282 joinsel=5772.000000 cpages=87 prefetch=N iosize=2
replace=LRU lp=502164 pp=87 corder=95

NEW PLAN (total cost = 87632):

varno=0 (pt_sample) indexid=0 ()
path=0x20e66920 pathtype=sclause method=NESTED ITERATION
outerrows=1 rows=5772 joinsel=1.000000 cpages=243 prefetch=N iosize=2
replace=LRU lp=243 pp=243 corder=95

varno=1 (pt_tx) indexid=0 ()
path=0x20e64510 pathtype=join method=REFORMATTING
outerrows=5772 rows=7282 joinsel=5772.000000 cpages=87 prefetch=N iosize=2
replace=LRU lp=11544 pp=73 corder=0
jnvar=0 refcost=58370 refpages=2 reftotpages=73 ordercol[0]=1  ordercol[1]=1

 1 - 0 -


TOTAL # PERMUTATIONS: 2



TOTAL # PLANS CONSIDERED: 4


CACHE USED BY THIS PLAN:

      CacheID = 0:    (2K) 316    (4K) 0    (8K) 0    (16K) 0
```

```
FINAL PLAN (total cost = 87632):

varno=0 (pt_sample) indexid=0 ()
path=0x20e66920 pathtype=sclause method=NESTED ITERATION
outerrows=1 rows=5772 joinsel=1.000000 cpages=243 prefetch=N iosize=2
replace=LRU lp=243 pp=243 corder=95

varno=1 (pt_tx) indexid=0 ()
path=0x20e64510 pathtype=join method=REFORMATTING
outerrows=5772 rows=7282 joinsel=5772.000000 cpages=87 prefetch=N iosize=2
replace=LRU lp=11544 pp=73 corder=0
jnvar=0 refcost=58370 refpages=2 reftotpages=73 ordercol[0]=1  ordercol[1]=1
```

Again, this information at first glance appears a bit cryptic, but soon you'll learn the keys you need to wade through this information and to comprehend what is going on in the join processing phase of your query.

> **NOTE**
>
> The dbcc traceon (310) output has been modified slightly in System 11. Some of the changes are provided to make the output a bit more readable. Others are necessary additions to reflect changes to the optimizer in System 11, such as prefetch and buffer replacement strategies.
>
> Where there are notable differences between System 11 and earlier releases of SQL Server, they will be described.

## QUERY IS [NOT] CONNECTED

QUERY IS [NOT] CONNECTED indicates whether the proper number of join clauses have been specified to avoid a Cartesian product (that is, all rows in one table are joined with every row in the other table). You typically hope to see that the query is connected, because Cartesian products can be very expensive in terms of I/O, even on moderately sized tables.

## 0 - 1 - ...

If this is a multi-table query containing a join, this statement indicates the join order permutation that the query optimizer is determining the cost of. This information is repeated for each valid join order the optimizer considers (for example, 0 - 1 - 2, 2 - 0 - 1, and so forth). The numbers correspond to the tables as listed in the query's FROM clause:

   0 = first table in from clause (varno=0)

   1 = second table in from clause (varno=1)

and so forth.

# NEW PLAN (total cost = ######):

`NEW PLAN (total cost = ######):` is printed for each join permutation considered. The total cost indicates the total I/O cost calculated for this plan in milliseconds.

Following the NEW PLAN line is the cost information, which is repeated for each table in the query. The order in which they appear in the output is the order in which they are being joined for this permutation. The first table listed under NEW PLAN is being considered as the outermost table, the second table listed under NEW PLAN is the first inner table, the third table listed is the second inner table, and so on.

The output for this information in System 11 is as follows:

```
varno=0 (pt_sample_CIid) indexid=0 ()
path=0x20dd6120 pathtype=sclause method=NESTED ITERATION
outerrows=1 rows=5772 joinsel=1.000000 cpages=243 prefetch=S iosize=16
replace=MRU lp=243 pp=243 corder=1
```

The output for System 10 looks similar to the following example:

```
varno=0 indexid=0 path=0x2071d9ac pathtype=sclause method=NESTED ITERATION
outerrows=1 rows=5772 joinsel=1 cpages=243 lp=243 pp=243 corder=1
```

This information is somewhat cryptic, but once you learn to decipher it, it contains a bunch of useful information. Table 14.6 describes some of the useful variables.

## Table 14.6. Description of variables displayed by `dbcc traceon (310)`.

| Variable | Description |
|----------|-------------|
| varno | Table number as listed in the from clause (0, 1, ...). Matches the varno listed in the 302 output. (System 11 now also displays the table name.) |
| indexid | ID of the index being used on this table for this permutation:<br>0 = base table<br>1 = clustered<br>>1 and <= 250 = nonclustered<br>(System 11 now also displays the index name.) |
| path | Bitmap representation of the pathtype. Can be ignored. |
| pathtype | Access path being used for this table for this permutation:<br>sclause—search clause (using index or table scan to find matching rows)<br>join—join clause<br>orstruct—OR strategy (using dynamic index) |

*continues*

### Table 14.6. continued

| Variable | Description |
|----------|-------------|
| method | Search method used to process this table:<br>NESTED ITERATION—standard method for reading from table making one or more passes (iterations)<br>REFORMATTING—using reformatting strategy (building temporary clustered index on-the-fly)<br>OR OPTIMIZATION—using OR strategy (that is, dynamic index) |
| outerrows | Number of iterations to be performed on this table; corresponds to number of rows in outer table. For the outermost table, outerrows will be 1. |
| rows | Estimated number of matching rows in this table. This information comes from the search clause processing phase and is based on the index statistics or built-in statistics. The value here corresponds with the value reported in the 302 output for this table using the specified index. |
| joinsel | Best cost join selectivity as reported by the 302 output for this table using the specified index. For the outer table, this will be 1. |
| cpages | Estimated number of page I/Os per lookup (index + data pages). |
| lp | Estimated number of logical page reads. This value is equal to the number of pages per lookup (cpages) times the number of iterations (outerrows). |
| pp | Estimated total number of physical page reads. For the outer table, this equals the total number of pages scanned for the single pass of the table. For an inner table, this equals the total number of pages physically read after all iterations. Note that if the inner table is larger than the available cache space, all iterations on the inner table are physical reads. In this case, pp equals lp. |
| corder | ID of the most significant sort column for this table for this query (corresponds to colid in syscolumns for this table). |

#### The following values are displayed when an index is used on the inner table or the reformatting strategy is considered:

| Variable | Description |
|----------|-------------|
| jnvar | Equals varno of the table the inner table is being joined from using the index. |
| refcost | Estimated I/O cost in terms of milliseconds to apply the reformatting strategy (0 if reformatting is not applied). Refer to Chapter 12 to see how this value is determined. |
| refpages | Number of pages per lookup using the temporary clustered index (0 if reformatting is not applied). |

| Variable | Description |
|----------|-------------|
| reftotpages | Total number of pages to be accessed for this table when the reformatting strategy is applied (0 if reformatting is not applied). |
| ordercol[#] | Indicates the column ID of the column in the inner table (# = 0) and the column ID it is joining against in the outer table (# = 1). |

### The following values are displayed only in System 11:

| Variable | Description |
|----------|-------------|
| prefetch | Indicates whether the prefetch strategy is being applied for this table. |
| iosize | Size of a physical I/O for this table. |
| replace | Buffer replacement strategy to be applied. |

The I/O cost for each table (total cost as displayed in the NEW PLAN line) is determined as follows:

(total logical page reads (lp) for all tables * 2 ms)

+ (total physical page reads for all tables (pp) * 18 ms)

# Ignoring Permutations

At times, the optimizer determines that some permutations are so unlikely to cost less than any plans examined thus far that it will ignore those permutations altogether. This saves processing time for the optimizer, but at times, it may possibly make the wrong assumption and ignore a plan that might possibly be cheaper.

When a permutation is ignored, you see just the join order listed (for example, 1 - 0) but no NEW PLAN costs generated.

If you want to verify that the optimizer isn't ignoring a plan that may be cheaper, reverse the order of the tables in the FROM clause. This causes the optimizer to process the table permutations in the reverse order and estimate the I/O cost for the previously ignored permutation. For example, consider the following query:

```
select company, amount
   from pt_sample s, pt_tx
   where t.id = s.id
```

Here is a portion of the 310 output for this query:

```
QUERY IS CONNECTED

0 - 1 -
NEW PLAN (total cost = 1010754):

varno=0 (pt_sample) indexid=0 ()
path=0x20e66920 pathtype=sclause method=NESTED ITERATION
```

```
outerrows=1 rows=5772 joinsel=1.000000 cpages=243 prefetch=N iosize=2
replace=LRU lp=243 pp=243 corder=95

varno=1 (pt_tx) indexid=0 ()
path=0x20e66b80 pathtype=sclause method=NESTED ITERATION
outerrows=5772 rows=7282 joinsel=5772.000000 cpages=87 prefetch=N iosize=2
replace=LRU lp=502164 pp=87 corder=95

NEW PLAN (total cost = 87632):

varno=0 (pt_sample) indexid=0 ()
path=0x20e66920 pathtype=sclause method=NESTED ITERATION
outerrows=1 rows=5772 joinsel=1.000000 cpages=243 prefetch=N iosize=2
replace=LRU lp=243 pp=243 corder=95

varno=1 (pt_tx) indexid=0 ()
path=0x20e64510 pathtype=join method=REFORMATTING
outerrows=5772 rows=7282 joinsel=5772.000000 cpages=87 prefetch=N iosize=2
replace=LRU lp=11544 pp=73 corder=0
jnvar=0 refcost=58370 refpages=2 reftotpages=73 ordercol[0]=1  ordercol[1]=1

  1 - 0 -


TOTAL # PERMUTATIONS: 2
```

Let's first break out the individual components of this output.

The first join order examined is from pt_sample to pt_tx (0 - 1). The first plan considered for this join order (NEW PLAN (total cost = 1010754)) is a table scan on the outer table, pt_sample (varno=0, indexid=0), and a table scan on the inner table, pt_tx (varno=1, indexid=0). The total cost of the first plan considered is 1,010,754 milliseconds.

The processing method used on both tables in the first plan considered is the normal query processing (NESTED ITERATION). Because the outer table, pt_sample, is scanned only once (outerrows=1), the number of logical page reads (lp=243) is the same as the physical reads (pp=243, cpages=243 × outerrows=1). The total I/O cost for the pt_sample table is the following:

> 243 logical page reads × 2 ms  = 486 ms
> + 243 physical page reads × 18 ms = 4,374 ms
> = 4,860 ms

Next, the optimizer determines the total I/O cost for the pt_tx table (varno=1).

The total number of pages per iteration on pt_tx is 87 pages (cpages=87) because a table scan would also be performed for each iteration. The total number of iterations performed is 5,772 (outerrows=5772). This value equals the total number of rows in the outer table, pt_sample (varno=0, rows=5772). Therefore, here is the total number of logical page reads:

> 5,772 iterations × 87 pages per iteration = 502,164 total logical page reads

The total I/O cost for the `pt_tx` table is this:

> 502,164 logical page reads × 2 ms = 1,004,328 ms
>
> + 87 physical page reads × 18 ms = 1,566 ms
>
> = 1,005,894 ms

The total I/O cost for the first plan is estimated to be 1,010,754 milliseconds, or nearly 17 minutes.

That's quite a long time for some rather small tables. Because neither of these tables has a usable index for this query, the optimizer considered applying the reformatting strategy on the `pt_tx` table (`varno=1, method=REFORMATTING`). This is the second plan considered (`NEW PLAN (total cost = 87632)`). The costs for the outer table, `pt_sample` (`varno=0`) are the same for this plan, but the cost for `pt_tx` are the costs associated with applying the reformatting strategy on `pt_tx`.

The reformatting strategy itself has an estimated I/O cost of 58,370 milliseconds (`refcost=58370`). The number of pages per lookup using the temporary clustered index is 2 (`refpages=2`) and the total number of pages accessed is 73 (`reftotpages=73`). Because you now have a clustered index on the table and do not have to read the entire table into cache, the number of physical page reads is the same as the number of pages accessed, 73 (`pp=73`). The total number of logical I/Os is the following:

> 2 pages (`refpages=2`) × 5,772 iterations (`outerrows=5772`)
>
> = 11,544 logical page reads

The total I/O cost for the `pt_tx` table, including the cost of reformatting, is this:

> 11,544 * 2 ms = 23,088
>
> + 73 * 18 ms  = 1,314
>
> + 58,370 ms (cost of reformatting)
>
> = 82,772 ms

This plus the I/O cost on `pt_sample` (4,860 ms) is a more reasonable 87,632 milliseconds, or 1.3 minutes. Quite obviously, the cost of using the reformatting strategy is considerably less than the cost of joining via a table scan on the inner table. However, at this point, the optimizer makes the assumption that the reformatting plan is the lowest plan to be found and ignores the alternative permutation of `pt_tx` as the outer table and `pt_sample` as the inner table. Just for fun (and because I am always somewhat skeptical) let's force the optimizer to evaluate this alternative, first by switching the order of the tables in the FROM clause:

```
select company, amount from pt_tx t, pt_sample s
where t.id = s.id
```

Here is the 310 output for this example:

```
QUERY IS CONNECTED

 0 - 1 -
NEW PLAN (total cost = 3545166):

varno=0 (pt_tx) indexid=0 ()
path=0x20dd8920 pathtype=sclause method=NESTED ITERATION
outerrows=1 rows=7282 joinsel=1.000000 cpages=87 prefetch=N iosize=2
replace=LRU lp=87 pp=87 corder=95

varno=1 (pt_sample) indexid=0 ()
path=0x20dd8b80 pathtype=sclause method=NESTED ITERATION
outerrows=7282 rows=7282 joinsel=5772.000000 cpages=243 prefetch=N iosize=2
replace=LRU lp=1769526 pp=243 corder=95

NEW PLAN (total cost = 172252):

varno=0 (pt_tx) indexid=0 ()
path=0x20dd8920 pathtype=sclause method=NESTED ITERATION
outerrows=1 rows=7282 joinsel=1.000000 cpages=87 prefetch=N iosize=2
replace=LRU lp=87 pp=87 corder=95

varno=1 (pt_sample) indexid=0 ()
path=0x20dd7078 pathtype=join method=REFORMATTING
outerrows=7282 rows=7282 joinsel=5772.000000 cpages=243 prefetch=N iosize=2
replace=LRU lp=14564 pp=448 corder=0
jnvar=0 refcost=133320 refpages=2 reftotpages=448 ordercol[0]=1  ordercol[1]=1

 1 - 0 -
NEW PLAN (total cost = 87632):

varno=1 (pt_sample) indexid=0 ()
path=0x20dd8b80 pathtype=sclause method=NESTED ITERATION
outerrows=1 rows=5772 joinsel=1.000000 cpages=243 prefetch=N iosize=2
replace=LRU lp=243 pp=243 corder=95

varno=0 (pt_tx) indexid=0 ()
path=0x20dd7210 pathtype=join method=REFORMATTING
outerrows=5772 rows=7282 joinsel=5772.000000 cpages=87 prefetch=N iosize=2
replace=LRU lp=11544 pp=73 corder=0
jnvar=1 refcost=58370 refpages=2 reftotpages=73 ordercol[0]=1  ordercol[1]=1


TOTAL # PERMUTATIONS: 2



TOTAL # PLANS CONSIDERED: 4



CACHE USED BY THIS PLAN:

    CacheID = 0:     (2K) 316     (4K) 0     (8K) 0     (16K) 0
```

```
FINAL PLAN (total cost = 87632):

varno=1 (pt_sample) indexid=0 ()
path=0x20dd8b80 pathtype=sclause method=NESTED ITERATION
outerrows=1 rows=5772 joinsel=1.000000 cpages=243 prefetch=N iosize=2
replace=LRU lp=243 pp=243 corder=95

varno=0 (pt_tx) indexid=0 ()
path=0x20dd7210 pathtype=join method=REFORMATTING
outerrows=5772 rows=7282 joinsel=5772.000000 cpages=87 prefetch=N iosize=2
replace=LRU lp=11544 pp=73 corder=0
jnvar=1 refcost=58370 refpages=2 reftotpages=73 ordercol[0]=1  ordercol[1]=1
```

Note that the total plan I/O cost of applying the reformatting strategy on the pt_sample table with pt_tx as the outer table is 172,252 milliseconds, or approximately 3 minutes. This plan is about twice as expensive as the cheapest plan estimate in the previous example with pt_tx as the outer table. Note also that the optimizer in this case continued and evaluated the reformatting strategy for the other permutation. So, when it skipped looking at using pt_tx as the outer table before, it was making the correct assumption that it would be more expensive.

In this example, the order of the tables in the FROM clause did not affect the choice of the best query plan.

## TOTAL # PERMUTATIONS: N

TOTAL # PERMUTATIONS: *N* represents the total number of possible join orders to be considered. Refer to Chapter 12 for a discussion of how SQL Server evaluates all possible join permutations. For two tables, the number of permutations is 2. For four tables, the number of permutations is 24.

## TOTAL # PLANS CONSIDERED: N

TOTAL # PLANS CONSIDERED: *N* represents the total number of all possible query plans the optimizer might have evaluated to determine the lowest query cost. This is the sum of all possible query plans that could have been evaluated for each permutation considered.

## FINAL PLAN (total cost = ##):

FINAL PLAN (total cost = ##): merely reiterates the costing information for the permutation with the lowest estimated I/O cost. This is the "final" plan, which will be used to process the query. It is the information that is interpreted and displayed by the showplan output.

## OR Strategy Example

Just for fun, let's take a look at the dbcc traceon (302) and (310) output for a query with an or clause:

```
select * from pt_sample_CIid
where id = 1000
or id = 100000
```

Let's break out the 302 and 310 output into parts and try to understand what's being evaluated and estimated at each point:

```
********************************
Entering q_score_index() for table 'pt_sample' (objectid 16003088, varno = 0).
The table has 5772 rows and 243 pages.
Scoring the SEARCH CLAUSE:
    id EQ

Base cost: indid: 0 rows: 5772 pages: 243 prefetch: N
    I/O size: 2 cacheid: 0 replace: LRU
Unique clustered index found--return rows 1 pages 2

Cheapest index is index 1, costing 2 pages and
    generating 1 rows per scan, using no data prefetch (size 2)
    on dcacheid 0 with LRU replacement
Search argument selectivity is 0.000173.

********************************


********************************
Entering q_score_index() for table 'pt_sample' (objectid 16003088, varno = 0).
The table has 5772 rows and 243 pages.
Scoring the SEARCH CLAUSE:
    id EQ

Base cost: indid: 0 rows: 5772 pages: 243 prefetch: N
    I/O size: 2 cacheid: 0 replace: LRU
Unique clustered index found--return rows 1 pages 2

Cheapest index is index 1, costing 2 pages and
    generating 1 rows per scan, using no data prefetch (size 2)
    on dcacheid 0 with LRU replacement
Search argument selectivity is 0.000173.

********************************
```

Because the OR clause is on the same column, and a unique clustered index exists on the column, the optimizer evaluates the cost of applying the OR strategy and performing two separate lookups on pt_sample using the unique clustered index on id. This cost is compared against a table scan that would cost 243 pages.

By using the unique clustered index in two separate lookups, it would cost two pages per lookup to find both qualifying rows for a total of four pages.

This is the end of the search clause processing phase. Even though there is no join in the query, there is still a join processing phase to estimate the total I/O cost using the cheapest access method determined during the search clause processing. The 310 output for this query is as follows:

```
QUERY IS CONNECTED
```

```
  0 -
NEW PLAN (total cost = 80):

varno=0 (pt_sample) indexid=0 ()
path=0x20d90e80 pathtype=orstruct method=OR OPTIMIZATION
outerrows=1 rows=2 joinsel=1.000000 cpages=4 prefetch=N iosize=0 replace=LRU
lp=4 pp=4 corder=0



TOTAL # PERMUTATIONS: 1



TOTAL # PLANS CONSIDERED: 1



CACHE USED BY THIS PLAN:

    CacheID = 0:     (2K) 4      (4K) 0      (8K) 0      (16K) 0

FINAL PLAN (total cost = 80):

varno=0 (pt_sample) indexid=0 ()
path=0x20d90e80 pathtype=orstruct method=OR OPTIMIZATION
outerrows=1 rows=2 joinsel=1.000000 cpages=4 prefetch=N iosize=0 replace=LRU
lp=4 pp=4 corder=0
```

This shows that the optimizer is using the OR strategy (method=OR OPTIMIZATION) rather than a table scan or normal single scan index retrieval. Notice that the total physical page reads are 4 (pp=4) and the total logical page reads are 4 (lp=4). This is the sum of the I/O cost for the two separate lookups using the clustered index. Four pages is significantly less than 243 pages, which would have been the I/O cost if a table scan were performed.

# Using *statistics io* and *statistics time*

To this point, you've seen how the optimizer evaluates your queries and estimates the number of I/Os and the I/O processing time and picks what it determines is the cheapest query plan. The decisions the optimizer makes are based on index statistics and row estimates.

You may next want to compare the optimizer estimates against the actual number of I/Os and actual query processing time to verify the estimates being generated by the optimizer.

## *statistics io*

SQL Server supplies a set option that causes the actual logical and physical page reads incurred by the query to be displayed. This option is the statistics io option and is turned on by executing the following command:

```
set statistics io on
```

> **TIP**
>
> If you've been viewing showplan and dbcc trace flag output, make sure you turn noexec off before running a query with statistics io on. The statistics io values are actual I/O counts generated when the query is executed. If noexec is on, the query won't run and no I/O statistics will be generated.

The statistics io option displays the total logical page reads per table, the total physical page reads per table, the scan count (that is, number of iterations) for each table, and the total writes performed to process the query. (Unless a worktable is required, the total writes for a select statement typically is 0.) The following is a query and a sample of the statistics io output generated for it:

```
select sum(amount) from pt_sample_CIid s, pt_tx_CIid t
where s.id = t.id

---------------------------
501,590,426.59

Table: pt_sample_CIid  scan count 1,  logical reads: 243,  physical reads: 243
Table: pt_tx_CIid  scan count 5772,  logical reads: 11667,  physical reads: 118
Total writes for this command: 0
```

In this example, pt_sample_CIid is the outer table and is scanned once (scan count 1). pt_tx_CIid is the inner table and is scanned 5772 times. SQL Server performed 243 logical reads and 243 physical reads on pt_sample_CIid, and 118 physical reads and 11667 logical reads on pt_tx_CIid. Because every physical page read requires a logical page read for SQL Server to process the page, the count of physical page reads will never exceed the number of logical page reads. However, you can experience a high number of logical page reads and few or zero physical page reads. If physical reads are 0, the table was entirely in cache when the query was executed.

## Scan Counts

Any single table query that uses a table scan or a single index scan will report a scan count of 1. Scan counts can be higher than 1 for tables that are inner tables in a join or for a table that is accessed by using the OR strategy (more than one index scan performed).

There are also times you may see a scan count of 0. This is reported for queries that use temporary tables or queries that perform deferred updates. In addition, the scan count on worktables for order by or distinct queries may report a scan count of 0.

## Using *statistics io*

One good use of the statistics io output is to evaluate the effectiveness of the size of your data cache. By turning this option on you can monitor the logical versus physical reads to see how much of your table(s) are staying in cache over time. If the physical page counts are consistently as high as the logical page reads, the table is not staying in cache, and you may need to modify the SQL Server configuration to increase data cache size (see Chapters 30, "Configuring and Tuning the SQL Server," and 31, "Optimizing SQL Server Configuration Options").

> **NOTE**
>
> In System 11, the `physical reads` count for a table may be less than `logical reads` if the optimizer takes advantage of System 11's capability of prefetching extents when doing sequential page reads. `physical reads` is not a count of pages read but a count of the number of times SQL Server must access the disk.
>
> If a query is able to take advantage of "prefetching" (that is, performing sequential reads), SQL Server will be able to recognize this and make use of the `prefetch` mechanism to minimize individual physical page accesses.
>
> For example, if the query uses 16KB I/Os, it reads eight pages at a time. If it performs 10 physical I/Os, it will have read 80 pages.
>
> Let's run the following query using 16KB I/O and see what the I/O results are:
>
> ```
> select count(company)from pt_sample_CIid (index idx1 prefetch 16 lru)
> go
> ```
>
> ```
> Table: pt_sample_CIid   scan count 1,   logical reads: 243,   physical reads: 31
> Total writes for this command: 0
> ```
>
> Using 16KB I/O, this query performed only 31 physical reads to read into cache 243 pages ($8 \times 31 = 248$).
>
> Additionally, the buffer replacement strategy used by the query in System 11 will affect `physical reads` for subsequent executions. If the MRU strategy is used, pages are read in near the wash marker and may be flushed from cache very quickly, so a second execution of the query will generate high physical I/Os. If the LRU strategy is used, pages are read into the beginning of the MRU/LRU chain and stay in cache longer. Subsequent executions of the query may incur little or no physical I/Os.

The other common use of `statistics io` is to evaluate the page estimates generated by the query optimizer for a query plan. If the actual numbers differ significantly from the optimizer's estimates for number of pages estimated by the optimizer, it indicates that the optimizer is making an inaccurate estimate. This could be due to a bug or weakness in the optimizer's costing algorithm, or to statistics that are woefully out of date. You should probably try updating statistics first and rerunning the command with `statistics io` on before you call Tech Support with a complaint about the query optimizer.

> **NOTE**
>
> In my experience, the SQL Server optimizer does a pretty good job of estimating page I/O. Obviously, because they are estimates based on index statistics, they are not typically going to match the actual page I/Os exactly. I wouldn't suspect an optimizer problem unless the estimates were substantially different from the actuals—probably any difference greater than 1,000 pages or more than a 10 percent margin of error.
>
> Compare only the logical I/O counts reported by `statistics io` against the SQL Server estimates. When the optimizer is making its I/O estimates, it makes no assumptions about any data that may already be in cache. Rather, it takes the more pessimistic view that all initial page reads on a table will be `physical reads`.

Let's take a look at the final plan displayed by the `dbcc traceon (310)` command, along with the `statistics io` for the following query, and compare the page estimates against the actual I/O statistics generated:

```
select sum(amount) from pt_sample_CIid s, pt_tx_CIid t
where s.id = t.id

FINAL PLAN (total cost = 30072):

varno=0 (pt_sample_CIid) indexid=0 ()
path=0x20f27120 pathtype=sclause method=NESTED ITERATION
outerrows=1 rows=5772 joinsel=1.000000 cpages=243 prefetch=N iosize=2
replace=LRU lp=243 pp=243 corder=1

varno=1 (pt_tx_CIid) indexid=1 (tx_CIid)
path=0x20f25590 pathtype=join method=NESTED ITERATION
outerrows=5772 rows=8338 joinsel=5041.153847 cpages=2 prefetch=N iosize=2
replace=LRU lp=11544 pp=118 corder=1
jnvar=0 refcost=0 refpages=0 reftotpages=0 ordercol[0]=1  ordercol[1]=1

 --------------------------
501,590,426.59
Table: pt_sample_CIid  scan count 1,    logical reads: 243,   physical reads: 64
Table: pt_tx_CIid  scan count 5772,   logical reads: 11667,  physical reads: 40
Total writes for this command: 0
Total writes for this command: 0
```

The optimizer estimated that there would be 243 total logical page reads on the outer table `pt_sample_CIid` (varno=0, lp=243). This matches exactly with the actual I/O count generated by `statistics io`. For `pt_tx_CIid` (varno=1), it estimated 11544 logical page reads and 5772 iterations. It did perform 5772 iterations on the `pt_tx_CIid` table, but it performed 11667 logical page reads—a difference of 123 pages and an error margin of only 1 percent. Using the optimizer estimate of 2 milliseconds per page, this is only about .25 seconds—not a significant amount of time.

Speaking of time, how closely do the time estimates generated by the optimizer correspond to the actual execution times?

# statistics time

To display the total CPU and elapsed time to execute a query and the time to parse and compile the query, turn on the `statistics time` option with the following command:

```
set statistics time on
```

> **TIP**
>
> Again, make sure you turn `noexec` off before running a query with `statistics time` on or the query will not be executed and no time statistics for execution of the query will be generated. However, the query will still be parsed and compiled, so time statistics for those will be generated.

Parse and compile time is reported as the number of CPU ticks required to parse, optimize, and compile the query. Execution time is the number of CPU ticks taken to execute the query. SQL Server CPU time is the number of CPU ticks to execute the query.

The following formula can be used to convert CPU ticks to milliseconds:

$$( \text{CPU ticks} * \text{clock rate} ) / 1000$$

To determine the value for clock rate in System 11, execute `sp_configure "sql server clock tick length"`. This option is configurable in System 11 as described in Chapter 30. In System 10, it is not configurable or viewable with `sp_configure`. You can see the value for the clock rate by running the following command:

```
buildmaster -d master_device -yall
```

This command gives a dump of the config block for the master device. The clock rate is the value reported for the configuration option `cclkrate`.

Elapsed time is the total time to process a query based on the operating system clock.

# Using statistics time

Let's use `statistics time` to compare the actual elapsed time reported with the estimated I/O times generated by the optimizer for the following query:

```
select sum(amount) from pt_sample_CIid s, pt_tx_CIid t
where s.id = t.id

Parse and Compile Time 1.
SQL Server cpu time: 500 ms.

--------------------------
501,590,426.50
```

```
Table: pt_sample_CIid  scan count 1,  logical reads: 243,  physical reads: 64
Table: pt_tx_CIid  scan count 5772,  logical reads: 11667,  physical reads: 40
Total writes for this command: 0
Total writes for this command: 0

Execution Time 7.
SQL Server cpu time: 3500 ms.  SQL Server elapsed time: 3540 ms.
(1 rows affected)
```

The times estimated by the SQL Server optimizer can be viewed with the dbcc traceon (310) trace flag:

```
FINAL PLAN (total cost = 30072):

varno=0 (pt_sample_CIid) indexid=0 ()
path=0x20f27120 pathtype=sclause method=NESTED ITERATION
outerrows=1 rows=5772 joinsel=1.000000 cpages=243 prefetch=N iosize=2
replace=LRU lp=243 pp=243 corder=1

varno=1 (pt_tx_CIid) indexid=1 (tx_CIid)
path=0x20f25590 pathtype=join method=NESTED ITERATION
outerrows=5772 rows=8338 joinsel=5041.153847 cpages=2 prefetch=N iosize=2
replace=LRU lp=11544 pp=118 corder=1
jnvar=0 refcost=0 refpages=0 reftotpages=0 ordercol[0]=1  ordercol[1]=1
```

In this example, the SQL Server time estimate (30072 ms) is significantly higher than the actual elapsed time of 3540 ms. But in this case, the SQL Server estimated a greater number of physical reads than actually occurred. Let's apply the I/O time estimates against the actual logical and physical page counts:

> 0 physical reads * 18 ms = 0 ms
>
> + (11,667 + 243) logical reads * 2 ms = 23,820 ms
>
> = 23,820 ms

This value is still considerably higher than the actual elapsed time. In addition, the query optimizer's time estimate does not factor in network I/O times. If you have a moderately large result set, the time to send the results across the network can exceed the actual query processing time. The elapsed time reported by statistics time is the total time from when the query execution was initiated to when the final DONE packet is sent to the client application. It includes all time spent by the query to send results to the client, any time spent waiting for CPU cycles, time spent performing physical I/O, plus any time spent waiting for a lock request to be granted.

In other words, don't expect the estimated time displayed by the dbcc traceon (310) trace flag to match the actual elapsed time to execute the query. The optimizer time estimates are primarily for comparison purposes by the optimizer. The time estimates for logical and physical page access times, 2 ms and 18 ms, respectively, are hard-coded values and don't necessarily represent actual I/O rates for the platform on which you are running.

The real useful purpose for the statistics time option is to record the actual CPU and elapsed time values for queries and transactions to benchmark and compare execution times. You also can use the output to identify queries with high parse and compile times. Some queries may even have higher parse and compile times than execution times. These would be good candidates to place in stored procedures to reap the benefits of reusable query plans residing in procedure cache and avoid the expensive parse and compile steps for each execution.

## A Minor Anomaly with *statistics time*

Before you finish exploring `statistics time`, it is worthwhile to point out a slight difference in the way the CPU time is calculated versus how the elapsed time is calculated. This can sometimes result in odd-looking values, such as cases where CPU time is greater then elapsed time, or when CPU time is 0 and there is substantially more elapsed time.

The elapsed time is based on the system time. It is determined by subtracting the system time when the query initially started execution from the system time when SQL Server sends the final DONE packet to the client application.

The CPU time is factored as the number of CPU ticks tallied for the query, converted to milliseconds. A CPU tick is the time interval between clock interrupts on a system. The number of milliseconds per CPU tick is determined by dividing the clock rate by 1,000.

Figure 14.2 shows the first scenario where CPU time exceeds elapsed time.

**FIGURE 14.2.**

*Example of how CPU time can exceed elapsed time.*

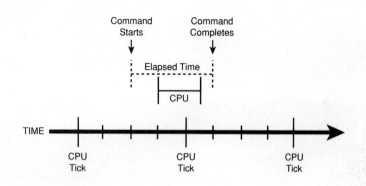

Notice how the command starts CPU processing just prior to a clock tick and completes just after. Because it was doing CPU processing at the time of a clock interrupt, a CPU tick was tallied for that process. If you assume that a CPU tick translates to 100 ms, the CPU time recorded for this process is 100 ms. However, the actual elapsed time from start to finish for the command appears to be only about 75 ms. Thus, the reported CPU time is more than the elapsed time.

Let's now look at a second scenario: a CPU time of 0 with substantially more elapsed time.

**FIGURE 14.3.**

*Example of how zero CPU time can be accounted.*

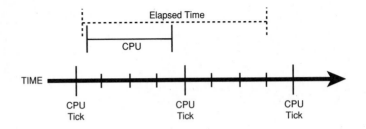

Scale: CPU Tick = 100 ms

In this example, the command starts CPU processing just after a CPU tick and completes prior to the next CPU tick. Since a CPU tick was not encountered, no CPU time is recorded. The total elapsed time from start to finish for this command appears to be around 175 ms. Here is a case where the reported CPU time is 0, even though the process did incur CPU processing time.

# Summary

SQL Server provides a number of tools to view and evaluate the query plans being generated by the query optimizer. You can use the showplan option to view the query plan chosen by the optimizer and the DBCC TRACEON (302, 310) trace flags to determine how the optimizer chose that query plan. You can use the statistics io and statistics time options to evaluate the actual performance of queries and validate the cost estimates of the query optimizer.

Through the use of these tools, you may sometimes discover that the optimizer is choosing the wrong plan, or at other times, you may simply want to force the optimizer to process a query differently than it chooses to. In Chapter 16, we'll examine some methods for forcing particular query plans and the conditions for when you may wish to do this.

# Locking and Performance

**15**

# SQL Server Locks Defined

In any multi-user database, there must be a consistent set of rules for making changes to data. The rules may be "there are no rules," but that still is a rule. For a true transaction processing database, the database management system is responsible for resolving potential conflicts between two different processes that are attempting to change the same piece of information at the same time. Such a situation cannot occur, because the atomicity of a transaction cannot be guaranteed. For example, if two users were to change the same data at approximately the same time, whose change would be propagated? Theoretically, the results would be unpredictable, because the answer is dependent on whose transaction completed last. Because most applications try to avoid "unpredictability" with data wherever possible (imagine your payroll systems returning "unpredictable" results, and you'll get the idea), there must be some way to guarantee the sequential, and atomic, nature of data changes.

The responsibility for ensuring conflict resolution between users falls on the SQL Server locking manager. Locks are used to guarantee that the current user of any resource (data page, table, index, and so on) has a consistent view of that resource from beginning to end of a particular operation. In other words, what you start with has to be what you work with throughout your operation. Nobody can change what you're working on in mid-state; in effect, intercepting your transaction.

Without locking, transaction processing is impossible. *Transactions*, being defined as complete units of work, rely on a constant state of data, almost a "snapshot in time" of what they are modifying, in order to guarantee their completion. Transactions and locking, therefore, are part of the same whole—ensuring the completion of data modifications.

# SQL Server Lock Granularities

Historically, all SQL Server locking management has been internal to SQL Server: there was no application-level of locking granularity or control. While there now is some control over lock behavior, as covered later in this chapter, the granularity for SQL Server locks still is fixed.

Lock granularity is the minimum amount of data that is locked as part of a query or update. Locking can be performed at the level of a server, a database, a table, a row, or even a column. The smaller the lock size, the greater the number of potential concurrent users—but the greater the overhead in maintaining those locks. The greater the lock size, the less overhead that is required to manage locks—but the less concurrency. Figure 15.1 illustrates these trade-offs between performance and concurrency.

The SQL Server balances performance and concurrency by locking at the page level or higher, and all locking is done implicitly by SQL Server—that is, the right type of lock is applied automatically to ensure data consistency in a multiuser environment.

**FIGURE 15.1.**

*Trade-offs between performance and concurrency, depending on lock granularity.*

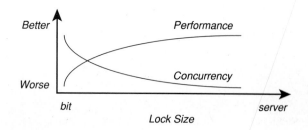

The smallest unit of work for any SQL Server operation, including locking, happens at the 2KB data-page level. In other words, SQL Server locks all of the rows on a particular page when that page is read or changed. For efficiency purposes, SQL Server also can use extent locks, but it uses these only to allocate new space for data tables. For queries that affect large percentages of available rows, SQL Server may choose to upgrade a collection of page locks to a table lock. In effect, SQL Server "trades in" a collection of locks of a smaller granularity for one of larger granularity. Any lock, regardless of granularity, consumes the same quantity of resource overhead. Therefore, a single table lock is more efficient than 5,000 individual page locks, even though this does introduce a concurrency issue.

# SQL Server Lock Types

The SQL Server relies on a variety of lock types and lock granularities in its work. Here are the three basic lock types:

- Shared locks—used by processes that are reading pages. Multiple shared locks can be held on any page; a single shared lock prevents any exclusive lock from being acquired. Shared locks typically are held only for the duration of the read on a particular page. If holdlock is specified, shared locks are held until the completion of the command or the transaction it is in.

- Update locks—used by processes that update or delete data, but have not yet done so. Update locks are acquired as the set or rows to be updated or deleted is being determined. Update locks are read-compatible with shared locks during the premodification phase, but no other update lock or exclusive lock can be acquired on the page. Update locks automatically are updated to exclusive locks when the data change occurs.

- Exclusive Locks—used by processes that currently are adding information to, changing information in, or deleting information from, data pages. Exclusive locks prevent any other type of lock (exclusive lock, update lock, or shared lock) from being acquired. Exclusive locks are held on all affected pages until an explicit transaction is complete, or until the command in an implicit transaction (a transaction that has no explicit begin tran/commit tran pair in its statements) is complete.

Table 15.1 summarizes the lock types and levels for SQL statements.

**Table 15.1. Lock types and levels for SQL Server commands.**

| Statement | Index Used Table Level | Page Level | Index not Used Table Level | Page Level |
|---|---|---|---|---|
| select | Shared intent | Shared | Shared intent | Shared |
| select holdlock | Shared intent | Shared | Shared | |
| update | Exclusive intent | Update, then exclusive | Exclusive | |
| insert | Exclusive intent | Exclusive | Exclusive intent | Exclusive |
| delete | Exclusive intent | Update, then exclusive | Exclusive | |

# Shared Locks

The SQL Server uses shared locks for all read operations. A read lock is, by definition, not exclusive, meaning that a theoretically unlimited number of shared locks can be on any page at any given time. In addition, shared locks are unique in that the particular page being locked is locked only by a process for the duration of the read on that page. For example, a query such as

```
select * from authors
```

locks the first page in the authors table when the query starts. After the first page is read, a lock on the second page is acquired and the lock on the first page is released. After the second page is read, a lock on the third page is acquired and the lock on the second page is released, and so on until all pages have been read.

To force a table-level lock or page-level lock to be held for the duration of a transaction, you can specify the holdlock keyword. For example, the query

```
select * from authors holdlock
```

acquires a table-level shared lock holding all pages until either the select complete or the transaction containing the select is committed or rolled back. In this fashion, a select…holdlock query returns a snapshot of data from the table, and that table data cannot be modified during such a read operation. If an index is used to satisfy the query, SQL Server starts out with page-level shared locks and holds them until the select, or transaction containing the select, completes. If the page locks are held and the lock-escalation threshold is exceeded, SQL Server may escalate to a table-level lock. (More on this later.)

Shared locks are "compatible," to use SQL Server terminology, with other shared locks, as well as with update locks. In this way, a shared lock does not prevent the acquisition of shared locks and update locks on a given page. Those user connections requesting shared locks or update locks are not prevented from acquiring them if a shared lock already exists on a page. However, shared locks do prevent the acquisition of exclusive locks.

For all releases of SQL Server prior to version 10.1, SQL Server prevented the ability to perform "dirty reads." *Dirty reads* are the ability to read data that currently is being modified but is not yet committed. The read is considered "dirty" because the actual data value being returned by the read query could be the value before the change, or it could be the value after the change, or the value read could be subsequently rolled back. The result itself is dependent on the timing of the operations involved. Because this is, by definition, an unpredictable result, SQL Server prevented such things from occurring, using shared locks to prevent any exclusive locks from being acquired. However, in versions 10.1 and later, you can override this behavior at the session level, query level, or both, as you see later in this chapter.

> **NOTE**
>
> SQL Server actually disables the locking manager, and any locking capabilities, for databases that have the read only option turned on using sp_dboption. If your database is read-only, using this option yields both the easiest database maintenance and the best performance improvement available.

## Update Locks

Update locks are used to mark pages that a user process is about to modify. An update lock is compatible with shared locks, in that both can be acquired on a single data page. Update locks are partially exclusive, in that only one update lock can be acquired on any page. In effect, an update lock signifies that a user wants to change a page while keeping out other connections that also want to change that page. As a result, update locks are useful in avoiding deadlock, a situation I discuss in detail later in this chapter. In the situation in which there are existing shared locks on a page and a user connection acquires an update lock, the update lock waits for all of the shared locks to be released. At that point, SQL Server automatically promotes the update lock to an exclusive lock, allowing the data change to proceed.

If the user connection sending the data-change request has done so through an explicit transaction (by including begin tran/commit tran statements in the submitted batch), the exclusive lock is held for the duration of the transaction; that is, until either a commit tran or rollback tran is encountered, or the server is stopped and restarted in the case of an aborted transaction.

If the user connection sending the data-change request has not defined an explicit transaction, the newly acquired exclusive lock is released immediately after that particular statement has completed.

# Exclusive Locks

Exclusive locks are used for those operations that are changing data. Exclusive locks are prevented when a data page is being read and, by default, all data reads are prevented during data modifications. In this way, exclusive locks prevent dirty reads. Later in this chapter, I discuss methods of modifying this default behavior for SQL Server.

Exclusive locks are incompatible with any other lock type. If a page has shared, update, or exclusive locks on it by another process, the exclusive lock request is forced to wait in a queue for the page to become available. If an exclusive lock is on a page, any read or update requests by other processes are similarly queued until the exclusive lock is released.

Exclusive locks are held for the duration of an explicit transaction, or for the duration of a statement in a simple batch.

# Transact-SQL Statements and Associated Locks

Different Transact-SQL operations affect locking in different ways, and the different ways you combine SQL statements also can have an impact.

select queries always acquire shared locks. As I described earlier, those shared locks are acquired and released in sequential order as pages are read. The only exception to this is to use the holdlock keyword. holdlock forces SQL Server to hold the shared page locks for the duration of the select, or the transaction containing the select. If the holdlock keyword is specified and the query must be satisfied by a table scan, SQL Server attempts to acquire a table-level shared lock.

insert statements always acquire exclusive page-level locks. update and delete queries always acquire some type of exclusive lock to perform data modifications. If the query first has to collect the set of rows to be modified before actually updating them, or if a select statement has shared locks on the pages, a delete or update statement first acquires an update lock, which subsequently is upgraded to an exclusive lock once the row updates are processed. If the query is an update or delete of the whole table, or if the query requires a table scan to process the update or delete, SQL Server automatically attempts to acquire a table-level exclusive lock that, once acquired, is held for duration of the statement or transaction.

# Table-Level Locks

SQL Server generally tries to lock at the page level to maximize concurrency. While a process has page-level locks on a table, SQL Server also gives the process a corresponding intent lock on the table.

An *intent lock* indicates, at the table level, the types of locks that are being acquired at the page level. The SQL Server applies an intent table lock when a process acquires a page-level shared or exclusive lock. The intent lock is used to prevent another process from acquiring a shared or exclusive table-level lock in case the current process has to escalate to a table-level lock. Intent locks are held for as long as a process holds a page-level lock on the table.

As the number of page locks on a table increase for a single command, SQL Server may escalate to a table-level lock. If an update or delete statement contains search arguments (SARGs) that the query optimizer can use to estimate the number of rows, and therefore pages, to be updated or deleted, SQL Server will begin by acquiring page-level locks. If the number of page locks acquired subsequently exceeds the lock escalation threshold, the SQL Server will attempt to escalate the page-level locks to a table-level lock. If an update or delete command does not contain a valid SARG, SQL Server automatically grabs a table-level lock.

There are two types of table-level locks: shared and exclusive. A *shared table-level lock* permits other processes to read at the page or table level, but prevents any exclusive locks at the page or table level. A shared table-level lock is acquired:

- When a nonclustered index is created on a table
- For certain DBCC commands (for example, dbcc checktable)
- When a select statement specifies the holdlock keyword and any of the following is true:

  There is no valid SARG in the query.

  The SARG does not match an available index.

  The number of pages locked by the select with holdlock statement exceeds the lock-escalation threshold.

Consider the following queries:

```
select * from titles holdlock

select * from titles holdlock where price > $10
```

The first query automatically acquires a shared table-level lock because the entire table is scanned (there is no SARG the optimizer can use to limit the query). For the second query, if there were no index on price, SQL Server would acquire a shared table-level lock. If there were an index on price, the query would initially acquire shared page locks and a shared intent lock on the table. Should the number of pages locked exceed the lock-escalation threshold, SQL Server would attempt to escalate to a shared table-level lock, as long as there were no conflicting page-level locks (that is, exclusive page locks) on other pages in the table.

An exclusive table-level lock prevents any other type of lock from being acquired at the page or table level. SQL Server applies an exclusive table-level lock:

- During creation of a clustered index
- For update and delete statements, when any of the following is true:

    There is no valid SARG in the query.

    The SARG does not match an available index.

    The number of pages locked by the update or delete statement exceeds the lock-escalation threshold.

Consider the following queries:

```
update titles set price = price * 1.10
```

```
delete titles where price < $10
```

The first query automatically acquires an exclusive table-level lock because the entire table is scanned (there is no SARG the optimizer can use to limit the update). For the second query, if there were no index on price, the query would acquire an exclusive table-level lock. If there were an index on price, the query would initially acquire update page locks and an exclusive intent lock on the table. Should the number of exclusive page locks acquired exceed the lock-escalation threshold, SQL Server would attempt to escalate to an exclusive table-level lock, as long as there were no conflicting page-level locks (that is, shared or exclusive page locks) on other pages in the table.

## Demand Locks

If a process is attempting to acquire an exclusive lock on a page that currently has one or more shared locks on it, the process must wait in the lock queue until the shared locks are released. However, before the last shared lock is released, another process could come along and also acquire a shared lock on the page. Before that process releases its shared lock, yet another process could come along and acquire a shared page lock, and so on. This situation would cause the process trying to acquire an exclusive lock to wait indefinitely, significantly affecting update performance.

Fortunately, SQL Server has a mechanism to detect this situation and issue a demand lock for the process trying to acquire an exclusive lock. After waiting on several different read transactions, SQL Server issues a demand lock, preventing other read transactions from acquiring shared locks. As soon as the existing read transactions finish, the process trying to update the page is granted the exclusive lock and allowed to proceed. Any other read processes then wait for the write transaction to release its exclusive lock before proceeding.

> **NOTE**
>
> Demand locks are SQL Server internal processes, and cannot be examined using the `sp_lock` stored procedure.

# Locking with Cursors

While all this seems simple, one area that directly affects locking and data changes centers on the use of cursors. Because cursors perform row-at-a-time operations on tables, a single row may be associated with many rows on a single page. Hence, attempts by multiple processes to update different rows on the same page using cursors can cause concurrency problems as the different processes fight for the same data page. Understanding how cursors implement locking can prevent application developers from writing queries that improperly use SQL Server's updatable cursors.

For cursors that are declared `for ready only`, SQL Server uses a shared lock on the current page being read by the cursor. In other words, a `fetch` from a cursor result set causes SQL Server to put a shared lock on the page containing the row that was fetched. The shared lock is held for the duration of the `fetch` operation. All of the other pages that the cursor is browsing are unlocked during the execution of the cursor until a row is fetched from the page.

For cursors that are declared `for update`, SQL Server uses an update lock on the page containing the current row being fetched. That update lock is held for the duration of the `fetch` operation. If the data row being fetched is modified, the update lock is upgraded to an exclusive lock and held as an exclusive lock for the duration of the transaction. If the `update` statement that changed the data page is not part of a multi-statement transaction, or is not part of an explicitly defined transaction, the exclusive lock reverts to an update lock after the change is complete. The update lock then is released when `fetch` operations move to another page. If the `update` statement involved is part of an explicitly defined or multi-statement transaction, the exclusive lock on the page is held for the duration of the transaction, and then released.

Cursors that are declared `for update` can use shared locks instead of update locks if they are declared with the `shared` keyword. Using the `shared` keyword after a table name in the cursor declaration statement allows SQL Server to use shared locks instead of update locks on that table for updatable cursors. The implication of this is that, because a cursor is using a shared lock, it's possible for a different operation to acquire an update lock. Remember, only one update lock is allowed for any given page. Using `shared` allows multiple connections running multiple cursors to fetch rows that may be updated simultaneously, enhancing concurrency. The shared locks used when the `shared` keyword is specified automatically are upgraded to exclusive locks when a cursor row is updated. This process is identical to the upgrade and downgrade process for update locks and updatable cursors.

This option is particularly useful for multi-table cursors. If you are updating only one of the tables, using the shared keyword enables you to avoid putting update locks on all the tables involved in the cursor set, because you can modify only one of the tables at any given time. For example, consider the following multi-table cursor:

```
declare title_pub_cursor cursor
   for select title_id, title, price
         from titles t, publishers p SHARED
         where t.pub_id = p.pub_id
            and p.state = "NY"
   for update of title, price
```

For the cursor defined, only the titles table is updated, so the shared keyword is specified on the publishers table. This allows other user processes to acquire update locks on pages in the publishers table.

# Lock Escalation for Large Data Sets

The SQL Server attempts to conserve locking resources by upgrading page-level locks to table locks when certain lock-escalation thresholds have been reached. Historically, that threshold has been to upgrade page locks to table locks when 200 page locks have been acquired on any given table for a single command. Note that a multi-statement transaction may acquire a total number of page-level locks on a single table that exceeds the lock-escalation threshold, but a table-level lock is not granted if no one command individually exceeds the threshold.

When the lock-escalation threshold is crossed by a single command, SQL Server releases the individual page locks and allocates a single table lock for the transaction, if a table lock can be acquired. If a table lock cannot be acquired at that time (due to other processes holding conflicting page-level locks on the table), the process continues acquiring page-level locks until the table-level lock becomes available. When this happens, it's possible for a process to eventually exhaust all available locks in SQL Server, requiring you either to configure SQL Server to allow more locks (covered later in this chapter) or to rewrite your transactions to better allow escalation to table-level locks when needed.

## Setting Lock-Escalation Thresholds in System 11

In System 11, you can define the lock-escalation point at the table, database, or server level. Setting the lock-escalation thresholds overrides the default behavior of escalating from page-level to table-level locks when more than 200 page locks are acquired by a single statement.

There are three lock promotion thresholds that can be set in System 11:

- ■ lock promotion hwm (high water mark)
- ■ lock promotion lwm (low water mark)
- ■ lock promotion pct (percentage)

The `lock promotion HWM` sets a discrete maximum number of locks that can be held on a table. When an individual command exceeds this value, SQL Server attempts to acquire a table-level lock. Setting this value higher than 200 decreases the likelihood of a process acquiring a table-level lock, especially for larger tables. Setting this value lower than 200 increases the likelihood of a table-level lock. A lower HWM value can be useful in situations where a process needs exclusive use of a table for which there is little or no contention.

The `lock promotion LWM` sets a discrete minimum number of locks allowed on a table before SQL Server attempts to acquire a table lock. The SQL Server does not attempt to escalate page-level locks to a table-level lock whenever the number of locks held is less than the LWM setting. The `lock promotion LWM` setting must be less the `lock promotion HWM` setting. Setting the LWM higher decreases the likelihood of a process acquiring a table-level lock, causing it to use more page-level locks for the duration of the transaction. This could lead to the process exhausting the available locks on the server.

The `lock promotion PCT` sets the percentage of locks based on the table size above which SQL Server attempts to escalate page-level locks to a table-level lock. The `lock promotion PCT` value is checked when the number of locks on a table is between the LWM and HWM. Setting the `lock promotion PCT` lower increases the likelihood of a process acquiring a table-level lock. This percentage is calculated as follows:

```
(PCT * number of rows in table) / 100
```

Setting the `lock promotion PCT` higher decreases the likelihood of a process acquiring a table-level lock causing it to use more page-level locks for the duration of the transaction. This could lead to the process exhausting the available locks on the server.

You can set the default lock-escalation thresholds for all tables in SQL Server, using either the `sp_configure` or the `sp_setpglockpromote` stored procedure. The syntax for setting lock escalation thresholds is as follows:

```
sp_configure "{lock promotion HWM ¦ lock promotion LWM ¦ lock promotion PCT}",
➥value
```

For example, to set the high water mark for the entire server to 500 by using `sp_configure`, execute the following:

```
sp_configure "lock promotion HWM", 500
```

The syntax for setting the server defaults by using the `sp_setpglockpromote` procedure is as follows:

```
sp_setpglockpromote "server", NULL, new_LWM, new_HWM, newPCT
```

The following example sets the default HWM value to 1000 pages, the LWM to 200 pages, and the PCT to 75:

```
sp_setpglockpromote "server", null, 200, 1000, 75
```

The lock-promotion thresholds are intended to maximize concurrency for large tables. With smaller tables, escalating to a table-level lock at 200 pages was not much of an issue. But for a 1GB table with 500 concurrent users, do you want to escalate to a table-level lock when one user process acquires only 200 out of 512,000 pages? Probably not.

If you have only a few large tables in your SQL Server, you may want to leave the server-level lock thresholds at the default settings and increase the thresholds specifically for the database containing those tables, or for the tables themselves. The following two commands set the HWM value to 1,000 pages, the LWM to 200 pages, and the PCT to 75 for a database and table, respectively:

```
sp_setpglockpromote "database", pubs2, 200, 1000, 75

sp_setpglockpromote "table", titles, 200, 1000, 75
```

Any settings at the table level override the database and server settings.

To remove table or database lock-promotion settings, use the sp_droplockpromote stored procedure.

> **NOTE**
>
> For more information on configuring lock escalation thresholds, refer to Chapters 30, "Configuring and Tuning the SQL Server," and 31, "Optimizing SQL Server Configuration Options."

# Index Locking

The SQL Server locks indexes differently than it locks tables. As you learn throughout this chapter, SQL Server's locking, by default, is internally managed. There are some ways to modify locking behavior, but only for user-defined queries on user tables. Index-locking issues are entirely internal, and actually use a substantially different mechanism.

Because SQL Server uses B-tree indexes, all SQL Server indexes have a single root page. As queries use indexes to retrieve rows, that root page receives more than its fair share of attention. As a result, locking this page during index scans and index-based reads would create high levels of contention for the index. Instead of locking all index pages for an index-based read, SQL Server locks and unlocks index pages as they are read through the index tree. In this way, a lock is held on an index page only as long as necessary to scan the key values for that page.

With B-tree indexes, there's always the possibility of page-splitting to accommodate index and table growth. (Refer to Chapter 10, "Understanding SQL Server Storage Structures," for more information about B-trees in general, and to Chapter 11, "Designing Indexes for Performance," for information about how SQL Server uses them.) When page splits occur, both index pages receive exclusive resource locks that are held for the duration of the transaction. After the data modification is complete, the exclusive locks are released and the index is rebalanced, if necessary.

The use of resource locks in indexes allows transactions to "read through" an exclusive lock on an index page in attempts to access data rows contained on data pages not exclusively locked by another transaction. This behavior helps to improve query performance by not forcing a select to wait for an update on one or more data rows to be committed before being able access data rows contained on different data pages. Figure 15.2 illustrates how resources locks are used in index pages.

**FIGURE 15.2.**

*How resource locks are used in index pages.*

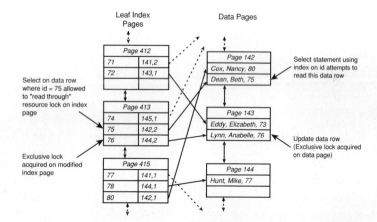

# Using Transaction Isolation Levels in SQL Server 10.0 and Later

The SQL Server is directly responsible for the management of individual locking tasks. As you find in this chapter, there are some provisions for manually overriding the locking behavior in some circumstances. However, there is another aspect to locking and lock management that is directly tied to transactions: SQL Server also provides for the management of transaction isolation levels. *Transaction isolation levels* are categories of locking behavior within transactions that are defined by ANSI. ANSI has described four different classes of transaction isolation levels, and each implements a different behavior regarding user concurrency versus data consistency.

Transaction isolation level 1, which is descriptively referred to as READ COMMITTED, is the default SQL Server behavior, and has been so through all versions of Sybase SQL Server. With READ COMMITTED as the transaction isolation level, read operations can only read pages where transactions have already been committed; that is, no "dirty reads" are allowed.

Transaction Isolation Level 0, which is named READ UNCOMMITTED, allows SQL Server to read pages that currently are being modified—in effect, this is support for "dirty reads." This feature was first provided in SQL Server versions 10.1 and 11.0. In versions prior to these, no reads of uncommitted changes were allowed outside of the transaction making the changes. To allow "dirty reads," SQL Server does not attempt to acquire read locks on data pages for a `select`, so the `select` command is not blocked by any exclusive locks. In addition, because no read locks are acquired, no update operations attempting to acquire exclusive locks are blocked by the read operation.

> **NOTE**
>
> Even if the `transaction isolation level` is set to `0`, certain utilities (like `dbcc` and `create index`) still acquire shared locks for their scans. This is because these commands must maintain the database integrity by ensuring the correct data is read before modifying it.

Transaction Isolation Level 2, REPEATABLE READS, allows a single page to be read many times within the same transaction and guarantees that the same value is read each time. This option prevents other users from updating a data row that has been read until the transaction in which it was read is committed or rolled back.

Transaction Isolation Level 3, SERIALIZABLE READS, is designed to prevent "phantom reads"; that is, preventing another transaction from updating, deleting, or inserting rows for pages previously read within a transaction. If the first transaction attempts to read the same rows again using the same search criteria, a different result set would be returned.

All of these options can be configured at the session level using the `set transaction isolation level` command. This set option determines the default locking behavior for that user session. By default, SQL Server uses level 1 (READ COMMITTED) for all sessions. READ UNCOMMITTED is available as an option for allowing dirty reads by setting the `transaction isolation level` to `0`. Levels 2 and 3 are similar under SQL Server: setting `transaction isolation level` to 3 will provide both REPEATABLE READS or SERIALIZABLE READS. Levels 2 and 3 cannot be set independently, because both are implemented similarly. Essentially, SQL Server enforces levels 2 and 3 by applying a `holdlock` to all `select` and `readtext` operations in a transaction.

> **NOTE**
>
> Remember, using the `set` command to change how SQL Server processes queries remains valid only for the duration of the user connection. If a user logs out and reconnects, the new connection reverts to SQL Server's standard behavior, which is READ COMMITTED.

You can determine the current isolation level of a user connection by using the command

```
select @@isolation
```

This command returns the number of the current transaction isolation level, as enabled by set transaction isolation level command.

When you're running queries in isolation level 1, you can simulate level 3 by using the holdlock keyword in a select statement. Conversely, when you are running queries in isolation level 3, you can simulate level 1 behavior by using the noholdlock keyword in the select statement. If you're running at isolation level 0, the holdlock, noholdlock, and shared keywords are ignored because no locks are acquired by a select statement.

## Query Isolation-Level Setting in System 11

System 11 also provides the capability to specify the isolation level to be used for a specific select or readtext command. To specify a different isolation level than the session default, use the at isolation clause in the select or readtext command. The allowable options for the at isolation clause are read committed (isolation level 1), read uncommitted (isolation level 0), and serializable (isolation level 3).

The following two examples execute queries on the same table using isolation levels 0 and 3, respectively:

```
select * from titles
    at isolation read uncommitted

select * from titles
    at isolation read serializable
```

The at isolation clause affects only the single select, readtext, or cursor in which it is specified. In addition, if you specify the read uncommitted option, you cannot also specify holdlock.

# Examining Current Lock Activity

SQL Server provides two stored procedures for monitoring locking and troubleshooting problems: sp_lock and sp_who. The sp_lock stored procedure supplied by SQL Server returns a snapshot-in-time of all currently allocated locks being managed by SQL Server. This information is obtained from the syslocks table in the master database. sp_who displays all current running processes within SQL Server and indicates whether a process is being blocked by another process due to conflicting lock requests.

The sp_lock stored procedure is useful only for the particular instance in which it runs, as locks are allocated and deallocated dynamically by SQL Server. For example, the following execution of sp_lock shows all current locks within SQL Server at the time sp_lock is run:

```
sp_lock
go
```

The class column will display the cursor name for locks associated with a
cursor for the current user and the cursor id for other users.

| spid | locktype | table_id | page | dbname | class |
|------|----------|----------|------|--------|-------|
| 6 | Sh_intent | 400004456 | 0 | master | Non Cursor Lock |
| 6 | Sh_table | 16003088 | 0 | testdb | Non Cursor Lock |
| 6 | Ex_intent | 48003202 | 0 | testdb | Non Cursor Lock |
| 6 | Ex_page | 48003202 | 576 | testdb | Non Cursor Lock |
| 6 | Ex_page | 48003202 | 586 | testdb | Non Cursor Lock |
| 6 | Ex_page | 48003202 | 608 | testdb | Non Cursor Lock |
| 6 | Ex_page | 48003202 | 611 | testdb | Non Cursor Lock |
| 6 | Ex_page | 48003202 | 612 | testdb | Non Cursor Lock |
| 6 | Ex_page-blk | 48003202 | 610 | testdb | Non Cursor Lock |
| 7 | Sh_intent | 16003088 | 0 | testdb | Non Cursor Lock |
| 7 | Sh_page | 16003088 | 800 | testdb | Non Cursor Lock |
| 7 | Sh_intent | 48003202 | 0 | testdb | Non Cursor Lock |

This sample output shows that process 7 has a shared intent lock on the table with ID 16003088, a page-level shared lock on page 800 for the table with ID 16003088, and a shared intent lock on table 48003202 in the testdb database. Process ID 6 has a shared intent lock on the table with ID 400004456 in the master database, a table-level lock on the table with ID 16003088 in the testdb database, and an exclusive intent lock and various exclusive page locks on the table with ID 48003202 in the testdb database. The output also shows an exclusive page block on page 610 in the table with ID 48003202.

The locktype column encodes the following information:

- The type of the lock: Shared locks are assigned a prefix of Sh_, while exclusive locks receive Ex_. Update locks are assigned a type of Update.

- The level at which the lock is assigned: table, page, or extent. (Remember, extent locks are used only for space allocations, not for normal querying operations.)

- Whether the lock is an intent lock; that is, whether this process wants to acquire a shared or exclusive lock on the table at some point.

- If the locktype value has a suffix of _blk, it is blocking another process; a user connection cannot access the unit of work held by this lock.

The class column displays whether the locks were acquired within a cursor. A page value of 0 indicates a table-level lock. A page value other than 0 indicates a lock on a table or index page. To determine whether the page is an index or table page, you must use the dbcc page command. Use of this command and its syntax is described in Chapter 10.

> **NOTE**
>
> The sp_lock stored procedure always displays at least one shared intent lock on the table with ID 400004456 in the master database. This is the spt_values table. The sp_lock procedure acquires the shared intent lock because, to display a lock type name in the output, it must join the syslocks table with the spt_values table.

To determine what table specifically is being locked, you can use the `object_name()` function to display the name of the table. You can run the following `select` statement to determine the name of the table with ID 48003202:

```
select object_name(48003202)
go
```

```
------------------------------
authors
```

For this command to work, you would have to be in the `testdb` database. However, there is a little-known second parameter to the `db_name()` function in SQL Server version 10.0 and later, which allows you to specify the database ID as well. This parameter lets you determine the table name without having to change the current database context. The full syntax is

```
select object_name (objectid, dbid)
```

For example, you could run the following command to determine the name of the table with ID 16003088:

```
select object_name(16003088, db_id('testdb'))
go
```

```
------------------------------
titles
```

What is somewhat baffling is why Sybase doesn't take advantage of this feature within `sp_lock` to display the table name instead of the table ID, because the `syslocks` table (from which `sp_lock` retrieves its information) contains the table and database IDs. If you want, you can run your own `select` against the `syslocks` table and convert the table name from its ID in the results, as follows:

```
select spid, locktype = convert(char(12),name),
dbname = convert(char(15), db_name(dbid)),
"table" = convert(char(15), object_name(id, dbid)),
page,
class = convert(char(15),class)
from master..syslocks l, master..spt_values v
where l.type = v.number
and v.type = "L"
order by spid
```

| spid | locktype | dbname | table | page | class |
|------|----------|--------|-------|------|-------|
| 6 | Sh_table | testdb | titles | 0 | Non Cursor Lock |
| 6 | Ex_intent | testdb | authors | 0 | Non Cursor Lock |
| 6 | Sh_intent | master | spt_values | 0 | Non Cursor Lock |
| 6 | Ex_page | testdb | authors | 576 | Non Cursor Lock |
| 6 | Ex_page | testdb | authors | 586 | Non Cursor Lock |
| 6 | Ex_page | testdb | authors | 608 | Non Cursor Lock |
| 6 | Ex_page-blk | testdb | authors | 610 | Non Cursor Lock |
| 6 | Ex_page | testdb | authors | 611 | Non Cursor Lock |
| 6 | Ex_page | testdb | authors | 612 | Non Cursor Lock |
| 7 | Sh_intent | testdb | titles | 0 | Non Cursor Lock |
| 7 | Sh_intent | testdb | authors | 0 | Non Cursor Lock |
| 7 | Sh_page | testdb | titles | 800 | Non Cursor Lock |

This sample output indicates that process 6 is holding a lock that is blocking another process. In order to track down the locking contention between user processes, use the sp_who stored procedure in conjunction with sp_lock. The sp_who procedure displays, in the blk column, the process ID of a process holding locks that are blocking another process.

```
spid    status        loginame       hostname     blk    dbname      cmd
------  ------------  -------------  -----------  -----  ----------  -----------------
1       recv sleep    sa             WINBOOK1     0      testdb      AWAITING COMMAND
2       sleeping      (null)                      0      master      NETWORK HANDLER
3       sleeping      (null)                      0      master      CHECKPOINT SLEEP
4       sleeping      (null)                      0      master      MIRROR HANDLER
5       sleeping      (null)                      0      master      SHUTDOWN HANDLER
6       running       sa             WINBOOK1     0      testdb      SELECT
7       lock sleep    sa             WINBOOK1     6      testdb      SELECT
```

This output indicates that process 6 is holding a lock that is blocking process 7, and that process 7 currently is in a "lock sleep" state, attempting to run a select command. By examining the sp_lock information (as shown in the preceding example), you can determine that the locking contention is on page 610 of the authors table.

# Configuring SQL Server Locking

SQL Server offers a configuration option, the locks parameter, for controlling the total number of locks that SQL Server can allocate at any given time. A lock of any type consumes a fixed amount of overhead (that is, each lock, regardless of size requires a single lock structure to manage it), so the lock type is unimportant from this perspective.

The default setting for locks is 5000. This means that SQL Server can grant up to 5,000 concurrent lock requests before it runs out of available lock structures. For most environments, the default setting is sufficient.

As a general rule of thumb for your own environment, you should start by configuring SQL Server with a ratio of approximately 20 locks per user connection. (Using the sp_configure stored procedure to configure the locks parameter is discussed in Chapter 30.) If applications running against SQL Server do large numbers of scanning operations, or affect large percentages of tables with individual queries, you will want to monitor lock activity closely. Increasing numbers of users, increasing numbers of rows affected by queries, or both, may result in the current number of available locks being insufficient. In System 11, setting your lock escalation thresholds higher may also result in SQL Server running out of available locks.

I recommend keeping the locks configuration option at its default setting. If you start getting "out of available locks" errors in your applications, you should first ascertain why you are running out of locks before arbitrarily increasing the locks configuration setting. In many cases, the increased number of locks is a result of poor transaction design or increased locking contention. You should first look into ways to minimize locking contention.

# Minimizing Locking Contention

To maximize concurrency and performance, you should minimize locking contention between processes as much as possible. Some general guidelines to minimize locking contention include the following:

- Keep transactions as short and concise as possible: the shorter the period of time locks are held, the less chance for lock contention. Keep commands not essential to the unit of work being managed by the transaction outside the transaction (for example, assignment selects, selects of updated rows, and so on).

- Keep transactions in a single batch to eliminate unnecessary delays between the begin tran and commit tran commands.

- Consider running transactions in stored procedures, because stored procedures typically run faster than commands executed from a batch.

- Commit updates in cursors frequently and as soon as possible. Cursor processing is much slower than set-oriented processing, and causes locks to be held longer.

> **NOTE**
>
> Cursors sometimes can be used to minimize locking contention for mass updates and deletes. To use cursors this way, update a large number of rows, one row at a time, with page-level locks rather than a potential table-level lock as might be acquired by a normal update or delete operation. Make sure you frequently commit changes to release the locks acquired.

- Use the lowest level of locking required by each process. For example, if dirty reads are acceptable, consider using level 0. Use level 3 or holdlock only if absolutely necessary.

■ Consider breaking one large table into multiple tables using a logical horizontal or vertical partitioning scheme. This minimizes the chances for table-level locks being acquired, and increases concurrency by allowing multiple users to go against multiple tables rather contending for access to a single table. (Horizontal and vertical table partitioning is covered in more detail in Chapters 17, "Database Design and Performance," and 35, "Administering Very Large SQL Server Databases.") For heap tables in System 11, consider using heap-table partitioning to spread a heap table across multiple page chains. (Heap table partitioning is covered in more detail in Chapter 18, "Database Object Placement and Performance.")

■ Avoid "hot spots" in a table. See the following section, "Avoiding Hot Spots," for more on this.

■ Reduce page-locking contention by reducing the number of rows per page. See the following section, "Decreasing the Number of Rows per Page," for more about this.

■ Never allow user interaction between a begin tran and a commit tran because this causes locks to be held for an indefinite period of time. If a process must return rows for user interaction and then update one or more rows, consider using optimistic locking in your application. You learn about this in the section on "Optimistic Locking."

# Avoiding Hot Spots

A *hot spot* occurs when multiple processes attempt to modify the same page in a table. For example, a table with no clustered index (that is, a heap table) has all new rows inserted to the last page in the table. Likewise, a table with a clustered index on a sequential key, with rows inserted in sequential-key order, has all rows inserted to the last page in the table.

One method to minimize hot spots is to create the clustered index on a column that will spread the insertions throughout the table. Some candidates for clustered index keys to randomize your data include the following:

■ Date of birth

■ Last name, first name

■ Zip code

■ A random hash key (a popular random hash key is one based on user ID)

In System 11, hot spots can be minimized by using heap table partitioning. A partitioned heap table contains multiple page chains, each with its own "last" page. Multiple insert processes can be inserted into different page chains concurrently, minimizing locking contention and "hot spots" for heap tables. (For more information on heap table partitioning, see Chapter 18.)

# Decreasing the Number of Rows per Page

If you're trying to minimize locking contention for inserts, you can consider using a low fill factor when creating the clustered and nonclustered indexes on the table. A low fill factor has a favorable effect on concurrency by spreading existing data rows across a greater number of pages, leaving extra free space on existing pages for new rows. This reduces page splits as well as page contention. (For information on setting the fill factor, refer to Chapters 10 and 30.)

By reducing page splits, you cause fewer exclusive page locks to be acquired in the index pages. This helps to improve overall performance in inserts and updates.

A low fill factor, however, is not a permanent solution. Once you begin inserting or modifying data, the fill factor is lost. It does not maintain a consistent number of rows per page. If you actually desire a method that explicitly limits the number of rows per page, or that simulates row-level locking in SQL Server to minimize page contention between processes updating different rows, you need a more permanent solution. The next section discusses how to simulate row-level locking in SQL Server.

# Simulating Row-Level Locking

Because SQL Server performs all locking at the page level, the issue of concurrency is complicated when attempting to address row-level access. Certain applications may require row-level access to support highly transactional systems, and workarounds are required to make those systems work in SQL Server. With the release of System 11, there now are two ways to address the issue of row-level locking. One method, which works in all versions, is row padding. The other is setting the maximum number of rows per page. This section discusses both.

## Row Padding

*Row padding* is based on a simple concept: If SQL Server locks at the page level, make rows big enough so that only one row fits on a page. Presto! Magnifico! Row-level locking, right? The answer, of course, is a bit more complex. Yes, you will have only one row locked at any given time if that data page is locked. However, the storage requirements to support this are substantial. Each row, even though it only has to be 1,009 bytes wide—half of the space available on a page: (2,016 bytes/2 = 1,008 bytes) plus one extra byte—the rows will effectively be 2,048 bytes in size. The reason? Only one row can fit on each page. That makes for a very, very big row. In addition, remember that SQL Server assesses the I/O cost and optimizes queries based on the number of pages involved. That number has just increased substantially, because the number of pages matches the number of rows.

Depending on the application and the business needs at hand, row padding could well be a viable alternative to page-level locking. However, carefully consider your database size and growth, and your application needs, before implementing this solution! Row-level padding can improve performance for OLTP applications by minimizing page contention, but it can degrade performance for data retrieval by increasing the number of pages that need to be accessed.

# Setting the Maximum Rows per Page in System 11

Instead of your having to artificially pad data rows to achieve a desired number of rows per page, System 11 lets you specify the maximum number of rows per page for a table or index. You can specify the max_rows_per_page setting during table or index creation. Unlike `fillfactor`, the max_rows_per_page value is maintained when inserting and deleting data.

For example, to configure the `salesdetail` table to allow only a single row per page, issue the following command:

```
create table salesdetail
    (stor_id  char(4),
     ord_num  varchar(20),
     title_id char(6),
     qty      smallint,
     discount float)
  with max_rows_per_page = 1
```

If you set max_rows_per_page on a table and subsequently create a clustered index on it, the index inherits the max_rows_per_page setting. If you create a clustered index and specify a max_rows_per_page value, that value is applied to the data pages as well.

If you want to apply a max_rows_per_page setting to existing data, use the sp_chgattribute system-stored procedure. This affects all future operations on the table, but does not change existing pages. To apply max_rows_per_page to a table immediately, either drop and re-create the clustered index specifying the max_rows_per_page value, or perform the following steps:

1. Use bcp to copy the data out of the table.
2. Truncate the table.
3. Set the max_rows_per_page with sp_chgattribute.
4. Use bcp to copy the data back into the table.

To display the current settings for max_rows_per_page, use the sp_helpindex command. The max_rows_per_page value is stored in the maxrowsperpage column in the sysindexes per table.

As in padding data rows, using a lower value for max_rows_per_page can improve performance for OLTP applications by minimizing page contention. However, doing so also can degrade performance for data retrieval by increasing the number of pages that must be accessed, increasing cache-memory requirements for tables, and incurring a greater number of locks per transaction.

Because a greater number of page locks may be held, this can increase the likelihood of page-level locks escalating to table-level locks, somewhat defeating the purpose of spreading the data out in the first place. In conjunction with setting the max_rows_per_page for a table, you may also have to increase the lock-escalation threshold to minimize escalation to table-level locks. If your processes start acquiring table-level locks, you've effectively lost any improvements in concurrency you originally sought to obtain by spreading out rows in the first place.

# Optimistic Locking

A method commonly used to implement a form of row-level locking is to use *optimistic locking*. Optimistic locking also allows for user interaction within transactions without holding read locks indefinitely, because locks are not used to manage the update consistency of retrieved data rows. Optimistic locking is achieved by putting a timestamp column on a table. Any applications must then use a "read-then-update" process, driven from the client application, in order to modify rows using optimistic locking.

In order to implement optimistic locking, some table structure prerequisites must be met. First, the table must have a primary key or unique index, so that rows can be uniquely identified in a where clause. Second, the table must have a timestamp column. The timestamp column is a special column that SQL Server updates automatically to a guaranteed unique value whenever a row is modified.

Instead of simply updating a row directly, an application must first read the row from the database without using the holdlock command. The value of the timestamp column for each row must be retrieved and stored in the client application.

When the application is ready to update a row, it submits a new query to change the row. However, the update statement must include a where clause that compares the timestamp value held in the client application with the timestamp value on disk. If the timestamp values match (that is, if the value that was read is the same as the value in the database), no changes to that row have occurred since it was read. As such, the change attempted by the application proceeds. If the timestamp value in the client application does not match the value in the data table, that row has been changed since the read operation occurred. This means that the row the application is attempting to modify is not the same as the row that currently exists. As a result, the change cannot occur because of the "phantom values" problem.

To compare the timestamp values, the update statement itself must make use of the tsequal function in the where clause of the update statement. The tsequal function compares the timestamp value returned by the read (and held in a buffer on the client application) with the timestamp value in the data table. If they match, the update proceeds. If not, the update fails because the where clause cannot be satisfied.

This sample illustrates how this works:

1. The client reads a row:

   ```
   select * from data_table where primary_key_field = <value>
   ```

2. The client prepares an update statement with new data values for this row.

3. The client submits the following update statement:

   ```
   update data_table set data_field_1 = "foo"
       where primary_key_field = 1234
       and tsequal (timestamp, 0x13590813570159017)
   ```

In this step, the update statement is using the same where clause as the select statement—identifying the same row using the same primary key or unique key value. This is required to make sure you get the same row, and explains why a primary or unique key is necessary for this to occur. However, in addition to specifying the primary key, the where clause also uses the tsequal function.

tsequal takes two distinct timestamp values and compares them for equality. In this case, the update statement is comparing the timestamp field of data_table with an explicit value, 0x13590813570159017. This value was retrieved when the row was first read by the application.

If tsequal evaluates to true, the row has not been modified since it was retrieved, and the update can occur. If the tsequal function evaluates to false, the row has been modified since it was retrieved, and the update fails with an error message similar to the following:

```
Msg 532, Level 16, State 1
The timestamp (changed to 0x000000001000013b7) shows that the row has been
updated by another user.
Command has been aborted.
```

At this point, it's up to the client application to decide what to do. Typically, the new version of the row is retrieved to determine whether the update should be applied.

> **NOTE**
>
> Take note that the following where clause
> ```
> where primary_key_field = 1234  and timestamp = 0x13590813570159017
> ```
> is not treated the same as
> ```
> where primary_key_field = 1234
>     and tsequal (timestamp, 0x13590813570159017)
> ```
> With the first where clause, if the timestamp values don't match, a data row is not found that matches both search criteria so no row is updated. However, no error message is issued to indicate why the row was not updated.
>
> Use the tsequal function to generate the specific error message to indicate that the timestamps do not match. Your client application error handler then can trap error code 532 and perform specific error handling for a mismatched timestamp value.

Although optimistic locking is a more efficient method of minimizing locking contention (in terms of disk resources) than row padding, sending multiple query statements back and forth across a busy network simply moves the additional overhead off the disk subsystem and into the network and processor subsystems. As a result, there is no way to implement row-level locking without incurring additional overhead somewhere in the application.

This last point is an important one to remember, as it defines SQL Server's page-level locking as the most efficient method for the greatest variety of applications. You should carefully examine row-level locking requirements to determine their necessity, as the overhead cost may outweigh the benefits.

# Deadlocking

Deadlocking is the interesting circumstance of having two different user connections fighting for the same resources. The situation is similar to what happens at major corporations every morning. One person brings in coffee; the other brings in doughnuts. The person with the doughnuts wants the coffee, but before having to give up the doughnuts. The person with the coffee wants the doughnuts, but before having to give up the coffee. In effect, you have two people trying to keep what they have and grab what the other has at the same time. Welcome to deadlocking.

In the case of SQL Server, deadlock uses this metaphor with a slightly more technical implementation. One user connection acquires a lock on a particular page. The next step is to acquire a lock on the next page affected by a transaction. However, a different user connection already is locking that page and requesting a lock on the page the first user connection has locked. In this situation, neither user connection can continue until the other has finished, and neither can finish until the other has continued—we have a deadlock. Figure 15.3 illustrates a deadlock.

The SQL Server continually checks for deadlocks and automatically aborts one of the conflicting transactions. The transaction that is aborted is the transaction belonging to the process that has accumulated the least amount of CPU time since the start of its session, not the amount of CPU time for the specific transaction.

The user process that is chosen has its transaction aborted, but not its batch, and is sent the following error message:

```
Msg 1205, Level 13, State 2
Your server command (process id 1) was deadlocked with another process and has
 been chosen as the deadlock victim. Re-run your command
```

**FIGURE 15.3.**

*Diagram of a deadlock.*

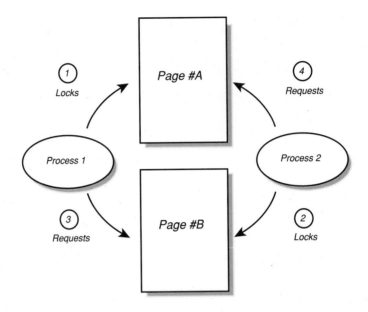

All SQL Server applications that use transactions should check for error number 1205, or for stored procedure return status of -3. Both of these error values indicate the transaction was aborted as the result of deadlock. If either is detected, typically an application should respond by simply resubmitting the transaction. Because the other user connection involved has been allowed to continue, it probably will have released its locks by the time the transaction is resubmitted.

Unfortunately, the nature of multi-user databases ensures that deadlock can only be avoided, not entirely eliminated. As a result, in addition to checking for deadlocks within applications, application developers also should write transactions so that deadlock can be minimized.

## So How Do I Minimize the Chance for Deadlock?

The steps involved in avoiding deadlock are easy in principle, but may be more difficult to implement, depending on the needs of your application.

The easiest way to avoid deadlock is to put all transaction-based SQL code into stored procedures. The performance advantages of stored procedures become most apparent here, because stored procedures allow a transaction to be completed in a dramatically shorter timeframe than would be possible submitting SQL statements as a batch. As a result, the amount of time that locks are held within transactions is similarly reduced, which reduces the potential for deadlock.

> **WARNING**
>
> Application developers using client application-development environments that use their own database API should allow the development tool to create stored procedures for SQL Server databases wherever possible. Tools such as PowerBuilder, Visual Basic, Enterprise Developer, and so on all implement their own abstraction-layer APIs, which shield developers from directly making database-specific SQL calls. As a result, these tools are much more portable—but at a cost. Behind the scenes, each is submitting "dynamic" or "naked" SQL statements to SQL Server.
>
> As a result, application-development tools that do not provide a means to access SQL Server–specific features typically encounter problems with highly transactional systems. If, for example, you're using PowerScript, Visual Basic's Data Access Objects, or the ODBC API directly, you should use whatever options exist that provide access to stored procedures. This is not necessarily a consideration for decision-support systems. For transaction-based systems on SQL Server, however, it can make a substantial difference in performance and concurrency.

Another method of speeding transactions is to avoid putting queries that return data in a transaction. The data read simply allocates additional read locks that extend the time frame that update locks are held, increasing the probability of deadlock. Instead, limit explicitly defined transactions to what they were intended for: changing data. If read operations are part of a batch, put them outside the `begin tran`/`commit tran` pair. They only add locking overhead and needlessly extend lock duration.

Whether using stored procedures or submitting dynamic SQL, it's ideal to use the minimum locking level needed to complete the transaction. Although `holdlock` and isolation level 3 are useful options for maintaining shared locks and for implementing repeatable reads, excessive use of these features is a common cause of deadlock. Consider using optimistic locking, or having the transaction first acquire an exclusive lock.

For example, one of the most common deadlock culprits is the sequential number generator. Often, it's written as follows:

```
begin tran
select new_id from keytab holdlock
update keytab set new_id = new_id + 1
commit tran
```

If two users run this transaction simultaneously, they both acquire the shared lock and hold onto it. When they both attempt to acquire an exclusive lock on the keytab table, they deadlock. To avoid this situation, rewrite the transaction as follows:

```
begin tran
update keytab set new_id = new_id + 1
select new_id from keytab
commit tran
```

Written this way, only one transaction is able to acquire the exclusive lock on keytab. The other process waits until the first transaction is complete, but a deadlock has been avoided.

If read repeatability is necessary within a transaction, consider writing the transaction to initially obtain an exclusive lock on the resource and then read the data. For example, if a transaction has to retrieve the average price for all books in the titles table and ensure it doesn't change before the update is applied, you can trick the query optimizer into giving you an exclusive table lock. Consider the following SQL code:

```
begin tran
update titles set title_id = title_id
    where 1 = 2
if (select avg(price) from titles) > $15
begin
    /* perform some additional processing */

end

update titles set price = price * 1.10
    where price < (select avg(price) from titles)

commit tran
```

In this transaction, it's important that no other process modifies price for any rows in the table, or the value retrieved at the end of the transaction will be different from the value retrieved at the beginning. Notice the update at the beginning of the transaction. The where clause looks kind of funny, doesn't it? Well, believe it or not, it's a perfectly valid where clause as far as the query optimizer is concerned, even though it always evaluates to false. When the optimizer processes the query, it doesn't recognize any valid SARGs; its query plan forces a table scan with an exclusive table lock. When executed, though, the where clause immediately evaluates to false, so no table scan actually is performed. However, the process still is granted an exclusive table lock.

Because the process now has an exclusive table lock, you can guarantee that no other transaction modifies any data rows, giving you the read repeatability you need while avoiding the potential for deadlock that holdlock would cause. Avoiding the deadlock does not come without a trade-off however. By using the table lock to minimize deadlocks, you also increase lock contention on the table. Therefore, before implementing this solution, you must consider whether deadlock avoidance is more important than allowing concurrent access to the table.

Finally, one of the best methods for minimizing deadlocks is the simple matter of referencing tables in the same order within all transactions. Some possible methods used for ensuring the reference order for a table include sorting alphabetically by name, numerically by table ID, or by some other common sorting order. As a result, if tables always are accessed in similar order, the very issue of two connections requesting conflicting resources is obviated. Locks are acquired and deallocated in relatively sequential order, preventing deadlocks by avoiding conflicting resource requests.

# Tracing Deadlocks

Because a user transaction is aborted when a deadlock occurs, any locking information that could be returned by sp_lock no longer is available for that transaction. The user connection with the aborted transaction had all of its locks deallocated by the SQL Server when the transaction was aborted. Additionally, the transaction that was allowed to continue has likely committed its changes and freed up any locks held, as well.

So how can you determine where the deadlock occurred, and which processes it occurred between? Fortunately, SQL Server provides a way to generate deadlock trace information in the SQL Server errorlog when a deadlock occurs.

The deadlock trace information is generated by turning on a couple of DBCC trace flags: 1204 and 3605. You can turn them on for a running SQL Server by issuing the dbcc traceon command in an SQL Server session as follows:

```
dbcc traceon (1204)
dbcc traceon (3605)
```

The 1204 trace flag tells SQL Server to generate deadlock trace information when a deadlock occurs. The 3605 trace flag tells SQL Server to send the output to the errorlog. You must be logged in as sa, or a login with the sa role, to turn these trace flags on. If you want to have these trace flags on all the time, you can add them as SQL Server command-line parameters using the -T command-line switch:

```
dataserver -d /dev/rsd0 -s SYBASE -e /home/sybase/install/errorlog
    -i /home/sybase/interfaces -M /home/sybase -T1204 -T3605
```

In System 11, this trace flag can also be turned on using the sp_configure stored procedure:

```
sp_configure print deadlock information, 1
```

> **WARNING**
>
> Setting the deadlock trace flag on can seriously degrade SQL server performance. Only use this option when attempting to debug the cause of deadlocks within a database. Do not leave it on all the time.

Once you have turned on these options, then SQL Server prints information to the errorlog file, similar to that listed below. This information documents the conflicting processes, the pages or tables on which they deadlocked, and which process was chosen as the victim:

```
Deadlock detected.  2 processes were involved in the deadlock.
Process 6 belongs to user 'sybstu3'.
Process 6 was executing a SELECT command at line 1.
Process 1 belongs to user >sybstu2=.
Process 1 was executing a SELECT command at line 1.
Process 1 was waiting for a >shared page= lock on page 489 of the >authors=
table in database 6 but process 6 already held a >exclusive page= lock on it.
Process 6 was waiting for a >shared page= lock on page 505 of the >titles=
table in database 6 but process 1 already held a >exclusive page= lock on it.
Process 1 was chosen as the victim.  End of deadlock information.
```

In this example, user processes 1 and 6 are noted as being involved in a deadlock. Process 1 is requesting a shared lock on page 489 of the authors table, but is being blocked by an exclusive page lock by process 6. At the same time, process 6 is waiting for a shared page lock on page 505 of the titles table, but is being blocked by an exclusive page lock held by process 1. In this case, process 1 was chosen as the deadlock victim.

# Deadlock Checking in System 11

In versions of SQL Server prior to System 11, SQL Server begins checking for deadlocks as soon as a process begins waiting for a lock. This deadlock checking incurs unnecessary, and time-consuming, overhead for processes that wait without a deadlock occurring. If you expect your processes to deadlock infrequently (for example, you've written your applications to minimize deadlock contention), System 11 allows you to configure the minimum amount of time, in milliseconds, a process will wait on a lock request before SQL Server initiates a deadlock check. You set this value server-wide using sp_configure. For example, the following line tells SQL Server to "wait at least 1,000 milliseconds before checking for a deadlock:

```
sp_configure "deadlock checking period", 1000
```

The default setting is 500 milliseconds. Setting the checking period higher than 500 produces longer delays before deadlocks are checked. This allows SQL Server to grant lock requests without incurring the deadlock-checking overhead. Unless you expect your processes to deadlock very infrequently, the default setting of 500 milliseconds should suffice.

When setting the deadlock-checking period, a process may actually wait longer before SQL Server checks it for a deadlock. This is because SQL Server performs deadlock checks for all processes at the same interval. Only those processes that have exceeded the deadlock-checking interval are checked at this time. If a process completes its designated interval after SQL Server already has completed a round of checks, it must wait until SQL Server performs the next round of checks. Therefore, a process actually could wait $N$ to $N \times 2$ milliseconds (where $N$ = the deadlock checking period) before SQL Server performs deadlocking checks on it.

# Summary

Up to SQL Server 10.0, all locking of all resources, except for using `holdlock`, was controlled solely by SQL Server. Version 10 provided the capability to modify locking behavior at the session level with the `set transaction isolation level` command. With Version 11.0, more control over locking behavior is provided through locking options at the query level, or by using specific configuration options. The SQL Server's smallest lock unit of work is the 2KB page, meaning that SQL Server does no row-level locking. While row-level locking can be simulated, it comes at the cost of potentially substantial overhead and space requirements.

Understanding that deadlock can only be minimized—but never eliminated—and understanding how to minimize deadlock are important in making the applications you develop on SQL Server both more reliable and faster. To minimize performance problems related to locking, use stored procedures, use the least-restrictive lock type possible, and make your transactions run as quickly as possible. A well-designed application on insufficient hardware almost always is faster and more reliable than a poorly designed application on a killer box!

# Overriding the SQL Server Optimizer

# 16

# Why Override the Optimizer?

SQL Server uses a cost-based optimizer to determine the most efficient query plan to process a query. The optimizer uses a number of algorithms to examine a query and determine the most efficient access path and join order to solve the query. Chapter 12, "Understanding the Query Optimizer," details this process.

The algorithms and computations the optimizer uses to determine query costs were developed by people. Because people are fallible, it stands to reason that the computations the optimizer uses might be fallible as well. At times, you may truly find that the optimizer is picking the wrong query plan. At other times, you may simply want to force the query optimizer to use a different plan just to validate whether the plan it chose on its own truly was the cheapest plan. For this reason, SQL Server provides some methods for manually overriding the query optimizer's decisions.

How often does SQL Server require manual intervention to optimally execute a query? Considering the overwhelming number of query types and circumstances in which those queries are run, SQL Server does a surprisingly effective job of query optimization. My own testing and testing by others has typically shown that SQL Server's optimizer is quite clever, and really, really good at wringing the best performance out of any hardware platform. For that reason, you should treat this chapter as a collection of exception handles: methods that you should use only where other methods of optimizing a query already have failed, or only when doing performance testing.

# Cautions on Overriding the Optimizer

Before applying the techniques discussed in this chapter, remember one important point: used indiscriminately, these features can effectively cover up serious, fundamental design flaws in your database or application. And, in fact, if you are tempted to use these features (with a few more moderate exceptions), it should serve as an indicator that there may lie problems elsewhere in your application. Before suspecting that the query optimizer is improperly optimizing the query, first try to determine why. Use the tools discussed in Chapter 14, "Analyzing Query Plans," to examine why an index isn't being used (for example, out-of-date statistics, nonoptimizable SARGs, and so on), or why the wrong join order is chosen (for example, invalid row and page estimates used in cost-evaluating a join). See if you can rewrite the query in a way that helps the optimizer choose the correct plan.

Having determined that no such flaws exist, and that SQL Server really is improperly optimizing your query, this chapter can show you how to override the two most important decisions the optimizer makes: choosing the index, if any, to solve the query, and choosing the most efficient join order for tables. In addition, for System 11, we will also examine how to force a specific, prefetch size and cache-buffer replacement strategy.

> **WARNING**
>
> If you haven't already read the previous four chapters on understanding query optimization, stored procedure optimization, analyzing query plans, and locking, I'd strongly encourage you to do so now. If you are new to SQL Server, I'd suggest you go back through those chapters again and make sure you have a solid grasp of the topics that they cover. Understanding how SQL Server behaves "normally" is paramount to making it behave for a particular exception!
>
> SQL Server's optimizer is quite good. SQL Server has a reputation for fast performance, and that reputation is owed in no small measure to the query optimizer. Remembering this as you peruse these chapters will help you keep perspective on how selective you should be in applying these concepts.

Throughout this chapter, one point must remain clear in your mind: these options are considered "exception cases" that are meant to cope with particular problems in particular queries in particular applications. As such, there are no "global rules" or "rules of thumb" to speak of, because the application of these features by definition means that normal SQL Server behavior doesn't work—these cases are "exceptional."

The practical result of this idea is that you should test every option in your environment, with your data and your queries, and use the techniques discussed in the previous four chapters to optimize your queries. The fastest performing query wins, so don't be afraid to experiment with different options. However, don't think that these statements and features are globally applicable or fit general categories of problems, either! There are, in fact, only three rules: test, test, and test!

> **NOTE**
>
> If, in the course of your testing, you do confirm that the optimizer is choosing the wrong query plan, use the methods described here as a workaround to solve the problem, but also put in a call to Sybase Technical Support to report the problem and get a case logged. This will allow the SQL Server engineers to address and, hopefully, fix the problem in a subsequent release of SQL Server.

# Forcing Index Selection

In versions of SQL Server prior to System 11, there was an officially undocumented, but commonly known, method to force index selection on the optimizer. If you included the index ID number after the table name in a query, SQL Server would use that index to satisfy the query. With System 11, there is now a documented method that you can use to specify, by name, the index SQL Server should use.

In order to use either method, you need to know the index names and IDs. The following `select` statement is an example of one that displays the names of tables and the index names and IDs for those tables:

```
select "table"=o.name, "index"=i.name, indid
from sysindexes i, sysobjects o
where i.id = o.id
and o.type = "U"    /* user tables only (no system tables) */
order by 1, 2, 3
go
```

```
table                      index              indid
-----------------------    ---------------    -----
pt_sample                  pt_sample              0
pt_tx                      pt_tx                  0
pt_sample_CIkey2           CIkey2                 1
pt_sample_CIcompany        CIcompany              1
pt_sample_CIidNCk          CIid                   1
pt_sample_CIidNCk          NCk                    2
pt_tx_CIamountNCamount     CIamount               1
pt_tx_CIamountNCamount     NCamount               1
pt_tx_NCamount             pt_tx_Ncamount         0
pt_tx_NCamount             NCamount2              2
pt_tx_CIid                 tx_CIid                1
```

Once you have the index names and IDs, you can use them to specify the index to be used by the query. Remember, an index ID of 0 reflects a table with no clustered index; an index ID of 1 is for the clustered index; 2–250 are the nonclustered indexes; 251–254 are reserved; and 255 indicates that the table contains a text or image column. Remember also that there will be a 0 or a 1, but not both, listed here.

We'll use `showplan` to observe the index the server will use to resolve several queries. In this query, the server has three meaningful options for identifying the correct result rows: a table scan, a clustered index search, or a nonclustered index search.

```
set showplan on
go

select *
from pt_sample_CIidNCk
where id between 1 and 500 and
key2 between 30000 and 40000
go
```

Left to its own devices, the optimizer selects the clustered index on `id` because this is what it determines to be the most efficient index to solve the query:

```
STEP 1
The type of query is SELECT
FROM TABLE
pt_sample_CIidNCk
Nested iteration
Using Clustered Index
```

To force selection of a specific index, you can specify the index ID for the index you want SQL Server to use in parentheses, after the name of the table in the `from` clause. In this example, we will force the use of the nonclustered index, `NCk`, by specifying the index ID of 2 (see the list of tables and indexes previously):

```
select *
from pt_sample_CIidNCk (2)
where id between 1 and 500
and key2 between 30000 and 40000
go
```

As you instructed it to, the optimizer uses the nonclustered index to find rows matching the query:

```
STEP 1
The type of query is SELECT
FROM TABLE
pt_sample_CIidNCk
Nested iteration
Index : Nck
```

Using the same method, you can force the optimizer to use the clustered index by selecting an ID of 1:

```
select *
from pt_sample_CIidNCk (index = 1)
where id between 1 and 500
and key2 between 30000 and 40000
go
```

```
STEP 1
The type of query is SELECT.
FROM TABLE
pt_sample_CIidNCk
Nested iteration
Using Clustered Index
```

In this example, we've forced the clustered index. To force a table scan, specify an index ID of 0:

```
select * from pt_sample_CIidNCk (0)
where id between 1 and 500
and key2 between 30000 and 40000
go
```

```
STEP 1
The type of query is SELECT
FROM TABLE
pt_sample_CIidNCk
Nested iteration
Table Scan
```

In System 11, you can now specify the name of the index you want the optimizer to use rather than the index ID. Do this using the special `(index indexname)` clause for `select`, `update`, and `delete` statements. This clause appears immediately after the table name in the `from` clause. For example, to force the use of the nonclustered index `NCk` in System 11, execute the following:

```
select *
from pt_sample_CIidNCk (index NCk)
where id between 1 and 500
and key2 between 30000 and 40000
go
```

To force a table scan, provide the table name rather than an index name in the index clause. If you have a nonclustered index with the same name as the table, specifying the table name causes the index to be used. To override this, use the older method of specifying the index ID.

> **NOTE**
>
> In versions of SQL Server prior to System 11, providing the index ID was the only method—and unsupported at that—of forcing index usage. This method still works in System 11, but still is not the supported method. The problem with using index IDs is that they might change if your nonclustered indexes are dropped and re-created in a different order.
>
> Because you specify an explicit name for an index when you create the index, you are safer specifying an index name than an index ID in System 11.

Let's look at the performance of this query given each of these choices. To do that, run the query with the set statistics io option turned on, and examine the reported number of logical I/Os used to process the query using the different indexes (see Table 16.1). Viewing physical I/Os is problematic because it varies depending on whether any of the table is in cache and values are not consistent.

**Table 16.1. Summary of logical I/Os to resolve the query using various indexes.**

| Index | Logical I/Os |
| --- | --- |
| Clustered: CIid (1) | 7 |
| Nonclustered: NCk (2) | 632 |
| Table Scan (0) | 243 |

In this case, you can see that the optimizer clearly found the most efficient path (using the clustered index) to process this query.

# A Case Study

Let's look at a case study in which a user might decide to try to outguess the optimizer.

Table 16.2 shows the table structure for a simple transaction table, pt_tx.

## Table 16.2. Partial output from transaction table `sp_help pt_tx`.

| Column | Data type | Length |
|--------|-----------|--------|
| id     | int       | 4      |
| amount | money     | 8      |
| date   | datetime  | 8      |

The table has a nonunique, nonclustered index created on the date column.

Consider this query, which retrieves the sum of amount for all entries where the date is a Sunday:

```
select sum(amount)
from pt_tx
where datename(dw, date) = "Sunday"
```

The output from showplan and statistics io shows that SQL Server has chosen a table-scan strategy for this query, at a cost of 88 logical reads:

```
STEP 1
The type of query is SELECT
Scalar Aggregate
FROM TABLE
pt_tx
Nested iteration
Table Scan
STEP 2
The type of query is SELECT

- - - - - - - - - - -
     37892

Table: pt_tx scan count 1, logical reads: 88, physical reads: 0
Total writes for this command: 0
```

Here is the actual data distribution for the data in the date column, by the day of the week:

```
select datename(dw, date) "day of week", count(*) "num rows"
from pt_tx
group by datepart(dw, date), datename(dw, date)

day of week     num rows
- - - - - - - - - - - -   - - - - - - - - - -
Sunday          25
Monday          1236
Tuesday         1185
Wednesday       1220
Thursday        1248
Friday          1289
Saturday        1079
```

As you can see, the optimizer is performing a table scan of 7,282 rows to find only 25 rows. This is because the optimizer doesn't recognize the search argument on the date column as a valid search argument, because the query is performing a function on the date column. Because it's not considered a SARG, the optimizer doesn't consider using the index on date.

If you were to run a covered query (see Chapter 12 for a discussion of index covering) against this table using the nonclustered index on date, you find that a nonclustered index scan will cost 55 logical I/Os.

The question is, did the optimizer fail to find the best path? If the server was able to scan the entire nonclustered index (at a cost of 55 I/Os) and then convert the date value in the index before deciding whether to read a data page, it would need to read only a page from the table itself 25 times (once for each row where the day of week is Sunday). The total cost of the query using the nonclustered would be

| | |
|---|---|
| Index scan cost | 55 |
| Data read cost | +25 |
| Total cost | 80 |

This is less than the cost of the table scan by 9 percent (80 versus 88).

Based on this reasoning, let's force the use of the nonclustered index and look at the total I/O cost and see if this assumption is correct:

```
select sum(amount)
from pt_tx (index = date_ix)
where datename(dw, date) = "Sunday"
```

The cost of this query is 7,337 logical I/Os, or almost 100 times the cost of a simple table scan. This is because SQL Server did *not* evaluate the value of the function before deciding whether to read a page from the table. Instead, for each value in the nonclustered index, SQL Server retrieved the corresponding page from the table, and only then determined whether the row matched the search condition.

In this case, it does not pay to force the use of the nonclustered index due to the way SQL Server processes the query, and it is obvious again that the optimizer found the most efficient path (a table scan) to process this query.

## Cautions on Forcing Index Selection

Forcing index usage in a query can be useful when you suspect that the optimizer, for one reason or another, is not choosing the best query plan. However, whenever you use this option, always use the set statistics io option to verify whether there was an I/O savings over the optimizer's choice. Also, if the query is a range retrieval, test the query with a variety of range values, as the size of the range can result in different query plans depending on the number of values within the range. Make sure that the index specified still is the most efficient for all range retrievals. Because you are now forcing the use of a specific index, the optimizer cannot re-evaluate your decision based on the number of rows in a range or on updated index statistics.

Once testing confirms that the query performs better using the specified index, you may consider including the option in the queries in your applications. However, you should also periodically check to make sure that the query plan using the specified index still is the most efficient one. Changes in data distribution may, over time, cause the forced index to become less efficient than other choices.

Another disadvantage to forcing index selection is that, if you drop a specified index, all queries specifying that index will generate a warning message that the index could not be found, and the optimizer then will evaluate and choose the best available index or other access method. In addition, if you are using the index ID method for specifying a nonclustered index, and you drop and recreate the indexes in a different order than they originally were in, you may get some truly undesirable performance from queries by specifying what is now the wrong index ID.

Because all queries specifying an index must be checked periodically to confirm performance, and may need to be modified if you change your indexes, the maintenance cost will increase for those applications. In addition, new releases of SQL Server may contain fixes to the problem that led you to force index selection in the first place. When upgrading to a new release, you should check all queries forcing indexes to see if the forced index still is the most efficient method. If the optimizer has been fixed to eliminate the previous problem, you should remove index forcing from the query.

For these reasons, always treat forcing an index as a last resort to solve performance problems. Instead of forcing an index, you usually should focus your time on why an incorrect index is being picked. A likely culprit is out-of-date statistics, or a nonoptimizable SARG. Use the `dbcc traceon (302)` command (described in Chapter 14) first to determine why the index is not being used before indiscriminately forcing index usage.

# Forcing Join Order

Forcing join order is another technique to get presumably better performance from SQL Server. We have seen that the order of the joins is as important to performance, if not more so, than index selection. When determining the best query plan for a multi-table query, the optimizer analyzes all possible join orders to determine the most efficient order in which to process the tables. Typically, the order the optimizer chooses is different from the order in which the tables are specified in the `from` clause.

We are then tempted to ask ourselves, "If we change the join order from the one the server selected, can we pick a better one?"

> **NOTE**
>
> Just like forcing indexes, consider forcing join orders as a way to debug whether the optimizer is choosing the wrong join order. Verify your results using the `set statistics io` option to see if you actually reduce logical I/Os.

(I have to admit that, in the past, I typically haven't been able to outguess the SQL Server optimizer very effectively on the best join order, but I've certainly been able to pump up the volume of logical I/Os.)

You force join order with the `forceplan` option:

```
set forceplan {on ¦ off}
```

With the `forceplan` option turned on, the optimizer still evaluates the best access path to use for each table (unless you've also forced index selection), but now joins the tables in the order specified in the `from` clause.

> **NOTE**
>
> When you specify the join order for the optimizer to use, the optimizer may use different indexes on the tables than it would have with a different join order, or no indexes at all on some tables. Remember from Chapter 12 that during the join order processing phase all join orders are evaluated using the various indexing strategies available on the tables. Certain indexes may not be useful for certain join orders.

In the following query, the optimizer found that the most efficient join order was the reverse of the order of the tables in the `from` clause:

```
set showplan on
set statistics io on
go

select * from titles, publishers
where titles.pub_id = publishers.pub_id
go
```

The `showplan` output indicates that the join order is `publishers` as the outer table and `titles` as the inner table:

```
STEP 1
The type of query is SELECT.
FROM TABLE
publishers
Nested iteration
Table Scan
FROM TABLE
titles
Nested iteration
Table Scan
```

The total I/O incurred by this query is as follows:

```
Total writes for this command: 0
Table: titles scan count 3, logical reads: 9, physical reads: 0
```

```
Table: publishers scan count 1, logical reads: 1, physical reads: 0
Total writes for this command: 0
```

> **TIP**
>
> You also can verify the join order by looking at the scan count value for each table in the statistics io option output. In the previous example, a scan count of 1 indicates that the table was the outer table and incurred one iteration, and the scan count of three indicates that table was the inner table and incurred three iterations. Therefore, publishers was the outer table and titles was the inner table.

Now let's force a different join order by turning on the forceplan option.

> **TIP**
>
> As a matter of tidiness, make sure you set the forceplan option to off when you are done with it. Otherwise, you may get undesirable and unexpected performance for subsequent queries.

Turn the forceplan option on as follows:

```
set forceplan on
go

select * from titles, publishers
where titles.pub_id = publishers.pub_id
go

set forceplan off
go
```

In the previous example, the forceplan option instructs the server to execute the query using the join order listed in the from clause (with the titles table as the outer table and the publishers table as the inner table), and to skip trying to pick a better join order. You can see this by examining the showplan output:

```
STEP 1
The type of query is SELECT.
FROM TABLE
titles
Nested iteration
Table Scan
FROM TABLE
publishers
Nested iteration
Table Scan
```

The total I/O for this query is displayed by the statistics io option as follows:

```
Table: titles scan count 1, logical reads: 3, physical reads: 0
Table: publishers scan count 18, logical reads: 18, physical reads: 0
Total writes for this command: 0
```

You can see from this output that reversing the join order more than doubles the amount of logical reads to resolve the query. In join operations between large tables, choosing the wrong join order can degrade performance by several orders of magnitude.

## When to Force Join Orders

In most cases, you do not want to force join orders for the optimizer, as doing so doesn't allow the optimizer to change the join order if your data changes significantly. Typically, you want to override the optimizer only when you've proven, through thorough testing, that the optimizer clearly is choosing the wrong plan.

Another instance in which you may want to force a join order is when the optimizer is picking the proper join order, but is taking a considerable amount of time to determine the best join order. This is likely in join operations involving more than six tables. In some cases, it is entirely conceivable that it could take the optimizer longer to determine the query plan than it does to actually execute the query plan. What you can do in a case where the optimizer is taking too long to optimize the query is to let it run a number of times and determine the best join order. Once you are convinced that it is consistently picking the same join order, list the tables in that order in the query's from clause and set forceplan to on when running the query. This results in a time savings because the optimizer skips looking at all the other join permutations. However, be careful and keep a close eye on this query for changes in the data and indexes, which could result in the forced plan no longer being the optimal one.

## Cautions on Forcing Join Orders

While forcing a join order can be useful for testing or as a workaround for optimizer problems, there are some drawbacks to its use.

One issue is that, when you force a specific join order, as the data distribution changes over time, the optimizer is not able to reevaluate the join order decision and choose a better join order. While the optimizer notices when index statistics are updated, you will have to remember to go and change all of the code that is forced to use a specific join order, and reorder the tables or turn off the forceplan option. This increases the maintenance cost of applications using the forceplan option.

As with forcing indexes, if you are using forceplan to work around an optimizer problem, subsequent releases of SQL Server may have eliminated the problem that led you to force a specific join order in the first place. You should check all query plans forcing join orders after installing a new SQL Server release and test them to see if it is still the most efficient join order.

Forcing the wrong join order can lead to expensive queries, and can be somewhat risky due to the issues discussed here. Before you indiscriminately use the forceplan option, first consider the obvious causes that may lead to invalid query plans being used. These include the following:

- Index statistics that are out-of-date
- SARGs that are invalid
- One or more indexes required to support a particular join order are not available
- A datatype mismatch between join columns

To track down the problem, use showplan to see if indexes are being used as expected, and use the dbcc traceon (302,310) trace flags to determine why a particular query plan is being chosen. Forcing join order to solve a problem query should be the last resort to improving performance. Before taking this measure, try to exhaust all other avenues (for example, adding additional join clauses) for tricking or helping the optimizer first.

# Overriding the Optimizer in System 11

In System 11, the optimizer makes decisions beyond index selection and join order on how to process a query. It now also considers the I/O prefetch size and the cache buffer strategy to efficiently process a query. Just as when you select join orders and indexes, System 11 provides options that allow you to override the optimizer's decisions for the new features as well.

## Increasing the Number of Tables in Join Permutations

In Chapter 12, I discussed how the optimizer processes queries with more than four tables by breaking it up into all possible combinations of four tables and considering the permutations for four tables at a time. If you suspect that an inefficient join order is being chosen using this approach, you can increase the number of tables examined at a time using the set table count option. Here's the syntax:

```
set table count number_of_tables
```

You can specify an integer value between 1 and 8. If you decrease the value, you reduce the chances of the optimizer finding the most efficient query plan. Increasing the value increases the number of tables the optimizer considers at one time to evaluate join orders. However, it also may increase the amount of time it takes to optimize the query. For example, for a query joining eight tables, the optimizer would look at 3,024 total permutations using the four-tables-at-a-time approach, but would have to examine 40,320 permutations examining all eight tables at a time.

Typically, you want to use the set table count option only when the time saved executing the query exceeds the additional time it takes to optimize the query. You can use the statistics time and statistics io options to verify any improvement in parse, compile, and execution times, or any reduction the total logical and physical I/Os. If processing with a higher table count does result in a better query plan, but increases query processing time unacceptably, consider rewriting the query listing the tables in the optimal order in the query's from clause, then using forceplan when running the query.

# Overriding the *prefetch* Size

Another performance improvement introduced in System 11 is the capability for the optimizer to determine the optimal I/O size for processing a query, as long as the SQL Server has been configured to use large I/Os (see Chapters 30, "Configuring and Tuning the SQL Server," and 31, "Optimizing SQL Server Configuration Options," for more detailed discussions of how to configure this option). Large I/Os can improve performance for queries that retrieve a large number of sequential pages by minimizing the number of disk I/O requests and prefetching pages into cache. Queries that can benefit from large I/Os include the following:

- Table scans
- Range queries using clustered indexes
- Queries covered by a nonclustered index

If the cache space used by the table or index is configured for large I/Os, SQL Server can prefetch up to eight pages at a time when a single page is requested from disk, and put the remaining pages into cache. (Refer to Chapters 30 and 31 for more detailed discussions of configuring named data caches.)

To specify an I/O size for processing a query, add the `prefetch` statement to the `index` clause of a `select`, `update`, or `delete` operation. Valid values for I/O size are 2, 4, 8, and 16 (that is, 2KB multiplied by the number of pages). To perform a `prefetch` on data pages, specify the table or clustered index name in the `index` clause. To perform `prefetch` on nonclustered leaf pages, specify the nonclustered index name. For example, the following query uses a `prefetch` size of 16KB (eight pages) when scanning the table:

```
select * from pt_sample (index pt_sample prefetch 16)
   where id > 500
```

> **NOTE**
>
> If there isn't a cache pool in the data cache configured to support a specified `prefetch` size, or if the cache pool configured for that I/O size has no available buffers, SQL Server uses the next smallest available I/O size.
>
> In addition, if SQL Server finds one or more of the pages in cache for the current I/O request, it skips using the `prefetch` size and performs normal 2KB I/Os on the other pages in the I/O request.

You may want to experiment with prefetch sizes to see whether or not a larger `prefetch` size saves physical I/O. To verify this, use the `set statistics io` and `showplan` options. For example, the following query by default uses 16KB I/Os because it performs a table scan:

```
set showplan on
set statistics io on
select count(*) from car_sales
```

> **TIP**
>
> If you are testing different `prefetch` sizes and using `statistics io` to confirm physical I/O savings, you need to make sure that none of the table is in cache before each execution of the query. The drastic way to do this is to shut down SQL Server, which flushes everything from cache.
>
> A more graceful, yet more tedious and time-consuming, way is to run queries on other tables or on one large table, which causes all pages for the table in question to be pushed out of data cache.
>
> The easiest way in System 11 is to bind the table to a named data cache. Between tests, you simply unbind and rebind the table from the named cache. Unbinding a table from a named caches causes all of its pages to be flushed from cache. For example, to flush all data pages from cache for the `car_sales` table in this example, I ran the following:
>
> ```
> sp_unbindcache testdb, car_sales
> go
> sp_bindcache "default data cache", testdb, car_sales
> go
> ```
>
> Setting up named data caches in System 11 and binding and unbinding objects to a named data cache is covered in more detail in Chapters 30 and 31.

Looking at the `showplan` output, you can confirm that the query is using 16KB I/Os:

```
STEP 1
        The type of query is SELECT.
        Evaluate Ungrouped COUNT AGGREGATE.

        FROM TABLE
            car_sales
        Nested iteration.
        Table Scan.
        Ascending scan.
        Positioning at start of table.
        Using I/O Size 16 Kbytes.
        With MRU Buffer Replacement Strategy.

    STEP 2
        The type of query is SELECT.
```

By viewing the `statistics io` output, you can determine the actual logical and physical I/Os:

```
Table: car_sales  scan count 1,  logical reads: 334,  physical reads: 54
Total writes for this command: 0
Total writes for this command: 0
```

As you can see, using 16KB I/Os, the SQL Server performed only 54 physical reads.

Now let's try running the query as follows and force it to use 2KB I/Os:

```
set showplan on
set statistics io on
select count(*) from car_sales (index car_sales prefetch 2)
```

In this case, `showplan` confirms that it will use 2KB I/Os:

```
STEP 1
The type of query is SELECT.
Evaluate Ungrouped COUNT AGGREGATE.

FROM TABLE
    car_sales
Nested iteration.
Table Scan.
Ascending scan.
Positioning at start of table.
Using I/O Size 2 Kbytes.
With LRU Buffer Replacement Strategy.

STEP 2
The type of query is SELECT.
```

Examining the `statistics io` output, you can see that this approach incurred as many physical as logical reads using a 2KB I/O size:

```
Table: car_sales  scan count 1,  logical reads: 334,  physical reads: 334
Total writes for this command: 0
Total writes for this command: 0
```

> **NOTE**
>
> If you wish to turn off prefetching for all queries in System 11 for the rest of your user session, use the `set prefetch off` statement. By default, `prefetch` is set to on. If you want to disable prefetching for a specific table, use the `sp_cachestrategy` stored procedure. For example, to turn off prefetching for the `car_sales` table, execute the following:
>
> ```
> sp_cachestrategy car_sales, "prefetch", off
> ```

Overall, the optimizer typically appears to use the appropriate I/O size for the type of query executed. So when would you want to override it? Well, it's pretty much dependent on your application.

If you have a mix of users doing random 2KB I/O and users doing sequential 16KB I/O, the users attempting to perform 16KB I/O will fall back to using 2KB I/O if any of the pages they are trying to read are already in cache from the users doing random I/Os. This can lead to a problem if the 2KB buffer pool is not large enough to handle the number of pages being retrieved by the users doing large reads. This results in wasted memory in the 16KB buffer pool, and excessive I/Os to the 2KB buffer pool. To avoid this, you may want to force the random reads to perform 16KB I/O. This allows both sets of users to work from the same cache pool, and prevents the large I/O users from constantly flushing the pages from the 2KB I/O pool.

# Forcing a Cache Strategy

One other new feature for System 11 is the capability of the optimizer to determine whether or not to use a fetch-and-discard strategy for pages read in from disk. In previous releases of SQL Server, all pages read in from disk went onto the most recently used (MRU) end of the cache chain. As you read more pages into memory, other pages would be pushed off the least recently used (LRU) end of the chain. This would hurt performance when a large table scan would fill up the data cache, pushing frequently needed pages out of memory and requiring physical I/Os to read them in again.

System 11 overcame this problem by determining whether to put the pages read in at the beginning or end of the chain, depending on the type of the query. If the optimizer determines that the query is a fetch-and-discard type of query (that is, one in which it reads the data in once and doesn't need to access it again), it puts the page near the end of the cache chain so that the page doesn't push out pages that should remain in cache.

The types of queries to which the optimizer applies the fetch and discard (MRU) strategy include the following:

- Table scans
- Range queries using clustered indexes
- Covered queries that scan nonclustered leaf pages
- The outer table of a join (only a single scan required)
- The inner table of a join if the table is larger than the available cache space

> **NOTE**
>
> The names Sybase chose for the different cache strategies seem a bit confusing. You would think that if you wanted a page to go at the LRU end of the cache chain, you would specify the LRU strategy. However, the LRU strategy actually puts the page at the MRU end of the chain. It seems that they named it the LRU strategy because the available page comes from the end of the LRU chain, a "clean" page that has already had any modifications written to disk. When the MRU strategy is applied, the page still comes from the end of the LRU chain, but is placed at the end of the MRU side of the cache chain just before the wash marker, so it goes back to the LRU side of the cache chain sooner (see Figure 16.1).
>
> For more information on the workings of the data cache chains and how to configure them in System 11, please see Chapters 30 and 31.

**FIGURE 16.1.**

*LRU strategy places clean page at beginning of MRU chain; MRU strategy places clean page just before the wash marker.*

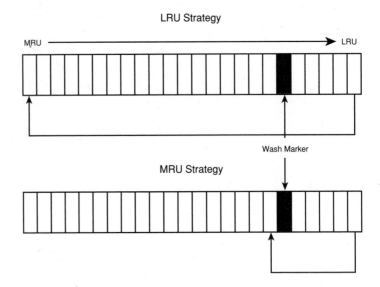

You can override the optimizer decision to use the MRU or LRU strategy by specifying the strategy you want it to use in the index clause of a select, update, or delete statement. For example, the following query tells SQL Server to use 16KB I/Os and apply the LRU strategy to keep the pages in cache longer:

```
select * from pt_sample (index pt_sample prefetch 16 lru)
    where id > 500
```

Looking at the showplan output, you can confirm that it's using the LRU strategy:

```
STEP 1
        The type of query is SELECT.
        FROM TABLE
            pt_sample
        Nested iteration.
        Table Scan.
        Ascending scan.
        Positioning at start of table.
        Using I/O Size 16 Kbytes.
        With LRU Buffer Replacement Strategy.
```

Being able to force a specific buffer-replacement strategy is useful for cases where you are performing a table scan and want to keep the table in cache memory (for example, "priming" the data cache), or when you don't want to keep pages in cache for queries that the optimizer typically would apply the LRU strategy for.

If you wish to turn off the use of the MRU strategy for all queries on a specific table, use the sp_cachestrategy stored procedure. For example, to turn off the MRU strategy for the car_sales table, execute the following:

```
sp_cachestrategy car_sales, "mru", off
```

# Summary

SQL Server provides a number of facilities for forcing optimizer behavior. Indiscriminate use of forcing indexes and forcing join orders often causes more harm than good, but it can be a useful tool for overcoming query-optimization problems or for testing different scenarios. System 11 provides even more options for fine-tuning and tweaking query performance.

For all topics discussed in this chapter, it can't be stressed enough that you should always test these options thoroughly before implementing them in an application. Also, if you don't have a thorough understanding what's really going wrong with a query, using these options often will make life much more painful, not less so. However, with thorough testing, these hints can help alleviate performance problems due to optimizer limitations, and let your client applications work more effectively.

# Database Design and Performance

**17**

The purpose of a logical database design is to understand and describe your data.

Logical database designers are very good at drawing diagrams explaining the relationship of the data within an organization and even explaining the diagrams in front of a group. Usually, they can even take the logical design to the next few steps, most notably assigning attributes to their entities (that is, identifying which columns go into which tables).

Many shops swear by this design, and require this logical design to be the physical design, simply because it is easy to understand.

This is not a good approach. A logical design does not have the same purpose as a physical design. *The primary purpose of a physical design is performance.*

Designing databases for performance, however, requires an understanding of the underlying DBMS. You have learned much from the preceding chapters in this book. This chapter explores physical database design techniques for improving SQL Server performance.

# Database Design Issues

There are three primary design issues to consider when developing a physical database design:

- Data integrity
- Ease of use
- Performance

When developing a physical database design, you want the design to support your data consistency and *referential integrity* (RI) requirements easily. If a data element is represented exactly once within a database, it is easier to track and maintain than if it is represented multiple times. Referential integrity must also be maintained and, if possible, enforced at the server level.

> **TIP**
>
> One of the more frequently asked questions is whether to handle integrity checking (of all sorts) at the client level or at the server level. The ideal answer is to check in both places. Check at the client level because it is cheaper and faster; check at the server level to guarantee database integrity across all applications uniformly, including those that might not perform integrity checks.

A DBA also should consider ease of comprehension in a physical database design. Tables should be browsable so that end users can easily find the data they need and know what data a table contains.

Finally, the DBA typically wants to make database access and modification fast. Speed of data retrieval and update is usually the yardstick used to measure the success of a physical database design. Often, designing a database for access speed or to improve update performance requires modifying the physical design of the database—for example, duplicating or partitioning frequently used data from infrequently used data.

Unfortunately, it is often impossible to design for all three criteria (data integrity, ease of use, and performance) because they tend to be mutually exclusive. For example, breaking up a table to improve access speed makes it harder to browse and pull data together for the end users. During physical database design, decisions need to be made regarding balancing these objectives.

# What Is Logical Design?

*Logical database design* is the process of defining end users' data needs and grouping elements into logical units (for example, tables in an RDBMS). This design should be independent of the final physical implementation. The actual physical layout of the tables, access paths, and indexes is provided at physical design time. Database design tradeoffs have ramifications in physical design and performance because an RDBMS can not detect a poorly designed database and compensate accordingly.

Logical design is intended to reduce (eliminate) redundant data and thereby minimize row size. This has the effect of increasing the number of joins required to pull related data elements together. The ultimate goal of logical design is to make it easy for a user to grasp a gestalt of his data and for the DBA to design the physical database.

## Normalization Conditions

In order to understand how to change the database in the physical design to suit your performance needs, you first need to understand relational database *normalization*, which is the end result of logical database design. Here's a review of the basic terminology and conditions of normalization:

- An *entity* (table) consists of *attributes* (columns) that define *properties* about each *instance* (row) of the entity.
- Each instance of data refers to a single event.
- There is a way of uniquely identifying each row, which we call a *primary key*. The primary key enables you to decide which row you want to reference.
- The primary key can be a single column or multiple columns (a *compound* or *composite* key).
- Primary keys cannot be null (if there is no way of uniquely identifying a row, it does not belong in a relational database).

# Normal Forms

There are up to five levels of normalization, or five *normal forms*, in the logical design process. The idea behind normalization is to provide data and keys to find the data and to ensure that the data exists in only one place. In this book, third normal form is considered a normalized database because it is pretty much the level the industry considers a normalized database.

## First Normal Form

In order for a database to be in *first normal form*, all repeating groups have to have been moved into separate tables; one column contains exactly one value.

This example is not in first normal form because it has a repeating group of titles; there are many titles for the single `Publisher` row:

| Publisher | Title1 | Title2 | Title3 |
|---|---|---|---|
| Smith Publishing | The Tale of... | Cooking with... | Computer and ... |

The following example is in first normal form. There are now several rows for `Publisher`, one for each `Title`:

| Publisher | Title |
|---|---|
| Smith Publishing | The Tale of... |
| Smith Publishing | Cooking with... |
| Smith Publishing | Computer and... |

## Second Normal Form

When *second normal form* is met, nonkey fields must depend on the entire primary key. A database without compound primary keys is automatically in second normal form (if first normal form is met).

This example is not in second normal form because the key is `Publisher` and `Title`, but `Publisher Address` relates only to one part of the key field (`Publisher`) but not to `Title`:

| Publisher | Title | Publisher Address |
|---|---|---|
| Smith Publishing | The Tale of... | New York, NY |
| Smith Publishing | Cooking with... | New York, NY |
| Smith Publishing | Computer and... | New York, NY |

To correct the example, break the table into two parts. Publisher-specific information belongs in the `Publisher` table:

| Publisher | Publisher Address |
|---|---|
| Smith Publishing | New York, NY |

Title-specific information belongs in the `Title` table:

```
Publisher           Title

Smith Publishing    The Tale of...
Smith Publishing    Cooking with...
Smith Publishing    Computer and...
```

# Third Normal Form

*Third normal form* dictates that nonkey fields must not depend on other nonkey fields.

This example table is not in third normal form because the `Location` column depends on the department, not the employee, even though `Employee` is the key field:

```
Employee            Dept            Location

Smith               10              Bldg C
Jones               10              Bldg C
Thomas              10              Bldg C
Alders              8               Bldg D
```

To bring the table into third normal form, break it into two parts, one for `Employee` that indicates the department:

```
Employee            Dept

Smith               10
Jones               10
Thomas              10
Alders              8
```

and the other for `Dept`, indicating the location:

```
Dept                Location

10                  Bldg C
8                   Bldg D
```

# Benefits of Normalization

A normalized database reduces redundancy and, therefore, storage requirements in the database. Data integrity also is easier to maintain in an environment where you have to look in only one place for the data, where each entity is represented only once.

In addition, when the database is normalized, the rows tend to get narrower. This enables more rows per data page within SQL Server, which can speed up table scanning and queries that return more than one row, improving query performance for single tables.

# Drawbacks of Normalization

There are some drawbacks to a normalized database design, however, mostly related to performance. Typically, in a normalized database, more joins are required to pull information together from multiple tables (for example, to get employees along with their current location requires a join between the Employee table and the Dept table).

Joins require additional I/O to process, and are therefore more expensive from a performance standpoint than single-table lookups.

Additionally, a normalized database often incurs additional CPU processing. CPU resources are required to perform join logic and to maintain data and referential integrity. A normalized database contains no summary data, because summary data violates normalization in two ways: it is redundant information and it has no independent business meaning. To calculate summary values requires aggregating multiple rows of data, which incurs both greater CPU processing and more I/O.

# Normalization and the Database Design Picture

Normalization provides a good place to start a physical database design because data is logically grouped and consistent. (I once had a student request to put those first seven words in writing and sign my name. Apparently, his shop didn't understand the difference between the purposes of the two designs.) Third normal form should always be applied to all database design, at least initially. Denormalization is something that is done intentionally—and with malice and forethought—for the purpose of performance.

Remember, however, *normalization can cause substantially more I/O than a denormalized database*. Redundancy can reduce physical I/O, which might be judged to be more expensive than storage costs. Redundancy, however, incurs additional cost at update time.

# Denormalizing the Database

*Denormalizing* is the process of taking a normalized logical design and intentionally disobeying the rules for the purpose of increasing performance. To denormalize effectively, you must understand the bias of the data that is to be loaded into the database and how the data will be accessed.

## Advantages of Denormalization

Denormalization can help minimize joins and foreign keys and help resolve aggregates. Because these are resolved within the database design, you might be able to reduce the number of indexes and even tables to process them.

# Guidelines

Here are some basic guidelines to enable you to determine whether it is time to denormalize your database design:

- Balance the frequency of use of the data items in question, the cost of additional storage to duplicate the data, and the acquisition time of the join.
- Understand how much data is involved in the typical query; this affects the amount of redundancy and additional storage requirements.
- Remember that redundant data is a performance benefit at query time, but is a performance liability at update time because each copy of the data needs to be kept up-to-date. You typically write triggers to maintain the integrity of the duplicated data.

# Basic Denormalization Techniques

Be aware that denormalization is a technique for tuning a database for a specific application, and as such tends to be a last resort when tuning performance. Adding indexes to a table is a tuning method that is transparent to your end users and applications; modifying the database schema is not. If you change the database design, your application code that accesses that database needs to be modified as well.

A variety of denormalization methods can be used to modify the physical database design in an effort to improve performance:

- Adding redundant data by duplicating columns or defining summary data
- Changing your column definitions by combining columns or shortening existing columns
- Redefining your tables by combining tables, duplicating entire tables or portions of a table, and partitioning tables into multiple tables.

# Redundant Data

Redundant data helps performance by reducing joins, or computations, which in turn reduces I/O and CPU processing, respectively. It tends to be either an exact copy of the data or summary data.

Duplicate data should be of exactly the same name, type, and domain, and have the same integrity checking as the original data. Triggers should be used to maintain integrity between the original and the duplicate data. Note that the more volatile the data, the more often you will incur overhead to maintain the duplicate data. You need to balance frequency of use and the cost of the acquisition join against the frequency of modification and the cost of the extra update.

It is occasionally a good idea to duplicate static data to avoid joins. In Figure 17.1, moving the title to the `salesdetail` table saves you from having to perform a lookup when you need that data for, perhaps, a report on sales by title. Is this a good candidate for duplication? The advantage is that it will improve performance, and the title is a *nonvolatile* data attribute (that is, it won't change much). The disadvantage is it might make the `salesdetail` table a lot larger.

**FIGURE 17.1.**

*Duplicating the* `title` *column from the* `titles` *table in the* `salesdetail` *table.*

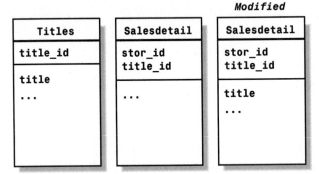

Why is this denormalized? Because there is redundant data and `title` does not depend on the entire key (`stor_id`, `title_id`) of the `salesdetail` table.

## Foreign Key Duplication

Another candidate column for duplication is a foreign key to reduce the number of joins required to retrieve related information.

Figure 17.2 shows a normalized version of a database, requiring a three-table join to retrieve the name of the primary author for a title. If you want to be able to know the primary author for a book 80 percent of the time you retrieve the title, how can you reduce the joins? The easiest way is to add the author ID or author name for the primary author to the `titles` table. (See Figure 17.3.) Author name or author ID is a good candidate for duplication because it is unlikely to change very often.

**FIGURE 17.2.**

*In a normalized version of this database, a three-table join is required to retrieve the name of the primary author.*

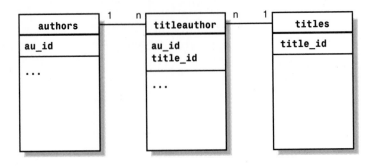

**FIGURE 17.3.**

*Duplicating the primary au_id value in the titles table reduces that to a two-table join for better performance.*

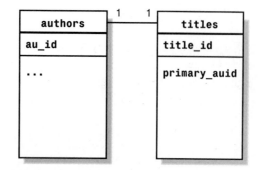

# Derived or Summary Columns

*Derived* columns contain data that is duplicated for the purpose of avoiding repeated calculations. This is called *summary data.*

In any environment, application designers have recognized that certain summary values need to be maintained and available constantly in order to speed their retrieval. If you store frequently accessed sums, averages, and running tallies, reports and queries can run substantially faster, but data modification is slowed somewhat.

Figure 17.4 shows the titles table with a derived column, total_sales, which contains a sum of the qty column from the salesdetail table for the rows related to that title. The total_sales is updated automatically every time a qty is inserted or modified in the salesdetail table. This speeds data retrieval, but adds overhead to modifications on salesdetail.

**FIGURE 17.4.**

*Storing a derived value in the titles table, total_sales, which is the sum of qty for the corresponding rows in the salesdetail table.*

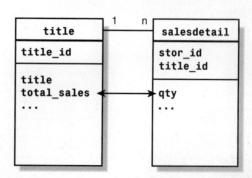

In this example, it is less expensive to maintain a running total_sales column than it is to calculate the total sales every time it is needed. This decision is based on comparing the frequency of the request for the quantity information with the additional cost of the update on salesdetail.

When defining summary data, triggers should be used on the detail tables to maintain the integrity of the summary data, and the summary data needs to be used often enough to justify the update-time overhead created by the triggers.

# Changing Column Definition

You've seen that adding redundant columns and derived columns can enhance performance. You can also see an improvement in performance when you shorten critical columns by using two strategies:

- Contrived columns
- Shortening long columns

When the columns get narrower, a narrower index enables more keys to be searched with fewer I/O operations. The corresponding data rows can also wind up being smaller, enabling more rows per data page, which minimizes the number of I/Os required to scan the data.

## Contrived Columns

A *contrived* column is typically a substitute for a long key; it has no business use of its own.

In Figure 17.5, is there enough information in the customer table to make rows unique? Is Name unique enough? City? State? Zip? Address? Maybe not. George Foreman presumably lives with each of his five sons, all named George, making six George Foremans (Foremen?) at one residence. How about Social Security Number? Some people haven't got one. Some people lie. Sometimes the Social Security Administration makes a mistake and issues a duplicate number. What do you do? What makes sense for a foreign key in the order table? Unfortunately, not necessarily any of the existing columns do.

**FIGURE 17.5.**

*The* customer *table has no easily identifiable primary key for the* order *table to reference. A contrived key can be used as both primary key in* customer *and foreign key in* order.

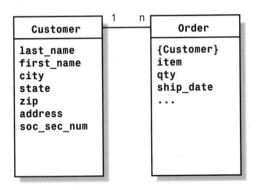

To use a contrived column, add the contrived key to the table and treat it as the primary key for all purposes. Use it as a foreign key in all related tables. This is most helpful in long or multicolumn key situations. You will save storage in the short *and* long run. Using a contrived column will result in a much shorter key than trying to decide how many columns guarantee uniqueness and using all those columns as the foreign keys.

Access performance also improves because index columns are narrower, speeding up individual lookups and joins. In addition, a contrived key is a column that generally doesn't change, so you don't have to worry as much about maintaining the foreign key values. If the customer name is part of the key and is used as a foreign key, any name change has to be cascaded to all foreign key entries as well, increasing the overhead on updates to customer. With a contrived key, you can update customer information without affecting the primary and foreign keys.

# Redefining Tables

Creating duplicate tables tends not to be the only solution, and it is frequently not the best solution. It is, however, a viable method of reducing I/O and search speed for specific types of queries.

There are two basic methods of duplicating tables: subsets and partitioning.

*Subsets* are duplicates of the original data—by row, column, or both. (Note that the replication server can do this across SQL Servers automatically!)

# Data Partitioning

Data *partitioning* takes on two basic varieties:

- Vertically, by separating infrequently used columns
- Horizontally, by separating infrequently used rows

Not all data are good candidates for duplication or partitioning.

If the data is fairly stable, it might be useful to consider duplicating or partitioning a table; volatile data is less likely to work well. The more volatile the data, the more you have to double your work. Triggers are necessary for maintaining data consistency and integrity of duplicate data, which incurs additional overhead on data modifications. In addition, if both tables of a partition must be checked to satisfy a query, additional code must be written (either a union or a join) to bring the results together into a single result set.

Duplicate data also means that you will incur an additional storage expense. On the other hand, you might need to scan less data to derive the same results. In addition, your joins will be faster (because the tables are smaller), and you might gain a benefit by archiving some of your historical, infrequently accessed data.

Although the potential benefits of duplication and partitioning might be large, the amount of extra maintenance might be correspondingly large.

## Vertical Partitioning

Vertical partitioning is a denormalization technique by which you split a table, by columns, into two or more tables. This technique is typically used to minimize the size of the primary table, or to move infrequently accessed columns to a separate table. Consider the following situation:

> "Our invoicing job will not fit in the overnight batch window. We need to reduce join time between orders and items."

In Figure 17.6, a table with several descriptive columns can be partitioned vertically. The information needed for the active processing is all in the `Item_Active` table; less-used information is stored in the `Item_Inactive` table. The `Item_Active` table is considerably smaller and has a higher row density (rows per page). Given this implementation, order-entry operators can still look at descriptions, take orders, and so forth by performing a simple join between `Item_Active` and `Item_Inactive`. Because these are point queries, retrieving one row at a time, the additional cost of the join is negligible. However, the nightly batch process that needs to scan a large number of item numbers and prices at a time speeds up significantly.

**FIGURE 17.6.**

*Vertically partitioning a table creates an active set of data with substantially higher row density.*

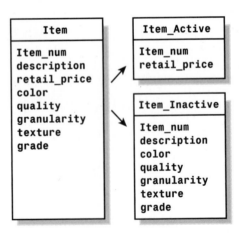

The advantage, if you choose to partition columns, is that the number of locks held on tables might be reduced, and table scans might be faster. However, if excessive joining takes place between vertically partitioned tables, and it adversely impacts performance, you might need to reevaluate your decision.

# Horizontal Partitioning

Table scan time grows proportionally with table size. When activity is limited to a subset of the entire table, it makes sense to isolate that subset. This is useful not only for production, but for test tables. Horizontal partitioning is a method of splitting a table at the row level into two or more tables.

The method used to partition the rows horizontally varies depending on how the data is used. The most common method used is by date, partitioning the most current, active data from the historical, inactive data. Other partitioning options include partitioning by activity, department, business unit, geographical location, or a random hash value.

Consider the following situations:

> 98 percent of the time we are using 5 percent of the rows; the rest of the rows are getting in our way.

or

> The most recent 15 percent of the data is being used 85 percent of the time. Why perform statistics updates on the whole 200,000,000 rows when only a part of the table is volatile?

Figure 17.7 illustrates an orders table partitioned horizontally, with active rows in one table and inactive rows in another.

**FIGURE 17.7.**

*You can reduce scan time, index size, and index levels by partitioning a table horizontally.*

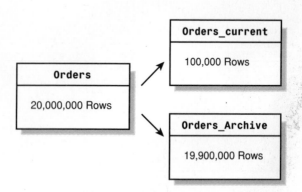

One of the main drawbacks to consider when horizontally partitioning tables is that retrieving data from more than one table as a single result set requires the use of the UNION statement. If you use a random hashing scheme to partition the data, it also is harder for end users to determine where the data resides, making the database less browsable.

## Views as a Partitioning Tool

One advantage of vertical partitioning over horizontal partitioning is that the vertical partitioning can be hidden from the end user or application developer through the use of views. If you split a table by columns, a view can be created that joins the two table partitions. Users can then select from the view as if it were a single table.

Views cannot be used to hide horizontal partitioning from end users or applications, because in the current releases of SQL Server, the UNION statement is not permitted in views.

# Summary

A fully normalized database, although easier to maintain, does not necessarily lend itself to optimal performance. To determine whether the database design needs to be modified to improve query performance, identify the problem queries and look at the base tables on which the queries rely. Identify any potential join problems due to column widths and types or due to the large quantity of rows that need to be accessed. Then consider modifying columns or creating derived, summary, or contrived columns where they might be helpful. Additionally, identify any potential scanning problems in the base tables and consider partitioning tables if there are no alternatives. Due to the impact on end users and application developers, the first choice for query optimization tends to be adding additional indexes, rather than modifying the physical database design.

# Database Object Placement and Performance

# 18

A database in SQL Server may reside on many devices (see Figure 18.1). In addition, a device can contain many databases.

**FIGURE 18.1.**

*A single database may span several logical devices. The create database statement here allocates 100MB on each device for use by the database,* perftune.

```
create database perftune
    on device_1 = 100,
    on device_2 = 100,
    on device_3 = 100
```

Here, then is the $64 question: When you create and/or load a table, where does it go? In this chapter, we will discuss the location of physical data, how to manage its location, and the performance ramifications of choosing from different database and object storage and placement options.

# Database Segments

Within SQL Server, you can define and use named segments to manually place objects onto particular disk devices and database fragments. SQL Server provides this feature, because it was the best way to maximize the use of multiple fixed disks and disk controllers on hardware platforms that may be incapable of presenting those hard disks as a single logical volume.

When you create a table, where will the table reside? Let's break this question into two parts:

■ Where will the table *structure* reside?
■ Where will the table *data* reside?

The official answer is that the location will be completely random. (In practice, we'll see that it is slightly less than random.) Unless segments are defined, you cannot exert control over which devices your tables will reside on. (See Figure 18.2.)

A *segment* is a pointer to a device allocated to a database. This is quite different from a *fragment*, which is a section of a database on a particular device. Segments and fragments are interrelated in that a segment points to a fragment or fragments—meaning it points to one or more specific devices. When creating a segment, you define the name of the segment (how you will refer to it when using it for object creation), and the device that the segment points to. A single segment can point to one or more devices at a time. When first created, segments point to a single device, but can subsequently be moved or "extended." For example, segment "foo" can start out pointing to device DATA_DEV_1, and then be extended to also point to DATA_DEV_2.

**FIGURE 18.2.**

*When you don't use segments, allocation of space to a table among several devices is unpredictable.*

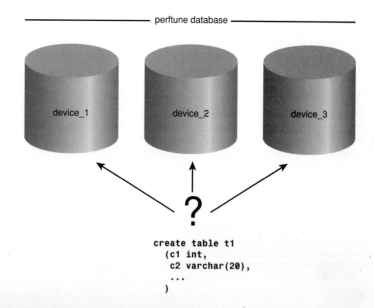

```
create table t1
    (c1 int,
     c2 varchar(20),
     ...
    )
```

> **NOTE**
>
> If you are unfamiliar with the concept of segments and how to define and manage them, read Chapter 26, "Defining, Altering, and Maintaining Databases and Logs," before reading further in this section.

There are three predefined segments in every database: `system`, `default`, and `logsegment`. The `system` segment is where the system tables in the database are stored. The `logsegment` is where the transaction log (the `syslogs` system table) allocates its space from. All other database objects (that is, your tables and indexes), are created on the segment named `default` if no specific segment is specified when the table or index is created.

In addition to the predefined segments in a database, the DBA can also define additional segments within a database to exert finer control over the placement of tables and indexes within a database.

# Why Define and Use Segments?

One reason you might want to use segments is control. An object cannot grow beyond its segment. As a result, you can limit the growth of potentially explosive tables by placing them on a segment which includes only that space you wish to allocate to the table. Typical uses are the database log (the `syslogs` table, which resides on the `logsegment` segment, and which typically goes on its own device), and volatile tables such as those with live data feeds. Examples of these include tables of stock ticker information and tables of physical monitoring data, as from shop floor and pollution control equipment. You want data accumulated, but if a huge number of data points suddenly feed into the database on orders of magnitude higher than typical/expected, you might consider losing some data points in exchange for the entire database not filling up unexpectedly.

The other reason for defining segments is performance. The most typical bottleneck in all of data processing is the limitation of speed imposed by disk drives and their corresponding controllers. If you split your I/O across disk drives, you should be able to increase performance by increasing the bandwidth of the I/O bottleneck. Spreading I/O across disk drives can also improve throughput for queries and transactions by spreading reads and writes across devices. Some objects, specifically logs and indexes, are hit so heavily that you might want to put them on their own devices. This can be accomplished using segments.

> **WARNING**
>
> Segments are not for everybody. As a guess, only about one in ten shops actually use them. About one in three of those shops actually needs them. This is bad news for the other two shops, because additional administrative overhead is required to maintain segments, as we will discuss in a moment.

> **TIP**
>
> Before going to the extra trouble of using segments, first identify positively that there is an I/O bottleneck. You may be able to do this with operating system tools that your operating system administrator can provide for you (and help you run). If you cannot identify I/O to a specific table as a bottleneck, I strongly advise you look for performance gain solutions elsewhere, and not to segments.

## Using Segments to Improve Performance

Typically, when segments are used to improve performance, the segments point to SQL Server devices that are mapped to different physical disk drives. The performance improvements typically seek to distribute database activity across disks (and controllers). (See Figure 18.3.)

Here are some examples of how activity can be distributed:

- Active tables can be placed on different segments to spread I/O across multiple devices.
- Nonclustered indexes can be stored on one segment, while the table itself is stored on another. This can improve both read and write performance because index I/O can run parallel to table I/O.

**FIGURE 18.3.**

*Using segments to spread I/O across database devices to minimize contention.*

I/O Contention for a single database device

Segments help spread I/O across devices

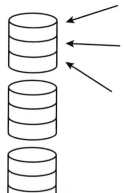

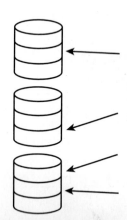

- A large table can be divided among segments (and disks) to allow different parts of the table to be read at one time.

- Text and image data (*Binary Large OBjects*, or BLOBs) can be placed on a segment, apart from the standard data pages. This may improve read performance when the table is heavily used.

# Placing Tables on Segments to Spread I/O

Defining segments provides a mechanism to identify and reference individual devices defined for databases. Now, we can assign objects to these devices to spread I/O for those objects across the devices.

Let's consider a database with two very active tables, table_a and table_b. This database also supports an OLTP application with a high transaction rate, so the transaction log is very active. The log should be placed on a separate device when the database is created. If the database is also allocated space on two other devices, we can place table_a and table_b by defining segments and placing the tables on those segments when we create them. For example, consider the following session:

```
create database testeb on dev1 = 100, dev2 = 100 log on logdev = 50
go
use testdb
```

```
go
sp_addsegment seg1, testdb, dev1
sp_Addsegment seg2, testdb, dev2
go
create table table_a (a int, b varchar(255) null) on seg1
create table table_b (a int, b varchar(255) null) on seg1
go
```

Let's take a look at what this code is doing. First, the log is placed on a separate device, `logdev`, when the database is created. Next we define `seg1` to point to `dev1`, and `seg2` to point to `dev2`. Finally, we create `table_a` which will reside on `seg1`, and `table_b` which will reside on `seg2`. This will separate the I/O for `table_a` from the I/O for `table_b`, minimizing contention between concurrent processes that access both tables.

## Placing Indexes on Segments

In SQL Server, when you `insert`, `update`, or `delete` data rows, if there are any nonclustered indexes on the table, the index rows may also be updated. This can lead to contention between index row updates and data row updates. Segments can be used to place nonclustered indexes on a device separate from the device where the data resides, thereby minimizing contention. The following example creates `table_a` on `seg_1` and its nonclustered index, `idx1`, on `seg_3`:

```
create table table_a (a int, b varchar(255) null) on seg1
go
create index idx1 on table_a(a) on seg3
go
```

> **NOTE**
>
> You cannot place a clustered index on a separate segment from its table because the leaf level of the clustered index is the table data pages. If you create a clustered index on a segment, the entire table moves to the segment with the index. This is actually a neat way to move a table to a new device. If you have created a table and loaded the data, and then decide you want the table on a different device, just define the appropriate segment and drop and re-create the clustered index on that segment.

## Splitting a Table Across Devices to Increase Throughput

To minimize I/O contention between multiple processes against a single table, you want to spread that table across multiple devices.

Creating a table on a segment that spans multiple devices won't help because SQL Server will use all available space on the first device before it starts allocating space on the second device. To split a table across devices, you need to define a segment for each device (see Figure 18.4) and spread the table across both devices using `sp_placeobject` as described in Chapter 26. In a nutshell, `sp_placeobject` controls *future* allocation of space for an object.

**FIGURE 18.4.**

*When you want to spread out the contents of a table across many devices, define a segment for each device and then create a segment that spans all relevant devices.*

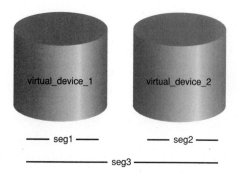

First, create segments as appropriate in your database. For example, the setup in Figure 18.4 could have been created as follows:

```
use perfdb
go

exec sp_addsegment seg1, perfdb, virtual_device_1
exec sp_addsegment seg2, perfdb, virtual_device_2
exec sp_addsegment seg3, perfdb, virtual_device1
exec sp_extendsegment seg3, perfdb, virtual_device2
```

Next, create your table and clustered index on the segment where you want to load the first portion of the data:

```
create table spread_table (a int, b varchar(255)) on seg1
create clustered index index1 on spread_table (a) on seg1
```

> **WARNING**
>
> Remember, if you create your clustered index later, you will move all of your data to the new segment!

Once you have created the table, use bcp (or other load facility) to load in the first portion of data.

Once the data is loaded, instruct the server to allocate all new pages from the other segment using sp_placeobject:

```
sp_placeobject seg2, spread_table
```

Now load the next portion of data. Repeat the last two steps (data load and sp_placeobject) for any additional segments.

Finally, place the table on the segment, seg3, that spans all devices.

> **NOTE**
>
> Please note that this technique helps to distribute selects, updates, and inserts across all defined segments as long as these operations occur on pages already allocated to the table. For any operation that requires additional pages to be allocated to the table, as an insert typically does, all new pages will come from the first device in the segment. This will not help as much to minimize I/O contention on inserts, and over time, with a substantial number of inserts, your table may not be spread evenly across all devices.
>
> If you have a real need to spread inserts across multiple devices, consider partitioning the table manually by modifying the database design to partition the table horizontally into multiple tables (see Chapter 17, "Database Design and Performance").
>
> If you are running System 11 SQL Server, you may want to consider using heap table partitioning to spread inserts across devices, as described later in this chapter.

# Placing Text/Image Data on a Different Segment

When a table contains text or image columns, the text/image data is stored on a separate page chain from the table. By default, this page chain is placed on the same segment as the table. Reading and writing text/image data requires, at a minimum, two page I/Os, one to read/write the data page and one to read/write the text/image page.

If you read or write text/image data frequently, you can improve I/O performance by placing the text/image chain on a separate physical device. Ideally, you want to place the text/image chain on a device that is not busy with other table/index access operations. This will minimize I/O contention between text/image reads and writes and other table/index reads and writes.

If you want to place the text/image page chain on a separate device from the table, use `sp_placeobject`. When you create a table with a text/image column, a row is added to the `sysindexes` system table in that database for that table, similar to an index row but with an index ID of 255. The name in the `name` column in `sysindexes` for the text/image column is the table name prefixed with a `t`.

> **NOTE**
>
> If a table contains multiple text/image columns, only a single text/image chain is created for the table. All text/image columns will read/write to the same text/image page chain.

If our table with a text column is called `authors`, the name of the text/image chain row in `sysindexes` would be `tauthors`. To move the text/image chain to a new segment, use the following commands:

```
sp_addsegment textseg, perfdb, dev4
go
sp_placeobject textseg, "authors.tauthors"
go
```

Preferably, you want to perform these commands before loading data into the table. If the table contains rows of text or image data before you execute `sp_placeobject`, only future allocations will go to the new segment. Existing text/image data will continue to reside on the same segment as the table until the data is deleted and the pages deallocated from the table.

# Using RAID as an Alternative to Segments

*RAID*, or Redundant Arrays of Inexpensive Disks, is a relatively new technology that debuted near the end of the 1980s. The concepts behind RAID are not new. RAID just provides a structured framework in which to discuss those concepts. The most basic concept is simple: Instead of using a single hard disk to store data, use multiple disks simultaneously and in parallel. By doing so, you can make your I/O operations much faster, because the read and write operations happen in parallel across multiple read-write heads on multiple hard disks, rather than across a single read-write head on a single disk. Such simple parallelization of I/O has demonstrated immediate and drastic performance improvements. SQL Server has traditionally used segments to achieve this same result, by breaking up a table across multiple disks. RAID technology provides a simpler method, from a DBA point of view.

## Introduction to RAID Technology

Six common classes of RAID technology are currently defined:

- RAID Level 0
- RAID Level 1
- RAID Level 2
- RAID Level 3
- RAID Level 4
- RAID Level 5

## RAID Level 0

A RAID Level 0 device provides data striping across multiple disks without providing any mechanism for data redundancy (see Figure 18.5). The data is divided into the appropriate number of chunks and striped across all disks in the array. All data reads and writes are handled asynchronously.

The advantages of RAID Level 0 are the high I/O rate due to the small block size, and the capability to read from and write to multiple disks at once. The transfer time for a data request to a RAID Level 0 device is proportional to the number of devices participating in the array.

**FIGURE 18.5.**

*RAID Level 0 diagram.*

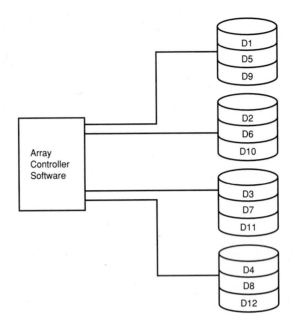

# RAID Level 1

RAID Level 1 is a traditional hardware-level disk mirroring configuration (see Figure 18.6), with no data striping. RAID Level 1 devices provide the highest level of reliability of all the RAID devices while providing a high I/O rate because of the small block sizes. RAID Level 1 devices support small reads and writes with performance nearly equivalent to that of a single disk, especially if the array performs mirrored writes concurrently. Data access time can also be improved if the controller software allows simultaneous read requests to be spread over both disks.

RAID Level 1 devices often provide a faster and more efficient mirroring mechanism than SQL Server software-level mirroring.

One disadvantage to RAID Level 1 is that there is no built-in mechanism for data striping— it is up to the database designer/DBA to spread tables and indexes across devices using segments to spread the I/O. RAID Level 1 also requires the greatest number of disks of any of the RAID architectures (each disk requires an equivalently sized duplicate to provide data redundancy).

As far as performance, large writes to a RAID Level 1 device will generally execute more slowly than writes to a single spindle because of the overhead of maintaining a duplicate copy of the data. RAID Level 1 offers no performance improvement over a single disk when writing data, and will definitely be slower if a separate controller is not used for the mirror drive. Read performance, however, will be the same or better than reads from a single spindle. This is because requested data can be read from either side of the mirrored pair and does not normally need to be read from both disks. With some RAID Level 1 devices, intelligent controller software can improve read performance by reading from the device closest to the requested data, or by splitting concurrent read requests across both devices.

**FIGURE 18.6.**

*RAID Level 1 diagram.*

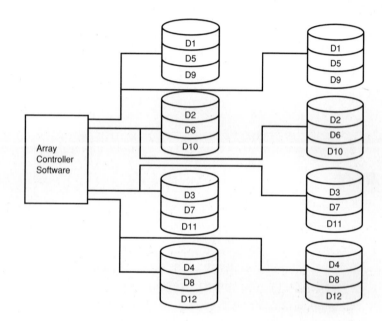

# RAID Level 2

A RAID Level 2 device is a parallel access array. All disks are accessed and written concurrently for every access to a RAID device. RAID Level 2 uses a bit-level interleaving scheme to spread a data chunk across all data disks in the array (see Figure 18.7). Data redundancy is implemented by spreading the corresponding check bits across check disks.

The advantages of using a RAID Level 2 array are that error detection and correction are handled by the array rather than by individual disks, and the cost of redundancy in terms of drives is less. Redundancy is maintained using check bits of the data rather than an exact copy. The disadvantage of RAID Level 2 is that failure of one disk shuts down the entire array.

**FIGURE 18.7.**

*RAID Level 2 diagram.*

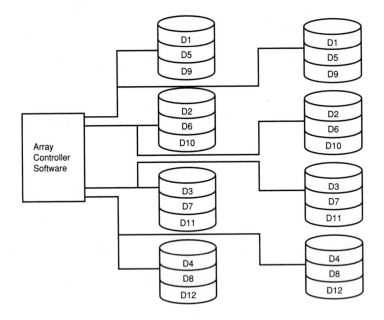

# RAID Level 3

RAID Level 3 also implements a parallel access array. It differs from RAID Level 2 in that data blocks are spread across devices. A single disk contains parity information (XOR) in order to rebuild a failed device in the array (see Figure 18.8).

The advantages of RAID Level 3 are that the synchronized parallel access supports fast large data transfers, and the cost of maintaining redundancy in terms of the number of devices required is lower than for Level 1. Level 3 also allows hot-swapping of a failed data drive (that is, the array does not have to be shut down in order to replace a failed device). The failed device can be swapped out on the fly and the contents will be re-created on the replacement from the contents of the parity disk.

The primary disadvantages of using a RAID Level 3 device are that the single parity disk is a bottleneck for the entire array, and failure of the parity disk disables the entire array. Also, because of the parallel access architecture, RAID Level 3 is not efficient for small block reads.

**FIGURE 18.8.**
*RAID Level 3 diagram.*

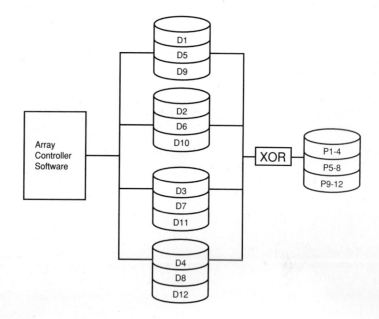

# RAID Level 4

A RAID Level 4 device is an independent array. Unlike the parallel access arrays, a single I/O request does not require concurrent access to all disks in the array. Data blocks in a RAID Level 4 device are striped across all data devices in the array. A single disk contains the parity information (XOR) necessary to rebuild a failed device (see Figure 18.9).

The primary advantage of RAID Level 4 over Levels 2 and 3 is that an independent array can process multiple data requests simultaneously. The disadvantage of RAID Level 4 is that write performance is compromised by the overhead of maintaining the disk parity.

To maintain the parity information, the controller software must read parity information to internal buffers, compute the new parity information, and then write the updated parity information as well the data to the appropriate devices. This is commonly referred to as the read/modify/write sequence. In addition, the single parity disk creates an I/O bottleneck in the array as well as a single point of failure.

**FIGURE 18.9.**

*RAID Level 4 diagram.*

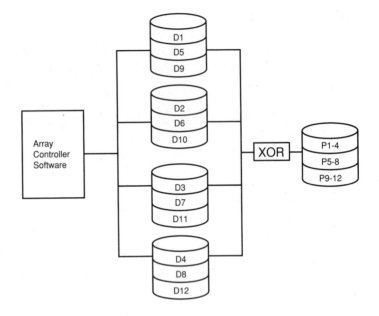

## RAID Level 5

RAID Level 5 is similar to RAID Level 4 except that it doesn't maintain a single parity disk. Instead, parity information for the data contained on one disk is spread across the other disks in the array (see Figure 18.10).

The advantage to this approach is that it eliminates the bottleneck and single-point-of-failure problems caused by having a single parity disk. The disadvantage of RAID Level 5 is the slower write performance caused by the read/modify/write sequence required to maintain the data redundancy.

## SQL Server and Storage Device Performance

SQL Server typically performs small block reads and writes, reading data in 2KB chunks at a time. Because of this, you may not experience the performance gain you'd expect when using storage devices designed to improve performance by using larger block sizes or caching controllers that buffer large block reads.

> **NOTE**
>
> You may be able to take better advantage of the performance of devices that perform large block reads if you configure the prefetch capabilities of SQL Server as described in Chapters 30, "Configuring and Tuning the SQL Server," and 31, "Optimizing SQL Server Configuration Options."

However, reading larger blocks of data at a time will only help improve performance if the data pages in a table are physically in sequential order. This is rarely the case in OLTP environments because modifications to your data cause page splits, fragmenting your tables (for more on page splits and how data is stored in SQL Server, see Chapter 10, "Understanding SQL Server Storage Structures"). As your tables become more fragmented, large block reads become less efficient because the next page required is not found within the block. SQL Server ends up incurring more large block reads.

To improve performance, you will need to defragment the table. This is accomplished by dropping and re-creating the clustered index on the table to repack the data rows into a sequential chain of pages. Applying a lower fill factor when creating the clustered index will leave free space for future inserts, preventing page splits initially so the table doesn't quickly become fragmented again.

**FIGURE 18.10.**

*RAID Level 5 diagram.*

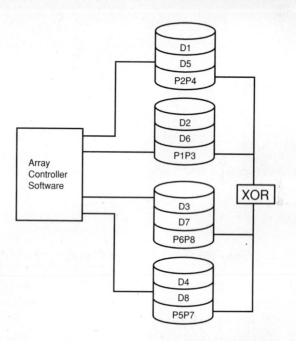

DSS and Data Warehouse–type applications may benefit from large block devices if these applications perform large sequential reads of adjacent data pages. OLTP applications generally perform operations on small blocks of data that are spread randomly across devices; therefore, they benefit more from devices that perform small block I/O efficiently.

# Which RAID Device to Use

There are three trade-offs involved in choosing a RAID device:

- Cost
- Performance
- Reliability

All three factors tend to be mutually exclusive:

- High performance equals higher cost and lower reliability.
- High reliability equals higher cost and lower performance.

If looking into a RAID solution, you will need to choose the strategy that best matches your desired goal of performance, reliability, and cost, and make trade-offs where necessary.

DSS and Data Warehouse implementations require good read performance and high availability. In an OLTP environment, the goal is both high device reliability and maximum write performance. A `tempdb` device requires high read and write performance, but not, typically, high reliability.

# RAID Levels Commonly Used with SQL Server

The three RAID levels most commonly implemented in a SQL Server environment are RAID Levels 0, 1, and 5. RAID Level 0 typically provides the best read/write performance of the RAID devices for the lowest cost, but with the trade-off of the lowest reliability. A RAID Level 0 device might be a good device to use for a large `tempdb` to help minimize `tempdb` I/O contention.

RAID Level 1 provides the highest reliability of RAID devices and high performance for small block I/O operations. Typically, RAID Level 1 provides the best trade-off between reliability and performance and is a good candidate for log devices and critical OLTP databases.

RAID Level 5 provides high reliability and excellent performance for reads, but lower performance for writes. It also requires fewer devices than RAID Level 1 to maintain redundancy. RAID Level 5 is typically a good candidate for DSS and Data Warehouse databases where OLTP activity is at a minimum and most of the activity is read oriented.

# SQL Server and RAID—Additional Notes

When setting up the log and data devices for a SQL Server database, you want to try to put the log and data on separate I/O devices, preferably on completely separate I/O channels so there is no contention between log writes and data reads and writes. This will give you the best I/O performance for your database. Because of the striping nature of RAID Level 0 and RAID Level 5 devices, if you mix the SQL Server log and data on these devices, both the log and the data will be striped across the same set of disks. Although striping reduces the chances of a log write going to the same disk at the same time as a data read or write, there is no guarantee that log and data I/O will always be going to separate physical disks. To eliminate any I/O contention between the log and the data, and to get the best performance when using RAID, we recommend that you use separate RAID devices for the data and the log.

For a transaction log, you may also want to consider using a mix of RAID Levels 0 and 1, essentially a striped set of mirrored disks. This gives you the best of both worlds—the highest level of reliability (RAID Level 1) with the highest write performance for concurrent writes (RAID Level 0).

RAID devices provide flexible alternatives for storage devices requiring large volumes, high performance, or high reliability. Choosing the appropriate RAID device requires balancing cost versus performance versus reliability in order to find the proper fit.

# Software-Based versus Hardware-Based RAID Subsystems

With today's operating systems, there are often two sets of options for using RAID technology: You can use O/S volume manager features to set up software-based RAID devices, or you can use a hardware-based RAID disk subsystem.

Hardware-based RAID, while more expensive than software-based RAID, can also be more reliable. For mission-critical transaction processing applications, you should be using hardware-based RAID. With hardware-based RAID systems, everything should be duplicated, and hot-swappable. Disk drives should be hot-swappable, and most manufacturers of high-quality RAID subsystems have additional disks already plugged into the cabinet, waiting to be turned on in the event of a disk failure. The disks themselves should be hot-swappable, meaning the physical disk can be removed and replaced without turning off the server or disk subsystem.

Power supplies should also be hot-swappable, and a redundant power supply should already be in the cabinet. Should the active power supply fail, the backup should be set to take over immediately, preventing service interruptions. Most hardware-based RAID systems also use dual controllers—one for managing the disk interface to the computer, the other for managing the striping of data. If possible, both of these controller types should also be duplicated, to prevent either controller from becoming a single point of failure. Swappable controllers are obviously more complicated, so understand that massive controller failure is still going to keep you up late trying to repair it.

Hardware-based RAID subsystems also often outperform software-based solutions. Many RAID subsystem vendors now incorporate caching mechanisms and intelligent controllers in their subsystems to improve read and write performance to RAID devices.

With all RAID Level 5 implementations, remember that approximately 25 percent to 30 percent of the rated disk capacity will be consumed by the parity bit information. This is important when planning capacity for databases. Putting a 5GB database on a 5GB RAID array will lead to disappointing results—for a 5GB database, count on needing a 7GB or 8GB array!

## RAID versus Segments

Segments provide functionality outside of parallel I/O and fault tolerance. RAID subsystems can't control the growth of objects by limiting that growth to a particular device. If your database requires this level of control, segments are your only option.

If you are using segments purely as a performance enhancement, however, you may find that RAID is not only faster, it is more reliable and cheaper to administer. A RAID volume will present itself as a single logical disk. By creating a disk device and database on that disk, you have immediately paralleled I/O, and fault tolerance as well.

# Heap Table Partitioning in System 11

SQL Server, by default, stores a table in a single page chain. Without a clustered index on the table, it is stored as a heap structure—all inserts go to the last page in the table. This approach works well for tables that do not receive a high number of inserts since, without a clustered index, SQL Server doesn't have to sort the new rows and the new rows can be added quickly at the end of the table. With multiple processes attempting to insert into the table concurrently, however, there would be locking contention on that last page. The first insert command would get an exclusive lock on the page, blocking other inserts until it completes.

As we saw earlier in this chapter, segments can be used to minimize I/O contention between concurrent reads and updates from a table if the segments are used to spread the table across multiple devices, and if the reads and updates are distributed across the segments as well. Remember though that new page allocations come only from the first device with available space. Therefore, multiple inserts that require new pages to be allocated will incur I/O contention on writes to the table.

Heap table partitioning, a new feature of System 11 SQL Server, gives you the ability to create multiple page chains for tables.

## Benefits of Heap Table Partitioning

The main benefits of heap table partitioning are to improve performance for concurrent inserts by reducing contention for the last page in a table, and to distribute table I/Os randomly across multiple devices.

Heap table partitioning creates multiple page chains for a table, which results in multiple last pages for insert. This helps to reduce page contention for multiple insert processes. Figure 18.11 illustrates the I/O contention for the last page in a single page chain between multiple insert processes. With the table partitioned into multiple page chains, SQL Server randomly assigns each insert transaction to one of the table partitions. This minimizes the chances for concurrent inserts to block one another. (See Figure 18.12.)

**FIGURE 18.11.**

*Page contention between multiple insert processes on a heap table.*

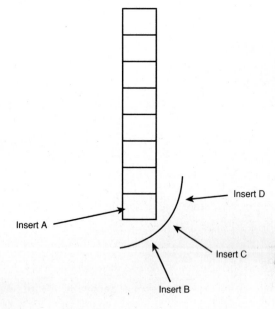

**FIGURE 18.12.**

*Page contention between multiple insert processes is minimized when the table is partitioned into multiple page chains.*

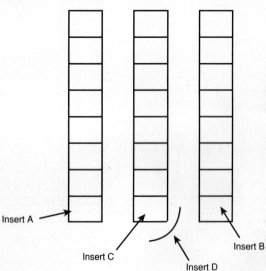

Heap table partitioning can also help to minimize I/O contention between multiple processes if the partitioned table's segment is spread across multiple drives. When a segment spans more than one physical disk, SQL Server distributes the table partitions across those disks. When SQL Server reads or writes to disk, I/Os assigned to different partitions can occur in parallel.

Read performance using heap table partitioning will be most improved when the data is spread evenly over the physical devices in the segment. For this reason, it is recommended that you partition the table *before* inserting the data. This will randomly distribute the data over the devices. If you partition the table after loading the data, most of the data remains in the first partition.

Partitioned heap tables are managed transparently to users and applications. A partitioned table will appear and behave just like a single page chain table when queried or viewed with most utilities.

# How to Partition Tables

Here are the basic steps for partitioning a table:

- Define a segment in a database (optionally, the segment can span multiple disks to minimize I/O contention).
- Create or place the table on the segment.
- Use the `alter table` command to define the number of table partitions.

Here is the `alter table` syntax:

```
alter table table_name partition #_of_partitions
```

For example, let's create an `orders` segment across three devices in our database and create an `orders` table on that segment with three partitions:

```
sp_addsegment orders_seg, salesdb, dev1
sp_extendsegment orders_seg, salesdb, dev2
sp_estendsegment orders_seg, salesdb, dev3
go

create table orders (order_id int,
                     item_num int,
                     qty      int,
                     date     datetime)
on orders_seg
go

alter table orders partition 3
```

The `create table` command creates a table on the segment with a single partition. The `alter table` command creates additional page chains for the number of partitions requested. SQL Server will create the specified number of partitions and spread those partitions evenly over the number of devices in the segment. You can define more partitions than devices, or have more devices than defined partitions. Table 18.1 illustrates how SQL Server assigns six partitions to three, six, and twelve devices.

## Table 18.1. Assigning six partitions to a different number of devices.

| Partition | 3 | 6 | 12 |
|---|---|---|---|
| | **Number of Devices** | | |
| 1 | dev1 | dev1 | dev1, dev7 |
| 2 | dev2 | dev2 | dev2, dev8 |
| 3 | dev3 | dev3 | dev3, dev9 |
| 4 | dev1 | dev4 | dev4, dev10 |
| 5 | dev2 | dev5 | dev5, dev11 |
| 6 | dev3 | dev6 | dev6, dev12 |

The number of partitions should be a multiple of the number of devices on the segment (for example, three partitions to three devices, or six partitions to three devices, or nine partitions to three devices, and so on). Following this convention spreads the page chains most evenly.

## Getting Information on Heap Table Partitions

SQL Server manages the partitions with the database's syspartitions table. The syspartitions table contains a row for each defined partition along with the location of the first page in the partition page chain, the address of the control page for the partition, and other status information. The control page works like the root column for a nonpartitioned heap table—it keeps track of the last page in the page chain.

To view the partition information for a specific table, use the sp_helpartition stored procedure:

```
sp_helpartition orders

partitionid firstpage   controlpage
----------- ----------  -----------
1           2361        2362
2           2384        2385
3           5377        5378
4           2400        2401
5           5384        5385
6           2408        2409
```

The output from sp_helpartition shows the partition IDs, the location of the first page in the partition page chain, and the address of the control page. To see the contents of the control page (for example, to find out what is currently the last page in the chain), use the dbcc page command, specifying a print option of 3 to format the control page information (for more information on dbcc page, refer to Chapter 10). The following code examines the control page for partition 4 in the preceding example (page 2401).

```
dbcc traceon(3604)
dbcc page ("default data cache", perftune, 2401, 3)

DBCC execution completed. If DBCC printed error messages, contact a user with
 System Administrator (SA) role.
 (-1 rows affected)


PAGE:
Page found in cache.

BUFFER:
Buffer header for buffer 0x20530dc0
    page=0x20531000 bdnew=0x0 bdold=0x0 bhash=0x0 bmass_next=0x0
    bmass_prev=0x0 bvirtpg=0 bdbid=0 bkeep=0
    bmass_stat=0x0800 bbuf_stat=0x0000 bpageno=2401
    bxls_pin = 0x00000000 bxls_next = 0x00000000b
    bxls_flushseq 0 bxls_pinseq 0

PAGE HEADER:
Page header for page 0x20531000
pageno=2401 nextpg=0 prevpg=0 objid=368004342 timestamp=0001 0000405f
nextrno=0 level=0 indid=0  freeoff=32 minlen=60
page status bits: 0x1,

Control Page Data:
lastpage=2482
slicenum=4
alloccount=10
 device affinity map count=1
lstart=0
size=5120
DBCC execution completed. If DBCC printed error messages, contact a user with
 System Administrator (SA) role.
```

The first part of this information is the standard page header data. We are interested in the information at the end—the control page data: information. From this output, we can see that the location of the last page for this partition is page 2432 (lastpage=2432). This is where the next insert to this partition will go. The total number of pages currently allocated on this partition is 10 (alloccount=10). In addition, the output indicates that this partition maps to only one device (device affinity map count = 1) and the size of the device it maps to is 5,120 pages, or 10MB (size = 5120). To determine specifically which device this partition is mapped to, we can map the lstart value (0) back to the sysusages and sysdevices tables in the master database. The following query gets this information:

```
select name from master..sysdevices d, master..sysusages u
where u.lstart = 0
and u.vstart between d.low and d.high
and u.dbid = db_id("perftune")

name
---------------------------------
perfdev
```

In addition, when a table is partitioned, `dbcc checktable` reports the number of pages allocated per partition. This information can be used to determine how well the data is balanced across partitions. The `orders` table we have been using in our examples contains 5,000 rows that were inserted one at a time, each as a single transaction. To see how well SQL Server balanced the inserts across partitions, we'll run `dbcc checktable` on the `orders` table:

```
dbcc checktable (orders)

Checking orders
The total number of pages in partition 1 is 10.
The total number of pages in partition 2 is 10.
The total number of pages in partition 3 is 10.
The total number of pages in partition 4 is 10.
The total number of pages in partition 5 is 10.
The total number of pages in partition 6 is 10.
The total number of data pages in this table is 66.
Table has 5000 data rows.
```

From this output, we can see that the data is distributed evenly across all six partitions, 10 pages each. The additional six pages are the control pages, one per partition.

## Notes on Heap Table Partitioning

A table defined for partitioning cannot have a clustered index defined on it (with a clustered index, it is no longer a heap table). In addition, the following operations cannot be performed on a partitioned table:

- `create clustered index`
- `truncate table`
- `drop table`
- `sp_placeobject`
- Changing the number of partitions

To perform any of these operations on a partitioned table, you must first unpartition the table using `alter table`:

```
alter table tablename unpartition
```

Only the table pages are partitioned across multiple page chains when you partition a table—nonclustered indexes on a partitioned table are not partitioned, and each resides in a single page chain.

Tables containing text or image columns can be partitioned, but the text and image data will remain on a single page chain.

If a partition runs out of space on its assigned device, SQL Server performs *page stealing* by trying to allocate space from any device in the table's segment. This avoids an out-of-space error on the insert, but is undesirable for performance reasons. Page stealing requires searches of the Global Allocation Map (GAM—refer to Chapter 10) to find available pages, and it results in destroying the physical continuity of the data within a partition. Also, two partitions are no longer spread over separate devices.

## Tips on Heap Table Partitioning

To determine candidate tables for partitioning, monitor sp_who and sp_lock for consistent blocking on one or more specific tables. If a table is blocking repeatedly, it is a possible candidate for partitioning. Obvious candidates for partitioning are "append only" tables that many transactions must write to, such as a history or audit log table, or tables with sequential keys that insert data in sequential key order.

Partitioning is designed primarily to improve concurrent insert performance by reducing page contention. The greater the number of partitions, the more reduced the chances for contention. Don't be afraid to create 30 to 60 partitions for a key heap table. This design could conceivably support up to 60 concurrent inserts without blocking.

Spreading partitions out across multiple disks will further improve insert performance by minimizing I/O contention. You may also experience improved performance on selects due to the ability of SQL Server to parallelize reads across devices.

SQL Server randomly assigns a transaction to a specific table partition. All insert statements within that transaction will go to the same partition. You cannot explicitly assign a transaction to a specific partition. To make sure your data is spread evenly, you want to break the inserts up into multiple transactions. This applies to bcp loads as well. To get bcp to insert into multiple partitions, it must be broken up into multiple batches. Each bcp batch is treated as a separate transaction; therefore, each batch will be randomly assigned to a different partition.

# Minimizing I/O Contention Between Databases

To minimize the I/O contention between your application databases and system databases that incur heavy I/O (tempdb and sybsecurity), place tempdb and sybsecurity on separate physical disks from your application databases. (For a discussion of how to move tempdb off the master device, see Chapter 21, "Miscellaneous Performance Topics.")

Also, be sure to place transaction logs for multiple databases on separate physical disks to spread the log writes across devices and minimize I/O contention between databases. Use segments and multiple devices to spread activity for high-use tables across devices, keeping in mind which other databases use those devices and how. If you have active tables in different databases, the goal is to allocate your devices and set up your segments in such a way as to balance the I/Os for all your databases evenly across all available devices. When the number of available devices is limited, you may have to balance things out by placing relatively quiet tables from one database on the same device as an active table for another database.

# Summary

The key to improving I/O performance, beyond buying the fastest devices available, is to minimize I/O and page contention as much as possible. Segments are one alternative for spreading I/O across devices in a database, but for truly mission-critical, high-transaction-volume applications, hardware-based RAID is the best choice for both performance and data fault tolerance. Neither of these alternatives is going to minimize locking contention for inserts. Heap table partitioning, available in System 11, provides a method for setting up multiple page chains for tables, providing multiple insert points.

# Application Design
# for Performance

**IN THIS CHAPTER**

Sometimes it seems as though there are a thousand ways to make your application run slowly. In this chapter, we will review various elements of system design and implementation that affect application performance, then we will focus on application design characteristics that also have an impact on system performance.

At the most general level, several components determine system performance:

- Server resources, including fast CPU, sufficient memory, and fast disks
- Network configuration, including sufficient bandwidth for the traffic
- Client configuration, including fast CPU and sufficient memory

Specifically, a bad database or application design can render a good hardware configuration useless. For example, a database design requiring repeated scans of a very large table can bring a powerful server to its knees.

> **NOTE**
>
> There is a theory of systems that states that all systems will ultimately fail. Systems that fail to gain acceptance obviously fail; but those that gain acceptance always grow in usage and demand until they can no longer handle the load and ultimately fail.
>
> No matter how powerful your hardware and software configuration, it makes sense to build an optimal system to delay the time when your configuration is no longer able to handle the demands on the system.

Here are the obvious areas on which to focus when building efficient SQL Server systems:

- Logical database design, to keep data as concise as possible and improve update performance
- Physical database design, to improve query performance
- SQL query syntax, to take advantage of server capabilities
- Proper balance of client and server workload

This last item is the focus of the chapter.

# Considerations in Balancing Performance

What you are looking for as you build client/server applications is the perfect mix of client processing and server processing. You need to understand the special strengths and weaknesses of servers and clients to predict how to distribute operations.

# Servers

When properly optimized and configured, an SQL Server is most efficient at "finding a needle in a haystack." It can find a handful of rows in a huge table or perform hundreds of concurrent modifications on a large table. It is efficient at performing fairly complex data modifications, and its deadlock detection and resolution scheme are acceptable if deadlocks are not too frequent. The server is acceptably efficient at scanning a medium-sized table and evaluating complex search criteria. The SQL Server can efficiently enforce fairly complex business rules within a database. Overall, the server is best suited to handle set-based data retrieval and modification operations in your system.

An SQL Server is extremely *inefficient* at executing thousands of operations in a loop (as with a cursor). It can be inefficient at scanning an enormous table (though no more inefficient than other relational database systems). Large data loads on tables having dozens of indexes will run slowly.

# Clients

A properly configured client workstation is most efficient at displaying complex user interfaces, handling data formatting and column- or row-specific data validation. The client can process and display small and moderate-size result sets, and is efficient at handling row operations on those sets.

## Implications of Server and Client Capabilities

Understanding the fundamental strengths of the components, you need to make several decisions regarding application design. Some of those decisions are very straightforward and indisputable while other decisions are more difficult and involve trade-offs.

# The Network as Bottleneck

You should not disregard the importance of the network in client/server systems. In general, you should always treat the network as a primary bottleneck. Even if your system has sufficient *potential* bandwidth to handle a specific operation efficiently, network availability is by far the most unpredictable performance factor. Moreover, under load, operations that run well for a single user may be unacceptably slow when multiple users are running.

Let's look at ways to reduce network load and make applications more efficient.

# Reducing Query Size

SQL allows definition of a complex set of operations in a single statement. Consider the difference between the code required to modify a set of rows having a certain characteristic in a typical third generation language and SQL. Here is pseudo-code representing the work of a 3GL to search a set of rows and modify certain ones:

```
open file for update to filehandle
set up rowset
while not (eof)
begin
   lock next row
   read next row into rowbuffer
   if column1 = value
   begin
      update column2 = newvalue
      write rowbuffer
   end
   unlock this row
end
close file
```

Here is a sample SQL statement to perform the same work:

```
update tablename
set column2 = newvalue
where column1 = value
```

In and of itself, then, the SQL language provides a mechanism for reducing query size; however, complex batches can include hundreds of SQL queries. For example, the `sp_help` stored procedure is about 48KB of code. If every time a user needed to know table and column definitions he had to submit a 48KB query, the strain on the network can be substantial.

One useful way to reduce network traffic, then, is to use stored procedures instead of submitting large SQL queries. A stored procedure with several parameters seldom requires more than a small network packet (512 bytes) to transmit. If your system will have hundreds or thousands of users attached to a single server, using procedures instead of sending large SQL queries will improve network performance.

# Reducing Result Sets

The other major drag on the network is large result sets. This is a genuine problem in decision-support systems, which by their nature deal with very large data and often need to return large sets of rows. We will look at that in a moment.

On the other hand, I have seen many client systems where programmers fail to take advantage of the server and instead return large numbers of rows to the client and then process the rows on the client system in order to find the desired rows. For example, consider this query:

```
select last_name, first_name, m_init
from names
where upper(last_name) = "GREEN"
```

The query will probably run horribly (the upper function invalidates a SARG and requires a table scan) unless the table is quite small. There are several reasonable solutions, including this one:

```
select last_name, first_name, m_init
from names
where upper(last_name) = "GREEN"
and last_name like "G%" or last_name like "g%"
```

Now the query will use an index to identify the rows starting with a capital or lowercase G. This should substantially speed up the query, but a lot depends on exactly what the data looks like.

On the other hand, an inexperienced SQL programmer's reaction to the poor performance may be to return all rows to his application, then identify those rows matching his criteria locally, figuring that his local use of an upper () function will be faster than that on the SQL Server.

The inexperienced programmer in this case is wrong and this approach hurts his individual query and every other activity on the network while he monopolizes bandwidth to transmit data.

Certain applications, particularly decision-support applications, legitimately need to bring back enormous quantities of data to the user. It may still be possible to keep that data off the network by submitting the query from a connection established locally on the server. (Use isql/w or the command-based isql program to do this.) That connection can create a file containing the large result set, which can be transferred to another physical computer far more efficiently than transferal of a large set with the Transaction Data Stream (TDS, the basic data packaging mechanism used by SQL Server).

Remember that it is almost always more efficient for the server to prepare aggregates with group by than for the raw data to be passed to a workstation and processed there. In addition to the benefit of keeping the result set small, SQL Server also has access to indexes and caching mechanisms that make totaling easier and faster than on a client workstation.

# Row Processing

A major application question is how to perform row-by-row processing. SQL Server 6.0 introduces cursor processing for the first time, but the performance of cursor applications is a serious problem. There are several application problems (most often, batch update processes, complex reports, and logical integrity checks) that seem to call for processing by rows. It is worth looking pretty hard for alternative approaches because of the enormous performance penalty introduced by cursor processing. See Chapter 20, "Advanced Transact-SQL Programming," for a discussion of the problems and solutions to row cursor-based processing and for some alternatives.

# Data Validation Methods

An on-going debate in SQL Server applications is where and how to perform data validation. It was fairly simple in earlier software generations to decide how and where to do data validation. Applications enforced all business rules, from individual column values to interdependencies between columns in a row and complex interdependencies among several tables (including referential integrity).

One of the great benefits of SQL Server is the ability to implement rules, defaults, constraints, and triggers that define the data integrity and consistency requirements for a table or set of tables. At this time, the application designer has several methods of enforcing consistency.

## Application-Based Integrity

This is the traditional place to enforce business rules in a 3GL application, where the database has little or no capability to manage the content or consistency of data. There are correct ways to implement this approach to be certain that you have the desired effect and that locking and transactional problems don't completely lock up the system.

## Procedure-Based Integrity

All data modifications can be performed through stored procedures, allowing all validation to be implemented in those procedures. This is a fairly common choice because it allows a single set of code to manage all data. It's easy to maintain, and it can provide better performance if properly implemented. In this approach, transactions do not typically span procedures (and therefore batches), so fewer locks are held for a long time.

## Server-Based Integrity

This is integrity based on rules, constraints, defaults, and triggers. This is the only approach that allows users to update freely using standard SQL statements, even if they know nothing about the structure or data integrity requirements of the database. This approach is modular and efficient, but can sometimes be difficult to debug because of the interaction of code in different objects.

## Mixed-Model Integrity

This is integrity enforced at several levels. This is a very common approach, often allowing the best combination of performance, flexibility, and user interface.

Performance, code maintenance, and interface issues are associated with the method used to enforce business rules on the database. Code running at the client level will reduce the load on the server, but the client does not have access to other rows in the table or in other tables.

Enforcement objects at the server level will increase the load on the server and can create persistent blocking locks that can damage performance. Server-based enforcement objects apply to all applications and can keep application development simpler and more reliable. In addition, server-based objects permit changes to the rules applied to data shared among several applications with a single modification. Only application-based validation can provide useful column-level assistance during input and modification steps.

Let's look at each of these approaches and understand its long-term implications. Here are some examples of business rules that might need validation before a data modification is permitted.

> **NOTE**
>
> We need to start this discussion with the understanding that there is no right way to do this, although there are several wrong ways. Your choice of how to implement data validation will depend on your hardware and software configuration, application design and implementation philosophy, and usage and performance requirements.

# Rule 1: Items May Be Deleted Only if the In-Stock Value Is 0

Rule 1 may be implemented in a couple of ways. It would be incorrect to read the row and verify that the in-stock value is 0 locally, then delete the row with confidence:

```
select instock
from item
where item_no = 1343
go

/* check instock in a local program */
delete item
where item_no = 1343
go
```

Clearly, the problem is that someone else could jump in and modify the value of instock on the item between the time you retrieve the row and when you delete the row. You could solve this with a persistent lock using holdlock in a transaction:

```
begin transaction
select instock
from item
where item_no = 1343
holdlock
go

/* check instock in a local program */
delete item
where item_no = 1343
commit transaction
go
```

This solves the potential hole in data integrity, but it leaves a persistent page-level lock on the page while you do application-side processing (transactions held open across batches). This can result in "live" locks and deadlocks, both damaging to performance.

You could delete the row by simply including the application condition in your SQL code like this:

```
delete item
where item_no = 1343
and instock = 0
```

What if the delete fails to find any rows? Does that mean there is no item, or the item has a non-zero instock value?

There is a mechanism that provides sufficient data integrity without creating the locking problem introduced by transactions that cross batches. SQL Server provides an optimistic locking mechanism using timestamp values to guarantee that the version of the row being modified or deleted is the same one read:

```
select instock, timestamp
from item
where item_no = 1343
go

/* check instock in a local program */
delete item
where item_no = 1343
and tsequal(timestamp, 0x123456671312)
go
```

In this example, the programmer retrieved the binary timestamp value along with the instock value in the first step, then used that timestamp value in the tsequal() function to guarantee that the version of the row deleted is the same as the version retrieved. The important point about this function is how different error cases are treated: the server finds the row based on other conditions, then validates the version with the timestamp value. If the row is not found, the server returns 0 rows processed, as you would expect. If the row is found but the timestamp value fails to match, the server returns a specific error message (Error 532). For a more thorough discussion of the use of timestamp columns, see Chapter 4, "Transact-SQL Datatypes."

The approaches described so far would all work as well or better if performed during a stored procedure. All the locking windows would be narrower, substantially improving performance and reducing the potential impact on other users. Validation of the deletion could also be easily implemented in a trigger:

```
create trigger tr_item_del
on items for delete as
if @@rowcount = 0 return
if exists
     (select * from deleted
     where instock != 0)
```

```
begin
    raiserror 55555 "Error: attempt to delete non-zero instock value"
    rollback tran
end
return
```

The trigger simplifies the problem of an application programmer by handling the error case completely. The data is safe from errors made by individual application programmers who forget to apply the rule or do so improperly. The trigger does require some additional overhead during the deletion, and locks are held during trigger execution. The overall performance impact of enforcing Rule 1 using a trigger is probably less than that of the other approaches.

# Rule 2: Customer Status May Be *ACTIVE, INACTIVE,* or *PENDING* Only

Rule 2 establishes a list of valid values for an individual column. It is simple enough to enforce this rule in an application program, although there is a chance that a programmer will make an error and allow invalid entries in one program. In addition, users accessing the database using a simple SQL interface such as isql/w can put any value in the column using a simple insert statement. This approach has two specific benefits: First, the application can prompt the user immediately if an entry is invalid. (This immediate feedback is critical to good user interface.) A server-based validation technique will only prompt the user when the entire row is submitted to the server. Second, performing column-level validation at the workstation avoids unnecessary network traffic and unnecessary work by the server.

To get efficient use of shared resources (the network and server) and good user interface (field-level prompting) as well as protection against application errors and interactive SQL users, it is common to implement a combination of both client-based and server-based validation techniques. In the case of Rule 2, using both application level tools and a rule or constraint to validate customer status provides the best of both worlds; although it does require additional maintenance if the values change frequently.

Can you perform column-level validation in a stored procedure? Yes. It may be appropriate if all data modifications have been channeled through procedures. The benefit of using procedures instead of rules is that all database consistency requirements are defined in a single unit of code.

Can column-level validation take place in a trigger? It can, but it should not. Remember that triggers execute *after* the table modifications are performed. There may be a tremendous amount of disk activity (mostly reads, as modifications are made in memory until they are committed to disk) to support a data modification. Whenever you can, pre-validate work instead of waiting until the trigger fires, as long as that pre-validation does not require additional work (refer to Rule 1).

# Rule 3: Orders May Be Entered Only for Valid Customer IDs

This is classic referential integrity, in which the referencing table's foreign key (`order.cust_id`) must match a primary key in the referenced table (`customer.cust_id`). You can certainly write code to ensure that the customer exists, either in an application program or in a stored procedure. This will require the same kind of transactional and locking work we saw in Rule 1.

SQL Server provides two mechanisms for handling referential integrity more efficiently: constraints and triggers. Constraints will generally be more efficient because they are implemented in C code rather than SQL (see Chapter 20 for more on the difference in performance between native C and SQL code performance), so whenever possible we use constraints rather than triggers. (The most substantial limitation on constraint use happens when the customer is running an application on version 4.21 as well as version 6.0.)

## Rule 3a: Orders May Be Entered Only for Customers Having a Status of *ACTIVE*

Here is an example where referential integrity requirements are more complex than a constraint would completely handle. Here, a constraint could catch the first level of data integrity problems (only valid customers), but a trigger would be required to check the status of the customer:

```
create trigger tr_order_ins_upd
on orders for insert, update as
if @@rowcount = 0 return
if exists
    (select * from inserted i, customers c
    where i.cust_id = c.cust_id
    and c.status != "ACTIVE")
begin
    raiserror 55556 "Order entered for inactive customer"
    rollback tran
end
return
```

The trigger code is simplified because the constraint has already handled referential integrity. (Note that additional code is required to allow updates to orders already in the table if the customer status is now INACTIVE.)

A mixed approach taking advantage of the capabilities of many elements of the system usually provides the best results, but may entail more sophisticated documentation and maintenance than you want. On the other hand, most single-mode approaches require a compromise on performance or functionality, and sometimes both.

# Complex Transactions

Some applications require complex transactions to take place in real time (or as close to real time as possible). Complex transactions could be multi-row updates requiring concurrency, or they could involve a dozen tables in a chain of nested triggers. Here is what complex transactions have in common:

- A substantial number of pages must be locked, possibly in many tables
- A large number of log entries are generated

What is substantial? What is a large number? There are no firm numeric guidelines, but if running the transactions is causing serious locking or performance problems, your transactions are complex enough to address.

Consider an example of an update to a table that requires a dozen updates to related tables. The best case would be to include those updates as part of a single transaction, but currently the response time is unacceptable for users of the system. What is the best way to perform this complex application?

The first step is to guarantee that the application is properly coded and that the database design is fully optimized. (By now you certainly should know that too many indexes can slow update performance.) Problems with concurrency or performance can often be resolved using basic optimization techniques that allow transactions to happen in real time.

The resources that are stressed during execution of a long-running transaction are the locking system, the transaction log, and memory. Locking large numbers of pages will certainly result in blocking "live" locks as well as some number of deadlocks. If concurrency problems arise, you may be able to reduce them by decreasing the `fillfactor` on small, heavily used tables. Changing the clustered index on a table can sometimes resolve locking problems as well. Using a cursor can reduce locking contention, but at a terrible price in performance.

Transaction log problems are most common with very large transactions—large enough to fill the transaction log between a `BEGIN TRAN` and a `COMMIT`. But a smaller transaction can cause this kind of problem if sufficient numbers of users are running it at one time. Log capacity isn't the only issue, however. A single transaction could take a long time to commit. If the log is a serious bottleneck, consider moving it to a non-volatile RAM drive such as a solid state drive (SSD).

Memory can also cause problems with long-running transactions, and you should certainly allow sufficient space in memory for several users to run a complex transaction concurrently.

If long-running transactions continue to present a performance problem, the next step is to consider ways to perform the transaction in a batch mode during off hours. (Make certain that the operation fits in with the rest of your maintenance schedule.) If you cannot wait for a nightly batch, or if you are running a 7x24 shop, you will need to run a periodic sweep of worktables to perform these operations in the background.

# Multiple Server Transactions

There are several ways to implement transactions that span multiple servers. You should generally avoid two-phase commit applications in favor of using the built-in replication that comes with SQL Server. The most significant problem with two-phase commits occurs when one of the servers is unavailable: at that point, no transactions involving that server can proceed.

In a replication approach, transactions involving an unavailable server are recorded and subsequently delivered to that server once it becomes available. Avoid designs that require complete concurrency between servers for the looser coupling offered with replication.

# Some General Advice

Here are the things most likely to ruin application performance, in order:

- Bad database design
- Bad application design
- Bad SQL
- Bad server configuration

It may not be a coincidence, but that is also a list of things most difficult to fix in an application. So you need to tend to your database and application design first.

# Summary

SQL Server applications perform well when they achieve the right balance of client and server work, and when each of the individual components of the system performs well. Sometimes your design options will be constrained by the functional requirements of the application, especially when it comes to transaction implementation and data validation.

Here are some other considerations to keep in mind:

- Choice of application server and its associated tools, including operating system
- Choice of network protocol and topology
- Choice of front-end and third-party tools (if any)
- Choice of reporting tools

These all affect your application's design and performance. Needless to say, the design of your application is crucial. When designing your system, you should keep in mind the current requirements and objectives, as well as anticipate future needs and improvements.

A final point: Never forget that *perceived* performance is as important as actual performance. Users are usually far more sensitive to operations that are slow to *start* doing work or hang up their systems for a long time than they are to operations that take a long time but are unobtrusive.

# Advanced Transact-SQL Programming

**20**

**IN THIS CHAPTER**

This chapter addresses advanced SQL techniques, particularly for improving individual query performance by understanding the impact of specific syntactic structures on optimization and execution of a query. Specifically, we will

- identify problematic statements and queries in application designs before they are created on the server;

- find problematic or performance-hindering statements in queries and stored procedures, and test different methods for fixing these statements and queries.

# Who Is This Chapter For?

This chapter should be useful to almost anyone responsible for writing efficient SQL; however, you will feel more comfortable with the topics discussed here if you already know some SQL. Here are the general groups of users and developers who will benefit from this chapter:

- Application developers who write queries as part of their applications

- SQL Server developers who write queries and stored procedures for client application developers

- System administrators and DBAs responsible for writing stored procedures for client application developers

# Where Else Can I Look?

System administrators and DBAs who want to optimize SQL Server configuration options and physical database design should look at Chapters 9 through 22 for information on performance and tuning techniques.

# Aggregate Query Resolution

This section looks at how SQL Server uses worktables to resolve queries with group by and aggregate functions. In general, aggregate functions automatically require use of a worktable, which introduces some overhead. While this overhead cannot be avoided, the worktable also has functional implications for certain types of queries. We will look at the use of having with group by, compare having and where clauses, and consider some advanced issues related to the use of group by.

## *having* Clauses with *group by*

When used with group by, having restricts the *groups* that are returned by the query after the computation has been completed. When used without group by, having restricts the *rows* that are returned by the query after the computation has been completed (see the following section).

having does *not* affect the rows that "go into" a computation; it only affects the rows or groups that come out of a computation. In this example, the server filters the final results to remove rows containing an average price of less than $10:

```
select type, avg(price)
from titles
group by type
having avg(price) >= $10
```

Compare that query to the following one, in which the server filters out rows having a price of less than $10 prior to performing the averaging:

```
select type, avg(price)
from titles
where price >= $10
group by type
```

having is always be evaluated *after* the computation completes, but before rows are returned.

## where versus *having*

If where clauses and having clauses both restrict rows, why not use having all the time? If a query has no aggregate functions and no group by clause, SQL Server interprets a having clause as a where clause implicitly. If a query does have aggregate functions or a group by clause, having is interpreted literally as having, which forces SQL Server to use a worktable to resolve the query.

## Query Tracking: *having*

This query uses a having clause to retrieve only selected rows from an aggregate result. Let's look closely at how the server resolves the query in two steps, using a worktable.

> **NOTE**
>
> The following information is accessed using the SHOWPLAN option, in which SQL Server displays its intended access method for resolving a query. It also includes output from the STATISTICS IO option, which provides details about SQL Server physical and logical data access during actual execution. Later in this section we will also examine output from DBCC Trace flags. If you are unfamiliar with these methods of examining query performance, refer to Chapter 12, "Understanding the Query Optimizer."

```
select id, avg(amount)
from pt_tx
where id < 200
group by id
having avg(amount) > $20000
```

In the following SHOWPLAN output, the server plans to execute the query in two steps. In the first step, SQL Server builds the grouped aggregate; in the second step, it returns only those rows in the worktable that match the having criteria:

```
QUERY PLAN FOR STATEMENT 1 (at line 1).

    STEP 1
        The type of query is SELECT (into Worktable1).
        GROUP BY
        Evaluate Grouped COUNT AGGREGATE.
        Evaluate Grouped SUM OR AVERAGE AGGREGATE.

        FROM TABLE
            pt_tx
        Nested iteration.
        Table Scan.
        Ascending scan.
        Positioning at start of table.
        Using I/O Size 2 Kbytes.
        With LRU Buffer Replacement Strategy.
        TO TABLE
            Worktable1.

    STEP 2
        The type of query is SELECT.

        FROM TABLE
            Worktable1.
        Nested iteration.
        Table Scan.
        Ascending scan.
        Positioning at start of table.
        Using I/O Size 2 Kbytes.
        With MRU Buffer Replacement Strategy.
```

The output from STATISTICS IO shows that the worktable is scanned several times as the aggregate is prepared:

```
Table: pt_tx  scan count 1,  logical reads: 88,  physical reads: 0
Table: Worktable1   scan count 1,  logical reads: 87,  physical reads: 0
Total writes for this command: 0
```

# Grouping and Worktables

This section looks at advanced issues with group by and worktables. We will examine the role of the worktable and how it relates to order by and having clauses.

## Role of the Worktable

The worktable stores temporary results that cannot be evaluated, processed, or returned to the user until after the server has completed the current step. Worktables are used to prepare many kinds of results, including these:

### Vector Aggregate

```
select type, count(*)
from titles
group by type
```

### Ordered Result Set (No Useful Index)

```
select type, title
from titles
order by type, title
```

# How Does SQL Server Process Queries Involving a Worktable?

Figure 20.1 illustrates how the server uses a worktable in resolving a query. where and group by are resolved as the processor moves rows from the base table(s) to the worktable. having and order by are resolved as the processor builds a final result set based on the worktable.

**FIGURE 20.1.**

*where clauses and grouping take place between the source table(s) and the worktable; having and order by operate on the worktable in producing a final result set.*

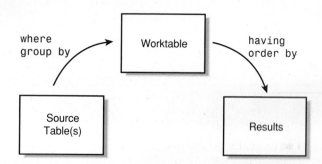

If the server can determine that the column value is dependent on the grouping value, it will perform the grouping properly (and probably derives the function on-the-fly when displaying results). Here's an example where the column in the select list (user_name(uid)) is dependent on the value of the group by column (uid):

```
select user_name(uid), count(*)
from sysobjects
group by uid
```

# Special Topics in Join Processing

In this section, we are going to look at some special topics in multitable optimization:

- Joins with or
- Overriding the optimizer
- Breaking up large queries

# Joins with or

A curious problem arises when you join three tables with two conditions, where a row is included in the result set if either join condition is true. Consider the set of tables shown in Figure 20.2.

**FIGURE 20.2.**

*In this three-way join, results include titles matching rows in* sales *or titles matching rows in* titleauthor.

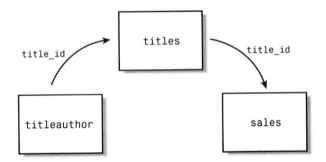

Here's an example of a query that joins three tables based on an or condition:

```
select title
from titles t, titleauthor ta, sales sa
where t.title_id = ta.title_id
or t.title_id = sa.title_id
```

On its surface, this query seems to request a list of all titles that have an author specified or that have been sold. We can observe a strange behavior with this type of query, however: When either of the optional join tables is empty, the server returns no rows. For example, consider this three-table join:

```
select count(*)
from A, B, C
where A.id = B.id or A.id = C.id
```

The contents of the three tables are shown in Table 20.1.

## Table 20.1. Contents of Tables A, B, and C.

| *Table A* | |
| --- | --- |
| ID | CA |
| 1 | 1 |
| 2 | 2 |

| *Table B* | |
| --- | --- |
| ID | CB |
| 1 | 1 |
| 2 | 2 |

| *Table C (empty table)* | |
| --- | --- |
| ID | CC |

Based on the contents of the tables, you would expect that the count would find two rows where Table A matched Table B. The query appears to work when all the tables contain at least one row, but it fails when any table is empty.

Actually, the query is incorrectly written and fails under all circumstances. Let's add a couple of rows to Table C, then try this query again:

```
1> insert C values (1, 21)
2> insert C values (2, 22)
3> go
(1 row affected)
(1 row affected)
1> select count(*) from A, B, C
2> where A.id = B.id
3> or A.id = C.id
4> go

 - - - - - - - - - -
          6

(1 row affected)
```

With only two rows in Table A, how did the server find six rows in the join? To understand better, let's look at the output of the join:

```
select A.id A, B.id B, C.id C
from A, B, C
where A.id = B.id or A.id = C.id
```

| A | B | C |
| --- | --- | --- |
| 1 | 1 | 1 |
| 1 | 1 | 2 |
| 1 | 2 | 1 |
| 2 | 1 | 2 |
| 2 | 2 | 1 |
| 2 | 2 | 2 |

When SQL Server does not understand your join condition or can find no path to optimize the join, it builds a Cartesian product (the set of all possible combinations), then tests the validity of each row against the search conditions provided. In this case, we have many duplicate rows, including rows where A is matched to an incorrect B or an incorrect C.

We need to restate the question as "How many rows in A have a match in B or a match in C?" Here is the proper way to write the query:

```
select count(*)
from A
where id in
    (select id from B)
or id in
    (select id from C)
```

This query becomes more problematic if you need to retrieve information from Tables B or C to be included in the final result set. Your method of resolving such a kind of query depends on your specific requirements, but you will probably need to use a temporary table, and to prioritize Table B or Table C.

In any case, avoid using or to connect join clauses because it creates duplicate and invalid data.

# Overriding the Optimizer

Here's a question: When might the optimizer be wrong?

We have looked at how to override the optimizer. Let's discuss some of the circumstances when this might be useful.

In general, you should override the optimizer if you are absolutely certain that you know something it does not. Here are some examples of when this might occur:

- Indexes did not exist at optimization time.
- Statistics are out of date.
- Actual device performance is different from assumed performance.

Let's look at each of these briefly.

# Indexes Did Not Exist at Optimization Time

When you create a temporary table inside a stored procedure, there are times when it is appropriate to index that temporary table so that you can access the table properly during a subsequent join, as in this example:

```
create proc p_temptable as

/* create a temporary table */
select title_id, au_id, title, au_fname, au_lname,
    au_ord, advance / royaltyper, price
into #temp_ta
from titles t, authors a, titleauthor ta
where t.title_id = ta.title_id
and a.au_id = ta.au_id

/* index the table for subsequent joins or other operations */
create unique clustered index on #temp_ta (title_id, au_id)
create nonclustered index on #temp_ta (title)

/* now execute queries ...
** will the procedure use the indexes or identify the best join order? */
select au_id, sum(qty)
from sales s, #temp_ta t
where s.title_id = t.title_id
group by au_id
order by 2 desc

... (other queries)

return
```

Stored procedure optimization occurs only once, so at procedure execution time, the temporary table indexes (as well as any index statistics, of course) are unavailable to queries like the aggregate query in the example. You may want to force a join order or identify a useful index on the temporary table to run the query.

# Statistics Are Out of Date

In most cases, the best cure for badly out-of-date index distribution statistics is to update your statistics. But updating takes time and locks tables. Remember that an index is extremely valuable, even if its statistics are incorrect. Statistics are only used to choose a path, not to execute it. Although you always want to update incorrect statistics, if you don't have time to do it and need to run the report right now, force the correct index choice and you may get good performance anyway.

Hard-coding a program to use a particular index path may cause trouble later on, however, when indexes are up-to-date. Forcing an index is best done with an *ad hoc* query when you know something specific about the current situation rather than about a global condition that may change over time. The optimizer is far better at adjusting to changing conditions than your programs are likely to be.

# Actual Device Performance Is Different from Assumed Performance

The optimizer assumes that the ratio of logical to physical read performance is 18 to 2. What is the effect of this assumption on a typical join? Consider the example shown in Table 10.2.

## Table 10.2. Sample table and index sizes.

| Table | Table A | Table B |
|---|---|---|
| Size | 10MB (5000 pages) | 2MB (1000 pages) |
| Rows | 1MB | 250KB |
| NCI levels / size | 4 levels, 500 pages | 3 levels, 100 pages |

Here is the query we are trying to optimize:

```
select count(*)
from A, B
where A.id = B.id
```

When the server estimates the work required to perform the join, it makes assumptions based on what will fit in cache. If an object will fit entirely in cache, the server assumes that one scan of a table or index will include a physical and a logical cost (number of pages to read × 18 milliseconds (ms) + 2ms), where any subsequent scan of the same object will require only a logical cost (pages to read × 2ms).

> **NOTE**
>
> Some of our calculations here are a little more crude than what the server's algorithm can handle. The server takes into account issues like the percentage of cache to use and considers index covering and reformatting strategies. We are only considering alternative join orders in performing a join.

Let's work out the estimated cost of performing the join, without assuming any specific values for logical and physical reads. Instead, we will carry two variables, LC (logical cost) and PC (physical cost), then look at how the ratio of those values affects actual performance.

First assume that A is the outer table and B is the inner table (A->B join order), and we will use a nonclustered index (NCI) on B to correlate tables. Also, assume that Table B and the nonclustered index fit in cache:

```
COST(A->B) = 5,000 pgs * PC
           + 1,100 pgs * PC
           + 1,000,000 rows * 4 levels * LC
         = 6,100 * PC + 4,000,000 * LC
```

In layman's terms, the cost equals

- the number of pages to read all of Table A times the physical cost of each read; *plus*
- the number of pages in the nonclustered index times the physical cost to read them; *plus*
- the number of rows in Table A times the number of index levels to traverse to find matching rows in Table B times the logical cost to read them once for each row in A.

Now let's assume a B->A join order, using a nonclustered index on A to correlate rows. Assume that the nonclustered index of Table A (but not the data pages) will fit in cache:

```
COST(B->A) = 1000 pgs * PC
           + 500 pgs * PC
           + 250,000 rows * (4 levels * LC + 4 pages * PC)
         = 1,001,500 * PC + 1,000,000 * LC
```

If you substitute varying values for the ratio of performance between logical and physical reads, you get the graph shown in Figure 20.3.

**FIGURE 20.3.**

*Some plans are more sensitive to device speed than others. In this example, as the physical device gets faster with respect to memory, the cost of treating B as the outer table in a join is reduced dramatically. SQL Server assumes that the performance ratio of physical to logical reads is 18:2 (dotted line).*

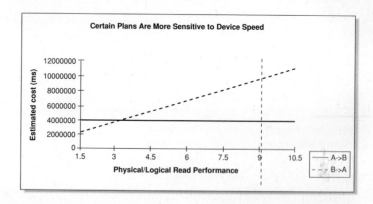

Clearly, the relationship between memory and disk speed will impact actual performance. Ordinarily, the ratio is more like 20 to 1 between memory and traditional disk storage, and much higher for nontraditional storage like WORM and CD-ROM drives, especially without aggressive caching strategies. It is reasonable for the optimizer to discount this benefit because of the effects of multiuser processing consuming available cache, requiring a fall-back to physical memory when memory is insufficient.

Are there times when the actual physical drive performance will be better than 9 to 1? If you set up tempdb in RAM or if you are using a solid state device (a nonvolatile RAM-based hard drive), you may see numbers substantially better than that. Also, new RAID devices include smart read-ahead strategies that could provide substantially better performance than we have experienced in the past. Finally, if you have limited cache space on your server, or if the cache is running over periodically into a swap space or paging file on a physical disk (a really, really awful situation, by the way), memory performance could be very bad.

528

The fact is that the type of device is as important as the access path in some instances. So you may find that drive performance is one area where you can out-guess the optimizer and force a specific order.

# Breaking Up Large Queries

This section examines how to break up large queries. We'll discuss the following topics:

- Defining large queries
- When to break up a large query
- How to break up large queries

## Defining Large Queries

A large multi-table query is a query consisting of many tables with sufficient rows in the table to make a join expensive. The critical issue in multi-table queries is join order. The server may not be able to find an efficient join order with all of the tables in the query. It may be necessary to break the query into multiple parts, using one or more temporary tables.

> **NOTE**
>
> The optimizer will not try this strategy.

It is not surprising that breaking up joins of six or eight tables is useful. What is surprising is that sometimes even a three-table join can benefit from the use of a temporary table. Here is a query to consider breaking into components:

```
select sum(t1.amount)
from A, B, C
where A.id = B.id
and C.id = A.id
and B.id = C.id
and C.key2 between 1000 and 15000
```

The SHOWPLAN shows that the server chose this join order: B -> A -> C.

```
STEP 1
The type of query is SELECT
Scalar Aggregate
FROM TABLE
B
Nested iteration
Table Scan
FROM TABLE
A
Nested iteration
Using Clustered Index
FROM TABLE
C
```

```
Nested iteration
Using Clustered Index
STEP 2
The type of query is SELECT
```

The problem is that Table C, the innermost table, has two separate, fairly selective indexes that might be useful for this query, a clustered index to use with a SARG, and a nonclustered index that could support the join. Because of the join selectivity estimates, the server has determined (correctly) that using the clustered index at the innermost level is the most efficient approach to this three-table join.

Here are the statistics for each table, retrieved using SET STATISTICS IO ON:

```
Table: A  scan count 7282,  logical reads: 14755,  physical reads: 0
Table: B  scan count 1,  logical reads: 88,  physical reads: 0
Table: C  scan count 11308,  logical reads: 34404,  physical reads: 0
```

# How to Break Up a Query

You want to break up queries to allow SQL Server to get the best effect out of all candidate indexes. In the case under discussion, only one of the two useful indexes on Table C is being used, while Table B is being scanned. Here is what we do to make this work:

- Separate the query into components that each have an effective strategy.
- Try several approaches to see which gives the lowest total STATS IO values.
- Use one or many temporary tables to store and rejoin values, especially when you have a highly selective index.

Typically, when breaking up a query will be useful, one of the SARGs in the query will be fairly selective (it will significantly reduce the number of relevant rows in a single table). The best SARGs will use a clustered index.

At the first step in breaking up a query, you want to take advantage of that selective index to reduce the overall number of rows in play, partly to reduce the complexity of subsequent steps but also to reduce the size of your temporary table.

> **NOTE**
>
> This approach to large queries is likely to be less effective if the entire temporary table will not fit in cache.

```
select C.id, B.amount
into #temp
from B, C
where C.id = B.id
and C.key2 between 1000 and 15000
```

Here is the SHOWPLAN output for the first step in the plan. The clustered index on the inner Table C is used to dramatically reduce the cost of each scan on that table:

```
STEP 1
The type of query is TABCREATE
STEP 2
The type of query is INSERT
The update mode is direct
Worktable created for SELECT INTO
FROM TABLE
B
Nested iteration
Table Scan
FROM TABLE
C
Nested iteration
Using Clustered Index
TO TABLE
#temp
```

In the second step, we join the remaining table(s) with the temporary table to get a result:

```
select sum(t.amount)
from A, #temp t
where t.id = A.id

drop table #temp
```

The server will choose to use the permanent Table A as the inner table if the index on id is sufficiently selective and if indexes fit in cache. Otherwise the temporary table, if small enough, will be the inner table. You may want to test this out, examining statistics, outputs, and optimization plans to make certain the server finds the most effective plan. You might want to force a join order or the use of an index if the server is not making the best choice. (See the section on forcing an index earlier in this chapter.)

The optimization plan for the second part of the query shows that the server is scanning the new temporary table as the outer table and then using the index on A to build the final result:

```
STEP 1
The type of query is SELECT
Scalar Aggregate
FROM TABLE
#temp t
Nested iteration
Table Scan
FROM TABLE
A
Nested iteration
Using Clustered Index
STEP 2
The type of query is SELECT

STEP 1
The type of query is TABDESTROY
```

Figure 20.4 shows the original and revised join orders. You can see that the join order presented after the query was broken up allows the server to make the most efficient use of the indexes available. The more tables involved in a query the more likely you can find a better optimization strategy by breaking up the join into more than one step.

**FIGURE 20.4.**

*Breaking up a query into many parts allows more flexibility in identifying an efficient join order.*

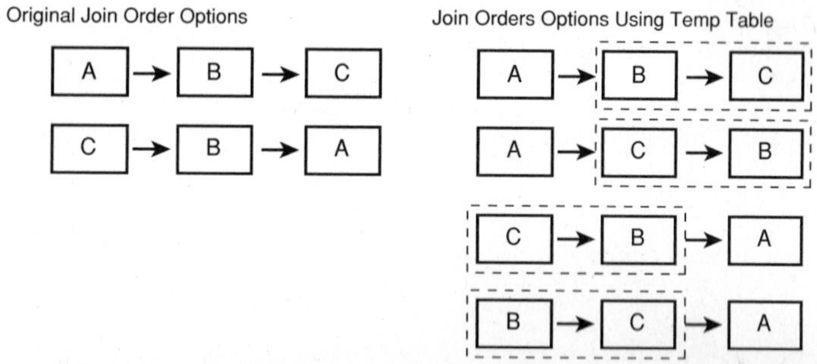

Original Join Order Options

Join Orders Options Using Temp Table

Here is the STATISTICS IO output from the query. The cost of the original query was about 48,000 logical reads. This query required less than half that many reads to complete:

```
Table: B  scan count 1,   logical reads: 88,   physical reads: 0
Table: C  scan count 7282,  logical reads: 22152,  physical reads: 0
Table: #temp_____000024884F  scan count 0,  logical reads: 554,
     physical reads: 0
Table: A  scan count 550,  logical reads: 1109,  physical reads: 0
Table: #temp_____000024884F  scan count 1,  logical reads: 5,
     physical reads: 0
```

## Recommendations

Here are some recommendations for how to break up query tables:

- Understand outer/inner processing with multitable joins, and use the first step to reduce *dramatically* the number of rows involved, if you can.
- Look for situations where the optimizer does not use all available indexing resources.
- Look for situations where nested scans of large tables are occurring.
- Break up queries by building temporary result sets.
- Try to encourage the optimizer to make use of many indexes.

# Summary

This chapter has provided some ideas on how to get better performance from difficult or large queries with special characteristics. Some of the recommendations include the following:

- In most cases, when using the output from the query diagnostic tools SHOWPLAN, TRACE, and STATISTICS IO, focus on logical and physical I/O and scan counts. These measures are the most reliable and durable measures of query performance.

- Understand how the server uses worktables, and find techniques to keep those worktables small.

- Override the optimizer with large, ad-hoc queries to improve performance. Remember the optimizer's fundamental assumptions and only plan to override *when you know something it does not.*

- Break up large joins by using temporary tables if you can reduce the number of scans on inner tables.

There are other techniques to improve query performance as well as the ones mentioned here, many of which you will be able to apply to your applications. Develop a good testing methodology that provides reliable, predictable information about the work required to complete a query. Build useful test data sets that mimic the performance of the actual system if you don't have access to (or can't hang up!) the live data.

Above all else, be an aggressive tester. SQL Server has its quirks and characteristics that make it do better with one approach to a problem than another, even though the two approaches may seem similar to you.

# Miscellaneous
# Performance Topics

# 21

There are a number of issues in SQL Server related to performance that both the programmer and the dba/sa need to consider. Many of these topics do not fit neatly into the previous chapters on understanding and tuning the performance of SQL Server. This chapter presents a selection of these topics, discussing the various performance implications of each and providing tips and guidelines to alleviate or avoid some of the performance problems.

# *bcp* and Performance

The bulk copy program (bcp) is a command-line utility that copies SQL Server data into or from an operating-system file. The operating system file is defined in a user-specified format.

The bcp program is a very useful utility for transferring data from SQL Server and non–SQL Server data sources into SQL Server (for example, loading a DB2 data extract into a SQL Server database). bcp is the fastest way to insert data into a SQL Server table. This is because during load, bcp does not enforce rules, triggers, or constraints as a normal insert statement does. In addition, if the appropriate conditions are met, bcp also can avoid logging the rows being inserted, greatly reducing the overhead involved and resulting in much faster load times.

When there are no indexes or triggers on a table, bcp performs a "fast" bcp load. The actual data rows being inserted into the table are logged as they would be by a normal insert statement. Only the new pages allocated to that table are logged.

> **NOTE**
>
> In addition to having no indexes and triggers on the table, the database must also be configured for select into/bulkcopy operations or bcp will fail to load any data into that database. It does not default to running in "slow" mode if all other criteria for "fast" bcp are met but the select into/bulkcopy option is not on.
>
> If a table you are inserting into is marked for replication, the individual rows need to be logged for the replication process to replicate them. This results in a slow, logged bcp.
>
> Surprisingly, even though triggers are not fired by a bcp load process, the presence of a trigger on a table results in the slower logged version of bcp being invoked. Watch out for existing triggers on a table into which you are performing a bcp. You have to drop all triggers on the table to invoke a fast bulkcopy.

> **WARNING**
>
> Setting the `select into/bulkcopy` option on disables transaction log dumps for that database. After completion of a nonlogged activity (`select into`, fast `bcp` load), a full database dump should be executed.

# Minimizing Data Load Time

In addition to performing fast versus slow `bcp` loads, there are a number of other methods of tweaking the `bcp` load performance.

## Network Packet Size

Network packet size determines the number of bytes, per network packet, sent to and from the SQL Server. Your SQL Server configuration determines the minimum packet size allowed. However, this option can be overridden on an individual basis with the `-A` option to `bcp`.

Increasing packet size may enhance performance on bulkcopy operations. The default network packet size used by `bcp` when copying data into an SQL Server is 512 bytes. 512 bytes is the smallest network packet size. If a larger packet is requested but cannot be granted, `bcp` defaults to the next largest packet size that can be granted (the performance statistics generated at the end of a `bcp` run show the actual packet size used). Most testing has found that packet sizes between 4,096 and 8,192 typically provide the fastest performance for `bulkcopy` operations. The most efficient packet size, however, may depend on the largest allowable packet size by your network protocol.

## *bcp* Load and Indexes

Generally, there are two reasonable sequences of events for initial loading of data into SQL Server:

*Sequence 1:*

1. Create the clustered index.
2. Load the data.
3. Create any nonclustered indexes.
4. Update your statistics on the clustered index.

*Sequence 2:*

1. Load the data.
2. Create the clustered index and nonclustered indexes.

Typically, sequence 2 is the most efficient method. Although the cost is high to build all indexes after the data is loaded, the total elapsed time is substantially less then the time it takes to perform a slow bcp into a table with the indexes in place.

Remember, however, that you need 120 percent of the size of the table as free space *within that database* for SQL Server to be able to sort the data and build the clustered index. Due to database size constraints, you may need to use sequence 1 and load the data with the clustered index in place.

> **TIP**
>
> If the source data file is in clustered index order, you can load the data into the table without the clustered index. Once the data is loaded, create the clustered index with the sorted_data option. This option creates the clustered index without applying the merge sort. The contents of the table are still copied and the fill factor applied, so you still need the 120 percent free space. If, during the creation of the clustered index with the sorted_data option, it detects a row out of order, the index create will fail. You are then forced to run a standard clustered index create and have the necessary free space available.
>
> If you must load the data with the clustered index in place, the load will proceed more quickly with the source file data in clustered index order than with unsorted data.

Regarding nonclustered indexes, it is always faster to drop the nonclustered indexes, load the data, and re-create the nonclustered indexes than to load the data with the indexes in place. This is due to the significant amount of overhead that is incurred to maintain those indexes during the data load. However, it depends entirely on whether you are performing a complete refresh of the data on an incremental data load as to whether it is feasible to drop all indexes prior to running bcp.

Another advantage to creating indexes after the data load is that the index statistics will be "up-to-date" because the indexes are created with data in the table. It is not necessary to run the update statistics command.

## Incremental Loads versus Full Loads

If you are replacing all data for a table, it is faster to drop all nonclustered indexes and truncate the table prior to the data load. Once the data is loaded, you then re-create the nonclustered indexes. Be aware, however, that if data volumes are high, index creation time can be substantial. In some cases, if the index rebuilds take an excessive amount of time (several hours), it may pay to absorb the overhead of leaving the nonclustered indexes in place during the data load. This typically applies when performing incremental data loads.

If you are making substantive increases in the amount of data being added to the table (approximately 20 percent or more as a rule of thumb), it generally is faster to drop the nonclustered indexes, load the data, and rebuild the indexes.

> **WARNING**
>
> Because rules, triggers, and constraints are not applied during bcp load, integrity controls are bypassed. You should ensure that the data is completely valid to avoid violating any data or referential integrity conditions (more on this later). For this reason, bcp is often not used for incremental data loads.

If you are not significantly increasing the amount of the data in the table, there are a variety of methods for performing an incremental bcp load.

One alternative is to run the bcp load with all indexes on the table. Although the bcp load is the slowest, you don't have to re-create the indexes, but you will need to update statistics on the table subsequent to the load.

A second alternative for incremental loads is to drop all nonclustered indexes and load with just the clustered index in place. This approach speeds up the bcp load, but the table still is essentially unusable by applications that depend on the nonclustered indexes for access performance until the indexes are re-created. Depending on the size of the table, index creation could take hours or even days.

The third option is to run the incremental bcp load with no indexes on the table. This allows the fastest load process, but the longest index creation time. The re-creation of the clustered index acquires an exclusive table lock, which must be completed before the creation of nonclustered indexes can commence. It also prevents any user access to the table until the clustered index creation completes. Unless you are adding over 25 percent of the data (that is, adding 500MB to a 2GB table), the time needed to re-create the clustered index and all nonclustered indexes is prohibitive.

## Multiple Concurrent *bcp* Loads

If you have to load multiple tables, and the tables are on different physical devices, you may want to consider running multiple bcp loads concurrently, one into each table. This should help increase overall bcp throughput over running them in serial. Be aware that there will still be contention for the log unless each table is in a separate physical database.

In System 11, if a heap table is partitioned, you can run multiple concurrent inserts into a single table (see Chapter 18, "Database Object Placement and Performance," for details on how to set up heap table partitioning).

When a heap table is partitioned, SQL Server randomly assigns a transaction to a specific table partition. Each bcp batch is a separate transaction, and is therefore randomly assigned to a table partition. With a random distribution of bcp insert processes, there should be little or no contention between multiple concurrent bcp loads into the table. If you don't break the bcp up into multiple batches, it is treated as a single transaction and will be assigned to a single partition for the duration of the load. Also, if batches are not used, or too large a batch is used, the bcp load may escalate to a table-level lock, preventing other bcp loads to continue on the table until the table level lock is released.

> **TIP**
>
> To get the best performance on concurrent bcp loads into a partitioned table, consider creating twice as many partitions as you'll have concurrent bcp load processes. This will decrease the likelihood of two bcp loads going into the same partition.
>
> Also, configure your batch size to coincide with the configured lock escalation point for the table to prevent a batch from escalating to a table-level lock and holding it for a substantial duration. Be careful also not to use too small of a batch size—this will result in excessive logging overhead as each batch is committed, and performance gains might not be realized.
>
> Lastly, concurrent bcp loads will be fastest if table partitions are also spread across multiple physical disks. This will minimize I/O contention as well as lock contention.

## Slow *bcp* and Logging

When running a slow bcp load, the individual data rows are being logged. Remember, for each row being inserted into the table, a corresponding row is being inserted into each existing nonclustered index on the table. This can result in a significant number of log records being generated. Large logged bcp loads are notorious for filling up the transaction log. Because the bcp load, by default, is treated as a single batch transaction, the bcp records in the log cannot be truncated until the bcp process completes.

To avoid having the log fill up, you can use the -b option to break the bcp load into multiple batches. At the completion of a batch, SQL Server commits the inserted rows and checkpoints the database. The log records for those inserted rows can now be removed from the log. If you also turn on the trunc. log on chkpt. option for the database, the log is automatically truncated. The size of the bcp batch is dependent on the size of your transaction log and the amount of other logged activity occurring at the same time.

> **NOTE**
>
> Using the -b option causes bcp to run slower due to the multiple commits and check-points that occur during the load. When the log gets truncated, all update and insert activity is suspended until the truncate completes. However, this alternative is much preferred over having the log fill up.

One other advantage of using the -b option for large data loads is that should the bcp load process fail at some point, you can restart the bcp load from the first row of the batch being loaded at the time the bcp failed. All rows for the previous batches will be committed and checkpointed. Check the load statistics reported at the end of the failed bcp to determine how many rows were copied. If 40,000 rows were copied into the table using a batch size of 10,000, you can restart the bcp load at row 40,001 by using the -F option as follows:

```
bcp acctg..customers in customer.bcp -Usa -P -c -b10000 -F40001
```

# bcp and Data Integrity

bcp does not invoke any data integrity checks during load, such as triggers, rules, or constraints—even in "slow" mode. Your data and referential integrity checks are completely bypassed. When bulk-copying data into a table with triggers, rules, or constraints, you need to decide how you are going to resolve this issue.

To make sure that new data is valid, you should run SQL code after the bcp load process completes to check the data validity and decide how invalid rows are to be handled. For example, to check that the loaded data meets your referential integrity constraints, you could run the following code:

```
select cust_id, line_no
from purchase
where cust_id not in
    (select cust_id from customers)
```

This query lists all rows with invalid foreign key values in cust_id.

Because bcp does not invoke rules or check constraints, you need to write SQL to check that all values in a column match your rules or constraints:

```
select order_id, item_num
from orders
where price <= $0.0
```

This query returns all rows that do not meet the rule or constraint that price must be greater than zero. You can then make the determination whether to change the rule, remove the rows, or change the invalid data.

Sometimes, triggers are also used to keep summary values in sync. For example, consider an `item` table that has a `total_sales` column that contains the sum of the `qty` column in the `orders` table for that item. In this case, your trigger code is structured to handle the incremental adding of data. The overall total value for `total_sales` cannot be determined by the trigger code. You may have to recalculate all summary values fully for the detail rows in the `orders` table. Determine the SQL necessary to accomplish this task and execute the code, similar to the following example, that uses a correlated subquery:

```
update item
set total_sales =
    (select sum(qty)
    from orders
    where item.item_num = orders.item_num
    group by orders.item_num)
```

How does all this relate to performance? Any corresponding speed gains achieved by running a `bcp` load are offset by the performance hit the system takes when you have to run these queries. If your tables are large, the processes to validate your data integrity can take hours. These processes are very I/O- and CPU-intensive and cause other concurrent processes to run more slowly. They also may lock tables from updates or retrievals until the process completes. Some of these processes can essentially bring the SQL Server to its knees.

You may at times find it more beneficial to use a standard `insert` process to add data to your table. This way all data integrity checks and trigger code are applied for each individual row inserted. True, there is more overhead on the `insert` process itself, but it enables other processes to continue to run only slightly hindered.

# Database Maintenance and Performance

The main issue to address regarding data maintenance and performance is that data maintenance tasks tend to be very resource-intensive, and although you can run many of the SQL Server maintenance tasks on-line, there may be a significant impact on performance.

One of the main culprits is the DBCC command. The database consistency checker validates your table allocation pages and page linkages. In order to do this, DBCC performs a huge amount of physical I/O and locks tables from update activity while running. As a result, it can be very time-consuming and have a severe impact on on-line performance. Table 21.1 summarizes the performance impact of the DBCC commands. For a detailed discussion of DBCC, refer to Appendix B, "The Database Consistency Checker."

**Table 21.1. Summary of DBCC commands and performance implications.**

| Command Option | Locking and I/O | Performance |
|---|---|---|
| CHECKTABLE, CHECKDB | Shared table lock(s), heavy I/O | Slow |

| Command Option | Locking and I/O | Performance |
|---|---|---|
| CHECKALLOC, TABLEALLOC, INDEXALLOC | Shared table locks, heavy I/O | Slow |
| CHECKCATALOG | Shared page locks on system tables | Fast |

In an effort to minimize the total amount of time spent running the DBCC commands, you may want to consider running some of them in parallel. Database consistency checks, when broken down with CHECKTABLE, TABLEALLOC, and INDEXALLOC, can be executed in parallel. For example, you can try running the DBCC CHECKTABLE and DBCC TABLEALLOC commands concurrently for a particular table. Performing consistency checks on different tables can be done in parallel, decreasing overall completion time. However, you need to determine what the break-even point is on your server for running DBCC processes in parallel before the combined contention between the multiple processes causes them to run slower than if they were run sequentially.

Other data maintenance commands that affect performance adversely are index creation and UPDATE STATISTICS. Both UPDATE STATISTICS and nonclustered index creates acquire shared locks on the affected tables. This prevents updates for the duration of the command. Clustered index creation acquires an exclusive lock on the table until completion, preventing any access by other processes.

> **TIP**
>
> The update statistics command updates statistics for all indexes on a table unless you specify a specific index name:
>
> ```
> update statistics table_name [index_name]
> ```
>
> When UPDATE STATISTICS is run specifying just the table name, the index statistics are updated for each index on the table sequentially. By running it on individual indexes, you can run multiple UPDATE STATISTICS processes concurrently, lowering the total time to update the statistics for a table and releasing the shared locks quicker.
>
> Keep in mind that the index statistics are used only for nonunique searches. For unique indexes used only for single-row retrieval (*not used for range searches*), the distribution page is not used. Therefore, it is not critical to update statistics on that index as frequently, if at all.

# *tempdb* and Performance

All users within SQL Server share the same tempdb database for worktables and temporary tables, regardless of the database in which they are working. This makes tempdb a potential bottleneck in any multi-user system. The primary bottleneck in tempdb is disk I/O, but there can also be locking contention on the `tempdb` system tables' processes between multiple processes that are creating/dropping temporary tables and indexes.

There are three basic techniques for eliminating `tempdb` as a bottleneck:

1. Add memory to SQL Server.
2. Put `tempdb` on faster devices.
3. Disseminate disk resources.

# Add Memory to SQL Server

Adding more memory to SQL Server helps improve `tempdb` performance by enabling more of the `tempdb` activity in `tempdb` to take place in the SQL Server data cache. The main disadvantage to this approach is that it doesn't help much for `inserts` into temporary tables in `tempdb` because the modified data pages still have to be written to disk upon `commit`. Therefore, there is still an I/O bottleneck on writes to `tempdb`. There also is no guarantee that additional cache will be used exclusively for `tempdb`, because the default data cache is shared by all databases in the system.

> **TIP**
>
> With System 11, you can define a named data cache and bind it exclusively to `tempdb`. This will avoid the problem of `tempdb` objects and other database objects competing for cache space. For more information on configuring named data caches, see Chapters 30, "Configuring and Tuning the SQL Server," and 31, "Optimizing SQL Server Configuration Options."

# Faster Devices for *tempdb*

One other way to minimize I/O contention in `tempdb` is to place `tempdb` on faster devices. These could be high-speed disk devices, disk devices with caching mechanisms, or—if supported by the operating system—solid state disk (SSD) devices. SSD devices are essentially nonvolatile RAM devices that appear to the operating system and SQL Server as standard storage devices. SSDs contain a built-in backup mechanism to maintain their contents following a system or power failure. I/O rates to SSD devices are roughly equivalent to reads and writes from system memory.

> **TIP**
>
> If you are running in a UNIX environment, you might want to consider using a file system device for `tempdb` rather than a raw device. The built-in caching capability of the UNIX operating system can, in some cases, greatly improve `tempdb` I/O. Some

customers have reported `tempdb` performance on file system devices up to 10 times faster than `tempdb` on a raw device. Because you don't care about the integrity of `tempdb` data in the event of a system crash, the typical concerns of putting databases on UNIX file system devices rather than raw devices don't apply.

By speeding up I/O operations in `tempdb`, you not only minimize the I/O bottleneck, you also minimize the potential for locking contention in `tempdb`. The shorter the amount of time it takes to create and insert data into a temporary table, the less time a lock is held on the system tables.

A customer once reported that they were experiencing deadlocking problems in `tempdb`. Further research determined that the deadlocking was occurring on the system tables due to the number of users concurrently creating and dropping temporary tables. By creating `tempdb` on an SSD device, I/O operations were speeded up considerably and the deadlocking problem went away.

# Disseminating Disk Resources

The goal of disseminating resources is to place the databases and logs within SQL Server across devices in such a way as to spread the I/O and minimize I/O contention. In an ideal world, you would have an unlimited supply of disk drives available so that you can place databases, logs, and objects on their own physical devices when needed. However, very few of us, if any, live in such a world. You frequently have to make do with existing hardware.

The first 2 MB of `tempdb` exists by default on the `master` device. If `tempdb` activity is high, you may wish to move this 2MB fragment off the `master` device so that `tempdb` I/O doesn't conflict with other activity on the `master` device. Unfortunately, SQL Server enables us to expand `tempdb` onto another device only, but not move it off the `master` device. How do you get rid of the 2MB slice of `tempdb`?

If you are squeamish about directly modifying SQL Server system tables, you can simply drop the `default` and `logsegment` segments from the `master` device for `tempdb` after you alter it to another device. This prevents any temporary tables or worktables and the `tempdb` log from reading or writing the `master` device. However, the `system` segment is still there, and system table reads and writes still go to the `master` device. To move the `system` segment, you need to define a user-defined segment in `tempdb` on the `master` device first, because SQL Server requires that there be at least one segment defined on a database device.

With the previous solution, you can effectively get all of `tempdb` off the `master` device, but you still have a 2MB slice of the `master` database that is essentially unused. To move `tempdb` completely off the `master` device, you need to modify the system tables.

> **WARNING**
>
> Modifying the system tables requires that you have sufficient knowledge of the information contained in the system tables. Once you start playing around with system tables, you risk corrupting your system if you modify or delete the wrong information.
>
> It is *strongly* recommended that you perform all system table modifications within a transaction. This way, you can verify your modifications before they are committed. If you really mess up your system tables, you can merely issue a `rollback` statement and be back at square one to try again or call in more experienced help.

The general steps to move `tempdb` off of `master` are as follows:

1. Start SQL Server in single-user mode to prevent users from attempting to access `tempdb`. Booting in single-user mode also allows updates to the system tables.
2. Log in as sa.
3. Make a backup of the `master` database in case something goes horribly wrong and you need to restore `master`.
4. Create a dummy database on the desired device at the size you want `tempdb` to be. (You will first need to create the device as well if the device does not already exist.)
5. Begin a transaction so you can roll back system table changes if an error is made.
6. Delete all references to the existing `tempdb` database from the `sysusages` and `sysdatabases` tables (that is, where `dbid = 2`).
7. Get the database ID for the dummy database and modify the `sysusages` and `sysdatabases` tables accordingly to change the dummy database references to `tempdb` (that is, change `dbid` in `sysusages` and `sysdatabases` to 2 and change the name in `sysdatabases` to `tempdb`).
8. Run `selects` against `sysusages` and `sysdatabases` to verify your changes to the system tables. If everything looks okay, commit the transaction; otherwise, roll back the transaction. Review the steps you performed to determine the cause of the problem and try again.
9. Shut down and restart SQL Server for the changes to take effect.

> **WARNING**
>
> This procedure should only be used on the `tempdb` database and not on any other database. Attempting this procedure on any database other than `tempdb` will corrupt that database. It only works on `tempdb` because `tempdb` is rebuilt each time the SQL Server is rebooted. Also be aware that incorrectly modifying the system tables can cause serious problems within the SQL Server.

The following code example displays a sample session. In this example, the new database which we are going to make tempdb will be called newtemp. The size of the new database will be 200MB. We will create it on an existing device called newdevice. A dump device called masterdump has previously been defined as the dump device for the master database. The server has already been booted in single user mode to allow updates to the system tables and you are logged in as sa:

```
/* backup the master database */
dump database master to masterdump
go

/* create the database called newtemp on the device called newdevice */
/* This will eventually become the new tempdb */
create database newtemp on newdevice=200
go

/* remember to begin a transaction before modifying system tables!! */
begin tran
go

/* remove tempdb references for tempdb (dbid = 2)
   from sysusages and sysdatabases */
delete sysusages from sysusages u, sysdevices d
where vstart between low and high and dbid = 2
go

delete sysdatabases where dbid = 2
go

/* get the database id for the new database */
select name, dbid from sysdatabases
where name = 'newtemp'
go

name                                 dbid
-----------------------------------  ------
newtemp                                 10

/* modify the system table references to the dummy database
   to make it look like tempdb (set dbid = 2 and change name to tempdb) */
update sysusages set dbid=2 where dbid = 10
go

update sysdatabases set name='tempdb',dbid=2
where name =  'newtemp'
go

/* verify your modifications by checking sysdatabase and sysusages */

select name, dbid, suid, crdate from sysdatabases
where name = 'tempdb'
go
```

```
name                                dbid   suid   crdate
----------------------------------  -----  -----  ---------------------
tempdb                                2      1     Dec  8 1994 10:36AM


select * from sysusages where dbid = 2
go

dbid   segmap      lstart       size        vstart
-----  ----------  -----------  ----------  -----------
    2           7            0       51200     16793600
(1 row affected)

/* Everything looks okay, commit the changes */
commit tran
go

/* shutdown and restart SQL Server for changes to take effect */
shutdown with nowait
go
```

# Other *tempdb* Performance Tips

When using temporary tables for storing intermediate values, select only the columns actually required by the subsequent SQL statements into the temporary table. This helps reduce the size of the temporary table and speeds access of data within the temporary table as more rows fit on a data page, reducing the number of data pages that need to be accessed by the query. With a large number of users, this can help minimize the amount of I/O and I/O contention within tempdb.

If any tables in tempdb are going to be accessed frequently, consider creating indexes on tempdb tables where appropriate. The investment in time and space to create the index may be more than offset by the time and I/O savings that can be realized using the indexes when the table is frequently accessed or used in joins. The index also can be used to satisfy the queries rather than table scans if index covering can be performed.

## TIP

SQL Server enables you to create temporary tables and indexes within a stored procedure and subsequently reference them within the same stored procedure. Unfortunately, at the time the queries are optimized, there is no data in the temporary table for the query optimizer to estimate the index usefulness. By default, it assumes the table has 100 rows on 10 pages. On execution of the procedure however, SQL Server will recompile a new query plan for the stored procedure after the table is created and populated. This incurs extra query optimization overhead for the stored procedure.

If you want to have SQL Server optimize the query based on actual data and index statistics initially, create the temporary table prior to executing the stored procedure that references it. You can do this easily by creating master and subprocedures as follows:

```
create proc p1 as
select * into #tmp1 from customers
create index idx1 on #tmp1 (cust_id)
exec p2
return
go
create proc p2 as
select * from #tmp1 where id = 1001
return
go
```

The only thing to remember when implementing this solution is that the temporary table must also exist at the time all stored procedures that reference it are created so that they can resolve the table's name; otherwise, the creation of the procedure will fail. To do this, add a command in the stored procedure script file that creates the table. Only the table definition must exist at procedure creation time, not any data in the table. You can use a where clause, which doesn't return any data rows, to create the temporary table template:

```
select * into #tmp1 from customers where 1 = 2
```

# Cursors and Performance

SQL was originally designed as a set-oriented processing language. Queries, updates, and deletes operate on sets of data. The set may contain a single row or multiple rows. The where clause specified indicates which rows are included in the set.

What if you want to examine the row contents and, based on the values, execute an appropriate action? Within the original SQL language, this would require running multiple update processes, specifying different conditions in the where clause.

What if you have this situation?

- Increase the price of all items by 10 percent where price is less than $50.
- Decrease the price of all items by 15 percent where price is greater than or equal to $50.

If you try to run these as two separate update statements, you could potentially update a row twice, regardless of the order in which you run the queries. If an item is priced at $49.95, the first update increases its price to $54.95, and it will be updated again by the second update. Obviously, you have a dilemma.

Cursors were designed to give us the ability to handle these types of situations. Cursors give us a way of performing operations on a row-by-row basis.

However, this method of row-by-row access incurs significant processing overhead due to the looping constructs needed to step through the cursor result set one row at a time. The slower processing of cursors can result in increased locking contention between concurrent users due to the longer time locks are held. It can, in other instances, minimize table-level locking contention since the cursor operates a row at a time and will not escalate to a table-level lock as a set-oriented update may.

Be careful—because of the additional overhead and slower processing, use cursors only when absolutely necessary. Often, cursor processing can be replaced by normal SQL set-oriented processing. Standard SQL set-oriented processing typically runs faster than a cursor performing equivalent operations—even if it requires multiple table scans.

For example, consider the following cursor:

```
declare curs cursor for
select price from titles for update of price
go
declare @price money
open curs
fetch curs into @price
while (@@sqlstatus !=2)
begin
   if @price > $50
      update titles set price = price * $1.10
         where current of curs
   else if @price > $25
      update titles set price = price * $1.20
         where current of curs
   else
      update titles set price = price * $1.30
         where current of curs
fetch curs into @price
end

close curs
deallocate curs
```

The previous example does not need to be performed as a cursor, because the result sets do not overlap. It can be replaced with the following code:

```
update titles set price = price * $1.10
   where price > $50
update titles set price = price * $1.20
   where price > $25
update titles set price = price * $1.30
   where price <= $25
```

In testing against a 5,000-row table, the second example has been observed to run approximately 2.5 times faster than the same processing performed as a cursor.

> **NOTE**
>
> Although cursor processing is slower than set-oriented processing, there are times when row-by-row processing can improve the concurrent access to the data.
>
> Consider an update to price for all rows in the items table. With normal set-oriented processing, this requires a table-level lock, locking out all other access to the table until the update completes. With a cursor, locking is performed at the page level. This enables access to other pages in the table by other user processes. If each row is committed as a single transaction, the cursor typically locks only a single page at a time.
>
> Committing each row individually can generate significantly more log records, however.

# *text* and *image* Columns and Performance

Inappropriate datatype selection is a common error for database designers new to Sybase. One of the more common mistakes made is the inappropriate use of the text or image datatype.

Recall from Chapter 4, "Transact-SQL Datatypes," that text and image columns are stored as a 16-byte pointer in the data row, pointing to a separate linked chain of pages to store the text/image data.

Often, the database designer decides, "We need a column for 4 to 5 lines of free-format comments. char doesn't get big enough, so let's use text."

The problems with text and image columns should cause you to think twice before using them. These problems range from potentially enormous space consumption to a serious performance impact. Let's look closely at the drawbacks, then consider some alternative implementations for storing large text and image data.

Text and image columns can demand a substantial amount of storage overhead in your database. Each row in the table storage itself includes a 16-byte pointer to the first page in a page chain. (If the data in the text or image column is null, the pointer is null as well.) To store the actual text or image data, the SQL Server allocates space for text/image data in each row in a linked chain of 2KB pages.

> **NOTE**
>
> This is an extremely important point. The server will not pack `text` data to use space efficiently. If the `text` column in a row contains the string, `"Hello, World!"`, those 13 characters occupy an entire 2KB data page. One million rows' worth of `text` columns like that takes up 2GB; they would take up only 13MB if stored in a conventional `varchar` column.
>
> See Chapter 10, "Understanding SQL Server Storage Structures," for the details of `text` and `image` storage.

When you update a row containing a `text` column, the amount of information logged can create a serious performance problem. `text` columns can be updated without logging by using the `writetext` command, but this has an impact on the recoverability of your database because the `text` data inserted is not logged.

> **NOTE**
>
> Enabling nonlogged modifications such as a `writetext` requires that the `select into/bulkcopy` option be turned on for that database. This disables transaction log dumps.

In addition, any read of `text`/`image` data requires a minimum of two page I/Os (one read of the data page to get the `text`/`image` pointer, and at least one page read to read the `text`/`image` data).

There are some basic workarounds to avoid the problems of `text` and `image` datatypes:

- *Store it somewhere else.* This is not as dumb as it seems. Lots of applications store only the pathname to an operating-system file containing the `text` or `image` data. The path is returned to the application, which in turn executes an operating system `file open` command to read the data. (Lots of commercial applications are written this way. There are some intricacies in implementing security, but the database application may run more smoothly.)

- *Use `varchar(255)` or `varbinary(255)`.* Stringing together a set of `varchar` or `varbinary` columns from a sequential set of rows takes a little extra application work, but eliminating the overhead of the `text`/`image` columns may provide better performance. (For an example of this, look at how SQL Server stores the text of stored procedures, views, triggers, rules, and defaults in the system table, `syscomments`.) An alternative is to break the `text`/`image` data across multiple `varchar(255)` or `varbinary(255)` columns within a single row. Again, your application program needs to break the data into the appropriate columns on `insert` and combine them on retrieval.

This approach can help improve performance by reducing search time for `like` strings, reducing storage overhead, and reducing I/O. The multi-column approach is not feasible if your data rows would exceed the SQL Server maximum allowable row size of 1962 bytes.

■ *Store the* `text` *or* `image` *information in a related table.* In the `pubs` database, the `pub_info` table stores `text`/`image` data separate from the actual `publishers` table. This improves the performance of updates on the `publishers` table, and the `pr_info` (text) and `logo` (image) columns can be placed in a table on a separate database enabling a nonlogged `writetext`.

# Summary

There are a number of performance issues to be addressed when working with SQL Server besides server configuration and query tuning. You've looked at only a subset of those issues in this chapter, those that are most common within standard environments. Generally, these are items and issues that you need to be aware of when working in an SQL Server environment so that you can prevent potential performance problems or can address them accordingly if problems should arise.

# Common
# Performance and
# Tuning Problems

**22**

When you tune the performance of SQL Server, there are a number of esoteric features that can be tweaked and tuned to improve overall performance. However, when you try to diagnose existing performance problems, a number of items can be potential culprits. How do you know where to begin to look to track down the performance problem?

Having a good understanding of the preceding performance-and-tuning chapters helps you understand how SQL Server processes queries so that you can identify the causes of performance problems and ways to improve them. However, it's one thing to understand the technology, and another to know how to apply it.

In my years as an SQL Server consultant, I've been called in on a number of occasions to track down performance problems. I've learned that the majority of performance problems have similar causes, typically the types of mistakes made by developers and database administrators who are new to SQL Server and don't have a full understanding of how SQL Server optimizes queries. Admittedly, I made many of those same mistakes in the past.

It helps to identify the common causes of performance problems before delving into areas such as spreading I/O across devices or denormalizing the database. In this chapter, you take a look at some of the more common causes of performance problems and the ways to work around or prevent them.

# Out-of-Date or Unavailable Statistics

A couple of years ago I was at a customer site conducting a performance evaluation of an application when the manager of another application-development group in the department asked if I could spend a few minutes with one of their developers to take a look at a performance problem they were experiencing. I had some free time later in the afternoon and decided to take a look at it.

The programmer's description of the problem was that initially the queries that populated the screen used to return values with subsecond response time, but over time, the application was getting slower as data was added to the tables. This behavior prompted me to ask the obvious question—a question so obvious I was almost embarrassed to ask it. "When was the last time you ran update statistics?" His answer was, "What is that?"

The moral of this story is, don't neglect to ask the obvious question. We ran update statistics on the entire database and, like magic, all queries were now back to subsecond response time. The problem was solved in about five minutes total time from diagnosis to solution.

What tipped me off was that the behavior the programmer described was textbook behavior of a database with out-of-date statistics or no statistics at all. (Refer to Chapter 12, "Understanding the Query Optimizer," for a detailed discussion of index statistics and how they are used by the optimizer.) This often occurs in development environments or newly created production databases. Remember, if indexes are created on empty tables, no index statistics are generated.

Without valid statistics to use, the query optimizer must use built-in statistics to estimate index usefulness, which often leads to invalid row and page estimates and may result in the wrong index or a table scan being used to process the query. A table scan may not present a noticeable performance problem when the table is only a few data pages, but as data is added and the table grows, performance begins to degrade. When you see this behavior, it's a good indicator that index statistics need to be updated.

> **TIP**
>
> If you update the statistics on your tables or indexes, don't forget to run `sp_recompile` on those tables. Any existing stored procedures in the procedure cache have a query plan associated with them based on the table statistics the first time they were run. To force them to generate a new query plan based on the updated statistics, run the `sp_recompile` stored procedure on the tables. All stored procedures that reference those table(s) will compile a new query plan on the next execution.

# Search Argument Problems

It's the curse of SQL that there are a number of ways to write a query and get the same result sets. However, some queries may not be as efficient as others. A good understanding of the query optimizer helps you avoid writing search arguments (SARGs) that SQL Server cannot optimize effectively. This section highlights some of the common "gotchas" encountered in SQL Server SARGs that can lead to poor or unexpected performance.

## No SARGs

Watch out for queries where the SARG may have inadvertently been left out:

```
select title_id from titles
```

An SQL query with no search argument (that is, no where clause) always performs a table scan unless a nonclustered index can be used to cover the query. (Refer to Chapter 11, "Designing Indexes for Performance," for a discussion of index covering.) If you don't want the query to affect the entire table, be sure to specify a valid SARG that matches an index on the table in order to avoid table scans.

## Negative Logic

Any negative logic (!=, <>, not in) always results in a table scan being performed, unless index covering can be applied:

```
select * from orders
where price != $10.95
```

The `not in` or `not equal` (`!=` or `<>`) statement is not considered an optimizable SARG by the SQL Server optimizer and is not evaluated for index matching. This typically results in a table scan to resolve the query. When faced with a `!=`, consider any possible ways to rewrite the query. For example, if you know, based on your data integrity rules, that `price` cannot be less than `0`, the following query

```
select * from orders
where price != 0
```

or

```
select * from orders
where price is not null
```

can be written and may perform better if written as this:

```
select * from orders
where price > 0
```

This query may perform better than either of the previous two because it avoids the negative logic and is treated as a SARG. The supplied constant value enables SQL Server to examine the distribution page to estimate the number of rows to be returned. This determines whether an index can be used to satisfy the query rather than a table scan.

## Operations on a Column in a *where* Clause

Any operation on the column side of a `where` clause causes it not to be treated as a SARG by SQL Server. Therefore, an index cannot be used to match the SARG with an index, and a table scan is performed to satisfy the query. Here are two examples of this type of `where` statement:

```
select * from orders
where price * 2 < $50.00

select * from customers
where substring(last_name, 1, 1) = "P"
```

These two queries could be rewritten as this:

```
select * from orders
where price < $50.00/2

select * from customers
where last_name like "P%"
```

As rewritten, the queries return the same result set, but the `where` clauses are now treated as SARGs. The optimizer can now consider using an index to satisfy these queries rather than having to perform a table scan. The query against the `customers` table uses the distribution steps to estimate the number of rows where `name` begins with `'P'`. The query against the `orders` table, however, isn't able to use the distribution steps, because although the mathematical expression resolves to a constant value, its value is determined at runtime, not at query compile time. In this case, the optimizer uses the index density to estimate the number of matching rows and evaluate the index usefulness. This is much better than limiting the optimizer to a table scan because the optimizer cannot treat the expression as an optimizable SARG.

# Unknown Constant Values in a *where* Clause

The previous discussion brings up an interesting point regarding how the optimizer treats constant expressions where the value isn't known until runtime. These are statements such as mathematical operations, string concatenation, SQL Server functions, subqueries, or local variables. The SQL Server treats these as SARGs but cannot use the distribution steps because it doesn't have a value to compare against the steps at query compile time. In this situation, it uses the density information that is also stored on the distribution page for the index. The density information is used to estimate the average number of rows that would match against any given value. The index density value is based on the uniqueness of the index. A less unique index will have a higher index density—that is, a greater percentage of rows may match any given value. (For an in-depth discussion of index density and distribution steps, please read Chapter 11.)

The optimizer will generally be able to better estimate the number of rows affected by a query when it can compare a known value against the distribution steps than when it has to use the index density to estimate the average number of rows that match an unknown value. This is especially true if the data in a table is not distributed evenly. When you can, you should try to avoid using constant expressions that cannot be evaluated until runtime so that the distribution steps can be used rather than the density value.

To avoid this situation, you might consider putting the queries into stored procedures and passing in the expression as a parameter. SQL Server evaluates the expression when the stored procedure is optimized. For example, create the following procedure:

```
create proc proc1 (@var1 money)
as
select * from orders
where price < @var1
```

and execute it as follows:

```
declare @var1 money
select @var1 = $50.00/2
exec proc1 @var1
```

In this example, @var1 is evaluated and a query plan generated for the stored procedure using a known value, so the distribution steps are used rather than the index density.

When working with stored procedures, if you want to have the optimizer use the distribution steps to optimize the queries within the procedure rather than the density information, make sure you don't perform any operations on the parameter in the SARG. If you need to perform an operation on a parameter, do it in an assignment select statement prior to the query. For example, the following two procedures optimize differently:

```
create proc proc1 (@var1 money)
as
select @var1 = @var1 * 2
select * from orders
where price < @var1

create proc proc2 (@var1 money)
```

```
as
select * from orders
where price < @var1 *2
```

The first procedure, proc1, optimizes the query by using the distribution steps based on the value of @var1 when passed into the stored procedure. proc2 has to use the index density because of the expression @var1 * 2. Keep in mind, however, that the query plan generated in proc1 is based on the value of the input parameter when the stored procedure is executed, not the value it may contain at actual query execution. This can result in an unexpected query plan being generated, but is typically a better alternative than forcing the optimizer to use the index density.

---

**TIP**

If you need to maintain the original value of a parameter for use later in the procedure, save it in a local variable and reassign it back to the parameter when needed, as in the following example:

```
create proc proc3 (@var1 money)
as
declare @initval money

select @initval = @var1

select @var1 = @var1 * 2
select * from orders
    where price < @var1

select @var1 = @initval
select * from orders
    where price > @var1
```

---

# Datatype Mismatch

Datatype mismatch was a problem in earlier releases of SQL Server, but appears to have been improved in current releases of SQL Server. Previously, if the value being compared against the column was of a different datatype, the index statistics couldn't be used. This was especially easy to do in stored procedures when a char or varchar parameter was being used in a SARG compared against a char or varchar column.

---

**NOTE**

Remember, SQL Server stores a char column that allows nulls as a varchar. Therefore, to match a parameter datatype to a column defined as char(10) null, you need to make sure you define the parameter as varchar(10) for the datatypes to match.

---

In examining the index selection process in SQL Server using the `dbcc traceon (302)` trace flags (as described in Chapter 14, "Analyzing Query Plans"), it was observed that SQL Server now converts the search value to the datatype of the column prior to checking the index statistics, as long as an implicit conversion between the datatypes can be performed. (For example, `float` converts to `int`, but `char` doesn't convert to `int`.) The only exception to this appears to be the comparison of a `char` to a `varchar`. These still are considered incompatible datatypes by the query optimizer and the distribution steps are not used—index density is used instead to estimate the number of matching rows.

To be on the safe side, it is recommended that you always try to match the datatype of the constant expression with the column datatypes.

## OR Logic in a *where* Clause

An `OR` clause may cause a worktable to be created if the optimizer chooses to apply the `OR` strategy to create a dynamic index (refer to Chapter 12 for a discussion of the `OR` strategy). The dynamic index is created and used to satisfy the query rather than a table scan if the I/O cost of creating and using the dynamic index is less than the I/O cost of a table scan.

> **NOTE**
>
> Remember, an `in` clause is treated like an `or` clause by SQL Server. For example, this
> ```
> select * from titles
> where title_id in ("BU3075", "BU1025")
> ```
> is the same as this:
> ```
> select * from titles
> where title_id = "BU3075" OR title_id = "BU1025"
> ```

If any one of the search clauses must be resolved by a table scan, a single table scan is performed to resolve the query. If the resulting cost of using the dynamic index is estimated to exceed the cost of a table scan, a table scan is performed.

If you are trying to avoid table scans when you have or clauses in your queries, make sure that all clauses involved in the or can be supported by an index and that the index is selective enough to avoid a table scan.

# Other Query-Related Issues

The majority of performance-related problems are a result of the way a query is written. The SQL language allows a number of additional clauses and keywords to sort and group the data in different ways. Unfortunately, this incurs extra work and may cause queries to run more slowly. This section identifies some additional performance issues you need to be aware of when writing SQL queries and offers some tips to improve query performance.

# The *distinct* Keyword

The `distinct` keyword causes a worktable to be created in `tempdb` for sorting and removing duplicate rows. This can seriously impact performance if the query returns a large result set. The entire result set is copied into a worktable in `tempdb`, sorted, and the duplicates removed before SQL Server sends the results to the client application. This can seriously add to the response time of the query and increases the amount of I/O performed on `tempdb`.

For single-table queries, if all columns of a unique index are included in the `select` list, the unique index guarantees that each row is unique and the worktable can be avoided. For multi-table queries, both tables must also have a unique index on the join columns.

---

**TIP**

Watch out for overuse or misuse of the `distinct` keyword. I was once at a client site where they were complaining about query response time in their applications. It was several minutes before any rows were being returned to the client application, even for single-table queries. As it turned out, they were using the `distinct` keyword in every query being issued, even for join queries where no duplicate rows were being returned because one of the tables had a unique index that was being retrieved. Dropping the `distinct` keyword from the queries resulted in data results being returned to the client application in seconds rather than minutes.

Be aware of instances where a unique index avoids duplicate rows in your result set, but the optimizer still insists on using a worktable to ensure that no duplicates are returned. Avoid using `distinct` unless absolutely necessary.

---

# The *count()* Function

The `count(*)` function, without a `where` clause, results in a table scan unless there is a nonclustered index on the table that can be used to cover the query. For the following query,

```
select count(*) from customers
```

the smallest nonclustered index can be used to satisfy this query because SQL Server can determine how many rows are in the table by counting the number of rows in the smallest nonclustered index. However, if the query contains a `where` clause, a clustered or nonclustered index must exist on one of the SARGs to avoid a full table scan.

**TIP**

If you wish to determine only the existence of a row in a table, without needing to know the exact count, use the `if exists` … statement rather than `select count(*)` …. `if exists` … discontinues processing as soon as a matching row is found, whereas `select count(*)` … continues processing to look for all matching rows.

**NOTE**

The `count(colname)` function counts all non-`NULL` values for a column in a table. Unlike `count(*)`, a query with a `count(colname)` function avoids a table scan only if a nonclustered index covers the query. The following query will avoid a table scan if there is a nonclustered index defined on `price`:

`select count(price) from titles`

If an index does not cover the query, SQL Server must scan the entire table if no `where` clause is specified, even if the column is defined as `NOT NULL`.

Whether an index can be used to satisfy a `count()` function or not, a single-column, single-row worktable is still created in `tempdb` for the purpose of calculating and storing the count.

## Aggregate Clauses

Aggregates such as `avg`, `min`, `max`, and `sum`, without a `where` clause, generally cause table scans unless the query can be satisfied by index covering. Here is an example:

```
select sum(qty) from orders
    where order_num = "3124"
```

If an index exists on the `orders` table that contains the `order_num` column, the query could be satisfied by finding the data rows via the index and calculating the sum of `qty`. If an index exists on the `order_num` and `qty` columns, the query could be satisfied by scanning the index rows without having to access the actual data rows at all.

The following query is also covered by the index and avoids a table scan if the index is created on the `qty` column:

```
select sum(qty) from salesdetail
```

If you expect an index to cover an aggregate query, but the query optimizer is performing a table scan, make sure that the query truly is covered by the index. All columns in the select list as well as all columns in the where clause must be included in the index definition.

As with the count() function, SQL Server creates a single-column, single-row worktable in tempdb for each aggregate function in the query for the purpose of calculating and storing the aggregate value. Be aware of the increased I/O that occurs from writing to tempdb and tempdb performance considerations. (Refer to Chapter 21, "Miscellaneous Performance Topics," for a detailed discussion of tempdb performance issues.)

---

**TIP**

If you want to retrieve the max and min values for a table on an indexed column, it is actually cheaper, in terms of total I/O and processing time, to run them as separate select statements rather than to combine them in a single statement. This is because SQL Server cannot walk an index structure in two different directions. For example, to resolve the following query on customers with a nonclustered index on id, such as this:

```
select min(id), max(id) from customers
```

the query is covered by the index, but finds the min(id) by reading the first row on the first page of the leaf level of the index. To find the max(id), it has to scan the entire leaf level of the index until it finds the last row on the last page. Based on the index in Figure 22.1, it would cost five page reads to find the min and max in a single query.

However, if you run a query to retrieve just the min value, it costs only one page. SQL Server merely reads the first row on the first page in the leaf level. (Recall from Chapter 10, "Understanding SQL Server Storage Structures," that the location of the leaf page is stored in the sysindexes table, so SQL Server does not need to traverse the index tree to find the leaf page.)

To retrieve the max value, SQL Server starts at the root page and traverses the index tree, following the last row on the last page at each level until it gets to the last row on the leaf level. If you refer to Figure 22.1 again, this costs two page reads (the root page plus the last leaf index page).

Therefore, the total number of pages read for two separate queries is only three pages read (versus five pages read). In this example, you save only two pages, but in much larger tables and indexes, the I/O savings can be substantial.

**FIGURE 22.1.**

*Finding the* MIN *and* MAX *values in the leaf pages of a nonclustered or clustered index.*

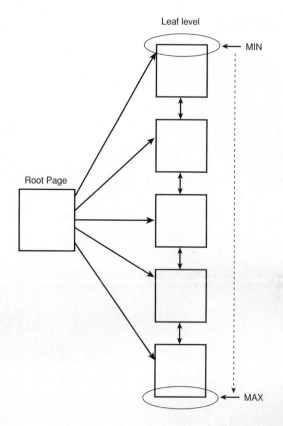

# order by and group by

The order by and group by clauses need to use tempdb as a work area for sorting or grouping the result set. When processing a small result set, the response should be subsecond. When a large result set is returned, response time can increase significantly due to the increased I/O in the tempdb database.

With the order by clause, a worktable can be avoided under two circumstances. The first is when there is a clustered index on the table and the result set is being sorted in clustered index order. Due to the nature of the clustered index, SQL Server knows the data is already sorted in clustered index order if it is retrieved using the clustered index or a table scan.

> **WARNING**
>
> If you are ordering by the clustered index but have a search argument on a column that has a nonclustered index on it and the nonclustered index is used to resolve the query, a worktable needs to be generated to sort the result set. This is because the result set is being retrieved in nonclustered index order rather than in clustered index order.

A worktable can also be avoided for an order by if the order by clause matches the SARG and the SARG can be satisfied by a nonclustered index, as in the following:

```
select * from customer
    where id between 10 and 20
    order by id
```

Because the result set is already being retrieved in nonclustered index order, additional sorting is not required.

> **WARNING**
>
> If you have an order by … DESC clause in your query, a worktable must be generated to do the sorting because SQL Server is unable to retrieve the data in descending sort order.

If you have any group by clauses in your queries, a worktable must always be generated to perform the grouping and the calculation of the aggregate(s) for each group.

## Join Clauses

When running troublesome queries with the showplan option on, watch out for the following message: "Worktable created for REFORMATTING". This indicates that no useful indexes were available to satisfy this query. The optimizer therefore, has determined that it is more efficient to build a temporary clustered index on the inner table in tempdb on the fly rather than incur the I/O and processing cost of joining via iterative table scans.

> **WARNING**
>
> This can be a very costly solution in terms of additional I/O and tempdb usage. It is better to provide queries with the appropriate indexes rather than to let the optimizer generate one on the fly. If you see the reformatting message in the showplan output, you should perform a query analysis and reexamine your indexing strategy.

You also want to watch out for and avoid Cartesian products (that is, when each row in one table joins with every row in the other table) between tables in a join due to a missing join clause. Remember, as a general rule of thumb, if there are *N* tables in a query, there should be at least *N-1* join clauses.

## Provide All Join Options

You can improve join performance in joins of three or more tables sharing a key by providing all join keys.

The key to fast joins is selecting an efficient join order. (When the server joins, it gets a value from one table, then looks for corresponding values in the other. Which table is first or "outer" and which is second or "inner" determines the amount of work required to answer the query.)

The server uses the information you provide about the tables to define the universe of possible orders. For example, if you write the following:

```
select *
from titles t,salesdetail sd,titleauthor ta
where t.title_id = sd.title_id
and sd.title_id = ta.title_id
```

you have the following two possible join orders:

| | | | | |
|---|---|---|---|---|
| titles | ← | salesdetail | ← | titleauthor |
| titleauthor | ← | salesdetail | ← | titles |

These two join orders are possible with two join conditions in the query.

Add the third leg of the triangle (t.title_id = ta.title_id) to the query to provide more possible join orders. (See Figure 22.2.)

**FIGURE 22.2.**

*By adding the third join clause, you complete a triangle of join tables and give the server complete freedom about the most efficient join order.*

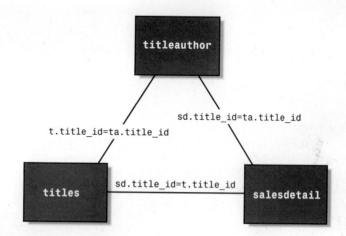

```
select *
from titles t,salesdetail sd,titleauthor ta
where t.title_id = sd.title_id
and sd.title_id = ta.title_id
and t.title_id = ta.title_id
```

Logically, you haven't added anything (you will get the same result), but you have provided more possible join orders. There are three join conditions specified, so there are now six possible join conditions:

| | | | | |
|---|---|---|---|---|
| titles | ← | salesdetail | ← | titleauthor |

```
titleauthor   ←   salesdetail   ←   titles

titles        ←   titleauthor   ←   salesdetail

titleauthor   ←   titles        ←   salesdetail

salesdetail   ←   titleauthor   ←   titles

salesdetail   ←   titles        ←   titleauthor
```

This means that with the additional join clause, you can actually triple your potential number of join orders. You won't necessarily always get a faster result, but you do improve your chances of getting a faster result.

# SQL Server Configuration

SQL Server configuration has an impact on overall system performance. One of the most important configuration issues to examine when tracking down performance problems is SQL Server memory configuration.

> **NOTE**
>
> For a more detailed discussion about memory configuration and some of the more esoteric SQL Server configuration parameters and how they affect SQL Server performance, refer to Chapter 31, "Optimizing SQL Server Configuration Options."

## Memory

Memory is probably the most important SQL Server configuration variable in relation to performance. The more data that can be accessed and worked on in data cache, the faster the system will perform. You want to make sure that sufficient data cache has been configured for the databases and queries being run. Don't assume that memory has been configured properly.

One time at a customer site during a performance-and-tuning engagement, I asked how much memory was on the machine. It was reported that there was 48MB available. Mistakenly, I assumed that was how much they had configured for SQL Server.

One query in question was taking approximately six hours to retrieve 50,000 records. I tried running it with the noexec option on, and the query plan indicated it was using the expected index. I turned off the noexec option and let the query run. I then noticed it was performing a significant amount of physical I/O.

At this point, I decided to take a look at the SQL Server configuration and discovered that the SQL Server was configured at only 8MB of memory. No one had reconfigured it after installation.

We increased the memory configuration to 32MB, which allowed all data pages required by the query to remain in memory. This also helped significantly reduce the runtime of the query. Overall, the time required to run the query was cut from about six hours down to approximately 20 seconds!

# Physical Database Design

The physical design of a database can have an impact on overall database performance. This section identifies some of the more common physical-design issues to consider when tracking down performance issues or tuning the performance of a database.

## Indexes

Watch out for missing indexes. You should verify that all indexes have been created as defined in design documentation. A common performance problem results from developers writing queries based on expected indexes that may have been created differently or not created at all. This results in the queries not using the expected index and adversely affecting performance.

## Overindexing

Avoid overindexing your tables whenever possible in an OLTP (on-line transaction processing) environment. Perform a thorough transaction and query analysis to map out carefully which indexes are really needed. You typically want to identify the most critical, high-priority transactions, which should be supported by indexes.

## Index Selection

Poor index selection is another tuning item you should examine. Chapter 11 contains a detailed discussion about index selection and usefulness. The following are a few things to keep in mind:

- For the SQL Server optimizer to consider using a composite index to process a query, at least the first ordered column in the index must be specified in the where clause.

- The first element in the index should be the most unique (if possible) and index order in general should be from most to least unique in a compound key, but remember that selectivity doesn't help if you don't use the first indexed column in your where clause.

- Choosing the clustered index for the primary key is correct only some of the time. A much more useful application is to choose the column(s) that will be accessed by ranges of data ("Give me all the consumers whose ages are between 25 and 45") or for grouping ("Give me sales by customer").

# Clustered Indexes

Are clustered indexes being effectively used? Any tables, if they have only one index, should typically have a clustered index before a nonclustered index, because the overhead involved with maintaining clustered indexes is less than nonclustered indexes. The space required for clustered indexes is also significantly less than a nonclustered index, because the clustered index typically has one level less than a similar nonclustered index. Using clustered indexes improves query performance because it results in one less page read per row lookup than a nonclustered index does on the same column.

Examine your clustered indexing strategy closely. Too often, the clustered index is automatically assigned to the primary key. This is fine if it is the exclusive access path to that table and is used frequently in joins. However, there are instances where it may be more efficient to create the clustered index on a different column(s) and create a nonclustered unique index to maintain and support the primary key.

Other possible candidates for a clustered index include the column or columns that are used most frequently to access data in the table, columns that are frequently specified in order by clauses, and columns that are frequently used for range retrievals.

> **TIP**
>
> Clustered indexes support range retrievals well because the data within the range is grouped, minimizing the number of data pages that need to be accessed to retrieve the data rows. For further discussion on selecting clustered versus nonclustered indexes, refer to Chapter 11.

# Avoiding Hot Spots

Watch out for potential hot spots when inserting or updating data. Hot spots occur when the most recently inserted rows are clustered together. This typically occurs in tables without a clustered index, because SQL Server inserts all new data rows at the end of the table. It also can occur with a clustered index if the clustered index exists on a sequential key and data is inserted in sequential key order.

If the most recently inserted rows are also the most often accessed, there can be locking contention and potential deadlock problems on those data/index pages between multiple users. Consider implementing a clustered index that spreads the data throughout the table, avoiding hot spots. For example, if you have an orders table with a sequential key on order_id and data is inserted in sequential order, you may consider creating a nonclustered index on order_id and placing a clustered index on product_id so that the new order entries are spread randomly throughout the table by product_id.

# DSS versus OLTP

Try to avoid mixing Decision Support System (DSS) activities with high-load on-line transaction processing (OLTP) activity. DSS queries are often long-running and CPU-intensive, causing a slowdown of other transaction activity. In addition, DSS queries and reports typically require a large number of supporting indexes. The greater the number of indexes, the greater the overhead to maintain all those indexes during update processing.

If possible, consider setting up a separate server on a separate machine, with duplicate data for performing DSS tasks. This way, the DSS system can be indexed as heavily as needed and the DSS reports won't affect the OLTP activities.

> **NOTE**
>
> This topic is covered in more detail in Chapter 17, "Database Design and Performance," and Chapter 35, "Administering Very Large SQL Server Databases."

# Historical versus Active Data

Is a large amount of historical data that is rarely accessed being kept on-line with the recent, more active data? Consider moving historical data into a separate table or database to make the active table smaller. This reduces the number of data and index pages that need to be searched as well as reduces the overhead of index maintenance by making the index trees smaller.

> **NOTE**
>
> This topic is covered in more detail in Chapters 17 and 35.

# Locking Issues

Watch out for obvious locking contention problems that can severely impact system performance. The following are some of the more likely culprits:

- Disconnected client processes that have left a session in SQL Server that is still holding locks
- Transactions that allow user input, causing locks to be held for indeterminate periods of time
- Nested transactions that don't fully commit properly, leaving locks held within a session

> **TIP**
>
> For a complete discussion of locking issues and solutions, please refer to Chapter 15, "Locking and Performance."

# Maintenance Activities

Watch out for maintenance activities such as dump, load, and dbcc, which can occur during normal processing periods. They are very I/O- and CPU-intensive and can have considerable impact on the performance of other online activities.

# Summary

There are a number of potential causes and solutions to performance problems within SQL Server. If you have a good understanding of the performance issues and SQL Server operations, you are effectively equipped to address and solve performance problems. You should now also have a good feel for the more likely culprits to look out for to identify and solve performance problems quickly.

If you've considered and looked into the common problems addressed in this chapter and ruled them out as the cause of your performance problems, it may be time to dig a little deeper into SQL Server. Just remember, when all else fails, feel free to give Tech Support a call. Who knows? You may have been one of the lucky(?) souls to uncover a bug or "undocumented feature" within SQL Server. Believe me, I've seen my share of those in the years that I have been working with SQL Server.

# PART

# IV

# System Administration

# Overview of System Administration

23

In this chapter, you look at the roles and responsibilities of a Sybase system administrator and at how they differ from or overlap with those of a database or operating system administrator. You learn critical terminology and explore the following key concepts:

- Roles (as defined by the system)
- System tables
- System stored procedures

# Components of SQL Server

The SQL Server environment consists of clients, servers, and a network that enables them to communicate. Let's review each of these components to understand the broad spectrum of administration required to keep SQL Server operational.

Client components include the following:

- Workstation hardware
- Network interface card (NIC)
- Operating system
- Network software
- Network library software
- Database library software (ct-library/DB-library)
- Application software

These are the network components:

- Server and client NIC
- Network software
- Hubs, routers, and concentrators
- Cable

The following are server components:

- Server hardware
- NIC
- Operating system
- Network software
- Network library software
- Server library software
- SQL Server software

- Audit Server
- Backup Server

As the SQL Server system administrator, you are probably only *officially* responsible for the SQL Server software and the various client libraries, but consider a different question. When the server becomes unavailable, which of these components could be the culprit? The answer: Any of them. Client/server configurations require mastery of several disciplines to maintain solid, reliable performance day in and day out.

As system administrator, you need to muster a team of experts—in client software, server software, and all the networking layers in between. As you work through this chapter, map the examples to your environment; this will enhance your ability to troubleshoot problems as they arise.

> **NOTE**
>
> People who are worried about job security in the client/server world should think about all the areas of expertise that are required to make a complex system such as SQL Server really work. Here's a very brief list of specializations:
> - Project manager
> - Analyst
> - Relational database designer
> - SQL Server administrator
> - Server OS (for example, UNIX) administrator
> - Network administrator
> - Help-desk staff
> - Database administrator
> - Client OS (for example, Windows) specialist
> - Applications programmer

# SQL Server Versions

SQL Server has been around for a number of years, and many releases and versions are in production in companies around the world. The most current release for Sybase SQL Server is System 11. The most current release for Microsoft SQL Server is version 6.0, which is the next release subsequent to 4.21.

System 11 is mostly a performance-related release, geared towards heavy volume OLTP (online transaction processing) shops and VLDB (very large database) applications. Sybase's System 10 and later releases offer a variety of important features for system administrators; the most visible of these are enhanced, faster backup capabilities, roles, and auditing capabilities. (This book points out features of System 10 and later; older versions of SQL Server and Microsoft releases will not include these advanced features.)

SQL Server runs on several operating platforms, including UNIX, NetWare, Windows NT, OS/2, and Open VMS. UNIX is by far the dominant platform for Sybase SQL Server, but Microsoft is selling thousands of servers on Windows NT. As of this writing, the major UNIX flavors of SQL Server are Sun, HP, IBM, DEC, and AT&T. Sybase's stated policy has been to provide concurrent major releases on each of these platforms, with releases for other platforms following closely behind.

SQL Server clients can run on any of the server platforms. In addition, development libraries are available on MS-DOS, Windows, and Macintosh. It is even possible to develop client software that operates in the MVS environment to enable mainframe terminals to execute applications to modify SQL Server data. (For organizations with well-developed WANs running over mainframe connectivity components, this approach enables a much smoother transition from a centralized to a client/server model. Over time and as appropriate, specific sites can convert to intelligent workstations. Until then, users can still operate from existing terminals and over existing lines.)

# System and Database Administration

In some organizations, no distinction is drawn between administration of SQL Server and its resident databases. A single individual or group is responsible for all these issues. Certainly, overall system responsiveness and integrity requires good coordination between the system and its databases, but there are distinctions between Sybase server and database administration. The systems administrator keeps the server available and focuses on the relationship between the server and its operating system. The database administrator focuses on database query performance, transaction throughput, and concurrency. The section on performance and tuning looks closely at database administration issues; this section of this chapter concentrates on server administration issues.

# The System Administrator (*sa*) Login and Roles

Prior to the System 10 release, all administrative responsibilities had to be executed by an individual logged in—literally—as sa, for system administrator. System 10 introduced the concept of *roles*. Now specific user logins can be assigned components of the administrative responsibility, which aids in the tracking and auditing of administrative activities.

The three roles are the sa_role (systems administrator) for administrative tasks, the sso_role (site security officer) for security tasks, and the oper_role (operator) for backup and recovery tasks. See Chapter 27, "Security and User Administration," for more on roles.

# Responsibilities of the System Administrator

The Sybase system administrator is responsible for the overall performance and reliability of SQL Server. In System 10 and subsequent releases, a system administrator is considered any login that has been granted the sa_role. (Note that the sa login is automatically granted the sa_role upon server installation.) For the purposes of this section, the use of sa really refers to any login granted that role. Here's a list of some of the responsibilities of the system administrator. (As you review this list, it's probably a pretty good time to start defining the job description of an sa for your organization or workgroup.)

## Server Installation and Upgrade

The system administrator installs the software on the server. (When performing an installation, assistance from a person skilled in the server operating system is always helpful.) A Sybase user must be added to the operating system to perform the SQL Server installation. This user is also responsible for applying patches and bug fixes to SQL Server, and for performing major version upgrades. Once installation is complete, the system will contain a login for the sa.

## Physical Device Configuration

Sybase uses underlying system resources, including disk, memory, and network resources. The system administrator needs to identify physical storage areas, then define logical mappings to those areas.

## Database Creation

After identifying logical devices, the sa creates databases on those devices and then often assigns ownership (and administrative responsibility) to another login.

## System Configuration Settings

The system administrator manages system configuration settings, including the amount of server memory and how it is allocated, the number of concurrent user connections and open databases, and the number of locks and system devices. These settings affect system availability and performance.

# Backup and Maintenance of the System Databases

The master database is a crucial resource where system-wide information is recorded. Model is the template database for all subsequent database creations. All stored procedures are maintained in the sybsystemprocs database. As system administrator, you guarantee the availability and integrity of these databases.

# Server Startup and Shutdown

Only the system administrator is permitted to start and stop the server process. You may require periodic shutdowns to change system parameters or to repair broken equipment.

In addition, the system administrator is the backup database administrator (dbo) for all databases.

# Responsibilities of the Site Security Officer

The site security officer (sso) is responsible for adding logins and administering the sa_role and the sso_role, as well as the audit system (if installed). The sso is considered to be any login that has been granted the sso_role. (Note that the sa login is also automatically granted the sso_role upon server installation.) The following tasks are handled by the sso:

- System security
- Management of site security and operator roles
- Management of the audit system

## System Security

SQL Server provides several levels of security: server login security, database security, and object security. A user with the sso_role is responsible for server-level security.

## Management of Site Security and Operator Roles

Only a user with the sso_role may grant others that permission or grant or revoke the operator role.

## Management of the Audit System

The sso is responsible for server auditing. The sso may grant others permission to use and query the audit tables, but only the sso can control what databases, objects, and users are audited.

# Operator Responsibilities

An operator is able to back up and load all databases. An operator is considered to be any login that has been granted the oper_role. Note that an operator can even back up and load databases that he cannot access in any other way. For example, a login with the oper_role may not be able to use a database or access any of the underlying objects, but still has the ability to perform a database backup or load.

# System Tables

SQL Server stores almost all configuration, security, and object information in its own *system tables*. There are system tables within each individual database, as well as in the master database.

**NOTE**

The system tables are sometimes referred to as the system catalog or data dictionary. It's crucial to remember that system tables are stored within each individual database (including the master database). *Additional tables* appear in the master database to store system-wide information.

## Database-Level System Tables

These tables are stored in every database, *including the* master *database:*

| | |
|---|---|
| sysalternates | Contains user "aliases" for logins whose database access is granted through another login. |
| sysattributes | Defines attributes for databases, tables, indexes, users, logins, and procedures. |
| syscolumns | Contains names and characteristics of every column in every table and view in the database, as well as parameters for stored procedures. |
| syscomments | Contains the creation text of every view, rule, default, trigger, and procedure. This text is accessed through sp_helptext. |
| sysconstraints | Contains names and characteristics of object constraints. |
| sysdepends | Describes relationships between dependent objects (views to tables, stored procedures to tables, and so forth). |
| sysindexes | Contains index and space allocation information for every table. |
| syskeys | Contains the documented keys for each table. |

| | |
|---|---|
| `syslogs` | Contains the transaction log, a record of each logged modification performed within the database (this is the only system table stored in the log segment—see Chapter 26, "Defining, Altering, and Maintaining Databases and Logs," for more on segments). It is stored in an internal format and is not useful for anything else. |
| `sysobjects` | Contains object (definitions tables, views, procedures, triggers, rules, defaults, constraints). |
| `syspartitions` | Contains internal information about partitions for individual tables in a database. |
| `sysprocedures` | Contains preparsed optimization trees for code-based objects (views, procedures, triggers, rules, defaults, constraints). |
| `sysprotects` | Describes permissions for users on objects (tables, views, procedures). |
| `sysreferences` | Contains names and characteristics of each referential integrity constraint declared on a table or column. |
| `sysroles` | Maps the server-wide roles to local database groups. |
| `syssegments` | Describes database partitions for storing different types or categories of objects and managing object growth below the level of the entire database. |
| `systypes` | Contains system- and user-defined datatypes available for columns when creating tables. |
| `systhresholds` | Contains information on each threshold defined for the database. |
| `sysusermessages` | Contains user-defined messages, added with `sp_addmessage`, for use with the `raiserror` statement (this is the only system table that is stored in a user data area). |
| `sysusers` | Describes the logins authorized to access the database. |

**NOTE**

Don't confuse the keys in `syskeys` with index columns or primary and foreign keys in constraints. Index columns determine the contents of an index, as well as the physical sort order of data (if clustered) and a unique identifier (if unique). Primary and foreign key constraints define an enforced referential integrity relationship between tables.

Keys recorded in `syskeys` (established with `sp_primarykey`, `sp_foreignkey`, `sp_commonkey`) define the structure of tables *as system documentation only*. Their only real use comes when an application examines these values to suggest a join or to learn about the structure of the tables, but the keys defined in `syskeys` are never enforced by SQL Server itself.

# System-Level System Tables

These tables are stored in master:

| | |
|---|---|
| syslogins | Contains name, password, and configuration information about each server login. |
| sysloginroles | Describes administrative roles for each login. |
| syslogshold | Contains information about the oldest active transaction and Replication Server truncation point for each database. |
| syssrvroles | Describes available administrative roles. |
| sysconfigures | Contains system configuration values to be used at next system startup. |
| syscurconfigs | Contains current system configuration values. |
| sysdatabases | Contains database name, owner, status, and other information. |
| sysdevices | Describes physical storage resources available to SQL Server (both active database devices and backup devices). |
| sysusages | Contains data allocations and mappings of physical storage areas to individual databases. |
| sysengines | Contains information about available CPUs (primarily for the SMP version of SQL Server). |
| sysprocesses | Contains process IDs, login information, and current status of each logged-in user. |
| syslocks | Contains current locks (this is a memory table only—if the server goes down for any reason, all locks are released). |
| syslanguages | Describes installed language sets (in the U.S., this is usually only us_english). |
| syscharsets | Describes installed character sets. |
| sysmessages | Contains server-wide error messages. |
| sysservers | Describes all servers involved in remote procedure calls. |
| sysremotelogins | Contains mappings and login identifiers for users logging in from remote SQL Servers. |

# Auditing System Tables

These tables are stored in sybsecurity:

| | |
|---|---|
| sysauditoptions | Contains global auditing option settings. |
| sysaudits | Contains detailed audit information. |

# System Stored Procedures

SQL Server enables the database developer to store SQL routines within the database; these are *stored procedures.* Stored procedures provide faster performance, reduced network traffic, better control for sensitive updates, and modular programming.

Although stored procedures often support user table processing, Sybase provides several stored procedures called *system stored procedures,* which support system table processing. For example, the `sp_helpdb` stored procedure returns a complete listing of all system tables. Other system stored procedures (for example, `sp_addlogin` and `sp_bindrule`) modify system tables.

> **NOTE**
>
> True story: When I first encountered SQL Server, I called a technical contact to find out how to retrieve the columns from a table. I'm not quite sure what she thought I was asking (she must have thought I knew more than I did), but this is what she told me to type:
>
> ```
> select c.name, c.colid
> From syscolumns c, sysobjects o
> where c.id = o.id
> and o.name = "employers"
> ```
>
> The query worked, but I couldn't help thinking that it was an awfully inconvenient way to get table information. I didn't learn about the `sp_help` stored procedure until several days (and lots of typing!) later.

## Special Characteristics

Names of system stored procedures start with `sp_` and are stored in the `sybsystemprocs` database. By naming a stored proc with `sp_` and storing it in `sybsystemprocs`, you can create your own system stored procedures.

> **NOTE**
>
> Users of SQL Server prior to System 10 should note that earlier versions stored system stored procedures in the `master` database.
>
> By moving system stored procedures out of `master`, Sybase enables `master` database backups to run more quickly and leaves more room in the `master` database for system configuration information.

When you execute a stored procedure whose name starts with `sp_`, the server first looks in your current database to find the procedure. If the procedure is not found in your current database, the server looks for it in `sybsystemprocs`.

Ordinary stored procedures are interpreted in terms of the current database when the procedure is created. For example, if you create a stored procedure in a user database, the stored procedure is immediately bound to the tables within the database. Note that in the following examples, any characters embedded inside a /* and */ are interpreted as comments and are ignored by SQL Server:

```
/* create proc in user1db */
use user1db
go
create proc show_objects
as
select name, user_name(uid)
from sysobjects
go
```

You can execute this procedure from any database, but you will always see a listing of objects in user1db, the database the procedure was created in. To invoke a procedure in one database from a different database, you must qualify the procedure name. The format is *database.owner.procedure*. If the database name is not provided, the object is assumed to be in the current database. If the owner is not provided, the system will first look for an object owned by you; if you do not own an object of that name, it will then look for an object owned by the user dbo, the database owner. Assuming the previous procedure was created by dbo, you would execute the procedure in the following manner:

```
/* sample execution of procedure from database user9db */
use user9db
go
user1db..show_objects
go
```

System procedures are always interpreted in terms of the current database *when the procedure is executed*. Create a similar system procedure in sybsystemprocs:

```
/* create this proc in sybsystemprocs */
use sybsystemprocs
go
create proc sp_show_objects
as
select name, user_name(uid)
from sysobjects
go
```

When the procedure runs, the system returns the contents of sysobjects in the current database at execution time. Remember, you don't need to fully qualify the procedure name with its database and owner if you have prefixed it with sp_.

```
/* sample execution from user9db */
use user9db
go
sp_show_objects
go
```

> **NOTE**
>
> With some practice, you will be creating these stored procedures yourself, without giving it much thought. Do not forget, however, that a stored procedure must be prefaced by execute (or exec) if it is not the first command in a batch. Here is an example:
>
> ```
> /* From user9db, execute the */
> /* show_objects proc in user1db */
> /* AND the sp_show_objects proc */
> use user9db
> go
> user1db..show_objects
> exec sp_show_objects
> go
> ```

# Useful System Procedures

The following are system procedures you will find useful:

| | |
|---|---|
| sp_who | Lists current logins and operations (from sysprocesses in master database). |
| sp_lock | Lists current locks and table identifiers (from syslocks in master database). |
| sp_help | Lists objects in the database or detailed object information (from sysobjects, syscolumns, sysindexes, syskeys, systypes). |
| sp_helpdb | Lists databases on the server (from sysdatabases in master database). |
| sp_configure | Lists or modifies current system configuration settings (from syscurconfigs, sysconfigures in master database). |
| sp_helpdevice | Lists physical storage and backup devices on the server (from sysdevices in master database). |

> **TIP**
>
> If you plan to write your own system stored procedures, you probably want to identify your procedures to avoid future versions of SQL Server from overwriting important, working ones with new standard system procedures. For example, if your company name is "ABC Corp.," you may want to prefix all your developed stored procedures with sp_abc_.

# Summary

As an administrator of a Sybase SQL Server, you have several areas of responsibility. These responsibilities can be assigned to other logins using roles. System tables record configuration and object information, and system stored procedures enable you to query and modify those system tables. (Although it is possible to update the system tables by hand, Sybase strongly recommends against bypassing the system stored procedures to make changes directly to system tables unless instructed to do so by Sybase Technical Support.)

In the coming chapters, you examine the many responsibilities of the system administrator, explore the system tables involved in maintenance, and learn the proper usage of most system stored procedures.

# SQL Server
# Installation and
# Connectivity

# 24

In this chapter you take a look at installation and connectivity with SQL Server. You explore some broad guidelines and learn about the traps at this stage. This chapter does not give detailed instructions because so many of the choices you have to make relate to your specific environment: your version of SQL Server, your platform, and your choice of client operating system. There are, however, several areas that may be of immediate interest:

- If you are trying to decide on a database server environment for your organization, see the section titled "Server Selection and Configuration."

- If you've already decided on your environment and are ready to perform an installation, you can find out some things to look out for in "Server Installation."

- If the server is already installed, but you want more information on how to bring the server up or down, see "Server Startup, Login, and Shutdown."

- Of course, you can't ignore the client side of "client/server." Preparing clients to communicate with the server is often an area of much confusion for many people. See "Client Installation" for more information.

- If you have the client and the server but want to know how they communicate, see "Networking and Connectivity" for an overview on the various protocols used in the industry.

- Look's like all the bases are covered, right? The system is going to work the first time and every time. It's always nice to be optimistic—but, just in case, we've included a "Troubleshooting" section to help you identify the problem and get the system running again.

- Even if your system is up and you haven't changed a thing, do not leave this chapter without reviewing "Changing Defaults: the Top 10 Items to Address as Soon as You Log In." You'll be glad you did.

- Finally, at the end of the chapter is a "Checklist" of the items that are part of a normal installation.

# Server Selection and Configuration

Before setting up SQL Server, you must understand the version and platform on which you are running—the characteristics of SQL Servers, the various operating systems they run under, and the versions of SQL Server that have been released in the last several years.

This is not meant to be a buyer's guide to Sybase versions; your choices depend most on the following crucial organizational issues:

- What operating systems are installed? If you already are running 500 NetWare servers in your organization, you should take a long, hard look at SQL Server NLM (The Novell operating system—NetWare Loadable Modules). If you are an all-UNIX shop, you should consider a UNIX implementation of SQL Server. New operating systems create new problems for MIS staffs, but a particular version of SQL Server may integrate connectivity features that help in other aspects of your project.

- What network protocols are installed? If you've already networked heavily with TCP/IP, using the UNIX version of the SQL Server won't add complexity or create new RAM problems on client workstations. If you're using Named Pipes to communicate with Windows NT servers, you might consider a Windows NT implementation.

- What are the required performance characteristics? At the time of this writing, there are limitations in the capabilities of Intel-based hardware for providing effective *symmetric multiprocessing* (SMP), and the bus architecture continues, for the most part, to be inappropriate for applications that move big blocks of data.

- How large are the databases you will implement? For a *very large database* (VLDB), you should consider the availability, cost, and reliability of very large storage devices for your platform.

- What other Sybase products do you plan to implement? Some newer products, such as Replication Server and Navigation Server, were available only for UNIX at the time this book went to press. If your architecture might benefit from these capabilities, you may find it easier or more manageable to bring up all Sybase applications under a single operating system.

- What is your budget? If your budget is tight, you might want to look at one of the Intel-based versions (NetWare, SCO UNIX, or Windows NT).

## Server Hardware Characteristics

SQL Server itself must be fast enough to handle the work of several users concurrently and to manage all the overhead involved in running a complex product. The speed of the bus is critical: data must move quickly between memory, CPU, disk, and network.

The memory capacity also is critical. Once Sybase has set aside the minimal memory it needs for users, devices, and databases, the remaining server memory is used for cache. There is a simple rule about Sybase and memory: more is better. The larger your tables, the more indexes you plan to create, and the more users you expect, the greater the memory you should plan to install.

Here are some quick RAM guidelines:

- Development systems can run with only 16MB of actual RAM in the system, although occasionally that is not enough memory even to start the server.

- Production systems can have as much as 1GB.

- On Intel-based systems, the lowest reasonable RAM is probably 32MB.

# SQL Server Platforms

Sybase runs as a process under several operating systems. The encouraging part is that, aside from installation, disk configuration, and setup of the backup devices, SQL Server is the same across all releases.

This chapter looks at installation in general, and some of the common environments. First, here's a review of the major platforms on which SQL Server is available.

The one critical difference between the platforms is that UNIX enables Sybase devices to be mapped directly to unformatted, "raw" physical drives or drive sectors. If you can't write to a raw device, your devices are mapped to the operating system's file system. For example, Sybase on a NetWare server maps physical devices to specific pathnames in the *NetWare file system* (NFS). Most environments enable you to optimize the system to avoid additional overhead and to turn off *cached writes*. (Cache writes are additional caching between SQL Server and the drive, which can cause data-integrity problems if the server goes down.) If you use file-system devices, it is critical that you explore these issues to guarantee both performance and data integrity.

## UNIX: Where It All Began

The Sybase SQL Server was first released under UNIX, and continues to be the first operating system (or set of operating systems) for which new releases are developed. Sybase focuses on five primary UNIX flavors when developing new versions, with other flavors of UNIX appearing in a second wave, along with other major platform releases. These are the five mainstream UNIX flavors:

- Sun OS and Solaris (Sun)
- HP/UX (Hewlett-Packard)
- AIX (IBM)
- Ultrix (Digital)
- UNIX System V (AT&T/NCR)

Nearly all hardware vendors in the UNIX arena can tell you about major Sybase applications running on their products. When choosing your hardware platform for a UNIX implementation, your criteria must include performance benchmarks, customer referrals, and internal experience with the UNIX product.

> **WARNING**
>
> Customer referrals are important. The critical issue in client/server architecture (as in all open, multivendor architectures) is the compatibility and supportability of all the

components. Ask vendors for names of others running Sybase on their platforms. Call those users and get detailed configurations: What specific products are you using? How are you using them? Do they work well together? Is each vendor's technical support group aware of the other products you use?

The fact is, there's no way to avoid being a pioneer in at least some part of your work with client/server architecture. You will use at least one new, untested product, or a new version, or a unique combination of products and features. Every implementation is a little different.

The critical point is to know in advance which elements are new or experimental and to make time for testing, experimentation, and even some backtracking if critical elements fall short.

# Windows NT

Windows NT is a portable operating system that runs on a variety of hardware platforms, from small, single-processor PC clones to large, multiprocessor RISC systems. SQL Server ports along with Windows NT to all those platforms, although it probably is even more important to be certain that another organization has tried to make your planned configuration work.

You can use SQL Server for Windows NT exclusively for in-house development. It is inexpensive to implement on an Intel box, and the server also can run other work at the same time. This is the only Intel environment in which SQL Server runs well even when users are doing other work at the same time.

Microsoft also sells a version of SQL Server for Windows NT. For more about that version, see the section in this chapter titled "SQL Server Versions" and its subsection titled "Microsoft SQL Server."

# OS/2

The original version of SQL Server for OS/2 presented an interesting problem. It provided all the features of other versions, but if you tried to do anything else in OS/2 while SQL Server was running, problems in the way that early versions of OS/2 handled multitasking resulted in either extremely poor performance or complete server lockup. It was discouraging.

Preliminary work with the System 10 implementation shows that Sybase has really addressed the OS/2 market with a solid product. You should still be aware of serious performance degradation when running another process on the server while the server is handling queries, however.

Most organizations that have implemented SQL Server on OS/2 chose it because of the following:

- They are 100-percent IBM shops.
- They need the promised integration between OS/2 and their existing mainframes.
- They like the low cost (compared to UNIX).
- They have a fear and loathing of UNIX.

## NetWare

Organizations with thousands of NetWare servers like the fact that the Sybase implementation of SQL Server uses IPX/SPX, meaning that client systems do not have to add another protocol. The proprietary NLM architecture does mean that client/server applications that do more than query a static SQL Server are harder to write, but the server is fairly reliable, provides acceptable performance, and supports a moderate size work group.

> **WARNING**
>
> Do not use the server for file services, print services, or anything else if it's a production SQL Server. Performance will be atrocious.

## Open VMS

For organizations with large networks of VAXs and strong organizational experience with DEC, Sybase on Open VMS might make sense. VMS is a capable multitasking environment, and many of the systems provide good throughput. This environment has proven itself to be reliable and easy to manage and network. On the other hand, it's rare to find any organization interested in buying into a new VAX to run SQL Server.

## SQL Server Versions

We're focusing here on the Sybase SQL Server, which has evolved substantially from its inception. Every once in a while you meet somebody with the impressive bragging rights of having worked with SQL Server since version 1 or 2. Also, every once in a while, you meet somebody with the sad credentials of maintaining a version 2 server. (This is very unusual.) Currently, it is very, very unusual to see a system earlier than 4.2.

# The Sybase SQL Server

Sybase is intended to be a fully operational, on-line transaction processing (OLTP) database. Organizations that implement OLTP systems in SQL Server are understandably nervous about upgrades to the server. Sybase is no different from any other software vendor when it comes to new releases; along with all the fabulous new features come all the fabulous new bugs.

Here are a few of the important Sybase releases you may encounter, along with the important features introduced with the release:

- Version 4.2 (released around 1989) introduced unions.
- Version 4.8 (1990) introduced multiprocessor architecture.
- Version 4.9x (1992) introduced stable, symmetric multiprocessing, and some maintenance features were introduced in anticipation of System 10.
- System 10 (1993) introduced server cursors, auditing, improved security, better maintenance features, and a backup server.

> **NOTE**
>
> What's with those version numbers—4.1, 4.2, 4.8, 4.9, System 10? The rumor is that Sybase was preparing for the big release of System 5 after version 4.9. (According to a Sybase engineer, it even says it's version 5 in the code!) Oracle released their version 7, however, and the rest is history.

Microsoft and Sybase cooperated for years on the SQL Server product line. Microsoft was responsible for Intel versions of the software (OS/2 and later Win NT); Sybase handled everything else. The products were based on the same core code and their architectures were identical. Microsoft releases typically trailed Sybase releases by about six months. From the standpoint of developers and users, it was ideal: there was a straightforward path from less expensive, less capable servers from Microsoft to more expensive, fire-breathing systems from Sybase.

Things got confusing when Sybase started selling an NLM version, because this armed Novell to compete with Microsoft in certain circumstances. It all fell apart in early 1994 when Sybase and Microsoft agreed to disagree. Microsoft has announced that it will remain compatible with the 4.2/4.8 release of SQL Server, but that it will feel free to provide enhancements to that product.

Sybase has already introduced a slew of enhancements, including new keywords and subtle variations from the 4.2/4.8 platform. The differences between the Microsoft and Sybase products will continue to grow.

Which version is right for you? That call is getting harder with the release of Windows NT on high-end RISC boxes. Microsoft has rewritten some of the multitasking and multiprocessing code in the SQL Server to take better advantage of the multithreading architecture of Windows NT. On the Intel platform, there have been dramatic performance improvements with NT over Sybase on the same platform; with limited memory and CPU resources, Microsoft can provide startlingly good performance. As of this writing, however, Sybase continues to offer a more mature product, with better features and solid performance across a range of platforms.

Which company will ultimately win? Never bet against Microsoft in this industry. It remains in both companies' best interests to continue to maintain compatibility. Both companies probably will continue to benefit so long as the uneasy cease-fire between them can hold.

# Server Installation

All the activities in this section vary dramatically from platform to platform. The installation routines and utilities vary, and the methods of identifying the server and defining its environment are completely different among the various implementations of SQL Server. Starting and stopping the server sometimes is performed by typing a command, sometimes by clicking an icon.

On UNIX platforms, you typically have to type a series of commands at the console. In Windows NT, you execute a set-up program and follow the onscreen instructions.

Nevertheless, the fundamental installation procedures and the information you must provide are fairly similar.

When you install an SQL Server, you follow the explicit instructions provided in the installation guide for your server.

### WARNING

The instructions should indicate the version of SQL Server provided, as well as the expected version of the operating system you are using. If your version of SQL Server or the operating system is different from the version specified by the installation manual, it is likely that some of the information in the manual is incorrect.

It's possible that you might install the 4.2.2 version of SQL Server on NetWare version 3.12, and have documentation for a 3.11 version of NetWare. Certain very specific instructions will be incorrect, and others unnecessary and misleading.

Sometimes you can find installation supplements, or some other document that helps you determine in what way your environment differs from the expected environment.

Just keep in mind that SQL Server places extreme demands on operating systems. There often are patches, utility updates, or other materials that enable the operating system to function properly. The best way to ensure smooth installation and operation is to call Sybase to get information about patches, releases, and other fixes to make your system work. It's also helpful to find another user with exactly your set of product releases, and find out what that user went through to accomplish an installation. A good place to find these users is in the Sybase Forum (GO SYBASE) on CompuServe. It is an excellent arena for posing questions, accessing information, and communicating with other Sybase users. This forum is monitored by Sybase employees and can be an alternative source of technical or general information. You can also access America Online, the usenet newsgroups on the Internet, and various WWW sites, including Sybase's.

Server installation consists of four steps: understanding o/s access, gathering information, copying files, and installing the software.

# Operating System User Privileges

Sybase needs access to specific user privileges in each operating system environment. Your documentation will tell you the user requirements for your server. On UNIX, you may be able to install SQL Server as the root, but you inevitably will have problems, and ultimately will have to rerun the entire installation as sybase. Create the sybase user and log in as sybase to run the installation.

On most other platforms (NT and NetWare, for example), SQL Server runs as a process owned by the administrative login (SUPERVISOR in NetWare, administrator in NT). The installation directories are owned by the administrative login.

# Filling Out the Forms

When you run the installation program, the server asks whether you have completed all the forms before beginning installation. If you answer "No," the server exits the installation program. (The typical next step is to answer "Yes" without filling in the forms.)

The installation program is going to ask you for some detailed information about your server. If you are the system administrator (sa) for the operating system where you are installing the SQL Server, go ahead and run without filling in the forms. Chances are good that you will know the answers as the questions arise.

> **NOTE**
>
> When I first installed SQL Server on HP/UX, I knew absolutely nothing about HP UNIX, or about the specific system on which I was running. My first step was to find someone who really knew UNIX well (and had root authorization) and could help me get the answers I needed. It's normal and efficient to seek help in defining the values you need to complete the installation.

## SQL Server Installation Path

Installation copies a number of files to the operating system file system, including the installation program, the server software itself, installation scripts, and utility files. You must tell the server where this installation path is in your directory structure.

In UNIX, you have to grant the full set of rights to the directory to the sybase user. On other platforms, the administrator should have sufficient privileges to run the installation. (Later, you may choose to grant users access to the utility programs, the error log, or other parts of the server environment that they might find helpful.)

## Master Device Location and Size

The next value required by the server is a location and size for the master device. Under UNIX, the master device can be mapped to a file or raw device; in Open VMS, this is a foreign device. Generally, mapping to a raw device provides better integrity and performance. On all other platforms, the master device is a file in the file system.

Mirror the master device. (For more information on how to do this, see Chapter 25, "Defining Physical and Mirror Devices.") You may have to make a provision for a small raw partition to mirror the master device under UNIX. If you are using a file system, the master device probably should be set apart from the other devices, in its own directory. Secure the directory to prevent other users from stumbling on the master device. Name the file master.dev, or something similar that makes its purpose unmistakable.

> **TIP**
>
> How large should the master device be? It's really hard to expand the master device, so it has to be large enough for everything that will ever be installed on the device.
>
> Typically, the only databases residing on the master device are master, model, and the first 2MB of tempdb. The model database, unless you expand it, also is 2MB. How large will the master database grow? The answer depends on your version of SQL Server.

The growth of the master database was a serious problem prior to the release of System 10. In earlier versions, the system stored procedures were stored in the master database. With each release, there were more and larger stored procedures, and master was stretched to its absolute capacity. There was no way to keep the size of the master database under control.

With System 10, Sybase has moved all the system stored procedures into a separate database, sybsystemprocs, which you should almost always install separately on its own device. This will avoid the hassle of having to move sybsystemprocs once you begin to run out of space in the master device. The contention for space in the master database has been resolved.

The official minimum size of the master device is 17MB. The master device should be no smaller than 30MB, and it certainly doesn't have to be larger than 40MB unless you're planning to write a lot of large, complex system-stored procedures in a pre–System 10 server (or if the sybsystemprocs database is created on the master device).

## Server Name

The default server name is SYBASE. This name is appropriate only for the first server you install on your hardware. Many sites have several servers installed, but they usually are on their own, dedicated hardware. Decide on a distinct server name now (see Chapter 34, "Defining Systems Administration and Naming Standards," for recommendations). The name can be no longer than 30 characters, although a shorter name probably is easier to type and remember. The name is installed in the interfaces file for your server.

## Port Number or Named Pipe

Depending on your network protocol (TCP/IP, IPX/SPX, or Named Pipes), you must decide on a listening port within the server. Processes that communicate with SQL Server send a message to the host operating system network address. The message is keyed with the internal address of the SQL Server process. The address that you establish is used by every client and every server having to communicate with this SQL Server.

In the Named Pipes protocol, the internal address of the process is a pipe name—usually, the following:

`\\SERVERNAME\PIPE\SQL\QUERY`

where *SERVERNAME* is the published name of the host computer.

In IPX/SPX, the server is assigned a standard port address within NetWare. There is a default value (normally, 0x08bd) included with the server installation. If that value already is assigned,

Sybase provides several other values you can try. (It's unlikely that you will encounter any other process with that identifier. Novell has assigned that number to Sybase for SQL Server processes, and you will never find two SQL Servers running on a single NetWare Server.)

In TCP/IP you identify a single integer port address within the server. For UNIX installations, contact an administrator for a value to use.

> **TIP**
>
> If you are installing many SQL Servers at your organization, it's helpful to install Sybase with the same port address everywhere, for the sake of consistency. If you choose not to standardize port addresses, publish port addresses to help those who do workstation setup and administration.
>
> You can use 5000, for example, unless that number is used. If you are installing several SQL Servers on the same hardware, increment this number by 100 for each new server. (Check with the administrator to ensure that each value is available.)

## *sybsystemprocs* Size and Path

The sybsystemprocs database (System 10 versions only) contains the system stored procedures. The database has to be at least 10MB, although the rate of growth of Sybase stored procedures from version to version indicates that 20MB may be more appropriate. You must provide a name and location for the device where sybsystemsprocs should be stored.

## Backup Server Name

You must provide a name and port address for the backup server as well. You must install a local backup server on the system where the SQL Server is to run. Even if the actual tape device to which the data is recorded is attached to a remote server, you still must install a local backup server to perform any database or transaction dump. In UNIX, the default name is SYB_BACKUP, which should be satisfactory.

## File Transfer

On UNIX servers, the first step of the installation is to load the installation program from the tape. On other systems, the installation program is directly executable from the SQL Server distribution disk or CD-ROM.

When installing on UNIX, log in as the sybase user so that all the files transferred from the tape will have the correct ownership. Follow your installation instructions closely to unload the installation files from the tape.

# Installation

The installation program has several names, depending on the platform. On UNIX platforms, it normally is called sybinit, although sybconfig or sybinstall sometimes are used, especially in earlier versions of the server. On NetWare, the program is called setup.nlm.

The Windows NT install program is named setup.exe.

The installation program prompts you for the information you recorded in Step 0. After you provide this information, it executes the following:

- Initializes the master device
- Creates four databases (three prior to System 10)
- Runs installmaster to set up the master database (or sybsystemprocs database in System 10)
- Runs installmodel (to set up the model database)
- Starts the server
- Starts the backup server, if installed
- Sets up the system tables (master, model, and sybsystemprocs) in each of the installed databases

When the installation step is complete, the server is up and running.

# Server Directories

The installation program copies several files into directories beneath the Sybase directory. The following sections explore some of the important files.

## The Sybase Root Directory

The Sybase root directory is the reference point for the other directories that follow. One important file in this root directory is the interfaces file. It lists the names and access paths for the server and backup server. You can run sybinit to add additional servers to the interfaces file, or you can add them manually.

> **TIP**
>
> Maintain a single interfaces file with a listing of all the servers in your organization. Copy the file to all your servers to simplify maintenance. (If you do not want the users on a particular server to be capable of accessing certain servers, remove those entries from the file.)

# The install Directory

The install directory contains files commonly used to start the server, as well as a file to house messages from the SQL Server. The contents of the install directory are as follows:

| | |
|---|---|
| startserver (or sqlsrvr) | The normal program for starting the server. |
| runserver | A file with detailed information about how to start a server. There probably are two runserver files in the install directory: one for the server, one for the backup server. The SQL Server runserver file invokes the dataserver executable; the backup server runserver file invokes the backupserver executable. |
| errorlog | The file in which the server records important changes to the server's configuration, and lists critical error messages. The errorlog file can be installed in a different directory, be given a different name, or both, if desired. The -e parameter to the dataserver executable dictates the name and location. (Note: although dataserver can be called from the command line, it normally is called from the runserver file. This is where you should verify the correct directory and name of the errorlog file.) |

# The bin Directory

The following are tools installed in the bin directory.

| | |
|---|---|
| isql | An interactive utility used to submit queries to the server and read results |
| bcp | The high-speed data-load utility |
| buildmaster | Provides access to less-used configuration options; critical if you must restore the master database |
| defncopy | Enables you to export the definition of Sybase objects from the server |
| dataserver | The executable used to invoke an SQL Server |
| backupserver | The executable used to invoke a backup server |

# The scripts Directory

The scripts directory provides SQL scripts that can be executed with the isql utility. The following are three of the install scripts:

| | |
|---|---|
| `installmaster` | Installs the `master` database during installation |
| `installmodel` | Installs the `model` database during installation |
| `installpubs2` | Optional; installs the `pubs2` database during installation or later |

# Backup Server Installation (System 10)

The installation of the backup server is optional during normal installation, but it's a good idea to go ahead and install a backup server when you install SQL Server. Otherwise, you later will have to rerun the installation program to enable the server to be able to backup.

> **NOTE**
>
> Remember, all backups for System 10 and later require a local backup server, whether you are backing up locally (to a locally connected tape drive or disk file) or remotely (to a tape drive or disk file on another system on your network).

To install the backup server, you must specify a name for the backup server and a listening port. (See the earlier section titled "Port Number or Named Pipe.") By default, the name of the backup server is SYB_BACKUP in UNIX, Novell, and Open VMS. In Windows NT, the name used is the same as the SQL Server name, with an extension of _BS. For example, if the server name is ACCOUNTING, the backup server name is ACCOUNTING_BS.

## Server Environmental Values

Although the implementation varies from platform to platform, SQL Server always has to be able to find mappings to other servers, including the backup server. Environmental values help SQL Server find a list of servers and addresses (usually stored in an interfaces file on UNIX systems), and enable it to identify itself within that list. Those same values are used to enable client programs to map to servers as well. (See the section titled "Client Installation," later in this chapter, for more on this topic.)

# Server Startup, Login, and Shutdown

Once the server is installed, there are a few activities you'll perform frequently in the normal use of SQL Server. You'll have to be able to start the server, log in to the server once it is up and running, and shut down the server.

# Starting the Server

Your installation manual gives the name of the server startup program. Here are the startup methods for four major platforms:

| Platform | Startup Method(s) |
|---|---|
| UNIX (logged in as sybase user) | `startserver -f <run_servername>` |
| NetWare | `load sqlsrvr` |
| Windows NT | `sybase.bat` |
| Open VMS | `startserver/server = <servername>` |

In the UNIX and Window NT cases, you call an operating system batch or script file from the operating system prompt. You also can execute the literal statements that are in the named script file. For example, in the case of Windows NT, the sybase.bat batch file provides the parameters required to start a server on any platform:

```
d:\SQL10\bin\sqlsrvr.exe -dd:\SQL10\data\master.dat -sSYBASE
        -ed:\SQL10\install\errorlog -id:\SQL10\ini -Md:\SQL10
```

> **NOTE**
>
> The command does not fit on one line, but you must type it on a single line.

The components of the `startup` command are as follows:

- The SQL Server executable (sqlsrvr.exe)
- The name and location for the master device (`-dd:\SQL10\data\master.dat`)
- The name of the server (`-sSYBASE`)
- The name and location of the errorlog (`-ed:\SQL10\install\errorlog`)
- The location of the interfaces file (`-id:\SQL10\ini`)
- The location of the SYBASE directory (`-Md:\SQL10`)

## Automatic Startup

In most environments, you can automatically execute the startup program as part of the operating system startup procedure. For example, you can insert the `load sqlsrvr` statement into the AUTOEXEC.NCF in NetWare, or insert each of the explicit statements in the runserver file in the automatic startup file in UNIX. (In Windows NT, use the Control Panel Services Manager to set the Sybase SQL Server to automatic startup.)

There are three potential problems with automatic startup:

- On UNIX servers, the SQL Server process must be started by the sybase user, not the root user. Because the root user is running the startup procedure, you must su (in UNIX, swap user) to sybase during startup in order to make the process start properly.

- On some servers, the network may not be completely started before SQL Server attempts to access it. If that happens, the SQL Server process fails to start.

- If the SYBASE process tries to start up before drives are really available (for example, if an external drive array takes a minute or two to power up), the automatic startup may try to access the drives too early. If that happens, any databases on those drives are marked as suspect, and you must remove that flag by directly modifying the sysdatabases table and restarting SQL Server. (See Chapter 30, "Configuring and Tuning SQL Server," on enabling updates.)

Obviously, you don't get much benefit from an automatic start if more than half the time you have to shut down and restart the server manually. If you experience this problem, you have a couple of options.

First, you can always start the server manually. However, although it's no problem to execute the startserver statement manually in the middle of a weekday afternoon, answering a page in the middle of a weekend night after a power interruption can be irritating.

Second, you can establish a protocol for starting the drives first and enabling them to warm up for thirty seconds before starting the server. This is useful, but also may not work in an automated environment.

Third, and probably best, start SQL Server last of all services, guaranteeing the most possible time to enable other devices and services to fully install. If necessary, insert a brief delay in the startup; 30 seconds ought to do it in most cases.

## Verifying with *showserver*

On character-driven systems such as UNIX, Open VMS, and NetWare, there is a command-line utility to determine whether SQL Server is running (for example, the UNIX showserver utility returns a list of SQL Server processes). On graphical systems, there is an icon-driven program to display the status of SQL Server, Backup Server, and SQL Monitor.

# Time to Log In!

You've installed the SQL Server. The server is running. It's time to log in, look around, and see what's left to do. You use the isql (interactive SQL) command on the server to log in. (For additional information on isql, see Chapter 14, "Analyzing Query Plans.") Your installation guide should tell you how to start isql if your platform is not listed here:

| Platform | Starting isql |
| --- | --- |
| UNIX (logged in as sybase user) | `isql -Usa -P` |
| NetWare | `load isql -Usa -P` |
| Windows NT | Double-click the isql icon in the SQL Server group. Press Enter when prompted for a password. |
| Open VMS | `isql /username = "sa"` |

> **NOTE**
>
> The only initial, usable login on the server is sa, which has no password upon installation. (See the section titled "Changing Defaults: the Top 10 Items to Address as Soon as You Log In," later in this chapter.)

You must get the capitalization right in the isql statement. Notice that the U means user, and it must be uppercase, but sa is a user name, and it must be lowercase. If the isql command works, within a few seconds you see the standard isql prompt:

```
1>
```

Run sp_who to see a list of connections. Enter these commands (not the numbers—the system provides those):

```
1> sp_who
2> go
```

You should see your own login listed, as well as three or four system connections.

Now log out of SQL Server:

```
1> quit
2> go
```

Congratulations: you have installed SQL Server!

## If the Login Didn't Work

When isql running on the server fails to work, there are a few simple problems to check, based on the error message you receive.

Because SQL Server is case-sensitive, the most common problem in invoking isql is an error in capitalization. Try retyping the isql command, carefully checking how you spell and capitalize each word.

The easiest message to resolve is Login Incorrect or Login Failed. Both of these messages mean that you found the server, but your combination of name and password were entered incorrectly. If you just installed the server, you probably typed something wrong. If you installed the server a while ago, the sa password may have changed, or the sa login may have been disabled. If you really can't get in, make sure the SQL Server process is running. In the worst case, you might have to reinitialize the master database. To do so, run buildmaster -m in UNIX. This is an extreme measure, and likely will require a reload of master!

Another common message is, Unable to Connect: the SQL Server is not available or does not exist. SQL Server probably is not running. Run the showserver command to see the status of SQL Server. If necessary, restart the server and try again.

> **NOTE**
>
> This really is a more difficult message to interpret. Troubleshooting the Unable to connect message is discussed in detail later in the chapter, but most of the issues there relate to proper addressing and network connectivity. When you execute isql from the physical SQL Server and cannot find the server process, the usual problem is that the server process is not started yet.

If you still are stumped, see the "Troubleshooting" section later in this chapter. There may be a useful hint there on how to resolve the problem.

## Shutting Down with *shutdown*

To shut down the server, you (as a systems administrator) execute the SQL statement shutdown after connecting to the server.

> **NOTE**
>
> There is no operating-system command to shut down the SYBASE process gracefully (except for the stop server command in Open VMS). You can kill the SYBASE process with the UNIX kill command (or the equivalent on other platforms), but this is not an orderly shutdown; as far as SQL Server is concerned, it's really no different from pulling the plug out of the wall, and could result in data-integrity problems, especially if you are using file devices. There are times when SQL Server hangs and must be killed from the operating system. Sometimes, the UNIX kill command does nothing, or the hardware itself hangs, requiring you to reboot the hardware.
>
> This situation is not normal and, if it occurs frequently, may indicate a serious problem with your system. Do not consider occasional hangups to be normal,

expected, or acceptable. Contact technical support and report the problem. They may direct you to new patches or versions or help you identify a configuration problem.

The shutdown command instructs the server to

1. Disable all logins except sa.
2. Wait for currently executing transactions and procedures to complete.
3. Checkpoint all databases.
4. Exit the server executable process.

This is an orderly shutdown, which manages data integrity before downing the server.

The shutdown with nowait command shuts everything down immediately, without regard to process status. Transactions are not allowed to continue to completion and are rolled back upon restart. Databases are not checkpointed and must do additional work to recover. This is not considered an orderly shutdown; data integrity is not damaged by a shutdown with nowait.

If you execute the shutdown statement and remain logged in while it proceeds, you lose your connection when the server shuts down. Your application program notifies you of the dropped connection. Other users are not notified until the next time they try to use their connection. To avoid user panic and annoying calls, inform users before executing a shutdown.

Although SQL Server is considered a round-the-clock, 24×7 server, there are some common administrative tasks requiring a server shutdown:

- Changing configuration options. There are a handful of dynamic configuration options that can change while the server is up. Most configuration options require modifications in the allocation of memory or resources that can be made only when the server is restarted.

- Removing aborted transactions from the log. If a client disconnects leaving a noncommitted, non-rolled-back transaction in the log, that transaction may prevent a truncation of the database log. During the database recovery, aborted transactions are marked for rollback, and the server is free to clean up the log.

- Setting server trace flags. Server trace flags enable you to access DBCC and monitoring features. You must set them during server startup. (Sybase Technical Support will instruct you on setting trace flags.)

- Configuring the mirroring of the master device. The mirror parameter must be supplied to the dataserver executable before startup.

- Killing certain user connections. The SQL Server kill statement can kill certain user processes, but other connections (for example, sleeping processes in earlier versions of SQL Server) simply cannot be killed without restarting the server.

# Client Installation

Getting workstations ready for client/server is a big job, and the more workstations there are, the more logistic problems overshadow technical ones. If you have existing workstations that require work before they are ready for SQL Server, you have a more complicated problem in making changes to workstation configurations without impacting current capabilities.

In this section, you look at the Open Client and Open Server implementations to understand how SQL Server provides application programmers with openness, portability, and modularity. You learn the differences between programming in DB-Library and ct-library, and discuss when to implement either one. Finally, you review some of the installation and application issues with some of the major client platforms.

It's important to realize that you must install completely the appropriate Open Client product on your server as well as your client workstations. For example, if you are running a UNIX server with Windows clients, you must install the UNIX Open Client on the server for two reasons:

- You are likely to have to run utilities from the server (isql, bcp). Without Open Client, these tools cannot access the server.

- The server also is capable of accessing other servers. To do that, it maintains hooks to Open Client itself.

## Open Client and Open Server

Sybase provides network transparency, code portability, and modularity with the Open Client and Open Server components of SQL Server. Figure 24.1 shows a single set of application code using Open Client function calls: that code can port easily between Windows and UNIX.

**FIGURE 24.1.**

*ct-library provides code portability to the application developer.*

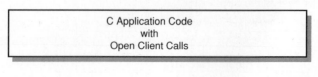

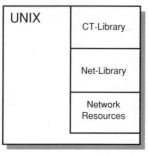

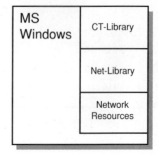

> **NOTE**
>
> Just how portable is SQL Server application code from UNIX to Windows to Macintosh to DOS? SQL Server code is completely portable. The function calls and their parameters are the same. There are fine differences in datatypes between the environments that probably can be handled with varying header files.
>
> The real portability problem comes in the application itself. Anyone who has made the transition from UNIX or DOS to Windows or Macintosh knows that the environments are completely different. So you can speak all you want about code portability; the fact is, you still have some work to do to make your application look even vaguely familiar to an experienced user of the system.

Open Server provides the same measure of code portability and openness as Open Client. Application programmers can write Open Server programs to handle the special needs of client programs.

> **NOTE**
>
> The most interesting Open Server programs can interact directly with real-time devices, such as scientific test equipment, stock tickers, and pagers. Other Open Server applications are able to interact with non-Sybase database sources, including mainframe flat-file databases and other, similar systems.

## DB-Library and ct-Library

Every SQL Server application uses Open Client calls to interact with the server. A typical Open Client application performs the following tasks:

1. Get a pointer to a login structure (a memory-resident record stored as a variable).
2. Set up the login structure.
3. Submit the login structure to a named server to get a pointer to a connection structure.
4. Set up a query in a buffer of the connection structure.
5. Submit the query to the server.
6. Process results sets (processing results rows).
7. Close the connection.

Each numbered item corresponds to a specific C function call (or set of calls).

If you already are running an SQL Server application, or have started to program one using a product such as PowerBuilder, Visual Basic, or Access, you did not see the Open Client function calls. All these products provide a transparent mapping between their own database functions (for example, login to server) and the SQL Server function (steps 1, 2, and 3). Whether it's your product or theirs, however, somewhere along the way, a client application is issuing an explicit function call to Open Client.

The original Open Client interface was called DB-Library, and it still is in use in almost all SQL Server installations. With the release of System 10, Sybase introduced ct-Library to take advantage of newer features of System 10, and to provide a better application architecture. Sybase also released a System 10 version of DB-Library that is able to access some of the advanced features of System 10.

## DB-Library Components

The following two components comprise DB-Library:

- db-lib
- net-lib

db-lib is the set of functions directly accessible to the application, including calls to set up information in the login record (`dbsetluser`), log in (`dbopen`), store a query in the buffer (`dbcmd`), execute the command (`dbsqlexec` or `dbsend`), and process result rows (`dbresults`, `dbnextrow`).

db-lib is implemented differently on different platforms. UNIX and DOS applications call a LIB file in a mapped directory; Windows applications use resources in a dynamic link library (W3DBLIB.DLL for Windows version 3.*X*).

net-lib provides network transparency, as illustrated in Figure 24.2. There typically are several net-libs available for each supported client operating platform. The net-lib receives the name of a Sybase server from DB-Library and transforms that into a full address and port identifier (or named pipe) for network communication. Applications written for DB-Library name only the server; the rest of the network implementation is managed entirely through net-lib.

**FIGURE 24.2.**

*Net-lib provides network transparency to the application developer.*

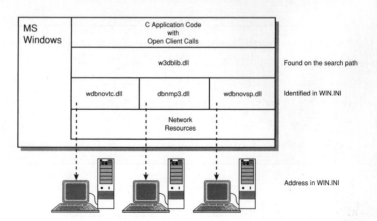

Each net-lib applies to a specific protocol and, if appropriate, a version of that protocol. For example, there is a specific net-lib for Windows for several different versions of TCP/IP (Novell, FTP, Microsoft, and so forth), as well as net-libs for Named Pipes and IPX.

## ct-Library Components

Sybase released ct-Library with System 10. ct-library ultimately will replace DB-Library as the standard method of writing applications to communicate with Sybase SQL Server, although there is no indication yet whether Microsoft SQL Servers will support the advanced features of ct-Library.

ct-Library offers many improvements over DB-Library, mostly in application structure. Sybase also adds substantial improvements in asynchronous architecture and support for server-side cursors within Client-library:

- Client-library is a collection of routines for writing client applications, and provides the same code portability as does DB-Library.
- CS-library (Client/Server library) is a collection of routines for writing both client and server applications. All client-library applications call at least one CS-library function to access a structure stored within CS-library.
- Net-library is a collection of network routines for handling the accessing of a specific network type. Net-library corresponds to net-lib, and provides the same benefit of network transparency to the application programmer.

## DB-Library or ct-Library?

For programmers, the choice of library depends on applications experience and system requirements, so the answer is fairly straightforward. Most programmers are using ct-Library whenever possible. On the other hand, the answer is not completely cut-and-dried for administrators.

The problem is that applications meant to run with DB-Library do not work with ct-Library, and vice versa. You must install the library used by the programmers or referred to by the application. Expect to have to install both DB-Library and net-library until early 1997 (at least).

Remember, the installation depends on your client configuration. Open Client is shipped with an installation manual, which is your best resource. If you have questions about your configuration, contact Sybase or seek help from another user.

Once the installation is complete, you must make certain that all the configuration settings are in place to enable a client to communicate with the server.

# UNIX

UNIX clients use a combination of text files and environmental variables to find a server address. The SYBASE environmental variable points to the location of the SYBASE home directory; this variable should be set up in your .profile or .cshrc file:

```
SYBASE=/home/sybase
```

Stored in the Sybase home directory is the interfaces file, a map to all the Sybase servers on the network. Here is a fragment from an interfaces file:

```
A sample interfaces file
#
SYBASE_1
        query tcp sun-ether rose 5000
        master tcp sun-ether rose 5000
DEVEL
        query tcp sun-ether tulip 5000
        master tcp sun-ether tulip 5000
```

> **WARNING**
>
> Be careful when you modify the interfaces file, if you do. The query and master entries must each be prefaced with a tab character, or DB-Library will interpret the line as a new server name.

The DSQUERY environmental variable identifies a default server entry within the interfaces file. If the user fails to specify a server name when logging in, the application logs in to the server named in DSQUERY.

For example, a user has a SYBASE variable of /home/sybase and a DSQUERY value of Devel. Now the user logs into isql, but does not specify a server name:

```
isql -Ujoey
```

Using this example, the client library identifies the Devel section of the interfaces file and uses the server address provided in the query line for Devel to find port 5000 in a server named tulip, using TCP/IP over Sun's version of Ethernet. To work with the server running on the rose server, the user types this:

```
isql -Ujoey -SSYBASE_1
```

By naming the server at startup, the user overrides the default server name and finds the correct SQL Server.

> **NOTE**
>
> Remember, even if you are using UNIX only as SQL Server and using some other OS for client workstations, you still must install and maintain an Open Client for UNIX clients.

# Windows

Under Windows, you record the names of servers in a text file in the format of a Windows initialization file. With DB-Library, you store server names and addressing schemes in the WIN.INI file (in the Windows directory) under the heading [SQLSERVER]. Figure 24.3 illustrates this.

**FIGURE 24.3.**

*DB-Library uses the WIN.INI section, [SQLSERVER], as a central resource to locate servers.*

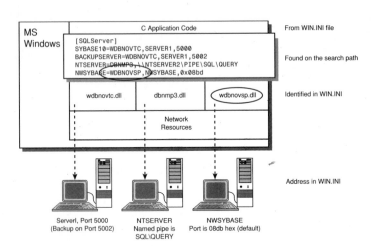

If you have a DSQUERY value listed in the INI file, it is used by default if no server is named. Here is the SQLSERVER section from a sample WIN.INI file:

```
[SQLServer]
DSQUERY=DBNMP3,\\SYB2\PIPE\SQL10\QUERY
BACKUPSERVER=DBNMP3,\\SYBASE_10\PIPE\SQL10\BACKUP
MSSQLV4_2=DBNMP3,\\SYBASE_10\PIPE\SQL\QUERY
```

With ct-Library, server names and addresses reside in the file SQL.INI (in the INI subdirectory within the SYBASE directory). Here is a sample SQL.INI file:

```
[SQLSERVER]
WIN3_QUERY=WNLWNSCK,SYBASE_10,5000
[SQL10NMP]
WIN3_QUERY=WNLNMP,\SYBASE_10\PIPE\SQL10\QUERY
[SQL10IPX]
WIN3_QUERY=WNLNOVSP,SYBASE_10
```

# Macintosh

Recall that Macintosh uses an interfaces file, identical in form and content to the UNIX interfaces file, to map login attempts to servers. The interfaces file is stored in the System folder and can be accessed through the control panel. There is no DSQUERY value, so all logins must specify a server. Macintosh has no isql utility.

# Networking and Connectivity

Let's start with an agreement: if you are not a "networking person," you are going to have to make friends with one pretty soon. Client/server is as dependent on the network as on any other component, and networks are a huge mystery to most Sybase administrators. In this section, you get up-to-speed on some of the important terms and concepts, but you are going to know enough only to be entertaining at cocktail parties, or a little dangerous.

Like most client/server products, SQL Server is open, modular, and flexible about its networking options.

## Network Types

You probably won't have to choose the network type; that decision will have been made by your LAN administrator. Just keep in mind that when you talk network type (Ethernet, Token Ring, or something else) you are talking about hardware: network interface cards in PC clients and servers, network cabling, central hubs, concentrators, routers, and other specialized equipment to improve performance.

The world is made up of three kinds of people: Ethernet people, Token Ring people, and everyone else.

## Ethernet

Ethernet people think you ought to keep Big Brother out of networking. If you want to send a message, see whether anyone's on the line and send your message. If two systems try to send a message at the same time, they cause a collision and both back off for a brief (but random) period. While they are backed off, they jam the network to keep other users not involved in the collision from jumping in front.

Ethernet is a freewheeling approach to networking, wherein moderate numbers of users sending large amounts of data from time to time get outstanding performance. However, performance tends to fall off rapidly if too many users send data too often and generate huge numbers of collisions.

Don't get the wrong idea. Ethernet can support networks of hundreds and thousands of users without problems, but performance under very high load can sometimes be problematic. It really depends on your configuration. With the correct combination of routers to localize traffic, Ethernet is a highly effective and simple network type.

> **TIP**
>
> If you want to impress the network administrator, ask what frame type you are using with Ethernet. (Not that you'll know what to do with that information!)

Ethernet is the standard network type for most UNIX systems. The exception is IBM RS/6000, which also supports Token Ring.

## Token Ring

Token-passing environments are more structured. A token is passed from user to user, with each connection having the chance to send a message. There are no collisions because you never transmit if you don't hold the token. Token Ring is only one implementation of a token-passing environment, but it is by far the most common.

Token Ring provides adequate performance with few users and low volume, but it really shines when there are many users, all transmitting frequently. The lack of collisions provides much steadier and more predictable throughput than Ethernet under load. Token Ring can feel slow when compared to Ethernet.

If your organization uses Token Ring, you may find the implementation easiest if you use OS/2, Windows/NT, NetWare, or AIX (IBM's flavor of UNIX, running on the RS/6000). If you want to use another UNIX system with Token Ring, talk to your hardware salesperson first, then to the Sybase representative or another Sybase customer already using it.

## Network Protocols

Network protocols provide an addressing and data-packaging method for sending information between systems. There are lots of network protocols out there, but only a few major players. The choice of a protocol also probably is not yours, but note that your choice of a server may be closely linked to internal policies about network protocols. Let's look at the primary protocols used to talk to SQL Server, and the implementation issues with each.

Protocols are implemented through software. Often, software to support a standard protocol is provided by the manufacturer of the hardware. Specialized software to support nonstandard protocols may be purchased separately.

# TCP/IP

Terminal Control Protocol/Internet Protocol (TCP/IP) is getting a lot of press nowadays. Just a few years ago, it looked as if TCP/IP's days were numbered, but then lots of people started hooking into the Internet and there was a resurgence of support for this stately, old method of interacting with the world.

TCP/IP requires that you manually assign addresses to each network connection. A classic problem in TCP/IP arises from duplicate addresses. Manage addresses carefully to avoid this error.

TCP/IP grew up on UNIX, so the networking software is part of the standard system. Novell started supporting and routing TCP/IP in the 3.1x versions. (Check to see whether it is included or provided at an additional charge.) Windows NT includes TCP/IP at no additional charge.

On DOS and Windows clients, however, you must find third-party TCP/IP software to enable you to communicate with a TCP/IP network. Some of the TCP/IP software comes from Novell (LAN WorkPlace for DOS), NetManager (Chameleon and Newt), and FTP (PC/TCP).

If you plan to have Macintosh workstations or UNIX servers, TCP/IP is your best bet.

# IPX/SPX

Novell invented Internetwork Packet Exchange/Simple Packet Exchange (IPX/SPX) to provide a simple method of transporting packets quickly across interconnected networks. Today, there are millions of workstations using IPX in existing Novell networks.

Certainly, the capability of communicating using IPX was a major factor in the selection of NetWare-based SQL Servers for many organizations. Changing the network configuration of hundreds and thousands of workstations is not something a LAN administrator does lightly.

IPX is fast and efficient, but support for IPX among UNIX systems still is fairly weak. Windows NT, DOS, and Windows for Workgroups all provide support for IPX right out of the box.

# Named Pipes

Named Pipes enables interprocess communication over networks. It was originally implemented as part of LAN Manager and OS/2, and is the easiest protocol to implement on small Windows NT networks.

Named Pipes is supported on Novell servers, although you usually are better sticking with IPX.

## Others (DecNet, SNA, AppleTalk)

There are other protocols available, but their use in SQL Server systems is rare. If you plan to do something out of the ordinary, remember to find others who have already been successful with your planned combination of pieces.

# Troubleshooting

Client/server works great—once you get it working. Then it works until someone changes something.

Troubleshooting client/server is no different from troubleshooting any other kind of system, except that the vendors are unbelievably non-useful. Why? Because there are simply too many products (and too many combinations of products) for them to be smart about all of them.

You must be single-minded about isolating the problem:

- Is the problem on the server, the client, or the network?
- Is the problem in the workstation application or the operating system?
- Is the problem in the connectivity software or the equipment?

And so forth. We're not going to troubleshoot performance, locking, or other such problems here. Here's the stated problem: "I can't log in." Or, "I can log in, but I can't send a query." Or, "I can log in, but periodically, my connection hangs." This section presents some of the steps you can take to isolate this problem.

## Step 1: Does SQL Server work?

Let's start simple. Run showserver. If the server isn't started, you can't log in. If the server was started but isn't showing up, it may not be able to start. Look at the error log.

## Step 2: Can you access SQL Server from *isql*?

The server is working, so now let's see whether anyone can log in. Remove the network and all the client issues, and try to log in from the server. Log in to the hardware where SQL Server resides and invoke isql. (See how to log into the server using the server-based isql program earlier in this chapter.) If you can't log in, you may be out of maximum connections; the message for this is quite specific.

You also may have a problem in your addressing on the server itself. Remember the port to which you assigned the server when you ran the installation? That's also how your client addresses the server. Look in the interfaces file (or the equivalent) on the server to make sure that the port address listed there is correct. You also may have to set server environmental variables to make this work.

> **TIP**
>
> In UNIX, you should set the environmental variables SYBASE and DSQUERY in your .profile or .cshrc file for your login. If you change these files, you may have to log out and log back in to change your session settings.

At any rate, don't bother trying to get a client process to talk to the server over the network until an `isql` session can communicate with the server locally.

## Step 3: Can you talk to the physical server at all over the network?

If a client is having a problem initiating a SQL Server session, first try to initiate a non-SQL Server connection. If you are using NetWare or Windows NT, try to access the file or print services of the server. Run `slist` in NetWare to see whether the Sybase server is listed. If you are running Windows and Named Pipes, see whether an NT server shows up in your workgroup under File Manager's Disk Connect Network Drive option.

In UNIX, use the TCP/IP `ping` utility. (This is shipped with every TCP/IP toolset; *ping* comes from the sonar method of detecting ships underwater.) The utility sends a packet to a specific address. If a network node is using that address, it returns an acknowledgment packet.

If you can't find, or ping, the server at the operating-system level, you have a network problem. The problem could be a loose or bad cable connection, a bad Ethernet card, out-of-date or incompatible network software, incorrect Ethernet frame types, bad packet sizes—well, you get the idea. This is the part where you call your networking friend and say, "Fix it. It's broken."

Again, don't bother continuing to try to log in to SQL Server until this problem is solved.

## Step 4: Can you ping SQL Server?

The next step is to make certain that you can ping SQL Server. Every Open Client product comes with a `dbping` (or `sybping`, `wsybping`, or `wdbping`) utility to perform at SQL Server level what I just described at the server level.

If you can connect to the physical box, and SQL Server is running, you should be able to connect to SQL Server. Period. If it doesn't work, the problem is in DB-Library or ct-Library and net-library.

The easy solution may be in your interfaces file (or the equivalent) on the workstation. Look for addressing problems or even missing references. The addresses should match what you see in the server interfaces file. If they do not, you almost certainly won't connect.

The worst problems can be with old or incompatible versions of DB-Library and net-library in Windows. The DB-Library program, W3DBLIB.DLL, has gone through dozens of interim releases. It's likely that you have a couple of different versions of DB-Library on each of your workstations, with varying sizes and release dates.

The question is, which DB-Library is being used? Ideally, you should have the same release on each workstation, and it should be the latest release.

> **NOTE**
>
> There has been a case where a single workstation needed access to two different versions of DB-Library to work well with two applications, but that is the exception. Generally, use only one version of DB-Library throughout the organization.

First, inventory all versions of SQL Server. Then test them in order, starting with the most recent version first.

> **NOTE**
>
> Sybase has just begun to talk freely about version control with DB-Library. DBAs have known for a long time about the importance of these versions. There are SQL Server DBAs with a disk having six or seven versions of DB-Library, just in case something new arises.

## Step 5: It worked yesterday—what changed?

This is one of the most perplexing problems you will face. It is especially problematic in Windows.

A Windows workstation worked yesterday, does not work today, but the user swears nothing changed. ("What did you do?" "Nothing." "Are you sure??" "Well, I did install Excel—" Aha!)

Microsoft (like a lot of other vendors) ships DB-Library with many of its products. (Some vendors ship really old, horrible versions.) If the installation program also changes the workstation search path (which, unfortunately, is common), the new DB-Library jumps to the front of the path and sabotages any attempt to find the SQL Server.

## Step 6: Can you log in to SQL Server?

If you can't log in, first check the capitalization and spelling of your name and password. Your SSO (site security officer, in charge of SQL Server security) should be able to give you a new password if that appears to be the problem. If you are the SSO, you have bigger problems.

## Step 7: Does it happen only when the number of users increases?

One of the simplest solutions to occasional server lockups or problems with logins is duplicate client TCP/IP addresses. These conflicts cause the server to go completely berserk, so manage those addresses carefully.

# Changing Defaults: The Top 10 Items to Address as Soon as You Log In

There are some things you should do as soon as you can log in. SQL Server is a great product, but sometimes you have to wonder. Some default settings are just senseless, and you must change them just as soon as you log in as sa.

## Securing System Administrator Access

The system administrator has no password and complete control over the server. You must fix that—pronto. (For more on security, see Chapter 27, "Security and User Administration.")

Prior to System 10, sa privileges were nontransferable, so you merely set a password. Log in as the sa and execute the following command:

```
sp_password null, my_secret
```

With System 10 and later, you put a password on the sa account. Then read about the `sa_role` and `sso_role` and grant those roles to actual logins for named administrators. When those roles are set up, disable the sa account.

## Turning Off the Master Device Default Status

If you don't change this value, you can mistakenly install user databases on the master device. Ultimately, this could mean a painful database recovery if you have to reinitialize the master device, and you may have to free up the space later to make additional room for the master database.

To turn this value off, use the following:

```
sp_diskdefault master, defaultoff
```

For more on default disks, see Chapter 27.

When you back up to `diskdump`, the backup is amazingly fast and equally fruitless. Nothing is backed up because there is no physical device attached. To avoid tragic mistakes, remove the `diskdump` device:

```
sp_dropdevice diskdump
```

# Increasing the Size of *tempdb*

You probably don't know how large tempdb will have to be yet, but 2MB certainly won't be enough. Use `disk init` to set up a logical device for `tempdb` (see Chapter 27) and alter the database to extend `tempdb` onto the new device (see Chapter 26, "Defining, Altering, and Maintaining Databases and Logs"). For now, 20MB might be a good place to start.

# Naming the Server

Although installation records the name of the server in the interfaces file, it might not set that name up in the sysservers table (you should do this if you are using remote access):

```
sp_addserver GEORGE, local
```

Other settings to enable remote server management are reviewed in Chapter 33, "Remote Server Management." You must set up remote servers to enable backups.

# Setting Obvious Configuration Settings

In Chapter 32, you review the configuration and tuning settings in detail, but here are three values that always are wrong:

- Open databases
- Memory
- User connections

Databases don't consume much server memory, so use the following to set this value near the maximum number of databases you expect to create on the server, with additional room for `master`, `model`, `tempdb`, and `sybsystemprocs`:

```
sp_configure "open databases", 20
 go
```

The memory setting probably has to be changed. The correct value depends on your server. Don't forget that memory is specified in 2KB pages (10240 = 20MB).

Set connections as low as reasonable because connections do consume memory (about 50KB each in System 10). Use the following:

```
sp_configure "user connections", 25
```

# Setting Up the Model Database Objects, Users, and Datatypes

You may want to set up the model database with all the objects (rules, defaults), users (guest, others) and user-defined datatypes you will want in every database on this server. This is optional.

If this is the first server in your organization, it is really unlikely that you have made any of these decisions yet. If you have other servers, you may already have a set of standards. Make certain you create everything in model before you create your first user database. Otherwise, you must copy everything manually into both model and the user database(s) later on.

## Installing the *pubs2* Database

The pubs2 database is provided with every server, and you should install it on most servers. pubs2 contains sample tables, views, and data that you can query to observe how the SQL works, or how to implement special objects or concepts. This also is optional. All of the examples in the Sybase documentation—and in most articles you read—use pubs2 objects.

## Installing the *sybsyntax* Database

SQL Server can provide help on Transact-SQL syntax with the sp_syntax stored procedure. Detailed help and syntax information is stored in the optional system database, sybsyntax, which you install with a script in the scripts directory; the script name depends on your operating system. This also is optional. To install the sybsyntax database in Windows NT, use the following:

```
isql -Usa -iinssyndb -oinssyndb.out
```

> **TIP**
>
> You may want to modify the pubs2 and sybsyntax scripts slightly to change the device where the database is installed. Otherwise, the database will be installed on your default device (which should not be the master device). For more on devices, see Chapter 4.

# Summary

If you have already decided on the SQL Server, you still must find all the pieces to make it work. Think of client/server as a scavenger hunt. One medium-size client eventually bought more than 100 products from more than 40 vendors to build a client/server system.

Your client/server installation will depend on your ability to find high-quality components and knit them together into a seamless system. It's not a one-day job; it's a continuous process of building a reliable, functional, simple system.

Use the Checklist at the end of this chapter to make sure you have addressed all of the major points covered in this chapter.

# Checklist

Deciding on Your SQL Server Environment

✓ Server operating system (UNIX, NetWare, NT, OS/2, Open VMS)

✓ Server vendor and configuration (IBM, Sun, HP, Compaq, DEC, and so on)

✓ Network type (Ethernet, Token Ring)

✓ Network protocol (TCP/IP, IPX, Named Pipes)

✓ Network operating system (NetWare, UNIX, NT, VINES)

✓ Client workstation operating system (UNIX, OS/2, DOS, Windows, Macintosh)

✓ Client workstation configuration (CPU, Speed, RAM, and so on)

✓ Client development and reporting products (PowerBuilder, Visual Basic, C++, Forest & Trees, ReportSmith, Clear Access, and so on)

✓ Server administration tools (Aurora)

✓ Network administration tools

# Defining Physical and Mirror Devices

# 25

The server is installed. Now what? In order for the server to be useful, you must be able to create and load user databases. On a Sybase SQL Server, you must first define the physical area that is to be used for the databases; you do this with the disk init statement. Figure 25.1 illustrates this.

**FIGURE 25.1.**

*You must set up devices before setting up databases.*

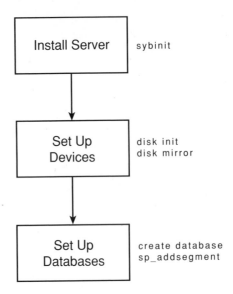

In this chapter, you explore device mirroring at the software level. When you mirror devices, Sybase keeps an exact copy of each used page from one device on another that you specify. You set up mirroring with the disk mirror statement. You also compare advantages and disadvantages of hardware-level mirroring, software-level mirroring, and RAID (Redundant Array of Inexpensive(!) Devices) devices.

# Disk Initialization with *disk init*

Chapter 26, "Defining, Altering, and Maintaining Databases and Logs," discusses database creation and configuration. Before you can set up databases, Sybase has to map logical device names to physical disk resources. The logical names you assign here (device names) are used again at database creation (and segment placement) time.

> **NOTE**
>
> Upon server installation, you will have a device initialized to house the `master`, `model`, `tempdb`, and (optionally) `sybsystemprocs` databases. The logical name of this device varies from platform to platform, but some common names are `master` and `the_master_device`. Although you can create user databases on this device, it is strongly recommended that you use this device only for these three (or four) named databases, especially for production servers.

Several databases can reside on a single physical device, and storage for a single database may span many devices. Also, a single physical disk can contain several devices. Figure 25.2 illustrates the many-to-many relationship between devices and databases (discussed at length later in this chapter).

**FIGURE 25.2.**

*A physical device is defined to Sybase as a logical device, on which may reside no, one, or many databases. A database can span several physical devices.*

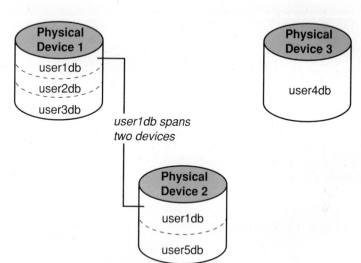

The `disk init` statement provides the server with a method of mapping databases to physical drives. You will use databases to contain (that is, to provide a context for) data objects such as tables, indexes, and stored procedures.

> **NOTE**
>
> Because `disk init` is used only when defining physical resources to the server, it's easy to forget the syntax. If you are unsure, look it up rather than guess at it.
>
> When working with the parameters, remember that the tricky parts are getting the physical name right, making sure the `vdevno` is unique on the server, and stating the size parameter in pages (not megabytes).

# Syntax

```
disk init
name = 'logical_name_of_device',
physname= 'os_location_of_device',
vdevno= virtual_device_number,
size=size_of_device_in_pages
[, vstart = virtual_address, cntrltype= controller_number]
[, contiguous]
```

# Parameters

The first parameter for disk init is the logical name:

```
name = 'logical_name_of_device',
```

The *logical name* of the device is the name you use to refer to the device when creating or altering a database on it, mirroring it, or using the sp_diskdefault command to make it a default disk for database creation. (Mirroring and the use of sp_diskdefault are covered later in this chapter.)

Device names must be unique within a Sybase SQL Server. Limitations on device names are the same as with any other Sybase SQL Server object: the name must be unique among devices and 30 characters in length, with no spaces or punctuation (for example, data_device, log_device, index_device). Don't forget that the server treats device names (like other meaningful identifiers) as case-sensitive.

The second parameter is the physical name:

```
physname = 'os_location_of_device',
```

The *physical name* of the device is its actual location within the operating system. The address here may be a raw partition (UNIX) or foreign disk (Open VMS), a file system name, or an address of some other type of device. Raw-partition and file-system devices are discussed later in this chapter.

> **NOTE**
>
> Until recently, the Sybase SQL Server used only disk devices. Third-party vendors created other media addressable by Sybase, including optical disk jukeboxes (for archival purposes) and solid-state disk (memory) devices.

The third parameter of disk init is the virtual device number:

```
vdevno= virtual_device_number,
```

The *virtual device number* is a unique identifier used by SQL Server to identify unique page numbers. (This is the high-order byte of an address; hence, the 255-device limitation on the servers.) These addresses are used to help map the many-to-many relationship between the system tables, sysdevices, sysusages, and sysdatabases.

The virtual device number must be less than the devices parameter in the sysconfigures system table. If, for example, you configure devices to 10, as follows, the device number must be 9 or less:

```
sp_configure "devices", 10
```

Device numbering begins with 0, and device 0 is set at installation time to be the master device.

> **TIP**
>
> Memory is assigned for devices at server startup. This means that if you configure for 255 devices, memory is allocated for 255 devices, even if you use only two. Devices normally require around 0.5KB of memory (which is not terribly significant). However, on certain Sybase platforms, you can externalize your I/O devices. This requires a process (a thread) that normally requires 50KB of memory: 100 times as much! If this is the case, over-configuring the number of devices can be a significant waste of memory—20 devices would require 1MB of memory—which could be better used for cache. (See Chapter 30, "Configuring and Tuning the SQL Server," for more about this.)
>
> If you must add more devices, change the devices parameter with sp_configure, then restart the server. Note that the server does not free up dropped virtual device numbers until the server is restarted. This applies even to many failed disk init statements. You may have to restart the server to free up a virtual device number after disk init fails.

The fourth parameter is the size, which is the size of the device in pages:

```
size=size_of_device_in_pages
```

(A page is 2KB on all platforms except Stratus, where it is 4KB.) It also has been rumored that the page size will be variable in the future.

> **TIP**
>
> Sybase generally is excellent at performance, throughput, and a host of other things, but leaves much to be desired in its consistency with administration commands. Sometimes turning flags on means setting them to 1; sometimes it means setting them to true, sometimes it means setting them to defaulton, and so forth.

In this case, note that size is in pages. At installation time, depending on version and platform, you may have been prompted for the size of your master device in megabytes, pages, or sectors. When you create a database, the sizes are in megabytes.

If you are unsure about the units, then you should refer to your manual. There is a reference card in the back of this manual to help you figure out what SQL Server is looking for in many situations.

The sixth line of `disk init` specifies these parameters:

```
[, vstart = virtual_address, cntrltype= controller_number]
```

It is unusual to have to specify this set of parameters; they default to zero. Leave them alone unless directed by Sybase Technical Support.

The final option is the following:

```
[, contiguous]
```

This option (in Open VMS only) is used to enable software mirroring of a disk file.

The following example of `disk init` creates a raw partition device in the UNIX environment:

```
disk init
name = 'data_device_1',
physname = '/dev/rsd03',
vdevno=3,
size = 512000
```

In this example, the `disk init` statement creates a device with a logical name of `'data_device_1'`. The device is mapped to physical location `'/dev/rsd03'` (which is likely to be a raw partition, but this is something that you would have to verify at the operating-system level). The virtual device number is 3, and its size is 1GB (= 512000 × 2KB).

How long does `disk init` take? That varies with your version of SQL Server. At one point in its evolution, `disk init` would zero out every page and could take hours. With more recent releases of the server, a `disk init` of 2GB takes only a couple of minutes.

**NOTE**

In the case of many SQL Server commands (`disk init` is one of these), no news turns out to be good news. If there is an error with a `disk init` statement, you hear about it. If the command appears to take a few seconds and there is no error, it probably worked. Just run `sp_helpdevice` to make sure. (See an example later in this chapter.)

After a while, you get used to it. For now, just make a note: if you don't get an error message, it probably worked.

# Raw Partition and File System Devices

What is the difference between a raw partition and an operating-system file—besides the fact that raw partitions are more difficult to create?

With a file system, when you write a page, SQL Server instructs the operating system to write a page. Figure 25.3 illustrates the relationship between SQL Server and a file system device.

**FIGURE 25.3.**

*When SQL Server requests data from a file system device, the request must pass through the operating system's I/O process.*

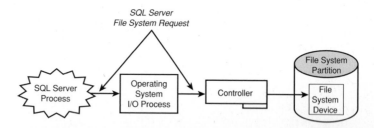

**FIGURE 25.4.**

*SQL Server requests from a device on a raw partition go directly to the controller.*

With a raw partition, SQL Server instructs the controller to write a page. Figure 25.4 illustrates the relationship between SQL Server and a raw partition.

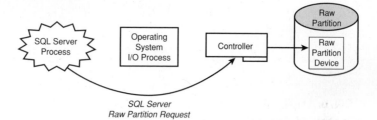

In addition to the overhead and performance penalty of writing through the OS, the use of a file system device introduces a level of risk in the SQL Server commit process. The problem is that operating systems cache I/O (both reads and writes in some cases) for efficiency. This would be fine if your only concern was speed, and you didn't care about losing data. But for writes, you have the following scenario:

>   Sybase: Here, write this page.
>
>   [Operating System writes the page to cache.]
>
>   Operating System: OK. It's written.
>
>   [Is it really written? Not necessarily.]
>
>   Sybase: Thank you.

Before the operating system has the chance to write from its internal cache to a disk device, any number of catastrophic events could occur. The OS could crash, there could be a power surge or blackout, or SQL Server itself could come down. When SQL Server comes back up, the page will not have been written by the operating system.

For a single page, this problem may be surmountable. But what happens when thousands of pages are written to the operating system, and the OS manages to write only some of these before a crash? There is no guarantee that they were written to disk in the order that Sybase requested, or that that would help anyway.

Referential integrity probably is lost and, if the wrong pages were lost, data could be orphaned or destroyed.

> **NOTE**
>
> Oddly, the most common problem in using file systems is index corruption.

Use your operating system's equivalent of a raw partition, if it's available. It's safer in the long run, and you probably will get better performance.

> **WARNING**
>
> Be sure to use an appropriate partition on UNIX. If you use the c partition (meaning the whole disk), most versions of the server overwrite the UNIX disk label (partition a), reinitializing the disk. When the server goes down and then comes back up, the disk will be unaddressable.

If you still are determined to use a disk file as your device, you must meet two criteria:

- The file must not already exist. (It will be created by the disk init process.)
- The file must be writable by the process that is running SQL Server. This means that if you started the server while logged in as the sybase user, as you normally would, the sybase user would have to have write permission in the directory, and file permission on the file after creation. It is irrelevant (and probably a bad security idea) to enable access to the file at the operating system level to any user other than sybase or any process other than the SQL Server dataserver process (including the sa who issued the disk init command!).

In the next example, a file system disk of 40MB (20,480 pages) is created on a UNIX file system. A file of 40MB is created during initialization and an entry is made in the sysdevices system table:

```
disk init
name = 'data_device_2',
physname = '/home/user/sybase/diskfile/data_dev1.dat',
vdevno=4,
size = 20480
```

**NOTE**

Errors from file system `disk init` statements normally are not very descriptive, for example:

```
Error 5123: DISK INIT encountered an error while attempting to open/create the
physical file. Please consult the SQL Server errorlog (in the SQL Server boot
directory) for more details.
```

When you do consult the errorlog, you usually find one of three errors:

- The directory or filename is invalid.
- The file already exists.
- There is not enough space to create the file.

Here are some sample errorlog entries after a `disk init` error:

```
94/10/29 13:26:30.25 kernel   udcreate: Operating system error 112
(There is not enough space on the disk.) encountered

94/10/29 13:26:38.61 kernel   udcreate: Operating system error 80
(The file exists.) encountered
```

Normally, you can delete a physical file that was created during a failed `disk init`. If you can't delete it, SQL Server failed to release the locks on the file. To delete the file and reclaim the space, you may have to cycle the server and try again. Before doing that, make absolutely certain that the `disk init` didn't actually work. You may be trying to delete a valid device!

# Effects of *disk init*

The `disk init` command can be performed only by the sa or by a login with the sa_role. After the disk initialization is complete, the space described by the physical address is available to SQL Server for storage, and a row is added to the `sysdevices` table in the master database.

Figure 25.5 shows the contents of a small `sysdevices` table (use `select * from sysdevices`).

The `sysdevices` table contains one row for each device that the server can access. (*Devices* include disks for data storage, and tape and file devices for backups.) Relevant columns in `sysdevices` include the name of the device (and its mirror, if it has one—you learn about that later), device status, and page range. Can you find the virtual device number? It's actually the high-order byte of the `low` column.

The status is a bitmap describing what the device is used for and what options have been set (if any). Table 25.1 provides the layout of the status byte.

**FIGURE 25.5.**

*The contents of the* sysdevices *table in an Aurora Utilities window.*

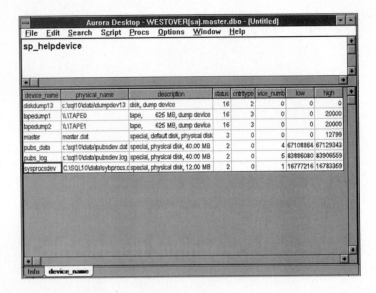

**Table 25.1. Bitmap values for the** status **column of** sysdevices**.**

| Decimal | Hex | Description |
|---------|-------|-----------------------------|
| 1 | 0x01 | Default disk |
| 2 | 0x02 | Physical disk |
| 4 | 0x04 | Logical disk |
| 8 | 0x08 | Skip header |
| 16 | 0x10 | Dump device |
| 32 | 0x20 | Serial writes |
| 64 | 0x40 | Device mirrored |
| 128 | 0x80 | Reads mirrored |
| 256 | 0x100 | Secondary mirror side only |
| 512 | 0x200 | Mirror enabled |

For instance, the status of the master device is 3 (= binary 00000011), which corresponds to "database device" and "default disk" (1 + 2 = 3).

By far the easiest way of decoding the status bit and virtual device number is to use the system stored procedure sp_helpdevice.

Here is the syntax of sp_helpdevice:

```
sp_helpdevice [<logical_device_name>]
```

You can use `sp_helpdevice` without parameters to get a list of defined devices. Figure 25.6 shows two devices for data storage (`master` and `data_device_2`):

**FIGURE 25.6.**

*The* `master` *and* `data_device_2` *devices in an Aurora Utilities window.*

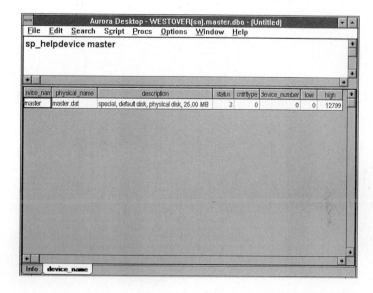

Pass `sp_helpdevice` the name of the disk device to get information on a specific disk. Figure 25.7 shows the information retrieved.

**FIGURE 25.7.**

*Specific disk information in an Aurora Utilities window.*

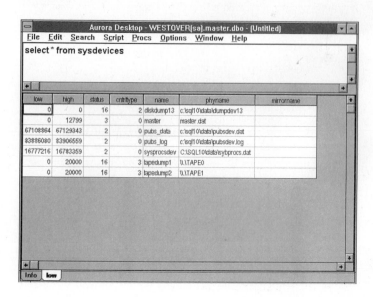

The master device status is 3 (disk device + default device), its controller type is 0 (a device for storage, not backup), its virtual device number (device) is 0, and its low and high values represent the logical page numbers that define the space to be used on the device (12,800 pages = 25MB).

## Removing Devices with *sp_dropdevice*

Once a device has been defined, it remains permanently in the data dictionary in the master database until you decide that it has served its purpose and should be removed. A typical reason for this might be that you are replacing a small or slower, older device with a newer one.

Devices cannot be removed if databases have been defined on the device; any databases must be dropped first. (The server checks sysusages for any allocated fragments for the device.)

You can drop a device by using the sp_dropdevice command.

## Syntax

```
sp_dropdevice <logical_device_name>
```

## Example

```
sp_dropdevice data_device_1
```

If your device was created as an operating system file, you must execute the necessary commands to remove the file; dropping the device does not automatically delete the file. Also, to be able to use that space, you must shut down and restart the server to release its pointer to the device.

# Default Disks

The point of defining disks with disk init is to store data on them. The data is stored in databases, which actually allocate space on disks for tables of data, their indexes, and related objects; database transaction logs; and so on. At database creation time, a database must have a disk to reside on. If there are no devices available (that is, no space left on any defined device), a database cannot be created.

When creating a database, you can (and usually do!) specify the devices where the database will reside. In some cases, you may want the server to determine the devices where the database will reside. In those cases, the server may use only the disks that you have indicated to be default disks. In other words, if you create a database and do not specify a device, each default disk may be used as a database device. In a moment, you see more closely how the server decides which default disk(s) to use.

# Syntax of *sp_diskdefault*

```
sp_diskdefault "device_name", {defaulton ¦ defaultoff}
```

# Examples of *sp_diskdefault*

```
exec sp_diskdefault data_device_1, defaulton
exec sp_diskdefault master, defaultoff
```

> **NOTE**
>
> You use execute or exec before any stored procedure that is not the first statement on the batch. This is a rule for the Sybase parser.
>
> In the previous example, in which you issue two procedure requests in a single batch, the first use of exec is optional. The second is required.

In the first example, you instruct the server that data_device_1 may be used as a default device.

In the second example, you tell the server that you do not want to use database space on the master device unintentionally. This does not mean the master cannot be used; it does mean that the space cannot be used unless it is specifically allocated.

> **NOTE**
>
> The only device for which default status automatically is on is the master device. (master is the "default default device.") This means that if you issue a simple create database command and do not specify a device, the database may end up on the master device.
>
> You do not want the master device cluttered up unintentionally. (It's a real problem if the master device becomes full—especially if you need to increase the size of the master database.) So turn off the default bit of your master database right now!

Because the sp_diskdefault command affects server-wide resources, it is limited to systems administrators only (those with the sa_role, which I discuss in Chapter 27, "Security and User Administration").

The net effect of the sp_diskdefault command is that the $2^0$ bit in the status bit of the sysdevices table for that device is set to 1 (if defaulton is set) or 0 (if defaultoff is set).

In most systems, a default is the single option chosen when no selection is made by the user. Because you can set the default bit on or off independently for each device, you can end up with several default disks, or none.

It probably seems a little strange to have several default devices. How does the server decide which default device to use? Space on default devices is assigned to databases alphabetically, exhausting all space on each default device, then proceeding to the next, until all requested space is allocated.

For example, consider the following `create database` command, which requests that 100MB be assigned to database `newdb` on a default device:

```
create database newdb on default = 100
```

Assume that you have the default disks and available space on each as outlined in Table 25.2. (OK, it doesn't follow the Greek alphabet correctly, but neither does SQL Server.)

**Table 25.2. Default disks.**

| Disk Name | Available Space |
|-----------|-----------------|
| alpha_disk | 10MB |
| beta_disk | 10MB |
| delta_disk | 10MB |
| gamma_disk | 1,000MB |

Where will the server place `newdb`? The obvious answer is "There is room on the gamma_disk, so it will go there." But this is not the way default disks are allocated. Remember: space on default disks is assigned to databases alphabetically.

Here's what happens:

- 10MB is allocated on the alpha disk.
- 10MB is allocated on the beta disk.
- 10MB is allocated on the delta disk.
- The remaining 70MB is allocated on the gamma disk.

The net effect is the same as if you had issued the `create database` command:

```
create database newdb
  on alpha_disk = 10,
     beta_disk = 10,
     delta_disk = 10,
     gamma_disk = 70
```

and the effect on the disks is the following:

| Disk name | Available space |
|-----------|-----------------|
| alpha_disk | 0MB |
| beta_disk | 0MB |
| delta_disk | 0MB |
| gamma_disk | 930MB |

Note that this is not necessarily a performance problem. In fact, it is an advantage to spread active tables across disk controllers.

> **TIP**
>
> If you want to find out whether a specific device is a default device, you can check the device status bit in sysdevices: if the status is odd, the $2^0$ bit is set and it is a default device. Alternatively, use the sp_helpdevice command. It specifies whether the device is a default device.
>
> It's normally not a good idea to use default disks. Whatever work it saves you in remembering physical device names is nullified by the enormous pain you must endure to fix one bad command. Turn off all your default statuses and specify device names in your create database statements.
>
> In fact, it is unusual to have default disks defined. Systems administrators tend to want to keep tight control of physical server resources.

# Disk Mirroring

Occasionally, devices fail. You can ensure against problems caused by device failures by instructing the server to mirror two devices, keeping them in complete synchronization at all times. You can mirror devices at the hardware, operating-system, or SQL Server level. In the last case, SQL Server handles all the disk-mirroring work.

> **WARNING**
>
> Disk mirroring at the hardware level may work, and may reduce the load on the CPU, but you must stress-test the hardware mirroring before counting on it to work with SQL Server in a production environment.

You should mirror, at a minimum, the master device and all your log devices. A failed master device without backup is agony; a failed master device with backup is merely a pain in the backside. (You learn more about this in the "Recovery" section in Chapter 29, "Backing Up and Restoring Databases and Transaction Logs.") Failed log devices cook the database; if the log devices do not fail, data device failures can be mitigated at least through log recovery (again, more in Chapter 29).

If you mirror devices across controllers as well as across physical disks, you reduce potential single points of failure. Figure 25.8 illustrates mirroring across devices and controllers.

**FIGURE 25.8.**

*Mirroring across devices still leaves you vulnerable to a controller failure. Mirroring across controllers protects against controller failures as well.*

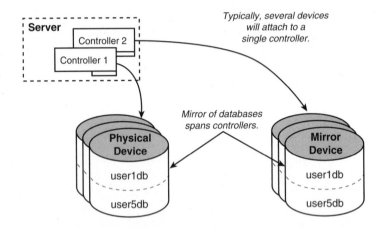

> **NOTE**
>
> Pages are written to both devices, synchronously or asynchronously, at your choice; the default is synchronously. Prior to System 10, reads could be across both devices using an option called mirrored read (splitting reads across both disks of a mirrored pair). This option was removed for System 10, because Sybase technical support and development determined that mirrored reads did not yield a substantial improvement in performance.

Sybase currently has a limitation of 255 physical devices. Mirroring does not take up any of these device connections. (Note the syntax.)

Finally, please note that a mirror device must be at least as large as the device it is mirroring.

## Syntax

```
disk mirror
name = 'logical_device_name',
mirror = 'physical_device_name'
[ , writes = {serial ¦ noserial } ]
[ , contiguous ]
```

In the disk mirror syntax, `logical_device_name` is the name of the device you initialized (on which you used the `disk init` command). The `physical_device_name` is the device that holds the contents of the mirror. Serial writes ensures that, in the case of a power failure, the write goes to at least one of the physical devices if the mirrors are on separate physical devices (as they should be). Serial writes is the default. The `contiguous` option is available on Open VMS only.

## Example

```
disk mirror
name = 'data_device_1',
mirror = '/dev/rsd05'
```

In the example, you mirror a device that you initialized and to which you assigned the logical device name `data_device_1`. A copy of all writes to the disk also are written to the physical device at address `/dev/rsd05`.

## Sequence of Events

There are three steps in the disk mirror sequence of events:

1. The secondary device (mirror device) is initialized.
2. All used pages on the primary device are copied to the secondary device. Note that, as expected, this is not a fast process.
3. Bits are set in `sysdevices`, bit $2^6$ (device mirrored) and $2^9$ (mirror enabled).

### WARNING

Sybase mirrors at the device level, not the database level. If a database is spread across many devices, and any one database is not mirrored, the database is at risk from a physical failure. For a database to be fully protected, every device associated with that database must be mirrored.

## Disk Mirroring Information

The easiest way to check on disk mirroring for a device is with the `sp_helpdevice` command.

Alternatively, you can identify all the disk devices using the SQL statement:

```
select * from sysdevices where cntrltype = 0
```

(Disk devices are those with cntrltype 0; others are backup devices.)

> **WARNING**
>
> With some versions of the server (prior to System 10), sp_helpdevice does not report disk-mirroring information with 100-percent accuracy. If you suspect the values in sp_helpdevice, you must select the row from sysdevices and decode the data bits.
>
> Alternatively, rewrite sp_helpdevice and fix it.

# Deactivating Disk Mirroring

Devices become unmirrored in two ways:

- You, as the sa or using the sa_role, issue the disk unmirror command.
- Sybase, in an attempt to write to a primary or secondary device of a mirror pair, is unable to write to one of the devices.

The server maintains the bit flags within the device status in sysdevices to report on the status of the mirror. When mirrors fail or are disabled for any reason, the server updates the bit flags to indicate which mirror failed. Table 25.3 summarizes the bit flags as they relate to mirror devices. Note that other status flags (default or reads mirrored) could be set in addition to the flags described in the table.

**Table 25.3. Status flags relating to mirror devices.**

| State of Mirror | Status Value | Decoded Status |
| --- | --- | --- |
| Not mirrored | 2 (2) | Physical disk |
| Mirrored | 578 (2+64+512) | Mirrored, mirror enabled |
| Secondary failed | 66 (2+64) | Mirrored |
| Primary failed | 322 (2+64+256) | Mirrored, half mirrored |

Unmirroring a device has the effect of modifying status bits and instructing the server to write to only one specific device of a mirrored pair.

If the mirroring is automatic, the server checkpoints the master database so that changes in the sysdevices table are permanently reflected on the disk. Additionally, any processes that are awaiting a mirrorexit event are enabled.

> **NOTE**
>
> waitfor is a Transact-SQL enhancement that is effectively an event handler. Here is an example:
>
> ```
> waitfor mirrorexit
> print "A mirror primary or secondary device has failed! Take action."
> ```
>
> In this example, the process executing the SQL sleeps until the event specified (the waitfor command) occurs. For more information, see the waitfor command in Volume One of the *SQL Server Reference Manual*, because a discussion of waitfor is beyond the scope of this book.

## Syntax

```
disk unmirror
name = 'logical_name'
[ , side = { "primary" ¦ secondary } ]
[ , mode = { retain ¦ remove } ]
```

The parameter *logical name* is the device that you initialized with the disk init command; the "primary" side is the device that you initialized; the secondary is the mirror that you specified. You may unmirror either the primary or the secondary device.

The defaults are secondary and retain. If you specify retain, the names of the unmirrored devices are kept in the sysdevices table indefinitely, and you may remirror. (You see how to remirror shortly.) Automatic unmirroring uses the retain option.

## Example

```
disk unmirror
name = 'data_device_1',
side = 'primary',
mode = remove
```

In the example, you're telling the server that you want to permanently remove the definition of the primary device from the data_device_1 device. The effect is that the mirror side becomes the primary (only) device:

```
disk unmirror name = 'data_device_1'
```

In this example, the server unmirrors the secondary device, and keeps the definition of the device in sysdevices. In this case, you can use the disk remirror command.

# Disk Remirroring

After a device becomes unmirrored automatically, or manually with `mode` = `retain`, you, the sa, can instruct the server to restart the software mirroring. The `disk remirror` statement will fail unless the device was previously mirrored and the definition remains in `sysdevices`.

## Syntax

```
disk remirror name = 'logical_name'
```

Note that it is not necessary to specify anything else. If the `logical name` in `sysdevices` does not already has the necessary information in the row, the command will fail (and you should have used the disk mirror command instead).

## Example

```
disk remirror name = 'data_device_1'
```

> **NOTE**
>
> Regardless of the elapsed time of the disk unmirror (one second unmirrored, with no updates occurring!), an unmirrored disk is considered to be out of synchronization with the primary, and the mirroring process begins anew. This means that the entire device is recopied onto the mirror (or primary, if that was the side unmirrored). Remember that this is not a fast process.

What happens when you have an older device that is being replaced because it is too old, small, or slow? What if you have several databases on the device (or parts of several databases on a device)? One technique is to execute the following steps:

1. Dump all the databases.
2. Drop all the databases. (You cannot drop a device if a database is on it.)
3. Drop the "old" device.
4. Cycle the server. (Remember, the device numbers are not reusable.)
5. Recreate the device.
6. Recreate the databases.
7. Reload the databases.

This is a lot of work. It also has to be done when your users are not on the system (and you'd rather be home in bed). It's possible to use the disk-mirroring commands to migrate data from one device to another. This may be extremely useful.

Here is the easy way, illustrated in Figure 25.9:

1. Mirror the current disk onto the new disk (or an appropriate slice of the new disk).

2. Unmirror the device, side = primary, mode = remove.

**FIGURE 25.9.**

*It usually is more efficient to migrate data with mirroring than with a backup and restore.*

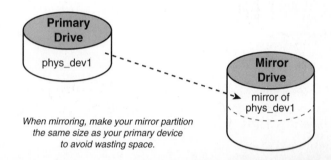

When mirroring, make your mirror partition
the same size as your primary device
to avoid wasting space.

You should mirror at least the master device and all log devices. With the low cost of disk space, there is little excuse not to mirror everything. Think about the cost of having the system down, compared to the cost of a 2GB SCSI drive. When it comes time to mirror the master device, there are two steps to follow:

1. Mirror the device like any other.

2. At startup, the dataserver command must be made aware that it has another place to look if the primary master device is unavailable. You can do this with the -r option on the dataserver command in the RUNSERVER file. Here is an example of a UNIX RUNSERVER file:

```
/sybase/bin/dataserver -d /dev/rsd06 -r /dev/rsd08
```

There are a few things to note about this command. First, even if your master device has failed, you must specify the master device before the mirror device to enable the server to recognize the mirrored master device properly.

Second, every platform or version offers subtle variations on maintaining a mirror on master; check your installation manual and troubleshooting guides for more information.

Third, mirroring the master device is important. If you lose master after a substantive change to your system configuration (but before a backup), you have to piece it back together. If you can't piece it back together, you may lose all contact with your user database(s).

# Software Mirroring, Hardware Mirroring, and RAID

Sybase mirrors data at the software level to ensure that mirroring is possible, regardless of hardware platform or configuration. There are alternatives, however. Many hardware vendors enable mirroring at the controller level. Alternatively, RAID provides an alternative to mirroring every device, along with a concurrent performance throughput benefit. What are the advantages and disadvantages of each?

## Software Mirroring

Software mirroring guarantees database stability against hardware failure. It is guaranteed by Sybase, so if there's a problem it is handled by Sybase Technical Support. In addition, software mirroring enables you to mirror across controllers, minimizing single points of failure.

However, software mirroring requires additional writes, which require more CPU cycles. Sybase does not admit to a substantial performance degradation, but other vendors talk about a 10 percent performance hit from software mirroring.

## Hardware Mirroring

Hardware mirroring reduces CPU work. (Hardware mirroring is handled by the controller.)

However, hardware mirroring is guaranteed by the hardware vendor. This means that if the mirroring does not work out, the hardware vendor will blame the software vendor, and the software vendor will blame the hardware vendor. This is not a pretty picture when all you want is your data back.

> **TIP**
>
> If you're going to mirror at the hardware level, be sure to test the mirroring. When the server is under load, pull out one of the drives and see what happens. After mirroring is reenabled, pull the other drive out and see what happens. (If you smell smoke or ozone, consider software mirroring.)
>
> One point about this: network administrators have been pulling the plug on uninterruptible power supplies (UPSs) for years, to make sure the server can run even when the UPS has suffered a lapse in power from the power company. However, when you pull the power cord on the UPS, you can sometimes damage the UPS—and it stops working immediately.

## Redundant Array of Inexpensive Devices (RAID)

With RAID, there typically are five devices: four contain data and the fifth has redundant hash information. If any device fails, the RAID notifies the operator, and acts as if nothing happened as far as data transmission goes. The operator replaces the bad drive with a "hot" backup. The RAID automatically brings the new device up to speed.

RAID architecture handles all mirroring automatically, and at the hardware level. It is a nifty technology.

However, RAID is expensive. You might spend some time looking into the advantages at the different RAID levels that you can set. You may decide that performance advantages are outweighed by an inconvenience factor.

Typically, you have to set RAID to level 5 to get the protection you want, and on many platforms you may find that SCSI was faster after all.

# Device SQL

It can be important to determine what devices are available, how much space is initialized on the devices, and how much space actually is utilized. This SQL returns that specific information in a neat report:

```
select 'Database device name' = name,
'In use by databases' = sum (size / 512),
'Space initialized' = (high-low+1)/512
from sysdevices, sysusages
where vstart between low and high
and cntrltype = 0
group by name
```

> **WARNING**
>
> Some Sybase documentation incorrectly states that sysdevices and sysusages are joined with lstart. vstart is correct.

# Summary

You've learned how to implement storage devices using SQL Server and looked at the use of internal and external mechanisms to provide fault tolerance and to ensure data reliability and availability. In the next chapter, you'll create databases using the space created on these devices.

# Defining, Altering, and Maintaining Databases and Logs

# 26

This chapter addresses how to create and maintain databases and database logs. You will learn several approaches to managing disk space on various versions of SQL Server. You also will learn about Sybase segments. If you are familiar with the term *segment* from a different database management system, disregard your preconceived definition when reviewing this chapter. It is likely that what is defined as a segment for some other database management system differs from what Sybase defines as a segment.

# What Is a Database?

The database concept is central to almost all implementation and administration tasks in SQL Server. During the database design phase of a project, you define the tables of interest to your organization. From a logical perspective, these related tables are collectively considered a single database. From a physical perspective, however, you can implement these tables in one or many Sybase databases. The Sybase database is important because it determines how data is stored physically—how data is mapped to physical devices. Physical space is assigned to a database during database creation, and additional space can be assigned to the database when the need arises.

Several key areas are based at the database level. All Sybase objects must exist within the database—often referred to as "in the context of a database." Therefore, the limits on how large an object can grow depends on the amount of space allocated to the database. (At a detailed level, limits on object growth truly are dependent on the amount of space available to a segment in the database, which is described in the section titled "Segments and Object Placement," later in this chapter.) The database also is an important element in your security strategy, because you must be a user of a database to be able to access objects within it. Some analysis tools, such as the Database Consistency Checker (DBCC) act at the database level. Also, backups are conducted only at the database level, which means that a database is the only unit of recovery available in Sybase. (Table-level backups currently are not supported.)

## Databases and Space Management

Logical devices (see Chapter 25, "Defining Physical and Mirror Devices") make space usable to the SQL Server, and databases organize that space, making it available to Sybase tables and their indexes, as well as other objects. Databases cannot span physical SQL Servers, nor can tables and their indexes span databases. Therefore, the size of a database limits the size of any tables and indexes it contains. However, if a table or index grows too large, you can increase the size of the database on-the-fly.

> **NOTE**
>
> Later in the chapter, you will look at database segments and how they are used to manage table and index sizes within the database. Although people usually refer to the size of the database as determining the maximum size of a table or index, this is not completely accurate. Each object is created on a segment in a Sybase database, and objects cannot span segments. Therefore, it is the amount of space available to the segment that determines the maximum size of an object.

# Databases and Security

The owner of a database maps a system login to a database user. This is accomplished in one of four ways, described in detail in Chapter 27, "Security and User Administration." Permission to access objects is granted to a database user (either explicitly—to the user, or implicitly—to a user group. See Chapter 27 for more information.) Therefore, if you do not allow an SQL Server login to be associated with a database user, you have eliminated the ability for that user to access the objects within that database.

# Databases and Backups

You will see later that Sybase utilities enable you to back up only a database. This can either be a full backup (a copy of the entire database) or an incremental backup (a copy of the transactions that have occurred since the last backup). Because transactions are logged in a table within a database, you must be careful when creating related tables in different databases.

For example, consider a table called `customer` in the `customerdb` database and a table called `purchase` in the `purchase_db` database. As part of a transaction, you add a new customer to the customer table and that customer's purchases to the purchase table. Each database logs the addition of rows in its own transaction log. If a disaster occurred, and you lost the `customer_db` database, you may be forced to reload this database from a backup. (Assume the `purchase_db` database was fine.) It is possible that you would not be able to restore the `customer_db` database to the point at which the disaster occurred. Therefore, the purchase table would contain purchases for customers that are not in the customer table.

When you decide how to distribute related tables in different databases, remember that you are possibly putting your data integrity at risk.

# System Databases

A *system database* is a database created to support the operation of the server or a Sybase facility. When the SQL Server is installed, it creates at least three system databases: master, model, and tempdb. In a System 10 installation, there is a fourth database created, called sybsystemprocs. However, you also can install other system databases to support additional capabilities. There is a new syntax database, sybsyntax, which allows the user to execute the sp_syntax command (System 10). Also, if you install auditing, the sybsecurity database is added. Each of the four primary databases has a purpose:

- The master database records all of the server-specific configuration information, including authorized users, devices, databases, system configuration settings, and remote servers.

- The model database is a template database. The contents of model are copied into each new database created after the system is installed.

- The tempdb database is the temporary database. This database is used as an interim storage area. The server automatically uses it to resolve large or multi-step queries, or to sort data before returning results to the user (if a query contains an order by clause). Programmers also can use it programmatically to provide a worktable to support application processing.

- The sybsystemprocs database contains all system stored procedures, such as sp_who, sp_helpdevice, sp_help, and sp_dropdevice.

> **NOTE**
>
> Before the release of System 10, system stored procedures were stored in the master database.

# Database Creation

A primary task of the system administrator is to create databases. In this section, you'll learn the syntax of the create database statement, as well as some of the implementation issues involved with database creation.

> **TIP**
>
> As you implement databases, remember that database creation can take a long time. Creation time depends mostly on your physical disk speed—the server initializes every

page in a database—and can take between 20 and 60 minutes per gigabyte, depending on your platform. If you are implementing a very large database, this could impact your project schedule.

# Syntax for *create database*

```
create database <db_name>
[on <device_name> [= <size>] [, ...]]
[log on <device_name> [= <size>] [, ...]]
[for load]
```

When creating a database, you must provide a database name. Database names must be 30 characters or less, cannot include punctuation or other special characters, and must be unique within the server.

> **NOTE**
>
> The naming conventions for database names vary widely between organizations. Some shops limit themselves to four or eight characters so that the database can easily map to DOS or MVS filenames. Others use long, descriptive names. Some shops standardize on encoded names, such as ACTV94TST01 (for "1994 activity test 1").
>
> Database names are case-sensitive. (For example, you could create two databases, customer_db and CUSTOMER_DB.) Many organizations standardize on uppercase—for database names and object names—to allow easier portability to other environments. (I prefer to use lowercase because writing in all uppercase usually looks like someone is shouting at me.)
>
> I recommend that you keep database names short. After all, people will have to type them. And keep them meaningful and memorable. Names like AU149305 don't mean much to most mortals. Use names like accounting or acctg, which are easy to remember and easy to type, so your users and programmers won't be cursing you six times a day. For more on naming standards, see Chapter 34, "Defining Systems Administration and Naming Standards."

A database is created on one or more physical devices. Specifying the device is optional—but highly recommended. When indicating the device, you use the logical name you specified as part of disk init. (See Chapter 25 for more on setting up database devices.)

> **NOTE**
>
> If you do not specify the device on which to create the database, a default device is used. (See the section titled "Default Disks" in Chapter 25.) Most DBAs like to know up front where a database is going to be placed. Therefore, always supply the device on which you want to create the database.

You also can specify the size of the database, in megabytes. If you do not indicate a size, the server uses the larger of the default size (a configurable value, set to 2MB upon installation) or the size of the model database (because the contents of model are copied into each new database created). It's good standard practice always to provide size to create database.

> **NOTE**
>
> You specify disk size in pages, but you specify database size in megabytes.

If you request more megabytes than are available on a device, the server allocates all remaining space on the device, as long as there is enough room to make a complete copy of the model database.

## Examples of *create database*

The following are some sample create database statements.

> **NOTE**
>
> Examine how the SQL has been written to improve readability: each individual device is listed on its own line. This does not affect how the command works, but it certainly makes it easier to read later on. And don't forget that you're saving all create statements in a script in case you have to execute them later.

The first example sets up a 12MB (8 + 4) database called marketing. In this database, 8MB is allocated for tables, indexes, system tables, and other objects (all of which are broadly classified as "data"), and 4MB is allocated for the transaction log.

> **NOTE**
>
> The transaction log is used by Sybase to log certain activity within a database. Examples of logged activity include creating objects; adding or deleting database users; or adding, deleting, or modifying data in tables.

```
create database marketing
on data_device_1 = 8
log on log_device_4 = 4
```

> **NOTE**
>
> In general, you should set up your log segment on a separate drive and controller, if possible. Performance will be better, you will be able to perform incremental backups, and you will be better able to recover after a disaster. Please see Chapter 28, "Database Logging and Recovery," for more on transaction logs.

The next example sets up a 30MB (12 + 8 + 10) database called accounting. It provides 20MB for data and 10MB for the transaction log.

```
create database accounting
on data_device_1 = 12,
data_device_2 = 8
log on log_device_1 = 10
```

This create database statement includes several devices and sizes. If you include several devices, SQL Server acquires, on each device, a fragment of the size you specify. If there is not enough space on any single device listed, SQL Server allocates as much space as it can on the device.

The next example includes the keywords for load. Create a database for load if you are creating the structure for the sole purpose of restoring a database from a backup, where the structure does not exist. For example, consider the situation in which you have encountered a database corruption and are forced to load from a backup copy. Normally, a corrupt database must be dropped; that is, completely removed from the physical device(s). However, you must load the backup copy into an existing database. Because the load process is going to replace the existing structure with the data in the backup, there is no need to go through the time-consuming activity of initializing all the database pages. See Chapter 29, "Backing Up and Restoring Databases and Transaction Logs," for more information on restoring databases.

```
create database newdb
on data_device_3 = 12,
data_device_4 = 8
log on log_device_2 = 10
for load
```

After a create database … for load, the only permitted operation on the database is load database, the SQL Server method of restoring a database from backup.

# What Happens When You Create a Database?

The server performs the following actions when you create a database:

1. Immediately allocates database space.

2. Inserts one row in sysdatabases (a system table in the master database) for the database. You will have a row in sysdatabases for every database in a server.

3. Inserts one row in sysusages (master database) for each device fragment.

4. Physically marks each extent. An *extent* is comprised of eight data pages (pages are normally 2KB, except on Stratus hardware where the page size is 4KB). This activity is what takes the bulk of the elapsed time for a database creation.

5. Copies the model database into the new database.

If the database is created for load, the server allocates the space from the specified devices, but does not mark the extents or copy the contents of the model database into the structure. The actual marking of extents is an automatic part of the restore process (load database). If you do not create the database for load, you are performing the most time-consuming part of the create process needlessly.

> **NOTE**
>
> A hospital system using Sybase experienced a database corruption. Minimizing downtime was critical. By using for load, I was able to create the database structure in a few minutes—instead of performing a "normal" database create, which had originally taken over seven hours. This allowed the system to be up and running almost a full business day sooner than if I had not used for load.

Here are the steps to take when you specify for load:

1. Immediately allocate database space.

2. Insert one row in sysdatabases for the database.

3. Insert one row per device fragment in sysusages.

4. Set the database status bit 5 (value = 32), indicating that the database was created for load.

# Sizing Databases

By definition, the size of the database is the size of all data fragments plus the size of all log fragments. The data area must be large enough to hold all of the system tables and your user tables, as well as any indexes. The log must be large enough for the transaction log.

# Minimum Size

The minimum database size is the greater of the setting in sp_configure (2MB is the default value) or the size of the model database (also 2MB, by default). If the model database will not fit into the allocated space, the database creation fails.

# Default Devices and Sizes

You don't have to specify a device name or a size. If you don't specify the size, the default size is the greater of the size of the model database and the value of database size in sysconfigures. For example, if database size is 2MB, but the model database is 8MB, the default database size is 8MB.

> **NOTE**
>
> To change the minimum database size, you can either increase the size of the model database (with alter database; see the section titled "Making Databases Larger" later in this chapter) or change the configured value (this is the recommended approach).
>
> To change the configuration setting to 8MB, use the sp_configure stored procedure:
> ```
> sp_configure "database size", 8
> reconfigure
> ```
> You must restart your server before the new setting takes effect.

# How Big Should the Database Be?

When you create a database, remember that the data area must be large enough to contain the system tables, user tables, and all indexes. You probably want to leave about 25 percent free space in your database as well. To estimate the eventual size requirements of tables, use the stored procedure sp_estspace.

> **NOTE**
>
> Use sp_estspace whenever you must estimate how large a table and its indexes will grow. The stored procedure is shipped with System 10, and is available on the Sybase CompuServe forum, OpenLink. You also can find the script on the CD-ROM with this book; look for the file named estspace.sql.

It is important to remember that databases can get larger—you see how in a moment—but they cannot get smaller. If you oversize a database, the only way to recover the additional space is to drop the database and re-create it, re-create all the database objects, then reload each table individually. The general approach is to start the database small and let it grow as necessary.

# How Big Should the Log Be?

The transaction log records all database modifications. If the log is full, no further modifications are permitted in the database. Under ordinary production circumstances, the only time SQL Server clears the transaction log is after an incremental backup.

The factors influencing log size are database activity level, the frequency of incremental backup, and the volume of simultaneous updates. Because these factors vary dramatically from one system to another, it is impossible to establish firm guidelines on sizing a database log. As a starting point, you may want to consider creating logs that are between 10 and 25 percent of the database size for an OLTP database.

Long-running transactions also influence log size. If your system will be updating large amounts of data in a single transaction, the log must be large enough to hold the entire transaction. In that case, you may need the log to be 200 percent or more of the size of the data. If you want your logs to be smaller, you must break up large updates into smaller transactions (which usually is a good idea anyway), then dump the transaction log in between the transactions to free up space in the log.

---

### SETTING UP A SEPARATE AREA FOR THE TRANSACTION LOG

Most of the examples of database creation in this chapter include a separate allocation for the transaction log. This is accomplished by providing `log on` information to `create database`. Transaction logging and log management are discussed in great detail in Chapter 28, but it's important to understand now some of the characteristics of transaction logs.

A Sybase transaction log is a record of all modifications made to a database. Every object creation, every security implementation, every row modification (`insert`, `update`, `delete`) is logged in a transaction log. (There are a handful of non-logged activities, which I discuss later. However, in a true production environment all activities are fully logged.)

The transaction log is a *write-ahead log,* which means that logged activity is written to the transaction log before the modifications are made to the tables and indexes themselves. In most cases, the only information that is written to disk at the time of update is the logging information; the data is brought up to date only at checkpoint time. (For more about checkpoints, see Chapter 28.)

There are several crucial benefits to separating your log from your data in your `create database` statement.

First, Sybase incremental backups actually are just copies of the transaction log. If the data and log areas are not separated, the server cannot perform incremental backups; all backups for database with integrated log and data areas are full backups.

Second, you can get some performance benefits by separating log and data activity, especially if the devices are attached to separate physical disk drives in the server.

Third, without separate logs, recovery is more difficult. One implication of writing the log first is that the log is the unit of data integrity in Sybase. If you lose your data but have your log, up-to-the-transaction recovery is possible (even likely). If you lose your log but still have your data, up-to-the-minute recovery is not possible, and you can only recover up to the point of your last backup.

The best method of ensuring fault tolerance is to mirror all the devices, but sometimes that's not feasible. If you can mirror at least your log devices (which are always smaller than all database devices), you can ensure recoverability. If any log device fails, you still have an alternative device from which you can work. (See Chapter 25 for more information on mirroring.)

## How Big Should You Make *tempdb*?

The `tempdb` database is a temporary work area used by the SQL Server to resolve large queries or queries requiring the creation of a worktable. (Queries that may need a worktable include those with `order by` or `distinct` clauses. The `group by` clause always uses a worktable.) Users also can direct SQL Server to create temporary tables with `create table` or `select … into` statements.

Temporary tables are identified by the number sign (#) in the first character. For example, the following statement creates a temporary table, `#authors_and_titles`, in `tempdb`:

```
select au_lname, au_fname, title
into #authors_and_titles
from authors a, titleauthor ta, titles t
where a.au_id = ta.au_id
and ta.title_id = t.title_id
```

The size of the temporary table depends on the size of the tables (`authors`, `titleauthor`, and `titles`) referenced in the query.

You cannot restrict users from creating temporary tables. A temporary table persists until the user explicitly drops the table (`drop table #authors_and_titles`) or until the user creating the temporary table logs out. Temporary tables created by stored procedures are dropped when the procedure ends.

Sizing `tempdb` depends on a number of factors: how often users create ad hoc temporary tables, whether application programs or stored procedures create temporary tables, how many concurrent users will have to create these tables at one time, and so on.

> **TIP**
>
> The typical motivation for a programmer to use a temporary table is to avoid a second pass through a large table. By copying a small subset of the data to another location, the user can save many disk operations and improve performance. In general, you want to encourage programmers to think this way because it improves overall system performance.
>
> If you properly select indexes on the primary tables, it may not be necessary to create a worktable to resolve a query. For example, a programmer may want to retrieve data from a table in a particular order. If there was a clustered index created on the columns by which the programmer wants to order the data, the data could be retrieved directly from the primary tables. (A clustered index on a column, or columns, of a table physically stores the data in the table in the sort order specified.)

> **NOTE**
>
> If `tempdb` runs out of space, the transaction aborts and an error is reported in the error log.

At first, make `tempdb` about 25 percent of the size of your largest database, unless you have reason to expect you will need substantially more.

# Database Creation Authority and Database Ownership

Normally, databases are created by the system administrator—who, historically, has logged into the server as sa. In System 10, however, the capabilities of the system administrator can be granted to individual logins through the use of Sybase roles. The sa_role is granted to an individual login, enabling the server to treat that login as a system administrator. Any login that has been granted the sa_role is permitted to perform database creations.

Whoever creates a database owns it. However, ownership of a database can be transferred.

## Allowing Others to Create Databases

Someone other than the system administrator can create a database if the system administrator grants that person the ability to execute the create database command. (See the section titled "Command Permissions" in Chapter 27 for more information.)

Ordinarily, you do not assign the database-creation ability to others, and you should not. Because database creation allocates system resources, you want to manage this task carefully and thoughtfully. Database creation should be a "system administrators only" task.

If you really have to allow others to create databases, do the following:

1. Use the `master` database:
   ```
   use master
   go
   ```

2. Add a database user in the `master` database for the particular login:
   ```
   sp_adduser john
   go
   ```

3. Grant the `create database` privilege to the user:
   ```
   grant create database to john
   go
   ```

## Transferring Database Ownership

Whoever creates a database is designated as its owner. It is common to transfer ownership of a database to another user, once the database is created. Database ownership often is transferred to distribute responsibility—a person other than the sa is responsible for the normal operations of the database (adding users, granting permissions, and so on).

> **NOTE**
>
> The database is the only object that can change ownership. If you try to change the ownership of a table or other object, the system usually marks the entire database "suspect," and you will have to drop the database and restore from tape. I know: I tried it.

# Making Databases Larger

Use the `alter database` command to make databases larger. You can enlarge a database while the system is online and the database is in use.

> **NOTE**
>
> Don't forget that databases can get larger, but not smaller.

## Syntax for *alter database*

The `alter database` command is similar to `create database`:

```
alter database <db_name>
[on device_name [= size], [...]]
[log on device_name [= size]]
```

Specify the additional amount of space to be allocated, not the ultimate size of the database. The default increment is 2MB. You cannot allocate less than 1MB at a time.

Consider the following example of `create` and `alter database`:

```
create database market_db
on device1 = 50,
device_2 = 100
log on logdev1 = 35

alter database market_db
on device1 = 50
```

In this example, a 185MB database is created on three devices. The `alter database` command adds an additional 50MB, for a total of 235MB.

# Adding Log Space

Adding log space to a database requires the `log on` keywords (found in System 10 only) in the `alter database` statement:

```
alter database market_db
log on logdev2 = 35
```

This statement adds 35MB of space to the log of the `market_db` database.

# Assigning Space to the Log

Typically, you assign log space with the `log on` clause in the `create database` or `alter database` statement. It also is possible to assign database space on a specific device to the log retroactively (that is, after a `create` or `alter` statement) with the `sp_logdevice` stored procedure, as in the following:

```
sp_logdevice <databasename>, <devicename>
```

Consider the following examples:

```
create database test_db
on device1 = 50,
device2 = 100
log on logdev1 = 35

alter database test_db
on newdevice = 50
```

After the `alter` statement, the database is 235MB, with 200MB of space for data and system tables (50MB on `device1`, 100MB on `device2`, and 50MB on `newdevice`); and 35MB of space for the transaction log (on `logdevice1`).

The space allocation on additional database devices is assumed to be used for data in SQL Server versions 4.8 and later. In the preceding example, the allocation on `newdevice` is for data, because there was no previous allocation of space for the database on the device. If you want to make `newdevice` a log device, use the `sp_logdevice` statement:

```
sp_logdevice test_db, newdevice
```

> **NOTE**
>
> In the previous example, the `create database` statement sets aside 35MB on `logdev1` for the transaction log. All subsequent allocations of space on that device also will be used for the log. The `sp_logdevice` procedure sets aside any space allocations on `newdevice` for the log as well.
>
> This really is the crucial point about space utilization: space is assigned for data or the log by device. This is a special case of the general use of database segments, which I examine in detail a little later in this chapter.

# Exploring Databases

It's useful to get down under the covers when it comes to databases, particularly if you ever have to do creative work with the system tables to enable a recovery. In the next sections you explore databases using standard stored procedures, then examine the system tables in more detail.

## sp_helpdb

The system-stored procedure, `sp_helpdb`, provides information about databases on the server. If you don't provide a parameter, the system provides a list of all databases on the server, as in the following example:

```
sp_helpdb

name            db_size     owner   dbid    created         status
fred            4.0 MB      sa      9       Jan 18, 1995    no options set
master          3.0 MB      sa      1       Jan 01, 1900    no options set
model           2.0 MB      sa      3       Jan 01, 1900    no options set
perftune        15.5 MB     sa      6       Jan 06, 1995    select into/bulkcopy
pubs2           2.0 MB      sa      8       Nov 23, 1994    no options set
sybsecurity     8.0 MB      sa      7       Nov 10, 1994    trunc log on chkpt
sybsystemprocs  20.0 MB     sa      4       Nov 05, 1994    trunc log on chkpt
tempdb          2.0 MB      sa      2       Jan 05, 1995    select into/bulkcopy
testdb          4.0 MB      sa      5       Nov 07, 1994    no options set
```

If you provide a parameter, you get detailed information about a single database, as in the following example:

```
sp_helpdb pubs2

name              db_size      owner      dbid   created        status
pubs2             2.0 MB       sa         8      Nov 23, 1994   no options set

device_fragments             size       usage                free kbytes
master                       2.0 MB     data and log         480
```

The detailed information from sp_helpdb includes a list of database fragments, which are specific allocations of space on each device.

# Database System Tables

When you create and modify databases, three system tables in the master database are involved: sysdatabases, sysusages, and sysdevices, as illustrated in Figure 26.1.

**FIGURE 26.1.**
*The* sysusages *table resolves the many-to-many relationship between* sysdatabases *and* sysdevices.

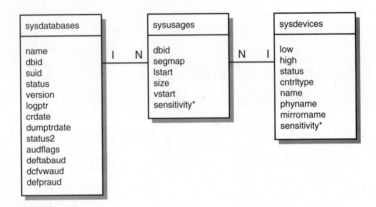

## sysdatabases

The server adds a row to sysdatabases for each new database. The user specifies the name, but the server automatically selects the next available integer ID for dbid. There are several important columns in sysdatabases:

| | |
|---|---|
| name | The name of the database, assigned by the database creator. |
| dbid | The system-assigned identifier for the database. |
| suid | The ID of the database owner; at database creation time, this is set to the ID of the login that issued the create database statement. To change the database owner, use the sp_changedbowner stored procedure. |
| status | An integer consisting of several control bits with information about the database. See the section titled "Database Status Flags" later in this chapter. |

dumptrdate    The date of the last dump transaction. The server marks this date on the next transaction dump to ensure that all dumps are loaded in order during a restore from backup.

> **NOTE**
>
> The sysdatabases table has additional columns used to record audit settings for the database itself, as well as default audit settings for tables, views, and procedures.

## sysdevices

The create database statements do not affect the sysdevices table, but each named device must exist in sysdevices. Information in sysdevices is used to build detailed rows in sysusages, so it is useful to look at sysdevices now. The important columns for this discussion are cntrltype, low, high, and name.

The maximum size of a device on SQL Server is 16 million pages (32GB). A unique range of 16 million pages is allocated to each device upon allocation; these are *virtual page numbers*.

> **NOTE**
>
> The virtual page range is determined by multiplying the virtual device number assigned in the disk init statement by $2^{24}$, or approximately 16 million.

Here is a description of some of the important columns in sysdevices:

cntrltype    This differentiates between dump devices and database devices. A value of zero is assigned to all database devices.

low    This is the first virtual page number available on the device.

high    This is the last virtual page number available on the database device. Although the system reserves the entire range of 16 million pages to the device, the high value reflects the device's actual capacity. To determine the number of pages on a device, use high − low + 1. To determine the number of megabytes, use (high − low + 1) / 512.

name    This is the logical name of the device.

The following is a sample listing from the sysdevices table for all physical database devices (cntrltype = 0).

```
select cntrltype, low, high, name
from sysdevices
where cntrltype = 0
order by low
```

```
cntrltype low          high        name
--------- ----------   ----------  ------------------------------
0         0            12799       master
0         16777216     16787455    sysprocsdev
0         33554432     33558527    sybsecurity
0         67108864     67112959    testdevice
0         100663296    100665343   test_dev
0         1342177728   134230015   introdev
0         150994944    151000063   instruct2_data
```

Values in the `low` column are even multiples of 16777216.

> **TIP**
>
> To determine the virtual device number, divide the `low` value by 16777216; the virtual device number for `testdevice` is 4.
>
> The size of the `testdevice` is (67112959 − 67108864 + 1) = 4,096 pages = 8MB.

## sysusages

The `create database` statement automatically adds one row in sysusages for each allocation of space on a device. For example, the `create database` command,

```
create database market_db
on DATA_1 = 100, DATA_2 = 100
log on LOG_1 = 50
```

allocates space on three devices, DATA_1, DATA_2, and LOG_1. Each of these allocations is recorded in a separate row in sysusages.

Take a closer look at the useful columns in sysusages:

dbid    This is the database identifier. This is used to relate information in sysusages to sysdatabases. (the `dbid` column exists in sysdatabases as well.)

segmap  This is used to map database fragments to segments. (See the section "Segments and Object Placement," later in this chapter).

lstart  This is the first logical database page number; the logical page starts within the database.

size    This is the number of contiguous pages.

vstart  This is the starting virtual page number, which enables you to map the database fragment to a specific virtual device. The fragment is located on the device if the vstart value falls between the `low` and `high` page numbers for the device in sysdevices.

# Using SQL to Query the System Tables

The trick to joining sysdevices, sysdatabases, and sysusages is to understand how virtual device numbers in sysdevices are mapped to the vstart column in the sysusages table.

The following output displays the rows in sysusages for a single database. There are three fragments in the database, all on the same virtual device. sysusages includes one row per device fragment per database.

```
select *
from sysusages
where dbid = 9
order by lstart
```

| dbid | segmap | lstart | size | vstart   | pad | unreservedpgs |
|------|--------|--------|------|----------|-----|---------------|
| 9    | 7      | 0      | 1024 | 67110912 |     | 664           |
| 9    | 7      | 1024   | 512  | 67111936 |     | 512           |
| 9    | 7      | 1536   | 512  | 67112448 |     | 512           |

The vstart value for each fragment falls between the low and high page numbers (67108864 and 67112959) for testdevice, so each of these fragments is stored on testdevice.

The actual SQL used to join sysusages to sysdevices uses a between test, as in the following fragment:

```
where sysusages.vstart between sysdevices.low and sysdevices.high
  and cntrltype = 0
```

> **NOTE**
>
> Some older Sybase documentation tells you to join sysusages to sysdevices with the lstart column. This is wrong. Use vstart to make the join to sysdevices.

Here is the SQL used to list allocations of space on devices for each database:

```
select 'Database' = d.name, 'Device' = v.name, u.size
from sysdatabases d, sysusages u, sysdevices v
where d.dbid = u.dbid
  and u.vstart between v.low and v.high
  and cntrltype = 0
order by d.name
compute sum(u.size) by d.name
```

# Database Space Usage

Use sp_spaceused to determine the amount of space used (and space available) in your database. If the database runs out of space for objects, you cannot add data to tables or indexes. You may not be able to add new views or procedures, either, depending on where the space shortfall occurred.

The database runs out of space only when it tries to allocate a new extent to an object. For example, the server determines that a page split is required in an index, but the current extent is full. At that time, the server attempts to allocate a new extent (eight pages, which usually is 16KB) to the index. If all extents for the segment are reserved, the update fails and rolls back, and the server reports an error out of space on segment….

You usually want about 25 percent free space in your database at any time. This will help you avoid major work stoppages when you are hurrying to add additional space to the database.

The sp_spaceused procedure can report on the space allocated to a table, if you pass the tablename as a parameter (sp_spaceused *tablename*). However, you should be more concerned with database space usage and availability at this time. No parameters are required to get database space usage for the current database, as in the following example:

```
sp_spaceused

database_name                database_size
--------------------------   --------------------
master                       8 MB
(0 rows affected)

reserved       data         index_size      unused
-------------  -----------  --------------  --------------
5230 KB        4232 KB      208 KB          790KB
(0 rows affected)
```

> **WARNING**
>
> sp_spaceused can be off by as much as two extents per table.

The output from the procedure can be somewhat misleading, so review it closely. Database size is the total database size, including data and log allocations, but the reserved value is based only on data usage (not logs). If you have allocated data and log separately, you can subtract from the total database size the space allocated to the log to get the total data allocation.

To determine how much space is reserved for objects within the data allocation, take the reserved value in the previous example (5230) and subtract the pages reserved for the log (run sp_spaceused syslogs). That is the space reserved for objects.

To arrive at the space available for allocation to objects, subtract from the total allocation for data the amount reserved for objects.

In the case of the master database, where you cannot separate the data and log segments, you may have to add the space reserved by syslogs to the reserved value to get a total for the space being utilized. Then subtract the total space utilized from the total size of the database to get the amount of space available for allocation.

# Database Options

Use `sp_dboption` to enable or disable a database option for a database. Internally, this command sets a status flag for the database. The following list contains several options you can use to define standard processing or to support special requirements:

| | |
|---|---|
| `abort tran on log full` | Enables the database administrator to determine whether transactions should be placed on hold or rejected when the free-space threshold is crossed in the transaction log. For more on the free-space threshold, see Chapter 29. |
| `allow null` | Permits the database owner to decide whether columns that do not specify nullability permit nulls. For example, the following `create table` statement does not specify whether `col_1` permits nulls or not.<br><br>`create table table_1 (col_1 int)`<br><br>Normally, `col_1` would not permit nulls. If you set `allow null` to `true` before executing the `create table` statement, the column will permit nulls. |
| `auto identity` | While this option is true, a 10-digit `IDENTITY` column is defined in all new tables created without specifying either a primary key, unique constraint, or `IDENTITY` column. This column is not made visible with a `select *`, but must be mentioned using the `SYB_IDENTITY_COL` column name in the select list. |
| `dbo use only` | After setting a database to `dbo use only`, only the database owner (`dbo`) may issue the `use` statement for this database. |
| `ddl in tran` | Permits the use of `create`, `drop`, `grant`, and `revoke` statements within `begin tran ... commit tran` structures. |
| `identity in nonunique index` | Automatically includes an `IDENTITY` column in a table's index keys, if the table has an `IDENTITY` column. This makes all indexes unique. |
| `no chkpt on recovery` | Prevents a checkpoint record from being written to the log after the recovery process is complete. |
| `no free space acctg` | Suppresses free-space accounting and execution of threshold actions for non-log segments. This option does not affect log segments. |

| | |
|---|---|
| `read only` | Enables database users to select from the tables, but prevents all modifications. This option may provide a performance enhancement to decision-support systems. |
| `select into/bulkcopy` | Enables fast, non-logged actions in a database, including `select … into`, non-logged `writetext`, and fast `bcp`. |
| `single user` | Limits database access to one user at a time. |
| `trunc log on chkpt` | Automatically truncates the transaction log after every system-generated checkpoint. |

---

### WARNING

I have experienced a curious problem with `trunc log on chkpt` on certain systems. A checkpoint clears a portion of the cache to free space or updates the data segments of the database. There are three kinds of checkpoints:

- Checkpoints explicitly requested by the database owner
- Checkpoints generated by the server to free space in the cache
- Checkpoints issued by the server-checkpoint process based on the server-recovery interval

On some SQL Server platforms, the `trunc log on chkpt` option truncates the log only after the third kind of checkpoint—a manual checkpoint did not truncate the log.

For more about checkpoints, see Chapter 28. For now, recognize this potential problem with truncation.

Consider a long-running transaction, like an update of all rows in a large table.

```
update titles
set price = price * 1.02
```

In this transaction, the `titles` table contains several million rows. The transaction is likely to be larger than the total capacity of the transaction log. You have two choices: you can increase the size of the log (ignore that choice), or you can try to run the transaction in smaller pieces, presumably clearing the log after each statement, as in the following:

```
update titles
set price = price * 1.02
where title < "P"
checkpoint
update titles
set price = price * 1.02
where title >= "P"
```

If the checkpoint results in a truncation, all is well. On some servers, the `dbo`-initiated checkpoint does not truncate the log, and the log fills up. What's worse, the explicit checkpoint reduces recovery time, further delaying the server-generated checkpoint that would otherwise have truncated the log.

# Default Database Options

Upon server installation, the following items are true concerning database options:

- All database options are set to `false` in the `model` database and in all user databases.
- No options can be set for the `master` database (and `master` has no options set).
- `select into/bulkcopy` is always `true` in the `tempdb` database.
- Any option enabled in the `model` database at the time a new database is created also is enabled for this new database.

# Setting Database Options

To set database options, use `sp_dboption`.

## Syntax

```
sp_dboption <databasename>, <option>, {true ¦ false}
```

## Example

```
sp_dboption market_db, "select", true
```

## Notes

- You must be using the `master` database when you execute the `sp_dboption` stored procedure.
- You can abbreviate the name of the database option, as long as the server can distinguish the option from all others. Note that all keywords (such as `select`) must be placed in quotation marks when they are passed as a parameter to a stored procedure.
- You can set options to `true` or `false`.
- If you attempt to enable a database option for the `master` database, the command will have no effect; no options can be set for the `master` database.
- You must explicitly checkpoint the database after setting an option.

- `sp_dboption` without parameters lists all possible parameters.
- Only the `dbo`, `sa`, or `sa_role` may set database options. `dbo` aliases may not set options.

Typically, changing an option involves the four steps shown in the following code:

```
use master  /* only set options in the master database */
go
sp_dboption market_db, "select into/bulkcopy", true
go
use market_db /* issue the checkpoint from within the target database */
go
checkpoint
go
```

## Examining Database Status

Use `sp_helpdb` to determine the value of status flags on a database. The status values are decoded to the far right in the output, and you may have to scroll to the end of the report to see the information.

## Database Status Flags

The `status` column in `sysdatabases` (and `status2` in System 10) records information about a database in a bit field. Table 26.1 displays the bit representations of the `status` column. Table 26.2 displays the bit representations of the `status2` column.

**Table 26.1. `status` column bit representation.**

| Value | Status |
|-------|--------|
| 4 | Select into/bulkcopy |
| 8 | trunc log on chkpt |
| 16 | No chkpt on recovery |
| 32 | Crashed during load or created for load |
| 256 | Database suspect |
| 512 | ddl in tran |
| 1024 | Read-only |
| 2048 | dbo use only |
| 4096 | Single user |
| 8192 | Allow nulls by default |
| 16384 | dbname has changed |

## Table 26.2. `status2` column bit representation.

| Value | Status |
| --- | --- |
| 1 | Abort tran on log full |
| 2 | No free space acctg |
| 4 | Auto identity |
| 8 | Offline |

# How to Turn Off the *SUSPECT* Flag on a Database

If you start the SQL Server before giving external storage devices a chance to warm up, or if, perhaps, a drive came unplugged, the server detects a failure of the device and marks all databases mapped to that device as SUSPECT (status column, bit value 2^8 = 256). That value in the status column prevents the server from ever trying to recover that database. In order to regain access to the database, you must turn off the bit and restart the server.

In a moment you learn how to manually update the sysdatabases table and remove the SUSPECT bit. Before you do anything unreasonable, though, you should check to make sure that you correctly understand the problem. If the server is up, run sp_helpdb on your database. Is the SUSPECT flag set? If not, but you still cannot access your database, you have a different problem.

If the database is marked SUSPECT, take a look at the errorlog. You want to see, fairly early in the server startup process, that it failed to start the device where the database is loaded. If you find this message, you're ready to roll. If not, keep reading and try to understand why the database was not recovered.

You must log in as sa, or with a login granted the sa_role, in order to be allowed to manually update the sysdatabases table. The following example shows the necessary commands to enable you to directly update the status bit in the sysdatabases table:

```
use master
go
sp_configure "allow updates", 1
reconfigure with override
go
update sysdatabases
set status = status - 256
where dbname = "your database name here"
and status & 256 = 256
go
sp_configure "allow updates", 0
reconfigure
go
```

Now shut down and restart the server. If the drives are working, the system should come right up and the databases should be available.

# The *model* Database

Whenever a database is created, the contents of the model database are copied to the new database. It is typical to place in the model database any objects that you intend to be located in all databases. Typically, model contains rules, defaults, user-defined datatypes, and any logins (for example, guest) that will be created in all databases.

> **TIP**
>
> User-defined datatypes are stored in systypes in each individual database. As new types are created in each database, each type is assigned a new integer identifier.
>
> For example, if ssn_type was the first user-defined type created in one database and age_type was first in another, each would be assigned the same identifier: 100. This would create a problem when you move information between databases, especially when you use the select … into command, where the datatype identifier (the numeric value) is copied to the new table structure.
>
> The same problem is more severe in tempdb, where the lack of any matching type identifier typically causes sp_help to fail.
>
> I recommend that you define user-defined types first in the model database before creating any user databases. Then, when the user database is created, the user-defined types are copied to this new database. I further recommend that as individual databases have to add further datatypes, you should create these datatypes in the model database first, then re-create them in each user database.
>
> Bear in mind that tempdb is created every time the server restarts. When tempdb is created, it also gets a copy of the model database, which means that it gets a complete library of user-defined datatypes.

You should consider creating a system-stored procedure to handle centralized functions, rather than creating a procedure in the model database to be propagated to all databases. You also should consider placing lookup tables in a single, central database, rather than propagating lookup tables into every database.

# Dropping Databases

To drop a database, simply issue the drop database command:

```
drop database <database_name>
```

Dropping a database removes all of the appropriate entries from the various system tables, and the structure is removed—making that space available to other databases. Only the dbo (or sa, or sa_role) can drop a database, and nobody can be using it at the time it is dropped.

When you drop a database, you remove all objects, all data, and all logs associated with the database. The server removes all references to the database in sysdatabases and sysusages.

Sometimes you aren't able to drop a database; for example, SUSPECT databases cannot be dropped. To remove a corrupt or damaged database, use dbcc dbrepair, as in the following:

```
dbcc dbrepair (<db_name>, dropdb)
```

The following is an example of how to remove a corrupt database called corrupt_db:

```
dbcc dbrepair (corrupt_db, dropdb)
```

# Segments and Object Placement

If you have a database with space allocated for data on two different physical devices, it is important to understand where the server places tables, indexes, and other objects as they are created and expanded. For example, a database was created on devices DATA_1 and DATA_2 as follows:

```
create database market_db
on DATA_1 = 100, DATA_2 = 100
log on LOG_1 = 50
```

When you create a table in the database, as in the following example, where does the server place the table, on DATA_1 or DATA_2?

```
create table Customer
(name char(30) not null,
 address char(30) not null)
```

The simple answer is, "If you haven't set up any segments in your database, it doesn't matter." The server allocates space freely within the data area of the database until all of the allocations for data are full.

> **NOTE**
>
> By specifying in the create database statement that the 50MB on LOG_1 was for log use only, you have already set up a *log segment*, a predefined segment that is for the exclusive use of the syslogs table. In this section you learn how to create your own user-defined segments for storing tables you want to isolate.

A *segment* is a label that identifies a set of storage allocations within a database. By using segments, you can control where the server places database objects, enabling those objects to expand only within specifically defined areas within the database. Segments can provide two broad benefits: improved performance, and greater control over object placement and growth within the database.

> **NOTE**
>
> Segments are not widely used in the SQL Server community. An estimate is that less than 5 percent of all SQL Server sites use any segments beyond those provided as part of SQL Server. (See the section on "Predefined Segments," later in this chapter.)
>
> Consider the following discussion and look at the examples before deciding to implement segments. They provide some benefit, but require a little more administrative attention and can sometimes complicate database restores.

## Segments for Performance

Typically, when segments are used to improve performance, the segments point to Sybase devices that are mapped to different physical disk drives. The performance improvements typically seek to distribute database activity across disks (and controllers). Here are some examples of how activity can be distributed:

■ Nonclustered indexes can be stored on one segment, while the table itself is stored on another. This can improve both read and write performance, because index I/O can run parallel to table I/O.

Note that clustered indexes always reside on the same segment as the table indexed. This requirement arises because the leaf level of the clustered index is the table itself.

■ A large table can be divided among segments (and disks) to allow different parts of the table to be read at one time.

■ Text and image data (Binary Large OBjects, or BLOBs) can be placed on a segment, apart from the standard data pages. This may improve read performance when the table is heavily used.

## Segments for Control

Segments also enable you to manage the size of objects within the database. Without segments, each object can grow to the full size of the data allocations in the database, contending for space with all other objects. In the previous example, the Customer table and its indexes could grow to 200MB, unless other objects also were consuming space in the database.

When you use segments, objects can grow only to the size of the segment. In addition, by implementing segments, you can place thresholds on each segment, and define the necessary action when the objects in a segment come near to filling the segment.

## Segment Definition

Use the sp_addsegment stored procedure to add a new segment to a database. Use sp_extendsegment to add other device allocations for the database to an existing segment.

## Syntax

```
sp_addsegment <segmentname>, <databasename>, <devicename>
sp_extendsegment <segmentname>, <databasename>, <devicename>
```

## Examples

```
sp_addsegment Seg1, market_db, DATA_1
sp_extendsegment Seg1, market_db, DATA_2
```

Take careful note of the parameters of the `sp_addsegment` and `sp_extendsegment` stored procedures: segment name, database name, and device name. There are two characteristics you must understand about segments:

- Segments are database-specific. When you create a segment, you establish a mapping to the usage of space on a specific device or set of devices for a database. Fragments of other databases on that device are not part of that segment.

- Segments refer to all fragments on a device or set of devices for a database.

Take a look at two examples. In the first example, the accounting database is 240MB, with 200MB for data, 40MB for log. The first segment, `Seg1`, includes 50MB on DATA_1 and 100MB on DATA_3. The second segment, `Seg2`, includes 50MB on DATA_2 and 100MB on DATA_3.

```
use master
go
create database acctg_db
on DATA_1 = 50, DATA_2 = 50, DATA_3 = 100
log on LOG_1 = 40
go

use acctg_db
go
exec sp_addsegment Seg1, acctg_db, DATA_1
exec sp_addsegment Seg2, acctg_db, DATA_2
exec sp_extendsegment Seg2, acctg_db, DATA_3
exec sp_extendsegment Seg1, acctg_db, DATA_3
go
```

## Notes

- Segment definitions are database-specific, so `Seg1` for `acctg_db` does not conflict with `Seg1` for `market_db` (see last section, "Examples").

- Segment definitions are database-specific, so the fact that `Seg1` in `acctg_db` extends to the DATA_3 device does not affect the mapping of the similarly named segment in `market_db`. Figure 26.2 illustrates this.

**FIGURE 26.2.**

*A segment is database-specific. Two segments, each with the same name, are created for different databases. They uniquely identify usages on devices for that database.*

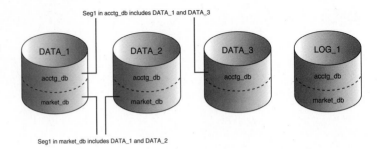

Seg1 in acctg_db includes DATA_1 and DATA_3

Seg1 in market_db includes DATA_1 and DATA_2

In the next example, add an additional 50MB to `acctg_db` on `DATA_3`. Now `Seg1` includes 50MB on `DATA_1` and 150MB on `DATA_3`.

```
alter database acctg_db
on DATA_3 = 50
```

## Additional Notes

Segments refer to all fragments on a device or set of devices for a database. When you add 50 additional megabytes to the database on `DATA_3`, the additional space automatically is incorporated into every segment that refers to that device for the database. Figure 26.3 illustrates this.

**FIGURE 26.3.**

*Segments refer to all fragments on a device or set of devices for a database. Additional space allocated on a device already mapped to a segment becomes part of that segment.*

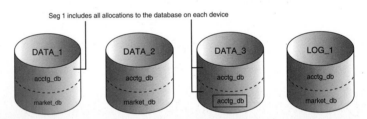

Seg 1 includes all allocations to the database on each device

> **NOTE**
>
> There is a many-to-many relationship between segments and devices. A single segment can include mappings to many devices. A single device can be part of many segments, even within a single database. The section "Segment System Tables," later in this chapter, talks about how this mapping is recorded in the `sysusages` table.

## Predefined Segments

Whenever you create a new database, the server automatically creates three segments in the database:

■ `default`, for tables and indexes

- system, for system tables (including all object definitions)
- logsegment, for storing syslogs

The default and system segments are mapped to all data allocations. The logsegment segment is mapped to any allocations for log. For example, in the first example you looked at:

```
create database market_db
on DATA_1 = 100, DATA_2 = 100
log on LOG_1 = 50
```

the allocations on DATA_1 and DATA_2 were mapped to the default and system segments. Allocations for LOG_1 were mapped to the logsegment segment. Figure 26.4 illustrates this.

**FIGURE 26.4.**

*Creating a database automatically defines the* default, system, *and* logsegment *segments.*

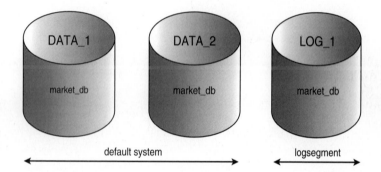

## Placing Objects on Segments

Every object is placed on a segment when the object is created. System tables (except syslogs) are placed on the system segment and the transaction log (syslogs) is placed on the logsegment segment. Everything else (specifically, tables and indexes) automatically is placed on the default segment.

To create an object on a specific segment, add

on <segmentname>

to your create statement. The following example places the Customer table (market_db database) on Seg1. As the table grows, it will use space on DATA_1 and DATA_2, the devices mapped to Seg1.

```
create table Customer
(name char(30) not null,
 address char(30) not null)
on Seg1
```

The next example creates a nonclustered index on Customer on a different segment, Seg2. A table and its nonclustered indexes can be on separate segments.

```
create index Customer_nci1
on Customer(name)
on Seg2
```

The final example explicitly places a table on the `default` segment:

```
create table lookup
(code int not null,
 value varchar(20) not null)
on "default"
```

> **NOTE**
>
> The word *default* must be enclosed in quotes: `default` is a keyword referring to a type of system object.

## Changing an Object's Segment

Use `sp_placeobject` to place all of an object's future growth on a specific segment.

> **NOTE**
>
> SQL Server allocates space to objects in eight-page (usually 16KB) extents. `sp_placeobject` instructs the server that all future extent allocations should come from devices mapped to the new segment. It does not prevent newly inserted rows from being added to pages that have already been mapped to the earlier segment.

## Syntax

```
sp_placeobject <segmentname>, <objectname>
```

## Example

```
sp_placeobject Seg3, Customer
sp_placeobject Seg3, "Customer.Index03"
```

After these statements are issued, all additional space allocations to the `Customer` table and to the `Customer` table `Index03` index come from `Seg3`.

> **NOTE**
>
> Placing the clustered index on a different segment, as in the following:
>
> ```
> sp_placeobject Seg3, "Customer.ClusteredIndex"
> ```
>
> has the same effect as placing the table on the new segment: all future space allocations to the table or clustered index come from devices mapped to `Seg3`.

One way to use segments is to spread a large table across several devices. To distribute the table evenly, you must create the table on one segment, load a segment of the data, then run `sp_placeobject` to point to the next segment, as in the following example:

```
create table spread_table ( ... ) on Seg1
```

Now load 50 percent of the data:

```
sp_placeobject Seg2, spread_table
```

Now load the rest of the data. At this point, the data is evenly distributed between the two segments.

```
sp_placeobject Seg3, spread_table
```

All future allocations will come from `Seg3`.

> **NOTE**
>
> The interesting question is, when should the clustered index be created? If you create the clustered index after the last `sp_placeobject`, the entire table resides on the `Seg3` segment. So you must create the clustered index early and enable it to grow across all three segments. To optimize the load, you probably will choose to create the clustered index after you load the first half of the data, but before you place the table on `Seg2`.

# Moving an Object to a New Segment

The method you use to move an object to a new segment, including all existing allocations, depends on the object. To move a table without a clustered index to a new segment, create a clustered index on the new segment, then drop the index. The first statement in the following code moves the table to `New_Seg`, and builds a clustered index along the way. The second statement drops the index (if the sole use of creating the index was to enable you to move the table).

```
create clustered index temp_index on Table1(key) on New_Seg
drop index Table1.temp_index
```

> **NOTE**
>
> Whether this is an efficient way to move a table to a new segment or not depends, in part, on the size of the table and the resources you have available to you. It may be faster to create a new table on the desired segment, insert rows from one table to the other, and then drop the old table and rename the new one. It may also be faster to use `bcp` to copy the data out, then in.

Keep in mind that you cannot use the clustered index method to move a table that contains fully duplicate rows: clustered index creation will fail if duplicate rows are discovered in the table.

To move a table that has a clustered index, drop the clustered index first and then re-create it on the new segment:

```
drop index Table1.clustered_index
create clustered index clustered_index on Table1(key) on New_Seg
```

To move a non-clustered index to a new segment, drop the index and re-create it on the new segment:

```
drop index Table1.nc_index
create index nc_index on Table1(nckey) on New_Seg
```

### TIP

Try to remember that `sp_placeobject` affects only the future growth of an object; it does not affect existing allocated space.

# Removing a Device from a Segment

Use `sp_dropsegment` to remove a device from a segment definition, or to remove a segment from a database. Remember: every object is created on a segment. If you remove a device from a segment definition, you control which objects can exist on a physical device.

There are some limitations to using `sp_dropsegment`:

- You cannot drop the last segment from a device.
- You cannot use `sp_dropsegment` on a segment if you have previously created or placed objects there.
- You cannot completely drop the predefined segments.

When you create a database, all data allocations are mapped to the `default` and `system` segments. When you create a new segment for a specific device, you probably want to remove the `default` and `system` segment mappings to that device to ensure that only objects explicitly placed there use the segment device(s).

For example, to create a segment to use with indexes in this database, you would create the `index` segment, then drop the `default` and `system` segments from the device, as in this example:

```
create database market_db
on DATA_1 = 50, DATA_2 = 50
log on DATA_3 = 25
```

```
exec sp_addsegment index_segment, market_db, DATA_2
exec sp_dropsegment "default", market_db, DATA_2
exec sp_dropsegment "system", market_db, DATA_2
```

Figure 26.5 illustrates the segment mappings at the end of this process.

**FIGURE 26.5.**

*You can drop the* default *and* system *segments from a data device once you have created a new segment on that device.*

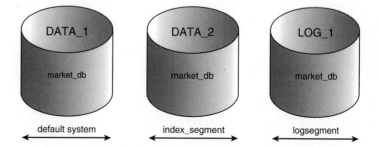

Getting Information on Segments

Use sp_helpsegment to get information about segments in your current database. If you do not pass the segment name parameter, sp_helpsegment lists all segments in the database. If you pass the name of a segment as a parameter, you get detailed information about the segment, including a detailed list of fragments on devices and the fragment size, as well as a list of all objects stored on the segment.

> **TIP**
>
> Don't forget that default is a keyword. To find out about the default segment, pass the name in quotes:
>
> ```
> sp_helpsegment "default"
> ```

# Segment System Tables

Segment changes have an impact on system tables in both the current database (syssegments and sysindexes) and the master database (sysusages).

## syssegments

When you create a segment, the server makes an entry in the syssegments table in the database. The entry consists of a *segment*, a *name*, and a *status*.

segment    A unique integer value assigned by the system. The maximum value is 31, and there can be no more than 32 segments in a database.

name    A unique name you assign with sp_addsegment.

status    A bit column indicating the default segment.

The following example shows the contents of syssegments. There is one row in syssegments per segment in the database; syssegments is a database-level system table.

```
segment name                              status
------- ----------------------------      ------
0       system                            0
1       default                           1
2       logsegment                        0
3       indexes                           0
```

## sysusages

Creation of a segment also has an impact on sysusages. The segmap column in sysusages is a bitmap of segments mapped to that device fragment.

| Segment Number | 0 | 1 | 2 | 3 | 4 |
|---|---|---|---|---|---|
| Bitmap Value | $1\ (2^0)$ | $2\ (2^1)$ | $4\ (2^2)$ | $8\ (2^3)$ | $16\ (2^4)$ |
| Segment Name | system | default | logsegment | Seg1 | index_segment |
| Value | 0 | 0 | 0 | 8 | 16 |

The value of segmap for the row in sysusages corresponding to DATA_2 is $(0 + 0 + 0 + 8 + 16) = 24$.

## sysindexes

Object placement is recorded in the segment column of sysindexes. sp_help displays the segment in which an object is stored.

## SQL to Query syssegments

To join syssegments to sysusages, you must select on dbid and perform a "bitwise and" (&) between the segmap column in sysusages and the segment values in the database. Your where clause should look like this:

```
where segmap & power(2, segment) > 0
  and db_id() = dbid
```

For example, to determine the number of fragments and the total megabytes allocated to each segment, execute the following command:

```
select s.name, count(*) "fragments", sum(size)/512 "allocation"
from master..sysusages u, syssegments s
where segmap & power(2, segment) > 0
  and db_id() = dbid
group by s.name
```

Segments are overlapping. In this database, there is a 3MB allocation to default, logsegment, and system on the same device, as shown in the following output:

```
name                              fragments   allocation
-------------------------------   ---------   ----------
default                           1           3
logsegment                        1           3
system                            1           3
```

# Thresholds

For any of the segments in your database, you can define a threshold procedure to monitor the free space that is available. Thresholds are new in System 10. The threshold tells the server to monitor a particular segment in a database. Once the threshold is crossed (meaning that the space available has fallen below a certain level), a stored procedure that you create is executed.

This procedure can expand the segment, dump the transaction log, write to the error log, or execute a remote procedure call. A remote procedure call could be to an Open Server, enabling you to send electronic mail, or even to page the person responsible for the system. You can define up to 256 thresholds in each database.

## Adding a Threshold

You use the sp_addthreshold command to add a threshold:

```
sp_addthreshold database_name, segment_name,
      space_left_in_pages, procedure_name
```

Here is an example of this command:

```
sp_addthreshold CustomerDB, "default", 10240, CustDefaultSegWarning
```

## Simple Procedure Code: *CustDefaultSegWarning*

Here is a simple procedure to alert you that you are running out of space in the CustomerDB database:

```
create procedure CustDefaultSegWarning
as
print "WARNING: The default segment in the CustomerDB database"
print "    Add more space to the database ASAP!!!"
go
```

> **NOTE**
>
> You must be using the database to which you are adding the threshold when executing `sp_addthreshold`. This is redundant, but required.

In the preceding example, when the available space in the default segment of the `CustomerDB` database falls below 20MB, the server automatically executes the `CustDefaultSegWarning` procedure. (The print messages are directed into the errorlog.) Your daily review of the errorlog would alert you to the need to alter the `CustomerDB` database.

## User-Defined Segments

Create a threshold or thresholds for every user-defined segment in your database. Reporting on free space for a user-defined segment is not particularly easy. `sp_spaceused`, often used to report on available space, may indicate you have 1GB of space available in the database. User-defined segments, unlike `default`, normally only apply to a small portion of the fragments available to your database. Users may receive "no space available" messages and call you to investigate. If you were not aware that the table in question was on a user-defined segment, you might execute `sp_spaceused` and be confused by the results.

## @@thresh_hysteresis

Once a threshold has been crossed, it is not executed again until the amount of free space in the segment increases by `@@thresh_hysteresis` pages (normally, 64). Therefore, in the "Example," the amount of free space that must be available before the threshold is crossed and the stored procedure kicks in would be 20MB + 128KB. (The example put a threshold at 10,240 pages, which is 20MB. Given that `@@thresh_hysteresis` normally is 64 pages, and pages are normally 2KB, the amount of space available would have to vary greater than 128KB from the point of the threshold for the procedure to be re-executed.) This prevents the procedure from executing repeatedly when the free space hovers around the threshold.

Each additional threshold added to a segment must be at least two times `@@thresh_hysteresis` away from other thresholds (2 × 64 = 128 pages; for 2KB pages, this total is 256KB). This means thresholds must have at least $1/4$MB of space (256KB) between them.

> **NOTE**
>
> Hysteresis, from the Greek *husteresis* ("shortcoming"), refers to the failure of something that has been changed by an external agent to return to its original value when the cause of the change is removed.

# Modifying Thresholds

Use sp_modifythreshold to change threshold information. You can associate a different stored procedure, change the free space value, or associate the threshold with a different segment. You can drop the threshold and create a new one based on the new information provided, as follows:

```
use database_name
go
sp_modifythreshold database_name, segment_name, free_pages
    [, new_procedure [, new_free_space [, new_segment ] ] ]
go
```

The three required parameters (database_name, segment_name, and free_pages) identify the threshold; the three optional parameters (new_procedure, new_free_space, and new_segment) indicate the change. You can use null if a parameter does not change (or you can simply provide the previous value). To change the threshold from the previous example to point to the system segment, execute the following code:

```
use CustomerDB
go
sp_modifythreshold CustomerDB, "default", 10240, null, null, "system"
go
```

# Dropping a Threshold

Use sp_dropthreshold to drop an existing threshold. You must provide enough information to identify the threshold:

```
use database_name
go
sp_dropthreshold database_name, segment_name, free_pages
go
use CustomerDB
go
sp_modifythreshold CustomerDB, "system", 10240
go
```

# Displaying Threshold Information

Use sp_helpthreshold to report on all thresholds in a database, or the threshold associated with a particular segment:

```
use database_name
go
sp_helpthreshold [segment_name]
go
```

# Summary

Databases are the main storage and allocation structure in the SQL Server. Databases provide a way for you to logically and physically store data and to perform backups and recovery with full transactional integrity. Databases also are a useful security mechanism, as you see in the next chapter.

Segments improve database performance and let you control the growth of objects more carefully than a database alone can. Thresholds make segments far more useful, because they enable the system administrator to monitor the capacity and space availability of each storage unit.

# Security and User Administration

# 27

Implementing a security and user administration plan in a Sybase SQL Server is not terribly difficult once you have designed an approach. This chapter offers several approaches, but first explores some basics to help you implement your plan correctly.

# Overview

To access server data, a user needs to clear four security levels (see Figure 27.1):

- The operating system
- The Sybase server
- The Sybase database
- The Sybase object

Think of each level as a door to a room: the door either needs to be unlocked, or you need a key to open it. You can set up a virtually unlimited number of doors to secure data within a database. Let's look at each level independently.

**FIGURE 27.1.**

*SQL Server security consists of four access levels.*

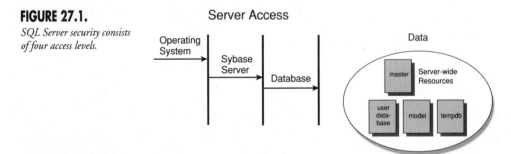

# Operating System Security Issues

A user may require some access to several operating systems to run a typical client/server application. For example:

- A client workstation and its file, disk, and presentation resources.
- A network operating system for the client/server application (as well as mail, file, and print services).
- The SQL Server host operating system where SQL Server is running.

Normally, each of these processes—client, network, SQL Server—runs on a distinct system; in some cases, however, the client application actually runs on the same host system as the SQL Server process (this is far more common in the UNIX and Open VMS environments than on other SQL Server systems).

A user does not require a login on the host machine where the Sybase server is running *unless the user's client process is also hosted by the same system.* To enable database access without requiring operating system logins, the SQL Server is network-port addressable. The client can connect directly to the SQL Server without logging in to the database server hardware first. (See Chapter 24, "SQL Server Installation and Connectivity," for a detailed discussion of network port addresses.)

You require an operating system login for a sybase user. This login owns the directories where SQL Server is installed and all the disk or file resources used by the data server process. You need to log in to the host as sybase to restart the server manually and to run maintenance programs such as buildmaster. The sybase login also is required to perform all upgrades.

> **NOTE**
>
> Remember, this is the operating system process that is actually running the SQL Server.

Operating system security is the responsibility of the OS administrator and varies dramatically between environments, so further discussion is beyond the scope of this book.

> **NOTE**
>
> In SQL Server for Windows NT, there is a closer integration between OS security and SQL Server security. By default, OS administrators have administrative access to SQL Server. Users can inherit privileges to the server through their Windows NT login or group. (The documentation refers to this as *integrated* or *mixed security.*)
>
> This integration between host and server security is not standard to SQL Server implementations. If you are staging your development or test systems on NT but planning to migrate to a Sybase server for production, build your security around the standard Sybase security mechanisms to avoid problems in portability.

# Sybase Server Security: Logins

Access to an SQL Server is controlled through a server login and password. (Logins are discussed in the Sybase Server Logins section later in this chapter.)

Once a user has entered the server door (gained access to the server), there are a variety of database doors available.

The door to the master database is always unlocked, and a person will end up in that room if you don't specify a different default when setting up the login, or if the user's default database is unavailable. (We'll discuss this in detail later in this chapter.)

However, there are several other doors to consider, including doors to other system databases and to any user databases that have been created.

# Sybase Database Security: Users

After you create a user login, you provide access to a Sybase database in one of the following ways:

- Adding a user to a database (giving the user a key);
- Telling the database to treat a user as some other valid user (an alias—giving the user a copy of someone else's key);
- Creating a guest user (unlocking the door and propping it open);
- Making that login the owner of the database.

Once inside a database, a user is able to see definitions for the objects contained in that database. This is because definitions are stored in the system tables, which any user of a database has select access to (except for certain sensitive columns). The user still needs permission to access each database object. (Database users are discussed in the "Database Access" section later in this chapter.)

# Object-level Security: Permissions

When you create an object (a table, a procedure, or a view), SQL Server automatically assigns ownership to you. Object ownership confers complete control over the object—its access, integrity, and administration. By default, only the object owner may select from a table until access is granted to others.

Object-level security is the last level of security. To provide access to an object, you must grant the user *permission* to use it. For example, a user can select from a table once the owner has granted select permission. If the user does not have the necessary permission, access will be denied.

Although this is the last main level in your security scheme, object security can contain several sublevels. (Later in this chapter, in the "Permission Approaches" section, we'll discuss how the use of dependent objects can tighten the security in your system.)

For example, you can grant permission to a view, but not to its underlying (base) tables. This enables an administrator to deny direct access to tables, but allow access to the data through the view. This same concept applies to stored procedures and triggers.

Sybase offers a variety of ways to control access to data. SQL Server login and database user approaches affect the way in which a permissions strategy is implemented.

At the object level, most sites grant broad permissions and then limit or grant specific access as needed to minimize the administrative overhead in implementing a permissions plan. This usually involves granting permissions to `public` or to a user-defined group, then revoking or granting specific permissions to a user-defined group or a specific user.

# Sybase Server Logins

An SQL Server login provides access to the SQL Server. Logins are usually the first line of defense for the DBA in a security plan. (Remember: OS passwords are usually the responsibility of the OS administrator.) When you grant a login, the user can connect to the server and can use the `master` database (you'll learn why in the security section).

An SQL Server login usually requires a password, although there are exceptions. For example, upon initial installation, the sa login has no password. On pre–System 10 servers, you can add new logins without a password (password is null). We urge you to require passwords on all servers, even on a pre–System 10 server. Without passwords, it is difficult to implement any meaningful security on SQL Server.

Add logins with `sp_addlogin`:

```
sp_addlogin login_name, password [ , defdb [ , deflanguage  [ , fullname ] ] ]
sp_addlogin rbrown, shake#crown
```

In versions prior to System 10, `sp_addlogin` reports `login added`. In System 10 and later, you get these messages:

```
Password correctly set.
Account unlocked.
New login created.
```

The next example shows the contents of `syslogins` after running `sp_addlogin` (adding a row to the `syslogins` table in the `master` database):

```
select suid, name from syslogins

suid    name
___ ___  ___ ___ ___ ___ ___ ___ ___ ___
1       sa
2       probe
3       mon_user
4       testuser1
5       jeff
6       rbrown
```

Let's take a look at each of the parameters of `sp_addlogin`. You pass parameters to stored procedures by name or by position. Passing by position is more common, especially when dealing with system procedures such as `sp_addlogin`.

In this example, the login of `joe` gets the default values for `defdb` and `deflanguage`:

```
sp_addlogin joe, "secret", null, null, "Joe Smith"
```

If no value is provided, `defdb` defaults to `master database` and password defaults to `NULL`.

When passing by name, you can specify any parameters you choose, in any order. To retrieve the names of the parameters, use `sp_help`:

```
sp_help sp_addlogin
go
```

The other method of displaying proper syntax for stored procedures (and all other SQL statements) is to use the `sp_syntax` procedure (System 10 only):

```
sp_syntax {command ¦ fragment} [, modulename [, language]]
```

The parameters of `sp_syntax` define the syntax requests. *command* or *fragment* is the command (or portion of a command) for which you require syntax. *modulename* is the name or partial name of the module or utility to which the syntax applies. *language* is any valid installed language on your server. (The `sybsyntax` database is loaded from an installation script that—in all likelihood—hasn't been run on your server.) For more information, see Chapter 24.

Use `sp_syntax` with no parameter to list installed modules.

Once you have the full syntax for the command, including the names of all parameters, you can run the procedure, passing parameters by name instead of position. Here's the same example, this time passing parameters by name:

```
sp_addlogin @fullname = "Joe Smith", @loginame = "joe", @passwd = "secret"
```

The unspecified parameters (`defdb` and `deflanguage`) get a default value.

You also can mix parameter-passing methods, but *once you start naming parameters, you cannot stop*. In the following example, *name* and *password* are passed by position, but *fullname* is passed by name:

```
sp_addlogin joe, secret, @fullname = "J. Smith"
```

In System 10 and later, only *login_name* and the password are required; prior to System 10, the password was also optional. *login_name* must be unique for the server and must not be more than 30 characters long. Passwords must be between 6 and 30 characters long.

You can define a default database for each login. The default database does not grant any inherent privilege to use a database; it merely tells SQL Server to *attempt* to use the defined database at login time. If the login does not yet have access to the default database, the server issues an error message; the user is logged in and the current database is the `master` database. A login that does not have a default database specified will also default to the `master` database.

> **TIP**
>
> It's important to assign a default database and provide access to that database for each login in your system.

In a well-secured system, a user can't really do any damage to the master database—rattle around, select from the system tables, make a general nuisance of himself, maybe, but not do any real damage without the sa password.

To be safe, don't leave users in master. Set valid default databases for users so they don't end up defaulting to master.

## WHY CAN'T I USE THE DATABASE?

There are times when you have done everything right, but users still end up pointed to the master database when they log in. Here is a list of some of the most common errors you'll see as a result, their probable causes, and their solutions, starting with the obvious and moving toward the obscure.

Each of the specific error messages you receive is followed by this general error message:

```
Error 4001: Cannot open default database 'testdb'.
```

*Error received:*

```
Message 916: Server user id 6 is not a valid user in database 'testdb'.
```

*Diagnosis:*

The login has not been added as a user to this database.

*Action required:*

Add the user to the database with sp_adduser, sp_addalias, or sp_changedbowner, or add the guest user to the database.

*Error received:*

```
Error 930: Database 'testdb2' cannot be opened because either an earlier system
termination left LOAD DATABASE incomplete or the database is created with 'for
load' option. Load the database or contact a user with System Administrator
(SA) role.
```

*Diagnosis:*

The database cannot be used until a restore from backup is complete.

*Action required:*

Restore the database from backup. The user must wait until the restore is completed.

*Error received:*

```
Error 905: Unable to allocate a DBTABLE descriptor to open database 'testdb'.
Another database must be closed or dropped before opening this one.
```

*Diagnosis:*

Your system configuration settings need to enable more concurrently open databases.

> *Action required:*
> Increase the open databases setting with sp_configure. Meanwhile, a database needs to be closed before this database is available.

The default language option (deflanguage) is used at sites that have loaded other character sets besides us_english (the language that is always available to the server). If this parameter is provided, the user receives all system messages in the language selected.

The *fullname* parameter (System 10 only) provides the capability of associating a user's full name with the login name.

Note that the optional parameters (defdb, deflanguage, and fullname) can be updated later using the sp_modifylogin (System 10) or sp_defaultdb (pre–System 10) procedures, which are described later in this chapter.

Of course, your users may ask whether they can change their own default database or password. A user can change his or her password using sp_password. Passwords should be changed frequently—about once a month is appropriate. Also, users can change their default database with the sp_modifylogin or the sp_defaultdb command.

# Special Logins

There are two special logins created during the installation of SQL Server: sa and probe.

## sa

The sa login owns the server, although you can use roles to transfer sa authority to other logins. The sa login owns the system databases (master, model, tempdb, sybsystemprocs, and any others installed by the sa). The sa login is the database owner (dbo) within those databases because it is the login that literally is mapped to the dbo user (more on dbo later in this chapter). (When an individual—a login—creates a database, the server records the suid column from the server's row in syslogins as the database owner in sysdatabases). Regardless of actual database ownership, the sa is seen as the dbo of any user database. It is important to note that in System 10, the sa login has its capabilities as a result of *roles* that have automatically been granted to the login as part of an installation. The roles granted to the sa are sa_role and sso_role. See the Roles section later in this chapter for more information.

## probe

There also is a probe login provided as part of SQL Server installation. This login is used between servers to manage two-phase commit activities.

# Generic Logins

Some sites add a general login, such as `templogin` or `sybguest`, to be used by temporary users of a server for in-house training or self-study. Often the logins have no password, or the password is the same as the login name. Of course, many administrators prefer an individual login for each user of a server; this provides better control and permits auditing of work by individual if necessary.

# How Logins Work

When a new login is created, a row is added to a system table called `syslogins` in `master`. Each login is assigned a unique system user ID (`suid`), an integer that identifies that user uniquely in the server. During login, the server matches the name passed in the login structure against the `name` column in the `syslogins` table. If a match is found and the password matches, the `suid` is stored in the memory allocated for the new connection.

The login name is not stored in any table except `syslogins`. The `suid` is the key used in all other tables that relate to a person's login, including system tables assigning roles and those relating server access to database access.

> **TIP**
>
> To retrieve a list of `suid`s and login names:
>
> ```
> select suid, name from syslogins
> ```
>
> Although you can select the password column if you are the sa, the values are encrypted in System 10 and above. Prior to System 10, the `password` column is plainly readable by the sa:
>
> ```
> select suid, name, password from syslogins
> ```

The system functions `suser_name()` and `suser_id()` convert login IDs to names and vice versa. For example:

```
select suser_name(2)
```

returns the value `probe` (because `probe` is always the second user inserted in the `syslogins` table). Conversely, the following:

```
select suser_id("probe")
```

returns the value 2. When the functions are used without arguments, they return the login name or ID for the current user.

**NOTE**

These system functions are most useful in accessing data from system tables, where they enable you to decode a name or ID without needing to specify a join, as in the following example. These system functions are also frequently used in the Sybase-provided system stored procedures.

```
use master
go
select spid, suid, suser_name(suid) "name"
from sysprocesses
order by suser_name(suid)
go

spid   suid   name
------ ------ ------------------------------
2      0
3      0
4      0
5      0
6      6      rbrown
1      1      sa
```

Notice the rows in sysprocesses with an suid of 0 and no name. These processes are system processes in charge of mirror, network, and checkpoint handling. In System 10, an additional handler—a shutdown handler—has been added.

# Modifying Login Information

Again, don't worry if you don't have all the login information at the time a login is added. It always can be changed using sp_modifylogin (System 10) or sp_defaultdb (pre–System 10):

```
sp_modifylogin login_name, option, value
```

The options are defdb (default database), deflanguage (default language), and fullname (user's full name):

```
sp_defaultdb login_name, default_db
```

# Displaying Login Information

Login information can be displayed using the sp_displaylogin procedure. sp_displaylogin reports information on a login's suid, the system login name (login name), the full name, any roles that have been configured for that login, an indication of whether the account is locked, and the date of the last password change. The syntax for sp_displaylogin is:

```
sp_displaylogin [ login_name ]
```

Only users who have been granted the sa_role or the sso_role can provide a login name as an argument. For all other users, the procedure must be executed without a login name. For those users who execute sp_displaylogin without providing login names, the login information for their logins is displayed.

# Passwords

A password is used to verify the authenticity of a login. Prior to System 10, passwords were not required, but they must be provided for System 10 and later versions. Passwords must now be at least six characters in length. There was no minimum password length prior to System 10. Passwords can include any printable characters, including A–Z, a–z, 0–9, or any symbols.

> **TIP**
>
> Add symbols or mix the case to make it difficult to guess a password.

## Changing Passwords

Passwords can be changed by the user or by the site security officer (a login with the sso_role, known hereafter in this book as sso). Change passwords with sp_password:

```
sp_password caller_password, new_password [ , login_name ]
```

To change a password, a user passes the current password and the new password. If a user without the sso_role passes a login_name to sp_password, the system returns an error message.

An sso changing another user's password passes the sso password, the new user password, and the login name. If the sso omits the login name, the sso password will be changed!

## Password Expiration

Periodic changes to passwords improve system security. Users have a nasty habit of sharing their passwords with others rather than encouraging their colleagues to get proper permission from the system administrator. When passwords change, the residual security breach caused by shared passwords is reduced.

By setting the configuration option password expiration interval (unfortunately, System 10 only), you can set passwords to expire periodically. The server warns users of a pending password expiration; if a user fails to modify the password before it expires, the sso needs to change the password and let the user know the new value. This example reconfigures the server to set the password expiration for three weeks:

```
/* configure password expiration for three weeks */
sp_configure "password expiration interval", 21
```

The default value, `0`, indicates no password expiration. Possible values range from 0 to 32,767 days, although a reasonable time is probably 45 to 60 days.

You can determine the day your password will expire by adding the password expiration interval to the `pwdate` column in `syslogins` (the date the password was originally set). Find the number of days to expiration (expiration date × current date).

Find the ratio of days until expiration (days to expiration/password expiration interval).

If the ratio is less than 25 percent or days to expiration is less than 7, the system notifies the user that the password will expire in $N$ days.

```
Error 4023: Your password will expire in 5.0 days.
```

If your password has expired, you may connect to the server, but the only command you can execute is `sp_password`. All other actions receive this error message:

```
Error 7742: You must change your password using the sp_password system stored
procedure before you can continue.
```

> **NOTE**
>
> The decision to implement password expiration is usually based on organizational security regulations. We have seen SQL Server sites where password expiration is not implemented because the application developers would need to build a password change subsystem, and there's no budget for it. Naturally, that is not the best reason for not forcing password changes, but it is often the excuse.
>
> If possible, password expiration should be configured to make your site as secure as possible.

# Database Access

After server login security, the next level of security is database access. You manage database access by establishing a link between logins (stored at the server level) and users (stored at the database level). User access to a database is required to use the database (change your current context to the database); it also is required to access any object stored in the database.

> **NOTE**
>
> This information is also added to the memory structure set up for a connection or process, and a review of `sysprocesses` (built dynamically) shows the `uid` and database ID (`dbid`) for a process.

The uid is used to identify ownership of objects within a database. Although the ID assigned to an object is used to relate that object with other tables, there is a unique index on the combination of an object name and a uid (database user ID). This is why more than one user can have an object with the same name, and this concept is very important when determining a development approach.

# Adding Users

You grant access to a database by adding a user to the database. Use sp_adduser to add users; it adds an entry in the database-level sysusers table. Here is the syntax of sp_adduser:

```
sp_adduser login_name [ , name_in_db [ , grpname ] ]
```

To add rbrown to the testdb database, use the following:

```
use testdb
go
sp_adduser rbrown
go
```

At the completion of the sp_adduser procedure, a row is placed in the sysusers table in the database where the user was added. The following example shows the contents of the database-level table, sysusers, after rbrown has been added to the database testdb:

```
use testdb
go
select suid, uid, name
from sysusers
go

suid   uid    name
------ ------ -------------------------------
-16389 16389  replication_role
-16388 16388  navigator_role
-16387 16387  sybase_ts_role
-16386 16386  oper_role
-16385 16385  sso_role
-16384 16384  sa_role
-2     0      public
1      1      dbo
4      3      testuser1
6      4      rbrown
```

**NOTE**

The six roles are defined in the sysusers table, in addition to the users and logins defined by the dbo. These roles are new with System 10. See the "Roles" section later in this chapter for more information.

The only required parameter is `login_name`, which is checked against the `name` column in the `master..syslogins`. (The login name must already exist in the `syslogins` table.) `login_name` is used to derive the `suid` to be placed into the `sysusers` table.

The `name_in_db` parameter is infrequently used in real life, and its purpose is not to be confused with true aliasing (`sp_addalias`). This parameter is inserted in the `name` column in the `sysusers` table.

---

**TIP**

Normally, the default value for this parameter is the string specified for the `login_name`, and—unless you have a very good reason—you should always keep them the same. It makes the matching of database users to server users much simpler. In fact, if a value is not specified or a value of `null` is provided, it defaults to the `login_name`.

---

The `grpname` parameter defines the group for the user. By default, a user is placed in the group `public`, which has a group ID (`gid`) of `0`, although the word `public` can be specified for this parameter. Groups are discussed later in this section.

Use `sp_helpuser` to get a list of users in a database or to see specific information about a single user, as in this example:

```
Users_name        ID_in_db Group_name       Login_name          Default_db
---------------   -------- ---------------  ----------------    --------------
dbo               1        public           sa                  master
rbrown            4        public           rbrown              testdb2
testuser1         3        public           testuser1           master
```

## Special Users

There are two special users that can exist in a Sybase database, `dbo` and `guest`.

## dbo

The `dbo` is the database owner. `dbo` is added to the `model` database during installation; hence the `dbo` exists in all databases in a server. The `dbo` can never be dropped from a database and always has a database user ID (`uid`) of `1`.

---

**NOTE**

It is unusual for the user ID (`uid` in `sysusers`) and the login ID (`suid` in `master..syslogins`) to have the same value. The values are predictably the same only for the `sa`, who is `dbo` in all databases.

---

## *guest*

The guest user is provided to grant database access to anyone who logs in to the server. The guest user must be explicitly added to a database using sp_adduser (or added to the model database before a subsequent database creation).

The presence of a guest user means that anyone logged in to the server can access the database. This is a catch-all to enable access to a database when the login has not been explicitly added as a user of the database (or aliased to another user—see the next section). The guest user always has a uid of 2. Guest permissions default to the permissions granted to the group public.

> **TIP**
>
> Be careful about adding the guest user to the model database, because this means the guest user will exist in any new database that is created. This could weaken your security strategy.

# Adding Aliases (Alternates)

To use a database, a user does not necessarily have to be added explicitly as a separate user of the database. Sybase provides the capability to relate a login to another login that is already a user of the database.

For example, every database has a user dbo, whose name can be found in the name column in the sysusers table. The sysusers row for dbo includes an suid, and a database uid (which is always 1 for dbo). The value specified in the suid column for dbo determines the login ID of the actual database owner—the individual who has all administrative privileges within that database. You can provide database access to additional users *as dbo* by defining aliases within the database for each such user.

> **TIP**
>
> The most common user privilege to be shared with aliases is dbo, which enables several logins to divide the responsibility for database implementation, evolution, and maintenance. This is most common in a development environment, where several users share responsibility for object creation and maintenance.

sp_addalias adds an entry to the sysalternates table, enabling an additional login to access a database as that user:

```
sp_addalias login_name, name_in_db
```

In the next example, mwhite is added as an alias to rbrown in the testdb database; now mwhite receives all the access and permissions granted to rbrown within this database:

```
sp_addalias mwhite, rbrown
```

Both *login_name* and *name_in_db* are required. *login_name* must be a valid entry in syslogins with no suid entry in sysusers or sysalternates in the current database. *name_in_db* must be a valid user name within the database.

sp_addalias adds a row to the sysalternates table. The login ID of *login_name* is stored in the suid column. The login ID of the actual login mapped to *name_in_db* is stored in the altsuid column.

> **NOTE**
>
> I'd like to meet the comedian who decided that aliases should be added with sp_addalias but stored in the sysalternates table!

Execute sp_helpuser with a user name to get detailed information about a user, including aliases, as in this example:

```
sp_helpuser rbrown

Users_name        ID_in_db Group_name       Login_name         Default_db
---------------- -------- ---------------- ----------------- -------------
rbrown            4        public           rbrown             testdb2

Users aliased to user.
Login_name
------------------------------
mwhite
```

If you examine the contents of the three system tables (syslogins, sysusers, and sysalternates) after adding an alias, you can understand the mapping of logins, users, and aliases.

Syslogins and sysusers join on suid. Syslogins and sysalternates also join on suid. Sysusers and sysalternates join on suid and altsuid, respectively (see Figure 27.2).

The values from sample versions of sysusers, sysalternates, and master..sysobjects show the correspondence between suid, uid, and altsuid among the tables:

```
select suid, uid, name
from sysusers
where uid > 0
select *
from sysalternates
select suid, name
from master..syslogins

sysusers
suid    uid     name
```

```
------ ------ --------------------------------
1      1      dbo
4      3      testuser1
6      4      rbrown
( 10 rows affected)

sysalternates
suid   altsuid
------ ------
7      6
( 1 row affected)

master..syslogins
suid   name
------ --------------------------------
1      sa
2      probe
3      mon_user
4      testuser1
5      jeff
6      rbrown
7      mwhite
( 7 rows affected)
```

**FIGURE 27.2.**

*The relationship between the login, user, and alias entities is built on a system user ID (suid) column in the syslogins tables.*

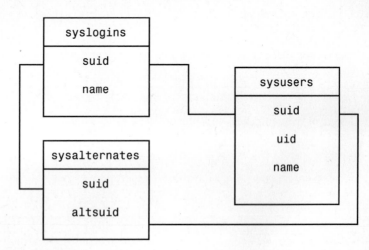

Notice these features of these tables:

- The dbo of the database is the sa (suid of the dbo in sysusers = 1).

- Besides dbo, there are two users of the database—rbrown (suid 6 in syslogins corresponds to suid 6 in sysusers) and testuser1.

- mwhite (suid 7) is aliased to rbrown (suid 6) in this database.

# How Database Access Works

So what does the server do when trying to determine access to a database? When a person tries to use a database, the server looks for an entry in sysusers and sysalternates to decide whether to grant access. It first looks in the sysusers table to see whether a match can be made on the suid.

A row will be found in sysusers for an suid if the following conditions exist:

■ The user has been added through the sp_adduser procedure (normal user addition).

■ The user created the database (suid matches with uid of 1, the dbo).

■ Ownership of the database has been transferred to the user.

After trying to find a match for the suid in the sysusers table, the server then tries to match the suid column in the sysalternates table.

If a match is found for the suid column in sysalternates, the server determines the suid that is found in the altsuid column. This value is matched against the suid column in the sysusers table, as before. Then the uid that corresponds to that suid is used by the user for activities conducted in the database.

If a match is not found in sysalternates, the server looks at the sysusers table again to see whether the special user guest has been added. If it has, the person assumes the uid of guest within that database.

The database access validation procedure is outlined in Figure 27.3.

If none of these matches can be made, the person is denied access.

**FIGURE 27.3.**

*SQL Server database permissions depend on user mappings or the presence of a guest user in the database.*

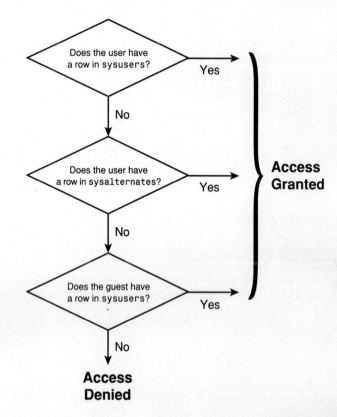

## Groups

Groups can be used as part of an effective database security strategy. Object and command permission are granted to users, groups, or roles. A user who is a member of a group inherits all the permissions granted to the group.

You can assign a user name to a group with sp_adduser (discussed earlier) or sp_changegroup. Assigning users to groups is a dbo responsibility. There is a detailed discussion of how to implement groups into your permission strategy in the "Permissions" section, later in this chapter.

---

**NOTE**

SQL Server allows a user to belong to only one group. (Actually, this isn't strictly true: A user may belong to one group in addition to public.)

The interesting question is why this limitation exists. It's clear that the structure of the system tables plays a role in this requirement—after all, a user's group membership is recorded in the gid column in sysusers. Permissions are granted to entries in

---

sysusers. Because groups are stored in sysusers alongside users, all permissions checks require that only two tables be read: sysprotects and sysusers.

In order to enable multiple group memberships, SQL Server needs to have a separate associative table where the many-to-many relationship between users and groups would be resolved. Needing to join a third table during permissions checks hurts performance. (Remember that every attempt to access a database object requires a permissions check.) One guess is that Sybase kept this part of the system simple to improve performance.

## *public* Group

Every user in a database is a member of the public group.

> **CAUTION**
>
> Don't forget that if you add a guest user to a database, any person that has a valid server login can use that database. The guest user will, of course, be able to perform any functions that have been granted to public.

It is common for an administrator to grant permissions to the public group rather than to each individual user. For example, if you have 500 users of a database, and all users need to select from the customer table, an administrator could execute a grant statement once for each user (500 statements) or a single select permission to the public group.

The public group is found in the sysusers table in each database with a uid of 0, and you cannot delete it.

> **WARNING**
>
> Prior to System 10, revoking permissions from the public group also revoked the object owner's permission.

## Adding Groups

Although the public group is a convenient way to grant universal access to database objects, it is inappropriate to use public when you need to grant different permissions to discrete sets of users. You may need to create additional groups to represent different permissions requirements. Add groups with sp_addgroup:

```
sp_addgroup groupname
```

For example, to add a group, marketing, to the current database, use the following:

```
sp_addgroup marketing
```

This procedure adds a row to the sysusers table with a uid of 16384 or larger.

> **NOTE**
>
> As part of the implementation of roles in System 10, each role actually takes up a row in sysusers as a group, so new groups are usually added with a uid of 16390 or greater.

## Determining Groups in a Database: *sp_helpgroup*

To determine the groups that exist in a database, or for more information about an individual group within a database, use sp_helpgroup:

```
sp_helpgroup [ groupname ]
```

Without any parameters, this procedure reports on all groups in a database. sp_helpgroup reports all groups in the database. Note that in System 10 each of the roles is recorded as a group in the sysusers table:

```
sp_helpgroup
```

| Group_name | Group_id |
| --- | --- |
| marketing_group | 16390 |
| navigator_role | 16388 |
| oper_role | 16386 |
| public | 0 |
| replication_role | 16389 |
| sa_role | 16384 |
| sso_role | 16385 |
| sybase_ts_role | 16387 |

There are already entries for each of the system-wide roles (sa_role, sso_role, oper_role, navigator_role, replication_role, sybase_ts_role), public, and the new group, marketing. Pass the *groupname* as a parameter to list all users in a group:

```
sp_helpgroup marketing_group
```

| Group_name | Group_id | Users_in_group | Userid |
| --- | --- | --- | --- |
| marketing_group | 16390 | rbrown | 4 |
| marketing_group | 16390 | testuser1 | 3 |

Drop groups with `sp_dropgroup`, but only if that group does not contain any users:

```
sp_dropgroup groupname

sp_dropgroup marketing_group
```

Use `sp_changegroup` to change a user's group membership. Only the `dbo` may execute `sp_changegroup`:

```
sp_changegroup groupname, name_in_database

sp_changegroup marketing_group, rbrown
```

## How Groups Work

`sp_addgroup` adds a row to the `sysusers` table. The `uid` and group ID (`gid`) are assigned the same value (16834 or greater). When you add users to a database without specifying a group name, the group ID of `0` (`public`) is assigned to that person. When you specify a group (either as a parameter in `sp_adduser` or with `sp_changegroup`), the `gid` of that group is placed in the `gid` column for that user.

> **NOTE**
>
> After you assign a user to a group, the user is no longer explicitly assigned to the `public` group. Nevertheless, any permissions assigned to `public` will apply to that user. The `public` group always encompasses all people.

# Login Approach

There are several approaches to security in Sybase systems; the following are the major ones:

- Sybase login equals the operating system/application (OS/App) login;
- Sybase login is independent of the OS/App login;
- A single login for all users of an application or user type.

## Sybase Login = OS/App Login

This is a fairly maintainable approach to logins. A user is given a login to the operating system. (The operating system could be the client workstation login, network login, or the user login to the server, if the client application runs on the server.) The operating system sets environment variables for the user name (and possibly the password) during its login process. Applications read the environment information when logging into SQL Server.

For example, SQL Server facilities such as isql and bcp look for the environment variables USER and PASSWORD when connecting to the server. When the user does not need to specify the " -U" option for isql, the application passes the user name from the environment when connecting to the server.

Administering OS/SQL Server logins is easier because you can develop administrative or automated procedures to keep these user (login) names and passwords in sync.

One drawback of this approach is that users do occasionally need to access an application with a different SQL Server login. Applications still must provide a facility for a different login name and password from the one stored at the operating system level.

# Sybase Login Independent of OS/APP Login

To enable separate OS and SQL Server login IDs, applications must include a login function. (Often, when there is some correspondence between Sybase and OS login IDs, applications automatically populate the login screen with information drawn from the environment.)

This approach is more difficult to administer and maintain than the previous one, but it can provide additional security.

# Single Sybase Login

The single Sybase login approach is often used by sites that want a single point of control for logins to the Sybase server. It is simple, but its simplicity has drawbacks.

Only one login exists for an entire application or for each major application piece. When a person invokes the application, the application connects to the server using hard-coded values for the login name and password. This approach has some benefits:

- Users do not need to log in to the server explicitly.
- A password-changing routine does not have to be written into the application to accommodate password changes. (Applications that use individual logins with the capability of changing passwords often integrate a password-changing application to shield users from having to connect to the server by using another interface to change their passwords.)
- The administration activity required to manage logins and passwords is extremely low.

However, drawbacks to this approach include the following:

■ A database administrator often executes sp_who to see who is logged into the SQL Server. Part of the output from this command is the login name. If all users log in to the SQL Server with same name, the output of sp_who will contain numerous processes with the same login name. If a problem is encountered, determining the actual user associated with a process becomes almost impossible. (To overcome this problem, applications pass the OS login ID as a hostname value when logging in to SQL Server. Hostname values are also included in the sp_who display.)

■ Auditing user activity is meaningless. Because every person would be the same application user, you can track only application activities and not individual user activities.

■ If an outside source is able to determine the application login and password, they have free rein on the server. As mentioned previously, auditing cannot be used to target suspects. The application has to change its password, which may require recompilation of the application—not always a desirable thing to do when in production.

Because of these drawbacks, this approach is not recommended. It can be used, however, if you determine that the reduction in flexibility is worth the reduction in administrative activity.

### SEPARATE LOGIN IDS FOR APPLICATION WORK VERSUS *ad hoc* QUERY

Users often require access to a system through an *ad hoc* query generator or other front-end tool, in addition to regular access through an application. If you allow the user to use an application login when running an *ad hoc* tool, you may find the user updating tables or running stored procedures without the protection or validation normally ensured by the application.

For example, a user who normally uses the application to delete a row from the ten-billion-row sales_history table by retrieving it and pressing a delete button (complete with are you sure? messages!) may be surprised when the delete sales_history statement removes every row from the table.

Unfortunately, you can't restrict most tools from enabling updates to tables or executing stored procedures. Worse, SQL Server never knows whether the user requesting a deletion is running a carefully written application in PowerBuilder or using isql after taking a one-day video course on SQL.

What's the solution?

You could try removing all the neat and interesting front-end products, but you bought SQL Server so that those products would run.

You could try to not tell anyone how to insert, update, or delete, but that usually doesn't work.

You could require that all updates, inserts, and deletes use a stored procedure (related objects and permissions are discussed later in this chapter), but even that isn't fool-proof; if the user can run the procedure from the application, it can be run from a command-line interface such as `isql` as well.

One approach is to have two sets of logins: one for running neat and interesting front-end tools, the other for using applications that are permitted to perform updates. The first set of logins and passwords is known to the users; the second set is based on the user name, but known only to the updating applications.

For example, a user `mdoe` with a password `littlelamb` would have an application user name `mdoe_app` and a password `littlelamb_00946`. The login names for the application are visible from `sp_who`, so the passwords need to be difficult to guess. (You may want the password to be derived from the user password and some hashed version of the `uid`. Keeping your password derivation method secret is critical here.)

Following this approach to assigning logins and passwords is not easy. To make it work, you prevent users from running `sp_password`, so password administration becomes your problem. But with perseverance you can have a system that is safe from the errors of a persistent and uneducated user.

# Password Approach

There are several standards that companies use when identifying a password administration plan. These usually fall into one of three categories:

- Password same as login
- General application login and password
- Password independent of login

Whether or not you use a login approach of "Sybase Login = Application Login," you still must determine whether the password for that login will be dependent or independent of the login.

## Password = Login

At many sites, passwords are identical to logins. Realistically, this is as close to having no password as you can get—the password for a user is the same as the login name. Therefore, a login for `user1` has a password of `user1`. With this approach, it would be very easy for a person to find a way to access the server because only a login name must be determined. Many sites also use a standard for naming logins to a system—for example, `market01` through `market99`, with passwords of market01 through market99, respectively. This is the least secure approach to user password administration (second only to having a null password, which is not permitted in System 10). It is also one of the least flexible, because login name and password must remain the same, denying the capability of using password expiration (System 10).

> **NOTE**
>
> When you talk to hackers about methods they use to guess passwords and break into systems, they invariably tell you that the first password to guess is the login name. (After that come the literal words, "password" and "secret.")

# General Application Login and Password

There are other sites that use a general application login for all users of an application. This means that users access an application, and when the application is connected to the database, it is connected as a single general user, regardless of the number of connections it opens. This approach results in a severe reduction in the capability of linking activities to users. When sp_who is executed, for example, all user names are the same. This makes it very difficult to track down who executed a certain command. Fortunately, this approach often enables changing the general user password, depending on whether the application reads its password information from a configuration file or is hard coded in the application itself.

# Password Independent of Login

This approach is the most secure. Each user has a distinct password not related to the login name in any way. The user can change the password periodically, and the use of the "password expiration interval" forces the issue. This approach is normally selected at sites that have regulations (federal) regarding their applications or at sites that are most worried about unauthorized access to the database.

Because each user has a password and the ability to change it, access to sp_password is required. Unfortunately, many sites want to keep users shielded from database operations because they are not usually accustomed to dealing directly with a database. Because of this, a command-line interface (isql) is not an acceptable alternative. As a result a user administration module is usually created to allow users to change passwords. This increases overall application complexity somewhat, but shields users from database operations.

This is naturally the preferred approach by secure sites, and is recommended if your environment is structured to handle the administrative complexities.

# Permissions

Permissions are used to control access within a database. This is accomplished through the use of the grant and revoke statements. Any permission that can be granted can also be revoked, so when the word "grant" is used within this section, it can be thought of in the broader sense of controlling access (granting *or* revoking).

The granting of permissions results in the addition of rows to the sysprotects system table. Each database contains the sysprotects table, which means that permissions are database specific. Because permissions are granted to database users, not server logins, there is no way to grant general access to a login (except through the use of roles).

## Users

Permissions are used to control access by users of a database. In this context, a user is essentially any uid that exists in the sysusers table. The sysusers table initially contains rows for the database owner (dbo), the public group (public), and the six roles that can exist within a Sybase server (sa_role, sso_role, oper_role, navigator_role, replication_role, and sybase_ts_role). Additional users of a database are added with sp_adduser, and additional groups in a database are added with sp_addgroup. Therefore, the list of users that permissions can be granted to actually contains users, groups, and roles.

## Object Permissions

Granting of permissions on objects is performed using the grant command syntax:

```
grant  {all [ privileges] ¦ permission_list }
  on { table_name [ ( column_list ) ]
  ¦ view_name [ ( column_list ) ]
  ¦ stored_procedure_name }
  to{ group_name ¦ user_name ¦ role_name}
[ { , {next_user_group_role } } ...]
  [ with grant option ]
```

Revoking of permissions on objects is performed using the revoke command syntax:

```
revoke [ grant option for ]
  {all [ privileges] ¦ permission_list }
  on { table_name [ ( column_list ) ]
  ¦ view_name [ ( column_list ) ]
  ¦ stored_procedure_name }
  to{ group_name ¦ user_name ¦ role_name}
[ { , {next_user_group_role } } ...]
  [cascade ]
```

## READING sysprotects

When you grant or revoke permissions on a table, SQL Server records that information in a database-level table, sysprotects. Every database includes explicit lines granting permission to system tables to public. (As of this writing, there were 17 rows of default system table permissions in the most recent version.)

Let's add some permissions and see how they affect sysprotects. The following command adds permissions entries:

```
grant all on marketing_table to public
```

Look at the contents of sysprotects after the grant statement:

```
select id, uid, action, grantor
from sysprotects
where id = object_id("marketing_table")
go

id          uid    action grantor
_____       ___    ___    ___
144003544   0      151    1
144003544   0      193    1
144003544   0      195    1
144003544   0      196    1
144003544   0      197    1
```

The id column identifies the table in the database.

The uid column indicates the user (or group) ID to whom permission is granted.

The action column specifies the type of action affected by the permission. You can decode the action value by referring to the spt_values table in the master database. Permissions actions are identified with the type "T". The output that follows lists all the permission action codes as of System 10:

```
use master
go
select name, number, type
from spt_values
where type = "T"
and number > 0
order by 2
go

name                    number    type
_____           _____    __
References              151       T
Select                  193       T
Insert                  195       T
Delete                  196       T
Update                  197       T
Create Table            198       T
Create Database         203       T
Grant                   205       T
Revoke                  206       T
Create View             207       T
```

```
Create Procedure          222        T
Execute                   224        T
Dump Database             228        T
Create Default            233        T
Dump Transaction          235        T
Create Rule               236        T
```

grantor records the ID of the user who executed the grant statement.

The object owner grants or revokes permissions on objects to control access to objects within a database. These objects include tables, views, and stored procedures. Permissions default to the object owner, which is why a user who creates an object does not have to grant permissions to himself. However, any other user of the system, except for users with the sa_role, would have to be granted permission on an object.

**NOTE**

sa object permissions are not checked. You do not need to grant object permissions to users with the sa_role—ever.

The types of permissions that can be granted/revoked to these objects include select, update, insert, delete, references, and execute. select and update can have a column list specified (to control access at the column level), references applies only to tables (and can contain a column list), and execute applies only to procedures. Table 27.1 summarizes how object permissions can be granted.

## Table 27.1. Object permissions.

| Permission | Specify Columns? | Can Grant On |
|------------|------------------|--------------|
| select     | Yes              | Tables, views |
| update     | Yes              | Tables, views |
| insert     | No               | Tables, views |
| delete     | No               | Tables, views |
| references | Yes              | Tables |
| execute    | N/A              | Stored procedures |

select, insert, update, and delete are pretty straightforward. They indicate whether a user can issue that type of command with a table or view listed in the from clause (a normal select or an insert, delete, or update with a join clause) or as the object of the action (update table or view, insert table or view, or delete table or view).

> **NOTE**
>
> Text and image columns enable use of the READTEXT and WRITETEXT commands:
>
> - The ability to use the WRITETEXT command is transferred through update permission.
> - The ability to use the READTEXT command is transferred through select permission.

execute permission is granted on a stored procedure to enable a user to execute the procedure. This can have very powerful implications because a system can be implemented when access is granted completely to procedures and not to the underlying tables or views.

The references permission is part of System 10 systems, and applies to the ability to use declarative referential integrity. When implementing declarative referential integrity, the create table or alter table statements can include a references clause to indicate the relationship between tables. This permission needs to be granted only when objects owned by two different users have referential integrity considerations (a user that owns both objects automatically has references permission). It is not likely that references permission would have to be granted in a production system, because most production systems have all objects owned by the same user name (dbo).

A permission list can contain a comma-delimited list of permissions or the word all (or all privileges). If all is specified, only the permissions that apply to the type of object the permission is being granted on are actually granted.

The with grant option (System 10 only) *enables the ability to grant permission* to be transferred to another user. For example, if select permission is granted on table customer to jsmith with the with grant option, jsmith then can grant select permission on customer to other users in the database. This option has ramifications, however, because exclusive control of permissions on an object is no longer in effect.

To revoke permissions on an object to a user, the revoke command is used. If an object owner wants to deny further granting of permissions on an object to a user who was granted access with the with grant option, the revoke command is used with the grant option for option. When the revoke grant option for ... command is used, it tells the server to deny the specified user(s) the capability of granting the specified permissions. For example, user1 can execute this statement:

```
grant select on table from user1 with grant option.
```

The user then can revoke the ability to grant select on all columns by revoking the ability to grant on selected columns. This is accomplished by executing this statement:

```
revoke grant option for select on table(column2) from user1
```

To revoke all permissions from the user *and all users who were granted permission by that user,* add the keyword `cascade`. Here is an example of this statement:

```
revoke select on table from user1 cascade
```

# Command Permissions

By default, the `dbo` is the only user who may create objects and perform backups. In some environments, users are granted access to these commands. These are called *command permissions.*

> **NOTE**
>
> It's important to differentiate between command and object permissions. *Command permissions* enable users to create objects themselves. This is rarely granted. *Object permissions* enable users to access objects that already exist. This permission must be granted to enable a system to operate.

Command permissions are granted to users by executing the following `grant` syntax:

```
grant  {all [ privileges] ¦ command_list }
  to{ group_name ¦ user_name ¦ role_name}
[ { , {next_user_group_role } } ...]
```

Here is the syntax for revoking the same command permissions:

```
revoke  {all [ privileges] ¦ command_list }
  on { table_name [ ( column_list ) ]
  ¦ view_name [ ( column_list ) ]
  ¦ stored_procedure_name }
  from{ group_name ¦ user_name ¦ role_name}
[ { , {next_user_group_role } } ...]
```

Command permissions are granted to and revoked from users to control access to certain commands within a database. These commands include:

- `create database` (master database only)
- `create default`
- `create procedure`
- `create rule`
- `create table`
- `create view`

These permissions are most often granted in a development environment to enable developers to create objects in the course of developing a system. In a production environment, these permissions are not usually needed.

**WARNING**

Usually, you should not grant the create database permission to users. create database authority should be reserved for those logins with the sa_role.

If you really need to grant the create database permission, don't give it to the guest user in the master database! Add the login as a new user in the master database, then grant create database permission to that new user.

A command list can contain a comma-delimited list of commands or the word all (or all privileges). If all is specified, only those commands that can be executed in that database are granted. This is only an issue with create database; you may grant permission to create database only within the master database. Note the following about command permissions:

- The creation of databases usually is performed by the system administrator (or person with the sa_role), and normally is not granted.

- The creation of temporary tables is permitted by any user and does not need to be specifically granted.

## Permission Approaches

You should establish the access requirements of tables, views, and stored procedures during the design phase of a system. As each object is identified, the documentation should contain notes on what types of users need what types of access. It is easier to develop an effective permissions plan if you start gathering this information early.

First, define the users of a system. Try to group them logically, based on job description, department, or responsibility (for example, managers, clerks, marketing personnel, billing personnel, and so forth). Often, you will develop systems knowing only the broad user classifications; you will fill in names of users later on. In any case, determine what logical groups will be using a database and define what access is needed to which tables, views, and procedures by each group and by the database user community as a whole.

**NOTE**

As you can see, any approach to permissions is deeply associated with a specific login and user approach. Permissions are granted to either users, groups, or roles. Granting permissions to roles does not usually play a part in production systems, except where objects are created for use by logins with a certain role. Most permission plans focus on controlling access to users.

It generally is easiest to grant broad permissions and then limit access to specified users. The easiest way to implement broad permissions is to grant them to groups. Users assigned to a group automatically have the permissions granted to that group. Recall that a group can be any group that is specifically added to a database or the system group `public` (which includes all users of a database).

## public

The `public` group is a special group that all users belong to, even when they are specifically added to a user-defined group. It is important to remember that the guest user is, of course, also a member of the `public` group. If you grant permissions to `public`, you allow anyone who has access to the database to receive the permissions specified to `public`.

If individual users are added to a database (not guest), you have substantial security at the database level. If you are satisfied with database-level security, granting to `public` allows all the users in the database to perform those functions specified. Using `public` is a good approach even when you have several user-defined groups in a database.

Often, several groups exist requiring special access to a select number of tables. Most other tables are available to all users of a database.

Take the example of a database with 100 tables and 10 user-defined groups. If you want to grant `select` permission on all the tables to all users, granting to each user-defined group requires 10 grant statements for each table. If all groups need `select` access to all tables, it is easiest to grant `select` permission to `public` for each table. This requires only one grant statement per table. If one group needs insert, update, and delete access to a table, additional permission can be granted on that table to only that group.

## public and guest

As indicated earlier, the `public` group contains all users, even the guest user. Adding a guest user to a database and using `public` as a means for defining permissions should only be done by those sites that are extremely confident with the security enforced at the server level. Once a person gains access to the server, that user has access to any database that has a guest user defined, and consequently can perform any activities granted to `public`.

Addition of the guest user invalidates control of access at the database level. However, you can grant permissions to `public` and revoke permissions from guest to curb the activities the guest user can perform.

> **WARNING**
>
> Do this in the correct order, please! Sybase permissions obey one simple rule:
>
> *Whatever happened last takes effect.*
>
> If you revoke from guest, then grant to public, guest receives the permission because guest is a member of public. *There is no hierarchy of permissions.* That is, user permissions do not take priority over group permissions, or vice versa.
>
> The safest way to manage permissions is to maintain a script of all the permissions for a particular database. Every time you need to make a change, insert the permission statement into the correct part of the script and *re-execute the entire script.* In this way, you can avoid unexpected consequences from grant and revoke statements.
>
> Be careful! You probably shouldn't run your big permissions script when users are online. You may end up revoking permissions while users are processing. The only safe way to implement this approach during active hours is to run the script in a transaction or set of transactions, with begin tran and commit tran. However, this can really slow processing dramatically because of locks placed on the system tables.

## Granting to User-Defined Groups

Beyond the use of the public group, granting permissions to user-defined groups is the next easiest way to implement a permission strategy. Of course, this approach is often combined with granting to public or to specific users. The approach is to define logically the access that applies only to a specific group and then to grant or revoke permissions to that group.

For example, if only the marketing group needs to be able to perform select, insert, update, and delete on marketing tables, you can add a marketing group and execute this command:

```
grant all on market_table to marketing
```

for each of the marketing tables. If you have billing tables that only billing personnel needed all permissions to, you add a billing group and execute the following for each of the billing tables:

```
grant all on billing_table to billing
```

What if billing personnel need to select from marketing tables and marketing personnel need to select from billing tables? You can grant select permission on each table to the appropriate group or use the public group by granting select permission on each table in a database to public:

```
grant select on billing_table to public
grant select on marketing_table to public
```

# Granting to Specific Users

Granting permissions to specific users requires the most administration but offers the greatest control. Normally, it is not used exclusively in a permission strategy because the addition of each new user requires executing individual grant statements for each object wherein access is needed. Granting and revoking to users is most commonly used in combination with granting to public or user-specified groups.

For example, all marketing users can select, insert, and delete on all marketing tables, but only the user super_market_user can update information in the database. In this case, you execute these commands:

```
grant select, insert, delete on market_table to marketing
grant update on market_table to super_market_user
```

(This assumes that the super_market_user is also a member of the marketing group.)

# Object Dependencies

Many organizations use dependent objects (views, procedures, and triggers) to implement advanced security structure. Recall the following from earlier chapters:

■ Views can restrict access to specific rows and columns of data.

■ Procedures can restrict and validate all data modifications.

■ Triggers can perform related updates or update substantive audit records.

In each of these cases, users need indirect access to the dependent object at a high level, but should not have comparable direct access to the dependent object.

If object ownership is distributed among several database users, implementing any of these types of advanced security schemes is fruitless. For example, in Figure 27.4, John wants to select from a view owned by Bob, but Mary owns the base table.

The permissions required for this scheme include:

```
[Mary:]grant select on basetable to bob
[Bob:]grant select on viewname to john
[Mary:]grant select on basetable to john
```

The final grant statement, in which Mary permits John to read the table directly, undermines the effect of a view intended to enforce security.

If both the base and dependent objects are owned by a single user, the user needs to grant permission to the user only for the dependent object. Because there is no change in ownership between the dependent and base objects, *permissions are not checked.*

In Figure 27.5, Mary owns both objects, and John wants access to the view.

This scheme requires only a single permission statement:

722

```
[Mary:]grant select on viewname to john
```

Because Mary owns both objects, John's permissions are checked only at the view level but not at the table level. With no change in ownership, permissions are not checked.

**FIGURE 27.4.**

*When the owner of an object and a dependent object are different, permissions must be granted explicitly on both objects.*

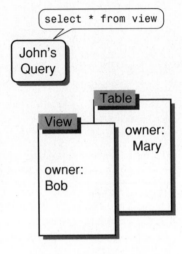

**FIGURE 27.5.**

*When the owner of an object and a dependent object are the same, permissions on the base object are not checked.*

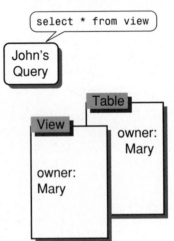

# Roles

Roles were introduced in System 10 to give Sybase sites the ability to distribute certain activities and identify the users performing these activities. Although there are six roles defined for a Sybase server, only three are used heavily. These three are sa_role, sso_role, and oper_role.

# System Administrator (*sa_role*)

The sa_role was introduced to enable the activities historically conducted by the system administrator (sa) login to be executed by people who access the server with login names other than sa.

> **WARNING**
>
> As noted earlier, the sa login can perform system administration functions only because that login has been granted the sa_role (and sso_role) upon server installation. A system administrator is essentially *above the law*, because the sa operates outside of normal command and permission checking. This is an important ability for a system administrator to have to maintain absolute control of the system and be able to perform almost any function in the system at any time.

The sa_role should not be granted without carefully considering the extreme capabilities a system administrator has. Types of activities that can be conducted by the system administrator:

- Installing SQL Server and/or specific SQL Server modules
- Managing allocation of physical storage to the server
- Tuning configuration variables such as memory and connections
- Creating user databases and transferring ownership
- Performing any activities as the database owner of any database the system administrator uses

It is obvious that controlling system administrative functions is of paramount importance to the function of a SQL Server. Anyone who is granted the sa_role is seen as the system administrator, and has all the capabilities associated with that role.

Historically, if several users needed the ability to perform system administration functions, they all logged into the SQL Server using the sa login. People familiar with pre–System 10 servers can attest to how annoying it was to execute sp_who and see five or ten processes with a login of sa.

By using roles, each of these processes appears in sp_who with the login used to access the server. If a situation develops where a process needs to be killed, you can easily determine who owns the specific process. This accountability is important in graceful administration of processes on the server. If auditing is installed, one can issue commands that require the sa_role to provide an audit history of which system administrators performed certain activities.

About the only difference between the capabilities of the sa login in pre–System 10 servers and of System 10 users with the sa_role is that users with the sa_role are not able to add or manage logins to the server. This activity has been distributed to the sso_role, described later. A person with the sa_role can grant the sa_role to other logins in the system, but is unable to grant any of the other roles available to the server.

The server will not enable the revocation of the sa_role from the last login that possesses its capabilities. This ensures that at least one login is active which can function as the system administrator at all times. The server will, however, enable a user with the sa_role to revoke the sa_role from the sa login! This is odd, but in System 10 the sa can be made to look like any other user by the revocation of certain roles (sa_role and sso_role).

You shouldn't strip sa of all powers. If the intent is to require system administrators to log in to the server as a user other than sa, the recommended approach is to lock the sa login (using sp_locklogin) once the necessary logins have been granted the sa_role.

## Site Security Officer (*sso_role*)

The site security officer (sso) role is used to give a specific login the ability to perform functions associated with adding logins and auditing a SQL Server. The sso_role was introduced to satisfy the needs of many large corporations in which the addition of logins to operating systems and databases is centralized in a group separate from database administration. A user that has been granted the sso_role has the ability of performing functions such as the following:

- Adding logins to the server
- Administrating passwords
- Configuring password expiration intervals
- Managing the audit system
- Granting all roles except the sa_role

The server will not enable the revocation of the sso_role from the last login that possesses its capabilities. This ensures that at least one login will be active at all times that can add new logins to the system and manage the audit system, if installed.

It should also be noted that the sa login has the ability to perform site security officer functions only because that login has been granted the sso_role upon installation. The sso_role can be revoked from the sa login.

## Operator (*oper_role*)

The operator (oper) role is used to give a specific login the ability to manage the backup and recovery system. The operator role was introduced to satisfy corporations in which the backup and recovery function is performed by a group other than database administration or by a select group within database administration that doesn't need the capabilities defined by database ownership (dbo).

Historically, a user was aliased to the dbo in a database to be able to dump and load a database. (Prior to System 10, the dump database command was transferable by the dbo, but the load database command was not.) Therefore, that user had far-reaching capabilities in a database, which resulted in potential exposure to sabotage and/or accidental modifications in a database.

A user that has been granted the oper_role can perform only the following commands:

- dump transaction
- dump database
- load transaction
- load database

Therefore, a user with the oper_role can perform backup and recovery on any database in a server without having to have more capabilities than needed to perform the tasks.

## Other Roles

It can be seen in the system tables that a navigator_role, replication_role, and sybase_ts_role can also be granted using the sp_role procedure.

The navigator_role is granted to users who manage the navigation server, and the replication_role is granted to users who manage the replication server.

The Sybase technical support role (sybase_ts_role) is a role whose use may not be readily apparent. The sybase_ts_role must be granted to execute certain dbcc (database consistency checker) commands that are considered outside the realm of normal system administration tasks. An example of dbcc commands that may require the sybase_ts_role include dbcc help, dbcc page, and dbcc traceon. However, as newer versions of the server are introduced, additional dbcc commands might be executed by users that have only the sa_role. The command dbcc page falls into this category. In version 10.0 of the server, that command could be executed only by a person with the sybase_ts_role, but in version 10.0.1, a person with only the sa_role is able to execute that command.

When executing undocumented dbcc commands (not strongly recommended, unless you know what you are doing), it is often a good idea to have the sybase_ts_role granted to your login. The other roles can be granted only by a user possessing the sso_role.

## Granting and Revoking Roles

Roles are granted to (and revoked from) users through the sp_role system procedure:

```
sp_role { "grant" ¦ "revoke" } ,
{ sa_role ¦ sso_role ¦ oper_role
 ¦ sybase_ts_role ¦ replication_role ¦ navigator_role } ,
login_name
```

You can grant a role only to an active login account (an account that is available for login). If the user executes the `sp_displaylogin` procedure, it reflects the newly granted role as part of the Configured Authorization, but the `select show_role()` command will not show that role as active. An active login that has been granted a role is able to perform in that role only if the `set role` command is used.

A role can be revoked, however, only if the specified login name is not currently active. This means that if you want to revoke a role from a person, that user must log off before you can revoke that role. (Of course, you can always kill the user's process, if you're in a bad mood!)

## set role

The `set role` command is used to turn a role on or off for an active login:

```
set role "role_name" { on ¦ off }
```

where `role_name` is `sa_role`, `sso_role`, `oper_role`, `sybase_ts_role`, `navigation_role`, or `replication_role`.

Roles can be set on at any time, but the ability to set a role off depends on the possibility of existing within a database without that role. For example, if you have a database called `testdb` in your server, a person that has been granted the `sa_role` can use that database and consequently is seen as the database owner with a `uid` of 1 (system administrators become the `dbo` user in any database they use). If the person is using that database and tries to execute this command:

```
set role "sa_role" off
```

the server displays an error, because that user would not be able to use the database if it were not for the `sa_role` (assuming there is not a `guest` user).

## Displaying Configured Role Information: *sp_displaylogin*

The roles configured for a login are reported by `sp_displaylogin`. The `sp_displaylogin` command reports a range of information, including a list under Configured Authorization of the roles that have been configured for a specified login. Note that this is different from the `show_role()` function, which reports on active roles for a specified login (based on an individual connection). Here is the syntax for `sp_displaylogin`:

```
sp_displaylogin [ login_name ]
```

The output from `sp_displaylogin` is not set up as a table of result values:

```
sp_displaylogin jeff

Suid: 5
Loginame: jeff
Fullname:
```

```
Configured Authorization: sa_role sso_role
Locked: NO
Date of Last Password Change: Nov  8 1994  1:28PM
```

Only users that have been granted the sa_role or the sso_role can provide a login name as an argument. For all other users, the procedure must be executed without a login name. For users who execute sp_displaylogin without providing a login name, the information for their login is displayed.

## Displaying Active Role Information: *show_role*

The function show_role() displays the active current roles for the login associated with a specific process. Here is the syntax for this statement:

```
select show_role( )
```

This command produces a list of the active roles for the login associated with a specific process. This is an important point, because a single login that is configured for the sa_role, sso_role, and oper_role roles could have three separate connections to the server. For each of the connections, the user can turn off any role that has been configured for the login. Therefore, one process may return sa_role, a second process may return sso_role, and a third process may show oper_role and sa_role as output to the command select show_role().

On the other hand, the execution of the sp_displaylogin procedure reports on configured roles for a login and returns identical information for each process. The Configured Authorization is "sa_role, sso_role, and oper_role," because sp_displaylogin reports on the actual login, and the select show_role() statement reports the roles active for a specific connection.

## Roles and Stored Procedures: *proc_role*

Although the permission to execute a certain procedure can be granted to a specific role, a user that does not have a specified role may also execute that procedure. If an extra level of checking is needed, a stored procedure can be created to check for a certain role before the code contained within the stored procedure is executed. This is accomplished by using the proc_role function. Here is the syntax for this function:

```
proc_role ( "role_name" )
```

where *role_name* can be any of the roles configured for a server.

Consider a situation where you have a table called archive_database_info. This table contains information about customers that have been archived from the active customer database to an archive database. You want to create a procedure called get_archive_names to retrieve the information from this table. However, you only want operators (users granted the oper_role) to be able to execute the code contained in this procedure. You could use the proc_role function to test whether the person executing this code has the appropriate role. Here is an example of how this function might be used in a procedure:

```
create proc get_archive_names
(@name char(30) = null )
as
if ( proc_role ( "oper_role" ) = 1 )
begin
select name, tape_location
from archive_database_info
where name = @name
return 0
end
else
begin
print "You are not a user with the Operator Role !!!"
return - 1
end
```

> **NOTE**
>
> Oddly enough, if a user has a specified role, the value 1 is returned. If the user does not have a specified role, a value of 0 is returned. This seems backwards, because most functions in Sybase return a value of 0 when execution is successful, and a non-zero value when there is a problem.

# Approaches

It is conceivable that a site can continue to operate a System 10 server in the same manner as a pre–System 10 server. Essentially, all activities can be conducted by the single sa login, with no accountability for the actions of that user.

However, you should use roles as they were intended. This means that users who need to perform system administration functions are granted the sa_role, users who need to add logins to the system are granted the sso_role, and users who will be performing backup and recovery operations are granted the oper_role. A recommended checklist for setting up roles includes the following tasks:

- Identify each individual user that needs to perform system administration functions.
- Grant each user the sa_role by the sa login.
- Identify each individual user that is responsible for adding logins, managing password administration, and managing system auditing (if installed).
- Grant each user the sso_role by the sa login.
- Identify each individual user that needs to be able to dump and load any database in the server.
- Grant each user the oper_role by the sa login.
- Enable the sa login to be locked by one of the other users with the sa_role.

At this point, any systems administration activities have to be performed by a login other than the sa login, and the activities of that user can be audited.

# Summary

SQL Server security is implemented in four layers: the operating system, the Sybase server, the Sybase database, and the Sybase object. Each allows greater or lesser control, depending on your requirements.

Sybase offers a variety of ways to control access to data. Server login and database user approaches affect the way in which a permissions strategy is implemented.

At the object level, most sites grant broad permissions and then limit or grant specific access as needed to minimize the administrative overhead in implementing a permissions plan. This usually involves granting to public or to a user-defined group, then revoking or granting specific permissions to a user-defined group or a specific user.

In System 10, roles added important capabilities, especially for large organizations that distribute the traditional sa tasks between several groups. Through roles, you can identify real logins by using sp_who, and an administrator's activities can be audited when the audit system is enabled. With roles in place, individual logins can be limited to the access they need to perform expected tasks.

# Database Logging and Recovery

# 28

Sybase uses a write-ahead log and automatic forward recovery to maintain up-to-the-transaction data integrity, even in the case of erratic or unexpected server shutdowns. This chapter explores how the Sybase transaction log works, and how it manages recovery. You'll understand commits and checkpoints, and how the server manages data integrity through various server events.

Sybase's use of terms may differ from your experience with computer systems. For example, you may think of recovery or disaster recovery as the administrative process of getting back to work after a catastrophe, but it means something quite different in the SQL Server world. You need to first nail down the meaning of the crucial Sybase terms.

- A *transaction* is a unit of work. Transactions can be long or short, and they can involve changes to millions of rows of data or only one. SQL Server promises that every transaction, no matter how long or complex, will either run to completion or be completely reversed for any reason. The transaction log is the system component responsible for transactional data integrity.

- *Recovery* is the automatic process of reconciling the log and the data. Recovery occurs when the server is started. We'll examine the recovery process in detail in this chapter.

- A *backup* is a physical copy of the database or transaction log. The Sybase term for a backup is a "dump," and dump is the Transact-SQL command used to initiate backups.

- *Restoration* is the process of taking a backup of the database from storage and copying it back onto the server (restore).

  Backup and restore are the topic of Chapter 29, "Backing Up and Restoring Databases and Transaction Logs."

# What Is a Transaction?

A *transaction* is a set of operations to be completed at one time, as though they were a single operation. A transaction is either completed or not performed at all. Standard examples of transactions include bank transfers (withdraw $500 from checking, add $500 to savings) and order entry systems (write an order for five widgets, remove five widgets from inventory).

All SQL statements are inherently transactions, from grant and create statements to the data modification statements, insert, update, and delete. Consider the following update example:

```
update titles
set price = price * 1.02
```

This statement modifies all rows in the titles table. SQL Server guarantees, regardless of the size of the titles table, to process either all rows or no rows. What if half of the rows are modified and the server fails? When the server comes back up (but before the database is available for use) it rolls back the incomplete transaction, removing all evidence that it ever began. That's part of the recovery process discussed later in this chapter.

SQL Server also includes transaction control syntax to group sets of SQL statements together into single logical work units:

- `begin transaction` starts a unit of work.
- `commit transaction` completes a unit of work.
- `rollback transaction` cancels a unit of work.

The following example enters an order and depletes inventory in a single transaction:

```
begin transaction
   update inventory
      set in_stock = in_stock - 5
      where item_num = "14141"
   insert orders (cust_num, item_num, qty)
      values ("ABC151", "14141", 5)
commit transaction
```

SQL Server guarantees that the inventory will not change unless you enter the order.

Look at the same example, but with the `rollback transaction` statement instead of `commit`:

```
begin transaction
   update inventory
      set in_stock = in_stock - 5
      where item_num = "14141"
   insert orders (cust_num, item_num, qty)
      values ("ABC151", "14141", 5)
rollback transaction
```

When the server encounters the `rollback` statement, it discards all changes in the transaction and returns the data to the state it was in before work began.

This chapter examines the mechanism used by SQL Server to manage data integrity (`rollback` and `commit`) in transactions.

# What Is the Transaction Log?

The transaction log is the database-level system table, called `syslogs`. The `syslogs` table contains a sequential list of all modifications to every object in the database, as well as any information required to maintain data integrity. It is managed exclusively by the SQL Server.

The transaction log is

- shared by all users of a database;
- modified in cache, and only flushed to disk at commit time;
- written first (a write-ahead log).

The log is not

- usefully manipulated or read with SQL;
- readable in any useful format.

> **NOTE**
>
> There are now third-party utilities that do access the log, allowing some direct interaction with the log and providing some measure of "undo" functions. However, nothing in the standard SQL Server suite will allow you to interact directly with the log.

# A Write-Ahead Log

*Write-ahead* means that the log is written before the data any time a query modifies data. The SQL Server buffers read and write operations to all tables, including the syslogs table, in a memory area called the data cache. The cache is made up of pages.

> **NOTE**
>
> In addition to standard SQL data modification statements (insert, update, delete), all create statements, permission statements (grant and revoke), and many system-stored procedures (such as sp_adduser and sp_bindrule) change the contents of *system* tables. The server logs each of these data modifications as well.

When modifying data, the server takes the following steps:

1. Writes a begin tran record in the log (in cache).
2. Records the modification in the log (in cache).
3. Performs the modification to the data (in cache).
4. Writes a commit tran record to the log (in cache).
5. Flushes all "dirty" (modified) log pages to disk.

## commit

commit flushes all "dirty" (modified) log pages for that database from cache to disk. Figure 28.1 shows the state of the data after the transaction is complete and the commit has taken place.

The server does all of the work in RAM first, before making changes to disk, to improve processing speed. When the process is complete, the only work that is written to disk is a change to the log. However, RAM is volatile. If the server goes down unexpectedly, or if someone pulls the plug out of the wall, you lose changes to data stored only in memory, right? That's where the transaction log earns its keep.

Remember, the log contains each modification. At recovery time (after the server goes down and restarted), committed transactions not written to the data area are rolled forward into the data. This is *forward recovery*, or *roll forward*. If the commit tran executes and the write to the log made to disk, the server guarantees data recovery if the server fails.

**FIGURE 28.1.**

*The* commit *process only writes log changes to disk.*

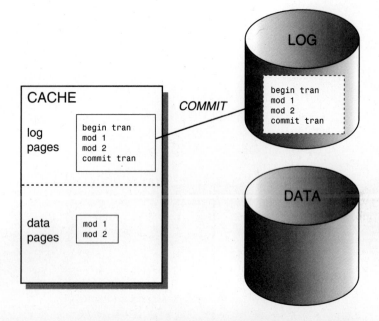

It is interesting to note here that the log is really the part of the database that matters when it comes to recovery and restore. If the data disk catches fire, you can use the information in the log, in combination with your backups, to restore the system up to the last complete transaction. On the other hand, if the log disk gets wet while you are putting out the fire, you will only be able to restore up to the time of the last backup.

Moral: Let the data disk burn to a crisp, but save the log disk (and keep your backups safe).

Serious moral: If you have to choose between mirroring logs and mirroring data, choose to mirror the logs.

At recovery time, uncommitted transactions (begin tran markers without a commit tran) roll back. All data modifications associated with the transaction are reversed. This is rollback. How do uncommitted transactions get into the log in the first place?

Frequently, when transactions overlap (that is, many user processes are creating simultaneous transactions), the commit tran will flush uncommitted, as well as committed, work to disk.

Identify uncommitted work by a `begin tran` entry in the log with no corresponding `commit tran`. Figure 28.2 illustrates a `commit` that writes both committed and uncommitted work to the log.

**FIGURE 28.2.**

*The `commit` process writes all dirty log pages for the database to disk, including those with incomplete transactions.*

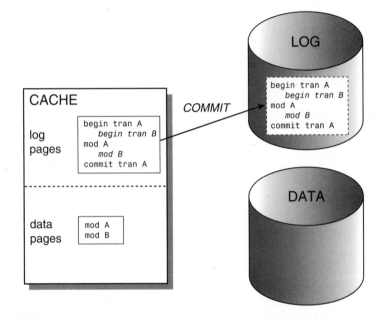

Why should you write both committed and uncommitted work with every `commit`? Keep in mind that Sybase always performs I/O at the page level or higher. Entries in `syslogs` are sorted by a consecutive timestamp value and so transactions processing concurrently are intermingled on a single page.

Remember that the `commit` process is the crucial bottleneck for an on-line system. The user is waiting and pages are locked until the `commit` is complete. By writing out `commits` at the page level without first weeding out any uncommitted work, the server can streamline `commits`. If the uncommitted work is subsequently rolled back, the server can record that fact in a later row in `syslogs`.

New for System 11, the server creates a separate log cache for each user. This is a performance enhancement intended to reduce the log bottleneck for incomplete transactions. This default size for this cache is 2KB, which you can reconfigure using the `sp_configure` command and `User log cache size` parameter. This means that with System 11, you *do not* end up with uncommitted transactions in the log.

## *checkpoint*

The log is the part of the database that keeps track of data integrity, transaction control, and recoverability. For the server to guarantee data integrity, it needs only to make certain that the log writes to disk. However, if enough transactions pile up in the log without being recorded on the data disk, it will take weeks to recover all of the committed transactions after the server fails. When is the data updated while the server is running? Update occurs during a `checkpoint`.

A `checkpoint` writes all dirty pages for the database from cache to disk, starting with the log (see Figure 28.3). A `checkpoint` reduces the amount of work the server needs to do at recovery time.

**FIGURE 28.3.**

*The* `checkpoint` *process writes all dirty pages for the database, starting with the log.*

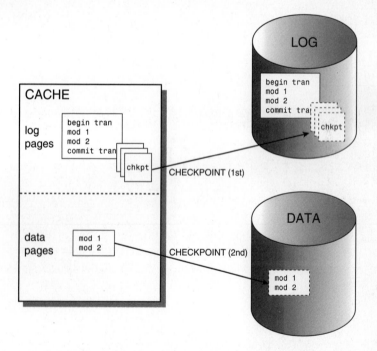

A `checkpoint` occurs under three different circumstances:

- The `dbo` issues the `checkpoint` command.
- The server needs additional cache space.
- The server recovery interval is exceeded.

Before the checkpoint starts, the server first notes in the log that a checkpoint has been performed in the database. The checkpoint marker enables the server to assume that all committed work recorded in the log prior to the checkpoint marker is reflected in the data.

If there are long-running transactions underway when the checkpoint begins, uncommitted work may be written to the log and to the data (see Figure 28.4). The recovery process uses the checkpoint marker in the log to identify work in incomplete transactions written to the data disk by a checkpoint.

**FIGURE 28.4.**

*The* checkpoint *marker indicates where the last update to the data took place. Recovery will roll back incomplete work written by a* checkpoint *and will recover transactions that completed after the* checkpoint *began.*

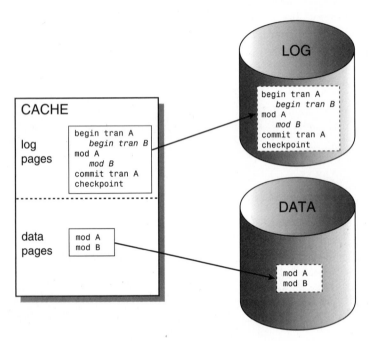

## *recovery*

recovery is an automatic process that verifies that completed transactions are in the data and that incomplete transactions are removed from the data. recovery guarantees that any completed transaction is reflected in the data. During the recovery process, the server does the following:

- Checks syslogs for each database, backing out incomplete transactions and rolling forward completed transactions not in the data.
- Checkpoints the database.
- Drops and re-creates tempdb.

# Recovery Interval

The sa can set the approximate amount of time per database he will wait for the SQL Server to start up using the `recovery interval` configuration option. For example, to set the server recovery interval to 12 minutes per database, use the following:

```
sp_configure "recovery interval", 12
```

`recovery interval` is a dynamic configuration setting, so the new value will take immediately. Here's how it works. Once a minute, one of the system processes listed in `sp_who` (you have seen it listed there—it always seems to be stuck on `CHECKPOINT SLEEP`) wakes up and examines each database in turn. Based on the amount of work recorded in the log for each database, the process determines whether it will take longer than the recovery interval to restore the database. If so, the system process issues an automatic checkpoint. Finally, if the database is set for truncate log on checkpoint, the system process truncates the log.

The length of time it will take your server to recover completely after an unexpected shutdown depends on your recovery interval and the number of databases on the server. The worst-case answer is that it could take (recovery interval × number of databases) minutes (In other words, 12-minute recovery interval × 20 databases = 4 hours!)

You will seldom encounter the worst case, but even if you do, you can access your own database as soon as recovery is complete. (Databases are recovered in order by dbid.)

> **NOTE**
>
> Don't forget that the `shutdown` statement includes an automatic `checkpoint` on every database. If you issue `shutdown with nowait`, the system skips the `checkpoint` and shuts down immediately. Server recovery is much faster after a `shutdown` than after a `shutdown with nowait`.

It's tempting to set the recovery interval low to ensure a quick recovery after any shutdown, but the checkpoint process creates overhead when you are running a high volume of transactions through the server. Set the configuration setting to the highest tolerable value.

# Recovery Flags

Use the `recovery flags` setting with `sp_configure` to display the names of transactions during recovery. If you use transaction names in SQL code, the names will display in the errorlog if the transaction is rolled back or brought forward during recovery:

```
sp_configure "recovery flags", 1
```

> **NOTE**
>
> Restart the server after this option to have the recovery flags take effect. Transaction names are not listed during the first restart. Subsequent restarts will display transaction names as transactions are processed.

Setting recovery flags enables you to determine exactly which work actually made it into the server before a shutdown. To make good use of the error log information, there needs to be a correlation between SQL Server transaction names and batch or work unit identifiers in the manual process. For example, if the batch number is 17,403, the transaction name might be B_17403. Pass the transaction name to the server with the begin tran statement, as follows:

```
begin tran B_17403
    ...
commit tran
```

# When the Transaction Log Fills Up

If the transaction log fills for any reason, all data modifications to the database will fail immediately. Most standard maintenance measures (dump the log, resize the log) will fail as well. The only reliable way to clear the log is to issue the dump tran … with no_log statement and dump the entire database.

# Thresholds and the Transaction Log

A "last-chance" threshold is provided for the logsegment for any database that has the log on a separate device. This is to prevent the log from completely filling up. The amount of free space available when the last chance threshold is reached is approximately the space needed to write the log records necessary to dump the transaction log.

The server executes sp_thresholdaction, written by you, when reaching the threshold.

## Creating *sp_thresholdaction*

The last-chance threshold procedure can be extremely simple (print a notification message in the log) or very complex (create a temporary dump device and dump the transaction, or send a pager notification through open server). Normally, you should create a dump device to use for emergencies, or code the procedure to dump to the device you would normally use for the database. The type of device depends on your environment. If you have automatic tape facilities, you could dump to your normal devices without worry. If the tape drive is unavailable, use a disk device.

> **NOTE**
>
> Unless you add a notification process, it is up to you to read the error log and discover that sp_thresholdaction was executed on the database. If you backed up the data to a disk during your threshold procedure, copy the data to a tape as soon as you realize what has happened.

Remember, this is emergency processing. The database locks for updates and remains that way until space in the log is available.

You need to decide whether you will have a single threshold procedure for all databases, or specific procedures for databases with special characteristics. You should certainly create one sp_thresholdaction in sybsystemprocs for all databases. Later, you can create specific procedures in individual databases. When crossing the last-chance threshold in a database, the server first looks for sp_thresholdaction in that database; it only looks for the procedure in sybsystemprocs if not found in the database.

The server always includes four parameters when it calls a threshold procedure:

- @dbname, varchar(30), is the name of the database.
- @segmentname, varchar(30), is the name of the segment. In the last-chance threshold, this value is always "logsegment."
- @space_left (int) is the number of pages available.
- @status (int) indicates whether this is a last-chance threshold (1), or not (0).

Here is an example of a simple last-chance threshold procedure that performs a backup to an emergency backup device and prints a warning message in the transaction log. For this procedure to work, the Emergency_Device must already exist (set it up with sp_addumpdevice):

```
create procedure sp_thresholdaction
    @database_name varchar(30),
    @segment_name varchar(30),
    @free_space_in_pages int,
    @status int
as
dump transaction @dbname to Emergency_Device
print "WARNING: Last Chance Threshold crossed!"
print "Transaction log for the %1! segment in the %2! database ", @segment,
@database
print " was dumped to the Emergency_Device!!!"
go
```

# Suspended Transactions

Once the last-chance threshold is crossed, processes that add rows to the log will either abort or suspend, depending on how you have configured the database. (By default, the processes will be suspended. You can verify that processes are suspended with sp_who.)

`sp_thresholdaction` normally dumps or expands the transaction log, freeing up space for the suspended transactions. The suspended transactions will awaken and should execute normally. If a process does not awaken on its own, use `lct_admin` to unsuspend all suspended processes for a database, as in the following example:

```
select lct_admin ("unsuspend", db_id)
```

You should call Sybase Technical Support before using this facility, because all processes should wake up when space is available in the log.

## Aborting Processes

If you have not written `sp_thresholdaction`, configure the database to abort transactions when the log is full. Otherwise user processes will appear to hang until you realize that the log is full. You must be in the master database to issue the `sp_dboption` command and change this value, as in the following example:

```
use master
go
sp_dboption database_name, "abort tran on log full", true
go
```

## Additional Log Thresholds

I recommend that you create several additional thresholds in your database log to allow you the time to act proactively. Thresholds are defined by the percentage of remaining space in the segment. Create thresholds so that you are warned periodically before log space is in crisis. I like to place thresholds at 50 percent available, 25 percent available, 10 percent available, and 2 percent available, depending on the size of the log.

# Summary

Transactions ensure consistency of database integrity to manage simultaneous updates and to ensure recovery after a server shutdown. All SQL statements are transactions themselves, and many SQL statements can be combined into a larger transaction.

You need to manage the transaction log, either with thresholds or by regularly monitoring the amount of available space in the log.

# Backing Up and
# Restoring Databases
# and Transaction Logs

Backup is common to any database environment. A *backup* is a copy of a database (or portion of a database) stored on some type of media (tape, disk, and so on). A *restore* is the process used to return a database to a point in time. In Sybase, a backup is normally referred to as a *dump* and a restore is normally referred to as a *load*, because these are the names of the commands for backing up and restoring.

It takes work to define an effective backup and recovery plan. This is particularly true in *very large database* (VLDB) environments because of the magnified complexity of administrative activities. Timing of activities quickly becomes an issue. For large tables and databases, consistency checks (dbcc), updating index statistics, and index creation can take several hours to *days*. Plans for automating backups must consider the impact of these activities as well as application activities.

The backup media you choose also can affect your plan. Dumping to tape devices means management of the physical tapes, which you must consider in your plan. Additionally, when a tape is full, a subsequent backup would fail, which could affect your entire backup and recovery process. When dumping to file devices, you must consider the organization of the directory structure as well as management of the backup files.

# Why Back Up?

Backups are a hassle. Why bother? (Why do you have car insurance?) Backups are the easiest and most foolproof way to ensure you can recover a database. Without a backup, all data might be lost and have to be re-created from the source. This is normally an option only for *decision support systems* (DSS), because its data normally originates in some other system. For *online transaction processing* (OLTP) systems, the majority of data originates on the server. The lost data *might not* be reproducible.

Backups can guard against table or database corruption, media failure, or user error. They should be performed as frequently as necessary for effective data administration. You can perform SQL Server backups while the database is in use, but it is generally more effective to back up during nonpeak activity periods.

# Roles and Responsibilities

The ability to execute the dump and load commands defaults to the dbo of the database. The dbo could be the login who created the database (anyone with a dbo alias in the database) or the sa login (the sa becomes dbo in any database the sa uses).

Logins granted the oper_role have the ability to dump and load *any* database in the server.

> **NOTE**
>
> Sybase added the concept of roles in System 10—a good idea! As with many of the enhancements in System 10, roles address the needs of large organizations.
>
> The sa normally performed backups for most sites using versions previous to System 10. In small organizations, this approach was adequate because the DBA was responsible for *all* activities on the server.
>
> Larger organizations often distribute database administration functions. Separate groups usually exist to manage logins, conduct backups, and configure and administer the server. Operators logging in as sa had inappropriate server access for executing simple backups and restores, but it was the only practical way to access those features.
>
> The oper_role solves these problems.

You should identify who is responsible for performing backups in your organization. For each of these individuals, create a login and grant the operator role:

```
sp_role "grant", oper_role, login_name
```

As always, the sa or dbo has the ability to dump and load the database.

# Types of Backups

There are two types of backups: full and incremental. A *full backup* is a copy of all the allocated pages in your database, including all system tables. (See Figure 29.1.) The system tables include syslogs, normally referred to as the transaction log. The transaction log is dumped to ensure that all transactions are in the backup.

**FIGURE 29.1.**

*A database backup (dump database* acctg_db*) copies the entire database, including log and data.*

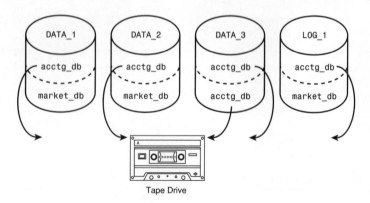

Tape Drive

> **WARNING**
>
> Full backups do not truncate the transaction log, which often is confusing and sometimes disastrous for new DBAs. Even if all your backups are complete backups, you must run the incremental backup process periodically to clear the transaction log. Otherwise, you'll certainly fill up your log, and processing on that database will halt until you clear the log. (See "Dumping Database Logs," later in this chapter.)

> **WARNING**
>
> Transaction log dumps do not truncate the log prior to the oldest open transaction. In earlier releases of SQL Server, aborted transactions could also have a similar effect.
>
> With System 11, you can check the `syslogshold` table in the `master` database. It will contain the oldest active transaction in a database, and you may be able to determine, based on the transaction time, whether this will effectively truncate your log. If it won't, you may have to kill users or even cycle the server (shut it down and restart it).

An *incremental backup* is simply a copy of the transaction log (see Figure 29.2). The transaction log contains the transactions that have occurred since the last `dump transaction` command. This is similar to incremental backups of file systems, where only the files that have changed are included. Dumping the transaction log truncates the log, unless you specify the `with no_truncate` option.

**FIGURE 29.2.**

*An incremental backup (*`dump transaction acctg_db`*) copies only the transaction log.*

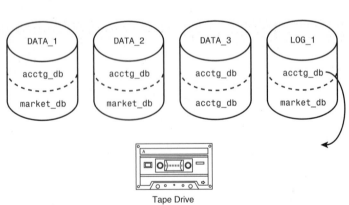

Tape Drive

# Dump Devices

A dump device is created for the exclusive use of the `dump` and `load` commands. When dumping a database or transaction log, you must tell it where to create the backup. Creating a dump device enables you to associate a logical name with the physical backup media. The two most common types of media are tape devices and disk devices.

# Tape Devices

A tape device records backups to removable tapes. Tape drives can be used alone, or several can be used at one time in parallel. Purchase as many drives as you can afford, based on the needs of your backup and recovery strategy. Tape devices are inherently more secure than disk devices because the media (tape) is removable and portable. Tape capacity has increased dramatically over the last five years. In 1990, a standard ¼-inch cartridge held only 150MB of data. Now, smaller cartridges (4mm or 8mm are common sizes) hold over 50 times the amount of data (8GB). The size and compactness of tapes will almost certainly continue to progress.

Most production sites use tape devices. Tape devices provide a removable source of backup media that can easily be moved off site for additional security. A tape device adapts to changing database size much more gracefully than disk devices. Dumping a 50MB database to disk is easily managed by your file system. As the database grows to 50GB however, a disk dump will probably prove impossible, because most sites do not have that amount of free space in the file system. Additionally, to move the dump off site, you must back up the dump files *to tape*.

# Disk Devices

A disk device is just a file in a directory, usually stored in the file system of your database server. Dumping to a disk device is faster than dumping to a tape device. When you dump to a disk device, you actually can see the file grow if you check the file size at intervals during the dump.

> **NOTE**
>
> One important fact to remember is that a dump to a disk device overwrites an existing file unless you specify a number of days to retain the file as part of the `dump` command. This is an important distinction between dumping to tape devices and dumping to file devices—overwrites are automatic.

A dump to a tape device will not overwrite any other dumps on the tape *unless you tell it to* (with the `init` option). A dump to a disk device has one of three results:

- The dump to the device creates a brand new file. This is the ideal situation.
- The dump to the device replaces or overwrites an existing file. This is potentially disastrous, because the "good" dump file from last night easily could be overwritten by a corrupt dump. *Make sure you specify the* `with retaindays = #_of_days` *option to avoid overwriting a dump.*

- The dump to the device fails. This may cause an interrupt in your backup and recovery schedule. Database backup scripts rarely —if ever—perform retries if the dump fails (normally, retry also will fail anyway). What if you can back up only once a week? This essentially means an entire backup may be missing from your backup schedule. This is not an ideal situation for most environments.

If you assume a file will be created (new or replacing an existing file), you must ensure that any file created as part of a production dump is not overwritten until after you make a copy of the file. This normally results in writing automation scripts to dump a database to a file immediately followed by either of the following:

- Moving that file to a different filename, clearing the way for the next dump.
- Backing up that file to a tape drive, which means the existing file could be overwritten without worry.

For these reasons, many people will tell you "Don't use disk drives for backups!" This is another of those "rules of thumb" that has several exceptions.

There are situations in which disk devices are appropriate. One normal environment in which you might back up to disk drives is a development environment, where backups are conducted often by developers. There is a major production system in the United States where disk devices are used in production because the dump is completely automated and requires no user intervention. Another reason has to do with the added baggage from tapes. Tapes must be managed. It is likely you'll need to hire an operator or make a significant purchase (a tape silo) to manage the process.

## Adding Dump Devices

Use `sp_addumpdevice` to add a new dump device to an SQL Server.

## Syntax

```
sp_addumpdevice "tape", logicalname, physical_name, size
sp_addumpdevice "disk", logical_name, physical_name
```

**TIP**

In System 10, you don't have to add dump devices with `sp_addumpdevice`. The physical name can be provided as part of the `dump` syntax.

I learned this the hard way by misspelling the logical name of a dump device in the `dump` command:

```
dump tran my_db to dumpdev1
```

It should have been `dump_dev1`. Imagine my surprise to find a file, dumpdev1, in the /home/sybase/install directory!

## Logical Name

After executing this command, you can use the logical name for all dumps and loads; a good practice is to choose the logical name based on the type of device being added. For tape devices, use a general name for the tape (Tape1, Tape2, and so on). For disk devices, use a logical name indicating the database and dump type (`CustomerDB_dump` or `CustomerDB_tran`, for example).

## Physical Name

The physical name is normally predefined for tape devices. Tape devices should be specified as dictated by your hardware. A common example of the physical name is /dev/nrst0. (Check the documentation for your specific hardware environment.) The following example adds a nonrewinding `"/dev/n..."` tape device called `"Tape1"` with a capacity of 8GB. This device will recognize any ANSI tape labels:

```
sp_addumpdevice "tape", "Tape1", "/dev/nrmt0", 8000
```

For file devices, it is a good idea to organize a directory structure for all your databases. For example, the root directory may be called /dbdump. Each database in your server would be a subdirectory. The CustomerDB subdirectory would be /dbdump/CustomerDB. The filename created is based on the dump type. Therefore, the two dump devices for the `CustomerDB` database would be created in the following manner:

```
sp_addumpdevice "disk", "CustomerDB_dump",
    "/dbdump/CustomerDB/CustomerDB_dump", 2

sp_addumpdevice "disk", "CustomerDB_tran",
    "/dbdump/CustomerDB/CustomerDB_tran", 2
```

By standardizing your structure, you can now write scripts that accept a database name as a parameter. The entire `dump` command can be created dynamically. The location of the dump is known, enabling you to immediately rename the dump file and avoid having it overwritten.

## Size

The `size` parameter specifies the tape capacity in number of megabytes. Use the maximum size allowable for your tape device.

Do not be stingy with the number of dump devices added. Using dump devices helps standardize your dump approach; particularly for disk devices.

# Backup Server

Backups for System 10 and later releases require backup server, an open server process that directly queries the controller and is approximately seven times faster than pre–System 10 technology. The SQL Server instructs the backup server, via remote procedure calls, to back up a specific database. The backup server handles I/O, rather than using SQL Server resources. The use of the backup server has several advantages:

- Backups can be *striped* (portioned), enabling you to specify up to 32 separate devices for dumping or loading a database. The backup server breaks the database into approximately equal portions and dumps those portions in parallel.

- Backups can be performed remotely, enabling you to dump your database or a portion (stripe) of your database to a device on hardware *other* than the hardware where your SQL Server resides.

- Backups can be dumped to multiple tapes without using the console program.

- Several backups may be recorded on the same tape. Subsequent reloads locate only the file necessary to recover.

- Tape options are expanded.

- Messages may be sent to the session initiating the dump or load, or to an operator console.

Backup server is a separate server process from your SQL Server and therefore requires enabling remote access before issuing commands. A "local" backup server *must* be available on the same hardware as your SQL Server. The local backup server listens on a different port number from the SQL Server. (You can easily confirm this by viewing your interfaces file.) You can dump to your local backup server, a remote backup server, or both.

## Remote Backup Server

The SQL Server can instruct a backup server, located on separate hardware from your SQL Server, to back up a specific database using remote procedure calls. In order to perform dumps with System 10, you must have a local backup server process running on the same physical server as SQL Server. The local backup server sends the necessary packets of data across the network to the remote backup server, which stores the data to a dump device. (See Figure 29.3.)

There are special instances where a remote backup is appropriate. In most circumstances, the increased load on the network, the poor performance of the dump itself over the network, and the logistics of remotely managing multiple-server backups imply that a local backup is more effective.

However, all these problems may be overcome if the specific business case warrants the investment of time and money. Certainly, remote backup is feasible—it is just more complex.

**FIGURE 29.3.**

*The local backup server can perform backups itself, or it can communicate over the network with other backup servers on other equipment to perform remote dumps.*

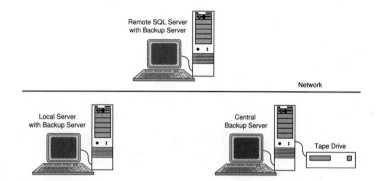

# Adding a Server

Sybase looks for an entry for the backup server name in the interfaces file. The backup server is named SYB_BACKUP by default. The entry for the backup server is added to the interfaces file and to the SQL Server with sybinit. You must make remote backup servers known to your SQL Server by using the sp_addserver command.

## Syntax

```
sp_addserver remote_backup_name, null, network_name
```

The *network_name* may be copied from your interfaces file.

# Starting a Backup Server

Start a backup server with startserver, which receives a startup script that invokes backupserver. This is similar to starting an SQL Server, except the startup script invokes dataserver. The startup script is automatically created by the sybinit procedure and is named SYB_BACKUP by default. At the operating system command line, you execute the following:

```
startserver -f SYB_BACKUP
```

If you want to shut down a backup server, provide the name of the backup server to the shut-down command (the backup server is normally shut down using isql):

```
shutdown [backup_servername] [ with {wait ¦ nowait} ]
```

Here is an example:

```
shutdown SYB_BACKUP with nowait
```

The with wait option is the default. It brings down backup server gracefully by enabling all current dumps or loads to complete. No new backup or dump requests are honored. The with nowait option immediately shuts down the backup server, even if a dump or load is in progress. *Do not specify the* with nowait *option unless it is really necessary.*

# Dumping and Loading

Now that the basics are defined, you need to take a close look at the dump and load commands. At this point, you should have backup server up and running and you should identify your dump devices. Let's look at the dump and load options for the entire database and for the transaction log.

## Dumping the Database

Use dump database to make a full copy of your database. The simplified syntax for the dump database command is the following:

```
dump database databasename to devicename
```

This command is valid in all environments. In System 10, however, the backup is handled by a backup server that has several other options, including remote backup, striped backups, and tape handling specifications. Here is the full format for the dump database command:

```
dump database databasename
    to stripe_device [ at backup_server_name ]
        [ density = density_value,
          blocksize = number_of_bytes,
          capacity = number_of_KB,
          dumpvolume = volume_name ]
    [ stripe on stripe_device ...]
    [ with {
          [ dismount ¦ nodismount ],
          [ nounload ¦ unload ],
          retaindays = number_of_days,
          [ noinit ¦ init ],
          file = file_name,
          [ notify = { client ¦ operator_console } ]
          }
    ]
```

Table 29.1 presents detailed descriptions of each parameter of dump database.

**Table 29.1.** dump database **parameters.**

| Parameter | Description |
| --- | --- |
| databasename | This is the name of the database you are attempting to dump. |
| stripe_device | When dumping locally, this is either the logical or physical name of the dump device. When dumping remotely, you must specify the *physical* name. |
| backup_server_name | Use this option when specifying a remote dump device. |

| Parameter | Description |
|---|---|
| density<br>blocksize<br>devicecapacity | These parameters relate to the physical characteristics of the tape you are using. Assume the defaults unless instructed otherwise. |
| retaindays = #_of_days | This is a UNIX option that can be used for any type of dump device. It does not allow the dump to be overwritten until the number of days specified has passed. This is an important option for any production backup strategy. |

There are several other options that focus on how to conduct the dump, regardless of the physical device characteristics. These options should be incorporated into your backup strategy.

Note that the options in the next six sections apply only to tape devices.

## dumpvolume

The option Specify dumpvolume for production dumps labels your dump, which can be specified during a load. For example, specify a dumpvolume of your database name and the date (CustomerDB_Jan07). Then, if you have dumps for January 7 through 10 on a single tape, you can easily reload the January 7 dump by specifying dumpvolume as part of the load.

## dismount | nodismount

The dismount ¦ nodismount option is valid only on platforms that support logical dismounts (OpenVMS). It determines whether the tape will be available for future dumps. By default, the dismount option is used. Specify nodismount to enable the tape to be used for subsequent dumps.

## nounload | unload

The nounload ¦ unload option controls the rewinding of the tape. nounload should be used, unless this is the last dump you wish to have on the tape.

## noinit | init

The noinit ¦ init option determines whether the dump will be appended to the tape or reinitializes the entire tape volume. Use init when dumping to a tape for the first time or to reuse an old tape. You might use noinit to allow for multiple dumps to a single tape.

# file = file_name

Use the `file = file_name` option to specify a filename of up to 17 characters in length. This option normally is not specified. By default, backup server names the file by concatenating the last seven characters from the database name, the two-digit year, the Julian day (1 through 366), and a hex representation of the time.

# notify = {client | operator_console}

Volume change messages are sent, by default, to the operator console if available. If unavailable, the messages are sent to the client initiating the request. Specify this parameter only if the default function is not desired. In UNIX systems, the messages are sent to the client. Specify `operator_console` to route the messages to the terminal on which the backup server is running. For OpenVMS, the messages are sent to the operator console. Specify `client` to send the messages to the client initializing the dump.

The following is an example of striped dumps:

```
# Dump the CustomerDB database across 4 dump devices (Tape1-4).
# Name each volume, initialize the tapes, do not rewind,
# prevent other dumps from overwriting this dump for 2 weeks,
# and send the messages to the client terminal.
dump database CustomerDB to Tape1 dumpvolume = Volume1
     stripe on Tape2 dumpvolume = Volume2
     stripe on Tape3 dumpvolume = Volume3
     stripe on Tape4 dumpvolume = Volume4
     with init, nounload, retaindays=14, notify=client
```

This is an example of remote dumps:

```
# Dump the CustomerDB database across 2 remote devices on two
# different backup servers. Append to the tapes, do not rewind,
# prevent other dumps from overwriting this dump for 1 week
dump database CustomerDB to "/dev/nrmt0" at REMOTE_BACKUP1
     stripe on "/dev/nrmt0" at REMOTE_BACKUP2
     with noinit, nounload, retaindays=7
```

Here is an example of multiple dumps to a single tape:

```
# Dump the CustomerDB, ProductDB, and SecurityDB to Tape1
# For the first dump, initialize the tape but do not rewind.
# Dump the second database after the first.
# After the third database is dumped, rewind the tape.
# (Send the messages to the client terminal.)
dump database CustomerDB to Tape1 dumpvolume = CustVol1
     with init notify=client
dump database ProductDB to Tape1 dumpvolume = ProdVol1
     with notify=client        /* no unload is the default */
dump database SecurityDB to Tape1 dumpvolume = SecVol1
     with unload, notify=client
```

You can dump a database while the server is in use. It impacts performance to some degree. Striping dumps decreases the total amount of time required to execute the dump, decreasing the duration of the impact. You should benchmark user response times with and without a dump process running to determine the impact on your system.

# Dumping Database Logs

Use dump transaction to make a copy of the transactions that have occurred against your database since the last transaction log dump. This is the simplified syntax for the dump transaction command:

```
dump transaction databasename to devicename
```

This command is valid in all environments. In System 10, however, the options available to the dump database command are also available to the dump transaction command. Transaction log dumps can occur remotely, be striped across several devices, and have the same tape handling facilities. Dump transaction has a few other options used for special purposes. Here is the full format for the dump transaction command:

```
dump tran[saction] databasename
    {with {truncate_only ¦ no_log } ¦
    to stripe_device [ at backup_server_name ]
        [ density = density_value,
          blocksize = number_of_bytes,
          capacity = number_of_KB,
          dumpvolume = volume_name ]
    [ stripe on stripe_device ...]
    [ with {
          [ dismount ¦ nodismount ],
          [ nounload ¦ unload ],
          retaindays = number_of_days,
          [ noinit ¦ init ],
          file = file_name,
          no_truncate,
          [ notify = { client ¦ operator_console } ]
          }
    ]
    }
```

The special-purpose options are in bold letters. These options are truncate_only, no_log, and no_truncate.

## *truncate_only and no_log*

The truncate_only and no_log options are used to prune the transaction log without making a copy of it. As you can see from the format of the command, you either specify one of these options or indicate a device to which to dump the transaction log. Use truncate_only to truncate the log gracefully. It checkpoints the database before truncating the log. Use no_log when your transaction log is completely full. no_log does not checkpoint the database before dumping the log.

Either of these options throws away the log. Once the command has been executed, you are exposed. If a disaster occurs before you can dump the database, you will not be able to recover *any* data that added since the last dump. The frequency of dumping transaction logs determines the scope of your exposure.

Any database that does not have its transaction log on a separate device cannot dump the transaction. Every system has a database meeting this characteristic. This is usually discovered when the transaction log for the master database is full.

Because master must fully reside on the master device, the database space is shared between data and log, negating the capability of dumping the transaction log.

To avoid this problem, periodically prune the transaction log with truncate_only (or no_log, if completely full). Make sure you dump the database after logged operations (database creation, user addition, and so on). For databases that do not require up-to-the-minute recovery, and for databases with no separate log segment, set the trunc log on chkpt option on for the database and dump frequently.

## no_truncate

The no_truncate option is exactly opposite of the previous two options. no_truncate makes a copy of your transaction log, but *does not* prune it. Use this option when you have a media failure of a device being used by your database. *The* master *database must be available.* This option enables the server to dump the transaction log, but does not try to touch the database in any way. (In a normal dump tran, a checkpoint is executed. If a database device is unavailable, the checkpoint process cannot write the dirty pages. no_truncate simply backs up the transaction log, without checkpointing.)

Dumping the transaction log is disabled after nonlogged operations such as writetext, select into, and fast bcp. You can dump a transaction log while the server is in use. The impact on performance should be minimal. It is common to dump transaction logs even during normal business hours.

# Loading the Database

Use load database to load a backup into an existing database. The database can be the database used to create the dump, but this is definitely not a requirement. The simplified syntax for the load database command is the following:

```
load database databasename from devicename
```

This command is valid in all environments. Most options available to the dump command may be used in the load. This is the full format for the load database command:

```
load database databasename
     from stripe_device [ at backup_server_name ]
          [ density = density_value,
            blocksize = number_of_bytes,
            dumpvolume = volume_name ]
     [ stripe on stripe_device ...]
     [ with {
          [ dismount ¦ nodismount ],
          [ nounload ¦ unload ],
          file = file_name,
          listonly [ = full ],
          headeronly,
          [ notify = { client ¦ operator_console } ]
          }
     ]
```

All options listed are identical to the dump command *except* for the listonly and headeronly options. If you specify either of these options, information is displayed but no data is loaded. Use these options *immediately after* a database dump to verify that the load process can read the dump. It may be used for tape or file devices.

## listonly

Use listonly to obtain a listing of all dump files on a tape volume. The output contains database name, device name, and date and time of the dump. The = full option provides additional information.

## headeronly

Use headeronly to display information about a single dump file. If the device specified is a tape device, information about only the first file on the dump is displayed, unless you specify the file parameter.

> **NOTE**
>
> No one can use the database while load is being executed, including the person executing the load command.

Here are some loading examples. The first shows striped loads:

```
# Load the CustomerDB database across 4 dump devices (Tape1-4).
# Indicate each volume, rewind the tape after the load, and notify
# the client terminal
load database CustomerDB from Tape1 dumpvolume = Volume1
     stripe on Tape2 dumpvolume = Volume2
     stripe on Tape3 dumpvolume = Volume3
     stripe on Tape4 dumpvolume = Volume4
     with unload, notify=client
```

The following is an example of using fewer devices to load:

```
# Load the CustomerDB database which was dumped across 4 devices
# with only 3 dump devices (Tape1-3).
# Indicate each volume, rewind the tape after the load, and notify
# the client terminal
load database CustomerDB from Tape1 dumpvolume = Volume1
     stripe on Tape2 dumpvolume = Volume2
     stripe on Tape3 dumpvolume = Volume3
     with unload, notify=client
# Once the first three stripes have loaded, a message will be
# sent to the operator to load the fourth.
# After placing the 4th tape in the Tape2 device, execute:
load database CustomerDB from Tape1 dumpvolume = Volume4
     with unload, notify=client
(e)Striped remote loads
# Load the CustomerDB database from 2 remote devices on two
# different backup servers. Rewind the tape upon completion.
load database CustomerDB from "/dev/nrmt0" at REMOTE_BACKUP1
     stripe on "/dev/nrmt0" at REMOTE_BACKUP2
     with unload
```

The load database command loads all used pages from the dump into the target database and runs recovery of syslogs to ensure consistency. Any unused pages are initialized by the load process. (This is the primary reason why a load can take significantly longer than a dump. The time required to dump a database is proportional to the used pages in the database; the time required to load a database is proportional to the overall number of pages in the database. Therefore, a 50GB database with 20MB of data may take only a few minutes to dump, but the load could take several hours or days.)

Dumps are conducted to be able to restore a database to a point in time. A load is executed to restore a database, normally after a corruption or user error occurs. If you are loading for a reason other than a disaster, the current database structure can be used to load the database dump. This does not require any extra work other than ensuring tapes are loaded (or files are in the correct locations).

## Restoring after a Disaster

If the load is a result of a disaster, the database must first be dropped. The drop database may not execute in the case of a corruption. For corrupt databases, use dbcc dbrepair:

```
dbcc dbrepair(database_name, dropdb)
```

A new structure must be created. If you are creating a database for the exclusive purpose of loading, use the for load option to create database.

## Creating for *load*

Creating a database for load allocates the structure but does not initialize the pages. Using this option takes *significantly* less time than a normal create. The database will not be usable except for running a `load`. The database must be created in the same fashion as the dumped database. For example, if you initially created the `CustomerDB` database with 1GB for data and 100MB for log and subsequently altered the database by 500MB for data, execute the following commands:

```
use master
go
create database CustomerDB on DataDevice1 = 1000,
     log on LogDevice1 = 200
     for load
go
alter database CustomerDB on DataDevice2 = 500 for load
go
load database CustomerDB from CustomerDB_dump
go
```

The easiest way to ensure the correct order is to save each `create` or `alter` command in a single `create` script as the commands are executed. If you have not saved your scripts, you can retrieve this information from the sysusages table in the `master` database:

```
select segmap, "Size in MB"=size/512
from sysusages
where dbid = db_id ("database_name")

segmap     Size in MB
3          1000
4          200
3          500
```

The `segmap` column refers to the segments defined in your database. Initially, there are three segments in your database: system, default, and logsegment. If you convert the `segmap` number to binary, you can determine how the `segmap` relates to segment names:

$2^0$ = system segment
$2^1$ = default segment
$2^2$ = logsegment
$2^3$ = first user-defined segment
$2^4$ = second user-defined segment

The segment mapping for the example database is the following:

| | log | data | sys | |
|---|---|---|---|---|
| segmap 2^3 | 2^2 | 2^1 | 2^0 | size |
| 3 | 0 | 0 | 1 | 1 | 1000 |
| 4 | 0 | 1 | 0 | 0 | 200 |
| 3 | 0 | 0 | 1 | 1 | 500 |

Therefore, a `segmap` of 3 indicates a data device (default + system), and a `segmap` of 4 indicates log only.

If you have added user-defined segments (and possibly dropped the default and system segments from a fragment), there are indicators in the $2^3$ column and greater. Create these fragments as data fragments. Because segments are database-specific, the database system tables containing the user-defined segment definitions are loaded in the `load` process, which resolves the segment mapping within the database.

> **NOTE**
>
> If you created your database with the log on a separate device, the log fragments should have a 1 in the log column ($2^2$) only.

## Loading into a Different Database

Occasionally, you may want to create an exact copy of a database in your system. First, dump the existing database. Then create a new database to load with this dump. The database does not have to be the same size as the original. The only requirement is that the destination database must be at least as large as the dumped database and have the same beginning fragments as the original database. For example, consider loading the dump from the previous database into a database of 3GB. The command to create this database might be the following:

```
use master
go
create database NewCustomerDB on DataDevice2 = 1000
     log on LogDevice2 = 200
     for load
go
alter database NewCustomerDB on DataDevice2 = 500 for load
go
alter database NewCustomerDB on DataDevice3 = 300 for load
go
alter database NewCustomerDB on DataDevice4 = 1000 for load
go
load database NewCustomerDB from CustomerDB_dump
go
```

> **NOTE**
>
> I have been told that the `create database … for load` command will not work in System 10 under NetWare but have not tried it myself. It's always worth a try when you are restoring a database. At worst, the command will not work in your environment, meaning you will need to drop the new, corrupt database and try again.

## Loading a Transaction

Use `load transaction` to load a transaction log backup. Transaction logs must be loaded in the order dumped. During a `load database`, the data in the dump is copied over the database. After the load is complete, the database contains all the data in the database at the time of the dump. The loading of a transaction log is different than loading a database. The transaction log load copies the contents of the dump over the current syslogs definition. Once the log is loaded, a recovery takes place. The server marches through the log applying changes in the log that are not reflected in the database (normally, all records in the log are new transactions). The simplified syntax for the `load database` command is the following:

```
load transaction <databasename> from <devicename>
```

This command is valid in all environments. Most options available to the `dump` command can be used in the `load`. This is the full format for the `load transaction` command:

```
load tran[saction] <databasename>
    from <stripe_device> [ at <backup_server_name> ]
        [ density = <density_value>,
          blocksize = <number_of_bytes<,
          dumpvolume = <volume_name> ]
    [ stripe on <stripe_device> ...]
    [ with {
        [ dismount ¦ nodismount ],
        [ nounload ¦ unload ],
        file = <file_name>,
        listonly [ = full ],
        headeronly,
        [ notify = { client ¦ operator_console } ]
        }
    ]
```

Most options listed are explained in the "`dump database`" section, except for the `listonly` and `headeronly` options, which are explained in the "`load database`" section.

The load of a transaction log dump requires significantly less time than a `load database`, because the size of the log is normally much smaller than the size of the database itself. No modifications can be made to the database between a `load database` and a `load transaction` (or between transaction log loads).

# Additional Considerations

The pieces of the puzzle are starting to fall in place. You have defined the groundwork necessary to begin development of your backup and recovery approach. Now you must consider several issues that can impact your plan.

## Automatic Backups

Sybase does not provide any facilities to automate the backup (or recovery) of your databases. Recovery is usually not automated due to the nature of recovery. You hope that recoveries are something you never have to perform. Recovery is normally performed when a catastrophe has occurred, and the setup necessary to begin a restoration *should* involve DBA interaction. Develop procedures to address recovery, but *do not* automate this procedure.

Backups, however, should be planned and scheduled. Investigate third-party tools once you have developed your backup plan. Off-the-shelf tools can automate backups, but may not address all the elements in your plan. If the tool does not have scripting extensions, it is to your advantage to develop your own facility.

*Write my own facility?* It is not as daunting as it sounds. Virtually all operating systems have scripting languages, and most have scheduling facilities (that is, UNIX crontab) or these facilities can be purchased. Scripts can range from simple (10 or 20 lines of code) to complex (1,000+ lines of code). The scope varies based on the functionality, error checking, and reporting requirements. Consider the following simple script:

```
[text file - custdump.sql]
use master
go
select "Start Time"=getdate()
go
dump database CustomerDB to CustomerDB_dump
go
select "End Time"=getdate()
go
[shell script - custdump.ksh]
#!/usr/bin/ksh
isql -U oper_login -P oper_password -e < custdump.sql > custdump.out
[crontab entry]
# Dump the customer database every day at 10 PM
# Format is minutes, hour, year, month, day, script
# See your manual page for more information
# Minutes - 0 (on the hour)
# Hour - 22 (10 PM, military time)
# Year - * (every year)
# Month - * (every month)
# Day - * (every day)
# Script (full path) - /home/dba/scripts/custdump.ksh
0 10 * * * /home/dba/scripts/custdump.ksh
```

# Frequency of Dumps

As mentioned previously, dumps should be executed as frequently as necessary for effective database administration. This is intentionally vague, because the frequency of dumps varies based on your requirements. The true driver is *the duration of time your business can afford for the database to be unavailable after a disaster.*

The total time to restore a database is the sum of database load time plus the transaction log load time. The database load is atomic; it happens only once during a recovery of a database. The transaction log loads, however, are dynamic. The time to load transaction logs depends on the amount of activity since the database dump.

Consider the difference between a database dumped yearly versus a database dumped weekly, with transaction logs dumped every day between dumps for both. The yearly dump scenario has 364 transaction log dumps between database dumps; the weekly dump scenario has six transaction log dumps. If a disaster occurs on January 4th, the time to recover in both cases is identical. Each scenario has a database load (January 1 database dump) and three transaction log loads (January 2, 3, and 4 transaction log dumps). Consider the worst case scenario, however. A yearly dump approach could result in having to load a full year's worth of activity, one day at a time. The weekly dump approach would have a maximum of only a week's worth of activity to load.

Therefore, dump your database as often as possible. Ideally, database dumps should occur with no activity on the system. Although this is not a requirement, it ensures that the dump contains the state of your database before *and after* your dump. If this is not possible, execute your dumps when activity is as light as possible.

Dumps can be executed during normal business hours, but will have an effect on your system's performance. Database dumps in System 10 are much less devastating to performance than in earlier versions. This is due to code changes in the implementation of the database dump as well as increased speed of the process, the capability of striping dumps, and the implementation of backup server as a separate process from SQL Server.

Transaction log dumps are often scheduled during normal business hours, but low (or no) activity periods are obviously preferred. Dumping a transaction log takes significantly less time than a database dump. The time required is based solely on the amount of data in the log (which is based on modifications since the last dump transaction). A backup plan for a production system should include transaction log dumps to provide up-to-the-minute recovery. Development environments normally do not dump transaction logs because this type of recovery is unnecessary. Fairly frequent database dumps usually suffice.

## Striping Dumps

Dumps can be striped across as many as 32 parallel devices in System 10. This can significantly reduce the time required to dump or load your database or transaction logs.

In spite of the performance improvement, try to avoid striping. Each stripe can be a possible point of failure. If one of the stripes is unreadable, the load will fail. Consider striping when you decide the time required to dump to a single device is too great to fit the activity in your administration window.

## Locking

The dump process locks pages differently in System 10 and version 4.*x*. In version 4.*x*, you cannot modify pages not yet read by the dump process. It is like a virtual shared lock on these pages—users can read, but not write (insert, update, or delete).

In System 10, the dump process consists of three distinct phases. During the first two portions, the dump process dumps all the used pages in your database (log first, data second). The third phase dumps the new log pages created by modifications during the first two phases. Any modifications that take place during this last activity are not reflected in the dump. This is a significant improvement over the version 4.*x* process because the dump process does not require a single, locked, consistent version of the database while running.

> **NOTE**
>
> Many administrators using version 4.*x* of SQL Server need a database dump that includes transactions occurring during the dump itself (like System 10 database dumps provide automatically). To do that, dump the transaction log immediately after the database dump is complete.

## Capturing Statistics

Capture as many statistics as possible about the dump and load processes. It will be invaluable in estimating durations and give you real statistics about the performance of your system. Here are important statistics to gather:

- Total database size (`sp_helpdb`)
- Total number of used pages (for information about sp_spaceused, see Chapter 26, "Defining, Altering, and Maintaining Databases and Logs")
- Total execution time (wrap the `dump` or `load` command with `select getdate()`)

For dumps, the time to execute is fairly linear based on used pages. For loads, the time to execute depends on total database size and used pages.

You need to understand and monitor database size and usage when planning backup regimens for databases that have not leveled off in size. During the early stages of a system, data volume can be low. Data is added over time. This increase levels off once your purge and archive criteria are active.

For example, a 15GB database may be created to support your production system. Initially, it may be loaded with only 2GB of base information (used pages). If your application adds 5GB of data each year and data is purged when it is two years old, the database size levels off at 12GB. Your statistics may show that the 2GB database dumps in one hour. If you have a four-hour dump window, you have to start investigating alternative approaches once your database reaches 8GB. By capturing statistics, you would be able to forecast this problem *a full year* in advance.

## Configuring Tape Expiration

The `retaindays` option to the `dump` command is not the only way to prevent your tapes from being overwritten. Use the `tape retention` configuration option to set a default retention value:

```
/* Configure the default retention to 3 weeks */
use master
go
sp_configure "tape retention", 21
go
```

This value is initially set to 0, which enables tapes to be overwritten by default. Note that the retaindays option to the dump command overrides the configuration value.

# Transaction Logging

It is important to prevent the transaction log from running out of space. When the transaction log fills, no other logged operation is executed until space is available in the log. This is disastrous in production systems. In version 4.*x*, however, it was a fairly common experience. The DBA had to pay close attention to the available space in the log, executing a dump transaction before the log ran out of space.

Over time, database activity stabilizes and system activity time can be estimated. You should know the amount of time your system can be active, under normal conditions, before the transaction log completely fills. Based on the amount, schedule transaction log dumps often enough to prevent this situation from occurring. (Dump transaction logs when they are about one-half to three-quarters full.)

Even though you may have dump transaction activities scheduled, the system may experience peak activities (end of quarter, fiscal year end, and so forth) that cause the log to fill at a greatly accelerated rate. Version 4.*x* users must monitor the log to be proactive. System 10 users can use the threshold facility to set an indicator to automate the monitoring of available space.

## Monitoring Available Log Space

Sybase offers the following two tools to monitor space availability. Use either to get a report on the syslogs table:

- sp_spaceused
- dbcc checktable

sp_spaceused checks the reserved column to see how many pages are in use. Relate this to your overall log size to determine availability.

dbcc checktable checks each page in a table and provides an accurate reporting of the number of data pages used. As with sp_spaceused, relate this value to overall log size to determine availability. If your log is on a separate device, the output is easier to analyze. It reports statistics regarding space used and space free in megabytes as well as percentage:

```
dbcc checktable (syslogs)
```

Thresholds are an excellent facility that should be exploited. Make sure you create `sp_thresholdaction` to minimize the possibility of completely filling the log. Always create a threshold on the default segment. The default segment can (by default) use any nonlog fragment in the database. Therefore, a default threshold reports on available database space in most cases. If you use user-defined segments, thresholds are also a must. Stage your thresholds to provide increasingly harsh messages and review your error log daily. By following these suggestions, you may never run out of space again!

# Developing Your Backup and Recovery Plan

Consider *all* your databases when developing the backup and recovery plan. System databases have *different* requirements than user databases.

## System Databases

There are four system databases created as part of server installation: `master`, `model`, `tempdb`, and `sybsystemprocs` (three for version 4.*x*—no `sybsystemprocs`). `tempdb` is temporary and by definition is exempt from backups. All other system databases should be backed up, however.

## Threats

There are two things to watch out for with system databases:

- Database or table corruption
- Damage to the master device

If a corruption occurs, follow the steps to rebuild that individual database. Reinitialize the master device if it is damaged. This affects the `master`, `model`, `tempdb`, and possibly the `sybsystemprocs` databases (which can exist on the master device or an alternate device).

### *master*

The `master` database is not a high-activity database. It is created on the master device and is fairly small with a default allocation of about 18MB. This size is adequate for most small installations, but the requirements of larger installations quickly mandate an increase in size. Because the `master` database is on a single device, data and log compete for available space and the transaction log cannot be dumped. It cannot grow beyond the confines of the `master` device.

The following activities result in the insertion or modification of rows in various system tables:

- Creating, altering, or dropping the database
- Using `disk init`
- Adding or dropping logins or users
- Adding or dropping dump devices
- Adding servers

Because `master` controls the server, a database corruption or the loss of the master device can be devastating. The server is unavailable until the `master` database is repaired. Not having a current backup of `master` can be fatal (or at least quite painful). *Back up the* `master` *database whenever commands are executed that insert, update, or delete rows in the system tables.* The importance of this database backup cannot be over emphasized. Trying to re-create `master` from scratch can be extremely difficult, especially if you have not saved the data from the system tables.

> **NOTE**
>
> The master database has no separate log segment, so all backups are full database dumps. Also, be *sure* to back up the `master` database, just as you do all of the other databases.

## Detecting the Problem

If you lose the master device, the server goes down alerting you to the problem. The normal method of detecting corruption in any database is the suite of DBCC commands. If a corruption does occur in the master device, the system likely will be instantaneously affected. Often, the server goes down and does not come up, or major errors appear in the error log (page faults, I/O errors, and so on).

> **TIP**
>
> If a `dbcc` detects corruption in `master`, log a call to Sybase Technical Support. Corruption in `model` or `sybsystemprocs` may not be as serious on the surface, but could be indicative of a problem with the underlying master device. If you are confident you can solve the problem yourself, start executing the steps in the recovery process.

You must be proactive to avoid a painful recovery. First of all, avoid striping the `master` database dumps, even if it is a standard for your user databases. Make sure all of the `master` dump can fit on a single tape or in an operating system file. (Based on the normal size of the master database, this should not be a problem.) SQL Server must be started in single-user mode to begin the recovery process. If the load requires a volume change, you cannot open another connection to tell backup server that the new tape is in place.

## Mitigating the Risk

`master` should be dumped regularly, probably on the same schedule as your user databases. If you make a change and you don't want to wait for the backup scripts to run, execute it by hand. As always, you should have scripts saved for every activity that modifies `master`. To be extra safe, bulkcopy the data from the following files:

- sysdatabases
- sysdevices
- sysusages
- syslogins
- sysloginroles

You might have to reinitialize `master` using `buildmaster -m`. At the completion of this command, you'll have the vanilla master created when you install SQL Server. At this point, `master` has no knowledge of any user databases in your system, including `sybsystemprocs`. You have to execute one of the following:

- Loading your *current* `master` backup (preferred)
- Transferring the data, using `isql` or `bcp`
- Re-creating items from DDL scripts

You should have all the resources to undertake any of these approaches at any time. It is the only way to ensure that the `master` database (and the server) will be available when you need it.

## model

The `model` database is copied into any database created with `create database`. It houses those items you want available across all databases (rules, defaults, user-defined datatypes, and users). If you have made any modifications to model, save all DDL files and back up the database after changes are made.

If you detect corruption only in the `model` database, re-create it using the `-x` option to `buildmaster` (make sure you shut down the SQL Server first). The end result is the vanilla model database. Run DBCCs to ensure the corruption no longer exists. If you still find corruption after re-creating `model`, call Sybase Technical Support. It likely is a problem with the master device. If `model` is free of corruption and you have not made any changes, the recovery process is complete. If you have made modifications to `model`, reload it from backup or rerun your DDL scripts.

## sybsystemprocs

If `sybsystemprocs` exists, check to see whether you can execute system stored procedures (run sp_who). If you are unable to use it, drop the database and re-create the structure (at least 10MB). After the structure is in place, load the backup (if you have one) or run `installmaster`:

```
isql -Usa -P < installmaster
```

This loads the Sybase-provided system stored procedures. If you have created any of your own, reload the DDL files.

# User Databases

Your business requirements define whether a database backup is needed. Backups are normally a requirement for production systems. Your approach should define the following:

- *Who?* Identify the person or group responsible for backup and recovery.
- *Name?* Outline your naming standards for database names and dump devices.
- *Which databases?* Identify the databases in your system to be backed up.
- *Types of dumps?* Identify whether you will dump the database only or whether you also will dump the transaction log.
- *How?* Identify whether dumps will use disk or file devices and whether the dump is a single process or striped.
- *Frequency?* Identify the schedule for dumping the database and the transaction logs.
- *Execution?* Determine whether dumps will be initiated by hand or automated. If automated, detail whether it is conducted by an off-the-shelf tool or custom developed. Include all code (dump script and scheduler, if applicable) and make sure it is commented extremely well.

For database recovery, detail the procedures involved in loading each database. If using a tool, outline its use.

# VLDB Considerations

When developing a backup and recovery plan for VLDB environments, several items must be considered. The challenge of a VLDB is its sheer size—everything is larger. Tables are measured in gigabytes, and databases are measured in tens or hundreds of gigabytes. The fact that several Sybase VLDBs exist in industry today gives credence to the product's capability of handling vast amounts of data. VLDBs are not easy to implement, however, for a variety of reasons. Here are the top ten VLDB issues:

1. Impact of corruption
2. Time for recovery

3. Time of backups

4. Time to perform initial load of data

5. Time to update statistics of indexes

6. Time to perform database consistency checks

7. Time to create indexes

8. Impact of incremental batch data-loading routines

9. Impact of online activity

10. Backup media capacity and backup facilities

Based on these items, you need to make several database architecture choices. These choices include the following:

- Physically implementing a single, logical database as several smaller, physical databases
- Segmenting tables horizontally and/or vertically
- Table or index placement
- Log size and placement
- `tempdb` size and placement

Let's consider the issues list in regard to your choices. The time required to perform database dumps, loads, updates of statistics, and creation of indexes increases linearly with size. Follow these steps:

1. First, consider the amount of time you are willing to be "down" while performing a recovery (impact of corruption). If you need to recover a database within eight hours, determine the size of a database that can be recovered in that time. Note that the load process is much slower than the dump process. Assume that 4GB is the maximum database size that can be reloaded in the defined window.

2. Taking 4GB as a baseline, analyze table estimates for your database. If you have a 40GB logical database, you may need to implement 10 4GB databases. Are any tables greater than 4GB? How many tables can you fit in a database? Are any tables candidates for segmentation based on this determination alone?

3. Develop your utopian administration schedule. For every day during a month, determine what time periods may be dedicated to administrative activities. Weekends might be available, but this is not always the case. For instance, suppose you determine that you have five hours each night to perform administrative activities. You need to then determine what activities must be completed and whether they can be distributed over your available administration time.

4. Determine the rate of the dump process. Take into consideration backup media capacity, speed, and number. Benchmark several scenarios. Create a database and load with about 2GB of data. Perform several database dumps, a varying number of dump devices (striped dumps), and a number of dump processes that can occur in parallel.

5. Determine periodic activity timings for each of your tables. This should be a matrix with table names down one axis and activities (dbcc, update statistics, index creation) across the other axis. Once you develop a baseline for these activities, you easily can group tables together to determine the total amount of administration time needed for a certain combination of tables.

6. Determine which activities must take place in a batch window. If you want to perform database consistency checks immediately prior to dumping a database, the time required to perform both activities can be determined from your timings. Assume a dump takes three hours and a DBCC takes two hours. Although this fits in your five-hour window, it does not consider the fact that you have ten of these activities to complete during the course of a week. Perform activities in parallel to determine concurrent processing times. Can you DBCC and dump two databases in a five-hour period?

7. Finalize your schedule and document accordingly.

# Summary

Development of a backup-and-recovery approach is not a trivial process. You must consider internal and external forces and determine their impact. In the end, you should document your approach so it is clear how you plan to handle these activities. Make sure to gather statistics on all activities, and use those statistics to predict future performance.

Although building a good backup and recovery plan seems like a tremendous amount of work, it is worth it in the long run. Project plans must allocate time to create the plan and it should be in place *before* you make your production database available.

# Configuring and Tuning the SQL Server

**30**

SQL Server contains a number of user-definable configuration parameters that control its behavior. In this chapter, you will look at these configuration parameters and examine the aspects of SQL Server that they control, their defaults, and the range of values for which they can be configured. Chapter 31, "Optimizing SQL Server Configuration Options," looks more in depth at those configuration parameters that have the greatest impact on performance and provides guidelines for tuning them to optimize SQL Server performance.

# Using *sp_configure* in System 10 and Earlier

You can view the configuration settings and change the SQL Server configuration with the sp_configure stored procedure. The syntax for sp_configure for SQL Server version 10.*x* and earlier is as follows:

```
sp_configure [option [, value]]
```

The sp_configure stored procedure, when executed without any parameters, lists all options for the current version of SQL Server. For example, the following sp_configure output is from a System 10 SQL Server running on Windows NT:

```
sp_configure
go
```

| name | minimum | maximum | config_value | run_value |
| --- | --- | --- | --- | --- |
| recovery interval | 1 | 32767 | 0 | 5 |
| allow updates | 0 | 1 | 0 | 0 |
| user connections | 5 | 2147483647 | 0 | 25 |
| memory | 3850 | 2147483647 | 0 | 4096 |
| open databases | 5 | 2147483647 | 0 | 12 |
| locks | 5000 | 2147483647 | 0 | 5000 |
| open objects | 100 | 2147483647 | 0 | 500 |
| procedure cache | 1 | 99 | 0 | 20 |
| fill factor | 0 | 100 | 0 | 0 |
| time slice | 50 | 1000 | 0 | 100 |
| database size | 2 | 10000 | 0 | 2 |
| tape retention | 0 | 365 | 0 | 0 |
| recovery flags | 0 | 1 | 0 | 0 |
| nested triggers | 0 | 1 | 1 | 1 |
| devices | 4 | 256 | 0 | 10 |
| remote access | 0 | 1 | 1 | 1 |
| remote logins | 0 | 2147483647 | 0 | 20 |
| remote sites | 0 | 2147483647 | 0 | 10 |
| remote connections | 0 | 2147483647 | 0 | 20 |
| pre-read packets | 0 | 2147483647 | 0 | 3 |
| upgrade version | 0 | 2147483647 | 1002 | 1002 |
| default sortorder id | 0 | 255 | 40 | 40 |
| default language | 0 | 2147483647 | 0 | 0 |
| language in cache | 3 | 100 | 3 | 3 |

```
max online engines              1          32               1       1
min online engines              1          32               1       1
engine adjust interval          1          32               0       0
cpu flush                       1          2147483647       200     200
i/o flush                       1          2147483647       1000    1000
default character set id        0          255              2       2
stack size                      20480      2147483647       0       28672
password expiration interval    0          32767            0       0
audit queue size                1          65535            100     100
additional netmem               0          2147483647       0       0
default network packet size     512        524288           0       512
maximum network packet size     512        524288           0       512
extent i/o buffers              0          2147483647       0       0
identity burning set factor     1          9999999          5000    5000
(38 rows affected)
```

To see the setting for a specific configuration parameter, pass the name of the parameter, or a substring of the name that can uniquely identify the parameter, to sp_configure. For example, to see the current setting for additional netmem, you can issue either this command:

```
sp_configure "additional netmem"
```

or this:

```
sp_configure "netmem"
```

The descriptions of the columns in the output are as follows:

- parameter name is the description of the variable.

- minimum is the minimum allowable configuration setting.

- maximum is the theoretical maximum value to which the configuration option can be set. Note that the actual maximum value is going to be dependent on the platform and available resources to SQL Server.

- config_value reflects the value in the sysconfigures table.

- run_value reflects the value in the syscurconfigs table.

## The *sysconfigures* and *syscurconfigs* Tables

The sysconfigures and syscurconfigs tables store the configuration parameters. When the server comes up, the values in the permanent table, sysconfigures, are copied into the memory-only table, syscurconfigs. Note that not all the values are necessarily going to be the same between sysconfigures and syscurconfigs. The sysconfigures table stores the current configuration settings as set by sp_configure. The syscurconfigs table stores the values with which the SQL Server is currently running.

A list of all configuration options, with their maximum and minimum values are stored in spt_values, a lookup table in the master database. Rows related to configuration values in spt_values are marked with a type of 'C'.

# Setting Configuration Values

To set a configuration option with sp_configure, provide both the option name and the value to which you want to set it. You must be a system administrator to modify configuration settings. A user with the sso_role can execute sp_configure to modify security-related options such as password expiration and audit queue size.

The following example sets the recovery interval to seven minutes:

```
sp_configure "recovery interval", 7
```

To make the configuration options take effect, you need to run the reconfigure command, which performs a sanity check on the modifications to the configuration settings and installs the changes. The syntax is as follows:

```
reconfigure [with override]
```

The with override option is necessary if you want to force the SQL Server to accept configuration options it deems invalid (such as configuring more user connections than you have available memory to support) or when you want to force the SQL Server to enable updates to the system tables.

If for some reason, you manage to change the configuration options in such a way that the SQL Server will not start up anymore, you have to run the buildmaster command (at the operating system level) with the -r option. This resets the configuration parameters to the defaults.

# System 11 Configuration Changes

Sybase has made a number of improvements for managing the SQL Server configuration in System 11. To begin with, there are a number of additional configuration parameters available to better fine-tune the behavior and performance of SQL Server. The configuration options are also now grouped into logically related groupings to make it easier to manage and view configuration options.

You no longer need to issue the reconfigure command when you run sp_configure to change configuration settings. sp_configure itself validates and installs configuration changes. The reconfigure command still exists for compatibility with pre–System 11 script files, but performs no action.

The primary change in System 11 is that now the configuration settings are stored in an external ASCII text file. This provides a number of benefits, as you shall soon see.

# Viewing Configuration Settings in System 11

The sp_configure command is still used in System 11 to view and change configuration settings. When executed without any parameters, sp_configure displays all current configuration settings:

Group: Configuration Options


Group: Backup/Recovery

| Parameter Name | Default | Memory Used | Config Value | Run Value |
|----------------|---------|-------------|--------------|-----------|
| allow remote access | 1 | 0 | 1 | 1 |
| print recovery information | 0 | 0 | 0 | 0 |
| recovery interval in minutes | 5 | 0 | 5 | 5 |
| tape retention in days | 0 | 0 | 0 | 0 |

Group: Cache Manager

| Parameter Name | Default | Memory Used | Config Value | Run Value |
|----------------|---------|-------------|--------------|-----------|
| memory alignment boundary | 2048 | 0 | 2048 | 2048 |
| number of index trips | 0 | 0 | 0 | 0 |
| number of oam trips | 0 | 0 | 2 | 2 |
| procedure cache percent | 20 | 19958 | 5 | 5 |
| total data cache size | 0 | 365616 | 0 | 365616 |
| total memory | 7500 | 409600 | 204800 | 204800 |

Group: Disk I/O

| Parameter Name | Default | Memory Used | Config Value | Run Value |
|----------------|---------|-------------|--------------|-----------|
| allow sql server async i/o | 1 | 0 | 1 | 1 |
| disk i/o structures | 256 | 33 | 256 | 256 |
| number of devices | 10 | #30 | 75 | 75 |
| page utilization percent | 95 | 0 | 95 | 95 |

Group: General Information

| Parameter Name | Default | Memory Used | Config Value | Run Value |
|----------------|---------|-------------|--------------|-----------|
| configuration file | 0 | 0 | 0 | /sybase/SYB |

Group: Languages

| Parameter Name | Default | Memory Used | Config Value | Run Value |
|----------------|---------|-------------|--------------|-----------|
| default character set id | 1 | 0 | 1 | 1 |
| default language id | 0 | 0 | 0 | 0 |
| default sortorder id | 50 | 0 | 50 | 50 |
| number of languages in cache | 3 | 4 | 3 | 3 |

Group: Lock Manager

| Parameter Name | Default | Memory Used | Config Value | Run Value |
|---|---|---|---|---|
| address lock spinlock ratio | 100 | 0 | 100 | 100 |
| deadlock checking period | 500 | 0 | 1000 | 1000 |
| freelock transfer block size | 30 | 0 | 30 | 30 |
| max engine freelocks | 10 | 0 | 10 | 10 |
| number of locks | 5000 | 4688 | 50000 | 50000 |
| page lock spinlock ratio | 100 | 0 | 100 | 100 |
| table lock spinlock ratio | 20 | 0 | 20 | 20 |

Group: Memory Use

| Parameter Name | Default | Memory Used | Config Value | Run Value |
|---|---|---|---|---|
| additional network memory | 0 | 150 | 153600 | 153600 |
| audit queue size | 100 | 42 | 100 | 100 |
| default network packet size | 512 | #248 | 512 | 512 |
| disk i/o structures | 256 | 33 | 256 | 256 |
| event buffers per engine | 100 | #1172 | 3000 | 3000 |
| executable codesize + overhead | 0 | 4919 | 0 | 4919 |
| max number network listeners | 15 | 1202 | 15 | 15 |
| max online engines | 1 | 1661 | 4 | 4 |
| number of alarms | 40 | 1 | 40 | 40 |
| number of devices | 10 | #30 | 75 | 75 |
| number of extent i/o buffers | 0 | 1605 | 100 | 100 |
| number of languages in cache | 3 | 4 | 3 | 3 |
| number of locks | 5000 | 4688 | 50000 | 50000 |
| number of mailboxes | 30 | 1 | 30 | 30 |
| number of messages | 64 | 1 | 64 | 64 |
| number of open databases | 12 | 395 | 12 | 12 |
| number of open objects | 500 | 512 | 500 | 500 |
| number of remote connections | 20 | 33 | 20 | 20 |
| number of remote logins | 20 | 22 | 20 | 20 |
| number of remote sites | 10 | 801 | 10 | 10 |
| number of user connections | 25 | 7989 | 100 | 100 |
| partition groups | 1024 | 21 | 1024 | 1024 |
| permission cache entries | 15 | #63 | 15 | 15 |
| procedure cache percent | 20 | 19958 | 5 | 5 |
| remote server pre-read packets | 3 | #32 | 3 | 3 |
| stack guard size | 4096 | #568 | 4096 | 4096 |
| stack size | 36864 | #5113 | 36864 | 36864 |
| total data cache size | 0 | 365616 | 0 | 365616 |
| total memory | 7500 | 409600 | 204800 | 204800 |

Group: Network Communication

| Parameter Name | Default | Memory Used | Config Value | Run Value |
|---|---|---|---|---|
| additional network memory | 0 | 150 | 153600 | 153600 |
| allow remote access | 1 | 0 | 1 | 1 |
| default network packet size | 512 | #248 | 512 | 512 |
| max network packet size | 512 | 0 | 4096 | 4096 |
| max number network listeners | 15 | 1202 | 15 | 15 |

```
number of remote connections          20          33          20          20
number of remote logins                20          22          20          20
number of remote sites                 10         801          10          10
remote server pre-read packets          3         #32           3           3
tcp no delay                            0           0           0           0
```

Group: O/S Resources

| Parameter Name | Default | Memory Used | Config Value | Run Value |
| --- | --- | --- | --- | --- |
| max async i/os per engine | 2147483647 | 0 | 2147483647 | 2147483647 |
| max async i/os per server | 2147483647 | 0 | 2147483647 | 2147483647 |
| o/s asynch i/o enabled | 0 | 0 | 0 | 0 |
| o/s file descriptors | 0 | 0 | 0 | 2000 |
| tcp no delay | 0 | 0 | 0 | 0 |

Group: Physical Resources


Group: Physical Memory

| Parameter Name | Default | Memory Used | Config Value | Run Value |
| --- | --- | --- | --- | --- |
| additional network memory | 0 | 150 | 153600 | 153600 |
| lock shared memory | 0 | 0 | 0 | 0 |
| shared memory starting address | 0 | 0 | 0 | 0 |
| total memory | 7500 | 409600 | 204800 | 204800 |

Group: Processors

| Parameter Name | Default | Memory Used | Config Value | Run Value |
| --- | --- | --- | --- | --- |
| max online engines | 1 | 1661 | 4 | 4 |
| min online engines | 1 | 0 | 1 | 1 |

Group: SQL Server Administration

| Parameter Name | Default | Memory Used | Config Value | Run Value |
| --- | --- | --- | --- | --- |
| allow nested triggers | 1 | 0 | 1 | 1 |
| allow updates to system tables | 0 | 0 | 1 | 1 |
| audit queue size | 100 | 42 | 100 | 100 |
| cpu accounting flush interval | 200 | 0 | 200 | 200 |
| cpu grace time | 500 | 0 | 500 | 500 |
| deadlock retries | 5 | 0 | 5 | 5 |
| default database size | 2 | 0 | 2 | 2 |
| default fill factor percent | 0 | 0 | 0 | 0 |
| event buffers per engine | 100 | #1172 | 3000 | 3000 |
| housekeeper free write percent | 1 | 0 | 1 | 1 |
| i/o accounting flush interval | 1000 | 0 | 1000 | 1000 |
| i/o polling process count | 10 | 0 | 10 | 10 |
| identity burning set factor | 5000 | 0 | 5000 | 5000 |
| identity grab size | 1 | 0 | 1 | 1 |
| lock promotion HWM | 200 | 0 | 200 | 200 |

```
lock promotion LWM                   200         0       200       200
lock promotion PCT                   100         0       100       100
number of alarms                      40         1        40        40
number of extent i/o buffers           0      1605       100       100
number of mailboxes                   30         1        30        30
number of messages                    64         1        64        64
number of open databases              12       395        12        12
number of open objects               500       512       500       500
number of pre-allocated extent         2         0         2         2
number of sort buffers                 0         0       800       800
partition groups                    1024        21      1024      1024
partition spinlock ratio              10         0        10        10
print deadlock information             0         0         0         0
runnable process search count          3         0         3         3
size of auto identity column          10         0        10        10
sort page count                        0         0       160       160
sql server clock tick length      100000         0    100000    100000
time slice                           100         0       100       100
upgrade version                     1100         0      1100      1100
```

Group: User Environment

| Parameter Name | Default | Memory Used | Config Value | Run Value |
| --- | --- | --- | --- | --- |
| default network packet size | 512 | #248 | 512 | 512 |
| number of pre-allocated extent | 2 | 0 | 2 | 2 |
| number of user connections | 25 | 7989 | 100 | 100 |
| permission cache entries | 15 | #63 | 15 | 15 |
| stack guard size | 4096 | #568 | 4096 | 4096 |
| stack size | 36864 | #5113 | 36864 | 36864 |
| systemwide password expiration | 0 | 0 | 0 | 0 |
| user log cache size | 2048 | 0 | 2048 | 2048 |
| user log cache spinlock ratio | 20 | 0 | 20 | 20 |

The descriptions of the columns in the output are as follows:

- `parameter name` is the description of the variable.

- `default` is the default configuration value.

- `memory used` displays the amount of memory (in kilobytes) required by the parameter at its current setting.

- `config_value` reflects the value in the `sysconfigures` table—the most recent value to which the option has been set.

- `run_value` reflects the value in the `syscurconfigs` table—the value with which the SQL Server is currently running.

Notice how the output is now displayed in logical groups. The `sp_configure` command will still take a single parameter name to view the settings, or optionally, you can specify a group name to display all the configuration settings for a group. For example, to see all configuration settings related to "user environment", execute the following:

```
sp_configure "user environment"
```

When viewing configuration settings, you can set the level of detail that SQL Server displays by using the `sp_displaylevel` command. There are three levels of display: `basic`, `intermediate`, or `comprehensive`. The default level is `comprehensive`, which displays all configuration options. `basic` shows just the most basic configuration options, those appropriate for general server tuning. The syntax for `sp_displaylevel` is as follows:

```
sp_displaylevel login_name" [,"basic" ¦ "intermediate" ¦ "comprehensive"]
```

## Changing Configuration Settings

There are two ways to modify configuration settings in System 11. You can use the `sp_configure` command as in previous releases, or you can edit the configuration file directly by using your favorite text editor.

When you run `sp_configure` in System 11, it now updates `sysconfigures` and `syscurconfigs` if it is a dynamic option and writes the change to the configuration file. The configuration file is typically located in the Sybase home directory. Each time you make a modification with `sp_configure`, a new copy of the configuration file is generated. The configuration file with the suffix of .cfg is the file that SQL Server will use on startup. Previous versions are stored using the naming convention of *filename.001*, *filename.002*, and so forth.

The advantages of having an external configuration file include the following:

- The ability to replicate standard configurations across multiple servers by simply copying the configuration file.
- The ability to create multiple configuration files and switch between them on SQL Server startup as your resource needs change (for example, DSS versus OLTP).
- If SQL Server won't start, you can modify the offending option in the configuration file and try again.
- The ability to set up a sample configuration in a configuration file and use `sp_configure` to validate it without having to set the values in SQL Server.

## Using Configuration Files with *sp_configure*

The syntax for using configuration files with `sp_configure` is as follows:

```
sp_configure "configuration file", 0, "action", "filename"
```

The `"configuration file"` parameter specifies that `sp_configure` is to take an action on a configuration file. The `0` is included for backward compatibility with `sp_configure` (it's the position of the value parameter for the normal option setting). The `"filename"` parameter specifies the full pathname of the configuration file on which you want to take one of the following four actions:

- `verify` performs a validation check on the configuration file.

- ▪ `read` performs a validation check on parameters in the file and loads those that pass validation into SQL Server.
- ▪ `write` creates a configuration file, using the specified file name, based on the currently running values. If the file already exists, a message is written to the errorlog and the existing file is renamed.
- ▪ `restore` creates a new file with the values in the `sysconfigures` table.

The following example verifies the configuration file called `test.cfg`:

```
sp_configure "configuration file", 0, "verify", "$SYBASE/test.cfg"
```

# Editing Configuration Files Directly

The configuration file is an ASCII file that can be edited by using any text editor that can save the file in ASCII format. The format for each parameter in the file is the following:

```
parameter_name={value ¦ default}
```

If `default` is specified, SQL Server applies the default configuration setting for that parameter.

When hand-editing a configuration file, there is no way to validate the settings until you re-start the SQL Server. It is recommended that you use the `sp_configure` command to verify changes to a configuration file prior to shutting down SQL Server.

The following shows an example of the contents of a configuration file:

```
##########################################################################
#
#                 Configuration File for the Sybase SQL Server
#
#                 Please read the System Administration Guide (SAG)
#                 before changing any of the values in this file.
#
##########################################################################


[Configuration Options]

[General Information]

[Backup/Recovery]
        recovery interval in minutes = DEFAULT
        print recovery information = DEFAULT
        tape retention in days = DEFAULT

[Cache Manager]
        number of oam trips = 2
        number of index trips = DEFAULT
        procedure cache percent = 5
        memory alignment boundary = DEFAULT
```

```
[Named Cache:default data cache]
        cache size = DEFAULT
        cache status = default data cache

[16K I/O Buffer Pool]
        pool size = 100.0000M
        wash size = DEFAULT

[Named Cache:lookup_01]
        cache size = 2M
        cache status = mixed cache

[Named Cache:syslog_01]
        cache size = 2.00M
        cache status = log only

[4K I/O Buffer Pool]
        pool size = 512.0000K
        wash size = DEFAULT

[Named Cache:system_tables_01]
        cache size = 1.00M
        cache status = log only

[Named Cache:temp_db]
        cache size = 50M
        cache status = log only

[Disk I/O]
        allow sql server async i/o = DEFAULT
        disk i/o structures = DEFAULT
        page utilization percent = DEFAULT
        number of devices = 75

[Network Communication]
        default network packet size = DEFAULT
        max network packet size = 4096
        remote server pre-read packets = DEFAULT
        number of remote connections = DEFAULT
        allow remote access = DEFAULT
        number of remote logins = DEFAULT
        number of remote sites = DEFAULT
        max number network listeners = DEFAULT
        tcp no delay = DEFAULT

[O/S Resources]
        max async i/os per engine = DEFAULT
        max async i/os per server = DEFAULT

[Physical Resources]

[Physical Memory]
        total memory = 204800
        additional network memory = 153600
        lock shared memory = DEFAULT
        shared memory starting address = DEFAULT
```

```
[Processors]
        max online engines = 4
        min online engines = DEFAULT

[SQL Server Administration]
        number of open objects = DEFAULT
        number of open databases = DEFAULT
        audit queue size = DEFAULT
        default database size = DEFAULT
        identity burning set factor = DEFAULT
        allow nested triggers = DEFAULT
        allow updates to system tables = 1
        print deadlock information = DEFAULT
        default fill factor percent = DEFAULT
        number of mailboxes = DEFAULT
        number of messages = DEFAULT
        number of alarms = DEFAULT
        number of pre-allocated extents = DEFAULT
        event buffers per engine = 3000
        cpu accounting flush interval = DEFAULT
        i/o accounting flush interval = DEFAULT
        sql server clock tick length = DEFAULT
        runnable process search count = DEFAULT
        i/o polling process count = DEFAULT
        time slice = DEFAULT
        deadlock retries = DEFAULT
        cpu grace time = DEFAULT
        number of sort buffers = 800
        sort page count = 160
        number of extent i/o buffers = 100
        size of auto identity column = DEFAULT
        identity grab size = DEFAULT
        lock promotion HWM = DEFAULT
        lock promotion LWM = DEFAULT
        lock promotion PCT = DEFAULT
        housekeeper free write percent = DEFAULT
        partition groups = DEFAULT
        partition spinlock ratio = DEFAULT

[User Environment]
        number of user connections = 100
        stack size = DEFAULT
        stack guard size = DEFAULT
        systemwide password expiration = DEFAULT
        permission cache entries = DEFAULT
        user log cache size = DEFAULT
        user log cache spinlock ratio = DEFAULT

[Lock Manager]
        number of locks = 50000
        deadlock checking period = 1000
        freelock transfer block size = DEFAULT
        max engine freelocks = DEFAULT
        address lock spinlock ratio = DEFAULT
        page lock spinlock ratio = DEFAULT
        table lock spinlock ratio = DEFAULT
```

# SQL Server Configuration Options

There are two kinds of configurable values, dynamic and nondynamic. *Dynamic values* are those parameters that, when modified, take effect immediately. Some examples are `recovery interval`, `password expiration interval`, and `default language`. Any variables that are not explicitly dynamic will not take effect until the server is cycled (shut down and started up again). In the following review of the configuration settings, the dynamic variables are flagged with asterisks (*).

> **NOTE**
>
> Don't forget! You need to shut down and restart the SQL Server for nondynamic options (those without an asterisk) to take effect.

The configuration options in this section are grouped the same way that SQL Server does in System 11. Configuration options that are only available in System 11 will be noted. Also, many of the configuration options in System 11 and previous versions are the same, but the names have changed. For the sake of simplicity, and because the new names are more descriptive, we will use the configuration option names as they appear in System 11. For versions prior to System 11, refer to Table 30.1 to match the old names with the new.

**Table 30.1. System 10 configuration option names versus System 11 configuration option names.**

| System 10 Option Name | System 11 Option Name |
| --- | --- |
| recovery interval | recovery interval in minutes |
| allow updates | allow updates to system tables |
| user connections | number of user connections |
| memory | total memory |
| open databases | number of open databases |
| locks | number of locks |
| open objects | number of open objects |
| procedure cache | procedure cache percent |
| fill factor | default fill factor percent |
| time slice | time slice |
| database size | default database size |

*continues*

**Table 30.1. continued**

| System 10 Option Name | System 11 Option Name |
| --- | --- |
| tape retention | tape retention in dayt |
| recovery flags | print recovery information |
| nested triggers | allow nested triggers |
| devices | number of devices |
| remote access | allow remote access |
| remote logins | number of remote logins |
| remote sites | number of remote sites |
| remote connections | number of remote connections |
| pre-read packets | remote server pre-read packets |
| upgrade version | upgrade version |
| default sortorder id | default sortorder id |
| default language | default language id |
| language in cache | number of languages in cache |
| max online engines | max online engines |
| min online engines | min online engines |
| engine adjust interval | N/A |
| cpu flush | cpu accounting flush interval |
| i/o flush | i/o accounting flush interval |
| default character set id | default character set id |
| stack size | stack size |
| password expiration interval | systemwide password expiration |
| audit queue size | audit queue size |
| additional netmem | additional network memory |
| default network packet size | default network packet size |
| maximum network packet size | max network packet size |
| extent i/o buffers | number of extent i/o buffers |
| identity burning set factor | identity burning set factor |

# Backup and Recovery Group

This set of parameters affects the operation of the dump and restore processes, as well as the way memory is configured.

# allow remote access*

**Units:** 0 or 1 (flag)

**Default:** 1 (yes)

The `allow remote access` variable determines whether this server can communicate with another one. With System 10, it is imperative that you have this option turned on. The backup server is another server, so you cannot perform a backup without remote access. Only a login with the `sa_role` can modify `remote access` values. This option is only dynamic in System 10 and later versions.

# print recovery information

**Units:** 0 or 1 (flag)

**Default:** 0 (no)

If this option is turned on, at startup time the server will list in the errorlog detailed information on each individual transaction that is rolled forward or backward during the recovery process. If the option is off, only the database name and quantity of transactions rolled forward or backward is listed. Turning this option on can be helpful to determine which transactions may have been rolled back following a system crash.

# recovery interval in minutes*

**Units:** Integer number of minutes

**Default:** 5

`recovery interval in minutes` is the maximum number of minutes per database that the server will take during the recovery process. This value affects how often the SQL Server checkpoints databases.

On SQL Server startup, the recovery process examines the transaction log to determine the oldest active transaction since the last time a checkpoint occurred in the database. A checkpoint synchronizes changes in the transaction log with the database on disk. The greater the number of records since the last checkpoint, the more transaction records that need to be processed by the recovery process to bring the log and database in sync before users can access the database.

It is a common misconception that the recovery interval is the number of minutes between checkpoints. This is simply not true. Rather, it is an estimate of the number of minutes recovery will take based on the number of records since the last checkpoint. SQL Server estimates it takes about one minute to recover 6,000 rows in the transaction log. Therefore, if the recovery interval remains set to the default value of five minutes, SQL Server will checkpoint the database when there are 30,000 records in the transaction log since the last checkpoint.

Notice that SQL Server doesn't take into consideration the type of transaction records in the log when estimating recovery time, only the number. Different types of transactions in the log could cause the recovery process to take substantially more or less time to complete recovery than that specified by the recovery interval in minutes setting.

> **NOTE**
>
> The checkpoint process "wakes up" approximately once a minute to examine the transaction log for each database to determine whether a checkpoint is required. If you have the trunc. log on chkpt. option on for a database, the checkpoint process automatically performs a checkpoint and truncates the log for that database each time it comes around to check the log.

## tape retention in days

**Units:** Integer days

**Default:** 0

When you attempt to overwrite a database or transaction log dump, the backup server checks to see how long ago this was dumped. The tape retention in days parameter is a safety feature that prevents you from overwriting your dumps prematurely. Operators may then manually override the retention time when they are prompted that there is a violation of the tape retention period, or by specifying the with init option when executing the dump command. You can also change the tape retention period for a particular dump by using the retaindays option on the dump command.

# Cache Manager Group

New for System 11, there exists more advanced configuration options for defining attributes for data and procedure cache.

## memory alignment boundary (New for System 11)

**Units:** Bytes in multiples of 2048

**Default:** 2048

memory alignment boundary sets the alignment boundaries for data caches. This parameter should be left alone unless you know that your machine performs I/O more efficiently on other boundaries. It should not be modified unless recommended by Sybase Tech Support.

# number of index trips* (New for System 11)

**Units:** Integer number of trips

**Default:** 0

This is the number of times an index page traverses the MRU/LRU chain before it is considered for swapping out to make room available in cache for other pages. If you increase this value, index pages will stay in cache longer. You may want to adjust this value upward in DSS systems to increase the likelihood of finding index pages in cache.

> **WARNING**
>
> Do not set this too high if your cache space is relatively small, because it may cause processes to time out waiting for cache space to become available. If you set it too low, index pages will be written to disk too often, which may result in poor performance.

# number of oam trips* (New for System 11)

**Units:** Integer number of trips

**Default:** 0

This is the number of times OAM pages will traverse MRU/LRU chain before being considered for aging out. OAM pages are used for controlling page allocation for tables and indexes (see Chapter 10, "Understanding SQL Server Storage Structures"). In systems that incur a significant amount of allocations (for example, large bulkcopy operations), keeping OAM pages in cache longer will improve performance.

> **WARNING**
>
> Do not set this too high if your cache space is relatively small, because it may cause processes to time out waiting for cache space to become available.

# procedure cache percent

**Units:** Integer percentage

**Default:** 20

Compiled stored procedure execution plans are stored in an area of memory called procedure cache. The balance of server memory, less that used by the server for its internal kernel and other variable elements, will be used by the server for data and procedure cache. The `procedure cache` configuration setting is the percentage of cache set aside for procedures. The larger the procedure cache, the more compiled plans can reside in memory.

At any given time, each user who executes a stored procedure needs his own executable procedure in cache. To establish an initial value for procedure cache, start by leaving enough room in cache to store at least one copy of your largest stored procedure for each concurrent user, plus a fudge factor. Here is an example:

100 concurrent users × 60KB (the largest stored procedure) = 6MB × 1.25 (fudge factor) = 8MB

Now you know how large to make the procedure cache, but the `procedure cache` setting doesn't require the size of the procedure cache; you need to indicate what percentage of cache should be set aside for procedures. If you have 50MB available for cache (run `dbcc memusage` to get available cache and procedure sizes), 8/50 = 16%. Note that if you use procedures heavily, you may want to increase cache capacity and also the percentage for procedures. For more information on configuring procedure cache for performance, see the following chapter, Chapter 31.

## total data cache size (New for System 11)

**Units:** N/A

**Default:** N/A

This is a calculated value that is not user-configurable. It represents the total amount of memory, based on the current configuration, that is available for data, index, and log pages.

## total memory

**Units:** Integer number of 2KB pages

**Default:** Varies depending on SQL Server platform

This is the most important configuration parameter you will tune. When the SQL Server comes up, it will request this amount of memory to be allocated from the operating system to SQL Server. If the allocation fails, the server will not come up, and an error is recorded in the errorlog.

The server needs this memory to manage devices, users, locks, databases, and objects. All the rest of the memory is used for cache. You can see how memory is used in `dbcc memusage`. Properly configuring memory to support SQL Server requirements and have enough available for sufficient data and procedure cache can have a large impact on performance. See Chapter 31 for a discussion on how to optimize your memory configuration.

# Disk I/O Group

This section defines parameters that affect SQL Server's disk I/O behavior. Many parameters that were not easily accessible prior to System 11 can now be tuned. Modify these parameters cautiously.

## allow sql server async I/O (New for System 11)

**Units:** Flag

**Default:** 1

This option enables SQL Server to run with asynchronous I/O. Both SQL Server and your operating system must have asynchronous I/O enabled.

Asynchronous I/O is almost always faster than synchronous I/O, unless you set up devices on block-oriented I/O operating system files. Using block I/O is *not* recommended, because SQL Server cannot guarantee data integrity in the event of a system crash.

## disk I/O structures (New for System 11)

**Units:** Control blocks

**Default:** 256

This is the number of disk I/O structures allocated on startup. This should be configured as high as your operating system allows to minimize the chance of running out of disk I/O structures (see your operating system documentation). Each user process will require its own disk I/O control block for SQL Server to initiate I/O request for that process.

## number of devices

**Units:** Integer quantity less than 256

**Default:** 10

This is the number of database devices that may be initialized with the `disk init` command. Virtual device numbers must be unique and must be less than the configured value. Devices require 512 bytes each. The master device uses `vdevno` of 0.

> **WARNING**
>
> Do not set this value less than the number of defined devices. On restart, SQL Server will be unable to initiate I/O to any devices with device numbers higher than `number of devices`, and any databases on those devices will be marked suspect and made inaccessible.

## page utilization percent* (New for System 11)

**Units:** Integer percentage

**Default:** 95

SQL Server compares the percentage of used-to-reserved (used plus unused) pages for a table, and if the page utilization percent setting is lower than the actual ratio, the Server allocates a new extent automatically instead of searching the OAM for free pages. A value of 100 instructs the server always to scan for free pages before allocating new extents. A lower page utilization percent setting will result in more unused pages. A high page utilization percent setting will result in slower page allocations for large tables.

> **NOTE**
>
> This parameter is ignored by bcp. bcp always allocates new extents until there are no more extents available in the database before it scans for free pages.

For a more in-depth discussion of page allocation and configuring page utilization percent, see Chapter 10.

# General Information Group

This group contains parameters that are not related to any specific behavior of SQL Server, and it currently contains only one configuration value.

## configuration file* (New for System 11)

This parameter specifies the location of the configuration file currently in use.

# Languages Group

This section lists the parameters that enable you to define the default language, sort order, and character set for SQL Server.

## default character set id

**Units:** Integer character set ID

**Default:** Varies depending on platform

This is the number of the default character set specified at installation time. This can be changed by the SQL Server installation utility.

## default language id*

**Units:** Integer language ID

**Default:** 0 (us_english)

This is the default language in which messages will be displayed, unless you override the default when you add logins with sp_addlogin or change the default language with sp_modifylogin.

## default sortorder id

**Units:** Integer sort order ID

**Default:** 50 (binary)

This displays the current sort order, but you cannot change this value with sp_configure. Your install utility provides a method for changing the server sort order. If you change your sort order, you will need to rebuild all indexes on the server manually, which is not necessarily a fast process.

The default value (50) provides the best performance for sorting and indexing data. Changing the sort order from binary causes approximately 10 percent overhead at sort/index creation times.

## number of languages in cache

**Units:** Integer quantity

**Default:** 3

This is the maximum number of languages that may be held in cache simultaneously.

# Lock Manager Group

This section contains the parameters that modify SQL Server locking behavior.

## address lock spinlock ratio (New for System 11)

**Units:** Integer ratio

**Default:** 100

This value specifies the number of rows in the address locks hash table (*hash buckets*) protected by one spinlock for SQL Servers running with multiple engines. A single-engine SQL Server uses only a single spinlock, because only that one engine can access the address locks hash table.

A spinlock is an internal locking mechanism that prevents a process from accessing a resource currently in use by another process (all processes must wait, or "spin," until the lock on the resource is released.

SQL Server manages the acquiring and releasing of address locks using an internal hash table. There are a maximum of 1,031 hash buckets, or rows, in this hash table. The default value for `address spinlock ratio` of 100 rows indicates that a maximum of 11 (1,031/100) spinlocks can concurrently be held on the address locks hash table.

Theoretically, the lower this setting, the better performance should be, because it will allow more spinlocks and, therefore, less contention. However, the default value is appropriate for most systems.

## deadlock checking period* (New for System 11)

**Units:** Integer number of milliseconds

**Default:** 500

This parameter specifies the number of milliseconds SQL Server waits to initiate a check for deadlocks for a process waiting for a lock to be released. Deadlock checking is a time-consuming process.

If you set this value higher, the deadlock checking overhead can be avoided if the lock request is granted before the waiting period expires. If you expect your applications will deadlock infrequently, you may see better performance by setting this value higher and avoiding the deadlock checking overhead for most processes. For more information on deadlocks and locking performance, see Chapter 15, "Locking and Performance."

## freelock transfer block size* (New for System 11)

**Units:** Integer number of locks

**Default:** 30

This parameter specifies the number of locks moved from the global freelock list to an engine's freelock list when an engine runs out of locks.

On a multi-engine SQL Server, each engine has its own freelock list to satisfy lock requests. If the engine freelock list runs out of locks, SQL Server will move locks from the global freelock list to the engine freelock list. When the number of locks in the engine freelock list exceeds its maximum (see the next parameter, `max engine freelocks`), SQL Server will move locks from the engine freelock list back to the global freelock list to make them available to other engines.

Setting this value higher will reduce the number of transfers between engine freelock lists and the global freelock list, thereby minimizing contention for the global freelock list. A higher value, though, will result in a process accessing more lock structures than it needs. The default setting should be sufficient for most systems.

## max engine freelocks* (New for System 11)

**Units:** Integer percentage

**Default:** 10

This parameter sets the maximum number of locks available to the engine freelock lists as a percentage of total number of locks. The greater the number of freelocks available to an engine, the fewer times it needs to access the global freelock list.

Setting this value too high could result in having insufficient freelocks available in the global freelock list. If an engine cannot acquire freelocks because they are all being held by other engines, you may see error message 1279, which indicates that an engine ran out of available locks. When you see this message, you may need to decrease max engine freelocks or to increase number of locks.

## number of locks

**Units:** Integer quantity

**Default:** 5000

This is the number of concurrent open locks that may be in simultaneous use. If you begin getting error messages that locks are unavailable, you may need to bump up the number of available locks by a thousand or two—the memory cost is very low (72 bytes per lock). However, before arbitrarily increasing the number of locks, you may first want to determine why your user processes are acquiring so many locks and see whether they can be rewritten to minimize locks.

## page lock spinlock ratio (New for System 11)

**Units:** Ratio

**Default:** 100

This value specifies the number of rows in the page locks hash table (hash buckets) protected by one spinlock for SQL Servers running with multiple engines. A single-engine SQL Server uses only a single spinlock, because only that one engine can access the page locks hash table.

A spinlock is an internal locking mechanism that prevents a process from accessing a resource currently in use by another process (all processes must wait, or "spin," until the lock on the resource is released).

SQL Server manages the acquiring and releasing of page locks using an internal hash table. There are a maximum of 1,031 hash buckets, or rows, in this hash table. The default value for `address spinlock ratio` of 100 rows indicates that a maximum of 11 (1,031/100) spinlocks can concurrently be held on the page locks hash table.

Theoretically, the lower this setting, the better performance should be, because it will allow more spinlocks and, therefore, less contention on the page locks hash table. However, the default value is appropriate for most systems.

## table lock spinlock ratio (New for System 11)

**Units:** Integer ratio

**Default:** 20

This value specifies the number of rows in the table locks hash table (hash buckets) protected by one spinlock for SQL Servers running with multiple engines. A single-engine SQL Server uses only a single spinlock because only that one engine can access the table locks hash table.

A spinlock is an internal locking mechanism that prevents a process from accessing a resource currently in use by another process (all processes must wait, or "spin," until the lock on the resource is released).

SQL Server manages the acquiring and releasing of table locks using an internal hash table. There are a maximum of 101 hash buckets, or rows, in this hash table. The default value for `address spinlock ratio` of 20 rows indicates that a maximum of 6 (101/20) spinlocks can concurrently be held on the page locks hash table.

Theoretically, the lower this setting, the better performance should be, because it will enable more spinlocks and, therefore, less contention on the page locks hash table. However, the default value is appropriate for most systems.

# Memory Use Group

This section of configuration parameters lets you set how SQL Server uses memory internally.

## additional network memory

**Units:** Bytes (should be in multiples of 2048)

**Default:** 0

When large network packets are being shipped, the client application can use a larger packet size than the default packet size of 512 bytes if the SQL Server is configured to allow using larger packet sizes. Larger packets will require additional memory for each user connection using the larger packets than is available in the standard user connection. This additional memory used for the larger network packets is taken from a separate pool of memory, allocated by `additional network memory`.

Each user connection uses three buffers within the SQL Server: a read buffer, a write buffer, and a read overflow buffer. Each buffer will be the size of the requested network packet size. To estimate the amount of additional network memory to configure, determine the number of concurrent processes that will use the larger packet sizes and multiply that value times the largest packet size times three buffers. Finally, factor in 2 percent overhead to manage the network buffers and round it up to the nearest multiple of 2,048.

The additional network memory required by 10 concurrent user processes using a 2KB packet size is the following:

3 (buffers/user) × 2048 (packet size) × 10 (connections) × 1.02 (overhead) = 62,668.8

with the total rounded up to the nearest multiple of 2,048 (65,536).

> **NOTE**
>
> Before any process can use the additional network memory, you first must configure the `max network packet size` allowed to be higher than the default of 512. (See the description of `max network packet size` in the Network Communication group, discussed later in this chapter.)

## audit queue size

**Units:** Integer quantity of audit records

**Default:** `100`

This is an option, configurable by a user with the `sso_role`, that instructs the server to retain a specific number of audit records in memory before they are written physically to the `sysaudits` table in the `sybsecurity` database. The larger this value is, the better your performance will be, because fewer physical writes occur and audited user processes will not be forced to sleep until space becomes available in the audit queue. Unfortunately, if the server is brought down unexpectedly, audit records stored in cache are lost permanently. `audit queue size` also affects memory, because the audit queue will set aside 424 bytes per configured record in the server kernel.

## default network packet size

**Units:** Bytes (should be a multiple of 512)

**Default:** `512`

This parameter determines the default packet size used by user connections that do not request a larger packet size. The default packet size is 512 bytes.

Each SQL server connection uses a read buffer, a write buffer, and a read overflow buffer, each of which requires a packet in memory. The memory allocated for a configured user connection includes three 512-byte buffers. If you increase the default network packet size, this will increase the memory requirements per configured user connection as follows:

$3 \times$ `default network packet size` (DNPS) $\times$ # user connections.

For example, if the default network packet size is configured to 1024, and you configure for 100 user connections, you would use the following equation to determine how much memory will be required for network packets:

$3 \times 1,024 \times 100 = 305,200$ bytes

If you increase the DNPS, you must also increase `maximum network packet size` to the same or higher value.

> **TIP**
>
> If you have any application programs or third-party products that were developed with earlier versions (prior to System 10) of Open Client and that use only 512-byte network packets, do not increase the default network packet size beyond 512 or these applications will not be able to connect to the SQL Server.
>
> To support larger packet sizes for applications that can take advantage of them, set `max network packet size` appropriately and have the applications request larger packets.

## disk i/o structures (New for System 11)

(See the description of `disk i/o structures` in the section "Disk I/O Group," earlier in this chapter.)

## event buffers per engine (New for System 11)

**Units:** Integer number of events

**Default:** 100

This specifies the number of events per SQL Server engine that can be monitored simultaneously. Monitor Server makes use of the events for monitoring SQL Server activity. The number of event buffers recommended is dependent on the number of engines in the SQL Server, the level of activity, and the types of applications. Setting it too low can result in a loss of event information. Consider setting it to 2,000 and above for most environments. The higher the value, the less Monitor Server will degrade SQL Server performance.

Each event buffer per engine consumes 100 bytes of memory. Multiply the configuration value by the number of SQL Server engines to determine the total memory requirements. If you are not going to be using Monitor Server, set event buffers to 1 to make memory available for other uses within SQL Server

## executable code size + overhead (New for System 11)

**Units:** Number of bytes

**Default:** N/A

This is the size of the SQL Server executable code and kernel structures for the current platform. It is not configurable.

## max number network listeners (New for System 11)

**Units:** Integer

**Default:** 15

Each master port defined in the SQL Server interface file requires a network listener. If your SQL Server defines multiple master ports to support multiple network interfaces, configure max number network listeners accordingly.

## max online engines

**Units:** Integer quantity

**Default:** 1

This is the number of engines you want the SQL Server to use in a Symmetric Multiprocessing (SMP) environment. An engine does not necessarily correspond with a physical CPU. It corresponds with the amount of work that would be performed by a physical CPU.

---

**TIP**

For the best performance, and to best utilize all resources, the number of engines should not exceed the number of available physical CPUs minus 1.

## number of alarms (New for System 11)

**Units:** Integer number of alarm structures

**Default:** 40

This is the number of preallocated alarm structures used by the server for event handling. Each configured alarm structure requires 20 bytes. Alarms are used by processes executing the `waitfor` command. If you have a large number of processes using `waitfor`, you may need to increase this value.

## number of devices

(See the description of `number of devices` in the section "Disk I/O Group," earlier in this chapter.)

## number of extent i/o buffers

**Units:** Integer quantity of eight-page extents

**Default:** 0

Index creation takes a huge amount of CPU and I/O resources. To reduce the load on the server during index creation, you can allocate additional memory in eight-page extents (16KB on most platforms) for the `create index` command to use.

The first `create index` command you issue will use all the defined extent I/O buffers allocated. Other simultaneous index creations will use standard I/O (reading and writing individual pages for intermediate sort results and index pages).

> **TIP**
>
> You may want to use a larger value here at initial load time so that when indexes are created they can take advantage of the extent I/O buffers. Then, reduce the value to 0 when you go to production and allow the memory to be used for cache instead.
>
> You have to experiment to find the optimal setting for your system. Most people have found that values between 40 and 60 provide optimum performance gains.
>
> *Do not* set the value higher than 100 or you will see performance degrade.

## number of languages in cache

**Units:** Integer quantity

**Default:** 3

This is the maximum number of languages that may be held in cache simultaneously.

## number of locks

(See the description of `number of locks` in the section "Lock Manager Group," earlier in this chapter.)

## number of mailboxes (New for System 11)

**Units:** Integer

**Default:** 30

These are structures used by the kernel for internal communication. This is a parameter that was occasionally changed using the `buildmaster -ycnmbox` command. Do not modify this parameter unless instructed to do so by Sybase Tech Support.

## number of messages (New for System 11)

**Units:** Integer

**Default:** 64

This is used, along with mailbox structures, by the kernel. Do not modify this parameter unless instructed to do so by Sybase Tech Support.

## number of open databases

**Units:** Integer number of open databases

**Default:** 12

This is the total number of databases for which SQL Server will build internal pointers in its kernel, and for which it can maintain simultaneous connections. This includes `master`, `model`, `tempdb`, `sybsystemprocs`, `sybsyntax`, `sybsecurity`, and any user databases that might be used concurrently.

> **TIP**
>
> If the process tries to exceed the configured number, you will typically get messages in the error log describing the incident. Unfortunately, the message reported to the user is fairly confusing. Avoid this problem by configuring the variable to equal the number of created databases within the SQL Server, and then forget about it. The amount of memory taken up is effectively insignificant.

# number of open objects

**Units:** Integer quantity

**Default:** 500

This is the number of concurrent open objects that may be in simultaneous use. If you begin getting error messages that object connections are unavailable, increase this number. The memory cost is low (40 bytes).

# number of remote connections

**Units:** Integer quantity

**Default:** 20

This is the total number of remote connections both to and from this SQL Server. For example, if this is set to 20 (the default), and there are 10 remote logins currently, only 10 outgoing connections may be made.

# number of remote logins

**Units:** Integer quantity

**Default:** 20

This is the total number of concurrent connections that can be made from this SQL Server to other servers. This value should be set equal to or less than number of remote connections.

# number of remote sites

**Units:** Integer quantity

**Default:** 10

This parameter controls the number of remote sites that simultaneously connect to SQL Server. SQL Server invokes a site handler for each site connecting to SQL Server. All access to SQL Server from a remote site is handled with a single-site handler.

# number of user connections

**Units:** Integer quantity

**Default:** 25

The `user connections` variable determines the number of concurrent connections that may be made to SQL Server at any given time. Every time a user logs in, it requires a single connection. (A single user could have dozens of connections at one time.)

The `user connections` variable has the most dramatic effect on configured memory. You need approximately 51KB of memory per user connection (this is higher if the stack size or default packet size is increased). In addition to actual users who are logged into the server, the server consumes user connections for the following:

- One per master network listener (each line for the master device in the interfaces file)
- One for standard output
- One for the errorlog
- One for internal use (if you are running on the VMS platform)
- One for each data device
- One for each mirror device
- One for the backup server
- One per active site handler
- One per remote server

The global variable `@@max_connections` is set to the absolute maximum server connections; the actual number of user connections allowed equals `@@max_connections` less the system connections in the preceding list.

Determining the number of user connections required depends on the number of concurrent users and the number of connections per user.

To determine how many connections are currently in use, execute `sp_who`.

## *partition groups* (New for System 11)

**Units:** Integer quantity

**Default:** 1024

When you partition a heap table (see Chapter 18, "Database Object Placement and Performance"), SQL Server needs internal memory structures to control access to individual partitions of the table. Each partition group will manage up to 16 partition caches, one for each table partition. If a table has more than 16 partitions, it will require more than one partition group.

The number of partition groups determines the number of open partitioned tables. If there are 64 partition groups, SQL Server is limited to 1,024 (16 × 64). If either of these values are exceeded, attempts to partition a table or access a table partition will fail.

## permission cache entries* (New for System 11)

**Units:** Number of 28-byte cache protectors

**Default:** 15

This parameter specifies the amount of permission cache used before the server has to check the sysprotects tables.

Information on user permissions is held in the permission cache. SQL Server checks the permission cache first when checking permissions before looking in the sysprotects table.

The permission cache gets wiped out with each grant and revoke. Don't spend a lot of time tuning this parameter, because the performance gains are negligible.

## procedure cache percent

(See the discussion of procedure cache percent in the section "Cache Manager Group," earlier in this chapter.)

## remote server pre-read packets

**Units:** Integer quantity

**Default:** 3

This is the number of packets the site handler may preread from a remote site. Because a site handler may be handling multiple users from a single remote site, the site handler can preread and keep track of data packets for each user process before it is ready to receive it. The default value is usually appropriate. Increasing it will increase memory requirements. Decreasing it may slow network traffic between servers.

## stack guard size* (New for System 11)

**Units:** Bytes, in an even multiple of your server's page size (usually 2KB)

**Default:** 4096 (multiple of 2KB)

The stack guard size is the size of the overflow stack area at the end of each stack. This area is used to monitor whether a transaction exceeds its available stack space. The stack guard helps avoid having a stack overflow overwrite other memory areas.

Typically the default size is appropriate. If you are having problems with stack overflow, you may better be served by increasing stack size.

Increasing stack guard size will increase the memory requirements per configured user connection accordingly.

## stack size

**Units:** Bytes, in an even multiple of your server's page size (usually 2KB)

**Default:** Varies depending on platform

Stack size is the capacity of the server's execution/argument stack. If you have queries with large numbers of arguments in the where clause or long select lists, or deeply nested stored procedures, you may get an error that says stack overflow or stack size exceeded. This is your clue to add a few kilobytes to this variable, or to break these large queries into smaller queries.

Increasing stack size will increase the memory requirements per configured user connection accordingly.

## total data cache size (New for System 11)

(See the discussion of total data cache size in the section "Cache Manager Group," earlier in this chapter.)

## total memory

(See the discussion of total memory in the section "Cache Manager Group," earlier in this chapter.)

# Network Communication Group

This section identifies parameters that affect network communications for SQL Server.

## additional network memory

(See the discussion of additional network memory in the section "Memory Use Group," earlier in this chapter.)

## default network packet size

(See the discussion of default network packet size in the section "Memory Use Group," earlier in this chapter.)

## max network packet size

**Units:** Bytes (should be a multiple of 512)

**Default:** 512

Some applications need to send large quantities of data across the network lines (bcp, for example). These applications can request larger packet sizes through client-library requests. When these requests are made, memory is allocated from the fragment acquired in the additional netmem variable. If no memory is available here, packet size will not increase.

If an application does not request the larger packet size, it uses the size specified in default network packet size (DNPS). The maximum network packet size should be at least as large as DNPS. If you increase max network packet size higher than DNPS, you will need to configure additional network memory to support the larger packets.

## max number network listeners (New for System 11)

**Units:** Integer

**Default:** 15

Each master port defined in the SQL Server interface file requires a network listener. If your SQL Server defines multiple master ports to support multiple network interfaces, configure max number network listeners accordingly.

## number of remote connections

**Units:** Integer quantity

**Default:** 20

This is the total number of remote connections both to and from this SQL Server. For example, if this is set to 20 (the default), and there are 10 remote logins currently, only 10 outgoing connections may be made.

## number of remote logins

**Units:** Integer quantity

**Default:** 20

This is the total number of concurrent connections that can be made from this SQL server to other servers. This value should be set equal to or less than number of remote connections.

## number of remote sites

**Units:** Integer quantity

**Default:** 10

This parameter controls the number of remote sites that simultaneously connect to SQL Server. SQL Server invokes a site handler for each site connecting to SQL Server. All access to SQL Server from a remote site is handled with a single-site handler.

### remote server pre-read packets

**Units:** Integer quantity

**Default:** 3

This is the number of packets the site handler may preread from a remote site. Because a site handler may be handling multiple users from a single remote site, the site handler can preread and keep track of data packets for each user process before it is ready to receive it. The default value is usually appropriate. Increasing it will increase memory requirements. Decreasing it may slow network traffic between servers.

### tcp no delay (New for System 11)

**Units:** Flag

**Default:** 0

By default, TCP bundles smaller logical packets into larger physical ones to improve network performance. Disabling this setting (which is the default) will enable packets to be sent regardless of size. This increases network traffic, but may improve performance in low-volume applications with small packet sizes.

# O/S Resources Group

This section lists configuration parameters that affect operating system parameters.

### max asynch i/os per engine (New for System 11)

**Units:** I/O quantity

**Default:** 2147483647

This parameter sets the maximum number of asynchronous disk I/O requests that may be outstanding for an engine. This should be set to your operating system limitation for maximum concurrent asynchronous I/O requests to avoid having the O/S reject SQL server requests. If an engine issues an asynchronous I/O request and either max asynch i/os per engine or max asynch i/os per server has been reached, SQL Server will delay sending the I/O request until enough outstanding I/O has completed to fall below the limit exceeded.

## max asynch i/os per server (New for System 11)

**Units:** I/O quantity

**Default:** 2147483647

This parameter sets the maximum number of asynchronous disk I/O requests that may be outstanding for a SQL Server, regardless of the number of engines. This should be set to your operating system limitation for maximum concurrent asynchronous I/O requests to avoid having the O/S reject SQL server requests.

## o/s asynch I/O enabled (New for System 11)

**Units:** N/A

**Default:** N/A

Indicates whether asynchronous I/O has been enabled at the operating system level. This is a read-only parameter and cannot be changed.

## o/s file descriptors (New for System 11)

**Units:** N/A

**Default:** N/A

Displays the maximum number of file descriptors available per process as configured for the operating system. This is a read-only parameter and cannot be changed.

## tcp no delay (New for System 11)

(See the discussion of tcp no delay in the section "Network Communication Group," earlier in this chapter.)

# Physical Memory Group

This section contains parameters that affect physical memory resources for SQL Server.

## additional network memory

(See the discussion of additional network memory in the section "Memory Use Group," earlier in this chapter.)

# lock shared memory (New for System 11)

**Units:** Flag

**Default:** 0 (off)

This parameter allows or disallows swapping of SQL Server pages to disk, and allows the O/S kernel to avoid the SQL Server's internal page locking code. This can reduce disk I/O.

Not all operating systems allow locking of shared memory.

# shared memory starting address (New for System 11)

**Units:** Physical address

**Default:** 0

This parameter identifies the location in memory where SQL Server starts its shared memory region. This is typically not modified unless Sybase Technical Support recommends it.

# total memory

(See the discussion of `total memory` in the section "Cache Manager Group," earlier in this chapter.)

# Processors Group

This section lists parameters for configuring processors in an SMP environment.

# max online engines

(See the discussion of `max online engines` in the section "Memory Use Group," earlier in this chapter.)

# min online engines

**Units:** Integer number of engines

**Default:** 1

Specifies the minimum number of SQL Server engines that should be online in a multiprocessor environment.

# SQL Server Administration Group

This group lists parameters that relate to general SQL Server Administration.

## allow nested triggers*

**Units:** 0 or 1 (flag)

**Default:** 1 (on)

If a trigger modifies a table that has a trigger, the trigger on the second table will fire if `allow nested triggers` is on (the value equals 1). Otherwise, it will not.

## allow updates to system tables*

**Units:** 0 or 1 (flag)

**Default:** 0 (no)

The `allow updates` option is a flag that directs the server to allow the `dbo` to modify system tables directly (that is, without using supplied system stored procedures).

> **WARNING**
>
> Turning on `allow updates` is a bad idea! The first few times I tried this, I permanently crashed the server. Do not do this without the safety net of having Sybase Technical Support on the telephone directing you to do so.
>
> If you do attempt to modify system tables, always back up the database first, and perform all system table modifications in a transaction. That way, if you really mess things up, you can issue a `rollback tran` command and get back to where you started.

> **NOTE**
>
> One reasonable time to `allow updates` is after inadvertent device failure. If a device is not available to the server (the power is down, for example) when the server comes up, any databases using that device will be recorded in `sysdatabases` as suspect. If you update the `sysdatabases` table (changing the SUSPECT bit), you may be able to bring the server down, power up the offending device, and reconnect to your database. The following shows the `update` statement you might issue to retry connecting to all suspect databases:
>
> ```
> update sysdatabases
> set status = status - 256
> ```

```
where status & 256 = 256
```
After you use the `allow updates` option, be sure you turn it off.

## audit queue size

(See the discussion of `audit queue size` in the section "Memory Use Group," earlier in this chapter.)

## cpu accounting flush interval* (New for System 11)

**Units:** Machine clock ticks

**Default:** 200

This is the frequency with which you want CPU usage accounting information dumped from `sysprocesses` to `syslogins`. This information can be gathered by using the `sp_reportstats` stored procedure and can be used for chargeback accounting. This information accumulates in `syslogins` until you use the `sp_clearstats` stored procedure.

How you set this option depends on how often you plan on running usage reports. Set it higher if you are running reports infrequently—for example, on a monthly basis. However, if you are doing periodic queries against `syslogins` to monitor CPU usage by process, set this lower to update the `totcpu` column in `syslogins` more frequently.

## cpu grace time (New for System 11)

**Units:** Milliseconds

**Default:** 500

This parameter sets the maximum amount of CPU time a process can use before the SQL Server aborts the process with a time-slice error. This feature, which can stop runaway processes, creates "Infected" processes.

## deadlock retries (New for System 11)

**Units:** Integer number of retries

**Default:** 5

Specifies the number of times a transaction will attempt to acquire a lock after it has been designated the deadlock victim. After failing the configured number of retries, the transaction is rolled back.

## default database size

**Units:** Megabytes

**Default:** 2

This is the size a database will be if you do not specify the size in the `create database` statement. This tends to be an infrequently adjusted variable, because you will almost always specify the size of your databases during creation.

## default fill factor percent

**Units:** Integer percentage

**Default:** 0

`fill factor` is the extent to which index pages should be filled (excluding the root) as indexes are created. This includes the data pages of clustered indexes. Note that this is a performance tool.

> **NOTE**
>
> The `fill factor` required by `sp_configure` is two words, but the `create index` statement keyword `fillfactor` is a single word.

Low fill factors cause index pages to be partially full, which in turn will create more index levels. The performance benefit comes at insert and update time, when row additions will be less likely to cause page splits. (Lots of page splits during updates are bad for performance.)

> **NOTE**
>
> A fill factor of 0 does not mean that pages will be empty. This is a special case. Clustered index data pages and nonclustered index leaf pages are 100 percent full, and some space is left in the intermediate levels (typically 75 percent full).

High fill factors fill the pages as much as possible. This reduces index levels and increases query performance.

> **NOTE**
>
> Fill factors are not maintained after index creation. To re-create indexes with the fill factors intact, you must drop and re-create the index. Some shops with intensive update applications do this on a nightly basis.
>
> Maintaining fill factors is typically the only reason you might periodically drop and re-create indexes, because SYBASE indexes tend to be self-maintaining and self-balancing.

## event buffers per engine (New for System 11)

(See the discussion of event buffers per engine in the section "Memory Use Group," earlier in this chapter.)

## housekeeper free write percent (New for System 11)

**Units:** Integer percentage

**Default:** 1

This parameter sets the maximum percentage by which the housekeeper task can increase database writes over normal database writes. When the frequency is set to 20, the housekeeper task can make the I/O only up to 20 percent busier by writing changed pages to disk.

When SQL Server has no tasks to process, the housekeeper task begins writing "dirty" pages from cache to disk. This helps improve CPU utilization and decreases the need for buffer washing during transaction processing.

The housekeeper task can be disabled by setting housekeeper free write percent to 0, or it can be made continuous by setting housekeeper free write percent to 100.

## i/o accounting flush interval* (New for System 11)

**Units:** Machine clock ticks

**Default:** 1000

This is the frequency with which you want I/O statistics information dumped from sysprocesses to syslogins. This information can be gathered by using the sp_reportstats stored procedure and can be used for chargeback accounting. This information accumulates in syslogins until you use the sp_clearstats stored procedure.

How you set this option depends on how often you plan on running usage reports. Set it higher if you are running reports infrequently—for example, on a monthly basis. However, if you are doing periodic queries against `syslogins` to monitor I/O statistics by process, set this lower to update the `totio` column in `syslogins` more frequently.

## i/o polling process count (New for System 11)

**Units:** Number of processes

**Default:** `10`

This parameter defines the maximum number of SQL Server processes that run before the SQL Server scheduler checks to see whether disk and/or network I/O tasks have completed. Tuning this will affect response time and throughput.

Increasing this value may increase throughput for applications with high disk/network I/O activity.

## identity burning set factor

**Units:** Percentage in decimal form × 10 million

**Default:** `5000` (represents .05 percent)

When you define a column as `identity` in a table (new for System 10), the server will auto-matically assign a unique, sequential number for that column in the table at row insertion time. To avoid excessive I/O, the SYBASE SQL Server keeps blocks of numbers available in memory, and writes `"Next available block"` information only to the database, rather than to each individual row. This is a performance enhancement.

The number of values in the block of information is controlled by the `identity burning set factor` variable. Note the units that are specified: `5000` means that .05 percent of the numbers will be made available. Because identity columns must be a numeric data type with a predefined precision, the server uses the possible range of values to determine which numbers are reserved with each available block. If the server is brought down unexpectedly, all numbers in the burning set memory block will be lost to each table that has an identity column. An orderly shut-down will not cause identity values to be burned.

For example, an identity column is defined as `numeric(7,0)` (values range from `1` to `9,999,999`). The burning set factor is the default value of `5000`, so .05 percent of the values are made available at a time. The worst case is that all the values in the available block are lost when the server shuts down, with a loss of 9,999,999 (max identity value) × .05% (burning factor) = 500 values.

> **TIP**
>
> If the server is going through an erratic phase (going up and down frequently and unexpectedly), which may happen in testing or early production before stability has been reached, or after a version upgrade, large sets of numbers may be used up. This moves you toward your maximum column value more quickly than you might have expected. Until things stabilize, set your burning factor lower, even if it means that performance takes a hit.

## identity grab size (New for System 11)

**Units:** Number of values

**Default:** 1

This is the number of identity values that each process may preallocate for its own use. The higher this value, the more potential gaps you will have in column values. The lower this value, the more often a process has to request identity values.

## lock promotion HWM* (New for System 11)

**Units:** Integer number of locks

**Default:** 200

Prior to System 11, lock escalation from page level locking to table level locking happened automatically at the 200-page lock level. Now, you can set a high water mark, which instructs the server not to escalate from page locking to table locking until this number of locks is obtained on a table.

For more information on locking and lock escalation, see Chapter 15.

## lock promotion LWM* (New for System 11)

**Units:** Integer number of locks

**Default:** 200

The server will never attempt to escalate locking when the number of table locks is below this level (low water mark).

For more information on locking and lock escalation, see Chapter 15.

## lock promotion pct* (New for System 11)

**Units:** Integer percentage

**Default:** 100

If the number of locks is between the HWM and the LWN, this is the percentage of page locks permitted before lock escalation.

For more information on locking and lock escalation, see Chapter 15.

## number of alarms (New for System 11)

**Units:** Integer

**Default:** 40

This is the number of preallocated alarm structures used by the server for event handling.

## number of extent i/o buffers

(See the discussion of extent i/o buffers in the section "Memory Use Group," earlier in this chapter.)

## number of mailboxes (New for System 11)

**Units:** Integer

**Default:** 30

These are structures used by the kernel for internal communication. This is a parameter that was occasionally changed using the buildmaster -ycnmbox command. This is not one to play with.

## number of messages (New for System 11)

**Units:** Integer

**Default:** 64

This is used, along with mailbox structures, by the kernel.

## open databases

(See the discussion of open databases in the section "Memory Use Group," earlier in this chapter.)

# open objects

(See the discussion of open objects in the section "Memory Use Group," earlier in this chapter.)

# number of preallocated extents (New for System 11)

**Units:** Integer quantity

**Default:** 2

This is the number of extents that bcp will preallocate during a single trip to the page manager. For bcp processes using large batches, a higher value will improve performance by reducing the number of allocation records that will be written to the log. However, if you are using small batches with bcp, a high value may result in the allocation of more pages than needed.

# number of sort buffers* (New for System 11)

**Units:** Integer quantity

**Default:** 0

This is the number of prereserved buffers used to hold pages read from the input buffer. When tuning the number of sort buffers in conjunction with extent i/o buffers, number of sort buffers should be set to eight times the value of extent i/o buffers. You should run benchmark tests to determine the optimal setting for this parameter. Be aware that setting sort buffers too high may result in slower performance.

# partition groups (New for System 11)

(See the discussion of partition groups in the section "Memory Use Group," earlier in this chapter.)

# partition spinlock ratio (New for System 11)

**Units:** Integer quantity

**Default:** 10

A spinlock is a simple mechanism to lock a partition cache in use by another process. This parameter specifies the ratio of spinlocks to internal caches.

> **NOTE**
>
> Although a 1:1 ratio of spinlocks-to-partitions might provide the least contention, the recommended ratio is 10 percent of the number of partitions in use.

## print deadlock information (New for System 11)

**Units:** Flag

**Default:** 0 (off)

This parameter instructs the server to print deadlock information to the error log for purposes of tracking down deadlocks. This is the information that was displayed in earlier releases of SQL Server using the dbcc traceon(1204) command (see Chapter 15 for information on how to use and interpret this output).

> **WARNING**
>
> Setting this option on can seriously degrade SQL server performance. Only use this option when attempting to debug the cause of deadlocks within a database. Do not leave it on all the time.

## runnable process search count (New for System 11)

**Units:** Integer quantity

**Default:** 3

This parameter determines the number of times an engine loops looking for a runnable task before relinquishing a CPU.

> **TIP**
>
> On single-processor systems, you should consider setting this parameter to 1. On multiprocessor systems, increasing the runnable process search count to 750–1250 may improve performance for CPU intensive applications; 50–200 may improve performance for I/O intensive applications.

## size of auto identity column (New for System 11)

**Units:** Bytes

**Default:** 10

If the database option auto identity is on, the server automatically appends an identity column to every table at creation time. This parameter specifies the default width of that column.

## sort page count* (New for System 11)

**Units:** Integer

**Default:** 0

This parameter specifies the maximum amount of memory a sort operation can use.

Because sorts require about 50 bytes per row while processing the input table, an optimal value for sort page count can be estimated by the following:

(# of sort buffers* rows per data page) / 50

This gives you a good starting point. You'll need to benchmark your applications with different settings to find the best value.

> **WARNING**
>
> Changing this parameter can cause dump incompatibilities between systems with different sort page count settings if a create index command is contained in the transaction log dump. To minimize this risk, always dump a database after creating indexes with large values configured for sort page count or number of sort buffers.

## sql server clock tick length (New for System 11)

**Units:** Microseconds

**Default:** 100000

This parameter enables you to specify the duration of the SQL Server's clock tick in microseconds.

**TIP**

In mixed-mode environments, decreasing this number can help performance for I/O-bound tasks. A recommended value is 20000. A lower clock tick length causes CPU-bound tasks to context switch more frequently, giving other processes more access to the CPU.

If your applications are CPU-bound, a higher clock tick length may improve performance by enabling CPU tasks to process longer between context switches.

## time slice

**Units:** Milliseconds

**Default:** 100

The time slice is theoretically the number of milliseconds the server allocates to each user process as the server does its own internal multithreading. In practice, the server uses time slice as a guideline, and may increase or decrease it (transparent to the configuration setting) if processes are taking too long to swap in and out.

If set too low, SQL Server may spend too much time switching between processes, which will hurt performance because context switching is expensive.

If set too high, CPU-intensive processes may monopolize the CPU, resulting in longer response times.

**TIP**

Leave the time slice alone, unless otherwise directed by Sybase Technical Support.

## upgrade version*

**Units:** N/A

**Default:** N/A

This is the version of the upgrade, automatically set by the installation software (and also the upgrade software). If you don't believe the number, try running the following to get a detailed report on your current version of Sybase:

```
select @@version
```

# User Environment Group

This group lists parameters that modify the user environments.

## default network packet size

(See the discussion of default network packet size in the section "Memory Use Group," earlier in this chapter.)

## number of preallocated extents (New for System 11)

(See the discussion of partition groups in the section "System Administration Group," earlier in this chapter.)

## number of user connections

(See the discussion of number of user connections in the section "Memory Use Group," earlier in this chapter.)

## permission cache entries* (New for System 11)

(See the discussion of permission cache entries in the section "Memory Use Group," earlier in this chapter.)

## stack guard size (New for System 11)

(See the discussion of stack guard size in the section "Memory Use Group," earlier in this chapter.)

## stack size (New for System 11)

(See the discussion of stack size in the section "Memory Use Group," earlier in this chapter.)

## systemwide password expiration*

**Units:** Integer number of days

**Default:** 0 (indicating that passwords do not expire)

Only a user with the sso_role can set this option, which dictates how often a login must change the current password. When the time interval is within 25 percent of the interval (or seven days, whichever is greater), users will get warning messages indicating they need to change the password. If a password has expired, a user can still log in to the server, but cannot execute any commands except sp_password (to change the password) until the password is modified.

## user log cache size (New for System 11)

**Units:** Bytes

**Default:** 2048

This parameter specifies the default size for user log caches.

There is one log cache for each configured user connection. SQL Server uses the log cache to hold transaction information for a single transaction for a single user. When a transaction commits, the contents of the log cache for that user are written to disk. By buffering each user's transaction records until the transaction completes, contention is reduced between multiple processes writing to the log.

> **TIP**
>
> It is a waste of resources to allocate more space for this value than your maximum server transaction length, because it is flushed on each commit.

## user log cache spinlock ratio

**Units:** Ratio

**Default:** 20

This specifies the ratio of user log caches per user log cache spinlock. SQL Server needs to use spinlocks to protect user log caches, because multiple processes can access the contents of a user log cache.

If you have a single-processor CPU, there will be only one log cache spinlock, regardless of the number of user connections.

# Configuration Variables That Require Substantial Memory

Several variables use a substantial amount of SQL Server memory. They are summarized in Table 30.2.

## Table 30.2. Variables that use substantial memory.

| Parameter | Bytes of Memory per Unit |
| --- | --- |
| user connections | Approximately 51KB (this is platform-specific) |
| devices | .5KB |
| open databases | 17KB |
| open objects | 40 bytes |
| locks | 72 bytes |
| audit queue size | 424 bytes |
| default network packet size | 3 × the number of user connections × DNPS (total, not per unit) |
| extent i/o buffers | 8 pages (16KB on most platforms) |
| procedure cache | Percentage of remainder of cache |

# Summary

SQL Server System 11 provides a number of configuration options for defining SQL Server behavior and tuning SQL Server performance. In the next chapter, you examine in more detail the configuration options that have the greatest impact on SQL Server performance and explore examples and guidelines for tuning them.

# Optimizing SQL
# Server Configuration
# Options

**31**

**IN THIS CHAPTER**

There are a number of configuration options within SQL Server that affect SQL Server performance. These include memory configuration, CPU configuration, network configuration, and lock configuration. The most important of these configuration variables in relation to performance is memory.

SQL Server 11 introduces an array of new configuration options that directly impact the performance of SQL Server. SQL Server 11 allows much finer control over memory configuration, lock resources and escalation, and I/O. Used properly, these configuration options can offer worthwhile increases in server performance. Used poorly, they can turn SQL Server into a performance dog just as quickly. Understanding what these configuration options define is just as important as understanding how to change them.

# Memory Utilization

Figure 31.1 represents physical memory on your server box. In this figure, all physical memory except for that set aside for the O/S kernel is allocated to SQL Server. The amount of memory allocated to SQL Server is configurable within SQL Server and should always be less than all available memory.

**FIGURE 31.1.**

*Physical memory allocated to the SQL Server is configurable, as is the distribution of cache between the procedure cache and data cache.*

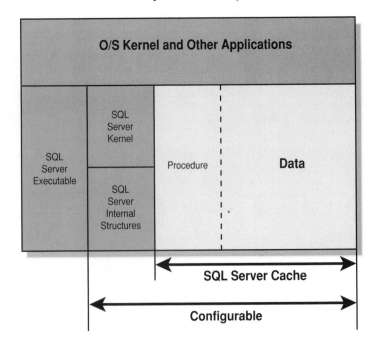

The first chunk of memory in physical memory is used by the operating system kernel. The amount of memory required by the O/S is typically defined by the operating system administrator (who is often not the SQL Server system administrator). It contains information about what can be done with memory, caching, connections, I/O, and other OS-specific activities. Occasionally at installation time, you may need to reconfigure the OS kernel to accommodate SQL Server memory and I/O needs. Don't forget to leave additional memory set aside within the O/S for other applications that may be running on the same server box (for example, Backup Server, Monitor Server, bcp, batch jobs, and so forth).

When the SQL Server starts up, it refers to a system configuration setting, memory, to determine the number of pages (remember, SQL Server pages are 2KB unless you are running on a Stratus system that uses 4KB pages) of real memory that the SQL server requests from the operating system when it comes up.

> **WARNING**
>
> If the server does not have enough memory to start properly, it will not start at all. (There is no partial server execution.) Prior to System 11, if you have misconfigured and the server is unable to get enough memory to start, you have to use buildmaster with the -r option to reconfigure all the memory settings to their default values (discussed later in this section). If that doesn't work, it is time to call Sybase Technical Support and probably have them rebuild the master for you one variable at a time (using the -y option of buildmaster).
>
> In System 11, you can simply edit the SQL Server configuration file and modify the offending configuration parameter, then try to start SQL Server again.

Within the block of memory allocated to SQL Server, the first chunk of memory is set aside for the SQL Server executable. SQL Server is software, which is executed within the operating system. The amount of memory needed for the SQL Server executable varies from about 1MB to about 4MB, based on the software version and the platform on which it is running.

The next block of memory is set aside for SQL Server's own internal kernel, the memory structures for managing user connections, open databases, open objects, locks, and so forth. How you configure kernel-related items determines how much memory the kernel requires. Whatever memory is left over at this point is available for data and procedure cache. For example, if you allocate 5,000 pages for memory and use 500 pages for the executable and 2,000 pages for kernel, there are 2,500 pages available for data and procedure cache.

Cache enables the server to read information repeatedly from memory rather than disk. Because memory is always much faster than disk, sufficient cache size is a critical element in server performance. Cache is effectively divided between data cache, which stores data pages being read or modified, and procedure cache, which stores the optimized, executable stored procedures.

# *dbcc memusage*

The Database Consistency Checker command (dbcc) can detail the current memory allocations within SQL Server, which will help you make the best use of memory resources. In order to see the dbcc memusage output, you need to direct the output to your terminal by using dbcc trace functions (trace flags). Several dbcc trace flags are talked about in this book; two very common values are 3604 and 3605.

Here are the important dbcc commands related to memory usage and what they do:

| | |
|---|---|
| dbcc traceon (3604) | Sends subsequent dbcc output to the local session |
| dbcc traceon (3605) | Sends subsequent dbcc output to the errorlog |
| dbcc traceoff (3604 ¦ 3605) | Terminates output to specified destination |
| dbcc memusage | Must be used with dbcc traceon (3604) if you want to see the output on your screen |

---

**TIP**

On some platforms or releases of the server, dbcc traceon (3604) must be in its own batch to take effect for the subsequent dbcc memusage command:

```
dbcc traceon (3604)
go
dbcc memusage
go
```

---

**WARNING**

If you are running SQL Server in an SMP environment with multiple engines configured, running dbcc memusage can cause other processes within the SQL Server to time out and die. Do not run dbcc memusage while other processes are active in a multi-engine environment.

---

## Memory Utilization

You can use dbcc memusage to determine how memory is being used within SQL Server and whether your memory allocations are appropriate. It provides extremely useful information about overall memory size, cache size, and the actual objects stored in the cache. This is the memory usage section of dbcc memusage:

```
Memory Usage:


                        Meg.        2K Blks         Bytes

    Configured Memory:400.0000       204800       419430400

          Code size:   3.4259         1755          3592296
    Kernel Structures:  5.9769         3061          6267212
    Server Structures: 13.9494         7143         14627040
         Cache Memory:357.0625       182816        374407168
         Proc Buffers:  0.6974          358           731272
         Proc Headers: 18.8848         9669         19802112
```

The first section of the output is the server kernel information. The following are things you want to look at and consider:

- Configured Memory. This should be the same as what you configured for total memory using sp_configure. Here, it is reported in megabytes (400.0000) as well as in 2KB blocks (204800).

- Code Size. This is the amount of memory required for the SQL Server executable.

- Kernel Structures and Server Structures represent the memory requirements for the fixed overhead and configurable options (for example, user connections).

- Cache Memory. This is the amount of memory available for data cache.

> **NOTE**
>
> In System 11, you can also use sp_configure to determine the amount of memory available for data cache. This is reported in the Memory Use group as total data cache size (see Chapter 30, "Configuring and Tuning the SQL Server").

- Proc Buffers and Proc Headers. This is the total amount of memory available as procedure cache. Proc Buffers represents the size of the memory structures set aside for managing compiled objects in procedure cache. Proc Headers is the actual amount of procedure cache space available.

> **NOTE**
>
> The amount of memory available for procedure cache can also be determined by viewing the SQL Server errorlog (this is discussed shortly).

# Data Cache Usage

The second part of dbcc memusage is a list of the 20 objects (tables and indexes) using the largest number of pages in data cache:

```
Buffer Cache Memory, Top 20:
```

| Cache | Buf Pool | DB Id | Object Id | Index Id | Meg. |
|---|---|---|---|---|---|
| default data ca |  | 5 | 400004456 | 0 | 1.8926 |
|  | 2K | 5 | 400004456 | 0 | 1.8926 |
| default data ca |  | 5 | 400004456 | 2 | 0.5000 |
|  | 16K | 5 | 400004456 | 2 | 0.5000 |
| default data ca |  | 5 | 48003202 | 0 | 0.1777 |
|  | 2K | 5 | 48003202 | 0 | 0.0059 |
|  | 16K | 5 | 48003202 | 0 | 0.1719 |
| default data ca |  | 1 | 36 | 0 | 0.0469 |
|  | 16K | 1 | 36 | 0 | 0.0469 |
| default data ca |  | 1 | 37 | 0 | 0.0156 |
|  | 16K | 1 | 37 | 0 | 0.0156 |
| default data ca |  | 1 | 2 | 0 | 0.0059 |
|  | 2K | 1 | 2 | 0 | 0.0059 |
| default data ca |  | 5 | 2 | 0 | 0.0039 |
|  | 2K | 5 | 2 | 0 | 0.0039 |
| default data ca |  | 1 | 2 | 1 | 0.0020 |
|  | 2K | 1 | 2 | 1 | 0.0020 |
| default data ca |  | 1 | 8 | 0 | 0.0020 |
|  | 2K | 1 | 8 | 0 | 0.0020 |
| default data ca |  | 1 | 30 | 0 | 0.0020 |
|  | 2K | 1 | 30 | 0 | 0.0020 |
| default data ca |  | 1 | 30 | 2 | 0.0020 |
|  | 2K | 1 | 30 | 2 | 0.0020 |
| default data ca |  | 1 | 33 | 0 | 0.0020 |
|  | 2K | 1 | 33 | 0 | 0.0020 |
| default data ca |  | 1 | 33 | 1 | 0.0020 |
|  | 2K | 1 | 33 | 1 | 0.0020 |
| default data ca |  | 2 | 2 | 0 | 0.0020 |
|  | 2K | 2 | 2 | 0 | 0.0020 |
| default data ca |  | 2 | 8 | 0 | 0.0020 |
|  | 2K | 2 | 8 | 0 | 0.0020 |
| default data ca |  | 2 | 14 | 0 | 0.0020 |
|  | 2K | 2 | 14 | 0 | 0.0020 |
| default data ca |  | 2 | 99 | 0 | 0.0020 |
|  | 2K | 2 | 99 | 0 | 0.0020 |
| default data ca |  | 3 | 8 | 0 | 0.0020 |
|  | 2K | 3 | 8 | 0 | 0.0020 |
| default data ca |  | 5 | 2 | 1 | 0.0020 |
|  | 2K | 5 | 2 | 1 | 0.0020 |
| default data ca |  | 5 | 8 | 0 | 0.0020 |
|  | 2K | 5 | 8 | 0 | 0.0020 |

The output shows not only the largest objects in cache, but also the named cache they belong to and the buffer pool within the cache they are using for I/O.

Unfortunately, the output only provides the IDs of the databases, tables, and indexes. You need to translate these to the names of the databases and tables you are familiar with by using the following steps:

1. To determine the name of the database, use the db_name() function to convert a database ID to a name:

```
select db_name(5)
go
```

```
. . . . . . . . . . . . . . . . . . . . . . . . . . .
perftune
```

2. Use the object_name() function to convert the object ID to an object name. The object_name() function takes the object ID and the database ID as parameters. For example, let's see which table is the largest one in the cache:

```
select object_name(400004456, 5)
go
```

```
. . . . . . . . . . . . . . . . . . . . . . . .
perftab
```

3. Using the index ID and the following table, you can determine what component of a table is cached:

| Index ID | Component of Table |
|----------|--------------------|
| 0 | Table itself |
| 1 | Clustered index |
| 2 to 250 | Nonclustered index |
| 255 | Text/image chain |

To determine which nonclustered index is cached when the index ID is greater than 1, use the following select statement from sysindexes:

```
select name
from sysindexes
where id = 400004456 /* object id from memusage */
and indid = 2 /* index id from memusage */
go
```

```
name
. . . . . . . . . . . . . . . . . . . . . . . . .
idx1
```

# Procedure Cache Utilization

The last part of dbcc memusage is a list of the 20 (or less if there are not 20 procedures currently in cache) largest stored procedures in cache, along with the size and number of compiled plans that are in memory for that procedure. An example of the third section is shown in the following output:

```
Procedure Cache, Top 8:

Database Id: 1
Object Id: 640005311
Object Name: sp_configure
Version: 1
Uid: 1
Type: stored procedure
Number of trees: 0
Size of trees: 0.000000 Mb, 0.000000 bytes, 0 pages
Bytes lost for alignment 0 (Percentage of total: 0.000000)
Number of plans: 4
Size of plans: 0.645847 Mb, 677220.000000 bytes, 332 pages
Bytes lost for alignment 10032 (Percentage of total: 1.481350)


 - - - -
Database Id: 4
Object Id: 1232007420
Object Name: sp_helpdb
Version: 1
Uid: 1
Type: stored procedure
Number of trees: 0
Size of trees: 0.000000 Mb, 0.000000 bytes, 0 pages
Bytes lost for alignment 0 (Percentage of total: 0.000000)
Number of plans: 1
Size of plans: 0.163151 Mb, 171076.000000 bytes, 84 pages
Bytes lost for alignment 2988 (Percentage of total: 1.746592)


 - - - -
Database Id: 4
Object Id: 1376007933
Object Name: sp_help
Version: 1
Uid: 1
Type: stored procedure
Number of trees: 0
Size of trees: 0.000000 Mb, 0.000000 bytes, 0 pages
Bytes lost for alignment 0 (Percentage of total: 0.000000)
Number of plans: 1
Size of plans: 0.156525 Mb, 164128.000000 bytes, 81 pages
Bytes lost for alignment 1633 (Percentage of total: 0.994955)


 - - - -
Database Id: 4
Object Id: 240003886
Object Name: sp_helpuser
Version: 1
Uid: 1
```

```
Type: stored procedure
Number of trees: 0
Size of trees: 0.000000 Mb, 0.000000 bytes, 0 pages
Bytes lost for alignment 0 (Percentage of total: 0.000000)
Number of plans: 1
Size of plans: 0.123927 Mb, 129947.000000 bytes, 64 pages
Bytes lost for alignment 363 (Percentage of total: 0.279345)

    . . . .
Database Id: 4
Object Id: 28527135
Object Name: sp_cacheconfig
Version: 1
Uid: 1
Type: stored procedure
Number of trees: 0
Size of trees: 0.000000 Mb, 0.000000 bytes, 0 pages
Bytes lost for alignment 0 (Percentage of total: 0.000000)
Number of plans: 1
Size of plans: 0.119993 Mb, 125822.000000 bytes, 62 pages
Bytes lost for alignment 2131 (Percentage of total: 1.693662)

    . . . .
Database Id: 4
Object Id: 1440008161
Object Name: sp_lock
Version: 1
Uid: 1
Type: stored procedure
Number of trees: 0
Size of trees: 0.000000 Mb, 0.000000 bytes, 0 pages
Bytes lost for alignment 0 (Percentage of total: 0.000000)
Number of plans: 1
Size of plans: 0.036139 Mb, 37895.000000 bytes, 19 pages
Bytes lost for alignment 412 (Percentage of total: 1.087215)

    . . . .
Database Id: 1
Object Id: 624005254
Object Name: sp_getmessage
Version: 1
Uid: 1
Type: stored procedure
Number of trees: 0
Size of trees: 0.000000 Mb, 0.000000 bytes, 0 pages
Bytes lost for alignment 0 (Percentage of total: 0.000000)
Number of plans: 1
Size of plans: 0.027714 Mb, 29060.000000 bytes, 15 pages
Bytes lost for alignment 54 (Percentage of total: 0.185822)

    . . . .
Database Id: 4
Object Id: 1872009700
Object Name: sp_who
Version: 1
Uid: 1
Type: stored procedure
Number of trees: 0
```

```
Size of trees: 0.000000 Mb, 0.000000 bytes, 0 pages
Bytes lost for alignment 0 (Percentage of total: 0.000000)
Number of plans: 1
Size of plans: 0.023154 Mb, 24279.000000 bytes, 12 pages
Bytes lost for alignment 175 (Percentage of total: 0.720788)

. . . .
DBCC execution completed. If DBCC printed error messages, contact a user with
System Administrator (SA) role.
```

> **NOTE**
>
> SQL Server's stored procedures are recursive and reusable, but not reentrant. If many
> processes want to run a procedure at one time, the server creates a new query plan for
> each concurrent execution. The size shown by dbcc memusage is the cumulative size for
> all plans. The size of an individual plan is the Size of plans/Number of plans. For
> example, in the previous output, the sp_configure procedure has 4 copies in cache
> using 332 pages. The size of a single plan therefore is 332/4 or 83 pages.
>
> The procedure size statistics reported in dbcc memusage refer to the largest plans in
> cache, but not necessarily the most frequently used. To find out which are the most
> frequently used, you can implement auditing to track procedure execution (see
> Appendix C, "Managing the Audit System").

# Using *dbcc memusage* Information

Run dbcc memusage regularly to understand how memory is being used in your server. Pay special
attention to these issues:

- Look at the overall memory figures to make certain that you have as much data cache
  as you expected.
- Look at data cache to see whether any particular object is monopolizing the cache at
  the expense of other objects, because it may be appropriate to take other tuning steps
  on that object.
- Look at how large stored procedures are, because smaller procedures compile and
  execute faster.

# Other Methods for Viewing Memory Utilization

There are two methods other than dbcc memusage that are used to examine the memory utilization within SQL Server: sp_configure and the SQL Server errorlog.

# Using *sp_configure*

In addition to providing a means for changing your SQL Server configuration, `sp_configure` also provides some reports on memory utilization within SQL Server.

An information-only configuration option, `total data cache size`, is available to view the total data cache memory available:

```
sp_configure "total data cache size"
go
```

```
Parameter Name                          Default     Memory Used Config Value Run Value
--------------------------------------  ----------  ----------- ------------ ----------
total data cache size                           0       365616            0     365616
```

For other memory-related configuration options—such as `procedure cache percent`, `number of user connections`, and `number of devices`—SQL Server reports in the `Memory Used` column the amount of memory required for the currently running configuration value.

## Using the Error Log

Another place to determine the amount of data and procedure cache available within SQL Server is the SQL Server errorlog. Scan the messages generated the last time the SQL Server was rebooted and look for lines similar to the following:

```
00:96/01/22 00:49:22.88 server  Number of proc buffers allocated: 709.
00:96/01/22 00:49:23.00 server  Number of blocks left for proc headers: 855.
00:96/01/22 00:49:24.60 server  Memory allocated for the default data cache cache: 2494 Kb
00:96/01/22 00:49:24.93 server  Size of the 2K memory pool: 1982 Kb
00:96/01/22 00:49:24.95 server  Size of the 16K memory pool: 512 Kb
00:96/01/22 00:49:24.97 server  Memory allocated for the perftune_cache cache: 5120 Kb
00:96/01/22 00:49:24.98 server  Size of the 2K memory pool: 5120 Kb
```

The `Number of blocks left for proc headers` value indicates the number of pages set aside for the procedure cache. `Number of proc buffers allocated` represents to the maximum number of compiled objects that can reside in procedure cache at one time—in this case, `709`.

The data cache space is broken out by named data cache. For example, the `default data cache` is `2494 Kb` in size and the `perftune_cache` is `5120 Kb`. The total data cache is the sum of these two values, 7,614KB. You will explore the meaning of memory pools later in this chapter.

# Configuring the Procedure Cache

Compiled stored procedure execution plans are stored in an area of memory called `procedure cache`. The balance of server memory, less that used by the server for its internal kernel and other variable elements, will be used by the server for data and procedure cache. The `procedure cache` configuration setting determines the amount of procedure cache set aside for procedures, triggers, and SQL batch executions. The larger the procedure cache, the more query plans that can reside in memory.

Stored procedure query plans in procedure cache are reusable, but not reentrant. This means that if more than one user executes a stored procedure or trigger simultaneously, multiple copies of the query plan are created in the procedure cache.

Query plans for stored procedures and triggers remain in cache after execution for subsequent execution by the same or other SQL Server users, providing there is sufficient cache space available for the query plan to remain in cache. If space needs to be made available, the oldest query plans in cache not in use are flushed out of cache to make room. If the stored procedure query plan is larger than available space in the procedure cache, (for example, all query plans are in use) and there is insufficient space to load another query tree or plan into procedure cache, the user will see the following error message:

```
Message 701: "There is not enough procedure cache to run this procedure,
trigger, or SQL batch. Retry later, or ask your SA to reconfigure SQL Server
with more procedure cache."
```

To avoid this error condition, and to have enough procedure cache space to avoid having frequently used query plans flushed from cache, make sure you configure procedure cache large enough. A good starting point for sufficient procedure cache space is to configure it large enough to store at least one copy of your largest stored procedure for each concurrent user, plus a fudge factor to accommodate other uses of procedure cache (trigger, rules, and so forth).

To derive this estimate, multiply the number of concurrent users executing stored procedures times the size of the largest stored procedure they will execute. You can determine the stored procedure size by using dbcc memusage, if the stored procedure is one of the 20 largest currently in procedure cache. Otherwise, you can get a rough estimate of the size of a procedure query plan by using the following select statement:

```
select (count(*) / 8) + 1
    from sysprocedures
where id = object_id("proc_name")
```

To get a report for all procedures and triggers in a database ordered by size, execute the following:

```
select o.name, "size in pages" = ((count(*)/8)+1)
from sysprocedures p, sysobjects o
where p.id = o.id
and o.type in ("TR", "P")
group by o.name
order by 2 desc
go

name                                size in pages
-------------------------------     -------------
storename_proc                      4
totalsales_trig                     4
deltitle                            3
title_proc                          3
```

```
history_proc                    3
storeid_proc                    3
titleid_proc                    3
insert_salesdetail_proc         3
byroyalty                       2
discount_proc                   2
insert_sales_proc               2
```

Let's assume there are 100 concurrent users, the largest stored procedure query plan is 60KB (30 2KB pages), and you need an additional 25 percent for other uses of procedure cache. The amount of memory then is calculated as follows:

> 100 concurrent users × 60KB (the largest stored procedure) = 6MB × 1.25 (fudge factor) = 8MB

This indicates that procedure cache needs to be at least 8MB. However, the procedure cache setting specifies the percentage of available cache memory to be set aside for the procedure cache.

The amount of memory available as cache space is the total memory configured for SQL Server minus the amount of memory required for the SQL Server executable and kernel and server structures. Use dbcc memusage to determine the amount of memory used for these purposes and subtract it from the total memory configured. If you have 50MB available for data and procedure cache, 8MB is 16 percent of that (8/50 = 16 percent).

Note that this is the minimum amount of memory you need for procedure cache to avoid an out-of-memory condition. If you use procedures heavily in your applications or use nested procedures, you may need to increase the procedure cache percentage to keep procedures in cache. Be careful not to overconfigure the procedure cache beyond what is needed because that wastes cache memory that can better be used as data cache.

# Tuning the Data Cache

For versions of SQL Server prior to System 11, tuning the memory configuration is fairly straightforward. You estimate your overall memory requirements for SQL Server executable, SQL Server Kernel, and other SQL Server structures (user connections, devices, open databases, locks, and so forth), and the amount of memory for procedure cache. Whatever is left is the amount of memory used for data cache. This data cache is used by all tables and indexes accessed.

In System 11, you estimate your total memory requirements in the same way, but the data cache management scheme is much improved. Rather than a single data cache shared by all databases, tables, and indexes, you can now partition the data cache into multiple buckets, or *named caches*, and bind databases and tables to specific cache areas. In this section, you learn how to configure and use named caches and the performance benefits.

# Estimating Total Memory Requirements

To estimate the total memory requirements, you first need to estimate how much data you want to keep in cache. Preferably, if you can keep an entire database in cache memory, your performance will be ideal. However, with most databases, this is simply not feasible. You need to size memory to improve your cache hit ratio. The cache hit ratio is the ratio of logical reads to physical reads, or in other words, the likelihood that a requested page will be found in data cache rather than having to be read from disk. For best performance, you want the cache hit ratio for your frequently used tables and indexes to be high.

> **NOTE**
>
> To determine your cache hit ratio, you can use the `set statistics io` option. This command displays the number of logical and physical page reads incurred when processing a statement against a table. Because every physical read incurs a corresponding logical read, the cache hit ratio is calculated as follows:
>
> logical reads – (physical reads × pages per I/O) / logical reads
>
> Prior to System 11, the number of "pages per I/O" was always a single page. In System 11, depending on how the cache buffers are configured within a named cache, SQL Server can perform reads up to 8 pages at a time (16KB using 2KB pages). Therefore, if SQL Server uses 16KB reads for a query and `statistics io` reports 20 physical reads, it actually reads 160 (20 × 8) pages. To determine the I/O method used by a query, you also turn on the `showplan` output:
>
> ```
> select count(*) from pt_tx_CIid
> go
>
> QUERY PLAN FOR STATEMENT 1 (at line 1).
>
>
>     STEP 1
>         The type of query is SELECT.
>         Evaluate Ungrouped COUNT AGGREGATE.
>
>         FROM TABLE
>             pt_tx_CIid
>         Nested iteration.
>         Index : idx2
>         Ascending scan.
>         Positioning at index start.
>         Index contains all needed columns. Base table will not be read.
>         Using I/O Size 16 Kbytes.
>         With LRU Buffer Replacement Strategy.
>
>     STEP 2
>         The type of query is SELECT.
>
> Table: pt_tx_CIid   scan count 1,   logical reads: 40,   physical reads: 3
> ```

> From this output, you see that SQL Server performed 3 physical reads, using 16KB
> I/O and 40 logical reads. The cache hit ratio is the following:
>
> `(40 - (3 * 8)) / 40 = 16 / 40 = 40%.`
>
> In other words, 16 pages, or 40 percent of the table, was found in cache.
>
> Remember, the first time you access a table, the cache hit ratio will be zero because
> none of the table will be in cache memory.

To improve the cache hit ratio for your frequently accessed tables and indexes, determine which tables and indexes you wish to fit in cache and size your data cache accordingly.

Let's assume you determine that you need at least 100MB of data cache to hold your frequently accessed tables and indexes. How much total memory do you need to configure SQL Server for?

First, you need to figure out how much memory you need for the SQL Server executable and kernel and server structures. This can be determined from the dbcc memusage output. If you don't have an SQL Server up and running yet, you'll have to estimate your memory requirements.

At the end of Chapter 30, there is a table of values indicating how much memory is required by certain SQL Server configuration values. The most important of these is user connections. At 51KB per configured user connection, this configuration variable requires the greatest amount of memory. The rest of the configuration parameter memory requirements are minimal in comparison.

Let's start adding things up with the assumption that you need 2MB for the SQL Server executable and 8MB for the procedure cache:

> 2MB (SQL Server executable)
>
> + 5.1MB (100 users × 51KB / user connection)
>
> + 5MB (rough estimate of other server and kernel memory requirements)
>
> + 8MB (procedure cache requirements)
>
> = 20.1MB

To have roughly 100MB of memory available for data cache, you therefore need to configure SQL Server for 120MB of memory. If you need 8MB set aside for procedure cache, calculate the procedure cache percentage as follows:

> 120MB
>
> - 12MB
>
> = 108MB for data and procedure cache
>
> 8MB / 108MB = 8%.

Therefore, procedure cache should be set to 8.

**NOTE**

If, in the future, you need to increase your memory allocation to increase data cache size, don't forget to adjust the procedure cache setting to accommodate. For example, if you are adding another 100MB to increase the data cache to 200MB and get more tables and indexes to remain in cache, you set the total memory configuration to 220MB.

However, if your procedure cache setting is 8%, you would have 17MB set aside for procedure cache. Your requirements for procedure cache are the same as before—only 8MB—because you haven't increased the number of users on the system or increased stored procedure sizes. You would waste 9MB of memory that might better be used for data cache (9MB could be enough memory for an entire table to remain in memory). After configuring total memory to 220MB, set the procedure cache setting down to 4% to make that 9MB of memory available to the data cache.

**WARNING**

Do not overconfigure the `total memory` parameter for SQL Server. If set too high—either more than the available physical memory or the available free memory within the O/S—the SQL Server will either not start at all or, if it does, may end up using virtual memory within the O/S. The paging in and out of virtual memory seriously degrades SQL Server performance.

# Buffer Management in SQL Server

After you install System 11 SQL Server, it contains a single data cache called the "`default data cache`" that will be used for all tables, indexes, and logs. This is similar to pre–System 11 SQL Server, which also had a single global data cache.

A pre–System 11 SQL Server data cache consists of a single MRU/LRU (most recently used/ least recently used) buffer chain (see Figure 31.2). As pages age out of cache, they move toward the wash marker. The wash marker ensures that pages past the marker at the LRU end of the chain are either clean (not modified) or are in the process of being written to disk. Clean pages are used for requested data pages not in cache and are moved to the MRU end of the chain as they are needed.

**FIGURE 31.2.**

*Pre–System 11 Data Cache MRU/LRU chain.*

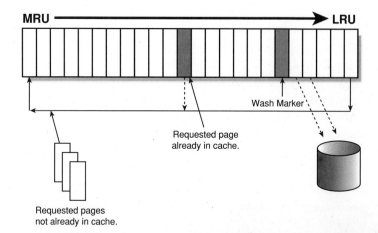

The MRU/LRU chain is a doubly linked list of 2KB pages. As cache space is needed and new data pages are read in, the least recently used pages are moved toward the wash marker. As a page crosses the wash marker, it is written to disk if it contains any data modifications not already written out previously. This is referred to as a "dirty" page. Once it is written out, it is then marked as clean and cycled back to the MRU end of the chain as new data pages are read in from disk to cache.

If a page already in cache is accessed again, it is moved back to the MRU end of the chain. This has the effect of keeping your frequently accessed data in cache memory.

## Indexes in the Data Cache

Indexes are treated slightly differently from data pages in the data cache in an effort to keep them in cache longer. Index pages can make multiple trips through the MRU/LRU chain. By default, the number of trips for an index page is 0, which results in index pages making only a single trip through the MRU/LRU chain. This can be modified by using the sp_configure command to change the setting for number of index trips. To keep index pages in cache longer, increase the number of index trips; reduce it to have them flush out sooner.

> **CAUTION**
>
> Do not set the number of index trips too high. In a high-transaction environment, the cache can flood with index pages that do not age out. This can cause processes to time out waiting for cache space to become available.
>
> Conversely, setting it too low causes index pages to age out too frequently, possibly resulting in poor performance if physical I/O is required too often to read index pages into cache.

# Pre-System 11 Buffer Management Performance

One shortcoming of a single data cache in SQL Server prior to System 11 is that all databases and user processes share the same data cache reading all data into the MRU end of the cache chain. This makes it difficult to ensure that frequently used tables will remain in cache, especially with queries on very large tables. If a process performs a table scan on a table that is larger than available cache space, the table can easily fill up the data cache, flushing other data and index pages out of the data cache. There is no way to prevent this from happening because there is no way to partition the cache or to modify how tables are read into cache.

This cache strategy can have an adverse impact on performance as smaller, frequently accessed tables that can easily fit in cache need to be read from disk again. In addition, it can increase the frequency of writes as modified pages get flushed out of cache by a large table scan.

# System 11 Enhancements to Buffer Management

System 11 offers you a number of enhancements to the buffer management scheme in SQL Server:

- The ability to partition the data cache into multiple caches—each with its own MRU/ LRU chain—and bind databases, tables, and indexes to specific caches
- The ability to configure multiple buffer pools within a data cache to support large I/Os
- The ability to use different cache replacement strategies for data that does not need to remain in cache

The rest of this section looks at ways of configuring and tuning SQL Server to take advantage of these improvements.

> **NOTE**
>
> The ability to create multiple data caches should not be seen as a substitute for proper indexing and optimizing queries using normal query optimization techniques. Splitting the data cache into multiple smaller caches can actually degrade performance if not configured wisely. For example, restricting a data cache area to a single table that is not accessed frequently takes away valuable data cache space for other objects that could have used that memory.

# Configuring Named Data Caches in System 11

One of the biggest enhancements System 11 offers is the ability to partition the data cache into multiple named data caches and binding databases or database objects to specific data caches.

Named data caches can help improve performance in a number of ways:

- Multiple data caches can minimize data cache contention in an SMP environment. With a single data cache, there is contention between multiple processes attempting to access the cache concurrently. SQL Server places a "spinlock" on the cache when one process makes changes to the cache, which can cause contention in a high-transaction environment, even though the spinlocks are held for a very short duration. With multiple caches, each has its own spinlock, which can increase concurrency if user processes are accessing objects in different caches.

- You can configure a named cache and bind critical tables and indexes to it to keep them in cache.

- Tables in a VLDB environment can be assigned to data caches configured to support large I/Os to improve table scan and large query performance. This also prevents large table scans from flushing other pages required by OLTP applications out of cache.

- Active tables can be assigned to a different cache than its indexes to increase concurrency.

- Transaction logs can be bound to separate cache from the data to reduce contention for cache space between the data and the log.

- tempdb can be bound to its own cache area to minimize contention for cache space between tempdb and user databases. If configured large enough, physical I/O in tempdb can be avoided completely, greatly improving tempdb performance.

## Creating Named Data Caches

Before setting up named data caches, you should try to configure SQL Server with as much memory as possible. Use dbcc memusage or examine the value reported for total data cache size by sp_configure to determine the amount of memory left in your SQL Server configuration for data cache. As you create additional named data caches, you will be reducing the size of the default data cache that will be used by databases and tables not bound to a specific cache.

To create a named cache, use the sp_cacheconfig stored procedure.

### Syntax

```
sp_cacheconfig [cachename, [cachesize[P¦K¦M¦G] [, logoonly ¦ mixed]]]
```

- cachename is the name you want to assign to the data cache. It must be unique within the SQL Server.

- cachesize specifies the size of the named cache in Pages, Kilobytes, Megabytes, or Gigabytes.

- logonly or mixed indicates whether the cache can be used for only log pages or data and log pages, respectively.

Without any parameters, sp_cacheconfig reports on all configured caches within SQL Server. Specifying only *cachename* will report on the configuration of the specified cache.

Changes made by using sp_cacheconfig will not take effect until SQL Server is restarted. At that time, the size of the default data cache will be decreased accordingly to accommodate the new named cache.

## Examples

Let's create a 5MB cache called perftune_cache:

```
sp_cacheconfig "perftune_cache", "5M"
go

- - - - - - - - - - -
0
The change is completed. The SQL Server must be rebooted for the change to take
effect.
```

Before restarting, let's examine what the cache configuration looks like:

```
sp_cacheconfig
go
```

| Cache Name | Status | Type | IO Sz | Wash Sz | Config Value | Run Value |
|---|---|---|---|---|---|---|
| default data cache | Active | Default | | | 0.00 Mb | 7.48 Mb |
| default data cache | Active | Default | 2 Kb | 512 Kb | 0.00 Mb | 6.98 Mb |
| default data cache | Active | Default | 16 Kb | 160 Kb | 0.50 Mb | 0.50 Mb |
| perftune_cache | Pend/Act | Mixed | | | 5.00 Mb | 0.00 Mb |
| | | | | Total | 5.00 Mb | 7.48 Mb |

Note the difference between the Config Value and the Run Value as well as the current size of the default data cache. Cache configuration changes that are not in effect yet have a status of Pend/Act. Now let's restart the SQL Server and execute sp_cacheconfig again:

```
sp_cacheconfig
go
```

| Cache Name | Status | Type | IO Sz | Wash Sz | Config Value | Run Value |
|---|---|---|---|---|---|---|
| default data cache | Active | Default | | | 0.00 Mb | 2.44 Mb |
| default data cache | Active | Default | 2 Kb | 512 Kb | 0.00 Mb | 1.94 Mb |
| default data cache | Active | Default | 16 Kb | 160 Kb | 0.50 Mb | 0.50 Mb |
| perftune_cache | Active | Mixed | | | 5.00 Mb | 5.00 Mb |
| perftune_cache | Active | Mixed | 2 Kb | 512 Kb | 0.00 Mb | 5.00 Mb |
| | | | | Total | 5.00 Mb | 7.44 Mb |

Note that the perftune_cache is now active and its type is mixed. It is currently configured only for 2KB I/Os (IO Sz) and its wash marker (Wash Sz) is 256 pages (512KB) from the LRU end of the page chain. Notice also how the default data cache has been reduced in size to allocate the 5MB to the perftune_cache. Currently, all the space is assigned to the 2KB buffer pool. You'll see how to change the buffer pool configuration shortly.

If you want to set a minimum size for the default data cache, use sp_cacheconfig and specify a size. For example, to ensure that the default data cache is always at least 10MB in size, execute the following:

```
sp_cacheconfig "default data cache", "10M"
```

> **NOTE**
>
> The default data cache is the only cache space used during SQL Server recovery. The smaller the default data cache, the longer it can potentially take for recovery to complete. If you have a high-transaction-rate environment, make sure the default data cache is large enough for recovery to occur in a reasonable period of time.

## Using the Configuration File to Configure Named Caches

In addition to using sp_cacheconfig to set up named caches, you can also set up named caches in the configuration file that will take effect the next time SQL Server is restarted. The configuration file syntax is as follows:

```
[Named Cache:cachename]
    cache size = {size[P¦K¦M¦G] ¦ DEFAULT}
    cache status = {mixed cache ¦ log only ¦ default data cache}
```

> **WARNING**
>
> Unlike when using sp_cacheconfig, editing the configuration file directly doesn't verify the cache settings. If you configure a named cache larger than you have available cache space, SQL Server will not restart. You have to modify the configuration file to reduce the named cache size(s) or increase the total memory configuration variable. For this reason, it is recommended that you use the sp_cacheconfig procedure when setting up named caches.

## Defining Buffer Pools

By default, SQL Server performs 2KB I/Os (the size of a data page) when retrieving data from disk into cache. A named cache is initially set up with a 2KB buffer pool to perform 2KB I/O only. If you want to support larger I/Os within the named cache, you need to configure additional buffer pools within the cache. This includes the default data cache as well.

The benefit of large I/Os is better read performance for queries retrieving large amounts of contiguous data. Types of queries that can benefit from large I/Os include table scans, large range retrievals using a clustered index, nonclustered index leaf level scans, text/image retrievals, bulkcopy operations on heap tables, and update statistics. If 16KB I/O is supported in a named cache, eight pages can be read per I/O request, significantly reducing the amount of read requests required.

Buffer pool configuration within a cache is dynamic. You can create buffer pools or modify buffer pools without having to restart SQL Server.

Creating buffer pools divides the memory within a cache area into multiple slices, one for each I/O size. To set up buffer pools, use the sp_poolconfig procedure.

## Syntax

sp_poolconfig *cachename* [, "*memsize*[P¦K¦M¦G]", "*poolK*" [, "*affectedpoolK*"]]

- ■ *cachename* is the name of the data cache for which you are configuring a buffer pool.
- ■ *memsize* is the amount of memory within the cache to allocate to the specified buffer pool.
- ■ *poolK* specifies the buffer pool being configured.
- ■ *affectedpoolK* (optional) is the buffer pool that space will be taken from for the *poolK* buffer (the default is the 2KB buffer pool).

Note that the 2KB buffer pool cannot be reduced smaller than 512KB.

## Example

Let's set up a 16KB buffer pool in the perftune_cache that's 3MB:

```
sp_poolconfig "perftune_cache", "3M", "16K"
go

sp_cacheconfig "perftune_cache"
go

Procedure  sp_cacheconfig
```

| Cache Name | Status | Type | IO Sz | Wash Sz | Config Value | Run Value |
|---|---|---|---|---|---|---|
| perftune_cache | Active | Mixed | | | 5.00 Mb | 5.00 Mb |
| perftune_cache | Active | Mixed | 2 Kb | 512 Kb | 0.00 Mb | 2.00 Mb |
| perftune_cache | Active | Mixed | 16 Kb | 608 Kb | 3.00 Mb | 3.00 Mb |
| | | | | Total | 5.00 Mb | 5.00 Mb |

You now have a 3MB, 16KB buffer pool configured that can be used for large I/O operations such as a table scan.

# Using Buffer Pools

When the optimizer optimizes a query, it knows whether the table or index is bound to a named cache, the size of the named cache, and whether any buffer pools in the named cache are configured for large I/Os. If the optimizer determines that large I/Os would improve performance for the method used to access the table and there are cache buffers available in the named cache to support large I/Os, it will attempt to use large I/Os as long as there are sufficient buffers available within the pool.

If the optimizer attempts to perform 16KB I/O and there are no 16KB buffers available, SQL Server attempts to use the next available smaller I/O size to process the query.

In addition to the optimizer automatically choosing to use large I/Os, the user can force a specific I/O size by using the `prefetch` clause in a query. For more information on forcing the `prefetch` size, refer to Chapter 16, "Overriding the SQL Server Optimizer."

# Changing the Wash Area for a Named Cache

The *wash area* is an area in the buffer pool where once dirty pages cross the wash marker, SQL Server will write the pages out to disk. Once the write completes, the page is marked as clean and is made available in the LRU end of the cache chain. This process ensures that queries that need clean pages in the data cache will find them at the LRU end of the memory pool.

In most cases, the default size of the wash area will provide the best performance. Tune all other aspects of the system before you play around with the wash area. If you set the wash area too high, pages will reach the wash marker too quickly, causing it to be written to disk. This will increase the number of writes for the database, especially if the page remains in the wash area and is modified again and needs to be written to disk. Setting the wash size too low may result in insufficient clean pages being available. This may result in a process requiring a clean page to have to wait until a dirty page is written to disk. This can significantly degrade performance.

To change a pool's wash size, use `sp_poolconfig`:

```
sp_poolconfig cache_name, "io_size", "wash=size[P¦K¦M¦G]"
```

For example, to set the wash size for the 2KB buffer pool in the `perftune_cache` at 400KB from the end of the LRU chain, execute the following:

```
sp_poolconfig perftune_cache, "2K", "wash=400K"
```

# Binding Databases and Objects to Named Caches

Once you have the named caches configured, the next step is to bind databases and database objects to the named caches to make use of them. Databases and objects can be bound to a named cache by using the `sp_bindcache` procedure.

# Syntax

```
sp_bindcache "cachename", dbname [, "tablename[.indexname]" [, text]
```

- *cachename* specifies the named cache to which you want to bind the database or object.
- *dbname* specifies the database or the database the object belongs to that you are binding to the cache.
- *tablename* specifies the table you are binding, unless *indexname* is also specified.
- *indexname* specifies the name of the index for the specified table being bound to the named cache.
- text allows binding of the text/image data for a table to the named cache.

When binding a database to a named cache, you must be in the master database. To bind tables or indexes, you must be in the database where they are stored.

# Examples

Let's first bind the pubs2 database to the perftune_cache:

```
sp_bindcache "perftune_cache", pubs2
```

'Next, bind the pt_tx table to the perftune_cache:

```
sp_bindcache "perftune_cache", perftune, pt_tx
```

Finally, bind the NCamount2 index for the pt_tx_NCamount table to the perftune_cache as well:

```
sp_bindcache "perftune_cache", perftune, "pt_tx_NCamount.NCamount"
```

If you ran a query against the pt_tx table requiring a table scan, it should now use the 16KB memory pool in the perftune_cache. You can confirm this with the set showplan on option:

```
set showplan on
go
select count(*) from pt_tx
go


QUERY PLAN FOR STATEMENT 1 (at line 1).


    STEP 1
        The type of query is SELECT.
        Evaluate Ungrouped COUNT AGGREGATE.

        FROM TABLE
            pt_tx
        Nested iteration.
        Index : idx2
        Ascending scan.
        Positioning at index start.
        Index contains all needed columns. Base table will not be read.
```

```
Using I/O Size 16 Kbytes.
With LRU Buffer Replacement Strategy.

STEP 2
    The type of query is SELECT.


----------
7282
```

## Dropping Cache Bindings

To drop a binding of a table from a named cache, use the sp_unbindcache procedure:

```
Sp_unbindcache dbname [, tablename[.indexname] [, text]
```

To remove all bound databases and objects from the data cache, use sp_unbindcache_all:

```
sp_unbindcache_all "cachename"
```

> **NOTE**
>
> When you unbind an object from a cache, all pages for that object are flushed from cache. This can be a useful technique when you want to test physical I/O performance of your SQL Server (for example, comparing the performance difference using 2KB or 16KB I/Os). The first time you access the table, its pages are read into cache. The next time you run your test you will perform logical I/O. To force physical I/Os, unbind the table from its named cache and then rebind it. This causes the table to be flushed from cache so that SQL Server will perform physical I/O on the next test.

## Getting Information on Named Cache Bindings

You saw earlier in this chapter how you can get basic size information on named caches by using the sp_configure and sp_cacheconfig stored procedures. To determine which objects are bound to a named cache, use the sp_helpcache procedure.

### Syntax

```
sp_helpcache ["cachename"]
```

### Example

```
sp_helpcache "perftune_cache"
go
```

```
Cache Name                     Config Size     Run Size     Overhead
----------                     -----------     --------     --------
perftune_cache                    5.00 Mb       5.00 Mb      0.27 Mb

----------------- Cache Binding Information: -----------------

Cache Name            Entity Name                Type            Index Name
----------            -----------                ----            ----------
perftune_cache        perftune                   database
perftune_cache        pubs2                      database
perftune_cache        perftune.dbo.pt_tx_NCamount index          NCamount2
perftune_cache        perftune.dbo.pt_tx         table
```

# Tuning the Private Log Cache

Another cache-related enhancement in System 11 is the introduction of the Private Log Cache (PLC). The PLC provides a separate user log cache for each user process. The user log cache is where log records are cached for a user's transaction before they are written to disk. The PLC is automatically enabled for all user connections within the SQL Server.

Prior to version 11, significant contention could occur between multiple user processes trying to write their log records to the end of the syslogs table. With the advent of a private log cache for each user in System 11, the log records for a given process are cached in their own private log space first, rather than being written to the log immediately. This minimizes contention for log writes, especially in multiprocessor environments where greater contention for the log tends to occur.

Another advantage of the PLC is that if the begin tran for a long running or open transaction is in the PLC rather than the transaction log, the log can still be truncated.

The PLC is flushed to the transaction log whenever any one of the following events occur:

- The next log record won't fit in the PLC.
- The transaction commits or aborts.
- The transaction modifies an object in another database (that is, internal two-phase commit).
- A modified data page must be written to disk (log records must always be written to disk before data pages).
- A checkpoint occurs.
- A trigger is executed for the transaction (the PLC is flushed to the transaction log before the trigger).

The default and minimum size of the PLC is 2,048 bytes. You can configure the size of the user log cache by using the sp_configure stored procedure:

```
sp_configure "user log cache size", 4096
```

This example sets the user log cache to 4,096 bytes. Be careful not to configure the user log cache size greater than the maximum amount of log information written by an application's largest transaction. Because the SQL Server flushes the user log cache when the transaction completes, any additional memory not used within the user log cache will be wasted. Don't configure the user log cache for large, long-running transactions because it is more likely for one of the other system events to occur before the transaction completes (see the previous list). This flushes the cache early and wastes user log cache memory.

Avoid setting the user log cache too small for your transactions. This causes the user log cache to be written to disk more than once per transaction, increasing the contention for the transaction log.

## Estimating Transaction Size

How do you estimate the transaction size? One way to do this is to add up the size of the rows modified by the transaction plus the log overhead (54 bytes per row). Inserts and deletes log a single transaction record for each row inserted or deleted. An update generates an insert and a delete record for each row modified (unless an update in place occurs). Use the following formula to estimate transaction size:

Number of inserts × (row size + 54)

+ Number of deletes × (row size + 54)

+ Number of updates × 2 × (row size + 54)

For example, if a transaction inserts 3 rows 50 bytes wide, updates a 200-byte row, and deletes 10 100-byte rows, the following is an estimate of the transaction size:

(3 × 104)

+ (10 × 154)

+ (1 × 2 × 254)

= 2,360 bytes

In this example, if this is the largest transaction, and it is not a long-running transaction, you may want to bump up your user log cache size to 2,500 bytes to fit this transaction in user log cache.

An alternative method is to use the dbcc log command (see Appendix B, "The Database Consistency Checker," for full syntax and description of dbcc log) and view the log records for your transactions. One of the fields displayed for each log record is the length of the log record (len=#). Match all the records for a transaction (those where sessionid is the same) and add up the lengths of each record to determine the transaction size. For example, examine the following records from a transaction log:

```
BEGINXACT     (3652,0)
attcnt=1 rno=0 op=0 padlen=2 sessionid = (3652,0) len=60 status=0x0000
masterxsid=(empty)
```

```
xstat=XBEG_ENDXACT,
spid=1 suid=1 uid=1 masterdbid=0 mastersite=0
name=$ins   time=Jan 17 1996 12:37PM

INSERT      (3652,1)
attcnt=1 rno=1 op=4 padlen=2 sessionid = (3652,0) len=72 status=0x0000
oampg=2360 pageno=2419 offset=1660 status=0x00 cid=0
old ts=0x0001 0x0000426d   new ts=0x0001 0x00004273
xrow:
2094808c:  004a0100 00000100 00000100 00000789  .J.............
2094809c:  0000f320 d000                         ... ...

ENDXACT     (3652,2)
attcnt=1 rno=2 op=30 padlen=0 sessionid = (3652,0) len=28 status=0x0000
endstat=COMMIT time=Jan 17 1996 12:37PM
```

Adding up the `len=` values shows this transaction is 160 bytes in size.

# Guidelines for Cache Configuration in System 11

To configure named caches in SQL Server properly, analyze your databases, database objects, I/O patterns, and queries to determine whether there are situations that will benefit from named caches and cache binding. Consider the following items:

- The size of any frequently accessed tables you want to keep entirely in cache.
- If `tempdb` is heavily used, determine the size of cache needed for `tempdb` and consider placing `tempdb` into a separate named cache.
- On multi-CPU systems, consider spreading your busiest tables and indexes across multiple caches to minimize cache contention.
- Make sure you leave a large enough default data cache for activity on unbound tables and indexes. In addition, the recovery process uses only the 2KB buffer pool in the default data cache. If this is too small, recovery will run slowly.
- Don't try to micromanage the data caches for every index and table. You'll probably end up wasting cache space and hurting performance rather than helping it.
- Overpartitioning the cache space can result in no cache large enough to keep moderately sized tables in cache. This can cause poor performance.

When setting up buffer pools, follow these guidelines when deciding whether to configure for large I/Os to improve performance:

- Determine whether you have queries that can benefit from large I/Os such as table scans on large tables that are scanned frequently, scans of large nonclustered indexes whose leaf level is scanned frequently, and range queries on clustered indexes that retrieve a large number of rows.
- Be careful not to leave too little space for the 2KB buffer pool. Many queries and types of data do not need large I/O (for example, single-row retrievals using an index). In addition, some tasks use only 2KB I/Os (for example, `disk init`, certain `dbcc` commands, and `drop table`).

■ Consider reconfiguring buffer pools to match workload requirements. For example, increase the smaller buffer pools (that is, 2KB and 4KB pools) during the day when performing OLTP activities. Reconfigure them for a larger 16KB buffer pool for DSS activities run at night. (Remember, you do not need to reboot the SQL Server to change buffer pool configuration.)

■ Consider the `syslogs` table and the amount of update activity. In addition, the I/O size for transaction logs is 4KB by default. To get the best log performance, make sure that the data cache the log is bound to has a 4KB buffer pool.

> **NOTE**
>
> Over time, with inserts and updates and the corresponding page splits, a table that initially took advantage of large I/Os to minimize the number of I/O requirements, may lose some of its performance gains as the table becomes more fragmented. Large I/Os provide the greatest benefit when the pages are sequential—that is, each page in the page chain points to the next physical page in the extent. If the page pointers cross extent boundaries, it could take up to 40 separate reads, rather than five 16KB reads, to read in 40 pages.
>
> To correct this situation, you can drop and re-create the clustered index on the table. This makes the data pages contiguous again. If you use a low fillfactor when creating the index, you make the table larger than it needs to be at first, but it helps slow down fragmentation by leaving available space on the data pages for new data rows.
>
> If you don't have room to create the clustered index with the data in the table, bcp the data out in sorted order and drop and recreate the clustered index. Then load the data into the table in the clustered index order and the data should be relatively sequential.

# Lock Escalation Configuration

SQL Server performs locking at two different levels for query processing. A single query can lock individual data pages within a table, or it can lock the entire table, depending on the number of pages being read. The "magic number" for lock escalation prior to System 11 was always 200 pages. In other words, any query was allowed to allocate 200 page locks on a table. As soon as that query attempted to allocate page lock 201, SQL Server's locking scheme would attempt to upgrade from 200+ individual page locks to a single table lock.

Although this mechanism introduced efficiency into the algorithms of the locking manager, its impact on query performance, particularly with large numbers of users, is not quite so obvious. The figure of 200 pages is unyielding. Whether a table has 400 or 4,000,000 pages, a single query acquiring 200 locks will attempt to escalate to a table level lock. As a result, a single query reading 250 pages (500KB of data) from a table containing 5,000,000 pages (a 10MB table), would lock the entire table. This is even more problematic in very large databases where individual table sizes can be measured in gigabytes.

With SQL Server 11, there are now three configuration options available that enable an administrator to adjust the thresholds for lock escalation. These options can be set globally at the SQL Server level or at the database or table level. The following are the three lock promotion thresholds that can be set in System 11:

- `lock promotion HWM` (high water mark)
- `lock promotion LWM` (low water mark)
- `lock promotion PCT` (percentage)

The `lock promotion LWM` configuration option sets the minimum number of page locks that SQL Server must acquire on a table before it will consider the option of upgrading to a table lock. In effect, it is the "on switch" for lock escalation.

The `lock promotion HWM` configuration option sets the maximum number of page locks a query can acquire before it is escalated to a table lock. The `lock promotion HWM` value is absolute and does not change based on activity or query size. As a result, this value may mean that smaller tables never receive table locks when needed, and very large tables may incur substantial blocking as table locks are applied where they shouldn't be.

The problem of relating lock escalation to table size is solved by using `lock promotion PCT`. The `lock promotion PCT` sets the number of page locks based on a percentage of the overall table size at which SQL Server will attempt to escalate page level locks to a table level lock. The `lock promotion PCT` value is checked when the number of locks on a table is between the `LWM` and `HWM`. Setting `PCT` lower increases the likelihood of a process escalating to a table level lock. This percentage is calculated as the following:

(PCT × number of rows in table) / 100

Setting `PCT` higher decreases the likelihood of a process acquiring a table level lock, causing it to use more page level locks for the duration of the transaction. This could lead to the process exhausting the available locks on the server.

The decision hierarchy that SQL Server uses to define the actual point of lock escalation is as follows:

1. If the `lock promotion LWM` value is never reached—that is, a table scan operation does not generate *at least* the `lock promotion LWM` number of page locks—SQL Server will not escalate to a table lock.

2. If the LWM threshold is reached, SQL Server upgrades page locks to a table lock based on which of the remaining configuration options is encountered *first*:

   If the high water mark is encountered before the percentage, page locks are escalated to table locks.

   If the percentage is encountered before the high water mark, page locks are escalated to a table lock.

# Setting Lock Thresholds at the SQL Server Level

The default values for both `lock promotion LWM` and `lock promotion HWM`, are 200 pages, and the default for `lock promotion PCT` is 100 percent. This mimics the lock escalation behavior of versions of SQL Server prior to System 11.

There are two ways to set the default lock escalation thresholds for all tables in the SQL Server: `sp_configure` (see Chapter 30) and the `sp_setpglockpromote` stored procedures. The lock thresholds are dynamic options that take effect immediately.

## Syntax

```
sp_configure "{lock promotion HWM ¦ lock promotion LWM ¦ lock promotion PCT}",
value
```

```
sp_setpglockpromote "server", NULL, new_LWM, new_HWM, newPCT
```

## Examples

To set the high water mark for the entire server to 500 by using `sp_configure`, execute the following:

```
sp_configure "lock promotion HWM", 500
```

To set the server defaults by using the `sp_setpglockpromote` procedure, specify the `"server"` option as the first parameter. The following command sets the default HWM value to 1000 pages, the LWM to 200 pages, and the PCT to 75:

```
sp_setpglockpromote "server", null, 200, 1000, 75
```

# Setting Lock Thresholds at the Database or Table Level

The server level lock promotion thresholds may not be appropriate for all databases or tables in the server. For a finer level of control over lock escalation at the database or table level, you can configure them specifically by using `sp_setpglockpromote`.

For example, if you have only a few large tables in your SQL Server, you may wish to leave the server level lock thresholds at the default settings and increase the thresholds, specifically for the database containing those tables or the tables themselves. Any settings at the table level will override the database and server settings.

To remove table or database lock promotion settings, use the `sp_droplockpromote` stored procedure.

856

## Syntax

```
sp_setpglockpromote "{database | table}", {dbname | tablename},
new_LWM, new_HWM, newPCT
```

## Examples

The following two commands set the previous server level options at the database and table levels, respectively:

```
sp_setpglockpromote "database", pubs2, 200, 1000, 75
```

```
sp_setpglockpromote "table", titles, 200, 1000, 75
```

> **NOTE**
>
> For a detailed discussion on locking and performance issues, refer to Chapter 15, "Locking and Performance."

# Tuning Network I/O for Performance

In a client/server environment, the network must always be treated as a potential bottleneck. In order to minimize the bottleneck, you want to move as little information across the network as possible. This typically means avoiding performing large batch work (backups, bcp) across the network, especially when other users are working, or using stored procedures to minimize the SQL transmitted to the SQL Server.

In this section, you will examine some configuration options available in SQL Server to improve network performance. However, although the options discussed here will help to improve performance on the network, the real key to removing the network as a bottleneck is to minimize the amount of network traffic as much as possible.

## SQL Server and the Network

All communication between SQL Server and clients occurs via the network. Requests for data from clients, and data and responses to those requests, are sent via packets. On the client and server side, the information is first put into Tabular Data Streams (TDS) packets. TDS packets are a network-independent protocol for passing information between a client and a server. This is what gives SQL Server its network independence. It is the Net-Library's responsibility in the client and server applications to wrap the necessary network-specific information around the TDS packets to route them on the network to the proper destination (see Figure 31.3).

**FIGURE 31.3.**

*Communication between SQL Server and an Open Client application is done via Tabular Data Streams (TDS) packets.*

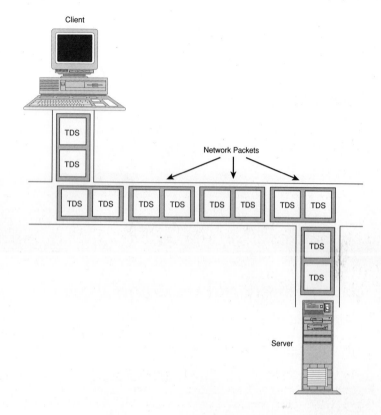

Sybase SQL Server was built on a network based client/server architecture and, as such, was designed to minimize network traffic as much as possible. However, it still uses the network exclusively for communication with clients, and the more optimally you can tune the network, the better the performance will be.

## Configuring Network Packet Size

By default, SQL Server uses a packet size of 512 bytes. This is appropriate for OLTP type environments where most transactions are short queries with small result sets. Many OLTP processes rarely even fill a packet. In DSS environments, however, queries typically return much larger result sets. In addition, both environments often have special processing requirements for large data loads or text processing. These types of processes can benefit from using larger packets to reduce the number of server reads and writes to the network by making each read or write more efficient.

You also may be able to improve performance by matching the TDS packet size to the network packet size, reclaiming unused space in the underlying networks.

Using larger packets also helps to improve network performance by reducing the number of packets sent between the client and the server. In most cases, the number of packets is more important than the size of the packets. The overhead to process the packets will typically affect performance the most.

In System 10, Sybase introduced the ability to configure the network packet sizes as a way to improve network performance. You can increase the default network packet size and/or configure additional network memory and the maximum network packet size to be used by applications requiring larger network packets for best performance.

> **NOTE**
>
> For details on how to configure and size the network configuration variables, refer to Chapter 30.

## default network packet size (DNPS)

`default network packet size` specifies the smallest packet size all clients will use to communicate with the SQL Server. By default, this is 512 bytes. If you increase the default packet size, remember to also increase the maximum packet size accordingly.

Each user connection structure includes 3 buffers, each the size of `default network packet size`, to support network communications between the client and the server. Increasing `default network packet size` increases the memory requirements for each configured user connection accordingly. If not all applications need the larger packet sizes, you are wasting memory. You may choose to leave `default network packet size` at 512 and configure `max network packet size` and `additional network memory` to allow applications that can better take advantage of the larger packet sizes to request them (for example, bcp can specify larger network packet sizes using the `-A` option).

> **WARNING**
>
> If you increase `default network packet size` above 512, older applications using pre-System 10 Open Client libraries will not be able to connect to SQL Server. Until it is definite that third-party applications are using System-10-or-later Open Client libraries, leave `default network packet size` at 512. Configure `max network packet size` and `additional network memory` to allow those applications that can use large packet sizes to request them.

## max network packet size (MNPS)

Some applications have special needs for sending large quantities of data across the network lines (bcp, for example). Setting `max network packet size` allows these applications to request larger packet sizes up to `max network packet size` as needed via client-library requests. Memory for larger network packets does not come from the three buffers set aside for each configured user connection, however. Memory for using the larger packets is allocated from the fragment acquired in the `additional network memory` variable. If sufficient memory is not available here, the requested packet size will not be granted. Instead, the largest network packet size that can be supported by `available network memory` will be used.

## additional network memory

The additional memory used for the larger network packets is taken from a separate pool of memory outside the memory allocated to SQL Server by the `total memory` parameter.

## tcp no delay

In TCP/IP networks, by default, SQL Server performs packet batching, briefly delaying sending partially full logical packets over the network by batching them into single larger physical packets. The purpose is to improve network throughput for terminal emulation environments. Disabling `tcp no delay` by setting this configuration variable on may help improve performance for applications that send and receive small TDS packets, allowing them to be sent immediately regardless of size. However, this will increase your network traffic volumes.

# Network Performance Tips

Although larger packet sizes can improve performance for applications performing large data transfers, there is eventually a point of diminishing returns. Unfortunately, there is no reliable method for predicting where this point is. The best method is to vary the network packet size and benchmark the I/O rates. Plot them until you find the point where performance is optimal.

Although you may see performance improvement for some applications using larger packet sizes, the greatest performance gains will come from optimizing network communications. Some optimization methods to consider include the following:

- Use stored procedures to reduce overall network traffic.
- Filter data at the server rather than the client to avoid sending unnecessary data across the network.
- Minimize the impact of other network-intensive activities (for example, network backups, bcp loads) by running them on a separate network or running them during periods when user activity is at a minimum.

# Speeding Up Index Creation

System 10 SQL Server introduced the `number of extent i/o buffers` variable, which allows you to set aside an area of memory exclusively for index creation. Extent I/O buffers allow SQL Server to use eight-page (16KB) buffers for reading and writing intermediate and final results when creating indexes.

Only one user process can take advantage of the `extent i/o buffers` when creating an index. Other simultaneous index creations use standard I/O (reading and writing individual pages for intermediate sort results and index pages).

The optimal setting for `number of extent i/o buffers` appears to vary depending on your system and the size of your tables. Many have found that values between 40 and 60 provide optimal performance. You may want to experiment with different settings to find the optimal setting for your environment. Do not set it too high, however. Setting `number of extent i/o buffers` over 100 has been found to degrade index creation performance, possibly due to the additional overhead of managing the buffers.

You may want to use a large value for `number of extent i/o buffers` at initial load time, so when indexes are initially created on your system they can take advantage of the extent I/O buffers to minimize index creation time. Once the system is loaded and indexes created, reduce the value to zero to make the memory available for data cache instead.

If you have ample memory available and frequently re-create indexes, you may want to set `number of extent i/o buffers` permanently. Otherwise, you can reconfigure the SQL Server during off-hours to use extent I/O buffers and run your index creates then.

# Tuning an SMP Configuration

The SQL Server Symmetric Multiprocessing (SMP) architecture is a Virtual Server Architecture running one to 32 cooperating SQL Server processes in parallel. Each process is referred to as an engine. There is no master processor.

The SQL Server SMP architecture is a "shared everything" architecture. The engines share the same SQL Server resources (memory, disk, and so forth). SQL Server performs its own task management, scheduling SQL Server tasks onto available engines. Tasks are not bound to a specific engine. When an SQL Server engine requires CPU resources, the operating system schedules the engine onto an available CPU. Engines are not bound to CPUs keeping the processing load symmetrically balanced.

Figure 31.4 demonstrates the scheduling of the following tasks within SQL Server:

1. As a client login request is received, SQL Server initially handles the request on engine 0, then passes it to the engine handling the fewest number of user connections (Note that in System 11, network traffic can be handled by all engines, not just engine 0.)

2. The task is then put to sleep in the sleep queue waiting for the client process to send a request.

3. When a request is received, the task is then put at the end of the runnable queue.

4. When the task reaches the front of the queue, it gets scheduled on the next available engine.

5. The SQL Server engine then requests CPU cycles from the operating system, and the operating system assigns it to an available CPU.

6. The task processes on the engine until it blocks on disk I/O or a lock request, or exceeds its time slice.

7. If the task is blocked waiting on a resource, it goes into the sleep queue where it remains until the request is satisfied.

8. The process then moves back to the end of the runnable queue.

9. When the task reaches the front of the queue, it gets scheduled on the next available engine and the process continues until the task finishes.

10. The task is then put onto the sleep queue waiting for a client request.

**FIGURE 31.4.**

*SQL Server SMP task management.*

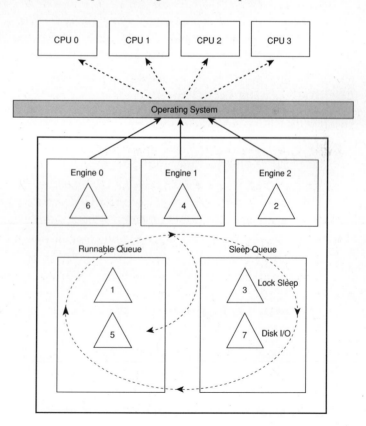

# Configuring Multiple Engines

SQL Server is initially configured for a single engine. If current performance is not up-to-par and you determine that the SQL Server is CPU-bound, you may want to increase the number of engines if you have additional CPUs available. Use a tool such as Sybase SQL Monitor or an operating system utility to monitor CPU utilization. Generally, if the average CPU utilization is greater than 85 percent, adding an additional engine may improve performance.

> **TIP**
>
> When measuring CPU performance, you may want to disable the housekeeping task within SQL Server to prevent its operations from skewing the CPU measurements. You can disable the housekeeper task with the following command:
>
> ```
> sp_configure "housekeeping free write percent", 0
> ```

You can reconfigure the number of available engines with the `sp_configure` command:

```
sp_configure "max online engines", 3
```

This is not a dynamic configuration value. A reboot of SQL Server is necessary for it to take effect.

# Engine Tuning Guidelines

Consider the following guidelines when configuring `max online engines`:

- Never have more engines than usable CPUs (if a CPU fails, remember to reconfigure the number of engines within SQL Server).
- Have only as many engines as usable CPUs. If there is a lot of processing by another application within the O/S, one engine per CPU is excessive. Leave at least one CPU available for the O/S and other applications.
- Start with what you think will be the minimum number of engines required, then monitor CPU usage and increase the number of engines slowly until CPU utilization falls to the desired level.

# Application Design Issues in an SMP Environment

As you increase the number of engines, the number of concurrent activities increases as well because more than one process can run simultaneously. This may increase contention for locks, I/O, network, and other SQL Server resources. To reduce contention in an SMP environment, follow these application development guidelines:

- Minimize the number of indexes on the tables. The greater the number of indexes, the greater overhead and the number of locks held during updates, increasing potential for contention.

- Spread your disk I/O across multiple databases to reduce I/O contention between the multiple concurrent processes.

- Use a lower fillfactor when creating indexes. This minimizes page splits temporarily and improves insert performance, thereby minimizing page and locking contention. The effect of fillfactor, however, will be lost as data is inserted and updated.

- Set the max_rows_per_page attribute on heavily accessed tables as a permanent means to spread rows out across multiple pages and to minimize page contention.

- Consider using heap table partitioning to set up multiple page chains to minimize locking and I/O contention on heap tables with concurrent insert activity. (See Chapter 18, "Database Object Placement and Performance," for a discussion on heap table partitioning.)

- Keep transactions short and as concise as possible so that locks are held for as short a period as possible.

# Summary

The main configuration parameter that affects SQL Server performance is the memory configuration. SQL Server 11 introduces some new options for fine tuning the memory configuration. Other configuration options can be tuned to improve SQL Server performance as well.

SQL Server 11 implements more varied and flexible configuration options than previous releases. This gives an administrator finer control over the SQL Server performance, but also the ability to configure incorrectly and possibly make the performance worse. Be careful when playing around with configuration options you don't fully understand.

Finally, keep in mind that although you may see performance improvement by tweaking the SQL Server configuration, the greatest performance gains are typically realized through proper database and index design and writing efficient SQL code. For example, you may see a 10 percent performance improvement by tuning your network configuration but a 100 percent or better performance improvement through proper index design.

# Measuring Performance

# 32

Sybase SQL Server runs on so many platforms that Sybase doesn't really try to provide a "be-all, end-all" tool for monitoring performance. Sybase does have a tool available, SQL Monitor, which is an add-on. I don't know of many shops that are using it—many have evaluated the product and decided it was lacking in too many areas.

Most shops use operating-system level utilities (vmstat, for example) to monitor disk and CPU utilization. Because these are operating system-specific, this text does not present them. Instead, you will focus on what to measure and why.

# Initial Benchmark

It is important to determine expected results for specific activities on specific platforms. The key element of a benchmark is that it will reflect the actual quantity of work you intend to perform, as well as enough documentation so that the benchmark is repeatable. If you are unable to run the same tests in six months and get the same results, you will never know what your problems are. For example, if performance suddenly drops off and your benchmark still runs the same, you know that your problem is DBMS-related. If your benchmark drops off, you want to be able to measure the component of the benchmark (disk, CPU, network, and so forth).

In order to understand your system's performance, you should be able to do the following:

- Estimate query times
- Understand physical I/O speed
- Understand logical I/O speed (page reads from cache)

## Estimating Query Times

The basic method of query resolution is a table scan, which is a sequential read of every data page in a table. This *should* be the worst-case cost (total elapsed time) for query resolution. Table scans are used if there is no appropriate index or if an index would slow down the process. If your query costs more than a table scan, you have problems (probably index statistics that are not up-to-date).

The time required for a table scan is directly proportional to the size of the table in pages. If you want to get exact I/O counts, you can set statistics io on prior to running a query.

Knowing the amount of time a table scan will take is useful for index selection, as well as for determining maximum expected query execution time. To do this, you need to understand the page access speed of your system. As of this writing, typical physical page access speeds are between 200 and 1,000 pages per second.

For example, for a 1,333,334-page table, you have the following:

    1,333,334 / 200 = 6667 seconds = ~ 111 minutes

> **TIP**
>
> To calculate disk access speed, follow these steps:
>
> 1. Identify a large table that is not in cache.
>
> 2. Cycle the server (shutdown followed by a startserver) to clear the cache.
>
> 3. Execute the following:
>    ```
>    set statistics io on
>    set statistics time on
>    select count(*) from identified table
>    ```
> 4. Read the results.

Here is a sample session to calculate physical I/O rates for SQL Server:

```
select count(*) from pt_sample_CIcompany
go
(Msg 3613) Parse and Compile Time 0.
SQL Server cpu time 0 ms.

--------
5772
(1 row affected)

(Msg 3615) Table: pt_sample scan count 1. logical reads: 317. physical reads: 317
(Msg 3614) Total writes for this command: 0

(Msg 3612) Execution Time 1.
SQL Server cpu time: 500ms. SQL Server elapsed time: 4173 ms.
```

In this example, 317 physical reads were accomplished in 4173 ms, for ~76 physical page reads per second.

Logical I/O speed can be calculated the same way, except that you want pages read from cache rather than disk. A good method is to run the previous test twice in succession. With luck, and an adequately sized cache, you can identify that the first set of reads is from disk and the second from cache, and calculate accordingly.

# Determining Access Speed

You may notice that at times, read performance times may be substantially different. This is not an "expected result." When measuring raw numbers, it is important to ensure that you are alone in your request for system resources (to isolate your numbers from other requests) and your tables are of adequate size to minimize the effect of system overhead and of a sleeping process (such as checkpoint or audit) kicking in at an inauspicious moment.

There are several ways of improving table scan time. Adding an index is the easiest and typically the first choice, in the hopes of avoiding the table scan in the first place. When the table scan cannot be avoided, frequently it helps to spread I/O across multiple disks and controllers. Horizontal or vertical partitioning can reduce the amount of data to be scanned. Cache can be increased so that more I/O is logical rather than physical (a 20:1 performance ratio, at this writing).

Faster drives or faster disk access methods might help (raw partitions may be 40 to 50 percent faster than file systems on a UNIX box).

# Ongoing Benchmarking

It is important to monitor, on an ongoing basis, activity on your server so that you can understand the growth or decline (normally growth) of the load on your system. At a minimum, you should monitor the following:

- CPU by engine
- I/O by virtual device
- Concurrency
- Throughput
- Batch effect

## CPU by Engine

SQL Server automatically balances loads across CPU engines, which is beyond your control. One server engine may manage many processes, but one process will never span engines (unless you're using Navigation Server). Engine zero handles all network requests. If this engine is running hard and other engines are not running, you have a load balancing problem (and likely a server bug). It also is comforting to watch the various engines at work. Prior to System 11, using more than 6–8 engines had a neutral-to-negative impact on performance. With System 11, you should be able to scale up to 16 processors comfortably.

## I/O by Virtual Device

When you are I/O bound, there are likely to be many possible culprits. You need to be able to monitor how hard each individual physical disk is being hit. This can be done not by physical disk, but by virtual device. If you cannot identify I/O by virtual device, you are probably not able to describe your data flow accurately. Hardware technicians claim that I/O cannot be bottlenecked through a controller—it is too fast.

# Concurrency

For the number of user connections you configure, the kernel uses memory that might otherwise be used for cache. As a result, you want to monitor how many connections are in use at average and peak times so that you can configure properly.

# Throughput

Monitor transaction rates to verify that, over time, a consistent maximum is available. As your throughput increases, look for additional resources for the point where it becomes necessary.

# Batch Effect

Be aware that batch processing can (and usually does) have a negative effect on performance. The "time slice" configuration parameter is the theoretical amount of time an engine gives a process. In practice, as processes last longer and take up more resources, the server may determine that swap time approaches or exceeds time slice. This can have the effect of giving long-running processes increasingly bigger time slices, causing a negative effect on OLTP processes.

# Rollout

Stress-testing your physical database design is an important step in understanding whether your system is up to the challenge of a rollout. It is important to establish required performance benchmarks.

By table, you should establish the following:

- Inserts per second
- Updates per second
- Concurrent selections

Profile all queries. Is response time acceptable for each query under load? Define your required response time under load for the following:

- Single row, single table lookups
- Inserts
- Multi-table queries

You also need to stress and observe activity on these:

- Objects
- Databases
- Server
- Network

# Stress-Testing Approach

Maximize performance at each level, in the following order, before addressing the larger issues:

1. Objects
2. Databases
3. Server

Optimization at each level may require revision (usually further streamlining) to prior levels. This process is iterative.

At the object level, you should stress tables and procedures.

At the table level, benchmark the following:

- Inserts
- Updates
- Deletes

Update many records concurrently, distributing updates across the table; then try to modify many records in the same area (with similar clustered index values). Update clustered and nonclustered index values to observe index page modifications. Look for problems in index selection, because indexed values are frequently updated. Watch for index page splits during updates.

Delete many records that are distributed across the database by several users concurrently. Watch for page level locks and locks in indexes that slow or block the delete process.

Monitor trigger performance. Perform concurrent modifications that call the same trigger. Watch performance when locks are required and held. Complex triggers create chains of locks; watch for deadlocks here and for performance hits as update and exclusive locks encounter page read locks on the same table.

On tables, perform large (many-row) and small (single-row) queries alone, then during updates. Try covered queries during updates and deletions. See whether select response time is affected by frequent updates (this depends on whether the select encounters locks in a table scan or in the index).

At the procedure level, test procedure response time with many users running the procedure concurrently. Does the procedure run quickly enough in memory? Do you max out procedure cache when a certain number of concurrent users accesses the procedure?

Understand how frequently the procedure is called. Execute procedures repeatedly, with widely varying parameters, to identify the benefit (cost?) of running redefined plans. What is the performance penalty (if any) for procedure creation or execution with recompile?

## Database Level Elements

Monitor the growth of the log under heavy table modification. Estimate the time before the log fills. Is the log itself a bottleneck? You may have to consider bundling statements together into larger transactions to get fewer log writes. If the log continues to be a bottleneck, you may need to reduce the number of indexes to reduce the amount of logged work.

## Server Stress Testing and Tuning

Check overall server performance. Model standard usage on the server and test the response time for all standard queries. If server response time is insufficient, look at these factors:

- CPU may be maxed out (look at sp_monitor).
- tempdb activity may be a bottleneck.
- Cache hit rate under load: you may need to add more data cache.
- Procedure cache hit rate: if you are constantly recompiling procedures, you should increase your procedure cache percentage.
- Virtual device level statistics tell you whether a database device needs to be split into two devices because of a heavy load of physical activity on that device.

The essential idea is to benchmark the following:

- Anything you will do on a regular basis
- Anything you need to do for project rollout

# Notes on Measuring Performance

Always keep in mind platform-related issues when measuring performance or benchmarking system performance. Always benchmark and test queries, bcp loads, and database maintenance tasks on your own system. Use the numbers you gather to estimate performance. Do not rely on vendor-provided information.

872

# Summary

You need to measure and monitor performance to anticipate system needs and isolate system functionality. This allows you to understand the changes in your system.

In this section we talked about benchmarking, estimating query times, ongoing benchmarking, and rollout.

# Remote Server Management

## 33

This chapter presents the definition and management of remote servers, privileges, and security.

As your systems grow in size, complexity, or geographic distribution, you may find it necessary to enable your servers to communicate with each other directly. Remote server access in a multi-server environment enables applications to share data (in a limited way) and to access data and functions on other SQL Servers and Open Servers (see Figure 33.1).

**FIGURE 33.1.**

*Remote servers include SQL Servers and Open Servers such as Net Gateway, OmniSQL Gateway, and others. Open Server processes require the same remote server administration as SQL Servers.*

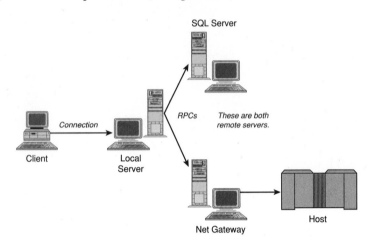

Because the remote server interface can access Open Servers, it also is the mechanism for connecting heterogeneous data sources, including mainframe databases from DB/2 to IMS to VSAM flat files, other non-Sybase databases, and nontraditional data sources. The most interesting applications involve the integration of real-time devices (stock tickers, news sources, and data-collection devices).

By definition, a remote server is a server you access as part of a client process without opening a distinct, direct client connection. Sybase SQL Server manages communications between servers using remote procedure calls (RPC). You call a remote procedure the same way you call a local procedure; the only difference is that you need to qualify the name of the procedure fully with the name of the server. Here is the syntax:

```
execute remote_server_name.db_name.owner_name.procedure_name
```

You've already used this syntax, with the exception of *remote_server_name*.

No matter what type of external data source you want to access, you need to implement remote servers. With Systems 10 and 11, all servers require remote access because the backup server (your backup technique) is accessed via RPC.

# Definitions

Let's consider a case in which the client is directly connected to an SQL Server, but needs to send and retrieve periodic information to a remote server using an RPC (see Figure 33.2).

**FIGURE 33.2.**

*The remote server is accessed through the local server, and the client maintains only a single connection to the local server.*

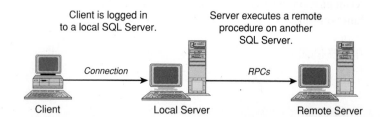

Client is logged in to a local SQL Server.

Server executes a remote procedure on another SQL Server.

Connection     RPCs

Client     Local Server     Remote Server

First, refresh your memory with a few definitions:

- A *local server* is the server you have logged in to.
- A *remote server* is another server to which you would like to connect from the local server.
- *Remote access* means connecting to a remote server.

To illustrate the configuration of remote servers, here is an example of two servers: a local server (near_server) and a remote server (far_server), as in Figure 33.3.

**FIGURE 33.3.**

*In this example, the name of the local server is* near_server*. The remote server is named* far_server*.*

Client     near_server     far_server

# Remote Access Cookbook

Ensuring remote access is not complicated, but it is complex. There are several steps to get just right:

1. Name the local and remote servers on both servers.
2. Configure each server for remote access.
3. Add all servers to the local interfaces file.
4. On the remote server, define the method for mapping logins and users to its own logins and users.
5. Set remote options, if necessary.

Let's go through each step in detail. Step 1 names the servers on each server. Until you start working with remote access, server names seem pretty arbitrary. For example, although you specify a named server when logging in, that server name is transformed into an address and port (or an address and named pipe) long before a packet goes out on the network. The server name you use on your local workstation does not need to correspond to the name in the interfaces file at the server.

With remote servers, the names are relevant to the communication; the names of servers must be defined consistently on each server or communication will not work properly.

Use sp_addserver to add a server name to the sysservers table in the master database. Prior to System 10, this was an sa-only task. With Systems 10 and 11, this became an sso-only task because it involves system access. You need to execute sp_addserver once for the local server name and once for each of the remote servers, as in the following example:

```
sp_addserver local_server_name , local
sp_addserver remote_server_name
```

Note that the local flag distinguishes the name of the local server.

As an example, on the local server (near_server), execute the following:

```
exec sp_addserver near_server, local
exec sp_addserver far_server
```

On the remote server (far_server), execute this:

```
exec sp_addserver far_server, local
exec sp_addserver near_server
```

Step 2 configures each server for remote access. The syntax is the following:

```
sp_configure 'remote access', 1
```

> **NOTE**
>
> In Systems 10 and 11, this setting is the default at server installation. If you are not currently configured for remote access and need to execute this step, you have to cycle your server (bring it down and back up) so that memory is reallocated for the remote connections. (See Chapter 30, "Configuring and Tuning the SQL Server," for a full discussion of memory allocation.)

As an example, on the local server (near_server), execute the following:

```
sp_configure 'remote access', 1
```

On the remote server (far_server), execute this:

```
sp_configure 'remote access', 1
```

Don't forget to shut down and restart each server.

Step 3 updates the interfaces file on the local machine to reflect the names and addresses of all servers to be accessed.

> **TIP**
>
> It is a good idea to have a single interfaces file with complete references for every server and propagate it throughout your network.

This is probably an sa task. At the operating system level (where the interfaces file resides), only the Sybase user can modify the file. For more on the interfaces file, see Chapter 24, "SQL Server Installation and Connectivity."

As an example, on each server, add both servers to the interfaces table:

```
near_server
      query tli sun-ether near_box ...
far_server
      query tli sun-ether far_box ...
```

Step 4, on the remote server, maps remote logins and users to the local environment. Here is the syntax:

```
sp_addremotelogin remote_server_name [, local_name [, remote_name]]
```

As an example, on the remote server (far_server), execute this:

```
sp_addremotelogin near_server
```

Step 5 sets remote options as necessary. Here is the syntax:

```
sp_remoteoption remote_server, login_name, remote_name, option_name, {true ¦ false}
```

As an example, on the remote server (far_server), execute this procedure to set up logins without requiring synchronized passwords between servers:

```
sp_remoteoption near_server, near_server_login, null, trusted, true
```

# Adding Servers with *sp_addserver*

Use the sp_addserver procedure to populate the sysservers table. The names in the sysservers table are mapped to the names in the interfaces file. Here is the syntax:

```
sp_addserver server_name [ { local ¦ null } [, network ]]
```

The local keyword identifies the name of the server into which you are signed. (There can be only one local server.) You can verify this by selecting the @@servername global variable. Note that this does not take effect until the server is cycled; until then, RPCs will not work. In this example, you add a local server, near_server, and a remote server, far_server:

```
exec sp_addserver near_server, local
exec sp_addserver far_server
```

The network parameter is the name of the server within the interfaces file, in case you want the names to be different. This permits server name aliasing. The following example adds a remote server, `extremely_far_server` (listed as such in interfaces), as `server17` in sysservers.

```
exec sp_addserver server17, null, extremely_far_server
```

As of System 10, at least one remote server—the backup server—is added automatically at installation time.

To remove a server from the sysservers table, use `sp_dropserver`. Here is the syntax:

```
exec sp_dropserver server_name [ ,droplogins ]
```

The `droplogins` keyword also instructs the server to remove all corresponding entries from sysremotelogins (discussed next). The following example removes the entry for `server17`, created previously, and removes all associated logins:

```
sp_dropserver server17, droplogins
```

# Adding Remote Logins with *sp_addremotelogin*

Remote logins enable you to map requests to a remote server to that server's local set of privileges and authorizations. *Remote logins are established on the remote server.*

The next three sections explore the three methods for mapping remote logins to local logins on the remote server.

## Using the Remote ID as the Local ID

Use this syntax to map the remote ID as the local ID:

```
sp_addremotelogin remote_server_name
```

This is the simplest mapping method. It presumes that the logins are the same on both servers, and maps login to login.

> **TIP**
>
> If users from the remote server need access on your server, don't forget to add them with `sp_addlogin`.

The following example (executed on far_server) requires each remote login on near_server to have a corresponding entry in syslogins on far_server:

```
sp_addremotelogin near_server
```

## Using a Single Local Login for All Remote Logins

If you want a single local login for all remote logins, use this syntax:

```
sp_addremotelogin remote_server_name, local_name
```

This is another straightforward mapping method. Any legitimate user on a server listed in sysservers will be mapped to a single login. In the following example, all logins originating from the server named near_server map to login near_server_user. (You need to run sp_addlogin near_server_user before running sp_addremotelogin.)

```
sp_addremotelogin near_server, near_server_user
```

## Using a New Local Name for All Remote Users

Here is the syntax for using a new local name for all remote users:

```
sp_addremotelogin remote_server_name, local_name, remote_name
```

The following is an example:

```
sp_addremotelogin near_server, selected_server_user, mdoe
```

In this example, the login named mdoe on near_server can access far_server using the login selected_server_user. (You still need to run sp_addlogin selected_server_user.)

# Removing Logins with *sp_dropremotelogin*

To remove a remote login after adding it, use the sp_dropremotelogin procedure. Here is the syntax:

```
sp_dropremotelogin remoteserver [, loginname [, remotename ] ]
```

The following drop statements remove the remote logins added previously:

```
sp_dropremotelogin near_server
sp_dropremotelogin near_server, near_server_user
sp_dropremotelogin near_server, selected_server_user, mdoe
```

# Remote Options

A variety of options can be set for specific servers, logins, and remote names. These define the way the server deals with the specific logins. Here is the syntax:

```
sp_remoteoption [remote_server [, login_name [, remote_name]], option_name, {true ¦
false}]
```

The options are listed in Table 33.1.

**Table 33.1. Options available for use with `sp_remoteoption`.**

| Option | Task |
|--------|------|
| trusted | Passwords are not rechecked. |
| net password encryption | Passwords are encrypted at both ends of the network. |
| timeouts | The server times out the connection after one minute of inactivity. |

In the next example (run on `far_server`), logins from the `near_server` do not need to retransmit passwords:

```
sp_remoteoption near_server, near_server_user, null, trusted, true
```

> **NOTE**
>
> If the trusted option is not turned on, you need to establish and maintain synchronized passwords between servers. Very few applications include the capability of transmitting a distinct remote password when necessary.

# Getting Information on Remote Servers

For information on remote servers defined for your server, you can use the `sp_helpserver` procedure. This procedure reads and decodes information from the `sysservers` table in the master database. Here is the syntax:

```
sp_helpserver [server_name]
```

Use `sp_helpserver` without a server name to list all servers defined on your system.

The following example includes two servers: the primary server and the backup server. The backup server is normally installed as part of Systems 10 and 11:

```
sp_helpserver

name            network_name    status                                  id
-------------   -------------   -------------------------------------   --
SYB_BACKUP      SYBASE_BS       no timeouts, no net password encryption 1
SYB_PRIMARY     SYB_PRIMARY                                             0
```

For information on individual logins for a server, use the sp_helpremotelogin command:

```
sp_helpremotelogin [remoteserver [, remote_name] ]
```

For a list of remote logins, execute sp_helpremotelogin without a parameter. In the following example, the server has two remote logins for two distinct servers. One remote login maps all logins from SYB_BACKUP to a similarly named login on this server. The second remote login maps all logins from near_server to a single local login, near_server_login. All remote logins are trusted so passwords are not verified:

```
sp_helpremotelogin

server                 remote_user_name        local_user_name        options
--------------------   --------------------    --------------------   --------------
SYB_BACKUP             ** mapped locally **    ** use local name **   trusted
near_server            ** mapped locally **    near_server_login      trusted
```

# Summary

Making your server accessible to other servers and able to access other servers requires a number of simple steps. Follow the cookbook, and remote access should work.

If you think you followed the cookbook, and remote access is not working, you probably forgot to shut down and subsequently restart the server.

# Defining Systems Administration and Naming Standards

# 34

**IN THIS CHAPTER**

As the number of applications you deploy on SQL Server increases, you will need to develop standards that enable you to administer your servers in a consistent manner. Most companies that successfully implement SQL Server have good standards in place. Standards are created to provide a foundation for administrative tasks and often result in establishment of the infrastructure necessary to enable the creation of procedures and scripts to automate activities.

What if you don't have standards in place? The cost of application development without standards is usually very high. The price is paid in effort and delay, as well as credibility. Let's face it—client/server is really no different from any other application environment. Success comes from the right mix of discipline and creativity. Thoughtful standards provide the discipline within which creativity can thrive.

This chapter focuses on those core standards needed to enable you to further develop procedures in your environment. You will look at two core activities: first, approaches to organizing databases and servers, especially regarding the development environment; and second, naming standards, from both the SQL Server and operating-system levels. Once you decide on names, a directory structure, and how you are going to approach development, you can start building those site-specific procedures and scripts to automate activities in your organization.

# SQL Server Environment Approach

You must approach development in an SQL Server environment in a consistent fashion, or each development project is destined to waste time performing certain activities. The approach should be focused on providing flexibility for the developer and structure for the database administrator. It also should be built to enable portability of code from the development environment to the potentially many levels of your test environment, and eventually to the production environment.

# Defining Environments

Most people who purchase SQL Server are using it to develop new *production* applications. When developing production software, you should assume there will be a development environment, at least one test environment, and a production environment. You must decide how each environment will be supported by SQL Server.

> **NOTE**
>
> Typical environments include development, system test, volume/stress test, user acceptance test, and production. Because there can be several test environments, this book considers them conceptually as a single environment called "test."

For each environment, you must determine the following:

- Is the environment supported by a separate (dedicated) SQL Server or does it share the SQL Server with some other function?
- How are the databases organized on the SQL Server? Is there a database per environment rather than an SQL Server per environment?

The most restrictive environment is a single SQL Server with databases for development, test, and production. As the detail will show, the needs of each environment conflict with other environments. The development environment may require rebooting the SQL Server often, but the production environment is likely to have up-time as an important business requirement. The testing environment often is constructed to be able to gather performance statistics. The activity of the development and production environments, however, might skew these performance statistics, and testing might ruin performance for production. It is *strongly recommended* that development, test, and production activities take place on separate SQL Servers.

# Development Environment

The development environment requires the maximum flexibility for developers while enabling the necessary control structures to provide for consistent promotion of code. In designing this environment, several issues should be considered:

- The SQL Server used for development may or may not be dedicated. A dedicated SQL Server is *strongly preferred* because "bouncing" (shutdown and restart) of the SQL Server is a *very* common activity in development. If the SQL Server is shared by several development groups, frequent reboots of the system may have a significant impact on the productivity of developers.
- The SQL Server may or may not be running on dedicated hardware. Dedicated hardware is preferable because the database hardware must be occasionally rebooted. Although dedicated hardware provides developers maximum control, it may not be cost-effective. Because this environment is used to unit-test individual modules for *functionality* and not performance, dedicated hardware is not a requirement.
- Although flexibility is at a maximum for the developer, so is developer responsibility. A developer has much more responsibility for administrative activities. Developers often create their own objects (tables, indexes, procedures, triggers, and so on) in the pursuit of satisfying a business problem. Developers often are responsible for managing their own test data. Organized database administration (the DBA group) still has some responsibilities, however. A DBA may create a base set of objects or manage a core set of data. As always, DBAs still get calls about any problems a developer cannot handle (killing processes, adding space, and so on).
- Developers must have a set of tables to use when developing. Define how many tables will be organized to meet the needs of all developers. (This is discussed in detail in the following section.)

■ Occasionally, a single logical database is physically implemented as several SQL Server databases in production. The distribution of tables to databases should match the production model. (Remember that relating tables from two different databases requires that at least one of the table names be qualified by the database name. If the development environment does not have the same database structure, the SQL has to be modified before production implementation, which is likely to introduce new bugs.) Your development environment should look *exactly* like the production environment in the base structure (database, tables, and objects).

If other projects share the development server, create a document to provide information about all groups. It should contain information such as project name, manager, contact name, phone, and specific instructions. Development environments are volatile. You may need to reboot the server to continue development. Because a reboot affects all users on the system, you should contact user representatives to prepare them for this situation.

# A Detailed Approach

The development environment is the area where developers first attempt to create new modules of an application. Development is an iterative process. Multiple revisions of code are normally created in the process of correctly satisfying design requirements. Consequently, the code may have unexpected results on tables. During the refinement of a module, database activities such as delete, insert, or update may need several modifications before they are deemed to work correctly. This requires the developer to create test conditions to test individual pieces of functionality. Additionally, new requirements may necessitate the addition or deletion of columns from tables to test the new pieces of code. These changes may become permanent modifications to the existing structures, validated by the iterative testing of an application. The development environment needs to be structured to minimize contention between developers.

Due to the nature of development, it is assumed that the development environment will use an SQL Server separate from the test and production environments. Based on that assumption, you can then determine an approach to development at a database and object level.

There are three main approaches to development in an SQL Server environment. The differences between the approaches depend on whether the developers share a database or have their own copies of objects and data.

The development approach is greatly impacted by the number of *actual* SQL Server databases used to represent the single logical database. An initial approach is to put all tables in a single database. However, experience shows that grouping tables into several databases can have significant performance and administrative benefits. The definition of databases in the development environment should be identical to the ultimate production environment to minimize code changes from development to production. If the production environment is organized using several databases, the development environment should also contain several databases.

Let's look at these three approaches to handling development in an SQL Server environment.

# Shared Database and Shared Objects and Data

In the shared database/shared objects and data approach, a single database (or databases) exists for development. All developers use the same objects and data. This approach is sometimes used in very small developments (one or two developers). When the number of developers increases, this approach quickly breaks down.

## Advantages

- It simplifies administration. There are fewer objects (tables, indexes, stored procedures, triggers, and so on) to manage.
- There are reduced storage requirements. There is only one database and one copy of objects and data.
- It is a viable option if your tables are grouped into multiple databases. The development environment is assumed to use a separate SQL server. The names used for databases can be *identical* between development, test, and production environments. Therefore, code that is developed does not have to be modified to be promoted to the next level.

## Disadvantages

- There is an almost unavoidable contention for data. Developer 1 might be testing a delete activity on the same row that Developer 2 is using to test an update activity. Development will be impeded as confusion results from "unexpected" changes to data.
- There is a significant decrease in a developer's capability of changing the underlying structure to support a hypothesis or test condition. Additionally, Developer 1 might want to add a column that would negatively affect Developer 2's testing.
- Development flexibility is greatly reduced.

# Individual Database and Individual Objects and Data

With the individual database/individual objects and data approach, each developer has a dedicated database for development. Because objects are created in the context of a database, the developer has a personal copy of all objects and data. Normally, developers are responsible for all activities with their databases, including data creation and backups.

## Advantages

- The developer has the capability to change data or structures without affecting other developers.

■ Because object names are created in the context of a database, all the SQL can be created to assume the database name and contain only object names.

## Disadvantages

■ If tables are grouped into several databases, using this development approach likely will require code changes to promote code to production. In a single database approach, code is consistent from development to production because there is never a need to *qualify* the name of a table with the database name. In a multiple-database scenario, if a query is executed that refers to tables in different databases, at least one of the tables has to be qualified with the database name.

Consider an example with five developers. The first developer writes code against customerdb_1 and purchasedb_1, the second developer writes code against customerdb_2 and purchasedb_2, and so on. The following is an example of SQL access across databases:

```
select *
from customerdb_1..customer c, purchasedb_1..purchase p
where c.cust_id = p.cust_id
```

Migrating this code into the test or production environments requires changes because these environments likely would contain different database names (customerdb, purchasedb). You have to modify the code to arrive at the following statement:

```
select *
from customerdb..customer c, purchasedb..purchase p
where c.cust_id = p.cust_id
```

Changing code from one environment to the next is not recommended. Do not use the private database approach for multiple database implementations.

■ The amount of space required to support development increases. Each database will require the space necessary to hold a copy of all objects, procedures, and data. In addition, the minimum size of any SQL Server database is the larger of the default database size (normally configured for 2MB) or the size of the model database.

■ The number of databases in the server increases. This complicates administrative tasks. It also can affect the recovery process because SQL Server recovers databases sequentially in database ID order.

> **NOTE**
>
> I was teaching a class once when the SQL Server was rebooted. Our training databases had database IDs of 70 to 80. It took about an hour for our training environment to become usable.

# Shared Database and Individual Objects and Data

In the shared database/individual objects and data approach, a single database (or databases) is used for development. Developers do not share objects or data. Each developer is a true user of the database. Objects are created, *and owned,* by the developer. The production objects are created by the user dbo. Code written by the developer does not refer to user name. The normal SQL Server procedure of looking for an object owned by you before looking for an object owned by dbo is leveraged. The SQL that is written acts against the developer's tables when executed in the development environment and against the dbo's tables when executed in the test and production environments.

## Advantages

- Each developer has an individual set of data. A developer has complete freedom to update, delete, and insert data without affecting other developers.

- Migration from the development environment to the production environment is easier. All developers work with the same database and object names. This ensures that any SQL created is identical in all environments. No code change due to different database or object names is necessary.

- Systems spanning multiple databases do not require modifications to promote to production (unlike the private database development approach) because the development environment database structure is identical to the production database structure.

## Disadvantages

- The number of tables in a single database can be large. A system with 100 tables and 10 developers will have 1,000 tables in the development database.

- Storage requirements are magnified by the number of developers as compared to the shared object approach.

#### NOTE

Each table and index requires 16KB (one extent) regardless of the amount of data in the table. Therefore, the storage requirements between a private database and a shared database/individual object approach should be equal.

In a private database approach, however, each developer database has its own free space. On average, the total amount of free space required in the private database approach is much greater than the shared free space in the shared database/individual objects approach.

Normally, a shared database/individual objects and data approach to development is recommended for multiple and single database installations. The individual database/individual objects and data approach is recommended for single database installations only.

> **WARNING**
>
> Your production requirements may not surface until after development has started. This approach does not work with a multiple database installation. If the decision to implement with multiple databases occurs after development starts, the shared database/individual objects and data approach can be adapted more easily to the new structure. You may be forced to change your development environment structure completely if you choose the individual database approach. Choose your approach carefully.

# Test Environment

There can be several test environments used in the software development life cycle (SDLC). You will test for function or performance. *Functional testing* is used to confirm that elements of an application or several distinct applications can work together. *Performance testing* is conducted to verify how the database performs under peak numbers of users, data size, or both.

## Functional Testing Environment

Most functional testing can be handled by a single SQL Server. Consider the following when planning this environment:

- An SQL Server used only for testing is *strongly preferred* because SQL Server should be configured for testing, and the configuration for your application may be different from the configuration needed for the testing of some other application.

- The hardware in which the SQL Server is running may or may not be dedicated. Dedicated hardware is useful in analysis because performance statistics gathered at the hardware level can be related easily to SQL Server, but you are testing functionality and usability across modules here, not performance.

- Objects are created by database administration. Often the files necessary to build the database's structures (DDL scripts) are part of a source code control system.

- There is only one copy of each object necessary to support the system. (A development environment may have several copies of each table.)

- If the tables in the system are physically organized into several databases for performance, recovery, or security reasons, there is only one copy of each database.

- All objects should be owned by the database owner (dbo). This supports the seamless migration of code from the development to the testing environments.

- A core set of data is created that is representative of production data. The amount of data does not need to represent production volumes, because it will be used to support feature, integration, and system testing.

- Logins and users of the test system should be representative of production users. This enforces the testing of the system in the same manner as it would be used by the actual production users. By simulating real users, potential problems such as improper permissions can be identified.

Development logins can be added to enable developers to add specific system test data or to assist in the creation of a core set of data. However, developers *should not* have the capability of changing the structure of tables or adding, dropping, or modifying any other existing object. Although developers may have access to tables to add or modify data, testing should be conducted using the logins of users representative of production users.

## Performance Testing Environment

Performance (or stress) testing should be handled by a different SQL Server than your functional testing environment. This environment will have similar features to the functional test environment, except for the recommendations for servers, hardware, and data:

- The SQL Server used for testing must be configured as it would be in production. Using an identically configured SQL Server is *necessary* because performance data captured is used to estimate production performance.

- The hardware wherein SQL Server is running should be configured identically to the production hardware so that statistics gathered can be considered representative of production performance. This environment is used to validate the system's capability of handling production loads.

- A core set of data, *representative of production volumes and content,* is created and loaded. The data in this environment is used to test the performance of the system under varying loads. To capture performance and load statistics that are representative of production, production type data must be used.

- Development logins are normally *not* added to the performance testing server. Logins are representative of production, and all modifications (data or structure) are conducted by database administration.

# Production Environment

The production environment is the last and most important environment in the SDLC. The production environment is under maximum control of database administration, and all defined production controls must be implemented and observed. This environment should have the following features:

- The SQL Server and database hardware used for production should be dedicated. A dedicated SQL Server is *preferred* because it greatly simplifies analysis of performance statistics captured at the SQL Server or hardware level. Most production implementations use dedicated hardware for the production SQL Server.

- An initial load of data may be required. Database administration normally is responsible for loading the core supporting data (code tables) as well as any other production data needed to support production use of the application.

- Logins and users are the actual production users. The only other logins added to this server should be for administration reasons. All modifications (data or structure) are conducted by database administration. Security standards and procedures are in place and enforced.

# Naming Standards

What's in a name? The answer to this simple question often takes organizations months—or even years—to define. Names should be chosen in a consistent manner across all SQL Server systems in your organization; for example, a word should not be abbreviated two different ways in two different places. Consistency with names is one of the building blocks of an infrastructure to which employees and users can become accustomed. Consistent naming enables employees to move from system to system (or software to software) and have basic expectations regarding names. This can help in the transition when learning a new environment.

> **NOTE**
>
> Naming standards are like filing standards: You have to think about the person who is storing the information and the person who will retrieve it. For the person defining the name, the choice should be automatic. For the person retrieving or accessing an object, the name should completely define its content without ambiguity.

Naming standards can be broken into two areas: SQL Server names and operating system names. *SQL Server names* are the names you specify in the SQL Server environment (databases, objects, and so on). *Operating system names* are the names you specify for files and directories.

## SQL Server Names

In SQL Server, you are responsible for naming the server, each user database, each object in the database (tables and columns, indexes, views) and any integrity constraints (rules, defaults, user datatypes, triggers, declarative constraints). Device names (disk and dump) have different parameters governing their names because they can be somewhat operating system–related.

Capitalization standards must be defined for each type of name. (Should names be in all capital letters, all lowercase letters, or mixed case?) This decision can be different for different groups of names (for example, server names could be in all capital letters and object names could be in mixed case).

Consider also whether to use an indicator of the item being named. For example, does the word database or the abbreviation DB get included in a database name? In the end, your standard should identify whether the customer database will be named `Customer`, `CUSTOMER`, `CustomerDB`, or `CUSTOMERDB`. For most database objects, the structure of names is the personal preference of the person writing the standard.

> **NOTE**
>
> A naming convention often debated within many shops is whether to use the underscore (_) character between descriptive words and/or indicators (for example, `sales_detail`) or mixed case (for example, `SalesDetail`). This author typically prefers using underscores, because it is, in my opinion, more readable and easier to type. Others tend to prefer the latter because it saves one character per word, which can help to keep names shorter and within size limitations without having to abbreviate as often. It also saves them from having to search for the underscore key on their keyboards. (If only we could convince computer manufacturers to design a standard keyboard with an underscore character that you don't need to use the Shift key to type, life would be near bliss!)
>
> The method you choose is entirely up to you and your (or your organization's) own preference. Throughout this chapter, I will attempt to switch between alternatives in the examples so as not to alienate either camp in this ongoing battle; I will provide you the opportunity to see both methods so you can decide which you prefer.

## Indicators

An *indicator* is a string of characters embedded in a name to indicate something about the type of object. In SQL Server, they are often used to indicate an object type. For example, `CurrDate_Def` could be used as a name for a default setting a column to the current date and time. There are two schools of thought on the use of indicators:

- An indicator is unnecessary because it can be retrieved from the system tables (the `type` column in the `sysobjects` table) or is indicated by the table from which you are selecting (`sysdatabases`, `sysservers`). Including it in the name is redundant and a waste of valuable characters. SQL Server limits names to 30 characters. Naming conventions may often further limit them to ensure compatibility with existing guidelines or other systems (for example, object names within a DB2 environment are limited to 18 characters). An indicator can easily take four or five characters (`_tbl` or `_view`, for example). This limits the number of available characters in an object name. Indicators can propagate (`Customer_Tbl_CIdx`), further reducing the number of available characters. When users need to use a name frequently, indicators also mean extra typing.

■ An indicator is needed because it simplifies reporting—a DBA can tell the type of object from just a listing of object names. Application designers are aware of what type of objects they are accessing (for example, the name tells them whether they are selecting from a table or a view). Indicators also enable you to use similar, meaningful names for two objects, once with each indicator (for example, `price_rule` and `price_default`).

> **NOTE**
>
> All object names within a database must be unique for the owner. In other words, the `dbo` may own only one object of any name. If you have a rule named `price_check`, you cannot create a constraint named `price_check`. This restriction applies to tables and views as well as rules, defaults, constraints, procedures, and triggers. Use indicators to avoid being constrained by these names, especially for objects with which users do not interact and whose names they will never type (rules, defaults, constraints, and triggers).
>
> Entries in `sysindexes` and `syscolumns` must be unique by table (only one index per table named `name_index`, only one column per table named `price`).
>
> User-defined types are not objects: they are stored in `systypes` instead. Names of types will not clash with objects, but it makes sense to qualify them by type.

If you decide to put an indicator in a name, it is best to make that indicator as short as possible. For object names based on an underlying table (constraints, triggers, indexes), the length of the indicator has an effect on the number of available characters used for the table name. For example, if you decide insert triggers will be identified by adding the indicator `_InsertTrigger` after the table name, the number of available characters that can be used for the table name can be no greater than 16 (30 characters minus 14 for the indicator). To give as much flexibility to the naming of an object, consider using an abbreviated indicator (such as `_tri`).

Indicators are sometimes placed at the beginning of the name, but you do not usually use this approach. Given an indicator of `tbl_`, a list of all object names groups the tables together. Although it's sometimes useful to list objects by type, you can do that in your SQL:

```
select name, type
from sysobjects
order by type
```

Table 34.1 lists the most common indicators used by SQL Server installations throughout the world. Consider that many sites choose no indicators at all.

## Table 34.1. Common SQL Server indicators.

| Item | Possible Indicators | Preferred |
|------|--------------------|-----------|
| Server | Server, _Server, _SERV, _serv, SERV, SRV | None |
| Database | _Database, _DATABASE, _DB, DB | DB |
| Table | Table, TABLE, T, TBL, _TBL, _tbl, _t, _T | None |
| Column | _col | None |
| Index | Clustered: ClusIdx, Cidx, _clus, _C, _CI, CI | |
| | Nonclustered: _Idx[#], Idx[#], NCIdx[#], NCI[#], _I[#] | _CI, _Idx[#] |
| View | V_, _V, _View, _VIEW | None |
| Rule | _Rul, _rul, _RUL, _rule, _RULE, R, _R, | _Rul |
| Default | _Def, _def, _DEF, _default, _DEFAULT, D, _D | _Def |
| User-defined datatype | _TYPE, _Type, TYPE, Type, _TYP, _Typ, TYP, Typ | _TYPE |
| Stored procedure | _Proc, _PROC, _Pr, _PR | _proc PROC, Proc, PR |
| Trigger | InsertTrigger, InsTrig, | _ITrg ITrg, _ITrg |
| Check constraint | _Check, _constraint, | _Check _con, _CkCon, _Chk |
| Primary key constraint | _PK, PK, _Pk, Pk | _PK |

*continues*

**Table 34.1. continued**

| Item | Possible Indicators | Preferred |
|------|---------------------|-----------|
| Unique constraint | _UniqueCons, _Unique, | _Uniq<br>_Uniq, _UN, _UQ |
| Foreign key constraint | _FK, RI | _FK |
| Data device | _DISK[#], _Disk[#],<br>_DATA[#], _Data[#],<br>_LOG[#], _Log[#], _IDX[#],<br>_Idx[#] | _Data1, _Log1,<br>_Idx1 |
| Dump device | TAPE[#], _Dump, _Tran,<br>_Log, _Tape[#], _Disk,<br>_DUMP, _TRAN, _LOG,<br>_TAPE[#], _DISK | _Dump, _Tran,<br>TAPE[#] |

# An Overall Approach

One approach is outlined in Table 34.2. You can use these standards at your site or develop your own. *Make sure you produce a matrix such as this to distribute to application development projects.*

**Table 34.2. Sample SQL Server name standards.**

| Item | Capitalization | Include Type Name? | Example |
|------|----------------|--------------------|---------|
| Server | ALL CAPS | No | CUST_DEVEL |
| Database | Mixed case | Yes | CustomerDB |
| Table | Mixed case | No | CustomerPurchase |
| Column | Mixed case | No | Age, Name, Address,<br>FaxNumber, HomeNumber |
| Index | Mixed case | Yes | (Format<br>of"TableName[C]Idx[#]" )<br>CustomerCIdx (clustered)<br>CustomerIdx3 (3rd nonclus) |

| Item | Capitalization | Include Type Name? | Example |
|---|---|---|---|
| View | Mixed case | No | `CaliforniaCustomer,` `PartialCustomer` |
| Rule | Mixed case | Yes | `ValidSSN_Rul,` `NonNegative_Rul` |
| Default | Mixed case | Yes | `Zero_Def, CurrDate_Def,` `CurrUser_Def` |
| User-defined datatypes | ALL CAPS | Yes | `SSN_TYPE, ADDRESS_TYPE,` `NAME_TYPE, PHONE_TYPE,` `COMMENT_TYPE, STATE_TYPE,` `ZIP_TYPE` |
| Stored Procedure | Mixed case | Yes | `Update_Customer_Proc,` `CheckInventory_Proc` |
| Triggers | Mixed case | Yes | `Customer_ITrg,` `Customer_DTrg,` `Customer_UTrg` |
| Constraints | Mixed case | Yes | `NonNegative_Check (check),` `Customer_Uniq (Uniqueness),` `Customer_PK (Primary Key),` `CustomerPurchase_RI (RI)` |
| Data devices | Mixed case | Yes | `Customer_DATA1,` `Customer_LOG1,` `Customer_Data1,` `Customer_Log1,` `DISK1, DATADISK1, LOGDISK1` |
| Dump devices | Mixed case | Yes | `Customer_Dump,` `CustomerDB_Tran,` `TAPE1` |

The standards outlined in this table are used throughout this chapter.

> **NOTE**
>
> It is probably not a good idea to use indicators in the names of tables or views. Many sites use the table name in the name of other objects. The inclusion of _tbl increases the number of redundant characters in the dependent object name (trigger, index, and so on). In addition, views exist to give users the feel that their queries are acting against a real table, although they actually are accessing a view. Therefore, the names should be identical in format, and should not contain anything that would distinguish one from the other (_tbl or _view, for example).

Your standards likely will be different, but the important thing is to be consistent in your implementation of names. Knowing the standards up front can save you days or weeks of costly name conversion changes (with SQL code, administration activities, and so on).

> **WARNING**
>
> In pre–System 10 versions of SQL Server, Sybase allowed you to use keywords such as primary, reference, user, and key as object identifiers. Because these are now keywords in version 10 and later of SQL Server, they can no longer be used. Be sure to check the list of reserved keywords for the release of SQL Server you are installing and avoid usage of these words as object identifiers.

## Naming the Server

Name servers according to function. For example, you would much rather have a server named DEVELOPMENT than a server named RSR8_AB100. Several companies name their servers according to cartoons or movies. There are Snow White servers (DOPEY, GRUMPY, DOC, and so on), Batman servers (BATMAN, ROBIN, JOKER, PENGUIN), and Mickey Mouse servers (MICKEY, MINNIE, GOOFY, DONALD). Although these names are fun, they should be used only for development or general server names as they don't convey any information as to the purpose of the server. Servers intended to support applications should be named in a consistent manner across *all* applications. The following is a good format:

systemname_environmentname

For the development of a Customer system, you might use CUST_DEVEL, CUST_TEST, and CUST_PROD servers.

## Naming Databases

Name databases according to their contents—for example, the type of data (customer or product) or activity (security or administration). A database containing security tables could be named

SecurityDB, and a database that contains customer data could be called CustomerDB. The name selected should be intuitive. (If a document is required to relate a database name to its contents, the name is probably not intuitive.) Some databases are named using a letter followed by three numbers. Would you rather have a database named B123 or ProductDB? *Avoid nondescriptive database names.*

## Tables, Views, and Columns

Table and view names should be representative of the underlying data. A customer table should be called Customer; a view of the California customers should be called CaliforniaCustomer. Some organizations like to use nondescriptive table names (TBL0001, for example). *Again, avoid nondescriptive table and view names.* If a name is not intuitive, a decode document may be required to relate the table name to its content. This delays development and makes it harder to write SQL statements. Column names should indicate the data in the column. Name a column containing the age of a customer Age or CustomerAge.

## Indexes

A table can have one clustered index and up to 249 nonclustered indexes. Index names should contain the table name and an indicator of the type of index. Some DBAs like to include the column as part of the index name, but compound indexes make this naming scheme difficult to implement. The following are examples of possible index names for the Customer table:

| Index Type | Identifier | Index Name |
|---|---|---|
| Clustered (max of 1) | _CIdx | Customer_CIdx |
| Nonclustered (up to 249) | _Idx[#] | Customer_Idx1, Customer_Idx2 |

**TIP**

Some application-development tools enable you to perform database administration activities. These tools may already have standard ways to construct names of indexes. Check whether you can modify the format or change your standards to accommodate this new format.

## Rules and Defaults

Rules and defaults are implemented at the database level and can be used across tables. Their names should be based on the function they are providing. A rule that checks for a valid age range could be called ValidAge_Rul, and a default placing the current date in a field could be called CurrDate_Def.

## User-Defined Datatypes

Here is a good format for user-defined types:

CONTENTS_TYPE

Because user-defined datatypes normally are targeted at certain types of columns, the name should contain the type of column for which it is used (SSN, PRICE, ADDRESS) followed by the indicator _TYPE.

## Stored Procedures

The name of a stored procedure should be meaningful and descriptive enough to indicate what actions are performed by the SQL statements within the stored procedure. For example, a stored procedure that inserts new entries into the Customer table would be called Insert_Customer_Proc.

SQL Server also allows the definition of customized system stored procedures. These must be created in the master database and begin with sp_. However, user-defined stored procedures should be named in a way to avoid conflict with existing or future Sybase-supplied system stored procedures. This prevents confusion as to whether a system stored procedure is a standard or user-defined stored procedure. It is recommended that an additional prefix be added to the procedure name after the sp_ to distinguish it from standard system stored procedures. This prefix is often an abbreviation of the company name. For example, a custom system stored procedure to display device usage by database for the XYZ Company would be named sp_XYZ_disk_usage. The XYZ indicator identifies this system procedure as one created by the XYZ Company and prevents it from conflicting with Sybase-supplied stored procedures.

## Triggers

Trigger names should consist of the table name and an indicator of the trigger action (insert, update, delete). A good format is TableName_[IUD]Trg, as shown in the following example:

| Object Type | Object Name |
| --- | --- |
| Table name | Customer |
| Insert trigger | Customer_ITrg |
| Delete trigger | Customer_DTrg |
| Update trigger | Customer_UTrg |
| Update and delete trigger | Customer_UDTrg |

> **NOTE**
>
> The indicator consists of seven characters maximum (_IUDTrg, for example). To avoid abbreviation problems, no table name should be greater than 23 characters (30–7).

## Constraints

Constraint names vary based on the scope of the constraint. Constraints can be used to check for valid values, add unique or primary keys, and establish relationships between tables (foreign keys).

A *check constraint* checks for valid values in a column or number of columns. Its name should indicate the column(s) and type of check.

*Unique* and *primary key constraints* are based on a table and should contain the table name and an indicator (_PK or _Uniq).

A *foreign key constraint* implements referential integrity between two tables. Its name should contain the tables or columns involved in the relationship and an indicator (_FK or _RI). Table 34.3 shows a sample list of constraint indicators and names for the customer table.

**Table 34.3. Sample constraint indicators and names.**

| Constraint Type | Indicator | Name Based On | Constraint Name |
|---|---|---|---|
| Check constraint | _Check | Column(s) | ValidAge_Check |
| Primary key constraint | _PK | Table | Customer_PK |
| Unique key constraint | _Uniq | Table | Customer_Uniq |
| Foreign key constraint | _FK | Related tables and/or columns | CustomerPurchase_FK |

> **WARNING**
>
> Remember that constraints are objects; for an owner, their names must be unique among all objects within the database. You may want to qualify the constraint name by including the table name as well. (In Table 34.3, different tables might contain columns named `ValidAge` and their check constraint names would clash.) If you decide to include table names in your constraint names, you face a serious limitation in the length of table and column names.
>
> For example, if you have a table called `Institution` and a check constraint on the column `Date_of_Enrollment`, the constraint might be named with the following:
>
> ```
> Institution_Date_of_Enrollment_Check
> ```
>
> This is much longer than the name length limit. The only realistic solution is to abbreviate the name, but that requires having the person creating the constraint and the person retrieving information about it both knowing the abbreviation rules. You may wish to implement standards for abbreviations as described later in this chapter.
>
> Table-level constraints can evaluate many columns. Include in your naming standard the method of naming table-level constraints. For example, the constraint requiring an invoice amount to be greater than zero whenever the type is `"SALE"` might look like this:
>
> ```
> constraint Invoice_AmtType_Check
> check ((amt > 0) or (type <> "SALE"))
> ```
>
> Keep table and column names fairly short, yet descriptive, particularly if you plan to use table names in check constraints.

# Database Device Naming Standards

A *database device* is physical space that is initialized with the `disk init` command. Once initialized, a device is available for use by any database (except for `master` and `model`). Selecting the logical name for a device is dependent on what *may* exist on that device and a DBA's confidence factor of the eventual use of that device. Devices can be named generically, by database, or by database contents.

## Generic Name

Devices can be named generically according to their number or general contents. For example, if you want to name a device according to number, you can use `DEVICE1`. This approach is flexible because any part of any database can be placed on the device without confusion. Tracking the databases created on a certain device cannot be easily inferred, however. It often is useful in performance analysis if the device can be easily mapped to a database, type of activity, or type of activity for a database.

Devices can be generically named to represent the *type* of data that will exist on that device (DATA1, LOG1, INDEX1). This provides the DBA with a guideline as to what portion of a database to place on each device. However, indicating the type of data expected on the device in the name can cause confusion if space constraints force you to create the data portion of a database on a device named LOG1.

> **NOTE**
>
> Once you begin placing database log segments on a device, the SQL Server prevents you from mistakenly placing database data segments on that same device. Go ahead and call a device "log-something" if you are planning to put a log on it immediately.

## Database Name

Devices can be named to represent the *database* that will be using the device. The device name can consist of the database name and a device number. For example, the four devices for the customer database might be named CustomerDB_dev1, CustomerDB_dev2, CustomerDB_dev3, and CustomerDB_dev4. The name indicates the database intended to be created on the device, but does not indicate the *type* of data. Therefore, log, data, and index data can be created on a device without confusion based on the device name. However, indicating the database expected on the device in the name can cause confusion if space constraints force you to create a different database on that device.

## Database Contents

Devices can be named to represent the *database* and the expected *contents* to be created on that device. The device name can consist of the database name and the type of contents (data, log, index). For example, the four devices for the customer database could be named CustomerDB_Data1, CustomerDB_Data2, CustomerDB_Log1, and CustomerDB_Idx1. The name indicates the database and the type of data expected to exist on the device. This naming scheme requires you to be *very* confident about the placement of databases.

> **NOTE**
>
> Experience has shown that early estimates of index, log, and data requirements are usually way off.

Name devices appropriately for your environment, based on the number of databases, whether certain data is placed on separate devices (log, index, data, and so on), and your confidence that the intended use of the device will not change. (It's probably best if a device named `CustDB_Data1` not be used for expansion of the `ProductDB` database.) VLDB environments are more likely to use the database-contents approach to naming, because databases normally span multiple disks and there is more flexibility for placement.

## Dump Device Naming Standards

Recall from Chapter 29, "Backing Up and Restoring Databases and Transaction Logs," that a dump device is created within the Server Manager or by using the `sp_addumpdevice` stored procedure. A *dump device* is used to back up an entire database or transaction log of a database to some type of media. Normally, this media is a local disk or a local tape device. You are required to provide the logical name and physical name of each dump device. The logical name is linked to the physical name. When dumping a database or transaction log, you can dump the database to the logical name (although the physical name can be supplied). The following are examples of three dump commands for the `CustomerDB` database:

```
dump database CustomerDB to CustomerDB_Dump
dump transaction CustomerDB to CustomerDB_Tran
dump database Customer DB to TAPE1
```

The logical name given to a dump device is normally based on the device type—tape or disk.

## Tape Devices

A tape device is usually attached or integrated with your database server hardware. These devices normally take 8mm or 4mm tapes, and the tape capacity can be as great as 8GB. Tape devices have simple names. The string TAPE followed by a number is a common approach to a generic tape device name. For example, if you have three tape devices, they could be named TAPE1, TAPE2, and TAPE3.

## Disk Devices

Disk device names should be selected with care. Dumping a database or log to disk creates a file on your file system. Each time a dump is executed to a disk device, a new file is created whether or not a file previously existed. If you have not moved the previous dump to a new filename, the file will be overwritten and *lost*. Databases or logs dumped to disk should be copied to a tape. Disk devices are often used in a development situation, due to the frequency of dumps and the inconvenience of tapes.

It is wise to create two disk dump devices for each database in your system—one for database dumps and one for transaction log dumps. Use the following format for the logical name:

```
DatabaseName_Dump
DatabaseName_Tran
```

Therefore, the `CustomerDB` database would have two dump devices created: `CustomerDB_Dump` and `CustomerDB_Tran`. Here is an example of the possible commands used to create these devices:

```
/* create a disk dump device for database dumping
** of the CustomerDB database*/
sp_addumpdevice "disk", CustomerDB_Dump,
    "/dbdumps/CustomerDB/Customer_DB.dmp"

/* create a disk dump device for transaction log dumping
** of the customer database*/
sp_addumpdevice "disk", CustomerDB_Tran,
    "/dbdumps/CustomerDB/Cust_DB.trn"
```

This approach has a number of benefits. Each database will have separate names for each type of dump. This eliminates the possibility of accidentally dumping the `CustomerDB` dump over the `ProductDB` dump. Additionally, a consistent naming standard enables you to more easily automate the backup process. Using uniquely named individual dump files for each database prevents a subsequent database dump from overwriting a dump file for another database should the SQL Executive Task Scheduler fail to move or rename the file for some reason.

# Operating System Names

You need to establish a naming standard for operating system files and directories. This standard is normally needed to organize DDL files. You need a DDL file for *every* important action and object that exists in SQL Server. This includes device creation, configuration changes (`sp_configure`), adding users and logins, creating and altering databases, creating objects (tables, views, indexes, and so on), and granting permissions. Place the files in directories organized to enable you to re-create an entire environment from scratch.

When creating directory and file names, you may have to abbreviate the names of databases or database objects in order to meet file naming restrictions of your operating system. In order to consistently name your objects and provide for understandable directory/file names, you will need to establish some standard for abbreviating names into filenames. Refer to the "Abbreviation Standards" section, later in this chapter.

## Directory Naming Standards

Specifying and organizing directory names should be based on your environment. Here are some important questions to answer:

- How many environments are you supporting (`CUSTOMER_DEVEL`, `CUSTOMER_SYSTEST`, `CUSTOMER_PERF`)?
- How many user databases exist in each server?
- Is there only one database or are multiple databases supported by the server?
- What is the approach to handling Data Definition Language files?

■ Are all the creation statements in a single file or is there a file per object?

■ Are index creation statements located in the same file as table creation statements?

■ How do you intend to grant permissions?

Assume the greatest complexity and level of detail, and devise a directory structure that can handle multiple SQL Servers and individual creation files for each object.

## Base Directory: Server Name

All DDLs for a server/environment should be stored relative to a base directory named according to the server name. For example, if you have three SQL Servers named CUSTOMER_DEVEL, CUSTOMER_TEST, and CUSTOMER_PROD, the base directories would be /CUST_DEV, /CUST_TEST, and /CUST_PROD, respectively.

The base directory should contain every necessary DDL statement to re-create the entire SQL Server. Separating the files from different SQL Server environments by directory enables different environments to contain different versions of the same file. This is helpful in regression testing.

## First Subdirectory: Database Name

Under the base directory for the server are subdirectories for each of the databases supported by the server. This includes all user databases *and* the system databases (master, model, and sybsystemprocs).

## User Databases

User databases are created to support applications. The name of the subdirectory should be identical to the database name. For the CustomerDB database in the CUST_DEV server, this is the directory name:

/CUST_DEV/Cust_DB

For each user database in the server, there are a number of subdirectories that can be created to hold the various DDL files. Table 34.4 lists possible subdirectories under the user database subdirectory.

## Table 34.4. Sample subdirectory names.

| Object or Activity | Subdirectory Name |
| --- | --- |
| Table | ../tbl |
| Index | ../idx |
| View | ../view |
| Rule | ../rul |
| Default | ../def |
| User-defined datatypes | ../type |
| Triggers | ../trg |
| Constraints | ../con |
| Permissions | ../grant |
| Stored procedure | ../proc |
| Remote procedure | ../rproc |
| Users | ../user |
| User-defined error messages | ../error |
| Threshold | ../thresh |

The directory containing the table creation statements for the `CustomerDB` database in the `CUST_DEVEL` server is the following:

```
/CUST_DEV/Cust_DB/tbl
```

The number of subdirectories under the database subdirectory is based on the level of granularity of your DDL files. Some sites like to put all creation statements in a single file. This gives you the least amount of control. To change the creation statement for a particular index, you might have to edit a 70,000-line file. The portion of the file for the index creation is copied into a temporary file or directly into an `isql` session for execution.

The next level of granularity is to put all creation statements of a particular type into a file, all the table creates in one file, and the index creates in another file. You still have the same problems with modification and execution, but you have a greater level of control (object type).

The last approach is to have a separate operating system file for each object in your system. This provides you with the maximum amount of control. Sites that use this approach normally save DDL files in a source code control system.

# The *master* Database

The master database subdirectory should contain all files necessary to re-create the base server and all user database structures. After the execution of the scripts in this subdirectory, the server is configured, disk devices are initialized, dump devices are added, logins and users are added, and all user databases are created.

You can use the following subdirectories for the master database:

| Object or Activity | Subdirectory Name |
| --- | --- |
| Configuration commands | ../config |
| Device creation (disk and dump) | ../device |
| Database creation, altering, and setting of options | ../dbcreate |
| User defined system stored procedures | ../sysprocs |
| Addition of logins and users | ../user |

The file to create the dump devices in the CUSTOMER_DEVEL server is /CUST_DEV/Cust_DB/device/ Custo_DB.dmp.

# The *model* Database

The model database subdirectory should contain all files necessary to re-create any applicable objects and/or users. The model database normally contains generic users, rules, defaults, user-defined datatypes, and user-defined error messages. These are the types of items you might want propagated to a new database.

You can use the following subdirectories for the model database:

| Object or Activity | Subdirectory Name |
| --- | --- |
| Rules | ../rul |
| Defaults | ../def |
| User-defined datatypes | ../type |
| User-defined error messages | ../error |
| Generic users | ../user |

You should be able to implement these guidelines, in some form, in your own organization. Note that user databases are handled differently than system databases.

# File Naming Standards

Name DDL files identically to the object names they are creating, with a concatenated indicator. Of course, the name of the DDL file should be based on its contents. The content of each file is based on the granularity of control needed in your system. A file that contains the create statements for all the objects in a database should not be run to re-create the Order table only. All DDL statements that do not pertain to Order should be deleted before running the script. However, if you have individual files for each object in your system, the Order table can be re-created easily. For example, a file containing the create statement for the Order table in the CustomerDB database in the development environment has this full path filename:

```
/CUST_DEV/Cust_DB/tbl/Order.sql
```

## File Extensions

It is common in some organizations to name a file with an extension indicating the type of object or activity. The philosophy is similar to indicators in SQL Server names. The extension may be redundant because you know the type of object being created by the name of the subdirectory (../tbl, ../rul, and so on). However, a file extension is normally provided as a matter of habit. The filename should be the concatenation of the object name and the extension. A rule called Price_Rul has a filename of PriceRul.rul. Notice the triple redundancy. A rule is created in the ../rul subdirectory with a filename of ValidPrice_Rul and a file extension of .rul. Consider that some sites do not use file extensions to indicate file type. Table 34.5 lists examples of filenames and extensions.

**Table 34.5. Sample filenames and extensions.**

| Object or Activity | Subdirectory Name | Extension |
|---|---|---|
| Table | ../tbl | .tbl |
| Index | ../idx | .idx |
| View | ../view | .vew |
| Rule | ../rul | .rul |
| Default | ../def | .def |
| User-defined datatypes | ../type | .typ |
| Triggers | ../trg | .trg |
| Constraints | ../con | .con |
| Permissions | ../grant | .gnt |
| Stored procedure | ../proc | .sp |

*continues*

## Table 34.5. continued

| *Object or Activity* | *Subdirectory Name* | *Extension* |
| --- | --- | --- |
| Remote procedure | `../rproc` | `.rpc` |
| Users | `../user` | `.usr` |
| User-defined error messages | `../error` | `.err` |
| Threshold | `../thresh` | `.thr` |
| Configuration commands | `../config` | `.cfg` |
| Device creation (disk and dump) | `../device` | `.dsk` `.dmp` |
| Database creation, altering, and setting of options | `../dbcreate` | `.cre, .alt,` `.opt` |
| Addition of logins and users | `../user` | `.lgn` `.usr` |

This author typically prefers letting the directory name indicate the type of object or activity the script file is associated with and using a generic extension of `.sql` or `\`. This is because most query or script management tools out there that run in the Windows environment look for and save files with one of those two extensions by default. It also makes it easier to set up an association between your script files and your query/script management tool of choice within the Windows or Windows NT File Manager.

## Source Code Control

Source code control software has been used for a number of years in the development of software to manage changes to application code (COBOL, C, and so on). Source code control software also can be used to manage changes to DDL. It often acts as a logbook, enabling only one person to check out a file at a time. Checking in a file normally requires text to be provided to indicate why the file was checked out. The version number of the file is incremented each time a file is checked in. Some sites decide to cross-reference the check-in statement with a database change request document.

Capabilities of "cutting a version" of a group of related files should be available. For example, 20 different source code files (each having its own revision number based on the number of times it was changed) can be used to create a C application. Cutting a version relates these 20 files together and logically groups them. Database changes happen for a reason. These changes usually parallel application changes that can be listed as part of the check-in comment.

Source code control gives DBAs a mechanism to manage different versions of the database effectively. Through using this tool, a DBA can identify what versions of DDL files to load to re-create a specific version of a database, object, or stored procedure.

# Abbreviation Standards

Due to limitations on the lengths of filenames and database object names, it often is necessary to abbreviate descriptive components of file and object names. It is recommended that abbreviation standards be included in your standards definitions so that all users and developers are using a consistent method of abbreviation to avoid confusion.

Some guidelines for applying abbreviations and keeping names shorter yet descriptive are as follows:

- Avoid the use of prepositions in the name (for example `BIRTH_DT` instead of `Date_of_Birth`)
- When abbreviation is necessary it is most beneficial to drop the least informative descriptors and abbreviate those which lend themselves most naturally to abbreviation.
- A common method of abbreviation is to remove all vowels from a word, similar to what you see on some vanity license plates.
- Use abbreviations consistently for common identifiers as defined by a master list of common abbreviations, similar to the example provided in Table 34.6.

**Table 34.6. Common abbreviations.**

| Base Word | Abbreviation |
| --- | --- |
| NAME | NM |
| NUMBER | NUM |
| CODE | CD |
| COUNT | CNT |
| AMOUNT | AMT |
| DATE | DT |
| TEXT | TXT |
| ADDRESS | ADDR |
| FLAG | FL |
| PERCENT | PCT |
| TIMESTAMP | TS |
| IDENTIFIER | ID |

# Summary

There are a number of SQL Server names to be defined in your environment. Too many SQL Server customers approach development without standards. This is likely to result in costly rework to bring an existing system up to standard once the standards are defined. Sometimes, customers decide not to change the database due to the cost of conversion. This results in a nonstandard SQL Server implementation in your environment.

Application standards are also important, but are not the focus of this chapter. You need to develop application standards to be able to build high-performing SQL Server applications consistently. The construction of SQL statements can have striking effects on query performance, and the uniform implementation of triggers, procedures, rules, defaults, and constraints is important in providing a consistent approach to developing SQL Server systems. This enables developers to develop more efficiently because a base structure is provided. It is important that you define standards as early as possible and monitor adherence.

It also is important to define naming standards as early as possible and stick with them. Naming standards apply to the operating system as well as to SQL Server. With a consistent approach to naming, you can build upon the underlying structure. Scripts can be written to automate activities on the server, decreasing the overall workload.

# Administering Very Large SQL Server Databases

# 35

When administering a very large database (VLDB) environment, you should consider and re-examine a number of items in light of the special issues facing a VLDB. The main challenge of a VLDB is that everything is larger and maintenance tasks take considerably longer. VLDBs provide unique challenges that sometimes require unique solutions to administer them effectively.

# What Is a VLDB?

The first question most people ask about VLDBs is, "What actually is a VLDB?" When does a database become a VLDB?

For some people, it depends on how you define *very large*:

- A fixed size (for example, 2 GB, 20 GB, 200 GB, 4,000 GB)?
- When database restore time exceeds a certain threshold (for example, four days)?
- When you're not sure whether to order 25 or 30 more 2GB drives?

Generally, there is no easy way to quantify at what point a database becomes a VLDB. Possible definitions may include quantifiable parameters, but these tend to be rather subjective.

In our experience with VLDBs, we've come to prefer the following definition:

> A very large database is any database in which standard administrative procedures or design criteria fail to meet business needs due to the scale of the data.

In other words, whenever the size of the database causes you to redesign your maintenance procedures or redesign your database to meet maintenance requirements, you are dealing with a VLDB.

# VLDB Maintenance Issues

VLDBs present a number of issues for the database administrator. Here are the top issues regarding maintenance of a VLDB:

1. Time required to perform dumps and loads
2. Time required to perform necessary database consistency checks
3. Time and effort required to maintain data (that is, update statistics, re-establish fill factors, incremental data loads)
4. Purging/archiving data
5. Managing partitioned databases

In this chapter, we'll explore these issues and present guidelines for implementing solutions.

# Managing Database Dumps and Loads

Database dumps are necessary to provide recoverability in case of disaster. While disk mirroring is a viable method to protect you from data loss and system downtime due to disk failure, it doesn't protect you from other types of failures that can cause data loss. You still need database dumps in addition to disk mirroring to protect you from the following problems:

- Physical server failure
- SQL Server failure
- Database failure/corruption
- Table/index corruption
- Controller/disk failure
- User error

The main issue with database dumps and VLDBs is the duration of the database dumps. An SQL Server dump makes a physical copy of all of the used pages in a database; therefore, dump time is proportional to the amount of data in the database.

If the time required to backup a database is excessive, the time to restore it is even more so. During a database restore, SQL Server will replace all data pages in the existing database with the contents of the dump and initialize or "zero out" those pages not loaded. As a result, the load time is proportional to the size of the database.

The typical ratio between dump and load duration is approximately between 1:1.5 and 1:3. That is, if it takes 1 hour to dump the database, it could take up to approximately 3 hours to restore it.

> **NOTE**
>
> Dump time is proportional to the amount of used pages in the database and load time is proportional to the total size of the database. If you have a database defined that is 100 GB, but you are only storing 100 MB of data in it, the dump time will be the time it takes to dump 100 MB of data. The load time, however, includes the time it takes to load 100 MB of data plus the time it takes to "zero out" the other 9,900 MB of data pages. Therefore, the ratio between dump and load time could be substantially greater than the expected.
>
> This is often a good argument for not creating an oversized database. Keep it only somewhat larger than the existing data capacity, and increase the size as needed on available logical devices. This will help to reduce database load and run times of other maintenance operations such as dbcc checkalloc, which performs full database checks.

When developing a backup and recovery plan for VLDB environments, several items must be considered:

- What is the impact of corruption or database loss on the application, end users, or company?
- What is the allowable and anticipated duration for database recovery?
- What is the allowable and anticipated duration of database dumps?
- What is the allowable and anticipated time to perform database consistency checks?
- How large are the database dumps going to be, and what are your backup media types and capacities?
- Can database dumps be completed within defined maintenance window?
- Can the database be restored within an acceptable or required time frame?

The most important of these items will be the duration of dumps and loads. If you have an available maintenance window of 4 hours per evening to perform your database dumps and a full database dump takes 12 hours, what do you do? Conversely, if you have a requirement that the system, in the event of failure, be backed up and running within 2 hours, and a full database load takes 24 hours, how do you meet the recoverability requirements?

As stated earlier, because you're dealing with a VLDB, you'll need to take a more creative approach to database dumps and loads in order to meet your requirements.

The first thing we want to take a look at is how to speed up database dumps. One method available in SQL Server 10.0 and later is striping of database dumps to multiple dump devices. If you have four dump devices available and a full database dump to a single device takes 8 hours, dumping to four dump devices concurrently will take just over 2 hours.

Another issue to consider is whether dumps are performed locally or across the network. Dumps across the network will be inherently slower than a dump to a locally attached database device. For a VLDB, you'll want to dump locally.

Another approach often adopted by organizations working with VLDBs is to physically implement a single logical database as several smaller physical databases by partitioning the data. There are two advantages to this approach:

- Database dumps for multiple databases can be performed in parallel, minimizing total database dump time.
- Your unit of recovery is the size of one smaller failed database—a single 2GB database will load much faster than a 12GB database.

In order to meet your required dump/load times, you may need to make several database architecture choices. These choices include whether to horizontally or vertically partition your data across databases. This approach essentially breaks a VLDB into a number of "databaselets." Here are the advantages to multiple databases:

- If a database failure occurs in one of the databases, database activity may be able to continue in unaffected databases.

- Even if activity cannot continue in the event of a single database failure, the entire system can be up and running faster since the unit of recovery is smaller—only the smaller single database needs to be restored since other databases are unaffected.

- Dump load times can be reduced by allowing concurrent dumps of multiple databases.

- Static or archival data that doesn't need to be backed up on a daily basis can be segregated from online.

- It helps to avoid the need to change tapes if database size is less than tape capacity.

The disadvantages to partitioning a VLDB into multiple databases include the following:

- If there are any relationships between tables in different databases, activity may not be able to continue in unaffected databases.

- If there are any referential integrity constraints between tables in separate databases, you may lose referential integrity in event of a database failure.

- Spreading tables across multiple databases may require application changes to fully qualify table references.

# Developing a VLDB Backup/Restore Procedure

The following is a set of steps to follow in order to design and implement a backup/restore procedure for a VLDB:

1. Consider the amount of time you are willing to be "down" while performing a recovery (that is, what is the allowable impact of corruption or database loss).

   - If you need a database to be recovered within 8 hours, determine the size of a database that can be recovered in that amount of time.

2. Estimate table sizes for your database to determine partitioning sizes and options.

   - If you have a 40GB logical database, you may need to implement ten 4GB databases.

   - Are any single tables greater than 4 GBs?

   - How many tables can you fit in a database?

   - Are any tables candidates for partitioning based on this determination alone?

3. Develop your utopian administration schedule.

   - For every day during a month, determine what periods of time can be dedicated to administrative activities.

   - Hopefully, weekends will be available, but this is not always the case.

   - If you determine you have 5 hours per night to perform administrative activities, you need to determine what activities must be completed and then how they can be distributed over your available administrative time.

4. Determine the rate of the dump process.

   - Take into consideration backup media capacity, speed, and number.

   - Benchmark several scenarios.

   - Perform several database dumps, varying the number of dump devices (striped dumps) and the number of dump processes that can be performed concurrently.

5. Finalize your schedule and document accordingly.

# Checking Database Consistency

The database consistency checker (dbcc) is a systems administration tool that verifies (and, if necessary, repairs) pointers internal to a database and its structures. It is highly recommended that dbcc checks be run prior to any database dump to avoid dumping a corrupt database. The worst time to realize you have a bad page pointer is during recovery of a critical database and have the load process fail due to the inconsistency. (This would probably be a good time to update your resume!)

The dbcc commands will typically lock user tables, indexes, system tables, and/or databases when running. Certain dbcc commands, such as dbcc checkdb/checktable, are very I/O intensive. The more I/O required, the longer dbcc will take. These are the main issues with running dbcc in VLDBs.

Suppose you follow the recommendations and run your dbcc commands prior to a database dump. If you have a daily administrative window of 8 hours, but the dbcc commands run for 4 hours and the database dump runs for 6 hours, how do you get everything to run within your administrative window?

In addition, although SQL Server allows dbccs to run while activity is ongoing in the database, the locking and I/O overhead incurred by dbcc activity may severely impact online performance. If the dbcc commands take several hours to run, this will more likely force you to run them online, negatively impacting system performance.

# Developing a Consistency Checking Plan

Your database may contain tables with very different processing requirements. While it is somewhat of a mystery how table corruption occurs, a static table is much less likely to encounter allocation problems than a highly active table with ongoing allocations/deallocations.

To develop a plan for effectively checking your database consistency in a VLDB, you first need to analyze your tables and rank them in order of importance. For example, where would a corruption have the most serious effect on your system?

Next, analyze each non-clustered index on your table and rank them in order of importance to determine which indexes are most important to check.

Plan to check your high activity tables as close to your dump as possible, because these tables are more likely to encounter allocation problems. You want to verify the consistency of these tables as close to the dump as possible. Static tables should only need to be checked after data loads. It is unlikely that corruption will occur once the data is loaded and indexes created. Therefore, it shouldn't be necessary to check the static tables on a daily basis.

You should always run `dbcc checkcatalog` immediately prior to the database dump. This `dbcc` command is relatively inexpensive to run and runs quickly, even on large databases. However, due to time constraints, the duration of your `checkalloc` and `checkdb` commands may not allow them to be run immediately before the dump.

Run `dbcc checkalloc` and `dbcc checkdb` for each database in your system to estimate execution times for your `dbcc` commands. Note the time needed for completion, running them serially (one after the other) and in parallel (multiple databases at the same time). It is probable that `dbcc checkalloc` and `dbcc checkdb` using either of these two methods cannot be completed in a reasonable time for most VLDBs. Thus, you'll need to develop a plan that breaks activities into smaller pieces.

Gather data into a table or spreadsheet, recording various `dbcc` times for your tables. Only the large tables in your system need this data. All others, such as code tables, may be grouped and are considered fairly negligible. Here are the commands you need to record times for:

- `dbcc checktable` for each large table
- `dbcc checktable`, skipping the checking of non-clustered indexes
- `dbcc tablealloc` for each large table
- `dbcc indexalloc` for each index on the large tables

Next, categorize each table as either "static" or "active." *Static tables* are tables that are not updated (or rarely updated) by the application (for example, tables containing only historical data). *Active tables* are tables where rows are inserted, updated, or deleted by the application on a regular basis. Rank the active tables based on importance to the overall success of the system.

In ranking the importance and criticality of a table, consider if the data exists only in SQL Server (is created as part of the application) or if it can be re-created or reloaded from other sources. For example, a purchase table may be updated continuously throughout the day by the application, but a product table may be re-created from a source table on a host machine.

For your static tables, list the frequency that data is added (for example, weekly, monthly, or yearly). This will determine the frequency with which you'll need to run your `dbcc` commands on the static tables.

If a non-clustered index is corrupted, it can be dropped and re-created as long as the base table is okay. Therefore, consistency of non-clustered indexes is of secondary priority. However, each index is used differently. For example, one index may be used in 80 percent of the queries, but another index may be used in only 3 percent of the queries. The frequently used index is much more important to the system and is a higher priority for checking than the infrequently used index.

Determine the amount of time you have to perform consistency checks in the batch window when you perform database dumps. You will use this period of time to determine which tables to check in that window. To be confident that a table is free of corruption, you'll need to run `dbcc checktable` and `dbcc tablealloc` on the table. Determine the time to perform both of these activities starting with the highest ranked activity table and work downward to determine which tables can be checked within your batch window.

If you can perform `dbccs` on all activity tables (`tablealloc` and `checktable`) within the batch window, start adding in the highest ranked index on each table and continue downward through the indexes until you determine which tables and indexes can be checked in the window before the dump. Also consider the possibility of running `checktable` and `tablealloc` on different tables concurrently as a way to accomplish more tasks in a limited time period.

If all active tables cannot be checked within a batch window, then during the next maintenance window, start with the point you left off during the last window. This way, over a certain time period (for example, two days, one week), you'll have checked all the critical, active tables in the database. Also plan to work in checks on your static tables as needed (weekends are a good time to run full checks on all tables).

When putting a consistency checking plan together, it is easy to concentrate on your application tables and forget about the system tables. It is possible for corruption to occur in system tables and is essential that you run `dbcc` commands on the system tables periodically as well.

Also, if you break up your `dbcc` commands by using `dbcc tablealloc` and `dbcc indexalloc`, these commands only look at the allocation pages in use for each table and index in the database. At some point, you'll want to run `dbcc checkalloc`, which checks all allocation pages in the database, including any allocation pages not currently in use, for any allocation page problems.

# Data Maintenance

In addition to performing database dumps and checking database consistency on a VLDB, there are other data maintenance commands that need to be performed on a database. These include updating statistics and purging/archiving data.

## Updating Statistics

SQL Server uses index statistics to choose the correct access path at query optimization time. SQL Server creates a statistics page for every index in the database at index creation time, but they are not kept up-to-date by SQL Server as data values change or data is updated or deleted.

The DBA will need to update statistics when the data distribution changes to ensure valid information is contained on the statistics page.

## Update Statistics Scheduling

Typically, you'll update statistics on your tables using the `update statistics` command on a table as follows:

```
update statistics customer
```

However, this would update the index statistics serially. The `update statistics` command requires a shared lock on the table for the length of time it takes for completion. This makes the table unavailable for update. On a very large table, this could be a significant period of time.

To speed up the `update statistics` process, you can update statistics concurrently on multiple indexes by executing `update statistics` commands in parallel.

For example, if you had a `customer` table with a clustered index named `customer_clus` and four non-clustered indexes named `customer_idx1`, `customer_idx2`, `customer_idx3`, and `customer_idx4`, create five files as such:

```
/* file 1*/
declare @starttime datetime
select @starttime = getdate()
update statistics customer(customer_clus)
select "The number of minutes to update statistics for customer_clus is:",
      datediff(mi, @starttime, getdate())
go
```

Create a similar file for each of the other four indexes and run the five `update statistics` processes in parallel. This will reduce the overall amount of time necessary to update statistics for all indexes on the table, making the table available to users quicker.

> **NOTE**
>
> If you are not using SMP-capable hardware, this may cause considerable strain on a single CPU system—be aware of other activities that are running during the same time period!

Determine possible periods during the week when the statistics can be updated with little or no impact to online users. For OLTP systems, this will likely be after business hours (during the maintenance window). For DSS/Data Warehouse systems, the activity is primarily read-only, so `update statistics` may be scheduled during business hours.

In a VLDB, you may not be able to update the statistics for all indexes on a table in a single maintenance window. With that in mind, consider spreading the updating of statistics across several days as part of your overall maintenance plan. In addition, you may want to put together an index maintenance plan based upon the usefulness and purpose of each index.

The distribution page is used by the query optimizer for estimating the number of matching rows for non-unique searches or range searches. If you have a unique index on a table and an SARG with an equality (=) operator, the optimizer knows one and only one row will match a single value. The distribution page is not used to estimate matching rows. For non-unique or range searches, the distribution page is used to estimate the number of matching rows within the range of values.

Indexes used in range retrievals will be your highest priority for updating the statistics. For a unique index used in single row lookups, the statistics will not need to be updated as often, if at all.

Consider a `customer` table with the following indexes:

1. `customer_id`: unique, non-clustered. Used for enforcement of uniqueness and single row searches by `customer_id`.

2. `state`, `last_name`: non-unique, clustered. Used to spread contention (activity is by `state`) and for 20 percent of the name searches.

3. `last_name`, `first_name`: non-unique, non-clustered. Used for 65 percent of the name searches.

4. `city`, `state`: non-unique, non-clustered. Used primarily for management reporting at the end of the month.

5. `phone`, `last_name`: non-unique, non-clustered. Used for 15 percent of online searches.

The maintenance plan for updating the index statistics might be this:

- Every Sunday, update indexes 3, 2, and 5 (or update index 3 on Sunday, index 2 on Tuesday, and index 5 on Friday) since these indexes are used on a regular basis.

- On the 25th of each month, update index 4 to support the execution of the monthly report.

- Updating statistics for index 1 is not required since the index statistics are not used by the optimizer for any of the queries using that index.

# Purge/Archive Procedures

At some point, the data in a VLDB may grow to a size approaching or exceeding the available database size. At this point, the decision will need to be made either to expand the database or, in order to purge or archive data, to free up space.

When purging or archiving data, a number of issues need to be addressed:

- Locking implications
- Performance implications
- Storage or retrieval of archived data

There are typically two ways of dealing with historical data, purging or archiving. *Purging* is the process of removing data from its current location via a delete process. *Archiving* is the process of moving data from its current location to an archival area via a delete and insert process.

To develop a purge or archive strategy, you'll need to project database growth over the expected life of your system. Is the database 100 GB in size, growing by 100 MB per year, or is it 500 GB in size, growing by 100 GB per year? Over 10 years, the first system would only grow to 101 GB. The second system, however, would grow to 1,500 GB. Considering physical limitations and the cost of dumps and dbccs, purging/archiving of data is absolutely critical.

If your growth estimates necessitate the need to remove data from your system periodically, you must decide whether to purge or archive. Here are the questions you must answer:

- Do current business requirements indicate which data is no longer of use to the company?
- Are there any legal requirements regarding data retention?
- Is it possible that data requirements may change in the future?
- Can the data be re-created from another source?

You must be able to identify the rows within a table to be purged or archived to be able to purge or archive data from your system. Some common data characteristics used to purge or archive data include:

- Time-based: Data is removed after a certain period of time. Common data elements that can be used are creation date or date of last activity.
- Non-time-based: Data is removed based on some element other than time—for example, geography (state), or a customer or product list (generated from some source).

Many systems are often designed, developed, and put into production with no regard to purge/ archive criteria. If the purge/archive process is not incorporated into the original system design, retrofitting a system to handle purge/archive criteria once it is in production can be extremely difficult and expensive. The time to identify purge/archive criteria is during the requirements analysis of a system, since it is possible that your purge/archive requirements will influence the database design.

To put together your purge/archive requirements and design your purge/archive process, you'll need to identify the following:

- How long data should remain in the table
- The frequency with which data will be purged/archived
- The element (column) in the table used to identify the rows to purge/archive

Whether you are purging or archiving data, rows must be deleted from the current table. There are four main areas of concern in purge/archive activities that also need to be factored into the design of the purge/archive process:

- Locking
- Logging
- Referential integrity
- Transactional integrity

## Locking and Performance Considerations

When deleting a large amount of data from a table, you must consider the locking implications of the delete and its impact on other online activities. SQL Server will escalate page level locks to a table level lock when the configured lock escalation point is reached by a single command during a transaction. Extensive archiving also acts as a batch process (which it is, in effect) and will grab an increasing share of a single processor's resources. Additionally, the I/O utilization for the affected disks can potentially create a bottleneck.

One way to avoid locking problems is to perform archival activities when users are not using the system. Other alternatives to avoid table level locks include the following:

- Using cursors to restrict rows being modified to one at a time
- Using the set rowcount option to affect a limited number of rows at a time
- Using some other site- or table-specific value to limit the number of pages being modified to less than the lock escalation threshold

If the clustered index is on the element used to identify the rows to purge in a table, the necessary rows will be organized in clustered index order on the data pages. The number of rows that may be deleted before a table lock is acquired is dependent upon the lock escalation threshold settings. The number of pages to be locked will need to be less than the lock escalation point to avoid a table level lock.

In SQL Server version 10.*x* and earlier, the lock escalation point was fixed at 200 pages. If a scan for a single command exceeded 200 page level locks on a table, SQL Server would attempt to escalate the page level locks to a table level lock. To prevent table level locks from being acquired during a `delete` process, it was necessary to write the `delete` process in such a way as to keep the `delete` command from exceeding 200 pages.

The number of rows that can be deleted in a pre–System 11 SQL Server before page level locks are escalated to a table level lock if the pages are contiguous would be this:

```
200 * (# of rows per page)
```

To be on the safe side, and to account for pages that are not completely filled, you should probably use a value less than 200 in the calculation, such as 150.

In SQL Server version 11.*x*, it is now possible to configure the lock escalation point at the server, database, or table level (see Chapters 15, "Locking and Performance," and 31, "Optimizing SQL Server Configuration Options" for more information on setting lock escalation thresholds) rather than having page locks escalate to table level locks at an arbitrary 200 pages. Two hundred pages is still the default escalation point.

If configured at the server or database level, a table level lock will not be requested unless a single command acquires more locks than configured by the lock promotion high water mark (HWM) or the lock promotion percentage (PCT), whichever is reached first.

The lock escalation point may also be configured at the table level in System 11 as well. This is accomplished using the `sp_setpglockpromote` stored procedure. This procedure allows you to configure a lock escalation point for a specific table that is different from the server defaults. When performing a deletion from a table for purge/archive purposes, you could reconfigure the escalation point higher for that table prior to running the `delete` process. This will help prevent a table level lock from being acquired and will improve concurrency on that table.

For example, to set the lock escalation point for the `pt_sample` table at 2,000 pages, issue the following command:

```
sp_setpglockpromote "table", pt_sample, null, 2000, 100
```

This sets the high water mark to 2,000 pages, leaves the low water mark at its current setting, and sets the percentage to 100. Therefore, a table level lock will not be requested until more than 2,000 pages are locked for the table.

> **WARNING**
>
> When increasing the lock escalation point for a table, database, or server, remember to make sure that the total number of allowable locks configured for the server is high enough to support the greater number of page locks that will be acquired so that SQL Server doesn't run out of available lock structures (see Chapter 30, "Configuring and Tuning the SQL Server").

Assuming that the lock promotion pct is left at the default of 100 (or 100 percent), then the number of rows that can be deleted in System 11 without a table lock escalation if the pages are contiguous would be this:

```
lock promotion hwm * (# of rows per page)
```

Again, you may wish to use a value less than the configured lock promotion hwm value to ensure that a table level lock is not acquired.

If the data is not clustered on the element you are using to find the rows to purge, then the pages to be locked are likely not to be contiguous, possibly a different page for each row. Therefore, you should assume that the number of rows that can be safely deleted at a time before a table lock is acquired is less than either 200 rows if you are running on System 10, or the lock promotion hwm if you are running on System 11. Again, assume fewer pages than the threshold to allow for index page locks in addition to data page locks and to prevent a table level lock from being acquired.

## Logging Considerations

Rows being deleted from a table are logged in the transaction log. You'll need to determine if your transaction log is large enough to handle the deletion of a large number of rows in a single transaction. Also, to minimize I/O contention, your log should be placed on a separate disk to distribute the I/O.

Also, although your transaction log may be large enough to handle a single deletion of 500,000 rows from a table, those records will remain in the log until they are dumped. Your purge/archive process should be designed to dump the transaction log after the completion of the purge process. This clears the log for the next purge process or normal system activity.

If your log is not large enough to handle the deletion as a single transaction, you will need to break the deletion into multiple transactions, dumping the log in between each.

## Referential Integrity Considerations

Data to be purged or archived may be spread across multiple related tables. You should consider the referential integrity implications when designing your purge/archive process.

If referential integrity is maintained via triggers, cascading delete triggers may exist on a table where data is to be removed. This could cause the deletion of rows from one table resulting in the deletion of even more rows from a related table. Even though your log may be able to handle the delete from the first table, the cascading effects could fill your log, causing the purge to fail. It could also lead to exclusive table locks throughout your system.

Alternatively, if declarative RI is used to enforce referential integrity or a delete trigger is designed to disallow the delete activity if rows exist in a related table, you'll be forced to delete from related foreign key tables first. Design the purge/archive activity to delete from the tables furthest removed from the base table and work inward to the base table.

If the purge/archive process is a batch job run during administrative periods, you could drop the triggers or RI constraints before running the purge/archive. If the purge/archive process is to be conducted during business hours, you will probably need to leave the triggers in place on the affected tables.

If there are cascading `delete` triggers, you'll need to perform deletes in small quantities, with regard to the number of rows deleted in each table in the relationship, in order to avoid table level locks being acquired by the purge/archive process.

## Transactional Integrity Considerations

A *transaction* is a logical unit of work. All activities in the transaction must complete successfully or they all should fail. During an archive process, you'll likely insert data into a table in a different database and remove the data from its current location. If an error occurs preventing the process form inserting the data into the new database, your archive process must not delete the data from its current database. Therefore, the insert/delete activity should be conducted in a transaction.

When archiving data with relationships across multiple tables, the design may require you to write transactions that transfer the data from all of the related tables before deleting any of the rows. You'll need to make sure your design considers multi-table relationships.

## Storage/Retrieval of Archived Data

To decide how and where you'll archive the data, you'll first need to answer some questions:

- How available does the archived data need to be?
- Does the system need close to real-time access to the data?
- What is the maximum amount of time your business can wait before having access to the data?
- What are any legal requirements for storage and security?

The answers to these questions will dictate whether the archived data must be stored online or can be saved into external storage locations such as `bcp` files.

Typically, the reason systems are designed with archive mechanisms is to separate infrequently accessed data from the frequently accessed data. With VLDBs, this is often required in order to be able to backup the active data in a reasonable time period, or to improve performance for the application that uses the most frequently accessed data.

"Old" data can often be handled on an exception basis; therefore, a delay in accessing the data may be acceptable to the business and the historical data need not be stored online.

# Possible Archive Solutions

If the data is accessed periodically (for example, more than several times per day), the data should be stored online. The data could be stored in a separate table in the same database or in a separate database.

If the data is accessed infrequently (for example, several times per month), the data can be stored externally with a mechanism to make the data available within a certain time period (minutes, hours, days).

If the data is rarely, if ever, accessed but must be maintained for legal purposes, some form of external storage is appropriate. The data could be stored in a database dump or in flat files.

# The Archive Process and Changes to Database Design

In addition to the problems and issues already discussed with purge/archive processes, another very important concern commonly overlooked is the structural changes to your database over time. Most databases will change over a period of time, even after the system is in production. It would be imprudent to ignore this fact when designing the purge/archive process.

Structural changes have much less of an impact on purge-only applications. If new columns are added to existing tables, they should have no effect on your purge application unless the field added is to become part of the key. If new tables are added to the schema, it should be fairly straightforward to accommodate the new table(s).

Structural changes can have a major effect on archive applications. Archived data must be accessible at a later point in time. You need to insulate your process against schema changes as much as possible. If archiving to flat files, also create a file with the table schema in place at the time of the archive so you have a record of the existing table structures. If you use version control software, you may be able to associate the version of the script file used to create the table with the archived table.

If you are using a database approach to archive data, design your application such that it detects a difference between the current application schema and the archive schema.

# Storage Alternatives for Archived Data

There are a number of options for storage of archival data. You can use any of the following media types for storing archived data:

- Tape
- Disk
- Optical Disk

There are advantages and disadvantages for each type of storage media. A possible solution is a combination of more than one device type, for example, storing recently archived data on disk and moving older data to tape or optical disk.

The advantages of archiving to tape include the "unlimited" capacity of tape storage, the reusability and low cost of tape storage, and the security and reliability of data stored on tape. However, databases archived to tape will take the longest to restore to an online state and it is more difficult to locate and access files on tape than on disk or optical disk.

The advantage of archiving to disk is that it provides the fastest access to archived data and makes archived files easy to locate. However, disk storage is the most expensive archival solution and the files are less secure. You'll still need to back up the disk to tape or optical disk to protect against data loss due to disk failure.

Archiving to optical disk provides the advantages of high reliability, secure storage, and easier access to archive files than tape. However, unless you use the more expensive re-writeable optical disk, disk platters can be used only once, and access times are slower than disk devices.

Data to be archived can be stored on any of the media types in any of the following formats:

- Database dumps
- bcp files
- Database device files

Database dumps are the simplest method of archiving an entire database. However, to restore the data, the destination database must be same size or larger than original database dumped and only the entire database can be restored, not individual tables.

bcp files provide an easier method to restore data to individual tables, and the data can be loaded into non–SQL Server databases if necessary.

One approach sometimes used for archiving data is to archive the device file(s) containing the database to be archived. Here are the typical steps to archiving a database using file system devices:

1. Freeze update activity on the database, set it to read-only, and checkpoint it.
2. Shut down SQL Server.
3. Copy the device file(s) containing the database to optical disk or another location on disk.
4. Restart SQL Server.

Here's how to restore a version of the database:

1. Shut down SQL Server.
2. Copy the device file(s) from optical disk or magnetic disk to the location of the archive database device(s).

3. Restart SQL Server.

4. You should now be working with an archived version of the database.

Dumping device files becomes a more complex procedure if a database spans multiple devices and it requires a shutdown of SQL Server to copy or replace a device file. This is probably not a viable approach in a production system. The advantage of this approach is that it is typically the fastest way to bring archived data online.

> **NOTE**
>
> Copying device files is not a backup method that is generally supported. It is presented here as it has been successfully implemented by a number of SQL Server customers.

# Data Partitioning Options

> **NOTE**
>
> The discussion of data partitioning in this section is related to logically partitioning your data and tables by modifying the database design. Do not confuse this with System 11 heap table partitioning, which is a way of physically partitioning a heap structure into multiple page chains. The logical database design is unaffected by this method of partitioning because it is considered one table in a single database. The advantage of physically partitioning page chains is to minimize I/O and page contention between multiple concurrent insert, update, and delete processes. Chapter 18, "Database Object Placement and Performance," presents this topic in more detail.

When dealing with VLDBs it may become necessary to partition the database due to SQL Server size limitations or in order to meet your backup and recovery or data maintenance requirements. Partitioning a database does come with some disadvantages. You'll need to consider these when considering database partitioning.

On the administrative side, you'll have more databases to track and backup and more databases to which you'll need to add users and setup permissions. Also, if any referential integrity exists between tables in different databases, you'll need some way to maintain referential integrity between databases during dump/load or if a database is unavailable.

There are two primary ways of partitioning databases: vertical partitioning and horizontal partitioning.

Vertical partitioning of data is the process of drawing imaginary lines through a database schema, and placing individual tables in different databases (see Figure 35.1). Alternatively, it may also involve partitioning individual tables by columns in order to separate the frequently accessed columns from infrequently accessed columns and placing the resulting tables in the same or different databases.

**FIGURE 35.1.**

*An example of vertical partitioning a large database across multiple databases to minimize the size of each individual recovery unit.*

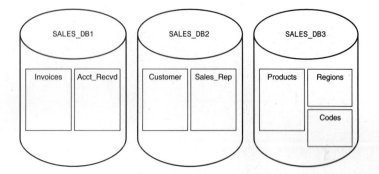

Horizontal partitioning of data involves breaking up tables into logical subsets and placing them into the same or different databases.

# Vertical Data Partitioning

The benefit of vertical partitioning over horizontal partitioning is that it simplifies administration because all data for a given table will be in a single table in a single database. Additionally, navigation and data access are simplified for end users since they do not need to know which portions of a table are in which database.

Another advantage of vertical partitioning is that you can hide the vertical partitioning from the end user or application developer through the use of views. If you split a table by columns (see Figure 35.2), you can create a view that joins the two table partitions. Users can then select from the view as if it were a single table. This approach also allows for the database containing the text table to have the `select into`/`bulkcopy` option on to allow for nonlogged text operations.

Also, no additional work is needed to join across databases other than full name qualification (a standard programming practice in many shops anyway). You need no additional programming to handle multi-database transactions because SQL Server automatically synchronizes transaction logs across databases if necessary in a single-server environment.

The drawback to vertical partitioning is that if you break up a database by drawing lines through the schema, and if relational integrity must be maintained across those lines, recovering an individual unit may be tricky or impossible while maintaining the referential integrity between units. Backups must be orchestrated and coordinated between databases to maximize RI and minimize recovery time.

**FIGURE 35.2.**

*An example of a vertical partitioning of a table to separate the infrequently accessed text data from the primary table data.*

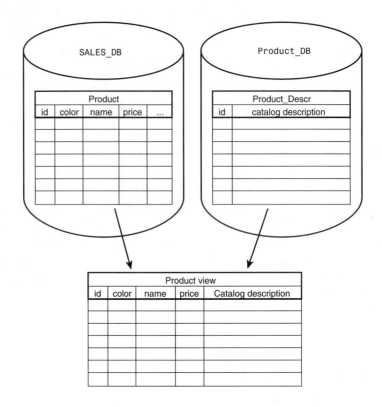

Also, the loss of a single database may cause navigational problems across the entire database or application if necessary tables are not accessible.

When partitioning vertically, you must identify which are the most heavily accessed components of the database in order to spread them across databases or devices. This will enable you to gain maximum performance by minimizing I/O contention.

---

**TIP**

While moving tables around different databases to balance I/O, application developers will be required to modify their code to properly reference the tables.

You might want to consider creating a lookup table containing a list of tables and the databases in which they reside. Application programmers can use this lookup table in their code to dynamically qualify the table names.

Another alternative is to create views in a single database that hides the actual location of the tables from the end users and developers.

# Horizontal Data Partitioning

One of the primary reasons for and advantages of horizontal partitioning in a VLDB is to separate active data from historical or inactive data. This helps to speed access of the active data by keeping it in a smaller table. Users do not need to wade through a lot of historical data to access the current data they need most frequently.

Alternatively, tables may need to be partitioned horizontally to spread activity across databases or devices, minimize locking overhead and contention, or to improve performance for table access. Horizontal partitioning can also serve as a security mechanism by allowing access to specific subcomponents of data through database security.

The main drawback to horizontal partitioning is that to retrieve data from more than one table as a single result set requires the use of the UNION statement. For example, if you partition an orders table by year into separate databases, pulling data together for a three-year period would require the following command:

```
select name, state, order_num
    from address a, customer c, db1994.orders o
    where a.custid = c.custid
    and c.custid = o.custid
union
select name, state, order_num
    from address a, customer c, db1993.orders o
    where a.custid = c.custid
    and c.custid = o.custid
union
select name, state, order_num
    from address a, customer c, db1992.orders o
    where a.custid = c.custid
    and c.custid = o.custid
    order by state, name, order_num
```

Unlike vertical partitioning, you cannot hide horizontal partitions from the end user using views. The UNION is not allowed in a view. Queries requiring data from multiple tables will have to explicitly include the UNION statement. If you redefine your partitions and move tables around, your users and application developers will need to update their queries or application code to reflect the changes.

Horizontal partitioning is usually structured using a logical boundary such as a datetime field, geographical location, department number, or other logical grouping value (see Figure 35.3). The advantage to this approach is that it is easy to determine the location of data. However, logical groupings may not provide an even breakup of your tables or certain logical groupings may be more active than others. If you want to spread your data out evenly and randomly spread the access, you might consider using a random *hash partitioning* scheme.

The approach shown in Figure 35.3 allows for the previous year's inactive and static data to be stored in a database separate from the active, current year data that needs to be backed up nightly. At the end of the fiscal year, the current database is renamed and made a historical database, and a new SALES_CURR_DB database is created.

**FIGURE 35.3.**

*An example of a horizontal partitioning of sales data by year across databases.*

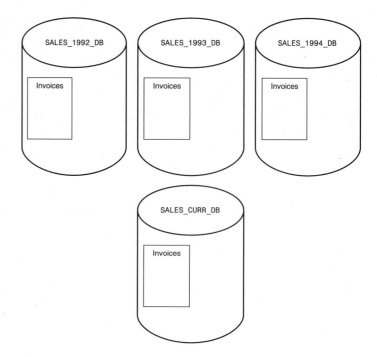

Hash partitioning is a horizontal partitioning scheme based on a derived hash key, rather than along logical boundaries. The hash key is usually generated by using an algorithm to generate some random value. The benefits of a hashing approach are realized if you are experiencing performance problems with hot spots in your data. Hashing the table is a way of randomly spreading the data across resources, balancing the I/O and data access.

The main drawback to a hashing scheme is that it is harder for end users to determine where the data resides. It is also more difficult to determine the logical recovery unit if a single partition is lost. When using a logical boundary for partitioning your data—for instance, by fiscal year—in the event of loss of a single table, you can rebuild the table by loading the data for that fiscal year. With a hash partition, it is more difficult to determine which rows were lost, and rebuilding the table may require reloading data from multiple source files.

# Summary

Although not originally designed as a data warehousing system, SQL Server is capable of handling large data volumes. The proof is in the fact that a number of people have successfully implemented VLDBs in SQL Server. This is not to say that there aren't a few bumps in the road to making a VLDB work. It will require some advance planning, and at times, creative solutions to deal with the size-related limitations of SQL Server. Fortunately, the current releases of SQL Server have begun to address the VLDB issues and problems with features like heap table partitioning, improved dbcc performance, and configurable lock escalation thresholds. This will make your job as an SQL Server administrator of a VLDB a little bit easier.

# Introduction to Open Client Programming

**V**

**PART**

# DB-Library Programming

# 36

In this chapter and the following two chapters, we'll discuss how to create client applications that interact with SQL Server. These chapters are by no means a complete resource; the intention is to introduce you to the basics of DB-Library, ct-Library, and ODBC programming.

DB-Library is an older technology that is still useful today. A DB-Library application is capable of talking to any version of Sybase (or Microsoft) SQL Server, from the early 4.*x* releases to the newest System 11. ct-Library allows the newer capabilities of System 10 and System 11 to be utilized by an application developer. Client-side cursor support and larger packet sizes are two examples of the functionality granted by this newer library. ODBC is a proposed Microsoft standard that allows a single application to talk to many different kinds of databases, from a Sybase System 11 server running on a UNIX box to a local Access database to an old xBase file on the network. ODBC incurs additional overhead using the Sybase ODBC driver, but gives applications great flexibility.

Examples will be provided in Visual Basic. There are some limited examples provided in C. Visual Basic examples are created using Visual Basic v3.0, with the Microsoft VBSQL object as the interface to DB-Library. C examples have been compiled using Visual C++ v1.5 for the 16-bit Windows environment. The development platform is an NT workstation running v3.51 build 1057.

# Essential Pieces of a DB-Library Client

Each DB-Library program has several essential pieces: entry code, opening a connection to the server, a message handler to process messages from the server, an error handler to process errors from the DB-Library, submitting queries to the server, processing results, and exit code. Examples of all of these pieces will be provided as we progress in this chapter.

In Figure 36.1, note that the message and error handler do not connect directly to the main program. This is because these routines are called directly by the DB-Library layer. In C, the functions are registered with DB-Library and pointers to the functions are passed into the DB-Lib layer. When a message occurs, it is passed from the server to the DB-Lib layer, which, in turn calls the message handler. When errors occur, the DB-Library detects them and fires the error handler. In VB, these functions are registered during initialization, and an event is fired from the VBSQL object. In either case, processing picks up where it left off after the appropriate function exits. See the sections titled "The Message Handler" and "The Error Handler" for a more detailed discussion on these handlers.

**FIGURE 36.1.**

*A flowchart of a simplified DB-Library program.*

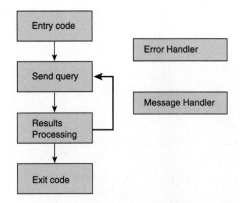

# Entry Code

Entry code is very short and simple. The first step is to initialize the Library. In VB, this also registers the message and error handlers.

In C, registration occurs separately, and is made more complex with the introduction of the two callback functions. Registration of the message and error handlers can occur at any time after calling dbinit(), although typically all three of these functions are grouped together. A good place to call the initialization code is after receiving the WM_CREATE message for your application's main window. (For those of you who are new to Windows programming, the following C code would appear in the function named in your CreateWindow() call inside of WinMain().)

Here's the code for VB:

```
VersionInfo$ = SqlInit()
```

Here's the code for C:

```
static FARPROC lpdbwinMessageHandler;
static FARPROC lpdbwinErrorHandler;
switch (message){
case WM_CREATE:
(...other window creation code here...)
        if (dbinit() == FAIL) return (-1)
 /* Returning -1 from WM_CREATE indicates Window creation failed */;

    lpdbwinMessageHandler = MakeProcInstance((FARPROC)dbwinMessageHandler,
    ➥hInst);
    lpdbwinErrorHandler = MakeProcInstance((FARPROC)dbwinErrorHandler, hInst);
    dberrhandle(lbdbwinErrorHandler);
    dbmsghandle(lpdbwinMessageHandler);
    break;
```

> **WARNING**
>
> If `dbinit()` returns `FAIL` or `VersionInfo$` = `""`, initialization of DB-Library has failed. A well written program must anticipate this and exit gracefully. Calling other DB-Lib functions before successfully initializing the library will be fatal.

# Opening a Connection

Once initialization has been done, it's time to open a connection to the server. Up to 25 connections are available by default. Microsoft's VBSQL object can manage up to 45 separate connections from a single object by calling `SqlSetMaxProcs()`. In C, this number may be increased with `dbsetmaxprocs()`.

When opening a connection to the server, a login record is first allocated within your local DB-Library. This login record holds several pieces of information relevant to the connection, which must be set inside of your application. Two of these parameters are required: the user name and the password. Optionally, a host name and application name can be provided. Finally, after the login structure has been populated, a connection can be opened to the server.

We'll go through each of these steps slowly. The complete code listing for opening a connection is shown at the end of this section. The following are code snippets that demonstrate allocation of a login structure.

Here's the code for VB:

```
ptrLogin% = SqlLogin%()
If ptrLogin% = 0 Then          ' some error encountered
     MsgBox "Error: cannot allocate a pointer to a login"
End If
```

Here's the code for C:

```
static LOGINREC *ptrLogin;
/* create a pointer to a login structure */
DBLOCKLIB();
/* Lock Windows DB-Lib; pre 10.0.3 lib only */
if((ptrLogin = dblogin()) != (LOGINREC *)NULL){
/* If ptrLogin is null, allocation has failed. */
(...)
     }
else
     MessageBox(hWnd, "Error: Cannot allocate a pointer to a login structure",
     "Example 1", MB_ICONSTOP);
DBUNLOCKLIB();     /* Unlock DB-Library */
```

> **NOTE**
>
> Locking and unlocking of the DB-Library is an operation peculiar to the Windows environment. After the release of Open Client v10.0.3, this was no longer necessary. Calling `DBLOCKLIB()` and `DBUNLOCKLIB()` has no net effect when using this client library.

Once a login structure has been allocated within DB-Library, you must set some of the parameters within the structure prior to opening a connection to the server. Both the user's name and password are required to login. It's a good idea to set the host name and the application name, too. The host name will show up in the output from sp_who, and is, according to general practice, the network name of the machine running the client application. Both the host name and the application name will appear in the sysprocesses table while this connection remains active. Well-behaved apps identify themselves to the SQL Server so that processes are easily identifiable.

Here, we set the user name, password, host name and application name. If any of the calls fail, it will return a zero, thus setting the whole logical expression to zero. The second example shows a simpler implementation, without extensive error checking.

Here's the code for VB:

```
If SqlSetLUser%(ptrLogin%, "sa") * SqlSetLPwd%(ptrLogin%, "ringding")
➡ *  SqlSetLHost%(ptrLogin%, "\\WESTOVER")
➡ *  SqlSetLApp%(ptrLogin%, "Example 36.1") = FAIL Then
      MsgBox "Error: cannot update login structure"
      SqlFreeLogin (ptrLogin%)    ' free the login structure
      Exit Sub
End If
```

Here's the code for C:

```
    DBSETLUSER(ptrLogin,(LPSTR)"sa");
/* set user name to sa*/
    DBSETLPWD(ptrLogin,(LPSTR)"ringding");
/* set the sa password in the login structure */
    DBSETLHOST(ptrLogin, (LPSTR)"\\WESTOVER");
/* set host name to the name of your machine, for example */
    DBSETLAPP(ptrLogin, (LPSTR)"Example 36.1");
```

After setting the appropriate values in the login structure, you're ready to ship it off to the server and establish a connection. This is very straightforward:

Here's the code for VB:

```
  SqlConn% = SqlOpen%(ptrLogin%, ServerName$)
  If SqlConn& = 0 Then MsgBox("Error: Cannot login to the server.",
➡"Example 1", MB_ICONSTOP)
  SqlFreeLogin (ptrLogin%)     ' free the login structure
```

Here's the code for C:

```
/* Open a connection to the SYBASE server.  NULL indicates failure. */
if((dbproc = dbopen(ptrLogin,(LPSTR)"SYBASE")) == (DBPROCESS *)NULL)
    MessageBox(hWnd, "Error: Cannot login to the server.",
    "Example 1", MB_ICONSTOP);

/* Deallocate login structure in DB-Library */
dbfreelogin(ptrLogin);
```

After opening a connection to the server, the information in the login structure is no longer needed, and the memory space that was allocated can be returned by calling `SqlFreeLogin()`/`dbfreelogin()`. Note that if several connections need to be opened at one time, the login space can be reused. For example, if `dbopen()` is called three times in succession, then three separate connections would be created based on the information in `ptrLogin`.

> **TIP**
>
> If you are using an old version of DB-Library, that is, prior to the Microsoft/Sybase split, you can retrieve a list of server names by calling the `SqlServerEnum()` or `dbserverenum()` function. This function can search locally or on the network for available servers. An example is provided later in the chapter, in the section titled "Cool Tricks and Handy Functions."
>
> Sybase stopped supporting this function in its newer clients. Calling it will return success immediately, but the server list will contain a single entry called "not support."

The following is a complete code listing containing everything in the "Opening a Connection" section of this book.

Here's the code for VB:

```
Dim VersionInfo$, ptrLogin%, SqlConn%

VersionInfo$ = SqlInit()

ptrLogin% = SqlLogin%()
If ptrLogin% = 0 Then        ' some error encountered
    MsgBox "Error: cannot allocate a pointer to a login"
End If

If SqlSetLUser%(ptrLogin%, "sa") * SqlSetLPwd%(ptrLogin%, "ringding")
➥* SqlSetLHost%(ptrLogin%, "\\WESTOVER")
➥* SqlSetLApp%(ptrLogin%, "Example 36.1") = FAIL Then
    MsgBox "Error: cannot update login structure"
    SqlFreeLogin (ptrLogin%)     ' free the login structure
    Exit Sub
End If
```

```
SqlConn% = SqlOpen%(ptrLogin%, ServerName$)
If SqlConn& = 0 Then MsgBox("Error: Cannot login to the server.",
➥"Example 1", MB_ICONSTOP)
SqlFreeLogin (ptrLogin%)    ' free the login structure
```

Here's the code for C:

```
static LOGINREC *ptrLogin;
/* create a pointer to a login structure */
DBLOCKLIB();
/* Lock the Windows DB-Library */
if((ptrLogin = dblogin()) != (LOGINREC *)NULL){
/* If ptrLogin is null, allocation has failed. */
    DBSETLUSER(ptrLogin,(LPSTR)"sa");
/* set user name to sa*/
    DBSETLPWD(ptrLogin,(LPSTR)"ringding");
/* set the sa password in the login structure */
    DBSETLHOST(ptrLogin, (LPSTR)"\\WESTOVER");
/* set host name to the name of your machine, for example */
    DBSETLAPP(ptrLogin, (LPSTR)"SQL Server Unleashed Example");
    /* Open a connection to the SYBASE server.  NULL indicates failure. */
    if((dbproc = dbopen(ptrLogin,(LPSTR)"SYBASE")) == (DBPROCESS *)NULL)
      MessageBox(hWnd, "Error: Cannot login to the server.",
      "Example 1", MB_ICONSTOP);
    dbfreelogin(ptrLogin);
/* Deallocate login structure in DB-Library */
    }
else
    MessageBox(hWnd, "Error: Cannot allocate a pointer to a login structure",
    "Example 1", MB_ICONSTOP);
DBUNLOCKLIB();                              /* Unlock library */
```

# The Message Handler

Defining a message handler is not necessarily required, but it is an essential part of even the simplest DB-Library applications. The message handler deals with messages from the server to the client, or in this case, from SQL Server to your application. The message handler will be fired whenever a print statement is executed by the server, or to report a problem to the client. Using print is common inside stored procedures to pass user-defined messages back to an application.

> **NOTE**
>
> Some common messages are Login failed and Incorrect syntax near…. You can view all system messages by running the query select * from sysmessages from the master database.

To better understand the relationship of the client program, DB-Library, and SQL server, consider the diagram shown in Figure 36.2.

**FIGURE 36.2.**

*Channels between SQL Server and your client application.*

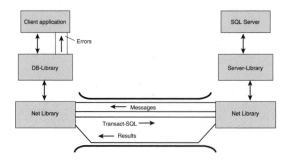

When your message handler is invoked, several parameters are passed in to it: the connection number, the message number, the error state number, the severity level, and the message text.

The connection number will correspond to the value returned by SqlOpen(). It is possible to receive a message that has either an invalid connection number or a connection number equal to zero. In this case, the connection is dead, and steps should be taken to disable it.

The message numbers can be used to trap particular messages. They are also useful for trouble-shooting: if a user is getting a particular message, he is more likely to report the message number verbatim than a message description. After you've received the message number, you can look it up yourself by issuing a select * from sysmessages where error=<msgnumber> query.

---

**TIP**

There are some messages that you'll want to trap and hide from your users. The first, 4002, is Login Failed. This message is followed directly by DB-Lib error number 10003. Only one of these should be displayed. Another message, 5701, is informational only. This message lets you know when your database context has changed. Usually, this message is less informative than annoying.

In the newest release of their client software, Sybase inexplicably changed the message numbers that DB-Library returns. Therefore, to ensure compatibility, you must also check for the new error numbers. These error numbers bear the same message text, but they are numbered in a different order and start at 20000.

---

Messages are also assigned a severity level. The severity level is either zero, or between 10 and 26. Severity levels describe the seriousness of the message. Informational messages are assigned a severity level of zero. The most serious messages (for example, Lock hash table linkage has been corrupted.) have a severity level of 26. Based on this, your program could, for example, pop a message box with an ICON_EXCLAMATION if the severity is over 18, pop an ICON_INFORMATION if the severity is between 10 and 18, or put the message on a status bar if the severity is zero.

One thing that you should be sure to do within your application is to detect deadlocks. If a deadlock occurs, and your process is chosen as the deadlock victim, message number 1207 will be passed into your handler. When this occurs, you may either resubmit the previous work or notify your user that a deadlock has occurred and allow the user to take action. Usually, simply resubmitting the work is the best option since this makes deadlocks, often a source of irritation, completely transparent to your users.

The following is an example of a simple message handler. This handler will display any non-informational message in a message box. It ignores the `Login failed` message and the `Database context has changed to...` message.

```
Sub vbsql_Message (SqlConn As Integer, Message As Long, State As Integer,
➡ Severity As Integer, MsgStr As String)
    Dim msg$, Title$, res%
    If Message <> 4002 And Message <> 5701 Then
        If Severity <> 0 Then
            Title$ = "Sql Server Message: Message=" & Message &
            ➡ " State=" & State & " Severity=" & Severity
                res% = MsgBox(MsgStr$, MB_ICONINFORMATION Or MB_OK, Title$)
        End If
    End If
End Sub
```

# The Error Handler

The error handler receives errors from DB-Library. These errors may report that an SQL server cannot be found, or that the connection has been broken, or that not enough memory is available for a connection to be opened. A list of errors is included in the VBSQL.BI constants file, or the sybdb.h include file.

The error handler, like the message handler, is passed a number of parameters. These parameters are the connection number causing the error, the severity of the error, the error number, and the error description.

Sometimes an error will occur from a dead connection. In this case, it is important to take steps within your handler to disable the connection. Attempting to send queries to a dead connection will fail.

> **TIP**
>
> One message that you should always trap and discard is number 10007, `General SQL Server Error`. This message will always be followed immediately by a message, which can be dealt with inside the message handler. It is often quite bothersome to users to recognize the same error twice within a client application. In the newest client release, the error number is 20018.

The following is a sample error handler. This error handler ignores the general error, checks for dead connections, and attempts a resynch with the SQL Server if a non-fatal error has occurred:

```
Sub vbsql_Error (SqlConn As Integer, Severity As Integer,
➥ErrorNum As Integer, ErrorStr As String, RetCode As Integer)
Dim msg$, Title$, ix%, res%

    ' suppress error message for general SQL Server error
    If ErrorNum <> 10007 and ErrorNum <> 20018 Then
        ' if the error killed the connection
        If SqlDead(SqlConn%) Or (SqlConn% = 0) Then
            Title$ = "Sql Server Error: Severity=" & Severity
            ➥& " ErrorNum=" & ErrorNum & " RetCode=" & RetCode
            MsgBox ErrorStr, MB_ICONEXCLAMATION, Title$
                ' Change the login icon to logged out
                frmMain.cbLogin.Value = False
            ' Set connection number to 0 for our array.
            ' Other routines will test SqlConn for zero
                SqlC(0).SqlConn% = 0
        End If
    Else
        ' connection is not dead, so just do
        ' normal message handling here

        ' set up and send a message box
    Title$ = "Sql Server Error: Severity=" & Severity
    ➥& " ErrorNum=" & ErrorNum & " RetCode=" & RetCode
        res% = MsgBox(ErrorStr, MB_ICONEXCLAMATION Or MB_OKCANCEL, Title$)
        End If

        Select Case ErrorNum
        Case SQLEBTOK     ' 10008 BAD TOKEN
        Case SQLETIME     ' 10024 CONNECTION TIMED OUT
        Case SQLEOOB      ' 10027 OUT OF BAND DATA
        Case SQLERPND     ' 10038 RESULTS PENDING
        Case SQLECSYN     ' 10039 SYNTAX ERROR IN SOURCE FIELD
        Case Else         ' ALL OTHER ERRORS
            Exit Sub            ' AVOID attempting a resynch
        End Select

        ' try resynch-ing with SqlOK%
        ' if both succeed then we're A-OK and running.
        If SqlOK%(SqlConn%) Then
          If SqlCancel%(SqlConn%) = FAIL Then
            ' logout
            frmMain.cbLogin.Value = False
          End If
        Else ' Sql not ok.
          frmMain.cbLogin.Value = False
        End If
    End If
    End If
End Sub
```

# Sending Queries

Once DB-Library has been initialized and the handlers have been defined, it is time to issue a query to the server. The first step in this task is accomplished with the SqlCmd() function:

```
res% = SqlCmd%(SqlConn%, " select * from sysmessages")
```

`SqlCmd` places SQL statements into the buffer inside DB-Library. This buffer is maintained until after a query is sent using `SqlExec` or `SqlSend` (see the code example). The next call to `SqlCmd()` after either of these function calls will clear the command buffer, unless the `SQLNOAUTOFREE` option is on.

Note that in the previous example, there is a space at the beginning of the query. This is simply defensive programming; if a query has been issued with `SqlCmd()`, and later in the code another `SqlCmd` puts more data into the command buffer, then the two queries could end up slapped together, as in `select * from sysmessagesselect getdate()`. A space never does damage, but it could prevent a silly error.

After placing the commands into the command buffer in DB-Library, they must be sent to the server. There are two functions to accomplish this: `SqlExec` and `SqlSend`.

Very simple query sending can be accomplished through the use of the `SqlExec()` function. When this function is called, the command buffer is sent, and the function waits until after the server has begun to return results before itself returning:

```
If SqlExec%(SqlConn%) = SUCCEED Then
(Do results processing here)
```

One of the problems with `SqlExec` is that it ties up your application while waiting for the SQL Server to return its results. During the time `SqlExec` is waiting, no other activity occurs inside your application, and the performance of other programs within Windows is affected. Also, if the results are not ready within the timeout period (by default, 60 seconds) `SqlExec` will give up on SQL Server and return `FAIL`.

To get over this problem, use `SqlSend`. `SqlSend` will send the command buffer and instantly return. You have assumed the responsibility for polling the server to determine if results are ready, but in the meantime your application (and your system) is free to do other things:

```
res% = SqlSend(SqlConn%)
```

### TIP

Use `SqlSend` to do most of the work in your application. `SqlExec` should be used for only the simplest queries.

# Retrieving Results

After sending the query, you must poll for results. One way to do this is inside a timer loop; call the timer once a second, or once every half second. Inside, use `SqlDataReady()` to determine whether results are prepared. If they are, call `SqlOK()` to begin retrieving results. An `SqlSend` immediately followed by an `SqlOK()` is the same thing as an `SqlExec()`:

```
If SqlDataReady%(SqlConn%) Then
        If SqlOk%(SqlConn%) Then
```

## WHY A TIMER IS BETTER THAN A LOOP

Under Windows, many processes are running together. Whether they're running in a multithreaded environment, like NT, or in a multitasking environment, like Windows for Workgroups or the standard Windows 3.1, your process is not alone. If you create a loop like this one:

```
While SqlDataReady(SqlConn%) = FAIL
Loop
```

you are fooling Windows into believing that your application has important work to do. This is bad. Using a timer (which, by the way, is a limited resource in the 16-bit Windows world) allows you to check for results now and then, and lets the rest of the system get on with whatever else it has to do.

After sending the query, regardless of the method you used, you must call a series of functions to retrieve the results of your query. First, call `SqlResults()`. This prepares the first result set for processing. Create a loop, like the one shown here:

```
res% = SqlResults%(SqlConn%)
Do Until res% = NOMORERESULTS or res% = FAIL
' Loop through each result set

    RowType% = SqlNextRow%(SqlConn%)
' RowType gets type of row

    Do Until RowType% = NOMOREROWS or RowType% = FAIL
' Loop through each row in the result set

        For Col% = 1 To NumCols%
            ColType% = SqlColType%(SqlConn%, Col%)
' ColType gets datatype of column

TheData$ = SqlData$(SqlConn%, Col%)
        ' TheData$ gets Result data
        Next Col%
    Loop
Loop
```

Of course, this code fragment doesn't actually use the data: something has to happen inside the column loop. You've probably noticed that all data returned using `SqlData()` is in the form of character data. What about numerical data? Well, for that, you need to use VB conversion functions such as `Val()`. All the data you receive will be in character format.

In the third line, we make a call to `SqlNextRow` to retrieve the data in the row. The return value of `SqlNextRow` will indicate whether this is a REGROW (regular row) or a compute row, in which case the value will be the (positive) identification number of the compute row. If `SqlNextRow` returns -2, or NOMOREROWS, the result set is exhausted.

> **NOTE**
>
> Empty result sets will still cause the creation of a result set and will return SUCCEED from
> SqlResults(), but they will return NOMOREROWS immediately when SqlNextRow() is
> called.

## Exit Code

After using the DB-Library, shut it down properly. Before exiting, make sure to call SqlWinExit().
It is also good practice to call SqlExit() prior to calling SqlWinExit(). SqlExit() closes all open
connections and frees all allocated login structures. It is identical to calling SqlClose() and
SqlFreeLogin() for each open connection and login structure.

> **TIP**
>
> Closing your connections prevents SQL Server from believing that your application is
> still running, and is proper etiquette for any application making use of SQL Server.
> Failing to close all connections before exiting will result in Null DB Process Pointer
> errors the next time a DB-Lib application runs. Often, this can lead to
> W3DBLIB.DLL becoming confused (corrupted in memory) and will force a Windows
> restart.

When you call SqlWinExit(), you inform the VBSQL object that your application is exiting.
The library releases the memory it used to track your application. In C, call dbwinexit() and
dbexit().

# Cool Tricks and Handy Functions

During the time that I've been programming DB-Library applications using Visual Basic, I've
come across some interesting and challenging problems. In this section, I'll discuss a few of the
most interesting functions I've added to my toolbox to solve these problems. My hope is that
you'll find these functions useful. Write me at 102101.164@compuserve.com and tell me how
you improved them.

## *GetServerList()*

One of the first functions I wrote for my VB/SQL toolbox was GetServerList(). This function populates a drop-down combo box with a list of all servers detected locally and/or on the
network. "Locally" here means either in WIN.INI or SQL.INI, depending on the version of
DB-Library being used. It returns the number of servers found:

```
Function GetServerList (cbx As ComboBox, mode%) As Integer
      ' Retrieves the list of servers from Win.INI
      ' or SQL.INI and/or the network
      ' parameters are ...
      ' cbx  = a combobox to be filled with server names
      ' mode = LOCSEARCH
      '          NETSEARCH (scan the network)
      '          LOCSEARCH + NETSEARCH (both)

      Dim RetVal%, Entries%, ix%, Char0$, Pos%, Length%
      Dim Buffer As String * 255
      Char0$ = Chr$(0)

      ' *** this function sets up the server names in the combo box ***
      ' if you use LOCSEARCH + NETSEARCH, both are searched, but if a
      ' server is available in both lists, it appears twice.

      ' clear the combo box if enumerating servers
      cbx.Clear

    Do
          RetVal% = SqlServerEnum%(mode%, Buffer$, Entries%)
          If RetVal% > 1 Then Exit Do      ' can't enumerate if > 1: error

          ' scan the buffer looking for Entries%
          Pos% = 1                         ' start in the first position
          For ix% = 1 To Entries%
                ' look for chr$(0) in String, which delimits server names
                Length% = InStr(Pos%, Buffer$, Char0$) - Pos%
                If Length% <= 0 Then Exit For ' this is an error case
                cbx.AddItem Mid$(Buffer$, Pos%, Length%)
                Pos% = Pos% + Length% + 1
          Next ix%
    Loop While RetVal% = MOREDATA%

      ' don't crash if there's no SQL Server entries!!
      If cbx.ListCount > 0 Then
            ' Set the list to the first server and
            ' return the # of servers found
            cbx.ListIndex = 0
            GetServerList = cbx.ListCount
      Else
            GetServerList = 0
      End If
End Function
```

If you install any of the utilities on the CD-ROM in the back of the book, you'll see this function every time you login to a server. All the work occurs inside the Do…Loop, where SqlServerEnum() is called.

**WARNING**

Many DB-Libraries will report an out-of-memory condition while calling SqlServerEnum(). This fires your error handler with error number 10000.

# GetTimeFromServer()

Sometimes it's useful to retrieve the time from the SQL Server. Once the time has been retrieved, it is possible to set the time on a client station to match that of the SQL Server, for example. Another good use for this function gives your application a dependable source of date and time for a log file. The SQL Server is a much better source for date and time than a PC client, since the PC is subject to the whims of the user and the state of the PC's battery.

The function accepts a connection number (returned from SqlOpen()) and an operation. The operation is just a fancy add-in that isn't critical to the workings of the function; it allows for different formats of the getdate() string. If the query fails for any reason, it's designed to return the client time. This might not be the best solution to failure; replace the error code with something else if you would like to be aware of failures from calling procedures:

```
Function GetTimeFromSQLServer (SqlConn%, nOp%) As String
Dim Query$, res%
' Accepts connection number and operation.
' The connection number must be established prior to calling
' this function.
' Operation is one of the following:
' SQLTM_ALL = 0      Return complete getdate() string
' SQLTM_DATE = 1     Return date portion only
' SQLTM_TIME = 2     Return time portion only
' SQLTM_ALL2 = 3     Differently formatted ALL;
'                    mm/dd/yy hh:mm (military)
'
    Select Case nOp%
        Case SQLTM_ALL
            Query$ = "select getdate()"
        Case SQLTM_DATE
            Query$ = "select convert(char(8), getdate(), 1)"
        Case SQLTM_TIME
            Query$ = "select convert(char(8), getdate(), 8)"
        Case SQLTM_ALL2
            Query$ = "select convert(char(8), getdate(), 1)"
              ➥ & " " & "convert(char(5), getdate(), 8)"
    End Select

    res% = SqlCmd%(SqlConn%, Query$)
    If SqlExec(SqlConn%) = FAIL Then GoTo GOErr:
    ' message handler fires here if there's an error
    res% = SqlResults%(SqlConn%)
    Do While res% <> NOMORERESULTS And res% <> FAIL
        res% = SqlNextRow%(SqlConn%)
        Do While res% <> NOMOREROWS And res% <> FAIL
            GetTimeFromSQLServer = SqlData(SqlConn%, 1)
            res% = SqlNextRow%(SqlConn%)
        Loop
        res% = SqlResults%(SqlConn%)
    Loop
Exit Function

GOErr:
    GetTimeFromSQLServer = Now
    Exit Function
End Function
```

# Retrieving Object Information

Another project I wrote required the application to retrieve the names of all databases available on the connected SQL server. From this list, the user selected one database, which caused the application to retrieve a list of tables in the selected database. This was repeated for indexes in the table.

Retrieving information like this can be extremely useful inside your applications. The following is code that populates a combo box. I placed the query to issue in the box's tag prior to calling `LoadCombo()`.

If you have ever run a copy of the Aurora Distribution Viewer, you can now grin smugly whenever you use it—you now know how we did the interface work! A screen shot of the Distribution Viewer follows this code snippet:

```
Sub LoadCombo (SqlConn%, Box As ComboBox)
On Error GoTo LCHandler
    If SqlCmd(SqlConn%, CStr(Box.Tag)) Then
        If SqlExec(SqlConn%) Then
            If SqlResults(SqlConn%) <> NOMORERESULTS Then
                Box.Clear
                Do Until SqlNextRow%(SqlConn%) = NOMOREROWS
                    Box.AddItem SqlData(SqlConn%, 1)
                Loop
                If Box.ListCount > 0 Then Box.ListIndex = 0
            End If
        End If
    End If
Exit Sub

LCHandler:
If Err = 7 Then
' Out of memory: Some yahoo with over 32,767 tables,
' databases, or indexes.
    Dim t$
    Select Case Box
        Case Box Is frmMain.cbxDatabase
            t$ = "databases"
        Case Box Is frmMain.cbxTable
            t$ = "tables"
        Case Box Is frmMain.cbxIndex
            t$ = "indexes"
    End Select
    MsgBox ("Only the first 32,767 " & t$ & " will appear in the combo box.")
End If
Exit Sub
End Sub
```

**FIGURE 36.3.**

*The Aurora Distribution Viewer, using the code described in* `LoadCombo()`.

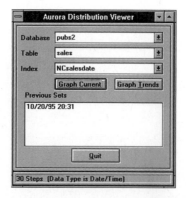

The queries attached to the combo boxes are listed in the following code. The database selected by the user is used so that it is the current database for each of the queries. Note that in the last query, the `object_id` for the table specified in `cbxTable` is used, which must be passed to SQL Server in quotes:

```
cbxDatabase.Tag = "select name from master..sysdatabases"
cbxTable.Tag = "select name from sysobjects where type = 'U' order by name"
cbxIndex.Tag = "select name from sysindexes where id=object_id(" +
➥QUOTE + CStr(cbxTable) + QUOTE + ") and indid > 0 order by indid"
```

# Programming Pitfalls

When programming DB-Library, there were a few things I ran into on the highway of VB code—some of them at 120 MPH. Listed here are a few of the specific things about which a beginning DB-Library programmer should be aware.

- *Versions of SQL Server behave differently.* This is a simple, but important, issue to the beginning DB-Library programmer. The version of the SQL Server can be retrieved by issuing a `select @@version` query and parsing the results.

- `NULL DBPROCESS` *pointers can surprise you.* If another application has mistreated DB-Library, or if one of your own applications terminates unexpectedly, (a General Protection Fault, for example) a `NULL DBPROCESS` pointer error can occur. This is error number 10001. When your application starts, if a `NULL DBPROCESS` error occurs, it will fire your error handler as soon as it is installed. Anticipate this by either making the 10001 error transparent or treating it as a special case, or both.

- *The connection to the SQL Server flows only one way at a time.* Recall the diagram in Figure 36.2. In this diagram there is a pipe between the client and server, along which flows SQL commands and query results. Now, keep in mind that if results are flowing through the pipe, no commands can be sent until all results have been processed. Any attempt to do so will cause error number 10038, `Attempt to initiate a new SQL`

`Server operation with results pending.` Following this error, DB-Library often becomes unstable. You should take pains in every DB-Lib project to avoid sending queries on a connection that is currently waiting for results.

■ *The versions of the DB-Library and the net-library .DLLs are heavily dependent upon one another.* Both Sybase and Microsoft have their own versions of the Windows 16-bit DB-Library, named W3DBLIB.DLL. There are lots of these around; one is bundled with the Visual Basic VBSQL.VBX, one comes with the Sybase Open Client installation, one comes with the Microsoft Client Installation, many third party apps include versions, etcetera ad infinitum.

Now, take this problem and square it, because the same thing has happened with net libraries. There are net libraries for named pipes, TCP/IP Windows Sockets, Novell SPX, and many others.

This mess is complicated by the fact that, as a third party, your ability to redistribute these libraries is severely restricted. Simply finding a pair of libraries that can live in peace is not enough; afterward, you need to find a way to get your users to install similarly agreeable libraries. The solution I use is to distribute no libraries and let the user take care of it on his end. Overwriting a library that worked before is an experience no technical support person wants.

# Summary

DB-Library applications are relatively simple to create. Once the basics of the library are clearly understood, creating simple DB-Lib apps is easy. After that, all that is left to do is to create an interface.

Using Visual Basic to go against data on an SQL Server is a smart decision. If your applications are performing CPU-intensive operations, externalize them in a .DLL written in C for maximum speed. Using VB to program your DB-Lib apps ensures a simpler interface for development and maintenance.

Write clever message and error handlers to manage errors generated by SQL Server and the DB-Library itself. The ability to define these handlers allows your application to account for most eventualities.

This concludes our overview of DB-Library. Whether to use DB-Library, ct-Library, or ODBC is a question that we'll discuss in the next chapters.

# ct-Library
# Programming

# 37

Sybase has developed and released a newer, more powerful, more flexible, but more complicated API to allow access to data on Sybase servers. If applications are being designed for use strictly with System 10 or later Sybase servers, ct-Lib offers many advantages over the older DB-Library. Some examples of these advantages are the capability to use larger packets to communicate with the Sybase SQL Server, improved support for client-side cursors, and the capability to define multiple, reusable command structures for each connection.

Examples in this chapter have been written in C. They have been tested on a Windows PC, but using QuickWin, so that other platforms (notably UNIX) can easily use this code. A complete code listing appears at the end of the chapter, from which pieces have been drawn to illustrate each segment of a ct-Lib program.

# Essential Pieces of a ct-Library Program

Figure 37.1 shows the basic steps involved in constructing an Open Client application. We'll go through each of these steps and demonstrate, with pieces from the sample program, how each of these steps is written.

**FIGURE 37.1.**

*A flowchart of a simplified ct-Library program.*

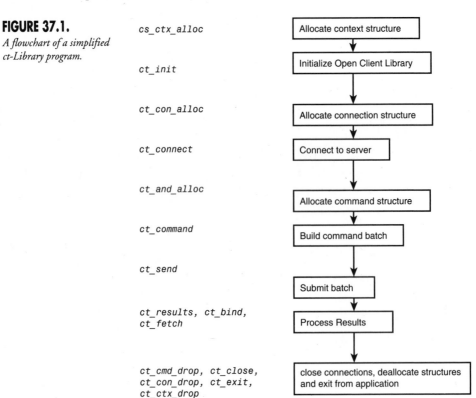

| | |
|---|---|
| `cs_ctx_alloc` | Allocate context structure |
| `ct_init` | Initialize Open Client Library |
| `ct_con_alloc` | Allocate connection structure |
| `ct_connect` | Connect to server |
| `ct_and_alloc` | Allocate command structure |
| `ct_command` | Build command batch |
| `ct_send` | Submit batch |
| `ct_results, ct_bind, ct_fetch` | Process Results |
| `ct_cmd_drop, ct_close, ct_con_drop, ct_exit, ct_ctx_drop` | close connections, deallocate structures and exit from application |

# What Is a Context?

Every ct-Lib application has a context. The context provides information about the connections that belong to the context. Connections can also have properties, many of which are unique to a connection and do not relate to the context. (For example, CS_CON_STATUS, which gives the status of the connection.)

Table 37.1 lists properties that can be set at the context level by using the ct_config() function.

**Table 37.1. Context-level properties.**

| Property | Description |
|---|---|
| CS_EXTRA_INF | Extra information relating to the message handler. |
| CS_LOC_PROP | Locale-specific information. Allows language, character set, and formats for datetime and money to be set. |
| CS_MESSAGE_CB | Installs a message handler (message callback). |
| CS_VERSION | Version of Client-Library (read only). |

# The Big Picture: How Commands, Connections, and Contexts Relate

Every program that sends information to a Sybase SQL server must have a context, a connection, and a command structure. Figure 37.2 illustrates how these constructs relate to each other.

**FIGURE 37.2.**

*Relationship of necessary structures in ct-Library.*

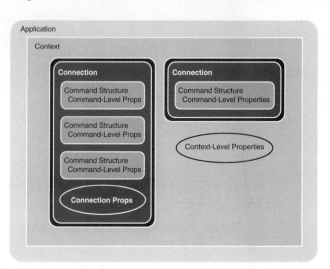

# Allocating a Context Structure

The first step in a ct-Library program is allocation of a context structure. There are two functions available to accomplish context init: cs_ctx_alloc() and cs_ctx_global(). The first function will allocate a new context each time it is called, while the second allocates a global context and returns a pointer to this context structure after subsequent calls.

After allocating a context structure, call ct_init() to initialize the library.

The following code listing allocates a context structure and initializes it. If any routine fails, shutdown is initiated and the program returns a failure code:

```
CS_CONTEXT      **context;

int main(){
    if(cs_ctx_alloc(CS_VERSION_100, context) != CS_SUCCEED)
        return CS_FAIL;
    if(ct_init(*context, CS_VERSION_100) != CS_SUCCEED){
        cs_ctx_drop(context);
        return CS_FAIL;
    }
```

# Allocating a Connection Structure

Once the context structure has been initialized, connection structures can be allocated as members of a context. Connection structures have a great many properties that can be set; a complete list can be obtained from the *Sybase Open Client Client-Library/C Programmer's Guide* (pages 5–18). Use ct_con_props() to set and retrieve these values.

An example of a connection property is CS_USERNAME, which must be set to the login name used to connect to a Sybase server prior to logging in. The function ct_con_props() takes six parameters. In the following example, the parameters are a pointer to the connection structure, an action to take (either CS_SET, CS_GET or, rarely, CS_CLEAR), the property to set, a pointer to the buffer containing the value of the property, the length of the buffer (the use of CS_NULLTERM in the example removes the need to calculate length), and, finally, the length of the output buffer, which the function sets if CS_GET is used as the second parameter.

After allocating the connection structure and setting the appropriate properties, call ct_connect() to connect to the server. These steps are illustrated in this example. Notice that ct_con_alloc() requires the context to which the new connection belongs as a parameter. After returning, *con will point to a new connection structure, or NULL in the case of an error. Here's the example:

```
CS_CONNECTION *con;
int buf;
/* Allocate connection structure */
if(ct_con_alloc(context, &con) != CS_SUCCEED){
    cs_ctx_drop(context);
    return CS_FAIL;
    }
```

```
/* Set connection properties */
ct_con_props(*con, CS_SET, CS_USERNAME, "sa", CS_NULLTERM, NULL);
ct_con_props(*con, CS_SET, CS_PASSWORD, "TMQ496Ae4", CS_NULLTERM, NULL);
ct_con_props(*con, CS_SET, CS_APPNAME, "Example 37", CS_NULLTERM, NULL);
ct_con_props(*con, CS_SET, CS_HOSTNAME, "\\WESTOVER", CS_NULLTERM, NULL);
ct_con_props(*con, CS_SET, CS_NETIO, CS_SYNC_IO, CS_UNUSED, NULL);
/* Packet size */
buf=2048;
ct_con_props(*con, CS_SET, CS_PACKETSIZE, &buf, CS_UNUSED, NULL);

if (ct_connect(*con, "SYBASE", CS_NULLTERM) != CS_SUCCEED){
    ct_con_drop(con);
    cs_ctx_drop(context);
    return CS_FAIL;
    }
```

# Allocating a Command Structure

Just as a connection belongs to a context, so too does a command belong to a connection. When commands need to be sent to the server, allocate a command structure, fill it, and submit it. This method has advantages over the method used by DB-Library. In DB-Library, each connection has a single buffer to which all commands need to be written, sent, then resubmitted. Using the Client-Library method, many command structures can be constructed ahead of time, then sent in quick succession through one or many connections. It saves work when commands are known ahead of time, or when they will be reused.

> **NOTE**
>
> Analogous to the `ct_cmd_alloc()` and `ct_command()` command structure functions is the `ct_cursor()` function. This creates a client-side cursor. Client-side cursor processing is beyond the scope of this chapter, but is worth investigation. ct-Library provides many advantages over DB-library with regard to these constructs.

The following code describes how to allocate a command structure. Note that the first parameter to this command is the connection to which the command structure belongs:

```
CS_COMMAND *cmd;
if(ct_cmd_alloc(connection, &cmd)) != CS_SUCCEED){
    ct_con_drop(con);
    cs_ctx_drop(context);
    return CS_FAIL;
    }
```

# Constructing a Command Batch

Once a command structure has been allocated, use `ct_command()` to put data into the structure.

The following code demonstrates a simple query being sent to the server. This query retrieves a list of names of all user-defined tables in the current database. The parameters to ct_command are a pointer to the command structure, the type of command (bulk copy; a regular command, called a *language command,* and so on), a pointer to the buffer containing the data to be set, the length of the buffer, and any options associated with the command. For language commands, there are no options. Here's the code:

```
if (ct_command(cmd, CS_LANG_CMD,
    "select name from sysobjects where type = 'U'",
    CS_NULLTERM, CS_UNUSED)) != CS_SUCCEED){
    ct_cmd_drop(cmd);
    ct_con_drop(con);
    cs_ctx_drop(context);
    return CS_FAIL;
    }
```

# Submitting a Batch

To this point, much of the work has been done. To send the batch, call ct_send(). It takes a single argument: a pointer to the command structure. After sending the batch, we will progress to the methods necessary for retrieving results. Here's the code:

```
if(ct_send(cmd) != CS_SUCCEED){
    ct_cmd_drop(cmd);
    ct_con_drop(con);
    cs_ctx_drop(context);
    return CS_FAIL;
}
```

# Processing Results

In the simple example provided, only a single result set can be returned. In events where there could be variable numbers of result sets, design a while loop to run ct_results until it returns CS_END_RESULTS.

The function places the result of the command in the second parameter. This value is usually placed in a switch/case statement where the different return values are handled. In the event of command failure, be sure to call ct_cancel to cancel the results and the command before attempting to proceed with the command structure.

Inside the results loop, we wait until we receive a CS_ROW_RESULT return value, which tells us that results are ready to be processed. Using ct_bind, results are bound to column variables. The data is then fetched with ct_fetch() and printed out using the standard C printf() command. Here's the code:

```
typedef struct _ex_column_data
{
    CS_SMALLINT      indicator;
    CS_CHAR          *value;
    CS_INT           valuelen;
} EX_COLUMN_DATA;

CS_INT res;
CS_DATAFMT *datafmt;
EX_COLUMN_DATA *coldata;
/*
res stores the result of ct_results.
The last two variables are used to store result data
*/

while(ct_results(cmd, &res) == CS_SUCCEED){
    switch(res){
    case CS_CMD_SUCCEED:
    case CS_CMD_DONE:
    case CS_CMD_FAIL:
        /* We are done processing rows */
        break;
    case CS_ROW_RESULT:
        /* Regular result row: Things are progressing smoothly */
        /* Allocate memory for the column info */
        coldata = (EX_COLUMN_DATA *)malloc(sizeof (EX_COLUMN_DATA));
        datafmt = (CS_DATAFMT *)malloc(sizeof (CS_DATAFMT));
        if (coldata == NULL || datafmt == NULL){
            /* Malloc error */
            ct_cancel(NULL, cmd, CS_CANCEL_ALL);
            ct_cmd_drop(cmd);
            ct_con_drop(con);
            cs_ctx_drop(context);
            return CS_FAIL;
            }

        /* Use ct_describe to get fill datafmt with col info */
        /* The 1 denotes the col # */
        ct_describe(cmd, 1, &datafmt);

        /* Allocate memory for the incoming data */
        coldata.value = (CS_CHAR *)malloc(datafmt.maxlength);
        if (coldata.value == NULL){
            /* Malloc error */
            ct_cancel(NULL, cmd, CS_CANCEL_ALL);
            ct_cmd_drop(cmd);
            ct_con_drop(con);
            cs_ctx_drop(context);
            return CS_FAIL;
            }

        /* Bind result columns to variable */
        if (ct_bind(cmd, 1, &datafmt, coldata.value, CS_NULLTERM, NULL)
```

```
            != CS_SUCCEED){
                 ct_cancel(NULL, cmd, CS_CANCEL_ALL);
                 ct_cmd_drop(cmd);
                 ct_con_drop(con);
                 cs_ctx_drop(context);
                 return CS_FAIL;
                 }

            /* Print column header */
            printf("%s\n", datafmt.name);

            /* ct_fetch loop, gets results */
            /* Middle parms currently unused by API */
            /* Results are printed until fetch returns CS_END_DATA */
            while (((ct_fetch(cmd, CS_UNUSED, CS_UNUSED, CS_UNUSED, &res))
            == CS_SUCCEED)
                 printf("%s\n",coldata.value);

            /* Finished processing rows. Free memory.*/
            free(coldata.value);
            free(coldata);
            free(datafmt);
            }
    }

/* We're finished.   */
```

Results-processing often makes up the bulk of a ct-Lib program.

# Cleanup

After processing results, all that remains is for the program to close connections, deallocate all of its structures, and exit. This is easily accomplished with the list of functions in the next code segment:

```
ct_cmd_drop(cmd);
ct_close(con, CS_UNUSED);
ct_con_drop(con);
ct_exit(context, CS_UNUSED);
ct_ctx_drop(context);
```

> **NOTE**
>
> If results have not been fully processed, `ct_close()` will fail unless the `CS_FORCE_CLOSE` option is used. This option treats the server poorly, however, and often leads to a phantom process on the server. It should be used only in error conditions, when `ct_close()` fails using the first method.
>
> The same is true for `ct_exit()`, which allows a `CS_FORCE_EXIT` option to be passed.

# Summary

ct-Library is a newer library for use with Sybase that allows the programmer more flexibility and power at the expense of added complexity. The basics of Client-Library have been discussed here, but much more remains to be examined.

Listing 37.1 is the complete code listing for the program discussed in this chapter.

## Listing 37.1. A complete code listing of the program discussed in this chapter.

```
CS_CONTEXT      **context;
typedef struct _ex_column_data
{
    CS_SMALLINT     indicator;
    CS_CHAR         *value;
    CS_INT          valuelen;
} EX_COLUMN_DATA;

int main(){
CS_CONNECTION *con;
CS_COMMAND *cmd;
CS_INT res, buf;
CS_DATAFMT *datafmt;
EX_COLUMN_DATA *coldata;

    if(cs_ctx_alloc(CS_VERSION_100, context) != CS_SUCCEED)
        return CS_FAIL;
    if(ct_init(*context, CS_VERSION_100) != CS_SUCCEED){
        cs_ctx_drop(context);
        return CS_FAIL;
    }

/* Allocate connection structure */
if(ct_con_alloc(context, &con) != CS_SUCCEED){
    cs_ctx_drop(context);
    return CS_FAIL;
    }

/* Set connection properties */
ct_con_props(*con, CS_SET, CS_USERNAME, "sa", CS_NULLTERM, NULL);
ct_con_props(*con, CS_SET, CS_PASSWORD, "TMQ496Ae4", CS_NULLTERM, NULL);
ct_con_props(*con, CS_SET, CS_APPNAME, "Example 37", CS_NULLTERM, NULL);
ct_con_props(*con, CS_SET, CS_HOSTNAME, "\\WESTOVER", CS_NULLTERM, NULL);
ct_con_props(*con, CS_SET, CS_NETIO, CS_SYNC_IO, CS_UNUSED, NULL);
/* Packet size */
buf=2048;
ct_con_props(*con, CS_SET, CS_PACKETSIZE, &buf, CS_UNUSED, NULL);

if (ct_connect(*con, "SYBASE", CS_NULLTERM) != CS_SUCCEED){
    ct_con_drop(con);
    cs_ctx_drop(context);
    return CS_FAIL;
    }
```

```
if(ct_cmd_alloc(connection, &cmd)) != CS_SUCCEED){
    ct_con_drop(con);
    cs_ctx_drop(context);
    return CS_FAIL;
    }

if (ct_command(cmd, CS_LANG_CMD,
    "select name from sysobjects where type = 'U'",
    CS_NULLTERM, CS_UNUSED)) != CS_SUCCEED){
    ct_cmd_drop(cmd);
    ct_con_drop(con);
    cs_ctx_drop(context);
    return CS_FAIL;
    }

if(ct_send(cmd) != CS_SUCCEED){
    ct_cmd_drop(cmd);
    ct_con_drop(con);
    cs_ctx_drop(context);
    return CS_FAIL;
}

/*
res stores the result of ct_results.
The last two variables are used to store result data
*/

while(ct_results(cmd, &res) == CS_SUCCEED){
    switch(res){
    case CS_CMD_SUCCEED:
    case CS_CMD_DONE:
    case CS_CMD_FAIL:
        /* We are done processing rows */
        break;
    case CS_ROW_RESULT:
        /* Regular result row: Things are progressing smoothly */
        /* Allocate memory for the column info */
        coldata = (EX_COLUMN_DATA *)malloc(sizeof (EX_COLUMN_DATA));
        datafmt = (CS_DATAFMT *)malloc(sizeof (CS_DATAFMT));
        if (coldata == NULL || datafmt == NULL){
            /* Malloc error */
            ct_cancel(NULL, cmd, CS_CANCEL_ALL);
            ct_cmd_drop(cmd);
            ct_con_drop(con);
            cs_ctx_drop(context);
            return CS_FAIL;
            }

        /* Use ct_describe to get fill datafmt with col info */
        /* The 1 denotes the col # */
        ct_describe(cmd, 1, &datafmt);

        /* Allocate memory for the incoming data */
        coldata.value = (CS_CHAR *)malloc(datafmt.maxlength);
        if (coldata.value == NULL){
            /* Malloc error */
            ct_cancel(NULL, cmd, CS_CANCEL_ALL);
            ct_cmd_drop(cmd);
```

```
        ct_con_drop(con);
        cs_ctx_drop(context);
        return CS_FAIL;
        }

    /* Bind result columns to variable */
    if (ct_bind(cmd, 1, &datafmt, coldata.value, CS_NULLTERM, NULL) !=
➥CS_SUCCEED){
        ct_cancel(NULL, cmd, CS_CANCEL_ALL);
        ct_cmd_drop(cmd);
        ct_con_drop(con);
        cs_ctx_drop(context);
        return CS_FAIL;
        }

    /* Print column header */
    printf("%s\n", datafmt.name);

    /* ct_fetch loop, gets results */
    /* Middle parms currently unused by API */
    /* Results are printed until fetch returns CS_END_DATA */
    while (((ct_fetch(cmd, CS_UNUSED, CS_UNUSED, CS_UNUSED, &res)) ==
➥CS_SUCCEED)
        printf("%s\n",coldata.value);

    /* Finished processing rows. Free memory.*/
    free(coldata.value);
    free(coldata);
    free(datafmt);
    }
    }

ct_cmd_drop(cmd);
ct_close(con, CS_UNUSED);
ct_con_drop(con);
ct_exit(context, CS_UNUSED);
ct_ctx_drop(context);
return CS_SUCCEED;
}
```

# ODBC Programming

# 38

Now that we've taken a look at programming using DB-Library, we'll look at something Microsoft would much rather have you use: ODBC, or the Open Database Connectivity, interface. This chapter discusses the concept behind ODBC, then provides some sample Visual Basic code using the ODBC API. There are many good, exhaustive ODBC books on the market, and any serious programmer planning to write to the ODBC interface should be armed with them accordingly.

Generally, ODBC allows a single application to talk to a variety of database systems from a single code set, using SQL as a portable method for manipulating data. It accomplishes this through the use of interchangeable ODBC drivers on the client machine. ODBC takes care of some of the things that DB-Lib programmers still need to handle, such as login screens and server lists.

If you are using Visual Basic to create applications, Microsoft has taken steps to make programming to the ODBC layer as easy as possible. Later in this chapter, we'll look more closely at how to create simple ODBC applications.

# What Is ODBC?

For starters, ODBC allows a single application to make a standard set of calls that are then translated, through the use of an ODBC driver, into statements on the target Database Management System (DBMS). It is also possible to use SQL passthrough simply to quote, to the server, SQL statements that are passed without being altered by the driver.

This second method has some merit. Although simply quoting SQL to the server can, in some ways, limit your application to a specific set of SQL, VB's Jet engine gives us, compared to the DB-Lib layer, a blindingly simple way to get at our data. Technical issues concerning the interaction of the Jet engine and ODBC should be reviewed by anyone attempting this route. There are other books describing how to approach a project in this manner. We will be using the ODBC CLI (Call Level Interface) through Visual Basic.

# ODBC Interface

The actual interactions that occur behind the ODBC interface are interesting to explore. There are four discrete layers in the ODBC implementation. (See Figure 38.1.)

Sitting on top of the whole thing is an application. Of course, the application can be anything. It is responsible for all results processing. The application talks to the ODBC driver manager. The driver manager decides which individual drivers to call when an application asks for a connection to a data source. Each data source is configured by the user before running the application, and the driver manager handles the interface between the actual driver and the application.

**FIGURE 38.1.**

*Discrete components comprising the ODBC architecture.*

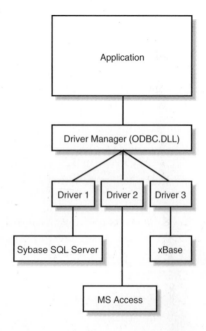

This includes, most importantly, loading the driver. It also includes validation of parameters passed to the driver functions, so that the driver need not concern itself with that task. Finally, the driver manager performs some of the ODBC initialization routines. Later on in the chapter, when we present our sample program, we'll point out where the driver manager does some actual, observable work.

The drivers do most of the work in the ODBC model. They accept ODBC function calls and translate them into things that the particular data source can understand.

The data sources, themselves, never know that they are being accessed by ODBC.

# API Conformance Levels

When an ODBC driver is written, its creators must adhere to a bare minimum of functionality. Enforcing this conformity is the job of an industry standard, such as ODBC, and it is a good thing.

Microsoft defines three sets of conformity for ODBC drivers. Each higher level includes the restrictions of the previous level. This is partly due to the inherent differences in data sources; an Xbase database has much less functionality than an SQL Server database. An Xbase ODBC driver would likely not support Level 2 functionality, because the underlying data source cannot support many of the features mandated by Level 2 conformity.

When product managers start a project that writes to the ODBC API, they must make a decision about which level of driver conformance will be required to run their software. To achieve maximum compatibility, PMs may decide to call only Core level API functions. To gain more functionality, PMs could allow their programmers to call Level 1 or Level 2 API functions.

## Core API

Core level API functions provide a method for doing most of the work in an application. These functions provide the following:

- Allocating and freeing handles for environment, connections, and statements
- Establishing connections to data sources and using multiple statements on a connection
- Preparing and executing SQL statements over an established connection
- Assigning storage variables for holding parameters in SQL statements and for holding column data in result sets
- Retrieving result set data as well as information about a result set
- Committing or rolling back transactions
- Retrieving error information returned by data source

## Level 1 API

The Level 1 API functions are listed below. Most ODBC applications in existence today demand that a driver support Level 1 conformance. The functions that fall into Level 1 are useful extensions of Core level functions or logical extensions of functionality not provided for in the Core level API. In some cases, they offer additional information about the data source that cannot be retrieved with Core level functions.

- Connecting to data sources with driver-specific dialog boxes
- Sending all or only part of a result column value (useful for long data values)
- Sending all or only part of a parameter value
- Retrieving catalog information about database items (for example, columns, special columns, statistics, and tables)
- Setting options for statements and connections and inquiring about current option settings
- Retrieving information about driver and data source capabilities, such as supported data types, scalar functions, and ODBC functions

## Level 2 API

Level 2 functions are more advanced functions. They provide ways to send and receive stored procedure parameters, use a backward-scrolling cursor, or retrieve information stored in the SQL system tables, such as indexes or a user's privileges. Below is a list of the tasks that Level 2 API functions provide.

- Browsing connection information to search for and list available data sources
- Assigning parameter values to arrays and sending them for use with stored procedures
- Retrieving information on stored procedure parameters, including the number of parameters and parameter descriptions
- Retrieving result column values into arrays
- Retrieving additional catalog information stored in system tables (for example, privileges, keys, and procedures)
- Defining and using scrollable cursors
- Retrieving native SQL statements generated
- Calling a translation DLL, which could translate information between the driver and the data source

# Using VB to Build a Simple ODBC Application

We will be calling functions directly from the ODBC.DLL for all the examples in this chapter. Note that we are not using a Visual Basic Data Access Object; although this approach is valid, direct ODBC calls allow us to get closer to the API and demonstrate its usefulness, while avoiding the overhead of the VB Jet Engine.

In Chapter 36, "DB-Library Programming," we used the VBSQL.VBX object to take care of the message and error handlers and initialization, then used the CLI to call functions from the VBX. Here, we will be doing much the same thing by calling all API functions directly from ODBC.DLL.

One difference you'll notice immediately is that return values exist for every function in the DLL. In other words, every function in ODBC.DLL returns a status code. In Table 38.1, the values from each function is listed with its predefined constant and the associated meaning.

## Table 38.1. ODBC.DLL function calls.

| Return Value | Constant | Explanation |
| --- | --- | --- |
| -2 | SQL_INVALID_HANDLE | An invalid connection handle was passed into the function. |
| -1 | SQL_ERROR | An error occurred with no additional information. |
| 0 | SQL_SUCCESS | Success. |
| 1 | SQL_SUCCESS_WITH_INFO | Function ran successfully, but there is additional information available. |
| 99 | SQL_NEED_DATA | A stored procedure was called without the necessary parameters supplied. |
| 100 | SQL_NO_DATA_FOUND | Returned when a function has no more data to return, for example, when calling SQLError() and no unprocessed errors exist. |

To receive values, (for example, a connection number) ODBC changes the value of a passed parameter. This is a much more refined way to do business. In the next example, compare the difference between the DB-Lib SqlOpen() and the ODBC SqlAllocConnect(). SqlOpen() returns the sought-after value (SqlConn) where SQLAlloc() returns a result code and places the sought-after value (the connection handle, hdbc&) in the second parameter:

```
SqlConn% = SqlOpen%(ptrLogin%, ServerName$)
```

```
res% = SQLAllocConnect(henv&, hdbc&)
```

Of course, these two statements would not appear in the same program.

> **NOTE**
>
> We will be writing to the ODBC 2.0 API; where 2.0 functionality differs from 1.0, it will be noted.

The example provided in this chapter was done using Visual Basic 3.0. It will work just as well with the newer 4.0 release. Before we start, you'll need a Visual Basic module that declares all the functions in the ODBC.DLL that we'll be using. If you have ODBC.BAS, it can be used with some modifications. The declarations we'll be using are the following:

```
Rem Core level API
Declare Function SQLAllocConnect Lib "odbc.dll" (ByVal env As Long, hdbc As
➥ Long) As Integer
Declare Function SQLAllocEnv Lib "odbc.dll" (env As Long) As Integer
Declare Function SQLAllocStmt Lib "odbc.dll" (ByVal hdbc As Long, hstmt As
➥Long) As Integer
Declare Function SQLExecDirect Lib "odbc.dll" (ByVal hstmt As Long, ByVal
➥sqlString As String, ByVal sqlstrlen As Long) As Integer
Declare Function SQLFetch Lib "odbc.dll" (ByVal hstmt As Long) As Integer
Declare Function SQLFreeConnect Lib "odbc.dll" (ByVal hdbc As Long) As Integer
Declare Function SQLFreeEnv Lib "odbc.dll" (ByVal env As Long) As Integer
Declare Function SQLFreeStmt Lib "odbc.dll" (ByVal hstmt As Long, ByVal
➥EndOption As Integer) As Integer
Declare Function SQLDisconnect Lib "odbc.dll" (ByVal hdbc As Long) As Integer


Rem Level 1 API
Declare Function SQLDriverConnect Lib "odbc.dll" (ByVal hdbc As Long,
➥ByVal hwnd As Any, ByVal szCSIn As String, ByVal cbCSIn As Integer,
➥ByVal szCSOut As String, ByVal cbCSMax As Integer, cbCSOut%, ByVal f As Integer)
As Integer
Declare Function SQLGetData Lib "odbc.dll" (ByVal hstmt As Long, ByVal col
➥As Integer, ByVal wConvType As Integer, ByVal lpbBuf As String,
➥ByVal dwbuflen As Long, lpcbout As Long) As Integer
```

You will also need to have ODBC drivers for your data sources. You should be confident about their proper installation before continuing.

> **WARNING**
>
> Readers familiar with either C or calling Windows API functions will already know about this, but if you do not have any experience calling functions directly from DLLs, be aware that a return code of 0 is a customary return value for success. The RETVAL values for SQL_ERROR and SQL_SUCCESS are the opposite of what you might expect: If a function returns -1, it means False, or SQL_ERROR, and if it returns 0, it means True, or SQL_SUCCESS.

# A Sample Program

The sample program we'll write will be a simple one. We will initialize the ODBC library, ask for a list of ODBC data sources to be presented to the user, open a connection to the selected server, ask for a simple, single-column, single-row result set, and output the result to the Debug device. Because we'll be writing to the debug device, run this in Development mode inside Visual Basic. The complete example is provided at the end of this section.

To run this program, you'll need to add the defines, shown previously, to a BAS module. We also need to create a dummy form from which our ODBC driver will obtain a parent hWnd handle. In the Form_Load procedure, place a single call to Example381(). Insert the code listed into a subroutine called Example 381.

# Initializing ODBC

There are three types of handles defined in the ODBC API (see Table 38.2).

## Table 38.2. Handle types in an ODBC application.

| Handle Type | Definition | Some Functions Referencing |
| --- | --- | --- |
| Environment | Memory storage for global information, such as connection handles. There is only one environment handle per application. | SQLDataSources() |
| Connection | Memory storage for each individual connection. Each connection is managed by the environment. There may be many connections in a single application, each of which is descended from an environment. | SQLConnect(), SQLConnectOption() |
| Statement | Memory storage for an SQL statement. Each statement is managed by its connection. There may be many statements in a single connection. Most of the actual work that occurs in an application will reference the statement handle. | SQLGetData(), SQLPrepare() |

To execute an SQL statement, a statement handle must be allocated, which requires and references a connection handle, which requires and references an environment handle. First, we'll define some variables we'll need in the program, load the form, and paint it. Figures are provided at each step to show what you should be getting. In Figure 38.2, the example is shown after the `Form1.Refresh` call. If you try this at home, step through the program with F8 to see how each statement works. Merely running this is pretty uninteresting:

```
Sub Example381()
' Result code storage, Handle to Database Connection, Handle to Environment, Handle
to Statement.
Dim res%, hdbc&, henv&, hstmt&

' Fixed length buffer to hold Connection String
Dim ConnectionStr As String * 255

' Work variables
Dim ConnStrlen%, outputlength&
Dim t As String * 255

Form1.Show
Form1.Refresh
```

**FIGURE 38.2.**

*Code example after painting the sample form, shown here with a background bitmap to avoid programmer boredom.*

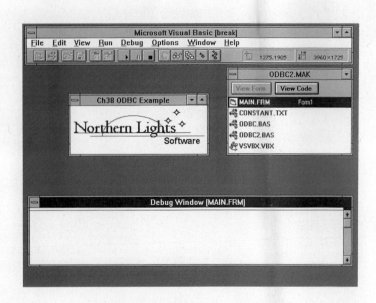

Now we need to allocate an environment handle and connection handle:

```
' Allocate environment
res% = SQLAllocEnv(henv&)

' Allocate connection
res% = SQLAllocConnect(henv&, hdbc&)
```

Note that in the `SQLAllocConnect()` call, the environment handle is used to let the ODBC API know which application is requesting a connection handle. The new connection handle is passed back in the `hdbc&` variable.

Once we have a connection available to us, we can open a connection to our server.

> **NOTE**
>
> There are several functions available that enable us to create a connection. For example, the simplest, `SQLConnect()`, is a Core level ODBC API function. This means that the function is guaranteed to work in all Core level–compliant (which is to say, all) ODBC drivers. `SQLBrowseConnect()` is a Level 2 function, the highest. The function featured here is a Level 1 API function.

Open a connection with the following line of code. After executing this function, you should see a dialog box appear as displayed in Figure 38.3. Your dialog box may differ in appearance depending on the version and manufacturer of your ODBC driver:

```
res% = SQLDriverConnect(hdbc&, CInt(Form1.hWnd), "", 0, ConnectionStr,
➥ 255, ConnStrlen%, SQL_DRIVER_PROMPT)
```

**FIGURE 38.3.**

*The call to* `SQLDriverConnect()` *creates this dialog box. Your dialog box will contain the ODBC sources you have set up in your particular environment.*

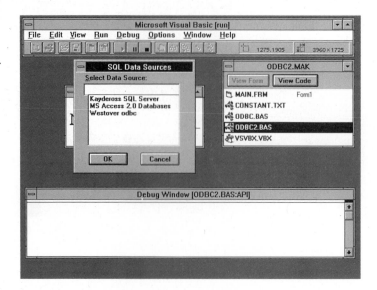

This dialog box is actually launched by the ODBC driver manager. (Refer to Figure 38.1 for a schematic of the call level involved.) Because a data source hasn't yet been selected, a driver can't be chosen; because a driver hasn't been chosen, the driver manager needs to do this work.

Once you select a data source, the `SQLDriverConnect()` function causes the actual driver (SQLSRVR.DLL, for instance) to create a new dialog box in order to get login information from the user. Again, there are lots of ways to get connections to the server; we're showing only one way to do this. It's certainly possible, and infinitely useful, to create connections based on predefined parameters behind the scenes. (You could update a graph once per minute to reflect changes in a table, for example.)

In Figure 38.4, notice that the driver has loaded a dialog box to retrieve user information. Observant readers may notice that the driver has titled the dialog box "Logon to System 10." System 10 ODBC drivers from Intersolv work just fine with System 11.

**FIGURE 38.4.**

*After selecting a data source, the ODBC driver manager loads the respective source's driver, which, in turn, presents this dialog box.*

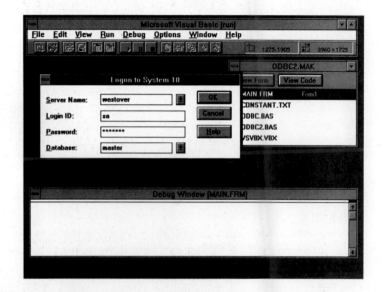

Because we are connecting to an SQL Server, the driver translates our SQLDriverConnect() call into a request for a login, password, and starting database. Once the user has supplied the necessary information, the driver uses it to log us in to the server.

After establishing a connection, we are ready to submit a query. To do this, we need to get a statement handle:

```
' Allocate a statement handle
res% = SQLAllocStmt(hdbc&, hstmt&)
```

Once the statement handle is allocated, we prepare one of our work variables, t, (for temporary string) with the text of our SQL query. For those of you playing along at home, you can change this query to anything that returns a one-column, one-row result set—for example, select getdate(). This query is sent to the server using the SQLExecDirect() function:

```
t$ = "select count(*) from d1..t1"
res% = SQLExecDirect(hstmt&, t$, Len(t$))
```

If you're stepping through the code, you may notice some latency after executing this function. On our machine, the ODBC connection we're using has been configured to process results synchronously in order to produce this behavior. This may not be the most desirable behavior, but it is excellent and simple for the purposes of our demonstration.

After results are ready, we need to go out and get them. We accomplish that here with SQLFetch() and SQLGetData(), although, like connecting to the server, the ODBC API offers several possible ways to retrieve and format results:

```
' Get a row
res% = SQLFetch(hstmt&)

' Get data from the row's first column
res% = SQLGetData(hstmt&, 1, SQL_C_CHAR, t$, 255, outputlength&)

' Print results to the debug device
Debug.Print Left$(t$, CInt(outputlength&))
```

SQLFetch() takes the statement handle and performs a row fetch on that handle. After executing a fetch, the statement structure contains what can be considered a pointer to a row in the result set. The arguments to SQLGetData() include the statement handle, the column number (SQLGetData() allows retrieval of a single column of data at a time), the type of data (although we're retrieving a numeric result, fetching character data is easier), the variable in which the data should be placed, the allocated length of the output buffer, and the reported length of the data according to SQLGetData().

This information is used in the format string passed to the Print statement. The remainder of the buffer contains nulls (chr$(0)) and looks dreadful in the Debug window. Thus, we take only the valid data from the buffer and place it in the Debug window. Notice that it is necessary to pass a long to the API function, but that the Left$() call requires an integer. Results are displayed in Figure 38.5.

**FIGURE 38.5.**

*A sample program with results displayed in the Debug window.*

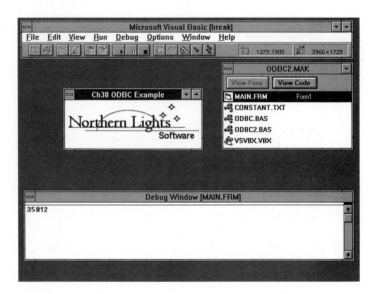

All that remains is to clean up our handles and close connections. We accomplish this with a series of simple functions:

```
res% = SQLFreeStmt(hstmt, SQL_DROP)
res% = SQLDisconnect(hdbc)
res% = SQLFreeConnect(hdbc)
res% = SQLFreeEnv(henv)
```

# Summary of Programming Example

This sample program demonstrated a very simple way to connect to an SQL Server by using the ODBC Call Level Interface. Using simple API calls, and leveraging the resources available to us in the driver and ODBC driver manager, we presented the user with dialog boxes to find and connect to a server, issue a predefined query, and retrieve and print results. The following is the complete code example discussed in this chapter:

```
Sub Example381()
' Result code storage, Handle to Database Connection, Handle to Environment, Handle
to Statement.
Dim res%, hdbc&, henv&, hstmt&

' Fixed length buffer to hold Connection String
Dim ConnectionStr As String * 255

' Work variables
Dim ConnStrlen%, outputlength&
Dim t As String * 255

Form1.Show
Form1.Refresh
' Allocate environment
res% = SQLAllocEnv(henv&)

' Allocate connection
res% = SQLAllocConnect(henv&, hdbc&)
res% = SQLDriverConnect(hdbc&, CInt(Form1.hWnd), "", 0, ConnectionStr, 255,
➥ConnStrlen%, SQL_DRIVER_PROMPT)
' Allocate a statement handle
res% = SQLAllocStmt(hdbc&, hstmt&)
t$ = "select count(*) from d1..t1"
res% = SQLExecDirect(hstmt&, t$, Len(t$))
' Get a row
res% = SQLFetch(hstmt&)

' Get data from the row's first column
res% = SQLGetData(hstmt&, 1, SQL_C_CHAR, t$, 255, outputlength&)

' Print results to the debug device
Debug.Print Left$(t$, CInt(outputlength&))
res% = SQLFreeStmt(hstmt, SQL_DROP)
res% = SQLDisconnect(hdbc)
res% = SQLFreeConnect(hdbc)
res% = SQLFreeEnv(henv)
```

# Summary

ODBC provides another way to access data on a Sybase SQL Server. Writing applications in ODBC enables a programmer to use the drivers to accomplish some of the grunt work. The CLI provides a way for the programmer to access all of the functions in the ODBC library. Using ODBC is relatively simple from programming environments such as Visual Basic.

# Appendixes

**VI**

**PART**

# Sybase Tools Reference

**A**

There are three major tools provided by Sybase for administering, maintaining, and accessing the SQL Server:

- bcp is used to import and export data between an SQL Server table and an operating system file.
- defncopy is used to import and export object-creation statements for views, triggers, rules, defaults, and procedures.
- isql is the standard interface provided by Sybase, which also is often used for batch program execution.

You may have used several of these utilities in the past, but it can be helpful to understand their full capabilities. For example, did you know you could encrypt your SQL Server password when using tools such as bcp, defncopy, and isql? Or that you can increase the network packet size to make the bulk copying routine perform faster? This appendix provides a reference to getting the most out of the Sybase utility programs.

> **NOTE**
>
> You can execute all these tools from the operating system where SQL Server resides. Some (isql and bcp, in particular) can be run from client workstations as well.
>
> As with everything else about SQL Server, the syntax for the tools may vary slightly among host operating systems, and will certainly provide different capabilities with different release levels. You must check the detailed release information that came with SQL Server to be sure about the names, syntax, and capabilities of the utilities you have installed.

# The Bulk Copy Program

The bulk copy program (bcp) is a tool that transfers data between a table and an operating system file at high speeds. It is the most common way to load large amounts of data into an SQL Server table. It also is frequently used to transfer data from other database vendors, spreadsheet applications, and other SQL Servers. Often, bcp is fully integrated into an overall system design. Initially, bcp is used to load existing data from other data sources. Incremental data then is bulk-copied on a nightly, weekly, or monthly basis using a scheduling program (crontab in UNIX).

The bcp program has over 25 options available. It is important to understand the capabilities and shortcomings of bcp, especially if you plan to use bcp as part of a production system sdesign.

# Syntax

```
bcp [ [ database_name.]owner.]table_name { in ¦ out } datafile
[ -m maxerrors ] [ -f formatfile ] [ -e errfile ]
[ -F firstrow ] [ -L lastrow ] [ -b batch_size_in_rows ]
[ -T text or image size ] [ -n ] [ -c ]
[ -t field_terminator ] [ -r row_terminator ]
[ -U username ] [ -P password ] [ -I interfaces_file ]
[ -S server ] [ -a display_charset ] [ -q datafile_charset ]
[ -J client_charset ] [ -z language ] [ -v ] [ -A size ] [ -E ] [ -X ]
```

# Options

Table A.1 presents detailed descriptions of each parameter of bcp.

## Table A.1. bcp parameters.

| Flag | Option | Description |
| --- | --- | --- |
| | database name | This is the database in which the table exists. |
| | owner | This is the owner of the table name table. |
| | table name | This is the name of the table to import or export. |
| | in ¦ out | This indicates the direction of data flow: out to copy rows from a table to a file, in to copy rows from a file to a table. |
| | datafile | This is the name of the source or target data file (depending on whether the bcp is in or out). It should include a complete pathname and file specification. |
| -A | size in bytes | This changes the network packet size for this bcp session. The network packet size boundaries are determined from the configuration options default network packet size and maximum network packet size. The value must be a multiple of 512. This option is used on large bulk copy operations to improve performance. |

*continues*

## Table A.1. continued

| Flag | Option | Description |
|------|--------|-------------|
| -b | *batch size in rows* | This specifies the number of rows to be used for each batch; the default is all rows. Use this option when copying large amounts of data so that the checkpoint process has a chance to remove rows in the log. Use this option with a batch size of one row if you want each row to be treated separately. See the section on "Batches," later in this chapter, for more on batch sizes. |
| -c | | This indicates that bcp should send or receive data in character format. The output file contains readable data. Fields are separated by a tab (\t), with a newline at the end of the row (\n). This probably is the easiest way to use bcp, but beware of conversion issues. |
| -e | *error file* | This is the file (full path or relative) where the bcp program stores rows that failed to be copied into a table. The types of errors usually are conversion problems (can't convert from int to datetime, for example). Duplicate rows rejected by an index are not considered errors, so they are not placed in the error file. |
| -E | | This tells bcp to recognize the identity column; use this option only if the table contains an identity column. |
| | | When you specify -E, the identity value is copied into the output file during a bcp out. During a bcp in, bcp uses the identity value in the file, if it exists, or prompts you for a value for each row in the file. (Don't forget that there is a maximum identity value dictated by the number of numeric digits specified for the identity column at creation time.) |

| Flag | Option | Description |
|------|--------|-------------|
|      |        | Without the -E option, bcp ignores the identity column during a bcp out so that it will not be part of the output file. During a bcp in, bcp sets the identity value, starting with 1 for the first row in the file. |
| -f   | *format file* | This indicates that you have an existing format file, which probably was created earlier, during a bcp out without the -c or -n options. This file normally is created in the directory from which you invoke bcp, although you could provide a full pathname. (See more on the topic of format files in the section called "Interactive bcp.") |
| -F   | *first row number* | This is the number of the first row in the file or table to copy; the default is 1. This can be used for both bcp in and bcp out, and usually is combined with the -L option to specify file boundary (bcp in) or table boundary (bcp out). |
| -I   | *interface file* | This is the name of the interface file to use when trying to find a server to connect to. If this option is not provided, bcp looks for a file named interfaces in the directory identified by the $SYBASE environment variable (the SYBASE home directory). |
| -J   | *client charset* | This is the character set to use on the client machine. bcp filters all rows in or out, translating between the SQL Server character set and the client character set. (This option is seldom used. |
| -L   | *last row number* | This is the last row for bcp to copy; the default is the last row. This can be used for both bcp in and bcp out, and usually is combined with the -F option to provide a specific boundary. |

*continues*

## Table A.1. continued

| Flag | Option | Description |
| --- | --- | --- |
| -m | *maximum errors* | This is the number of errors before bcp aborts a batch; the default is 10. |

> **TIP**
>
> If you want to make sure all rows in a batch are tried, set maxerrors equal to batch size in rows.)

| Flag | Option | Description |
| --- | --- | --- |
| -n | | This indicates that bcp should send or receive data in native format. bcp does not prompt for input. The output file is in operating system format and is not easily readable. |
| -P | *password* | This is the password for the login name specified. If this option is not specified, bcp prompts for it. |
| -q | *datafile charset* | This tells bcp that a file to be created or read uses a character set other than the client character set. (This option is seldom used.) |
| -r | *row delimiter* | This specifies the delimiter used for the end of a row; the default is a newline character (\n). This is useful if you are copying data from another product and the rows are terminated with a character other than newline. |
| -S | *server name* | This is the name of the server to which to connect. If the server name is not provided, bcp uses the DSQUERY value, if it exists, or SYBASE. This name must be found in the interfaces file used by bcp. The location of the interfaces file is explained in the -I option. |
| -t | *field delimiter* | This specifies the delimiter used to indicate the end of a field; the default is a tab (\t). This is useful if you are copying data from another product and the fields are separated with a character other than a tab. |

| Flag | Option | Description |
| --- | --- | --- |
| -T | *text or image size* | This is the size (in bytes) of text or image data; the default is 32KB. The value provided to bcp is converted to a 2KB increment. If data is longer than the value provided (or larger than 32KB if no value is provided), bcp does not send any data after the maximum has been reached. |
| -U | *login name* | This is the login name for bcp to use when connecting to the server. The default is the user name identified by your environment. |
| -v | | This options displays the version number of bcp and copyright information. |
| -X | | This is for password encryption. If -X is specified, bcp attempts to connect to the server and requests an encryption string. The server sends the encryption code to the client and the client encrypts the password using the provided code. The client sends the encrypted password to the server, where it is decoded and verified. Use this option if security needs dictate. |
| -z | *language name* | This tells bcp to put messages and prompts in a language other than the default language for the server. |

## Notes

You should use the *database_name* option to specify a database. You can rely on the default database mechanism for a login. However, if a name is not provided to bcp, a connection is made to the server and bcp looks for the table in the current database only. The current database is the designated default database (or master, if none is specified in syslogins).

You rarely use the *owner* option. Remember that the server identifies objects first by looking for a table owned by the database user's name (determined when the database is "used"), then for a table owned by the database owner (dbo). Therefore, the owner name does not have to be provided, unless the object you want is owned by someone other than yourself or dbo.

One of the few places you specify an owner is during development, when two different users of a database own identically named tables and want to transfer data between them. To transfer data from a table owned by "mark" to a table owned by "dave," you specify mark on the bulk copy out and dave on the bulk copy in.

The *login name* parameter is critical, because your *login name* can be mapped to a user name within a database. For data being copied out, the user must have select permission. For copying data in, the user must have insert permission.

The interfaces file is seldom specified, except in those cases where DBAs create a "super" interface file for administrative use and the default interface file contains only a subset of entries.

# Character Sets

If the -J option is included without a value, bcp assumes that the client uses the same character set as the default SQL Server character set. If no value is specified, bcp assumes a default for the platform of the client where bcp is running (remember that bcp can run on the server itself or on a network-connected client). There are four default character sets:

| | |
|---|---|
| iso_1: | Sun, DEC, Pyramid, NCR, others |
| roman8: | HP |
| cp850: | RS6000/aix and OS/2 |
| mac: | Apple Macintosh |

# Modes of Operation

The bcp program has two modes of operation: fast and slow. Modes of operation apply only to bulk copying data into a table, because a bcp out essentially executes a select operation.

The fast bcp does not log the insert of individual rows into the transaction log. It logs only the allocation of pages and extents. To achieve fast bcp, several conditions must apply:

- The select into/bulkcopy option must be set on for the database.
- The table in question cannot have triggers or indexes.
- The rows inserted by the bcp are not recoverable. Transaction logs cannot be dumped after nonlogged bcp; you must use dump database instead.

Slow bcp is used when a table has one or more indexes or triggers. Each insert is logged, but triggers are not kicked off. Log activity may be intense. If you are using slow bcp to import a large file, the log must be dumped frequently. Either set the truncate log on checkpoint option on or have a script dump the transaction log at short intervals (every five or ten minutes).

> **NOTE**
>
> Setting `truncate log on checkpoint` automatically prunes the transaction log every time the system issues an automatic checkpoint. Manual checkpoints issued by the dbo do not truncate the transaction log.

Here is an example:

```
/* SQL to dump the transaction log
   of the customer database every 5
   minutes until 4:00 PM. */
while (getdate() < "1/1/95 4:00:00 PM)
begin
     dump transaction customer with truncate_only
     waitfor delay "00:05:00"
end
```

# Formats

You can run the bulk copy program interactively, or you can execute it at the command line. An interactive bcp prompts you to enter information about each column. An interactive bcp also gives you an option to save your selections in a format file. You can use this format file for later imports or exports to avoid having to respond to prompts every time you want to copy data. There also are two default formats that act in a predefined manner: native and character.

You can specify the field terminator using the -t option, and the row terminator using the -r option. If the interactive mode is used, the values you supply using the -t and -r options are used as the default input value for the field. In character (-c) or native (-n) mode, these values override the default values of the tab character for the end of a field and the newline indicator for the end of a row. For example, if you want to copy the data out of the titles table in native format with ¦ as the field terminator and a carriage return (\r) as the row terminator, this is the command:

```
bcp pubs2..titles out titles.bcp -Uuser1 -Ppasswd -n -t\¦ -r \\r
```

> **NOTE**
>
> Because the pipe character (¦) and the backslash (\) have special meanings in UNIX and other operating systems, the first backslash is required as an "escape" character so that the second backslash character is treated literally. In some environments (such as MS-DOS or Windows NT), you may need to put quotes around special characters. For example, in Windows NT, to use the pipe character (¦) as a field terminator, specify -t "¦".

# Interactive *bcp*

If you do not specify native format (·n) or character format (·c), or if you do not provide a format file (·f *format_filename*), bcp enters interactive mode. Interactive mode prompts you for the storage type, prefix length, storage length, and field terminator for each column in a table. Interactive mode therefore provides flexibility for importing and exporting data.

## File Storage Type

The file storage type tells bcp how to store (or retrieve) the data in a file. You can select from any of the valid SQL Server datatypes. bcp writes the data to the file in an operating system format, and noncharacter data is not readable. bcp provides default storage-type values as part of the prompt. The datatype specified by bcp matches the column datatype and usually provides the most compact way to store your data.

Accept the default datatype values if possible. If you specify a datatype different than the default, make sure the datatype can accommodate the value without truncation. During bcp in, if the type is too small, bcp prints an overflow message and aborts the insert of the row.

## Prefix Length

When using native format files, bcp precedes each variable length field with one or more bytes that indicate the length of the data field. Fixed length fields do not require any prefix bytes. The prefix length option is used to specify the number of bytes used to indicate the length of a field. Use the default value, if possible. The prefix length defaults are shown in Table A.2.

**Table A.2. Prefix length defaults for datatypes when used with bulk copy.**

| Datatype | Prefix Length |
| --- | --- |
| Fixed-length columns | 0 |
| Variable-length characters | 1 |
| Text or image columns | 4 |
| Binary or varbinary column (defined in table) and character data in file | 2 |

Note that prefix lengths are stored in a native (noncharacter) format, causing the output file to have nonprintable characters.

If a prefix length of 0 is specified, the data fields will be stored at the full width specified by the storage length option.

# Storage Length

The storage length always refers to the operating system file. When specifying this value, be aware that this is the number of bytes bcp uses to represent the data in your operating system file.

> **TIP**
>
> Use the default storage length, if possible, because making this number too small can lead to truncation and loss of data or overflow errors in the output file.

# Field and Row Terminators

A terminator marks the end of a column. The terminator for the last column is considered the row terminator. The terminator can be any printable character, or string of characters, as well as null terminators (\0), a backslash (\), a carriage return (\r), a newline (\n), or a tab (\t). The default terminator for character data is the tab character (\t). Your terminator should be something that does not appear in your data (for example, ¦ or ,). bcp looks for this terminator to determine whether it is at the end of a field or at the end of a row.

Do not forget which column is the last in your table. bcp asks you to Enter field terminator, even though this terminator actually does double duty by specifying that it is the end of the row. A newline (\n) normally is used to terminate a row, although carriage return (\r) sometimes is used.

# Format Files

After you answer all the questions about how to store each column of data, bcp asks whether you want to save these values in a format file. Unless this is a one-time bulk copy, you should save your values for later use. If you save your format file, you can run a later bcp without having to enter field-by-field information. Merely specify the -f option followed by the name of the format file.

> **TIP**
>
> Format files usually are created by running a bcp out from the target table into an operating system file. Once the file is created, you know that any data you copy out using that file can be read in using that file.
>
> I usually create a format file by running a bcp out that copies only a single row out of the table. This can be accomplished with the -F *firstrow* and -L *lastrow* options,

using a value of 1 for each. This copies out only the first row in the table. Believe me, it is much easier to create a format file this way than to try and do it from scratch. If you do need to modify the format file to accommodate your data file (for example, if the fields in the data file are not in the same order as your table columns), you now have a template file to work with.

If you do not create your format file using the SQL Server bcp utility, make sure you understand how input files are formatted before creating your own from scratch or starting an interactive bcp in.

Listing A.1 is a sample bcp session run on a Windows NT System 10 SQL Server. In the example, the user is retrieving (out) data from the pubs06..publishers table into a file named publ.out. The user is the system administrator. Because no password is provided, the bcp program prompts for one.

After each column is defined, the utility prompts for a filename for the format file. Finally, the copy starts.

### Listing A.1. Sample bcp session output.

```
C:\users\default>bcp pubs06..publishers out publ.out -Usa
Password:

Enter the file storage type of field pub_id [char]:
Enter prefix-length of field pub_id [0]:
Enter length of field pub_id [4]:
Enter field terminator [none]:

Enter the file storage type of field pub_name [char]:
Enter prefix-length of field pub_name [1]:
Enter field terminator [none]:

Enter the file storage type of field city [char]:
Enter prefix-length of field city [1]:
Enter field terminator [none]:

Enter the file storage type of field state [char]:
Enter prefix-length of field state [1]:
Enter field terminator [none]:

Do you want to save this format information in a file? [Y/n]
y
Host filename [bcp.fmt]: publ.fmt

Starting copy...

3 rows copied.
Clock Time (ms.): total = 1      Avg = 0      (3000.00 rows per sec.)
```

Here's the format file automatically generated by bcp:

```
11.0
4
1       SYBCHAR    0    4        " "    1    pub_id
2       SYBCHAR    1    512      " "    2    pub_name
3       SYBCHAR    1    512      " "    3    city
4       SYBCHAR    1    512      " "    4    state
```

There are seven columns in the format file:

- Position of data field in the operating system file
- Datatype of the data field
- Prefix length
- Data length of the data field
- Column terminator (if no terminator is specified, the data fields in the data file are fixed width)
- Position of the column the data maps into the SQL Server table
- Column name in the SQL Server table

# Native Format

If you want your data in operating system-specific format, and want the server to make all the default choices for file storage type, prefix length, and storage length, use the -n option to indicate native format. Native format files do not use field and row terminators. The prefix length specifies the data width of each data field.

# Character Format

Bulk copying data in character format is one of the easiest and least troublesome ways to bulk copy data. When you specify the -c option, it tells bcp that all data is to be represented in character format. Fields are terminated with tabs, and rows are terminated with the newline. Data in character format can be easily read and modified using text editors. This makes it easy to change the data in the input file, which can help when creating test data. Terminators are the defaults (tab for field, newline for row) unless the -t or -r options are specified.

# Native Versus Character Format

Use native format (-n option) when copying data between tables within the same SQL Server or SQL Servers running on the same platform. Native format files will load faster than character format files because no data conversion is necessary. However, if the data is to be loaded into a table within a SQL Server running on a different platform, the native formats between the two platforms might not be compatible. In these instances, you'll need to use character format files.

# Batches

A bcp batch is a logical unit of work. The entire batch is treated as a transaction. If you do not use the -b option, the entire data set is considered a single transaction. Encountering a fatal error results in having the entire load aborted and rolled back. By setting the batch size, you enable bcp to commit fewer rows per transaction. Fatal errors during bcp sessions may still enable partial results; you can fix the problem and continue where you left off.

If you set your batch size properly, log entries pertaining to the bcp load can be deleted when the log is truncated, even while the bcp is still running. If you do not set the batch size, your transaction log must be able to accommodate the logging of all rows added to your table in a session.

> **TIP**
>
> If your batch size is too large, you must rerun large amounts of data when you encounter a fatal error. If your batch size is too small, the additional overhead in managing more numerous, smaller transactions slows bcp down noticeably. Experiment with batch sizes between 100 and 50,000, depending on your requirements to find the optimal batch size.

# Permissions

The permissions needed to run bcp depend on whether you are copying data in or out. If you are copying data into a table, you must have insert permission on that table. If you are copying data out of a table, you must have select permission on that table (as well as select permission on sysobjects, syscolumns, and sysindexes, and the permission to create the operating system file).

# Text or Image Data

When copying data out to an operating system file, bcp attempts to enable enough characters to handle any possible value in a field. That is why variable-length character fields are stored as their maximum value. Text and image columns, however, can be of almost unlimited length. At present, a single column of this type can contain over two billion characters per row.

By default, the server limits how much data to copy out of a text or image column to 32KB per row. Any data after 32KB is not copied to the output file. If it is possible that your fields contain more than 32KB (16 pages) of data, override the default value by specifying a new maximum value with the -T option.

# Network Packet Size

Use the -A option to specify the size of the network packet to use when transferring data between SQL Server and the operating system file. The default network packet size is determined by the configuration variable, default network packet size, and the maximum network packet size is determined by the value of maximum network packet size. The size specified must be between these values and must be a multiple of 512. This packet size is used only for the duration of the bcp.

> **TIP**
>
> Benchmark your system by executing a large bcp several times, using different values for network packet size. This helps determine what value is appropriate for your architecture.

# Error Files

Error files are used to store rows that bcp is unable to copy. To create an error file, specify a filename after the -e flag. If you don't provide a full path, bcp attempts to create the error file relative to your current directory. An error file is created only if an error is encountered. The error file contains information on the row number and the type of error encountered on one line and the actual data on a separate second line. The data itself is copied in the default character format: file data is in character format and readable, the field terminator is the tab, and the row terminator is the newline. You should always specify the -e option because the error file can be helpful in analysis.

The error file actually can be used as an input file for a future bcp. Because the data is in character format, you can determine the reason the insert failed, and modify the error file with data that is acceptable. You can delete the information lines inserted by bcp, either by hand or by using an operating system facility to exclude data (grep -? in UNIX). You then can copy the file into the table using bcp, but make sure to specify the -c option.

## Errors During *bcp in*

When you copy data to a table, these are the types of errors you might encounter:

- Data conversion errors (input data of 000000 for a datetime field; bcp cannot format a valid date from this string and the insert fails)
- Nullability errors (no value in the input file; column defined as not null)
- Format errors (too many or too few fields in the input file than were expected by bcp, improperly defined format file, field terminators contained in the data, or improper terminators specified)

Duplicate rows are not discovered until the batch is submitted, and they are caught by SQL Server, not bcp. Duplicate data is not written to the error file. If the ignore_dup_key option is specified for the index, bcp does not interpret the rejection of that row as a fatal error. Additionally, the rejection is not included in the count of errors for the batch. There is a message indicating that there were duplicate rows in the batch. Set this option when creating the index if duplicate data is not considered to be a serious business error warranting the aborting of a batch.

> **TIP**
>
> Specify the -m option for the maximum number of errors. The default value of 10 is not always adequate if you want to insert all the input rows. Set the value for -m equal to the value of -b (batch size) to ensure that all input rows are attempted.

## Errors during *bcp out*

When copying data out of a table, the -e option is not as useful. The types of output errors you might encounter include the following:

- Data conversion errors
- I/O errors in writing to the host bcp output file

These errors are somewhat rare, especially when using the -n or -c options.

> **NOTE**
>
> This book does not cover the following issues:
>
> - Translations based on differences in languages or terminal types. See the -J, -a, -q, and -z options in your *SQL Server Utility Programs* manual for more information on this problem.
> - Programming using the bcp DB-Library and ct-Library routines. There are several bcp functions available in the DB-Library to enable you to write your own programs to handle the bulk transfer of data. Your programs will have access to the same bcp functions as the bcp utility. See the Open Client DB-Library or ct-Library reference manual for more information.

# Data Integrity Issues

When you are running bcp, you must be aware of several data-integrity issues. These issues are most important if you are loading data directly into existing tables that are used in production. Here are the highlights, then we will look at each issue in detail. During a bcp:

- Triggers are not fired.
- Rules are not enforced.
- Constraints are not enforced.
- Defaults are enforced.
- Money columns are truncated to two decimal places during a bcp out when using the -c option.

> **NOTE**
>
> Many organizations bulk copy data into intermediate load tables, then use insert statements to load the data into the production tables. In that case, any integrity that works for common insert statements works with an insert from the load table.

## bcp and Triggers

bcp does not fire triggers, even in slow mode, so your trigger code is completely bypassed. (Interestingly, even though bcp doesn't fire triggers, the presence of a trigger on a table causes the slower, logged version of bcp to run—more on this in the section "Is Fast bcp Really Possible?" later in this chapter.) Triggers often are used to implement referential integrity, complex rule, or default enforcement, or for keeping derived values in sync with detail records. When bulk copying data into a table with triggers, decide how you are going to resolve this issue. To make sure the new data is valid, run the trigger code as SQL code to validate the referential integrity of the loaded data, to apply complex rule and default enforcement, or to keep summary and detail values in sync. Decide how invalid rows are to be handled.

Validate the bcp data by executing the integrity pieces of the pertinent trigger SQL after a bcp. This enables you to validate the existing data. For example, if you have a trigger on the table named purchase indicating that a customer_number inserted into that table must exist in the customer table, execute the SQL code necessary to validate all customer numbers that exist in the purchase table. The SQL code to find any rows that violate referential integrity might look like this:

```
select cust_id, line_no
from purchase
where cust_id not in
   (select cust_id
    from customers)
```

Sometimes triggers are used to keep summary values in sync. For example, the `pubs2` database has a `salesdetail` and a `titles` table. The quantity value (qty) in the salesdetail table for a particular title is summarized to establish the total sales for a book (the `total_sales` column in the `titles` table). In this case, your trigger code is structured to handle the incremental adding of data. The overall total value for the sales cannot be determined by the trigger code. You may have to recalculate fully all summary values for detail rows. Determine the SQL necessary to accomplish this task and execute the code. Here is the SQL statement to reestablish the relationship between `titles.total_sales` and `salesdetail.qty`:

```
update titles
set total_sales =
   (select sum(qty)
   from salesdetail sd
   where titles.title_id = sd.title_id
   group by sd.title_id)
```

## bcp and Rules

`bcp` does not invoke rules. Compare the count of rows that match the domain criteria to the total number of rows in the table. For example, the following query checks to see if any rows in the `drivers` table are not of legal driving age (16 years or older):

```
select count(*)
from drivers
where age < 16
```

If the count is greater than zero, then there are values in the table that do not conform to the business rules. The next step is to determine which rows violate your rule criteria and decide whether to change the rule, remove the rows, or change the invalid data.

## bcp and Constraints

`bcp` does not invoke constraints, which were introduced in System 10. Handle check constraints as you would rules and referential integrity constraints (primary key or foreign key declaration) as you would referential integrity code in triggers.

## bcp and Truncation

A bcp out of data using the character mode (-c) automatically rounds money columns to two decimal places. If this is unacceptable, do use the -c option to copy out any tables that contain money columns.

A bcp in of character values larger than the column definition will be automatically truncated without warning.

# *bcp* and Defaults

A bcp in does apply column defaults if the bcp input file contains no data in a row for a data field.

# *bcp* and Character Conversion

When using the -c option to specify character data, it is important to know what your input file contains for those unknown pieces of data. bcp reads characters until it detects a delimiter. The default delimiter is the tab character (\t), although you can specify a different delimiter if you wish (¦, @, #, and so forth). All the characters up to the delimiter are considered part of that field. Many programmers (mainframe programmers especially) are accustomed to padding a field with spaces if no data exists at the source. Note that SQL Server considers spaces to be different than null. The spaces are converted to the appropriate column datatype:

- For numeric datatypes, spaces convert to a 0 equivalent (0 for int, 0.00 for float, and so forth).
- For datetime datatypes, spaces convert to the default SQL Server date of 1/1/1900.
- For character datatypes, a string of spaces is inserted as a single space.

### NOTE

SQL Server stores actual data length (not maximum length) in variable length and nullable columns.

If you truly want no value for a column (null), do not pad the field with any characters. Merely follow a delimiter with another delimiter. bcp interprets this as no data, and the row is inserted with that field being null.

### WARNING

Don't learn the date-conversion issue the hard way! It's frustrating to find out that 40 percent of your customers were born on January 1, 1900, after you have loaded 10 million customer records.

# Format Files versus Standard Format

One of the key elements in the everyday use of bcp is whether format files are used. Format files are used when the input or output file must exist in a format other than the standard character or native formats.

When exporting data using bcp, you must export all columns from a table unless you define a format file that skips table columns. The identity column, available in System 10 and later, is the only exception to this rule (see the -X option). When importing data using the -n or -c option, you are also required to copy all columns from the input file into the table (except the identity column, as the exception still applies). If you want to skip columns when copying data into or out of SQL Server using bcp, you must use a format file and specify a 0 for the column number of the column you want to skip.

You'll also need to use format files when the order of the columns in the input file differs from the order of the columns in the table. For example, the following format file maps the third data column in the input file to the fourth column in the table and the fourth column in the input file to the third table column:

```
11.0
4
1    SYBCHAR    0    4     "\t"    1    pub_id
2    SYBCHAR    0    40    "\t"    2    pub_name
3    SYBCHAR    0    2     "\t"    4    state
4    SYBCHAR    0    20    "\n"    3    city
```

# Is Fast *bcp* Really Possible?

The fast mode for bcp is attempted when data is copied into a table with no indexes or triggers. It requires the select into/bulkcopy option to be set to on for the database. It is the fastest way to load data, but it often is difficult to use this mode when importing data. The issues that affect your approach are table distribution within databases and data availability to users. It is important to consider these issues based on whether the load is of initial data or incremental data.

## Initial Load

Initial load data must be considered when the SQL Server is to contain information that exists in some other source. Consider a new customer-support application. You may require that all existing customers be copied into the customer table as part of the necessary startup data for the application. When a customer calls in, the record already exists in the SQL Server table. Your initial load of the customer table includes all customers as of a certain point in time. You write programs or use an export facility to copy the data from the source into an operating system file. This file is then loaded into the customer table using bcp.

Initial load data implies that the table is not truly usable until the data is loaded. The table is not accessed until the load is finished. This gives you the luxury of deciding how the data will be loaded, because data availability is not an issue.

# Incremental Load

Incremental data is data that represents a roll-up of existing data. Incremental data is any new data that has been added to a source since a point in time (the time of the initial extract or last incremental extract of data).

Incremental data implies that the table is currently being used and must be available for business use. Therefore, availability of the data is the big concern. Normally, there is a certain period of time in which to load incremental data without worrying about people using the system. This is normally referred to as the "batch window."

Another major concern, especially for production databases, is recoverability. Rows inserted using slow bcp are logged like a normal insert. Fast bcp does not log row inserts, and causes the dump transaction capability to be turned off. Fast bcp may not be prudent, because the capability of recovering up to the minute is jeopardized.

# Achieving Fast *bcp*

To achieve fast bcp, the table cannot have triggers or indexes. Almost every table you deal with in a production environment contains at least one index (for uniqueness) and probably a trigger (especially if used to enforce referential integrity). The trigger is not executed, but forces a slow bcp. In addition, you'll need to write code to apply your trigger checks after the data is loaded. (See the sections on "Data Integrity Issues" and "bcp and Triggers" in this chapter for information on how to handle trigger code.) Indexes have a much greater impact on your ability to use fast bcp.

Indexes are needed on the table for the application to perform in a reasonable amount of time. Therefore, all indexes should be created before users access the table. Indexes have three important issues to be addressed:

- **Creation time**—The creation of an index can take a great deal of time, which is proportional to the amount of data on the table and size of the index. The time to create all indexes easily can be greater than the actual time available in a batch window.

- **Space requirements**—Creating clustered indexes requires available database space estimated at 120 percent of the size of the table. If the table you're copying data into is the only table in a database, it may not be possible to create the index after the data is loaded. For example, take a 2GB table. If you want to use fast bcp, you need 2GB for the table and 2.4GB for the creation of the index. You then have to size the database to at least 4.4GB (without accounting for the size of the log). If this table is not going to grow over time, the additional 2GB will never be used. If disk space is at a premium, this is not a valid option.

■ **Locking**—Nonclustered indexes acquire shared locks on a table, and clustered indexes acquire exclusive locks. During clustered index creation, the table will not be available to users. Because clustered index creation can take a lot of time, fast bcp is not normally an option for an incremental load of data. Although nonclustered indexes can be created while the system is in use, on-line modifications of the data may conflict with the index creation.

A summary of what mode to use based on the type of data to be loaded is shown in Table A.3.

### Table A.3. A comparison of bcp modes.

| Mode | Initial Load Data | Incremental Load Data |
|---|---|---|
| Fast bcp | Use if there is no clustered index on the table or if space required for clustered index is not an issue. | This usually is not possible due to space availability constraints caused by index creation. Use only on small tables, or tables where indexes could be recreated in the available time. |
| Slow bcp | Use if space restrictions require that the clustered index exists before data is loaded. | This is the normal mode. Distribution of data in the table can be affected by the bulk load of data. The distribution statistics for the indexes on the table should be updated using the update statistics command. |

---

**TIP**

Be sure the input file data is sorted in clustered index order if a clustered index already exists. This avoids page splits and decreases the amount of time and space needed for the load.

# Dealing with No Terminators

Often an input file contains data in fixed-length character format with no terminators. In this case, use interactive bcp to specify the format of the input file. The prefix length for each field should be 0, indicating the absence of a value for the width of the row. The storage datatype should be character, and the length should be the number of characters specified for that field in the input file.

# Updating Statistics

The query optimizer uses the distribution page for an index to determine the number of rows affected by an operation. The distribution page is used to determine the query plan, which specifies the order in which the tables are accessed and the index used to retrieve the data. The distribution page is created at index-creation time, and is updated only when the update statistics command is executed.

During initial load, space conditions may mandate that data be loaded into a table with an existing index. This implies that the index was created when the table was empty. If so, no distribution page is created. If you load data into an empty table with an existing clustered index, run the update statistics command after the data is loaded. This creates the statistics page for the clustered index.

During incremental loads, tables usually have existing indexes (clustered, nonclustered, or both). An incremental load can change the actual distribution of data in a table. It's a good idea to run the update statistics command after an initial load to ensure that the table has valid statistics. Because this activity may take a long time, consider updating the statistics when the batch window is larger (weekends or holidays).

# Replacement Data

When adding data to a table, you must ensure that all data is "new," meaning that it is a new row to be added to the table. If the input file contains data for existing rows, bcp does not have the capability of replacing the existing row with the row in the bcp input file. To replace a row in a table with a record in a file, you must use a different facility, or write a data-loading routine to perform the delete and insert or update of the row.

# The Definition Copy (*defncopy*) Utility

The defncopy utility can be used to copy object-creation statements from the database system tables into an operating system file or to create an object in a database using an existing file. defncopy can be used to copy defaults, rules, stored procedures, triggers, or views, but cannot be used for tables or indexes. defncopy works on all those objects on which you can perform an sp_helptext—that is, those objects whose source code is stored in the syscomments table. Remember, you can copy any objects you create "as" SQL statements (create default as 5, create rule as @value > 0, and so forth).

This tool is invoked much like bcp: on the command line with a variety of options. However, the database name is listed separately for defncopy, unlike bcp, which accepts a database name only as part of fully qualifying the name of a table. defncopy in assumes an object does not exist, and defncopy out assumes an object does exist.

## Syntax

```
defncopy [ -U login_name ] [ -P password ] [ -S server ] [ -v ]
[ -I interfaces_file ] [ -a display_charset ]
[ -J client_charset ] [ -z language ] [ -X ]
{ in ¦ out } datafile database_name
{ [owner.]object_name [ [owner.]object_name] ...}
```

> **NOTE**
>
> Specify object names for defncopy out only.

## Options

Table A.4 presents detailed descriptions of each parameter of defncopy.

**Table A.4. defncopy parameters.**

| Flag | Option | Description |
|------|--------|-------------|
| | database name | When copying out, this is the database where the object resides. For copying in, this is the target database where you want the object copied. |
| | owner | This is the owner of the object (out only; rarely used). The mechanism used to identify objects is first to look for a table owned by the database user name (determined when the database is "used"), then to look for a table owned by the database owner (dbo). Therefore, the owner name does not have to be provided unless the object you want is owned by someone other than yourself or dbo. |
| | in ¦ out | This indicates the direction of data flow: out to copy definitions from a database to a file, in to create an object using a creation script as input. |

| Flag | Option | Description |
|------|--------|-------------|
| | datafile | This is the fully qualified path name of the data file to be created (in) or used as a source (out). |
| | object name | This is used to identify the object name to copy out (out only). defncopy first searches sysobjects to determine whether it is a valid object; then it extracts the definition from the syscomments table. Regardless of the number of objects listed, their creation statements are copied into the indicated output file. |
| -a | display charset | This is the character set used by the display device. The defncopy program can be running on a different machine than the display. This normally is used with the -J option to specify the complete conversion information. Use -a without -J if the client character set is the same as the default. (This option is seldom used.) |
| -I | interfaces file | This is the name of the interface file to use when trying to find a server to which to connect. If this option is not provided, defcopy looks for a file named interfaces in the directory identified by the $SYBASE environment variable (the SYBASE home directory). |
| -J | client charset | This is the character set to use on the client machine. defncopy filters all definitions in or out, translating between the SQL Server character set and the client character set. (This option is seldom used.) (See the section on "Character Sets" under "Bulk Copy (bcp)" for more on character sets.) |
| -P | password | This is the password for the login name specified. If this option is not specified, defncopy prompts for it. |
| -S | server | This is the name of the server to which to connect. If the server name is not provided, it uses the $DSQUERY value, if it exists, or SYBASE. This name must be found in the interfaces file used by defncopy. The location of the interfaces file is explained in the -I option. |

*continues*

**Table A.4. continued**

| Flag | Option | Description |
|------|--------|-------------|
| -U | *login name* | This is the login name for `defncopy` to use when connecting to the server. The default is the username identified by your environment. |
| -v | | This is used to display the version number of `defncopy` and copyright information. |
| -X | | This is for password encryption. If `-X` is specified, `defncopy` attempts to connect to the server and requests an encryption string. The server sends the encryption code to the client and the client encrypts the password using the provided code. The client sends the encrypted password to the server where it is decoded and verified. Use this option if security needs dictate. |
| -z | *language* | This tells `defncopy` to put messages and prompts in a language other than the default language for the server. |

## Notes

Note that the login name is critical, because your login name can be mapped to a user name within a database (or you can be a guest). For definitions being copied out, the user must have select permission on `syscomments` and `sysobjects`. For copying definitions in, the user must have `create` *object* permission, where *object* is either `default`, `rule`, `trigger`, `procedure`, or `view`.

The interfaces option (`-I`) is seldom used, except in those cases where DBAs create a "super" interface file for administrative use and the default interface file contains only a subset of entries.

## Permissions

When copying a definition out of a table, you do not need the capability of accessing the object in question. `defncopy` first identifies the existence of an object based on the database (required), owner (optional), and object_name (required). Using this information, `defncopy` queries the `sysobjects` table to determine whether an object exists in the database with the specified name. It searches for only the following types:

- V (view)
- R (rule)

- D (default)
- TR (trigger)
- P (procedure)

If a match is made, defncopy captures the internal object_id and selects the definition from the syscomments table. Therefore, you need select permission only on the sysobjects and syscomments tables, which normally is granted to public by default.

When using defncopy to create an object based on an existing file, you must be able to perform that function within the specified database. For example, if your script has a rule-creation statement, you must have create rule command permission in the target database. The types of command permissions that may be needed include create view, create rule, create default, create trigger, and create procedure.

## Dealing with Comments

defncopy constructs an output file from the data in the syscomments table. When commenting creation text, people often place all comments before the create statement. When there are more than 100 characters of text before a create statement, defncopy may fail, or it may construct a script that cannot be used without modification. To avoid this problem, embed all comments inside your create statement or keep comments before a create statement to a minimum.

defncopy places a comment in all the scripts it creates. This comment must end the definition for defncopy to be able to execute the script. If you are creating your own scripts to use with defncopy, make sure you place the following comment at the bottom of your script:

```
/* ### DEFNCOPY:  END OF DEFINITION  */
```

If your script file does not have this comment at the bottom, defncopy is unable to execute your code. Note that any defncopy scripts can also be executed in isql or other SQL script execution utilities.

## Tips

You can easily use isql to create a defncopy command to create backup scripts for most existing objects (rule, default, trigger, view, and procedure) other than tables or indexes. Because you can list your current objects by querying the sysobjects table, you easily can concatenate a string to generate the necessary creation syntax.

For example, suppose you are given a database called marketdb and standards such as the following:

- Trigger script files should have a suffix of .trg.
- Procedure script files should have a suffix of .prc.

- Rule script files should have a suffix of `.rul`.
- Default script files should have a suffix of `.def`.
- View script files should have a suffix of `.vew`.

You can execute the following code:

```
1>  use marketdb
2>  go
1>  set nocount on
2>  go
1>  select "defncopy -Uuser1 -Ppasswd out " + name + ".trg marketdb " + name
2>  from sysobjects where type = 'TR'
3>  and uid = user_id()
4>  go
1>  select "defncopy -Uuser1 -Ppasswd out " + name + ".prc marketdb " + name
2>  from sysobjects where type = 'P'
3>  and uid = user_id()
4>  go
1>  select "defncopy -Uuser1 -Ppasswd out " + name + ".rul marketdb " + name
2>  from sysobjects where type = 'R'
3>  and uid = user_id()
4>  go
1>  select "defncopy -Uuser1 -Ppasswd out " + name + ".def marketdb " + name
2>  from sysobjects where type = 'D'
3>  and uid = user_id()
4>  go
1>  select "defncopy -Uuser1 -Ppasswd out " + name + ".vew marketdb " + name
2>  from sysobjects where type = 'V
3>  and uid = user_id()
4>  go
```

The output from these five `select` operations can be used to create an operating system script to run the necessary `defncopy` commands. This is an easy way to give yourself a warm, fuzzy feeling about your ability to recreate an object in the case of a problem.

# The Interactive SQL (*isql*) Utility

`isql` is the generic interactive SQL execution utility for SQL Server. It often is referred to as "working at the command line." `isql` is used to execute activities such as creating objects, testing, inserting data, and selecting information. However, it is somewhat limited in its formatting and scrolling capabilities (essentially, it has none). `isql` often is run as a batch command interpreter rather that an interactive tool. Files are created that are read into `isql` for processing, with the output being directed to the terminal or an operating system file. `isql` also has no command history capability, and editing scripts is accomplished by invoking an operating system editor (and then you can only edit the current SQL batch or the just previously executed SQL batch).

# Syntax

```
isql [ -U login_name ] [ -P password ] [ -S server ] [-H hostname ]
[-E editor] [ -I interfaces_file ] [-y sybase_dir]
[-c command_end ] [-h headers] [-s col_separator]
[-w column_width] [-i inputfile ] [-o outputfile] [-m errorlevel]
[ -J client_charset ] [ -a display_charset ] [ -z language ]
[-l login_timeout] [-t timeout] [ -A size]
[-e] [-F] [-p] [-n] [-v] [-X] [-Y]
```

# Options

Table A.5 presents detailed descriptions of each parameter of isql.

### Table A.5. isql parameters.

| Flag | Option | Description |
|------|--------|-------------|
| -a | display charset | This is the character set used by the display device. The isql utility could be running on a different machine than the SQL Server. This is used normally with the -J option to specify the complete conversion information. Use -a without -J if the client character set is the same as the default. (This option is seldom used.) |
| -A | size | This is used to specify the network packet size for this connection. The value provided must be a multiple of 512 and between the configured values for default network packet size and maximum network packet size. |
| -c | command end | This is used to specify a command terminator other that the word go. For example, if you have a script that uses a semicolon to indicate the end of a command, invoke isql with the argument -c;. |
| -E | editor | This is used to specify an editor other than the default editor. For example, if vi is the default editor and you want to use emacs, invoke isql with the argument -E emacs. |
| -F | | This is used to enable the FIPS flagger, which alerts the user to any SQL that is considered non-ANSI standard. |

*continues*

## Table A.5. continued

| *Flag* | *Option* | *Description* |
|---|---|---|
| -J | client charset | This is the character set to use on the client machine. isql filters all definitions in or out, translating between the SQL Server character set and the client character set. (This option is seldom used.) |
| -h | headers | This is used to identify the number of rows to print between column headings. The default mode of operation is to list column headers only once for the entire result set. |
| -H | hostname | This is used to set the host name for the client. |
| -i | inputfile | This is the name of a file to be read into isql for processing. This file must contain command terminators (go or a character specified by -c option). |
| -I | interfaces file | This is the name of the interface file to use when trying to find a server to which to connect. If this option is not provided, isql looks for a file named interfaces in the directory identified by the $SYBASE environment variable (the SYBASE home directory). |
| -l | login timeout | This specifies the maximum timeout value allowed when connecting to the SQL Server. The default value is 60 seconds. |
| -m | errorlevel | This is used to set the minimum level of error required to print error data on your screen. Currently, all errors go to your screen. If you want to suppress messages below an error level of 17, specify the value -m 17. |
| -n | | This removes the prompt (line number and >) from input lines. |
| -o | outputfile | This is the name of the file to use for standard output of the isql commands. This is normally used with the -i option. |
| -p | | This tells isql to print out performance statistics after completion of each batch. It lists the total clock time from sending the query to receiving results and the average time per transaction (clock time/# of commands). |

| Flag | Option | Description |
|------|--------|-------------|
| -P | *password* | This is the password for the login name specified. If this option is not specified, isql prompts for it. |
| -s | *col separator* | This specifies a column separator other than the default (space). |
| -S | *server* | This is the name of the server to which to connect. If the server name is not provided, isql uses the $DSQUERY value if it exists or SYBASE. This name must be found in the interfaces file used by isql. The location of the interfaces file is explained in the -I option. |
| -t | *timeout* | This specifies the number of seconds before a command times out. If you do not set a value for this option, a command can run indefinitely. |
| -U | *login name* | This is the login name for isql to use when connecting to the server. The default is the username identified by your environment. |
| -v | | This displays the version number of isql and copyright information. |
| -w | *column width* | This is used to set the screen width for output. This is often used so that output is not broken into several lines. Good values to use are 120 or 160. |
| -X | | This is for password encryption. If -X is specified, isql attempts to connect to the server and request an encryption string. The server sends the encryption code to the client, and the client encrypts the password, using the provided code. The client sends the encrypted password to the server where it is decoded and verified. Use this option if security needs dictate. |
| -y | *sybase dir* | This is the directory in which to look for the interfaces file, if other than the default $SYBASE directory. |
| -Y | | This tells SQL Server to use chained transactions (required for some application development environments—might be helpful in testing embedded SQL code). |

*continues*

**Table A.5. continued**

| Flag | Option | Description |
|------|--------|-------------|
| -z | language | This tells isql to put messages and prompts in a language other than the default language for the server. |

## Notes

The login name is critical, because your login name can be mapped to a user name within a database (or you can be a guest).

The interfaces option (-I) is seldom used, except in those cases where DBAs create a "super" interface file for administrative use and the default interface file contains only a subset of entries.

## Option Recommendations

isql has about as many options as bcp (25+). Aside from the familiar ones, such as -U and -P, there are several other options that can help you use isql:

■ Use the -e option to echo input when reading in files. This option is useful when you are using isql as a batch command interpreter. There are several commands that you can execute in SQL Server that do not have output or in which the output does not contain enough information to define fully the activity that encountered the error. When you are working interactively, you know what commands an error applies to because the error information is displayed after you type go to execute the query. When you're working with files, however, it can be frustrating trying to determine which commands the errors belong to, especially when you are rebuilding the database or performing an activity across a number of tables. By specifying the -e option, isql echoes input lines after they are read by SQL Server. Your output file then contains all input commands, which may make the output file more readable and useful.

■ The -w option is used to change the column width of your output from 80 characters to a user-defined value. This command is often used when the output from a command such as sp_help tablename is broken across several lines and is difficult to read. By increasing the column-width size, the server uses that number of characters when deciding how much of a line of output can fit on a screen. The value should not exceed the maximum screen display width or the lines might be truncated or end up wrapping anyway.

- The -c option is used to specify a command terminator other than go. This is extremely useful for those people migrating to an SQL Server environment from some other database vendor. Often a semicolon (;) is used to indicate the end of a command, even in GUI development tools such as PowerBuilder. A script exported from such an environment has a semicolon to indicate the end of each command. Rather than editing all your source files, turning each ; into go, you can simply invoke isql and provide the terminator using -c.

- The -X option is important for any sites concerned about security. Because a knowledgeable person with a network sniffer is able to capture a userid and password from the raw network packets, it is important to encrypt passwords to make an environment more secure. The -X option requests that encryption be used. Provide a command alias to redefine isql to isql -X if security is an issue.

- The -A option may provide some performance gains if you are sending or receiving large amounts of data in isql. Use this option when you are executing readtext or writetext commands or when you are extracting a lot of information using isql in a batch mode.

# Important Commands

When using isql, there are several commands that have special meaning. These words are typed at the isql command line and are interpreted by the isql program (see Table A.6).

**Table A.6. Important isql commands.**

| Command | Description |
|---|---|
| go [#] | This indicates to the server that the contents of the buffer are to be sent to the server. The word go must be on a separate line from the other statements in the batch and start at the first character on the line. A number can be specified after the word go to indicate the number of times to execute the SQL in the batch. For example, go 100 tells the server to execute the SQL in the buffer 100 times. |
| reset or <cntrl>-C | This clears the command buffer, and is used when you want to clear your work and start over. It is sometimes used to clear the buffer before invoking a text editor. |
| vi (or other) | This enters an editing session using the contents of the command buffer. The UNIX default is vi, but other editors can be used by defining the EDITOR environment variable or the -E option to isql. |

*continues*

**Table A.6. continued**

| Command | Description |
|---------|-------------|
| quit, exit | This is used to break the connection to SQL Server and end the isql process. This word must be the only command on the line and can be typed at any time. |
| !!os_cmd | This is used to shell out to the operating system to run a command at the operating-system level. For example, if you want to see what scripts you have in the current directory, execute !! ls (UNIX) or !! dir (DOS) to obtain a listing of files in the current directory. Upon completion of the operating system command, you still will be at the same isql command line as before execution. |
| :r filename | This reads the contents of the filename into the command buffer. The buffer is not displayed. For example, if you have a file with 10 lines in it, and you read in that file starting at line 1 in isql (1> :r filename), you immediately see an indicator of the 11th line (11>) showing that isql read in 10 lines and is awaiting additional input. This file cannot contain a command terminator (go). If your files contain terminators, you must edit the buffer contents using an editor before executing the query. |

# Command-Line Redirection

Often isql is used as a batch interpreter, where input and output files are specified as isql options or using standard redirection syntax. To use the isql options, specify -i for the input file and -o for the output file. When using normal redirection commands, use < to direct a file into isql and > to direct the output into an output file. Therefore, the following two commands are equivalent:

```
isql -Uuser1 -Puser1 -i mytext.sql -o mytext.out
isql -Uuser1 -Puser1 < mytext.sql > mytext.out
```

> **NOTE**
>
> If you use the < method to redirect input to isql and do not provide a password with the -P parameter, SQL Server expects to find the password as the first line of the input file. This feature can be useful if you do not want to type the password on the command line (which is visible to all the world on a UNIX machine via the ps command) or be prompted for a password by isql. If you put the password in the input file, you'll want to be sure to protect the input files from prying eyes!

There also is a way to tell isql to accept data as input until a certain character or combination of characters is detected. This normally is used as a scripting technique, although it can be used interactively. When used interactively, it essentially acts like the word quit or exit. Note this example, where isql is invoked at the command line with the option telling it to look for the string !@! as an indicator to exit isql:

```
% isql -Uuser1 -Puser1 << !@! > outputfile
use pubs2
go
select * from titles
go
!@!
```

Clearly, this is not as useful on an interactive basis—it is much easier to type quit or exit. This capability is wonderful for scripting, though. It can be used in a shell script to invoke isql and pass data without having to deal with an input file.

# Summary

The SQL Server administrative utilities are a nuisance to learn, and most administrators only learn what they need to know to get by. It's especially difficult for administrators who are unaccustomed to the UNIX command style to learn to use these commands well.

It's important to use utilities to simplify the tasks that are performed by the basic SQL Server utilities. Using bcp properly can save you hours in a load, and knowing how to automate scripts with isql can allow you to simplify administrative tasks that previously were impossible.

bcp is a good, basic tool to use for extracting and importing data. It does have shortcomings (for example, rules, defaults, and constraints are bypassed—perhaps this should be an option), but with some extra work you can feel confident about the integrity of your data. It is important to understand how loading large amounts of data affects table distribution.

defncopy gives you the capability of recreating the creation text for most objects in your database. bcp can be used for data, and third-party tools are available to recreate your table and index creation syntax (Erwin and so forth). If you do not currently have your object-creation scripts stored away, the SQL shown in this chapter can have you covered in a matter of minutes. You can decide whether to use defncopy or a third-party tool, but make sure you have a way to recreate your database at any point in time.

isql is a tool that is used heavily in the industry. It is the standard means of interactive access, and often is a critical part of a DBA's toolset. It doesn't have a great deal of formatting capabilities, but it does a good job as a standard interface, especially for batch oriented processing.

# The Database Consistency Checker

B

Here is the list of Database Consistency Checker (dbcc) commands that are used by database administrators to perform consistency checks against items within a Sybase SQL Server. These commands run at different levels, including database, table, index, and page. Most of these checks are used to ensure that a database is not corrupt before dumping it; however, some of these commands are executed as part of a language upgrade, to target suspected items, or to just get more information.

> **NOTE**
>
> There are a wealth of other, undocumented dbcc commands used by Sybase Technical Support personnel to assist in database analysis and fixing corruption problems. Some of the more useful (and non-destructive!) commands are presented for your reference in this appendix because I have found them to be very helpful.

# Preventive *dbcc* Commands

Table B.1 briefly summarizes many commonly used dbcc commands. The remainder of this appendix describes each command in detail, along with its syntax and examples of usage.

**Table B.1. Preventive dbcc commands for table and page consistency checks, and other actions.**

| Command | Action |
| --- | --- |
| *Table Consistency Checks* | |
| checkcatalog* | Check system tables |
| checkdb* | Check all tables for a database |
| checktable | Check a specific table's consistency |
| *Page Allocation Consistency Checks* | |
| checkalloc* | Check page allocations |
| indexalloc | Check index page pointers |
| tablealloc | Check table allocation pointers |
| *Other dbcc Commands* | |
| dbrepair | Drop a corrupt database |
| fix_text | Upgrade text to multi-byte character set, language upgrade |
| help | Display syntax help for dbcc commands |
| memusage | Review memory-usage information |
| reindex | Correct indexes as part of sort-order conversion |

| Command | Action |
| --- | --- |
| log | Display contents of transaction log |
| page | Review header (and possible contents) of a page |
| pglinkage | Display page chain linkage information |
| prtipage | Display index row pointer information |
| traceon/traceoff | Set trace flags on or off for a session |

**TIP**

Sybase recommends that you perform at least those dbcc commands marked with an asterisk (*) before backing up (dumping) the database or transaction log.

# Table Consistency *dbcc* Commands

Because bad data tends to snowball, it pays to periodically verify that your data has integrity. Also, when you suspect table corruption (because messages are in the errorlog or queries do not act as expected), it's nice to be able to tell the server to go take a look.

## checkcatalog

The dbcc checkcatalog command checks for consistency problems between system tables and within a system table in a database. For example, some of the checks performed include:

- Verifying a table or view in the sysobjects table has at least one row in the syscolumns table (all tables or views must consist of at least one column).
- Verifying that a type in the syscolumns table has a row in the systypes table (each column must be defined with a valid type).
- Checking that the last checkpoint in the syslogs table is valid.
- Checking the segment definitions in the syssegments table.

checkcatalog performs these types of checks for all of the system tables within the specified database or the current database.

## Syntax

```
dbcc checkcatalog [ ( database_name ) ]
```

## Examples

```
dbcc checkcatalog /* check system tables for current database */
dbcc checkcatalog (master) /* check system tables for master database */
```

## *checkdb*

The dbcc checkdb command performs a dbcc checktable on each of the tables within a database.

## Syntax

```
dbcc checkdb [ ( database_name [ , skip_ncindex ] ) ]
```

## Examples

Check tables in current database:

```
dbcc checkdb
```

Check tables in database pubs2:

```
dbcc checkdb (pubs2)
```

Check database pubs2, skip checking of non-clustered indexes:

```
dbcc checkdb (pubs2, skip_ncindex)
```

The dbcc checkdb command performs a dbcc checktable for every table in the specified database. See the next section for a description of what dbcc checkdb performs.

The skip_ncindex parameter enables you to skip the checking of nonclustered indexes. Use this option, especially in an EIS/DSS environment, to check only the data and ignore potentially huge nonclustered indexes. Use this option on large databases to speed up dbcc time when you are performing dbccs before dumping a database. It enables you to shorten your maintenance window so you can perform at least a minimal check of the database before dumping it.

## *checktable*

The checktable command (and, correspondingly, checkdb for each table in the database) verifies the following information for a table:

- Page linkages: making sure previous page, current page, and next page are consistent throughout the page linkage
- Index sort (that is, making sure indexes are in the correct order)
- Consistency of all pointers (that is, the index pointer to the page and row are valid)
- Data rows on each page have entries in an object allocation map (OAM) page

The OAM pages in SQL Server maintain information on rows and pages used by the tables. The `checktable` command also updates the information in the OAM pages that potentially can become inaccurate (see Chapter 10, "Understanding SQL Server Storage Structures," for a discussion on OAM pages and the information they contain).

> **NOTE**
>
> The built-in `rowcnt()` function, used in the system procedure `sp_spaceused`, reads the OAM page to provide quick counts. The `dbcc checktable` command ensures that the OAM page is accurate, providing better data for `sp_spaceused`.

In System 11, `checktable` reports page linkage information on table partitions (see Chapter 18, "Database Object Placement and Performance," for a discussion of heap table partitioning).

## Syntax

```
dbcc checktable ( { table_name ¦ table_id } ) [ , skip_ncindex ] )
```

The `skip_ncindex` parameter enables you to skip the checking of nonclustered indexes. This may be quite a useful option, especially in an EIS/DSS environment, because it enables you to check only the data and ignore potentially voluminous non-clustered indexes. It is recommended for large sites so that you can check tables quickly.

## Examples

Check table `syslogs`, ID is 8:

```
dbcc checktable (8)
```

Check table `titles`:

```
dbcc checktable (titles)
```

Check `titles` table, skip checking of nonclustered indexes:

```
dbcc checktable (titles, skip_ncindex)
```

Check `authors` table in the `pubs2` database from a different database:

```
dbcc checktable ("pubs2..authors")
```

# Page Allocation *dbcc* Commands

Use the page allocation dbcc commands to check allocation information. These commands check allocation pages to ensure that pages that are allocated actually are a part of a page linkage, and that pages in a page linkage have been marked as allocated.

Object allocation map problems seemed most prevalent in SQL Server Version 4.9.1 and early 4.9.2. They would crop up for no apparent reason, which was often a source of DBA frustration. Eventually, Sybase fixed whatever error was causing the problems, which are once again unusual—but still annoying when they crop up.

If an OAM page error does crop up, you must run the page allocation dbcc commands with the fix option to attempt to correct them. To do so, the database must be in single user mode.

## *checkalloc*

The dbcc checkalloc command checks to see if the page allocation for a database is consistent. It basically executes the following command for every table and index in your database:

```
dbcc tablealloc ( table_name, full, nofix )
```

(See the section "dbcc tablealloc" for a discussion on that command.) dbcc checkalloc checks to see that all pages have been correctly allocated, that no page is allocated that is not part of a page linkage, and that no page is part of a page linkage that has not been marked as allocated. In addition to checking page allocation for all tables, checkalloc also checks all allocation pages in a database to ensure that they contain valid information (see Chapter 10 for a description of allocation pages).

The output of checkalloc can be useful, because it reports the number of pages and extents that have been allocated to the table (indid of 0, or 1 if the object is a clustered index) and any nonclustered indexes. For example, it reports information such as *n* Data Pages in *n* extents. A DBA could use this information to see if there has been significant shrinkage of data in a table. Each extent represents eight pages. If you divide by eight the number of pages reported and round to the next-highest integer (finally, a use for the built-in ceiling function), you will have the minimum number of extents that would be required to hold the specified data pages. If the number you come up with is off by a large margin from the number of extents reported, you probably have had page shrinkage.

Output such as 100 Data Pages in 25 extents indicates that 15 extents have been allocated to the table, but there may be an overabundance of free pages. Optimally, only 13 extents would be needed to hold 100 data pages, with four pages available for use:

$$13 \times 8 = 104 \text{ pages}$$
$$104 - 100 = 4$$

If you are using 25 extents, that means you have a total of 200 pages allocated ($8 \times 25 = 200$), of which only 100 are in page linkages. Logic would dictate that the reason the extents are only half full is because of page shrinkage (voluminous deletes) or the table was created with a low fill factor. If space is an issue, you may want to consider dropping and re-creating the clustered index on this table (if one exists), or creating a "dummy" clustered index that you drop after creation. Either of these methods will consolidate your data into the minimum number of needed extents.

## Syntax

```
dbcc checkalloc [ ( database_name [ , fix ¦ nofix ] ) ]
```

The `fix` option fixes allocation errors, as described in the section "tablealloc" later in this chapter, but it is not recommended that you use this option as part of `checkalloc`. Because `dbcc checkalloc` checks system tables, it needs the database to be set to single-user mode. Setting a database to single-user mode for the duration of a `checkalloc`, especially for large databases, is prohibitive. Use `checkalloc` to locate errors, and then use `tablealloc` to fix errors. This will help limit the amount of time a database is unavailable to a user.

## Examples

Check allocation for current database:

```
dbcc checkalloc
```

Check allocation for database `pubs2`, default is "`nofix`"

```
dbcc checkalloc (pubs2)
```

Check allocation for database `pubs2`, fix allocation errors—not recommended (database must be in single-user mode)

```
dbcc checkalloc (pubs2, fix)
```

## *indexalloc*

The `dbcc indexalloc` command applies to a single-index structure. It can check (with the `full` option) that all pages have been correctly allocated, that no page that is not part of a page linkage is allocated, and that no page is part of a page linkage that has not been marked as allocated. It also can check only certain pieces of an index structure, as described in the "Options" section.

## Syntax

```
dbcc indexalloc ( {table_name¦table_id}, index_id [, {full¦optimized¦fast¦null}
    [ , { fix ¦ nofix ] ] )
```

## Options

The dbcc indexalloc command is much more flexible than the dbcc checkalloc command, which essentially executes a dbcc tablealloc for all of the tables, and dbcc indexalloc for all of the indexes in a database. The dbcc indexalloc command enables you to target an index by itself, which is helpful in segmenting dbcc activity. The following options are available to dbcc indexalloc:

| | |
|---|---|
| full | Widest scope, checks all pages for all types of allocation errors. This is the method used by dbcc checkalloc. |
| optimized | Checks only allocation pages referenced in the OAM pages. An extent not referenced in the OAM page is not detected. This is the default option if null is specified or this option is omitted. |
| fast | Checks whether all index pages that are part of page linkages have been allocated. |
| fix | Fixes allocation errors detected by the consistency check. This option is the default for indexes on user tables. If you select fix for indexes on system tables, the database must be in single-user mode. |
| nofix | Does not fix any allocation errors. This is the default for indexes on system tables. |

## Examples

Check index allocation pages (defaults to "optimized") of index with an ID of "2" on the titles table, fix errors (defaults to "fix" for user tables):

```
dbcc indexalloc (titles, 2)
```

Fully check index page allocation of the sysobjects table, fix errors (database must be in single user mode):

```
dbcc indexalloc (sysobjects, 2, full, fix)
```

Check index allocation pages for the sysobjects table, do not fix errors (null defaults to optimized and nofix is default for system tables):

```
dbcc indexalloc (sysobjects, null)
```

Check index OAM pages for the titleauthor table, fix errors:

```
dbcc indexalloc (titleauthor, 2, fast, fix)
```

# *tablealloc*

The dbcc tablealloc command applies to a single table structure. It can check (with the full option) that all pages have been correctly allocated, that no page is allocated that is not part of a page linkage, and that no page is part of a page linkage that has not been marked as allocated. It also can check only certain pieces of a table structure, as described in the "Options" section.

## Syntax

```
dbcc tablealloc ( {table_name ¦ table_id} [ , {full ¦ optimized ¦ fast ¦ null}
    [ , { fix ¦ nofix ] ] )
```

## Options

The dbcc tablealloc command is much more flexible than the dbcc checkalloc command, which essentially executes a dbcc tablealloc for all of the tables and dbcc indexalloc for all of the indexes in a database. The options available to dbcc tablealloc include the following:

| | |
|---|---|
| full | Widest scope; checks for all types of allocation errors. This is the method used by dbcc checkalloc. |
| optimized | Checks only allocation pages referenced in the OAM pages. An extent not referenced in the OAM page is not detected. This is the default option if null is specified or this option is omitted. |
| fast | Checks whether all pages that are part of page linkages have been allocated. |
| fix | Fixes allocation errors detected by the consistency check. This option is the default for user tables. If you select fix for system tables, the database must be in single-user mode. |
| nofix | Does not fix any allocation errors. This is the default for system tables. |

## Examples

Check allocation pages (defaults to "optimized") of titles table, fix errors (defaults to "fix" for user tables):

```
dbcc tablealloc (titles)
```

Fully check allocation of the syslogs table, fix errors (database must be in single user mode):

```
dbcc tablealloc (8, full, fix)
```

Check allocation pages for the `syslogs` table, do not fix errors (null defaults to optimized and nofix is default for system tables):

```
dbcc tablealloc (8, null)
```

Check OAM pages for `sales` table, fix errors:

```
dbcc tablealloc (sales, fast, fix)
```

## Segmenting the Allocation-Checking Workload

You can use the `dbcc indexalloc` command with `dbcc tablealloc` to effectively segment the workload performed by the `dbcc checkalloc` command. Because the `dbcc checkalloc` command sequentially checks each table (and its indexes) in object ID order, it is a serial process. To speed up an overall consistency check, a DBA could run several `dbcc tablealloc` or `dbcc indexalloc` commands in parallel. This has a negative effect on overall activity on the server, but can effectively reduce the overall amount of time you spend performing this type of consistency check. Hardware capable of Symmetric MultiProcessing (SMP) would definitely be helpful in this type of scenario.

# Other *dbcc* Commands

These `dbcc` commands are not used as often as the standard preventive maintenance batch, but you'll probably use them eventually.

## *dbrepair*

To drop a database that has become corrupt, use the `dbcc dbrepair` statement. This drops a database that you were unable to drop with a standard `drop database` command.

### Syntax

```
dbcc dbrepair (db_name, dropdb)
```

### Examples

```
dbcc dbrepair (customerdb, dropdb)
```

> **WARNING**
>
> Do not use `dbcc dbrepair` without first trying to dump the database, sending Sybase Technical Support the tape, and asking for an explanation as to why the problem occurred in the first place.

# fix_text

The dbcc fix_text command is used to upgrade text values after converting the server to a multi-byte character set. This command makes sure that any existing text fields work correctly with the new multi-byte character set.

## Syntax

```
dbcc fix_text ( { table_name ¦ table_id } )
```

## Example

```
dbcc fix_text (publishers) /* adjusts the publishers table */
```

# help

The dbcc help command probably is one of the more useful dbcc commands in SQL Server. dbcc help displays the syntax for a dbcc command passed as a parameter. This is helpful for commands such as dbcc log, which has a lot of esoteric options. Note that you need to issue the dbcc traceon(3604) command to send the output from dbcc help to the user terminal.

## Syntax

```
dbcc help (cmd_name)
```

## Example

```
dbcc traceon(3604)
dbcc help(log)
go

log( [dbid][,objid][,page][,row][,nrecords][,type={-1..36}],printopt={0¦1} )

DBCC execution completed. If DBCC printed error messages, contact a user with
System Administrator (SA) role.
```

# log

Another useful command is the dbcc log command. This command lets you view, in hex data format, the contents of your transaction log. One good use of the dbcc log command is to verify that updates in place are occurring.

> ### WARNING
>
> Do not run dbcc_log in a database if you have the trunc. log on chkpt. option set to true for that database. There apparently is a rare situation where, if you are running dbcc log at the same time that the SQL Server is attempting to truncate the log, you could end up with a corrupted transaction log, and your database is marked suspect.
>
> If your log ever gets corrupted, you'd better hope you have a fairly recent backup of your database. There is no way to fix a bad transaction log other than to restore your database to a point prior to the log getting corrupted.

## Syntax

```
dbcc log [( dbid ¦ dbname [,objid][,page][,row][,nrecords][,type={-
1..36}],printopt={0¦1} )]
```

To view the entire contents of the log, execute dbcc log with no options. Be forewarned, however, that if your transaction log hasn't been truncated recently, the output can be rather voluminous.

For this reason, you may want to use these additional parameters to limit the records retrieved:

- *objid*—Display only log records associated with the specified object. 0 indicates all objects.
- *page*—Display only log records associated with the specified page. 0 indicates all pages.
- *row*—Display only log records associated with the specified row ID. 0 indicates all rows
- *nrecords*—Display the specified number of records. 0 indicates all records.
- *type*—Display log records for the specified transaction operation type code. (See Table B.2 for a list of some of the more useful operation types.) A type of -1 indicates all records.
- *printopt*—Print all or part of the log record. A 0 indicates the entire log record; a 1 indicates only log record header information

### Table B.2. Transaction log operation type codes.

| Type | Description |
|------|-------------|
| 0 | BEGIN TRANSACTION |
| 4 | INSERT |
| 5 | DELETE |
| 6 | INSIND (indirect insert) |

| Type | Description |
|------|-------------|
| 7 | IINSERT (index insert) |
| 8 | IDELETE (index delete) |
| 9 | MODIFY (update in place) |
| 11 | INOOP (deferred insert) |
| 12 | DNOOP (deferred delete) |
| 13 | ALLOC (page) |
| 15 | EXTENT (allocation) |
| 16 | PAGE SPLIT |
| 17 | CHECKPOINT |
| 30 | END TRANSACTION (commit or rollback) |

## Examples

The first example shows dbcc log output with no parameters. The output has been edited down to help save a tree or two:

```
dbcc log
go

LOG SCAN DEFINITION:
    Database id : 5
    Forward scan: starting at begining of log

LOG RECORDS:
    BEGINXACT       (3652,0)
    attcnt=1 rno=0 op=0 padlen=2 sessionid = (3652,0) len=60 status=0x0000
    masterxsid=(empty)
    xstat=XBEG_ENDXACT,
    spid=1 suid=1 uid=1 masterdbid=0 mastersite=0
    name=$ins   time=Jan 17 1996 12:37PM

    INSERT          (3652,1)
    attcnt=1 rno=1 op=4 padlen=2 sessionid = (3652,0) len=72 status=0x0000
    oampg=2360 pageno=2419 offset=1660 status=0x00 cid=0
    old ts=0x0001 0x0000426d   new ts=0x0001 0x00004273
    xrow
2094808c:   004a0100 00000100 00000100 00000789  .J..............
2094809c:   0000f320 d000                        ... ...

    ENDXACT         (3652,2)
    attcnt=1 rno=2 op=30 padlen=0 sessionid = (3652,0) len=28 status=0x0000
    endstat=COMMIT time=Jan 17 1996 12:37PM

    BEGINXACT       (3652,3)
    attcnt=1 rno=3 op=0 padlen=2 sessionid = (3652,3) len=60 status=0x0000
```

```
     masterxsid=(empty)
     xstat=XBEG_ENDXACT,
     spid=1 suid=1 uid=1 masterdbid=0 mastersite=0
     name=$ins    time=Jan 17 1996 12:37PM


     INSERT        (3652,4)
     attcnt=1 rno=4 op=4 padlen=2 sessionid = (3652,3) len=72 status=0x0000
     oampg=2360 pageno=2474 offset=1638 status=0x00 cid=0
     old ts=0x0001 0x0000426e    new ts=0x0001 0x00004275
     xrow:
2094812c:  00490100 00000100 00000100 00000789   .I..............
2094813c:  0000fd20 d000                          ... ...

     ENDXACT       (3652,5)
     attcnt=1 rno=5 op=30 padlen=0 sessionid = (3652,3) len=28 status=0x0000
     endstat=COMMIT time=Jan 17 1996 12:37PM

     CHECKPOINT    (3652,6)
     attcnt=1 rno=6 op=17 padlen=0 sessionid = (3652,6) len=60 status=0x0000
     rows=0, pages=0 extents=0
     timestamp=0x0001 0x00004276  xstat=0x0040  no active xacts

 ...


Total number of log records 24
DBCC execution completed. If DBCC printed error messages, contact a user with
 System Administrator (SA) role.
```

The following example displays all log records for page 2,170:

```
dbcc log (perftune, 0, 2170)
go

LOG SCAN DEFINITION:
     Database id : 5
     Forward scan: starting at begining of log
     log records for page 2170

LOG RECORDS:
     IDELETE       (3652,12)
     attcnt=1 rno=12 op=8 padlen=1 sessionid = (3652,7) len=60 status=0x0000
     oampg=2184 pageno=2170 offset=516 status=0x00 cid=0
     old ts=0x0001 0x00001611    new ts=0x0001 0x00004277
     xrow:
209482c8:  00ee0300 000b0900 003c00             .........<..

     IDELETE       (3652,14)
     attcnt=1 rno=14 op=8 padlen=1 sessionid = (3652,7) len=60 status=0x0000
     oampg=2184 pageno=2170 offset=516 status=0x00 cid=0
     old ts=0x0001 0x00004277    new ts=0x0001 0x00004279
     xrow:
2094834c:  00ee0300 000b0900 003d00             .........=..

PREVIOUS PAGE:
     SALLOC        (3652,17)
     attcnt=1 rno=17 op=24 padlen=0 sessionid = (3652,7) len=92 status=0x0000
     Pagehdr: pageno=2162 nextpg=2172 prevpg=2170
          ts=0x0001 0x0000427e stat=130, objid= 240003886, oampg= 1992
```

```
        cid = 0
        old next ts=0x0001 0x00001611 new next ts=0x0001 0x0000427d
        old prev ts=0x0001 0x00004279 new prev ts=0x0001 0x0000427c
        extent oampage= 1992

        SPLIT          (3652,18)
        attcnt=1 rno=18 op=16 padlen=0 sessionid = (3652,7) len=52 status=0x0000
        oampg=2184 pageno=2170 offset=1022 status=0x03 cid=0
        old ts=0x0001 0x0000427c   new ts=0x0001 0x0000427f

        IINSERT        (3652,20)
        attcnt=1 rno=20 op=7 padlen=1 sessionid = (3652,7) len=60 status=0x0000
        oampg=2184 pageno=2170 offset=516 status=0x00 cid=0
        old ts=0x0001 0x0000427f   new ts=0x0001 0x00004281
        xrow:
209484dc:  00ee0300 000b0900 003c00              .........<..

        IINSERT        (3652,22)
        attcnt=1 rno=22 op=7 padlen=1 sessionid = (3652,7) len=60 status=0x0000
        oampg=2184 pageno=2170 offset=527 status=0x00 cid=0
        old ts=0x0001 0x00004281   new ts=0x0001 0x00004283
        xrow:
20948554:  00ee0300 000b0900 003d00              .........=..


Total number of log records 6
DBCC execution completed. If DBCC printed error messages, contact a user with
 System Administrator (SA) role.
```

Another good use of the dbcc log command is to determine how many page splits (op=16) are occurring in a database since the last time the log was truncated. To get a count of all the page splits, execute the following:

```
dbcc log (perftune, 0, 0, 0, 0, 16, 1)
go
LOG SCAN DEFINTION:
    Database id : 5
    Forward scan: starting at begining of log
    Log operation type SPLIT (16)

LOG RECORDS:
    SPLIT          (3652,18)
    attcnt=1 rno=18 op=16 padlen=0 sessionid = (3652,7) len=52 status=0x0000
    oampg=2184 pageno=2170 offset=1022 status=0x03 cid=0
    old ts=0x0001 0x0000427c   new ts=0x0001 0x0000427f


Total number of log records 1
DBCC execution completed. If DBCC printed error messages, contact a user with
 System Administrator (SA) role.
```

In this example, you can see that there is only a single page split in the transaction log. This is because I recently truncated it and have only run one update statement since.

## memusage

The dbcc memusage command output is extremely useful for validating your SQL Server memory configuration. dbcc memusage reports three pieces of information:

- The current allocation of memory within SQL Server
- Up to the 20 largest tables and/or indexes currently in data cache
- Up to the 20 largest stored procedures currently in procedure cache

The first section of output, the current memory allocations, provides the following information:

- Configured Memory. This should be the same as what you configured for total memory using sp_configure.
- Code Size. This is the amount of memory required for the SQL Server executable.
- Kernel Structures and Server Structures represent the memory requirements for the fixed overhead and configurable options (for example, user connections).
- Cache Memory. This is the amount of memory available for data cache.
- Proc Buffers and Proc Headers. This is the total amount of memory available as procedure cache. Proc Buffers represents the size of the memory structures set aside for managing compiled objects in procedure cache. Proc Headers is the actual amount of procedure cache space available.

You must use the dbcc memusage command with a traceon (3604) if you want to see the output on your screen.

---

**TIP**

On some platforms or releases of the server, dbcc traceon (3604) must be in its own batch to take effect for the subsequent memusage. If you can't get trace flag 3604 to send data to your screen, use 3605 to send the data to the error log.

---

## Syntax

```
dbcc memusage
```

## Example

```
dbcc traceon (3604)
go
dbcc memusage
go
```

Memory Usage:

|  | Meg. | 2K Blks | Bytes |
|---|---|---|---|
| Configured Memory: | 400.0000 | 204800 | 419430400 |
| Code size: | 3.4259 | 1755 | 3592296 |
| Kernel Structures: | 5.9769 | 3061 | 6267212 |
| Server Structures: | 13.9494 | 7143 | 14627040 |
| Cache Memory: | 357.0625 | 182816 | 374407168 |
| Proc Buffers: | 0.6974 | 358 | 731272 |
| Proc Headers: | 18.8848 | 9669 | 19802112 |

Buffer Cache Memory, Top 8:

| Cache | Buf Pool | DB Id | Object Id | Index Id | Meg. |
|---|---|---|---|---|---|
| default data c |  | 2 | 8 | 0 | 0.1035 |
|  | 2K | 2 | 8 | 0 | 0.1035 |
| default data c |  | 6 | 8 | 0 | 29.0000 |
|  | 2K | 6 | 8 | 0 | 29.0000 |
| default data c |  | 1 | 8 | 0 | 3.0000 |
|  | 2K | 1 | 8 | 0 | 3.0000 |
| default data c |  | 10 | 99 | 0 | 2.0000 |
|  | 2K | 10 | 99 | 0 | 2.0000 |
| default data c |  | 1 | 31 | 1 | 1.0000 |
|  | 2K | 1 | 31 | 1 | 1.0000 |
| default data c |  | 3 | 8 | 0 | 1.0000 |
|  | 2K | 3 | 8 | 0 | 1.0000 |
| default data c |  | 3 | 99 | 0 | 1.0000 |
|  | 2K | 3 | 99 | 0 | 1.0000 |
| default data c |  | 10 | 0 | 0 | 1.0000 |
|  | 2K | 10 | 0 | 0 | 1.0000 |

Procedure Cache, Top 6:

```
Database Id: 1
Object Id: 672005425
Object Name: sp_configure
Version: 1
Uid: 1
Type: stored procedure
Number of trees: 0
Size of trees: -0.000000 Mb, 0.000000 bytes, 0 pages
Bytes lost for alignment 0 (Percentage of total: -INF)
Number of plans: 4
Size of plans: -INF Mb, 667416.000000 bytes, 328 pages
Bytes lost for alignment 100832 (Percentage of total:
-30389485638527546835337216.000000)

....
Database Id: 4
Object Id: 1776009358
```

```
Object Name: sp_spaceused
Version: 1
Uid: 1
Type: stored procedure
Number of trees: 0
Size of trees: 0.000000 Mb, 0.000000 bytes, 0 pages
Bytes lost for alignment 0 (Percentage of total: 0.000000)
Number of plans: 1
Size of plans: 0.107710 Mb, 112942.000000 bytes, 56 pages
Bytes lost for alignment 8739 (Percentage of total: 7.737600)


    - - - -

Database Id: 4
Object Id: 1440008161
Object Name: sp_lock
Version: 1
Uid: 1
Type: stored procedure
Number of trees: 0
Size of trees: 0.000000 Mb, 0.000000 bytes, 0 pages
Bytes lost for alignment 0 (Percentage of total: 0.000000)
Number of plans: 1
Size of plans: 0.037201 Mb, 39008.000000 bytes, 20 pages
Bytes lost for alignment 1660 (Percentage of total: 4.255537)


    - - - -

Database Id: 1
Object Id: 656005368
Object Name: sp_getmessage
Version: 1
Uid: 1
Type: stored procedure
Number of trees: 0
Size of trees: 0.000000 Mb, 0.000000 bytes, 0 pages
Bytes lost for alignment 0 (Percentage of total: 0.000000)
Number of plans: 1
Size of plans: 0.028290 Mb, 29664.000000 bytes, 15 pages
Bytes lost for alignment 850 (Percentage of total: 2.865426)


    - - - -

Database Id: 4
Object Id: 1872009700
Object Name: sp_who
Version: 1
Uid: 1
Type: stored procedure
Number of trees: 0
Size of trees: 0.000000 Mb, 0.000000 bytes, 0 pages
Bytes lost for alignment 0 (Percentage of total: 0.000000)
Number of plans: 1
Size of plans: 0.023853 Mb, 25012.000000 bytes, 13 pages
Bytes lost for alignment 1059 (Percentage of total: 4.233968)


    - - - -

Database Id: 4
Object Id: 1728009187
Object Name: sp_server_info
Version: 1
Uid: 1
```

```
Type: stored procedure
Number of trees: 0
Size of trees: 0.000000 Mb, 0.000000 bytes, 0 pages
Bytes lost for alignment 0 (Percentage of total: 0.000000)
Number of plans: 1
Size of plans: -INF Mb, 9924.000000 bytes, 5 pages
Bytes lost for alignment 248 (Percentage of total:
-204377558912439736109353472.000000)

----
DBCC execution completed. If DBCC printed error messages, contact a user with
 System Administrator (SA) role.
```

> **NOTE**
>
> For a detailed discussion on using and interpreting the output of the dbcc memusage command for tuning your SQL Server memory configuration, refer to Chapter 31, "Optimizing SQL Server Configuration Options."

> **WARNING**
>
> If you are running SQL Server in an SMP environment with multiple engines configured, running dbcc memusage can cause other processes within the SQL Server to time out and die. Do not run dbcc memusage while other processes are active in a multi-engine environment.

## *page*

The dbcc page command enables you to view a page header and, optionally, the data on a page. It has limited use, but it can provide further insight during lock analysis by determining the exact type of page where locking occurred.

The page numbers you may want to check using this command are those indicated in the output of the sp_lock command. By using dbcc page, you can tell if a page is a data or index page (and which level it is in the index). The things to look for in the dbcc page command output include the following:

■ indid—The index ID, which indicates the type of page: 0 = data page, 1 = clustered index page, 2–250 = non-clustered index page, 255 = text/image page

■ level—the level within the index in which the page is found

There also is an indication of the previous page, next page, and current page. If a zero is listed for a previous page, you are looking at the first page in a page linkage. If a zero is listed for the next page, you are looking at the last page in the page linkage. (If zero is listed for both, this is the only page in the page linkage.)

You can determine page ranges for a database by looking in the sysusages table. Remember that the high-level byte of the low column is the virtual device number. Also, the sysindexes table provides values for the following:

| | |
|---|---|
| first | The first data page or leaf page in an index or table |
| root | The last page in a table linkage (table) or text chain (text/image), or the root index page if it is an index |
| distribution | The location of the distribution page for an index |

## Syntax

```
dbcc page( dbid¦dbname, pagenum [, printopt={0¦1¦2¦3} [, cache={0¦1} [,
logical={1¦0}
     [, cachename ¦ -1 ]]]] )
```

> **NOTE**
>
> If you've used dbcc page in the past, notice that the syntax has changed slightly for System 11. You now must provide the named data cache where the page can be found in memory. If you haven't set up named data caches, all pages come from the default data cache. If you provide the -1 option instead of a cache name, SQL Server will search all data caches to find the page in memory.

The display options (0, 1, 2, 3) determine how the page contents will be displayed. 0 is the default and displays only the page header without the page contents. 1 displays the page header and a hex dump of the page contents individually by row. 2 displays the same information as 1, but displays the page contents as a single block of data. 3 is used when displaying the contents of a control page for a partitioned table (see the "Heap Table Partitioning" section in Chapter 18 for more information on table partitions and control pages).

> **NOTE**
>
> You need to run the dbcc traceon(3604) command prior to running dbcc page, or dbcc page will print its output to the SQL Server errorlog rather than to the user's screen.

The *cache* option indicates whether to fetch the page from disk (0) or from memory (1, the default). The logical option indicates whether the page number specified is the virtual page number (0) or the logical page number in the database (1, the default).

# Examples

Check page header of page 402 in database 6:

```
dbcc page (6, 402)
```

Review page header and data, segmented by row, on page 402 in database 6, look for page in the default data cache:

```
dbcc page (6, 402, 1, 1, 1, "default data cache")
```

Review page header and data, rows displayed as a single block, on page 402 in database 6, search all data caches:

```
dbcc page (6, 402, 2, 1, 1, -1)
```

> **TIP**
>
> For more information on the contents of pages within SQL Server databases and interpreting the output of dbcc page, see Chapter 10.

# *pglinkage*

You can use this command to display the page chain and check the consistency of page pointers for a table or index page chain. You may find this command useful to traverse a page chain, or to determine whether the pages in the table are contiguous.

## Syntax

```
dbcc pglinkage ({dbid | dbname}, startpage#, #ofpages, printopt,
    target_page#, direction [, cachename | -1 ])
```

The startpage# option specifies the page number you want to start scanning the page linkage from. The #ofpages option specifies how many pages you want to scan in the linkage (0 scans to the end of the page linkage). The target_page# lets you specify a logical page address where you want the scan to stop (0 will cause prtipage to scan to the end of the page linkage or until #of pages value is reached). direction is either 0 (descending) or 1 (ascending).

Here are the available print options:

- 0—Print only a count of the pages in the chain.
- 1—Print the last 16 pages in scan.
- 2—Print each page number in scan.

## Example

This example examines the first eight pages for the `pt_sample_CIcompany` table, starting at the first page in the table (which you can get from the `sysindexes` table).

```
dbcc traceon(3604)
dbcc pglinkage (perftune, 1616, 8, 2, 0, 1)
go

Page : 1616
Page : 1617
Page : 1618
Page : 1619
Page : 1620
Page : 1621
Page : 1622
Page : 1623

8 pages scanned.  Object ID = 112003430.  Last page in scan = 1623.
```

This output shows that the pages belong to the `pt_sample_CIcompany` (`object ID = 112003430`), and that all eight pages are sequential, from 1,616 to 1,623.

## prtipage

You can use the `prtipage` command to display the page pointers for each row on a clustered index page or non-leaf nonclustered index page or the page and row pointers on a leaf level nonclustered index page.

## Syntax

```
dbcc prtipage (dbid ¦ dbname, object_id ¦ object_name, index_id, page_#)
```

## Example

To examine the pointers for the first leaf index page retrieved from the `sysindexes` table for the nonclustered index, `NCamount`, on the `pt_tx_NCamount` table in the `perftune` database, enter the following command:

```
dbcc traceon(3604)
dbcc prtipage (perftune, pt_tx_NCamount, 2, 2096)
```

The output appears as follows:

```
*** INDEX LEVEL 0 - PAGE # 2096

Leaf row at offset 32 points to data page 771, row number 67
Leaf row at offset 47 points to data page 771, row number 62
Leaf row at offset 62 points to data page 770, row number 18
Leaf row at offset 77 points to data page 771, row number 16
Leaf row at offset 92 points to data page 772, row number 22
```

```
Leaf row at offset 107 points to data page 771, row number 28
Leaf row at offset 122 points to data page 771, row number 47
Leaf row at offset 137 points to data page 771, row number 32
Leaf row at offset 152 points to data page 770, row number 17
Leaf row at offset 167 points to data page 771, row number 73
Leaf row at offset 182 points to data page 771, row number 52
...
```

From this output, you can determine which rows on which data pages the index rows on this index page point to.

## reindex

If the sort order of the server is changed, you should use the `dbcc reindex` command to make sure the indexes on a table are in sync with the new sort order of the system.

## Syntax

```
dbcc reindex ( { table_name ¦ table_id } )
```

## Example

Perform a "fast" version of `dbcc checktable`, and drop and rebuild any indexes that do not comply with the new sort order:

```
dbcc reindex ( publishers )
```

## traceon/traceoff

Many trace flags are covered in this book; two common ones are 3604 and 3605. The 3604 flag directs output to the local session. The 3605 flag directs output to the errorlog. These trace flags are used primarily for commands such as `dbcc memusage` and `dbcc page`. There are other trace flags, such as 201, 302, and 310, that you can set to display detailed information to augment performance analysis. Table B.3 provides a list of useful trace flags.

**Table B.3. Useful `dbcc` trace flags you can set with the `traceon/traceoff` option of `dbcc`.**

| Trace Flag | Information to Display |
| --- | --- |
| 200 | "Before" image of query tree |
| 201 | "After" image of query tree |
| 302 | Information on index selection |

*continues*

**Table B.3. continued**

| Trace Flag | Information to Display |
|---|---|
| 310 | Information on join selection |
| 317 | Complete information on join select |
| 1204 | Deadlock trace information |
| 3604 | Send output to screen |
| 3605 | Send output to the SQL Server errorlog |

## Syntax

```
dbcc traceon ( traceflag [, traceflag …] )
dbcc traceoff (traceflag [, traceflag …] )
```

## Examples

Send dbcc output to screen:

```
dbcc traceon (3604)
```

Send dbcc output to SQL Server errorlog:

```
dbcc traceon (3605)
```

Turn off trace flag output:

```
dbcc traceoff (3604)
```

Turn on printing of deadlock trace information to the SQL Server errorlog:

```
dbcc traceon (3605)
dbcc traceon (1204)
```

# Comparison of Commands

Table B.4 compares the various dbcc checking commands.

**Table B.4. Comparison of dbcc commands.**

| Command | Action | Usage |
|---|---|---|
| dbcc checkdb | Check all tables for a database | Run before a database dump (or if you suspect inconsistencies) |

| Command | Action | Usage |
|---------|--------|-------|
| dbcc checktable | Check a specific table's consistency | Run if a certain table is suspect, or as part of a maintenance plan (check half the tables on Sunday, the other half on Wednesday) |
| dbcc checkcatalog | Check rows in system tables for consistency | Run before a database dump (or if you suspect inconsistencies) |
| dbcc checkalloc | Check allocation for all tables and indexes in a database | Run before a database dump (or if you suspect inconsistencies) |
| dbcc tablealloc | Check allocation for a specific table (or clustered index) | Run with fix option when a table is identified by checkalloc, or as part of a maintenance plan (check half the tables on Sunday, the other half on Wednesday) |
| dbcc indexalloc | Check index page pointers | Run with the fix option when an index is identified by checkalloc, or as part of a maintenance plan (check half the tables on Sunday, the other half on Wednesday) |

Table B.5 shows the scope of the dbcc checking commands.

## Table B.5. Scope of dbcc checking commands.

| Command/Option | Scope of Check | Locking | Performance/Speed | Coverage |
|----------------|----------------|---------|-------------------|----------|
| checktable<br>checkdb | Page chains, sort order, data row checks for all indexes | Shared table lock, one at a time (lock A, release A, lock B, release B) | Slow | Full coverage |

*continues*

## Table B.5. continued

| Command/Option | Scope of Check | Locking | Performance/Speed | Coverage |
|---|---|---|---|---|
| checktable checkdb with skip_ncindex | Page chains, sort order, data rows for tables and clustered indexes | Same | Potentially much faster than without the skip_ncindex option, dependent on number of non-clustered indexes | Partial coverage, nonclustered indexes ignored |
| checkalloc | Page chains | No locks, heavy I/O, only allocation pages cached | Slow | Full coverage |
| tablealloc full indexalloc full | Page chains | Shared table lock, heavy I/O, only allocation pages cached | Slow | Full coverage, essentially distributed checkalloc |
| tablealloc optimized indexalloc optimized | Allocation pages | Shared table lock, heavy I/O, only allocation pages checked | | Medium Partial coverage: only allocation pages cached |
| tablealloc fast indexalloc fast | OAM pages | Shared table lock | Fast | Least coverage: only OAM pages checked |
| checkcatalog | System table rows | Shared page locks on system tables, released after data on page is checked; not much cached | Fast | Detailed check of consistency of rows of certain system tables |

# Managing the Audit System

**IN THIS CHAPTER**

The Audit System was introduced as part of the System 10 release. The Audit System is like Big Brother: with auditing enabled, you can keep tabs on most SQL Server activities. For years, Sybase system administrators have needed auditing to address security, data integrity, and performance questions.

If you are unfamiliar with auditing in Sybase, consider the following scenarios:

- You suspect there are people trying to break in to the SQL Server and wonder how they are trying to get in.

- Rows are being deleted from a table, but users all say they never delete rows. Who's been deleting these rows?

- Bob in marketing has not been himself lately. Management is nervous that he may try to sabotage the system. How can Bob's activities be monitored?

- Someone ran the purge procedure and deleted active data. Who committed this most grievous offense?

- The mix of activity on your consumer table is estimated at 80 percent selects, 10 percent inserts, 5 percent updates, and 5 percent deletes. Is this an accurate estimate?"

- Ellen is running ad hoc queries from a report generator that doesn't display any SQL to the user. The reports are taking forever and sometimes even providing questionable results. How can you find out the SQL actually being provided to the SQL Server?

The Audit System can provide answers to all of these questions, as well as many others. The capabilities available in the Audit System help a database administrator (DBA) understand how and when SQL Server is being used. These capabilities give DBAs a powerful new tool that they can utilize to gather historical information or to conduct point-in-time analysis.

The following shows some practical reasons to use auditing:

- To detect unauthorized attempts to log in to the SQL Server, use a database, or access objects within a database

- To track the use of potential "hot spots" or suspected trouble areas in the SQL Server

- To analyze applications by monitoring the execution of stored procedures or the use of objects

- To determine the effect of adding new views or tables to the system by tracking the access to those new objects to determine actual use

- To gather specific data on selects, inserts, updates, and deletes to a table to determine volatility

- To monitor a specific user's activities in SQL Server

> **NOTE**
>
> The introduction of the Audit System was welcome news to long-time administrators of SQL Server. This new capability has been needed for years.
>
> Analysis was a much more crude activity before the Audit System. In many cases, administrators would collect `iostat` data (I/O statistics from the UNIX operating system) from a disk on the database server, map that disk to a database device, and map those devices to tables on the database. Many administrators would try to infer how `iostat` data related to actual activity. As you can guess, this was an imperfect science.
>
> What's more, trying to track individual usage statistics was practically impossible. The Audit System can provide detailed answers to many database administrator questions.

This chapter covers the types of specific events that can be tracked by the Audit System. First, however, you learn what type of data is collected as part of an Audit System record. You can collect the following information for each audited event:

- The name of the user
- The action for the event (`select`, `insert`, `update`, and so on)
- The fully qualified name of the object (`dbname.owner.objectname`)
- The type of object
- The time the event occurred
- The authorization status (was it authorized?)
- The number of rows returned or affected
- The stored procedure arguments or command options provided (`grant/revoke`)

# Installing and Enabling Auditing

The Audit System normally is installed by the system administrator (sa) login as part of the `sybinit` program (or the equivalent on non-UNIX platforms) in an SQL Server installation. You can install auditing during the initial installation of the SQL Server or after the SQL Server is up and running.

> **TIP**
>
> At many sites system administrators choose not to install auditing during initial installation because they believe that auditing introduces overhead and hurts performance. Go ahead and install auditing during SQL Server installation: auditing only collects data (introducing overhead and requiring maintenance) when it is enabled.

> By installing auditing but not enabling it, you can experiment with the system and become familiar with its capabilities.

When you install the Audit System, a database called `sybsecurity` is created. The `truncate log on checkpoint` option is automatically turned on in the database. The transaction log in this database is somewhat useless, because the rows added to the `sysaudits` table are not logged. Also, the data added to the `sysaudits` table can be considered a much more detailed and readable version of the transaction logs from the other databases in your system. The rows added to the audit database are not considered critical because they report on activity, and are not essential to the integrity of the system.

Auditing is not enabled after you install the Audit System. To enable auditing, you must execute the `sp_auditoption` stored procedure, as in the following example:

```
sp_auditoption "enable auditing", "on" /* enable auditing */
```

You also can use `sp_auditoption` to disable the auditing system.

```
sp_auditoption "enable auditing", "off" /* disable auditing */
```

# The *sybsecurity* Database

When you install the Audit System, the `sybsecurity` database is automatically created. This database contains all database-level system tables (copied from the `model` database) and the `sysaudits` and `sysauditoptions` auditing tables. When you install the Audit System, several auditing stored procedures also are created in the `sybsystemprocs` database.

---

**NOTE**

Auditing also creates an *audit queue*, which is an in-memory holder of audit records used to buffer audit rows before they are written to the actual `sysaudits` table. For more about the audit queue, see the section titled "How Large Does the Audit Queue Have to Be?"

---

**WARNING**

Because the `sybsecurity` database is just another database, it is possible to create user objects (tables, procedures, views, and so on). Don't do it! Once you add user objects to the `sybsecurity` database, you may have to save the transaction log (normally marked `trunc. log on checkpoint`), which increases the complexity and maintenance requirements of this database.

# The *sybsecurity* Tables

You use only the following two tables when you do auditing:

- ■ sysauditoptions contains a row for each global audit option. (See the section on "sp_auditoption" for more information on sysauditoptions.)
- ■ sysaudits contains the records generated as part of audited activities.

When sysauditoptions is installed, it contains a row for each global option; the default value for each option is 0, which means "off." Change the value settings for each option with sp_auditoption. Table C.1 outlines the structure of the sysauditoptions table.

**Table C.1. The `sysauditoptions` table layout.**

| Column | Datatype | Description |
|--------|----------|-------------|
| optn | smallint | Option number. See Table C.3 for values and descriptions. |
| value | smallint | Current value configured. Initially set to 0. |
| min | smallint | Minimum valid value for this option. |
| max | smallint | Maximum valid value for this option. |
| name | varchar(30) | Name of the option, corresponds to the value in the column named optn. |
| svalue | varchar(30) | Short string description corresponding to the value of the val column. |
| comment | varchar(255) | Full description of the option. |

The value column defines the state of the auditing feature. It ranges from 0 to 3. The svalue column decodes value, as shown in Table C.2.

**Table C.2. `sysauditoptions`: `val` versus `sval`.**

| val | sval |
|-----|------|
| 0 | off |
| 1 | ok (nonfatal for optn=13) |
| 2 | fail (fatal for optn=13) |
| 3 | both (where applicable) |

# The *sybsecurity* System Procedures

There are six new system procedures used to manage the auditing system. This may not seem like a lot of new procedures, but each procedure accepts a wide variety of parameters and can have very wide implications. Each procedure enables you to audit activity at a specific level: the SQL Server, a database, an object, a stored procedure, or a login. You also can add a user-defined message to the sysaudits table.

The following are the auditing stored procedures:

| | |
|---|---|
| sp_auditoption | Enables server-level or "global" options |
| sp_auditdatabase | Enables database-level auditing options |
| sp_auditobject | Enables auditing for a particular object, all objects (tables or views), or all future objects in a database |
| sp_auditsproc | Enables auditing for a particular procedure, all current procedures, or all future procedures in a database |
| sp_auditlogin | Enables auditing of activity for specific logins to SQL Server |
| sp_addauditrecord | Creates a comment record in the sysaudits table |

# The *sp_auditoption* System Procedure

Use sp_auditoption to enable, disable, or report on server-wide auditing and global audit options. There are many options, and each has its place in an overall audit strategy. As discussed previously, this procedure enables the audit function. Typically, you set all of your audit options, then turn auditing on and off as necessary.

The format for sp_auditoption is

```
sp_auditoption ["option name" [, "value"] ]
```

If you do not provide the value parameter, this procedure reports on the particular option. Table C.3 gives a full list of options and acceptable value settings for sp_auditoption.

**Table C.3. Value settings for the stored procedure sp_auditoption.**

| Option | Values (if no value supplied, procedure reports on option) | Description |
|---|---|---|
| enable auditing | {on ¦ off} | Enable/disable auditing. |
| logins | {ok ¦ fail ¦ both ¦ off} | Enable/disable authorized and/or unauthorized login access to the system for all users. |

| Option | Values (if no value supplied, procedure reports on option) | Description |
| --- | --- | --- |
| `logouts` | `{on ¦ off}` | Enable/disable monitoring of normal logouts from the system and lost connections. |
| `server boots` | `{on ¦ off}` | Enable/disable logging of reboots to the system in the audit log. Works like an effective checkpoint in the log to indicate all future activity in the log was on a clean SQL Server (memory flushed, no users, and so on). |
| `rpc connections` | `{ok ¦ fail ¦ both ¦ off}` | Enable/disable logging of access to the SQL Server from other servers. |
| `roles` | `{ok ¦ fail ¦ both ¦ off}` | Enable/disable logging of authorized and/or unauthorized use of the `set role` command. Useful in determining who is using special roles (`sso`, `oper`, and so on). |
| `{ sa ¦ sso ¦ oper ¦ navigator ¦ replication}` commands | `{ok ¦ fail ¦ both ¦ off}` | Enable/disable logging of the use of commands that need the `sa_role`, `sso_role`, `oper_role`, `navigator_role`, or `replication_role` to execute. |
| `errors` | `{nonfatal ¦ fatal ¦ both ¦ off}` | Enable/disable logging of fatal and/or non-fatal errors in the SQL Server. Includes fatal errors by a client resulting in a restart of the client program, but not internal errors. |
| `adhoc records` | `{on ¦ off}` | Enable/disable capability to use the `sp_auditrecord` procedure, which adds user-defined records to the `sysaudits` table. |

*continues*

## Table C.3. continued

| Option | *Values (if no value supplied, procedure reports on option)* | *Description* |
|--------|----------------------------------------------------|--------------|
| all | {on ¦ off} | Enable/disable all of the preceding options except `enable auditing`. Options are set to on or both; options that can detect success or failure are set to detect both. |

## *sp_auditoptions* Recommendations

The following are some useful server-level audit settings:

- To audit unauthorized login attempts to the SQL Server: `sp_auditoption "logins", "fail"`

- To gather information on SQL Server logouts: `sp_auditoption "logouts", "on"`

  Although this command also reports on normal logouts, its real usefulness comes in capturing information on lost connections. This is almost impossible to track unless you audit it.

- To write a record in the audit log when you boot SQL Server: `sp_auditoption "server boots", "on"`

  You should set this on so you know that all activity that occurs after this record has happened after a fresh reboot of the SQL Server.

- To monitor remote access: `sp_auditoption "rpc connections", "ok"`

- To track fatal and non-fatal errors: `sp_auditoption "errors", "both"`

  This may be very helpful in problem analysis if these types of errors become a problem in your system.

- To allow user-defined records to be added to the `sysaudits` table: `sp_auditoption "adhoc records", "on"`

  Use this to set reference points in your audit log before you start a specific test, or to indicate that a certain option has been set on and why.

## Reporting on Server/Global Options

To report on server-wide and global options, you can execute either of the following two commands:

```
sp_auditoption
sp_auditoption "all"
```

The output from `sp_auditoption` indicates the state of each global audit option, as shown in the following example. No audit options are set for this SQL Server:

```
name                           sval
------------------------------ --------
enable auditing                off
logins                         off
logouts                        off
server boots                   off
rpc connections                off
roles                          off
sa commands                    off
sso commands                   off
oper commands                  off
navigator commands             off
errors                         off
adhoc records                  off
replication commands           off
```

If you only want information about a certain option, supply an option name but do not provide a value:

```
sp_auditoption "errors" /* report on the "errors" global option */
```

# The *sp_auditdatabase* System Procedure

Use `sp_auditdatabase` to report on database-level activity.

> **NOTE**
>
> `sp_auditdatabase` is not intended to focus on object access within a database. Use `sp_auditobject` for that purpose.

You can audit activities such as dropping objects, truncating tables, granting permissions to objects, and using the database (directly or indirectly). The format for this command is

```
sp_auditdatabase [ "db_name" [ , "value" [ ,"option(s)" ] ] ]
```

You can set the `value` parameter for successful attempts (`ok`), failed attempts (`fail`), all attempts (`both`), or turned off (`off`).

For example, to track both successful and unsuccessful grant statements in the `testdb` database, execute the following:

```
sp_auditdatabase "testdb", "both", "g"
```

where g indicates that grants and revokes should be tracked.

Database-level auditing information is stored in bit-map form in the `audflags` column of the `master..sysdatabases` table. The following query from `spt_values` returns a results set outlining the bitmap for the `audflags` column in sysdatabases:

```
select number, name
from master..spt_values
where type = "Q"
```

```
number      name
--------    --------------------------
-1          DATABASE AUDITING
1           successful drop
2           failed drop
4           successful use
8           failed use
16          successful outside access
32          failed outside access
64          successful grant
128         failed grant
256         successful revoke
512         failed revoke
1024        successful truncate
2048        failed truncate
```

The next example provides a listing of the `dbid`, `name`, and `audflags` from sysdatabases. Note that `audflags` for the system databases (`master`, `model`, `tempdb`) is null. This listing of databases shows only one database, `testdb`, with auditing enabled (`audflags` is not 0):

```
select dbid, name, audflags
from master..sysdatabases
```

```
dbid    name                              audflags
------  ------------------------------    ----------
1       master
3       model
7       sybsecurity                       0
4       sybsystemprocs                    0
2       tempdb
5       testdb                            192
6       testdb2                           0
```

The `audflags` value of 192 for `testdb` means that failed grant statements (128) and successful grants (64) are enabled. Table C.4 provides a full list of the options available to the `sp_auditdatabase` procedure.

**Table C.4. Options available to the `sp_auditdatabase` stored procedure, following `sp_auditdatabase "db name", "{ok ¦ fail ¦ both ¦ off}", ...`**

| Value | Description |
|-------|-------------|
| d | Audit dropping of tables, views, procedures, triggers, or the database itself by any user |
| u | Audit execution of the use `dbname` statement |
| g | Audit execution of the `grant` statement |
| r | Audit execution of the `revoke` statement |
| t | Audit execution of the `truncate table` statement |
| o | Audit execution of SQL that references this database (for example, a user in the `master` database executes a query that references the `pubs2` database: `select * from pubs2..publishers`) |

# Setting Options

When you execute `sp_auditdatabase`, you can set an option or list of options in a single statement. If you specify a database and a value (without any options), the procedure sets that value for all six options. Consider the following examples:

```
/* audit failed attempts of dropped objects in the pubs2 database */
sp_auditdatabase pubs2, "fail", "d"

/* audit all attempt to execute the use command, grants, and
revokes in the master database */
sp_auditdatabase master, "both", "ugr"

/* audit failed attempts for all options */
sp_auditdatabase pubs2, "fail"
     or
sp_auditdatabase pubs2, "fail", "dugrto"
```

# Reporting on Database Options

If no parameters are passed to `sp_auditdatabase`, it reports the audit status of all databases in an SQL Server:

```
/* report on all databases */
sp_auditdatabase
```

If you specify a database but do not provide the `value` and `option` parameters, the procedure reports all options set for that database:

```
/* report on the pubs2 database */
sp_auditdatabase pubs2
```

## *sp_auditdatabase* Recommendations

Here are a few options and values you should set as part of an auditing strategy in a production environment. Most of these options would create a high volume of fairly uninformative audit transactions in a typical development environment because these types of activities happen all the time (dropping objects, granting permissions, and so on). I like to set the following database-level settings in production systems:

- To log any attempts to drop objects within a database:

  ```
  sp_auditdatabase "dbname", "both", "d"
  ```

  This helps you determine how certain objects "disappear" (as in, "I don't know where it went, it just disappeared!") with no person to claim responsibility.

- To log any unauthorized attempts at using a database in a system:

  ```
  sp_auditdatabase "dbname", "fail", "u"
  ```

  This helps you identify users in your system who are trying to access databases they should not be able to access.

- To log any attempts to truncate a table within a database:

  ```
  sp_auditdatabase "dbname", "both", "t"
  ```

  Truncating a table in production is as serious as dropping a table. This provides data on the table that was truncated and the user who performed the action.

- To log failed attempts at accessing data within a database from some other database:

  ```
  sp_auditdatabase "dbname", "fail", "o"
  ```

  Use this command along with the command to audit failed attempts to use the database (`fail`, `u`). I like to audit only failed attempts, because this provides information on unauthorized access attempts.

# The *sp_auditobject* System Procedure

One of the most valuable capabilities of the Audit System is being able to audit access to objects. Use the `sp_auditobject` command to audit any or all of the four basic operations (SELECT, INSERT, UPDATE, or DELETE). You can monitor successful attempts (`ok`), failed attempts (`fail`), all attempts (`both`), or turn auditing of an object off (`off`).

You also can use `sp_auditobject` to define auditing for future tables and views. This can simplify your maintenance for auditing objects. For example, you may want to track deletes on all tables in your system. By defining the auditing parameters for future objects, you are assured that any new table or view will be tracked in the manner you define. The format for this command is

```
/* audit an existing object */
sp_auditobject object_name, db_name
 [, "{ok¦fail¦both¦off}" [, "{d i s u}" ] ]
```

```
/* audit a future object */
sp_auditobject {"default table"|"default view"}, db_name
 [, "{ok|fail|both|off}" [, "{d i s u}" ] ]
```

For example, to audit all successful selects from the table `testdb..product`, execute the following statement:

```
sp_auditobject "product", "testdb", "ok", "s"
```

You can use a single command to set several auditing values. For example, to audit failed and successful attempts to SELECT, INSERT, or UPDATE the `titles` table in the `pubs2` database, you would execute the following command:

```
sp_auditobject titles, pubs2, "both", "siu"
```

# Reporting on Object Options

If the access success (ok|fail|both|off) and access type (d i s u) parameters are not provided, this procedure reports on the options set for that object or future objects:

```
/* report on the titles table in the pubs2 database */
sp_auditobject titles, pubs2
```

```
/* report on future views created in the pubs2 database */
sp_auditobject "default view", pubs2
```

### NOTE

In the past, it was almost impossible—or a crude science, at best—to try to track activity on a table. You can implement limited object auditing capability by combining table design with triggers and a few built-in functions.

When I transform a logical model into a physical implementation, I add columns for `modified_by` and `modification_date` to each table. I then create triggers for `insert` and `update` to change the values in these columns to the login name (using the `suser_name()` function) and current date (using the `getdate()` function).

This approach enables you to use an insert trigger to record the name of the person adding the row and the date on which it was added. You then can use the update trigger to maintain these values, recording the user name and modification date.

This approach would at least let you track some information for the most recent activity to a row. It is limited because you are not able to track selects or deletes, and it provides only for the activity about that particular row, not overall activity to the table. This approach still is useful and can be combined with Audit System capabilities. However, `sp_auditobject` should satisfy most of your needs.

SQL Server stores object auditing information in a bitmap column, `audflags`, in `sysobjects`. A breakdown of that bitmap value is provided in the following output. This query retrieves the values of the bitmap flags in `audflags` in the `sysobjects` table:

```
select number, name
from master..spt_values
where type = "M"

number      name
---------   ----------------------------
-1          OBJECT/SPROC/TRIGGER
1           successful deletes
2           failed deletes
4           successful updates
8           failed updates
16          successful selects
32          failed selects
64          successful inserts
128         failed inserts
256         successful sproc/trigger
512         failed sproc/trigger
```

The following statement enables you to audit failed deletions and insertions (`di`) for the `marketing_table` in `testdb`:

```
sp_auditobject marketing_table, "testdb", "fail", "di"
```

The following output requests a listing of all objects except system tables. (This database includes a single table, `marketing_table`.)

```
select id, name, audflags
from sysobjects
where type != "S"

id           name                              audflags
---------    ------------------------------    ----------
144003544    marketing_table                   130
```

In the bit map provided earlier for `audflags` in the `sysobjects` table, the value of `130` in the `audflags` column means that failed inserts (128) and failed deletes (2) are tracked by the Audit System ($128 + 2 = 130$).

Keep the following in mind when you are auditing objects:

- An audit record is written only when command-line or application-embedded SQL is sent to the SQL Server. Auditing does not capture object access when the command is issued by a stored procedure.

- A user who accesses a view which, in turn, acts on an audited table generates an audit record only when permissions are different between the two objects.

- `sp_auditobject` might be too cumbersome to put on all tables or views. Specific volatile tables that need additional analysis are good candidates for auditing.

- Use sp_auditobject as part of an overall analysis approach by tracking specific tables for a short period of time (usually, one hour) during peak and normal operations. This gives you real distribution statistics and enables you to develop a benchmark plan for that table. A good benchmark test should produce data on normal operations as well as peak activity periods (the beginning of the day, the end of a shift, and the end of the day).

- Use sp_auditobject sparingly to gather statistics on specific, secure objects.

- Set the fail option for most auditable activities to provide data on possible unauthorized attempts to access data. To avoid the nuisance of having to execute this command for all existing tables and views, set the fail option on for all future tables before you create any objects in your database:

```
sp_auditobject "default table", dbname, "fail"
sp_auditobject "default view", dbname, "fail"
```

# The *sp_auditsproc* System Procedure

Use sp_auditsproc to audit access to stored procedures. It enables you to specify an existing procedure, all procedures, or any future procedure. The format for this command is

```
/* audit a specific (or all) existing procedure(s) */
sp_auditsproc [ proc_name ¦ "all", dbname
 [ , "{ ok ¦ fail ¦ both ¦ off }" ] ]

/* audit future procedures */
sp_auditsproc "default", dbname
 [ , "{ ok ¦ fail ¦ both ¦ off }" ]
```

## Setting Procedure Options

You can specify auditing for specific, all, or future stored procedures in a database. You can request audit records be generated for successful attempts (ok), failed attempts (fail), all attempts (both) or turn off auditing of stored procedures (off). Here are a few examples:

```
/* audit all attempts to execute the sp_addlogin command
 in the sybsystemprocs database */
use sybsystemprocs
go
sp_auditsproc sp_addlogin, sybsystemprocs, "both"
go

/* audit failed attempts to execute any existing procedure in customerdb */
sp_auditsproc "all", customerdb, "fail"

/* audit failed attempts to execute any future procedure in pubs2 */
sp_auditsproc "default", pubs2, "fail"
```

# Reporting on Procedure Auditing Options

You can report on procedure auditing options in a single database only. If the dbname parameter is not specified, the command reports on the current database you are using. The following code shows a few examples:

```
/* provide a list of all procedures being audited in the current db */
sp_auditsproc

/* report on the auditing status for all procedures in the current db */
sp_auditsproc "all"

/* report on auditing status for the sp_addlogin command */
use sybsystemprocs
go
sp_auditsproc sp_addlogin, sybsystemprocs
go
```

## *sp_auditsproc* Recommendations

You can use the sp_auditobject stored procedure to track SQL access to tables. Unfortunately, you cannot set this option to capture the access of a table through a stored procedure. I have administered several sites that dictate that all access to tables or views must be done through stored procedures. If you are using stored procedures to manage most or all access to objects, sp_auditobject becomes essentially useless at handling the brunt of activity, and you will have to use sp_auditsproc to audit stored procedure executions.

If you enable auditing of all stored procedures, you can gather actual usage statistics of the procedures in your database. This also is useful in developing a benchmark plan, because you can use these statistics to choose representative stored procedures for a test.

Keep the following in mind when you are auditing stored procedures:

- It might be too resource-expensive to continuously audit all stored procedures in your database, especially in an online transaction processing (OLTP) environment that makes heavy use of stored procedures. The overhead of recording a high volume of audit records could damage performance, or the sheer mass of audit records may turn out to be less useful than a simpler record of failed attempts.

- Set this option as part of an overall analysis approach by tracking all procedures for a short period of time (usually, one hour) during peak and normal operations. This gives you real usage statistics and enables you to develop a benchmark plan that includes a representative suite of stored procedures. Note that a good benchmark test should produce data on normal operations, as well as peak activity periods (the beginning of the day, the end of a shift, and the end of the day).

- The DBCC MEMUSAGE command is not as useful as sp_auditsproc in determining procedure distribution or usage. The DBCC MEMUSAGE command has a section for the top 20 stored procedures in memory. This, however, is the largest 20 stored procedures *currently* in memory, not the 20 most often accessed.

- Set this option sparingly to gather statistics on a particularly secure or sensitive procedure.

- Set the fail option for most auditing capabilities to provide data on unauthorized attempts:

  ```
  sp_auditsproc "all", dbname, "fail"
  ```

- If your database still is undergoing changes, it is useful to set the default option to ensure that any new procedures that are created will be audited:

  ```
  sp_auditsproc "default", dbname, "fail"
  ```

> **TIP**
>
> It's especially important to set sp_auditsproc to track future stored procedures while stored procedures are in development. Remember that stored procedures cannot be modified, but must be dropped and re-created. Make the resetting of sp_auditsproc part of the standard procedure creation script if you are not automatically enabling auditing for all new stored procedures.

# The *sp_auditlogin* System Procedure

Use sp_auditlogin to track the work of a specific individual. This is the most "Big Brother" of all the auditing functions; you normally execute this command when you have suspicions about the activities of a particular person in your organization.

Using login-level auditing, you can track table or view access. Here is an example:

```
audit access to tables or views by a particular login */
sp_auditlogin [ "login_name" [ , "table ¦ view"
 [ , "{ ok ¦ fail ¦ both ¦ off }" ] ] ]

/* audit failed table access by "user1" */
sp_auditlogin "user1", "table", "fail"
```

Using an alternative format, you can record every SQL batch issued by a user:

```
/* capture all SQL passed to the SQL Server by a login */
sp_auditlogin [ "login_name" [ , "cmdtext" [ , "on ¦ off" ] ] ]

'/* capture all SQL text sent by "mary" */
sp_auditlogin "mary", "cmdtext", "on"
```

# Reporting on Login Auditing Options

You can obtain a list of all logins being audited, the auditing status of a login, or whether a particular type of auditing is set for a login. Here are several examples:

```
/* provide a list of logins being audited */
sp_auditlogin

/* report on the auditing status for bob */
sp_auditlogin "bob"

/* determine if the SQL is being captured for mary */
sp_auditlogin "mary", "cmdtext"
```

# Login Auditing Recommendations

Keep in mind the following when you are auditing logins:

- Use this option when you have suspicions about the activities of a particular person.

- The `table` and `view` options usually are sufficient for initial tracking of a login. Because this only generates rows when a SELECT, INSERT, UPDATE, or DELETE is executed against a table, it does not cover stored procedure access. Use the `cmdtext` option when you are very concerned with a person's activities.

- The `cmdtext` option generates a row in the `sysaudits` table, and the SQL text is placed in the `extrainfo` column. I consider this high-maintenance auditing because you must search the `extrainfo` column to gather data about a person's activities.

### NOTE

Some products are so user-friendly that you can't figure out what they're doing. Companies purchasing third-party applications, report generators, or other front-end applications may find that they have too little control or understanding of the SQL being generated by these systems.

Tracking the `cmdtext` for a test user is a good way to observe the generated SQL from a closed application. It also is useful for catching datatype mismatches and other quirks that prevent good optimizations and slow performance.

You also may use the `cmdtext` option to find out who is generating queries that generate a Cartesian product (for example, a `join` query that fails to set sufficient `join` criteria). You can't suppress those queries, but finding out who is executing them is the next best thing.

The query in the following output examines some sample rows in sysaudits, after login-level auditing was established for the sa login so the system administrator could track all commands. This output displays all audit records related to the sa login:

```
select event, spid, suid, dbid, loginname, extrainfo
from sysaudits
where suid = 1
107    8    1    5    sa                            select * from
                                                    master..syslogins
107    1    1    4    sa                            use  sybsecurity
107    1    1    7    sa                            select user_name()
107    1    1    7    sa                            select * from sysaudits
```

> **NOTE**
>
> If the SQL command text is longer than the maximum 224 characters per audit record, the SQL Server breaks the command into multiple audit records to record the entire SQL statement.

# The *sp_addauditrecord* System Procedure

Use sp_addauditrecord to add a user-defined comment into the sysaudits table. The format for this command is

```
sp_addauditrecord [ @text = "message text" ]
[ , @db_name = "db_name" ]
[ , @obj_name = "object_name" ]
[ , @owner_name = "object_owner" ]
[ , @dbid = "database_id" ]
[ , @objid = "object_id" ]
```

Table C.5 shows a list of the available parameters, how to use them, and the affected columns in the sysaudits table.

**Table C.5.** sp_addauditrecord **parameters.**

| Parameter Name | Usage | Affected Column |
| --- | --- | --- |
| @text | The text of the message to be added. Should be descriptive and provide an understanding of why a message is added. This often is the only parameter specified. | extrainfo |

*continues*

**Table C.5. continued**

| Parameter Name | Usage | Affected Column |
|---|---|---|
| @db_name | The database to which the message applies. If the message applies to the server or to several databases, do not specify this parameter. | dbname |
| @obj_name | The object to which the message applies. If the message does not pertain to a single object, do not use this parameter. | objname |
| @owner_name | The owner of the object specified in @obj_name. Use only if the @obj_name parameter is specified. | objowner |
| @dbid | The database ID corresponding to the @db_name. Use only if the @db_name parameter is specified. | dbid |
| @objid | The object ID of the object specified in @obj_name. Use only if @obj_name is specified. | objid |

# Using *sp_addauditrecord*

Because you use sp_addauditrecord to add a user-defined message to the sysaudits table, the @text parameter is the most useful of the available parameters. You can use the other parameters, but they are not validated (the SQL Server does not verify object IDs, database names, and so on). Anyone can be granted permission to use this procedure, once both auditing and ad hoc records have been enabled as follows:

```
exec sp_auditoption "enable auditing", "on"
exec sp_auditoption "adhoc records", "on"
```

The following shows two examples of how to use sp_addauditrecord:

```
/* make a notation regarding temporary system-wide privileges */
sp_addauditrecord @text = "SSO privileges temporarily granted to Bob
between 10 and 11 AM", @db_name = "master"

/* enter a checkpoint before commencing system test */
sp_addauditrecord @text = "Beginning of system test.
All records to the next checkpoint are based on a system with 20 users
using the new billing application", @db_name = "test_db"
```

## sp_addauditrecord Recommendations

Use the sp_addauditrecord command for the following types of activities:

- To set a boundary when you are conducting a test. For example, if you are going to audit some activities during a stress test, add a record just before the test starts and after the test is complete to indicate that the records in the table between these entries pertain to that test.

- To enter a record before you grant a certain privilege as a reminder and/or log of the event. Use it before granting temporary sensitive access to a login. (For example, Bob needs sa_role capabilities to set up a database, but needs the access for only a short period of time.)

- To identify the point in time at which a certain auditing function is enabled (that is, to serve as a logbook entry for further reference).

# Managing the Audit Queue and sybsecurity Database

The audit queue is an in-memory area used to buffer audit rows that are to be added to the sysaudits table. The queue decreases the performance burden of auditing SQL Server activity by avoiding physical writes during transaction processing. You can set the audit queue size by executing the sp_configure procedure:

```
sp_configure "audit queue size', number_of_audit_records
```

The size of an audit record on disk can range from 22 bytes to 424 bytes, but in memory each audit record always requires 424 bytes. To determine how much memory auditing needs, multiply the configured number of audit queue records by 424 bytes.

The SQL Server stores audit records first in the audit queue, then writes them to a buffered page from sysaudits as time allows. No more than a single page of audit data remains in cache at any time, so buffered pages are flushed to the disk copy of sysaudits at least every 20 records, depending on the size of the audit records, as illustrated in Figure C.1.

**FIGURE C.1.**

*Audit records are stored in the audit queue until the system has time to write them to buffered audit pages. Audit pages are flushed after no more than 20 records are written from the queue.*

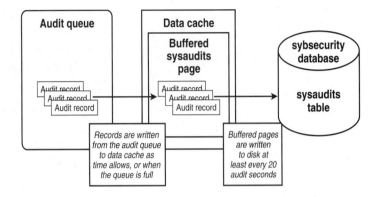

# How Large Does the Audit Queue Have to Be?

The trade-off in setting audit queue size is transaction performance versus the risk of losing audit data.

> **NOTE**
>
> There are situations in which audit data could be lost, but auditing does not change the transaction logging mechanism and should not put you at risk for actual production data loss. Keep this in mind throughout this discussion.

Although SQL Server writes transactions to disk as part of the commit process, audit records associated with your transaction are inserted in the audit queue. Audit queue records are written to the audit pages in buffer as the SQL Server has available time, or when it is necessary because the queue is full.

When the queue fills up, audited activities waiting for audit queue space are suspended until the queue can write to the buffer pages. This produces a serious domino effect:

- Any audited command or activity is suspended until space becomes available in the audit queue.
- If an audited activity is part of a transaction performing modifications on a table in a database, the implicit or explicit transaction involved in this modification remains open.
- Any locks that are acquired are held until the transaction is complete.
- The number of locks in the SQL Server may soon multiply, because other activities are likely to be blocked waiting for locks to release, causing their locks to be held.

Under load, it is clear that the audit queue could be a substantial bottleneck. To reduce the bottleneck, you could make the audit queue very large, enabling the system to prioritize transactions until there are enough cycles to move the queue to the buffer and flush the buffer.

The problem is, the larger the queue, the more audit records are in memory waiting to be written to disk. After an unmanaged SQL Server shutdown (for example, a power failure or system lock-up), the audit data will be lost. Your total exposure in any case is the number of records in the audit queue plus no more than 20 additional buffered audit records in the data cache.

The solution is to start with a small audit queue. After introducing auditing, if you see a steep performance drop-off under load, the audit queue is a bottleneck. Increase the size of the queue until the bottleneck is eliminated for your site. If audit integrity is critical to your site, you could try adding an additional CPU engine to an SMP version of SQL Server instead of increasing the size of the queue.

## Growth of Audit Tables on Disk

You must closely manage the available space in the sybsecurity database. When the sybsecurity database becomes full and no more records can be written from the in-memory audit queue, no further audited activities can be performed. The only way to re-enable auditing is to free up space in the sybsecurity database by truncating the sysaudits table, or altering the sybsecurity database to increase its size. Then the SQL Server needs to be shutdown and restarted to re-enable the audit process.

If no login with the sa_role or sso_role currently is logged in to the SQL Server, the sybsecurity database cannot be altered to allocate more space, and the sysaudits table cannot be archived to free up existing space. However, if logins are audited (sp_auditoption "logins"), no new connections to the SQL Server are granted. In addition, if activities by users with the sa_role are being audited (sp_auditoption "sa_role", "on"), the sa_role becomes powerless and the shutdown command cannot be executed.

## Is It the End of the World?

It is not the end of the world. The SQL Server automatically detects this situation and immediately makes changes to rectify the problem:

■ Any login with the sso_role gains executive privileges. The SQL Server does not generate audit records for any activity performed by a login with the sso_role, and a person with this role is able to log in to the SQL Server even if logins are audited.

■ A login with the sso_role then can archive and truncate the sysaudits table.

■ A login with the sso_role is able to shut down the SQL Server, normally a capability reserved for the sa (or login with the sa_role).

■ Error messages are written to the errorlog to document the situation.

# Recommendations for Managing the *sybsecurity* Database

Obviously a complete end to all audited work would be devastating to a production SQL Server. To prevent this, you must take necessary precautions. Here are some tips to help you prevent sybsecurity from filling up:

- Create a simple script to check the space available in the sybsecurity database. Run this script every day to track the growth in the sybsecurity database. Listing C.1 shows an example of a possible UNIX script.

**Listing C.1. This UNIX script tracks the growth of the objects in the** sybsecurity **database.**

```
#!/bin/ksh
/*      The following command will invoke isql
and input lines to the specified delimiter "!!".
The output will be placed in an output file.
You may need to list the full path of the isql executable,
located in the bin subdirectory of the SYBASE home directory.
If the SYBASE home directory is /usr/local/sybase,
the isql executable's full path is /usr/local/sybase/bin/isql

        The output file named "audit_space.out"
could also be given a full path filename.
Make sure this file is placed somewhere safe.
The ">>" is specified so the file will be
continuously appended to, to save the historical data */

isql -Uusername -Ppassword << !! >> audit_space.out
use sybsecurity
go
declare @curdate datetime
select @curdate=getdate()
print "-----------------"
print "Space Availability as of %1!", @curdate
go
sp_spaceused
go
print " "
print " "
!!
```

- To avoid the nuisance of having to run this script by hand, place it in a scheduling program to run at the same time each day. UNIX systems have a scheduling utility called crontab. Windows NT has a system scheduler. Other environments may need a client application to use its own timer to initiate a similar process.

- Gather enough data to establish a realistic growth rate for audit records in the sysaudits table. It is helpful to create a spreadsheet or document that lists the date and time, the size of sysaudits, and the growth from the previous day.

■ Divide the amount of space allocated for data for the sybsecurity database by the average growth rate (see previous tip). This gives you an estimate of the number of days you can audit activity before having to archive the sysaudits table. I recommend you archive this table before the database becomes 75 percent full, to insulate the system from sudden, unforeseen surges in audited activity.

# Using Thresholds

You can use the threshold facility to provide even more information about the space available in the sybsecurity database. A *threshold* is a marker you set in a segment to execute a stored procedure once a specified amount of available space has been crossed. I highly recommend that you install a threshold, because it is easy to do and provides the peace of mind of knowing that you have done all you can to insulate the system from a temporary catastrophe. For more on creating thresholds, see the section titled "Thresholds" in Chapter 26, " Defining, Altering, and Maintaining Databases and Logs."

To decide on the amount of space available when the threshold is crossed:

1. Determine how many days in advance you want to be notified about the filling of the sybsecurity database.

2. Multiply this number by the average growth per day using a method similar to that shown in Listing C.1.

3. Use this total to determine the value of the *free_pages* parameter for the sp_addthreshold procedure.

The format for this procedure is

```
sp_addthreshold dbname, segment, free_pages, proc_name
```

If you add 2MB of audit data per day, and you want four days notice, set the number of pages to

```
8MB x 512 2k pages/MB = 4096 pages.
```

Create a simple procedure to execute when this threshold is crossed and generate notification messages. When you are using thresholds, any print statements in a procedure are written to the SQL Server errorlog. Review the errorlog daily and use these comments to gauge an impending fill. A sample procedure is as follows:

```
create proc audit_fill
as
print "WARNING:  The sybsecurity database has only 8MB of space left!"
print "          This is enough space for about 4 days more of activity."
print "          Archive the sysaudits table as soon as possible!!!"
go
```

Now that you have the procedure (`audit_fill`) and the number of free pages (4,096), you can set the threshold. The database name is sybsecurity and the segment name is system (because the sysaudits table is a system table). To set up this threshold, execute the following system procedure:

```
sp_threshold sybsecurity, system, 4096, audit_fill
```

> **NOTE**
>
> For much more detail on setting up log and data space thresholds, see Chapter 26.

## Archiving the Audit Queue

The sysaudits table fills until it is truncated by a person with the sso_role. (Note that truncate is the only command you can use to remove rows from this table; you cannot use the delete command on the sysaudits table.) Before truncating this table, you can archive the data by doing any of the following:

- Insert the sysaudits data into a different table in another database. In the following example, the contents of the table are copied to an audit_archive table in the database archive_db:

```
use sybsecurity
go
select *
into archive_db..audit_archive
from sysaudits
go
```

(Of course, you could insert this data into a different table in the sybsecurity database, but that would defeat the purpose of freeing up space.)

- Bulk copy the archive data to an operating system file using the bcp command:

```
bcp sybsecurity..sysaudits out aud_archive.bcp -c -Usso_login -Ppswd
```

You then could save the operating system file to tape for long-term storage.

# Summary

The new auditing features of SQL Server provide a welcome facility to help manage a database, to look for problems before they become crises, and to monitor system usage. The many levels of auditing provide you with the flexibility to focus on a specific problem, or to get broad statistics about system use.

Be certain to decide in advance on the purpose of auditing, and make certain that the usefulness of the auditing outweighs the potential performance cost. Finally, don't forget that auditing requires its own maintenance as well.

# Transact-SQL Quick Reference

The tables in this appendix summarize the commands available in SQL Server for creating, managing, and accessing database objects and data. The following list indicates the syntax conventions used:

| Key | Definition |
| --- | --- |
| command | Command names, options, and other keywords |
| variable | Values you provide |
| {} | Indicates that you must choose at least one of the enclosed options |
| [] | The value/keyword is optional |
| () | Parentheses are part of the command |
| ¦ | Indicates that you can select only one of the options shown |
| , | Indicates that you can select as many of the options shown, separated by commas |
| ... | Indicates that the previous option can be repeated |
| expression | An expression that returns a single value; may be restricted to one of the following types: |
| | *char_expression* |
| | *constant_expression* |
| | *float_expression* |
| | *integer_expression* |
| | *numeric_expression* |
| | *binary_expression* |

## Table D.1. Data retrieval and manipulation.

| Task | Command |
| --- | --- |
| Retrieve rows of data from table(s) | `select [all ¦ distinct] select_list`<br>`[into table_name]`<br>`[from {table_name ¦ viewname} [alias]`<br>`    [(index indexname [prefetch size]`<br>`[lru¦mru])]`<br>`        [holdlock ¦ noholdlock]`<br>`        [,...] ]`<br>`[where search_conditions]`<br>`[group by [all] aggregate_free_expression]`<br>`[having search_conditions]` |

| *Task* | *Command* |
|---|---|
| | `[order by {col ¦ col_no}[{asc ¦ desc}]` |
| | `    [, …] ]` |
| | `[compute row_aggregate(column_name)` |
| | `      [, …]` |
| | `    [by column_name [, …]]]` |
| | `[at isolation {read committed ¦ read` |
| | `uncommitted` |
| | `                  ¦ serializable}]` |
| Add rows to a table | `insert [into] {table_name ¦ viewname}` |
| | `          [(column_list)]` |
| | `{values (constant_expression [, …])` |
| | ` ¦ select_statement}` |
| Modify rows in a table | `update {table_name ¦ view_name}` |
| | `set col_name1 = {expression ¦ NULL ¦` |
| | `                  (select_statement)}` |
| | `  [,col_name2 = {expression ¦ NULL ¦` |
| | `                  (select_statement)} ]` |
| | `[from {table_name ¦ view_name} [, …]]` |
| | `  [(index indexname [prefetch size]` |
| | `[lru¦mru])]` |
| | `[where search_conditions]` |
| Remove rows from a table | `delete [from] table_name` |
| | `  [from {table_name ¦ view_name} [, …]]` |
| | `    [(index indexname [prefetch size]` |
| | `[lru¦mru])]` |
| | `[where search conditions]` |
| Quickly remove all rows from a table | `truncate table table_name` |
| Read text/image data | `readtext tablename.colname text_ptr offset` |
| | `size` |
| | `  [holdlock]` |
| | `  [using {bytes ¦ chars ¦ characters}]` |
| | `  [at isolation {read uncommitted` |
| | `                    ¦ read committed` |
| | `                    ¦ serializabl}]` |
| Insert text/image data | `readtext tablename.colname text_ptr` |
| | `  [with log] data` |

## Table D.2. Tables and indexes.

| Task | Command |
|------|---------|
| Create a table | ```create table table_name``` |

```
create table table_name
(col datatype [ default constant_expression ]
   [ {identity | null | not null} ]
   [ [ constraint constraint_name ]
   {  check (search_condition)
   | references ref_table [(ref_col)]
   | {unique | primary key}
       [ {clustered | nonclustered} ]
       [with {fillfactor | max_rows_per_page} = #]
       [on segmentname]
   } … ]
[ , … ]
[ , [ constraint constraint_name ]
   {  check (search_condition)
   | {unique | primary key}
       [{clustered | nonclustered}] (col [, …] )
       [with {fillfactor | max_rows_per_page} = #]
       [on segmentname]
   | foreign key (column_name[, …])
           references ref_table [(ref_col[, …])] ]
   }
[ , … ]
)
[with max_rows_per_page = #] [on segmentname]
```

| Modify a table definition | ```alter table table_name``` |

```
alter table table_name
{ add column_name datatype [default constant_expr]
     {null | identity}
     [ [ constraint constraint_name ]
     {  check (search_condition)
     | references ref_table [(ref_col)]
     | {unique | primary key}
         [ {clustered | nonclustered} ]
         [with {fillfactor | max_rows_per_page} = #]
         [on segmentname]
     } … ]
   [ , … ]
| add [ constraint constraint_name ]
     {  check (search_condition)
     | {unique | primary key}
```

| Task | Command |
|------|---------|
| | [{clustered ¦ nonclustered}] (*col* [, …] )<br>[with {fillfactor ¦ max_rows_per_page} = #]<br>[on *segmentname*]<br>¦ foreign key (*column_name*[, …])<br>references *ref_table* [(*ref_col*[, …])]<br>}<br>¦ drop constraint *constraint_name*<br>¦ replace *column_name* default {*constant_expr* ¦ null}<br>¦ partition *#_of_partitions*<br>¦ unpartition<br>} |
| Drop a table | drop table *table_name* |
| Create a view | create view *view_name* [(*col_name*, …)]<br>as *select statement*<br>[ with check option ] |
| Drop a view | drop view *view_name* |
| Create an index | create [unique] [clustered ¦ nonclustered]<br>index *index_name*<br>on *table_name* (*column* [, …])<br>[with {{fillfactor ¦ max_rows_per_page} = #<br>¦ ignore_dup_key<br>¦ sorted_data<br>¦ [ignore_dup_row ¦ allow_dup_row]}]<br>[on *segmentname*] |
| Drop an index | drop index *table_name.index_name* |

## Table D.3. Other database objects.

| Task | Command |
|------|---------|
| | ***User-Defined Datatypes*** |
| Create a datatype | sp_addtype *type_name*, *system_type*,<br>{ null ¦ not null ¦ identity } |
| Remove a datatype | sp_droptype *type_name* |

*continues*

## Table D.3. continued

| *Task* | *Command* |
|---|---|
| **Rules and Defaults** | |
| Create a rule | `create rule rule_name as` |
| | `@variable operator constant_expression [{and¦or} …]` |
| Drop a rule | `drop rule rule_name` |
| Bind a rule to a column | `sp_bindrule rule_name,` |
| | `    'table.column_name'` |
| Unbind a rule from a column | `sp_unbindrule 'table.column_name'` |
| Create a default | `create default default_name as` |
| | `        constant_expression` |
| Drop a default | `drop default default_name` |
| Bind a default to a column | `sp_bindefault default_name,` |
| | `    'table.column_name'` |
| Unbind a default from a column | `sp_unbindefault 'table.column_name'` |
| **Stored Procedures** | |
| Create a procedure | `create proc procedure_name[; number]` |
| | `[(@parm_name datatype = default_value [output]` |
| | ` [, … ] )]` |
| | `[with recompile]` |
| | `as` |
| | `SQL Statements` |
| | `[return [integer_status_value]]` |
| Execute a procedure | `[exec[ute]] [@status =] procedure_name[; number]` |
| | ` [[@parm_name =] expression [output][, … ]]` |
| | `[with recompile]` |
| **Triggers** | |
| Create a trigger | `create trigger trigger_name` |
| | `  on table_name` |
| | `  for {insert ¦ update ¦ delete} [, …]` |
| | `as` |
| | `SQL_Statements` |
| | `[return]` |
| Check whether a column was updated/inserted | `if update (col_name)` |
| | `   [ { and ¦ or } update (col_name) …]` |
| Roll back a trigger and its statement | `rollback trigger` |
| | `[with raiserror error_num [error_msg]]` |

## Table D.4. Transact-SQL programming constructs.

| *Task* | *Construct* |
|---|---|
| | |

### *Flow Control*

| Task | Construct |
|---|---|
| Insert a comment | ```/* multi-line comment```<br>```[…]```<br>```*/``` |
| — | single-line comment |
| Exit a batch | ```return``` |
| Exit a stored procedure | ```return [```*return_status*```]``` |
| Declare a local variable | ```declare @```*variable_name datatype*<br>```[, …]``` |
| Set a local variable | ```select @```*variable_name* ```= expression```<br>```[, …] [from … [where …]]``` |
| Evaluate a condition | ```if ```*boolean_expression*<br>```        {statement ¦ statement_block}```<br>```[else```<br>```        {statement ¦ statement_block}]``` |
| Check for existence of rows | ```if [not] exists (select_statement)```<br>```        {statement ¦ statement_block}```<br>```[else```<br>```        {statement ¦ statement_block}]``` |
| Create a statement block with ```if``` or ```while``` | ```begin```<br>```  SQL_Statements```<br>```end``` |
| Execute repeatedly | ```while ```*boolean_condition*<br>```        {statement ¦ statement_block}``` |
| Restart ```while``` loop | ```continue``` |
| Exit ```while``` loop | ```break``` |
| Declare a label execute from a labeled spot | ```goto ```*label*<br>```…```<br>*label*```:``` |
| Wait for an event | ```waitfor {delay "```*time*```" ¦ time "```*time*```"```<br>```  ¦```<br>```  errorexit ¦ processexit ¦```<br>```mirrorexit}``` |
| Modify the environment | ```set ```*condition*``` {on ¦ off ¦ ```*value*```}``` |

*continues*

## Table D.4. continued

| Task | Construct |
| --- | --- |
| **Cursors** | |
| Define the query for a cursor | ```declare cursor_name cursor for     select select_list         from { table_name ¦ view_name }         [ holdlock ¦ noholdlock ]         [ shared ]         [ , … ]         [for {read only ¦ update             [ of column_name_list ]}]``` |
| Execute the query and set the row pointer to the first row | `open cursor_name` |
| Set the number of rows for a fetch | `set cursor rows num_rows     for cursor_name` |
| Retrieve a row or rows | `fetch cursor_name [ into variable_list ]` |
| Stop cursor processing and release locks | `close cursor_name` |
| Release cursor name and resources | `deallocate cursor cursor_name` |
| **Transactions and Locking** | |
| Start a transaction | `begin tran[saction] [tran_name]` |
| Complete a transaction | `commit tran[saction] [tran_name]` |
| Roll back a transaction | `rollback tran[saction] [tran_name]` |
| Mark a point in the transaction | `save tran[saction] save_name` |
| Turn on/off chained mode | `set chained {on ¦ off}` |
| Set transaction isolation level | `set transaction isolation level {0 ¦ 1 ¦ 3}` |
| **Generated Messages** | |
| Print a text string | `print {"character_string"¦@variable¦ @@global_variable} [, arglist]` |
| Raise an error message | `raiserror error_number     {character_string ¦ @variable}     [, arglist]` |
| Register an error message | `sp_addmessage msg_num, message_text` |
| Bind error message to constraint | `sp_bindmsg constraintname, msg_num` |

## Table D.5. Database commands.

| Task | Command |
|------|---------|
| Create database | `create database db_name`<br>`[ on device_name = size [, …]`<br>`[ log on device_name = size [, …]]]` |
| Alter database | `alter database db_name`<br>`[ on device_name = size [, …]`<br>`[ log on device_name = size [, …]]]` |
| Change current database | `use db_name` |

## Table D.6. Security and access control.

| Task | Command |
|------|---------|
| Add login | `sp_addlogin login_name, password`<br>`[, default_database [, default_language`<br>`[, fullname ] ] ]]` |
| Remove login | `sp_droplogin login_name` |
| Lock/unlock login | `sp_locklogin [login_name,"{lock ¦ unlock}"]` |
| Add user to database | `sp_adduser login_name [, name_in_db`<br>`[, group_name]]` |
| Remove user | `sp_dropuser user_name` |
| Grant object permissions | `grant {all ¦ permission_list}`<br>`on object[(col_list)]`<br>`to user_list [with grant option]` |
| Revoke object permissions | `revoke [grant option for]`<br>`{all ¦ permission_list}`<br>`on object[(col_list)]`<br>`from user_list [cascade]` |
| Grant command permissions | `grant {all ¦ command_list} to user_list` |
| Revoke command permissions | `revoke {all ¦ command_list} from user_list` |
| Display info on a specific login | `sp_displaylogin [login_name]` |
| List info on database users | `sp_helpuser [user_name]` |
| List security for object/user | `sp_helpprotect {object_name ¦ user_name}` |

## Table D.7. Useful system stored procedures.

| Task | Command |
|------|---------|
| Display information about an object | `sp_help {type_name ¦ procedure_name ¦`<br>`table_name ¦ view_name ¦`<br>`rule_name ¦ default_name}` |
| List indexes defined on a table | `sp_helpindex table_name` |
| Display creation text | `sp_helptext {rule_name ¦ default_name`<br>`¦ view_name ¦ procedure_name`<br>`¦ trigger_name}` |
| Rename an object | `sp_rename {old_name ¦`<br>`'table_name.old_col_name'},`<br>`new_name` |
| Display info on constraints | `sp_helpconstraint table_name [, detail]` |
| List all referenced objects | `sp_depends {trigger_name ¦`<br>`procedure_name}` |
| List all triggers and stored procedures that reference a table or view | `sp_depends {table_name ¦`<br>`view_name}` |
| View current locks | `sp_lock [spid]` |
| View current processes | `sp_who [login_name ¦ spid]` |
| List database(s) | `sp_helpdb [db_name]` |
| Add custom error messages | `exec sp_addmessage integer, text` |
| Bind messages to constraints | `exec sp_bindmsg constraint_name, msg#` |
| Define and display keys | `sp_primarykey table_name, col1 [, …]` |
| | `sp_foreignkey table_name, pk_table_name,`<br>`col1 [, col2, …]` |
| | `sp_commonkey table1_name, table2_name,`<br>`col1a, col2a [, col1b, col2b , …]` |
| | `sp_helpkey table_name` |

## Table D.8. SQL Server functions.

| Function | Description |
| --- | --- |
| **Row Aggregate Functions** | |
| sum ([all ¦ distinct] *expression*) | The total of the (distinct) non-null values in the numeric column |
| avg ([all ¦ distinct]) *expression*) | The average of the (distinct) non-null values in the numeric column |
| count ([all ¦ distinct] *expression*) | The number of (distinct) nonnull values in the column |
| count (*) | The number of selected rows |
| max (*expression*) | The highest value in the *expression* |
| min (*expression*) | The lowest value in the *expression* |
| isnull (*expr1, expr2*) | Replace *expr1*, if null, with *expr2* |
| **String Functions—Length and Parsing** | |
| char_length(*char_expr*) | Returns integer number of characters in *char_expr*, ignoring trailing spaces |
| substring (*expression, start, length*) | Returns part of string |
| right (*char_expr, int_expr*) | Returns *int_expr* characters from right of *char_expr* |
| upper (*char_expr*) | Converts *char_expr* to uppercase |
| lower (*char_expr*) | Converts *char_expr* to lowercase |
| space (*int_expr*) | Generates string of *int_expr* spaces |
| replicate (*char_expr, int_expr*) | Repeats *char_expr, int_expr* times |
| stuff (*char_expr1, start, length, char_expr2*) | Replaces *length* characters from *expr1* at *start* with *expr2* |
| reverse (*char_expr*) | Reverses text in *char_expr* |
| ltrim (*char_expr*) | Removes leading spaces |
| rtrim (*char_expr*) | Removes trailing spaces |
| **String Functions—Conversions** | |
| ascii (*char_expr*) | ASCII value of first character in *char_expr* |
| char (*int_expr*) | ASCII code-to-character conversion |

*continues*

## Table D.8. continued

| Function | Description |
|---|---|
| str (*float_expr* [, *length* [, *decimal*]]) | Numeric-to-character conversion |
| soundex (*char_expr*) | Returns soundex value of *char_expr* |
| difference (*char_expr1*, *char_expr2*) | Returns difference between soundex values of expressions |
| charindex (*char_expr*, *expression*) | Returns the starting position of the specified *char_expr*, else 0 |
| patindex ("*%pattern%*", *expression*) | Returns the starting position of the specified pattern, else 0 |

### Mathematical Functions

| Function | Description |
|---|---|
| abs (*numeric_expr*) | Absolute value of specified value |
| ceiling (*numeric_expr*) | Smallest integer greater than or equal to the specified value |
| exp (*float_expr*) | Exponential value of the specified value |
| floor (*numeric_expr*) | Largest integer less than or equal to the specified value |
| pi () | Returns the constant value of 3.1415926… |
| power (*numeric_expr*, *power*) | Returns the value of *numeric_expr* to the power of *power* |
| rand ([*int_expr*]) | Returns a random float number between 0 and 1, optionally using *int_expr* as a seed |
| round (*numeric_expr*, *int_expr*) | Rounds off a numeric expression to the precision specified in *int_expr* |
| sign (*int_expr*) | Returns the positive (+1), zero (0), or negative (-1) |
| sqrt (*float_expr*) | Returns the square root of the specified value |

### Date Functions (see Table D.9 for list of *dateparts*)

| Function | Description |
|---|---|
| getdate ( ) | Returns the current system date and time |
| datename(*datepart*, *date_expr*) | Returns a specified part of *date_expr* value as a string, converted to a name (for example, June) if appropriate |

| Function | Description |
| --- | --- |
| datepart(*datepart*, *date_expr*) | Returns a specified part of *date_expr* value as an integer |
| datediff(*datepart*, *date_expr1*, *date_expr2*) | Returns *date_expr2 - date_expr1* as measured by specified *datepart* |
| dateadd(*datepart*, *number*, *date_expr*) | Returns the date produced by adding specified number of dateparts to *date_expr* |

### Access and Security Information

| | |
| --- | --- |
| host_id ( ) | Current host process ID number of client process |
| host_name ( ) | Current host computer name of client process |
| suser_id (["*login_name*"]) | User's SQL Server ID number |
| suser_name ([*server_user_id*]) | User's SQL Server login name |
| user_id (["*name_in_db*"]) | User's ID number in database |
| user_name ([*user_id*]) | User's name in database |
| user | User's name in database |
| show_role() | Current active roles for user |
| proc_role ("sa_role", ¦ sso_role" ¦ oper_role") | Check whether user executing procedure has specified role |
| valid_user (*login_id*) | Returns 1 if specified *login_id* is a valid user or alias in at least one database |

### Database and Object Information

| | |
| --- | --- |
| db_id (["*db_name*"]) | Database id number |
| db_name ([*db_id*]) | Database name |
| object_id ("*objname*") | Database object id number |
| object_name (*obj_id* [, *db_id*]) | Database object name |
| col_name (*obj_id, col_id*) | Column name of column |
| col_length ("*objname*", "*colname*") | Length of column |
| index_col ("*objname*", *index_id*, *key #*) | Indexed column name |

*continues*

### Table D.8. continued

| Function | Description |
|---|---|
| valid_name (*char_expr*) | Returns 0 if *char_expr* is not a valid identifier |
| curunreservedpgs (*db_id*, *lstart*, *unreservedpgs*) | Used in query against sysusages; returns number of free pages on device fragment |
| data_pgs (*object_id*, {*doampg* ¦ *ioampg*}) | Number of data pages used by table (doampg) or index (ioampg) |
| reserved_pgs (*object_id*, *doampg* ¦ *ioampg*}) | Number of reserved pages for a table (doampg) or index (ioampg) |
| rowcnt (*doampg*) | Number of rows in a table |
| used_pgs (*object_id*, *doampg*, *ioampg*) | Total number of pages used by a table and its clustered index |
| lct_admin ({{"last chance" ¦ "logfull" ¦ "unsuspend"}, *database_id*} ¦ "reserve", *log_pages*) | Manages the last chance threshold for a transaction log |

#### Data Functions

| Function | Description |
|---|---|
| datalength (*expression*) | Returns length of *expression* in bytes |
| tsequal (*timestamp1*, *timestamp2*) | Compares timestamp values; returns error if timestamp values do not match |
| convert (*datatype*,*expression*,[*format*]) | Converts expression to datatype. *Format* specifies the display format for datetime values when converted to character string. |

### Table D.9. Date parts (for use with date functions).

| Date Part | Abbreviation | Value Range |
|---|---|---|
| year | yy | 1753–9999 |
| quarter | qq | 1–4 |
| month | mm | 1–12 |
| dayofyear | dy | 1–366 |
| day | dd | 1–31 |

| Date Part | Abbreviation | Value Range |
|---|---|---|
| week | wk | 1–54 |
| weekday | dw | 1–7 (1 = Sunday) |
| hour | hh | 0–23 |
| minute | mi | 0–59 |
| second | ss | 0–59 |
| millisecond | ms | 0–999 |

## Table D.10. Date conversion formats.

| Without Century | With Century | Format of Date in Converted String |
|---|---|---|
| | 0 or 100 | mon dd yyyy hh:miAM (or PM) |
| 1 | 101 | mm/dd/yy |
| 2 | 102 | yy.mm.dd |
| 3 | 103 | dd/mm/yy |
| 4 | 104 | dd.mm.yy |
| 5 | 105 | dd-mm-yy |
| 6 | 106 | dd mon yy |
| 7 | 107 | mon dd, yy |
| 8 | 108 | hh:mm:ss |
| | 9 or 109 | mon dd, yyyy hh:mi:ss:mmmAM (or PM) |
| 10 | 110 | mm-dd-yy |
| 11 | 111 | yy/mm/dd |
| 12 | 112 | yymmdd |

# System Administration Quick Reference

The tables in this appendix summarize the tasks and commands of the different roles. System functions and tables are also presented. The tables are as follows:

Table E.1. Basic sa tasks.

Table E.2. Database management.

Table E.3. Monitoring CPU and I/O usage.

Table E.4. Managing the Audit System (sso task only).

Table E.5. Basic dbo tasks.

Table E.6. System tables.

## Table E.1. Basic sa tasks.

### *Starting and Stopping the Server*

```
startserver -f runserver_file -c configuration_file [-m] [-p]
```

> f specifies the name of the runserver file.

> `runserver_file` contains the SQL Server command with appropriate options for locations of the master device, interfaces file, SQL Server name, and so on.

> d specifies the master device name.

> c specifies the name of the configuration file with which to boot.

> `configuration_file` contains configuration parameters to use upon SQL Server startup.

> m specifies the single user mode.

> p generates the password for the SSO account.

```
shutdown [with  nowait]
```

### *Granting Access to the Server*

```
sp_addlogin login_name, password [ ,default_db [ ,language]]
```

> `password` required, 6 characters minimum.

> *Note:* Only the user with the sso_role can add logins.

```
sp_password caller_password, new_password, [ , login_name]
```

> *Note:* Only the user with the sso_role should specify `login_name`.

```
sp_droplogin login_name
```

```
sp_locklogin login_name, {"lock ¦ "unlock"}
```

> Locks the specified `login_name`.

```
sp_configure "password expiration interval", #_of_days
```

> Sets the number of days before passwords will expire after they are changed. A value of 0 means no password expiration.

*Note:* Only the user with the `sso_role` can set the password expiration interval.

```
sp_modifylogin login_name, option, value
```

> `option` is defdb, deflanguage, or fullname.

## Defining Physical Resources

```
disk init name = 'logical_name', physname = "phys_name",
    vdevno = dev_num, size = dev_size
```

> `logical_name` must be unique throughout the server.

> `physname` indicates the disk location of the device.

> `dev_num` is the unique integer < `sp_configure` devices.

> `dev_siz` is the size in pages —2KB except Stratus (4KB).

```
disk reinit name = 'logical_name', physname = "phys_name",
        vdevno = dev_num, size = dev_size
```

> Rebuilds sysdevices to reestablish a database device after restoring a damaged master database, if the device was added since the last database dump of the master database.

```
disk refit
```

> Used after `disk reinit` to rebuild sysusages and sysdatabases to reestablish databases created or altered since the last database backup of the master.

```
disk mirror name = 'logical_name', mirror = 'phys_name'
```

> Keeps a copy of the device `logical_name` on `phys_name`.

```
disk unmirror name = "logical_name"
        [ , side = {primary ¦ secondary}]
        [ , mode =  {retain ¦ remove}]
```

> Defaults are side=secondary, mode=retain.

```
disk remirror name = "logical_name"
```

```
sp_adddumpdevice 'disk' ¦ 'tape', logical_name, physical_name, tape_size
```

> `logical_name` is the unique name within the server for the dump device.

> `physical_name` is the physical location of the device of the disk file.

> `tape_size` is the capacity of the tape dump device in megabytes.

```
sp_help device [logical_name]
```

> Reports information about the specified or all database and dump devices.

```
sp_diskdefault logical_name, defaulton ¦ defaultoff
```

```
sp_dropdevice logical_name
```

> Removes the device definition if the device is not in use.

## Table E.2. Database management.

### Basic Commands

```
create database db_name [on device_name = size [ , …] ]
            [log on device_name = size [, …] ]
            [with override]
            [for load]
```

with override allows the specification of the same device name for the on and log on clauses; enables dumping of the transaction log even though it is not on a separate device.

for load invokes a streamlined version of create database. Used when recovering from media failure, and database will be loaded from backup immediately following creation.

*size* is in megabytes.

*device_name* is any database device in sysdevices.

A separate log device is highly recommended.

```
drop database db_name

alter database db_name [on device_name = size [ , …]]
            [log on device_name = size [ , …]]
            [with override]
            [for load]

sp_changedbowner login_name

sp_dboption database, options, true ¦ false
```

*options* are select into/bulkcopy, read only, single user, dbo use only, no chkpt on recovery, trunc log on chkpt, abort tran on log full, allow nulls by default, ddl in tran, no free space acctg, and identity in nonunique index.

```
checkpoint
```

checkpoint a database (must be in database to be checkpointed).

```
sp_helpdb [database_name]
```

### Granting create database Permission

```
use master

sp_adduser login_name

grant create database to login_name
```

### Memory and Resource Allocation

```
sp_configure [option, [new_value] ¦ config_group_name]
```

*option* is any value in the description column of sysconfigures.

*new_value* is any value in the valid range for the parameter.

*config_group_name* is the name of the configuration parameter group.

`sp_configure` without arguments lists valid options and ranges.

`reconfigure [with override]`

Instructs the server to apply changes. Obsolete in System 11.

```
sp_configure "configuration file ", 0,
            {"write" ¦ "read" ¦ "verify" ¦ "restore"} "file_name"
```

Reads, validates, and writes configuration file settings.

`sp_bindcache namedcache, dbname, [, tablename[.indexname][, text]]`

Binds the database, table, index, or text/image objects to a named data cache.

`sp_cacheconfig [namedcache [, "cachesize[P¦K¦M¦G]"][,logonly ¦ mixed]]`

Creates, configures, drops, and provides information on named caches.

*cachesize* is specified in <u>P</u>ages, <u>K</u>ilobytes, <u>M</u>egabytes, or <u>G</u>igabytes.

`sp_cachestrategy object_name [, {prefetch ¦ mru}, "{on¦off}"`

Enables/disables `prefetch` and `mru` cache replacement strategy for tables, indexes, or text objects.

`sp_helpcache {namedcache ¦ "cachesize[P¦K¦M¦G]"]`

Displays information about objects bound to named caches or amount of overhead required for a specific cache size.

```
sp_poolconfig namedcache,
            { "memsize[P¦K¦M¦G]", "configpoolK" [, "affected_poolK"]
            ¦ "io_size", "wash=size[P¦K¦M¦G]" }
```

Creates, drops, resizes and provides information about memory pools within named caches.

*memsize* is the size of the memory pool or amount to move to a memory pool, specified in <u>P</u>ages, <u>K</u>ilobytes, <u>M</u>egabytes, or <u>G</u>igabytes.

*configpool* is the I/O size in the pool being configured. Valid sizes are 2KB, 4KB, 8KB, and 16KB.

*affected_pool* is the size of the I/O in the memory pool where the memory is being deallocated (default = 2KB pool).

`wash=` changes the location of the wash marker for the memory pool.

`sp_unbindcache dbname, [, tablename[.indexname][, text]]`

Unbinds a database, table, index, or text/image object from a named cache.

`sp_unbindcache_all cache_name`

Unbinds all objects bound to a named cache.

`sp_logiosize ["default" ¦ "size"]`

Sets the log I/O size for the current database to `size`.

`size` legal values are 2, 4, 8, 16, 32, 63, 128, 256, and 512.

## Table E.3. Managing CPU and I/O usage.

### Basic Commands

```
sp_monitor
```

Shows CPU usage, I/O usage, and so on, since server came up and also since last `sp_monitor` call.

```
set statistics io on ¦ off
```

Quantity of logical and physical I/O.

```
set statistics time on ¦ off
```

Elapsed system and CPU time for `parse`, `compile`, and `execute`.

```
set forceplan on ¦ off
```

### Managing Remote Access

```
sp_addserver server_name, {local ¦ null}, network_name
```

```
sp_dropserver server_name [ , droplogins]
```

```
sp_addremotelogin server_name [ , local_name [, remote_name]]
```

```
sp_remoteoption [server_name, login_name, remote_name, 'trusted', true ¦ false]
```

```
sp_serveroption [servername, options, {true ¦ false}]
```

*options* are net password encryption and time-outs.

```
sp_helpremotelogin [servername [, remotename]
```

### Managing System-Defined Roles

```
sp_role {"grant" ¦ "revoke"}, {sa_role ¦ sso_role ¦ oper_role ¦
      oper_role}, login_name
```

*login_name* must be a valid SQL Server login.

User must have sa_role to grant sa_role.

User must have sso_role to grant sso_role and oper_role.

sa_role performs SQL Server management tasks:

> Server configuration
> Manage database devices
> Create/drop databases
> Shut down SQL Server
> Kill processes

sso_role performs security-related tasks:

> Add/drop/lock logins
> Change passwords
> Set the password expiration interval
> Manage the auditing system

oper_role can back up and restore any database within SQL Server.

```
set role {"sa_role" ¦ "sso_role" ¦ "oper_role"} {on ¦ off}
```
Disables/enables the role for the current session.

## Table E.4. Managing the Audit System (SSO task only).

```
sp_auditoption
```
Enables/disables auditing and global audit options.

Without arguments, displays current global audit settings.

```
sp_auditoption "{all ¦ enable auditing ¦ logout ¦ server boots
            ¦ adhoc records}" [ , "{on ¦ off}"]

sp_auditoption " {logins ¦ rpc connections ¦ roles}"
            [ , "{ok ¦ fail ¦ both ¦ off}"]

sp_auditoption "errors" [ , "{nonfatal ¦ fatal ¦ both}"]

sp_auditoption "{sa ¦ sso ¦ oper} commands" [ ,
            "{ok ¦ fail ¦ both ¦ off }"]
```
`enable auditing` must be on before setting other audit options.

`ok` audits successful operations.

`fail` audits failed operations.

`both` audits successful/failed operations.

`on` turns on specified auditing.

`off` turns off specified auditing.

```
sp_auditdatabase [dbname [ , "ok ¦ fail ¦ both ¦ off" [,
            " { d u g r t o}"]]]
```
Enables auditing of events within database or object references within database from another database.

`d` audits dbo commands.

`u` audits execution of use *dbname*.

`g` audits grant commands.

`r` audits revoke commands.

`t` audits truncate table.

`o` audits outside access of *dbname*.

```
sp_auditobject table_name ¦ view_name, dbname [ ,
            "{ok ¦ fail ¦ both ¦off}" [ , "{d i s u }"]]
```
Enables auditing of access to existing tables/view.

`d` audits deletes.

*continues*

### Table E.4. continued

      i audits `inserts`.

      s audits `selects`.

      u audits `updates`.

```
sp_auditobject "default {table | view}", dbname [ ,
          "{ok | fail both | off}" [ , "{ d i s u}"]]
```

Enables auditing defaults for future tables/view created in *dbname*.

```
sp_auditsproc [proc_name | "all" | "default"], dbname [ ,
          "{ok | fail | both | off}"]]
```

Audits execution of existing stored procs/triggers or enables auditing defaults for future stored procs/triggers created in *dbname*.

```
sp_auditlogin [login_name [, "cmdtxt" [, "{on | off}"]]]

sp_auditlogin [login_name [,"table | view" [,
          "{ok | fail | both | off}"]]]
```

Audits commands and table/view access for a login.

```
sp_auditrecord [@text="msg text"] [ , @db_name="objowner"]
          [ , @obj_name="objname"] [ , @owner_name="objowner"]
          [ , @dbid=db_id] [ , @objid=obj_id]
```

Enters user-defined audit records.

```
sp_configure "audit queue size", #_audit_records
```

Sets the number of records to be held in the audit queue (default = `100`).

---

### Table E.5. Basic dbo tasks.
#### *User and Group Maintenance*

```
sp_adduser login_name [ , name_within_db [ , group_name]]
```

    *login_name* is from `syslogins`.

    *name_within_db* is an optional different name within the database.

    *group_name* is the name of the group in which to place the user. Specifying a group name requires specifying a non-null name_within_db.

    `guest` is a special case of user; it gives any nonuser database access.

    Adds a row to `sysusers`.

```
sp_addalias login_name, current_user
```

    *login_name* is the user to add to the database.

    *current_user* is the existing user to whom *login_name* will be aliased.

    Adds a row to `sysusers`.

```
sp_addgroup group_name
```

Adds the group *group_name* to sysusers.

```
sp_changegroup group_name, user_name
```

Places the user *user_name* in group *group_name*.

```
sp_dropuser user_name
```

Removes the user *user_name* from sysusers and any aliased users from sysalternates.

```
sp_dropalias login_name
```

Removes the *login_name* from sysalternates.

```
sp_dropgroup group_name
```

Removes the group *group_name* from sysusers.

```
sp_helpuser [user_name]
```

Displays a list of database users or detailed user information.

### Granting and Revoking Permission

```
grant {all ¦ permission_list} on object [(column_list)]
      to {public ¦ name_list ¦ role_name} [with grant option]

grant {all ¦ command_list} to {public ¦ name_list ¦ role_name}
```

*permission_list* may be any combination of select, insert, update, delete.T

*name_list* may be any combination of users and groups.

*command_list* may include any of the create commands (create rule/table/view/procedure/default).

with grant option enables the user to grant specified permissions to other users.

```
revoke [grant option for] {all ¦ permission_list ¦ execute}
      n object [ (column_list)]
      rom {public ¦ name_list ¦ role_name}
      cascade]

revoke {all ¦ command_list} from {public ¦ name_list ¦ role_name}
```

grant option for revokes users' permission to grant specified permissions.

cascade is required with grant option for if user has granted permissions to other users.

Revokes those permissions.

### Segments and Partitions

```
sp_addsegment segment_name, database, device_name

sp_dropsegment segment_name, database [ , device_name]
```

*continues*

## Table E.5. continued

### User and Group Maintenance

```
sp_placeobject segment_name, object_name
```

Controls future growth of an object.

```
sp_extendsegment segment_name, database, device_name
```

```
sp_helpsegment [segment_name]
```

```
sp_logdevice database, device_name
```

```
sp_helpartition table_name
```

### Space Monitoring

```
sp_spaceused [object_name]
```

```
dbcc checktable (table_name)
```

```
sp_estspace table_name, est_#_of_rows, [fillfactor [cols_to_max
          [ , textbin_length [ , iosec]]]]
```

*fillfactor* is the fill factor used on index create.

*cols_to_max* is a comma-separated list of the variable-length columns for which to use the maximum width of the columns rather than the average width.

*textbin_length* is the average size of text/binary columns.

*iosec* is the number of disk I/Os per second for the machine (default = 30).

```
sp_addthreshold dbname, segname, free_pgs, proc_name
```

```
sp_dropthreshold dbname, segname, free_pgs
```

```
sp_modifythreshold dbname, segname, free_pgs
          [ , new_proc] [ , new_free_pgs] [ , new_seg_name]
```

*free_pgs* is the number of free pages left in the segment where the threshold is placed.

*proc_name* is the stored procedure to execute when the threshold is crossed.

```
sp_helpthreshold [segname]
```

```
sp_thresholdaction @dbname, @seg_name, @space_left, @status
```

Stored procedure is automatically called when logsegment crosses the last-chance threshold.

This procedure must be defined by the sa or dbo.

### Updating Statistics

```
update statistics table_name [(index_name)]
```

Makes statistics pages current for specific table or index.

## Database Consistency Checker

```
dbcc checktable ({table_name ¦ table_id} [, skip_ncindex])
```
Table consistency.

```
dbcc checkdb [ (dbname [ , skip_ncindex] )]
```
Checks all tables in the database *dbname*.

```
dbcc checkalloc [ (dbname [ , fix ¦ no fix] ) ]
```
Checks page allocation.

```
dbcc checkcatalog [(dbname)]
```
Checks all system tables.

```
dbcc dbrepair (dbname, dropdb)
```
Removes the damaged database.

```
dbcc traceon ¦ traceoff  (3604)
```
Sends output for certain dbcc commands to screen.

```
dbcc memusage
```
Displays memory contents.

```
dbcc page( {dbid¦dbname}, pagenum [, printopt={0¦1¦2} [, cache={0¦1}
        [, logical={1¦0}[, cachename ¦ -1 ]]]] )
```
Displays page contents.

```
dbcc tablealloc ({table_name ¦ table_id}
                [ , {full ¦ optimized ¦ fast ¦ null}
                [ , fix ¦ nofix ] ] )
```
Checks page allocation of the specific table and its indexes.

```
dbcc indexalloc ({table_name ¦ table_id} , index_id
                [ , {full ¦optimized ¦ fast ¦ null}
                { , fix ¦ nofix ] ] )
```
Checks page allocation of the specific index.

fix option tells SQL Server to attempt to fix the allocation errors found.

```
dbcc reindex ( { table_name ¦ table_id})
```
Checks and fixes the index integrity.

```
dbcc fix_text ( { table_name ¦ table_id})
```
Upgrades the text values after a character set change to the multibyte charset.

```
dbcc engine (net [, {show [, engine_#] ¦ show_all ¦ netengine}])
```
Displays the network I/O engine affinities.

*continues*

## Table E.5. continued

### Backing Up and Loading Databases

```
dump database dbname to dump_device [at backup_server_name]
        [ , stripe on dump_device [ at backup_server_name] … ]
        [with { [ dismount ¦ nodismount],
                [ nounload ¦ unload],
                [ noinit ¦ init ],
                [retaindays = #_days] ,
                [file = file-name] } ]

dump tran[saction ] dbname to dump_device [ at backup_server_name]
        [ , stripe on dump_device [ at backup_server_name] … ]
            [ with { [dismount ¦ nodismount],
                     [nounload ¦ unload],
                     [retaindays = #_days],
                     [file = file_name],
                     [ { truncate_only ¦ no_log ¦ no_truncate}]]} ]

load database dbname from dump_device [at backup_server_name}
        [ , stripe on dump_device [ at backup_server_name]  … ]
        [ with { [ dismount ¦ nodismount] ,
                 [nounload ¦ unload],
                 [file = file_name],
                 [listonly [= full] ] ,
                 [headeronly] } ]

load tran[saction] dbname from dump_device [at backup_server_name]
        [ , stripe on dump_device [ at backup_server_name] … ]
        [ with {[ dismount ¦ nodismount] ,
                 [ nounload ¦ unload],
                 [ file = file_name],
                 [listonly [= full] ] ,
                 [headeronly] } ]
```

dismount/nodismount determines whether tapes remain mounted after dump/load.

nounload/load determines whether tapes rewind after dump/load.

no init/init determines whether dumps are appended to tape or tape is overwritten.

retaindays specifies the number of days that the Backup Server protects you from overwriting a dump.

file allows you to specify a name for the dump file on the tape.

listonly lists information about dump files on tape without loading.

headeronly displays header information for a single dump file without loading.

```
online database dbname
```

Makes the specified database available for public use following a load of the database.

### Managing User-Defined Messages

```
sp_addmessage msg_num, msg_text [ , language]
```

Adds user-defined messages to sysusermessages for use by `print` and `raiserror` calls and by sp_bindmsg.

```
sp_dropmessage msg_num [ , language]
```

```
sp_getmessage msg_num, @msg_var output [ , language]
```

*msg_num* is the user-defined message number; it must be > 20,000.

*@msg_var* is the variable to receive returned message text.

```
sp_bindsmg constraint_name, msg_num
```

Binds the stored message to a constraint.

```
sp_unbindmsg constraint_name
```

### Impersonating Users

```
setuser 'user_name'
```

```
sp_addalias login_name, name_in_db
```

## Table E.6. System tables.

| Table | Description |
|-------|-------------|
| **Database-Specific** | |
| sysalternates | Aliases defined |
| sysattributes | Database and object attribute definitions |
| syscolumns | Column descriptions for tables |
| syscomments | Original SQL definition of objects |
| sysconstraints | Referential and check constraints |
| sysdepends | Track procedure/table dependencies |
| sysindexes | One row for each table and index |
| syskeys | Keys defined (documentation only) |
| syslogs | Database transaction log |
| sysobjects | Pointers to all objects in db; types: U = User table, P = Procedure, R = Rule, V = View, S = System table, Tr = Triggers, D = Default |

*continues*

## Table E.6. continued

| *Table* | *Description* |
| --- | --- |
| syspartitions | Information on partitions of a partitioned table |
| sysprocedures | Parsed text of stored procedures |
| sysprotects | Protections granted and revoked |
| sysreferences | Primary/foreign keys defined in referential constraints |
| sysroles | Maps server role ids to local role ids |
| syssegments | Segment definitions |
| systhresholds | Thresholds defined in the database |
| systypes | System- and user-defined data types |
| sysusermessages | User-defined error messages |
| sysusers | Specifies who can use the database |

### Master Database Only

| *Table* | *Description* |
| --- | --- |
| syscharsets | Currently defined character sets |
| sysconfigures | Memory only, server-wide locks |
| syscurconfigs | Memory only, version of sysconfigures |
| sysdatabases | Defined databases |

| status | *Meaning* |
| --- | --- |
| 4 | Select into/bcp |
| 8 | Trunc log on chkpt |
| 16 | No chkpt on recovery |
| 32 | Database created for load |
| 64 | Crash during load |
| 256 | Suspect |
| 512 | ddl in tran allowed |
| 1024 | Read only |
| 2048 | dbo use only |
| 4096 | Single-user mode |
| 8192 | Allow nulls by default |
| 16384 | db_name change |

| status2 | Meaning |
|---------|---------|
| 1 | Abort tran on log full |
| 2 | No free space acctg |
| 4 | Auto identity |
| 8 | Identity in nonunique index |
| 16 | Database is offline |
| 32 | Database undergoing recovery |
| 32768 | Database does not have a dedicated log device |

`sysdevices`  Database and dump devices

| status | Meaning |
|--------|---------|
| 1 | Default disk |
| 2 | Physical disk |
| 8 | Skip header |
| 16 | Dump device |
| 32 | Serial writes |
| 64 | Mirrored device |
| 128 | Read-mirrored |
| 256 | Half-mirrored |
| 512 | Mirror-enabled |

| | |
|---|---|
| `sysengines` | SQL Server engines currently online |
| `syslanguages` | Available languages |
| `syslisteners` | Information for each type of network connection used by SQL Server |
| `syslocks` | Memory only, server-wide locks |
| `sysloginroles` | Maps logins to system-defined roles |
| `syslogins` | Specifies who has server access |
| `syslogshold` | Information about the oldest active transaction for each database |
| `sysmessages` | System messages |
| `sysprocesses` | Memory-only, current server processes |
| `sysremotelogins` | Specifies who has remote access |
| `sysservers` | Local and remote server names |
| `syssrvroles` | Contains all server-wide roles |
| `sysusages` | Maps databases to `sysdevices` |

# Legal Agreements Pertaining to the CD-ROM

By opening this package you are agreeing to be bound by the following agreement:

Some of the software included with this product is copyrighted, in which case all rights are reserved by the respective copyright holder. You are licensed to use software copyrighted by the Publisher and its licensors on a single computer. You may copy and/or modify the software as needed to facilitate your use of it on a single computer. Making copies of the software for any other purpose is a violation of the United States copyright laws.

This software is sold as is without warranty of any kind, either expressed or implied, including but not limited to the implied warranties of merchantability and fitness for a particular purpose. Neither the publisher nor its dealers or distributors assumes any liability for any alleged or actual damages arising from the use of this program. (Some states do not allow for the exclusion of implied warranties, so the exclusion may not apply to you.)

By opening this package, you are agreeing to be bound by the following agreement which applies to products supplied by Northern Lights Software:

Aurora is a copyrighted product of Northern Lights Software, Ltd., and is protected by United States copyright laws and international treaty provisions. Copyright 1994, 1995, 1996. All Rights Reserved. Aurora Utilities for Sybase, Aurora Desktop, Aurora Script Manager, Aurora Distribution Viewer, and Aurora Cost Retrieval DLL are service marks of Northern Lights Software. Sybase is a trademark of Sybase, Inc.

Period of evaluation. By installing the software, it is understood that the provided software is for the purposes of evaluation, only, and cannot be used beyond a period of thirty (30) days unless the software is registered. The software can be registered only by Northern Lights Software, Ltd., or its empowered agents.

Limited Warranty. Northern Lights warrants that the SOFTWARE will perform substantially in accordance with the written description delivered with the software, usually in the form of a readme.txt, for a period of ninety (90) days. Any implied warranties are limited to the same period of ninety (90) days.

Remedies. Northern Lights and its suppliers' entire liability and your exclusive remedy shall be, at Northern Lights' option, a refund of the price paid or repair or replacement of the software. This Limited Warranty is void if the failure has resulted from accident, abuse, or misapplication. These warranties are limited to the United States unless you can provide proof of purchase from an authorized non-U.S. source.

No Other Warranties. To the maximum extent permitted by applicable law, Northern Lights disclaims all other warranties, either express or implied, including but not limited to implied warranties of merchantability and fitness for a particular purpose. This limited warranty gives you certain rights. You may have other rights which vary by state and jurisdiction.

No Liability for Consequential Damages. To the maximum extent permitted by applicable law, in no event shall Northern Lights be liable for any damages whatsoever (including without limitation, damages for loss of business profits, business interruption, loss of business information or any other pecuniary loss) arising out of the use of or inability to use this product, even if Northern Lights has been advised of the possibility of such damages. Because some states do not allow the limit or exclusion of liability for consequential or incidental damage, the above limitation may not apply to you.

# INDEX

## SYMBOLS

## G

# Add to Your Sams Library Today with the Best Books for Programming, Operating Systems, and New Technologies

## The easiest way to order is to pick up the phone and call

# 1-800-428-5331

### between 9:00 a.m. and 5:00 p.m. EST.

### For faster service please have your credit card available.

| ISBN | Quantity | Description of Item | Unit Cost | Total Cost |
|------|----------|---------------------|-----------|------------|
| 0-672-30467-8 | | Sybase Developer's Guide (Book/Disk) | $40.00 | |
| 0-672-30700-6 | | Developing Sybase Applications (Book/CD-ROM) | $39.99 | |
| 0-672-30888-6 | | Sybase DBA Survival Guide, 2E (Book/CD-ROM) | $49.99 | |
| 0-672-30717-0 | | Tricks of the Doom Programming Gurus (Book/CD-ROM) | $39.99 | |
| 1-57521-041-X | | The Internet Unleashed 1996 | $49.99 | |
| 1-57521-040-1 | | The World Wide Web Unleashed 1996 | $49.99 | |
| 0-672-30706-5 | | Programming Microsoft Office (Book/CD-ROM) | $49.99 | |
| 0-672-30474-0 | | Windows 95 Unleashed (Book/CD-ROM) | $39.99 | |
| 0-672-30602-6 | | Programming Windows 95 Unleashed (Book/CD-ROM) | $49.99 | |
| 0-672-30791-X | | Peter Norton's Complete Guide to Windows 95 | $29.99 | |
| 1-57521-064-9 | | Teach Yourself Web Publishing with HTML 3.0 in a Week, 2E | $29.99 | |
| 1-57521-005-3 | | Teach Yourself More Web Publishing with HTML in a Week | $29.99 | |
| 0-672-30745-6 | | HTML & CGI Unleashed (Book/CD-ROM) | $49.99 | |
| | | Shipping and Handling: See information below. | | |
| | | TOTAL | | |

❏ 3 ½" Disk

❏ 5 ¼" Disk

Shipping and Handling: $4.00 for the first book, and $1.75 for each additional book. Floppy disk: add $1.75 for shipping and handling. If you need to have it NOW, we can ship product to you in 24 hours for an additional charge of approximately $18.00, and you will receive your item overnight or in two days. Overseas shipping and handling adds $2.00 per book and $8.00 for up to three disks. Prices subject to change. Call for availability and pricing information on latest editions.

**201 W. 103rd Street, Indianapolis, Indiana 46290**

**1-800-428-5331 — Orders     1-800-835-3202 — FAX     1-800-858-7674 — Customer Service**

Book ISBN 0-672-30909-2

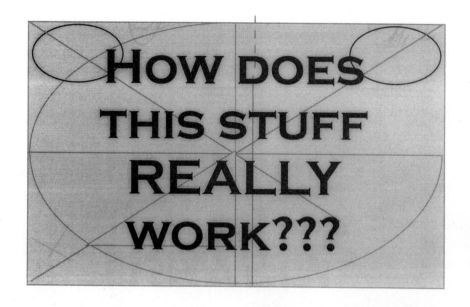

# HOW DOES THIS STUFF REALLY WORK???

SYBASE AND MICROSOFT SQL SERVER ARE POWERFUL CLIENT/SERVER TOOLS.

BUT THEY CERTAINLY AREN'T...INTUITIVE. EVEN BASIC TRAINING CAN LEAVE YOU IN THE DARK ABOUT THE "REAL WORLD" OF SYBASE AND MICROSOFT SQL SERVER.

LET NORTHERN LIGHTS CONSULTING, AN INTERNATIONALLY RECOGNIZED SQL SERVER TRAINING AND CONSULTING FIRM, HELP YOU GET WHERE YOU WANT TO GO.

WE HAVE A GREAT DEAL OF EXPERIENCE HELPING FIRMS MAKE THESE TOOLS *DO WHAT THEY WANT THEM TO DO!*

**BUILDING EXCELLENCE IN CLIENT/SERVER SYSTEMS**

# NORTHERN LIGHTS PRODUCTS & SERVICES

## BOOKS

✧ "SYBASE DBA SURVIVAL GUIDE, 2ND ED"
(GARBUS, SOLOMON, RANKINS, TRETTER),
*SAMS PUBLISHING, 1996*

✧ "SYBASE SQL SERVER
   11 UNLEASHED"
(RANKINS, GARBUS, SOLOMON, MCEWAN ),
*SAMS PUBLISHING, 1996*

✧ "MICROSOFT SQL SERVER 6
   UNLEASHED"
(SOLOMON, WOODBECK, RANKINS, GARBUS,
MCEWAN), *SAMS PUBLISHING, 1996*

## COURSES

✧ SQL FOR PROGRAMMERS
✧ INTRODUCTION TO SQL SERVER
✧ PRACTICAL SQL SERVER SYSTEMS ADMIN
✧ LOGICAL DATABASE DESIGN FOR SQL SERVER
✧ SQL SERVER PERFORMANCE AND TUNING
✧ WHAT'S NEW WITH SYBASE SYSTEM 10
✧ WHAT'S NEW WITH SYBASE SYSTEM 11
✧ SQL SERVER FOR SYSTEMS ADMINISTRATORS
✧ SQL SERVER FOR DATABASE DESIGNERS
✧ GUI DESIGN
✧ OPEN SYBASE
✧ VISUAL BASIC FOR SQL PROGRAMMERS

## NEW COURSES FOR 1996!!!

✧ **ADVANCED SQL TECHNIQUES**
(THREE-DAY COURSE) COVERS THE "HOWS AND WHYS" OF ADVANCED QUERY AND STORED
PROCEDURE WRITING, OPTIMIZING, AND DEBUGGING. FOR APPLICATION PROGRAMMERS
INTERESTED IN SERIOUS PERFORMANCE; INCLUDES WHEN TO BREAK UP QUERIES, FORCE A
QUERY PLAN OR INDEX, OR RESOLVE A COMPLEX QUERY, AMONG OTHER TOPICS.

✧ **DESIGNING AND IMPLEMENTING VERY LARGE DATABASES**
(FIVE-DAY COURSE) LEARN A METHODOLOGY FOR HANDLING VERY LARGE SQL SERVER
DATABASES. THIS COURSE INCLUDES A CLOSE INVESTIGATION INTO THE PHYSICAL
OPERATION OF SQL SERVER AND THE ADMINISTRATIVE IMPLICATIONS OF VLDBs.

**ALL NORTHERN LIGHTS COURSES ARE UPDATED FOR SYBASE SYSTEM 11
AND MICROSOFT SQL SERVER 6.0**

## AURORA UTILITIES

✧ AURORA DESKTOP
✧ PERFORMANCE MONITOR
✧ DISTRIBUTION VIEWER
✧ STRESS TESTER
✧ COST DLL
✧ SCRIPT MANAGER

## CONSULTING

✧ TUNING & OPTIMIZATION
✧ STANDARDS
✧ SYSTEM REVIEW
✧ OFF-SITE HELP DESK
✧ VLDB ARCHITECTURE

*PHONE: (800) 774-6764*
*FAX: (518) 581-9737*
*E-MAIL: 72702.373@COMPUSERVE.COM*
*WWW: WWW.NLIGHT.COM*

**Northern Lights**
Consulting

# Visible Analyst Workbench

## Integrated Enterprise CASE

*Planning - Analysis - Design - Construction - Re-Engineering/BPR*

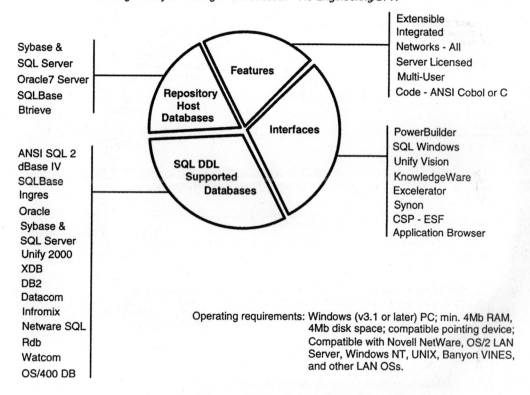

Sybase &
SQL Server
Oracle7 Server
SQLBase
Btrieve

Repository Host Databases

Features

Extensible
Integrated
Networks - All
Server Licensed
Multi-User
Code - ANSI Cobol or C

Interfaces

PowerBuilder
SQL Windows
Unify Vision
KnowledgeWare
Excelerator
Synon
CSP - ESF
Application Browser

SQL DDL Supported Databases

ANSI SQL 2
dBase IV
SQLBase
Ingres
Oracle
Sybase &
SQL Server
Unify 2000
XDB
DB2
Datacom
Infromix
Netware SQL
Rdb
Watcom
OS/400 DB

Operating requirements: Windows (v3.1 or later) PC; min. 4Mb RAM, 4Mb disk space; compatible pointing device; Compatible with Novell NetWare, OS/2 LAN Server, Windows NT, UNIX, Banyon VINES, and other LAN OSs.

The Visible Analyst Workbench® is an object based corporate workgroup CASE tool that combines data, process and objects in an integrated open repository. Powerful modeling support includes Business Modeling, Class Modeling, Entity Relationship Modeling, Data Flow Modeling, State Transition Modeling, and Program Modeling, which is synchronized and cross-balanced, allowing for all development in one singular OO environment. Migration of legacy systems, IEW/ADW and Excelerator data and designs to an OO world make for fast generation of new client/server applications.

Visible Systems Corporation
300 Bear Hill Road
Waltham, MA 02154
Phone: (617) 890-CASE (2273)  Fax: (617) 890-8909
Web Page/http://www.visible.com  Email: info.visible.com

Free trial copy available on CD-ROM

# Installing the
# CD-ROM

The companion CD-ROM contains sample programs developed by the authors, plus an assortment of third-party tools and product demos. The disc is designed to be explored using a browser program. Using Sams' Guide to the CD-ROM browser, you can view information concerning products and companies, and install programs with a single click of the mouse. To install the browser, here's what to do.

# Windows 3.x/NT Installation Instructions

1. Insert the CD-ROM disc into your CD-ROM drive.

2. From File Manager or Program Manager, choose Run from the File menu.

3. Type **<*drive*>\setup** and press Enter, where <*drive*> corresponds to the drive letter of your CD-ROM. For example, if your CD-ROM is drive D:, type **D:\SETUP** and press Enter.

4. The installation creates a Program Manager group named Sybase SQL Server. To browse the CD-ROM, double-click the Guide to the CD-ROM icon inside this Program Manager group.

# Windows 95 Installation Instructions

1. Insert the CD-ROM disc into your CD-ROM drive. If the AutoPlay feature of your Windows 95 system is enabled, the setup program will start automatically.

2. If the setup program does not start automatically, double-click the My Computer icon.

3. Double-click the icon representing your CD-ROM drive.

4. Double-click the icon titled Setup.exe to run the installation program. Follow the onscreen instructions that appear. When setup ends, double-click the Guide to the CD-ROM icon to begin exploring the disc.

Following installation, you can restart the Guide to the CD-ROM program by pressing the Start button, selecting Programs, then Sybase SQL Server and Guide to the CD-ROM.

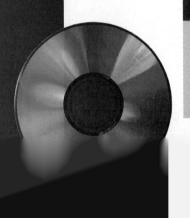

**NOTE**

The Guide to the CD-ROM program requires at least 256 colors. For best results, set your monitor to display between 256 and 64,000 colors. A screen resolution of 640 by 480 pixels is also recommended. If necessary, adjust your monitor settings before using the CD-ROM.